LOUIS E. BOONE

Ernest G. Cleverdon Chair of Business and Management
and Chair, Department of Marketing and Transportation
University of South Alabama

DAVID L. KURTZ

The R. A. and Vivian Young Chair of Business Administration
and Head, Department of Marketing and Transportation
University of Arkansas

Contemporary Marketing
SEVENTH EDITION

THE DRYDEN PRESS / A HARCOURT BRACE JOVANOVICH COLLEGE PUBLISHER

Fort Worth • Philadelphia • San Diego • New York • Orlando • Austin
San Antonio • Toronto • Montreal • London • Sydney • Tokyo

Acquisitions Editor: Rob Zwettler
Developmental Editor: Mary Beth Nelligan
Managing Editor: Cate Rzasa
Project Editor: Karen Steib
Art and Design Manager: Alan Wendt
Production Manager: Barb Bahnsen
Permissions Editor: Doris Milligan
Director of Editing, Design, and Production: Jane Perkins

Text and Cover Designer: Barbara Gibson
Copy Editor: Margaret Jarpey
Indexer: Sheila Ary
Compositor: The Clarinda Company
Text Type: 9½/12 Helvetica

Library of Congress Cataloging-in-Publication Data
Boone, Louis E.
    Contemporary marketing / Louis E. Boone, David L. Kurtz. — 7th ed.
        p.   cm.
    Includes bibliographical references and index.
    ISBN 0-03-054018-6
    1. Marketing.   I. Kurtz, David L.   II. Title.
HF5415.B53   1992
658.8 — dc20   91-11467

Printed in the United States of America
 23-032-98765432

Address orders:
The Dryden Press
Orlando, FL 32887

Address editorial correspondence:
The Dryden Press
301 Commerce Street, Suite 3700
Fort Worth, TX 76102

The Dryden Press
Harcourt Brace Jovanovich

Cover source: Courtesy of France Telecom.

To Our Families,

PAT, BARRY, AND CHRISTOPHER
DIANE, JENNIFER, KELLI, FRED, AND TOM

The Dryden Press Series in Marketing

Preface

Students who open the pages of the seventh edition of *Contemporary Marketing* can be assured that they are reading a classroom-proven text. In fact, one million students since 1974 have used *Contemporary Marketing* to begin their study of one of the most fascinating disciplines in the field of business.

What accounts for *Contemporary Marketing*'s success? With each successive edition it has introduced a number of "firsts" to bring marketing alive for students. The following innovations have established a benchmark that we believe will have a lasting effect on how the introduction to marketing course is taught:

□ *Contemporary Marketing* was the first marketing text to be based on marketing research; it is written the way instructors teach the course.

□ *Contemporary Marketing* was the first marketing text written to the student rather than to the professor. Many students tell us that *Contemporary Marketing* is the best text they have ever used. Why? It is written in a clear, concise style at a level students can comprehend and enjoy.

□ *Contemporary Marketing* was the first text to integrate computer applications into every chapter. This feature demonstrates a real-world purpose for all the computer instructions presented in other business classes.

□ *Contemporary Marketing* was the first text to respond fully to instructors' requests for video materials to be integrated with marketing concepts in the text. Every chapter in *Contemporary Marketing* includes a case study supported by a video designed specifically for that case.

Innovations in the Seventh Edition

As with any successful product, *Contemporary Marketing* is constantly evolving. Let's take a look at the highlights of the new edition.

Integration of Global Marketing: A First in Marketing Textbooks

Study after study (as well as accrediting association reports) have suggested that international concepts should be integrated into text discussions. Many books have attempted to do this by placing a chapter on international issues at the end of the text, where it becomes a logical candidate for omission if time runs short at the end of the term. Other texts have gone a step further by adding boxed examples on international topics to most chapters. Unfortunately, this is not what is meant when instructors plead for an internationally integrated text.

In response to this plea, the new edition of *Contemporary Marketing* has taken a truly global perspective. Hundreds of international examples are sprinkled throughout the book's 20 chapters. The major international examples are identified by a globe in the page margin, similar to the one that appears on this page. The international examples are not merely stories of U.S. firms that have sold something successfully overseas. The examples also focus on foreign marketers who sell their goods and services here as well as in other foreign markets. In this new approach, marketing is viewed from a truly global perspective rather than a narrow, nationalistic one.

As part of our strategy for making *Contemporary Marketing* the first global text for basic marketing classes, we have also moved the traditional "international" chapter up to Chapter 3. It is now treated as part of the general environment for marketing. Future marketers will have to think globally—beyond the "us versus them" orientation that is so prevalent in marketing education today.

More Emphasis on the Marketing of Services

The previous edition of *Contemporary Marketing* introduced a new chapter on services. The authors have rewritten this chapter to reflect the most current research in this field, much of which has been conducted in the past five years.

This chapter is also repositioned as part of the product section, which was suggested by many of our users. Furthermore, service examples have been increased significantly throughout the text. When combined with the global orientation mentioned above, it is clear that *Contemporary Marketing* continues to live up to its title. It is *the* contemporary marketing text for the 1990s.

Enhanced Integrated Video Cases

The Emmy Award-winning *Contemporary Marketing* videocase package has been enhanced for the seventh edition. Five of the videos are new, three are significantly revised, and another five include three- to five-minute updates at the end of the video. The written cases at the end of each chapter are either totally new or have been revised and updated.

A complete list by chapter of the *Contemporary Marketing* videos is given below. The new video cases are highlighted with an asterisk.

Chapter 1	McDonald's in Moscow*
Chapter 2	Mitsubishi Motor Sales of America
Chapter 3	Carl's Jr. and the Mikoshi Japanese Noodle House*
Chapter 4	Lakeway Resort*
Chapter 5	The Disney Channel
Chapter 6	Kawasaki Motors Corp.
Chapter 7	Skyfox Corp.
Chapter 8	Irvine Co.
Chapter 9	Carushka
Chapter 10	Robert Mondavi
Chapter 11	Azure Seas
Chapter 12	Famous Amos
Chapter 13	Northern Produce Co./Mushrooms, Inc.
Chapter 14	South Coast Plaza*
Chapter 15	Arrowhead Drinking Water Co.
Chapter 16	Apple Computer, Inc.
Chapter 17	Santa Anita Park*
Chapter 18	Lipton & Lawry's
Chapter 19	Yamaha Motorcycles
Chapter 20	Looking Good Calendar Co.

Each video has been reduced in length to between 15 and 20 minutes, the length preferred by most instructors. Video experts throughout the publishing industry acknowledge that nothing compares to *Contemporary Marketing*'s video cases. The current enhancement of this package sets a new standard for classroom videos.

An Oversized Format and Striking New Use of Color

The seventh edition of *Contemporary Marketing* has a strikingly different appearance from that of its predecessors. The new large text size and extensive use of color represent the commitment of The Dryden Press to continuous renewal and improvement in each edition. For additional clarity, some pedagogical elements are printed in a special fifth color. This feature is designed to improve student learning and comprehension in comparison to standard text treatments.

Instructional Resource Package

Contemporary Marketing is more than a text. The book you are reading is supported by the most comprehensive and usable instructional resource package in the field of marketing.

Instructor's Resource Manual

The two volumes of instructional materials contain the following sections for each chapter:

- ☐ Changes from the Previous Edition
- ☐ Annotated Learning Goals
- ☐ Key Terms
- ☐ Lecture Outline
- ☐ Lecture Illustration File
- ☐ Answers to Review Questions
- ☐ Answers to Discussion Questions
- ☐ Box Focus
- ☐ Answers to Video Case Questions
- ☐ Solutions to Computer Applications
- ☐ Guest Speaker Suggestions

A total of 100 suggested term paper topics are also included in the *Instructor's Resource Manual.* In addition, the volumes contain suggested class schedules, instructions on using the marketing videos, additional information on guest speakers, and instructions for the *Boone & Kurtz Marketing Disk.*

Test Bank

The completely revised 3,000-question *Test Bank* is available in a printed format and a computerized format for IBM PC, MacIntosh, and Apple II microcomputers. The *Test Bank* has been designed to aid the classroom learning experience with a wide range of testing alternatives. Each chapter includes application and knowledge-based multiple choice, true/false, and essay questions, as well as two minicases. The minicases, which are followed by multiple-choice questions, present a problem situation that requires a more thorough analysis and synthesis of information than typical multiple-choice questions. Students will also be tested on their knowledge of the Competitive Edge and Ethics box material. Each question is keyed to specific text page numbers and level of difficulty. No *Study Guide* questions appear in the test bank. The *Test Bank* was prepared by Professors Jonas Falik and Benjamin Wieder of Queensborough Community College. RequesTest™ is also available to instructors. This service allows instructors to order test masters by question and criteria via a toll-free telephone line. Contact your local Dryden sales representative for more information.

Study Guide

The *Study Guide* is a learning supplement designed to enhance students' understanding and to provide them with additional practice in applying concepts presented in the text. Each chapter includes a brief outline of the chapter, experiential exercises, a self-quiz, cases, short-answer questions, and computer problems. Also included are crossword puzzles at the end of each chapter, a marketing plan exercise, and three term projects. *Study Guide* solutions now appear at the end of the *Study Guide,* not in the *Instructor's Resource Manual.* The *Study Guide* was prepared by Professor Thomas S. O'Connor of the University of New Orleans.

Marketing Simulation Game

Microsim, a marketing simulation game written by Professor Steven Schnaars of Baruch College, is available for marketing instructors. The game asks students to assume the role of a marketing manager for a microwave oven company and manipulate fundamental marketing variables to maximize profits. It is designed for use with the IBM PC.

The Boone & Kurtz Marketing Disk

The *Boone & Kurtz Marketing Disk* contains complete programs for the computer applications problems in the text and *Study Guide.* It is available free to adopters for use with IBM PC microcomputers.

Contemporary Marketing Videos and Video Instructor's Manual

The 20 *Contemporary Marketing* videos are available at no cost to professors who use the text in their classes. The videos are available only in half-inch VHS format. In addition, a separate *Video Instructor's Manual* is provided with the videos.

Full-Color Overhead Transparencies

This innovative component includes a set of 150 original full-color transparency acetates, which are also available as 35mm slides. Without duplicating the presentation of material in the text, each transparency is a striking graphic illustration of a concept discussed in the text. One-half of the transparencies are advertisements illustrating marketing concepts. The set includes teaching notes for each transparency.

Transparency Masters

A set of approximately 100 transparency masters is available, consisting of key tables and figures from the text. The transparency masters have been chosen to illustrate important concepts and reinforce text material.

Acknowledgments

The authors gratefully acknowledge the following academic colleagues who reviewed all or part of the manuscript for earlier editions:

Keith Absher	Eugene M. Johnson	Arthur E. Prell
Dub Ashton	James C. Johnson	Bill Quain
Wayne Bascom	Harold H. Kassarjian	Gary Edward Reiman
Richard D. Becherer	Bernard Katz	Arnold M. Rieger
Tom Becker	Stephen K. Keiser	C. Richard Roberts
Richard F. Beltramini	James H. Kennedy	Patrick J. Robinson
Robert Bielski	Charles Keuthan	William C. Rodgers
Robert Collins	Donald L. Knight	William H. Ronald
Howard B. Cox	Philip Kotler	Bert Rosenbloom
Michael R. Czinkota	Francis J. Leary, Jr.	Carol Rowey
Kathy Daruty	Paul Londrigan	Ronald S. Rubin
Jeffrey T. Doutt	Lynn J. Loudenback	Rafael Santos
Sid Dudley	David L. Loudon	Bruce Seaton
Phillip E. Egdorf	Dorothy Maass	Howard Seigelman
John W. Ernest	James C. Makens	Jack Seitz
Gary T. Ford	Lou Mansfield	Steven L. Shapiro
Ralph M. Gaedeke	James McCormick	A. Edward Spitz
G. P. Gallo	Carl McDaniel	William Staples
Don Gibson	James McHugh	David Steenstra
James Gould	John D. Milewicz	Robert E. Stevens
Donald Granbois	Robert D. Miller	G. Knude Swenson
Paul E. Green	J. Dale Molander	Vern Terpstra
William Green	John F. Monoky	Howard A. Thompson
Blaine Greenfield	James R. Moore	John E. Timmerman
Matthew Gross	Colin Neuhaus	Rex Toh
John H. Hallaq	Robert T. Newcomb	Dennis H. Tootelian
Cary Hawthorn	Jacqueline Z. Nicholson	Fred Trawick
Hoyt Hayes	Robert O'Keefe	Toni Valdez
Sanford B. Helman	Sukgoo Pak	Dinoo T. Vanier
Nathan Himelstein	Gordon Di Paolo	Gayle D. Wasson
Robert D. Hisrich	Dennis D. Pappas	Fred Weinthal
Ray S. House	Constantine Petrides	Robert J. Williams
Michael D. Hutt	Barbara Piasta	Cecilia Wittmayer
Don L. James	Dennis D. Pitta	Julian Yudelson
David Johnson	Barbara Pletcher	Robert J. Zimmer

The seventh edition was no exception when it came to benefiting from quality reviewers' comments. The authors are extremely grateful for the many insightful comments of the following people:

Robert Bielski, Dean Junior College
Elizabeth Cooper-Martin, Georgetown University
Deborah L. Cowles, Virginia Commonwealth University
Michael R. Czinkota, Georgetown University
Robert F. Gwinner, Arizona State University
Debbora Heflin-Bullock, California State Polytechnic University, Pomona
Maryon King, Southern Illinois University—Carbondale
Edwin A. Laube, Macomb Community College
Faye McIntyre, University of Mississippi
Robert D. O'Keefe, DePaul University
Constantine Petrides, Borough of Manhattan Community College
Carolyn E. Predmore, Manhattan College
F. Kelly Shuptrine, University of South Carolina
Clint B. Tankersley, Syracuse University
Ruth Taylor, Southwest Texas State University
Susan B. Wessels, Meredith College
Nicholas C. Williamson, The University of North Carolina at Greensboro

We are also proud to have worked with the following people on the instructional resource package: Jonas Falik and Benjamin Wieder of Queensborough Community College on the *Test Bank;* Thomas S. O'Connor of the University of New Orleans, and reviewers James E. Hansz of Lehigh University and Matthew Gross of Moraine Valley Community College on the *Study Guide;* Steven Schnaars of Baruch College on *Microsim;* and Cindy Acker and Richard Vivona on the *Boone & Kurtz Marketing Disk.*

Special thanks go to our research associates, the folks who keep *Contemporary Marketing* contemporary. We sincerely appreciate the work and devotion of Judy Block, Ginger Honomichl, Jeanne Lowe, Nancy Moudry, Carolyn Smith, and Carole Stamps.

Last, but not least, we want to thank our good friends at The Dryden Press. Rob Zwettler, our acquisitions editor, Mary Beth Nelligan, our developmental editor, and Karen Steib, our project editor, have been most supportive and helpful. Other key Dryden professionals who made this edition possible include Barb Bahnsen, Kelly Gozdziak, Aimee Gosse, Susan Hartill, Rose Hepburn, Jan Huskisson, Jennifer Lloyd, Doris Milligan, Megan Mulligan, Susan Pierce, Cate Rzasa, and Alan Wendt. We also thank our marketing manager, Patti Arneson.

Louis E. Boone
David L. Kurtz

About the Authors

Louis E. Boone (Ph.D.) holds the Ernest G. Cleverdon Chair of Business and Management at the University of South Alabama. He formerly chaired the Division of Management and Marketing at the University of Tulsa and has taught marketing in Australia, Greece, and the United Kingdom.

Dr. Boone has been active in applying computer technology to marketing education. His research on marketing information systems has been published in the Proceedings of the American Marketing Association, Business Horizons, *and the* Journal of Business Strategy. *His marketing simulations include* Marketing Strategy *(Charles E. Merrill Publishing Company, 1971 and 1975) and* The Sales Management Game *(McGraw-Hill, 1989). His research has also been published in such journals as the* Journal of Marketing, Journal of Retailing, Journal of Business of the University of Chicago, Business, Health Marketing Quarterly, Journal of Business Research, *and the* Journal of Marketing Education. *He has served as president of the Southwestern Marketing Association and vice-president of the Southern Marketing Association.*

David L. Kurtz (Ph.D.) heads the Department of Marketing and Transportation at the University of Arkansas where he holds the R. A. and Vivian Young Chair of Business Administration. Dr. Kurtz has also taught at Seattle University, Eastern Michigan University, Davis & Elkins College, and Chisholm Institute of Technology (now part of Monash University) in Melbourne, Australia.

Dr. Kurtz has authored or coauthored 24 books and more than 70 articles, cases, and papers. His text Foundations of Marketing *(Louis E. Boone and Dale M. Beckman, coauthors) is the leading introductory marketing text in Canada. Dr. Kurtz has served as president of the Western Marketing Educators Association and vice-president of the Academy of Marketing Science.*

Brief Contents

Contents

PART **2**   Marketing Planning and Information   115

P A R T 3   Buyer Behavior and Market Segmentation   187

P A R T **4**   **Product Strategy   295**

CHAPTER 9   Product Strategy   296

PART 6   **Promotional Strategy**   523

CHAPTER 16   Introduction to Promotion   524

PART 7

Pricing Strategy   625

Source: Used with permission of Kraig Carlstrom, photographer, and The Coca-Cola Company.

This chalet in the Snowy River area of Australia is one of The Coca-Cola Company's 9 million customers—people who sell soft drinks and other products to consumers. For all marketers, understanding and satisfying the changing needs of customers have never been more important than in today's increasingly competitive global marketing environment.

PART **I**

The Contemporary Marketing Environment

....

I

Marketing in Profit and Nonprofit Settings

CHAPTER OBJECTIVES

1. To explain the types of utility and the role marketing plays in their creation.

2. To relate the definition of marketing to the concept of the exchange process.

3. To contrast marketing activities during the three eras in the history of marketing.

4. To explain the concept of marketing myopia.

5. To identify and briefly explain the types of nonprofit marketing.

6. To identify the basic elements of a marketing strategy and the environmental factors that influence strategy decisions.

7. To explain the universal functions of marketing.

8. To list three reasons for studying marketing.

The Mazda Miata, one of the most remarkable marketing success stories of the 1990s, is the result of a unique cooperative effort by a Japanese auto executive and a former American journalist. The Japanese is Kenichi Yamamoto, head of Mazda Motor Corp. and one of the industry's most creative thinkers. The American is Robert Hall, an automotive journalist who never forgot the joys of the rag-top two-seater sports cars of his youth. As Hall puts it, "My dad used to drive my twin brother and me all over California in little tea-bagger sports cars with the top down. My dad owned a red MG-TD, a Triumph TR2, and several Austin-Healeys. He taught my brother and me how to drive them in the Rose Bowl parking lot in Pasadena."

These relatively inexpensive British sports cars had disappeared by 1980. Their manufacturers simply failed to keep up with technological advancements, stronger safety requirements, and stiffer clean-air regulations. Hall met Yamamoto in 1978, seven years after living in Japan as an exchange student. The two men conversed about the world of transportation, and Hall suggested that Yamamoto experience the true joy of driving by taking the wheel of a Triumph Spitfire. Finally, they located a Spitfire in Japan to borrow. Yamamoto saw the marketing opportunity of a lifetime; he would create a blend of 1950s British styling with 1990s Japanese quality. He set up two competing study teams, one in Tokyo and one headed by Hall in Irvine, California.

Hall had specific ideas in mind for his team. The car would be a convertible because American buyers—the firm's primary target market—associate sports cars with openness. In addition, he wanted rear-wheel drive to create the feel of the 1950s-era roadsters. The low-slung, curvy exterior and the elliptical door handles and locks should create a unified styling theme reminiscent of the classic sports cars. Dozens of refinements in the engine and exhaust systems were made to produce the sound of the early roadsters. Rod Bymaster, a product planner at Mazda Motor of America chose the name *Miata* from an old German dictionary because of its sound and its meaning: "high reward."

A jury of Mazda executives concurred with Hall's concepts by selecting his design. The Mazda Miata was introduced to U.S. buyers at a retail price of $13,800. Buyer acceptance was overwhelming. Waiting lists appeared at Mazda dealerships, and classified ads began to appear with offers by purchasers to resell their Mazdas at prices as high as $10,000 above the retail purchase price. Mazda clearly succeeded in recognizing a consumer need and filling it.[1]

Photo source: Copyright 1990 Mazda Motor of America, Inc. Used by permission.

Chapter Overview

All organizations perform two basic functions: They produce a good, a service, or an idea, and they market it. This is true of all firms—from international giants such as Mazda to an exclusive French boutique. It is true of both profit-seeking firms and nonprofit organizations. Production and marketing are the essence of economic life in any society.

Increasingly, the marketplace is becoming globally oriented as the goods and services resulting from the performance of production and marketing functions are crossing national boundaries. By producing and marketing high-demand footwear products promoted by internationally recognized pop star Michael Jackson, L.A. Gear generates 15 percent of its annual sales outside the United States.[2] In 1990 Galeries Lafayette, France's largest department store chain, expanded to the United States by opening a store on Fifth Avenue in Manhattan.[3] Hong Kong diners craving American fast food can select from among 51 McDonald's restaurants located in the tiny British crown colony.[4]

utility
Want-satisfying power of a good or service.

Through the production and marketing of goods, services, and ideas, organizations satisfy a commitment to society, to their customers, and to their owners. They create what economists call **utility**—the want-satisfying power of a good or service. The four basic kinds of utility—form, time, place, and ownership—are shown in Table 1.1.

Form utility is created when the firm converts raw materials and component inputs into finished goods and services. Glass, steel, fabrics, rubber, and other components are combined to form a new Ford Probe or Acura Integra. Cotton, thread, and buttons are converted into Benetton shirts. Dancers, sheet music, musical instruments, musicians, a director, and concert hall facilities are used to create a performance by the Bolshoi Ballet. Although marketing inputs may be important in specifying consumer and audience preference, the actual creation of form utility is the responsibility of the organization's production function.

Time, place, and ownership utilities are created by marketing. *Time* and *place utility* are created when goods and services are available to consumers when and where they want to purchase them, respectively. *Ownership utility* is created when title to the good or service may be transferred at the time of purchase.

This chapter sets the stage for the entire text by examining the meaning of marketing and its importance for all organizations. It describes the development

---

Table 1.1   Four Types of Utility

Type	Description	Examples	Organizational Function Responsible
Form	Conversion of raw materials and components into finished goods and services	Club Med vacation; Hyundai Motors	Production[a]
Time	Availability of goods and services when consumer wants them	Domino's Pizza's 30-minute home delivery service; DHL Worldwide Delivery service	Marketing
Place	Availability of goods and services at convenient locations	Vending machines in office buildings; Pizza Hut outlets in Moscow, Melbourne, and Minneapolis	Marketing
Ownership (Possession)	Ability to transfer title to good or service from marketer to buyer	Retail outlets (in exchange for currency or credit card payment)	Marketing

[a]Marketing provides inputs related to consumer preferences, but the actual creation of form utility is the responsibility of the production function.

of marketing in our society and its contributions and introduces the marketing variables used in a marketing strategy.

What Is Marketing?

To survive, all organizations must create utility. The designing and marketing of want-satisfying goods, services, and ideas is the foundation for the creation of utility. However, the role of marketing in an organization's success has only recently been recognized. This is particularly the case in the USSR and Eastern European nations that are currently in the process of converting from state-controlled to market-driven business ventures. Management author Peter F. Drucker emphasizes the importance of marketing in his book *The Practice of Management:*

If we want to know what a business is, we have to start with its purpose. And its purpose must lie outside the business itself. In fact, it must lie in society since a business enterprise is an organ of society. There is one valid definition of business purpose: to create a customer.[5]

How does an organization "create" a customer? Professors Guiltinan and Paul explain it this way:

Essentially, "creating" a customer means identifying needs in the marketplace, finding out which needs the organization can profitably serve, and developing an offering to convert potential buyers into customers. Marketing managers are responsible for most of the activities necessary to create the customers the organization wants. These activities include:

☐ *Identifying customer needs*

☐ *Designing goods and services that meet those needs*

☐ *Communicating information about those goods and services to prospective buyers*

☐ *Making the goods or services available at times and places that meet customers' needs*

☐ *Pricing goods and services to reflect costs, competition, and customers' ability to buy*

☐ *Providing for the necessary service and follow-up to ensure customer satisfaction after the purchase.*[6]

A Definition of Marketing

Ask five persons to define marketing, and five definitions are likely to follow. Due to their continuous exposure to advertising and personal selling, most respondents are likely to link marketing and selling. Over a quarter-century ago, the American Marketing Association, the international professional association in the marketing discipline, tried to standardize marketing terminology by defining marketing as "the performance of business activities that direct the flow of goods and services from producer to consumer or user."

But this definition proved too narrow. It also implied that marketing begins at the end of a producer's loading dock by emphasizing the flow of goods and services that already have been produced. It failed to recognize marketing's crucial role in analyzing consumer needs and securing information designed to ensure that the goods or services created by the firm's production facilities would

Figure 1.1   Marketing Concepts Applied by Profit and Nonprofit Organizations

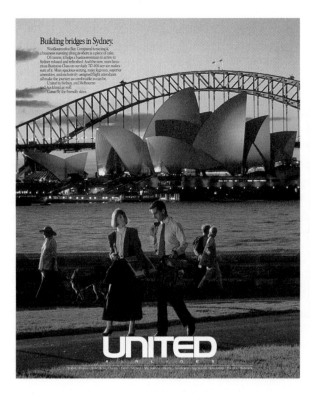

Source: Courtesy of United Airlines and TIME Environmental Challenge/Lord Einstein O'Neill & Partners: advertising agency (now known as Lord, Dentsu & Partners).

marketing

Process of planning and executing the conception, pricing, promotion, and distribution of ideas, goods, and services to create exchanges that will satisfy individual and organizational objectives.

match buyer expectations. The old definition ignored the thousands of nonprofit organizations that engage in marketing activities. A broader and more descriptive view was needed, one that would describe the firm or enterprise as an organized behavioral system seeking to generate output of value to consumers.

In 1985 the American Marketing Association replaced its antiquated definition with a broader one: **Marketing** is the process of planning and executing the conception, pricing, promotion, and distribution of ideas, goods, and services to create exchanges that will satisfy individual and organizational objectives.[7]

The expanded concept of marketing activities permeates all organizational functions. It assumes that the marketing effort will proceed in accordance with ethical practices and that it will be effective from the standpoint of both society and the organization. It also identifies the marketing variables of product, price, promotion, and distribution that are used to provide consumer satisfaction. In addition, it assumes that the consumer segments to be satisfied through the organization's production and marketing activities have been selected and analyzed prior to production. In other words, the customer, client, or public determines the marketing program. Finally, it recognizes that marketing concepts and techniques are applicable to nonprofit organizations as well as to profit-oriented businesses, as shown in the advertisements in Figure 1.1. United Airlines, a for-profit service firm, targets a select group—the international business traveler—by providing daily nonstop flights between the nations of the Pacific Rim and the United States. The ad represents United's marketing effort to capture more of the growing traffic to Australia and New Zealand. The "planets" ad illustrates how marketing concepts apply to nonprofit organizations. The sponsors of the Environmental Challenge Fund are seeking to heighten environmental awareness and to secure donations for scholarships to enable students to acquire the skills and training needed to protect the environment.

The Origins of Marketing

exchange process
Process by which two or more parties give something of value to each other to satisfy perceived needs.

The essence of marketing is the **exchange process,** in which two or more parties give something of value to each other to satisfy felt needs. In many cases, the item is a tangible good, such as a newspaper, a compact disk, or a pair of shoes. In others, intangible services, such as a car wash, a haircut, or a concert performance, are exchanged for money. In still others, funds or time donations may be offered to a Red Cross office, a church or synagogue, or a local recycling center.

The marketing function is both simple and direct in subsistence-level economies. For example, assume that a primitive society consists solely of Person A and Person B. Assume also that the elements of their standard of living are food, clothing, and shelter. The two live in adjoining caves on a mountainside. They weave their own clothes and tend their own fields independently. They are able to subsist even though their standard of living is minimal.

Person A is an excellent weaver but a poor farmer, whereas Person B is an excellent farmer but a poor weaver. In this situation, it would be wise for each to specialize in the work that he or she does best. The net result would be greater total production of both clothing and food. In other words, specialization and division of labor would lead to a production surplus. But neither Person A nor Person B would be any better off until each had traded the product of his or her individual labor, thereby creating the exchange process.

Exchange is the origin of marketing activity. In fact, marketing has been described as the process of creating and resolving exchange relationships. When there is a need to exchange goods, the natural result is a marketing effort on the part of the people involved. As Wroe Alderson, a leading marketing theorist, points out, "It seems altogether reasonable to describe the development of exchange as a great invention which helped to start primitive man on the road to civilization."[8]

While the cave dweller example is simplistic, it reveals the essence of the marketing function. A complex, industrial society has a more complicated exchange process, but the basic concept is the same: Production is not meaningful until a system of marketing has been established. Perhaps publisher Red Motley's adage sums it up best: "Nothing happens until somebody sells something."

Three Eras in the History of Marketing

Although marketing has always been a part of business, its importance has varied greatly. Table 1.2 identifies three eras in the history of marketing: (1) the production era, (2) the sales era, and (3) the marketing era.

Table 1.2 Three Eras in the History of Marketing

Era	Approximate Time Period in the U.S. and Other Highly Industrialized Economies	Prevailing Attitude
Production Era	Prior to 1920s	"A good product will sell itself."
Sales Era	Prior to 1950s	"Creative advertising and selling will overcome consumer resistance and convince them to buy."
Marketing Era	Last half of twentieth century	"The consumer is king! Find a need and fill it."

The Production Era

Until about 1925, most firms—even those operating in highly developed economies in Western Europe and North America—were production oriented. Manufacturers stressed production of quality products and then looked for people to purchase them. Pillsbury Company is an excellent example of a production-oriented company. Here is how the company's former chief executive officer, the late Robert J. Keith, described Pillsbury during its early years:

We are professional flour millers. Blessed with a supply of the finest North American wheat, plenty of water power, and excellent milling machinery, we produce flour of the highest quality. Our basic function is to mill high-quality flour, and, of course (and almost incidentally), we must hire [salespeople] to sell it, just as we hire accountants to keep our books.[9]

production orientation

Business philosophy stressing efficiency in producing a quality product; attitude toward marketing is "a good product will sell itself."

The prevailing attitude of this era was that a good product (defined in terms of physical quality) would sell itself. This **production orientation** dominated business philosophy for decades—indeed, business success was often defined solely in terms of production victories.

Although marketing had emerged as a functional activity within the business organization prior to the twentieth century, management's orientation remained with production for quite some time. In fact, what might be called industry's production era did not reach its peak until the early part of this century. The apostle of this approach to business operations was Frederick W. Taylor, whose *Principles of Scientific Management* was widely read and accepted. Taylor's approach reflected his engineering background by emphasizing efficiency in the production process. Later writers, such as Frank and Lillian Gilbreth, the originators of motion analysis, expanded on Taylor's basic concepts.

Henry Ford's mass-production line exemplifies this orientation. Ford's slogan, "They [customers] can have any color they want, as long as it's black," reflected a then prevalent attitude toward marketing. Production shortages and intense consumer demand were the rules of the day. It is easy to understand how production activities took precedence.

The "Better Mousetrap" Fallacy. The essence of the production era resounds in a statement made over 100 years ago by the philosopher Ralph Waldo Emerson:

If a man writes a better book, preaches a better sermon, or makes a better mousetrap than his neighbor, though he builds his house in the woods, the world will make a beaten path to his door.

But Chester M. Woolworth knows better. Woolworth, president of the nation's largest mousetrap producer, once designed a new mousetrap based on thorough research on the type of trap that would be most "appealing" to mice. The new model had a modern, brown plastic design, was completely sanitary, and was priced only a few cents more than the commonplace wood mousetrap. Also, it never missed!

But the better mousetrap failed as a new-product venture. While Woolworth's designers had created a quality product, they had forgotten the customer and the environment in which the purchase decision is made. The postmortem analysis of this marketing disaster went something like this. Men bought the majority of the newly designed plastic mousetraps. In most instances, it was also the responsibility of the male member of the household to set the trap before the family retired for the night. But the problem occurred the next morning when he failed to check the trap before leaving for work. Women were most likely to check the trap—during the morning in the case of wives not employed outside the home and in the afternoon after work in the case of working women. With the conventional wood trap, they would simply sweep both trap and mouse into a dustpan, minimizing the effort and time involved in this undesirable task. However, the new trap looked too expensive to throw away, even though it cost only a few cents more. Consequently, the wife was faced with first ejecting the mouse and then cleaning the instrument. In a short time, the new improved mousetrap was replaced with the traditional wood version.

The moral of the mousetrap story is obvious: A quality product is not successful unless it can be effectively marketed. Mr. Woolworth expressed it most eloquently when he said, "Fortunately, Mr. Emerson made his living as a philosopher, not a company president."[10]

The Sales Era

Between 1925 and the early 1950s, production techniques in the United States and other highly industrialized nations became more sophisticated, and output grew. Thus, manufacturers began to increase the emphasis on an effective salesforce for finding customers for their output. In this era, firms attempted to match their output to the potential number of customers for it. Companies with a **sales orientation** assume that customers will resist purchasing goods and services not deemed essential and that the task of personal selling and advertising is to convince them to buy.

Although marketing departments began to emerge during the sales era, they tended to remain in a subordinate position to production, finance, and engineering. Many chief marketing executives held the title of sales manager. Here is how Pillsbury described itself during the sales era:

We are a flour-milling company, manufacturing a number of products for the consumer market. We must have a first-rate sales organization which can dispose of all the products we can make at a favorable price. We must back up this sales force with consumer advertising and market intelligence. We want our sales representatives and our dealers to have all the tools they need for moving the output of our plants to the consumer.[11]

But selling is only one component of marketing. As Theodore Levitt has pointed out, "Marketing is as different from selling as chemistry is from alchemy, astronomy from astrology, chess from checkers."[12]

The Marketing Era

As personal incomes and consumer demand for goods and services dropped rapidly during the Great Depression of the early 1930s, marketing was thrust into a more important role. Organizational survival dictated that managers pay closer

sales orientation
Business philosophy assuming that consumers will resist purchasing nonessential goods and services; attitude toward marketing is that creative advertising and personal selling are required in order to overcome consumer resistance and convince them to buy.

The USSR's radical, painful transition from centralized controls to a market-driven economy is illustrated by this two-page Paketa watch ad. The tightly clenched fist surrounded with Russian copy contrasts with the wrist on the right that sports a Paketa watch and two fingers extended to form a peace sign. The ad's design spoofs the rigid Leninist propaganda posters of the 1920s, 1930s, and 1940s. The copy even carries a touch of tongue-in-cheek Russian attitude. The last line reads: "You will like them."

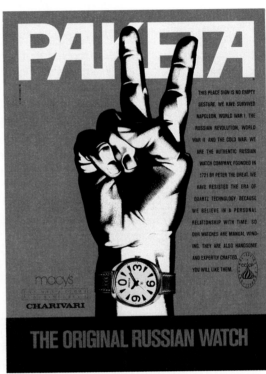

Source: Courtesy of Armando Testa Inc.

attention to the markets for their goods and services. This trend was halted by the outbreak of World War II, when rationing and shortages of consumer goods became commonplace. The war years, however, were only a pause in an emerging trend that gave a priority to the marketing concept.

Emergence of the Marketing Concept

What was the setting for this crucial change in management philosophy? Perhaps it can best be explained by the shift from a **seller's market**—one with a shortage of goods and services—to a **buyer's market**—one with an abundance of goods and services. When World War II ended, factories stopped manufacturing tanks and Jeeps and started turning out consumer goods again—an activity that had, for all practical purposes, stopped in early 1942.

The advent of a strong buyer's market created the need for a **consumer orientation** on the part of business. Goods and services had to be marketed, not just produced and sold. This realization has been identified as the emergence of the *marketing concept*. The recognition of this concept and its dominant role in

seller's market
Marketplace characterized by a shortage of goods and/or services.

buyer's market
Marketplace characterized by an abundance of goods and/or services.

consumer orientation
Business philosophy incorporating the marketing concept of first determining unmet consumer needs and then designing a system for satisfying them.

business dates from 1952, when General Electric's *Annual Report* heralded a new management philosophy:

[The concept] introduces the [marketer] at the beginning rather than at the end of the production cycle and integrates marketing into each phase of the business. Thus, marketing, through its studies and research, will establish for the engineer, the design and manufacturing [person], what the customer wants in a given product, what price he [or she] is willing to pay, and where and when it will be wanted. Marketing will have authority in product planning, production scheduling, and inventory control, as well as in sales, distribution, and servicing of the product.[13]

Marketing would no longer be regarded as a supplemental activity performed after the production process has been completed. The marketer would, for instance, now play the lead role in product planning. Marketing and selling would no longer be synonymous.

marketing concept
Companywide consumer orientation with the objective of achieving long-run success.

The **marketing concept** is a companywide consumer orientation with the objective of achieving long-run success. The key words are "companywide consumer orientation." All facets of the organization must be involved with first assessing and then satisfying customer wants and needs. The effort is not something to be left only to the marketers. Accountants working in the credit office and engineers designing products also play important roles. The words "with the objective of achieving long-run success" differentiate the concept from policies of short-run profit maximization. Since the firm's continuity is an assumed component of the marketing concept, companywide consumer orientation will lead to greater long-run profits than will managerial philosophies geared toward reaching short-run goals.

The marketing concept is a contemporary philosophy for dynamic organizational growth. But it has not been universally adopted. In centrally planned, developing nations such as the People's Republic of China, textile factory managers express amazement at such consumer garment favorites as white pants and stone-washed jeans. The production-orientation philosophies of such managers focus on more "practical" stain-hiding blue or brown colors on single styles produced in very large production runs.

Production-oriented firms can also be found in postindustrial societies characterized by high living standards. Consider Xerox Corporation President Paul Allaire's extensive internal study of operations for which outside marketing experts were hired to assess problems in different areas of the company. Results of the study pointed to marketing as the source of many problems and revealed that most functional areas of the company other than sales were operating with a production mentality. "We've done well as a technology-driven company," said William Spencer, director of corporate research, "but we need to become market-driven in order to continue the success we've had in the past. In order not to miss the large, new markets that are going to grow in the future, we've got to understand, firsthand, what their requirements are."

Xerox began a transition from being just a copier company to becoming a customer-driven systems company. A major part of the change involved instilling a marketing mindset in all functional areas of the company. William Lowe, head of a new development and manufacturing group, put it this way: "Part of becoming market-driven is that everybody's job is going to become marketing no matter where you are in the company." Implementing the marketing concept began at the top of the organization. Top managers became directly involved with customers by participating in a "customer officer-of-the-day" program, in which each executive, including Xerox chairman David Kearns, spends one day a month answering customer complaint calls and making sure that problems are

COMPETITIVE EDGE

NINTENDO DOMINATES THE TOY MARKET

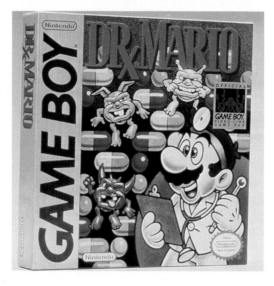

Today Nintendo is a household word, and video games are a staple of daily life in millions of American homes. But in 1983 most observers believed that the video game craze was over. While other manufacturers wrote it off and sought new ideas elsewhere, however, Nintendo took a closer look.

On the basis of careful marketing research, Nintendo determined that consumers were still interested in video games. The problem lay in the quality of the existing games. Consumers wanted better graphics and visuals, more interesting games, much more memory capacity, and better service. Nintendo developed a more sophisticated machine that could run more interesting graphics. In the process it helped establish a whole new medium: interactive entertainment.

The basic Nintendo unit is a small plastic box that is hooked up to a television set; interchangeable game cartridges are inserted into the box, and the players control the action with hand-held joysticks. By the 1990s, Nintendo units could be found in one out of three American homes, and sales of game cartridges had reached 50 million annually. The company controls a remarkable 80 percent share of the $5 billion video game market, and its Entertainment System is the best-selling toy in America—in 1990 it accounted for 21 percent of total U.S. toy sales.

Peter Main, Nintendo's vice-president for marketing, says the key to marketing success is to "accumulate knowledge. Talk to people. Listen carefully to their words." Nintendo makes a point of listening. Every week reports come in from stores equipped with scanners. Field reps with portable computers supplement the scanner reports with information about what they find on store shelves. Nintendo's professional game counselors—eighty video game wizards who answer calls from players—also contribute marketing insights. Main points out that the company is guided by "real-life consumer demand," not the perceptions or desires of retailers.

Nintendo's success has turned its name into a marketable commodity: There are Nintendo cereals, T-shirts, backpacks, jackets, bath towels, flashlights, even Halloween costumes. But as the market for video games approaches saturation, the company is seeking new ways to keep game players hooked. Competitors have already introduced more advanced game systems with improved graphics and sound, and Nintendo is following suit (reluctantly, since the more powerful machine makes the original version obsolete). The company has developed a hand-held system called Game Boy with stereo sound, multiplayer capacity, and interchangeable game cassettes. The NES Network modem system will enable customers to compete with other players throughout the nation. And Nintendo has donated $3 million to MIT's Media Laboratory in the hope that it will create games that stimulate thought.

Discussion Questions

1. Nintendo delayed the introduction of its second-generation entertainment system in the United States in order to keep players glued to its first-generation games. Meanwhile competitors introduced more powerful systems, accompanied by a few high-quality games. What were the risks in Nintendo's strategy?

2. As the video game market approaches saturation, Nintendo hopes that by creating more interest in educational games it can boost software sales. Educational games have never been very popular, however. What are Nintendo's chances of succeeding in this area?

Sources: Stephen Brookes, "Fanning Flames of Nintendo Fever," *Insight* (April 9, 1990), pp. 52–54; "But I Don't Wanna Play Nintendo Anymore," *Business Week* (November 19, 1990), pp. 52–54; Marco R. della Cava, "Nintendo Feels Heat from Advancing Competitors," *USA Today* (June 21, 1990), p. 4D; Matthew Grimm, "Nintendo Game Boy Heads into Adulthood," *Marketing Week* (October 29, 1990), p. 10; Cleveland Horton, "Nintendo Adopts Dual Strategy," *Advertising Age* (September 10, 1990), p. 40; Jon Berry, "Marketer of the Year," *Marketing Week* (November 17, 1989), pp. 14–15; Susan Moffat, "Can Nintendo Keep Winning?" *FORTUNE* (November 5, 1990), pp. 131–136; "The Newest Nintendo Will Take a Slow Boat to America," *Business Week* (July 2, 1990), p. 46; "The Nintendo Kid," *Newsweek* (March 6, 1989), pp. 64–68; Joseph Pereira, "Nintendo Looks to MIT for Brain-Teasing Video Games," *The Wall Street Journal* (May 15, 1990), p. B1; and Eric Lucas, "Nintendo Launches Video Games into Hyperspace," *Puget Sound Business Journal* (July 10, 1989), pp. 17, 24. *Photo source:* Courtesy of Nintendo of America Inc.

Figure 1.2   Converting Needs to Wants

Source: Courtesy of California Milk Advisory Board.

quickly solved. Xerox tied 50 percent of researchers' salary increases to how well they understood customer requirements. Product development became an integrative process, directly involving representatives from all functional areas —research, manufacturing, sales, service, administration, and distribution—as well as the customer.

One indication of the new market-driven attitude at Xerox is the way it measures customer satisfaction. In the past, Xerox asked customers how well its products performed. "Now we're asking how Xerox as a company is doing," says Allaire. "We're making sure customers are satisfied with our sales, installation, invoicing, service, and administrative processes in addition to the performance of our products."[14]

Converting Needs to Wants

Every consumer must acquire goods and services on a continuing basis to fill certain needs. The fundamental needs for food, clothing, a home, and transportation must be satisfied through purchase or, in some instances, temporary use in the form of rented property or hired or leased transportation. By focusing on the *benefits* resulting from these goods and services, effective marketing converts needs to wants. A need for clothing may be translated into a desire (or want) for designer clothes. The need for transportation may become a desire for a new Suzuki Samurai. The need for liquid refreshment may be satisfied with a product as basic as water or as expensive as Perrier. The California Milk Advisory Board advertisement shown in Figure 1.2 illustrates how marketing converts basic needs (satisfying thirst) into wants for specific goods (Extra Light 1% milk) by focusing on product benefits (trim torsos). Each black-and-white sportswear garment carries a hang tag telling the consumers about the nutritional value of milk and sports the slogan "Milk. It Does a Body Good." Consumer demand for this swimwear has been so strong that a line of "cow clothes" ranging from T-shirts and bike shorts to leotards and capri pants are now being offered for sale by such retailers as J.C. Penney, Nordstrom, and Macy's.[15]

Avoiding Marketing Myopia

marketing myopia
Term coined by Theodore Levitt in his argument that executives in many industries fail to recognize the broad scope of their businesses; according to Levitt, future growth is endangered because the executives lack a marketing orientation.

The emergence of the marketing concept has not been devoid of setbacks. One troublesome situation has been what Theodore Levitt calls *marketing myopia.*[16] According to Levitt, **marketing myopia** is management's failure to recognize the scope of its business. Future growth is endangered when management is product oriented rather than customer oriented. Levitt cites many service industries—dry cleaning, electric utilities, movies, and railroads—as examples of marketing myopia.

Changing marketplace conditions during the past decade, including deregulation, increased competition, and alternative sources of supply, have forced public utility managers to move from a product to a customer orientation. "We suffered from the same thing that other public utilities suffered from: myopia," said Mike Slota, vice-president of sales and marketing for Public Service Company of New Mexico, an Albuquerque-based electric utility firm. Tackling the problem of steadily declining profits, Public Service and many other utilities across the nation began conducting marketing research to better understand the needs and wants of commercial and residential customers. Based on their findings, they have developed innovative pricing programs to attract commercial customers and conservation programs that help customers use electricity more efficiently. Research conducted by Florida Power and Light showed that older citizens were concerned with safety. The utility responded by developing an outdoor security lighting program to help make communities safer. It not only made the citizens feel more secure, but also helped the utility use up some of its overcapacity.[17]

To avoid marketing myopia, organizational goals must be broadly defined and oriented toward consumer needs. British Airways, for example, has redefined its business as travel rather than just air transportation. The firm now offers complete travel services, such as hotel accommodations, credit, and ground transportation, in addition to air travel. Esprit de Corps, the San Francisco–based clothing designer and manufacturer, describes itself as a "lifestyle" company rather than a clothing firm and offers, in addition to clothing collections, accessories, shoes, kids' wear, eyewear, and bed and bath accessories. Revlon founder and president Charles Revson understood that a broader focus on benefits rather than on products is required. As Revson described it, "In the factory we make perfume; in the store we sell hope." Table 1.3

Table 1.3   Avoiding Marketing Myopia by Focusing on Benefits Provided by the Organization

Company	Myopic Description	Marketing-Oriented Description
British Telecom	"We are a telephone company."	"We are a communications company."
Burlington Northern	"We are in the railroad business."	"We are in the transportation business."
Royal Dutch Petroleum	"We are in the petroleum business."	"We are in the energy business."
Walt Disney Enterprises	"We are in the animated-film business."	"We are in the entertainment business."

illustrates how firms in a number of other industries have overcome myopic thinking with a marketing-oriented description of their businesses that focuses on consumer need satisfaction.

Broadening the Marketing Concept to Nonprofit Marketing

In the early 1960s, several writers suggested that marketing should be concerned with issues beyond the traditional profit-oriented domain. Marketing was beginning to be perceived as having a wider application than was formerly believed. A major breakthrough came two decades ago with the publication of Kotler and Levy's classic article arguing that the marketing concept should be broadened to include the nonprofit sector of society.[18] Marketing, they proposed, is a generic activity for all organizations. Thus, the **broadening concept** extended the marketing concept to nontraditional exchange processes.

broadening concept
Expanded view of marketing as a generic function to be performed by both profit-seeking and non-profit organizations.

The broadening concept was not accepted by all marketers. Some argued that it was an unwarranted extension of the marketing concept.[19] Others said the concept might be responsible for undesirable social changes and disorder.[20] But despite such dissent, the broadening concept has been widely adopted by nonprofit organizations. The Canadian armed forces use advertising to recruit volunteers; Red Cross and Red Crescent conduct marketing research to help charities attract donors around the world; and the San Diego Zoo employs a goodwill ambassador to promote and publicize the zoo's reputation worldwide.

During the past decade, financial pressures resulting from increased competition for donations and cutbacks in government funding have prompted more nonprofit organizations to adopt the marketing concept. Indeed, some nonprofit organizations have been forced to turn to marketing to ensure their survival. The Los Angeles Mission, for example, faced a major crisis when a county building inspector threatened to close down the mission's Skid Row facility unless the building was renovated to meet new earthquake safety standards. The renovation would have cost $500,000, four times the mission's annual budget of $125,000. Like many nonprofits, the mission had no marketing plan; it raised funds by simply contacting existing donors once or twice a year and asking for contributions. For more than 30 years the mission had used donor gifts to provide food and shelter for the city's hungry and homeless. But board members realized much more had to be done if the mission were to continue servicing the poor plus raise the additional capital for renovation. With the help of an outside marketing consultant, they developed a marketing strategy to maximize contributions from existing donors and attract new donors. Existing donors were sent monthly appeal letters, and a newspaper advertising campaign expanded the donor list. Funds generated by these marketing efforts resulted in a dramatic turnaround, enabling the mission not only to renovate its old building but to build a new $11 million facility to house 300 men, women, and children each night. Today, the mission's annual budget tops $6 million.[21]

Marketing in Nonprofit Organizations

Although a latecomer to the management of nonprofit organizations, marketing has become an important part of the operational environment of many successful nonprofit groups. A substantial part of every economy is made up of nonprofit organizations—those whose primary objective is something other than returning a profit to its owners. The 1.2 million nonprofit organizations operating in the

Table 1.4   Types of Nonprofit Marketing

Type	Brief Description	Examples
Person Marketing	Marketing efforts designed to cultivate the attention, interest, and preference of a target market toward a person	Celebrities (such as Arsenio Hall, Princess Diana, Gabriela Sabatini, and Luciano Pavorotti); political candidates ("Yeltsin for Premier," "John Major for Prime Minister")
Place Marketing	Marketing efforts designed to attract visitors to a particular area, improve consumer images of a city, state, or nation, and/or attract new business	"There's never been a better time to say G'day." (Australia) "The most surprising tropical island." (Singapore) "It all starts here." (Greece)
Idea Marketing	Identification and marketing of a cause or social issue to selected target markets	"Don't rubbish Australia." "Save the rain forest." "No Nukes!"
Organization Marketing	Marketing efforts of mutual-benefit organizations, service organizations, and government organizations that seek to influence others to accept their goals, receive their services, or contribute to them in some way	"Reach for the union label." "United Way Brings Out the Best in All of Us." "Army: Be All That You Can Be." "Feed the Children."

United States employ almost 11 million people (including volunteers) and generate an estimated $300 billion in revenues each year. The nonprofit sector is growing rapidly: two of every three nonprofits now operating were formed since 1960.[22] It includes religious and human service organizations, museums, libraries, secondary schools, many hospitals, colleges and universities, symphony orchestras, fraternal organizations, and thousands of other groups such as government agencies, political parties, and labor unions.

Nonprofit organizations operate in both public and private sectors. Federal, state, and local government units and agencies whose revenues are derived from tax collection have service objectives that are not keyed to profitability targets. The nation's Department of Defense, for example, provides protection; a state department of natural resources regulates conservation and environmental programs; and the local animal control officer enforces ordinances that protect people and animals.

The private sector has an even more diverse array of nonprofit organizations. Art institutes, the University of Miami's football team, labor unions, hospitals, private schools, the March of Dimes, the Rotary Club, and the local country club are all examples of private-sector, nonprofit organizations. Some, like Miami's football team, may return a surplus to the university that can be used to cover other activities, but the organization's primary goal is to win football games. The diversity of nonprofit groups suggests the presence of numerous organizational objectives other than profitability. In addition to organizational goals, nonprofit groups differ from profit-seeking firms in other ways.

Types of Nonprofit Marketing

Nonprofit organizations have a special set of characteristics that influence their marketing activities. Like profit-seeking firms, nonprofits may market a tangible good or an intangible service. The U.S. Postal Service, for example, offers stamps (a tangible good) and mail delivery (an intangible service). As Table 1.4 shows, four categories of nonprofit marketing can be identified: person marketing, place marketing, idea marketing, and organization marketing.

Figure 1.3   Place Marketing: The U.S. Virgin Islands

See what the world is like when nature takes care of itself.

Fascinating iguanas, rare turtles, fragile reefs and seagrass beds—they're all protected by law in the United States Virgin Islands. Two thirds of lovely St. John is a protected national park. So is St. Croix's incredible Buck Island. And St. Thomas' Magens Bay is called "one of the three most beautiful beaches in the world." Just think—all this natural beauty surrounds luxurious resorts, historic towns, world-class dining and world-class shopping.   See your travel agent.

St.Croix St.John St.Thomas
The American paradise. United States Virgin Islands
© 1990 United States Virgin Islands Division of Tourism: Atlanta, Chicago, LA, Miami, NYC & D.C.

Source: Courtesy of United States Virgin Islands Division of Tourism/Greengage Associates.

person marketing
Marketing efforts designed to cultivate the attention, interest, and preference of a target market toward a person (typically a political candidate or celebrity).

place marketing
Marketing efforts to attract people and organizations to a particular geographic area.

Person Marketing.   One category of nonprofit marketing, **person marketing,** refers to efforts designed to cultivate the attention, interest, and preferences of a target market toward a person.[23] Campaigns for political candidates and promotions for celebrities are examples of person marketing. In political marketing, candidates target two markets: They attempt to gain the recognition and preference of voters and the financial support of donors. Increasing numbers of campaign managers are using computerized marketing research to identify voters and donors and then design advertising to reach those markets. Other promotional efforts include personal handshakes, political rallies, fund-raising dinners, and publicity.

Place Marketing.   Another category of nonprofit marketing is **place marketing,** which refers to attempts to attract customers to a particular area. Cities, states, and countries publicize their tourist attractions to lure vacation travelers. The U.S. Virgin Islands Division of Tourism is attempting to entice tourists to visit this three-island Caribbean territory through marketing efforts such as the ad shown in Figure 1.3. Use of the slogan "American Paradise" in advertising messages (and on Virgin Islands auto license plates) is intended to communicate the fact that this vacation destination is, in fact, a U.S. territory, not a foreign land.

To stimulate economic growth within the United States, many states and cities launch marketing campaigns aimed at attracting new businesses. For

Figure 1.4   An Example of Idea Marketing

Source: Courtesy of the Alcoholism Council of Greater New York/Lord Einstein O'Neill & Partners: advertising agency (now known as Lord, Dentsu & Partners)/James Salzano: Photographer.

example, aggressive marketing has helped the State of Tennessee revitalize its economy. Tennessee's "Where the world comes to work" campaign takes an international approach by targeting both U.S. and foreign firms. To attract new businesses, Tennessee promotes its major strengths: its central location in the United States and, on a global scale, its convenient location between Tokyo and London; its travel/transportation system, such as major airline hubs and the axis of Federal Express; a capable work force; and the state's commitment to education, human services, and quality of life. Tennessee's marketing efforts have paid off. Businesses have opened or expanded in the state faster than one a day in a two-year period, including U.S. firms and companies from Japan, the United Kingdom, Germany, Sweden, Belgium, and Canada.

idea marketing
Identification and marketing of a cause to chosen consumer segments.

Idea Marketing.   A third category of nonprofit marketing, **idea marketing,** refers to the identification and marketing of a cause or social issue to selected consumer market segments. Idea marketing covers a wide range of issues, including literacy, physical fitness, gay and lesbian rights, family planning, prison reform, control of overeating, environmental protection, elimination of birth defects, prevention of child abuse, gun control, and punishment of drunk driving. The advertisement in Figure 1.4 is an example of idea marketing. This "Don't drink when you're pregnant" campaign, sponsored by the Alcoholism Council of Greater New York, aims to help prevent birth defects.

Due to the curtailment of government funding, an increasing number of nonprofit organizations are enlisting the help of for-profit firms in the marketing of causes and social issues. For example, Beatrice/Hunt-Wesson, a grocery products manufacturer, has joined the World Wildlife Fund in promoting the cause of saving endangered species. Through a program of coupon redemptions for Beatrice products, consumers can buy stuffed toy replicas of animals on the

Figure 1.5   An Example of Organization Marketing

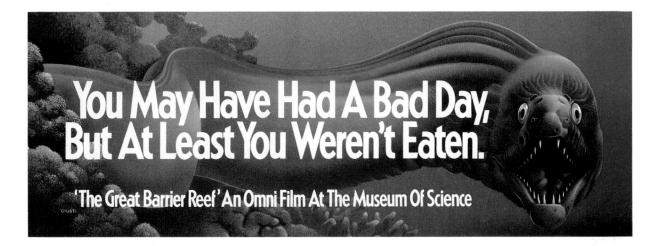

Source: Courtesy of Museum of Science, Boston.

endangered list. The World Wildlife Fund uses the funds from the purchases for the animals' preservation.[24]

Organization Marketing.

organization marketing
Marketing by mutual benefit organizations, service organizations, and government organizations that seek to influence others to accept their goals, receive their services, or contribute to them in some way.

Finally, the category of nonprofit marketing that we call **organization marketing** involves attempts to influence others to accept the goals of, receive the services of, or contribute in some way to an organization. For example, through billboard ads such as the one in Figure 1.5, the Museum of Science in Boston invites the public to visit the museum and experience the underwater world by viewing the Omni film *The Great Barrier Reef.* Organization marketing includes mutual benefit organizations (churches, labor unions, and political parties), service organizations (colleges and universities, hospitals, and museums), and government organizations (military services, police and fire departments, and the U.S. Postal Service). An example of organization marketing is Wisconsin Calling, a phonathon program set up by the University of Wisconsin Foundation that targets UW-Madison alumni. Through this fundraising program, student callers contact alumni across the country to solicit their financial support, update alumni records, and answer questions about the university.

Another example of organization marketing is the marketing efforts of public television stations. WTTW/Channel 11 in Chicago has a strong track record in marketing, which has helped the station increase its number of subscribers from 21,000 to 225,000 families. Viewer contributions are an important revenue source for WTTW, accounting for almost 50 percent of the station's annual income. The major challenge facing WTTW is getting viewers to contribute to the organization. William Natale, the station's director of publicity and promotion, says, "It's a constant struggle to try and get the money we need to put programs on. A lot of people watch us and don't feel obligated to pay for the programming." To boost subscriptions, WTTW holds several pledge drives a year and conducts an extensive direct mail campaign tied to a sweepstakes promotion. Another 25 percent of the station's income comes from production contracts. WTTW produces shows such as "The Frugal Gourmet" and "Sneak Previews" and markets them to other public television stations, and it creates pilot programs that it markets to cable channels such as Disney and HBO.[25]

Characteristics of Nonprofit Marketing

An important distinction between nonprofits and for-profit companies is that nonprofit organizations often market to multiple publics, which complicates decision making regarding the correct market to target. Political candidates, for example, target both voters and campaign contributors. One writer describes it this way:

Nonprofit organizations normally have at least two major publics to work with from a marketing point of view: their clients and their funders. The former pose the problem of resource allocation and the latter, the problem of resource attraction. Besides these two publics, many other publics surround the nonprofit organization and call for marketing programs. Thus, a college can direct marketing programs toward prospective students, current students, parents of students, alumni, faculty, staff, local business firms, and local government agencies. It turns out that business organizations also deal with a multitude of publics, but their tendency is to think about marketing only in connection with one of these publics, namely their customers.[26]

A second distinguishing characteristic of nonprofit marketing is that a customer or service user may wield less control over the destiny of a nonprofit organization than would be true for a profit-seeking firm. A government employee may be far more concerned with the opinion of a member of the legislature's appropriations committee than with that of a service user. Further, nonprofit organizations often possess some degree of monopoly power in a given geographic area. An individual might object to the United Fund's inclusion of a crisis center among its beneficiary agencies. But a contributor who responds to the United Fund appeal recognizes that a portion of total contributions will go to the agency in question.

Another potential problem involves the resource contributor, such as a legislator or financial backer, who interferes with the marketing program. It is easy to imagine a political candidate harassed by financial supporters who want to replace an unpopular campaign manager (the primary marketing position in a political campaign).

Perhaps the most commonly noted feature of the nonprofit organization is its lack of a *bottom line*—business jargon referring to the overall profitability measure of performance. Profit-seeking firms can measure profitability in terms of sales and revenues. While nonprofit organizations may attempt to maximize their return from a specific service, less exact goals, such as service-level standards, are the usual substitute for an overall evaluation. The net result is that it is often difficult to set marketing objectives that are aligned specifically with overall organizational goals.

A final characteristic is the lack of a clear organizational structure. Nonprofit organizations often refer to constituencies that they serve, but these usually are less exact than, for example, the stockholders of a profit-oriented corporation. Nonprofit organizations often have multiple organizational structures. A hospital might have an administrative structure, a professional organization consisting of medical personnel, and a volunteer organization that dominates the board of trustees. These people may sometimes work at cross-purposes and disagree with the organization's marketing strategy.

While some of the above factors may also characterize profit-seeking firms, they are particularly prevalent in nonprofit organizations. However, all organizations, both for-profit and nonprofit, must develop a marketing strategy to satisfy the needs and wants of consumers.

Elements of a Marketing Strategy

Figure 1.6 illustrates the basic elements of a marketing strategy: (1) the target market, and (2) the marketing mix variables of product, distribution, promotion, and price that are directed toward satisfying the needs of the target market. The outer circle in the figure lists environmental factors that provide the framework within which marketing strategies are planned.

The Target Market

Since the focal point of marketing activities is the consumer, market-driven organizations begin their overall strategies with detailed descriptions of their **target market:** the group of consumers toward whom the firm decides to direct its marketing efforts. For firms such as Sears, the target market consists of consumers purchasing for themselves or their families. Other companies, such as General Dynamics Corporation, market most of their products to government purchasers. Still other firms provide goods and services to retail and wholesale buyers. In every instance, however, marketers should be as specific as possible in delineating their target markets. Consider the following examples:

□   *Stouffer's Lean Cuisine frozen-food line is targeted at weight-conscious 25- to 45-year-olds willing to pay premium prices for high-quality, microwavable convenience foods with relatively few calories.*

target market
Group of people toward whom a firm markets its goods, services, or ideas with a strategy designed to satisfy their specific needs and preferences.

Figure 1.6

Elements of a Marketing Strategy and Marketing's Environmental Framework

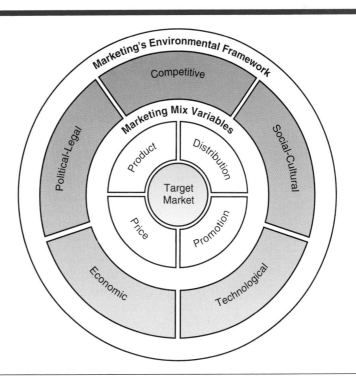

☐ *Contempo Casuals targets fashion-minded 18- to 25-year-old women.*

☐ *The Saab target market consists of well-educated, 30- to 40-year-old professionals and managers with household incomes of $50,000 to $100,000.*

Although the identification and satisfaction of a target market are subjects relevant to every chapter in this text, three chapters in Part 3 focus specifically on this subject. Consumer behavior is the subject of Chapter 6. Chapter 7 is devoted to the analysis of organizational buying behavior. Methods of segmenting markets are analyzed in Chapter 8.

The Marketing Mix Variables

After marketers select a target market, they direct company activities toward profitably satisfying that segment. Although thousands of variables are involved, marketing decision making can be divided into four strategies: product, pricing, distribution, and promotion. The total package forms the **marketing mix**—the blending of the four strategy elements to fit the needs and preferences of a specific target market. Each strategy is a variable in the mix. While the fourfold classification is useful in study and analysis, the *combination* of the variables determines the degree of marketing success.

The focus of the marketing mix variables on chosen consumer or organizational target markets is illustrated in Figure 1.6. In addition, decisions about product, price, distribution, and promotion are affected by the environmental factors in the outer circle of the figure. Unlike the controllable marketing mix elements, the environmental variables frequently are beyond the control of marketers. However, they may play a major role in the success of a marketing program and must be taken into consideration by marketers even if they cannot be controlled. It should also be stressed that the consumer is not a marketing mix component, since marketers have little or no control over the future behavior of present and potential consumers.

marketing mix
Blending the four strategy elements of marketing decision making—product, pricing, distribution, and promotion—to satisfy chosen consumer segments.

Product Strategy. In marketing, the word *product* means more than a good, service, or idea. Product is a concept that considers the satisfaction of all consumer needs in relation to a good, service, or idea. For example, Purina designed a new easy-to-reseal container for its Happy Cat moist catfood. Cardboard boxes often frustrate consumers because they are difficult to reseal. Purina's new package is a sturdy cardboard box with a hinged plastic top that is easy to open and close, keeping the contents fresh and moist. The package is also appealing to environmentally conscious consumers. When empty, it can be used to store nails, screws, and other small household items. Purina's new package is part of its product strategy aimed at satisfying consumer needs in relation to the product.[27]

Product strategy involves more than deciding what goods or services the firm should offer to a group of consumers. It also includes making decisions about customer service, package design, brand names, trademarks, warranties, product life cycles, positioning, and new-product development. General Motors' product strategy for its 1990 Oldsmobile models included a customer satisfaction program called the "Oldsmobile Edge." Designed to cultivate the loyalty of current customers, the program allows dissatisfied buyers of Oldsmobile cars and trucks to return them for full credit. Another part of the GM division's product strategy was upgrading the three-year vehicle warranty to cover repair for the entire car, not just the engine and transmission, and to provide emergency roadside service for any problem, including a dead battery or empty gas tank.[28] A product strategy chosen by Kraft, Inc., made it possible to extend the life cycle

product strategy
Element of marketing decision making comprising activities involved in developing the right good or service for the firm's customers; involves package design, branding, trademarks, warranties, product life cycles, and new-product development.

FOCUS ON ETHICS

COMMERCIALS IN THE CLASSROOM

. . . .

For schools struggling to cope with reduced budgets, Whittle Communications' offer is attractive: Whittle supplies about $50,000 worth of equipment, including a satellite dish, video recorder, and television sets, to schools that agree to show its 12-minute daily broadcast, Channel One, and keep records of the numbers of students watching.

Designed to appeal to teenagers, Channel One carries reports from journalists around the world, often accompanied by a map. The 10 minutes of news reporting are interspersed with 2 minutes of paid advertising. According to Christopher Whittle, founder and president of Whittle Communications, Channel One is a useful educational tool. According to critics, the program exploits a captive audience. The expensive equipment is loaned, not given, to the schools, while advertisers pay Whittle $150,000 for a 30-second commercial.

Channel One is just one of several approaches used by marketers in their efforts to reach the $250 billion youth market. Textbook covers, product samples, wall posters, and other devices are being used to convey commercial as well as educational messages to more than 45 million students enrolled in 102,000 elementary and secondary schools. The fact that educational settings are relatively free from advertising makes them especially tempting. Coupled with the temptation is a genuine concern for quality education; companies hardly need to be reminded that today's students are tomorrow's workers.

Educators, parent-teacher organizations, and consumer groups have leveled some harsh criticism at companies that advertise in the classroom. Consumers Union, for instance, has voiced opposition to teaching materials that mention products by brand, give incomplete or inaccurate information, or encourage purchasing via coupons, brand-specific recipes, or free samples. Channel One has come in for especially strong criticism, and several states have barred their school systems from purchasing the program. "Local school boards do not have the power to compel students to come to school to watch commercials," says an attorney involved in litigation over North Carolina's ban on Channel One. Despite the criticism, Whittle, who claims that "nobody is forcing anyone to watch anything," has managed to obtain commitments from 3,300 schools in 37 states.

Educators find themselves in a quandary on this issue. Many feel that school boards should have the right to screen course materials themselves, and they recognize the need for corporate commitment to education to fill the void left by decreased government support. "The majority of schools are unlikely to have the funds to fully equip their classrooms, especially with costly high-tech tools like computers and videodisc players," says one. The American Association of School Administrators has endorsed the use of corporate logos on equipment and materials provided to schools, but it does not support in-school advertising.

Discussion Questions

1. According to Campbell North America President Herb Baum, "There's nothing wrong with advertising to kids as long as you are truthful and do not use puffery." Does this extend to advertising in classrooms?

2. It has been argued that Channel One can be as useful an educational tool as *National Geographic*, which carries advertising and is available in schools. Is there a difference between these two types of educational materials?

Sources: John Birmingham, "Marketers—and Revisionists—Are Taking a Hard Look at Whittle," *Marketing Week* (April 9, 1990), pp. 20–28; Judann Dagnoli, "Consumers Union Hits Kids Advertising," *Advertising Age* (July 23, 1990), p. 4; Susan Dillingham, "The Classroom as a Marketing Tool," *Insight* (September 24, 1990), pp. 40–41; Joshua Hammer, "A Golden Boy's Toughest Sell," *Newsweek* (February 19, 1990), pp. 52–53; Laurie Petersen, "Risky Business: Marketers Make a Beeline for the Nation's Schools," *Marketing Week* (May 14, 1990), pp. 18–22; "Television at School: No Thanks," *The Economist* (April 14, 1990), p. 27.

of its Cheez Whiz process cheese spread by positioning it as a microwavable sauce available in convenient single-serve packages.

Three chapters in Part 4 deal with product strategy. Chapter 9 introduces the basic elements of product strategy, Chapter 10 discusses product mix decisions and new-product planning, and Chapter 11 focuses on strategies used in the marketing of services.

In some instances, marketers who design product strategies aimed at a specific target market find that their blend of product offerings and related services appeal to consumers around the globe. This is clearly illustrated by the world's largest McDonald's restaurant. The Moscow outlet is capable of seating 700 customers and is operated by 1,200 employees. Daily crowds of as many as 50,000 customers greeted its 1990 opening. Even today, the Soviet restaurant serves about 40,000 to 50,000 customers daily.

Source: Courtesy of Moscow-McDonald's.

pricing strategy

Element of marketing decision making that deals with the methods of setting profitable and justifiable exchange values for goods and services.

Pricing Strategy.   One of the most difficult areas of marketing decision making is **pricing strategy,** which deals with the methods of setting profitable and justifiable prices. It is closely regulated and subject to considerable public scrutiny.

One of the many factors that influence a marketer's pricing strategy is competition. Anheuser-Busch decided to change its pricing strategy when competitors Adolph Coors and Miller Brewing lowered the price of their beer. Attracted by the discounted prices, beer drinkers began buying Miller or Coors rather than Budweiser. Anheuser-Busch never had to compete on price in marketing its premium Budweiser brand, but as sales declined, the company decided to join the price war to keep its share of beer drinkers. Anheuser-Busch CEO August Busch said, "We don't want to start a bloodbath, but whatever the competition wants to do, we'll do. Everyone understands that market share is key in a mature industry." But price wars can be dangerous for marketers because once consumers get used to paying lower prices for a product they don't want to pay more. The decade-long price battle between Coke and Pepsi, for example, has kept soft-drink marketers from raising prices for more than eight years."[29]

Pricing strategy is the subject of Part 7. Chapter 19 analyzes the elements involved in determining prices. Chapter 20 covers the management aspect of pricing.

distribution strategy

Element of marketing decision making comprising activities and marketing institutions involved in getting the right good or service to the firm's customers.

Distribution Strategy.   Marketers develop **distribution strategies** to ensure that their products are available in the proper quantities at the right time and place. Distribution decisions involve modes of transportation, warehousing, inventory control, order processing, and selection of marketing channels. Marketing channels are made up of institutions such as retailers and wholesalers—all those involved in a product as it goes from producer to final consumer.

To illustrate the importance of distribution strategy, consider the problem Jolt Company, makers of Jolt cola, had in getting its product to consumers. Soft-drink

Figure 1.7   Advertising as Part of a Promotional Strategy

bottlers are the main distribution channel in the highly competitive soft-drink industry. When Jolt wanted to expand distribution beyond its regional Rochester, New York, base, the company realized it was locked out of many major markets because bottlers can carry only one cola. The small firm did not have the marketing clout or distribution channels of giant competitors such as The Coca-Cola Company and PepsiCo. So Jolt decided to use beer distributors instead. Because beer distributors were not accustomed to selling to Jolt's target market—the 21 and under age group—Jolt provided them with lists of target accounts, mainly convenience stores and pizza parlors on college campuses, where Jolt is sold in single cans rather than in multipacks. The distribution strategy worked. Jolt Company now has 330 beer distributors selling to accounts in all 50 states plus Canada, Japan, and Australia.[30]

Distribution strategy is covered in Part 5. Topics include channel strategy (Chapter 12), wholesaling (Chapter 13), retailing (Chapter 14), and physical distribution (Chapter 15).

Promotional Strategy. Promotion is the communication link between sellers and buyers. Organizations use many different means of sending their messages about goods, services, and ideas. The message may be communicated directly by salespeople or indirectly through advertisements and sales promotions. As the advertisement in Figure 1.7 illustrates, the Idaho Potato

promotional strategy
Element of marketing decision making that involves appropriate blending of personal selling, advertising, and sales promotion for use in communicating with and seeking to persuade potential customers.

Commission is emphasizing the taste and unique tradition of its potatoes. In developing a **promotional strategy,** marketers blend together the various elements of promotion that will communicate most effectively with their target market.

Promotional strategies serve different purposes and vary in size and scope. Procter & Gamble, which has been marketing only four products in the Soviet Union on a limited basis, aired a 12-minute commercial on Soviet television as its first major promotion in that country. The purpose of the long commercial was to introduce the company and its wide variety of household and personal care products, from Ivory soap to Crisco cooking oil, to the emerging market of 290 million Soviet consumers.[31] On a smaller scale, I Can't Believe It's Yogurt, a U.S. chain of frozen yogurt stores located mainly in shopping malls, uses a variety of promotions to get people to taste its product. The company hands out yogurt samples at local art fairs and sporting events and gives away premiums such as book covers, key chains, and balloons advertising the product. But the most effective promotion is the simplest, says Scott White, the company's director of marketing: "We'll make our best parfait and tell one of our employees to walk around the mall eating it. People come up and ask where they can get one."[32]

Promotional strategy is covered in Part 6. The concept of promotion is introduced in Chapter 16. Chapter 17 deals with advertising, sales promotion, and public relations. Personal selling and sales management are the topics of Chapter 18.

The Marketing Environment

Marketing decisions about target markets and marketing mix variables are not made in a vacuum. They must take into account the dynamic nature of the five dimensions of the marketing environment shown in Figure 1.6: competitive, political-legal, economic, technological, and social-cultural. Consider how the worldwide social and legal movement of environmentalism—the so-called "green revolution"—has influenced marketing decisions. Some firms are dropping products deemed harmful to the environment. DuPont, for example, decided to discontinue marketing chlorofluorocarbons (CFCs), an ingredient used in foam containers and cleaners, because of its potential hazard for destroying the earth's ozone layer.[33] Wal-Mart, the largest U.S. retailer, has launched an educational campaign to make consumers more aware of environmental issues. In-store posters in Wal-Mart retail outlets are part of the firm's effort encouraging consumers to recycle.[34] Other firms are designing products and packages that are biodegradable, recyclable, or take up less space in landfills. Colgate-Palmolive, for example, introduced new refill packages for Palmolive dishwashing detergent that take up "75 percent less space in landfills than bottles."

Even though disposable diapers account for only 1 percent to 2 percent of the nation's solid waste, they have been a focal point of environmental concerns. Procter & Gamble, whose Pampers brand represents almost 50 percent of the total market in the U.S., has invested millions in finding alternative diaper disposal methods. The photo of a tree seedling planted in accelerated-composting soil in Figure 1.8 reflects P&G's belief that composting is the answer to the environmental problems caused by used disposable diapers. Accelerated composting turns garbage into humus, an important element of fertile soil, in three to 14 days. Disposable diapers currently are about 80 percent compostable, but P&G is testing a 100 percent compostable disposable diaper.[35]

Figure 1.8

Addressing Environmental Concerns in Product Design

Source: @ Procter & Gamble; used by permission.

Dimensions of the marketing environment are discussed in more depth in Chapter 2. The significance of these dimensions in the global marketplace is presented in Chapter 3. The marketing environment is important because it provides a framework for all marketing activity. It influences the development of marketing plans and forecasts, which are described in Chapter 4, and the process of marketing research, the subject of Chapter 5. Marketers consider the environmental dimensions when they study consumer and organizational buying behavior, the topics of Chapters 6 and 7, respectively, and when they develop segmentation strategies, covered in Chapter 8.

Marketing Costs and Marketing Functions

Creation of time, place, and ownership utilities costs money. Numerous attempts have been made to determine marketing costs in relation to overall product costs and service costs, and most estimates have ranged between 40 and 60 percent. On the average, one-half of the costs involved in a product such as Pizza Hut pizza, an ounce of *Joy* perfume, a pair of Calvin Klein jeans, or even a European vacation can be traced directly to marketing. These costs are not associated with fabrics, raw materials and other ingredients, baking, sewing, or any of the other production functions necessary for creating form utility. What, then, does the consumer receive in return for this 50 percent marketing cost? What functions are performed by marketing?

As Table 1.5 reveals, marketing is responsible for the performance of eight universal functions: buying, selling, transporting, storing, standardization and grading, financing, risk taking, and securing marketing information. Some functions are performed by manufacturers, others by retailers, and still others by marketing intermediaries called wholesalers.

Table 1.5   Eight Universal Marketing Functions

Marketing Function	Description
A. Exchange Functions	
1. Buying	Ensuring that product offerings are available in sufficient quantities to meet customer demands
2. Selling	Use of advertising, personal selling, and sales promotion to match goods and services to customer needs
B. Physical Distribution Functions	
3. Transporting	Moving the product from its point of production to a location convenient for the purchaser
4. Storing	Warehousing products until needed for sale
C. Facilitating Functions	
5. Standardization and grading	Ensuring that product offerings meet established quality and quantity control standards of size, weight, and other product variables
6. Financing	Providing credit for channel members or consumers
7. Risk taking	Uncertainty about consumer purchases resulting from creation and marketing of goods and services that consumers may purchase in the future
8. Marketing information	Collection of information about consumers, competitors, and channel members for use in making marketing decisions

Buying and selling, the first two functions shown in Table 1.5, represent *exchange functions. Buying* is important to marketing on several levels. Marketers must determine how and why consumers buy certain goods and services. To be successful, they must seek to understand consumer behavior. In addition, retailers and other intermediaries must seek out products that will appeal to their customers. Since they are generating time, place, and ownership utilities through these purchases, they must make decisions concerning likely consumer preferences that will be expressed through purchases several months after orders are placed. *Selling* is the second half of the exchange process. It involves advertising, personal selling, and sales promotion in an attempt to match the firm's goods and services to consumer needs.

Transporting and storing are *physical distribution functions. Transporting* involves the physical movement of the goods from the seller to the purchaser. *Storing* involves the warehousing of goods until they are needed for sale. These functions frequently involve manufacturers, wholesalers, and retailers.

The final four marketing functions—standardization and grading, financing, risk taking, and securing market information—are often called *facilitating functions* because they assist the marketer in performing the exchange and physical distribution functions. Quality and quantity control *standards* and *grades,* frequently set by federal or state governments, reduce the need for purchasers to inspect each item. Specific tire sizes, for example, permit buyers to request a needed size and to know that they will receive a uniform size.

Financing is another marketing function because funds often are required for financing inventories prior to their sales. In many instances, manufacturers may provide financing for their wholesale and retail customers. In other cases, some types of wholesalers perform similar functions for their retail customers. Finally, retailers frequently permit their customers to make credit purchases.

The seventh function, *risk taking,* is part of most ventures. Manufacturers create goods and services based on their belief (and research studies) that a consumer need for them exists. Wholesalers and retailers acquire inventory based on similar expectations of future consumer demand. These uncertainties about future consumer behavior must be assumed by entrepreneurial risk takers when they market goods and services.

The final marketing function involves *securing market information.* Marketers gather information about their markets to obtain decision-oriented input about their customers—who they are, what they buy, where they buy, and how they buy. By collecting and analyzing market information, marketers also seek to understand why consumers purchase some goods and services and reject others.

The Study of Marketing

Marketing is a pervasive element in contemporary life. In one form or another, it is close to every person. Three of the most important things for students to know about marketing are as follows:

1. Marketing costs passed on to the consumer may account for the largest percentage of their personal expenditures. As pointed out earlier, approximately 50 percent of the total cost for the average product is for marketing.

   Cost alone, however, does not indicate the value of marketing. The living standards of citizens in highly developed nations are in large part a function of the country's efficient marketing system. When considered in this perspective, the system's costs seem reasonable. For example, marketing expands sales, thereby spreading fixed production costs over more units of output and reducing total output costs. Reduced production costs offset many marketing costs.

2. There is a good chance that many students will become marketers. Marketing-related occupations account for 25 to 33 percent of the jobs in the typical highly industrialized nation. History has shown that the demand for effective marketers is not affected by cyclical economic fluctuations.

3. Marketing provides an opportunity to contribute to society as well as to an individual company. Marketing decisions affect everyone's welfare. Further opportunities to advance to decision-making positions come sooner in marketing than in most occupations. (Societal aspects of marketing are covered in detail in later chapters.)

Why study marketing? The answer is simple: Marketing influences numerous facets of daily life as well as the future careers and economic well-being of almost everybody, to some degree. It is little wonder that marketing is now one of the most popular fields of academic study.

Each succeeding chapter in *Contemporary Marketing* includes detailed analysis and evaluation of at least one ethical issue. Different types of ethical dilemmas that may be confronted in marketing will also be examined.

Summary of Chapter Objectives

1. **Explain the types of utility and the role marketing plays in their creation.** Utility is the want-satisfying power of a good or service. There are four basic kinds of utility: form, time, place, and ownership. Form utility refers to the conversion of raw materials and component parts into finished products. Although marketing provides information about consumer wants

and needs, the actual creation of form utility is the responsibility of the production function. In contrast, marketing creates time, place, and ownership utilities. These utilities refer to making goods and services available when and where people want to buy them, and providing facilities for the transfer of title.

2. **Relate the definition of marketing to the concept of the exchange process.** The American Marketing Association has defined marketing as the process of planning and executing the conception, pricing, promotion, and distribution of ideas, goods, and services to create exchanges that satisfy individual and organizational objectives. The exchange process, by which two or more parties give something of value to each other to satisfy felt needs, is a critical aspect of this definition.

3. **Contrast marketing activities during the three eras in the history of marketing.** Firms were production oriented during the production era; the prevailing attitude was that quality products would sell themselves. Marketing was a secondary activity. In the sales era, the emphasis was on convincing people to buy. Marketing was, in essence, defined as selling. The marketing era saw the emergence of the marketing concept, a companywide consumer orientation with the objective of achieving long-run success.

4. **Explain the concept of marketing myopia.** Both production- and sales-oriented firms frequently do not achieve long-run success because they define the scope of their business around the product rather than customers' needs. The term *marketing myopia* was coined by Harvard marketing professor Theodore Levitt to describe this failure of the marketer to recognize the scope of the business. Future growth of an organization is endangered when management is myopic this way—that is, product rather than customer oriented.

5. **Identify and briefly explain the types of nonprofit marketing.** There are four types of nonprofit marketing. Person marketing focuses on an individual, such as a celebrity or political candidate. Place marketing attempts to attract people and/or businesses to a particular geographical area—city, state, or country. Idea marketing involves identifying and marketing a cause or idea to chosen consumer segments. Organization marketing refers to marketing efforts to influence others to accept the organization's goals or services or contribute to it in some way. Organization marketing is undertaken by (1) mutual-benefit organizations, such as churches, labor unions, and political parties; (2) service organizations, such as colleges, universities, hospitals, and museums; and (3) government organizations, such as the military services and police and fire departments.

6. **Identify the basic elements of a marketing strategy and the environmental factors that influence strategy decisions.** The two major variables in a marketing strategy are (1) analysis, evaluation, and selection of a target market and (2) the development of a marketing mix designed to satisfy the chosen target market. Marketing begins with an assessment of consumer wants and needs, the collection of information about potential consumer segments to be satisfied, and the ultimate choice of a consumer segment that will serve as the firm's target market. Once the target market has been selected, the marketing manager directs activities toward its satisfaction. The four strategy elements in marketing decision making are product strategy, pricing strategy, distribution strategy, and promotional strategy. The combination of these four elements is called the *marketing mix.* The five components of the marketing environment are the competitive environment, the political-legal environment, the economic environment, the technological environment, and the social-cultural environment.

7. **Explain the universal functions of marketing.** Marketing is responsible for the performance of eight universal functions as it creates time, place, and ownership utilities. Some of these functions are performed by manufacturers, others by retailers, and still others by marketing intermediaries such as wholesalers. The eight functions may be divided into three broad categories: (1) exchange functions (buying and selling); (2) physical distribution functions (transporting and storing); and (3) facilitating functions (standardization and grading, financing, risk taking, and securing marketing information).

8. **List three reasons for studying marketing.** Three basic reasons for studying marketing are (1) marketing costs may account for the greatest percentage of the consumer's personal expenditures; (2) there is a good chance that individual students will become marketers; and (3) marketing provides an opportunity to contribute to society as well as to an individual organization.

Key Terms

utility

marketing

exchange process

production orientation

sales orientation

seller's market

buyer's market

consumer orientation

marketing concept

marketing myopia

broadening concept

person marketing

place marketing

idea marketing

organization marketing

target market

marketing mix

product strategy

pricing strategy

distribution strategy

promotional strategy

Review Questions

1. Identify the types of utility created by marketing. What types are being created by the following examples?
   a. One-hour cleaners
   b. Blockbuster Video rental outlet
   c. Euro-Disneyland near Paris
   d. Annual boat and sports equipment show in a local convention center
   e. Regional shopping mall

2. Relate the definition of marketing to the concept of the exchange process.

3. Discuss the production and sales era. How does the marketing era differ from the previous eras?

4. Explain the concept of marketing myopia. Why is it likely to occur? What steps can be taken to reduce the likelihood of its occurrence?

5. What is person marketing? Contrast it with marketing of a consumer product such as magazines.

6. Why is idea marketing more difficult than place or organization marketing?

7. What did the General Electric annual report mean when it stated its plan to introduce the marketer at the beginning rather than at the end of the production cycle?

8. Identify the major variables of the marketing mix. Briefly contrast the mix variables in nonprofit marketing with those involved in for-profit marketing.

9. What are the components of the marketing environment? Why are these factors not included as part of the marketing mix? Is the target market a component of the marketing mix?

10. Categorize the following marketing functions as an exchange function, a physical distribution function, or a facilitating function. Choose a local retail store, and give an example of how it performs each of these eight functions:
    a. Buying
    b. Financing
    c. Securing marketing information
    d. Standardization and grading
    e. Selling
    f. Risk taking
    g. Storing
    h. Transporting

Discussion Questions

1. What type of nonprofit marketing does each of the following represent?
    a. International Brotherhood of Teamsters
    b. "South Korea: Land of the Rising Calm"
    c. British Museum
    d. Save the Whales Foundation
    e. National University of Singapore
    f. Girl Scouts
    g. Easter Seals

2. How would you explain marketing and its importance in the economy to someone not familiar with the subject?

3. Identify the product and the consumer market for each of the following organizations:
    a. Local cable television firm
    b. Montreal Expos baseball club
    c. Planned Parenthood
    d. Diet soft drink

4. Give two examples each of firms that you feel reflect the philosophies of the following eras. Defend your answers.
    a. Production era
    b. Sales era
    c. Marketing era

5. Choose a company in your area and briefly describe its target market. How are each of the marketing mix variables employed by this firm? Which of these variables appear to be emphasized in its marketing strategy?

Computer Applications

In this chapter, the origin of marketing activity was traced to the exchange process. Two of the eight fundamental marketing functions—buying and selling—are performed when suppliers exchange surplus goods or services for other items or money.

Figure 1 illustrates the most primitive form of exchange, in which producers contact one another directly to exchange surplus output. In this example of what might be termed *decentralized exchange,* the small barter economy consists of eight families living within a few miles of one another on a small island. At one time, each family was completely self-sufficient. Over time, however, each began to realize that it could increase its standard of living by specializing in the production of a limited number of products and then exchanging its surplus production for products produced

Figure 1

Decentralized Exchange
among Eight Families

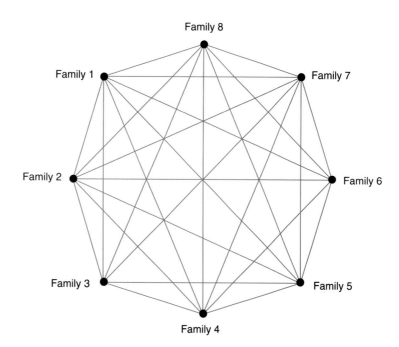

by the other families. Although the families were uncomfortable at first with the prospect of being dependent on others for products necessary for their own comfort and enjoyment, they gradually accepted this new approach to production and trade due to its ability to provide them with more goods and services than they could produce under the previous system of total self-sufficiency.

Although specialization produced benefits for the eight families, the decentralized exchange proved time consuming, since each family had to make direct contact with each of the other seven families to complete the process. Another source of complaint would occur when one family representative seeking to make an exchange with another family discovered that the second family had traveled to the residence of still another family to make an exchange, leaving no one at home.

Figure 1 illustrates the inefficiency of decentralized exchange by showing all of the connecting lines necessary for completing the transactions among the eight families — a total of 28.

Instead of resorting to drawing and then counting all the lines connecting the families, we can use the following formula to determine the number of transactions required to carry out decentralized exchange:

$$T = \frac{n(n-1)}{2},$$

where T is the number of transactions and n the number of producer families. In this case,

$$T = \frac{8(8-1)}{2} = \frac{8(7)}{2} = \frac{56}{2} = 28.$$

But what happens if the decentralized exchange economy is converted to a *centralized exchange system* through the introduction of some form of marketing intermediary such as a central market? The results are shown in Figure 2. The exchange process becomes much more efficient when a central market is created, because each family can contact the manager of the market directly to exchange surplus production for other needed products. The need to make direct contact with

Figure 2

Centralized Exchange among
Eight Families

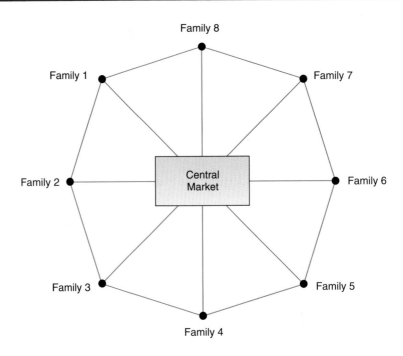

other families in order to facilitate exchange no longer exists. Instead of the 28 transactions required for decentralized exchange, only 8 transactions are needed when a marketing intermediary is introduced. The result is increased efficiency, since the marketing intermediary reduces the amount of work that must be done.

How much more efficient is centralized exchange than the former system of decentralized exchange? The following calculation provides the answer to this question:

$$\text{Percentage of Increased Efficiency} = \frac{\text{Number of Transactions with Decentralized Exchange}}{\text{Number of Transactions with Centralized Exchange}}$$

$$= \frac{28}{8}$$

$$= 350\%.$$

Directions: Use menu item 1 titled "Exchange Process" to solve each of the following problems.

Problem 1. Five small manufacturers were operating in close proximity to one another. Each manufacturer made purchases from and, in turn, sold products to the other four manufacturers. A marketing intermediary offered to serve as a linkage among the firms to reduce the time and costs involved in the old system of decentralized exchange. However, one of the manufacturers argued that the small number of firms was insufficient to justify a marketing intermediary. How much will efficiency increase if the intermediary is used?

Problem 2.   A group of nine families located in an isolated region near Nome, Alaska, have been engaged in decentralized exchange of surplus products for several years. They are considering opening a central market that would operate every Saturday in a conveniently located meeting place.

a.   How many transactions are involved under the present decentralized exchange system?

b.   How many transactions would be involved if the families decided to establish the central market?

c.   What effect would the central market have on efficiency?

Problem 3.   A small community of 75 farmers residing in a rural area of Wisconsin were considering the development of a central farmer's market for their exclusive use in trading with one another. How many transactions are currently necessary to conduct decentralized exchange among the 75 farmers? How many transactions will be necessary if the farmer's market is constructed and utilized by each farmer? What effect will the farmer's market have on efficiency?

Problem 4.   Thirty families emigrated to a small Pacific island located 800 miles east of Tasmania. Since they are completely dependent on trading surplus goods with one another, they have been actively engaged in a decentralized exchange system. Due to the problems involved in their current informal system of trade, they are considering a proposal to establish a central market.

a.   How many transactions are involved under the present system?

b.   How many transactions will be involved if the central market is established?

c.   Specify the impact of the central market in terms of increases in efficiency.

Problem 5.   Ten families currently reside on the small Caribbean island of Anta. Another eight families live on Benzille, another island three miles away. At the present time, the 10 families on Anta are engaged in decentralized exchange but do not trade with the residents of Benzille. Decentralized exchange is also in effect on Benzille. During recent trade discussions between a Benzille representative and an Anta resident, two proposals for increasing efficiency were presented:

a.   Establish two central markets, one located on Anta and the other on Benzille. Although a centralized exchange system would replace the previous system on both islands, no inter-island trade would be involved.

b.   Establish one large, central market on the currently uninhabited island of Centar, located midway between Anta and Benzille. Residents of both Anta and Benzille would utilize this market, and their original decentralized exchange systems would be eliminated.

Compare the current decentralized exchange systems on Anta and Benzille with the first proposal. How much will efficiency increase on Anta if the first proposal is implemented? On Benzille? How many transactions will be involved if the second proposal is implemented?

McDonald's in Moscow

Some companies are fortunate in their ability to attract a target market in nation after nation. The combination of benefits offered satisfies needs and wants present in people regardless of their income, language, or geographic location. Such a firm is McDonald's. World travelers are comforted in locating the familiar Golden Arches, realizing that they are assured of receiving known quality levels when they order a Big Mac, fries, and Coke in Milan, London, Tokyo, or Toronto. But could McDonald's succeed in the Soviet Union? George Cohon, president and CEO of McDonald's Restaurants of Canada, devoted part of his time during the last 14 years, despite his many other obligations and duties, ensuring just such a success.

During the 1976 Summer Olympics in Montreal, McDonald's loaned one of its buses to help transport visitors and officials to and from the games. Cohon noticed a group of Soviet officials on the bus, struck up a conversation, and ended by inviting them to dinner at the McDonald's across from the Montreal Forum. At the time, it was the busiest McDonald's in the world and Cohon could see that the Soviets were impressed with the efficiency of the operation.

This was the beginning of negotiations for opening a McDonald's in Moscow. The prospect of entering a market with 290 million potential customers drove Cohon to pursue his dream. Cohon was persistent in overcoming the political barriers, until finally he was able to negotiate a joint venture with the Moscow City Council to build and operate 20 McDonald's restaurants in Moscow. On January 31, 1990, the largest McDonald's in the world opened in Pushkin Square off Gorky Street. Opening-day sales set a new record for a single-day's operation, with 30,000 meals served.

At first glance, the Soviet Union did not appear to be a very desirable location for a quick-service operation, since food quality there does not always come up to Western standards, and McDonald's prides itself on quality ingredients in its products. Soviet tastes are also quite different from Western tastes and McDonald's could not be sure the Soviets would savor burgers and fries. Another formidable obstacle was that worker attitudes differ greatly in the Soviet Union, which potentially could slow the quick-service operation to a turtle's pace. Inefficient distribution systems also posed a potential problem, since ingredients and materials might not be available when needed. And probably the best known problem for Western firms establishing joint ventures was that it meant large capital sums would have to be invested in the Soviet Union.

One remaining obstacle — and certainly the one of most concern — was the ruble. By law, the ruble cannot be taken out of the Soviet Union, and it is not traded on the world market. Foreign investors who sell their products for rubles cannot get their profits out of the country. And, if the products are sold for dollars, nobody except foreign tourists and members of the Soviet elite can afford to purchase them.

So how did McDonald's of Canada expect to ensure that their Soviet product offerings would conform to McDonald's internationally uniform standards and also derive a profit from the venture? Since Soviet food shortages often have less to do with production than with distribution, the McDonald's Soviet operation could only succeed by organizing its own distribution system through its Moscow plant and trucks. The venture could achieve profits by taking a long-run approach. After all, the Soviet joint venture agreement called for the opening of an initial 20 restaurants in Moscow. McDonald's would pour dollars into the first outlet and into a vast production and distribution network necessary to support it, but the product would be sold for rubles. The rubles would be used to pay all current expenses, such as salaries and materials purchases, and to finance the next outlet. In the future, some of the restaurants would accept only dollars for purchases, and those dollars would be used to make any necessary foreign purchases and to help build McDonald's business in the Soviet Union. Remaining dollars would constitute a profit that could be utilized in long-term growth strategies in the Soviet Union.

This plan only made it *possible* to make a profit; it did not *guarantee* that a profit would be made. Cohon saw that what interested the Soviets was not only the food but also the know-how that made the operation efficient. McDonald's in Moscow would be an example of Western capitalism at its best, and Cohon knew that the Soviets wanted to experience this as well as taste Western food. While the meat-and-potatoes diet was familiar to them, the presentation and the preparation differed considerably from anything the Soviets had ever experienced.

Even though operations in the Soviet Union would resemble other foreign ventures in that the outlet would begin with a reduced line of foods (no chicken, no breakfasts, no salads), Cohon's task was formidable. McDonald's uses its own particular potato—the Russet Burbank, which has proven to be the best potato for McDonald's french fries. Since this type of potato was not indigenous to the Soviet Union, McDonald's french fry experts from Holland brought Russet Burbank seed potatoes to the Soviet Union and worked with farmers to develop a new crop of potatoes for McDonald's fries. Also, since some of garnishes that are an integral part of the American hamburger, such as mustard and ketchup, are not readily available in the Soviet Union, and, in fact, in some cases had never been introduced there, McDonald's had to import them initially.

As a result of the lack of some ingredients, distribution problems, and processing facility requirements, McDonald's built the McComplex, a 100,000-square-foot distribution center and processing plant in a suburb of Moscow. The facility includes a meat plant, a bakery, a potato plant, a dairy, and quality-assurance labs, as well as other offices and facilities. McComplex was the first such facility under one roof established by McDonald's to service its local operations.

When a single ad was placed for workers in Moscow, 27,000 workers applied for the 630 available jobs. The applicants selected were able to give the public an unaccustomed extra with their service—a smile. McDonald's brought four Soviet managers to Toronto for nine months of extensive training and then to Hamburger University in Oak Brook, Illinois, for two weeks. Upon graduation, all four of the trainees were on the dean's list and one was first in his graduating class. McDonald's strategy was to enable the venture to be Soviet-run and as self-sufficient as possible while operating to McDonald's standards.

The first 50 customers on opening day were children brought in by the Soviet Children's Fund, of which Cohon was made the first non-Soviet member and president of the North American chapter of the Soviet Children's Fund. The Children's Fund also received half that day's sales. Outside the restaurant, entertainers helped keep the waiting crowd happy, employees gave them McDonald's flags and pins, and brochures were passed out explaining the many services offered, including wheelchair facilities and diaper changing areas, as well as how to order. There were also instructions on how to eat what was ordered since Muscovites were totally unfamiliar with burgers and fries. The clean, brightly lit building was as much an attraction as the food. The eager Muscovites crowded in for a taste of the West's lifestyle—food, folks, and fun.

Approximately 15 million customers were served in the first year of operation. Escalating raw ingredient prices (for example, the 700 percent increase in beef prices, which forced McDonald's to raise its restaurant prices) failed to dent business, and the Pushkin Square outlet continued to serve approximately 50,000 customers every day. On opening day, Muscovites paid approximately 6 rubles for a McDonald's meal, consisting of a Big Mac, french fries, and a Coke. Although the cost was more than the prices charged in state-owned restaurants, McDonald's offered a unique, quality product at a good value for Soviet families.

Sources: Jeffrey M. Hertzfeld, "Joint Ventures: Saving the Soviets from Perestroika," *Harvard Business Review* (January–February 1991), pp. 80–91; Paul Hofheinz, "McDonald's Beats Lenin 3 to 1," *Fortune* (December 17, 1990), p. 11; Scott Hume, "How Big Mac Made It to Moscow," *Advertising Age* (January 22, 1990), pp. 16, 51; and Richard A. Melcher, "From Gung-Ho to Uh-Oh," *Business Week* (February 11, 1991), pp. 43–46. Updated information provided by Rem Langan, Senior Director of Marketing and Communications, McDonald's Restaurants of Canada, May 1991.

Questions

1. Relate McDonald's marketing efforts in the Soviet Union to each of the environmental factors described in Chapter 1.

2. Discuss the concept of a marketing mix as it relates to the marketing of Big Macs to Muscovites.

3. Relate each of the universal functions of marketing to this case.

2

Marketing: Its Environment and Role in Society

CHAPTER OBJECTIVES

1. To identify the five components of the marketing environment.

2. To explain the types of competition marketers face and the steps in developing a competitive strategy.

3. To describe how government and other groups regulate marketing activities and how marketers can influence the political-legal environment.

4. To outline the economic factors that affect marketing decisions and consumer buying power.

5. To explain the impact of the technological environment on a firm's marketing activities.

6. To explain how the social-cultural environment influences marketing.

7. To describe the role of marketing in society.

8. To identify the two major social issues in marketing.

The fur industry had its heyday not too many years back. Fur sales of $600 million in 1977 grew to $1.8 billion a decade later. Following a decade of spectacular growth, sales leveled off. Several forces in the industry's marketing environment influenced consumers' willingness and ability to buy furs. One reason sales stagnated was several years of mild winter weather. Buying a fur became more expensive after Congress put a 10 percent luxury tax on furs priced at more than $10,000.

The industry also suffered from overproduction. For example, the number of minks ranched worldwide increased from 35 million in the mid-1980s to 45 million by the end of the decade. With a falloff in consumer demand and overstocked inventories, many furriers slashed retail prices, some by as much as 70 percent. The three major U.S. fur retailers, Evans, Fur Vault, and Antonovich, and many smaller furriers experienced huge financial losses. Evans's stock price fell from a 1986 high of $18 a share to less than $1 a share in 1990. Fur Vault sold its fur operations to Jindo, a South Korean fur firm. Antonovich filed for Chapter 11 bankruptcy protection. Financial losses threatened the survival of many smaller fur retailers.

Added to furriers' woes was a growing social force of animal-rights activists. Groups such as People for the Ethical Treatment of Animals (PETA), Friends of Animals, and ARM! (formerly Trans-Species Unlimited), launched a massive advertising and public relations campaign to persuade people to stop buying and promoting furs. Contending that it is not right for an industry to profit from the suffering of animals, anti-fur groups created ads portraying the mistreatment of trapped and ranched animals. Public awareness increased as the media publicized anti-fur activities such as the Fur Free Friday marches held in cities nationwide on the day after Thanksgiving. A PETA member says, "As people realize this is a business of cruelty and greed, furs will go out of fashion."

Activists claim many victories for their efforts. After PETA waged a year-long letter-writing campaign, Merv Griffin Enterprises stopped using fur coats as prizes on *Wheel of Fortune.* A similar effort led American Express to discontinue selling furs in its gift catalogs. Anti-fur campaigners in Europe take credit for depressed fur

sales in the Netherlands, Western Germany, and Great Britain, where Princess Diana publicly stated she would no longer wear furs.

The fur industry, however, claims the anti-fur movement has had a negligible impact on sales but a major impact on the industry's attitude. "It's made us more aware of the need to know more about what's going on in the industry," says Tom Riley of the Fur Information Council of America. The industry was ill-prepared to deal with overproduction and economic and social changes. After years of ignoring the anti-fur campaign, FICA and other trade groups joined together and launched a multimillion dollar marketing campaign in 1990 designed to educate people in the industry and the general public. One part of the program addresses the charges of cruelty to animals. Riley says: "The industry has certainly become more responsive to the needs of animals, and we have a need to tell that story." The Fur Farm Animal Welfare Coalition, a rancher group, tells the story in a coloring book targeted at third graders. It explains how Farmer Bob raises mink: "He gives them good food and fresh water, cleans their cages, and calls the animal doctor when they are sick." Another part of the program targets fur owners and potential buyers. From consumer research, FICA learned that most people believe that wearing a fur should be a question of personal choice. So FICA created ads reassuring consumers of their right to choose what they wear. Saga, a Scandinavian fur producers' cooperative, used the same theme in its U.S. ad campaign. One ad says: "Some people are opposed to a very basic luxury: Your freedom of choice."[1]

Chapter Overview

Like fur producers and retailers, every type of organization is affected by outside forces. Increasing consumer demands for healthier foods led Kentucky Fried Chicken marketers to offer skinless "Lite 'n Crispy," a product with 39 percent fewer calories and 45 percent less fat than the firm's regular chicken. Beginning in 1992, all Swedish cigarette marketers were required to add a drawing to cigarette cartons of a skull and stories of smokers who died. Recent events in the Middle East led Nabisco marketers to yank a magazine ad claiming that Chips Ahoy! cookies are "richer than an OPEC nation." McDonald's, whose societal concerns were apparent at the company's beginnings, when founder Ray Kroc instructed the first franchisees to pick up all litter within a two-block radius of their stores (whether it was McDonald's litter or not), now has a vice-president of environmental affairs.[2]

All firms must identify, analyze, and monitor external forces and assess their potential impact on their goods and services. Although external forces frequently are outside the marketing manager's control, they must be considered together with the variables of the marketing mix in developing marketing plans and strategies.

This chapter begins by describing five forces in marketing's external environment: competitive, political-legal, economic, technological, and social-cultural. These forces, as shown in Figure 2.1, are important because they provide the frame of reference within which marketing decisions are made. The response of marketers to society in general through socially responsible and ethical behavior is also discussed in this chapter.

environmental management
Attainment of organizational objectives by predicting and influencing the competitive, political-legal, economic, technological, and social-cultural environments.

In some instances, marketers can influence the environment in which the firm operates. **Environmental management** is the attainment of organizational objectives by predicting and influencing the competitive, political-legal, economic, technological, and social-cultural environments. This influence can result from a number of activities by the firm's management. Political power in the form of lobbying among legislative groups and contributions by political action committees (PACs) may result in modifications of regulations, laws, or tariff restrictions.

The competitive environment can be affected by product innovation, joint ventures, and mergers. To compete in the global marketplace, many firms are forming alliances with foreign companies. For example, Corning International has strengthened its competitive position in the United States and abroad by forming joint ventures with more than 20 firms whose products complement those of Corning. Corning expanded the market for its optical fibers by teaming up with optical fiber producers in Australia, France, Great Britain, and Germany. Corning's business of making glass bulbs for television sets has declined along with the dwindling number of U.S. firms that produce television sets. To increase its presence in this market, Corning formed a joint venture with Asahi Glass of Japan, a supplier of TV glass to Japanese firms in the United States. "A lot of Japanese tubemakers have moved to the United States, and Asahi has good relationships with them that we want to take advantage of," explains John Loose, Corning's international vice-president and CEO of the joint venture. Joint ventures account for almost half of Corning's net income.[3]

Successful research and development efforts may result in changes in the technological environment. A research breakthrough may lead to reduced production costs or a technologically superior new product. While the marketing environment may exist outside the confines of the firm and its marketing mix components, effective marketers continually seek to predict its impact on marketing decisions and to modify it whenever possible.

In addition to its effect on current marketing decisions, the marketing environment, due to its dynamic nature, necessitates that management at every level continually reevaluate marketing decisions in response to changing conditions. Even modest environmental shifts can alter the results of marketing decisions.

Figure 2.1

Elements of the Marketing Mix as They Operate within an Environmental Framework

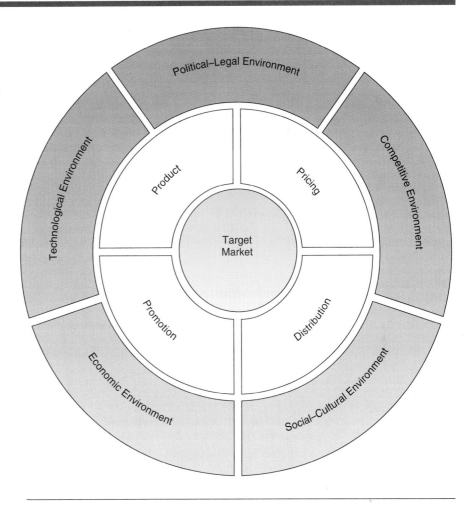

The Competitive Environment

The interactive process that occurs in the marketplace as competing organizations seek to satisfy markets is known as the **competitive environment.** Marketing decisions by an individual firm influence consumer responses in the marketplace. They also affect the marketing strategies of competitors. As a consequence, marketers must continually monitor competitors' marketing activities—their products, channels, prices, and promotional efforts.

In a few instances, organizations enjoy a monopoly position in the marketplace. Utilities, such as natural gas, electricity, water, and cable television service, accept considerable regulation from local authorities of such marketing-related factors as rates, service levels, and geographic coverage in exchange for exclusive rights to serve a particular group of consumers. Other firms, such as pharmaceutical companies, possess temporary monopoly as a result of patents.

Types of Competition

Marketers actually face three types of competition. The most direct form of competition occurs among marketers of similar products. Kinder-Care, Inc. competes with other day-care chains. Competitors in the personal computer industry include IBM, Apple, Compaq, and NEC of Japan. American Red Cross competes with United Way, among others, for charitable contributions.

competitive environment

Interactive process that occurs in the marketplace among marketers of directly competitive products, marketers of products that can be substituted for one another, and marketers competing for the consumer's purchasing power.

A second type of competition involves products that can be substituted for one another. In the transportation industry, Amtrak competes with auto rental services, airlines, and bus services. In the sending of documents, overnight express mail services and messenger services compete with facsimile (fax) machines. The growth of fax has put a huge dent in competitors' business. Federal Express, for example, has given up 20,000 documents a day to fax machines. "We can't compete with fax because it delivers within minutes," says a Federal Express spokesperson. Choice Courier, a large messenger service, lost 10 percent of its revenues in one year to fax. Not only do fax machines speed delivery, they also provide cost savings. The Russian Tea Room in Manhattan recouped its $2,000 investment in a fax machine in just seven months with savings on banquet contracts, press releases, and menu changes.[4]

In instances in which a change such as a price increase or an improvement in a product's strength occurs, demand for substitute products is directly affected.

The final type of competition occurs among all organizations that compete for the consumer's purchases. Traditional economic analysis views competition as a battle among companies in the same industry or among substitutable goods and services. Marketers, however, accept the argument that all firms compete for a limited amount of discretionary buying power. *Competition* in this sense means that a Mercury Sable competes with a ClubMed vacation and a Madonna compact disk competes with a Steve Martin movie for the buyer's entertainment dollar.

Because the competitive environment often determines the success or failure of a product, marketers must continually assess competitors' marketing strategies. New product offerings with technological advances, price reductions, special promotions, or other competitive variations must be monitored, and the firm's marketing mix may require adjustments with which to counter these changes. Among the first purchasers of any new product are the product's competitors. Careful analysis of its elements—physical components, performance attributes, packaging, retail price, service requirements, and estimated production and marketing costs—allows marketers to forecast its likely competitive impact. Adjustments to one or more marketing mix components may be needed in order to compete with a new market entry.

Developing a Competitive Strategy

All marketers must develop an effective strategy for dealing with the competitive environment. Some compete in a broad range of markets in many areas of the world. Others specialize in particular market segments, such as those determined by geographical, age, or income factors. Determining a competitive strategy involves answering three questions:

1. Should we compete?
2. If so, in what markets should we compete?
3. How should we compete?

The answer to the first question—should we compete?—must be based on the firm's resources, objectives, and expected profit potential. A firm may decide not to pursue or continue operating a potentially successful venture because it doesn't mesh with its resources, objectives, or profit expectations. Gulf & Western, for example, sold 50 businesses that were not operating profitably, did not show a satisfactory return on investment, or were not a good fit with its core businesses of financial services, publishing, and entertainment. Chicago-based Continental Bank decided to relinquish its consumer banking interests and build on its strengths in serving business customers.

Figure 2.2   Honda's Competitive Strategy: Expanding Beyond Motorcycles to the Automobile Market

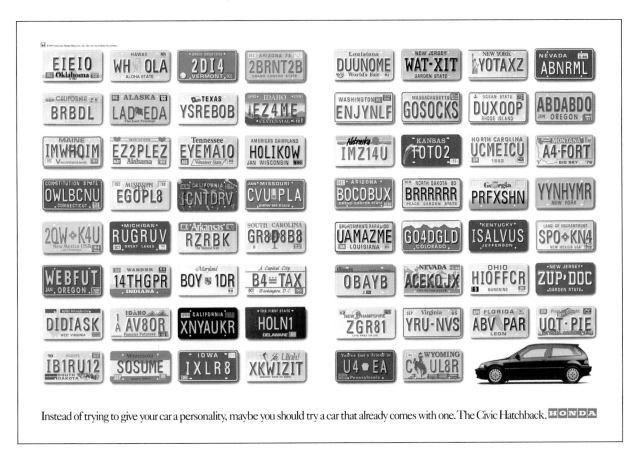

Source: Courtesy of American Honda Motor Co., Inc.

Answering the second question—in what markets should we compete?—requires acknowledging that the marketer has limited resources (sales personnel, advertising budgets, product development capability, and the like) and that these resources must be allocated to the areas of greatest opportunity. Too many marketers have taken a "shotgun" approach to market selection and thus have done an ineffective job in many markets rather than a good one in a selected few. For example, through acquisitions, General Mills diversified beyond its food business and tried to compete in 13 different industries, including retailing, toys and games, jewelry, and fashions. But General Mills learned that competing in markets unrelated to its core business spread the company's resources too thin. To prepare for the intensely competitive environment of the 1990s, General Mills reviewed its strategy and decided to sell its nonfood businesses and focus instead on the two markets it knows best: consumer foods and restaurants. As a smaller, more focused company, General Mills concentrates its resources on developing new products. Its goal is to be a top competitor, holding either the first or second market position in each of its food and restaurant product lines.[5]

After developing a strong reputation in Japan and other nations for its motorcycles, Honda decided to utilize its technology in the automobile market. Its match of organizational strengths and marketplace is one of the major successes of the past decade. Honda's Civic Hatchback model, shown in Figure 2.2, has been highly successful. Its Accord model ranked as the top-selling car—domestic or imported—in the United States during 1989 and 1990.

Answering the third question—how should we compete?—requires the marketer to make product, pricing, distribution, and promotional decisions that give the firm a competitive advantage in the marketplace. Firms can compete on a variety of bases, including product quality, price, and customer service. For example, retailer Nordstrom Inc. has gained a competitive advantage by providing superior customer service. With increased international competition and rapid changes in technology, a steadily growing number of firms are using time as a strategic competitive weapon. **Time-based competition** is a strategy of developing and distributing goods and services more quickly than competitors. Japanese firms, pioneers of time-based competition, have gained a competitive edge in industries such as automobiles and projection television by developing products in one-third to one-half the time as U.S. competitors. Toyota Motor Corporation reduced the time it takes to sell and distribute its cars from four to six weeks to just eight days by developing a computerized order-entry system that links salespeople directly to production scheduling. Italian retailer Benetton has achieved global success by using a time-based strategy to respond quickly to marketplace demands. After spotting a new trend, Benetton uses computer technology to design, produce, and deliver new fashion items to its stores in less than one month. The flexibility and speedy responsiveness of time-based competitors enables them to improve product quality, reduce costs, offer a broader variety of products that cover more market segments, and enhance customer satisfaction.[6]

time-based competition
Strategy of developing and distributing goods and services more quickly than competitors.

The Political-Legal Environment

Before you play the game, learn the rules! It would be absurd to start playing a new game without first understanding the rules. Yet some businesspeople exhibit a remarkable lack of knowledge about marketing's **political-legal environment**—the laws and interpretations of laws that require firms to operate under competitive conditions and to protect consumer rights. Ignorance of or noncompliance with laws, ordinances, and regulations can result in fines, embarrassing negative publicity, and possibly expensive civil damage suits.

political-legal environment
Component of the marketing environment consisting of laws and interpretations of laws that require firms to operate under competitive conditions and to protect consumer rights.

Considerable diligence is required for developing an understanding of the legal framework for marketing decisions. Numerous laws and regulations exist, many of them vague and legislated by a multitude of different authorities. Our existing legal framework was constructed on a piecemeal basis, often in response to concerns over current issues.

Regulations affecting marketing have been enacted at the federal, state, and local levels, as well as by independent regulatory agencies. They touch on all aspects of marketing decision making—designing, labeling, packaging, distribution, advertising, and promotion of goods and services. To cope with the vastness, complexity, and changing nature of the political-legal environment, many large firms maintain in-house legal departments, and small firms seek professional advice from outside attorneys. All marketers, however, should be aware of the major regulations that affect their activities.

Government Regulation

Government regulation in the United States can be divided into four phases. The first phase was the antimonopoly period of the late nineteenth and early twentieth centuries. During this era, major laws such as the Sherman Antitrust Act, Clayton

Act, and Federal Trade Commission Act were passed to maintain a competitive environment by reducing the trend toward increasing concentration of industry power in the hands of a small number of competitors. The second phase, aimed at protecting competitors, emerged during the Depression era of the 1930s, when independent merchants felt the need for legal protection against competition from larger chain stores. Federal legislation enacted during this period included the Robinson-Patman Act and the Miller-Tydings Resale Price Maintenance Act. The third phase focused on consumer protection. Although consumer protection is an underlying objective of most laws—the Sherman Act, FTC Act, and Federal Food and Drug Act are good examples—many of the major pro-consumer laws have been enacted during the past 40 years. The fourth phase, industry deregulation, began in the late 1970s and has continued to the present. This phase sought to increase competition in such industries as transportation and financial services by discontinuing many regulations and permitting firms to expand their service offerings to new markets.

Table 2.1 lists and briefly describes the major federal laws affecting marketing. Legislation affecting specific marketing practices, such as product warranties and franchise agreements, is discussed in later chapters.

Marketers must also be aware of state and local laws that influence marketing activities. The Exxtasy Channel, a New York-based cable channel that delivered adult movies to satellite dish subscribers who rented a descrambler device to receive the movies, was accused of violating Alabama's obscenity law. The case was settled when the firm agreed to give $150,000 to charity and not to offer its service to Alabama viewers. However, the resultant publicity caused satellite owners to refuse to provide transmission services, and the firm ceased operating in 1990.[7] In recent years, a number of states and cities have passed pollution-prevention legislation. A Minneapolis ordinance prohibits all food packaging at grocery stores and restaurants that is not biodegradable, returnable, or collectible. Suffolk County, New York, prohibited Styrofoam and other polystyrene plastics at fast-food restaurants. Similar laws have been passed in Berkeley, California, and Portland, Oregon.[8]

Government Regulatory Agencies

Federal, state, and local governments have established regulatory agencies to enforce laws. At the federal level, the Federal Trade Commission (FTC) has the broadest powers to influence marketing activities. It has the authority to enforce laws regulating unfair business practices and can take action to stop false and deceptive advertising. The scope of other agencies is narrower. The Federal Communications Commission, for example, regulates communication by wire, radio, and television. The Interstate Commerce Commission continues to monitor many of the rates of interstate rail, bus, truck, and water carriers. Other federal regulatory agencies include the Food and Drug Administration, the Consumer Products Safety Commission, the Federal Power Commission, and the Environmental Protection Agency.

The FTC uses several procedures to enforce laws. It may issue a consent order whereby a business accused of violating a law agrees to voluntary compliance without admitting guilt. For example, the FTC issued a consent order against Twin Star Productions for producing and airing three *infomercials,* the half-hour or hour-long commercials that promote various products. The FTC charged Twin Star with deceptive advertising, claiming that the infomercials for a baldness cure, a diet suppressant, and a male impotence cure carried false and unsubstantiated product claims and misled viewers into thinking the infomercials were consumer programs rather than paid advertisements. A Twin Star

Table 2.1   Major Federal Laws Affecting Marketing

Date	Law	Description
A. Laws Maintaining a Competitive Environment		
1890	Sherman Antitrust Act	Prohibits restraint of trade and monopolization; delineates maintenance of a competitive marketing system as national policy
1914	Clayton Act	Strengthens Sherman Act by restricting such practices as price discrimination, exclusive dealing, tying contracts, and interlocking boards of directors where the effect "may be to substantially lessen competition or tend to create a monopoly"
1914	Federal Trade Commission Act	Prohibits unfair methods of competition; established Federal Trade Commission, an administrative agency that investigates business practices and enforces the FTC Act
1938	Wheeler-Lea Act	Amends the FTC Act to further outlaw unfair or deceptive practices in businesses; gives FTC jurisdiction over false and misleading advertising
1950	Celler-Kefauver Antimerger Act	Amends the Clayton Act to include major asset purchases that will decrease competition in an industry
1975	Consumer Goods Pricing Act	Prohibits pricing maintenance agreements among manufacturers and resellers in interstate commerce
1980	FTC Improvement Act	Gives the Senate and House of Representatives joint veto power over FTC trade regulation rules; limits FTC power to regulate unfairness issues
B. Laws Regulating Competition		
1936	Robinson-Patman Act	Prohibits price discrimination in sales to wholesalers, retailers, or other producers; prohibits selling at unreasonably low prices to eliminate competition
1937	Miller-Tydings Resale Price Maintenance Act	Exempts interstate fair trade contracts from compliance with antitrust requirements
C. Laws Protecting Consumers		
1906	Federal Food and Drug Act	Prohibits adulteration and misbranding of foods and drugs involved in interstate commerce; strengthened by the Food, Drug, and Cosmetic Act (1938) and the Kefauver-Harris Drug Amendment (1962)
1939	Wool Products Labeling Act	Requires identification of the type and percentage of wool used in products
1951	Fur Products Labeling Act	Requires identification of the animal from which a fur product was derived
1953	Flammable Fabrics Act	Prohibits interstate sale of flammable fabrics
1958	National Traffic and Safety Act	Provides for the creation of safety standards for automobiles and tires
1958	Automobile Information Disclosure Act	Prohibits automobile dealers from inflating factory prices of new cars

spokesperson said the company "didn't do anything wrong" but nonetheless signed the consent decree under which it agreed not to air the infomercials again and to pay a $1.5 million fine.[9]

If a business refuses to comply with an FTC request, the agency can issue a cease-and-desist order, which is a final order to stop an illegal practice. Firms often challenge the cease-and-desist order in court. The FTC can require advertisers to provide additional information about products in their advertisements and can require firms using deceptive advertising to correct earlier claims with new promotional messages. In some cases, the FTC requires that firms give refunds to consumers misled by deceptive advertising.

State and local agencies also enforce laws and regulations concerning marketing practices. The Texas attorney general, for example, charged Volvo Cars of North America, a unit of AB Volvo of Sweden, with deceptive advertising. The ad in question showed a car-crushing event in which a monster truck drove over the tops of a row of cars, crushing all except the Volvo. This actually happened during a car-crushing exhibition in Vermont in 1988. However, when the ad was filmed in Austin, Texas, in 1990, the roof pillars of the Volvo were

Date	Law	Description
C. Laws Protecting Consumers—continued		
1966	Child Protection Act	Outlaws sale of hazardous toys; 1969 amendment adds products posing electrical, mechanical, or thermal hazards
1967	Fair Packaging and Labeling Act	Requires disclosure of product identification, name and address of manufacturer or distributor, and information on the quality of contents
1967	Federal Cigarette Labeling and Advertising Act	Requires written health warnings on cigarette packages
1968	Consumer Credit Protection Act	Truth-in-lending law requiring disclosure of annual interest rates on loans and credit purchases
1970	Fair Credit Reporting Act	Gives individuals access to their credit records and allows them to change incorrect information
1970	National Environmental Policy Act	Established the Environmental Protection Agency to deal with various types of pollution and organizations that create pollution
1971	Public Health Cigarette Smoking Act	Prohibits tobacco advertising on radio and television
1972	Consumer Product Safety Act	Created the Consumer Product Safety Commission, which has authority to specify safety standards for most consumer products
1975, 1977	Equal Credit Opportunity Act	Bans discrimination-in-lending practices based on sex and marital status (1975) and race, national origin, religion, age, or receipt of payments from public assistance programs (1977)
1978	Fair Debt Collection Practices Act	Prohibits harassing, deceptive, or unfair collection practices by debt collection agencies; exempts in-house collectors such as banks, retailers, and attorneys
1990	Nutrition Labeling and Education Act	Requires food manufacturers and processors to provide detailed nutritional information on the labeling of most foods
1990	Children's Television Act	Limits the amount of advertising to be shown during children's television programs—no more than 10.5 minutes per hour on weekends and not more than 12 minutes per hour on weekdays.
D. Laws Deregulating Specific Industries		
1978	Airline Deregulation Act	Granted considerable freedom to commercial airlines in setting fares and choosing new routes
1980	Motor Carrier Act and Staggers Rail Act	Significantly deregulated trucking and railroad industries by permitting them to negotiate rates and services
1980	Depository Institutions and Monetary Control Act ("Banking Act of 1980")	Significantly deregulated financial service industry by permitting all depository institutions to offer checking accounts, expanding the services and lending powers of savings and loan associations, and removing interest rate ceilings on customer deposits

reinforced and the pillars of other cars weakened. The Texas attorney general claimed the ad was deceptive because it did not state that the event illustrated was a staged dramatization, misleading consumers to believe it was a real contest. The ad copy said: "On June 12, 1990, a Volvo 240 ruined an otherwise perfect car-crushing exhibition. According to Fred Shafer, the monster truck driver, 'I tried everything. The darn thing just wouldn't give.' We couldn't ask for a better endorsement." Volvo settled with the Texas attorney general by agreeing to stop running the ads, to pay the state investigative costs, and to run ads in Texas and national newspapers explaining how the ad was filmed and giving details of the settlement.[10]

Other Regulatory Forces

Marketing activities are also affected by public and private consumer interest groups and self-regulatory organizations. Consumer interest groups have mushroomed in the past 20 years. Today hundreds of these organizations operate at the national, state, and local levels. Groups such as the National Coalition Against Misuse of Pesticides seek to protect the environment. Others attempt to advance the rights of minorities, elderly Americans, and other special-interest groups. The power of these groups has also grown. Pressure from anti-alcohol groups has resulted in proposed legislation requiring health warnings on all alcohol ads and stricter regulation of alcoholic beverage advertising.

Self-regulatory groups are industry's attempts to set guidelines for responsible business conduct. The Council of Better Business Bureaus is a national organization devoted to consumer service and business self-regulation. The Council's National Advertising Division (NAD) is designed to promote truth and accuracy in advertising. It reviews and resolves advertising complaints from consumers and business on a voluntary basis. If NAD fails to resolve a complaint, an appeal can be made to the National Advertising Review Board, which is composed of advertisers, ad agency representatives, and public members. In addition, many individual trade associations set business guidelines and codes of conduct and encourage members' voluntary compliance.

Controlling the Political-Legal Environment

In most cases, marketers comply with laws and regulations. Operating within the legal framework is both socially responsible and ethical. Besides, noncompliance can scar a firm's reputation and hurt profits. Velsicol Chemical Company agreed to the Environmental Protection Agency's demand to stop selling its two leading termite control chemicals until it could prove that the potentially cancer-causing products could be used safely. Velsicol's attorney said the company agreed to the pact because "it was getting killed in the marketplace" as a result of negative publicity about the chemicals' hazards.[11]

Marketers can, however, attempt to control forces in the political-legal environment. Individual firms and trade associations can influence public opinion and legislative action through advertising, political action committees, and political lobbying. In the advertisement in Figure 2.3, Amoco Chemical argues against the ban of plastics, promoting other alternatives such as recycling as solutions to the solid waste problem.

To influence the outcome of proposed legislation or change existing laws, many industry groups, trade associations, and corporations use political lobbying and political action committees. Lobby groups frequently enlist the support of customers, employees, and suppliers to assist in the lobbying effort. For example, when the banking industry wanted to repeal a law requiring banks to withhold taxes on savings account interest, it asked bank customers to join in the effort by writing to their Congressional representative. A deluge of 22 million letters and postcards prompted Congress to repeal the law before it went into effect.[12]

The Economic Environment

The health of the economy influences how much consumers spend and what they buy. It also works the other way: Consumer buying plays an important role in the economy's health — indeed, consumer outlays perennially make up some two-thirds of overall economic activity.[13] Since all marketing activity is directed toward satisfying consumer wants and needs, marketers must understand how economic conditions influence consumer buying power.

Figure 2.3   Use of Advertising to Influence the Political-Legal Environment

Do we really want to return to those good, old-fashioned days before plastics?

America is coping with the problem of too much garbage and too few places to put it.

Our nation is currently generating about 160 million tons of garbage a year. Our landfills have decreased from 18,500 to 6,000 during the past 10 years. About 2,000 more will close within the next five years.

Some people believe that banning plastics and substituting other materials will solve the problem. We don't think that they have all the facts.

If plastics were banned, we'd lose safety and convenience features such as closures for foods and medicines, shatter-resistant bottles, freezer-to-microwave packages, and wrappers that preserve food freshness.

A 1987 study shows that if paper and other packaging materials were to replace plastics, the energy needed to produce the packaging would double, the weight of packaging would increase four-fold, the packaging cost would double, and the volume of waste collected would increase about 2½ times.

Myth vs. Reality.

The thinking behind a ban on plastics is based on a number of myths.

Myth #1 is that plastics make up a major part of our solid waste. Fact: according to a recent study, plastics make up about 18% of the volume of solid waste in our landfills; paper and paperboard about 38%; metals, 14%; glass, 2% and other wastes, 28%.

Myth #2 is that paper and other products commonly considered biodegradable will decompose in a landfill, so it takes longer to fill up. Fact: recent excavations of some landfills have turned up newspapers buried 40 years ago—still perfectly readable.

Myth #3 is that plastics are not recyclable. Fact: plastics are among the easiest materials to recycle.

20% of all plastic soft drink bottles were recycled in 1987.

Recycling takes plastic items destined for disposal and turns them into useful new products. It can turn plastics into a "natural resource."

Recycling is growing.

At Amoco Chemical, we believe the solution must integrate recycling, source reduction, environmentally secure landfills and waste-to-energy incineration. Everything recyclable should be recycled—yard waste, paper, glass, metal and plastics.

Today, almost 200 companies are recycling millions of used plastic containers into everything from fiberfill for ski parkas to carpet yarn to "plastic lumber."

How Amoco Chemical is helping.

Amoco Chemical is sponsoring a program in New York demonstrating that used, polystyrene foam food service containers from schools and restaurants can be recycled into insulation board for commercial construction, cafeteria trays and office products.

We're participating in a consortium with other major plastics manufacturers involved in the construction of regional polystyrene recycling plants.

We're encouraging the start up of new recycling efforts, helping to find better ways to collect and sort recyclables, and supporting efforts to create markets for products made from recycled plastics.

At Amoco Chemical, we believe that recycling can play a major role in helping America solve its solid waste problem. Before we decide to return to the past, let's remember that the good old days were sometimes the not-so-good old days.

For a free copy of "Recycling, Do It Today For Tomorrow," write Amoco Chemical, Recycling BW, 200 East Randolph Drive, Chicago, IL 60601.

Recycling. Do It Today For Tomorrow.

Amoco Chemical

© 1989 Amoco Chemical Company

Source: Courtesy of Amoco Chemical Company.

economic environment
Factors that influence consumer buying power and marketing strategies, including stage of the business cycle, inflation, unemployment, resource availability, and income.

Marketing's **economic environment** consists of those factors that influence consumer buying power and marketing strategies. They include stage of the business cycle, inflation, unemployment, resource availability, and income.

Business Cycles

Historically the economy has tended to follow a cyclical pattern consisting of four stages: prosperity, recession, depression, and recovery. No depressions have occurred since the 1930s, and many economists argue that society is capable of preventing future depressions through intelligent use of various economic policies. Thus, a recession would be followed by a period of recovery. Consumer buying differs in each stage, and marketers must adjust their strategies accordingly.

In times of prosperity, consumer spending is brisk. Marketers respond by expanding product lines, increasing promotional efforts and expanding distribution to raise market share, and raising prices to widen their profit margins. During periods of prosperity, buyers often are willing to pay more for premium versions of well-known brands. But consumer buying power declines during a recession. The most recent recession in the United States and Western Europe occurred during the early 1990s. During recessions, consumers frequently shift their

Figure 2.4   Example of Marketing Strategy during a Recession

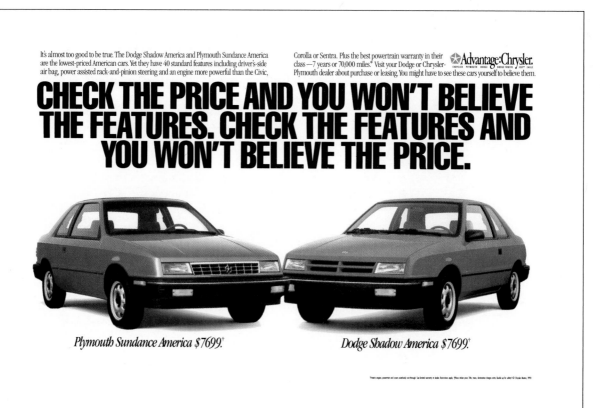

Source: Courtesy of Chrysler Corporation.

buying patterns to basic, functional products that carry low price tags. They spend more at hardware stores and do-it-yourself centers and less on restaurant meals and nonessential products such as convenience foods. Sales of low-priced, black-and-white-label generic grocery products and private-label goods rise. During recessions, marketers should consider lowering prices, eliminating marginal products, providing better customer service, and increasing promotional outlays to stimulate demand. They launch value-priced products that appeal to cost-conscious buyers. During the most recent recession, Campbell Soup Company introduced a new budget frozen food line, and Holiday Inn Worldwide developed budget-priced Holiday Express hotels. Promotional messages stress efficiency and value. Quaker Oats, for example, developed an advertising campaign in 1990 emphasizing the value of its oatmeal by saying that a serving "costs you one nickel and four pennies." Chrysler Corporation used a value-priced strategy for its 1991 Plymouth Sundance and Dodge Shadow compact cars, which cost less than $8,000 and came equipped with an airbag, power steering, and power brakes as standard equipment. Advertisements for the cars, such as the one in Figure 2.4, addressed consumer worries in a slow economy.[14]

Consumer spending is lowest during a depression. The United States has not suffered a depression since the late 1930s. Although a possibility always exists, the likelihood of another severe depression is slim. Through effective management of monetary and fiscal policies, the federal government attempts to control extreme fluctuations in the business cycle.

In the recovery stage, the economy emerges from a recession to prosperity and consumer purchasing power increases. But while consumers' *ability* to buy increases, their *willingness* to buy is often characterized by caution. Remembering the tougher times of recession, they may be more likely to save than spend or buy on credit. As the recovery strengthens, consumers become more indulgent, buying convenience-type products and higher-priced goods and services such as housecleaning and lawn care. Recovery is a difficult stage for marketers. It requires them to assess how quickly consumers make the psychological transition from recession to prosperity. Hartmarx Corporation misjudged the transition and had to readjust its marketing strategy. Hartmarx operates a chain of higher-priced clothing stores. In 1982, the firm acquired Kuppenheimer Men's Clothiers, a discount chain, to diversify into the lower-priced suit market and started expanding the number of Kuppenheimer stores. But demand for the cheaper suits lessened as consumers, emerging from the recession, began to buy higher-quality clothes. Hartmarx decided to reposition the no-frills stores by upgrading their merchandise and remodeling the stores to meet this changing consumer demand. The repositioning strategy was successful. Today Kuppenheimer is the leading quality specialty store operation in the value-priced field, and Hartmarx plans to continue expanding the concept throughout the 1990s.[15]

Business cycles, like other aspects of the economy, are complex and seem to be beyond the control of marketers. The key to success is developing flexible plans that can be adjusted to satisfy consumer demands during the various business cycle stages.

Inflation

A major constraint on consumer spending, which can occur during any stage of the business cycle, is *inflation,* a rising price level that results in reduced consumer buying power. A person's money is devalued in terms of what it can buy. The impact of inflation would be less restrictive if income kept pace with rising prices, but often it does not. The rate of inflation in the United States soared to double digits in the late 1970s and early 1980s, reaching 13.6 percent in 1980. Although the inflation rate dropped to the 4 percent range in the late 1980s, it later climbed to over 6 percent in 1991. Economists expect it to level off at a 5 percent annual rate. If consumer prices continue to rise at an annual rate of 5 percent until the year 2000, it will halve the dollar's current purchasing power by the end of the century.[16] Inflation increases marketers' costs, such as for purchasing materials for production, and may result in declining sales.

Unemployment

Unemployment is defined as the situation in which people who do not have jobs are actively looking for work. Unemployment rises during recessions and declines in the recovery and prosperity stages of the business cycle. Like inflation, unemployment affects marketing by modifying consumer behavior. Unless unemployment insurance, personal savings, and union benefits are sufficient to offset lost earnings, the unemployed have less income to spend. Even if people are completely compensated for lost earnings, buying behavior is likely to be affected. Instead of buying, they may choose to build their savings. Consumers, especially during periods of high inflation, become more price conscious in general. This can lead to three possible outcomes, all important to marketers. Consumers can (1) elect to buy now, in the belief that prices will be higher later (automobile dealers often use this argument in their commercial messages); (2) decide to alter their purchasing patterns; or (3) postpone certain purchases.

Resource Availability

Resources are not unlimited. Shortages—temporary or permanent—can be caused by several factors. A brisk demand may exceed manufacturing capacity or outpace the response time required to gear up a production line. Shortages may also be caused by a lack of raw materials, component parts, energy, or labor. The worldwide embargo that preceded the Persian Gulf War of the early 1990s produced shortages in Iraq illustrated by televised reports of Iraqi drivers lined up at gas stations, all fearful that the Iraqi government would ban auto fuel sales for private use. Regardless of the cause, shortages require marketers to reorient their thinking. One approach is **demarketing,** the process of reducing consumer demand for a product to a level that the firm can reasonably supply. Oil companies, for example, publicize tips on how to cut gasoline consumption, and utility companies encourage homeowners to install more insulation to reduce heating costs. Many cities discourage central business district traffic by raising parking fees and violation penalties and promoting mass transit and car pooling.

demarketing
Process of reducing consumer demand for a good or service to a level that the firm can supply.

Shortages present marketers with a unique set of marketing problems. In some instances, they force marketers to be allocators of limited supplies. This is in sharp contrast to marketing's traditional objective of expanding sales volume. Shortages require marketers to decide whether to spread a limited supply over all customers so that none are totally satisfied or to limit purchases by some customers so that others may be completely satisfied. During World War II, consumer demand for Wrigley gum increased while ingredient supplies diminished. Wrigley supplied large quantities of gum to the U.S. armed forces overseas. Since the company could not meet everyone's needs, it took its Spearmint, Doublemint, and Juicy Fruit brands off the civilian market and directed its entire output overseas. It marketed a special wartime brand, Orbit, for civilians but told the public that it wasn't quite good enough to carry the Wrigley label. Top-grade materials eventually became so scarce that Wrigley halted production and marketing of its established brands. But to keep the Wrigley name in buyers' minds, the company ran an advertising campaign showing an empty Wrigley's wrapper with the slogan "Remember This Wrapper." Wrigley's adaptive strategy worked. After being off the market for two years, the brands quickly regained and then exceeded their prewar popularity.[17]

Companies today have also devised ways to deal with increased demand for fixed amounts of resources. Reynolds Metal Company addresses the dwindling supply of aluminum through its recycling programs, including cash-paying vending machines. Such "reverse" vending machines allow recyclers to insert empty cans and receive money, stamps, and/or discount coupons for merchandise or services.

Income

Income is another important factor in marketing's economic environment, because it influences consumer buying power. Studying income statistics and trends helps marketers estimate market potential and develop plans for targeting specific market segments. Household incomes have grown in recent years and, coupled with a low rate of inflation, have resulted in added purchasing power for millions of American households. For marketers, a rise in income represents the

THE HELLFIGHTERS

. . . .

"This is really no different than any of the jobs we've ever gone to," says Joe Bowden, president of Wild Well Co. "It's just bigger."

Bigger indeed. Bowden is referring to the job of putting out oil well fires in Kuwait. In early 1991 virtually all the country's 1,000 or so wells were wrecked or set ablaze by retreating Iraqi troops, who made the job of putting out the fires even more difficult by lacing the landscape with booby traps and mines. The result is a nightmarish scene in which 400-foot plumes of flame release deadly gases into a smoky, soot-laden sky and produce heat so intense that it turns desert sand into liquid glass. While scientists worry about the environmental impact, Kuwaiti officials, upset at the vast quantities of oil that are going up in smoke, are scrambling to get the fires put out.

Wild Well Co. is one of a few U.S. firms that have been hired to combat the oil well fires. Others include Red Adair, Inc., and Boots & Coots. All three companies are headquartered in Houston and employ skilled firefighters who call themselves "hellfighters."

Some oil well fires can be fought with the same weapon that is used on more conventional fires: vast quantities of water. Tougher fires require a more drastic method. A crane mounted on a bulldozer approaches the well and suspends a barrel filled with explosives in the gap between the wellhead and the bottom of the flame. (Both the operator and the charge are cooled by a constant spray of water.) The charge is detonated electronically, and the explosion sucks all the oxygen away from the flame and smothers it. "It's like blowing out a candle," says one of the hellfighters.

Wild Well, Boots & Coots, and Adair stand to gain immensely from the Kuwaiti firefighting efforts, which are expected to continue for a year or more. Although company representatives decline to reveal their fees, it is likely that each company will make millions of dollars. Only a handful of companies are available to do one of the dirtiest, most dangerous jobs in the world and the Kuwaitis are not haggling over the price.

Discussion Questions

1. Are the firefighting companies taking unfair advantage of the Kuwaitis?

2. What risks (other than physical danger) do the firefighting companies face in taking on such an immense job?

Sources: William J. Cook, "Battle Under the Sand," *U.S. News & World Report*, March 11, 1991, p. 28; Philip Elmer-Dewitt, "A Man-Made Hell on Earth," *Time*, March 18, 1991, p. 36; "Hellfighters to the Rescue," *Newsweek*, March 25, 1991, pp. 27, 30. Photo source: © 1991 Peter Turnley/Black Star.

potential for increasing overall sales. However, marketers are most interested in *discretionary income*, the amount of money people have to spend after they have paid for necessities such as food, clothing, and housing.

Discretionary income varies greatly by age group and household type. Bureau of the Census statistics show that older people, for example, have a significant amount of buying power compared to other groups with higher incomes. Contributing to the elderly's buying power are smaller household size, the increased likelihood that children's education outlays will be completed, and

Figure 2.5   Marketing Targeted at the Over-50 Market

Source: Courtesy of General Mills.

the fact that most older people no longer make mortgage payments. Based on this information, many firms are aiming goods and services at this once neglected market. Levi Strauss, for example, produces slacks designed specifically for older customers, and Hyatt Corporation, the hotel chain, has developed Classic Residence, a senior rental retirement community. Firms whose products have a multigenerational appeal are tailoring advertising to older consumers' active lifestyles, such as the General Mills ad in Figure 2.5.[18]

The Technological Environment

technological environment
Applications to marketing of knowledge based on discoveries in science, inventions, and innovations.

The **technological environment** represents the application to marketing of knowledge based on discoveries in science, inventions, and innovations. New technology results in new goods and services for consumers, improved existing products, better customer service, and often lower prices through the development of more cost-efficient production and distribution methods. Technology can quickly make products obsolete—calculators, for example, wiped out the market for slide rules—but can just as quickly open up new marketing opportunities. Technology has spawned new industries: Computers, lasers, and xerography all resulted in the development of major industries in the past 40 years. Recent technological advances in superconductivity—the conducting of electricity with virtually no power loss—is expected to result in an annual $20 billion worldwide

Figure 2.6   Product Innovation through the Application of Technology

industry by the year 2000.[19] Scientists and researchers around the globe are working to convert superconductor technology into commercial applications. Superconductors have the potential to eliminate urban air pollution by making electrical cars practical, improve medical imaging systems that will give doctors sharper pictures, save the utilities billions of dollars, and enable computers to perform much more rapidly.

Technology sometimes provides the means of addressing societal concerns. Chrysler Corporation plans to introduce its battery-powered TE Van in 1995. Although the new van is almost identical to the firm's gasoline-powered minivans, the TE Van is powered by 30 six-volt batteries weighting 1,800 pounds. The new vans will first be sold in pollution-choked southern California to commercial users, such as delivery firms and utility companies. Although the TE Van has a top speed of 65 miles per hour and a 120-mile range before needing a nine-hour battery recharge on regular household current, the batteries add another $6,000 to its price, making it less attractive as a consumer vehicle.[20]

Applying Technology

Marketers must closely monitor the technological environment for a number of reasons. Applying technology may be the means by which a firm introduces major product breakthroughs that give it a competitive edge. After years of research, Procter & Gamble scientists succeeded in perfecting a formula for a combination shampoo and conditioner, introduced to the marketplace as Pert Plus. The brand became the leading shampoo in the United States, capturing 12 percent of the market, where it competes with more than 1,100 other products. P&G quickly distributed its innovation to foreign markets, where it is sold under various brand names such as Rejoy in Japan. Today it is the best-selling shampoo worldwide. Advertisements for Pert Plus, such as the poster in Figure 2.6 targeting college students, promotes the product's great hair performance combined with value of convenience to consumers.[21]

Applying new technology also gives marketers the opportunity to improve customer service. Breakthroughs in electronic communications have brought consumers the convenience of in-home shopping and 24-hour banking at automated teller machines. Otis Elevator Company uses an expert computer system and equips its maintenance personnel with laptop computers to speed customers' elevator repairs. Some restaurants provide faster service by equipping their waiters and waitresses with palmtop computers that transmit patrons' orders to the bar or kitchen. Many firms use computer-based communication systems to give customers information. A computer system at St. Joseph's Hospital and Medical Center in Phoenix, Arizona, enables patients to receive billing information by calling a computer and entering their account number.[22]

New technology can help marketers make decisions that will result in increased productivity and operating efficiency. Computer-aided design, super workstations, and computer-aided manufacturing speed up the process of bringing new products to market. Designing products by computer allows firms to thoroughly test products for potential problems, thus eliminating costly errors before the products go into manufacturing. Computerized mapping systems give marketers instant geographic and customer information simultaneously. General Motors creates color-coded maps to help determine optimal dealership locations, and 3M uses computer-generated maps to analyze its sales territories. Computer maps also help marketers in targeting markets, planning advertising, analyzing competitors, and distributing products. Advances in communications technology have created computer networks that allow marketers to share information with dealers, salespeople, and co-workers in such areas as finance and research and development. Pillsbury uses an electronic data interchange system to automatically transmit information on price changes, new products, and promotions to its 100 brokers and leading wholesalers.[23] Laptop computers and cellular phone technology have increased salesforce productivity, because salespeople do less paperwork and spend more time with clients and prospects.

Sources of New Technology

Industry, government, universities and colleges, and other nonprofit institutions all play a role in the development of new technology. In the United States, industry is a major source of technological innovation. In 1990 business spent $74 billion of the $108 billion the United States invested in civilian research and development (R&D). That is more than the combined R&D spending of Japanese and Western European firms. Important technology companies such as Hewlett-Packard, Allied-Signal, DuPont, IBM, AT&T, and Eastman Kodak employ thousands of researchers and invest large percentages of their sales revenues to develop new technologies and transfer them into commercial products. Hewlett-Packard, which derives more than half of its revenue from computer and electronic instrument products introduced in the past three years, invests about 10 percent of its net revenue in research and development each year and employs some 9,000 researchers and product developers.[24] Another major source of technology is the federal government. The geographic information system used in computer mapping systems stems from the first photographs taken by the government's Landsat spy satellites in the 1960s. The government's research in national defense and space programs has resulted in new technologies that the government encourages industry to apply in the private sector.

Although the United States has long been the world leader in research, competition from foreign rivals in Japan, West Germany, and France has intensified in recent years. Japanese firms, in particular, have taken the lead in several industries because of their ability to transfer basic technologies into commercial products. For example, the technology for videocassette recorders was developed by American firms, but two Japanese firms—Sony and JVC—commercialized the invention into one of the most successful new products of the last decade. To remain at the leading edge of technology, American firms have taken steps to improve technology transfer. Some firms are forming closer relationships between their researchers and marketing personnel. Hewlett-Packard (H-P) encourages its scientists to help promote products they invent. For example, an H-P physicist helped write a marketing brochure for a product he invented. Since 1984, when the U.S. government liberalized an antitrust law, some firms have begun to exchange ideas and research findings and pool their resources with other companies. IBM, AT&T's Bell Laboratories, and the Massachusetts Institute of Technology have formed a consortium to commercialize superconductivity. Included in the growing number of cooperative research activities are international alliances. Hewlett-Packard has established science centers in conjunction with the University of Tokyo and the University of Pisa in Italy where its corporate researchers work with their academic counterparts.[25]

The Social-Cultural Environment

social-cultural environment
Component of the marketing environment consisting of the relationship between the marketer and society and its culture.

Americans are on a health and fitness kick—eating more turkey and less red meat, drinking more bottled water and fewer alcoholic beverages, buying more low-salt, low-fat, and low-cholesterol substitutes, smoking less, and exercising more. We are concerned about the environment, buying products that are ozone friendly and reduce pollution. As a nation, we are becoming older and more affluent. Our birthrate is falling, and the population of our sub-cultures is rising. We value time at home with family and friends, watching videos and eating microwave popcorn. And we love goods and services that offer quality and convenience. These are the types of events that shape marketers' **social-cultural environment**—the relationship between marketing and society and its culture.

Marketers must be sensitive to society's changing values and shifts in demographics such as population growth and age distribution. These changing variables affect the way consumers react to different products and marketing practices. What may be out of bounds today may be totally acceptable in tomorrow's marketplace. Subjects that were once taboo—condoms and feminine hygiene products—are now commonly advertised. A change in national attitudes toward sex has altered the way some firms advertise their products. The ad for Calvin Klein's Obsession for Men shown in Figure 2.7 might have stirred public protest in the 1970s, but it contributed to the product's successful launch and was ranked as one of America's favorite advertising campaigns. Although society in general has become more accepting of such promotions, consumers tend to respond to a sexual approach only when the advertising is geared toward certain products, such as fragrances, fashion clothing, suntan lotions, and lingerie.[26]

Cultural diversity is another important element within society. The United States is a mixed society composed of various submarkets, each of which displays unique values and cultural characteristics and differs by age, place of residence, and buying behavior. For example, the Hispanic population, which is expected to grow from 21 million to 30 million over the next decade, is highly concentrated with respect to national origin and geography. Most Hispanics in the United States are of Mexican origin and live in the Southwest, while many

Figure 2.7

Society's Acceptance of
Sensuous Advertising

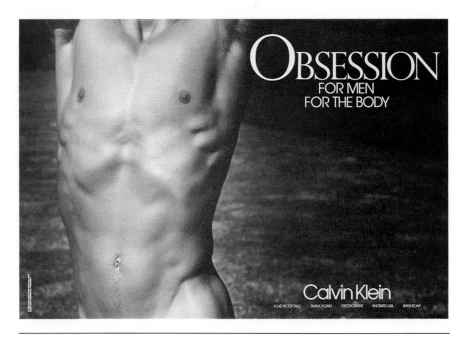

Source: Courtesy of Calvin Klein, Inc.

Americans of Puerto Rican descent live in the New York metropolitan area. In buying behavior, Hispanics tend to be very brand conscious and brand loyal. Advertising messages that appeal to Hispanics focus on values important to them, such as family relationships and goals.[27] Recognition of the size, growth rate, and buying power of this market and development of goods and services aimed at satisfying Hispanics' needs and wants can open up new marketing opportunities for many firms, large and small. The importance of culture in marketing is explored in more depth in Chapter 6; demographic considerations are discussed in Chapter 8.

Importance in International Marketing Decisions

The social-cultural context for marketing decision making often is more pronounced in the international sphere than in the domestic arena. Learning about cultural and societal differences among countries is paramount to a firm's success abroad. Marketing strategies that work in the United States often cannot be directly applied in other countries. In many cases, marketers must redesign packages and modify products and advertising messages to suit the tastes and preferences of different cultures. Consider the trouble The Coca-Cola Company has in marketing Coke in France, a market it has served for 70 years. Because of the cultural and health concerns, the French drink much less Coke than the British, Germans, Spaniards, and Italians. The preferred drink in France is bottled water, which the French drink 11 times more of than Coke. The French consider Coke "very chemical." One Parisian woman says: "In France, fine food is like religion, and Coke is like junk food. It's just not my culture." The soft-drink company has taken several steps to boost Coke sales in France, including buying the Coke franchise from a French spirits producer, increasing its salesforce, installing thousands of vending machines, and building concentrate and canning plants. The company recently introduced its diet soda, naming it Coca-Cola Light rather than Diet Coke because the word *diet* in French connotes a medicinal product. Advertising for the diet drink features a topless model in a black bikini, an approach that differs radically from the company's clean-image advertising in other countries. The French, like other European nations, are more accepting of nudity in advertising for a wide range of products than are the Americans.[28] The social-cultural aspects of international marketing will be discussed in more detail in Chapter 3.

Consumerism

Changing societal values have led to the consumerism movement. Today everyone—marketers, industry, government, and the public—is acutely aware of the impact of consumerism on the nation's economy and general well-being. **Consumerism** has been defined as a social force within the environment designed to aid and protect the buyer by exerting legal, moral, and economic pressures on business.[29] It is a societal demand that organizations apply the marketing concept.

In recent years, marketers have been beset by increasing consumer activism. The Defense of Animals has held demonstrations in 48 cities to encourage buyers to boycott Procter & Gamble products until the company stops using animal tests. Some television networks stopped running a Reebok International commercial for its Pump basketball shoe after receiving numerous consumer complaints. The ad showed two men plunging from a bridge with their feet attached to elastic bungee cords. The man with the Pump shoe survived, while the other man fell to his death. Viewers protested that death in advertising is not humorous, and Reebok finally pulled the ads, even though it claimed its target audience of male adults 18 and over reacted positively to the commercial. Under pressure from environmental groups and a growing consumer boycott of their products, the three largest U.S. marketers of canned tuna agreed not to sell tuna caught by nets that trap and kill dolphins. H.J. Heinz, which markets the Star-Kist brand, changed its packaging to include a "Dolphin Safe" logo. Even children have become active participants in the consumer movement. A student group called Kids Against Pollution, with 800 chapters in the United States and Europe, boycotted McDonald's stores and organized a letter-writing campaign to urge the company to stop using polystyrene clamshell packaging. McDonald's decided to replace the foam packages with paper.[30]

But not all consumer demands are met. A competitive marketing system is based on the individual behavior of competing firms. Our economic system requires that reasonable profit objectives be achieved. Business cannot meet all consumer demands if it is to generate the profits necessary for remaining viable. This selection process is one of the most difficult dilemmas facing society today. Given these constraints, what should the buyer have the right to expect from the competitive marketing system?

The most frequently quoted statement of **consumer rights** was made by President John F. Kennedy in 1962. While it was not a definitive statement, it is a good rule of thumb with which to explain basic consumer rights:

1. *The right to choose freely.* Consumers should be able to choose from among a range of goods and services.

2. *The right to be informed.* Consumers should be provided with enough education and product information to enable them to be responsible buyers.

3. *The right to be heard.* Consumers should be able to express their legitimate displeasure to appropriate parties—that is, sellers, consumer assistance groups, and city or state consumer affairs offices.

consumerism
Social force within the environment designed to aid and protect the consumer by exerting legal, moral, and economic pressures on business and government.

consumer rights
As stated by President Kennedy in 1962, the consumer's right to choose freely, to be informed, to be heard, and to be safe.

Mounting consumer protests against advertising of alcohol and tobacco products, especially those targeted at children and minorities, included the white-washing of billboards. The anti-alcohol and anti-tobacco crusade challenges the right of firms to sell products the activists claim destroy human life. Such protests led to the removal of tobacco and liquor ads in the vicinity of some schools and churches and to new self-regulatory guidelines from the outdoor advertising industry's trade groups.

Source: © Peter Freed.

4. *The right to be safe.* Consumers should be assured that the goods and services they purchase are not injurious with normal use. Goods and services should be designed in such a way that the average consumer can use them safely.

These rights have formed the conceptual framework of much of the consumer legislation passed in the last 40 years. However, the question of how best to guarantee these rights remains unanswered.

The social-cultural environment for marketing decisions at home and abroad is expanding in scope and importance. Today no marketer can initiate a strategy without taking into account the society's norms, values, culture, and demographics. Marketers must be aware of how these variables affect their decisions. The constant influx of societal issues requires that marketing managers place more emphasis on addressing these questions instead of concerning themselves with the standard marketing tools. Some firms have created a new position—manager of public policy research—to study the changing societal environment's future impact on the company.

Marketing's Role in Society

Another dimension that goes beyond the five environments described in the previous section is the role that marketing plays in society itself and the consequent effects and responsibilities of marketing activities.

Marketing's relationship to society in general and to various public issues is subject to constant scrutiny by the public. In fact, it may reasonably be argued that marketing typically mirrors changes in the entire business environment. Because marketing is the final interface between the business enterprise and the society in which it operates, marketers often carry much of the responsibility for dealing with various social issues affecting their firms.

Marketing operates in an environment external to the firm. It reacts to its environment and, in turn, is acted upon by it. Relationships with customers, employees, the government, vendors, and society as a whole form the basis of the societal issues that confront contemporary marketing. While they are often a product of the exchange process, these relationships are coincidental to the primary sales and distribution functions of marketing. Marketing's relationship to its external environment has a significant effect on the relative degree of success that the firm achieves. Marketing must continually find new ways to deal with the social issues facing our competitive system.

The competitive marketing system is a product of our drive for materialism. However, it is important to note that materialism developed from society itself. Most of the U.S. culture, with its acceptance of the work ethic, traditionally has viewed the acquisition of wealth favorably. The motto of this philosophy seems to be "more equals better." A better life has been defined in terms of more physical possessions, although that definition seems to be changing.

Evaluating the Quality of Life

One theme runs through the arguments of marketing's critics: materialism (as exemplified by the competitive marketing system) is concerned only with the quantities of life and ignores the quality aspect. Traditionally, a firm was considered socially responsible in the community if it provided employment for its residents, thereby contributing to its economic base. Employment, wages, bank deposits, and profits—the traditional measures of societal contributions—are quantity indicators. But what about air, water, and cultural pollution? The boredom and isolation of mass assembly lines? The depletion of natural resources? The charges of neglect in these areas go largely unanswered simply because we have not developed reliable indices with which to measure a firm's contribution to the quality of life.

Criticisms of the Competitive Marketing System

An indictment of the competitive marketing system would contain at least the following complaints:

1. Marketing costs are too high.
2. The marketing system is inefficient.
3. Marketers (the business system) are guilty of collusion and price fixing.
4. Product quality and service are poor.
5. Consumers receive incomplete and/or false and misleading information.
6. The marketing system has produced health and safety hazards.
7. Unwanted and unnecessary products are promoted to those who least need them.

Almost anyone could cite specific examples in which these charges have been proven. Because each of us has a somewhat different set of values, it should be recognized that we all evaluate the performance of the marketing system we experience within our own frames of reference.

Bearing this in mind and taking the system as a whole, we can evaluate the success or failure of the competitive marketing system in serving consumers' needs. Most of us will likely arrive at the uncomfortable and somewhat unsatisfying conclusion that the system usually works quite adequately, although there are some aspects of it that we would like to see changed.

Current Issues in Marketing

Marketing faces many diverse social issues. The current issues in marketing can be divided into two major subjects: marketing ethics and social responsibility. While the overlap and classification problems are obvious, the framework provides a foundation for systematically studying these issues.

Marketing Ethics

marketing ethics

Marketer's standards of conduct and moral values.

Environmental considerations have led to increased attention to **marketing ethics**—the marketer's standards of conduct and moral values. Ethics concern matters of right and wrong: the decision of the individual and the firm to do what is morally right. A discussion of marketing ethics highlights the types of problems individuals face in their roles as marketers. Such problems must be considered before we can suggest possible improvements in the marketing system.

People develop standards of ethical behavior based on their own systems of values. Their individual ethics help them deal with the various ethical questions in their personal lives. However, when they are put into a work situation, a serious conflict may materialize. Individual ethics may differ from the employer's organizational ethics. An individual may believe that industry participation in developing a recycling program for industrial waste is highly desirable, but his or her firm may take the position that such a venture would be unprofitable. In contrast, unethical behavior of employees may conflict with a firm's high standards of ethical conduct. Anheuser-Busch made it clear to all employees that questionable marketing practices would not be tolerated following a scandal involving allegations that three of its key marketing executives had taken kickbacks of more than $150,000 from a supplier.[31]

How can these conflicts be resolved? The development of and adherence to a professional ethic may provide a third basis of authority. This ethic should be based on a concept of professionalism that transcends both organizational and individual ethics. A professional peer association can exercise collective sanctions over a marketer's individual behavior. For example, the American Marketing Association, the major international association of marketers, has developed a code of ethics that includes a provision for expelling members who violate its tenets. The code is shown in Figure 2.8.

Marketers face a variety of ethical problems. While promotional matters tend to receive the greatest attention, ethical issues also relate to marketing research, product management, channel strategy, and pricing.

Ethical Problems in Marketing Research.   Marketing research has been criticized because of its alleged invasion of personal privacy. People today seek individual identity to a greater degree than ever before. Personal privacy is important to most consumers and therefore has become a public issue. With the proliferation of databases and renting of information lists among marketers, public concern about threats to personal privacy has increased. A survey revealed that in 1990 79 percent of respondents were concerned about invasion of their privacy compared to 64 percent in 1978. Without adequate protection from the government or an industry self-regulatory group, some buyers are taking action against marketers' invasion of their private lives. For example, when members of Private Citizens Inc., a privacy advocate group, receive an unsolicited survey or research call, they bill the marketers $100 for the use of their phone and time. Consumer demands for privacy protection have gained political support, and it is likely that by the mid-1990s federal legislation will restrict marketers' use and gathering of research information.[32]

Ethical Problems in Product Strategy.   Product quality, planned obsolescence, brand similarity, and packaging questions are significant concerns of consumers, managers, and governments. Competitive pressures have forced some marketers into packaging practices that may be considered misleading, deceptive, and/or unethical. Food marketers, for example, have been accused of putting unsubstantiated and misleading nutritional claims on their packages to appeal to health-conscious shoppers. Larger than necessary packages are used to gain shelf space and consumer exposure in the supermarket. Odd-size packages make price comparisons difficult. Bottles with concave bottoms give the impression that they contain more liquid than they actually do. The real question seems to be whether these practices can be justified in the name of competition. Growing regulatory mandates appear to be narrowing the range of discretion in this area.

Ethical Problems in Distribution Strategy.   A firm's channel strategy is required to deal with two kinds of ethical questions:

1. What is the appropriate degree of control over the channel?
2. Should a company distribute its products in marginally profitable outlets that have no alternative source of supply?

The question of control typically arises in relationships between manufacturers and franchised dealers. Should an automobile dealership, a gas station, or a fast-food outlet be coerced to purchase parts, materials, and supplementary services from the parent organization? What is the proper degree of control in the channel of distribution? The second question concerns marketers' responsibility to serve unsatisfied market segments even if the profit potential is slight. Should marketers serve retail stores in low-income areas, users of limited amounts of the firm's product, or a declining rural market? These problems are difficult to resolve, because they often involve individuals rather than broad segments of the general public. An important first step is to ensure that channel policies are enforced on a consistent basis.

Ethical Problems in Promotional Strategy.   Promotion is the component of the marketing mix that gives rise to the majority of ethical questions. Personal selling has always been the target of ethically based criticism. Early traders, pack peddlers, greeters, drummers, and today's used-car salespeople, for example, have all been accused of marketing malpractice ranging from exaggerating product merits to outright deceit. Gifts and bribes are common ethical abuses.

Advertisers now try to show women in varied situations, especially in nontraditional work roles such as bus driver, bank officer, and heavy-equipment operator.

Another ethical issue concerns advertising to children. Some critics fear that television advertising exerts an undue influence on children. They believe children are easily influenced by toy, cereal, and snack-food commercials. Correspondingly, there is the assumption that children in turn exert substantial

Figure 2.8   American Marketing Association Code of Ethics

Members of the American Marketing Association (AMA) are committed to ethical professional conduct. They have joined together in subscribing to this Code of Ethics embracing the following topics:

Responsibilities of the Marketer

Marketers must accept responsibility for the consequences of their activities and make every effort to ensure that their decisions, recommendations, and actions function to identify, serve, and satisfy all relevant publics: customers, organizations, and society. Marketers' professional conduct must be guided by:
1. The basic rule of professional ethics: not knowingly to do harm;
2. The adherence to all applicable laws and regulations;
3. The accurate representation of their education, training, and experience; and
4. The active support, practice, and promotion of this Code of Ethics.

Honesty and Fairness

Marketers shall uphold and advance the integrity, honor, and dignity of the marketing profession by:
1. Being honest in serving consumers, clients, employees, suppliers, distributors, and the public;
2. Not knowingly participating in conflict of interest without prior notice to all parties involved; and
3. Establishing equitable fee schedules including the payment or receipt of usual, customary, and/or legal compensation for marketing exchanges.

Rights and Duties of Parties in the Marketing Exchange Process

Participants in the marketing exchange process should be able to expect that:
1. Products and services offered are safe and fit for their intended uses;
2. Communications about offered products and services are not deceptive;
3. All parties intend to discharge their obligations, financial and otherwise, in good faith; and
4. Appropriate internal methods exist for equitable adjustment and/or redress of grievances concerning purchases.
   It is understood that the above would include, *but it is not limited to,* the following responsibilities of the marketers:

In the area of product development and management,
☐ Disclosure of all substantial risks associated with product or service usage;
☐ Identification of any product component substitution that might materially change the product or impact on the buyer's purchase decision;
☐ Identification of extra-cost added features.

In the area of promotions,
☐ Avoidance of false and misleading advertising;
☐ Rejection of high-pressure manipulations or misleading sales tactics;
☐ Avoidance of sales promotions that use deception or manipulation.

In the area of distribution,
☐ Not manipulating the availability of a product for purpose of exploitation;
☐ Not using coercion in the marketing channel;
☐ Not exerting undue influence over the reseller's choice to handle a product.

In the area of pricing,
☐ Not engaging in price fixing;
☐ Not practicing predatory pricing;
☐ Disclosing the full price associated with any purchase.

In the area of marketing research,
☐ Prohibiting selling or fundraising under the guise of conducting research;
☐ Maintaining research integrity by avoiding misrepresentation and omission of pertinent research data;
☐ Treating outside clients and suppliers fairly.

Organizational Relationships

Marketers should be aware of how their behavior may influence or impact on the behavior of others in organizational relationships. They should not demand, encourage, or apply coercion to obtain unethical behavior in their relationships with others, such as employees, suppliers, or customers. Marketers should:
1. Apply confidentiality and anonymity in professional relationships with regard to privileged information;
2. Meet their obligations and responsibilities in contracts and mutual agreements in a timely manner;
3. Avoid taking the work of others, in whole, or in part, and represent this work as their own or directly benefit from it without compensation or consent of the originator or owner;
4. Avoid manipulation to take advantage of situations to maximize personal welfare in a way that unfairly deprives or damages their organization or others.

Any AMA member found to be in violation of any provision of this Code of Ethics may have his or her Association membership suspended or revoked.

Source: Reprinted with permission from "AMA Adopts New Code of Ethics," *Marketing News* (September 11, 1987), pp. 1, 10; published by the American Marketing Association.

pressure on their parents to acquire these items. In recognition of this concern, the Canadian Association of Broadcasters has formulated a comprehensive broadcast code restricting advertising to children. No similar code exists in the United States; however, the work of Action for Children's Television has contributed to proposed legislation that would reduce the commercial time allowed on children's programming.[33]

Ethical Problems in Pricing.　Pricing is probably the most regulated aspect of a firm's marketing strategy. As a result, most unethical price behavior is also illegal. There are, however, some gray areas in the matter of pricing ethics. For example, should some customers pay more for merchandise if distribution costs are higher in their areas? Do marketers have an obligation to warn customers of impending price, discount, or return policy changes? All these queries must be dealt with in developing a professional ethic for marketing.

Social Responsibility

social responsibility

Marketing philosophies, policies, procedures, and actions that have the enhancement of society's welfare as a primary objective.

In a general sense, **social responsibility** is the marketer's acceptance of the obligation to consider profit, consumer satisfaction, and societal well-being of equal value in evaluating the firm's performance. It is the recognition that marketers must be concerned with the more qualitative dimensions of consumer and societal benefits as well as the quantitative measures of sales, revenue, and profits by which marketing performance is traditionally measured.

As Professors Engel and Blackwell point out, social responsibility is a more easily measured concept than marketing ethics:

Actions alone determine social responsibility, and a firm can be socially responsible even when doing so under coercion. For example, the government may enact rules that force firms to be socially responsible in matters of the environment, deception, and so forth. Also, consumers, through their power to repeat or withhold purchasing, may force marketers to provide honest and relevant information, fair prices, and so forth. To be ethically responsible, on the other hand, it is not sufficient to act correctly; ethical intent is also necessary.[34]

The locus for socially responsible decisions in organizations has always been an important issue. Who should be specifically accountable for the social considerations involved in marketing decisions? The direct sales manager? The marketing vice-president? The firm's CEO? The board of directors? Probably the most valid assessment is to say that *all marketers,* regardless of their stations in the organization, are accountable for the societal aspects of their decisions. At Gerber Products Company, a group of research and development people made a socially responsible decision by volunteering their off-work time to produce a special baby formula for a teenage boy. Since birth the boy has been allergic to all food except Meat-Based Formula, a product Gerber discontinued making in 1985, replacing it with soybean formula. Gerber gave the boy its remaining MBF stock until it ran out in 1990, when the R&D volunteers retooled a plant to produce MBF for a market of one.[35]

Marketing's Responsibilities.　The concept of business responsibility traditionally has concerned the relationships between the manager and customers, employees, and stockholders. Management had the responsibility of

A leader in pharmaceutical product innovation, Merck & Co., Inc., exemplifies the ideal of corporate social responsibility in advancing health care worldwide. Merck distributes free supplies of a new drug called "Mectizan" through the World Health Organization to people in Third World countries who suffer from river blindness. "Mectizan" prevents and kills the parasitic infection and could eliminate the disease in several years. Merck's socially responsible action is voluntary and costs the company millions of dollars in lost profits.

Source: Courtesy of Merck & Co., Inc.

providing a quality product at a reasonable price for customers, adequate wages and a decent working environment for employees, and an acceptable profit level for stockholders. Only occasionally did the concept involve relations with the government and rarely with the general public.

Today the responsibility concept has been extended to the entire societal framework. A decision to temporarily delay the installation of a pollution control device may be responsible in the traditional sense: Customers receive an uninterrupted supply of the plant's products, employees do not face layoffs, and stockholders receive a reasonable return on their investment in the company. But from the standpoint of contemporary business ethics, this is not a socially responsible decision.

Similarly, a firm that markets foods with low nutritional value may satisfy the traditional concept of responsibility, but such behavior is questionable in contemporary perspective. This is not to say that all firms should distribute only foods of high nutritional value; it means merely that the previous framework for evaluation is no longer considered comprehensive in terms of either scope or time.

Contemporary marketing decisions must include consideration of the external societal environment. A growing number of firms have decided to allocate a portion of their promotional budgets for social causes. Nike, for example, announced it would spend $5 million of its estimated $50 million advertising budget on television commercials that try to sell kids on the merits of a good education.[36] Marketing decisions must also account for eventual, long-term effects. Socially responsible decisions must consider future as well as existing generations.

MARKETING CIGARETTES ABROAD

. . . .

Should the U.S. government put pressure on foreign governments to ease restrictions on the sale and advertisement of American cigarettes while at the same time discouraging smoking in the United States?

The Reagan administration was able to persuade Japan, South Korea, and Taiwan to dismantle their government-sanctioned tobacco monopolies, and more recently negotiators have succeeded in doing the same in Thailand. Asian sales of American cigarettes have gone a long way toward offsetting the decline in U.S. sales, rising to over $2.5 billion in the late 1980s. But antismoking organizations and some members of the Bush administration believe that efforts to increase sales of American cigarettes in foreign nations are hypocritical. Former Surgeon General C. Everett Koop compared U.S. cigarette exports to Latin American cocaine exports. And the World Health Organization has expressed concern that sophisticated marketing techniques will increase rates of smoking among citizens of other nations, especially women and young people.

According to U.S. Trade Representative Carla Hills, "We are not pushing cigarettes on other countries, but where they allow cigarette consumption, we say they ought not to ban ours." Representatives of the tobacco industry point out that Asians are already heavy smokers: Between 50 and 60 percent of Asian men smoke, compared with about 30 percent of American men, and governments in those nations have done little to discourage their citizens from smoking. Moreover, Asian cigarette brands contain significantly more tar than American brands.

Several European nations have taken steps to ban tobacco advertising from both television and the print media, and there is a movement to ban such advertising throughout the European Community. A number of nations outside Europe, including Singapore, Kuwait, Canada, Norway, and New Zealand, have also enacted bans on tobacco advertising. Since the Canadian ban was passed in 1989, the smoking rate among Canadians has decreased by about 8 percent per year. Australia recently expanded its ban on tobacco advertising to cover print as well as electronic media, citing evidence of a link between tobacco advertising and number of smokers.

Discussion Questions

1. It has been suggested that instead of promoting American cigarettes overseas, the United States should use trade policy to reduce smoking everywhere, just as it does to save whales or oppose apartheid. Is such an approach likely or even possible?

2. It is argued that consumers everywhere should have the freedom to choose what they will buy and use. Does this justify the marketing of products that may be harmful?

Sources: Dan Koeppel, "RJR Charged with Violating Canadian Tobacco Law," *Marketing Week* (January 1, 1991), p. 6; Joanne Lipman, "French Plan to Ban Tobacco Ads Cheers Advocates of Same in U.S.," *The Wall Street Journal* (March 30, 1990), p. B6; Paul Magnusson, "Uncle Sam Shouldn't Be a Traveling Salesman for Tobacco," *Business Week* (October 9, 1989), p. 61; "Australia to Ban Cigarette Ads in Print," *Arkansas Democrat* (December 6, 1989), p. 8A; and James Drummond, "Hazardous to Whose Health?" *Forbes* (December 11, 1989), pp. 89–92.

Marketing and Ecology. Ecology—the relationship between organisms and their environments—has become one of the most important aspects of marketing in the 1990s. Industry and government leaders attending the World Economic Forum in 1990 ranked the environment as the number one challenge facing business. Environmental concerns of garbage disposal, acid rain, depletion of the ozone layer, global warming, and contamination of the air and water span the globe. They have influenced all areas of marketing decision making from product planning to public relations.[37] There are several aspects of ecology with which marketers must deal: planned obsolescence, pollution, recycling waste materials, and resource conservation.

The original ecological problem facing marketing was *planned obsolescence*—a situation in which a manufacturer produces items of limited durability. In some instances, products are made obsolete by technological improvements.

In others, physical obsolescence is intentional in that products are designed to wear out within a short time period. Marketers have responded to consumer demand for convenience by offering extremely short-lived products such as disposable diapers, pens, razors, and cameras. In still other products, such as the fashion industry, rapid changes in design produce obsolescence. Planned obsolescence has always represented a significant ethical question for the marketer. On one side is the need for maintaining sales and employment; on the other is the need for providing better quality and durability. A practical question is whether the consumer really wants or can afford increased durability. Many buyers prefer to change styles often and accept less durable items. Increased durability has an implicit cost. It may mean that fewer people can afford the product.

Pollution is a broad term that can be applied to a number of circumstances. It usually means "making unclean." The concern about polluting such natural resources as water and air has reached critical proportions in some areas. The marketing system annually generates billions of tons of packaging materials, such as glass, metal, paper, and plastics, that add to the worlds' growing piles of trash and waste. Efforts among marketers to improve their eco-responsibility are widespread. Oil producers are formulating cleaner fuels to reduce air pollution. Atlantic Richfield Co., the largest gas retailer in Southern California, introduced EC-1, a less polluting substitute for leaded gasoline. Benjamin Moore, Red Devil, and other paint companies developed new water- and acrylic-based paints and stains to replace previous products that used environmentally hazardous chemical solvents. Mercedes-Benz was the first automaker to introduce a car without chlorofluorocarbons in its air-conditioning system. Retailers and mail-order marketers are using popped corn as a packing material substitute for polystyrene peanuts. Consumer goods firms are reducing the materials used in their packaging. In an effort to help save the tropical rain forests, Ben & Jerry's Homemade Inc. launched Rainforest Crunch, a candy made with nuts grown in the Brazilian rain forest.[38]

Recycling—the processing of used materials for reuse—is another important aspect of ecology. The underlying rationale of recycling is that reprocessed materials can benefit society by saving natural resources and energy as well as by alleviating a major factor in environmental pollution. Marketers have stepped up their recycling initiatives to meet increased consumer demand for recyclable products and packaging. H.J. Heinz, Procter & Gamble, The Coca-Cola Company, and PepsiCo, Inc. have introduced recyclable plastic for their products. Consumer support of voluntary and mandatory recycling programs has produced a steady supply of recycled paper, plastics, glass, and other materials. As a result, marketers are working to find new uses and create new markets for recycled materials. Rubbermaid uses recycled plastic to produce its garbage containers. Eastman Kodak uses recycled paper for its film boxes and recycles its disposable cameras that consumers return to Kodak labs for processing. Under its McRecycle USA program, McDonald's uses recycled materials to build and remodel its restaurants and for furnishings and equipment. The advertisement in Figure 2.9 is an example of Dow Plastics' efforts to create new markets for recycled plastic waste. Some companies have developed programs to facilitate the collection of recyclable materials. General Electric, for example, buys back used plastic from customers such as computer-maker Digital Equipment Corporation and Domino's pizza, which distributes its pizza dough on plastic trays.[39]

Figure 2.9

Finding Uses for Recycled Plastic

Source: Courtesy of The Dow Chemical Company.

Controlling the Marketing System

When the marketing-economic system does not perform as well as we would like, we attempt to change it. We hope to make it serve us better by producing and distributing goods and services in a fairer way. Most people believe that the system is working sufficiently well to require no changes and that relatively minor adjustments can achieve a fair distribution.

Four ways in which we control or influence the direction of the marketing system and try to rid it of imperfections are by (1) helping the competitive market system to operate in a self-correcting manner; (2) educating the consumer; (3) increasing regulation; and (4) encouraging political action. The competitive market system operates to allocate resources and to provide most of the products we purchase to satisfy felt needs. While we may hear many complaints about the system, most of the goods and services we purchase or use flow through it with little difficulty. Competition works if the conditions of many buyers and sellers and other technical requirements of the free-market economic model allow it. We have attempted—sometimes with limited success—to restore competition where monopolies have reduced it.

Combined with the free-market system, consumer education can lead to wise choices. As products become more complex, diverse, and plentiful, the consumer's ability to make wise decisions must also expand. Educational programs and efforts by parents, schools, business, government, and consumer organizations all contribute to a better system. A responsible marketing philosophy should also encourage consumers to voice their opinions. Such comments can result in significant improvements in the seller's goods and services.

The marketing concept must include social responsibility as a primary function of the marketing organization. Social and profit goals are compatible, but they require the aggressive implementation of an expanded marketing concept. Explicit criteria for responsible decision making must be adopted in all companies. This is truly marketing's greatest challenge.

Summary of Chapter Objectives

1. **Identify the five components of the marketing environment.** The five components of the marketing environment are (1) the competitive environment—the interactive process that occurs in the marketplace as competing organizations seek to satisfy markets; (2) the political-legal environment—the laws and interpretations of laws that require firms to operate under competitive conditions and to protect consumer rights; (3) the economic environment—environmental factors resulting from business fluctuations and resultant variations in inflation rates and employment levels; (4) the technological environment—applications to marketing of knowledge based on discoveries in science, inventions, and innovations; and (5) the social-cultural environment—the component of the marketing environment consisting of the relationship between the marketer and society and its culture.

2. **Explain the types of competition marketers face and the steps in developing a competitive strategy.** The three basic types of competition marketers face are (1) direct competition among marketers of similar products; (2) competition among goods or services that can be substituted for one another; and (3) competition among all organizations that compete for the consumer's purchasing power.

   The development of a competitive strategy is derived from answers to the following three questions: (1) Should we compete? This question is answered on the basis of the firm's available resources and objectives as well as its expected profit potential; (2) If so, in what markets should we compete? This question acknowledges that the marketer has limited resources that must be allocated to the areas of greatest opportunity; and (3) How should we compete? This question requires the marketer to make the technical decisions involved in setting up a comprehensive marketing strategy.

3. **Describe how government and other groups regulate marketing activities and how marketers can influence political-legal environments.** Marketing activities are affected by federal, state, and local laws that require firms to operate under competitive conditions and to protect consumer rights. Government regulatory agencies such as the Federal Trade Commission enforce these laws and develop enforcement procedures for unfair marketing practices. Public and private consumer interest groups and industry self-regulatory groups also influence marketing activities. Marketers may seek to influence public opinion and legislative actions through advertising, political action committees, and political lobbying.

4. **Outline the economic factors that affect marketing decisions and consumer buying power.** The primary economic factors operating in the marketing environment are the stage in the business cycle, inflation and unemployment rates, resource availability, and income. All of these factors are vitally important to marketers because of their effects on consumers'

willingness to buy and consumers' conceptions regarding changes in the marketing mix variables.

5. **Explain the impact of the technological environment on a firm's marketing activities.** The technological environment consists of applications to marketing of knowledge based on discoveries in science, inventions, and innovations. This knowledge can provide both marketing opportunities and threats to current goods and services. The technological environment affects marketing in several ways: (1) It results in new products for consumers and improves existing ones; (2) it is a frequent source of price reductions through new production methods or materials; (3) it can make existing products obsolete virtually overnight; and (4) technological innovations can have significant impacts on consumers' life-styles, competitors' products, industrial users' demands, and government regulatory actions.

6. **Explain how the social-cultural environment influences marketing.** The social-cultural environment relates to the attitudes of members of society toward goods and services as well as pricing, promotion, and distribution strategies. Society demands that business be concerned with the quality of life, which has broadened the social impact of marketing. More specifically, the social-cultural environment has the following influences: (1) It influences the general readiness of society to accept a new marketing idea; (2) the public's trust and confidence in business as a whole influence legislation regulating business and marketing; and (3) although it affects domestic marketing, it is an even more critical factor in international marketing. Consumerism is the social force within the environment designed to aid and protect the consumer by exerting legal, moral, and economic pressures on business. Consumer rights include: (1) the right to choose freely; (2) the right to be informed; (3) the right to be heard; and (4) the right to be safe.

7. **Describe the role of marketing in society.** Marketing operates in an environment external to the firm. These environmental relationships exist with customers, employees, the government, vendors, and society as a whole. They form the basis of the societal issues that confront contemporary marketing. Marketing's relationship to its external environment has a significant effect on the relative degree of success the firm achieves. Marketers must continually find new ways to deal with the social issues facing our competitive system.

8. **Identify the two major social issues in marketing.** Current issues in marketing include marketing ethics and social responsibility. Marketing ethics are the marketer's standards of conduct and moral values. Social responsibility is the marketer's acceptance of the obligation to consider profit, consumer satisfaction, and societal well-being of equal value in evaluating the performance of the firm.

Key Terms

environmental management	technological environment
competitive environment	social-cultural environment
time-based competition	consumerism
political-legal environment	consumer rights
economic environment	marketing ethics
demarketing	social responsibility

Review Questions

1. Briefly describe each of the five components of the marketing environment. Give an example of each.

2. Explain the types of competition marketers face. What are the steps involved in developing a competitive strategy?

3. Government regulation in the United States has evolved in four general phases. Identify each phase and give an example of laws enacted during it.

4. Give an example of a federal law affecting
   a. Product strategy
   b. Pricing strategy
   c. Distribution strategy
   d. Promotional strategy

5. Explain the methods the Federal Trade Commission used to protect consumers. Which of these methods do you consider most effective?

6. What are the major economic factors affecting marketing decisions? How do each of these factors affect marketing decision making?

7. Identify the ways in which the technological environment and the social-cultural environment affect marketing activities. Cite examples of both.

8. What is consumerism's indictment of the competitive marketing system? Critically evalute these arguments.

9. Describe the ethical problems related to
   a. Marketing research
   b. Product strategy
   c. Distribution strategy
   d. Promotional strategy
   e. Pricing strategy

10. Identify and briefly explain the major avenues open for the resolution of contemporary issues facing the marketing system. Cite relevant examples.

Discussion Questions

1. Give an example of how each of the environmental variables discussed in this chapter might affect the following firms:
   a. United Airlines
   b. Local aerobics center
   c. Local cable TV franchise
   d. Tupperware products
   e. Sears catalog department
   f. Pizza Hut

2. Classify the following laws as (1) assisting in maintaining a competitive environment, (2) assisting in regulating competitors, (3) regulating specific marketing activities, or (4) deregulating industries. Justify your classifications and identify the marketing mix variable(s) most affected by each law.
   a. Miller-Tydings Act
   b. Staggers Rail Act
   c. Fair Packaging and Labeling Act
   d. Clayton Act
   e. Robinson-Patman Act

3. Cite two examples of instances in which the technological environment has produced positive benefits for marketers. Give two instances of the harmful impact of the technological environment on a firm's marketing operations.

4. Should the United States ban all advertising aimed at children? Explain.

5. Identify a critical social issue confronting your local community. How does this issue affect marketers in your area? Discuss.

Computer Applications

It is often possible to minimize the adverse effects of environmental factors on operations by predicting their occurrence and taking actions designed to maximize possible benefits resulting from their occurrence. In some cases, the marketer may be able to engage in environmental management and actually influence occurrences in the competitive, political-legal, economic, technological, and social-cultural environments.

A useful method for making decisions in an uncertain marketing environment is *decision tree analysis.* This is a quantitative technique used in identifying alternative courses of action, assigning probability estimates for the profits or sales associated with each alternative, and indicating the course of action with the highest potential profit or sales. The marketer must be able to estimate the likelihood of occurrence in each alternative. In addition, he or she must assign financial payoffs (sales, profits, or losses) for the various alternatives. The following example illustrates how decision tree analysis works.

The vice-president of marketing of a major bicycle manufacturer estimates a 60 percent likelihood that the federal government's Consumer Product Safety Commission will require added safety features on bicycles next year. If the new safety features are included in the basic designs now, they will add $10 to the cost of each bicycle produced. On the other hand, if they are not included and if the new safety requirements are enacted next year, the cost of adding them to the finished product will be $15 per bicycle. In addition, the inclusion of these features would involve additional time and would delay the shipment of finished bicycles from the manufacturer to its dealers. This would reduce next year's sales from current estimates of 800,000 units to 600,000 units. Per-unit profits with no changes in product design are estimated at $20. If the new features are built into product design at this time, estimated per-unit profits are $10 as compared with $5 if they must be added to the finished product as a result of new government regulations.

The problem can be illustrated as a type of decision tree lying on its side (see the figure on the following page). Each branch represents a different possible course of action. The expected profits from a decision to add the new safety features now are $8 million. This determination is made by first multiplying expected total profits ($10 per unit times the 800,000 units) by the .6 probability that the new regulations will be enacted. Next, the expected total profits ($10 per unit times the 800,000 units) are multiplied by the .4 probability that no new safety regulations will be enacted. Finally, the expected values of the two possible outcomes are combined for a total of $8 million.

The decision to defer installation of additional safety features produces a slightly larger net expected value of profits. Unless the firm's marketers are greatly concerned that the shipment delays would generate ill will among their retail dealers and customers should the proposed regulations be enacted, they should choose the second option.

Directions: Use menu item 2 titled "Decision Tree Analysis" to solve each of the following problems.

Problem 1. Sid Norris, director of marketing for Orlando-based FloridaFruit, recognizes more than most people the difficulty involved in producing time, place, and ownership utilities during winters, when the citrus industry often is devastated by unpredictable, killing freezes. Smudge pots and water spraying—the current methods of reducing the impact of low temperatures—are of little use when the temperatures dip below the 25°F mark. After carefully analyzing the test results of a newly developed citrus grove heating system, Norris is viewing his firm's technological environment in a most positive way. Not only did the new system appear to work; it could be leased on a year-to-year basis, thereby avoiding huge equipment outlays. Norris estimates the likelihood of a severe freeze at 20 percent for the upcoming season. He expects total revenues from next year's crop to reach $700,000 and earnings to amount to 9 percent of sales—as long as no severe freeze occurs. Norris estimates that if one occurs, sales will fall to $200,000 and profits to zero. Norris's calculations show that if FloridaFruit decides to lease the new system, the added

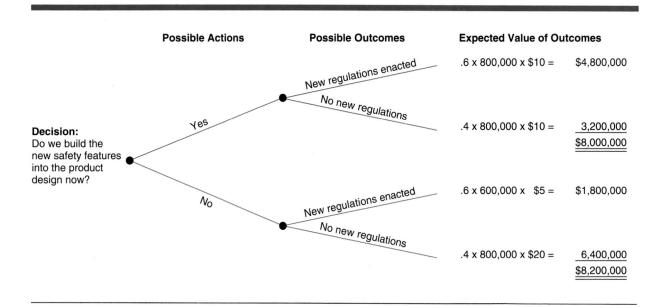

Possible Actions	Possible Outcomes	Expected Value of Outcomes	
	New regulations enacted	.6 x 800,000 x $10 =	$4,800,000
Yes	No new regulations	.4 x 800,000 x $10 =	3,200,000
			$8,000,000
No	New regulations enacted	.6 x 600,000 x $5 =	$1,800,000
	No new regulations	.4 x 800,000 x $20 =	6,400,000
			$8,200,000

Decision:
Do we build the
new safety features
into the product
design now?

leasing costs will trim profits to 5 percent of sales. However, should a freeze occur once the system is in place at FloridaFruit citrus groves, the increased price resulting from the reduced overall industry output would increase the firm's revenues from $700,000 to $850,000. Recommend a course of action for FloridaFruit.

Problem 2. Nancy Akers, vice-president of marketing at Philadelphia Industries, is confident that next year's sales will reach $36 million. However, she is worried about the impact of increased costs on her firm's profits during the coming year. Akers estimates a 70 percent likelihood of a major price increase in one of the petroleum-based raw materials used in the production of her firm's products. Akers feels that she would be unable to raise prices to cover these cost increases. Her major competitors recently have switched to a new, blended process that uses a small amount of petroleum in combination with synthetic materials. Akers projects next year's earnings at 10 percent of sales. If she converts to the new process, earnings are expected to be reduced to 7 percent of sales as a result of the changeover expenses. On the other hand, Akers feels that if she does not make the change and the price increase occurs, her earnings will be reduced to 2 percent of sales as a result of the price-cost squeeze. Recommend a course of action for Philadelphia Industries.

Problem 3. Virginia Beach WaterMania manager Norm Olsen is pleased with next year's $800,000 revenue forecast and projected earnings of 12 percent of sales. However, he is concerned about reports of a new waterslide park opening. In fact, he estimates a 50 percent likelihood that the new competitor will be open for business in time for next year's season. Olsen estimates that if the new park opens at the location under consideration and Virginia Beach WaterMania makes no competitive moves at this time, total revenues will plummet to $300,000 and earnings to only 2 percent of sales. If the competing park fails to materialize and Olsen reduces admission prices by 25 percent to match those charged in other cities by the potential competitor, overall sales revenues will increase to $900,000 and earnings will be 8 percent of sales. If Olsen lowers prices and the new park opens, WaterMania's competitive prices will be sufficient to generate $600,000 in revenues and earn profits of 6 percent of sales. Olsen prefers to postpone his decision until he is certain of his potential competitor's plans, but the need for a new, huge sign and the preparation of tickets, coupons, and advertising materials require him to make the decision now. Recommend a course of action for Olsen.

Mitsubishi Motor Sales of America

What seemed to be an astute marketing decision back in 1970 proved to be one that strategists at Japan's Mitsubishi Heavy Industries would later regret. Mitsubishi is Japan's largest company, a giant conglomerate whose product lines range from shipbuilding to rocketry. Its subsidiary, Mitsubishi Motors Corporation (MMC), is the oldest and third largest Japanese automaker, but its market share is far less than those of market leaders Toyoto and Nissan.

In 1970, MMC marketers discovered a low-cost, low-risk way to enter the huge U.S. market, a market they had previously ignored to the benefit of Honda, Nissan, and Toyota. Chrysler Corporation executives, seeking to add small cars to their product line, agreed to purchase a 35 percent share in MMC in return for an exclusive franchise to distribute Mitsubishi models in the U.S. under the Chrysler nameplate. As MMC spokesperson Tohei Takeuchi explains, the arrangement appeared to make sense in 1970, but proved less satisfactory after a few years: "It would have cost MMC a lot of money to expand in the U.S. . . . . Instead, we decided to use Chrysler's distribution network. But suddenly the American consumer liked Japanese cars. The market changed, and we no longer needed help from an existing channel."

Even though one million Mitsubishi cars and small trucks were sold in America between 1971 and 1981, they carried such nameplates as Dodge Colt, Challenger, and Plymouth Sapporo. American car buyers were not being educated about the strengths of Mitsubishi models. In addition, MMC marketers were dissatisfied with Chrysler's marketing efforts and felt that the U.S. firm was emphasizing its own small cars over the Mitsubishi-built Colts and Sapporos because selling its own product was more profitable. They were all too aware of the fact that MMC's market share in Europe, where they controlled their own distribution, was double their U.S. market share.

The opportunity to end Chrysler's exclusive U.S. marketing rights came in 1980. The U.S. firm, in the midst of a financial crisis, was struggling to avoid bankruptcy when Japan's major banks refused to continue their previous practice of financing Mitsubishi shipments to Chrysler. Mitsubishi executives agreed to provide their own financing for Chrysler, but only if the U.S. firm would allow MMC to sell a minimum of 30,000 Mitsubishi cars in the United States through its own dealer network. Chrysler executives had no viable alternative and agreed to the proposal in April, 1981. A new subsidiary, Mitsubishi Motor Sales of America (MMSA) based in Fountain Valley, California, was created to direct the firm's marketing efforts on the U.S. mainland.

Nineteen eighty-two was one of the worst times in automobile history to launch a new product line. The U.S. economy was in the midst of a severe recession further complicated by inflation. The high interest rates and economic uncertainty caused American consumers to postpone major purchases, and the auto industry was in a major sales slump. In addition, the growing share of the American auto market held by imports was prompting increasingly frequent demands for import quotas as a means of reducing the number of foreign cars sold in the U.S.

Japan's Ministry of International Trade & Industry responded by voluntarily limiting auto shipments to the U.S. to 1.68 million units annually. Each Japanese auto company's quota was based on average sales since 1976. While Mitsubishi was granted a quota of 112,500 cars annually, 82,500 of this total had to be shipped to Chrysler. MMSA faced the unenviable task of establishing a widespread distribution network with an annual nationwide sales ceiling of only 30,000 cars. While some auto industry representatives felt that the Voluntary Restraint Agreement would be lifted within a few years, no one knew for certain.

MMSA executives needed a marketing strategy that would produce sales and profit success in an environment filled with uncertainty. In addition to a low quota of cars and the need to create a strong dealership network, they also had to deal with such factors as well-known Japanese and U.S. competitors, low name recognition, and cultural differences that existed in this new market.

Richard Recchia, MMSA's executive vice president, recognized that the first task facing his firm in the highly competitive import market was to convince American consumers that Mitsubishi automobiles were special and unique. He decided to base his marketing strategy on the parent firm's demonstrated strengths.

We didn't want our products to be perceived as just another Japanese car. So the product line we selected and the price lines within those product lines that we established were aimed at placing our products a step above other Japanese car lines in the same segment so people would perceive Mitsubishi as having more features, more technology, more innovation at a better price than the competition.

Three models were selected: the two-door sport hatchback Cordia and the four-door Tredia sedan — both offered at approximately $10,000 — plus the sporty Starion turbo coupe designed to compete with the Mazda RX7 and Nissan's best-selling ZX sports car. In addition, MMSA decided to market a line of small trucks, a product category not included under the Voluntary Restraint Agreement.

Crucial to MMSA's U.S. success was its dealer network. By limiting distribution of the Mitsubishi models to a quality network of a few dealerships, MMSA could assure each dealer sufficient inventory to be successful in the market. Moreover, the presence of high-volume, exclusive Mitsubishi dealers in carefully selected markets would serve as tangible evidence to auto buyers that the new cars represented substantial competition for Toyota, Honda, and other companies that consumers associate with Japanese imports.

The dealerships were strategically placed in geographic areas where concentrations of Japanese car registrations were highest. Special computer programs were developed to create density maps that would pinpoint these locations for prospective dealerships. The first two years of U.S. operation saw Mitsubishi dealerships in only 22 metropolitan markets, but those markets accounted for 43 percent of total car sales in the entire nation.

MMSA marketers worked closely with these dealers to ensure marketplace success. Advertising expenditures were double the per-unit average of other Japanese automakers. Some dealers began to report consumer requests for a fuel-efficient subcompact model; others asked for a more luxurious sedan to compete with the Cressida, Maxima, and Audi. MMSA responded by introducing the subcompact Mirage and the Galant sedan in 1985, enabling Mitsubishi dealers to offer car buyers a complete product line for the first time. Four new models were added in the 1991 model year, including the 3000 GT sports car, Mitsubishi's highest-image car to date. Advertising was expanded to include national TV coverage; the 1991 advertising budget was $120 million, up 20 percent from the 1990 budget. Recchia explained that it is essential to advertise a new model heavily for the first 90 days, followed by six months of advertising to enhance the model's image. "You have to live with [that image] for the life of the product," he said.

During the late 1980s, Mitsubishi benefited from changing American transportation preferences. In 1960, U.S. consumers bought one truck for every ten cars. In 1987, they bought one truck for every two cars. Compact trucks, such as Mitsubishi's Mighty Max and Montero, are not governed by the Voluntary Restraint Agreement, and they actually outsold the firm's car models in the late 1980s.

To provide its dealers with additional models, Mitsubishi began importing the Hyundai Precis in 1987. Although the Precis (rhymes with "thesis") carries the Mitsubishi nameplate, its South Korean origin exempts it from the restraint quotas, thus permitting MMSA dealers to boost sales and profits without reducing imports of their own higher-priced and more profitable Japanese cars.

In the years since the creation of MMSA, Chrysler Corporation has continued to import and market Mitsubishi car and light truck models under its own nameplate. During the 1980s, Chrysler was more dependent on Japanese imports than the other U.S. automakers. About 11 percent of its cars and 40 percent of its light trucks were built by Mitsubishi.

Relations between Chrysler and Mitsubishi changed during the late 1980s as Chrysler reduced its share of ownership in MMC to 12.8 percent. Meanwhile, the two firms formed a joint venture to build a giant production facility in Bloomington—Normal, Illinois. The new plant can produce up to 240,000 cars a year, and both firms share the output. Its benefits are enormous for Mitsubishi, since domestic production provides a means of avoiding the sales ceilings imposed by the Voluntary Restraint Agreement. Moreover, it allows MMSA to reduce the headaches resulting from the huge exchange rate fluctuations between the Japanese yen and the U.S. dollar. American sales of MMSA products were expected to approach 250,000 units in 1990, eight times the 1982 totals.

Sources: Cleveland Horton, "Mitsubishi Maps Solo Success," *Advertising Age* (July 2, 1990), pp. 3, 33; Manning, Selvage & Lee; Takeuchi quotation from Lawrence Minard, "Just What Detroit Needs," *Forbes* (November 21, 1983), pp. 208, 210. See also "Mitsubishi Motors Corp.," *Advertising Age* (November 23, 1987), p. S-35; Andrew Tanzer, "Gentlemen, Start Your Engines." *Forbes* (April 8, 1985), p. 38; and Doug Carroll, "Buyers Keep on Trucking," *USA Today* (February 8, 1988), p. 10E.

Questions

1. Relate the material in this case to each of the elements of the marketing environment.

2. Give specific examples of environmental factors that were truly uncontrollable. How did MMSA marketing responses to these factors differ from those made in response to environmental variables that could be influenced by the firm?

3. What are the major differences between the MMSA marketing approach and the more typical approaches used by other marketers of imported automobiles? What modifications in the MMSA marketing approach do you expect to occur over the next five years.?

4. Isuzu Motors is another relatively recent entry in the U.S. auto market with an initial U.S. quota of 16,800 cars. Use the Mitsubishi experience to recommend a course of action for Isuzu.

3

Global Dimensions of Marketing

CHAPTER OBJECTIVES

1. To describe the importance of international marketing from the perspectives of the individual firm and the nation.

2. To identify the major components of the environment for international marketing.

3. To identify the various methods of entering international markets.

4. To differentiate between a global marketing strategy and a multinational marketing strategy.

5. To describe the alternative product and promotional strategies used in international marketing.

6. To explain the attractiveness of the United States as a target market for foreign marketers.

A major challenge facing marketers in the 1990s is to be successful in a globally competitive world. Cincinnati-based Procter & Gamble Company entered the decade as a global powerhouse. It has operations in 46 countries outside the United States—up from 22 countries in 1981—and markets 160 consumer brands in more than 140 countries. In 1991, Procter & Gamble purchased Revlon's Max Factor line and its German makeup and fragrance subsidiary, Betrix. Procter & Gamble CEO, Edwin Artzt, remarked at the time that the deal "speeds up

the global expansion of the company by at least five years."

P&G's success in the international marketplace didn't come easy. In the past, P&G marketed its products abroad in a distinctly American way, and the strategy didn't always work. In some cases it produced disastrous results. Consider, for example, how P&G erred in marketing disposable diapers in Japan, where the company lost $200 million before realizing its mistakes.

When P&G introduced Pampers disposable diapers to Japan in 1973, it quickly captured 90 percent of the market. In the early 1980s, though, Japanese competitors Kao and Unicharm introduced superabsorbent diapers. Japanese parents stopped buying Pampers in favor of the more absorbent products. By 1985 P&G's share of the diaper market dropped to 6 percent.

Anxious to turn around the money-losing venture, P&G conducted marketing research to gain a better understanding of Japanese consumers' needs and wants. P&G learned that Japanese parents change their babies' diapers more often than their American counterparts. Japanese consumers also said that better fit and comfort and less bulkiness are important considerations in the buying of diapers.

Armed with this knowledge, Artzt, then president of P&G International, created a product development team based in Japan. The Japanese team developed Ultra Pampers Plus, a thinner and more absorbent diaper than the American version. With this product, P&G regained its leadership position in Japan's diaper market.

In describing P&G's initial diaper product launch in Japan, Artzt says the company "stormed into the Japa-

nese market with American products, American managers, American advertising, and American sales methods and promotional strategies." The company cites its turnaround story in Japan as its biggest lesson in developing products for different cultures. Artzt says, "We are successful in Japan today because we learned some lessons about tailoring our products and marketing strategies to the local market. The learning from our experiences in Japan has had global reapplication."

P&G's product adaptation strategy is illustrated in the photo shown here. Laundresses at its Cincinnati research center test detergents in waters and washing machines from such countries as Peru, Mexico, Japan, and Venezuela where the products are marketed.

Whereas P&G once operated as an export-driven multinational—a U.S.–based firm that sold products in foreign markets—today it operates as a world marketer. It has globalized its sources of product innovation by establishing technology centers in Japan, Great Britain, Belgium, Mexico, and Germany. Artzt says P&G plans to continue its "world technology" strategy so that "products, wherever we develop them—whether we develop them in the United States, Japan, or Europe—can be sold throughout the world."

P&G entered the decade as a strong global competitor with 40 percent of its business coming from international sales. By pursuing its new global thrust, it plans to become a stronger competitor, poised to enter the twenty-first century with international sales accounting for 60 percent of its business.[1]

Photo source: © 1990 Louis Psihoyos/Matrix.

Chapter Overview

Increasing numbers of U.S. organizations are crossing national boundaries in search of markets and profits. For many of these firms, the international marketplace generates a sizable portion of total revenues and profits. Exxon receives 73 percent of its total revenue from its overseas operations, IBM 59 percent, Dow Chemical 54 percent, and ITT 43 percent. Mobil, Texaco, Merck, Eastman Kodak, and Digital Equipment derive more than 40 percent of their annual earnings from international business.[2] The Coca-Cola Company, the prime example of a global marketer, generates 77 percent of its nearly $9 billion in annual revenues from foreign sources, and its product is sold in 160 foreign countries.[3]

Overseas sales are also important revenue sources for many U.S. service firms. Citicorp earns about 52 percent of its revenues from foreign operations. Its financial services for global customers include the foreign exchange service described in the ad in Figure 3.1. Other service marketers that derive a substantial portion of total revenues from foreign operations include American Family Insurance, 73 percent; Pan Am, 71 percent; Woolworth, 43 percent; and McDonald's, 36 percent.[4]

Just as some firms depend on foreign sales, others rely on purchasing raw materials abroad for use in their domestic manufacturing operations. A furniture company's purchase of South American mahogany is an example.

Figure 3.1   Citicorp: An International Service Marketer

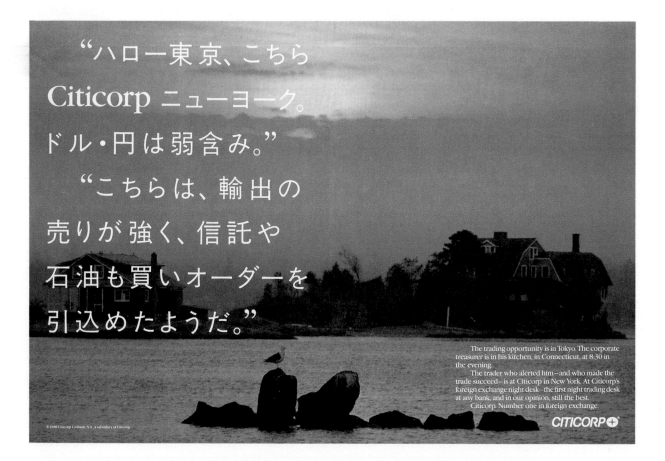

Source: Courtesy of Citicorp.

Components of a firm's international product line may be acquired through foreign purchases. Although Matsushita of Japan is one of the world's largest manufacturers of VCRs, the firm's marketers recognized that software is typically more profitable than hardware. In 1990 Matsushita agreed to pay almost $7 billion for MCA, home of such Hollywood blockbusters as *ET: The Extraterrestrial, Jaws,* and internationally famous recording artists such as Michael Jackson and New Kids on the Block. MCA will continue to produce movies and records to complement the sale of Matsushita's entire product line.

International marketing is valuable to the individual firm for other reasons. In some instances, the company discovers significant product innovations being offered by competitors in foreign markets. These improved offerings may be adapted for the firm's product line currently being offered in its home country, thereby providing a way to generate profitable new-product ideas. Another reason is that the global marketer may be able to meet foreign competition abroad before the latter infringes on home markets. After Japan's Makita Electric Works succeeded in capturing a 20 percent market share for professional tools in Europe over a three-year period by offering a highly standardized, low-priced product line, Black & Decker responded with a crash program designed to cut costs and tighten quality control to match the Japanese firm's retail prices. These corrective measures prevented Makita from expanding its European successes to the United States.

Foreign marketers, in turn, are becoming increasingly attracted to the huge U.S. market. Foreign product invasions are no longer limited to such industries as automobiles, electronics, and steel. Americans buy tires from Canada, jewelry boxes from Taiwan, golf balls from South Korea, vitamin C from Germany, and Gouda cheese from the Netherlands.

International trade is vital to a nation and its marketers for several reasons. It expands the market and makes production and distribution economies feasible. It also means more jobs at home: Each billion dollars of exports supports about 22,000 jobs.

exporting
Selling domestically produced goods and services in foreign countries.

importing
Purchasing foreign products and raw materials.

Foreign trade can be divided into **exporting**—selling goods and services abroad—and **importing**—purchasing foreign goods and raw materials. Major U.S. exports include transportation equipment, electrical and electronic equipment, specialty chemicals, computers, semiconductors, drugs, and food and related products. The United States is now the world's second leading exporter after Germany and the world's leading importer. Its formerly dominant role in the export of manufactured goods has diminished in recent years. The United States now accounts for slightly more than 10 percent of world trade in manufactured goods compared to 43 percent for the European Community, 13 percent for Japan, and 9 percent for Hong Kong, Taiwan, Singapore, and South Korea.[5]

Even America's distinction as a leader in high technology has diminished. With U.S. firms abandoning manufacturing and relying more on foreign companies for parts, Japan has acquired the leadership position in semiconductor manufacturing equipment. Instead of exporting components, Apple Computer uses major parts made by Sony in its Macintosh computers. In total, nearly three-quarters of the Macintosh is composed of foreign-made parts.[6] Despite this, many of our country's top exporters, including Boeing, IBM, United Technologies, McDonnell-Douglas, and Hewlett-Packard, deal in high-technology products. And as you can see in Table 3.1, many of our country's fastest-growing exports include high-technology equipment.

U.S. firms are important exporters of services. Companies like Toys "R" Us, Electronic Data Systems, Arthur Andersen, and the Fluor Corp. earned between 10 percent and 40 percent of their total sales abroad. The United States leads the world in the export of computer services (including data processing, custom software, and computer network integration), air courier services like those provided by Federal Express, and industrial construction.[7]

Table 3.1

Fastest-Growing U.S. Exports

Product	Growth Rate 1985–1989 (percent of change)	Amount July 1988–June 1989 (in billions)
1. Music, video, and computer tapes; floppy disks	32.3%	$ 2.5
2. Cigarettes and other tobacco products	30.4	3.2
3. Meat	30.0	2.7
4. Pulp and wastepaper	27.1	4.1
5. Synthetic resins, rubber, and plastics	27.1	7.9
6. Electronic components and parts	25.0	11.5
7. Electromedical and radiological equipment	23.3	2.7
8. Electrical machinery and equipment	19.8	4.9
9. Timber	19.3	2.3
10. Animal feeds	19.0	3.4

Source: Data from office of Trade Information and Analysis, Department of Commerce. Reported in *Fortune* (April 23, 1990), p. 90.

The foreign products Americans most often purchase include transportation equipment, electrical and electronic equipment, machinery, primary metals, petroleum and coal products, and apparel and other mill products. While the United States trades hundreds of thousands of products with many countries, its major trading partners are Canada, Japan, Mexico, the United Kingdom, and Germany. Currently, 99 percent of videotape recorders, 77 percent of footwear, 75 percent of telephones, 72 percent of televisions and video cameras, 45 percent of car radios, and 44 percent of automobiles sold in this country are made abroad.[8]

Foreign trade is less critical to the United States, however, than it is to many other nations. In fact, U.S. exports account for a modest 10 percent of the nation's gross national product. In contrast, exports comprise 72 percent of Japan's GNP, 23 percent of Canada's, 27 percent of Germany's, and 45 percent of the Netherlands'. The leading U.S. firms in volume of export sales are Boeing, General Motors, Ford, General Electric, and IBM.[9] Table 3.2 lists the most successful U.S. exporters in terms of exports as a percentage of total sales.

Since the marketing functions of buying, selling, transporting, storing, standardization and grading, financing, risk taking, and obtaining market information must be performed regardless of whether the market is domestic or global, a question arises about the wisdom of treating international marketing as a distinct subject. After all, international marketing is marketing—that is, the firm performs the same functions and has the same objectives in domestic or international marketing. Both similarities and differences in strategy for international and domestic marketing exist, however. This chapter examines the characteristics of the international marketplace, environmental influences on international marketing, and the development of an international marketing mix. It also discusses the sequence of steps that most firms use in entering the global marketplace.

The International Marketplace

Many U.S. firms never venture outside the domestic market, which, after all, is huge. Those that do venture abroad find the international marketplace far

Table 3.2

Successful U.S. Exporters of
Goods and Services

Company	Exports as a Percentage of Total Sales
Boeing	54%
Sun Microsystems	42
Compaq Computer	31
Intel	30
Caterpillar	30
Motorola	24
Unisys	24
Hewlett-Packard	22
Ethyl	22
McDonnell-Douglas	19

Source: Data from *Fortune* (July 16, 1990), p. 77.

different from the domestic one. Market sizes, buyer behavior, and marketing practices all vary, meaning that international marketers must carefully evaluate all market segments in which they expect to compete.

Market Size

In 1865 the world population was recorded at 1 billion. It now exceeds 5 billion, and forecasters predict that it will reach 6 billion by the year 2000. Although the United States has attained one of the highest standards of living in world history, its population is dwarfed by those of countries such as India and China. While one-fifth of the world's population lives in China, for example, only one-twentieth resides in the United States.

A prime ingredient of market size is population growth. Every day the world's population increases by about 200,000 people; hence, it is expected to be 8.2 billion by 2025. A review of these projections produces some important contrasts. Average birthrates are dropping, but death rates are declining even more rapidly. In the next 25 years, the population of more developed countries is expected to rise from 1.2 billion to 1.4 billion while that of less developed countries rises from 4 billion to 6.8 billion. Nearly 80 percent of the population in 2025 will live in less developed nations.

The world marketplace is increasingly an urban marketplace. By the year 2000, almost one of every two of the world's inhabitants will live in large cities. These cities are also growing in size: 39 of them currently have a population of 5 million or more. Mexico City, whose population of 18 million ranks it as the world's largest city, is expected to grow to 31 million by the year 2000. Increased urbanization will expand the need for transportation, housing, machinery, and services.

The increased size and growing urbanization of the international market-place does not mean that all foreign markets will offer the same market potential. Income differences, for instance, vitally affect any nation's market potential. India has a population of 830 million, but its per capita income of $150 is very low. Canada's population of 27 million, on the other hand, is only a small fraction of India's, but its per capita income is about $10,000.

Another factor influencing market potential is the stage of a nation's economic development. In *subsistence economies,* in which most people

Figure 3.2   Marketing to Affluent Consumers in Industrialized Nations

Source: Courtesy of Hermes, Paris.

engage in agriculture and per capita income is low, few opportunities for international trade exist. In *newly industrialized countries,* such as Brazil and South Korea, an increase in manufacturing creates more demand for consumer goods and industrial goods such as high-technology equipment. As nations become more developed, they give rise to an increasingly affluent and educated middle class, creating a need for more leisure goods and services ranging from sports equipment to child care. The middle class in India, for example, is almost as large as America's and is growing at a rate of 20 percent a year. This growth translates into increasing consumer demand: In 1978 Indian consumers purchased only 150,000 television sets as compared to 6 million a decade later. The *industrial nations* of North America, Western Europe, and Japan trade manufactured goods and services among themselves and export to less developed countries. Although these countries account for just 15 percent of the world's population, they produce more than 50 percent of its output.[10] With their large middle classes and high per capita incomes, industrial nations constitute attractive opportunities for international marketers. Luxury goods, such as the matching gloves and shoes promoted in the advertisement in Figure 3.2, are targeted at affluent consumers in industrialized countries. While affluent households exist in every nation, their concentration in industrial nations makes effective marketing programs implemented in these countries pay off in sales and profits.

Buyer Behavior

Buyer behavior differs among countries and often among different market segments within each nation. After the Iron Curtain fell in Eastern Europe, the California Walnut Commission, a group that represents 5,000 West Coast walnut growers, began investigating the export opportunities in Eastern Europe. The group's reasoning was linked to their study of buyer behavior: Eastern Europeans are well known for their love of nuts.[11]

Marketers must be careful to make their marketing strategies comply with local customs, tastes, and living conditions. Foreign-based companies, attempting to market goods and services to Japan, should be aware of some unique characteristics of Japanese consumers. For instance, marketers developing new sales campaigns for Japan should understand that the Japanese are uncomfortable using consumer coupons. Although coupons have been in Japan since 1976, most consumers are too embarrassed to redeem them at the checkout counter.[12] Additional analysis of buyer behavior reveals that since most Japanese women wash their hair daily, milder shampoos are more likely to sell. In addition, detergents must be suited for the cold, hard water found in most Japanese homes, and sugar, an expensive product in Japan, must be used sparingly in product manufacturing.[13]

An analysis of buyer behavior patterns in Western Europe tells U.S.–based food distributors to focus much of their marketing efforts on specialty stores. With the supermarket a relatively recent development in Western Europe, consumers traditionally shop for food daily, often visiting a number of specialty stores for different items. The result is that there are nearly four times as many food outlets in Europe than in the United States, meaning many more opportunities for U.S. firms distributing groceries abroad.

Food marketers exporting their products abroad or importing products to the United States must be particularly sensitive to local tastes. CPC International, a U.S.–based food company, learned that the popularity of marmite (a sticky, yeast-based spread) in England did not transfer to the United States. Conversely, although American kids love peanut butter, Italian kids hate it. However, the company has had success marketing peanut butter in Asia.[14]

Different buying patterns mean that marketing executives should do considerable research before entering a foreign market. Sometimes the research can be done by the marketer's own organization or a U.S.–based research firm. In other cases, a foreign-based marketing research organization is needed. Whoever conducts the research, investigators must focus on five different areas before advising a company to enter a foreign market.[15]

1. Whether foreign consumers need the company's good or service (demand).
2. How the market currently is being supplied (competition).
3. Whether indices of the nation's economic health are positive (the economic environment).
4. The legal restrictions that may make entering the market difficult (the legal environment).
5. The relationship between cultural factors and business opportunity (the cultural environment).

Environment for International Marketing

Various environmental factors can influence international marketing strategy. Marketers should be as aware of economic, social-cultural, and political-legal influences in foreign markets as they are of those in domestic ones.

Economic Factors

A nation's size, per capita income, and stage of economic development determine its feasibility as a candidate for international business expansion. Nations with low per capita incomes may be poor markets for expensive industrial machinery but good ones for agricultural hand tools. These nations cannot afford the technical equipment an industrialized society needs. Wealthier countries may be prime markets for many U.S. industries, particularly those producing consumer goods and services and advanced industrial products. Realizing that many European countries have faster growing economies than the United States, Citicorp, the parent of Citibank Visa, has targeted Europe's emerging middle class. With the charge volume of European Visa cards reaching an estimated $250 billion, a figure that surpasses Citicorp Visa's domestic business, this strategy makes sound business sense.[16]

Marketers thinking of doing business in the new free-market societies of Eastern Europe must be aware of the economic problems that plague the area. Ironically, these problems may be the result of the move away from the centrally planned economies that characterized the communist systems. In Poland, for example, the abolition of government subsidies and price controls brought unemployment to 400,000 people and reduced the purchasing power of some families by as much as 40 percent. Since Poland's own factories cannot sell everything they produce, the opportunity for foreign business may be limited.[17] Nevertheless, the positive benefits of the free-market economy are real: The inflation rate dropped from as high as 250 percent a month to 3.4 percent a month, and store shelves are well stocked.[18]

Another problem marketers face is that many Eastern European currencies are considered "soft" currencies, which cannot be readily converted into such "hard" Western currencies as the dollar, British pound, or German mark. Russian rubles, for example, are worthless in the West and may require exporters to engage in countertrade. (Countertrade is discussed later in the chapter.) Despite these and other hardships, many U.S. companies are flocking to Eastern Europe, believing that the first company to enter a market will hold a position of leadership.

Another economic factor that marketers must consider is a country's infrastructure. **Infrastructure** refers to a nation's communication systems (television, radio, print media, telephone services), transportation networks (paved roads, railroads, airports), and energy facilities (power plants, gas and electric utilities). An inadequate infrastructure may constrain marketer's plans to manufacture, advertise, and distribute goods and services. Marketers doing business in Romania, for example, will find the telephone system inadequate to meet their needs. The system, which was built in the 1930s, has only 38 phone lines to the United States.[19] Similarly, in Poland there is a 20-year waiting period for a phone, and one-third of all rural Soviet hospitals do not have running water.[20]

In contrast, concerted efforts to improve a region's infrastructure can make an area more attractive to marketers. Western Europeans will benefit from three transportation projects that will change the way they do business. These projects include a rail tunnel under the English Channel where trains will travel the 30 miles between Britain and France in as little as 20 minutes; a high-speed train network across continental Europe that will accommodate trains traveling between 120 and 200 miles per hour; and a bridge and tunnel that will unify the two halves of Denmark. All these projects are expected to be completed by the year 2005.[21]

Changes in exchange rates can also complicate international marketing. An **exchange rate** is the price of one nation's currency in terms of other countries' currencies. In the early 1980s the U.S. dollar was strong compared to other

infrastructure
A nation's communication systems, transportation networks, and energy facilities.

exchange rate
Price of one nation's currency in terms of other countries' currencies.

As soon as the Berlin Wall fell, The Coca-Cola Company sent delivery trucks to checkpoints and handed out thousands of samples of "the real thing." The speedy promotion, almost six months prior to reunification of the two Germanys, helped the company to be the first Western soft-drink marketer in East Germany, an important advantage in today's global competitive environment. East Germany's union with West Germany, its market size—a population of 16.6 million, and a high per-capita income make it an attractive emerging market for Coca-Cola and other consumer goods companies.

Source: Courtesy of The Coca-Cola Company.

currencies. For example, one dollar could be exchanged for 3.3 German deutschemarks or about 240 Japanese yen. During this period, German and Japanese consumer and industrial buyers considered U.S. products relatively expensive, while American shoppers thought foreign goods were attractively priced. Sales of many U.S. exporters therefore suffered. Some firms even withdrew from certain export markets due to lack of sales and profits. But by the end of the decade, the dollar had declined significantly against other currencies in the face of huge balance-of-trade deficits. By 1991 a mild recession coupled with the costs of the Persian Gulf War was accompanied by a decline in the dollar to 1.5 deutschemarks and 130 yen. The impact of these fluctuations was all too evident to U.S. travelers who discovered that it took twice as many dollars to purchase the same goods and services in Germany and Japan as it had less than a decade earlier. These exchange rate fluctuations helped ease the balance-of-trade problem because they resulted in less expensive U.S. products for German and Japanese shoppers and higher prices for products imported from these countries for U.S. buyers.

To head off currency-related problems, Minster Machine Co., an Ohio-based company that sells forming presses, strengthened its international sales organization, recruited multilingual engineers with the technical and linguistic ability to speak to clients in their native languages, boosted product development spending to improve company products, and cut expenses. The result was increased exports from 20 percent of company sales to 28 percent a year later in a rising-dollar environment.[22]

Companies with manufacturing facilities in the United States and overseas use these facilities in different ways, depending upon the strength of the dollar. For example, Air Products and Chemicals, Inc., of Allentown, Pennsylvania, a manufacturer of air-purifying equipment, has factories in Wilkes-Barre, Pennsylvania, and Acrefair, England. When the dollar is strong, the company centers its export manufacturing operations in England. In a weak-dollar environment, the Wilkes-Barre plant is the focus of the company's export business.[23]

Social-Cultural Factors

Before entering a foreign market, firms must study all aspects of a nation's culture, including language, education, social values, and religious attitudes. For example, a condom manufacturer might encounter social resistance if it tried to market its products in Spain. Despite the fact that by 1993 Spain will have Europe's highest number of AIDS cases, the strong conservative influence of the Catholic Church would make marketing this product difficult. As evidence, marketers need only look at the recent clash between the Church and Spain's socialist government over the government's attempt to promote the use of condoms through TV ads.[24]

Because languages frequently differ in international markets, firms must take pains to ensure that their communications are correctly translated and convey the intended meanings. A classic example of international miscommunication is PepsiCo's theme "Come Alive with Pepsi," which in German translates as "Come Alive Out of the Grave."

U.S. goods and services sometimes face consumer resistance abroad due to different cultural values. American credit card companies, for example, have found it difficult to overcome the reluctance of Germans to amass debt and to use revolving credit. This reluctance is such an ingrained part of the German culture that the German word for "debt"—*schulden*—also means "guilt." To deal with this problem, Citicorp Visa is using a marketing strategy that has positive connotations for consumers. Company ads use the phrase *Ruckzahl-Wahl*—"credit that empowers."[25]

Political-Legal Factors

Political factors often influence international marketing. Consider the effect of political turmoil in Iraq, the Philippines, Lebanon, and China. Sometimes political unrest results in acts of violence, such as destruction of a firm's property. In the late 1980s and early 1990s, Middle East terrorists have targeted U.S. corporate offices abroad. IBM, Pan American, and American Express have all been subject to terrorist threats and attacks.

Many U.S. firms have set up internal *political risk assessment* (PRA) units or turned to outside consulting services to evaluate the political risks of the marketplaces in which they operate. Sometimes marketing strategies must be adjusted to reflect the new situation. For example, after the 1989 Tiananmen Square massacre, such U.S. corporations as Chrysler, McDonnell-Douglas, and Occidental Petroleum put on hold many of the 600 joint ventures they planned in China. German-based Mercedes-Benz withdrew advertising from China after the massacre. Many U.S. corporations are also uneasy about their continuing relationship with Hong Kong, which on July 1, 1997, will become part of mainland China. Currently, more than 800 U.S. corporations have a presence in Hong Kong with capital investments totaling more than $6 billion.[26]

Many nations try to achieve political objectives through international business activities. Japan, for instance, has openly encouraged involvement in international marketing because much of its economy depends on overseas sales.

Legal requirements complicate world marketing. A law in France prohibits comparative advertising. In Malaysia, promotional contests are allowed only if they involve games of skill, not chance, while in Germany sales promotions are

As Philip Morris continues to fight political and legal attempts to restrict its marketing activities in the United States and other countries around the world, the company is also developing international strategies since worldwide cigarette consumption is growing in real terms. A large portion of this growth is generated in Japan, where ads like the one shown here have helped Philip Morris increase its share of the market to nearly 11 percent, more than all other foreign competitors combined.

restricted to full-value coupons.[27] All commercials in the United Kingdom and Australia must be cleared with the government in advance. In the Netherlands, ads for candy must show a toothbrush. Some nations have local content laws specifying the portion of a product that must come from domestic sources. Other governments require that package and labeling information be provided in local languages. In Canada, for example, packaging information must be in both English and French. In addition, an increasing number of countries have passed laws requiring businesses to meet strict environmental standards. The so-called Green movement in Western Europe has added greatly to the operating expenses of Ford and General Motors. Between 1989 and 1993, they were required to spend an extra $7 billion a year to install anti-pollution equipment in all their vehicles.[28] These examples show that managers involved in international marketing must be well versed in legislation affecting their specific industries.

The legal environment for U.S. firms operating abroad can be divided into three dimensions: (1) U.S. law, (2) international law, and (3) legal requirements of host nations. International law can be found in the treaties, conventions, and agreements that exist among nations. The United States has many **friendship, commerce, and navigation (FCN) treaties**—agreements that deal with various aspects of commercial relations with other countries, such as the right to conduct business in the treaty partner's domestic market. Other international business agreements concern worldwide standards for various products, patents, trademarks, reciprocal tax treaties, export control, international air travel, and international communication. The International Monetary Fund lends foreign

friendship, commerce, and navigation (FCN) treaties
International agreements that deal with many aspects of commercial relations among nations.

exchange to nations that require it in order to conduct international trade. These agreements facilitate the whole process of world marketing.

The legal requirements of host nations affect foreign marketers. For example, some nations limit foreign ownership in their business sectors. In others, laws governing the protection of trade secrets are markedly different than they are here. High-technology companies attempting to enter the Japanese market are faced with the fact that patents are made public 18 months after filing, although often they are not granted for four to six years. In contrast, in the United States, patents remain secret until they are granted. According to one expert, while the U.S. system protects proprietary secrets, the Japanese system exposes them. This difference alone may discourage U.S. companies that want to protect their high-technology patents from doing business in Japan.[29]

International marketers generally recognize the importance of obeying the laws and regulations of the countries within which they operate. Even the slightest violations of these legal requirements would set back the future of international trade. Smart marketers also realize that the legal requirements of host nations can provide important business opportunities. For example, Chubb Corp., the U.S.–based insurance company, is targeting foreign consumers, partially because insurance is subject to fewer regulations abroad than it is here. Currently, some 14 percent of the company's revenues came from foreign markets. By the year 2000, Chubb projects that one out of four premium dollars will be generated abroad.[30]

International marketing is subject to various trade regulations, tax laws, and import/export requirements. One of the best-known U.S. laws is the Webb-Pomerene Export Trade Act (1918), which exempts from antitrust laws various combinations of U.S. firms acting together to develop foreign markets. Its intent is to give U.S. industry economic power equal to that possessed by cartels, the monopolistic organizations of foreign firms. Companies operating under the Webb-Pomerene Act cannot reduce competition within the United States or use "unfair methods of competition." Generally, Webb-Pomerene associations have been insignificant in the growth of U.S. trade.

The Foreign Corrupt Practices Act of 1977, which makes it illegal to bribe a foreign official in an attempt to solicit new or repeat sales abroad, has had a major impact on international marketing. The act also mandates that adequate accounting controls be installed to monitor internal compliance. Violations can result in a $1 million fine for the firm and a $10,000 fine and five years' imprisonment for the individuals involved. This law has been controversial, mainly because it fails to clearly define what constitutes bribery. Efforts to amend the law to include more specific statements of prohibited practices are in progress. In a recent violation of this law, U.S.–based Young & Rubicam, one of the world's largest advertising agencies, was fined $500,000 after pleading guilty to making improper payments to a Jamaican businessperson in an attempt to gain the Jamaican government's tourism account.[31]

Trade Barriers.   Assorted trade barriers also affect global marketing. These barriers are most commonly implemented through **tariffs**—taxes levied against imported products. Some tariffs are based on a set tax per pound, gallon, or unit; others are calculated according to the imported item's value.

Tariffs can be classified as either revenue or protective tariffs. *Revenue tariffs* are designed to raise funds for the importing government. Most early U.S. government revenue came from this source. *Protective tariffs,* which are usually higher than revenue tariffs, are designed to raise the retail price of an imported product to match or exceed that of a similar domestic product. In 1983 Harley-Davidson Motor Company requested that the International Trade Com-

tariff
Tax levied against imported goods.

FOCUS ON ETHICS

WHEN IS A BRIBE NOT A BRIBE?

. . . .

The 1988 amendments to the Foreign Corrupt Practices Act have made it a little easier for U.S. firms doing business overseas to deal with international differences in definitions of bribery. Companies now break the law only if they knowingly make an illegal payment. Previously they were operating illegally if they "had reason to know" that a payment was illegal. Perhaps more important, under the new law it is proper to make payments that are allowed under the written laws of a foreign country. And if a company representative makes an illegal payment, the company is not liable if it does not know about it.

The Foreign Corrupt Practices Act is the law governing the business conduct of American citizens and companies abroad. It is intended primarily to prevent the payment of large bribes to officials of foreign governments. Payments to officials to "facilitate" routine government action, such as processing visas and licenses, are permitted.

For some American businesspeople, this is not enough. "U.S. companies still often find they can't engage in activities their local competitors do every day," says one. In Asian cultures the everyday payments that civil servants expect to receive are considered no more improper than the American business practice of taking a public official out to dinner. Moreover, foreign competitors often entertain prospective customers far more lavishly than U.S. companies can under the terms of the act.

Such differences in outlook can have major consequences. Consider the effectiveness of Iraqi President Saddam Hussein's campaign to buy friendly news coverage before his army invaded Kuwait in August 1990. Hussein's financial contributions and gifts of expensive cars to journalists throughout the Arab world won him favorable press coverage in the months before the invasion. According to Arab officials, lavish gift-giving is an ancient Bedouin tradition, and in Arab societies a gift cannot be refused.

Discussion Questions

1. Although the Foreign Corrupt Practices Act allows U.S. companies to make payments to "facilitate" government action, outright bribery is forbidden. How can American firms determine what is a bribe and what is an allowable payment?

2. Are there any circumstances in which the act could be beneficial to U.S. businesspeople overseas?

Sources: "Doing Business Abroad with Fewer Restraints," *The Wall Street Journal* (June 5, 1990), p. B1; Jane Mayer and Geraldine Brooks, "How Saddam Hussein Courted Mideast Press with Cars and Cash," *The Wall Street Journal* (February 15, 1991), pp. A1, A8; and Ford S. Worthy, "When Somebody Wants a Payoff," *Fortune* (Pacific Rim, 1989), pp. 117–122.

---

mission impose a protective tariff on large-size motorcycles imported from Japan. At the time, Japanese imports from Honda, Yamaha, Kawasaki, and Suzuki held 86 percent of the U.S. market while Harley's share had dropped from 21 percent in 1978 to 12 percent five years later and the firm was facing bankruptcy. The special tariff was set up on a sliding scale, adding 45 percent to the cost of Japanese imports in 1983 and gradually reducing the tariff to 10 percent in 1988. During that period, Harley implemented productivity improvements that made its products more competitive with imports. By the end of the decade, Harley had regained 19 percent of the market and asked the government to end the special protection.[32]

In the past, it was believed that a country should protect its infant industries by using tariffs to keep out foreign-made products. Some foreign goods did enter, but the high tariff payments made domestic products competitive in price. Recently it has been argued that tariffs should be raised to protect employment and profits in domestic U.S. industries.

In 1988 the United States passed the Omnibus Trade and Competitiveness Act in order to remedy what it perceived as unfair international trade situations.

Japan's protective tariffs on imported liquors once added as much as 220 percent to imported liquor products. Since the country revamped its liquor tax system, taxes on a bottle of a premium import have been cut in half. Foreign brands are now sold close to the prices for Japanese brands made by Suntory and Nikka. Foreign distillers have benefitted, as their share of the liquor market has grown from 14 percent to 25 percent after the protective tariff was lifted. More Japanese consumers can now afford to buy imported Scotch and bourbon and drink it the way they like—*on zah roku* (on the rocks).

Source: Parsons/Aria Pictures.

Under the so-called *Super 301* provisions of the law, the United States can now single out countries that unfairly impede trade with U.S. businesses. If these countries do not open their markets within a year and a half, the law requires the United States to retaliate through the imposition of tariffs or quotas on the offenders' imports into this country. The law was used to charge Japan with restricting the import of U.S. supercomputers, satellites, and lumber products. As a result, Japan announced that it would open its market wider in all three areas—a move that could create up to 20,000 more jobs in the Pacific Northwest's wood industry alone. How well Japan implements its pledge is still to be seen. Also charged under the provisions of the law are Brazil and India. Seventeen additional countries were cited for failing to safeguard U.S. copyrights and patents.[33]

Although in recent years Japanese markets have been opening to U.S. goods and services, the restrictions that remain are serious barriers to free trade. Critics charge that Japanese trade policy continues to push up the price of imports and to restrict access to the Japanese market. Chrysler chief Lee Iacocca summed up the attitude of many Americans when he said, "Japan is a rigged market. . . . I send a Jeep to Japan and the price goes up 70 percent to 90 percent—if I can find someone to sell it."[34] Another comparison shows the disadvantage American products have in Japan: While a Fischer-Price rattle costs the equivalent of $9.40, a nearly identical Japanese version costs only $6.15.[35]

Since 1947, the **General Agreement on Tariffs and Trade (GATT),** an international trade accord, has sponsored eight major tariff negotiations that have

General Agreement on Tariffs and Trade (GATT)
International trade agreement that has helped reduce world tariffs.

reduced worldwide tariff levels. The latest series of conferences, called the *Uruguay Round,* was begun in 1986 to discuss stabilization of currencies and prevention of protectionist legislation. These talks collapsed temporarily in December 1990 when the European Community (EC) refused to reduce sharply its farm subsidies so as to allow food-exporting nations like the United States, Canada, Argentina, and Australia access to European markets. The talks were revived several months later when the EC finally agreed to reduce farm supports. Also on the agenda for the 108 nations taking part in the talks are attempts to cut tariffs by one-third, improved patent and copyright protection, lower trade barriers for services, and improved methods for settling trade disputes.[36]

import quota
Trade restriction that limits the number of units of certain goods that can enter a country for resale.

Still other forms of trade restrictions exist. **Import quotas** limit the number of units of products in certain categories that can be imported. They seek to protect domestic industry and employment and to preserve foreign exchange. The ultimate quota is the **embargo**—a complete ban on the import of certain products. In the past, the United States has prohibited the import of items from some Communist countries. It has also used export quotas; in 1990 and 1991, for example, most of the world stopped trading with Iraq prior to and during the Persian Gulf war.

embargo
Complete ban on the import of specified products.

Foreign trade can also be regulated by exchange control through a central bank or government agency. **Exchange control** means that firms that gain foreign exchange by exporting must sell this exchange to the central bank or other foreign agency, and importers must buy foreign exchange from the same organization. The exchange control authority can then allocate, expand, or restrict foreign exchange according to existing national policy.

exchange control
Method used to regulate the privilege of international trade among importing organizations by controlling access to foreign currencies.

Dumping.   The practice of selling a product in a foreign market at a price lower than what it commands in the producer's domestic market is called **dumping.** It is often argued that foreign governments give substantial export support to their own companies. Such support may permit these firms to extend their export markets by offering lower prices abroad. In retaliation, the United States adds import tariffs to products that have been dumped on U.S. markets in order to bring their prices in line with those of domestically produced products. However, businesses often complain that charges of alleged dumping must undergo a lengthy investigative and bureaucratic procedure before duties are assessed. In an attempt to speed up the process in the steel industry, a trigger pricing system, which established a set of minimum steel prices, has been implemented based on Japanese production costs, the world's lowest. Any imported steel selling at less than these rates would trigger an immediate Treasury Department investigation. If the dumping were substantial, additional duties would be imposed. Charges of dumping have been leveled against foreign makers of such diverse items as hockey sticks, cement, and motorcycles in addition to steel and semiconductors.

dumping
Controversial practice of selling a product in a foreign market at a price lower than what it receives in the producer's domestic market.

Demands for protection against foreign imports are common in all countries, particularly during periods of economic uncertainty. Firms ask for protection against sales losses, and unions seek to preserve their members' jobs. Overall, however, the long-term trend is in the direction of free trade among nations. A recent example is the U.S.–Canada free-trade pact, between the world's largest trading partners, which will remove all tariffs between the two nations by the end of the century, eliminate all import and export quotas and taxes, and end minimum import and export price requirements. The trade accord covers services, energy, and investments in addition to manufactured goods. California wine growers are already enjoying the benefits of this free-trade agreement. Shipping wines into Canada is now simpler, enabling the companies to improve their systems of distribution.[37]

In 1990 President George Bush and Mexican leader Carlos Salinas de Gortari announced that they were seeking a U.S.–Mexico free-trade agreement similar to the U.S.–Canada agreement. When free trade is possible between Mexico to Canada, the result will be a $6 trillion North American trading bloc, made up of 350 million people, with economic power greater than the European Community.[38]

Multinational Economic Integration and World Marketing

A noticeable trend toward multinational economic integration has developed since the end of World War II. The Common Market, or European Community (EC), is the best-known multinational economic community and went into effect in 1992.

Multinational economic integration can be set up in several ways. The simplest approach is to establish a *free-trade area* in which participating nations agree to the free trade of goods among themselves, meaning all tariffs and trade restrictions are abolished. A *customs union* establishes a free-trade area plus a uniform tariff for trade with non-member nations. The EC is the best example of a customs union. A true *common market,* or *economic union,* involves a customs union and seeks to reconcile all government regulations affecting trade. The EC has been moving in the direction of an economic union.

Involving 12 countries, 325 million people, and a combined gross national product approaching $5 trillion, the EC is the world's largest common market. Under its provisions, all barriers to free trade will disappear among EC members, making it as simple and painless to ship products between England and Spain as it is between Missouri and Illinois. Also involved is the standardization of the regulations and requirements businesses must meet. Instead of having to comply with 12 sets of standards, manufacturers will have to comply with just one. Before 1992, varying regulations drove up the cost of doing business by eliminating the possibility of achieving economies of scale. For example, in France yellow headlights were required on all automobiles while in Italy white lights were standard. Belgian sausages were outlawed in Germany because of different fat-content requirements. And auto emissions standards were different for each country.

How will the changes in the European Community affect U.S. exporters? Although the European Community offers the attraction of a larger market, experts predict that the competition will be tougher for U.S. companies since European firms are expanding to meet the demands of their own market. In addition, U.S. firms that do not have European distributors or partners may find doing business more difficult. Although the standardization of European products ultimately will make it easier for U.S. exporters, companies may find themselves scurrying to meet the requirements of the nearly 300 directives that determine what the European market will and will not accept. (These directives cover the minutia of international trade including, among other things, the hormone content of beef, allowable noise levels of household appliances, and the size and shape of car windshield wipers.)[39]

Methods of Entering International Markets

About 15 percent of U.S. firms currently engage in international marketing. The U.S. Department of Commerce estimates that about 100,000 firms are now involved in exporting, up from 40,000 just three years earlier. Despite this

Figure 3.3

Building Overseas Business
by Entering New Markets

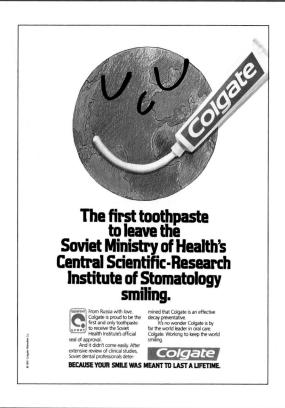

The first toothpaste
to leave the
Soviet Ministry of Health's
Central Scientific-Research
Institute of Stomatology
smiling.

From Russia with love. Colgate is proud to be the first and only toothpaste to receive the Soviet Health Institute's official seal of approval.
And it didn't come easily. After extensive review of clinical studies, Soviet dental professionals deter-   mined that Colgate is an effective decay preventative.
It's no wonder Colgate is by far the world leader in oral care. Colgate. Working to keep the world smiling.

Colgate
BECAUSE YOUR SMILE WAS MEANT TO LAST A LIFETIME.

Source: Courtesy of Colgate-Palmolive, © 1991.

dramatic increase, experts believe that many more firms, including small and mid-size businesses, could expand their operations into the export market. A Small Business Administration survey indicates that a significant number of small businesses now realize the potential overseas. Of the 5,000 firms surveyed, 11 percent said that although they do not export, they plan to start.[40]

One obvious reason for becoming involved in international marketing is that the world market is more than four times larger than the U.S. market. In addition, overseas markets in Europe and Asia are expanding at a faster rate than the domestic market. International marketing also gives firms greater flexibility during national recessions and helps minimize the need for plant closures and layoffs. Finally, doing business overseas provides the opportunity to discover new products and strategies, to recycle old ones in a new setting, and to learn about additional markets.[41]

An important part of Colgate-Palmolive's global marketing strategy is extending its existing products to new markets. The ad in Figure 3.3 announces the introduction of Colgate toothpaste in the Soviet Union. Other new markets for the toothpaste include Pakistan, Turkey, Saudi Arabia, and Eastern European countries. Blue Sky Natural Beverage Co., a producer of all-natural juices and sodas, began exporting when its home market of Santa Fe, New Mexico, was saturated. Company products met with immediate success in Japan where the concept of "all-natural" was not yet popular. In effect, Japan provided the same marketing opportunities available in the United States a decade earlier.[42]

A firm's reluctance to begin international marketing operations may stem from concerns about fluctuating foreign currencies, government regulations, cultural differences, or financial problems. These hurdles can be overcome by studying the information provided by such sources as the Small Business Administration, banks, local freight forwarding firms, export management com-

Figure 3.4

Levels of Involvement in
International Marketing

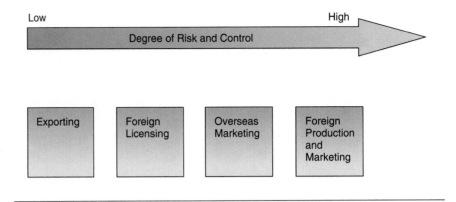

panies, and export trading companies. The U.S. Department of Commerce compiles detailed foreign market surveys that are available for a small fee. The U.S. and Foreign Commercial Service, a division of the Department of Commerce, has offices both abroad and throughout the United States. These offices offer businesspeople individual export counseling, market research guidance, sales leads, and information about relevant conferences.[43]

The more information marketers have before they begin exporting, the greater their chance of success. For example, it is important to realize what goods and services sell well abroad. According to a recent survey, ten industries make up 80 percent of all exports by small businesses: wholesale trade in durable goods, machinery equipment, wholesale nondurable goods, electrical equipment, instruments, fabricated metal, chemicals, miscellaneous manufactured goods, rubber and plastics, and transportation equipment.[44]

Firms interested in marketing their products abroad may choose from among four basic entry strategies: exporting, foreign licensing, overseas marketing, and foreign production and marketing. As Figure 3.4 indicates, the level of risk involved and the firm's degree of control over international marketing increases with greater involvement. Some firms market their products worldwide by using more than one of the entry approaches. Chicago-based Helene Curtis Industries, for example, markets its hair care products, toiletries, and salon appliances by exporting, through licensing arrangements and joint ventures, and via foreign subsidiaries.

Exporting may be direct or indirect. *Indirect exporting* means that a firm may export only occasionally to sell surplus or obsolete inventory or that part of its production is used in products made by another firm and then sold abroad. An example of indirect exporting is an electronics components firm whose output becomes part of a computer that is sold in foreign markets. *Direct exporting* occurs when a firm actually makes a commitment to seek export business. It is the most common form of international marketing. Direct exporters make a continuous effort to sell their merchandise abroad. For many firms, exporting is the first step in reaching foreign markets. Success in exporting often encourages marketers to move on to other entry strategies.

foreign licensing
Agreement in which a firm permits a foreign company to either produce or distribute the firm's goods in a foreign country or gives it the right to utilize the firm's trademark, patent, or processes in a specified geographic area.

Foreign licensing is an agreement in which a firm permits a foreign company to produce and distribute its merchandise or use its trademark, patent, or processes in a specified geographic area. Hasbro, for example, has licensing agreements with firms in Japan and Latin America to locally manufacture, distribute, and market Hasbro toys. Licensing offers several advantages over exporting, including availability of local marketing information and distribution channels and protection from various legal barriers. Because licensing does not

Through direct exporting, Boeing markets its commercial and military aircraft to foreign customers including Japan Air Lines, China's Civil Aviation Administration, and Korea Air Lines. The freshly painted Boeing 747s shown here are bound from Boeing's plant in Everett, Washington, to foreign airlines. The company agressively pursues overseas business to supply the strong worldwide demand for aircraft. With worldwide airline traffic expected to double by 2005, Boeing is likely to maintain its position as the leading U.S. exporter.

Source: © Harold Sund/The Image Bank.

require a capital outlay, it is an attractive entry method for many firms, especially small ones.

A firm that maintains a separate marketing or selling operation in a foreign country is involved in *overseas marketing.* Examples are foreign sales offices and overseas marketing subsidiaries. Production may be performed in one of the following ways:

1. The firm may set up its own production and marketing operation in the foreign country. Eastman Kodak operates its own film-processing labs in Hungary and Poland and is planning similar facilities in the Soviet Union.[45]

2. The firm may acquire an existing firm in the country in which it wants to do business. In an effort to expand its operations to Western Europe, Businessland, the largest personal computer dealer in the United States, bought computer retailers in Great Britain and Germany, and is attempting to purchase one in France.[46] In the United States, Matsushita purchased entertainment giant MCA.

joint venture

Agreement in which a firm shares the risks, costs, and management of a foreign operation with one or more partners who are usually citizens of the host country.

3. The firm may form a **joint venture,** in which it shares the risks, costs, and management of the foreign operation with one or more partners who are usually nationals of the host country.

In recent years, joint ventures have provided the vehicle for American companies to do business in Eastern Europe and the Soviet Union. Already some 3,000 joint ventures have been established in this region, with Hungary and Poland receiving the most Western attention.[47] Hearst Corp. proposed a joint publishing venture with *Izvestia,* the official Soviet government daily newspaper.[48] General Electric formed a joint venture with Tungsram, a Hungarian light-bulb manufacturer.[49] Also in Hungary, Ogilvy & Mather Worldwide set up a joint venture with Mahir, Hungary's oldest advertising agency.[50] Joint ventures can result as well in products being imported into the United States. When Chesapeake International, a Norfolk, Virginia, trading company, joined forces

COMPETITIVE EDGE

GLAXO HOLDINGS

. . . .

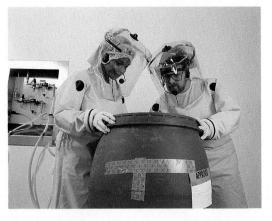

Decentralization and joint ventures have paid off for London-based pharmaceuticals giant Glaxo Holdings. Glaxo supplies its international operations with funding, legal services, insurance, and technical support. Managers of its 70 companies in 150 countries are free to set their own research and development and marketing goals. Glaxo has no reason to complain about the results: Since 1981 its annual sales have risen from about $1 billion to nearly $5.6 billion.

A key factor in Glaxo's success is its strategy of entering into joint ventures. Beginning in Japan in the 1970s, Glaxo has entered into marketing partnerships with companies in several countries, including Canada, South Korea, and the Soviet Union. In some cases it has formed alliances with competitors in which the companies market each other's products.

Glaxo's joint ventures are important in light of current trends in the pharmaceuticals industry. Until recently the key to profitability was discovering or developing new drugs like Glaxo's Zantac, which is used in the treatment of ulcers and is the world's best-selling drug. Today, however, the pace of technological change in the industry is so rapid that the profitable lifetime of

any single drug is much shorter than in the past. It is, therefore, advantageous for a company to be large enough so that it can sell new drugs in large volumes as rapidly as possible.

These conditions mean that selling drugs globally is now at least as important as investing in research and development. Glaxo's numerous joint ventures and marketing alliances enable it to launch a new drug in markets throughout the world, thereby profiting more quickly from the research and development efforts of its component companies.

Discussion Questions

1. In the United States, many hospitals are forming centrally run purchasing operations to buy medicines. How is this trend likely to affect Glaxo's marketing practices?

2. What risks does Glaxo face when it enters into an alliance with a competitor?

Sources: "The Doctors' Dilemma," *The Economist* (January 27, 1990), pp. 69–70; Christopher Elias, "Glaxo Is Swallowing Market for Prescription Drugs in U.S.," *Insight* (November 12, 1990), pp. 35–37. *Photo source:* © Will & Deni McIntyre.

with a Kiev manufacturer of dumpling-making machines, the result was Russian-style fast food on American shores.[51]

Even such secretive corporate giants as AT&T, IBM, and Boeing now accept that joint partnerships are among the most efficient way to develop a global strategy. AT&T operates jointly with many of the world's largest telephone and electronics companies. IBM has more than 40 joint partnerships worldwide. And Boeing has three Japanese partners as it works toward the 1995 deadline of producing the new 777, a long-range, wide-body jet.[52]

The Multinational Corporation Goes Global

multinational corporation

Firm with significant operations and marketing activities outside its home country.

A **multinational corporation** is a firm with significant operations and marketing activities outside its home country. Examples of multinationals include General Electric, Siemens, and Mitsubishi in the heavy electrical equipment industry; Caterpillar and Komatsu in large construction equipment; and Timex, Seiko, and Citizen in watches. The ten largest U.S. multinationals are listed in Table 3.3.

Table 3.3

Ten Largest U.S. Multinationals

Rank	Company	Foreign Revenue (in billions)	Total Revenue (in billions)	Foreign Revenue as a Percentage of Total
1	Exxon	$63,429	$ 86,656	73.2%
2	IBM	36,965	62,710	58.9
3	General Motors	33,768	126,932	26.6
4	Mobil	33,003[a]	50,976[a]	64.7
5	Ford Motor	31,964	96,146	33.2
6	Citicorp	19,877	37,970	52.3
7	E. I. du Pont de Nemours	14,152[b]	35,534[b]	39.8
8	Texaco	13,710	32,416	42.3
9	ITT[c]	10,944	25,271	43.3
10	Dow Chemical	9,516	17,600	54.1

[a]Includes other income.
[b]Includes excise taxes.
[c]Includes proportionate interest in unconsolidated subsidiaries and affiliates.
Source: Data reported in "The 100 Largest U.S. Multinationals," *Forbes* (July 23, 1990), p. 362.

Since they first became a force in international business in the 1960s, multinationals have evolved in some important ways. First, these companies are no longer exclusively U.S. based. Today it is as likely for a multinational to be based in Japan, Germany, or Great Britain as in the United States. Second, multinationals no longer think of their foreign operations as mere outsourcing appendages to carry out the design, production, and engineering ideas conceived at home. Instead, there is a constant exchange of ideas, capital, and technologies among all the multinational operational bases. Third, many multinationals, including IBM, Gillette, and Xerox, now make more than half their sales abroad. And many companies like General Motors earn more than half their profits from foreign operations. Fourth, multinationals now employ huge foreign workforces relative to their American employees. Four out of ten people who work for IBM, for example, are foreign. These workforces are no longer seen as merely a source of cheap labor. On the contrary, many multinationals center technically complex activities in locations throughout the world. Texas Instruments, for example, does much of its research, development, design, and manufacturing in East Asia. Fifth, U.S. multinationals are bringing products back to the United States from their foreign facilities. And finally, foreign-based multinationals see tremendous opportunity in the United States and are buying American companies that employ Americans. They are also manufacturing their products entirely in the United States. The Honda Accord station wagon, for example, was designed in Torrance, California, and built in Marysville, Ohio. This reflects the evolution of Japanese multinationals' strategy from first importing completed cars into the United States, to assembling them here, to becoming nearly autonomous U.S.–based producers. Today, aside from their corporate ownership, it is getting harder to tell the difference between Honda, Toyota, and Nissan on the one hand and General Motors, Ford, and Chrysler on the other.[53]

What has emerged are world, or global, corporations that reflect the internationalization of U.S. markets, the interdependence of world economies, the growth of international competition, and the globalization of world markets.[54] The worldwide operations of Matsushita, the Japanese electronics giant that is the parent of 163 different companies, illustrates the global strategy of all multinationals. Matsushita, whose brands Panasonic and Technics are popular in the United States, manufactures half its products in the countries in which they are sold. In the United States the company has ten factories and is building its largest facility in north-central Texas.[55]

Developing an International Marketing Strategy

Like domestic firms, international marketers must follow the steps in the marketing planning process described in Chapter 4. They should assess organizational strengths and weaknesses, study environmental factors, set marketing objectives, select target markets, and develop marketing mixes that will satisfy their chosen targets.

global marketing strategy
Standardized marketing mix with minimal modifications that a firm uses in all of its foreign markets.

In developing a marketing mix, marketers may choose from two alternative approaches: a global marketing strategy or a multinational marketing strategy. A **global marketing strategy** uses a standardized marketing mix, with minimal modifications, in all foreign markets. The advantage of this approach is that it enables marketers to realize economies of scale from their production and marketing activities. The Benetton advertisement in Figure 3.5 illustrates this strategy. Benetton's cosmetics, as well as its well-known line of Italian knitwear, targets the same type of consumer worldwide—young, affluent shoppers with trendy tastes. Benetton's international advertising has a common theme— "United Colors of Benetton"—and uses global visual images that appeal to its target audience whether in New York, Paris, or Tokyo. The only modification is translation of the copy into different languages. Other companies follow the same strategy. After Gillette combined its North American and European operations, it used the same ad campaign to market its new Sensor razor in 17 countries.[56] Similarly, Coca-Cola uses the same TV ads, adapted with local languages and other slight variations, in its 160-country world market. The idea of Coke's global approach is to have "one sight, one sound, one sell around the world."[57]

A global marketing perspective is appropriate for some goods and services and for certain market segments common to many nations. The approach works for products that have universal appeal, such as Coca-Cola and Levi's jeans, and for those that appeal to upscale consumers, such as Jaguar.

The global approach is particularly appealing to food marketers who hope to help define consumer preferences. They believe that if their foods are introduced to children, who do not yet have well-defined tastes, they are likely to be accepted. In addition, travel—especially in Europe—has created a willingness among adults to try different ethnic flavors. Certainly, some new product concepts, like fast-food restaurants and microwave meals, have been readily accepted in the absence of similar local offerings.[58]

multinational marketing strategy
Application of market segmentation to foreign markets by tailoring the firm's marketing mix to match specific target markets in each nation.

Most firms find it necessary to continue practicing market segmentation outside their home markets by tailoring their marketing mixes from country to country. This approach, called a **multinational marketing strategy,** assumes that different market characteristics and competitive situations among nations require the development of a customized marketing mix appropriate for each marketplace. For example, in a recent advertising campaign for Lux soap, ads that appeared in the United Kingdom showed a celebrity applying the soap in her bath. In Germany, the same ad showed the woman about to step into the shower. These two versions were necessary because while the British are more likely to bathe in a tub, the Germans prefer the shower. Kraft followed a similar multinational approach in its cheese advertisements. In Belgium, an ad shows a wedge of white cheese being spread on toast as part of a breakfast. In Spain, the same brand of cheese is in slice form and is being rolled around an asparagus stalk as an hors d'oeurve.

Figure 3.5 Implementing a Global Marketing Strategy

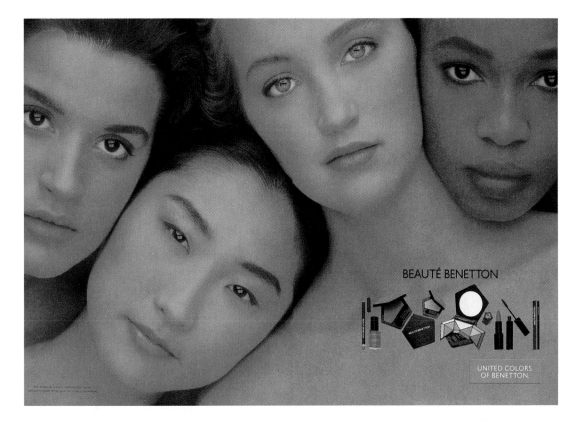

Source: Courtesy of Benetton Cosmetics Corporation.

Some marketers use a combined global and multinational approach. For example, when Scott Paper entered the European market, its marketing research convinced the company to create a consistently warm, cuddly advertising image. To implement this global concept, Scott created a series of ads that focused on a labrador puppy, an image that would tell consumers that Scott was "soft and strong." However, because Scott believed that its ads should reflect local markets, a series of ads were shot in different settings. In Great Britain, the puppy was shown in a traditional English country garden. In Spain, the setting was a living room with Spanish-style furniture. In Italy, an Italian living room was chosen. In addition, the background music varied by location.[59]

Product and Promotional Strategies

straight extension
International product and promotional strategy whereby the same product marketed in the home market is introduced in the foreign market using the same promotional strategy.

International marketers can choose from among five strategies for selecting the most appropriate product and promotion strategy for a specific foreign market. As Figure 3.6 indicates, the strategies center on whether to extend a domestic product and promotional strategy into international markets or adapt one or both to meet the target market's unique requirements.

The one-product, one-message **straight extension** strategy is typical for firms employing a global marketing strategy, such as PepsiCo and Benetton. This

Figure 3.6   Alternative International Product and Promotional Strategies

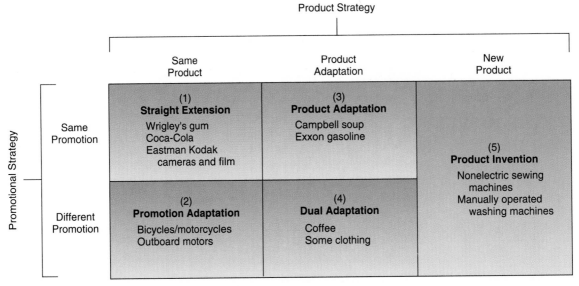

Source: Adapted from Warren Keagan, *Multinational Marketing Management* (Englewood Cliffs, NJ: Prentice-Hall, 1984), pp. 317–322.

strategy permits economies of scale in production and marketing and a universally recognized product for consumers traveling from country to country.

Other strategies call for **product adaptation, promotion adaptation,** or both. While products such as bicycles, motorcycles, and outboard motors are primarily recreational vehicles in the United States, they may represent important transportation modes in other nations. Consequently, the promotional message may be adapted even if the product remains unchanged. In contrast, a promotional theme such as Exxon's "Put a Tiger in Your Tank" may be successfully used in dozens of nations even though Exxon gasoline is reformulated to meet varying weather conditions and engine specifications in different countries. In still other instances, both the product and the promotional message may require a **dual adaptation** to meet the unique needs of specific international markets. Coffee marketers such as Nescafe develop different blends and promotional campaigns to match consumer preferences in different countries.

The final strategy alternative is **product invention.** In this case, the firm may decide to develop an entirely different product to take advantage of unique foreign market opportunities. For example, to match dissimilar foreign needs in developing nations, an appliance manufacturer might introduce a hand-powered washing machine even though such products have been obsolete in industrialized countries for many years.

Distribution Strategy

Distribution is a vital aspect of overseas marketing. Proper channels must be set up and extensive physical distribution problems handled. Transportation systems and warehousing facilities may be unavailable or of poor quality. International

product adaptation
International product and promotional strategy wherein product modifications are made for the foreign market, but the same promotional strategy is used.

promotion adaptation
International product and promotional strategy in which the same product is introduced in a foreign market with a unique promotional strategy for the new market.

dual adaptation
International product and promotional strategy in which modifications of both product and promotional strategies are employed in the foreign market.

product invention
In international marketing, the development of a new product combined with a new promotional strategy to take advantage of unique foreign opportunities.

marketers must adapt promptly and efficiently to these situations if they are to profit from overseas sales.

Distribution decisions involve two steps. First, the firm must decide on a method of entering the foreign market. Second, it must determine how to distribute the product within the foreign market once it has chosen an appropriate entry channel.

Distribution decisions are based on many factors, including the nature of the firm's products, consumer tastes and buying habits, and market competition. These considerations affected Anheuser-Busch's distribution strategy when it decided to market Budweiser beer in Europe. Europeans prefer their own brews and consider American beer weak and flavorless. For these reasons, American brewers have not attempted to sell their beer in Europe. Anheuser-Busch marketers, however, decided to try, largely because the potential market for European beer sales is four times that of the United States.

Because the British are considered the most discriminating beer drinkers, Anheuser-Busch marketers chose Great Britain as their first European target market. The company hoped that British acceptance of Budweiser would pave the way for marketing in other European countries. Most British pubs are owned by one of Britain's major breweries or operated under a franchise agreement. Anheuser-Busch signed a licensing agreement with Watney, Mann, and Truman, the country's largest brewer. Under the agreement, Budweiser is made at Watney's brewery and distributed throughout Watney's system of 5,000 pubs. This distribution approach enables Anheuser-Busch to reach a large part of the beer-drinking market and is an important element in helping the company attain its goal of making Budweiser the best-selling brand in Great Britain by the late 1990s.

As companies grow, their distribution systems often evolve. For example, when Sony and Panasonic first entered the U.S. market, they sold their products through importers, who assumed all the business risk. As their products gained popularity, they began doing business with exclusive distributors. In their current operations, both companies have eliminated the distributors' role and sell directly to the trade.[60]

Often, the key to a successful distribution strategy is realizing that systems often vary from country to country. In France, for example, 40 percent of all sales take place in *hypermarkets,* the football-field-sized stores that sell everything from groceries to auto parts. Although hypermarkets exist in Spain, half the population lives in rural areas and shops in smaller, specialized stores. And Germany has up to four distinct distribution channels that are heavily used.[61]

Pricing Strategy

Pricing in foreign markets can be a critical ingredient in overall marketing strategy. Considerable competitive, economic, political, and legal constraints on pricing exist. Global marketers must thoroughly understand these requirements if they are to succeed.

A pricing strategy that works in the United States does not always succeed abroad. In addition, an accepted strategy may change over time. For example, for years marketers believed that to succeed in Japan, foreign products must be priced high. Brown & Williamson Tobacco Corp., a division of London-based B.A.T. Industries, decided to test this conventional wisdom when in 1987 it dropped the price of a pack of Kent cigarettes to 220 yen (about $1.67) from 280 yen. No other major imported product had cut its price so drastically, and the strategy made front-page news in Japanese papers. Instead of losing sales, Kent became one of the fastest-selling cigarettes on the market. While high pricing had worked when the dollar was strong, it faltered in a weak-dollar environment. When the dollar hovered around 240 yen, exporters focused on low-volume, high-margin goods that were insensitive to high prices, and they priced mid-range products, including cigarettes and beer, in a similar way. However, as the value of the dollar fell, exporters found it easier to bring in products at competitive prices and compete in the mass market.[62]

An important development in pricing strategy for international marketing has been the emergence of commodity marketing organizations that seek to control prices through collective action. The Organization of Petroleum Exporting Countries (OPEC) is the best example of these collective export organizations, but many others exist.

Countertrade.   In a growing number of nations, the only way a marketer can gain access to foreign markets is through **countertrade**—a form of exporting whereby products are bartered rather than sold for cash. Countertrade enables less developed nations that lack the foreign currency with which to pay for goods and services they want or need from exporting countries to secure them by using an alternative form of payment. Such requirements are also used in some industrialized nations as a means of controlling balance-of-trade problems. To more than double the number of bottling plants in the Soviet Union from 24 to 50, PepsiCo agreed to a barter agreement involving shipments of Stolichnaya vodka and the sale or lease of ten or more Soviet-built freighters and tankers. Pepsi also used countertrade to enter Romania and Bulgaria, trading their products for wine.[63] Similarly, McDonnell-Douglas agreed to sell 34 F/A-Hornet 18 aircraft worth $1 billion to Switzerland in exchange for a "fruit basket of goods that contains everything from grass mats and door knobs to watches, snow skis, luggage, and tour packages."[64]

Countertrade comprises an estimated 30 percent of all world trade. The value of goods bought and sold in countertrade transactions is valued between $275 and $500 billion.[65] Many companies, including Sears, Citicorp, and General Electric, have special departments that focus on countertrade.

countertrade
Form of exporting whereby goods and services are bartered rather than sold for cash.

The United States as a Market for International Marketers

America is an inviting target for foreign marketers. It has a large population, high levels of discretionary income, political stability, an attitude generally favorable to foreign investment, and its economic ills are relatively controlled.

Foreign-owned assets in the United States total more than $1 trillion. In a recent year they grew by more than $219 billion. Public attention was drawn to these foreign investments when Sony acquired Columbia Pictures, and Mitsubishi took ownership of that landmark of American capitalism, New York's Rockefeller Center. Among the U.S. companies owned by foreigners are:

□ Saks Fifth Avenue, Tiffany & Co., and Color Tile (owner: Investcorp International, Bahrain)

□ A&P (owner: Tengelmann Group, Germany)

□ Pillsbury (owner: Grand Metropolitan, Great Britain)

□ Barnes & Noble and B. Dalton (owner: Vendex International, Netherlands)

This trend is likely to continue as foreign multinationals seek to produce goods locally and control channels of distribution.

U.S. marketers must expect to face substantial foreign competition in the years ahead both at home and abroad. The United States' high level of buying power will likely continue to attract foreign firms to enter the U.S. market, and the reduction of trade barriers and expanded international marketing appear to be long-run trends. U.S. marketers no longer have the choice of whether to compete with foreign firms. Their continued long-term success greatly depends on their ability to compete.

Summary of Chapter Objectives

1. **Describe the importance of international marketing from the perspectives of the individual firm and the nation.** Global marketing is important to many U.S. firms. The Coca-Cola Company, for example, depends on foreign markets for over three-quarters of its revenues. Others rely on imports as a source of raw materials and component parts. But foreign trade is less important to the United States than it is to many other nations. Only 10 percent of the U.S. gross national product is from exports. In other countries, the percentage is considerably higher.

2. **Identify the major components of the environment for international marketing.** A variety of environmental factors can influence marketing decision making in the international context. This chapter categorizes these factors as economic, social-cultural, and political-legal.

3. **Identify the various methods of entering international markets.** Several levels of involvement in world marketing are possible, including indirect or direct exporting, foreign licensing, overseas marketing, and foreign production and marketing.

4. **Differentiate between a global marketing strategy and a multinational marketing strategy.** Some firms use a global marketing strategy, in which they apply their domestic marketing strategies directly in foreign markets with little or no modifications. Marketers of products such as Coca-Cola feel that tastes around the world are sufficiently homogeneous to allow the effective use of their existing marketing strategies everywhere. In contrast, other firms employ a multinational marketing strategy whereby they employ different marketing programs to match the characteristics and requirements of buyers in each foreign market.

5. **Describe the alternative product and promotional strategies used in international marketing.** Alternative product and promotional strategies for international markets include (1) straight extensions, whereby the same product is introduced in the foreign market using the same promotional strategy as in the domestic market; (2) promotional adaptation, in which the same product is introduced with a unique promotional strategy designed for the specific market; (3) product adaptation, wherein product modifications are made but the same promotional strategy is used; (4) dual adaptation, in which modifications of both product and promotional strategies are employed; and (5) product invention, whereby the firm decides to develop an entirely different product and combine it with a new promotional strategy to take advantage of unique foreign opportunities.

6. **Explain the attractiveness of the United States as a target market for foreign marketers.** A number of factors contribute to the attractiveness of the U.S. market to foreign firms: its large population, high levels of discretionary income, political stability, general acceptance of foreign

investment, and relatively controlled economic ills. Recent declines in the value of the dollar relative to foreign currencies have also attracted many foreign marketers.

Key Terms

exporting

importing

infrastructure

exchange rate

friendship, commerce, and navigation (FCN) treaties

tariff

General Agreement on Tariffs and Trade (GATT)

import quota

embargo

exchange control

dumping

foreign licensing

joint venture

multinational corporation

global marketing strategy

multinational marketing strategy

straight extension

product adaptation

promotion adaptation

dual adaptation

product invention

countertrade

Review Questions

1. Why is the global marketplace so important to international marketers? Cite examples of firms that are highly successful in the global market. Why do you think these firms are successful?

2. How does the international marketplace differ from the domestic marketplace? In your answer, specifically examine market size and buyer behavior differences.

3. Name the major variables in the global marketing environment. Explain how each influences marketing decision making.

4. List the components of the legal environment for U.S. firms operating abroad. Specifically discuss FCN treaties, the Webb-Pomerene Act, and the Foreign Corrupt Practices Act.

5. What are the major barriers to international trade? Explain how trade restrictions may be used to either restrict or stimulate international marketing activities. Also explain the role of GATT.

6. Explain the practice of dumping. Why does dumping sometimes occur?

7. Describe the world's growing economic interdependence. Link this trend to the emergence of the EC.

8. Identify the basic entry strategies in international business. What factors should be considered in selecting an entry strategy?

9. Outline the basic premises behind the operation of a multinational corporation. Why have many of these organizations become global firms?

10. Differentiate between a global marketing strategy and a multinational strategy. In what ways is the international marketing mix most likely to differ from a marketing mix used in the domestic market?

Discussion Questions

1. Relate specific environmental considerations to each of the following aspects of a firm's international marketing mix:

        a. brands and warranties
        b. advertising
        c. distribution channels
        d. discounts to intermediaries
        e. use of comparative advertising

2. Give a hypothetical or actual example of a firm operating at each of the following levels of international marketing:
        a. indirect exporting
        b. direct exporting
        c. foreign licensing
        d. overseas marketing
        e. foreign production and marketing

3. Give a local example of each of the product and promotional strategy alternatives available to international marketers.

4. The Dutch swapped beads, trinkets, and cloth with native Americans in exchange for Manhattan. What international marketing concept described in this chapter did that business deal illustrate? Discuss.

5. Some people argue that foreign investment in the United States should be limited. Would you agree with a plan that would limit such investment by foreign firms or individuals in a particular firm to some specified amount? Explain.

Computer Applications

The versatility of solving different types of marketing problems has been demonstrated by the application of *decision tree analysis* (menu item 2) in Chapter 2. While this chapter focuses on global dimensions of marketing and compares domestic and international marketing decisions, the problems and decisions concerning international target market analysis and appropriate blending of marketing mix elements can be solved by applying the analytical techniques used by domestic marketers.

Directions: Use menu item 2 titled "Decision Tree Analysis" to solve each of the following problems.

Problem 1.   Las Vegas Industries is currently involved in international marketing through a licensing agreement signed five years ago with Singapore Exports, Ltd. The agreement expires at the end of this year, and the firm's management is considering establishing its own international marketing organization. Such a move would be particularly profitable if demand for the firm's products continues to grow. The following international demand estimates have been developed to help with the marketing decision at Las Vegas Industries:

        High Demand: Probability = 60%
        Moderate Demand: Probability = 40%

Forecasts for next year total $40 million in sales and a 10 percent earnings rate for a high-demand environment if the licensing agreement is renewed and $30 million in sales and an 8 percent earnings rate for a moderate-demand environment with the licensing agreement. In contrast, if Las Vegas Industries establishes its own international marketing organization and high demand occurs next year, sales will probably rise to $70 million and earnings to 8 percent of sales. However, if a moderate-demand environment exists, the cost of the new marketing organization will reduce profits to 2 percent of estimated sales of $30 million.

a. Review the discussion of decision tree analysis on page 75. Then use menu item 2 titled "Decision Tree Analysis" to recommend a course of action for Las Vegas Industries.

b. Would your recommendation change if the likelihood of high demand were reduced to 50 percent?

Problem 2.   Maria Fergamo, manager of the Fashion Perfect chain of fashion clothing stores headquartered in San Francisco, realizes that the success of her operations depends on the ability to monitor and predict changes in consumer tastes. Sales projections for next year total $4.2 million, with expected profits of 5 percent of sales. Several of Fergamo's managers, who make up the merchandise buying committee, have recommended a substantial purchase of a new, radical line of clothing that is enjoying huge sales in Europe. Although Fergamo is always concerned about significant inventory investments in unproven lines, she is aware of the consequences of missing major changes in shopper tastes. Fergamo makes the following notes as she listens to the presentation about the new line:

My guess is that the chances of a major consumer taste switch to the new line are 60 percent. If we don't get in on the bandwagon now, our sales next year could fall to $3 million, and at that level Fashion Perfect will earn only 2 percent on sales. On the other hand, if we place the orders and our inventory matches a change in buyer tastes, we could generate as much as $6 million in sales. If this happens, our profits should rise to 7 percent of sales. Even if we place the orders and no radical changes in consumer tastes occur, I think we could still push sales up to $5 million next year. Unfortunately, if tastes don't change as much as those in Europe, the extra inventory and sale merchandise that would result will depress earnings to 2 percent.

a. Recommend a course of action for Fergamo.

b. Would your recommendation change if Fergamo decreased the likelihood of consumer taste changes to 30 percent?

Problem 3.   The political-legal environment has been on Hans Nielsen's mind lately. Nielsen is managing director of Stockvagen Industries AB, a Swedish furniture manufacturer. Although the firm's sales projections are a healthy $14 million for next year, profits are estimated at 8 percent of sales. Nielsen is concerned about rumors that the Swedish government will ban the use of the filler material Stockvagen Industries uses in its furniture cushions. Although substitute filler materials are available (and, in fact, are used by many of the firm's major competitors), they are more expensive. Nielsen estimates that a switch to the alternative filler material would reduce profits to 4 percent of sales. On the other hand, if he decides not to switch now and the ban is enacted, the time involved in converting to the new materials next year is likely to represent a loss of $8 million in projected sales and a corresponding profit decline to 2 percent of sales. Nielsen feels there is a 30 percent chance that the ban will be enacted.

a. Recommend a course of action for Nielsen.

b. Would your recommendation change if Nielsen reduced his estimate of the likelihood of the ban's enactment to 20 percent?

> ## VIDEO CASE   3

. . . .

Carl's Jr. and Mikoshi Japanese Noodle House

Whether it is an American food being marketed abroad or a foreign food being marketed in the United States, fast-food franchises must make adjustments to the culture, ingredient availability, and taste preferences of the new market. The stories of two successful adjustments follow: Carl's Jr., which took its hamburger to Japan, and Mikoshi Japanese Noodle House, which brought its ramen dishes to Southern California.

In 1988 the Carl's Jr. restaurant chain had more than 600 outlets in California, and management decided that the time was ripe for expansion into the Far East. For some time, Friendly Corp. of Osaka had been pursuing Carl's Jr. for a franchise; several commissioned marketing studies indicated that Japanese tourists in California liked Carl's Jr. hamburgers. Carl's Jr. decided to offer Friendly's a Japan franchise, and the first overseas outlet opened in Osaka in 1989. By 1991 five outlets had been opened, and six more were scheduled for opening.

Because the idea was to give the Japanese a brief encounter with California life, it was necessary to preserve the ambiance and menu of the home chain as much as possible. However, both participants in the venture knew that changes would have to be made. Beef is a high-priced commodity in Japan, but the Japanese perceive the hamburger as a snack, so the size of the hamburger patty was reduced by 25 percent, keeping the cost within bounds while better matching the market's needs. Because quality beef patties were not available locally, they were initially imported from the United States. Subsequently, an agreement was made with a Japanese firm to process Japanese, Australian, and American beef for the franchises. Bacon proved to be a greater problem, however, because Japanese-produced bacon doesn't become crisp when it is fried. Since crisp bacon is an essential textural element of the Carl's Jr.'s menu, it is imported from the United States. Condiments such as ketchup and mustard were initially produced locally because Japanese laws ban many of the preservatives used in American products, but Carl's Jr. has reformulated the condiments and now ships them from the United States.

The physical environment also is different in Japan. Land generally costs more, so the physical size of the outlets is considerably smaller. Luckily, local building codes and the smaller average stature of Japanese customers allow smaller aisles, especially in the kitchen areas, decreasing wasted space. Efficient kitchen layout is important in the Carl's Jr. operation, and the home office retained control of the design, working closely with Japanese architects. While much of the equipment for the first outlets had to be shipped from the United States, the layout was successfully reduced to meet Japanese space constraints. Subsequent outlets are being fabricated in Japan, with only a few pieces of specialized equipment coming from the United States.

Carl's Jr. has since decided to expand into Malaysia and Mexico. Each of these locations calls for unique modifications of domestic operations. For instance, because of Malaysia's large Muslim population, beef must be slaughtered under the "halal" system. And because Muslims do not eat pork, bacon cannot be used. Experiments with soy bacon and beef bacon were tried, but neither proved entirely satisfactory. Rather than compromise the quality of the burger, Carl's Jr. decided to omit bacon altogether. The smoky taste of the sauce prevents the omission from affecting the burger's flavor significantly, although the texture is changed. When plans are made to expand into other Far Eastern countries such as Singapore, bacon can be reintroduced without debasing the Malaysian product.

The Mexican market is quite different from the Japanese and Malaysian markets. Because Mexicans crave larger amounts of meat, the size of the patty has not been changed. The bacon double cheeseburger is being heavily promoted and is selling well.

In all overseas locations, only a portion of Carl's Jr.'s original menu is offered. This makes it easier to start up new outlets and establish supply networks, but it also leaves room for future additions to the menu and for associated promotional campaigns. Other Far Eastern, European, and South American countries are being investigated as targets for expansion.

Mikoshi Japanese Noodle House

Satoshi Sakurada, founder of MOS Food Services, Inc. of Japan, also looked overseas for expansion opportunities. In fact, the home chain itself is partly a result of global marketing.

In 1962 Sakurada lived in Los Angeles and worked as a salesperson for the Japanese firm Nikko Securities. During this time he often lunched on a Southern California chili-and-beef concoction called the Tommy burger. Ten years later, when McDonald's had just opened its first restaurant in Japan, Sakurada decided that it was time to introduce his concept of the hamburger to Japan.

After working tirelessly to promote the idea of his hamburger and winding up in a hospital suffering from exhaustion, Sakurada developed a successful approach, which is summed up in the company acronym HDC, "hospitality, deliciousness, and cleanliness." There is no question about the intended market for the MOS burger and its siblings—the teriyaki burger, the soy burger, and the rice burger. Outlets are located in local neighborhoods, not in expensive tourist and business districts like Tokyo's Ginza. But the American slant of the food gives the chain enough of an international touch for it to outrank both Kentucky Fried Chicken and McDonald's with the most number of outlets in Japan—more than a thousand.

How, then, could Sakurada expand operations overseas? Bringing the transformed Tommy burger back to its birthplace didn't seem wise, especially in view of the tremendous competition in the American burger market and the health-related issues constantly being raised against fast foods. The answer was not to export the product itself but instead to export the business idea—a chain of small, clean, orderly outlets selling a quality product that was somewhat exotic but that could be tailored to the culture in which the outlet was located without destroying the integrity of the dish. For the United States, the solution was the noodle.

Soup and noodles, or ramen, are traditionally paired in Japanese cuisine. Relying on foodstuffs that can be prepared either in advance or rapidly prepared at the last minute, these dishes lend themselves to a high-quality fast-food operation. The basic dishes are low in animal fats and appeal to health-conscious consumers, an increasingly significant percentage of the population. These noodle dishes became the basis for the menu of Sakurada's venture, the Mikoshi Japanese Noodle House.

Southern California was chosen for the first outlets because a wide variety of exotic foods are available there and the sizable Asian-American community has created a food processing network that is sensitive to ramen's culinary requirements. Although rice flour was initially imported from Japan, local processors were eventually able to provide an acceptable product. As the traditional recipes have not required changes, the basic dishes have not been compromised. However, the toppings for the noodles, always open to some variation in the traditional cuisine, have been modified for American tastes. While a traditional topping based on roast pork is offered, the yakisoba greens harvest was developed specifically for this market. It consists of traditional yakisoba noodles topped by a fresh green salad with an oil-free dressing. The most popular dish is teriyaki chicken ramen. Teriyaki chicken would be served before or after, or possibly with, ramen in traditional Japanese cuisine.

Although respect for the ramen tradition was a central ingredient of the Mikoshi Japanese Noodle House plan, the chain had to establish itself visually as a high-quality fast-food outlet. Thus, Japanese tea-house decor was shunned in favor of California techno-pop. Orders are placed at a register, and the food is served at a table on real china. Americans are not accustomed to eating Japanese foods, so a card on the table gives instructions to enhance appreciation of the cuisine—for instance, the soup and noodles should be eaten together like hamburger and fries, not sequentially like hamburgers and pie. (Sakurada solved a similar problem in Japan: Because the Japanese are reluctant to touch food, the MOS burger is served wrapped in a napkin.)

Sakurada opened four Mikoshi outlets in California. For the present, the California outlets are owned by the American parent corporation, MOS Foods West, Inc., but future plans call for franchised outlets, as many as 100 a year, expanding first to San Francisco and then to the East Coast and the Sun Belt.

Sources: Christina Lee, "The International Burger," *Los Angeles Times* (January 28, 1991), p. D4; personal interview with Steve Kishi, Carl Karcher Enterprises, May 1991; Teresa Watanabe, "Exporting Fast Food," *Los Angeles Times* (January 7, 1991), pp. D1, D4; personal interview with Gretchen Booma, Dentsu Burson-Marsteller, representing the Mikoshi Japanese Noodle House, May 1991.

Questions

1. Compare the product-promotional strategies of Carl's Jr. and Mikoshi Japanese Noodle House with those shown in Figure 3.6.

2. Choose one of the two companies and explain why it would want to expand beyond its own national boundaries. Explain why it finds its particular foreign market attractive.

3. Explain how Carl's Jr. is exporting more than materials to its overseas franchises. Why is franchising more desirable for Carl's Jr. than overseas marketing or foreign production and marketing? Why would Mikoshi Japanese Noodle House want to open its first outlets itself instead of franchising them?

4. Why did Mikoshi choose California over other U.S. locations?

Source: Philip Saltonstall/ONYX.

Reebok International marketers ask consumers on a Los Angeles street corner what they think about a new athletic shoe style. The collection of such information is a research activity marketers conduct that facilitates effective marketing planning and decision making.

PART 2

Marketing Planning and Information

4

Marketing Planning and Forecasting

CHAPTER OBJECTIVES

1. To distinguish between strategic planning and tactical planning.

2. To explain how marketing plans differ at various levels in the organization.

3. To identify the steps in the marketing planning process.

4. To describe the concept of SWOT analysis in terms of its four major elements: leverage, problems, constraints, and vulnerability.

5. To explain how the strategic business unit concept, the market share/market growth matrix, and spreadsheet analysis can be used in marketing planning.

6. To identify the major types of forecasting methods.

7. To explain the steps in the forecasting process.

American air conditioner manufacturers did not have much to worry about, or so it seemed. They controlled the U.S. market, the world's largest, and had little interest in either foreign competitors or consumers. As revenues rolled in from Americans' insatiable quest for coolness, strategic planning for a global marketplace seemed unnecessary. This all changed when the Japanese began manufacturing and buying their own air conditioners.

Lack of planning made U.S. manufacturers blind to two simultaneous trends. First, the glory days of seemingly unending domestic growth were over. Indeed, the air conditioning industry expects no growth in the United States over the next five years. Second, at the same time U.S. demand was dropping, demand in the Far East and Europe was increasing at double-digit rates. The result, not surprisingly, is that the largest air conditioner market in the world is now Japan. While 37 percent of all air-conditioner sales are from the United States, 38 percent—an impressive $8 billion worth—are made in Japan.

To make matters worse, U.S. manufacturers have allowed Japan to take the lead in air conditioning technology. Due to the lack of planning, companies like Carrier, Lennox, and Trane find themselves unable to compete with Japanese technology, which is now the standard in Japan and making inroads in Europe. Japanese central air conditioning is based on a system called the ductless split, which, ironically, was first developed in the United States during the 1960s. A quieter system to operate and less expensive to install, the system puts the noisy motor outside and pumps refrigerant indoors, where it is then circulated throughout the house via fans. When more than one room requires cooling, the refrigerant is piped to a series of fans, in contrast to traditional systems that push the cooled air from room to room via ductwork. Unable to see the potential in this technology, U.S. manufacturers refused to invest in its research or development.

In Europe, the large number of older buildings that do not have existing ductwork make this technology extremely popular. These systems can be installed without the need for extensive—and expensive—renovations. In the Far East, Japanese systems dominate the market with a 55 percent market share compared to 22 percent for U.S. systems.

Where does this lack of planning leave U.S. manufacturers hoping to increase their export business? In a not very enviable position. Although Carrier boasts that it is the leading American air conditioner manufacturer in Japan, its market share totals less than 1 percent. The company's position seems even sadder in the light of history: After World War II, Carrier dominated Japan's air conditioning market, with a 90 percent market share.

Having learned from its mistakes, Carrier has doubled its research and development staff and committed $30 million a year to developing a competitive ductless split technology. Whether this translates into successful strategic planning decisions for what is now a global marketplace is yet to be seen.[1]

Photo source: © Keisuke Mizumoto.

Chapter Overview

□   "Will changing the performance time and date affect concert attendance?"

□   "Should we utilize company sales personnel or independent agents in the new territory?"

□   "Should discounts be offered to cash customers? What impact would such a policy have on our credit customers?"

The above questions are examples of the thousands of major and minor decisions that the marketing manager regularly faces. Continual changes in the marketplace resulting from changing consumer expectations, technological improvements, competitive actions, economic trends, and political-legal changes, as well as product innovations and pressures from channel members, are likely to have a substantial impact on the operations of any organization. Although these changes are often beyond the marketing manager's control, effective planning can help the manager anticipate many of them. Indeed, effective planning often means the difference between success and failure.

This and the next chapter provide a foundation for all subsequent chapters by demonstrating the necessity for effective planning and reliable information in providing a structure within which a firm can take advantage of its unique strengths. Both the choice of specific target markets and the most appropriate marketing mix to use in satisfying those markets result from marketing planning. This chapter examines marketing planning. Chapter 5 discusses marketing research and ways in which decision-oriented information is used to plan and implement marketing strategies.

What Is Marketing Planning?

planning
Process of anticipating the future and determining the courses of action necessary for achieving organizational objectives.

Planning is the process of anticipating the future and determining courses of action for achieving organizational objectives. As the definition indicates, planning is a continuous process that includes specifying objectives and the actions required for attaining them. The planning process creates a blueprint that not only specifies the means for achieving organizational objectives but provides checkpoints at which actual performance can be compared with expectations to determine whether current activities are moving the organization toward its objectives.

marketing planning
Process of anticipating the future and determining the courses of action necessary for achieving marketing objectives.

Marketing planning—the implementation of planning activities as they relate to the achievement of marketing objectives—is the basis for all marketing strategies. Product lines, pricing decisions, selection of appropriate distribution channels, and decisions relating to promotional campaigns all depend on plans formulated within the marketing organization.

Strategic Planning versus Tactical Planning

strategic planning
Process of determining an organization's primary objectives, allocating funds, and then initiating actions designed to achieve those objectives.

Planning is often classified on the basis of scope or breadth. Some plans are quite broad and long range, focusing on certain organizational objectives that will have a major impact on the organization for a time period of five or more years. **Strategic planning** can be defined as the process of determining the organization's primary objectives and then adopting courses of action that will eventually achieve them.[2] This process includes, of course, the allocation of necessary resources. The word *strategy* is derived from a Greek term meaning "the general's art." Strategic planning has a critical impact on the organization's destiny because it provides long-term direction for decision makers.

The Chevrolet division of General Motors developed a strategy to market its foreign imports under the Geo brand because of customer confusion about whether the division's cars were domestic or imported. Before the Geo strategy was developed, the Chevy Sprint, a subcompact built by Suzuki; the Spectrum,

Figure 4.1   Tactical Planning: Implementation of a Strategic Plan

built by Isuzu; and the Nova, built in California with Toyota, were marketed with the rest of the Chevrolet lineup. Although budget-conscious consumers were drawn to these models (their sticker prices were all under $10,000), these same consumers were confused by Chevrolet's claim that its Japanese imports represented the "Heartbeat of America."

So a strategy was developed to set these foreign imports apart from Chevrolet's domestic products. Geo advertising and product information told consumers that they were buying an "international" car. Initial plans were aimed at redesigning and renaming the new Geo lineup to make it appeal to younger buyers, improving consumer awareness of the brand, and increasing sales.[3] To execute this long-term strategy, the company developed a set of tactical plans.

tactical planning
Implementation of activities that are necessary for the achievement of the firm's objectives.

Tactical planning focuses on the implementation of those activities specified in the strategic plan. Tactical plans typically are more short-term than strategic plans, focusing more on current and near-term activities that must be completed to implement overall strategies. Resource deployment is a common decision area for tactical planning. Chevrolet's tactical plans included carrying out the strategy to redesign many of the Geo models, now renamed the Prizm, Storm, Tracker, and Metro. While the Spectrum was boxy, the Geo Storm is a sport coupe. While the Geo Metro is similar to the Sprint, a convertible top has been added to attract younger buyers. Chevrolet's tactical plans also included promoting the Geo under a separate framework from other Chevrolet models, as in the ad in Figure 4.1, in order to target the right buyers. Some Geo ads have

FOCUS ON ETHICS

MARKETING IN WARTIME

· ·

When Operation Desert Storm burst into the consciousness of Americans, other activities were set aside and attention focused on the war. During and after the war, marketing planners faced a number of difficult questions. Should they mention the war in their ads? Should they cancel or alter their existing advertising? Should they reduce or increase their spending? Where lay the boundary between patriotism and war profiteering?

Marketers responded to the war and its aftermath in a variety of ways. Some examples:

☐ Two days after the beginning of the war, Boeing Co. ran a commercial showing military people at work, with "America the Beautiful" playing in the background and a message supporting the troops.

☐ Walt Disney altered its Super Bowl commercial, instructing Giants MVP Ottis Anderson to "dedicate this win to the troops."

☐ Topps Co. Inc., maker of baseball cards, shipped a series of "educational" Desert Storm collectors' cards and stickers to retailers; the cards carried photos of U.S. military leaders and equipment, with appropriate facts on the back.

☐ A one-tenth scale model of the Patriot anti-missile missile, equipped with a launching pad and three solid-fuel engines, became the best-selling model rocket in the nation's toy stores and hobby shops; manufacturer Estes Industries was hard-pressed to keep up with the demand.

☐ Norwegian Cruise Line pulled an ad showing sailors on a U.S. naval vessel picking up another ship's signals, which turn out to be music from an NCL pleasure cruise.

☐ The makers of Moet & Chandon champagne ran a full-page ad in *The New York Times* containing its logo and the words. "Please tear this page into many small pieces and toss high into the air in celebration of peace."

According to some advertising experts, companies that ran ads or promoted products that played on the emotions created by the war did run the risk of being perceived as war profiteers—especially when the products were not related to the war. Consumers, they said, usually "see right through it" when advertisements invoke patriotism. Many companies were unwilling to run these risks at the beginning of the war, but as the war continued, war-related messages crept into their advertising. Some companies went to great lengths to avoid the charge of profiteering. Bulova Corp., for example, created a new line of watches called The Patriot but announced that profits from sales of the watches would go to the USO as long as the war continued.

Discussion Questions

1. Advertisers and advertising agencies expressed some confusion about whether commercials like Boeing's would be perceived as a form of war profiteering. What principles could they have applied in making decisions about wartime advertising?

2. Some companies insisted that the war would not change their marketing plans. What risks might be associated with such a policy?

Sources: "Advertisers Wary of Boosting Postwar Spending," *Marketing News* (April 1, 1991), pp. 1, 17; "A Patriot of Your Very Own," *U.S. News & World Report* (March 18, 1991), p. 66; and "War-Related Products Face 'Profiteering' Tag," *Marketing News* (March 18, 1991), p. 1.

focused on changing values as they have encouraged buyers to "Get to know Geo." For example, the tagline for an advertisement for the Geo Prizm is, "In a disposable world, some things are made to last." To target the young single market, Geo sponsored the World Surfing Championship in Hawaii and the Pro Beach Volleyball Championship. It also sponsored 11 episodes of a popular MTV sports program and ran tie-ins with the Hard Rock Cafe. Tactical plans also included making changes in dealer presentations. To differentiate Geo models from the domestic Chevrolets that were standing nearby in the same showroom, separate sections were set aside for each line of cars. Showroom signs clearly

Table 4.1 Planning by Different Management Levels

Managerial Level	Types of Planning Emphasized at This Level	Examples
Top Management Board of directors Chief executive officer (CEO) Chief operating officer (COO) Division vice-presidents	Strategic planning	Objectives of organization; fundamental strategies; long-term plans; total budget.
Middle Management General sales manager Marketing research manager Advertising director	Tactical planning	Quarterly and semiannual plans; subdivision of budgets; policies and procedures for each department.
Supervisory Management District sales manager Supervisors in staff marketing departments	Operational planning	Daily and weekly plans; unit budgets; departmental rules and procedures.

pointed customers to the Geos. Interestingly, Geo signs often were larger than the signs for the domestic Chevrolets. The Geo Metro, with its better than 50-mile-per-gallon gas mileage, was promoted heavily to young car buyers.[4]

Planning at Different Organizational Levels

Planning is a major responsibility for every manager, and managers at all organizational levels devote some of their workdays to planning. However, the relative proportion of time spent in planning activities and the types of planning vary. Top management—the board of directors, CEO, COO, and functional vice-presidents, such as the chief marketing officer—spend greater proportions of their time engaged in planning than do middle- and supervisory-level managers. Also, top management is likely to devote more of its planning activities to long-range strategic planning than are middle-level managers (such as the advertising director, regional sales managers, or the marketing research manager), who tend to focus on operational planning—creating and implementing narrow tactical plans for their departments. Supervisory personnel are more likely to engage in developing specific programs for meeting the goals in their responsibility areas. Table 4.1 indicates the types of planning involved at various organizational levels.

According to Edith Weiner, a prominent strategic planning consultant, planning should permeate every level of an organization. In Weiner's view, every employee should engage in some degree of strategic planning, marketing, and should also understand corporate profitability.[5]

Steps in the Marketing Planning Process

The marketing planning process begins with the development of objectives and then moves to procedures for accomplishing these objectives. The basic steps in the process—defining the organization's mission, determining organizational

Figure 4.2   The Marketing Planning Process

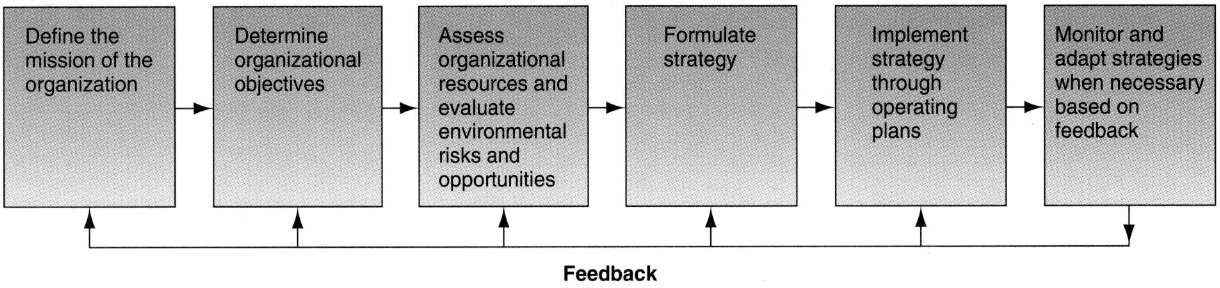

objectives, assessing organizational resources, evaluating environmental risks and opportunities, formulating a marketing strategy, implementing the strategy through operating plans, and using feedback to monitor and adapt strategies when necessary—are shown in Figure 4.2.

Defining the Organization's Mission

mission
General enduring statement of organizational purpose.

The starting point in the planning process is for the firm to define its **mission,** the essential purpose that differentiates the company from others. The mission statement specifies the organization's operational scope as illustrated in the following example.[6]

Johnson & Johnson's consumer products business is dedicated to achieving worldwide growth that is greater than its competitors. To fulfill this mission, Johnson & Johnson developed a four-part strategy to build leadership brands, to become more cost efficient, to focus on technology leadership, and to strengthen leadership with trade customers.[7]

Moreover, a subsidiary of a larger organization can have a mission statement of its own:

The mission of Saturn Corporation, a subsidiary of General Motors, is "to design, manufacture, and market vehicles to compete on a global scale, as well as re-establish American technology as the standard for automotive quality." It is the corporation's intent to win over small-car consumers who have been committed to the imports. "These young, well-educated car buyers are the customers who will be the key to our success."[8]

Mission statements provide general guidelines for future management actions. They can be adjusted to reflect a changing business environment and different philosophies of management. Intel's corporate mission is one that has changed over time. The Santa Clara, California firm withdrew from the memory-chip industry and now concentrates on microprocessors. Its current mission is "to become the premier building block supplier to the new computer industry." The firm's CEO, Andrew Grove, points out that any mission statement must provide a practical guide to management actions. Grove says that the test of whether a mission statement is effective is if it "helps a manager who is earning $60,000 or $80,000 a year actually do what he . . . [or she] . . . does."[9]

Resource strengths help The Coca-Cola Company implement its global growth strategy. One of the company's major assets is its exceptional distribution system. In emerging markets, it develops innovative and inexpensive delivery systems. To expand the availability of products in Indonesia, it uses pushcarts mounted with coolers, shown here. Per-capita consumption of company products in Indonesia is low, about four drinks per year, but the company expects to boost the level to ten by 1993 through increased distribution efforts. By capitalizing on its resource strengths, Coca-Cola has increased its international market share to 46 percent, four times that of any competitor.

Source: © Arthur Meyerson/The Coca-Cola Company.

Determining Organizational Objectives

The basic objectives, or goals, of the organization are derived from the mission statement. These objectives provide the basis from which marketing objectives and plans are developed. They vary among organizations. The goal of Toyota is to be the number three automaker in the United States, surpassing Chrysler with annual sales of 1.5 million cars and trucks by 1995.[10] The goal of Saturn is to attract eight out of ten buyers from consumers who own non-GM cars.[11] After years of internal trouble, the Italian retailer Gucci now defines its corporate goal in the following way: to reemerge as the world's leading retailer in leather goods and fashion accessories.[12]

Soundly conceived objectives should be specific ("a 12 percent increase in profits over last year"; "attain a 20% share of the market by 1996"; "15% increase in sales over last year"). In addition, they should specify the time period for their achievement.

Assessing Organizational Resources and Evaluating Risks and Opportunities

The third and fourth steps of the marketing planning process actually occur at about the same time in a back-and-forth assessment of strengths, risks, and available opportunities. As Figure 4.2 illustrates, marketing opportunities are affected by organizational resources and environmental factors. Both are important considerations in the planning process.

Organizational resources include production, marketing, finance, technology, and employees' capabilities. Organizations should pinpoint their strengths and weaknesses. Strengths help organizations set objectives, develop plans for meeting objectives, and take advantage of marketing opportunities. For example, The Coca-Cola Company identifies its strengths as having the world's best-known and most-admired trademark, financial soundness, a global soft-drink production and distribution system, marketing and advertising efficiency, new-product innovations, and a dedicated team of managers and employees.

The environmental dimensions discussed in Chapter 2—competitive, politi-cal-legal, economic, technological, and social-cultural—also influence marketing opportunities. Environmental factors can emerge both from within the organiza-tion and from the external environment. U.S. exports suffered for many years because the value of the dollar was so high; only when the dollar dropped in value could many U.S. firms compete. Similarly, as the economies of such Asian countries as Korea, Taiwan, Hong Kong, and Singapore grow stronger, these countries depend less on access to U.S. goods and services. With self-sufficiency comes decreased demand.[13] Internal environmental factors also influence operational success. For example, out-of-date production facilities of many U.S. steel mills have made it impossible for American companies to compete with fully modernized Japanese and South Korean companies. By contrast, the Coca-Cola Company was ready to take advantage of the political upheaval in Eastern Europe. With the demise of communism in East Germany came an opportunity for Coca-Cola to bring its products to a united Germany. The company's move into East Germany was made with a $140 million capital investment.[14]

SWOT analysis
Study of organizational resources and capabilities to assess the firm's strengths and weaknesses and scanning the external envi-ronments to identify opportunities and threats.

SWOT Analysis.   An important strategic planning tool, **SWOT analysis,** compares internal organizational strengths and weaknesses to external oppor-tunities and threats. (SWOT is an acronym for strengths and weaknesses, opportunities and threats.) This analysis provides management with a critical view of the organization's internal and external environment. It is useful in the fulfillment of the firm's basic mission.

The matching of internal strength with external opportunity produces a situation known as *leverage* for the organization (see Figure 4.3). The Red Adair Company—discussed in the Competitive Edge feature in Chapter 2—found itself with tremendous leverage immediately after the 1991 Persian Gulf War. Adair's organizational strengths included a trained workforce and specialized equipment. The firm also benefited from the fact that only a handful of other companies are equipped to do the job.[15]

A *problem* exists when environmental threats attack an organization's weakness. Eastman Kodak has long been hampered by an unwieldy manage-ment structure. Although the company has recognized this weakness and has reorganized four times since 1984 in an effort to resolve it, the corporate bureaucracy continues to obstruct marketing efforts. Kodak's difficulty has been compounded by the innovative marketing of Fuji, which brought out the first high-speed film for both indoor and outdoor use and positioned itself as a leader in the exploding easy-to-use 35mm camera market. Fuji's advantage over Kodak was obvious to consumers. Jacques Kauffman, president of IMAC International, a photo-industry consulting firm in Wilmette, Illinois, explains, "While 35mm cameras came in, Kodak continued to push the 110mm camera. For that reason, 35mm photographers tended to look to companies like Fuji for innovations."[16] While Fuji provided the environmental threat, Kodak's own bureaucracy ham-pered its marketing efforts.

Constraints refer to situations where organizations are unable to capitalize on opportunities because of internal limitations. For example, Eastern Airlines' failure meant that its gates in Atlanta would be available to any airline that wanted to compete against Delta. Northwest Airlines craved this opportunity but was limited in its ability to take advantage of it by its internal debt load.

COMPETITIVE EDGE

OPEL'S DRIVE TOWARD NUMBER ONE

. . . .

Capitalizing on its strengths, alert to its weaknesses, and tuned in to opportunities in the wide-open European automobile market, Opel is mounting a serious challenge to Volkswagen's number one position in Germany. One of the obstacles that the company must overcome is its past reputation. For years children chanted a derogatory rhyme that could be translated, "Every yokel drives an Opel." Recently Opel (a subsidiary of General Motors) revamped its

product line and introduced more aerodynamic models, like those shown here, that have helped improve its image. But Opel has benefited even more from some important strategic decisions.

While Volkswagen has made German customers wait as long as six months for new models, Opel has shifted supplies from sagging markets to satisfy German demand. In the first eight months of 1990 it captured 16.9 percent of the market in the former West Germany, compared to Volkswagen's 20 percent. In fact, Opel had a record 160,000 cars on order.

In an effort to cope with the increased demand, GM is building a new plant in the former East Germany, where land is cheap, wages are low, and demand for cars is expected to triple by the end of the decade. Opel's existing European plants are already running at full capacity. "We're sold out," says one company executive.

Opel's success in Germany has stimulated GM to seek additional markets in Hungary and other Eastern European countries. In 1987 it signed a five-year trade agreement with Hungary under which it buys components for Opels from a Hungarian manufacturer, Ràba.

In exchange, Hungary imports about 1,000 Opels per year. GM is optimistic about its prospects in Eastern Europe. The short-term opportunities are good, and if the economies of these countries improve, the long-term prospects may be equally good.

Discussion Questions

1. Customers now must wait four to six months for some popular Opel models, just as Volkswagen customers do. Can Opel maintain its momentum under these conditions?

2. What risks does GM run in building a new plant in the former East Germany?

Sources: Terence Roth and Bradley A. Stertz, "GM's Opel Is Closing in on Volkswagen as Top Selling Brand in German Market," *The Wall Street Journal* (October 4, 1990), p. A17; Shawn Tully, "Doing Business in One Germany," *Fortune* (July 2, 1990), pp. 80–83; Allan T. Demaree, "The New Germany's Glowing Future," *Fortune* (December 3, 1990), pp. 146–154; and "Eastern Europe Beckons," *Advertising Age* (November 20, 1989), pp. 1, 45. *Photo source:* Courtesy of General Motors Corporation.

An environmental threat to a current organizational strength is termed a *vulnerability.* Stamford, Connecticut, retailers viewed the news of the proposed expansion of the state sales tax with trepidation. No longer would they attract shoppers from nearby New York City who wanted to avoid New York's 8¼ percent sales tax on clothing. (Connecticut taxed only those clothing items costing $75 and more, at a rate of 8 percent.)

Figure 4.3   SWOT Analysis

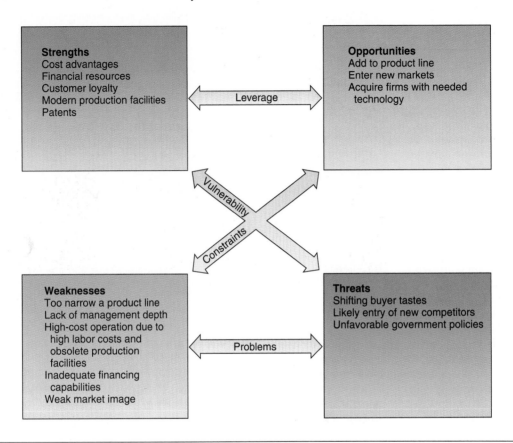

Source: Adapted from a discussion in Ramon J. Aldag and Timothy M. Stearns, *Management* (South-Western Publishing Co., 1991), pp. 199–201.

strategic window

Limited periods during which the "fit" between the key requirements of a market and the particular competencies of a firm is optimal.

The Strategic Window.   Derek Abell has suggested the term **strategic window** to define the limited periods during which the key requirements of a market and the particular competencies of a firm best fit together.[17] The devastation of Kuwait opened up a strategic window for many U.S. firms who were hired to help rebuild the country after the Persian Gulf War. Immediately after the liberation of Kuwait, Motorola was asked to supply thousands of portable telephones; Raytheon was awarded a $5.7 million contract to provide temporary air-control and communications equipment as well as runway lights for Kuwait International Airport; AT&T was contracted to install a satellite station that would enable residents of Kuwait City to make emergency long-distance phone calls; and Caterpillar was asked to provide diesel engines linked to electrical generators for emergency electrical power.[18]

A strategic window perspective offers a way of relating potential opportunities to company capabilities. Such a view requires a thorough analysis of (1) current and projected external environments, (2) current and projected internal company capabilities, and (3) how, whether, and when it will be feasible to reconcile the two by implementing one or more marketing strategies.

When Paris-based Source Perrier announced that it would recall 160 million bottles of its sparkling water after traces of benzene, a known carcinogen, were

ConAgra, a diversified food company, took a strategic window perspective when it launched Healthy Choice premium frozen dinners. Unlike other frozen dinners that are low in calories, Healthy Choice is also low in cholesterol, fat, and sodium. With Healthy Choice, ConAgra matched its capabilities in product innovation and supermarket distribution with consumers' desire for convenience food that answered health concerns. Healthy Choice caught competitors by surprise and quickly became the market leader in the premium frozen dinner market. ConAgra is building on the product's enormous initial success by extending the brand beyond frozen meals to canned and shelf-stable meals and children's frozen meals.

Source: © 1991 Crain Communications Inc./Photographer: Brooke Hummer.

discovered in water shipped to the United States, other bottlers recognized the strategic window created by the recall. Companies like San Pellegrino had the manufacturing capacity to meet expanded demand (dozens of distributors doubled their orders). And Evian, distributors of Evian and Saratoga brands, tried to capitalize on the situation by launching new advertising campaigns. Although competitors insisted that they would not wish Perrier's plight on anyone, they were quick to develop a strategic window perspective to take advantage of the changed marketing environment.[19]

Formulating a Marketing Strategy

The net result of opportunity analysis is the formulation of marketing objectives designed to achieve overall organizational objectives and help in developing a marketing plan. The marketing plan revolves around a marketing strategy that is resource efficient, flexible, and adaptable. **Marketing strategy** is the overall company program for selecting a particular target market and then satisfying consumers in that market through careful use of the elements of the marketing mix. The components of the marketing mix—product, pricing, distribution, and promotion—represent subsets of the overall marketing strategy.

marketing strategy
Selection of a target market and the related blending of marketing mix elements.

Implementing and Monitoring Marketing Plans

The sixth step of the marketing planning process consists of implementing the marketing strategy that has been agreed upon by management. The overall strategic marketing plan serves as the basis for a series of operating plans necessary to move the organization toward accomplishment of its objectives. Although marketing planning is discussed throughout this text in connection with the analysis and selection of a target market and the development of a marketing mix designed to satisfy the chosen market, detailed and intensive analysis of operating plans in specific areas of the organization must be dealt with in more advanced marketing texts.

At every step of the marketing planning process, marketing managers use feedback to monitor and adapt strategies when actual performance fails to match expectations. This is the seventh and final step in the marketing planning process. Methods of securing feedback are discussed in Chapter 5.

Tools Used in Marketing Planning

As more organizations have discovered the benefits resulting from effective marketing planning, a number of planning tools have been developed to assist in conducting this important function. These include the strategic business unit concept, the market share/market growth matrix, and spreadsheet analysis. In addition, the marketing audit is frequently used in evaluating marketing planning and marketing performance.

Strategic Business Units (SBUs)

Although smaller firms may offer only a few goods and services to their customers, larger organizations frequently produce and market numerous offerings to widely diverse markets. For example, Chemical Bank has a portfolio of banking-related businesses that includes consumer and corporate banking services in the New York/New Jersey metropolitan area, a wholesale banking business with corporate and institutional clients, a major banking presence in Texas through its Texas Commerce Bancshares subsidiary, and transaction and information services serving corporations and institutions worldwide.[20] The ad in Figure 4.4 illustrates the diverse businesses, ranging from oil production to animal nutrition, that comprise the corporate portfolio of the British Petroleum Company, p. l. c. Top management at major firms needs some method for determining the best way to evaluate these diverse businesses in order to distinguish the promising product lines that warrant additional resources from those that should be weeded from the firm's product portfolio. The concept of an SBU provides this method.

strategic business unit (SBU) Related product groupings of businesses within a multiproduct firm with specific managers, resources, objectives, and competitors; structured for optimal planning purposes.

Strategic business units (SBUs) are key business units within diversified firms. Each of these divisions has its own specific managers, resources, objectives, and competitors. A division, product line, or single product may be an SBU. Each SBU has its own distinct mission, and each is planned independently of other units in the organization.

Strategic business units enable company management to better respond to changing consumer demand. For example, the U.S. division of Reebok International is now split into two separate units to better respond to an increasingly segmented footwear market. The Performance Footwear Unit will focus on technology-based athletic footwear while the Lifestyle Unit targets fashion-conscious consumers.[21]

The Market Share/Market Growth Matrix

market share/market growth matrix Matrix that classifies a firm's products in terms of the industry growth rate and its market share relative to competitive products.

To evaluate the organization's strategic business units, some type of portfolio-performance framework is needed. The most widely used framework was developed in the early 1970s by the Boston Consulting Group. The **market share/ market growth matrix** is a four-quadrant matrix that plots market share—the percentage of a market a firm controls—and market growth potential. The market share, plotted on the horizontal axis, indicates the SBU's market share

Figure 4.4   Strategic Business Units

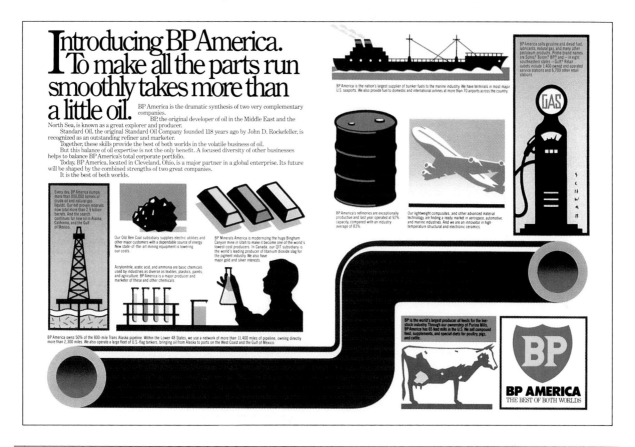

Source: Courtesy of BP.

relative to competitors in the industry. The market growth rate, plotted on the vertical axis, indicates the annual growth rate of that market. All of a firm's various businesses can be plotted in one of the four quadrants. As Figure 4.5 shows, the quadrants are labeled cash cows, stars, dogs, and question marks, and each requires a unique marketing strategy.

Stars represent high market share and high market growth. These products or businesses are high-growth market leaders. While they generate considerable income, even more cash flow is needed to finance their further growth. When Upjohn first discovered that its blood-pressure medication Minoxodil also had the potential to grow scalp hair, the product took its position as a corporate star.

Cash cows represent high market share and low market growth. Marketers want to maintain this status for as long as possible, because these businesses are producing a strong cash flow, but instead of heavily investing in promotions and production for them, the firm can use its funds to finance the growth of other SBUs with high growth potential. Chicago-based FMC Corporation operates a profitable business based on three cash cows: industrial chemicals, defense equipment, and machinery.[22] Cash cows are often the targets of other companies. Toyota wants to crack the U.S. market for full-size pickup trucks, which is now a cash cow of General Motors, Ford, and Chrysler.[23]

Question marks represent low market share and high market growth. These situations require marketers to make a decision on whether or not to pursue these products or businesses, since question marks typically require more cash

Figure 4.5

Market Share/Market Growth
Matrix

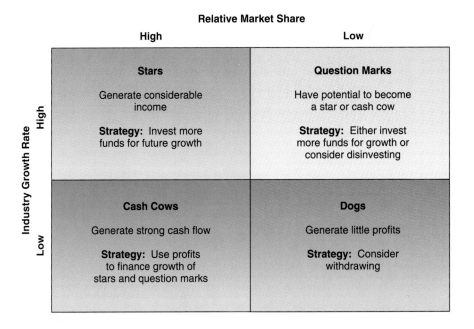

than they are able to generate. If question marks cannot be converted to stars, the firm should pull out of these markets and target markets with greater potential. Procter & Gamble made the "no go" decision when it cut spending on its fat substitute, olestra, focusing instead on such best sellers as superconcentrated Tide detergent and Pert Plus shampoo.[24]

Dogs represent low market share and low market growth. SBUs in this category have poor future prospects, and marketers should withdraw from these businesses or product lines as quickly as possible. Recent corporate dogs include RJR Nabisco's "smokeless cigarette" Premier; Anheuser-Busch's low-alcoholic brew, LA Beer; and Wegman's Foodmarkets UltraSofts diaper.[25]

Evaluating the Matrix Approach to Planning.   The market share/market growth matrix emphasizes the importance of creating market offerings that will position the firm to its best advantage. It also indicates that successful SBUs undergo a series of changes as they move through their life cycle. The successful product or business typically begins as a question mark, then becomes a star, and eventually drops into the cash-cow category, generating surplus funds with which to finance new stars. Ultimately it becomes a dog at the end of its life cycle and is eliminated from the firm's product offerings.

Spreadsheet Analysis

Spreadsheets are special computer software used in answering "what if" questions. Electronic spreadsheets are the computerized equivalent of an accountant's hand-prepared worksheet. The electronic spreadsheet, like its manual counterpart, is a rigid grid of columns and rows that enables the manager to organize information in a standardized, easily understandable format. The most popular spreadsheets include Lotus 1-2-3, Excel, Supercalc 5, Quattro Pro, and Wingz.

spreadsheet analysis
Marketing planning tool that uses a decision-oriented computer program to answer "what if" questions posed by marketing managers.

Spreadsheet analysis may be used to anticipate marketing performance given a specified set of circumstances. For example, a spreadsheet might be

Figure 4.6   Example of Spreadsheet Analysis

Fixed Costs				Per-Unit Variable Cost	Sales Price	Breakeven Point (Units)
Manufacturing	Marketing	R&D	Total			
$80,000	$100,000	$70,000	$250,000	$4	$8	62,500
$80,000	$200,000	$70,000	$350,000	$4	$8	87,500
$80,000	$100,000	$70,000	$250,000	$3	$7	62,500

used to determine the outcomes of different prices for a new product, as shown in Figure 4.6. In this example, the item will be marketed at $8 per unit and can be produced for $4 in variable costs. The total fixed costs of $250,000 include $80,000 for manufacturing-overhead outlays such as salaries, general office expenses, rent, utilities, and interest charges; $100,000 for marketing expenditures; and $70,000 for research and development for the product. The spreadsheet calculation, using the basic breakdown model, reveals that sales of 62,500 units are necessary in order to break even.

But what if a marketing manager convinces other members of the group to increase marketing expenditures to $200,000? As the second part of Figure 4.6 shows, the $100,000 marketing expenditure in the cell (the name of each point at which the rows and columns intersect) is changed to $200,000, and the newly calculated breakeven point is 87,500 units. As soon as an amount in one or more cells changes, all amounts are recalculated automatically by the spreadsheet software.

The final part of Figure 4.6 demonstrates the impact of a reduction in variable costs (by switching to the lower-cost materials) to $3 coupled with a $1 reduction in the product's selling price. The new breakeven point is 62,500 units.

This figure demonstrates the ease with which a marketing manager can use a microcomputer spreadsheet program to determine the potential results of alternative decisions. More complex spreadsheets may have as many as 50 or more columns, yet can make the new calculations as quickly as the manager changes the variables.

Marketing Audits

marketing audit
Objective evaluation of an organization's marketing philosophy, goals, policies, tactics, practices, and results.

If the marketing organization is to avoid the Persian Messenger Syndrome (the tendency to criticize or ignore people who provide negative information), it must institute periodic reviews of marketing plans and be willing to accept the objective results of the evaluations. For most organizations, this means using a **marketing audit**—a thorough, objective evaluation of an organization's marketing philosophy, goals, policies, tactics, practices, and results.[26]

(A periodic audit should (1) identify the tasks that the organization does well and (2) reveal its failures.) Such periodic review, criticism, and self-analysis are crucial to the vitality of any organization. They are particularly critical to a function as diverse and dynamic as marketing. Marketing audits are especially valuable in pointing out areas in which managerial perceptions differ sharply from reality.

Methods of conducting audits are almost as diverse as the firms that use them. Some audits follow informal procedures; others involve elaborate checklists, questionnaires, profiles, tests, and related research instruments.

The marketing audit goes beyond the normal control system. The control process for marketing essentially asks, are we doing things right? The marketing audit extends this question to, are we doing the right thing?

Marketing audits are applicable to all organizations—large or small, profitable or profitless, nonprofit or profit oriented. Audits are particularly valuable when performed for the first time or when conducted after having been discontinued for several years. While not all firms use marketing audits, an increasing number are recognizing their important role in evaluating strategies that will maintain competitiveness and profitability.

Sales Forecasting

sales forecast
Estimate of company sales for a specified future period.

A basic building block of marketing planning is the **sales forecast,** an estimate of the firm's sales or income for a specified future period. In addition to its use in marketing planning, the sales forecast plays a major role in new-product decisions, production scheduling, financial planning, inventory planning and procurement, product distribution, and determining personnel needs. An inaccurate forecast will result in incorrect decisions in each of these areas. The sales forecast is also an important tool for marketing control, because it produces standards against which to measure actual performance. Without such standards, no comparisons can be made. If no criterion of success exists, there can be no definition of failure.

Sales forecasts can be classified as short run, intermediate, or long run. Short-run forecasts usually include a period of up to one year, intermediate forecasts cover one to five years, and long-run forecasts extend beyond five years. The time frame of a forecast depends on many factors, including organizational resources, environmental factors, and the ways in which the forecast will be used.

Although forecasters use dozens of techniques to divine the future—ranging from computer simulations to the study of trends by futurists—their methods fall into two broad categories. *Qualitative* forecasting techniques are more subjective because they are based on opinions rather than exact historical data. *Quantitative* forecasting methods, by contrast, employ statistical computations such as trend extensions based on past data, computer simulations, and econometrics to produce numerical forecasts. As Table 4.2 shows, each method has benefits and limitations. Consequently, most organizations use a combination of techniques.

Qualitative Forecasting Techniques

As noted above, qualitative forecasting is judgmental or subjective in nature. Qualitative forecasting techniques include the jury of executive opinion, Delphi technique, salesforce composite, and survey of buyer intentions.

jury of executive opinion
Qualitative sales forecasting method that combines and averages the sales expectations of various executives.

Jury of Executive Opinion.
The technique called **jury of executive opinion** combines and averages the outlooks of top company executives from

Table 4.2   Benefits and Limitations of Various Forecasting Techniques

Technique	Benefits	Limitations
Qualitative Methods		
Jury of executive opinion	Opinions come from executives in many different departments; quick; inexpensive	Managers may lack sufficient knowledge and experience to make meaningful predictions
Delphi technique	Group of experts can accurately predict long-term events such as technological breakthroughs	Time consuming; expensive
Sales force composite	Salespeople have expert customer, product, and competitor knowledge; quick; inexpensive	Inaccurate forecasts may result from low estimates of salespeople concerned about their influence on quotas
Survey of buyer intentions	Useful in predicting short- and intermediate-term sales for firms that have only a few customers	Intention to buy may not result in actual purchase; time consuming; expensive
Quantitative Methods		
Market tests	Provides realistic information on actual purchases rather than on intent to buy	Alerts competition to new-product plans; time consuming; expensive
Trend analysis	Quick; inexpensive; effective when customer demand and environmental factors are stable	Assumes the future is continuation of past; does not consider environmental changes
Exponential smoothing	Same benefits as trend analysis but emphasizes more recent data	Same limitations as trend analysis but not as severe due to emphasis on recent data

such areas as finance, production, marketing, and purchasing. It is particularly effective when top managers are experienced and knowledgeable about situations that influence sales, open-minded about the future, and aware of the bases for their judgments. This method is quick and inexpensive and can be effectively used to forecast sales and develop new products. It works best for short-run forecasting.

Delphi Technique.

Delphi technique √
Qualitative sales forecasting method that involves several rounds of anonymous forecasts and ends when a consensus of the participants is reached.

While similar to the jury of executive opinion in that it involves soliciting the opinions of several people, the **Delphi technique** seeks opinions of experts outside the firm, such as university researchers and scientists, rather than relying completely on company executives. It is most appropriately used to predict long-run issues, such as technological breakthroughs, that could affect future company sales and the market potential for new products. The Delphi technique works as follows: A firm selects a panel of experts, then sends each a questionnaire relating to a future event. The answers are combined and averaged, and, based on these results, another questionnaire is sent to the experts. The process continues until a consensus of opinion has been reached. Although firms have successfully used Delphi to predict future technological breakthroughs, the method is both expensive and time-consuming.

Salesforce Composite.

salesforce composite √
Qualitative sales forecasting method in which sales estimates are based on the combined estimates of the firm's salesforce.

The technique of the **salesforce composite** is based on the belief that organizational members closest to the marketplace—those with specialized product, customer, and competitor knowledge—are likely to have better insight concerning short-term future sales than any other group. It is typically a bottom-up approach: Salespersons' estimates are first combined at the district level, then the regional level, and finally the national level to obtain an aggregate forecast of sales that reflects all three levels. Few firms rely solely on the salesforce composite, however. Since salespeople recognize the role of the sales forecast in determining sales quotas for their territories, they are likely to make conservative estimates. Moreover, their narrow perspectives on their limited geographical territories may prevent them from knowing about trends developing in other territories, forthcoming technological innovations, or the impact of major changes in marketing strategies on sales. Consequently, the salesforce composite is best combined with other forecasting techniques in developing the final forecast.

survey of buyer intentions
Qualitative sales forecasting method in which sample groups of present and potential customers are surveyed concerning their purchase intentions.

Survey of Buyer Intentions.   In the **survey of buyer intentions,** mail-in questionnaires, telephone polls, or personal interviews are used to determine the intentions of a representative group of present and potential customers. This method is more appropriate for firms with a limited number of customers. It is often impractical for those with millions of customers. Also, buyer surveys are limited to situations in which customers are willing to reveal their buying intentions. Moreover, customer intentions do not necessarily translate into actual purchases. These surveys may help predict short-run or intermediate sales, but they are time consuming and expensive.

Quantitative Forecasting Techniques

Quantitative techniques use a more scientific approach to forecasting sales. They attempt to eliminate the guesswork of the qualitative methods. Quantitative techniques include such methods as market tests, trend analysis, and exponential smoothing.

market test
Quantitative forecasting method in which a new product, price, promotional campaign, or other marketing variable is introduced in a relatively small test market location in order to assess consumer reactions.

Market Tests.   The quantitative technique of the **market test** is frequently used in assessing consumer response to new product offerings. The procedure typically involves establishing a small number of test markets with which to gauge consumer response to a new product under actual marketplace conditions. Market tests also permit the evaluation of different prices, alternate promotional strategies, and other marketing mix variations through comparisons among different test markets. Based on consumer responses in test markets, a firm can predict sales for larger market areas. Recently, McDonald's test-marketed an expanded menu in its Scranton, Pennsylvania, restaurants. In addition to its standard burgers and fries, spaghetti and lasagna, fettuccine and tortellini were also on the menu. The results in Scranton and other test-market cities were so positive that McDonald's decided to widen its traditional menu adding items that bring it closer to being a full-fledged family restaurant.[27]

The primary advantage of market tests is the realism they provide for the marketer. On the other hand, they are expensive and time-consuming and may communicate marketing plans to competitors before a product has been introduced to the total market. Test marketing is discussed in more detail in Chapter 10.

trend analysis
Quantitative sales forecasting method in which estimates of future sales are determined through statistical analyses of historical sales patterns.

Trend Analysis.   The technique of **trend analysis** involves forecasting future sales by analyzing the historical relationship between sales and time. It is based on the assumption that factors that collectively determined past sales will continue to exert similar influence in the future. When historical data are available, trend analysis can be performed quickly and inexpensively. For example, if sales were X last year and have been increasing at Y percent for the past several years, the sales forecast for next year would be calculated as follows:

$$\text{Sales Forecast} = X + XY.$$

In actual numbers, if last year's sales totaled 520,000 units and the average sales growth rate has been 5 percent, the sales forecast would be:

Ameritech frequently conducts market tests on new information and telecommunications goods and services to assess consumer response in the marketplace. An example is the test of the public facsimile (FAX) machine shown here at Detroit's Cobo Center. The machine is one of several being tested by Ameritech's Michigan Bell in partnership with PayFAX, Inc. If the trial of the machine is successful, Ameritech will introduce the service more widely.

Source: © Mark Joseph/Chicago.

$$\text{Sales Forecast} = 520{,}000 + (520{,}000 \times .05) = 546{,}000.$$

Of course, trend analysis cannot be used if historical data are not available, as in the case of new products.

The danger of trend analysis lies in its underlying assumption that the future is a continuation of the past. Any variations in the determinants influencing sales in the future will result in an incorrect forecast. In other words, this method is reliable only during periods of steady growth and stable demand. If conditions change, predictions based on the trend-extension method may become worthless. For this reason, forecasters have increasingly been using more sophisticated techniques and more complex mathematical models to take into account various possible changes in the future.

exponential smoothing
Quantitative forecasting technique that assigns weights to historical sales data, giving greater weight to the most recent data.

Exponential Smoothing. A more sophisticated approach to trend analysis, the **exponential smoothing** technique, assigns a weight factor to each year of sales data. Greater weight is given to the most recent years. For example, an exponential smoothing forecast based on five years of sales data might be weighted as follows:

Year	Weight
1987	.8
1988	.9
1989	1.0
1990	1.1
1991	1.2

Since those factors contributing to the most recent sales data are most likely to continue to interact similarly for the next time period, these data are assigned a greater weight than those of earlier years.

Steps in Sales Forecasting

Although sales forecasting methods vary, the most typical one begins with an environmental forecast of general economic conditions that marketers use to project industry sales and develop a forecast of company and product sales. This approach is referred to as the *top-down method.*

environmental forecast
Broad-based economic forecast that focuses on the impact of external factors on the firm's markets.

Environmental Forecasting.   The broad-based **environmental forecast** focuses on factors external to the firm that affect its markets, such as consumer spending and saving patterns, balance-of-trade surpluses and deficits, government expenditures, and business investments. These projections are combined to develop an overall economic forecast. The most common measure of economic output is the nation's gross national product (GNP), the market value of all final products produced in a country in a given year. Trend analysis is the most frequently used method of forecasting increases in the GNP. Since many federal agencies and other organizations develop regular GNP forecasts, a firm may choose to use their estimates, which are regularly reported in popular business publications.

Industry Sales Forecasting.   The general economic forecast is used with other relevant environmental factors in developing an industry sales forecast. Since industry sales often are related to GNP or some other measure of the national economy, a forecast may begin by measuring the degree of this relationship and then applying the trend extension method. Most industries have trade associations and publications that provide short-, intermediate-, and long-term forecasts. These forecasts are valuable because they combine an economic outlook with trends and environmental factors that influence specific industries.

Company and Product Sales Forecasting.   After the industry forecast has been completed, company and product forecasts are developed. This process begins with a detailed analysis of previous years' performances. The firm's past and present market share are reviewed, and product managers, as well as regional and district sales managers, are consulted about expected sales. Since an accelerated promotional budget or the introduction of new products may stimulate additional sales, the marketing plan for the coming year is also considered.

   Product and company forecasts must evaluate such factors as sales of each product; future sales trends; sales by customer, territory, salesperson, and order size; and financial resources. After the preliminary sales forecast has been developed, it is reviewed by the salesforce and by district, regional, and national sales managers.

Grass-Roots Forecasting.   An alternative approach to top-down forecasting is *grass-roots,* or *bottom-up,* forecasting. This forecasting method begins with sales estimates provided by each salesperson for his or her sales territory. These estimates are combined and refined at the divisional, regional, and national levels by sales and marketing managers. They are then submitted to the national sales manager and are combined into one sales estimate for the forthcoming time period. Proponents of the bottom-up approach to forecasting stress the improved employee morale and the motivational benefits that result when each member of the salesforce participates in developing the forecast that will be used as the primary basis for establishing sales quotas. In addition, the approach ensures inputs from each individual territory, and personal inputs from the salespeople who are in direct and continuing contact with the firm's customers.

One shortcoming of the grass-roots approach is the lack of perspective the individual salesperson has of the organization as a whole. Major trends, such as forthcoming market entries of competitive products, new products about to be introduced by the company, price changes, new promotional campaigns, packaging changes, and other variables likely to affect the marketplace, may not be reflected in the sales estimates for individual territories. In addition, since salespeople realize the relationship between the sales forecast and their sales quotas, they may be tempted to make relatively low forecasts that will be easy to exceed. Consequently, firms using the bottom-up approach depend heavily upon the compromises and final estimates that result from discussions at the divisional, regional, and national levels.

Since both the top-down and grass-roots approaches to sales forecasting possess strengths and weaknesses, it is not surprising that many marketers employ a combination of the two approaches to obtain the most realistic forecast possible.

New-Product Sales Forecasting.   Forecasting sales for new products is an especially hazardous undertaking since no historical data are available. Companies typically employ consumer panels to obtain reactions to the products and probable purchase behavior. Test market data may also be utilized.

Since few products are totally new, forecasters carefully analyze the sales of competing products that the new entry may displace. A new type of fishing reel, for example, will compete in an established market with other kinds of reels. This substitute method provides the forecaster with an estimate of market size and potential demand.

Summary of Chapter Objectives ✓

1. **Distinguish between strategic planning and tactical planning.** Planning, the process of anticipating the future and determining the courses of action needed for achieving organizational objectives, is the basis for all strategy decisions. Strategic planning is the broad, all-encompassing planning that involves determining the organization's primary objectives and adopting courses of action and allocation of resources necessary for achieving them. Tactical planning focuses on the implementation of activities specified in the strategic plan. Tactical plans typically are more short term than strategic plans, focusing on current and near-term activities that must be executed in order to implement overall strategies. Resource allocation is a common decision area in tactical planning.

2. **Explain how marketing plans differ at various levels in the organization.** Although all organization managers devote at least some time to planning, the relative proportion of time spent in planning activities and the types of planning vary at different organizational levels. Top management—the board of directors, CEO, COO, and functional vice-presidents (such as the chief marketing officer)—spend more time engaged in planning than do middle- and supervisory-level managers. Top managers are more likely to devote the bulk of their planning activities to long-range strategic planning. Middle-level managers (such as the advertising director, regional sales managers, or the marketing research manager) tend to focus on narrower, tactical plans for their departments. Supervisory managers are more likely to engage in developing specific programs designed to meet the goals for their areas of responsibility.

3. **Identify the steps in the marketing planning process.** The basic steps in the marketing planning process are mission definition, determination of organizational objectives; assessment of organizational resources; evaluation of environmental risks and opportunities; formulation of a marketing strategy; implementation of a marketing strategy through operating plans, and monitoring and adaptation based on feedback.

4. **Describe the concept of SWOT analysis in terms of its four major elements: leverage, problems, constraints, and vulnerability.** SWOT (an acronym for strengths, weaknesses, opportunities, and threats) analysis is a planning approach that focuses on the relationship between an organization's internal strengths and weaknesses and external opportunities and threats. Leverage exists if an external opportunity coincides with an internal strength. Constraints exist when an organization is unable to take advantage of opportunities because of internal limitations. Problems are the result of an environmental threat against an organizational weakness. Vulnerability involves an external threat to what has been perceived as an internal strength.

5. **Explain how the strategic business unit concept, the market share/ market growth matrix, and spreadsheet analysis can be used in marketing planning.** A number of very large, multiproduct firms use the strategic business unit (SBU) concept to aid in marketing planning. SBUs are divisions composed of key businesses within the firm with specific managers, resources, objectives, and competitors. Grouping company operating divisions into SBUs helps the firm focus on customer needs. Distinct strategies can be set up for each SBU based on the needs of its customer segments and its profit or growth potential. The market share/market growth matrix is a four-quadrant matrix that plots market share against market growth potential in the industry. Different marketing strategies may be appropriate for each segment of the matrix. The four segments are stars, cash cows, question marks, and dogs.

6. **Identify the major types of forecasting methods.** Sales forecasting is an important component of both planning and controlling marketing programs. Two basic categories of forecasting techniques exist: Quantitative forecasting utilizes statistical techniques such as trend analysis based on past data, exponential smoothing, and market tests to produce numerical forecasts of future events. Qualitative forecasting uses subjective techniques such as surveys of buyer intentions, salesforce composite, the jury of executive opinion, and the Delphi technique.

7. **Explain the steps in the forecasting process.** Although sales forecasting varies among individual firms, it is possible to divide the approaches into three general categories. With top-down forecasting, the firm begins with an environmental forecast of general economic conditions, which the marketer uses to forecast industry sales and then company and individual product sales. In bottom-up (or grass-roots) forecasting, the firm begins with sales estimates from individual salespersons. These estimates are combined and refined at the divisional, regional, and national levels by sales and marketing managers and then submitted to the national sales manager, at which point one sales estimate is developed for the forthcoming time period. Many firms combine the strengths of top-down and bottom-up forecasting to obtain the most realistic forecast possible. Forecasting sales for new goods or services can be especially difficult, since no historical data are available. Marketers of new products may have to base their forecasts on market tests or surveys of buyer intentions, which may not provide an accurate picture of actual purchase behavior. A substitute method in which forecasters carefully analyze

the sales of competing products that may be displaced by the new entry is also frequently used.

Key Terms

planning

marketing planning

strategic planning

tactical planning

mission

SWOT analysis

strategic window

marketing strategy

strategic business unit (SBU)

market share/market growth matrix

spreadsheet analysis

marketing audit

sales forecast

jury of executive opinion

Delphi technique

salesforce composite

survey of buyer intentions

market test

trend analysis

exponential smoothing

environmental forecast

Review Questions

1. How does strategic planning differ from tactical planning? Which type is more important at each level of management?

2. What are the basic steps in the marketing planning process? Give an example of a decision that might be made at each step.

3. Discuss how the analysis of an organization's external environment and an assessment of internal strengths and weaknesses can identify strategic opportunities and threats. Examine in your answer the concepts of leverage, problems, constraints, and vulnerability.

4. Explain the concept of the strategic window. Provide one example for a for-profit business and one for a nonprofit business.

5. Identify the two major components of a firm's marketing strategy. Why is it important that they be considered in a specific order?

6. Differentiate among stars, cash cows, question marks, and dogs in the market share/market growth matrix. Give two examples of products in each of the four quadrants of the matrix, and suggest marketing strategies for each product.

7. What are the potential dangers of rigid application of product portfolio models such as the market share/market growth matrix?

8. Explain how spreadsheet analysis can assist the marketing manager in planning and implementing marketing strategies.

9. Compare the major types of forecasting methods. Explain the steps involved in the most typical method.

10. Discuss the advantages and shortcomings of basing sales forecasts exclusively on estimates developed by the firm's salesforce.

Discussion Questions

1. Prepare a case history on the strategic plans of a company in your area. Information of this nature is often reported in the nation's leading business magazines.

2. The heads of each of General Electric's 13 businesses prepare annual charts or memos about the potential opportunities and pitfalls their industries might

encounter over the next two years. When Hungary authorized foreign ownership of state companies, General Electric quickly concluded an agreement to acquire Tungsram, the nation's leading lighting firm. The GE charts had been tracking Tungsram for several years.[28] Relate the above incident to the chapter's discussion of the marketing planning process.

3. Describe the following marketing situations in terms of SWOT analysis:
    a. A pharmaceutical company's patent for a market-leading drug is about to expire.
    b. A heavy-equipment construction company is located in a state that just passed a road-construction bond issue.
    c. A large commercial bank is known for its relationships with mid-size businesses, supplying loans and mortgages as well as a range of business accounts and services to them. Bank executives begin to worry when two smaller commercial banks in the region merge.
    d. Royal Crown Cola was the first to develop a low-calorie diet drink. But financial, distribution, and size constraints prevented the firm from exploiting its opportunities to capture and hold the market.

4. Domino's Pizza correctly predicted the launch of Operation Desert Storm against Iraq in 1991. Domino's managers noticed that pizza orders were up at both the White House and the Pentagon. At 5 am the next day, they predicted the attack would probably commence that day.[29] Domino's was correct, and thousands of Americans ordered a pizza and settled back to watch TV accounts of the war. Discuss the forecasting approach evident in this situation. Specifically relate this incident to the sales forecasting discussion in Chapter 4.

5. Which forecasting technique(s) do you feel is most appropriate for each of the following? Defend your answer.
    a. Ivory Soap
    b. Green Bay Packers
    c. Midas Muffler & Brake Shop
    d. *U.S. News & World Report*

Computer Applications

The sales forecast is a basic building block for marketing planning. A relatively simple quantitative forecasting technique that is frequently utilized for short-term forecasting during periods of steady growth is called *trend analysis*. This technique involves the extrapolation (or extension) of historical data into a specified future time period. This is accomplished by fitting a trend equation to past data on sales, market share, or earnings and using the equation to estimate a future time period. The equation for trend analysis is:

$$Y_c = a + bx$$

where

Y_c = predicted amount of sales, market share, or earnings for the specified time period

a = estimated amount of sales, market share, or earnings at the time period when $x = 0$

b = slope of the trend line, that is, average change in sales, market share, or earnings for each specified time period

x = time period (such as one year) used when forecasts are made

To use the trend analysis equation, the marketer must obtain estimates of a and b. These estimates are calculated from historical data using a technique called *least squares*. The following two equations are used for calculating a and b:

$$a = \frac{\Sigma Y}{n}$$

$$b = \frac{\Sigma xY}{\Sigma x^2}$$

The mathematical symbol Σ means "the sum of." The variable n refers to the total number of time periods.

Consider the following example. A small mail-order firm specializing in novelty items is seeking to forecast sales for next year. The firm's president feels that trend extension is an appropriate forecasting technique because of the relatively stable growth in company sales and the forecast's short-term nature. To calculate the needed data for the trend analysis equation, she has created the following table, beginning with a listing of annual sales for each year since the firm's establishment nine years ago:

n Time Period	y Sales (Thousands of Dollars)	x	xY	x^2
1	100	−4	−400	16
2	112	−3	−336	9
3	130	−2	−260	4
4	160	−1	−160	1
5	205	0	0	0
6	210	1	210	1
7	240	2	480	4
8	280	3	840	9
9	325	4	1,300	16
	$1,762		1,674	60

Since the firm has been operating for an odd number of years, the mid-year of Year 5 is coded 0. The years prior to Year 5 are coded −1, −2, and so on. The years following Year 5 are coded with positive 1, 2, and so on. If the data involve an even number of observations, the two mid-years are coded −1 and +1. The prior years are then coded in increments of −2 (−3, −5, −7, and so on); all years following the mid-years are coded in increments of +2 (+3, +5, +7, and so on). The analysis is completed by calculating ΣxY, Σx^2, and n. The first two values are determined by totaling the two columns labeled xY and x^2. Since the number of time periods included in this example is 9, the value of n is 9. The calculated values for a and b are:

$$a = \frac{1,762}{9} = 195.8$$

$$b = \frac{1,674}{60} = 27.9$$

Therefore, the trend line for this example is

$$Y_c = a + bx$$
$$= 195.8 + 27.9x$$

To forecast next year's sales for the mail-order firm, it is necessary to count from the Year 5 center value. Since the value for Year 9 is 4, the value for next year (Year 10) would be 5. The forecast is then made by substituting the value of 5 for x in the formula:

$$\text{Annual Sales Forecast for Next Year} = 195.8 + 27.9(5)$$
$$= 335.3$$
$$= \$335,300.$$

Directions: Use menu item 3 titled "Sales Forecasting" to solve each of the following problems.

Problem 1.   Total annual sales for each of the last seven years for a movie rental chain based in Evansville, Indiana, are shown below. Forecast sales for next year using the trend extension method.

Year 1	$ 1,000,000
Year 2	3,000,000
Year 3	6,000,000
Year 4	10,000,000
Year 5	11,000,000
Year 6	13,000,000
Year 7	14,000,000

Problem 2.   Career Path, a newly designed board game, was introduced eight months ago. Its sales have continued to grow each month even though it carries a healthy price tag of $32. Moreover, there appears to be no seasonal variation in sales. Monthly unit sales of the product are as follows:

August	14,000
September	16,000
October	23,000
November	24,000
December	28,000
January	29,000
February	33,000
March	36,000

How many unit sales of Career Path would you estimate for April? For May?

Problem 3.   During the first year of operation for Garden State University, enrollment totaled 1,200 students. The following year's enrollment grew to 2,100, and by the third year 2,800 students attended the university. Fourth-year enrollments totaled 4,200 students and the growth continued. A total of 4,400 students attended GSU in Year 5, 4,500 in Year 6, 4,800 in Year 7, 5,400 in Year 8, and 6,000 in Year 9. Use the trend extension method to estimate Garden State University enrollments for each of the next two years.

Problem 4.   The establishment of a "Birthday Surprise from Home" operation at Ohio State University has proven a market success for its founder, junior marketing major Nancy Wilkes. A direct-mail brochure was prepared and mailed to the parents of each on-campus OSU student offering to personally deliver a birthday cake, complete with a song and a personal message from the parents, on the student's birthday for $20. During the first seven months of operation, Nancy's part-time business has generated the following revenue:

September	$6,400
October	6,800
November	7,000
December	5,600
January	7,200
February	7,200
March	7,400

Forecast revenue for April using the trend extension method.

Problem 5. Ed Smithson set up "Quick Change Artist" (an automobile lubrication service) eight years ago. Since then his sales have grown rapidly. Annual sales revenues has been:

Year 1	$ 46,000
Year 2	78,000
Year 3	120,000
Year 4	132,000
Year 5	156,000
Year 6	190,000
Year 7	230,000
Year 8	278,000

Forecast "Quick Change Artist" revenues for each of the next two years.

Lakeway Resort

Services are the largest sector of the American economy. The dawning of the 21st century finds three of every four U.S. workers employed in the service sector and more than two-thirds of the gross national product produced by this sector. The shift toward services has been accompanied by increases in the proportions of single people, working women, and senior citizens in the population. At the same time, higher productivity and an increasing number of dual-income households have resulted in increased affluence.

Service providers must be sensitive to changing needs and desires if they are to remain competitive. In fact, this is truer for service providers than for manufacturers. A defective radio can be replaced, but a spoiled vacation is lost forever.

Lakeway Resort in Austin, Texas, has taken this dictum to heart. When Lakeway opened almost thirty years ago it quickly became a successful local destination resort. But after twenty-five years, its image and its occupancy rate had declined and it was faced with increased competition. However, the resort industry in general was experiencing rapid expansion because discretionary spending had been increasing throughout this period. It was apparent that Lakeway's marketing approach needed to be changed.

In 1987 the Dolce Company purchased Lakeway Resort as part of its strategy to develop a small network of high-quality conference facilities across the United States. Lakeway's location was an ideal complement to other Dolce facilities in New York, Chicago, California, and Florida. It contained full conference facilities to meet the needs of its business customers, championship golf and tennis facilities to attract recreational customers, a wide assortment of lodgings, and the scenic beauty of the Texas hill country.

Dolce wanted to turn Lakeway into a "world class resort" that would continue to attract its traditional Texas customers as well as national conference customers and families. In other words, it planned to rebuild its existing markets and penetrate new ones. To do so Lakeway would require investment to add new and maintain existing services with a strong commitment to outstanding service by the staff. Once these changes were implemented, Lakeway's target markets would have to be told about them.

The facilities were expanded and upgraded as planned. Ongoing addition of new services and expansion of existing services take a major place in the operational scheme at Lakeway. For instance, to attract families Lakeway began a "kids under 12 eat free" program and a "summer camp" program. A recreation department was created to develop new activities for all market segments, with a recreation director hired to run it. Because management was aiming for a Mobil's four-star rating, room service was introduced.

In the resort business it is essential to maintain a continuously high level of service. In employee–customer interactions, even brief lapses of service will discourage repeat patronage. Lakeway's staff has been trained in what Lakeway calls aggressive hospitality. Employees are encouraged to "go the extra mile" for their customers, and every month one employee is given an "aggressive hospitality award." The employee receives a lapel pin and a wall plaque, and his or her name is printed on all employees' pay checks for the following month.

At Lakeway, aggressive hospitality is not an empty phrase. Consider the actions of an employee in the conference services department. One morning, while checking out a conference room with a customer just before the latter's presentation was to begin, he was told that the customer needed a TV and a VCR that had not been ordered with the other services in advance. The employee said there would be no problem, and when he found that only the TV was available, he drove to his parents' home nearby and borrowed their VCR for the presentation. Such initiative is indicative of the quality of the employees that Lakeway has been able to recruit. According to CEO Andrew J. Dolce, "Our real challenge is to continue to attract real quality people."

Lakeway wanted to carry slightly different messages to each segment of its market. To former patrons, the message was that new ownership, new management, and upgraded and expanded services made the Lakeway "experience" better than ever. Potential new patrons were given a description of Lakeway's excellent facilities and superior hospitality.

Potential new clients comprise many diverse groups, including recreational clients throughout the nation, corporate business clients, and the conference segment known as "smurf"—social, military, religious, and fraternal organizations. To promote this message to all these clients, Lakeway has relied on personal selling and direct mail, the latter achieving a response rate of more than 8 percent, roughly three times the national average. Only 9 percent of Lakeway's marketing budget is spent on advertising, mostly in trade publications such as *Successful Meetings* magazine. Most of the business is generated by a force of highly talented salespeople who are keenly aware of each competitor's offerings, prices, and performance. Because of their skills, they have been successful at keeping prices and occupancy up in spite of poor economic times in Texas.

What has been the result of these changes? Occupancy was up even though the mix had shifted from 87 percent to 65 percent Texas residents. By forming a realistic long-term plan for market development, and sensitively adjusting its services in response to market changes, Lakeway has achieved its goal and has reestablished its competitive position.

Sources: Lakeway Resort, produced by The Dryden Press, 1991.

Questions

1. Relate the Lakeway decisions to the steps in the marketing planning process shown in Figure 4.2. Identify two examples in the case that reflect tactical planning. Give an example of strategic planning by Lakeway marketers.

2. Recommend an approach to sales forecasting for Lakeway marketers.

3. If Lakeway had been a private club before being purchased by the Dolce Company, how would Dolce's strategic plan for developing the resort have differed from the plan discussed in this case?

4. Given Lakeway's structure as discussed in this case, what are some ways in which market forecasts could be made?

A P P E N D I X

Developing a Marketing Plan

The natural outgrowth of the marketing process is a *marketing plan*—a detailed description of resources and actions necessary for achieving stated marketing objectives. Once this plan is formulated and implemented, it may be evaluated periodically to determine its success in moving the organization toward its stated objectives.[30]

Although the format, length, and focus of marketing plans may vary, they typically focus on identifying answers to the following three questions:

☐   Where are we now?

☐   Where do we want to go?

☐   How can we get there?

The following outline illustrates how marketing plans provide answers to each of these questions. The format may be used in a manufacturing, wholesale, retail, or service setting.

Components of the Marketing Plan

I. Situation Analysis: Where are we now?

    A. *Historical Background*

        ☐ Nature of the firm, sales and profit history, and current situation.

    B. *Consumer Analysis*

        ☐ Who are the customers this firm is attempting to serve?

        ☐ What segments exist?

        ☐ How many consumers are there?

        ☐ How much do they buy, and why?

    C. *Competitive Analysis*

        ☐ Given the nature of the markets — size, characteristics, competitive activities, and strategies — what marketing opportunities exist for this firm?

II. Marketing Objectives: Where do we want to go?

    A. *Sales Objectives*

        ☐ What level of sales volume can we achieve during the next year? During the next five years?

    B. *Profit Objectives*

        ☐ Given the firm's sales level and cost structure, what level of profits should it achieve?

    C. *Consumer Objectives*

        ☐ How will we serve our target market customers?

        ☐ What do we want present and potential customers to think about our firm?

III. Strategy: How can we get there?

    A. *Product Strategy*

        ☐ What goods and services should we offer to meet consumers' needs?

        ☐ What is their exact nature?

    B. *Pricing Strategy*

        ☐ What level of prices should be used?

        ☐ What specific prices and price concessions are appropriate?

    C. *Distribution Strategy*

        ☐ What channel(s) will be used in distributing our product offerings?

        ☐ What physical distribution facilities are needed?

        ☐ Where should they be located?

        ☐ What should be their major characteristics?

    D. *Promotional Strategy*

        ☐ What mix of personal selling, advertising, and sales promotional activities is needed?

        ☐ How much should be spent using what themes and what media?

    E. *Financial Strategy*

        ☐ What will be the financial impact of this plan on a one-year pro forma (projected) income statement?

        ☐ How does projected income compare with expected revenue if we do not implement the plan?

Sample Marketing Plan

The following excerpts from a marketing plan prepared for a motel, the Driftwood Inn, illustrate the value of such a plan in directing the organization's pursuit of its objectives.

Driftwood Inn Objectives

I. Short Term: 1993

    A. *Sales Objectives*
To experience an increase in food sales of 100 percent through increased awareness of the Driftwood Inn restaurant and changing consumer attitudes toward motel restaurants—especially the Driftwood Inn restaurant.

Basic Marketing Strategy Statement

I. Lodging

    A. Increase occupancy during seasonal and weekend "slack" periods through development and promotion of special "holiday packages."

    B. Attract participants and spectators to special events through direct mailing of promotional literature where names and addresses are available.

II. Food

    A. Develop an identity and image for the restaurant that are separate and distinct from the Driftwood Inn motel by (1) choosing a new name for the dining facilities, (2) developing a new menu, and (3) making minor changes in decor to create a distinctive dining atmosphere.

    B. Create awareness of the changes in the restaurant among local residents as well as motel guests by developing a complete promotional campaign and improving in-house promotions (such as lobby signs and promotional "tents" in rooms).

    C. Attract civic-group luncheons and rehearsal dinners through price dealing and personal selling.

III. Beverage

    A. Develop an atmosphere in the lounge that will complement and extend the restaurant image.

    B. Improve awareness of the lounge among local residents through a direct mail campaign.

Situation Analysis

I. General Market: Lodging, Food, and Beverage

Table A.1 shows the total sales for lodging and eating places between 1989 and 1992 in Baytown and Driftwood Inn's share of this market. The figures indicate that while total city sales increased 20 percent, the Driftwood Inn's sales increased only 15 percent.

II. Lodging

A breakdown of lodging sales for Baytown and Driftwood Inn is shown in Table A.2. The last column indicates the Inn's market share. Although the

Table A.1

Driftwood Inn's Share of
Baytown Area Market for
Lodging and Food by Year
(1989–1992)

Year	Baytown	Driftwood Inn	Market Share
1989	24,176,034	1,241,480	5.14%
1990	23,074,244	1,381,104	5.98
1991	24,942,588	1,423,842	5.70
1992	29,110,886	1,430,086	4.91

Table A.2

Driftwood Inn's Share of the
Baytown Lodging Market by
Year (1989–1992)

Year	Baytown	Driftwood Inn	Market Share
1989	5,354,172	803,112	14.99%
1990	5,209,544	935,658	17.96
1991	6,048,874	978,256	16.15
1992	7,094,854	953,208	13.44

Table A.3

Driftwood Inn's Share of the
Washington County and
Baytown Food Market by
Year (1989–1992)

Year	Washington County	Baytown	Driftwood Inn	Market Share for Washington County	Market Share for Baytown
1989	20,345,220	18,821,862	438,368	2.1%	2.3%
1990	22,546,924	17,846,700	445,446	1.9	2.4
1991	24,430,106	18,893,714	445,586	1.8	2.3
1992	27,989,222	22,016,032	476,878	1.7	2.1

Inn's lodging sales have increased substantially during the 1989–1992
period, its market share has fallen. This is due to an increase in total area
lodging sales and increased competition. It is worthwhile to note that the
Inn's market share fell to 13 percent between 1991 and 1992. The Inn's sales
fell slightly more than 2 percent in those two years, while area lodging sales
rose more than 17 percent.

III. Food Sales

Table A.3 presents a comparison of Washington County, Baytown, and
Driftwood Inn food sales. The last two columns represent the restaurant's
respective market shares. During the 1989–1992 period, county sales
increased almost 38 percent; city sales 17 percent; and the Inn's food sales
only 9 percent. New competitors are one possible explanation for these
losses of market share.

IV. Beverage

No sales data for alcoholic beverages are available for a trend comparison
on a state, county, or city level.

Table A.4

Driftwood Inn Lodging Market

	Individuals or Couples	Groups
Business	Salespeople Management personnel Special events On-premises business	Conventions Seminars, workshops Union negotiations National guard
Nonbusiness	Vacationers Military Moving through, in, or out	Tour groups Party groups Sports groups Reunions

Table A.5

Driftwood Inn Food Service Market

	Individuals or Couples	Groups
Guests	Vacationers Salespeople Family visits Relocation	Tour groups Conventions Sports groups Military
Nonguests	"Nights out" Special occasions Regular buffets	Tour groups Business meetings Rehearsal dinners Receptions Civic groups

Consumer Analysis

I. Lodging

Generally, the lodging market can be broadly divided into the segments shown in the market grid in Table A.4.

These distinct groups of potential customers represent the market that the Driftwood Inn must attract. The basic consumer characteristics most appropriate for analyzing the lodging market are the nature of the person's stay (business or nonbusiness) and the number of persons staying (individuals and couples or groups). Individuals on business might include salespeople on regular routes, management personnel on special supervisory trips, or people who wish to do business on a temporary basis from their rooms. Groups whose stay might be of a business nature include persons attending conventions, company seminars, and the like (see Table A.5).

Food sales may be derived from the public or private dining facilities. An analysis showed that although total food sales increased somewhat in recent years, the growth in food sales revenues was not sufficient to maintain the Inn's market share. Revenues from private dining are derived from three basic sources: wedding rehearsal dinners, wedding receptions, and civic-group luncheons. The potential revenues from these three sources are estimated at over $100,000 annually. The Driftwood Inn appears to have captured a large share of this market, but management recognizes that there are a limited number of competitors for the private dining market. It is believed that little marketing effort has been directed toward local civic organizations, which are important potential customers.

Assignment

Use the format described in this appendix to develop a marketing plan for one of the following:

a. Local retailer
b. Local service provider
c. Local shopping center
d. Nonprofit organization
e. College or university

5

Marketing Research and Information Systems

1. To describe the development and current status of the marketing research function.

2. To list the steps in the marketing research process.

3. To differentiate the types and sources of primary and secondary data.

4. To identify the methods of collecting survey data.

5. To explain the various sampling techniques.

6. To describe a marketing information system and to distinguish it from marketing research.

7. To explain the contributions of marketing decision support systems (MDSS).

The year was 1911. Film producer Thomas H. Ince was about to release *Custer's Fight,* an epic western. But first he wanted an audience to preview the film. The audience liked what they saw, and *Custer's Fight* went on to become a classic in the silent film era.

Ince's early use of marketing research set a precedent that has been followed in the movie industry ever since. Pre-release previews—called "recruited audience screenings" in the trade—are now used to measure audience satisfaction, spot flaws, and suggest improvements that can be made before the film is released to the general public.

Typically, recruited screenings begin with the distribution of free passes. Researchers favor people aged 15 to 39, the prime age target for movies. After the film is over, questionnaires are distributed to the audience. The questions tend to be very basic: Did you like the movie? What did you like about the movie? What did you dislike?

A small group of previewers are paid to stay for a focus group, where more detailed questions are asked and explored. Focus groups usually last 15 to 30 minutes. Maria Stark, vice-president of entertainment for Lieberman Research West in Los Angeles, explains the benefits of recruited audience screenings this way: "Market research helps in the actual finetune editing process of a film."

Movie endings are especially crucial. If audiences don't like the ending, they don't like the movie. For example, preview audiences did not like the original ending of *Fatal Attraction,* so Paramount spend $1.3 million re-doing it. *Fatal Attraction* went on to become a box office favorite and achieve critical acclaim.

The movie industry does a variety of other marketing research studies. These involve promotional items, newspaper advertisements, radio spots, television commercials, and previews of coming attractions. Research is also used in the development stages of a movie. The results of such research must be carefully evaluated, though. When the idea for *E.T.* was tested, it was rejected by consumers. Yet *E.T.* went on to become a blockbuster hit, largely because of its special effects that the original respondents could not visualize.

Which movies benefit the most from marketing research? Arnold Fishman, chairman of Lieberman Research West, says that poor films benefit more than good ones. According to Fishman, marketing research can increase the ticket sales of lesser movies by 50 percent, while already good movies might see only a 20 percent increase.

What happens to a movie in its final version? If the producers are confident that the movie will do well it is given a so-called "wide release." A recent example is *Robin Hood: Prince of Thieves* starring Kevin Costner. The second option is a "platform release," where the movie initially appears in only a few cities and selected theaters. In this case, the movie producer is counting on critical reviews and word-of-mouth to sell the film to movie-goers. An example of this type of release was *sex, lies, and videotape.* The least desirable option is used only when a re-edited and re-shot film continues to fare poorly in marketing research studies. In this unfortunate circumstance, the film goes straight to video release.

Marketing research clearly plays a major role in the movie industry. As Fishman commented: "Market research helps the studios stay in touch with the business side. America is a self-funded movie-making business. Not like Europe, where some projects are supported by the government. If there aren't any profits, then the company will not be around in the future."[1]

Source: Questionnaire courtesy of Arnold Fishman and Maria Stark: Lieberman Research West Inc.

Chapter Overview

The quality of all marketing management decisions depends on the quality of the information on which they are based. Good decisions require information of the right type and in sufficient quantity. A variety of sources for decision-oriented marketing data exist. Some are well-planned investigations designed to elicit specific information. Other valuable information may be obtained from salesforce reports, accounting data, and published reports. Still other information may be obtained from controlled experiments and computer simulations.

A major source of information for marketing planning takes the form of marketing research. The American Marketing Association defines *marketing research* as follows:

Marketing research is the function which links the consumer, customer, and public to the marketer through information — information used to identify and define marketing opportunities and problems; generate, refine, and evaluate marketing actions; monitor marketing performance; and improve understanding of marketing as a process. Marketing research specifies the information required to address these issues; designs the method for collecting information; manages and implements the data collection process; analyzes the results; and communicates the findings and their implications.[2]

For our purpose here, this definition may be simplified to the following: **Marketing research** is the collection and use of information in marketing decision making.

marketing research
Information function that links the marketer and the marketplace.

The critical task of the marketing manager is decision making. Decision making involves not only solving problems as they arise but also anticipating and preventing future problems. Often managers are forced to make these decisions with insufficient information. Marketing research aids the decision maker by presenting pertinent facts, analyzing them, and suggesting possible actions.

This chapter deals with the marketing research function, which is closely linked with the other elements of the marketing planning process. Indeed, all marketing research should be done within the framework of the organization's strategic plan.

Much of the material on marketing planning and forecasting in Chapter 4 and on market segmentation in Chapter 8 is based on information collected as a result of marketing research. Clearly the marketing research function is the primary source of the information needed for making effective marketing decisions.

The Marketing Research Function

Before looking at how marketing research is conducted, let's consider the activities it entails, the people and organizations it involves, and the background of how the field developed.

Marketing Research Activities

All marketing decision areas can benefit from marketing research investigations. However, efforts most often focus on determining marketing potential, market share, and market characteristics. Marketers conduct research to analyze sales and competitors' products, to gauge the performance of existing products and the degree of acceptance of new products and package designs, and to develop promotional campaigns. Saturn Corporation used marketing research in developing its new nameplate. As the advertisement in Figure 5.1 explains, Saturn Corporation used marketing research to find out car buyers' needs and wants.

Figure 5.1

Use of Marketing Research
in Product Development

WAYNE VIEIRA *first started sketching car designs at age 14. Which is understandable, when you consider that he grew up just six blocks from one of southern California's most famous custom car shops. That era of car design is over, but Wayne never stops thinking about cars and how they should look. Here, he talks about turning the design process upside down to find a fresh approach for the new cars Saturn is building in Spring Hill, Tennessee.*

"...When I started my first job as a car designer, my boss told me, 'Design the car the way you want it to be, not the way you think the customer wants it.'

Well, we've tried hard to make the Saturn just the opposite. I don't think you can get very far in the car business today by ignoring what people want.

In fact, we were out there talking to car buyers long before we had a car. Getting ideas from people. And that made a real impact on the kind of cars we designed. For instance, during one of our consumer research sessions, someone said he wanted the Saturn to look like a Ferrari, but cost no more than a Civic. A big dream of his, I guess. But I knew what he meant.

Small car buyers want something they can park in the driveway. Not something they have to hide in the garage.

As proud as I am of the way they look, everything about the design of our coupe and sedans is based on honesty. You won't find scoops on the hood of the car, for example, unless the engine really needs the extra air.

There's nothing about these cars that isn't a direct answer to what we heard people asking for. A want or a need expressed by the customer.

So if people find any surprises on these cars, I think they'll be pleasant ones. That's what I hope to hear, anyway, when we talk with our owners the next time around...."

A DIFFERENT KIND OF COMPANY. A DIFFERENT KIND OF CAR.
If you'd like to know more about Saturn, and our new sedans and coupe, please call us at 1-800-522-5000.

Source: Courtesy of Saturn Corporation, Troy, Michigan.

And follow-up research with Saturn owners is planned to help the company assess the acceptance of its products.[3]

Development of the Marketing Research Function

Marketing research is a relatively new field. More than a hundred years have passed since N. W. Ayer conducted the first organized research project in 1879. A second important milestone in the development of marketing research occurred in 1911 when Charles C. Parlin organized and became manager of the nation's first commercial research department at Curtis Publishing Company.

Parlin actually got his start as a marketing researcher by counting soup cans in Philadelphia's garbage! Parlin was employed as a sales representative for advertising space in the *Saturday Evening Post.* He had failed to sell advertising space to Campbell Soup Company because the firm believed that the magazine reached primarily working-class readers who preferred to make their own soup rather than spend 10 cents for a can of prepared soup. Campbell was targeting its product at higher-income people who could afford to pay for the convenience. So Parlin began counting the soup cans in the garbage of different neighborhoods. To Campbell's surprise, Parlin's research revealed that more canned soup was sold to the working class than to the wealthy, who had servants to make soup for them. Campbell's soup quickly became a *Saturday Evening Post* client.

It is interesting to note that garbage is still a good source of marketing research information. United Airlines has studied what passengers do not eat from the onboard meals. This research led United to stop serving canned fruit cocktail to coach flyers.[4]

Much of the early research was little more than written testimonials received from purchasers of firms' products. Research became more sophisticated during the 1930s as the development of statistical techniques led to refinements in sampling procedures and greater accuracy in research findings. However, mistakes still occurred. After the *Literary Digest* conducted a major national study of U.S. households selected at random from lists of telephone numbers and auto registration records, it reported that Alf Landon, not Franklin D. Roosevelt, would be elected president in 1936. The magazine's miscalculation resulted from its failure to realize that many voters (most of whom apparently were Democrats) had neither telephones nor automobiles in the midst of the Great Depression.

In recent years, advances in computer technology have significantly changed the complexion of marketing research. Computers not only have accelerated the pace and broadened the base of collecting data, they also have aided marketers in making informed decisions about problems and opportunities. Computer simulations, for example, allow marketers to evaluate decision alternatives by posing a number of "what if" questions. Marketing researchers at many consumer goods firms simulate product introductions on computers to help them decide whether to risk a real-world product launch or even subject a product to test marketing. For instance, Sara Lee used a simulation before launching its line of frozen Hearty Fruit Muffins.[5] Simulated test marketing is also widely used in Europe, where models are able to account for regional differences such as those between Northern and Southern Italy.[6]

While high-tech marketing research is common in many medium-size and large firms, smaller companies also find innovative—albeit less sophisticated—ways to research their markets. For example, toy maker Catco Inc. has a 14-year-old vice-president, Mary Rodas, who tries out toy prototypes with her eighth-grade friends in Union, New Jersey. "People give their straight opinion because I'm a kid," says Mary.[7]

Participants in the Marketing Research Function

According to the American Marketing Association, 77 percent of the nation's consumer goods manufacturers have a formal marketing research department. The comparable number for industrial products firms is 51 percent. Many smaller firms depend on independent marketing research firms to conduct their interviews, and they often contract out some research studies to independent agencies as well. The decision of whether to conduct a study through an outside organization or internally is usually based on cost. Another major consideration is the reliability and accuracy of the information collected by an outside organization.

A marketing research firm often is able to provide technical assistance and expertise not available within the firm. For example, as the advertisement in Figure 5.2 explains, the British Broadcasting Corporation chose Research International to conduct a difficult research project because of RI's worldwide expertise, global resources, and knowledge of local markets. The use of outside groups also helps ensure that the particular researcher is not conducting the study only to validate the wisdom of a favorite personal theory or preferred package design. A survey of marketing research by the American Marketing Association revealed that nearly two-thirds of the total marketing research budgets of consumer goods firms is spent on outside research. The comparable number for industrial products is 37 percent. Both were up significantly from a survey five years earlier.[8]

Marketing research companies range in size from single owners/managers to giant firms such as A. C. Nielsen, Arbitron, and IMS International. In recent years, total worldwide revenues of 50 leading marketing research firms were $2.6 billion. Over 30 percent of these revenues were earned outside the United States. In fact, A. C. Nielsen, the largest of the marketing research firms, received 56 percent of its revenues from abroad.[9]

Figure 5.2

Choosing a Research Firm
for Its Worldwide Expertise

Source: Courtesy of Research International. In the U.S. also DCI (Decisions Center)/Research
International and Cambridge Reports/Research International.

Marketing research companies can be classified as either syndicated
services, full-service suppliers, or limited-service suppliers, depending on their
primary thrust.[10] Some full-service organizations are also willing to take on
limited-function activities.

Syndicated Services.   An organization that provides a standardized set of
data on a regular basis to all customers is called a *syndicated service.*
Mediamark Research, for example, operates a syndicated product research
service based on personal interviews with 20,000 adults each year regarding
their exposure to advertising media. Clients include advertisers, advertising
agencies, magazines, newspapers, broadcasters, and cable networks.

Full-Service Research Suppliers.   An organization that contracts with a
client to conduct a complete marketing research project is called a *full-service
research supplier.* J.D. Power & Associates is a full-service firm that specializes
in the domestic and international automotive markets. Full-service suppliers
become the client's marketing research arm, performing all the steps in the
marketing research process (discussed in the next section).

Limited-Service Research Suppliers.   A marketing research firm that
specializes in a limited number of activities, such as providing field interviews or
data processing services, is called a *limited-service research supplier.* Working
almost exclusively for clients in the movie industry, The National Research Group
Inc. specializes in appraising entertainment facilities with audiences of movie-
goers, preparing studies for developing advertising strategies, and tracking for
awareness and interest. Syndicated services can also be considered limited-
service research suppliers.

Figure 5.3

The Marketing Research
Process

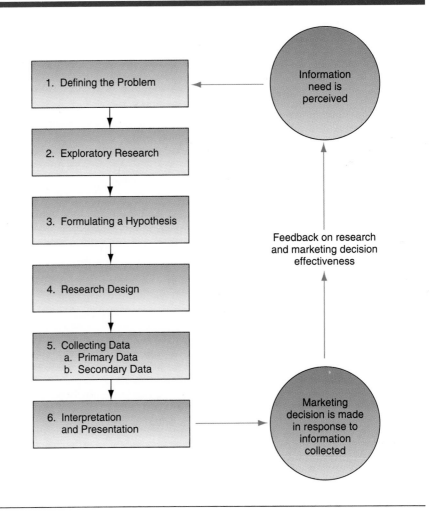

The Marketing Research Process

How is marketing research actually conducted? It depends, of course, on the type of information needed for a particular decision. Certain events create the need for certain decisions. For example, a firm that makes frozen pizzas would perceive an information need if the product's market share dropped from 8 to 5 percent in six months. Information is needed before the firm can decide what to do to reverse that decline.

The marketing research process can be divided into six specific steps:

1. Defining the problem.
2. Conducting exploratory research.
3. Formulating a hypothesis.
4. Creating a research design.
5. Collecting data.
6. Interpreting and presenting the research information.

Figure 5.3 diagrams the marketing research process from the emergence of the information need to the completion of the research-based decision. Emphasis shifts from one stage of the process to another depending on the global market. For example, the Japanese are sometimes viewed as spending more time on problem definition than American firms.

Problem Definition

Someone once remarked that well-defined problems are half-solved. A clearly defined problem permits the researcher to focus on securing just the information necessary for solving the problem. This makes the research process faster and more accurate. If we think of problems as barriers that prevent the attainment of organizational goals, we can see the importance of using marketing research to define them.

Consider the case of Welch's. Sales were declining while the industry volume was growing 2 percent per year. CEO Everett Baldwin asked Welch's advertising agency to define the problem. The resulting study determined that although consumers thought Welch's offered quality products, they perceived the company as strictly a grape juice and jelly company, giving it a very narrow market.

In response, Welch's was successfully repositioned as a fruit company. Labeling, packaging, even the company's letterhead was redesigned to reflect this new positioning.[11] Problem definition was the key to the successful change.

Researchers must not confuse symptoms with the problem itself. A symptom merely alerts marketers that a problem exists. For example, a falling market share is a symptom of a problem facing the pizza maker mentioned earlier. To define its problem, the firm must look for underlying causes of market share loss. A logical starting point would be the firm's marketing mix elements and target market. Suppose that the pizza maker has had no recent changes in its product, pricing, or distribution strategies but has adopted a new promotional strategy. A close look at the promotional strategy may reveal the source of the problem. Or perhaps the problem stems from the external environment in the form of new competitors entering the market with superior products and lower prices. The possible causes of problems are further explored in the next step of the marketing research process—exploratory research.

Problem Definition in International Markets

Correctly defining the problem is of particular importance in international markets. Suppose a marketing researcher wanted to study consumer behavior related to hot milk-based drinks. In this case, consumption patterns differ among nations. In the United Kingdom, hot milk-based drinks are considered an aid to sleep and are consumed prior to going to bed. By contrast, Thais consume the same drinks in the morning since they are believed to provide energy for the day. In the United States, hot milk-based drinks are associated with cold weather and can be consumed at any time of day.[12]

Exploratory Research

exploratory research
Process of discussing a marketing problem with informed sources within the firm as well as with outside sources such as wholesalers, retailers, and customers and examining secondary sources of information.

Searching for the cause of a problem, often called **exploratory research,** consists of discussing the problem with informed sources within the firm and with wholesalers, retailers, customers, and others outside the firm, as well as examining secondary sources of information. The idea is to focus on specific areas for study. Marketing researchers often refer to internal data collection as the *situation analysis* and to exploratory interviews with informed persons outside the firm as the *informal investigation.* Exploratory research usually involves evaluating company records, such as sales and profit analyses, and the sales and profits of competitors' products.

Table 5.1

Income Statement for
Venture Company for the
Year Ended December 31,
199X

Sales		$ 57,830,000
Cost of goods sold		−32,910,000
Gross margin		$ 24,920,000
Expenses:		
Selling expenses	$7,530,000	
Other expenses	3,010,000	−10,540,000
Profit before taxes		$ 14,380,000
Income taxes		−7,190,000
Profit after taxes		$ 7,190,000

Using Internal Data

An organization's sales records contain valuable sources of information. Analysis of these records should provide a basis for obtaining an overall view of company efficiency and a clue to the problem under investigation.

The main source of this information is traditional accounting data that is summarized on the firm's financial statements. Table 5.1 shows a simplified income statement.

Where nondetailed accounts are used, their main contribution is that of assisting the analyst in raising more specific questions. The income statement in Table 5.1 shows that the company earned a profit for the period involved, since selling expenses represented approximately 13 percent of sales:

$$\text{Cost/Sales Ratio} = \frac{\$7,530,000}{\$57,830,000} = 13\%.$$

Comparison of the 13 percent selling expense-to-sales ratio with ratios for previous years may hint at possible problems, but it will not specifically reveal the cause of the variation. To discover the cause, a more detailed breakdown is necessary.

Sales Analysis.   Table 5.2 shows a typical breakdown of sales by territory. This kind of breakdown becomes part of an overall sales analysis. The purpose of the **sales analysis**—the in-depth evaluation of a firm's sales—is to obtain meaningful information from the accounting data.

Easily prepared from company invoices stored on computer tapes, the sales analysis can be quite revealing for the marketing executive. As Table 5.2 shows, the salesforce in District 4 has a much higher cost/sales ratio than the salesforces in other districts.

sales analysis
In-depth evaluation of a firm's sales.

Table 5.2

Sales and Expense Analysis
of Selected Districts

District	Average Salary	Average Expenses	Average Sales Costs	Average Sales	Cost/ Sales Ratio
1	$33,600	$10,400	$44,000	$654,000	6.7%
2	31,900	12,800	44,700	534,000	8.4
3	37,200	13,100	50,300	790,000	6.4
4	35,200	12,300	48,000	380,000	12.6
5	34,200	11,700	35,900	580,000	7.9

Table 5.3

Sales Breakdown of Selected Sales Representatives in District 4

Salesperson	Quota	Actual	Performance as a Percent of Quota
Washington	$336,000	$382,000	114%
Ho	428,000	453,000	106
Shapiro	318,000	325,000	102
Chandler	446,000	360,000	81
Total	$1,528,000	$1,520,000	

In order to evaluate the performance of the salespersons in the five selected districts, the marketing executive must have a standard of comparison. District 4, for example, may be a large territory with relatively few industrial centers. Consequently, the costs involved in obtaining sales will be higher than for other districts.

The standard by which actual and expected sales are compared typically results from a detailed sales forecast by territory, product, customer, and salesperson. Once the **sales quota**—the level of expected sales by which actual results are compared—has been established, it is a simple process to compare the actual results with the expected performance.

Table 5.3 compares actual sales with the quota established for salespersons in District 4. Although Shapiro had the smallest amount of sales for the period, her performance was better than expected. However, the district sales manager should investigate Chandler's performance since it represented only 81 percent of quota.

The performance of the salespersons in District 4 provides a good illustration of the **iceberg principle,** which suggests that important evaluative information is often hidden by aggregate data. (The tip of an iceberg represents only one-tenth of its total size; the remaining nine-tenths lies hidden beneath the surface of the water.) Summaries of data can be useful, but sometimes they actually conceal more than they reveal. Had the sales breakdown by salesperson for the district not been available, Chandler's poor sales might have been partially concealed by the good sales performances of the others.

Other possible breakdowns for sales analysis include customer type, product, method of sale (mail, telephone, or personal contact), type of order (cash or credit), and size of order. Sales analysis is one of the least expensive and most important sources of marketing information.

Marketing Cost Analysis.

A second source of internal information is **marketing cost analysis**—the evaluation of such items as selling costs, warehousing, advertising, and delivery expenses in order to determine the profitability of particular customers, territories, or product lines.

Marketing cost analysis requires a new way of classifying accounting data. Functional accounts must be established to replace the traditional natural accounts used in financial statements. These traditional accounts, such as salary, must be reallocated to the purpose for which the expenditure was made. A portion of the original salary account, for example, would be allocated to selling, inventory control, storage, advertising, and other marketing costs. In the same manner, an account such as supply expenses would be allocated to the functions that utilize supplies.

sales quota
Level of expected sales against which actual results are compared.

iceberg principle
Theory suggesting that collected data in summary form often obscures important evaluative information.

marketing cost analysis
Evaluation of such items as selling costs, billing, and advertising to determine the profitability of particular customers, territories, or product lines.

Table 5.4

Allocation of Marketing Costs

Marketing Costs	By Customer		By District		
	Large	Small	A	B	C
Advertising	$140,000	$ 300,000	$200,000	$100,000	$140,000
Selling	520,000	620,000	380,000	380,000	380,000
Physical distribution	330,000	260,000	280,000	140,000	170,000
Credit	4,000	26,000	16,000	6,000	8,000
Total	$994,000	$1,206,000	$876,000	$626,000	$698,000

The cost allocated to the functional accounts will equal those in the natural accounts. But instead of showing only total profitability, they can show the profitability of, say, particular territories, products, customers, salespersons, and order sizes. The most common reallocations are to products, customers, and territories or districts. The marketing decision maker can then evaluate the profitability of particular customers and districts on the basis of the sales produced and the costs incurred in generating them. Table 5.4 shows how such cost reallocations can be made.

Table 5.5 indicates that District B is the most profitable and District A the least. Attention can be given to plans for increasing sales or reducing expenses in this problem district to make market coverage of the area a profitable undertaking.

Linking Sales and Marketing Cost Analysis to Other Forms of Marketing Research. Safeway provides an excellent example of how effective sales and marketing cost analysis can be used in conjunction with another form of marketing research—in this case, checkout scanner data. Safeway's management knows that each 1 percent increase in net margin earns $14 million in profits, or 13 cents per share. With annual sales of about $400 per square foot, a 4 percent increase in revenues will increase the bottom line by 21 percent. Such razor thin margins explain why Safeway teamed up with Procter & Gamble to test whether soap would sell better stacked by hand or dumped in a wire bin. Safeway's marketing research concluded that hand stacking increased soap sales by 5 percent. Procter & Gamble is now developing a system to deliver prestacked soap to stores.[13] For Safeway, the starting point of this exercise was knowing where its sales came from, and what their impact was on profitability.

Table 5.5

Income Statement for
Districts A, B, and C

	District			
	A	B	C	Total
Sales	$2,600,000	$2,000,000	$1,910,000	$6,510,000
Cost of sales	1,750,000	1,350,000	1,200,000	4,300,000
Gross margin	850,000	650,000	710,000	2,210,000
Marketing expenses	876,000	626,000	698,000	2,100,000
Contribution of each territory	$ (26,000)	$ 24,000	$ 12,000	$ 10,000

Exploratory Research in Japan

The Japanese tend to divide marketing research into soft and hard data. Soft data is the result of visits with dealers, while hard data includes items like a unit's sales history. The head of Matsushita's VCR division contrasted Japanese and U.S. marketing research in this fashion: "Why do Americans do so much marketing research? You can find out what you need by traveling around and visiting the retailers who carry your products."[14]

Formulating Hypotheses

hypothesis

Tentative explanation about some specific event; statement about the relationship among variables, including clear implications for testing it.

After the problem has been defined and an exploratory investigation conducted, the marketer should be able to formulate a **hypothesis**—a tentative explanation for some specific event. A hypothesis is a statement about the relationship among variables and carries clear implications for testing this relationship.

A decade ago, the rental car industry targeted the business traveler to the extent that Avis got 90 percent of its sales from this segment. Ten years later, Avis's sales breakdown was 60 percent business and 40 percent leisure. This changing business mix caused the company to launch a marketing research effort to determine what consumers wanted in a rental car company. Focus groups, in-depth interviews, and attitudinal studies were included.

Avis's hypothesis was based on conventional industry wisdom: customers wanted prompt checkout and check-in procedures. However, the research failed to confirm the hypothesis. Rental car customers—both business and leisure travelers—were more concerned about protection in varying trip conditions than about promptness.

The result of this marketing research was the "Avis Cares" plan that includes 24-hour emergency road service with an 800 number; a booklet about local driving regulations; a diagram for operating the model of car that is rented; and the *Avis Traveler,* a magazine featuring information on specific cities complete with restaurant and entertainment guides.[15]

Research Design

research design

Series of advanced decisions that, when taken together, comprise a master plan or a model for conducting marketing research.

The means for testing the hypothesis formulated about the problem is the **research design,** a series of decisions that taken together comprise a master plan or model for the conduct of the investigation. When Hallmark wanted to study the "any day" segment of the greeting card market—with its 25 percent annual growth rate—the Kansas City card giant designed an extensive two-year study with 6,500 respondents. Focus groups, national surveys, and personal interviews were used. The study concluded that this category of card buyers sought more message options, so Hallmark introduced its extensive "Just How I Feel Line."[16]

Sometimes published data are not enough. In that case, the research design must call for a direct test of the hypothesis. Published data, for example, indicate that people drink diet sodas because they want to control their weight. Accordingly, ads for Diet Rite, a Royal Crown cola product, previously focused on low-calorie content, taste, and lower price. But Diet Rite marketers decided they needed ads with an emotional appeal to help distinguish their product from competing Diet Pepsi and Diet Coke. The company interviewed dozens of women dieters and learned that they had poor self-images and felt that dieting was difficult and made them feel more vulnerable. Based on these interviews, Diet Rite decided against commercials showing slim, attractive women in bathing suits, because women with poor self-images do not relate to such models. Instead, the company developed a humorous campaign—one commercial featuring a slightly out-of-shape Tony Danza—that allows viewers to empathize with other dieters who also appear vulnerable.[17]

 Finally, marketers must ensure that the research design measures what is intended. *Reader's Digest* once conducted a study in Europe that concluded that people in France and Germany consume more spaghetti than those in Italy. This obviously incorrect measurement of total spaghetti consumption resulted from the way questions were asked about purchasing packaged and branded spaghetti. While the French and Germans buy spaghetti in this form, Italians tend to purchase it in bulk, but the format of the survey questions did not allow for this response.[18]

Data Collection

primary data
Information or statistics collected for the first time during a marketing research study.

secondary data
Previously published data.

A major part of research design is determining what data are needed for testing the hypothesis. Data are classified as primary or secondary. **Primary data** refers to data that are collected for the first time during a marketing research study. The Diet Rite interviews with women dieters is an example of primary research. **Secondary data** are previously published matter. They serve as an extremely important source of information for marketing researchers such as those who use census data to help decide on new store locations.

Collecting Secondary Data

Secondary data are not only important to the marketing researcher, they are also very abundant. The overwhelming quantity of secondary data available at little or no cost challenges the researcher to select only what is pertinent.

Secondary data consist of two types: internal and external. Internal data include sales records, product performances, salesforce activities, and marketing costs. External data are obtained from a variety of sources, including the government—local, state, and federal.

database
Collection of data that are retrievable through a computer.

Use of Databases.   Both external and internal data can be obtained from computerized databases. A **database** refers to any collection of data that are retrievable through a computer. A considerable amount of published information is available in this form. Some firms create their own databases that include sales and marketing cost records. DuPont is spending $200 million a year in an effort to set up an information network that will link the databases of its 80 business operations in 50 different countries.[19]

The growth in popularity of databases has led to an expansion of commercial services. Widely used commercial on-line database services include CompuServe, Data Resources Inc., Dow Jones News/Retrieval, Dialog, and The Source.

Government Data.   The federal government is the nation's most important source of marketing data. The most frequently used government statistics are census data. Although the U.S. government spent more than $2.5 billion

SPYING ON FOREIGN BUSINESSES

A controversy is raging over "economic intelligence." American firms could benefit immensely from knowledge about what foreign companies are doing economically both in the United States and in their home markets. This is especially true of small and medium-size businesses, which are eager for information about foreign export opportunities. As the domestic economy slows, they are increasingly interested in economic intelligence, regardless of how it is obtained.

An agency already exists to gather export intelligence. The U.S. Foreign & Commercial Service (USFCS) emphasizes product-specific and target market research, using publicly available sources such as foreign business journals and trade shows. But some analysts consider such information inadequate in an increasingly complex and competitive world market. They have suggested that the CIA might help track the activities of foreign firms.

Industrial espionage is nothing new. It is known, for example, that the French intelligence service has attempted to penetrate offices of American firms in France. But so far the CIA has limited its economic espionage to the economic prospects of countries—especially the Soviet Union—rather than individual companies.

Some experts are strongly opposed to the idea of having the CIA play an increased role in economic intelligence. According to Claude Barfield, director of sci-

ence and technology studies at the American Enterprise Institute, "There is no more stupid or pernicious idea. In any case, we have a Department of Commerce which has been looking for something to do for 50 years."

As policymakers in the United States become more concerned about whether U.S. companies are playing on a "level playing field" in world markets, they are likely to become more sympathetic to the idea of expanding the CIA's economic intelligence-gathering activities. In the meantime Congress has given additional responsibilities to the USFCS and the Department of Commerce. The Foreign Direct Investment and International Financial Improvement Act of 1990 allows the Bureau of Economic Affairs to obtain Census Bureau data on individual companies, though not to publicize information about foreign companies or hunt through Census Bureau files for additional information.

Discussion Questions

1. Should the CIA be authorized to spy on foreign companies?

2. Can U.S. firms compete effectively without specific information about the activities of foreign firms?

Source: Stephen Barlas, "Does CIA Have Role in Foreign Market Research?" *Marketing News* (January 7, 1991), pp. 2, 5.

conducting the 1990 Census of Population, census information is available for use at no charge to local libraries, or it can be purchased on computer tapes for instantaneous access. In addition to the Census of Population, the Bureau of the Census conducts a Census of Housing (which is combined with the Census of Population), a Census of Business, a Census of Manufacturers, a Census of Agriculture, a Census of Minerals, and a Census of Governments.

The Census of Population is so detailed that it breaks down population characteristics into very small geographical areas. The census breaks down population traits by city blocks or by census tracks in large cities. The population of nonmetropolitan areas is divided into *block-numbering areas* (BNAs). The BNAs and census tracts are important for marketing analysis because they show a population with similar traits, unlike that defined by political boundaries such as county lines. Marketers such as local retailers and shopping center developers can easily gather specific information about customers in the immediate neighborhood without spending time or money to conduct a comprehensive survey.

Of even greater value to marketing researchers is the government's computerized mapping database called TIGER—for Topographically Integrated

Geographic Encoding & Referencing. This system combines features such as railroads, highways, and rivers with census data such as household income. Marketers can buy digital tapes of the data from the Census Bureau.

The federal government produces so much information that marketing researchers often purchase summaries such as:

- *Monthly Catalog of the United States Government Publications.*
- *Statistical Abstract of the United States,* published annually.
- *Survey of Current Business,* updated monthly.
- *County and City Data Book,* typically published every three years, providing data on each county and city of over 25,000 residents.

State and city governments serve as other important sources of information on employment, production, and sales activities. In addition, university bureaus of business and economic research often collect and disseminate such information.

Private Data.   Many private organizations provide information for the marketing executive. Trade associations are excellent sources of data on activities in a particular industry. Advertising agencies continually collect information on the audiences reached by various media. A wide range of valuable data are found in the annual "Survey of Buying Power" published by *Sales & Marketing Management* magazine. Table 5.6 illustrates this source's 1994 projections for Illinois, which combine population, effective buying income (EBI), and retail sales into the "buying power index," a measure of a market's ability to buy. Illinois represents 4.67 percent of the nation's total buying power.[20]

Several national firms offer information to businesses on a subscription basis. Information Resources, Inc., the fourth largest marketing research firm, offers a national scanning service that tracks consumer purchases of every UPC-coded product sold in supermarkets. Called InfoScan, this system collects sales data from 2,700 supermarkets on a weekly basis and consumer purchasing data from 60,000 households on a daily basis. Recently it was introduced in the drug, mass merchandising, and convenience store sectors as well. InfoScan provides marketers with information on promotional conditions that affect consumer purchases by correlating consumer sales with newspaper ads, prices, in-store displays, and coupon redemptions. The integrated store sales and household purchase data give marketers information on their brands' buyers, store loyalty, and general shopping behavior. In addition, InfoScan has developed a PC work-station and special software that allow marketing researchers to analyze its data in ways that fit their unique information needs.[21]

Strengths and Weaknesses of Secondary Data

The use of secondary data offers two important advantages: (1) assembly of secondary data is almost always less expensive than collection of primary data, and (2) less time is involved in locating and using secondary data. Completing a research study requiring primary data typically takes about three to four months. Although the time involved in a marketing research study varies considerably depending on such factors as the research subject and the study's scope, an additional time and cost investment is required when primary data are needed.

The researcher, however, must be aware of several potential limitations of secondary data. First, published information can quickly become obsolete. A marketing researcher analyzing the populations of various California counties may discover that much of the 1990 census data are already out of date because

A TIGER IN YOUR COMPUTER?

. . . .

Imagine being able to chart every block in every county in the United States both topologically and demographically. The possible applications are endless. With such information at your fingertips, you could make deliveries more efficiently, keep track of customers more accurately, allocate resources more effectively, and target your marketing campaigns with a precision never achieved before.

The Census Bureau's TIGER —a detailed computerized map of the entire United States— is turning this dream into reality. The bureau began developing TIGER—Topographically Integrated Geographic Encoding and Referencing—in 1982 with the goal of enabling census takers to find specific addresses more easily. The project took seven years and cost $200 million. Although it was not intended to be a commercial product, TIGER's potential benefits to certain kinds of businesses soon became obvious, and it was placed in the public domain. Retailers, banks, franchisers, vehicle fleet operators, and direct-mail marketers rejoiced.

TIGER links addresses to specific city blocks; it also lists in digital form the geographic coordinates of every highway, street, bridge, and tunnel in the country. Paired with marketing research analysis software or with a database like the results of the 1990 census, it gives desktop computer users what could be called a cartographic spreadsheet. Though it does not actually produce maps, it allows users to create computerized maps that can be linked with data to produce visual profiles of highly detailed areas. Such maps can be used for a wide variety of purposes, including site selection, routing, and maintenance of data on subjects such as land use, public-utility consumption, crime patterns, and wildlife movements.

TIGER is part of one of the fastest-growing branches of computing: combining computerized data with automated mapmaking to create *geographic information systems* (GIS). GIS systems merge two databases, one containing maps and the other information such as demographic data or sales figures. Until recently the only way to keep track of different kinds of data about a particular geographic area was to use a map with a series of overlays presenting specific types of information. Now the information can be combined in

Reprinted from American Demographics magazine

a single, easily read map with a precision that was previously unattainable. As the advertisement shown here illustrates, Equifax Marketing Decision Systems offers firms a marketing information system that integrates TIGER with 30 other databases.

TIGER is not without problems. The digitizing process is costly, time-consuming, and subject to error. Trained personnel are required to install and operate a TIGER-based system, and some small businesses lack the necessary computer capacity. These difficulties are expected to be overcome in time, however. As one Census Bureau official points out, "Through use, the [TIGER] data will become current and represent what's actually on the ground." The cost of software is also likely to decrease.

Discussion Questions

1. Can you think of additional uses for TIGER besides those mentioned here?

2. The specially developed software that can be linked to TIGER may cost $2,500 or more and does not include the TIGER data. At that price, is it a worthwhile investment for a small business?

Sources: Eugene Carlson, "Businesses Map Plans for Use of Tiger Geographical Files," *The Wall Street Journal* (June 8, 1990), p. B2; Howard Schlossberg, "Census Bureau's TIGER Seen as a Roaring Success," *Marketing News* (April 30, 1990), p. 2; Richard Kern, "The 1990 Census: The Good, the Bad, and the Undercount," *Sales & Marketing Management* (July 1989), pp. 49–51; Gene Bylinsky, "Managing with Electronic Maps," FORTUNE (April 24, 1989), pp. 237–254; and Jeffrey Rothfeder, "These Maps Can Find Oil—Or Sell Burgers," *Business Week* (March 13, 1989), p. 134. *Photo source:* Courtesy of Equifax.

Table 5.6

Estimating the 1994 Buyer Power Index for Illinois

Illinois	12/31/94 Total Pop. (Thous.)	Average Household EBI 1994	Retail Sales Per Household 1994	Buying Power Index 1994
Aurora-Elgin	*386.0*	*56,727*	*27,660*	*.1609*
Kane	342.4	57,140	29,942	.1472
Kendall	43.6	53,404	9,303	.0137
Bloomington–Normal	*129.9*	*52,955*	*27,130*	*.0533*
McLean	129.9	52,955	27,130	.0533
Champaign–Urbana–Rantoul	*174.3*	*47,203*	*27,035*	*.0671*
Champaign	174.3	47,203	27,035	.0671
Chicago	*6,268.4*	*56,997*	*25,370*	*2.6375*
Cook	5,249.2	54,204	23,112	2.1021
Du Page	830.1	74,891	40,485	.4606
McHenry	189.1	57,815	23,074	.0748
Chicago–Gary–Lake County Consolidated Area	*8,333.9*	*57,159*	*25,331*	*3.4588*
Davenport–Rock Island– Moline	*358.5*	*50,268*	*22,583*	*.1404*
Henry	52.6	49,652	18,811	.0190
Rock Island	151.7	50,568	19,184	.0575
Scott, Iowa	*154.2*	*50,173*	*27,219*	*.0639*
Decatur	*120.6*	*50,620*	*22,690*	*.0477*
Macon	120.6	50,620	22,690	.0477
Joliet	*404.7*	*56,811*	*21,114*	*.1482*
Grundy	36.2	57,202	15,897	.0136
Will	368.5	56,768	21,693	.1346
Kankakee	*99.5*	*44,212*	*21,282*	*.0342*
Kankakee	99.5	44,212	21,282	.0342
Lake County	*542.7*	*71,761*	*34,227*	*.2603*
Lake	542.7	71,761	34,227	.2603
Peoria	*339.2*	*54,545*	*23,123*	*.1382*
Peoria	182.3	56,127	24,820	.0781
Tazewell	122.8	53,496	22,444	.0487
Woodford	34.1	49,308	15,793	.0114
Rockford	*286.6*	*50,239*	*24,209*	*.1131*
Boone	32.2	44,146	20,586	.0110
Winnebago	254.4	50,970	24,643	.1021
Springfield	*199.3*	*43,497*	*22,483*	*.0764*
Menard	12.8	35,588	9,772	.0033
Sangamon	186.5	43,995	23,283	.0731
Total Metro Counties	*9,756.9*	*55,655*	*25,114*	*4.0169*
Total State	*11,788.5*	*53,054*	*23,558*	*4.6723*

Source: Reprinted from "1990 Survey of Buying Power—Part II," *Sales & Marketing Management* (November 13,1990), p. 86.

of continued growth and changing demographics. Second, published data that were collected for a different purpose may not be completely relevant to the marketer's specific needs. For example, census data should not be adapted to inappropriate uses.

Collecting Primary Data

The marketing researcher has three alternatives in the collection of primary data: observation, survey, or controlled experiment. No single method is best in all circumstances, and any of them may prove the most efficient in a particular situation.

Observation Method.   Observational studies are conducted by actually viewing the overt actions of the subject. They may take the form of a traffic count at a potential site for a fast-food franchise, the use of supermarket scanners to record sales of certain products, or a check of license plates at a shopping center to determine where shoppers live.

American Airlines has used an observational approach in improving its service standards on international flights. American employees flew dozens of flights on major international carriers to observe how passengers were treated. As a result, well-known chefs, like Paul Prudhomme, were hired to improve American's menus; sheepskin-and-leather seats were installed in business and first-class areas; and even the cocktail nuts were heated to the recommended 98°F.

American employees were also trained to adjust to the national preferences of its international flyers. Flight attendants use formal titles like "Herr Doktor" in addressing German passengers. Attendants are also careful about accidentally touching Japanese passengers, who react negatively to such contact. Meal and beverage services are modified on some flights—for example, on flights to Latin America, beef is served more often than usual and French wines made available to accommodate passengers' observed preferences. The amenities of American's International Flagship Service resulting from the company's observational research is the focus of the airline's foreign and domestic advertising targeted at business travelers.[22] One of the ads is shown in Figure 5.4.

"People meters" are another observational technique. These electronic, remote-control devices record the television viewing habits of each household member. At one time, each person in the household was given his or her own button to push to signal television watching. Now, however, passive people meters that automatically record a person's preferences are now being introduced.[23] This information is sent overnight, via telephone wire, to the researcher's central computer, providing advertisers with timely and detailed data on audience viewing habits. The viewer information is used to measure a program's success and to set advertising rates.

Survey Method.   Some information cannot be obtained through observation. The researcher must ask questions to get information on attitudes, motives, and opinions. The most widely used approach to collecting such primary data is the survey method, which includes telephone interviews, mail surveys, and personal interviews.

Telephone Interviews.   Telephone interviews are an inexpensive and quick method of obtaining small quantities of relatively impersonal information. Telephone interviews account for an estimated 55 to 60 percent of all primary

Figure 5.4   Improved Service Resulting from Observational Research

marketing research in the United States. By contrast, telephone interviews are often difficult to conduct in many foreign countries. In Sri Lanka less than 3 percent of the people have telephones. In Cairo, up to half of the telephones are inoperable at any given time. Only a quarter of all dialed calls get through on the first try.[24]

Telephone interviews have other limitations. Simple, clearly worded questions must be used, and respondents cannot be shown a picture of the item under discussion. Also, it is extremely difficult to obtain information on respondents' personal characteristics by telephone. Finally, the results of the survey may be biased by the omission of households without phones or with unlisted numbers. The use of unlisted numbers is commonplace today: Over 27 percent of all phone numbers (56 percent in Los Angeles) are unlisted.[25] Such groups as single women, physicians, and others who do not wish to be disturbed at home choose to have unlisted numbers. As a result, a number of telephone interviewers have resorted to using digits selected at random and matched to telephone prefixes in the geographical area to be sampled in order to reach some unlisted numbers. However, several states have restricted random dialing, and others propose to do so. The ultimate technological feat in telephone interviewing is probably computerized dialing linked with a digitally synthesized voice doing the interviewing.

Two other obstacles to telephone surveys are answering machines and caller I.D. Answering machines are in 55 percent of all U.S. households.

Penetration is particularly high among younger people, who have adopted telephone answering machines as part of their lifestyle. A sixth of the people with answering machines use them to screen all incoming calls, effectively excluding marketing researchers.[26]

A related obstacle is "caller I.D.," a system that shows the telephone number of the person placing an incoming call, thus allowing receivers to ignore unfamiliar callers. By 1995 Bell Atlantic projects that caller I.D. will have achieved an 18 to 20 percent market penetration. In an early Pennsylvania case, however, a state court ruled that caller I.D. violated "the caller's privacy!" Congressional legislation was also introduced that would require caller I.D. vendors to offer a blocking service to callers who wished to evade the system.[27]

Mail Surveys.   Whereas the cost of personal interviews with a national sample may be prohibitive, a mail survey can contact each potential respondent for the price of a postage stamp. Cost figures can be misleading, though. Returned questionnaires may average only 40 to 50 percent depending on the questionnaire's length and respondents' interest. Some mail surveys even include money to gain the reader's attention, which further increases costs. Also, unless additional information is obtained from nonrespondents, the results of mail interviews are likely to be biased, since there may be important differences in the characteristics of respondents and nonrespondents. For this reason, follow-up questionnaires are sometimes mailed to respondents or telephone interviews are used to gather additional information.

Herman Miller, the Michigan-based manufacturer of furniture for offices and health care facilities, uses a simple, yet effective, system for ensuring that respondents answer the customer survey. Before the survey is mailed, Herman Miller contacts the respondent to stress the importance of the questionnaire and request cooperation. Later, the respondent is again contacted to be sure he or she has mailed the survey back to Herman Miller. This second call also provides an opportunity to clarify responses.[28]

Finally, it should be noted that mail surveys are often difficult or more costly to conduct in foreign markets. For example, in some countries it is difficult to mail to households because most homes are not numbered. Names like "Casa Rosa" are used instead.[29]

Personal Interviews.   The best means of obtaining detailed information is usually the personal interview, since the interviewer has the opportunity to establish rapport with each respondent and explain confusing or vague questions. Although mail questionnaires are carefully worded and often pretested to eliminate potential misunderstandings, they cannot answer unanticipated questions.

Personal interviews are slow and expensive to conduct. However, their flexibility and the detailed information they can provide often offset these limitations. Marketing research firms have rented locations in 170 U.S. shopping centers, where they have greater access to potential buyers of the product in which they are interested. These facilities sometimes have private interviewing compartments, videotape equipment, and food-preparation equipment for taste tests. Interviews conducted in shopping centers are typically referred to as *mall intercepts.* Ninety percent of all marketing researchers use mall intercepts in their work.[30] Downtown retail districts and airports are other on-site locations for marketing researchers.

Personal interviews are also often the best way to collect marketing research information abroad. However, there are some limitations. Mall intercepts in Saudi Arabia would produce all male respondents.[31] In Brazil, no one will admit to owning a foreign-made car because of government regulations.[32]

Case, one of the world's leading manufacturers of agricultural and construction equipment, conducts personal interviews with farmers in India to understand their needs and wants. From these interviews, Case also learns what farmers expect of equipment dealers. The market for agricultural equipment in India and other developing nations is vast and fast-growing.

Source: Used with permission of J I Case Company.

focus group interview

Information-gathering procedure in marketing research that typically brings eight to twelve individuals together in one location to discuss a given subject.

Focus group interviews are widely used as a means of gathering research information. In a **focus group interview,** eight to twelve individuals are brought together in one location to discuss a subject of interest. Although the moderator typically explains the purpose of the meeting and suggests an opening discussion topic, his or her main purpose is to stimulate interaction among group members in order to develop discussion of numerous points. Focus group sessions, which are often one or two hours long, are usually taped and frequently observed through a one-way mirror. A recent innovation is the FocusVision network of Newport Beach, California, which broadcasts focus groups live (in session) from independently owned focus facilities to a client's, an advertising agency's, and/or the company's own reception center. This process, shown in Figure 5.5, allows a variety of users to see the actual focus group and to remain in audio contact with the moderator.

Focus groups are used by a wide array of organizations for various purposes. Binney & Smith picked eight new colors and eliminated eight others for Crayola crayons this way.[33] Attorneys often use focus groups to test arguments before a trial. Nonprofit organizations use them to develop fund drives and improve their services. For example, focus groups revealed that many people did not know how United Way worked. As a result, a national television campaign was launched featuring stories of people who had been helped by a United Way agency.[34]

Figure 5.5

How the Focus Vision
Network Operates

Source: Reprinted from Cyndee Miller, "Network to Broadcast Live Focus Groups," *Marketing News* (September 3, 1990), p. 10.

experiment
Scientific investigation in which a researcher controls or manipulates a test group(s) and compares these results with those of a group(s) that did not receive the controls or manipulations.

Experimental Method.   The least used method of collecting marketing information is the controlled experiment. An **experiment** is a scientific investigation in which a researcher controls or manipulates a test group or groups and compares the results with that of a control group that did not receive the controls or manipulations. Although such experiments can be conducted in the field or in a laboratory setting, most have been performed in the field. To date, the most common use of this method by marketers has been in test marketing, a topic discussed in Chapter 10.

As Chapter 4 pointed out, marketers often attempt to reduce their risks by *test-marketing,* that is, introducing the product or marketing strategy into an area and then observing its degree of success. Marketers usually pick test areas that will reflect what they envision as the market for their product. For instance, Seattle and Milwaukee might be used as test markets for a new diet soft drink since these cities share the lead for the highest per capita consumption in this product category.

Consider the test-marketing approach used by Peacock Papers, Inc., an $8 million Boston-based producer of stationary, giftwrap, and party goods. Peacock's unique approach to test marketing is to operate a 600-square-foot store in Boston's urban mall, Faneuil Hall Marketplace. President Sharon Cavanough explains, "The store gives us a window through which we can figure out what works. When you're selling through reps or to store buyers, you can get removed from what is happening in the marketplace. The store allows us to stay on top of what is going on and lets us steer our customers—the buyers—toward products that are bestsellers." As a bonus, the Faneuil store is also "extremely profitable."[35]

The major problem with controlled experiments is that they cannot take into account all the variables in a real-life situation. How can the marketing manager determine the effect of, say, reducing the retail price through refundable coupons when the competition simultaneously issues such coupons? Experimentation may become more common as firms develop sophisticated competitive models. Simulation of market activities promises to be one of the great new developments in marketing.

Sampling Techniques

Sampling is one of the most important aspects of marketing research, because it involves the selection of respondents; and if these respondents do not accurately reflect the target market, the conclusions of the research will likely be wrong. Figure 5.6 illustrates just how important sampling is in marketing research.

Figure 5.6

Importance of Sampling in Marketing Research

population (universe)
Total group that the researcher wants to study.

census
Collection of data from all possible sources in a population or universe.

probability sample
Sample in which every member of the population has a known chance of being selected.

simple random sample
Basic type of probability sample in which every item in the relevant universe has an equal opportunity to be selected.

stratified sample
Probability sample that is constructed so that randomly selected subsamples of different groups are represented in the total sample.

cluster sample
Probability sample in which geographic areas or clusters are selected and all of or a sample within them become respondents.

The total group that the researcher wants to study is called the **population** (or **universe**). For a political campaign, the population would be all eligible voters. For a new cosmetic line, it might be all women in a certain age bracket. The *sample* is the representative group of this population. Information is rarely gathered from the total population during a survey. If it is, the results are known as a **census.** Unless the total population is small, the costs are so great for a census that only the federal government is able to afford it (and it uses this method only once every ten years).

Samples can be classified as either probability samples or nonprobability samples. A **probability sample** is a sample in which every member of the population has a known chance of being selected. Types of probability samples include a simple random sample, a stratified sample, and a cluster sample.

In the **simple random sample** every item in the relevant universe has an equal opportunity of being selected. The draft lottery of the Vietnam era was an example. Each day of the year, those males born on that day had the same chance of being selected, thus establishing a conscription list. In a **stratified sample** randomly selected subsamples of different groups are represented in the total sample. It differs from *quota sampling* (discussed shortly) in that the subsamples are drawn randomly. Stratified samples are efficient for such uses as opinion polls, in which various groups hold divergent viewpoints. In a **cluster sample,** areas (or "clusters") are selected from which respondents are drawn. This type of probability sample is very cost efficient and may be the best option where the population cannot be listed or enumerated. A good example is a market researcher who identifies various U.S. cities and then randomly selects supermarkets within those cities to study.

Figure 5.7

The Research Report and
Presentation Should Link the
Marketing Researcher and
the Research User

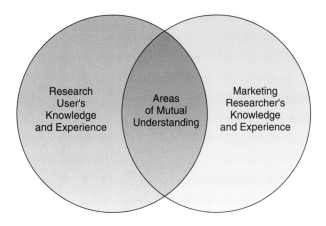

nonprobability sample
Arbitrary sample in which most
standard statistical tests cannot
be applied to the collected data.

convenience sample
Nonprobability sample based on
the selection of readily available
respondents.

quota sample
Nonprobability sample that is divided so that different segments
or groups are represented in the
total sample.

In contrast, a **nonprobability sample** is arbitrary and does not permit use of standard statistical tests. Types of nonprobability samples are the convenience sample and the quota sample. A **convenience sample** is a nonprobability sample based on the selection of readily available respondents. Broadcasting's "on-the-street" interviews are a good example. Marketing researchers sometimes use convenience samples in exploratory research, but not in definitive studies. A **quota sample** is a nonprobability sample that is divided so that different segments or groups are represented in the total sample. An example would be a survey of auto import owners that includes seven Hyundai owners, ten Honda owners, eight Volvo owners, and so on.

Interpretation and Presentation

Figure 5.7 illustrates how marketing researchers and marketing research users can sometimes differ in the way they interpret marketing research due to their differing backgrounds of knowledge and experience. Marketing researchers should target presentations at the area of mutual understanding. The cardinal rule is to understand that marketing research is intended to assist decision making, not be an end in itself.

It is imperative that marketing researchers and research users cooperate at every stage in the research design. Too many marketing studies go unused because marketing management becomes convinced by lengthy discussions of research limitations or unfamiliar terminology that the results are too restricted.

Marketing researchers must remember that their reports are directed toward management, not other research specialists. Consequently, they should spell out their conclusions in a clear, concise, and actionable fashion. Technical details of the research should be outlined in an appendix, if at all. This approach will increase the likelihood of management's utilizing the research findings.

International reports require special handling when a language other than English is involved. Many marketers suggest using "back translation," wherein a report is translated into the other language and then retranslated by a different person in order to catch problems. Consider the case of a soft drink firm that sought to use an Australian advertising theme in Hong Kong. "Baby, it's cold inside" was translated into Cantonese and then back to English. The slogan that appeared was, "Small Mosquito, on the inside it is very cold." ("Small mosquito" is a term used to refer to a small child in Hong Kong.)[36]

Marketing Information System (MIS)

Many marketing managers discover that their information problems result from an overabundance rather than a paucity of marketing data. Their sophisticated computer facilities may provide them with daily printouts on sales in as many as 30 market areas, in regard to 100 different products and 6,400 customers. Such data are not necessarily usable, since *data* and *information* are not synonymous terms. **Data** refers to statistics, opinions, facts, or predictions categorized on some basis for storage and retrieval. **Information** is data relevant to the marketing manager in making decisions.

To obtain relevant information, one can establish a **marketing information system (MIS),** which is a planned, computer-based system designed to provide managers with a continual flow of information relevant to their specific decision areas. The marketing information system is a subset of the firm's overall *management information system* (also often called an MIS) that deals specifically with marketing information.

A properly constructed MIS can serve as the company's nerve center, providing instantaneous information suitable for each management level. It can monitor the marketplace continuously, allowing management to adjust actions as conditions change.

Frito-Lay provides a good illustration of how an MIS should operate. Every day, some 10,000 Frito-Lay salespeople use hand-held terminals to update information on 100 Frito-Lay product lines in 400,000 stores. The information appears on Frito-Lay's computer screens in color chart form. Green means sales are up, red signifies a decline, and yellow suggests a possible slowdown. When its Tostitos tortilla chips' numbers turned red in San Antonio and Houston, Frito-Lay was quickly able to identify the problem. A competitor had introduced a well-received white corn tortilla chip. Within three months, Frito-Lay was selling a similar chip, and it won back its lost market share.[37]

data
Statistics, opinions, facts, or predictions categorized on some basis for storage and retrieval.

information
Data relevant to marketing decision making.

marketing information system (MIS)
Planned, computer-based system designed to provide managers with a continuous flow of information relevant to their specific decision areas.

Marketing Research and the MIS

Many marketing executives think their organizations are too small to have a marketing information system. Others contend that their marketing research departments provide adequate research data for decision making. Such contentions often result from a misconception of the services and functions performed by the marketing research department. Marketing research has already been described as typically focusing on a specific problem or project; its investigations have a definite beginning, middle, and end. Marketing information systems, on the other hand, are much wider in scope, involving the continuous collection and analysis of marketing information. Figure 5.8 indicates the various information inputs—including marketing research studies—that serve as components of a firm's MIS.

By focusing daily on the marketplace, the MIS allows a continuous, systematic, and comprehensive study of any deviations from established goals. The up-to-the minute information allows problems to be corrected promptly.

MDSS: A State-of-the-Art MIS

Marketing information systems have come a long way from the days when they were responsible primarily for clerical activities (and usually at an increased cost over the old method). Today managers have special computer programs,

Figure 5.8   Information Components of the Firm's Marketing Information System

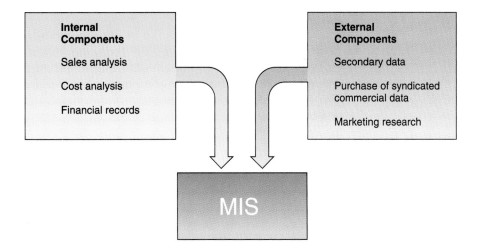

MDSS

Marketing decision support system that links a decision maker with relevant databases.

remote-access consoles, better data banks, and direct communication with computers, and can assign authority to computers for review and referral.

An **MDSS** (marketing decision support system) is an interactive communication network that links the decision maker with marketing information databases. The essential elements of an MDSS are outlined in Figure 5.9. It is dependent on special software that gathers, stores, retrieves, and processes the information relevant to a specific decision.

The Towel and Tissue Group of James River Corporation has upgraded its marketing information system to an MDSS designed to improve the firm's relationship with its retailer customers. The James River MDSS generates a profit and loss statement for each customer purchase. The retailer is then asked to lay out plans for selling the James River products, the costs of which are shared by the seller. The MDSS producer gets a budget from its database of James River's actual costs, and the MDSS identifies the tradeoffs that are involved in the sales support program. The result is an enhanced partnership relationship with the firm's customers.[38]

Figure 5.9   Model of a Marketing Decision Support System

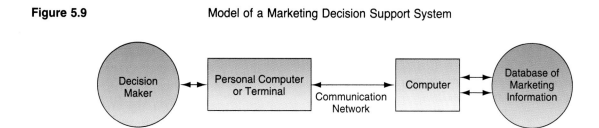

Source: Reprinted from Louis A. Wallis, *Decision-Support Systems for Marketing* (New York: The Conference Board, Inc., 1989), p. 2.

Summary of Chapter Objectives

1. **Describe the development and current status of the marketing research function.** Marketing research started when Charles C. Parlin, an advertising space sales representative for the *Saturday Evening Post,* counted empty soup cans in Philadelphia's trash in an effort to convince Campbell Soup Company to advertise in the magazine. Today the most common marketing research activities are (1) determining market potential, market share, and market characteristics and (2) conducting sales analyses and competitive product studies. Most large companies now have internal marketing research departments. However, outside suppliers still remain vital to the research function. Some of these outside suppliers perform the complete research task, while others specialize in a limited area or provide other data services.

   The American Marketing Association has defined marketing research as follows:

   Marketing research is the function which links the consumer, customer, and public to the marketer through information—information used to identify and define marketing opportunities and problems; generate, refine, and evaluate marketing actions; monitor marketing performance; and improve understanding of marketing as a process. Marketing research determines the information needed for these purposes, specifies and implements the data collection process, and interprets and communicates the results.

2. **List the steps in the marketing research process.** The marketing research process can be divided into six specific steps: (1) defining the problem, (2) conducting exploratory research, (3) formulating hypotheses, (4) creating a research design, (5) collecting data, and (6) interpreting and presenting the research information. A clearly defined problem allows the researcher to obtain the relevant decision-oriented information. Exploratory research refers to information gained both outside and inside the firm. Hypotheses—tentative explanations of some specific event—allow the researcher to set out a specific research design, which is the series of decisions that taken together comprise a master plan or model for the conduct of the investigation. The data-collection phase of the marketing research process can involve either or both primary data (original data) and secondary data (previously published data). After the data are collected, researchers must interpret and present them in a way that will be meaningful to management.

3. **Differentiate the types and sources of primary and secondary data.** Primary data can be collected by the firm's own researchers or by independent marketing research companies. Three alternative methods of primary data collection can be used: observation, survey, or experimental. Secondary data can be classified as either internal or external. Internal sources include sales records, product evaluations, salesforce reports, and records of marketing costs. External sources include the government and private sources such as business magazines and consulting services. Both external and internal data can also be obtained from computerized databases.

4. **Identify the methods of collecting survey data.** Survey data can be collected through telephone interviews, mail surveys, or personal interviews. Telephone interviews provide over half of all primary marketing research. It is a fast and inexpensive way to get small amounts of information but not detailed or personal information. Mail surveys allow market researchers to conduct national studies at a reasonable cost; their disadvantage is a

potentially inadequate response. Personal interviews are costly but allow researchers to get detailed information from respondents.

5. **Explain the various sampling techniques.** Samples can be categorized as either probability samples or nonprobability samples. A probability sample is a sample in which every member of the population has an equal chance of being selected. Probability samples include simple random samples, in which every item in the relevant universe has an equal opportunity to be selected; stratified samples, which are constructed such that randomly selected subsamples of different groups are represented in the total sample; and cluster samples, in which areas are selected from which respondents are drawn. A nonprobability sample is arbitrary and does not allow application of standard statistical tests. Nonprobability samples include convenience samples, in which readily available respondents are picked, and quota samples, which are divided so that different segments or groups are represented in the total sample.

6. **Describe a marketing information system and distinguish it from marketing research.** A marketing information system (MIS) is a planned, computer-based system designed to provide managers with a continuous flow of information relevant to their specific decision areas. While marketing research concentrates on a specific problem or project, a marketing information system is wider in scope, involving the ongoing collection and analysis of marketing information.

7. **Explain the contributions of marketing decision support systems (MDSS).** MDSS is the abbreviation for marketing decision support system. It is an interactive communication network that links a decision maker with marketing information databases. The MDSS depends on special software to gather, store, retrieve, and process the information relevant to a specific decision.

Key Terms

marketing research	population (universe)
exploratory research	census
sales analysis	probability sample
sales quota	simple random sample
iceberg principle	stratified sample
marketing cost analysis	cluster sample
hypothesis	nonprobability sample
research design	convenience sample
primary data	quota sample
secondary data	data
database	information
focus group interview	marketing information system (MIS)
experiment	MDSS

Review Questions

1. Outline the development and current status of the marketing research function. What role did Charles Parlin play in the development of marketing research?

2. List and explain the various steps in the marketing research process. Trace a hypothetical project through the various steps.

3. Distinguish between primary and secondary data. When should each type be used?

4. What are the major sources of secondary data? What are the advantages and limitations of using secondary data?

5. Compare and contrast sales analysis and market cost analysis. What is meant by the iceberg principle?

6. Collect from secondary sources the following information:
   a. Retail sales in Springfield, Ohio, for last year.
   b. Number of persons over 65 in Salem, Oregon.
   c. Earnings per share for Ford last year.
   d. Coal produced in West Virginia in a recent year.
   e. Consumer price index for last August.
   f. Number of households earning more than $80,000 in Oakland County, Michigan.

7. Distinguish among surveys, experiments, and observational methods of data collection. Cite examples of each method.

8. Explain the differences between probability and nonprobability samples. Identify the various types of each.

9. Define and give an example of each of the three methods of gathering survey data. Under what circumstances should each be used?

10. Distinguish among marketing research, marketing information systems, and MDSS. Give an example of each.

Discussion Questions

1. The Gallup organization polled 1,500 Soviet citizens about their lifestyles, consumer preferences, and perception of quality by country of origin.[39] If you had been one of Gallup's five clients, what would you want to know about Soviet consumers? Discuss.

2. Politicians throughout the country complained loudly that the 1990 census undercounted minorities, illegal aliens, and the homeless. Why was there so much concern about the census? In New York, for instance, each person counted is worth $150 in federal funds distributed on the basis of the census. The Census Bureau tried to minimize the problem by, among other things, sending enumerators out at night to count the homeless. Modern politicians might be interested to know that George Washington also complained of an undercount in 1790. He believed that Americans feared a tax based on the census.[40] Suggest ways in which the Census Bureau could address the undercount problem.

3. Nissan's California-based product strategy office has done some interesting cultural research on car buyers. Consumers were asked to cut out magazine pictures and make a collage of "who you are." On the basis of these results, Nissan classifies 9 percent of the population as "showy sophisticates"—people who cut out pictures of Porsches, lobster dinners, and American Express gold cards. Another 11 percent, categorized as "self-sacrificing escapists," clipped out Victoria's Secret lingerie advertisements along with pictures of baby food jars. By defining market segments like these two, Nissan researchers hope to discover what motivates various groups of people, then link these desires to future automobiles.[41] What does this research suggest about Japanese companies' approach to marketing? Can you think of other examples of where culturally oriented marketing research might be useful? Discuss.

4. Advertising agency McCann-Erickson has conducted a marketing research study in which 50 people were asked to draw the buyers of Pillsbury and Duncan Hines cake mixes. The Pillsbury buyer was consistently drawn as a grandmother type, apron and all, while a Duncan Hines customer was portrayed in a more

contemporary manner.[42] How could these research results be used by both Pillsbury and Duncan Hines? Discuss.

5. There are up to 10,000 different languages or dialects worldwide. The most common languages are as follows:[43]

Language	Number of Speakers
Chinese	More than 1 billion (500–825 million speak Mandarin)
English	300–450 million (official language in 87 nations)
Hindi	140–325 million
Russian	130–300 million
Spanish	125–320 million
Arabic	100–190 million (official language in 17 countries)
Bengali	100–180 million
Portuguese	100–170 million
French	100–150 million (official language in 37 nations)
Japanese	100–125 million
German	90–150 million
Urdu	40–90 million

How does this diversity in language influence marketing research? What actions can marketing researchers take to avoid potential language problems? Discuss.

Computer Applications

Sales analysis is defined in this chapter as the in-depth evaluation of a firm's sales. This information is obtained from the organization's sales reports, customer purchase orders, invoices, and other accounting data. The sales analysis concept is explained in detail on pages 160–161. The following problems deal with sales analysis.

Directions: Use menu item 4 titled "Sales Analysis" to solve each of the following problems.

Problem 1.   The salesforce of Associated Industries of Victoria, Texas, is divided into four sales zones. Average sales for representatives in the various zones are as follows: A—$440,000; B—$407,500; C—$436,000; D—$448,000. The average sales compensation in the four zones is: A—$36,000; B—$39,000; C—$41,000; D—$42,000. Average selling costs are relatively low, with zone D being the most expensive at $6,340. Other average selling cost figures are: A—$5,940; B—$6,380; C—$6,700. Determine the cost/sales ratios for each of Associated's four sales zones.

Problem 2.   A Detroit-based corporation organizes its sales force into three sales regions: A, B, and C. The average salaries in these regions are $40,000, $45,000, and $50,000, respectively. Region A sales personnel average $700,000 in sales; Region B, $640,000; and Region C, $945,000. Selling expenses average $12,000 in all regions. Calculate the cost/sales ratios for the three regions.

Problem 3.   Jackie Frost, a marketing consultant, has been hired to analyze the sales of a Pittsburgh firm. Management is particularly concerned with Division 4's average selling expenses of $26,400.

The Pittsburgh Firm Operates Five Divisions with the Following Average Sales Salaries:		Average Selling Expenses for Personnel in the Divisions Are:		Average Sales Per Representative in these Divisions Are:	
Division 1	$39,300	Division 1	$ 7,670	Division 1	$396,000
Division 2	42,840	Division 2	7,850	Division 2	480,000
Division 3	38,750	Division 3	10,025	Division 3	501,000
Division 4	39,050	Division 4	26,450	Division 4	604,000
Division 5	40,175	Division 5	13,000	Division 5	528,000

What should Frost tell management about the firm's cost/sales ratios?

Problem 4.   The Mid-Atlantic Division of a Hartford, Connecticut, company has a seven-person sales force to cover New York, Pennsylvania, and New Jersey. For the year, the following quotas were assigned according to the territory's sales potential:

Territory 1	$365,000
Territory 2	386,000
Territory 3	476,000
Territory 4	429,000
Territory 5	400,000
Territory 6	411,000
Territory 7	436,000

At the close of business on December 31, 19XX, the following annual sales volumes were reported:

Territory 1	$392,000
Territory 2	387,000
Territory 3	442,000
Territory 4	408,000
Territory 5	450,000
Territory 6	416,000
Territory 7	429,000

a.   Calculate the performance-to-quota ratios for each of the seven territories.

b.   What is the overall performance-to-quota ratio for the Mid-Atlantic Division?

Problem 5.   The Chicago Division of a Kirksville, Missouri, firm employs five sales representatives. All were assigned annual sales quotas of $450,000. The division manager, Duane Washington, is now preparing an analysis of how his people did this year. The actual sales results were as follows:

Snow	$415,000
Harris	468,000
Beck	389,000
Davis	414,000
Clark	453,000

a.   Calculate the performance-to-quota ratio for each of the sales representatives in the Chicago Division.

b.   What is the overall performance-to-quota ratio for the Chicago Division?

VIDEO CASE 5

The Disney Channel

In June 1985, The Walt Disney Company hired a new management team to revamp their then-fledgling pay television service, The Disney Channel. Having launched in April 1983, The Disney Channel had gained just under two million cable subscribers in the intervening two years, less than had been budgeted under the Channel's original business plan. Under new management, several strategies were devised to take advantage of the Channel's untapped growth potential.

First, the Channel's programming line-up was reconfigured to broaden the target audience beyond just children to appeal to adults as well. By 1986, a structured daypart programming schedule had been introduced that was designed to provide entertainment for different members of a subscribing household at different times of the day: preschoolers in the morning and early afternoon, older children in the late afternoon, families during the early evening, and adults after 9 pm. Programming from the Disney library, while remaining the centerpiece of the Channel's programming mix, was de-emphasized, with older Disney programs replaced with more contemporary, original, made-for The Disney Channel films and series.

Second, The Disney Channel's marketing activities were streamlined to focus on targeting the service's best subscription prospects. Free national previews, which allow basic cable subscribers to sample The Disney Channel's programming for up to a week, became the centerpiece of The Disney Channel's marketing program. Currently offered in conjunction with participating cable systems five times a year, each preview is preceded by national and local advertising as well as targeted direct mail to non-Disney Channel subscribers, encouraging them to tune in to The Disney Channel during the free preview period. Direct response television spots running on the Channel provide viewers with an 800-number to call if they are interested in having The Disney Channel installed in their homes. In this way, prospective new customers can be generated in a cost-effective manner for those cable systems that offer the preview to their subscribers. Marketing research is then used to monitor preview viewership and to assess the effectiveness of tune-in advertising so that improvements can be put into place for the subsequent national preview campaigns.

Third, The Disney Channel developed a new wholesale rate card, which allowed those cable operators that offered the Channel for a low retail price to consumers to benefit by paying lower wholesale rates for the service. Research had proven that demand for The Disney Channel was relatively price elastic, with cable systems that charged consumers lower retail prices for The Disney Channel generating significantly higher sales than those cable systems that offered The Disney Channel at a higher price. In addition, with Congress' enactment of the 1984 Cable Communications Policy Act, many cable operators were freed of regulating constraints that had prevented them from raising the retail price for basic cable service. As cable operators started to raise the retail price for basic cable to consumers, The Disney Channel's affiliate marketing staff was able to provide cable operators with a financial incentive to simultaneously reduce the price of The Disney Channel, thereby keeping the total price paid by the consumer for a subscription to basic cable and the Channel relatively unchanged.

These three major changes in strategy proved extremely effective in helping to propel The Disney Channel's subscriber growth between 1985 and 1990, while the other major pay television services, the Channel's prime competitors, were fighting to maintain their market share. As a basis of comparison, the Channel's subscribers grew 120%, to 5.6 million households, from December 1985 to December 1990, while the rest of the entire pay TV industry combined grew by only 27% during that same period of time.

Competition remains intense within the maturing pay television industry, and for The Disney Channel to continue to grow at a healthy rate, programming and marketing strategies must be continually reassessed. Marketing research plays an important role in this process. For example, Anne Hotchkiss, director of marketing research for The Disney Channel from 1984 to 1991, was faced during her tenure with the task of how to use research to help identify new areas of opportunity for the Channel. In one instance, in planning her budget for the year ahead, she had arranged to meet with one of the several firms that The Disney Channel used to conduct its marketing and programming research projects. Specifically, she wanted information on: (1) how to increase market penetration; (2) the various market segments to which the Channel appealed and whether programming changes could capture new segments; and (3) the price thresholds for The Disney Channel.

Sources: Personal interview with Tom Wszalek, Disney Channel, April 1991; personal interview with Dea Shandera, Disney Channel, May 1991.

Questions

1. Chapter 5 describes the marketing research process. What steps in that process are evident in this case?

2. What type of information does The Disney Channel require for developing its future marketing strategy?

3. How should The Disney Channel gather the information needed for making a decision?

Source: Paul Lowe/Network/Matrix.

Consumers worldwide, like this shopper at a Tesco supermarket in London, are basing buying decisions on the ecological friendliness of goods and services. Concern for the environment is one of many factors that influence buying behavior. Marketers' understanding of the factors that affect purchase decisions help them develop effective marketing strategies.

PART 3

Buyer Behavior and Market Segmentation

—

CHAPTER 6
Consumer Behavior

CHAPTER 7
Organizational Buying Behavior

CHAPTER 8
Market Segmentation

6

Consumer Behavior

CHAPTER OBJECTIVES

1. To explain the classification of behavioral influences on consumer decisions.

2. To identify the interpersonal determinants of consumer behavior.

3. To identify the personal determinants of consumer behavior.

4. To outline the steps in the consumer decision process.

5. To differentiate among routinized response behavior, limited problem solving, and extended problem solving.

Just two decades ago, the Hispanic population in the United States totaled 9 million; today it totals more than 23 million. That is a growth rate of 163 percent, compared to 23 percent for the U.S. population as a whole.

Advertisers and advertising agencies are scrambling to keep up. Spending on advertisements targeting Hispanics more than doubled in a recent five-year period and is expected to continue to grow at a rate of 25 percent per year. Some agencies have hired young marketers with Hispanic backgrounds in an effort to create specialists in Hispanic advertising; others have hired seasoned professionals from Latin American countries in the expectation that they will be more conscious of the similarities and differences among various sectors of the Hispanic market. Coors Brewing Company is attempting to raise its profile in the Hispanic community through campaigns promoting adult literacy and voting. And Volkswagen, M/S (hot sauce), Coca-Cola, and McDonald's are among the many companies that are launching Hispanic marketing campaigns.

Much of the marketing aimed at Hispanic consumers makes use of special events such as concerts, in-store parties, festivals, and trip giveaways. According to Tere Zubizaretta of Zubi Advertising in Miami, "Hispanics tend to be a little more relaxed; they enjoy music and getting together and dancing, so special events of that nature have a great deal more impact." PepsiCo has capitalized on this trait by contributing a huge piñata to the fiestas organized by Von's Tianguis markets in Southern California.

As the Hispanic market has grown and competition among advertisers has intensified, Hispanic campaigns

have become more sophisticated. Coors Light, for instance, has launched a slick campaign around the theme *Pura Vida* ("the good life"). Coors has also put together a touring exhibition that includes art from 16 Hispanic countries.

Marketers that want to reach Hispanic consumers need to be aware that the Hispanic population is not only growing but becoming more complex. New subsegments have been created as a result of changing flows of immigrants. Some Hispanics have become fully assimilated into American culture while others are completely unassimilated and still others have ties to both Hispanic and American cultures. In this crowded, complex market it is no longer enough to simply translate an ad into Spanish. Advertisers need to devote time and resources to learning the needs and nuances of the Hispanic market. As one program manager comments, "It takes a long time to understand a community."[1]

Photo source: Courtesy of Coors Brewing Company.

Chapter Overview

consumer behavior
All the acts of individuals in obtaining, using, and disposing of economic goods and services, including the decision processes that precede and determine these acts.

Consumer behavior consists of the acts of individuals in obtaining, using, and disposing of economic goods and services, including the decision processes that precede and determine these acts.[2] This definition applies to both the individual consumer and the industrial products purchaser. A major difference in the purchasing behavior of the two, however, is that the industrial buyers are subject to additional influences from within their organization. Chapter 7 will deal with those influences. This chapter assesses interpersonal and personal influences on individual consumer behavior.

Since the study of consumer behavior requires an understanding of human behavior in general, it is not surprising that consumer researchers borrow extensively from the areas of psychology and sociology. The work of Kurt Lewin, for example, provides a useful classification of influences on buying behavior (and is also used in motivation theory, which is part of the management discipline). Lewin's proposition is:

$$B = f(P,E),$$

where behavior (B) is a function (f) of the interactions of personal influences (P) and the pressures exerted on them by outside environmental forces (E).

This statement is usually rewritten for consumer behavior as follows:

$$B = f(I,P),$$

where consumer behavior (B) is a function (f) of the interaction of interpersonal determinants (I), such as reference groups and culture, and personal determinants (P), such as attitudes, learning, and perception. Both the individual's psychological makeup and the influences of others affect his or her consumer behavior. The relationship between the interaction of personal and interpersonal determinants and the consumer decision process is described later in this chapter.

Before examining the steps in the decision process in consumer purchasing, let us look at the interpersonal and personal influences on consumer behavior.

Interpersonal Determinants of Consumer Behavior

People often buy goods and services that will enable them to project a favorable image to others. Three categories of interpersonal determinants of consumer behavior are usually involved: cultural influences, social influences, and family influences.

Cultural Influences

Culture is the broadest environmental determinant of consumer behavior, so it is important for marketers to understand the culture they are dealing with. A lack of knowledge can lead to some embarrassing mistakes. For example, when one company placed an ad in a Chinese publication to wish the community a happy new year, the Chinese characters appeared upside down. As another example of advertising disaster, a footwear campaign showed Japanese practicing the ancient art of footbinding—something that was exclusive to China.[3]

culture
Complex of values, ideals, attitudes, and other meaningful symbols that help people communicate, interpret, and evaluate as members of society.

Culture can be defined as "a set of values, ideas, artifacts, and other meaningful symbols that help individuals to communicate, interpret, and evaluate as members of society."[4] It is a completely learned and handed-down way of life that gives each society its unique flavor and its values. To give just one example, the Japanese place such a high value on work that most workers do not take their

Figure 6.1   Advertisement That Appeals to a Core U.S. Value

Redhawk is the perfect place to teach your children about values. (And we don't just mean real estate values.)

Do you feel, like we do, that there's more to the appreciation of life than the appreciation in property values?

Then you've come to the right place. At just the right time.

This is a new 1300-acre, everything-in-one-place community in the Temecula Valley that we call Redhawk. You can call it home, for short.

Oh, don't misunderstand, you'll like the prices here. This is one of the best places left in Southern California, if you want a lot of house for your money. But it's even more perfect, if you want a lot of house for your family.

At the risk of sounding like a greeting card, this is the kind of place where you see parents tying long tails on kites, kids rolling down grassy hills on Saturdays, and children running through sprinklers.

The sort of place where you may have to explain to your kids that those strange noises they hear at night are things called crickets.

We hope you'll come out now, during our Preview Opening. You'll see homes from some of California's best builders. And a golf course you don't need to be a golfer to appreciate.

(And, in case you're wondering, no, those hot air balloons aren't part of our celebration. They're just part of another normal day in Temecula.)

For information, call 1-800-662-HAWK. REDHAWK

You reach Redhawk by travelling Interstate 15 to South 79, then continue on South 79 to Redhawk Parkway.

Source: Courtesy of Great American Development Company/Franklin Associates.

full annual vacations—one explanation, some say, for the low birthrate in Japan.[5]

Core Values in U.S. Culture. While some cultural values change over time, other basic core values do not. The work ethic and the desirability of accumulating wealth are two such core values in American society. Others are efficiency, practicality, individualism, freedom, youthfulness, activity, and human-itarianism. Each of these values influences consumer behavior. Consider Americans' value of activity—the notion that keeping busy is healthy and natural. This stimulates consumers' interest in products that save time and thus allow more activities, particularly leisure-time activities. The value of youthfulness stimulates a desire for goods and services that provide the illusion of youth.[6]

Another core American value—the importance of family—has survived cultural change even though the typical family structure and members' roles have changed. Marketing experts believe that family values will remain major factors in consumer behavior throughout the 1990s. The 35–54 age group will control 55 percent of disposable income by 2000, up from 42 percent in 1980. Geoffrey Greene of Data Resources, a research firm, commented: "The number of affluent consumers will grow, and many of them will be in the most intensely home-focused stage of the life cycle, settling down, raising children. For marketers of the nineties, home will be where the action is."[7] In other words, the modified Eisenhower-era values that are now in vogue again will no doubt continue thus for the decade. Figure 6.1 shows how Great American Development Company appeals to the American core value of family in promoting a new housing community.

An International Perspective on Cultural Influences.

Cultural differences are particularly important for international marketers. In the 1990s, as Europe becomes a single market in political and economic terms, marketers will have to find ways to reach a multi-cultural market with nine different languages and a multitude of lifestyles, cuisines, and product preferences.[8] Marketing strategies that have proven successful in one country often cannot be applied to other international markets because of cultural differences. General Foods positions Tang as a breakfast drink in the United States, but in France it is marketed as a refreshment since orange juice is rarely consumed with breakfast. Similarly, soup commercials would have to be adapted for Japan, where soup is drunk with breakfast.[9]

U.S.–based international marketers face competition from firms in Germany, France, Japan, and several other countries, as well as from firms in the host nation. Therefore, they must become familiar with all aspects of the local population, including its cultural heritage. This can be accomplished by treating each country as a distinct market segment that must be thoroughly analyzed before developing a marketing mix.

Subcultures.

subculture
Subgroup of a culture with its own distinct mode of behavior.

Cultures are not homogeneous entities with universal values. Within each culture are numerous **subcultures**—groups with their own distinct modes of behavior. The culture of the United States, in particular, is composed of significant subcultures based on such factors as race, nationality, age, rural versus urban location, religion, and geographical distribution.

Inhabitants of the southwestern United States have a lifestyle emphasizing casual dress, outdoor entertaining, and active recreation. Mormons refrain from buying tobacco and liquor. Orthodox Jews purchase kosher and other traditional foods. Understanding these and other differences among subcultures results in successful marketing of goods and services. Consider the marketing efforts of Winn-Dixie in South Florida. The bulk of the area's considerable Hispanic population is Cuban. However, Winn-Dixie marketers noted statistics that showed the population of Central Americans—particularly Nicaraguans—had increased fourfold in the past decade. One out of every six South Florida Hispanics is of Central American heritage. Winn-Dixie marketers knew that Nicaraguans and Cubans are culturally different, especially when it comes to food. The supermarket chain therefore developed television commercials featuring Nicaraguan dishes that were linked to weekly specials. Winn-Dixie's success with its Nicaraguan campaign led it to promote other national holidays and related dishes. The chain uses the slogan, "Dixie Tiene el Sabor de mi pais," or "Winn-Dixie has the flavor of my country."[10]

The three largest ethnic subcultures in the United States are blacks, Hispanics, and Asians. Together they account for about 20 percent of the total U.S. population. However, by the year 2056, whites will be in the minority. In fact, whites currently represent only 58 percent of all Californians. In San Jose's phone directory, there are 14 columns of Nguyens, a Vietnamese surname, and only eight columns of Joneses.[11]

Black Consumption Patterns.

Blacks represent the largest racial/ethnic subculture in the United States—some 31 million strong. They account for nearly 12 percent of the U.S. population and about $250 billion in purchasing power. The black market is also growing in terms of expendable income. One in three black families now have incomes of $35,000 or more. By the end of the decade, over half of all blacks will fall into the government's "middle-class" category.[12]

One important demographic difference distinguishes blacks from whites. Blacks are considerably younger, with a median age of 28 compared to 33 for whites. This difference is sometimes reflected in black consumption patterns.[13]

While marketers recognize that no group of this size can be considered a homogeneous market segment for all products, a number of marketing studies have compared consumption patterns of blacks and whites. One study revealed that the spending patterns of blacks and whites are quite similar in broad categories such as housing, transportation, and food. These categories claim two-thirds of yearly household expenditures for both groups. Blacks, however, spend less on tobacco, alcohol, entertainment, and personal care than do whites.[14] But within these broad categories, there are important differences in the consumer preferences of blacks and whites. A Conference Board study reported the following.[15]

☐   Although blacks and whites spend the same proportion of their incomes on transportation, blacks spend far less than whites on the purchase of trucks and vans and far more on mass transit and taxis.

☐   Blacks account for more than one-third of the money spent on rented televisions.

☐   Though, on average, blacks have less money than whites, they account for 10 percent of most expenditures in the television, radio, and sound equipment category.

☐   Blacks spend far less than whites for most kinds of reading materials, but they account for 17 percent of expenditures on encyclopedias and other reference books.

A general buying characteristic of black consumers is their brand loyalty. Blacks typically account for a disproportionate share of the purchases of many major national brands. This makes them an especially significant target market. Several national firms, including McDonald's, Wendy's, and Procter & Gamble, use black-owned advertising agencies to create advertising messages targeted at the black community. Anheuser-Busch has created brand loyalty among black consumers with the help of its fine collection of paintings by top African-American artists, "The Great Kings and Queens of Africa." The collection has appeared in newspapers and colleges around the world and has played a central role in the company's marketing to black consumers. Some firms are building their rapport with black consumers by being sensitive to concerns of the black community. Toyota, for example, shows support for the value of education in the black culture by donating 16 scholarships each year to the American Negro College Fund.[16] In addition to giving financial support to black colleges, General Foods promotes the value of an education at black colleges through advertisements such as the one in Figure 6.2.

Hispanic Consumption Patterns.   Accounting for over 8 percent of the U.S. population, Hispanics are the nation's second largest and fastest-growing subculture. There are twice as many Hispanics in the U.S. as there are in Cuba. The Bureau of the Census predicts that by the year 2010 Hispanics will have become a larger minority than blacks. Hispanics already constitute a majority of the population in cities like Miami, San Antonio, and El Paso. Hispanics' purchasing power was estimated at $172 billion in a recent year.[17]

Due to their variety of national origins, Hispanics are a more heterogeneous subculture than blacks. Mexico is the birthplace of 63 percent of the U.S. Hispanic population. Other primary places of origin are Puerto Rico, 11 percent; Cuba, 5 percent; and Central and South American countries, 12 percent.[18] Hispanics are geographically concentrated, with those of Mexican origin living

Figure 6.2   Marketing Program That Supports a Cultural Value

primarily in California and the Southwest, Puerto Ricans in the metropolitan New York area, and Cubans in South Florida.

One study revealed the following buying traits of U.S. Hispanics:[19]

☐ Hispanics prefer buying American-made products, and goods and services offered by firms that cater to Hispanic needs. More than 40 percent consider a firm's interest in or recognition of Hispanics when they shop.

☐ Hispanics are quality and brand conscious. They prefer to buy brand name products. Almost one-half of Hispanic consumers do not buy unfamiliar brands, even if they cost less. They buy products on a cost-value basis and are willing to pay a premium price for premium quality.

☐ Hispanics are very brand loyal. About 45 percent always buy their usual brands, and only 20 percent frequently switch brands. Brand loyalty stems from Hispanics' perception that buying what they consider to be the best brands is a way of doing their best for their families. Of particular importance to marketers is the youthfulness of the Hispanic market—the median age of Hispanics is less than 24 years, compared with 32 years for the U.S. population as a whole. This gives marketers the opportunity to capture Hispanics' loyalty at an early age.

PepsiCo, Inc. wowed Hispanic youngsters by unveiling the world's largest piñata at Carnaval Miami's "Calle Ocho" street festival. Participating in special events is one way PepsiCo targets the family-oriented and brand-loyal Hispanic consumer. Hispanics are an important segment for PepsiCo, as they consume one-third more soft drinks than the U.S. population as a whole. The company's promotions to Hispanics are successful because they are relevant to the Hispanic culture and to the company's product.

Source: © 1990 Brian Smith.

Another cultural characteristic of Hispanics is that they spend relatively more of their free time with their extended families than do other population segments. Shopping and movie-going, for example, are family outings. The focus on family was the rationale for a "diaper derby" staged by Huggies in Southern California's Tianguis stores: Five babies at a time crawled up a store aisle to their mothers. The first one there was given a box of diapers.[20]

Marketers are responding to the growing Hispanic market by targeting their advertising to Hispanics, establishing bilingual salesforces, and sponsoring special events in Spanish-speaking communities. Local firms welcome Hispanics by displaying "Aqui se habla espanol" ("Spanish is spoken here") signs in their shop windows. Spanish-language television provides yet another avenue for marketers to reach the Hispanic population.

As noted in the opening story, marketers are also placing increasing emphasis on special events aimed at Hispanic audiences. For example, Von's supermarkets in Long Beach, California, hosted a Hispanic food fair. More than 5,000 people, primarily Mexican-Americans, came to browse among booths set up by specialty companies like El Rey Sausage and Argas Tortillas.[21]

Asian Consumption Patterns.   Although a smaller market segment than blacks and Hispanics, the U.S. Asian population is expected to grow from 6 million currently to nearly 16 million by the turn of the century. The Asian market is particularly attractive to advertisers because median household income is higher than that of whites, blacks, or Hispanics. Total Asian buying power is estimated at $61 billion.

Like Hispanics, Asians are culturally diverse, maintain their own languages, and are brand conscious. The cultural diversity among Asians is marked. Accordingly, a television advertising campaign for the California State Lottery did separate commercials in Korean, Vietnamese, and two Chinese dialects. For example, the Korean version showed a family playing a game called "Yute" to pick its lottery numbers. The Chinese version showed a family seated at a table labeled "Table 8" and being served by a waitress with a "3" on her blouse. The ethnically correct commercial suggested the two numbers considered lucky by Chinese.[22]

The fact that many Asian consumers are recent immigrants further complicates marketing efforts to reach them. For example, the Asian community in the Central Valley of California is made up primarily of refugees from Southeast Asia. These immigrants generally distrust banks and are not very sophisticated about financial institutions. Bank of America therefore approached this market with the simple message, "Come See Us," printed in Asian-language newspapers.[23]

√ Social Influences

The second interpersonal determinant of consumer behavior consists of various social influences. Children's earliest group experience is their membership in the family. From this group they seek total satisfaction of their physiological and social needs. As they grow older, they join other groups—neighborhood play groups, school groups, Girl Scouts, Little League, and friendship groups, among others—from which they acquire both status and roles.

status
Relative position of any individual in a group.

roles
Behavior that members of a group expect of individuals who hold a specific position within it.

Status is the relative position of any individual member in a group; **roles** are what the other members of the group expect of individuals who hold specific positions within it. Some groups (such as Boy Scouts) are formal, and others (such as friendship groups) are informal. Both types of groups supply each member with both status and roles; in doing so, they influence that person's activities—including his or her purchase behavior. (Of course, family also continues to be a major influence, as will be discussed under the heading of "Family Influences.")

Asch phenomenon
The effect of a reference group on individual decision making.

The Asch Phenomenon.   Groups are often more influential in an individual's purchase decisions than he or she realizes. Most people tend to adhere in varying degrees to the general expectations of any group that they consider important to themselves—often without a conscious awareness of this motivation. The surprising impact that groups and group norms can exhibit on individuals' behavior has been called the **Asch phenomenon,** after research conducted by psychologist S.E. Asch. Purchase decisions ranging from the choice of automobile model and residential location to the decision to purchase at least one item at a home party sponsored by a direct seller are affected by this phenomenon.

√ reference groups
Group with which an individual identifies to the point where it dictates a standard of behavior.

Reference Groups.   Discussion of the Asch phenomenon leads us to the subject of **reference groups**—groups whose value structures and standards influence a person's behavior. Consumers usually try to keep their purchase behavior in line with what they perceive to be the values of their reference groups. The extent of reference-group influence varies widely. In order for the influence to be great on a purchase, two factors must be present:

1. The item being purchased must be one that can be seen and identified by others.

2. The item being purchased must be conspicuous; it must stand out, be unusual, and be a brand or product that not everyone owns.

Figure 6.3

Brand Decision Influenced by
a Reference Group

Source: Courtesy of L.A. Gear.

Reference-group influence would be significant in the decision to buy a Jaguar, for example, but would have little or no impact on the decision to purchase a loaf of bread. The influence of reference groups is especially strong on younger people. The L.A. Gear ad in Figure 6.3 capitalizes on reference-group influence in promoting its MJ footwear collection.

The status of the individual within a reference group produces three subcategories: a membership group which the person actually belongs to, such as a country club; an aspirational group which the person desires to associate with; and a dissociative group with which the individual does not want to be identified.

This concept helps explain the spending patterns of so-called yuppies, young urban professionals. Those with higher incomes are able to indulge their craving for six-bedroom homes, antique furniture, and whirlpool baths—the symbols of their membership group. Those with somewhat lower paychecks are struggling to follow suit, with the result that they have racked up more credit-card debt per capita than any other group in their generation.[24] They are people influenced by an aspirational group.

Reference-group influences can also be seen among young professionals in Taiwan, South Korea, and other Asian countries. With up to 20 times the spending power of their fellow citizens, many of these young people have adopted spending patterns like those of their counterparts in the West. For example, unlike their parents, they will spend money rather than putting it in a bank; they use credit cards; and their top priority is a car rather than a house.[25]

Figure 6.4   Alternative Channels for Communication Flows

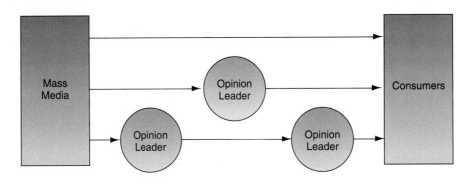

Social Classes.   Research conducted a number of years ago by W. Lloyd Warner identified a six-class system within the social structures of both small and large cities in the United States: upper-upper, lower-upper, upper-middle, lower-middle, working-class, and lower-class.

Class rankings are determined—variously—by occupation, income, education, family background, and dwelling area. Income is not always a primary determinant; pipe fitters paid at union scale earn more than many college professors, but their purchase behavior may be quite different. Thus, the adage "A rich man is a poor man with money" is sometimes incorrect from a marketing viewpoint. Also, sociological research has shown that people's perceptions of their social class persist even during an economic downturn or when unforeseen problems lower their income. When their expectations are not matched by reality, they are frustrated and may cut back on their spending, but they do not consider themselves to be members of a lower social class.[26]

The role of social class in determining consumer behavior, however, continues to be a source of debate in the field of marketing, and some have argued against using this classification at all, preferring to segment markets simply by income.

opinion leader
Individual in a group who serves as an information source for other group members.

Opinion Leaders.   Every group usually contains a few members who can be considered **opinion leaders,** or trendsetters. These individuals are likely to purchase new products before others. They then communicate their experience with the new products via word-of-mouth.

Generalized opinion leaders are rare; instead, individuals tend to be opinion leaders for specific goods or services due to their considerable knowledge and interest in that particular product. Their interest in the item motivates them to seek out information from mass media, manufacturers, and other supply sources and, in turn, transmit this information to their associates through interpersonal communications. Opinion leaders are found within all segments of the population.

In some cases, information about goods and services flows from radio, television, and other mass media to opinion leaders and then from opinion leaders to others. In other instances, the information flow is direct to all consumers. In still other instances, there is a multistep flow of information from mass media to opinion leaders and then on to other opinion leaders before being disseminated to the general public. Figure 6.4 illustrates the three types of communication flows.

Family Influences

One's family is perhaps the most important determinant of consumer behavior because of the close, continuing interactions among family members. Most people are members of at least two families during their lifetimes—the one they are born into and the one they eventually form as they marry and have children.

The establishment of a new household results in new marketing opportunities. The need for furniture, refrigerators, vacuum cleaners, and paintings for the living room depends not on the number of persons comprising a household but the number of households. The decline of household size is discussed in Chapter 8.

Another market is established by parents whose children have moved away from home. These people may find themselves with a four-bedroom residence and a half-acre of lawn to maintain. Lacking maintenance assistance from their children and no longer needing the large house, they become customers for townhouses, condominiums, and high-rise apartments in larger cities. Later they may become customers for retirement centers, supplemental medical insurance, off-season travel, and hearing aids.

Another important market is that of the single and divorced. Marketers have had some difficulty in figuring out how to approach this market. Campbell Soup Company discovered that its single-serving can of soup, offered under the name "Soup for One," had been dubbed "The Lonely Soup" by singles.[27]

Household Roles.   Historically, the wife made the majority of family purchases and the husband worked at a paying job most of the day. Although the preferences of children or husband may have influenced her decisions, the wife usually was responsible for food buying and most clothing purchases. Two forces have changed her role as sole purchasing agent for most household items. First, a shorter workweek provides each wage-earning household member with more time for shopping. Second, there is a large number of women in the work force. In 1950 only one-fourth of married women were employed outside the home; now nearly half have paid jobs. Studies of family decision making have shown households with two wage earners exhibit a larger number of joint decisions and an increase in night and weekend shopping.

The changing roles of household members are reflected in changes in purchasing behavior. A recent study found that men make more than half of their family's brand purchase decisions in several categories of foods including soups, cereals, and soft drinks.[28] Women, on the other hand, still do much of the shopping for clothing; they purchase 78 percent of men's sweaters, 71 percent of men's socks, and 70 percent of men's sport shirts.[29]

Although an infinite variety of roles can be played in household decision making, four role categories are most often used:[30]

1. *Autonomic,* in which an equal number of decisions is made by each partner.
2. *Husband-dominant,* in which the husband makes most of the decisions.
3. *Wife-dominant,* in which the wife makes most of the decisions.
4. *Syncratic,* in which most decisions are jointly made by both partners.

Personal-care items illustrate autonomic decisions; insurance, a typically husband-dominant purchase; children's clothing, a typically wife-dominant decision; and automobiles, a syncratic pattern.

Teenagers—The Family's New Purchasing Agent.   The role of children in purchasing decisions evolves as they grow older. Children's early influence generally centers around toys to be recommended to Santa Claus and

Figure 6.5   Advertising Aimed at the Youth Market

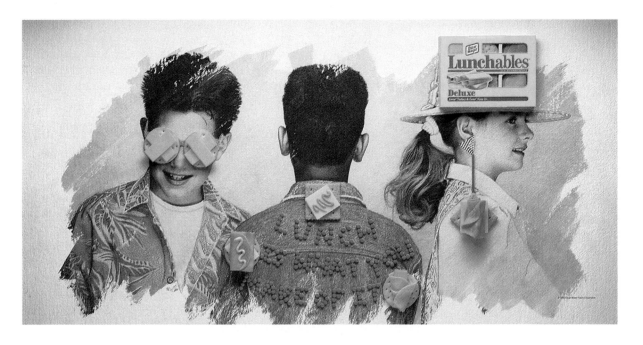

Source: Courtesy of Oscar Mayer & Co.

the choice of cereal brands. Younger children are also important to marketers of fast-food restaurants. Recognizing the role of children in this area—1.7 million children under the age of six eat at fast-food restaurants each day—Wendy's is trying to increase its appeal by offering more and better-quality toys in its promotions.[31]

Children under 12 represent an enormous market for video games. They spend over $10 billion annually on such games, much to the delight of Nintendo, which has revolutionized the U.S. home video game market. Toy marketers are also profiting from Americans' tendency to spend even greater amounts to amuse their children; Mattel's Barbie line brings in about $600 million a year.[32]

As children grow older, they increasingly influence their clothing purchases. Teenagers also become major consumers of sports equipment, movies, video rentals, and computers. The growing number of married and divorced mothers who work outside the home has had a decided impact on several household purchasing patterns. Teenage boys and girls now play an important role in their families' grocery purchases. Recent research has found that teenagers are also playing a greater role in the purchase of more expensive items such as cars and appliances. In some families, teenagers are viewed as the experts on purchases of high-technology items such as VCRs and compact-disk (CD) players.[33]

Yet surprisingly little advertising has been targeted at these important buyers, who represent an estimated $1 billion a week of buying power.[34] Research suggests that television, radio, and magazines, not traditional newspaper shopping sections, may be the best ways to reach them. The average young viewer is exposed to more than 100 minutes of television advertising each day. In promoting its Lunchables snack products, Oscar Mayer & Company accordingly developed a print campaign directed at the youth market. An example is the poster in Figure 6.5. Young shoppers are not only a sizable part of the current market for many products, they are also the future market. Brand loyalties built now may last for decades. A recent study of 40,000 college students found that the majority buy the same brand of toothpaste they used during high school.[35]

The role of children and teenagers in purchasing decisions is increasing throughout the world. In Asia, young people are also more affluent than ever before. Companies like McDonald's, Nike, and Coca-Cola are taking advantage of this trend with campaigns designed specifically for younger consumers in Asian nations.[36]

Personal Determinants of Consumer Behavior

Consumer behavior is a function of both interpersonal and personal influences. The personal determinants of consumer behavior include individual needs and motives, perceptions, attitudes, and self-concept. The interactions of these factors with interpersonal influences decide what is purchased.

Needs and Motives

need
Lack of something useful; a discrepancy between a desired state and the actual state.

The starting point in the purchase decision process is the recognition of a felt need. A **need** is simply the lack of something useful. It is an imbalance between the consumer's actual and desired state. Since people are typically confronted with numerous unsatisfied needs, a need must be sufficiently urgent before it can serve as a motive to buy something. Marketers attempt to arouse this sense of urgency, making a need "felt."

motive
Inner state that directs a person toward the goal of satisfying a felt need.

Motives are inner states that direct a person toward the goal of satisfying a felt need. The action is taken to reduce a state of tension and return to a condition of equilibrium.

Hierarchy of Needs. A. H. Maslow developed the theory that needs could be categorized and arranged in a hierarchy reflecting their importance to most people. Lower-level needs, according to this theory, had to be at least partially satisfied before higher needs could affect behavior.

Maslow's five-level hierarchy of needs begins with physiological needs and progresses to self-actualization needs. Table 6.1 illustrates products and marketing themes designed to satisfy each need level.

Physiological Needs. Physiological needs are primary needs for food, shelter, and clothing that must be satisfied before the individual can consider higher-order needs. After the physiological needs are at least partially satisfied, other needs enter the picture.

Safety Needs. The second-level safety needs include security, protection from physical harm, and avoidance of the unexpected. Gratification of these needs may take the form of a savings account, life insurance, purchase of radial tires, or membership in a local health club.

Social/Belongingness Needs. Satisfaction of physiological and safety needs leads to the third level—the desire to be accepted by members of the family and other individuals and groups, which is a social need. The individual may be motivated to join various groups, conform to their standards of dress and behavior, and try to obtain status in an attempt to gain such acceptance. In

Table 6.1

Marketing Strategies
Designed for Each Level in
Maslow's Needs Hierarchy

	Physiological
Products:	Limited in the United States. Generic foods, medicines, special drinks, and foods for athletes.
Specific themes:	☐ Campbell's Soup—"Soup is good food," with copy that stresses the nutritional benefits of soup.
	☐ Raisins—"Thank goodness I found a snack kids will sit for. And mothers will stand for."
	☐ Kellogg's All-Bran—"At last, some news about cancer you can live with," with copy that stresses the role of fiber in the diet.

	Safety
Products:	Smoke detectors, preventive medicines, insurance, social security, retirement investments, seat belts, burglar alarms, safes.
Specific themes:	☐ Sleep Safe—"We've designed a travel alarm that just might wake you in the middle of the night—because a fire is sending smoke into your room. You see, ours is a smoke alarm as well as an alarm clock."
	☐ General Electric—"Taking a trip usually means leaving your troubles behind. But there are times when you just might need help or information on the road. And that's when you need HELP, the portable CB from GE."
	☐ Alka-Seltzer—"Will it be there when you need it?"

	Belongingness
Products:	Personal grooming, foods, entertainment, clothing, and many others.
Specific themes:	☐ Atari—"Atari brings the computer age home," with a picture of a family using an Atari home computer.
	☐ Oil of Olay—"When was the last time you and your husband met for lunch?"
	☐ JC Penney—"Wherever teens gather, you'll hear it. It's the language of terrific fit and fashion. . . ."

	Esteem
Products:	Clothing, furniture, liquors, hobbies, stores, cars, and many others.
Specific themes:	☐ Sheaffer—"Your hand should look as contemporary as the rest of you."
	☐ St. Pauli Girl—"People who know the difference in fine things know the difference between imported beer and St. Pauli Girl. . . ."
	☐ Cadillac—". . . those long hours have paid off. In recognition, financial success, and in the way you reward yourself. Isn't it time you owned a Cadillac?"

	Self-Actualization
Products:	Education, hobbies, sports, some vacations, gourmet foods, museums.
Specific themes:	☐ U.S. Army—"Be all you can be."
	☐ U.S. Home—"Make the rest of your life . . . the best of your life."
	☐ Outward Bound School—"Challenges, adventure, growth."

Source: Reprinted by permission of the publisher from Del I. Hawkins, Roger D. Best, and Kenneth A. Coney, *Consumer Behavior,* 4th ed. (Homewood, IL: BPI/Irwin, 1989), pp. 357–358.

recognition of this need, Hallmark's line of "To Kids with Love" cards is designed to help adults and children maintain their social bonds in families that are undergoing changes such as divorce or remarriage.[37]

Esteem Needs.   The higher-order needs are more prevalent in developed countries, where a higher per capita income has allowed most people to satisfy the basic needs and thus concentrate on the desire for status, esteem, and self-actualization—more difficult needs to satisfy. The desire to feel a sense of accomplishment and achievement, to gain the respect of others, and even to better the performance of others, is an apparently universal human trait after lower-order needs are satisfied. Marketers can address this need in terms of giving buyers an opportunity to stand out from the crowd in some way.

Self-Actualization Needs. The top rung of the ladder of human needs is self-actualization—the need for fulfillment in realizing one's potential and fully using one's talents and capabilities. Satisfying this need may be beyond the marketer's scope.

Maslow points out that a satisfied need is no longer a motivator. Once the physiological needs are met, the individual moves on to the higher-order needs. Consumers are periodically motivated by the need to relieve thirst or hunger, but then their interests are immediately directed toward satisfaction of safety, social, and other needs in the hierarchy.

Critics have pointed out a variety of flaws in Maslow's reasoning. For example, some needs can be related to more than one level. However, the hierarchy continues to occupy a secure place in the study of consumer behavior.

Perceptions

perception

Manner in which an individual interprets a stimulus; the often highly subjective meaning that one attributes to an incoming stimulus or message.

Perception is the meaning that a person attributes to incoming stimuli received through the five senses—sight, hearing, touch, taste, and smell. Certainly a buyer's behavior is influenced by his or her perceptions of a good or service. And only recently have researchers come to recognize that what people perceive is as much a result of what they want to perceive as of what is actually there. It is for this reason that Saks Fifth Avenue is perceived so differently from K Mart and Godiva chocolates from Fannie May.

The perception of an object or event results from the interaction of two types of factors:

1. *Stimulus factors*—characteristics of the physical object, such as size, color, weight, or shape.

2. *Individual factors*—characteristics of the individual, including not only sensory processes but experiences with similar items and basic motivations and expectations.

Perceptual Screens. The average American today receives 17 more pounds of mail annually than ten years ago. Prime-time television is jammed with 15-second commercials. Products are advertised everywhere—even on TV monitors attached to self-service gasoline pumps.[38]

People are continually bombarded with many stimuli, including advertising of all kinds. Most of those stimuli are ignored, since in order to have time to function, people must respond selectively. Determining which stimuli they respond to is a problem for all marketers. The marketer's job is to entice the consumer to read the advertisement, listen to the sales representative, or react to the point-of-purchase display.

perceptual screen

Filtering process through which messages must pass.

Although studies have shown that the average consumer is exposed to more than 500 advertisements daily, most of these ads never break through people's **perceptual screens**—the filtering process through which messages must pass. Consider what happened in Salt Lake City during the 1984 Super Bowl. So many people flushed their toilets during a television commercial break that the city's main water line broke, leaving many homes without water. To prevent a similar occurrence during the 1991 Super Bowl, Buffalo's Erie County Water Authority

ADVERTISING TO CHILDREN

American children see an average of 100 commercials a day and between 30,000 and 40,000 a year. With so much competition, advertisers are looking for new ways to get their messages across. One approach that is coming into increasing use is the *informercial*—a commercial that is spliced into a show so seamlessly that children are unaware of the difference between commercial and program. This is the rationale for "Video Power," a syndicated show about video games in which a 14-year-old host named Johnny Arcade presents "news" about video games sandwiched between 10- and 20-second commercials.

This is just one of a variety of methods that are being used to slip commercial messages into TV programs, video cassettes, movies, and video games for young audiences. Product names and labels appear throughout these productions. In McDonald's *McTreasure Island,* for example, Ronald McDonald stars in a remake of the classic children's story. Another favored technique is "product placement," in which brand names are strategically worked into the action of movies. *Back to the Future II,* for instance, contained references to Toyota, Miller, Nike, AT&T, *USA Today,* Texaco, Pizza Hut, Pepsi, and others.

Critics of children's television are concerned about the trend toward blurring the line between advertising and programming. According to Michael Jacobson, ex-

ecutive director for the Center for Science in the Public Interest, the practice is "shameful and deceptive." Since disguised advertising on television is not currently banned, and films and videos do not come under the regulations of the Federal Communications Commission, there isn't much the critics can do about it.

Advertisers, on the other hand, note that children have a shorter attention span than adults and that they typically change channels during commercials. Blending advertising into programming is simply a way of keeping kids tuned in. "All we're trying to do is let the kid walk away remembering the commercial," says Alan Bohbot, the producer of "Video Power."

Discussion Questions

1. Should "informercials" aimed at children be banned?

2. Peggy Charren, head of Action for Children's Television, believes it is essential for commercials to be clearly distinguished from "editorial speech," that is, communication that has not been paid for by a sponsor. Do you agree?

Source: Joseph Pereira, "Kids' Advertisers Play Hide-and-Seek, Concealing Commercials in Every Cranny," *The Wall Street Journal,* (April 30, 1990), pp. B1, B6.

---

assigned two engineers to monitor the situation. Five million gallons of water were kept in reserve in case of a break in Buffalo's aging pipes.[39]

Breakthroughs can be accomplished in the printed media through large ads. Doubling the size of an ad increases its attention value by about 50 percent. Using color in newspaper ads in contrast to the usual black and white is another effective way to penetrate the reader's perceptual screen. Other contrast methods include using a large amount of white space around a printed area or using white type on a black background.

In general, the marketer seeks to make the message stand out, to make it different enough from other messages that it gains the prospective customer's attention. For example, two firms have developed technology to create print ads that make sounds ranging from a train whistle to the voice of John F. Kennedy.[40] The ad in Figure 6.6 is an excellent example of an attention-getting message. It encourages the involvement of readers in touching and tasting the product and motivates them to make a purchase decision to satisfy a need.

The psychological concept of *closure* is employed in creating a message that will stand out. Closure refers to people's tendency to produce a complete picture from an incomplete one. Advertisements that allow consumers to do this are successful in breaking through perceptual screens. Salem cigarettes once asked

Figure 6.6   Advertisement Breaking through Perceptual Screens

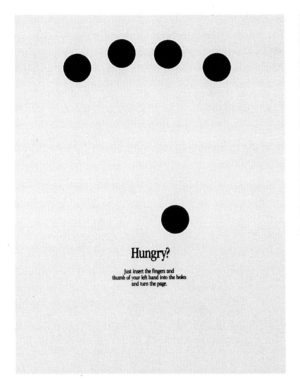

Hungry?

Just insert the fingers and
thumb of your left hand into the holes
and turn the page.

Get your hands on
à McD.L.T.®

Now bring it closer. Take a bite. CRUNCH!
(Watch your fingers!) Through the cool, crisp, crunchy
iceberg lettuce. Sinking further into a sweet, juicy slice
of tomato. And on into delicious American cheese.
Then into that piping hot 100% U.S. beef
Only McDonald's® could come up with something so unique, yet so simple. The McD.L.T.®
Now use your other hand to wave goodbye,
because you're going to McDonald's.®

GOOD TIME. GREAT TASTE.®

Source: Courtesy of McDonald's Corporation.

people to complete the advertising theme, "You can take Salem out of the country, but . . .". During a Kellogg campaign promoting the use of fruit with cereal, the company emphasized the point by replacing the letters "ll" in "Kellogg" with bananas. In a campaign featuring a 25-cent coupon offer, Kellogg emphasized the promotion by replacing the letter "o" in the brand name with a quarter.

With selective perception at work, it is easy to see the importance of the marketer's efforts to obtain a "consumer franchise" in the form of brand loyalty. Satisfied customers are less likely to seek information about competing products. Even when advertising by competitors is forced on them, they are less apt than others to allow it to pass through their perceptual filters. They simply tune out information that does not agree with their existing beliefs and expectations.

Subliminal Perception.   Is it possible to communicate with persons without them being aware of the communication? In 1956 a New Jersey movie theater tried to boost concession sales by flashing the words "Eat Popcorn" and "Drink Coca-Cola" between frames of Kim Novak's image in the movie *Picnic.* The messages flashed on the screen every 5 seconds for a duration of $\frac{1}{300}$ of a second. Researchers reported that these messages, though too short to be recognizable at the conscious level, resulted in a 58 percent increase in popcorn sales and an 18 percent increase in Coca-Cola sales. After the findings were published, advertising agencies and consumer protection groups became intensely interested in **subliminal perception**—the receipt of incoming information at a subconscious level.

subliminal perception
Receipt of information at a subconscious level.

Subliminal advertising is aimed at the subconscious level of awareness to circumvent viewers' perceptual screen. The goal of the original research was to induce consumer purchasing while keeping consumers unaware of the source of their motivation to buy. Further attempts to duplicate the test findings, however, invariably have been unsuccessful.

Although subliminal advertising has been universally condemned as manipulative (and declared illegal in California and Canada), it is exceedingly unlikely that it can induce purchasing except in those instances where the person is already inclined to buy. The reasons for this are:

1. Strong stimulus factors are required in order to even gain a buyer's attention.

2. Only a very short message can be transmitted.

3. Messages transmitted at the threshold of consciousness for one person will not be perceived at all by others.

In recent years, subliminal programming has spread to self-help cassette tapes. With these tapes, listeners hear on a conscious level relaxing music or the sound of ocean waves, and on a subconscious level, imperceptible to the ear, thousands of subliminal messages. Promoters of these tapes claim that they can help people stop smoking, lose weight, or achieve a host of other goals.

Attitudes

attitudes
One's enduring favorable or un-favorable evaluations, emotional feelings, or pro or con action tendencies.

Perception of incoming stimuli is greatly affected by attitudes. In fact, the decision to purchase a product is based on currently held attitudes about the product, store, or salesperson. **Attitudes** are a person's enduring favorable or unfavorable evaluations, emotional feelings, or pro or con action tendencies in regard to some object or data. They are formed over time through individual experiences and group contacts and are highly resistant to change.

Because favorable attitudes are likely to be conducive to brand preferences, marketers are interested in determining consumer attitudes toward their products. Numerous attitude-scaling devices have been developed for this purpose.

Attitude Components.   An attitude has cognitive, affective, and behavioral components. The *cognitive* component refers to the individual's information and knowledge about an object or concept. The *affective* component deals with feelings or emotional reactions. The *behavioral* component involves tendencies to act in a certain manner. For example, in making the decision to shop at a warehouse-type food store, the individual might obtain information about what the store offers from advertising, trial visits, and input from family, friends, and associates (cognitive). He or she might also receive input from listening to others about their experience of shopping at this type of store—whether they liked it or not (affective). Other affective information might lead the person to make a judgment about the type of people who seem to shop there—whether they represent a group he or she would like to be associated with. The consumer may ultimately decide to make some purchases of canned goods, cereal, and bakery products there but continue to rely on his or her regular supermarket for major food purchases (behavioral). All three components exist in a relatively stable and balanced relationship to one another and together form an overall attitude about an object or idea.

Changing Consumer Attitudes.   Given that a favorable consumer attitude is a prerequisite to marketing success, how can a firm lead prospective buyers to adopt such an attitude toward its products? The marketer has two choices: (1)

Figure 6.7

Developing a Product to Match Consumer Attitudes

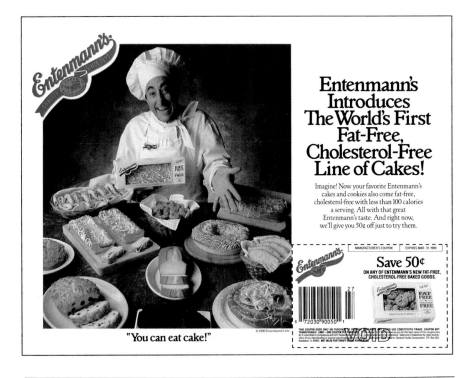

"You can eat cake!"

Source: Courtesy of Entenmann's Inc.

attempt to produce consumer attitudes that will motivate purchase of a particular product or (2) determine what existing consumer attitudes are and then make the product appeal to them.

If consumers view an existing product unfavorably, the firm may choose to redesign it with styling changes, different ingredients, or new package size or design. Or the firm might switch retail stores. Entenmann Bakery marketers realized that some health-conscious consumers had stopped buying desserts or cut down on their purchases of them. As an option for these consumers, the bakery introduced a new line of fat- and cholesterol-free baked goods made with all-natural ingredients. Figure 6.7 shows an example of Entenmann's advertising campaign introducing the new line, which attempts to recapture dessert eaters with the message "You Can Eat Cake."

The other course of action—producing consumer attitudes favorable to the product—is much more difficult. Consider Bic's failure to crack the fragrance market both here and in Europe. Bic successfully made pens and lighters disposable commodities but failed in its attempt to sell fragrances. Its disposable lighter-shaped packages were rejected by Americans and Europeans alike. A former Bic executive commented, "You can measure the amount of ink in a pen or how many times a lighter will light, but there are intangibles in the fragrance business that can't be measured."[41]

Modifying the Attitudinal Components. Attitude change frequently occurs when inconsistencies among the three attitudinal components are introduced. The most common inconsistencies result from changes in the cognitive component of an attitude as a result of new information. The Pepsi Challenge was launched in an attempt to convince consumers that they would prefer the taste of Pepsi to Coca-Cola if they compared the two. A Life Savers advertising campaign built around the theme that a Life Saver contains only 10

COMPETITIVE EDGE

GREEN MARKETING

. . . .

Marketers can gain a competitive edge by satisfying consumers' growing desire for "green," or "environmentally friendly," products. Market research and opinion polls are finding evidence of a sensitivity among consumers that goes beyond a demand for environmental-protection laws and regulations. Companies that can demonstrate that their production processes not only meet the laws against releasing toxic chemicals into the environment, but also have a minimal environmental impact at all, stand to gain.

The Bhopal and Chernobyl disasters, the *Exxon Valdez* and Persian Gulf oil spills, and medical waste washing up on beaches have contributed to creating this enhanced environmental awareness. So has the health and fitness movement: Concern for a healthy environment follows logically from concern for a healthy body. In short, consumers are undergoing a fundamental attitude change.

As behavior that ignores environmental impact becomes socially unacceptable, businesses that avoid facing environmental issues will suffer. Consumers are increasingly "voting at the cash register" for environmental responsibility. For example, they are beginning to avoid single-serving packaging and showing a preference for biodegradable and recyclable materials. Many are willing to pay more for products packaged with such materials.

A company that has turned environmental concern to its advantage is Toronto-based Loblaw Cos., which operates a chain of 340 supermarkets and a subsidiary that develops and markets household products. Convinced that "the disposable society is going to have to come to an end," Loblaw has developed a line of more than 100 environmentally friendly products. The products are packaged under the "GREEN" label and include such items as disposable diapers made from non-chlorine-bleached pulp, toilet paper made from recycled paper, phosphate-free detergents, recycled motor oil, rechargeable batteries, and high-efficiency lightbulbs, all in bright green packaging made from recycled paper. The products are priced competitively and sold in local supermarkets. Within the first year after they were introduced, many GREEN products became leaders in their categories, and Loblaw plans to expand the line.

Discussion Questions

1. Critics point out that switching to brands that are "environmentally friendly" will not solve the problem of overconsumption and that not all products marketed as "green" have been proven to be good for the environment. How can marketers deal with these criticisms?

2. Shoppers are willing to pay a premium for products they see as environmentally responsible. Should marketers take advantage of this attitude in pricing such products?

Sources: Carolyn Lesh, "Loblaws," *Advertising Age* (January 21, 1991), p. 38; Anita Manning, "Sales Are Ringing Up for Ecology-Friendly Products," *USA Today* (March 21, 1990), p. 5D; Howard Schlossberg, "Canadians Are Serious About Their Environment—and Ours, Too," *Marketing News* (March 19, 1990), p. 16; Richard P. Wells, "Environmental Performance Will Count in the 1990s," *Marketing News* (March 19, 1990), p. 22; Leonard A. Wood, "U.S. Consumers More Concerned with Economy Than Ecology," *Marketing News* (March 19, 1990), p. 20; and Laurie Freeman, "Consumers Thinking 'Green' Too," *Advertising Age* (August 21, 1989), p. 66. *Photo source:* Reprinted by permission of *Advertising Age.*

calories was designed to correct many consumers' misconceptions about the candy's high caloric content.

The affective component may be altered by relating the use of the new good or service to desirable consequences for the user. For example, AMF's advertising has described how walkers, dancers, and runners can burn off 30 to 300 percent more calories when they use Heavyhands.

The third alternative in attempting to change attitudes is to induce the buyer to engage in different behavior. Thus, a free sample of a product might be offered in the hope that trying the product will lead to an attitude change.

Learning

learning
Changes in behavior, immediate or expected, that occur as a result of experience.

drive
Strong stimulus that impels action.

cue
Any object existing in the environment that determines the nature of the response to a drive.

reinforcement
Reduction in drive that results from an appropriate response.

Marketing is as concerned with the process by which consumer decisions change over time as it is with the current state of such decisions. **Learning,** in a marketing context, refers to changes in consumer behavior, immediate or expected, as a result of experience. The learning process includes the component of **drive,** which is any strong stimulus that impels action. Examples of drives are fear, pride, desire for money, thirst, pain avoidance, and rivalry. Also involved in learning is a **cue,** that is, any object existing in the environment that determines the nature of the response to a drive. Examples of cues are a newspaper advertisement for a new French restaurant (a cue for a hungry person) and a Shell sign near an interstate highway (a cue for a motorist needing gasoline).

A *response* is the individual's reaction to cues and drive. Responses might include such reactions as purchasing a package of Gillette Sensor blades, dining at Burger King, or deciding to enroll at a particular college or university.

Reinforcement is the reduction in drive that results from a proper response. The more rewarding the response, the stronger becomes the bond between the drive and the purchase of the particular product. Should the purchase of Sensor blades result in closer shaves through repeated use, the likelihood of their future purchase is increased. Reinforcement is the rationale underlying "frequent buyer" programs, which reward repeat purchasers for their loyalty. Such programs, which are derived from the Green Stamp promotions of an earlier era, give consumers points for buying particular brands; the points can be redeemed for gifts like an electric can opener or a barbecue grill. Many consumers report that the programs have induced them to stick with certain brands.[42]

Applying Learning Theory to Marketing Decisions.
Learning theory has some important implications for marketing strategists, particularly those involved with consumer packaged goods.[43] A desired outcome such as repeat purchase behavior must be developed gradually. *Shaping* is the process of applying a series of rewards and reinforcements to permit more complex behavior to evolve over time. An example of the shaping process is illustrated in Figure 6.8. To help consumers learn about Lipton's new teas with honey, Thomas J. Lipton marketers use advertising to create awareness of their new product and encourage consumers to learn about it from direct experience by offering a free sample.

Both promotional strategy and the product itself play a role in the shaping process. Assume that marketers are attempting to motivate consumers to become regular buyers of a certain product. The first step is an initial product trial induced with a free sample package that includes a substantial discount coupon for a subsequent purchase. This example illustrates the use of a cue as a shaping procedure. The purchase response is reinforced by satisfactory product performance and still another (less substantial) coupon for the next purchase.

Figure 6.8

Marketing Application of
Learning Theory

Source: Courtesy of Thomas J. Lipton Company.

The second step is to entice the consumer to buy the product with little financial risk. The large discount coupon enclosed with the free sample prompts such an action. The package that is purchased has a smaller discount coupon enclosed. Again the reinforcement is satisfactory product performance and the second coupon.

The third step is to motivate the person to buy the item again at a moderate cost. A discount coupon accomplishes this objective, but this time there is no additional coupon in the package. The only reinforcement is satisfactory product performance.

The final test comes when the consumer is asked to buy the product at its true price without a discount coupon. Satisfaction with product performance is the only continuing reinforcement. Repeat purchase behavior literally will have been shaped by effective application of learning theory within a marketing strategy context.

The Promotion Marketing Association of America studied how consumers view certain kinds of promotions. The results of this research have implications for marketers using learning theory. Researchers found that consumers have become conditioned to respond to in-store bargains, offers of free merchandise, or high-value coupons. Some consumers refuse to buy a product unless it is attached to a promotion. Also, they have become more cynical about promotions that require them to work to obtain something that they do not consider worth the effort. (For example, promotions asking customers to mail in a request for a coupon are less successful.) The lesson for marketers is to offer a tangible and immediate benefit and avoid anything that will be perceived as deceptive.[44]

Self-Concept Theory

self-concept
Mental conception of one's self, comprised of the real self, self-image, looking-glass self, and ideal self.

The consumer's **self-concept**—or multifaceted picture of himself or herself—plays an important role in consumer behavior. One young man, for example, may view himself as intellectual, self-assured, talented, and a rising young business executive. He will be disposed to buy products that agree with this mental conception of himself. The response to direct questions, such as, "Why do you buy Obsession?" is likely to reveal a person's desired self-image.

The concept of self is the result of the interaction of many of the influences—both personal and interpersonal—affecting buyer behavior. The individual's needs, motives, perceptions, attitudes, and learning lie at the core of his or her conception of self in addition to the environmental factors of family, social, and cultural influences.

The self-concept has four components: real self, self-image, looking-glass self, and ideal self. The *real self* is an objective view of the total person. The *self-image*—the way individuals view themselves—may be a distortion of the objective view. The *looking-glass self*—the way individuals think others see them—may also be quite different from self-image, because people often choose to project a different image to others than that which they believe is their real self. The *ideal self* serves as a personal set of objectives since it is the image to which the individual aspires. In purchasing goods and services, people are likely to choose products that move them closer to their ideal self-image.

The Consumer Decision Process

Consumer behavior may be viewed as a decision process. As Figure 6.9 shows, the act of purchasing is merely one point in the process. To understand consumer behavior, we must examine the events that precede and follow the purchase.

The steps in the consumer decision process are:

1. Problem recognition
2. Search
3. Evaluation of alternatives
4. Purchase decision
5. Purchase act
6. Postpurchase evaluation

Consumers use the decision process in solving problems and taking advantage of opportunities. Such decisions permit consumers to correct differences between their actual and desired states. Feedback from each decision serves as additional experience on which to rely in making subsequent decisions.

Problem Recognition

The first stage in the decision process occurs when the consumer becomes aware of a significant discrepancy between the existing state of affairs and a desired state of affairs. Once the problem has been recognized, it must be defined so that the consumer may seek out methods for its solution. As a consequence of problem recognition, the individual is motivated to achieve the desired state.

Figure 6.9

An Integrated Model of the
Consumer Decision Process

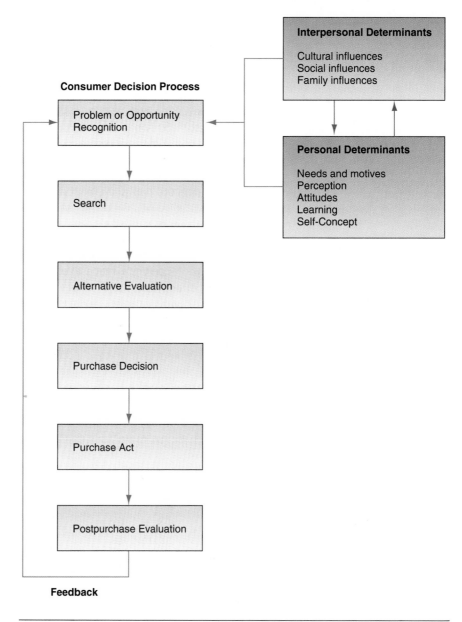

Source: James F. Engel, Roger D. Blackwell, and Paul W. Miniard, *Consumer Behavior,* 6th ed.
(Hinsdale, IL: The Dryden Press, 1990), pp. 26–33.

Perhaps the most common cause of problem recognition is routine depletion of the individual's stock of an item. A large number of consumer purchases involve the replenishment of products ranging from gasoline to groceries. In other instances, the consumer may possess an inadequate assortment of products. The gardening hobbyist may make regular purchases of different fertilizers, seeds, or gardening tools as the season progresses.

A third cause of problem recognition is dissatisfaction with the present brand or product type. This situation is common in the purchase of a new automobile, new furniture, or a new fall wardrobe. In many instances, the consumer's boredom with current products and a desire for novelty may be the underlying rationale for the decision process leading to new-product purchases.

Another important factor in problem recognition is changed financial status. The infusion of additional financial resources from such sources as a salary increase, a second job, or an inheritance may permit the consumer to make purchases that previously had been postponed.

Search

The second step in the decision is to gather information related to the attainment of a desired state of affairs. This searching stage permits the identification of alternative means of problem solution.

The search may be internal or external. Internal search is a mental review of stored information relevant to the problem situation. This includes both actual experiences and observations and memories of personal communications and exposures to persuasive marketing efforts.

External search is the gathering of information from outside sources, which may include family members, friends and associates, store displays, sales representatives, brochures, and product-testing publications such as *Consumer Reports.* Recent research has shown that the influence of advertising on shopper behavior has been decreasing, while that of in-store displays is increasing. Inspired by the successful L'eggs display, many firms have shifted their emphasis to in-store displays.[45]

Many times consumers solve problems through internal search—that is, by relying on stored information in making a purchase decision. Achieving favorable results using a certain car polish may sufficiently motivate a consumer to repurchase this brand rather than consider possible alternatives. Since external search involves both time and effort, consumers will resort to it only when adequate information is unavailable in memory.

evoked set
Number of brands that a consumer actually considers before making a purchase decision.

Alternative brands for consideration and possible purchase are identified during the search process. The number of brands that a consumer actually considers in making a purchase decision is known as the **evoked set.** In some instances, the consumer is aware of the brands worthy of further consideration; in others, the external search process involves the acquisition of such information. The actual number of brands included in the evoked set will vary in accordance with both situational and individual factors.[46] For example, an immediate need might limit the evoked set, as would a lack of knowledge about a product category.

Evaluation of Alternatives

The third step in the consumer decision process is to evaluate the alternatives identified during the search process. Actually, it is difficult to completely separate the second and third steps, since some evaluation takes place simultaneously with the search process as consumers accept, discount, distort, or reject incoming information as they receive it.

evaluative criteria
Features considered in a consumer's choice of alternatives.

Since the outcome of the evaluation stage is the choice of a brand or product in the evoked set (or possibly the search for additional alternatives should all those identified during the search process prove unsatisfactory), the consumer must develop a set of evaluative criteria for use in making the selection. **Evaluative criteria** may be defined as those features the consumer considers in making a choice among alternatives. These criteria can be either objective (government tests of miles per gallon) or subjective (favorable image of Donna Karen clothing). As the advertisement in Figure 6.10 suggests, the evaluative criteria used in making a decision about the purchase of a Harley-Davidson motorcycle is based on pure emotion rather than on rationality.

Figure 6.10   Basing a Purchase Decision on Subjective Evaluative Criteria

Source: Courtesy of Harley-Davidson, Inc.

Commonly used evaluative criteria include price, brand name, and country of origin.[47] Table 6.2 classifies evaluative criteria used in picking a retailer or other service establishment by cost, value-added, and quality factors. Such criteria can change over time. Today many of the leading automobile models receive high ratings for quality, making it more difficult for manufacturers to use superior quality as a selling point. In the 1990s the evaluative criteria for choosing an automobile are quite different from those of previous decades; safety, rather than quality or fuel economy, is at the top of the list.[48]

Purchase Decision and Purchase Act

The end result of the search and alternative evaluation stages of the decision process is the actual purchase decision and the act of making the purchase. In this stage, the consumer has evaluated each alternative in the evoked set, utilizing his or her personal set of evaluative criteria, and narrowed the alternatives down to one.

Another decision facing the consumer is the purchase location. Consumers tend to make store choices by considering such factors as location, price, assortment, personnel, store image, physical design, and services. In addition, store selection is influenced by the product category. Some consumers choose

Table 6.2   Examples of Evaluative Criteria

Category	Cost Components	Examples of Value-added Components	Quality Components
Bank	Service charges; interest rates	Variety of services; easy to understand services	Financial stability; personal interest in customers
Coffee shop	Low prices; specials	Hours open; take-out items	Cleanliness; taste of food
Convenience store	Reasonable prices	Items easy to find; variety	Clean interior
Discount store	Sales/clearances; low prices	Easy return; check cashing	Selection; well-known brands; pleasant atmosphere
Family steak house	Low prices; coupons	Salad bar; things for kids	Taste of steak; atmosphere
Furniture store	Credit policies; low prices; price ranges	Delivery; display method	Well-known brands; knowledgeable salespeople
Gas station	Low prices	Windshield cleaning equipment; speed of pumps	No alcohol in gas; octane rating
Ice cream	Low cost; specials; coupons	Container size	Taste; richness; amount of flavor; creaminess
Jewelry store	Sales; low prices; low interest rates	Personal interest in customers; fast service	Unique jewelry; custom designing
Pizza restaurant	Specials; coupons; promotions; low prices	Fast service; home delivery; take out; variety	Hot product; taste; consistent product
Psychiatric hospital	Low cost treatment	Comfortable rooms; visitor accommodations	Experienced physicians; innovative treatment
Specialty tune-up clinic	Reasonable cost; specials	Car ready when promised; fast service	Fixed right the first time; qualified mechanics
Supermarket	Low prices	Well-stocked; check cashing	Clean; selection; specialty departments

Source: Adapted from Tyrus C. Ragland, "Consumers Define Cost, Value, and Quality," *Marketing News* (September 25, 1989), p. 20.

the convenience of in-home shopping via telephone or mail order rather than completing the transaction in a retail store.

Postpurchase Evaluation

The purchase act results in either satisfaction to the buyer and removal of the discrepancy between the existing and desired states or dissatisfaction with the purchase. Consumers are generally satisfied if their expectations are met.

It is also common for consumers to experience some post-purchase anxieties, called **cognitive dissonance.** This psychologically unpleasant state occurs when an imbalance exists among a person's cognitions (knowledge, beliefs, and attitudes). For example, consumers may experience dissonance after choosing a particular automobile over several alternative models when some of the rejected models have some desired features not available with the chosen one.

Dissonance is likely to increase (1) as the dollar value of the purchase increases, (2) when the rejected alternatives have desirable features not presented in the chosen alternative, and (3) when the decision is a major one. The consumer may attempt to reduce dissonance by looking for advertisements or other information supporting the chosen alternative or by seeking reassurance from acquaintances who are satisfied purchasers of the product. The individual may also avoid information favoring the unchosen alternative. The Toyota purchaser is likely to read Toyota advertisements and avoid Nissan and Subaru ads.

cognitive dissonance
Post-purchase anxiety that results when an imbalance exists among an individual's cognitions (knowledge, beliefs, and attitudes).

Figure 6.11   Reducing Cognitive Dissonance

Source: Courtesy of Chrysler Corporation.

Marketers can assist in reducing cognitive dissonance by providing informational support for the chosen alternative. Automobile dealers recognize "buyer's remorse" and often follow up purchases with a letter from the dealership owner offering personal handling of any customer problems and including a description of the product's quality and the availability of convenient, top-quality service. Advertisements that stress customer satisfaction also help reduce cognitive dissonance. For example, the Chrysler Corporation ad in Figure 6.11 is a powerful testimony that reinforces the decision of consumers who purchase cars equipped with air bags as a safety feature.

A final method of dealing with cognitive dissonance is to change options, thereby restoring the cognitive balance. In this instance, the consumer may ultimately decide that one of the rejected alternatives would have been the best choice and vow to purchase it in the future.

The importance of keeping customers satisfied is evidenced by the growth spurt in marketing research firms that specialize in measuring customer satisfaction. Recognizing that it is far less expensive to keep an existing customer than to gain a new one, businesses throughout the nation are turning to such firms to evaluate the effectiveness of their service to customers. Even the New York Stock Exchange went to an outside marketing research firm to determine how well it was satisfying its "customers," the chief financial officers of companies listed on the exchange.[49]

Classifying Consumer Problem-Solving Processes

The consumer decision process varies on the basis of the problem-solving effort required. There are three categories of problem-solving behavior: routinized response behavior, limited problem solving, and extended problem solving.[50] The classification of a particular purchase according to this framework clearly influences the consumer decision process.

Routinized Response Behavior.   Many purchases are made on the basis of a preferred brand or selection from a limited group of acceptable brands. This type of rapid consumer problem solving is referred to as routinized response behavior. The routine purchase of a regular brand of soft drinks is an example. The evaluative criteria are set and the available options identified. External search is limited in such cases.

Limited Problem Solving.   Consider the situation in which the consumer has set evaluative criteria but encounters a new unknown brand. The introduction of a new shampoo is an example of a limited problem-solving situation. The consumer knows the evaluative criteria but has not used them to assess the new brand. A moderate amount of time and external search is involved in such situations. Limited problem solving is affected by the number of evaluative criteria and brands, the extent of external search, and the process by which preferences are determined.

Extended Problem Solving.   Extended problem solving results from situations in which the brand is difficult to categorize or evaluate. This first step is to compare the item with similar ones. The consumer needs to understand the item before evaluating alternatives. Most extended problem-solving efforts are lengthy and involve considerable external search.

Regardless of the type of problem solving involved, the steps in the basic model of the consumer decision process remain valid. The problem-solving categories described here relate only to the time and effort devoted to each step of the process.

Summary of Chapter Objectives

1. **Explain the classification of behavioral influences on consumer decisions.** The behavioral influences in consumer decisions are classified as either personal or interpersonal. These categories resulted from the work of Kurt Lewin, who developed a general model of behavior that has been adapted to consumer behavior.

2. **Identify the interpersonal determinants of consumer behavior.** There are three interpersonal determinants of consumer behavior: cultural influences, social influences, and family influences. Culture, the broadest of these influences, refers to behavioral values that are created and inherited by a society. The work ethic and the desirability of accumulating wealth were the original determinants of American culture. Some cultural norms change over time while others endure.

   Cultural influences are particularly significant in international marketing, but they are also crucial factors in domestic marketing. Increased attention is being devoted to the consumption behavior patterns of the U.S. subcultures of blacks, Hispanics, and Asians, which are rapidly growing market segments.

Social influences concern the nonfamily group influences on consumer behavior. Some marketers take into consideration the social influences of the class system in the United States that was postulated by W. Lloyd Warner years ago. Opinion leaders, or trendsetters, are another important social influence on consumer behavior. Marketers must make special efforts to appeal to these flagships of consumer behavior.

Family influences are the third interpersonal determinant of consumer behavior. Family purchasing patterns vary. In some cases the female is dominant, in others the male, and in still others, decisions are made jointly or separately. The traditional role for the female was that of family purchasing agent, but this situation is now in flux. For example, more teenagers are doing the household's shopping.

3. **Identify the personal determinants of consumer behavior.** The personal determinants of consumer behavior are needs and motives, perceptions, attitudes, learning, and self-concept. A need is the lack of something useful. Motives are the inner states that direct individuals to satisfy needs. A. H. Maslow proposed a hierarchy of needs that starts with basic physiological needs and proceeds to progressively higher need levels—safety, social, esteem, and self-actualization.

Perception is the meaning that a person assigns to stimuli received through the five senses. Because most incoming stimuli are screened or filtered out, the marketer's task is to break through these perceptual screens in order to effectively present the sales message.

Attitudes are a person's evaluations and feelings toward an object or idea. There are three components of attitudes: cognitive (what the person knows), affective (what the person feels about something), and behavioral (how the person tends to act).

Learning refers to changes in behavior, immediate or expected, as a result of experience. The learning-theory concept can be useful in building consumer loyalty for a particular brand. The self-concept theory has other important implications for marketing strategy, such as in the case of targeting advertising messages to agree with the ideal self-image of various groups of people.

4. **Outline the steps in the consumer decision process.** The consumer decision process consists of six steps: problem or opportunity recognition, search, evaluation of alternatives, purchase decision, purchase act, and post-purchase evaluation. The time involved in each stage of the decision process is determined by the nature of individual purchases.

5. **Differentiate among routinized response behavior, limited problem solving, and extended problem solving.** Routinized response behavior, limited problem solving, and extended problem solving are the three categories of problem-solving behavior. Routinized response behavior refers to purchase situations based on selection of a preferred brand or from a group of acceptable brands. When the alternative criteria are set but a new brand is encountered, limited problem solving takes place. Extended problem solving occurs when a new brand is difficult to evaluate or categorize. Extended problem-solving efforts are lengthy and involve considerable external search.

Key Terms

consumer behavior	perceptual screen
culture	subliminal perception
subculture	attitudes
status	learning
roles	drive
Asch phenomenon	cue
reference group	reinforcement
opinion leader	self-concept
need	evoked set
motive	evaluative criteria
perception	cognitive dissonance

Review Questions

1. What are the two primary determinants? How are these determinants sub-classified?

2. What is culture? How does it affect buying patterns?

3. Identify the subcultures most important to marketers in the United States today. Describe the unique consumer behavior characteristics of each.

4. Explain the social influences on consumer behavior. Examine the specific roles of the Asch phenomenon, reference groups, social class, and opinion leaders.

5. For which of the following products is reference-group influence likely to be strong?
   a. Corona beer
   b. Skis
   c. Shaving lather
   d. Eighteen-speed mountain bike
   e. Health club membership
   f. Soft contact lenses

6. Outline Maslow's hierarchy of needs. Cite examples for each need level.

7. Explain the concept of perception. Consider perceptual screens, selective perception, and subliminal perception in your explanation.

8. How do attitudes influence consumer behavior? How can negative attitudes toward a product be changed?

9. Differentiate among the four components of the self-concept: ideal self, looking-glass self, self-image, and real self. Which is the most important to marketers?

10. List the steps in the consumer decision process. Relate a recent purchase you made to this process.

Discussion Questions

1. Global marketers are often reminded of the importance of business cards in Japan. Marketers should give their card to the highest ranking Japanese executive first. Also, upon receipt of the Japanese businessperson's card, Americans are advised to study the card carefully before putting it in their pocket.[51] Relate this business rite to the material in Chapter 6.

2. Some Betty Crocker ads suggest that baking a cake is an expression of love for a person's family.[52] What does this theme say about American core values?

3. Poll your friends about subliminal perception. How many believe that marketers can control consumers at a subconscious level? Report the results of this survey to your marketing class.

4. Americans currently drink about 1.75 cups of coffee per day. This figure is approximately half of what it was three decades ago. The decline is attributed to younger consumers' preferences for soft drinks.[53] What attitude component is reflected in this trend? How might the coffee industry change current consumption patterns?

5. Moviegoers tend to watch less television than the typical American. Therefore, they have less exposure to commercials. In order to reach this group, some companies run advertisements at the beginning of movies. Others hand out samples in movie lobbies.[54] Relate this information to the chapter's discussion of learning theory.

Computer Applications

Two important concepts discussed in connection with the consumer decision process are evoked set and evaluative criteria. An *evoked set* is defined in this chapter as the number of brands a consumer actually considers in his or her search behavior. *Evaluative criteria* are those features the consumer considers in selecting a specific purchase option. Both concepts are described in detail on pages 213–214.

Consumers develop various methods for making purchase choices from alternative products or brands. For major purchases and cases involving considerable risk, potential buyers may score or rank the brands that comprise their evoked sets on the basis of various evaluative criteria. Then the question becomes how to best make the actual purchase decision. Approaches to this problem include the following:[55]

1. *Overall scoring method.* This approach uses the highest total score to select a brand from the evoked set. All of the evaluative criteria are considered equally important, and the brand with the highest overall score is chosen.

2. *Weighted scoring method.* This approach involves assigning different weights to the various evaluative criteria according to the consumer's perception of their relative importance. Once the variables are assigned their weighted scores, they are totaled and the brand with the highest score is selected.

3. *Minimum-score method.* This approach sets a floor for one or more evaluative criteria below which a brand will not be selected. For example, if the consumer decides that a brand must receive a ranking of 4 or more on "service availability," a brand ranked 3 for this criterion will be rejected even if it receives the highest overall score. The minimum-score method is frequently used in conjunction with either the overall scoring method or the weighted scoring method.

It should be noted that these methods represent quantitative approaches to a typically qualitatively oriented subject. Not all consumers behave in such a fashion. Moreover, those who do may differ significantly in their scoring evaluations. The following problems refer to a specific consumer's perceptions of a purchasing situation in which he or she has already determined the evaluative criteria and the evoked set.

Directions: Use menu item 5 titled "Evaluation of Alternatives" to solve each of the following problems.

Problem 1.   Pam Zimmer of Cincinnati is attempting to select a new car based on the following criteria: price, trade-in allowance, styling, riding comfort, and fuel economy. Earlier Zimmer had narrowed her decision to four models: Elegance,

Standard, Speedo, and Majestic. She then decided to rate each model on each evaluative criterion, using 3 to represent "excellent," 2 for "good," and 1 for "fair." Her rankings are as follows:

Evoked-Set Alternatives	Evaluative Criteria: Decision Factors				
	(A) Price	(B) Trade-in Allowance	(C) Styling	(D) Riding Comfort	(E) Fuel Economy
1. Elegance	2	2	3	3	2
2. Standard	2	2	2	2	3
3. Speedo	3	3	3	3	1
4. Majestic	3	3	1	1	3

a. Which model would Zimmer select using the overall scoring method?

b. Suppose Zimmer decides that fuel economy, price, and trade-in allowance are each 50 percent more important than the other two evaluative criteria. Which model will she select?

c. Suppose that using the overall scoring method Zimmer also decides she will not accept any model that is rated lower than "good" on fuel economy, price, and trade-in allowance. Which model will she prefer?

d. Would Zimmer's decision in question c change if she decided to use the weighted scoring method?

Problem 2. Like Pam Zimmer in Problem 1, Tom Jenkins is contemplating the purchase of a new car. In fact, he and Zimmer conferred before assigning the ratings for the Elegance, Standard, Speedo, and Majestic. However, Jenkins also considers another auto model, the Olympic, a viable option. His rankings are as follows:

Evoked-Set Alternatives	Evaluative Criteria: Decision Factors				
	(A) Price	(B) Trade-in Allowance	(C) Styling	(D) Riding Comfort	(E) Fuel Economy
1. Elegance	2	2	3	3	2
2. Standard	2	2	2	2	3
3. Speedo	3	3	3	3	1
4. Majestic	3	3	1	1	3
5. Olympic	3	2	2	2	2

a. Which model would Jenkins select using the overall scoring method?

b. Suppose Jenkins considers riding comfort and fuel economy 100 percent more important than styling and price and trade-in allowance 200 percent more important than styling. Which model will he select?

c. Suppose that using the overall scoring method Jenkins also decides that he will not accept a car that is rated lower than "good" on any variable. Which model will he select?

d. Would Jenkins' decision in question c change if he used the weighted scoring method?

Problem 3. Edna Fram, of Morristown, New Jersey, is considering the purchase of a new refrigerator. Her evoked set consists of five brands: Best Fridge, Chillmaster, Super Fridge, Excellence, and Keep Fresher. Fram's evaluative criteria are price, energy efficiency, appearance, ice-making feature, and reversible doors. She decides to use a seven-point rating scale in making her assessment. Scores range from 1 (unacceptable or feature absent) to 7 (perfect). Fram's scores are as follows:

	Evaluative Criteria: Decision Factors				
Evoked-Set Alternatives	(A) Price	(B) Energy Efficiency	(C) Appearance	(D) Ice-Making Feature	(E) Reversible Doors
1. Best Fridge	4	5	5	7	1
2. Chillmaster	7	5	7	7	1
3. Super Fridge	2	2	7	7	7
4. Excellence	3	4	2	7	7
5. Keep Fresher	7	7	4	1	7

a. Which model would Fram select using the overall scoring method?

b. Suppose Fram considers price and energy efficiency 100 percent more important than the other criteria. Which model would she select if she assigned this weight to price and energy efficiency?

c. Suppose that using the overall scoring method Fram decides that an ice maker and reversible doors are absolutely essential. What model will she select?

d. Would Fram's decision in question c change if she used a weighted scoring method?

Problem 4.   A Sacramento, California, consumer is considering four brands of washing machines: Master Wash, Washer Magic, Washing Wonder, and Super Wash. She has decided to evaluate the brands on the bases of price, quality, warranty, and service availability. She has also decided to give each model a score of 1 (poor) to 5 (best) on each evaluative criterion. Her rankings are as follows:

	Evaluative Criteria: Decision Factors			
Evoked-Set Alternatives	(A) Price	(B) Quality	(C) Warranty	(D) Service Availability
1. Master Wash	4	3	4	4
2. Washer Magic	4	4	4	4
3. Washing Wonder	2	5	5	5
4. Super Wash	5	5	4	2

a. Which model would the consumer select using the overall scoring method?

b. Suppose the consumer considers price 50 percent more important than any of the other evaluative criteria. Which model will she select?

c. Suppose that using the overall scoring method the consumer also decides that she will not accept any model scoring lower than 3 on any variable. Which model will she select?

d. Would your response to question c change if the consumer used the weighted scoring method?

Problem 5.   Al Ogden, director of purchasing for Granite Industries of Nassau, New Hampshire, is a very orderly decision maker. When he was asked to purchase a snowblower, Ogden developed a 100-point scoring system to evaluate different models on the bases of price, ease of use, power, warranty, and ease of maintenance. The maximum score is 100. Ogden's evoked set consists of five brands: Snow Tosser, White Energy, Super Blower, The Remover, and Expert Blower. His scores are as follows:

Evoked-Set Alternatives	Evaluative Criteria: Decision Factors				
	(A) Price	**(B)** Ease of Use	**(C)** Power	**(D)** Warranty	**(E)** Ease of Maintenance
1. Snow Tosser	70	75	65	60	70
2. White Energy	95	45	75	99	100
3. Super Blower	45	85	85	100	100
4. The Remover	75	75	80	45	60
5. Expert Blower	99	50	55	70	60

a. Which model would Ogden select using the overall scoring method?

b. Suppose Ogden considers price and power 100 percent more important than the other criteria. Which model will he select if he assigns this weight to price and power?

c. Suppose that using the overall method Ogden decides he will not accept any snowblower that scores less than 50 on any evaluative criterion. Which brand will he select?

d. Would Ogden's decision in question c change if he used the weighted scoring method?

VIDEO CASE   6

Kawasaki Motors Corp.

Santa Ana, California–based Kawasaki Motors Corp., U.S.A., is a wholly owned subsidiary of Japan's Kawasaki Heavy Industries Ltd. and sells about $375 million worth of motorcycles annually in the United States. Kawasaki offers American consumers two types of motorcycles—sports models and custom models—each of which appeals to a different group of buyers.

Kawasaki asked its advertising agency, Kenyon & Eckhardt, to develop a print advertisement that would appeal to buyers of both sports and custom models without alienating either group. The firm needed an advertisement that would stand out from the 2400 ads that every American consumer is exposed to each week, and that would break through the clutter that characterizes contemporary U.S. advertising.

To accomplish these objectives, Peter Goodwin, the account supervisor for Kawasaki, asked Renee Fraser, a psychologist and the agency's research director, to gather information about motorcycle owners to find out why they buy what they do. The agency's creative people—artists and copywriters—needed this information to create an advertisement that satisfied the needs of motorcycle buyers. The advertisement had to influence the purchase decisions of new buyers and also reassure current owners that they had made the right choice. This latter goal is known as alleviating cognitive dissonance, the post-purchase doubt that accompanies any major purchase.

Fraser understood the importance of her task. She remarked, "To make persuasive advertising we have to really understand what motivates the consumer." Fraser began by checking some databases to learn about the people who buy motorcycles. This secondary research produced considerable demographic statistics such as income, age, and so forth. But Fraser realized that this information was useless because it did not tell her what really motivated people to buy motorcycles.

As a result, Fraser decided to gather some primary data by using focus groups, personal in-depth interviews, and field research. In speaking to motorcycle owners, Fraser learned that the motorcycle buying audience consists of a wide range of people from many social classes—blue collar workers, professionals (doctors, engineers, lawyers), even movie stars. Owners are much more diverse than the stereotypical motorcycle rider.

The motorcycle owners interviewed shared many common traits: cycling gave them a sense of power, a sense of being in control, and a feeling of independence and freedom (which are core values discussed in the interpersonal determinants section of Chapter 6). They liked being outside, feeling the wind on their faces, and enjoyed the thrill and speed of riding, being able to control the risk and dangers involved. Owning and riding a motorcycle was important in their self-concept and in satisfying esteem needs. One of the people that Fraser interviewed expressed the feeling this way: "I sort of feel like a pioneer. . . ." Fraser herself commented: "It was almost as if there was a relationship between them and the bike; it was their thing."

In later meetings with other Kenyon & Eckhardt personnel, Fraser noted that motorcycle riders ". . . want to demonstrate to other people what they really are . . . it's almost like they take off their clothes and they are Superman underneath." The research director continued: "One of the fantasies these men have about themselves on the bike is that they are the lone cowboy . . . they identify very strongly with that image of themselves."

The Kenyon & Eckhardt staff decided that motorcycle riders in general are not so much concerned with vehicle performance as with the way the motorcycle looks and the way it makes them look. The challenge was to come up with a print advertisement that would appeal to this image and break through the advertising clutter discussed earlier.

The agency's art department eventually designed a print advertisement showing a lone rider rounding a bend with the bike leaning to the side and the rider's knee almost touching the ground. The rider's position had been suggested several times by the people Fraser interviewed. The Kawasaki advertisement captures the thrill of riding—the wind, the speed, the danger. It depicts the self-image of cyclists, projecting a positive relationship between the product and the buyer. Both types of cyclists—those who ride sports bikes and those who ride custom models—can see themselves in this ad.

Questions

1.   Which categories of the personal and interpersonal determinants of consumer behavior influence a person's decision to purchase a motorcycle?

2.   Use this video case to explain the relationship between marketing research and the study of consumer behavior.

3.   Discuss how you would respond to the Kawasaki print ad.

7

Organizational Buying Behavior

CHAPTER OBJECTIVES

1. To list and define the components of the business market (organizational market).

2. To identify the major characteristics of organizational markets and industrial market demand.

3. To describe organizational buying behavior.

4. To classify organizational buying situations.

5. To explain the buying center concept.

6. To outline the steps in the organizational buying process.

7. To compare government markets with other organizational markets.

Institutional buyers were opposed to Robert Bennett's product when he presented it. Who would want to encourage a practice that leads to over 1,600 fires a year? Still, Bennett persevered and he is now the CEO of a $15 million company.

Just a few years ago, Bennett was a Boston-area computer salesperson who dreamed of running his own firm. Eventually, he spotted a niche that he could target—people living in small quarters serviced by marginal wiring. So Bennett set off to build MicroFridge, an 87-pound combined microwave, freezer, and refrigerator that could fit in a space just 43.5 by 18.5 by 20 inches. Bennett's target market was college dormitories.

As noted above, collegiate administrators refused to consider Bennett's idea. They did not want to get into the business of leasing such a unit. In addition to the fire danger and institutional policies against cooking in dormitory rooms, the administrators cited the electricity demands and limited number of outlets in a dorm room.

Bennett used his sales skills to his best advantage. He hired a research firm to survey Massachusetts college students. The study concluded that despite institutional rules against cooking in their rooms, some 90 percent of students regularly used hot plates and the like. When presented with the MicroFridge concept, the majority of students said they would pay extra to have a unit in their room. While these were both powerful selling points, Bennett still needed to counter the administrators' other arguments.

To do so, Bennett also developed a unique switch that could be plugged into a single outlet and never use more than 10 amps of power. MicroFridge is able to limit its electricity use because the freezer/refrigerator

shuts off when the microwave is in use. By contrast, Underwriters' Laboratory estimates that a refrigerator and hot plate can draw up to 35 amps from the required two outlets.

Objections began to disappear. Bennett got Sanyo to produce MicroFridge, and thousands of dorm rooms now feature it. Schools lease the units to students for about $150 per year or sell them for $389.

Bennett then turned to a second market—budget hotels without restaurant facilities. Again his potential market resisted. Purchasing MicroFridge units would be a major capital outlay. Some hotels also did not like the idea of stocking food. Bennett overcame the first objection by getting GE Credit to finance the leasing or purchase of the units. He countered the second objection with another survey, this one showing that guests would be willing to pay $3 more for a room equipped with MicroFridge. Bennett also pointed out the profit opportunities available from food sales. Today many Comfort Inns, Travelodges, Best Westerns, and Howard Johnsons offer MicroFridges to their guests.

MicroFridges are marketed by a national network of distributors, independent sales reps, and direct sales personnel. Bennett is also eyeing other markets. The military has given preliminary approval to the units. Overseas, the Saudi Arabian housing authority is attempting to negotiate a 40,000 unit deal, and several Canadian distributors have expressed an interest. Finally, although Bennett wants to concentrate on the business market, he is also experimenting with retail sales. Some Staples office supply stores now carry Microfridge.[1]

Photo source: © Brian Smith.

Chapter Overview

In Chapter 6, we saw how attitudes, perceptions, family and social influences, and other determinants affect consumer buying behavior. Understanding these determinants is important for firms involved in consumer marketing, that is, selling goods and services to individuals for personal use. A somewhat different set of determinants is involved when goods and services are sold to other organizations rather than individuals.

Some firms focus entirely on business markets. Federal Signal Corporation makes warning lights and sirens that are purchased by police departments. Manpower provides temporary personnel services to firms that need extra workers. Methode Electronics manufactures controls, connectors, and printed circuits that it sells to more than 1,000 firms in the aerospace, automotive, and other industries. These companies use Methode's components in the manufacture of their own products. Other firms sell to both consumer and organizational markets. In addition to serving the consumer market, First Interstate Bank sells international banking, cash management, and lending services to a variety of large and small corporations. Kraft sells cheese and dairy products to consumers and food service institutions such as restaurants. Kraft also sells edible oil, snack seasoning, flavoring, and other ingredients to other food manufacturers.

In this chapter, we will discuss buying behavior in the *organizational market,* also known as the *business market.* The organizational market can be divided into four major categories: the industrial market (also known as the producer or commercial market), trade or reseller industries (wholesalers and retailers), government markets, and institutional markets.

The Nature of the Business, or Organizational, Market

industrial market

Individuals and firms that acquire goods and services to be used, directly or indirectly, to produce other goods and services.

The **industrial market** is the largest component of the organizational market, consisting of all individuals and firms that acquire goods and services to be used, directly or indirectly, in producing other goods and services. Northwest Orient's purchase of the new, fuel-efficient Boeing 757 aircraft, a wheat purchase by General Mills for its cereals, and the purchase of light bulbs and cleaning materials for an Owen-Illinois manufacturing facility all represent industrial purchases. Some products aid in producing another good or service (the new airplane); others are physically used up in the production of a product (the wheat); and still others are routinely used in the firm's day-to-day operations (the maintenance items). The commercial market includes manufacturing firms; farmers and other resource industries; construction contractors; and providers of such services as transportation, public utilities, finance, insurance, and real estate.

trade industries

Retailers or wholesalers that purchase products for resale to others.

The second component of the organizational market is **trade industries,** such as retailers and wholesalers that purchase for resale to others. In most instances, such resale products as clothing, appliances, sports equipment, and automobile parts are finished goods that are marketed to consumers in the selling firm's market area. In other cases, some processing or repackaging may take place. For example, retail meat markets may make bulk purchases of sides of beef and convert them into individual cuts for their customers. Lumber dealers and carpet retailers may purchase in bulk and then provide quantities and sizes to meet customers' specifications. In addition to resale products, trade industries buy cash registers, computers, display equipment, and other products required for operating their businesses. These goods (as well as maintenance items) and specialized services such as marketing research studies, accounting services, and management consulting all represent organizational purchases. Detailed

Japan's Matsushita Electric Industrial Company, Ltd. is one of the world's largest industrial corporations. The company's factory-automated products, such as the intelligent robot shown here, are purchased by other firms to use in the production of their goods and services. Because increasing productivity is a major concern of business decision makers in the industrial market, the demand for Matsushita's factory-automated products is growing. Matsushita is also tapping the growth potential of automation in the institutional market by developing an automated catering system for hospitals.

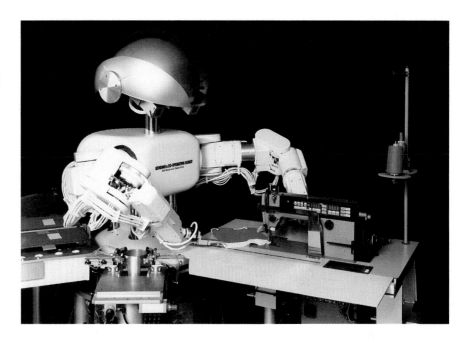

Source: Courtesy of Matsushita Electric.

discussions of the trade industries are presented in later chapters, wholesaling in Chapter 13, and retailing in Chapter 14.

Governments at the federal, state, and local levels represent the third category of organizational purchasers. This important component of the business market purchases a wide variety of products ranging from highways to F-16 fighter aircraft. The primary motivation of government purchasing is to provide some form of public benefit, such as national defense or public welfare.

Institutions, such as hospitals, universities, museums, and other nonprofit groups, comprise the fourth component of the organizational market. The purchasing behavior of the institutional sector is similar to that of the other components of the organizational market.

Differences in Foreign Business Markets

It should be noted that some industrial products must be modified for foreign markets. New Zealanders drive their trucks and industrial equipment on the left-hand side of the road. The electric wiring in many foreign companies differs from that in the United States. Australian business stationery is longer than the 11-inch U.S. equivalent. All of these circumstances could dictate product adaptation by U.S. manufacturers. However, on balance, the international marketing of industrial products is more similar than that for consumer products.[2]

Characteristics of the Organizational Market

The organizational market can be distinguished from the consumer market on the basis of three distinct characteristics: (1) geographic market concentration, (2) relatively small number of buyers, and (3) a unique classification system called *SIC codes.*

Table 7.1

State Rankings of Value
Added by Manufacturing

Ranking	State	Ranking	State
1	California	26	Maryland
2	New York	27	Kansas
3	Ohio	28	Colorado
4	Texas	29	Oregon
5	Illinois	30	Arizona
6	Michigan	31	Arkansas
7	Pennsylvania	32	Mississippi
8	North Carolina	33	Oklahoma
9	New Jersey	34	New Hampshire
10	Indiana	35	Nebraska
11	Massachussetts	36	West Virginia
12	Georgia	37	Maine
13	Wisconsin	38	Rhode Island
14	Florida	39	Utah
15	Virginia	40	Delaware
16	Tennessee	41	Idaho
17	Missouri	42	Vermont
18	Minnesota	43	New Mexico
19	Connecticut	44	South Dakota
20	South Carolina	45	Hawaii
21	Alabama	46	Montana
22	Kentucky	47	North Dakota
23	Washington	48	Nevada
24	Louisiana	49	Alaska
25	Iowa	50	Wyoming

Source: U.S. Bureau of the Census, *Statistical Abstract of the United States: 1990* (110th edition), Washington, D.C.

Geographic Market Concentration

The market for commercial items in the United States is more geographically concentrated than the consumer market. Table 7.1 ranks the states according to **value added by manufacturing,** the difference between the price charged for a manufactured good and the cost of the raw materials and other inputs. California is the state leader in value added, followed by New York, Ohio, Texas, and Illinois. On a regional basis, the East North Central sector (Ohio, Indiana, Illinois, Michigan, and Wisconsin), with 22.9 percent of the value added by manufacturing, is the biggest target market for business marketers. The next biggest industrial market is the South Atlantic area (Delaware, Maryland, District of Columbia, Virginia, West Virgina, North Carolina, South Carolina, Georgia, and Florida), with 15.5 percent of total value added. Close behind is the Middle Atlantic division (New York, New Jersey, and Pennsylvania) at 15.4 percent.

value added by manufacturing
Differences between the price charged for a manufactured product and the cost of the raw material and other inputs.

Limited Number of Buyers

In addition to geographic concentration, the industrial market is characterized by a limited number of buyers. Boeing has 54 percent of the world market for commercial airplanes.[3] Industrial purchasers at three companies—John Deere, Case-IH, and Ford—represent virtually all of the U.S. farm equipment output. The top three oil companies account for 55 percent of the ten leading gasoline brands' total volume.

The concentration of the business market—in terms both of the number of buyers and of geographic concentration—greatly influences the marketing strategies used in serving it. Some companies have set up a *national accounts* sales organization that deals solely with buyers at corporate headquarters. A separate field sales organization is then used to service buyers at regional production facilities. Wholesalers are used less frequently in the industrial field

Figure 7.1

Boston Digital's Replication of a Classic Statue

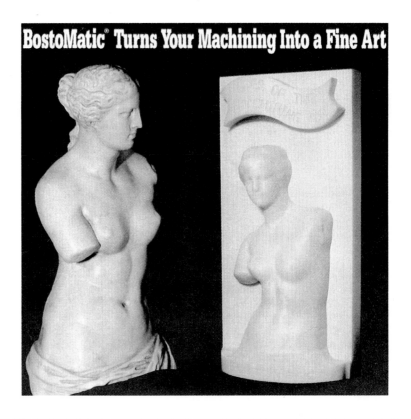

Source: Courtesy of Boston Digital Corporation

than in the consumer field, and the distribution channel for business goods is typically much shorter than for consumer goods. In addition, advertising plays a much smaller role in the business market. It is used primarily to enhance the image of the company and its products and to identify new prospects who are then contacted directly by the sales staff.

An ad that successfully generates leads does not necessarily result in significantly increased sales. For example, Boston Digital Corporation, a manufacturer of highly precise $75,000–$300,000 Computer Numerical Control machining systems, wanted to visually communicate its product's exceptional contouring capability. To do this, a cast model of the famous Venus de Milo statue was digitally mapped, creating a program that was used to machine a replica of the statue. The resulting ad, shown in Figure 7.1, produced a large number of leads, but unfortunately hardly any were legitimate prospects for the company's products. A typical respondent wanted a machine that cost about $2,500 to create novelty items. Capital equipment such as Boston Digital's product is marketed by an exceptionally complex personal selling process, with the time from initial contact to final sale typically requiring one to two years.[4]

Standard Industrial Classification (SIC) Codes

Marketers are aided in their efforts to reach the geographically concentrated and limited number of business buyers by a wealth of statistical information. The federal government is the largest single source of information. Every five years it conducts a Census of Manufacturers as well as a Census of Retailing and Wholesaling, which provide detailed information on industrial establishments,

Figure 7.2   Standard Industrial Classification System

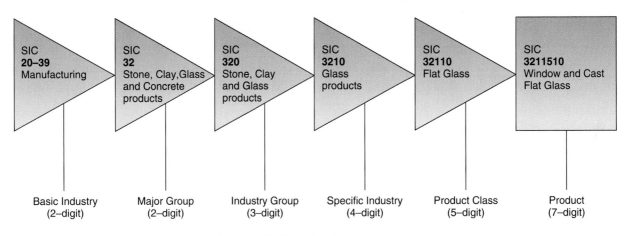

SIC 20–39 Manufacturing	SIC 32 Stone, Clay, Glass and Concrete products	SIC 320 Stone, Clay and Glass products	SIC 3210 Glass products	SIC 32110 Flat Glass	SIC 3211510 Window and Cast Flat Glass
Basic Industry (2–digit)	Major Group (2–digit)	Industry Group (3–digit)	Specific Industry (4–digit)	Product Class (5–digit)	Product (7–digit)

output, and employment. Specific industry studies are summarized in the annual *U.S. Industrial Outlook,* a government publication providing statistical data and discussing industry trends.

Trade associations and business publications provide additional information on the business market. Private firms such as Dun & Bradstreet publish detailed reports on individual firms. These data serve as useful starting points for analyzing business markets.

Standard Industrial Classification (SIC)

Government classification system that subdivides the industrial marketplace into detailed market segments.

The federal government's **Standard Industrial Classification (SIC)** system greatly simplifies the process of focusing on an industrial target market. This numbering system subdivides the industrial marketplace into detailed market segments. Its purpose is to standardize the collection and reporting of information on U.S. industrial activity. The code was revised in 1987 to reflect the many new industries that have developed in recent years. Additional SIC numbers were developed for the services, wholesaling, and manufacturing sectors. The SIC codes are divided into the following broad industry divisions: agriculture, forestry, fishing; mining, construction; manufacturing; transportation, communication, electric, gas, and sanitary services; wholesale trade; retail trade; finance, insurance, and real estate; services; public administration; and nonclassifiable establishments. Each major category within these classifications is assigned its own two-digit number; three- and four-digit numbers subdivide the industry into smaller segments. For example, a major group such as food and kindred goods is assigned SIC 20. A specific three-digit industry group such as meats is SIC 201. The next category, specific industries, would use the fourth digit; poultry slaughtering and processing, for example, is SIC 2015. Government operations and nonprofit organizations also have SIC numbers. For example, hospitals are SIC 8062.

In the Census of Manufacturers, the Bureau of the Census also assembles industrial data at two additional levels: five-digit product classes and seven-digit product or commodity categories. Figure 7.2 gives the seven-digit breakdown of the window and cast flat glass industry.

Using SIC Codes.   Since most published data on organizational markets utilize the SIC system, the SIC codes are invaluable tools in analyzing the business marketplace. The detailed information for each market segment provides the marketer with a comprehensive description of the activities of potential customers on both a geographic and specific-industry basis. For example, Dun & Bradstreet has worked on a new classification system called SIC 2+2 Enhancement, which would allow for more precise data at the eight-digit level.

Sales & Marketing Management magazine is another traditional data source. Until 1989 the magazine published an annual "Survey of Industrial & Commercial Buying Power" (SICBP). These reports included number and size of business establishments, employment, and shipments and receipts—all classified by four-digit SIC codes. Since 1989 Dun's has produced a similar volume that *Sales & Marketing Management* often reports and makes available upon request.

The following examples illustrate how marketers have used this type of data:

☐ A manufacturer of industrial metals used this information to get "a general feel for the size of a particular market" where it was suspected that penetration was limited. The data helped this manufacturer determine potential within certain target markets on a state-by-state basis.

☐ A major midwestern office-products manufacturer used these statistics to assign sales potential to targeted markets and to forecast demand for its manufacturing planning.

☐ The advertising manager of a business publication used these statistics to substantiate its coverage of certain industries, including the number of companies in those industries, the number of employees, and the dollar value of shipments/receipts.

☐ A consulting company found the data indispensable in setting up sales territories and quotas for an industrial client.[5]

Prioritizing Target Markets by SIC Data.   SIC data can also be used to prioritize target markets. *Sales & Marketing Management* recommends first calculating state location quotients (LQ). The formula is as follows:

$$\text{Location Quotient (LQ)} = \frac{X}{Y}$$

where

$$X = \frac{\text{Total manufacturing shipments in dollars (state)}}{\text{Total manufacturing shipments/receipts in dollars (state)}}$$

$$Y = \frac{\text{Total manufacturing shipments in dollars (U.S.)}}{\text{Total all shipments/receipts in dollars (U.S.)}}$$

If an LQ exceeds 1.0, manufacturers are producing a larger-than-average share of state output. This is the case in North Carolina, which has an LQ of 1.32. By contrast, Vermont, New Mexico, and Wyoming have LQs of less than 1.0.[6]

The use of location quotients allows business marketers to rank-order statewide markets. Figure 7.3 shows the rating of the 48 contiguous states on the basis of their location quotients. The top third are rated top prospects, the middle third middle prospects, and the bottom third poor prospects. A similar approach could be used to prioritize international markets.

Evaluating International Industrial Markets

Industrial purchasing patterns differ from one country to the next.[7] Researching these markets is a particular problem for business marketers. Secondary data is not available or reliable in many overseas markets.

Figure 7.3   Continental U.S. Divided by Location Quotients

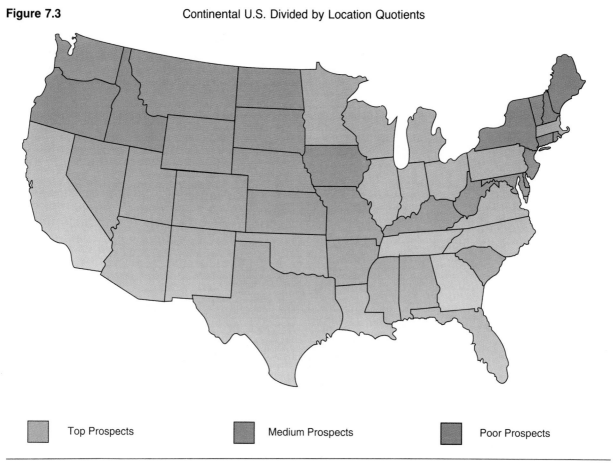

| | Top Prospects | | Medium Prospects | | Poor Prospects |

Source: Reprinted from Samuel Gilbert, "Who Your Customers Are: A Marketing Application," *Sales & Marketing Management* (June 1990), p. 136.

Still, a variety of information sources exist for international industrial markets. A few, like Dun & Bradstreet's *Principal International Businesses* and Predicast's *F&S Index,* even use SIC codes to classify data. Table 7.2 outlines the primary source of data in international business markets.

Characteristics of Industrial Market Demand

Considerable differences exist in the marketing of consumer and industrial products. The characteristics of the industrial market that create the need for such differences in marketing could be summarized as derived demand, joint demand, inventory adjustments, and demand variability (or volatile demand).

Derived Demand

derived demand
Demand for an industrial product that is linked to the demand for a consumer product.

The term **derived demand** refers to the linkage between the purchases of such needed items as machinery, component parts and materials, and raw materials by a business and the desires of customers for that business's output. For example, the demand for automated teller machines, an industrial product, is derived from customer demand for banking convenience. In recent years, purchases of ATMs by commercial banks have increased because more and more bank customers like the convenience of 24-hour banking by machine.

Table 7.2   Sources of Data on International Industrial Markets

Source	Regions/Areas Covered	Type of Data Provided
Business International	Eastern and Western Europe, Middle East, Latin America, Asia, Africa, Australia	Indicators of percent of growth over past 5 years, degree of concentrated purchasing power, measures of relative size of each national market as a percentage for its region
World of Information	Middle East, Africa, Asia, the Pacific, Latin America, the Caribbean	Annual surveys of general business environment in regions covered
Worldcasts	World, regions of the world, individual countries	Forecasts for 1-, 6-, 10-, and 15-year periods on commodities and industrial products
Global Market Surveys	Limited to top 20–30 best foreign markets	Detailed surveys for given industries such as graphics, computers, medical equipment, industrial equipment
Dun & Bradstreet's *Principal International Business*	135 countries of the world	Names, addresses, number of employees, products produced, and chief executive officer, up to 6 SIC classifications (4-digit) for each organization; over 144,000 business units classified by 4-digit SIC and alphabetical order
Dun & Bradstreet's *International Marketing Services*	133 countries of the world	Information similar to *Principal International Businesses* on over 500,000 businesses and subsidiaries
Moody's *International Manual*	5,000 major corporations in 100 countries	Company histories, descriptions of business, financial statistics, management personnel
Europe's 1500 Largest Companies	Europe	Companies by sales, profit, number of employees, country; classified by U.N. International SIC activity codes
Major Companies of Europe	Europe	Company names, addresses, telephone numbers, executives, principal products/activities, number of employees, sales size; classified by business activity codes 1 to 131
Predicasts's *F&S Index*	Worldwide	Company, product, and industry information from 750 publications; up to 7-digit SIC codes
Survey of Industrials	Canada	Company names, addresses, telephone numbers, product types, key personnel, sales size, and financial statistics
Overseas Business Reports	Worldwide	Monthly reports provide information for marketing to specific countries (e.g., "Marketing in Pakistan," "Marketing in Nigeria")
Foreign Economic Trends	Worldwide	Annual analyses of economic trends in specific countries, implications for U.S. companies
Business America	Worldwide	Published biweekly, provides statistics, success stories by U.S. firms, features on particular markets, trade show announcements

Source: Reprinted from Robert W. Hass, *Industrial Marketing Management* (Boston: PWS-Kent Publishing Company, 1989), p. 435.

Joint Demand

joint demand

Demand for an industrial product as related to the demand for another industrial product that is necessary for the use of the first item.

The <u>demand for some industrial goods</u> is related to the demand for other industrial goods to be used jointly with the former, a concept known as **joint demand.** For example, coke and iron ore are required for making pig iron. If the coke supply is reduced, there will be an immediate effect on the demand for iron ore.

Another example is the joint demand for aircraft and jet engines. The status of airplane orders at Boeing and McDonnell-Douglas can affect General Electric, United Technologies, Rolls-Royce, and other makers of jet engines. The General Electric advertisement in Figure 7.4 illustrates the concept of joint demand. The Soviet Union's Aeroflot, a global leader in air transportation, chose GE jet engines to power its new fleet of Airbus aircraft.

Figure 7.4   An Illustration of Joint Demand

Source: Courtesy of General Electric Company.

Inventory Adjustments

Changes in inventory policy can have an impact on business demand. Assume that a two-month supply of raw materials is considered the optimal inventory in a particular industry. Now suppose economic conditions or other factors dictate that this level be increased to a 90-day supply. The raw-materials supplier will then be bombarded with a tremendous increase in new orders.

A variety of factors can affect inventories. Consider the case of merchant shipping. Insurance and maintenance costs rise significantly after a vessel is 15 to 18 years old. Currently, approximately 65 percent of the world's fleet is at or nearing replacement. As a result, Lloyd's Maritime Information Services expects 20,000 ships to be built in the 1990s, as compared to only 6,000 in the previous decade.[8]

Just-In-Time Inventory Policies.   Just-in-time (JIT) inventory policies involve cutting inventories to an absolute minimum, and then requiring vendors to deliver the items as they are needed.[9] JIT has become a widespread practice, with a substantial impact on organizational purchasing behavior. One study reported that 80 percent of JIT buyers studied had cut the number of their suppliers.[10] In some cases, JIT leads to **sole sourcing** for some items—that is, the practice of buying an item from just one supplier.

sole sourcing

Using just one vendor in a purchasing situation.

Volatile Demand

Derived demand in the business market is linked to immense variability in industrial demand, or *volatile demand*. Assume the demand for a particular type of gasoline pump is derived from the consumer demand for a brand whose gallon volume has been growing at an annual rate of 5 percent. Now suppose that the demand for the gasoline brand has slowed to a 3 percent annual increase. Management might decide to delay its normal pump replacement program until market conditions are clarified. Therefore, even modest shifts in the demand for gasoline would greatly affect the pump manufacturer. This disproportionate impact that changes in consumer demand have on industrial market demand is called the *accelerator principle*.

Small Business's Role in Organizational Markets

While less than 1 percent of all small businesses regularly do business with large industrial firms, many organizational buyers seek out small vendors. It is estimated that 33 to 50 percent of large firms have specific programs for contacting small suppliers. There are a variety of reasons for this effort. One is the sheer complexity of many industrial products. For example, a Boeing 747-400 has 6 million parts, and it takes over 1,500 vendors to supply these items.[11] Another reason is that federal government suppliers are required to deal with specified numbers of small, minority, and female-owned businesses. For example, Northrup makes 53 percent of its purchases from firms defined as "small" by the Small Business Administration. In fact, Northrup's Aircraft Division maintains a Small/Socio-Economic Business Office to solicit small and disadvantaged vendors.[12]

The International Factor

Some small business procurement programs seek out overseas vendors. Ford is an example. In addition, some foreign firms seek out small U.S. suppliers. For instance, Nippon Telegraph & Telephone (NTT) regularly participates in U.S. procurement trade shows. The Japanese firm has even advertised in the *New York Times* for small suppliers. Some 20 percent of NTT's U.S. purchases are from small and medium vendors like GNB Industrial Battery of Langhorn, Pennsylvania, which sold 10,000 batteries to the Japanese firm.[13]

Basic Categories of Commercial Products

There are two general categories of commercial products: capital items and expense items. *Capital items* are long-lived business assets that must be depreciated over time. *Depreciation* is the accounting concept of charging a portion of a capital item as a deduction against the company's annual revenue for purposes of determining its net income. Examples of capital items include major installations such as new plants and office buildings as well as equipment.

Expense items, in contrast, are goods and services that are used within a short time period. For the most part, they are charged against income in the year of purchase. Examples of expense items include the supplies used in operating the business, ranging from paper clips to machine lubricants.

Chapter 9 presents a comprehensive classification of industrial products. The initial breakdown of capital and expense items is useful because buying behavior varies significantly depending on how a purchase is treated from an accounting viewpoint. Expense items may be bought routinely and with minimal delay, while capital items involve major fund commitments and are subject to considerable review by the purchaser's personnel.

The Make, Buy, or Lease Decision

Business buyers considering the acquisition of a new product have three basic options:

1. Make the purchase themselves.
2. Purchase it from another organization.
3. Lease it from another organization.

If the company has the capability for manufacturing the item itself, it may be desirable to do so. Considerable cost savings may be realized if the purchaser does not have to pay the manufacturing division all of the overhead or profit margin that would otherwise be charged to an outside buyer.

On the other hand, most organizational or industrial goods cannot be made internally. Therefore, purchasing them from an outside vendor is the most common choice. This option is discussed in the following section.

Leasing is a third possibility in many business marketing situations. Its popularity decreased as a result of the Tax Reform Act of 1986, which removed several tax-related advantages of purchasing.

Organizational Buying Behavior

Organizational buying behavior tends to be more complex than the consumer decision process described in Chapter 6. There are several reasons for this complexity:

1. Many persons may exert influence in business purchases, and considerable time may be spent in obtaining the input and approval of various organization members.
2. Organizational buying may be handled by committees, with greater time requirements due to the need for gaining majority or unanimous approval.
3. Some organizations attempt to utilize several sources of supply as a type of "insurance" against shortages. This policy is known as **multiple sourcing.**
4. Organizational buyers are influenced by both rational (cost, quality, delivery, reliability) and emotional (status, fear, recognition) needs not involved in individual consumer buying.

multiple sourcing
Using several vendors in a purchasing situation.

Most organizations have attempted to systematize their purchases by employing professional buyers—purchasing managers/buyers, or a buying committee (in the case of retailers and wholesalers). These technically qualified people are responsible for handling much of the organization's purchases and securing needed products at the best possible price. Unlike the ultimate consumer, who makes periodic purchase decisions, a firm's purchasing department devotes all its time and effort to determining needs, locating and evaluating alternative sources of supply, and making purchase decisions. Two of the tools purchasers use are value analysis and vendor analysis.

HEDGING BETS ON FUEL COSTS

. . . .

Jet fuel prices took off when the Persian Gulf crisis began in 1990, increasing by as much as 100 percent before falling to levels considerably higher than before the crisis. This created tough times for the airlines, which were already suffering from sluggish demand for travel. Many carriers cut back on passenger capacity and sold off major routes. But some concentrated on ways to make their fuel-purchasing operations more efficient.

Fuel is the airlines' second-highest expense after labor, so it should come as no surprise that airline managers are deeply interested in oil prices, which continue to fluctuate wildly.

United has carried that interest to an extreme. Its fuel-purchasing department operates around the clock, making deals in markets throughout the world. Whenever the price of oil shows signs of decreasing, United is ready to take advantage of any available opportunity. During periods when oil prices are low, it keeps inventories low. But when it foresees higher prices, it stocks up. United's storage tanks in Chicago and Denver and on the Gulf Coast can hold 3 million barrels of jet fuel, enough to keep its 400 jets flying for twenty days.

United's fuel-purchasing operations are among the most sophisticated in the industry. The airline makes use of a variety of creative financial strategies, such as an arrangement in which it buys heating oil contracts and exchanges them for delivery of jet fuel at some future date, thereby locking in a specific future price for jet fuel. Another tactic is known as fuel ferrying: Jets landing in states with low fuel taxes have their tanks filled with more fuel than they need to reach their next destination, enabling them to buy less in states where fuel is more expensive.

A variety of other techniques are used in efforts to control the price of fuel, including futures and options contracts, forward contracts, and commodity swaps. The basic thrust of these strategies is to minimize risk by hedging. Hedging does not reduce costs—hedgers often end up paying more when prices are low—but it does reduce risk when prices jump suddenly. More important, it allows managers to predict and manage costs better, possibly averting financial disaster later on.

Discussion Questions

1. A wrong guess about future fuel prices could be very expensive—for United, a penny a gallon more in fuel costs would mean $22.5 million in additional expense per year. Why, then, is United willing to take the risk?

2. Why does United's immense storage capacity give it an advantage over other airlines?

Sources: Dirk Beveridge, "High Fuel Costs Deal Airlines Serious Blow," *Arkansas Democrat* (October 25, 1990), pp. 1D, 8D; Doug Carroll, "United's Fuel Buyers Ride Currents," *USA Today* (September 17, 1990), pp. 1B, 2B; and "Some Fuel Users Hedge Against Price Run-Up," *The Wall Street Journal* (August 29, 1990), pp. B1, B5. *Photo source:* Courtesy of United Airlines.

Value Analysis

value analysis
Systematic study of the components of a purchase to determine the most cost-effective way to acquire the item.

Value analysis is an examination of each component of a purchase in an attempt to either delete the item or replace it with a more cost-effective substitute. For example, DuPont's Kevlar, a synthetic material, is now used in airplane construction because it weighs less than the product it replaced. The resulting fuel savings are significant for the buyers in this marketplace.

SELLING BUSINESS MACHINES TO WOMEN

Computer and copier ads used to portray women as sex objects or as targets of jokes. Take the ad that showed a pregnant woman and assured potential customers that "our optical readers can do anything your keypunch operator can do . . . well, almost."

Today, although sex remains a major theme in advertising, some makers of business machines have, somewhat belatedly, recognized that women constitute a large proportion of their customers. For example, a survey by Zenith Data Systems found that 65 percent of the people who said they were planning to buy a lightweight laptop computer were women.

Computer makers are now trying to attract women customers with more enlightened advertising messages. Examples: Zenith ads for laptop computers show a woman using the product; a TV ad for Apple's Macintosh shows a young professional woman deciding that she needs a computer; a Toshiba ad shows a woman directing a meeting in which the other participants are men. Computer companies are also buying more advertising space in women's magazines like *Working Woman* and *Redbook*.

This approach has its pitfalls, however. Men and women use computers in similar ways, making it difficult to develop distinctive advertising messages for the two sexes. Ads aimed at women also risk creating a backlash. One woman manager comments, "I probably would be turned off by a company that tried to market to me based on my sex."

Minolta's advertising seems to avoid these difficulties. After research showed that women constitute between 60 and 70 percent of its target audience, the company developed an advertising campaign featuring actress Pamela Bowen, who portrayed a productivity analyst demonstrating how Minolta equipment could solve mundane office problems such as time wasted waiting in line to use a copying machine. The advertising is informative, with a note of humor.

Ads like Minolta's point up the value of steering a middle course between the hazards of ignoring women, on the one hand, and pandering to them on the other. Above all, advertisers need to avoid making their gender-based pitches too obvious.

Discussion Questions

1. If men and women use computers in similar ways, what is the point of designing ads to appeal to members of one sex?

2. Can the recent advertising campaigns of makers of business machines be considered sexist even though they do not portray women as sex objects?

Sources: Mark Lewyn, "PC Makers, Palms Sweating, Try Talking to Women," *Business Week* (January 15, 1990), p. 48; and Alison Fahey, "Minolta Copier Line Aims Ads at Women," *Advertising Age* (May 5, 1989), p. 26.

J.I. Case Company, the Tenneco subsidiary that makes tractors, combines, backhoes, and other heavy equipment, relies extensively on value analysis. Al Mulvey, Case's vice-president for purchasing and administration, recalls a Japanese company that proposed a new transmission: "They said they could provide the electronics and save us thirty to forty percent. They're trying to provide us with more value down the road. Now, who would you want to do business with; a company that's causing you trouble, or one that's looking down the road?"[14]

Vendor Analysis

vendor analysis
Assessment of the supplier's performance in areas such as price, back orders, timely delivery, and attention to special requests.

Purchasing managers also use vendor analysis to evaluate potential suppliers. **Vendor analysis** is an ongoing evaluation of a supplier's performance in categories such as price, back orders, delivery times, and attention to special requests. A checklist set up along these lines helps purchasers determine the most effective supply source for a particular item. Figure 7.5 shows the vendor analysis form used by Chrysler.

Figure 7.5 Chrysler's Vendor Analysis Form

Supplier Rating Chart:

Supplier Name: _____   Commodity: _____
Shipping Location: _____   Annual Sales Dollars: _____

	5 Ex.	4 Good	3 Sat.	2 Fair	1 Poor	0 N/A
Quality 40%						
Supplier defect rates	___	___	___	___	___	___
SQA program conformance	___	___	___	___	___	___
Sample approval performance	___	___	___	___	___	___
Responsiveness to quality problems	___	___	___	___	___	___
Overall quality rating	___	___	___	___	___	___
Delivery 25%						
Avoidance of late or overshipments	___	___	___	___	___	___
Ability to expand production capacity	___	___	___	___	___	___
Engineering sample delivery performance	___	___	___	___	___	___
Response to fluctuating supply demands	___	___	___	___	___	___
Overall delivery rating	___	___	___	___	___	___
Price 25%						
Price competitiveness	___	___	___	___	___	___
Absorption of economic price increases	___	___	___	___	___	___
Submission of cost savings plans	___	___	___	___	___	___
Payment terms	___	___	___	___	___	___
Overall price rating	___	___	___	___	___	___
Technology 10%						
State-of-the-art component technology	___	___	___	___	___	___
Sharing research development capability	___	___	___	___	___	___
Capable and willing to provide circuit design services	___	___	___	___	___	___
Responsiveness to engineering problems	___	___	___	___	___	___
Overall technology rating	___	___	___	___	___	___

Buyer: _____   Date: _____

Comments: _____

Source: Chrysler Corporation; Michael D. Hutt and Thomas W. Speh, *Business Marketing Management* (Hinsdale, IL.: The Dryden Press, 1989), p. 95.

Consider the case of Okonite Company, a New Jersey–based insulated wire producer. Okonite has an in-house program that shows information on inventories, delivery dates, purchases by vendor, and other supply sources. Charles Romano, Okonite's director of purchasing, describes the firm's vendor analysis system this way: "If we've been buying from someone for any length of time, I'll be able to see how they've been performing, if they're delivering on time, and look at other sources of material and prices."[15]

Systems Integration

systems integration
Centralization of the procurement function within an internal division or external supplier.

One of the newest concepts in organizational purchasing is **systems integration,** or the centralization of the procurement function. Some firms have designated a lead division to handle all purchasing. For example, all of Boeing's airliner programs—the 747, 767, 757, and 737—handled their own purchasing needs. In the mid-1980s Boeing decided to centralize its purchasing into one division called the Material Division. Today this division buys $6 billion of goods and services each year from 3,500 suppliers. The material division now controls 40 percent of the cost of Boeing aircraft.[16]

An alternative approach to systems integration is to designate a major supplier, the systems integrator. This vendor is then responsible for dealing with all of the suppliers for a project and presenting the entire package to the buyer. Examples of system integrators include General Motors' Electronics Data Systems and the consulting division of Arthur Andersen, the CPA firm.[17]

Complexity of Organizational Purchases

Where major purchases are involved, negotiations may take several weeks or even months, and the buying decision may rest with a number of persons in the organization. The choice of a supplier for industrial drill presses, for example, may be made jointly by the purchasing agent and the company's production, engineering, and maintenance departments. Each of these principals may have a different point of view to be taken into account in making a purchase decision. As a result, sales representatives must be well versed in the technical aspects of the good or service and capable of interacting successfully with managers of the various departments involved in the purchase decision. In the chemicals industry, for instance, it takes an average of seven face-to-face presentations to make a sale. The UNISYS advertisement in Figure 7.6 suggests the various users that might be involved in the purchase of an information system.

Classifying Organizational Buying Situations

Organizational buying behavior is affected by situational variables involving the degree of effort exerted in making the purchase decision and the levels within the organization that are involved in the decision. There are three generally recognized organizational buying situations: straight rebuy, modified rebuy, and new-task buying.[18]

Straight Rebuy

straight rebuy
Recurring purchase decisions in which an item that has performed satisfactorily is purchased again by a customer.

A **straight rebuy** is a recurring purchase decision in which an item that has performed satisfactorily is purchased again by a customer. This organizational buying situation occurs when a purchaser is pleased with the good or service and with the terms of sale. The buyer therefore sees little reason to assess other options and so follows a routine buying format of repurchase. A straight rebuy is the business market equivalent of "routinized response behavior" in the consumer market.

Low-cost items such as paper clips and No. 2 pencils for an office are typical examples. If the purchaser is pleased with the products and their prices and terms, future purchases will probably be treated as a straight rebuy from the current vendor. Even expensive items specially designed for a customer's needs are treated as a straight rebuy in some cases. Harsco Corp.'s BMY Wheeled Vehicles Division in Marysville, Ohio, is currently fulfilling a Department of Defense contract for more than 16,000 military trucks. The M939A2 series was specially designed to operate in sand. Drivers can deflate the tires without

Figure 7.6   Advertising Suggesting the Complexity of an Organizational Purchase

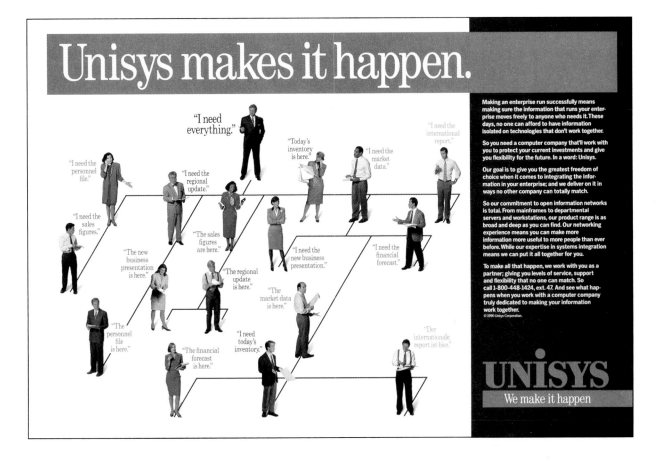

Source: Courtesy of UNISYS Corporation.

stopping. The tires can also be kept inflated even if they are punctured by gunfire.[19]

Marketers facing straight-rebuy situations should concentrate on maintaining a good relationship with the buyer by providing excellent service and delivery. Competitors will then find it difficult to present unique sales proposals that would break this chain of repurchases.

Modified Rebuy

modified rebuy
Situation in which purchasers are willing to reevaluate available options in a repurchase of the same good or service.

A **modified rebuy** is a situation in which purchasers are willing to reevaluate their available options. The appropriate decision makers feel that it may be to their advantage to look at alternative offerings using established purchasing guidelines. This might occur if a marketer allows a straight-rebuy situation to deteriorate because of poor service or delivery. Perceived quality and cost differences can also create a modified-rebuy situation. Modified rebuys are similar to "limited problem solving" in consumer markets.

Business marketers want to move purchasers into a straight-rebuy position by responding to all of their products and customer service needs. Competitors, on the other hand, try to move buyers into a modified-rebuy situation by raising issues that will make purchasers reconsider their decisions.

Figure 7.7   Example of New-Task Buying

We helped Dollar Dry Dock divide and conquer.

What do you call a bank that's everything you see here? Profitable.

Dollar Dry Dock had a new idea—to become a one-stop financial center. And that's where NYNEX® came in.

We gave them a digital network that makes their new identity possible. It hooks up over 1,000 terminals with instant information, so every teller can sell every product in the shop.

And with our 24-hour support, their one-stop center can go non-stop.

NYNEX would like to work with you, too. In

addition to the solutions our New York Telephone, NYNEX Business Information Systems and Telco Research Companies gave Dollar Dry Dock, we offer you the computer and tele-communications networks of New England Telephone, along with the software and services of the other NYNEX companies. Call us at 1 800 535-1535.

Once you've discovered the answer is NYNEX, you won't have to keep shopping around.

Need to communicate? Need to compute? The answer is

© 1990 NYNEX Corporation

Source: © NYNEX. Reprinted with permission.

New-Task Buying

New-task buying refers to first-time or unique purchase situations that require considerable effort on the decision makers' part. Alternative offerings and vendors are carefully considered in this situation. For example, a firm that enters a new field must seek suppliers of component parts that it did not purchase previously. Manufacturing firms moving into automated factory systems face the task of buying new equipment such as robots and computers. The advertisement in Figure 7.7 illustrates how Nynex provided a computer and telecommunication network that helped Dollar Dry Dock bank accomplish its new task of becoming a one-stop financial center. The consumer market equivalent of new-task buying is "extended problem solving."

Sometimes the buying situation shifts from one scenario to another. Consider the case of AT&T. For years it operated as a monopoly. The firm's purchasing policies reflected its protected environment. AT&T divisions were required to buy from other AT&T units where possible—essentially, a straight-rebuy situation. Today AT&T is no longer a monopoly. It competes with a variety of firms, such as MCI and Sprint. Its purchasing policies have also changed. AT&T buyers seek out the best deal regardless of the vendor—a new-task buying situation.

The Buying Center Concept

buying center
Participants in the organizational buying action.

The buying center concept is vital to the understanding of organizational buying behavior.[20] The **buying center** simply refers to everyone who is involved in some fashion in an organizational buying action. For example, a buying center may include the architect who designs a new research laboratory, the scientist who will use the facility, the purchasing manager who screens contractor proposals, the chief executive officer who makes the final decision, and the vice-president for research who signs the formal contracts for the project. Buying center participants seek to satisfy personal needs such as participation or status needs, as well as organizational needs in any purchase situation.

Buying centers are not part of the firm's formal organizational structure. They are informal groups whose composition varies among purchase situations and firms. Domestic buying centers typically include anywhere from 4 to 20 participants. They tend to evolve as the purchasing process moves through its various stages.

Buying Center Roles

Buying center participants play different roles in the purchasing process, as follows:

- *Users* are the people who will actually use the purchased good or service. Their influence on the purchase decision may range from negligible to extremely important. Users sometimes initiate the purchase action by requesting the product, and they may also help develop product specifications.

- *Gatekeepers* control the information to be reviewed by buying center members. Their information control may be in terms of distributing printed information or advertisements or deciding which salespeople will speak to which individuals in the buying center. For example, a purchasing agent might allow some salespeople to see the engineers responsible for developing specifications, but not allow others the same privilege.

- *Influencers* affect the buying decision by supplying information for the evaluation of alternatives or by setting buying specifications. Influencers are typically technical personnel such as engineers, quality control specialists, and research and development staff. Sometimes a buying organization hires outside consultants, such as engineers and architects, who influence the buying decision.

- *Deciders* actually make the buying decision, although another person may have the formal authority to do so. The identity of the decider is the most difficult role to determine: For example, a firm's buyer may have the formal authority to buy, but the firm's CEO may actually make the buying decision. A decider could be a design engineer who develops specifications that only one vendor can meet.

- *Buyers* have the formal authority to select a supplier and implement the procedures for securing the good or service. The buyer's power is often usurped by more influential members of the organization. The buyer's role is assumed often by the purchasing agent, who executes the administrative functions associated with a purchase order.[21]

The critical task for the organizational marketer is to determine the specific role and the relative buying influence of each buying center participant. Sales presentations and information can then be tailored to the precise role that the individual plays at each step of the purchase process. Business marketers also have found that while their initial—and, in many cases, most extensive—contacts are all with the purchasing department, the buying-center participants having the greatest influence often are not in that department at all.

An Illustration of How Buying Centers Work

LeCroy Corp. of Chestnut Ridge, New York, is a small electronic testing equipment company. LeCroy's traditional market was universities and research labs. Its 46-person salesforce had technical backgrounds suitable for calling on these research-oriented customers. LeCroy's president, Michael Bedesem, described the buying situation this way: "Our salespeople were used to visiting 'Herr Professor' or 'Herr Doktor' at the lab. They would talk to them about the instruments and projects and when it came time, the customers would buy from us."

While LeCroy was successful, management began to realize that its market was stagnating. As a result, LeCroy decided to enter the commercial market with $10,000 to $25,000 oscilloscopes that measure electronic waves. LeCroy was largely unknown in the new market, so it began to advertise in trade magazines and employ direct-mail promotions.

The biggest problem facing LeCroy was reorienting its salesforce to a new buying center. The sales organization had to be retrained to the faster-paced, more aggressive industrial marketplace. Alan Michalowski, LeCroy's sales vice-president, outlined the new buying center: "Their target was still the engineer, but they had to be aware of the purchasing agent and project supervisor, too. These people may not use the product, but they can slow down or stop the buying process."

LeCroy made this shift successfully. The firm established credibility by offering one-day and on-site service. As a result, sales nearly tripled in the four-year period after the oscilloscopes were introduced.[22]

International Buying Centers

Two distinct characteristics differentiate international buying centers from domestic ones. First, members of foreign buying centers are difficult to identify. In addition to the cultural differences in decision making, some foreign companies lack staff personnel. For example, in less developed countries, line managers may make most of the purchase decisions.

The second distinction is that the buying centers of a foreign company may be larger than U.S. versions. International buying centers can range from 1 to 50 people, with 15 to 20 participants being commonplace. This greater diversity must be considered by international marketers.[23]

Model of the Organizational Buying Process

The exact procedures used in buying industrial goods and services vary according to the buying situation confronted: straight rebuy, modified rebuy, or new-task buying. However, all industrial purchases follow the same general process, one that Herbert Brown and Roger Brucker have suggested can be viewed as the buying stream outlined in Figure 7.8. While this model was developed for an industrial purchasing situation, it has general application to any organizational buying process. The model's similarities to the individual consumer's decision process are also striking.

Figure 7.8   The Industrial Buying Stream

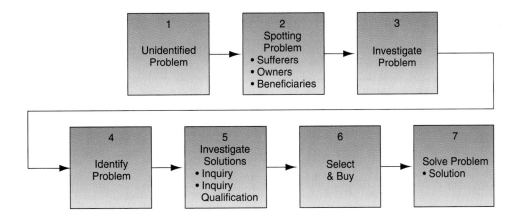

Source: Reprinted from Herbert E. Brown and Roger W. Brucker, "Charting the Industrial Buying Stream," *Industrial Marketing Management* (February 1990), p. 57.

Dissecting the Brown-Brucker Model

Approximately half of all industrial purchases are in response to specific problems. Therefore, the Brown-Brucker model considers the problem as the starting point in the industrial buying stream.

Brown and Brucker suggest that most problems are identified by problem sufferers, owners, or beneficiaries. A *sufferer* is someone like a sales manager who misses quota because of customer concerns about product quality. An example of a *problem owner* is a technical person assigned to fix the quality problem. A *beneficiary* is someone who benefits from the identification and correction of the problem. A salesperson striving for an annual bonus could be a beneficiary of an improved quality program.

The problem is then investigated and identified, and solutions are developed. Finally, a purchase decision is made by the buying center, and the initial problem is resolved.

Linking the Brown-Brucker Model to Organizational Buying Situations

Brown and Brucker view organizational buying as a stream of problem-solving adventures. They link their model to the standard organizational buying situation as follows:

It can be taken as given that a "new task" buy solves a problem, but it cannot be assumed that subsequent repurchases of a . . . [good] . . . or service are solving the same problem or are, in truth, either "modified" or "straight rebuys." One can see, in fact, that these latter categories are not even different kinds of buys. Instead, they are actually timing stages in a buy that continues successfully to solve a problem that would recur if buying stopped. Thus, a modified rebuy is actually one in which the "problem" that produced the original "new task" buy is modified, such as in response to a company cost-cutting campaign, poor performance of the original supplier, or redefinition of the problem or solution upstream. Similarly, the straight rebuy is an ongoing response to a "new task" problem solution that is perceived to be satisfactory and thus "unmodified".[24]

Reciprocity

A controversial practice in a number of organizational buying situations is **reciprocity**—the extension of purchasing preference to suppliers that are also customers. For example, an office equipment manufacturer may favor a particular supplier of component parts if the supplier has recently made a major purchase of the manufacturer's products. Reciprocal arrangements traditionally have been used in industries with homogeneous products with similar prices, such as the chemical, paint, petroleum, rubber, and steel industries.

Reverse reciprocity is the practice of extending supply privileges to firms that provide needed supplies. In times of shortages, reverse reciprocity occasionally emerges as firms attempt to obtain raw materials and parts with which to continue operations.

The practice of reciprocity suggests the close links among the various elements of the organizational marketplace. Although some reciprocal agreements still exist, both the Justice Department and the Federal Trade Commission view them as attempts to reduce competition. This view is not shared in many foreign markets. In Canada, for instance, reciprocity is viewed as both favorable and widespread by industrial buyers. In contrast to the U.S. legal position, the Canadian Combines Investigation Act has rarely been used.[25]

Government Markets

Government at all levels is a sizable segment of the business market. In addition to the federal government, with its 3.1 million civilian employees, the states employ another 3.5 million people, and the nation's 83,116 local governments another 8.6 million people.[26] Total spending for goods and services by all three levels of government—federal, state, and local—is in the trillions of dollars. The federal government alone buys 778 million paper clips a year, at a total price of $1.2 million. It also spends $500 million on automobiles, $105 million on athletic and recreational equipment, and $741 million on carpeting, which is enough to carpet everything inside the inner loop of Washington's Capital Beltway.[27]

Foreign governments are another business market. In some cases, governments dominate international trade. For example, 80 percent of all agricultural trade is done through government agencies.[28] The U.S. grain deals with the Soviet Union illustrate this type of agreement. Similarly, the Civil Aviation Administration of the People's Republic of China orders aircraft for Air China, Guangzhan CAAC, China Southwest Airlines, and other Chinese airlines.[29]

Construction and other infrastructure sales also typically involve the government in foreign markets. Examples would include airport and highway construction, telephone systems, and even equipment like mainframe computers. Arms sales are still another example of this aspect of business marketing.

Sales for foreign governments involve an array of regulations. For example, many governments, like the United States, limit foreign entry into the defense sector. Joint ventures and countertrade are also common, as are local content laws, which mandate that a certain percentage of an industrial product must be manufactured locally.

Selling to the Federal Government

By law, most government purchases must be made on the basis of **bids,** or written sales proposals, from vendors. As a result, government buyers develop **specifications**—detailed descriptions of needed items—for prospective bid-

June Collier (right) is president of National Apparel, a firm that supplies the federal government with chemical warfare suits. National Apparel is one of only four U.S. firms approved as a federal procurement source for chemsuits. The camouflaged clothing must meet exacting specifications to neutralize mustard-gas and nerve-gas agents from chemical warfare weapons. The Defense Department agency that buys National Apparel's products is the Defense Personnel Supply Support Center in Philadelphia. The agency's purchase of food, clothing, and medical supplies average about $3.5 billion a year.

Source: © Mike Clemmer.

ders. Some of these specifications are highly complicated. For example, the government specifications for athletic supporters runs 22 pages. The Defense Department offers 18 pages of specifications for the fruitcakes it buys. Federal purchases must comply with the Federal Acquisition Regulation (FAR), a 30,000-page set of standards originally designed to cut red tape in government purchasing. This effort has been thwarted by the issuance of the numerous exceptions outlined by various government agencies.[30]

The General Services Administration (GSA), through its Office of Federal Supply Service, buys many goods and services for use by other agencies. For example, it has contracted lodging with 12,000 hotels and motels nationwide. However, the GSA has delegated buying authority to a large number of other federal agencies. As a result, the federal government issued 22 million contracts in a recent year. Some 150,000 government procurement personnel and 5,000 contracting offices were involved.[31]

Another example of the government's attempts to introduce flexibility in its purchasing policies is the increased use of off-the-shelf buying. Consider the case of Wesley Bennefield, the manager of the Hindsville, Georgia, K Mart. When soldiers at nearby Fort Benning were deployed to Saudia Arabia in 1990, the Army ordered 5,550 bottles of suntan lotion and a similar number of bottles of skin lotion and cans of foot powder, along with 2,400 bottles of lip balm and 174,000 gallons of bottled water. Bennefield filled the off-the-shelf orders at no profit despite the fact that his K Mart does not carry bottled water.[32]

Business marketers confused by the government's purchasing maze should contact the GSA's Business Service Center for the latest information. In addition to its Washington office, Business Service Centers can be found in Chicago, Boston, New York, Philadelphia, Atlanta, Kansas City, Fort Worth, Denver, San Francisco, Los Angeles, and Seattle.

In addition to the information provided by GSA's Business Service Center, marketers should review the Commerce Department's *Commerce Business Daily,* a six-day-a-week listing of planned procurements, contract awards, and sales of surplus property. All planned purchases of $10,000 or more will appear in this listing. Business marketers have a minimum of 30 days before bids are opened.[33]

Problems and Opportunities.   Despite its immense size, the government market is often viewed as unprofitable by many suppliers. For example, the GSA once was unable to find three bidders for some $50,000 in purchases of facial tissues, filing cabinets, garbage cans, and table napkins. A survey conducted by *Sales & Marketing Management* reported that business marketers have registered a variety of complaints about government purchasing procedures. These include excessive paperwork, bureaucracy, needless regulations, emphasis on low bid prices, decision-making delays, frequent shifts in procurement personnel, and excessive policy changes.[34] Consider the case of the nation's largest shotgun shell manufacturer. The firm produces only 60 rounds a minute of military ammunition because of Defense Department requirements that mandate the use of a dozen outdated machines, each run by a separate employee and backed up by a 24-machine quality control system. By contrast, the firm can produce 240 commercial rounds per minute because one person operates three machines.[35]

On the other hand, marketers generally credit the government for being a relatively stable market. Once the government purchases an item, the probability of additional sales is good. Other marketers cite such advantages as the instant credibility established by contracts with the federal government, timely payment, excise tax and sales tax exemptions, acceptance of new ideas, and reduced competition. For example, the U.S. Postal Service spent two years and $700,000 on a study to develop the perfect stamp glue—one that could handle both humidity and high-speed sorting equipment. The Postal Service then sought a manufacturer to make the glue it developed.[36]

Selling to State and Local Governments

State and local purchasing is very similar to the federal situation. Most states—and many large cities—have created buying offices similar to the GSA. Specifications and open bidding are common at this level also. A unique feature of many state purchasing regulations is that preference is given to in-state vendors. For example, the state of Ohio allows a 5 percent preference to in-state bidders. The 5 percent preference is used to reduce the price upon which the in-state bidder is evaluated.

Summary of Chapter Objectives

1. **List and define the components of the business market (organizational market).** The organizational, or business, market is divided into four segments: the industrial (producer, commercial) market; trade industries, including wholesalers and retailers; governments; and institutions. The industrial market consists of individuals and firms that acquire products to be used, directly or indirectly, to produce other goods and services. Trade industries are organizations, such as retailers and wholesalers, that purchase for resale to others. The primary purpose of government purchasing at the federal, state, and local levels is to provide some form of public

benefit. The purchasing behavior of institutions, such as hospitals, universities, museums, and other nonprofit groups, is similar to that of the other components.

2. **Identify the major characteristics of organizational markets and industrial market demand.** The major characteristics of the industrial market are geographic market concentration, a relatively small number of buyers, and a classification system of SIC codes. Analysis of value-added-by-manufacturing data shows that over half of the industrial market is concentrated in just three census divisions. The limited number of buyers in the marketplace is illustrated by such industries as commercial aircraft, farm equipment, and oil. The Standard Industrial Classification (SIC) code system is the government's system of subdividing the organizational market place into more detailed industries or market segments.

   Industrial market demand is characterized by derived demand, joint demand, inventory adjustments, and volatile (or variable) demand. Derived demand means that the demand for industrial offerings is linked to the demand for consumer goods and services. Joint demand refers to the relationship of the demand for some industrial products to the demand for other industrial products that are used jointly with the first item. Changes in inventory policy also can have a significant effect on industrial demand. All these factors influence the nature and extent of industrial market demand.

3. **Describe organizational buying behavior.** Organizational buying behavior tends to be more complex than individual consumer behavior. More people and time are involved, and buyers often seek several alternative supply sources. The systematic nature of organizational buying is reflected in the use of purchasing managers for directing such efforts. Major organizational purchases may require an elaborate and lengthy decision-making process involving many people. Purchase decisions typically depend on a combination of such factors as price, service, certainty of supply, and product efficiency.

4. **Classify organizational buying situations.** Organizational buying situations differ. A straight rebuy is a recurring purchase decision in which an item that has performed satisfactorily is purchased again by a customer. A modified rebuy is a situation in which purchasers are willing to reevaluate their available options. New-task buying refers to first-time or unique purchase situations that require considerable effort on the part of the decision maker.

5. **Explain the buying center concept.** The buying center concept refers to everyone who is involved in some fashion in an organizational buying action. There are five buying center roles: users, gatekeepers, influencers, deciders, and buyers.

6. **Outline the steps in the organizational buying process.** The actual process of buying an industrial good or service consists of problem recognition, problem investigation, problem identification, investigation of solutions, buying decisions, and problem solution. A controversial practice that comes into play for some organizational purchasing situations is reciprocity, in which purchasing preference is given to suppliers that are also customers.

7. **Compare government markets with other organizational markets.** The government is a sizable organizational market that exhibits both similarities to and differences from other organizational markets. The government seeks to buy many of the same goods and services—for example, office equipment—but unlike other organizational markets, the government has numerous special regulations governing its purchasing behavior.

Key Terms

industrial market	vendor analysis
trade industries	systems integration
value added by manufacturing	straight rebuy
Standard Industrial Classification (SIC)	modified rebuy
derived demand	new-task buying
joint demand	buying center
sole sourcing	reciprocity
multiple sourcing	bids
value analysis	specifications

Review Questions

1. Outline the four components of the organizational market. Cite examples of each.

2. What are the characteristics of the industrial market? Show how each affects the marketing strategy used by firms serving it.

3. What are SIC codes? How are they used by organizational marketers?

4. Contrast organizational buying behavior and consumer purchasing behavior. What are the primary differences and similarities?

5. Distinguish between value analysis and vendor analysis. How do these concepts apply to industrial purchasing situations?

6. Give examples of how derived demand, joint demand, inventory adjustments, and the accelerator principle can affect industrial market demand.

7. Identify two different types of organizational buying situations. Give two examples of each.

8. Describe the roles involved in the buying-center concept. Identify the person in an organization who would most likely play each role.

9. In what ways is the government market similar to other organizational markets? How does it differ?

10. How does the extensive use of bids in government purchasing affect the marketing strategies employed in this market?

Discussion Questions

1. Comment on the following statement: "There is really no need to separate the study of organizational buying behavior and consumer buying behavior."

2. Explain in detail how an industrial marketer would use SIC codes.

3. Choose an industrial product, then analyze the foreign market potential for this item. Report your findings to the class.

4. Investigate the qualifications needed for being a purchasing manager in an industry located in your area. Discuss these qualifications in class. What generalizations can be reached from this discussion?

5. Identify the recent developments affecting the government market. How should business marketers deal with these developments?

Computer Applications

Because many organizational purchasers make buying decisions on the basis of competitive bids from alternative suppliers, determining the most appropriate bid is an important assignment for industrial marketers. One method of quantifying this task is to use the concept of *expected net profit (ENP)*. The formula for calculating ENP is as follows:

$$\text{Expected Net Profit} = P(\text{Bid} - \text{Costs})$$

where

P = probability of buyer accepting the bid

bid = bid price of product or project

costs = estimated total costs of product or project

Consider the following example. A firm is contemplating submission of a bid for a job that is estimated to cost $23,000. One executive has proposed a bid of $60,000 and another a bid of $50,000. Although it is impossible to determine the buyer's reactions to either bid, the firm's marketing director estimates a 40 percent chance of the buyer accepting bid 1 ($60,000) and a 60 percent chance of accepting bid 2 ($50,000). The two bids can be evaluated as follows:

- **Bid 1:**   ENP = .40($60,000 − $23,000)
  = .40($37,000)
  = $14,800.

- **Bid 2:**   ENP = .60($50,000 − $23,000)
  = .60($27,000)
  = $16,200.

The expected net profit formula indicates that bid 2 is better, since its expected net profit is $1,400 higher than that of bid 1.

The most difficult task in applying the ENP concept is estimating the probability that a certain bid will be accepted. However, this is not a valid reason for failing to quantify an estimate. Experience can provide the foundation for such estimates. The calculation of ENP is particularly useful in permitting organizational marketers to compare alternative competitive strategies. It is especially helpful in industries in which marketers must prepare and submit hundreds of bids as a regular component of their marketing programs.

Directions: Use menu item 6 titled "Competitive Bidding" to solve each of the following problems.

Problem 1.   Garden State Industries of Trenton, New Jersey, has developed a new industrial scrubber. Its marketing executives are actively working on a large sale to the leading firm in their target market, one whose purchase decisions are frequently imitated by other firms in the industry. One of Garden State's executives has proposed a price of $76,000 per unit, and another has suggested $85,000. Total costs of the scrubber average $50,000 per unit. Garden State's marketing research department has assigned a 58 percent probability of the buyer accepting the lower price and a 42 percent probability of purchase at the higher price. Use the ENP formula to recommend a bid price for the scrubber.

Problem 2.   Terp Industries of Baltimore has been supplying Columbus Manufacturing with a certain rivet for years. Columbus treats these purchases as what is referred to in this chapter as a *straight rebuy*. Terp's price of $350 per 1,000 rivets has remained unchanged for the past three years. But the cost of producing the rivet recently has risen from $275 to $300 per 1,000. Terp would like to pass the $25 cost increase along to Columbus Manufacturing in the form of a price increase. However, its marketing director expects that a 20 percent chance exists that Columbus would turn to a different supplier. At $350 per 1,000, the director is completely confident that Columbus will continue to be a Terp Industries customer. What would Terp's management do in this case?

Problem 3. Joe Bakens, director of marketing at HBC Corporation based in Cicero, Illinois, is considering offering a large industrial product to a local buyer at one of two possible prices: alternative A, $25,000, and alternative B, $30,000. Baken's total costs involved in producing the item amount to $15,000. Bakens believes that the likelihood of the customer accepting alternative A is 60 percent and of accepting alternative B, 40 percent. Use the ENP formula to recommend a course of action for HBC Corporation.

Problem 4. Hal Weissman is a sales representative for The Copy Store, an office equipment distributor in Portland, Oregon. Weissman currently is attempting to sell a small, low-volume copier to a local contractor. He believes that his best approach is to prepare a single proposal with a reasonable price. The firm's copier is available in two models: model A, which costs The Copy Store $1,200, and the slightly faster model B, which costs $1,300. Weissman's manager has given him authority to negotiate any price above $1,400 for model A and $1,500 for model B. Weissman has assigned an estimated probability of closing the sale at each of several alternative prices, shown in the accompanying table. Which model and price should Weissman propose to the contractor?

Alternative Prices	Probability of Sale
$1,500 for model A	30%
$1,500 for model B	35
$1,750 for model A	15
$1,750 for model B	25
$1,850 for model A	5
$1,850 for model B	15

Problem 5. A Georgia-based defense contractor has developed a new generation of fighter aircraft. The firm's marketing executives are in the process of completing the proposal and are discussing the price tag they should attach to each plane. Should the U.S. Department of Defense elect to purchase the fighter, the order would amount to 400 aircraft. Total costs in developing and producing the fighters are $8 billion. Management is considering two prices for the fighter: $25 million and $28 million. The executive board thinks the probability of the Pentagon accepting the first price is 60 percent and of it accepting the higher price is 40 percent. Use the ENP formula to determine which price the defense contractor should select.

. . . .

Skyfox Corp.

A first-time visitor to the annual Paris Air Show would be amazed at the capabilities and technical sophistication of the military aircraft on exhibit. Government buyers and military officers from all over the world view the latest aircraft, listen to company sales representatives, and make purchase decisions. A General Dynamics representative points out that the 32-foot-long F-16 Fighting Falcon can fly at twice the speed of sound at a ceiling of 50,000 feet. Next to the General Dynamics display, another sales representative is extolling the virtues of the United Kingdom's Mach 2.2 Tornado fighter with its two 27mm cannons and an assortment of Sidewinder and Sky Flash missiles.

But these high-tech military marvels carry a stratospheric price tag. It can easily cost a country over $1 billion to equip even the most modest air force. Additional millions are required for months of intensive training for the pilots who will fly these planes, spare parts inventory for maintenance, and similar training for ground personnel needed for maintaining the aircraft.

While heading up United Nations food airlifts to several famine-plagued areas, Russell O'Quinn realized that many less developed countries did not require the technologically advanced planes of modern aviation. O'Quinn, a former test pilot, thought specifically of the venerable T-33, which had been the standard jet trainer for air forces around the world since the 1950s. In fact, some 1,100 T-33s are still in service, and many more are in storage.

O'Quinn developed a plan for resurrecting the T-33. He envisioned a redesigned and upgraded aircraft that would be integrated with an original T-33 air frame, which is known for its virtually unlimited life. O'Quinn's configuration would offer potential buyers an aircraft that would be the match of today's sophisticated trainers at a considerably lower price. The new plane, dubbed Skyfox, would be fuel efficient and maintain the handling features of the old T-33. The target market for the Skyfox would be smaller nations with limited defense budgets.

Skyfox Corp. was set up in Mojave, California, to develop the prototype. The firm was financed with private capital. The resulting flight test plane differed markedly from the T-33 despite a 70 percent common structure. The T-33's single 4,600-pound-thrust Allison T-33 centrifugal force turbojet engine was replaced by two externally mounted, 3,700-pound-thrust Garett TFE-731-3 turbofan engines. This gave the Skyfox 60 percent more thrust while reducing its fuel consumption. The Skyfox also had the longest range of any plane in its category, because its external engine placement allowed extra fuel to be carried in the internal engine bay. The cockpit was also upgraded with a Stencil MK3 ejection seat, Canadian Marconi fiber optics instruments and display panels, and off-the-shelf Collins avionics.

Designing the Skyfox proved to be the easy part. Selling it was an entirely different matter. Securing consumer acceptance of a new product, particularly one in the $3-million-to-$3.5-million range, is always difficult. Buyers are wary of the risks associated with any new item. But in the case of Skyfox, 70 percent of the so-called new product was really an old product—the T-33.

After the testing of the Skyfox, O'Quinn's company benefited from considerable free publicity. The Skyfox project was described in several trade and popular publications. Still, Skyfox Corp. was unable to translate this publicity into actual orders; only Portugal expressed an interest.

O'Quinn began searching for a merger with a larger firm that would provide the needed financial and marketing clout. Eventually he concluded a licensary agreement with Boeing to produce and market the Skyfox. (A licensary agreement is an arrangement whereby a technology is transferred to another party in exchange for some specified type of payment.) Management at Boeing Military Aircraft Co. adopted a broader view of Skyfox's potential role. It saw the Skyfox as a multipurpose aircraft that could conduct a variety of missions, such as reconnaissance, maritime patrol, electronic warfare simulation, and target towing, in addition to serving as a jet trainer.

While Boeing estimated that only 700 T-33s were still in service (compared to Skyfox Corp.'s estimate of 1,100), it agreed with O'Quinn's original assessment of the product. The Skyfox appears to be a cost-effective way to extend an airplane's life by an additional 20 years. Boeing also broadened the target market for the Skyfox to include the U.S. Air Force/Air National Guard, Canada, South Korea, Greece, and Portugal.

After three years of efforts to market the Skyfox, the Boeing Military Aircraft Co. withdrew from the venture. Skyfox Corp. continued to develop the airplane, changing to larger, more powerful engines and expanding its performance range. Although well over 100 orders have been received, the company still seeks funding and production capabilities. Potential buyers require assurances of long-term support, especially availability of parts, which Skyfox is unable to provide at present. Two major firms with operations on the scale of Boeing's have expressed interest, so there is hope that the Skyfox project will eventually get off the ground.

Sources: Update interview with Russell O'Quinn, Skyfox Corp., April 1991; Brendon M. Greeley, Jr., "Boeing Markets New Acquired Skyfox Twin-Engine Jet Trainer," *Aviation Week & Space Technology* (August 11, 1986), pp. 54–55; "Skyfox Seeks Merger to Fund Production of Jet Trainer Aircraft," *Aviation Week & Space Technology* (January 21, 1985), p. 21; and Robert R. Ropelewski, "Skyfox Updates T-33 Trainer Effectively," *Aviation Week & Space Technology* (March 8, 1984), pp. 39, 42, 44, 46. Updated by Boeing Military Aircraft Co., (February 1, 1988). The information on the F-16 and Tornado is from Chris Bishop and David Donald, eds., *World Military Power* (New York: Military Press, 1986), p. 33.

Questions

1. Classify the organizational buying situation for the Skyfox. Why did you select this classification category?

2. Relate the buying center concept to the potential purchase of Skyfox.

3. How should Skyfox be marketed?

4. Would Skyfox be an attractive investment for another aircraft manufacturer?

8

Market Segmentation

CHAPTER OBJECTIVES

1. To explain what is meant by a market.

2. To outline the role of market segmentation in developing a marketing strategy.

3. To explain each of the four bases for segmenting consumer markets.

4. To describe the three bases for segmenting industrial markets.

5. To identify the steps in the market segmentation process.

6. To explain how target market decision analysis can be used in segmenting markets.

7. To discuss three alternative strategies for reaching target markets.

New York's Yellow Pages currently contains 11 pages of "Health Clubs & Gymnasiums," double the number of entries a decade ago. With this many competitors, health clubs are far from a homogeneous market. For marketers, a basic question is how to segment health club memberships.

Health & Tennis Corp., a division of Bally Manufacturing, has used market segmentation in each of its 51 markets. When the 320-unit chain decided to move into New York, it prepared to face a highly fragmented market with many competing health clubs.

Conventional wisdom in the industry is that health clubs compete against each other, not against home exercise equipment. Nearly 60 percent of all exercise equipment is used for 60 days or less. People join health clubs for the motivation factor. Health & Tennis's job was to identify why New Yorkers join a specific club.

A psychologist was hired to conduct in-depth interviews to this end. Arthur Quinby, Health & Tennis's vice-president and director of marketing, explains the results of these interviews:

We found that people chose a health club membership based on a "trigger." They can see ads for years without them having an effect. Then, all of a sudden, something clicks, making them want to buy a membership. What matters most to people, however, is time. They often pick one health club over another based on location, hours, and amenities. They want a good price-value relationship.

Quinby and his marketers decided that they could segment the New York market into the following categories: mass, mid-market, and first-class. The firm bought the existing Jack LaLanne chain and positioned it for the 25–30 age mass market. Many of these customers were first-time buyers of health club memberships. Research had revealed that the primary motivating factor among women buyers was weight control, and for men it was muscle tone. The LaLanne clubs are heavily advertised using celebrity endorsements by Don Johnson, Sheena Easton, and Glenn Frey. Pricing was based upon specific locations, hours, and club sections requested. Prices now range from $13 to $40 per month based on a 24-month contract.

Health & Tennis then acquired the 11-story Vertical Club on the trendy Upper East Side. A similar unit was later set up in the Wall Street area. The Vertical Clubs feature weight systems, lifecycles, pools, tennis courts, aerobics, and squash courts. Annual memberships for this first-class segment of the market were originally set at a flat $1,400. In contrast to the LaLanne clubs, Health & Tennis does only minimal advertising to support the high end of its market entries.

Quinby also had a strategy for reaching the so-called mid-market. His firm's three Manhattan Sports Clubs were positioned as semi-exclusive clubs located near subways and commuting facilities. The clubs were priced at $750 to $1,000 a year. Quinby and his fellow executives later decided that the Manhattan Sports Clubs were cannibalizing sales from their other units. Health & Tennis lacked the promotional budget to differentiate these mid-market clubs in the consumer's mind. As a result, the Manhattan Sports Clubs were upscaled to be on a par with the Vertical Clubs. This revised segment is now called the Vertical Club Collection, and customers can join more than one unit. Annual memberships now range from $118 to $1,598 depending on location and the number of clubs selected.

Health & Tennis has continued to use segmentation in its approach to the New York market. It now offers a corporate program that provides club memberships as part of a firm's health plan. Companies like Johnson & Johnson — among others — are including a health club membership as part of their fringe benefits for employees.[1]

Photo source: © Walter Urie/Westlight.

Chapter Overview

market
Group of people who possess purchasing power and the authority and willingness to purchase.

Before a marketing mix strategy can be implemented, the marketer must identify, evaluate, and select a target market. The starting point is to understand what is meant by a market. It is more than just people and institutions with a willingness to buy. To be a **market,** those people or institutions must have the purchasing power and authority to buy. A real estate salesperson would be unimpressed by news that 50 percent of a marketing class raised their hands in response to the question, "Who wants to buy a condominium in Aspen, Colorado?" More pertinent would be the answer to the question, "How many of you have $100,000 for the down payment and can qualify for the mortgage?"

A successful marketer quickly learns how to pinpoint which individual in an organization or household has the authority to make particular purchasing decisions. Without this knowledge, too much time may be spent convincing the wrong person to buy the product.

Types of Markets

consumer products
Products purchased by the ultimate consumer for personal use.

industrial products
Products purchased for use directly or indirectly in the production of other products for resale.

Products are often classified as either consumer products or industrial products. **Consumer products** are products purchased by the ultimate consumer for personal use. **Industrial products** are products purchased for use either directly or indirectly in the production of other goods and services for resale. Most products purchased by individual consumers—books, CDs, and clothes, for example—are consumer goods. Rubber and raw cotton are examples of products generally purchased by manufacturers and therefore classified as industrial products. Rubber is used in many products by producers such as Goodyear; textile manufacturers such as Burlington Industries convert raw cotton into cloth.

Sometimes the same product is destined for different uses. Spark plugs purchased for the family car constitute a consumer good, but spark plugs purchased by Chrysler for use on its four-wheel-drive line are an industrial product, since they become part of another product destined for resale. (Some marketers use the term *commercial products* to refer to industrial products not directly used in producing other goods.) The key to proper classification of products is determining the purchaser and the reasons for the purchase.

The Role of Market Segmentation

The world is too large and filled with too many diverse people and firms for any single marketing mix to attract everyone. Except in the case of an unbranded, descriptive-label product aimed at the mass market, an attempt to attract everyone may doom the marketer to failure. Even a seemingly functional product such as toothpaste is aimed at specific market segments. Crest and Colgate focus on tooth decay prevention; Close-Up hints at enhanced sex appeal; Gleem emphasizes teeth-whitening; Topol promises removal of smoking stains. As the ad in Figure 8.1 shows, Colgate Junior is designed to appeal to kids while satisfying parents' concerns for fluoride protection.

The often told story of Henry Ford's resistance to market segmentation is worth repeating here. Ford's continued reliance on the Model T cost his firm its leadership in the developing automobile industry. While Ford insisted that his Model T was all that car buyers needed, Alfred P. Sloan, Jr., of General Motors, developed specific models for different groups of customers. Sloan's segmentation strategy worked, and General Motors replaced Ford as the number one U.S. automaker.[2]

Figure 8.1

Targeting a Specific Market Segment

Source: Courtesy of Colgate-Palmolive Company.

market segmentation

Process of dividing the total market into several relatively homogeneous groups with similar product interests based on such factors as demographic or psychographic characteristics, geographic location, or perceived product benefits.

The division of the total market into relatively homogeneous groups is called **market segmentation.** This process requires marketers to identify factors that affect purchasing decisions, so that consumers can be grouped accordingly. Marketing mixes are then adjusted to meet the needs of each targeted segment. Market segmentation can be used by both profit-oriented and nonprofit organizations.

Koenig Corp., a Connecticut-based chain of art-supply stores, is an excellent illustration of a firm that has adapted its marketing mix to its target market. Since industry sources estimate that only 6 percent of the population are professional artists or active hobbyists, Koenig concentrates on people who have only a casual interest in painting. Koenig reaches this market through mall outlets rather than the freestanding stores common in the art-supply business. The firm's sales personnel are trained to let amateurs browse extensively, and to never ask potentially embarrassing questions like, "Are you interested in acrylics or oils?"[3]

Criteria for Effective Segmentation

Market segmentation cannot be used in all cases. To be effective, segmentation must meet the following basic requirements:[4]

1. The market segment must be measurable in terms of both purchasing power and size.

2. Marketers must be able to effectively promote to and serve the market segment.

3. Market segments must be sufficiently large to be potentially profitable.

4. The number of segments must match the firm's marketing capabilities.

If one or more of these factors is missing, the marketer should reassess any proposed market segmentation strategy. For example, Health & Tennis Corp. was unable to meet the second and fourth criteria in the mid-market the firm had defined. Therefore, it revised its segmentation strategy to include only two segments.

Segmenting Consumer Markets

Marketing segmentation results from the isolation of factors that distinguish a certain group of consumers from the overall market. These characteristics—age, sex, geographic location, income and expenditure patterns, and population size and mobility, among others—are vital factors in the success of the overall marketing strategy. Toy manufacturers such as Ideal, Hasbro, Mattel, and Kenner study not only birthrate trends but shifts in income and expenditure patterns. Colleges and universities are affected by such factors as number of high school graduates, changing attitudes toward the value of a college education, and increasing enrollment of older adults. The four commonly used bases for segmenting consumer markets are geographic segmentation, demographic segmentation, psychographic segmentation, and benefit-related segmentation. These segmentation bases can be important to marketing strategies provided they are significantly related to differences in buying behavior.

Geographic Segmentation

geographic segmentation
Dividing a population into homogeneous groups on the basis of location.

A logical starting point in market segmentation is the examination of population characteristics. **Geographic segmentation**—the dividing of an overall market into homogeneous groups on the basis of population location—has been used for hundreds of years. While homogeneity of consumer buying decisions does not occur within each geographic area, this segmentation approach is useful in spotting product-specific patterns as well as generalized purchase tendencies.

The U.S. population of over 250 million is not distributed evenly; rather, it is concentrated in states with major metropolitan areas. The 15 largest metropolitan areas are listed in Table 8.1.

States vary not only in population density but in population migration. Census data indicate two major population shifts over the past decade: to the Sunbelt states of the Southeast and Southwest, and to the West. Between 1980 and 1990, the population of the South increased by 15 percent and that of the West by 21 percent, compared to a modest 4 percent increase in the Northeast and only a 2 percent gain in the Midwest.[5] Foreign immigration has played a role in the rapid growth rate in the West. For instance, California, with 11 percent of the nation's population, gets 27 percent of legal immigrants, and an estimated even higher percentage of illegal immigrants.[6]

The U.S. population is expected to peak out at about 300 million in 2038. A third of the nation's remaining growth is expected before 2000.[7] California, Texas, and Florida are projected to account for more than half of the U.S. population growth during the 1990s.[8]

Population shifts have also occurred within states. Farmers have migrated steadily to urban areas since 1800, and the percentage of farm dwellers has dropped below 3 percent.

Similar patterns have developed in other countries. For instance, during the past 30 years, South Korea has gone from a 72 percent rural population to a 73 percent urban population. Korea's city dwellers are expected to rise to 80 percent by the end of this decade.[9]

Table 8.1

The Largest 15 Metropolitan Areas

Rank in 1990	Rank in 1980	Metropolitan Areas	1990 Population (in thousands)	Percent Change
1	2	L.A./Long Beach	8,771	17.3%
2	1	New York	8,625	4.2
3	3	Chicago	6,308	4.1
4	4	Philadelphia	4,973	5.4
5	5	Detroit	4,409	−1.8
6	7	Washington, D.C.	3,710	14.1
7	8	Houston	3,509	28.3
8	6	Boston	2,837	1.1
9	13	Atlanta	2,744	28.3
10	9	Nassau-Suffolk, NY	2,736	5.0
11	15	Dallas	2,615	33.6
12	10	St. Louis	2,511	5.6
13	14	Minneapolis/St. Paul	2,460	15.1
14	19	San Diego	2,375	27.6
15	12	Baltimore	2,352	6.9

Source: Reprinted from Diane Crispell, Thomas Exter, and Judith Waltrop, "Census '90," *The Wall Street Journal Reports* (March 9, 1990), p. R13.

The United States traditionally has been a mobile society. About one of every six Americans moves each year. However, this figure is down from one out of five persons a few decades ago. The slowdown is attributed to factors such as economic downturns, a higher percentage of home ownership, higher housing prices, and fluctuating mortgage interest rates.

The move from urban to suburban areas after World War II, primarily by middle-class families, created a need to redefine the urban marketplace. This trend radically changed cities' traditional patterns of retailing and led to a disintegration of many U.S. cities' downtown shopping areas. It rendered traditional city boundaries almost meaningless for marketing purposes.

In an effort to correct this situation, the government now classifies urban data using three categories:

Metropolitan Statistical Area (MSA)

Large, freestanding area for which detailed marketing-related data are collected by the Bureau of the Census.

□ A **Metropolitan Statistical Area (MSA)** is a freestanding urban area with an urban center population of 50,000 and a total MSA population of 100,000 or more. MSAs exhibit social and economic homogeneity. They are usually bordered by nonurbanized counties. Moorhead, Minnesota; Peoria, Illinois; and Sheboygan, Wisconsin, are examples.

Primary Metropolitan Statistical Area (PMSA)

Major urban area within a CMSA.

□ A **Primary Metropolitan Statistical Area (PMSA)** is an urbanized county or counties with social and economic ties to nearby areas. PMSAs are identified within areas of 1-million-plus populations. Long Island's Nassau and Suffolk counties would be part of the New York CMSA, Oxnard-Ventura part of the Los Angeles CMSA, and Aurora-Elgin part of the Chicago CMSA.

Consolidated Metropolitan Statistical Area (CMSA)

Major population concentration, including the 25 or so urban giants.

□ A **Consolidated Metropolitan Statistical Area (CMSA)** includes the 25 or so urban giants such as New York, Los Angeles, and Chicago. It must include two or more Primary Metropolitan Statistical Areas.

Using Geographic Segmentation.   There are many instances in which markets for goods and services may be segmented on a geographic basis. One instance is when consumer tastes vary among regions. For example, catfish has always been a Southern staple, but it has only recently been accepted in other areas of the country. Similarly, scrapple sells well in Pennsylvania and a few

Figure 8.2

High Purchase Rates for
Selected Products

Test Yourself

What would you guess?

Match the products on the left with the city or regions on the right in which these products have the highest purchasing rate.

1. Heinz ketchup		a.	Philadelphia
2. Fritos		b.	Salt Lake City
3. Twinkies		c.	Miami
4. ChunKing chow mein		d.	Seattle
5. Breyer's ice cream		e.	New York
6. Prune juice		f.	Pennsylvania
7. Skippy peanut butter		g.	Houston
8. Hash		h.	Portland, ME
9. Beef stew		i.	Pittsburgh
10. Sloppy Joe sauce		j.	Dallas
11. Bacon		k.	California
12. Bubblegum		l.	Chicago
13. Prince spaghetti		m.	Minnesota
14. Wine		n.	Boston
15. Canned soup		o.	Cleveland
16. Insecticide		p.	San Antonio
17. Frozen bagels		q.	Des Moines
18. Canned chili		r.	Louisville
19. Cajun food		s.	Columbus
20. Scrapple		t.	Richmond
21. Cold remedies		u.	South
22. Frozen pizza		v.	Southern California
23. Wonder bread		w.	East Coast
24. Snack nuts		x.	Grand Rapids
25. Cheerios		y.	Gulf Coast

Key:
1–i; 2–j; 3–l; 4–m; 5–a; 6–c; 7–q; 8–t; 9–r; 10–s; 11–u; 12–b; 13–n; 14–k; 15–x; 16–g; 17–w; 18–v; 19–y; 20–f; 21–p; 22–o; 23–e; 24–h; 25–d.

Source: Reprinted from Thomas W. Osborne, "An American Mosaic," *Marketing Insights* (June 1989), p. 79.

other spots, but the bulk of the country has rejected this Pennsylvania Dutch favorite.[10]

Some categories of products are more prone to regional preferences than others. Accordingly, some national firms develop products and marketing strategies aimed at specific regions while others do not. Most major brands get 40 to 80 percent of their sales from what are called *core regions.* For the rest of the national marketplace, the product is essentially a specialty brand. Figure 8.2 presents a quiz on cities or regions with the highest purchase rates of particular products.

Residence location within a geographic area is an important geographic variable. Urban dwellers may have less need for automobiles than their suburban and rural counterparts, and suburban dwellers spend proportionately more on lawn and garden care than do rural and urban residents. Both rural and suburban dwellers may spend more of their household incomes on gasoline and automobile needs than urban households.

Climate is another important factor. Chilly Grand Rapids, Michigan, is the nation's top-ranked soup market. In contrast, soups do poorly in the warmer

GEODEMOGRAPHIC SEGMENTATION

Your best bet is to market nationally, right? Not necessarily. Marketers are increasingly finding it profitable to focus on consumers in specific regions, local areas, and even individual neighborhoods. It's called *geodemographic targeting.*

The purpose of this approach is to cluster potential customers into lifestyle categories and then customize products and promotions for those categories. Sears has been doing this for several years. It "geo-codes" its credit-card customer base to identify growth segments and determine what merchandise is best suited to the needs of customers in a particular area.

Marketers have been slow to realize that many supposedly national brands get 40 to 80 percent of their volume from one region of the country and are viewed as specialty brands in other regions. They have tended to view the United States as a single, homogeneous mass market. Yet cities in the Northeast and the Southwest are as different from one another as cities in northern and southern Europe are. Their climates, cultures, demographics, and lifestyles are different, and so is the buying behavior of their inhabitants. To enter these different markets it is not necessary to learn a new language or get approval from a new government, but it can't hurt to learn their special characteristics. Only recently have marketers begun to realize that it would be worthwhile to develop a marketing plan or product line for, say, California or New York rather than trying to blanket the nation.

Sometimes called *micro-marketing,* geodemographic segmentation is used to identify strategic targets, assess the potential of market areas, develop an effective merchandise mix, select media, and find profitable new sites. It is also useful in store layout and stocking and in direct marketing. It is based on the recognition that "birds of a feather flock together"—that people who live in similar neighborhoods are likely to have similar consumption patterns and product preferences. It also takes into account the fact that the United States is becoming increasingly polycultural, with an increasingly diverse ethnic makeup.

To get an idea of how geodemographic factors shape markets, consider a few examples:

☐ The Arcadian people fled from France to eastern Canada and then to the area around New Orleans,

becoming the Cajuns. Their distinctive cuisine is popular in the South. On the other hand, the strong Italian heritage of Boston and other New England cities have made them the leading market for spaghetti sauce.

☐ Salt Lake City has the highest proportion of children in the nation and is the nation's largest consumer of bubblegum and Cracker Jacks. Prune juice sells best in Miami, with its high concentration of older retirees.

☐ The Twin Cities are characterized by cold weather, plenty of snow, and a tradition of active participation in winter sports. But the area is flat. Accordingly, it has a highly developed market in cross-country skiing.

☐ Insecticides sell best in Houston, least well in Denver.

A number of firms have developed systems for clustering consumers using geodemographic data. Each cluster presents a portrait of the residents of a particular type of neighborhood or town—especially their eating, drinking, working, and shopping habits. These portraits can be used to predict buying preferences and purchasing patterns. To create the clusters, demographic information and survey data about consumers (age, education, income, and numerous other factors) are correlated with the nation's 36,000 ZIP codes.

Discussion Questions

1. If people in different parts of the country have different lifestyles, is there any reason to market a brand nationally?

2. Geodemographic segmentation cannot answer all marketers' questions; for example, it does not explain why Wonder bread sells best in New York or why there is no logic to the pattern of peanut butter sales. Why might this be the case?

Sources: Lynn G. Coleman, "Marketers Advised to 'Go Regional,'" *Marketing News* (May 8, 1989), pp. 1, 8; Bob Laird, "Marketers Say Clusters Are Us," *USA Today* (March 16, 1989), pp. 1B, 2B, 4B; Thomas W. Osborne, "An American Mosaic," *Marketing Insights* (June 1989), pp. 76–83.

Figure 8.3

Use of Sex Segmentation in Advertising

southeastern markets. Similarly, Denver and Salt Lake City rank first and second in the country when it comes to purchase of skiing-related products.[11]

Geographic segmentation is useful only when regional preferences exist. Moreover, even then, geographic subdivisions of the overall market tend to be rather large and often too heterogeneous for effective segmentation without careful consideration of additional factors. In such cases, several segmentation variables may need to be utilized.

Demographic Segmentation

demographic segmentation
Dividing a population into homogeneous groups based on characteristics such as age, sex, and income level.

The most common approach to market segmentation is **demographic segmentation** — dividing consumer groups according to demographic variables such as sex, age, income, occupation, education, household size, and stage in the family life cycle. This approach is also sometimes called *socio economic segmentation.*

Vast quantities of data are available for assisting marketers in segmenting markets this way. The following sections describe the most commonly used demographic variables.

Segmenting by Sex.   Sex is an obvious variable for segmenting the markets for certain products that are sex-specific. In recent years, however, more industries have discovered marketing opportunities for sex segmentation. Beer advertising, for example, has been aimed at men in the past. By contrast, Figure 8.3 shows a recent Coors ad aimed at women.

Similarly, the automobile industry has recently turned to sex segmentation. In the past, cars were made for and sold mainly to men. Today women account for 44 percent of new car prospects in the United States. While the percentages differ in other countries, women worldwide are playing an increased role in the

FOCUS ON ETHICS

TARGETING CIGARETTES AT MINORITIES AND WOMEN

"Uptown's message is more disease, more suffering and more death for a group already bearing more than its share of smoking-related illness and mortality." It is a "cynically and deliberately targeted" product backed by "slick and sinister advertising." This sharp criticism by Louis W. Sullivan, secretary of Health and Human Services, dealt a death blow to Uptown, R. J. Reynolds' new menthol cigarette.

Uptown was developed, packaged, and marketed specifically for blacks. Reynolds had planned to test-market the cigarette in Philadelphia, where it had lost significant market share to Lorillard's Newport brand. But the protests of consumer groups, medical associations, and black community leaders forced it to back down.

Sullivan's attack marked the first time a secretary of HHS had singled out a particular cigarette brand for criticism. Concerned about the high rate of smoking-related illness among blacks, he concluded that blacks do not need any more encouragement to smoke. (Blacks have a 58 percent higher rate of lung cancer than whites and lose twice as many years of life as whites because of smoking-related diseases.)

Reynolds was stunned by the furor over Uptown. According to a company spokesman, it was merely trying to be honest about its intentions: "We developed a product based on research that shows that a significant percentage of black smokers are currently choosing a brand that offers a lighter menthol flavor than our other major menthol brand, Salem." Uptown was not the only brand of cigarettes targeted at minority consumers, but it was the first to be explicitly identified as a cigarette for blacks. The company issued a statement saying that pressure from "a small coalition of anti-smoking zealots" was limiting the choices of black smokers.

As cigarette consumption has declined in the United States, there has been increased pressure on tobacco companies to target specific groups, such as blacks,

women, and Hispanics. Forty-four percent of black adults smoke, compared to 37 percent of the white population, making blacks an attractive target market. Critics contend that Uptown, which contains 19 milligrams of nicotine, would have been RJR's second most potent cigarette and was designed to get smokers addicted quickly. They also note that Uptown is only the most visible of a number of products targeted toward minorities and women; Dorado, for example, is pitched toward Hispanics, and Dakota is aimed at "tough" women with a high school education. The critics are especially concerned about the new lower-priced brands, which they believe are an effort to entice minority children to smoke.

Discussion Questions

1. Civil rights activist Benjamin Hooks says that the protest against Uptown is based on "the rationale that blacks are not capable of making their own free choices." Is this argument sufficient to justify continued targeting of cigarettes toward black consumers?

2. Tobacco companies contribute large sums to minority political and social organizations, which accept the funds despite the high cancer rates among their constituents. Should such contributions be prohibited?

Sources: "Alcohol and Tobacco: Down for Something Positive in the Community," *Inside PR* (February 1991); Shaun Assael, "Why Big Tobacco Woos Minorities," *Marketing Week* (January 29, 1990), pp. 20–22, 26, 30; Associated Press, "RJR Cancels Test of 'Black' Cigarette," *Marketing News* (February 19, 1990), p. 10; "Don't Aim That Pack at Us," *Time* (January 29, 1990), p. 60; Dan Koeppel, "In Philadelphia, R. J. Reynolds Made All the Wrong Moves," *Marketing Week* (January 29, 1990), pp. 20–22; James R. Schiffman, "Uptown's Fall Bodes Ill for Niche Brands," *The Wall Street Journal* (January 22, 1990), p. B1; "The Secretary Who Snuffed a Cigarette," *U.S. News & World Report* (January 29, 1990), p. 12; Clemens P. Work, "Where There's Smoke," *U.S. News & World Report* (March 5, 1990), pp. 57–58.

car-buying decision. In Mexico, 55 percent of career women paid for their own cars. In Australia, 51 percent of career-oriented women, and 47 percent of other working women, made their own car-buying decisions.[12]

While widely criticized by health, consumer, and women's groups, U.S. tobacco companies have also used market segmentation to reach women. Like men, women are smoking less in the 1990s; but the decline for women is not as pronounced. More younger women are also starting to smoke than are comparably aged men. Some of the cigarette brands targeted at women are Virginia Slims (the original entry in this segment), Capri, SuperSlims, Newport Stripes 100, Chelsea, Spring Lemon Lights, and Eve Ultra Lights 120.[13]

Figure 8.4   Segmenting Markets by Age

Evelyn Kuhn, age 46.

Healthy, natural, wholesome.
Taste isn't the only reason for you to eat Yoplait*   Every day.

THE BEAUTY OF YOPLAIT.*

Source: Courtesy of Yoplait USA. Reprinted with the permission of Yoplait U.S.A., Inc. YOPLAIT is a registered trademark of Sodima, a French Company, used under license agreement with Yoplait U.S.A., Inc.

Segmenting by Age.   Many firms identify market segments on the basis of age. Indeed, some market products only to specific age groups. Gerber focuses on food for infants and toddlers. New Beginnings Adult Care offers medical treatment and recreational services for older people. The ad for Yoplait in Figure 8.4 is aimed at middle-aged people who want to maintain a youthful appearance.

Age distribution and projected changes in age groups are important to marketers because consumer needs and wants differ notably among age groups. Consequently, markets in declining age groups usually shrink. The traditional college-age population (18–25) has declined in recent years, resulting in a change from a seller's market to a buyer's market for colleges and universities. To attract students, colleges are spending more money on advertising and public relations and offering unique programs. Northeastern University in Boston offers a program that allows all full-time students to work every other quarter for one of 50,000 employers nationwide. Through its Adelphi-On-Wheels program, Adelphi University in New York offers business courses taught on commuter trains. Other institutions are targeting students age 25 and older and women—the two fastest-growing groups of college students.

The most notable trend in the U.S. population is referred to as the "graying of America." The elderly—those defined by the Bureau of the Census as 65 or older—have increased by 28 percent during the past decade, twice as fast as the general population.[14] Today, one American in eight falls in the 65-plus group; by the year 2030, more than one in five will.

The relative importance of older Americans is likely to increase in the years ahead. Currently, the 63 million Americans over 50 account for 50 percent of the U.S. discretionary income and control 77 percent of the nation's financial assets. While only a quarter of the U.S. population, the over-50 group is responsible for 40 percent of total consumer demand. In fact, some marketers now use the designation SOPPIES—for senior urban professionals—to refer to this market group.[15]

The aging of the American population has opened many marketing opportunities. For example, book publisher Doubleday & Company offers a large-print book club for older Americans. However, marketing experts say that selling to older Americans is made difficult by the fact that so many of them perceive themselves as 15 years younger than their actual age.[16] Although older Americans will respond to products and advertising that appeal to the changed interests, needs, and wants of their later years, they often reject approaches that use terms such as "senior citizen," "golden years," and "retirees." Older people, for example, did not take to Johnson & Johnson's initial advertising campaign for Affinity shampoo because it promoted the product as beneficial for older, brittle hair. Sales increased after the company repositioned Affinity as a product that would enhance the beauty of age and changed the advertising message to suggest that women can be alluring at any age.

A Global Perspective. The United States is not the only market with an aging population. While 13 percent of the U.S. population will be over 65 by the year 2000, the comparative Soviet Union figure is not much less—11.5 percent.[17] And Europe has some of the world's oldest populations. Sweden currently has over 20 percent of its population in the 60-plus category. The United Kingdom, Germany, and Italy will reach this milestone by the end of the decade.

Japan, with the longest life expectancies in the world, is aging more quickly than most nations. Currently, some 10 percent of all Japanese are 65 or older; but this figure is expected to rapidly climb to 20 percent. In fact, the Japanese government has already proposed an "Extended Leisure Stays Abroad" plan that would encourage Japanese to retire abroad. European resort areas are suggested.

Like Americans, elderly Japanese tend to reject certain appeals to their age. Marketers have learned not to use the word "silver" in their promotional appeals, which in Japanese has connotations of "helpless" or "feeble."[18]

Segmenting by Family Life Cycle Stage. Still another form of demographic segmentation employs the stages of the **family life cycle**—the process of family formation and dissolution. J. Walter Thompson (JWT), a $3.8 billion global advertising agency, has conducted extensive research on the family life cycle and has identified nine so-called *lifestages,* grouped under three general categories: new singles, new couples, and new parents.[19]

family life cycle
Stages of family formation and dissolution that can be used in demographic segmentation.

New Singles. JWT's research identified four types of new singles: *At-home singles* were young singles still living at home with mom and dad. *Starting-out singles* were young singles who had left home. *Mature-singles* were older never-married, separated, or divorced singles. *Left-alone singles* were seniors who had lost their spouse or were separated or divorced.

Table 8.2   Life-Stage Profiles

Lifestage	Mean Age	Percent of Adults	Purchase Patterns	Magazine Preferences
At-Home Singles	22	14	Prefer casual clothes; heavy buyers of personal-care items, entertainment, and sporting equipment	Rolling Stones, Seventeen, GQ, Mademoiselle, Hot Rod, Road & Track, Muscle & Fitness
Starting-Out Singles	26	4	Heavy buyers of household furnishings and related items	GQ, Ski, Muscle & Fitness, Shape, Rolling Stone, Vanity Fair, Cycle World
Mature Singles	45	5	Reject fashions and trends; frequent travelers	New York, New Yorker, Esquire, Playboy, Road & Track, Gourmet, Discover
Left-Alone Singles	70	7	Active investors; heavy mail-order buyers	Flower & Garden, House Beautiful, Prevention, Ladies Home Journal, Woman's Day, Sunset
Young Couples	29	7	Happiest lifestage; heavy buyers of personalized gifts, homes, power tools, furniture, and crystal ware	Glamour, Cosmopolitan, Car & Driver, Field & Stream, Country Living
Empty Nesters	62	19	Financially secure; most important leisure market; active investors; heavy buyers of motor homes, movie cameras, and self-cleaning ovens	Changing Times, Prevention, Consumer Digest, Creative Ideas for Living, Reader's Digest
Young Parents	32	17	Many purchases are influenced by their children	Parents, Working Mother, Family Handyman, Mother Earth News, Inc.
Mature Parents	47	20	Buyers of college tuition and other children-influenced purchases	Workbench, Sports Illustrated, Redbook, Fortune, Outdoor Life
Single Parents	41	7	Three out of four are women; contradictory purchase patterns; baby food, cigarettes, toys, alcoholic beverages, convenience foods, and designer jeans	Jet, Essence, Soap Opera Digest, Ebony, New Woman

Source: Adapted from *Lifestages* (J. Walter Thompson, June, 1989).

New Couples.   Two types of new couples were identified: *Young couples* were young, recently married couples with no children. *Empty nesters* were older couples whose children had grown up and left home.

New Parents.   Three types of new parents were identified: *Young parents* were married parents whose oldest child was a pre-teen. *Mature parents* were married parents whose oldest dependent child was a teenager or adult. *Single parents* were unmarried parents raising their own children.

Table 8.2 outlines important demographic characteristics of each lifestage, as well as the purchasing patterns and media preferences of each group. The underlying theme of the JWT research is that lifestages, not age per se, are the primary determinant of many consumer purchasers.

Segmenting by Household Type.

When the first census was taken in 1790, the average household had 5.79 persons.[20] Today the typical U.S. household has 2.62 persons. Florida and Oregon have the lowest household size, 2.46, while Utah, with 3.17, has the highest. The U.S. Department of Commerce cites several reasons for the trend toward smaller households: lower fertility rates; young people's tendency to postpone marriage or never marry; the increasing tendency among younger couples to limit the number of children or have no children; the ease and frequency of divorce; and the ability and desire of many young singles and the elderly to live alone.

Over 23 million people live alone today—about 25 percent of the 93.5 million U.S. households.[21] The single-person household has emerged as an important market segment with a special title: SSWD, for single, separated, widowed, and divorced. SSWDs are customers for single-serve food products, such as Campbell's Soup for One and Green Giant's single-serve casseroles and vegetables.

Married-couple families constitute 56 percent of all U.S. households, down from 61 percent a decade earlier. This figure is expected to decline to 53 percent by the end of the current decade. The number of unmarried individuals living together increased during this same time period. As a result, the Bureau of the Census has designated another category—POSLSQ—for unmarried people of the opposite sex living in the same quarters.

Finally, one of the most highly sought-after market segments in the 1990s are DINKs—dual-income couples with no kids. With a high level of spendable income, such couples are big buyers of gourmet foods, luxury items, and travel. DINKs have become one of the most important market segments to emerge in the last five to ten years.

An offshoot of the emergence of DINKs is the "cocooning" trend. The pressure of two careers has made DINKs more conscious of convenience and household comforts. Therefore, DINKs call Domino's Pizza frequently and are major purchasers of expensive home entertainment centers. They are staying at home more and more, and they are buying whatever makes their time at home more comfortable.

 A Similar Pattern Exists Abroad.   Pacific Rim countries, in particular, exhibit a similar pattern of shrinking household size. The average South Korean household size has gone from 5.13 in 1975 to 3.79 currently. Taiwan, Hong Kong, and Singapore report similar statistics. While household size is down, though, the number of households is up.[22]

Segmenting by Income and Expenditure Patterns.   Earlier we defined markets as people (or institutions) with purchasing power. Not surprisingly, then, a common method of segmenting the consumer market is on the basis of income. Mass-market retailers aim their appeals at middle-income groups. By contrast, fashionable specialty shops stocking designer clothing target high-income shoppers. Gucci, the Italy-based retailer of finely crafted leather goods and fashion accessories, targets upper-income consumers. Because consumers in Gucci's target market share the same income levels and are likely to travel, the company uses a single print advertising campaign to reach consumers in the United States, Great Britain, France, Japan, and Italy. The ads, such as the one for Gucci loafers in Figure 8.5, are consistent with Gucci's luxury-goods image. Perhaps the ultimate example of an upscale retailer is Amen Wardy of Newport Beach, California. Wardy's 30,000-square-foot store features the likes of $2,500 purses and $246,000 necklaces. However, for the ultimate of segmentation by income and expenditures, Wardy has equipped a mobile home with some 600 garments for personal showings. Wardy drives the vehicle—complete with a seamstress—to the homes of his wealthy clients on a regular basis.[23]

The opposite side of the income spectrum is targeted by Western Union Corp. This firm, which is synonymous with Western history, now concentrates on money-order and transfer services for the 25 percent of the U.S. population that do not have checking accounts. (The comparable figure for low-income people is 50 percent.) One recent Western Union (now New Valley Corp.) advertising

Figure 8.5   Segmenting Markets on the Basis of Income

Source: Courtesy of Gucci.

campaign depicted a college student waiting for a new cash infusion from home.[24]

Engel's Laws.   How do expenditure patterns vary with income? Over a century ago, Ernst Engel, a German statistician, published what became known as **Engel's laws**—three general statements based on his studies of the impact of household income changes on consumer spending behavior. According to Engel, as family income increases

Engel's laws

Three general statements on spending behavior: As a family's income increases, (1) a smaller percentage of income goes for food; (2) the percentage spent on household operations, housing, and clothing remains constant; and (3) the percentage spent on other items increases.

1.   A smaller percentage of expenditures goes for food.
2.   The percentage spent on housing and household operations and clothing remains constant.
3.   The percentage spent on other items (such as recreation and education) increases.

Are Engel's laws still valid? Recent studies say, essentially, yes, with a few exceptions. There is a steady decline in the percentage of total income spent on food, beverages, and tobacco as income increases. Although high-income families spend a greater absolute amount on food items, their purchases represent a smaller percentage of their total expenditures than is true of low-income families. The second law is partly correct, since the percentage of expenditures for housing and household operations remains relatively unchanged in all but the very lowest income group. The percentage spent on clothing, however, rises with increased income. The third law is also true with the exception of medical and personal care, which appears to decline with increased income.

Engel's laws provide the marketing manager with useful generalizations about the types of consumer demand that evolve with increased income. They can also be helpful for the marketer evaluating a foreign country as a potential target market.

Demographic Segmentation Abroad.   It is often difficult to obtain the data necessary for a global approach to demographic segmentation. Irregularity characterizes the census data of many nations.[25] The most recent Dutch count is now two decades old. West Germany skipped from 1970 to 1987, and France conducts a census only about every seven years. In contrast, Japan and Canada conduct censuses every five years; however, the mid-decade ones are not as complete as the end-of-decade counts.

While some of the foreign data addresses demographics not found in the U.S. Census (Canada collects information on religious affiliation, for instance), some of the most common segmentation data is not available abroad. Many nations do not collect income data. Great Britain, Japan, Spain, France, and Italy are examples. Similarly, family life cycle data is difficult to use in global demographic segmentation. Ireland uses only three marital statuses—single, married, and widowed—while Latin American nations and Sweden count their cohabitating population.

Psychographic Segmentation

Although geographic and demographic segmentation traditionally have been the primary bases for dividing consumer and industrial markets into homogeneous segments for use as target markets, marketers have long recognized the need for fuller, more lifelike portraits of consumers in developing marketing programs. In addition to the traditionally used variables of age, sex, family life cycle, income, and population size and location, lifestyle has proved equally significant.

lifestyle
The way people decide to live their lives, including family, job, social activities, and consumer decisions.

Lifestyle refers to the consumer's mode of living; it is how an individual operates on a daily basis. Consumers' lifestyles are regarded as composites of their individual psychological makeups—their needs, motives, perceptions, and attitudes. A lifestyle also bears the mark of many other influences, such as reference groups, culture, social class, and family members.

psychographic segmentation
Dividing a population into homogeneous groups on the basis of behavioral and lifestyle profiles developed by analyzing consumer activities, opinions, and interests.

AIO statements
Collection of statements in a psychographic study to reflect the respondents' activities, interests, and opinions.

What Is Psychographic Segmentation?   Although definitions vary among researchers, **psychographic segmentation** generally refers to the lifestyle profiles of different consumers developed from asking consumers to agree or disagree with **AIO statements,** which are a collection of several hundred statements dealing with activities, interests, and opinions.

Marketing researchers have conducted psychographic studies on hundreds of goods and services ranging from beer to air travel. Hospitals and other health organizations use such studies to assess consumer behavior and attitudes toward health care in general, to learn the needs of consumers in a particular marketplace, and to determine how consumers perceive individual institutions. For example, Marriott Corporation, Avon, and other businesses have turned to psychographics in an effort not only to learn what seniors need but to understand what becomes important to them as they grow older.

The NPD Group, a consulting organization based in Port Washington, New York, has conducted studies segmenting food and beverage consumers according to their attitudes and behavior.[26] This research was first done in 1983, with a follow-up study in 1989. NPD says there are now four psychographic segments in the food and beverage marketplace:

- □ *Traditional-taste group* (29 percent)—they like butter, sweets, fried foods and fast foods, and tend to discount health and nutrition considerations.
- □ *Health-maintainers group* (26 percent)—they combine the "nutritionally fit" and "restrictive dieters" segments.
- □ *Busy-urbanites group* (20 percent)—they value time and convenience and tend to eat out frequently; dominated by singles and families without children.
- □ *Moderates group* (25 percent)—first identified in the 1989 study, they lack consistency when it comes to food and beverage purchases, alternating between healthy and snack foods; moderates cross all demographic profiles.

Psychographic segmentation of this nature can help marketers better target specific consumer segments. Marketing variables such as advertising campaigns can then be adapted to these groups.

VALS 2

Commercially available psychographic segmentation system.

VALS 2.   The commercially available psychographic segmentation system called VALS, which stands for "values, attitudes, and lifestyles," was developed by SRI International, a consulting organization.[27] The original VALs scheme, developed in 1978, was based primarily upon values and lifestyle continuums. The segmentation was revised a decade later to reflect consumer resources and self-motivation. **VALS 2,** as the revised system is called, is outlined in Figure 8.6. The resource factor is considered vertically, while self-orientation is measured horizontally. The resource dimension measures income, education, self-confidence, health, eagerness to buy, intelligence, and energy level. Self-orientation is divided into three groups: *principle-oriented* consumers have set views; *status-oriented* consumers are influenced by what others think; and, *action-oriented* consumers seek physical activity, variety, and adventure.

Principle-oriented consumers include fulfillers and believers. *Fulfillers* are mature, home-oriented, well-educated professionals with relatively high incomes. They are value-oriented consumers who are open to new ideas. *Believers* are family- and community-oriented people of more modest means. They are brand loyal and favor American-made products.

The status-oriented groups are achievers and strivers. *Achievers* are work-oriented and successful. They have high job satisfaction, respect authority, and favor the status quo. Achievers like to demonstrate their success through their purchases. *Strivers* are lower-income people with values similar to the achievers. This group emulates achievers. Style is important in their lifestyle.

Experiencers and makers are the components of the action-oriented segment. *Experiencers* are the youngest people in the VALS 2 scheme. Their median age is 25. Experiencers are active in both physical and social activities. They are also avid consumers, who favor new products. *Makers* are the self-sufficient group. They are practical people who have little interest in most material possessions.

The two remaining categories are strugglers and actualizers. *Strugglers* have few resources and do not fit into the regular VALS 2 categories. Strugglers, however, are brand loyal to the extent possible. By contrast, *actualizers* have both high income and self-esteem. This allows them to indulge in a variety of self-orientations.

How Marketers Use VALS 2.   The revised format, VALS 2, is expected to make VALS more useful in industries such as packaged goods which have not been the traditional market for psychographic systems. In the past, systems like VALS were best used for ego-driven, big-ticket items like automobiles.

Figure 8.6

VALS 2 Groupings

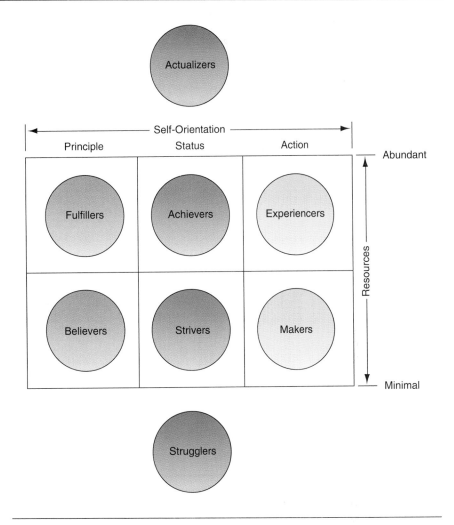

Marketers can subscribe to VALS 2. SRI, the organization that developed the system, will also analyze data for subscribers and characterize the respondents according to the eight VALS 2 groups. Subscribers also have access to other SRI research; and those who subscribe to selected databases can have this information classified by the VALS 2 format.

Psychographics — A Global Perspective.   Psychographics can also be applied on a global basis. Advertising agency Backer Spielvogel Bates Worldwide (BSBW) studied 15,000 people in 14 countries. Its report, *Global Span,* says that consumers tastes are becoming more materialistic and that differences between consumer groups will expand. BSBW also concluded that psychographics could be applied on a global basis. The five global segments that are believed to cross national and cultural barriers are as follows:[28]

☐   *Strivers* — young people (median age 31) who lead active lives. They are under stress most of the time and prefer goods and services that are sources of instant gratification.

☐   *Achievers* — about the same age as strivers, but have already found the success they seek. They are affluent, assertive, and serve as society's

Figure 8.7   Use of Psychographic Segmentation in Advertising

opinion and style leaders. Achievers value status and quality in the brands they buy, and are largely responsible for setting trends.

- *The Pressured*—mainly women, in every age group, who find it extremely difficult to manage all the problems in their lives. They have little time for enjoyment.
- *Adapters*—older consumers who live comfortably. They are content with themselves and their lives, and they recognize and respect new ideas without losing sight of their own values. They are willing to try new products that enrich their lives.
- *Traditionals*—those who embody the oldest values of their countries and cultures. They are resistant to change, and they are content with familiar products.

Using Psychographic Segmentation.   The marketing implications of psychographic segmentation are considerable. Psychographic profiles produce a much richer description of a potential target market than is otherwise possible, so they aid greatly in matching the company's image and product offerings with the type of consumer who uses the products. The *Food & Wine* ad in Figure 8.7 suggests that the magazine appeals to people with nontraditional interests.

Psychographic segmentation is a good addition to segmentation by demographic or geographic variables such as age, income, city, size, education, family life cycle stage, and geographic location. These more traditional bases give the marketer access to consumer segments through orthodox communications channels such as newspapers and radio and television. Psychographic studies may then be implemented to develop a more fully dimensional lifestyle profile of the consumers in the firm's target market.

When combined with demographic and geographic characteristics, psychographics help predict and understand consumer preferences. For example, people living in or near financial centers such as New York prefer darker-color automobiles. Bob Daily, color marketing manager at DuPont, observes, "A car is a form of expression. It either shows what people want or who they want to be."[29]

Benefit Segmentation

benefit segmentation
Dividing a population into homogeneous groups on the basis of benefits consumers expect to derive from a product.

Benefit segmentation—sometimes called behavioral segmentation—focuses on the attributes that people seek in a product and the benefits that they perceive existing products to have. Consider the detergent market. According to one study, 55 percent of consumers see little difference among laundry detergents, most of which are promoted as making clothes clean, bright, and fresh-smelling. In its search for a new benefit, Lever Brothers decided to target consumers concerned about body odor in clothes, a problem that has increased because more Americans are exercising and more clothing is being made of synthetic fibers that hold odors. Surf was formulated as a detergent with the new benefit of special odor-tackling properties. It quickly became the number two detergent brand in the country.[30]

Everest & Jennings International Inc. is another firm that markets products designed to offer a specific benefit. The Los Angeles–based firm sells a line of clothes targeted at wheelchair users. This clothing is specially designed to look good on a seated person.[31]

Sometimes it is impossible to identify and measure perceived benefits directly. In these cases, marketers turn to proxy variables such as *usage rate* and *brand loyalty.*

Usage Rates.   Relative usage rates are used for benefit segmentation this way: Heavy users in enterprises as diverse as lottery tickets, beer, fast food, and cosmetics are identified as the target market, and promotions are directed at them. For example, children consume more than a third of all ready-to-eat cereal in the United States. As a result, Kellogg has long used animated characters like Tony the Tiger to promote their cereals.[32]

Children are an even more important factor in some foreign markets. For example, the under-14 age group accounts for 38 percent of Malaysia's population. When Nestlé entered this market, it safely disregarded the adult market—which prefers rice porridge and pork soup for breakfast—and concentrated on children. Later, it introduced a less sugary cereal targeted at adolescents and young adults.[33]

Consider another example of how usage rates are employed: Since Indonesia bans television commercials for all but the 120,000 viewers of a subscriber channel (the population of Indonesia is 180 million), Auto 2000, the country's biggest Toyota dealer, developed a mailing list of existing customers and then used direct mail, a relatively new concept in Indonesia, to encourage repeat purchases and referrals by these customers.[34]

Usage rates can also be linked to other segmentation approaches, such as demographics and psychographics. One study of the sports activities of 14,000

Figure 8.8   Building Brand Loyalty through Relationship Marketing

Source: KRAFT CHEESE & MACARONI CLUB is a trademark of Kraft General Foods, Inc. Reproduced with permission.

Americans found that income and age were primary factors in determining the usage rates for each activity. For example, affluent people prefer tennis over fishing, and younger people favor skiing over golf.[35]

Brand Loyalty

Brand loyalty is another benefit-related segmentation variable. The classic example of this approach to segmentation is the frequent-flyer program. Originally targeted at heavy users—business travelers—frequent-flyer programs now help bind even occasional travelers to specific airlines. The success of these programs has resulted in similar efforts in the hotel industry and elsewhere.

Today brand loyalty is one of the most popular ways to segment markets. Once brand-loyal consumers are identified, such as by sending out application forms to be filled in, databases can be built that will allow marketers to communicate with customers through cost-effective direct mail. The newsletter and special promotions of frequent-flyer programs illustrate these marketing efforts.

Terms like *relationship marketing, affinity marketing, frequency marketing,* and *loyalty marketing* apply here. Examples are increasingly abundant. Kraft now has a "Cheese & Macaroni Club" for children, who receive a variety of fun premiums in exchange for proofs of purchase and a small fee. An advertisement for Kraft's relationship marketing effort is shown in Figure 8.8. Similarly, Burger King has a Kids Club, and Coors now has a Club Coors.[36] (This subject is discussed further in Chapter 17.)

Segmenting Business Markets

While the bulk of marketing segmentation is done for consumer markets, the concept is also sometimes used in the business or industrial sector. The overall process is similar. IBM has identified over 40 growth business markets for its dealers to target, and a segmentation strategy has proved very effective for Sears Business Centers of Chicago, who specifically target attorneys and the distribution industry. Richard Foster, the Sears regional general manager, explains his firm's approach this way: "If I am going to sell an expensive system to a customer, I'd better understand his [or her]. . . business. How can I do that if I'm selling to 20 different businesses?"[37]

Segmentation approaches used in business markets include geographic segmentation, customer-based segmentation, and segmentation by end-use application.

Geographic Segmentation

Geographic segmentation is useful in industries whose customers are concentrated in specific geographic locations. This approach is used effectively in the U.S. automobile industry, concentrated in the Detroit area, and the tire industry, centered in Akron. It might also be used where markets are limited to just a few locations. The oil field equipment market, for example, is largely concentrated in cities in Texas and Oklahoma.

Customer-Based Segmentation

customer-based segmentation
Dividing a business market into homogeneous groups on the basis of product specifications identified by organizational buyers.

Customer-based segmentation is often used in the business marketplace because industrial users tend to have much more precise product specifications than do ultimate consumers. Thus, business products often fit narrower market segments than consumer products. Designing an industrial good or service to meet specific buyer requirements is a form of market segmentation. Consider the problem confronting Chiquita in the marketing of its bananas. The company needed an adhesive for its banana labels that was resistant to the fruit's natural oils, stuck on more than just one type of banana, and withstood frequent temperature changes. Hercules, Inc., provided the solution. It developed a tackifying resin that met Chiquita's exacting specifications. A similar example is provided by Canadian-based Linear Technology. While Japanese and American firms dominate microchip markets, Linear Technology concentrated on satisfying the needs of just one industry. Linear is now the leading provider of audio amplifier chips for hearing aids.[38]

Segmentation by End-Use Application

end-use application segmentation
Dividing a business market into homogeneous groups on the basis of precisely how different industrial purchasers will use the product.

A third segmentation base is **end-use application segmentation,** which focuses on the precise way in which the business purchaser will use the product. For example, a manufacturer of printing equipment may serve markets ranging from a local utility to a bicycle manufacturer to the U.S. Department of Defense. Each end use of the equipment may dictate unique specifications for performance, design, and price. Instead of competing in markets dominated by large firms, many small and medium-size companies concentrate on specific market segments. Glassmaker AFG Industries receives 65 percent of its sales from specialty lines of tempered and colored glass. It makes 70 percent of the glass used in microwave oven doors and 75 percent of that used in shower enclosures and patio table tops.[39]

The Market Segmentation Decision Process

To this point, we have discussed the various segmentation bases used by consumer and business marketers. In both types of markets, marketing managers follow a systematic five-step decision process, which is outlined in Figure 8.9.[40]

Stage I: Identify Market Segmentation Bases

Segmentation begins when a firm seeks bases on which to identify markets. These bases are one or more characteristics of potential buyers that allow classification for further analysis. The idea is for segments to contain customers who respond similarly to specific marketing mix alternatives; customers in different segments respond differently. For example, it is not enough for Procter & Gamble to target Crest at large families. Management must first be confident that most large families are interested in preventing tooth decay and thus will be receptive to the Crest marketing offer.

In some cases, this objective is difficult to achieve. Consider the marketer seeking to reach the consumer segment that is over 50 years of age. Saturday evening television commercials can reach this group, but much of the expenditure may be wasted, since the other major viewer group is composed of teenagers.

Stage II: Develop Relevant Profiles for Each Segment

Once segments have been identified, marketers should seek further understanding of the customers in each segment. This deeper analysis of customers is needed for managers to more accurately match customers' needs with marketing offers. Characteristics that explain the similarities among customers within each segment as well as account for differences among segments must be identified. Thus, the task at this stage is to develop profiles of the typical customer in each segment. Such profiles might include lifestyle patterns, attitudes toward product attributes and brands, brand preferences, product-use habits, geographic location, and demographic characteristics.

Von's Grocery Co. spent 30 months developing a relevant profile of its targeted market segment before it opened Tianguis, a Los Angeles supermarket designed to appeal to Hispanics. Von's researchers concluded that Hispanic buyers have minimal refrigeration, are very concerned about freshness, and spend more on food than do other consumers. Hispanics are also heavy users of particular products, like fruit juices. Tianguis—the Aztec word for marketplace—has half its floor space dedicated to fresh food and carries large quantities of fruit juices. It also stocks automatic tortilla-makers.[41]

Stage III: Forecast Market Potential

In the third stage, market segmentation and market opportunity analysis continue to coincide to produce a forecast of market potential within each segment. Market potential sets the upper limit on the demand that can be expected from a segment and, when multiplied by market share, determines maximum sales potential. This step should be the preliminary go or no-go decision point for management, since it must determine whether the total sales potential in each segment is sufficient to justify further analysis.

Consider the toothbrush segment of the dental supplies and mouthwash market. This segment would more than double if a marketer could convince the

Figure 8.9

The Market Segmentation
Decision Process

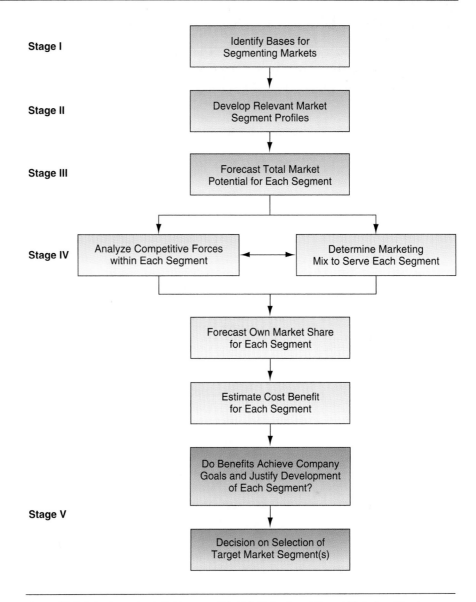

Stage I — Identify Bases for Segmenting Markets

Stage II — Develop Relevant Market Segment Profiles

Stage III — Forecast Total Market Potential for Each Segment

Stage IV — Analyze Competitive Forces within Each Segment ↔ Determine Marketing Mix to Serve Each Segment

Forecast Own Market Share for Each Segment

Estimate Cost Benefit for Each Segment

Do Benefits Achieve Company Goals and Justify Development of Each Segment?

Stage V — Decision on Selection of Target Market Segment(s)

Source: M. Dale Beckman, Louis E. Boone, and David L. Kurtz, *Foundations of Marketing,* 5th ed. (Toronto: Holt, Rinehart and Winston of Canada, 1991). The figure was originally prepared by Professor J. D. Forbes of the University of British Columbia and is reprinted by permission of the authors and publisher.

public to replace toothbrushes on a regular basis. Americans should buy 3 to 4 toothbrushes a year with average usage, but the current replacement rate is only 1.5 brushes annually.[42] Obviously a tremendous market potential exists.

A similar point can be made about Coca-Cola sales in Europe. While Americans drink an average of three and one-half cans of Coke a week, Germans consume only two cans and the French just half a can. These figures suggest the tremendous potential for the Coca-Cola Company abroad.[43]

Stage IV: Forecast Probable Market Share

Once market potential has been estimated, the proportion of demand that the firm may capture—its probable market share—must be forecasted. Competitors' positions in targeted segments must be analyzed and a specific marketing

Figure 8.10   Assessing Nonfinancial Factors in Market Selection

Source: GARFIELD: © 1978 United Feature Syndicate, Inc. Courtesy of Alpo Petfoods, Inc. and United Feature Syndicate, Inc. ALPO is a registered trademark of Alpo Petfoods, Inc..

strategy designed to serve these segments. These two activities may be performed simultaneously. Moreover, design of marketing strategy and tactics determines the expected level of resources, that is, the costs that will be necessary for tapping the potential demand in each segment.

When Perpetual Savings Bank opened a new branch in suburban Washington, D.C., management expected the unit to generate $3 million to $4 million of deposits in its first year. The bank used sophisticated demographic mapping systems to locate the branch, and then to target promotional literature. This approach significantly altered management's original market share projection. Perpetual's new branch generated $16 million in deposits during the first two months after it opened.[44]

Stage V: Select Specific Market Segments

The information, analysis, and forecasts accumulated through the entire market segmentation decision process allow management to assess the potential for achieving company goals and to justify the development of one or more segments. For example, demand forecasts, when combined with cost projections, are used to determine the profit and the return on investment (ROI) that can be expected from each segment. Marketing strategy and tactics must be designed to reinforce the corporate image and advance reputation goals yet keep within the unique organizational capabilities of the firm.

At this point in the analysis, the costs and benefits to be weighed are not only monetary; they also include many difficult to measure but critical organizational and environmental factors. For example, the firm may not have enough experienced personnel to launch a successful attack on what clearly promises to be certain monetary success. Similarly, a firm with 80 percent of the market faces legal problems with the Federal Trade Commission if it increases its market concentration. The assessment of both financial and nonfinancial factors is a difficult but vital step in the decision process. When Alpo Petfoods Inc. decided to enter the $2 billion cat food market segment, a major consideration was how the new 28-item line would be accepted by retailers, who were wary of adding another brand to an already crowded pet food aisle. Alpo marketers achieved wide trade acceptance by extending the Alpo trademark used on its dog food products to its new cat food line and by using the popular GARFIELD® cartoon character as its cat food spokesperson. The use of GARFIELD on all product packaging and introductory promotions, such as the ad in Figure 8.10, was a major selling point with retailers.[45]

There is no single answer to the market segmentation decision—nor should there be. The marketing concept's prescription for serving the customer's needs and earning a profit while doing so implies that the marketer must evaluate each potential marketing program on its ability to achieve both goals in the marketplace. By performing the detailed analysis outlined in Figure 8.9, the marketing manager can increase the probability of success in profitably serving consumers' needs.

Target Market Decision Analysis

target market decision analysis
Evaluation of potential market segments on the basis of relevant characteristics.

Target market decision analysis is a useful tool in the market segmentation process. Targets are chosen by segmenting the total market on the basis of a given characteristic.

Applying Target Market Decision Analysis

Consider the decisions of an Atlanta-based publisher that wants to produce its first travel magazine. Management hopes to eventually publish a series of regional travel magazines, but it decides to concentrate on just one area until it develops a successful format. Therefore, the first segmentation question is which region to select. The publisher picks the Southeast primarily because of its editorial staff's familiarity with the region. Figure 8.11 outlines this and subsequent segmentation decisions.

Management's initial research shows that age is a significant variable in travel decisions. Generally, older empty-nesters spend more time in leisure travel than younger people with children at home. As a result, the publisher decided to narrow the target market to empty-nesters in the 55–64 age group and retired persons. Of course, the target market is also limited to people in these age groups living in the Southeast.

Finally, management believed that both travel costs and the price of the magazine would influence subscribers. Therefore, family income level was considered as the third segmentation variable. People in the top two brackets of family income were considered to be the most likely to purchase the new magazine. The final target market profile consisted of Southeastern residents aged 55 and over with family incomes over $40,000.

While this illustration used geographic and demographic segmentation bases, benefit and psychographic segmentation can also be used in target market decision analysis. Similarly, geographic, customer-based, and end-use application segmentation bases can be used in targeting industrial market segments.

Strategies for Reaching Target Markets

Much of the marketing effort is dedicated to the development of strategies that will best match product offerings to the needs of particular target markets. An appropriate match is vital to the firm's market success. Three basic strategies for

Figure 8.11

Target Market Decision Analysis for a New Travel Magazine

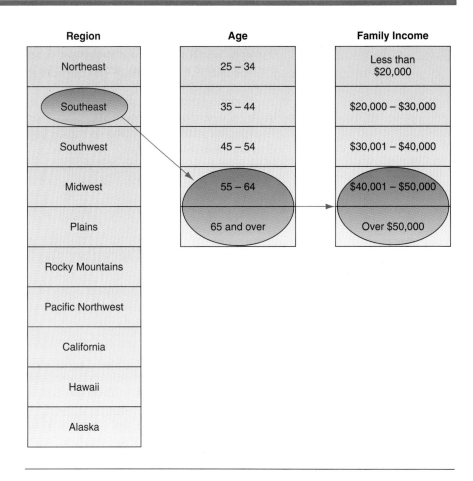

Region	Age	Family Income
Northeast	25 – 34	Less than $20,000
Southeast	35 – 44	$20,000 – $30,000
Southwest	45 – 54	$30,001 – $40,000
Midwest	55 – 64	$40,001 – $50,000
Plains	65 and over	Over $50,000
Rocky Mountains		
Pacific Northwest		
California		
Hawaii		
Alaska		

achieving consumer satisfaction are available: undifferentiated marketing, differentiated marketing, and concentrated marketing.

Undifferentiated Marketing

undifferentiated marketing
Strategy used by organizations that produce only one product and market it to all customers using a single marketing mix.

Firms that produce only one product or one product line and market it to all customers with a single marketing mix are said to practice **undifferentiated marketing.** This strategy is sometimes called *mass marketing.* Undifferentiated marketing was much more common in the past than it is today. As noted earlier, Henry Ford built the Model T and sold it for one price to everyone. He agreed to paint the car any color that consumers wanted "as long as it is black." Ford's only concession to more specific customer needs was to add a truck body for those Model T purchasers who needed more hauling capacity.

While undifferentiated marketing is efficient from a production viewpoint, there are inherent dangers in the strategy. A firm that attempts to satisfy everyone in the market with one standard product faces the threat of competitors offering specialized products to smaller segments of the total market and better satisfying each segment. Indeed, firms that implement a strategy of *differentiated marketing* or *concentrated marketing* (discussed in detail later) may capture enough small segments of the market to make the strategy of undifferentiated marketing unworkable for the competition. For this reason, The Arrow Company, despite its enviable reputation for quality dress shirts, added shirts of similar quality to appeal to more diverse segments of the shirt market, such as the casual-wear segment.

A firm that uses undifferentiated marketing may also encounter problems in foreign markets. The rugged Marlboro Man marketing campaign, so well received in the United States, never scored in Hong Kong. In fact, cigarette sales suffered because Hong Kong smokers perceived the Marlboro Man as a bum. Ads showed him with dirty fingernails, alone, and doing manual labor. A new campaign changed the Marlboro Man's image: He had clean fingernails, became a ranch owner, and owned a personal helicopter. The ad change resulted in Marlboro's emergence as the brand leader in Hong Kong, outselling the next two brands combined.[46]

For some products, though, tastes and preferences vary little among countries. Playtex successfully used a global approach in advertising its new WOW (WithOut Wire) bra. The product universally appeals to underwire-bra users because of the superior comfort of its plastic undershaper. Playtex launched WOW worldwide with identical advertising translated into seven languages and shown in eleven countries. The strategy was cost efficient: The global campaign cost about $250,000 to produce, about half the cost of creating individualized commercials for each country.[47]

Differentiated Marketing

differentiated marketing
Strategy employed by organizations that produce numerous products and use different marketing mixes designed to satisfy market segments.

Firms that produce numerous products with different marketing mixes designed to satisfy smaller segments are said to practice **differentiated marketing.** This strategy is still aimed at satisfying a large part of the total market, but instead of marketing one product with a single marketing program, the organization markets a number of products designed to appeal to individual parts of the total market. Reebok offers various walking shoes to satisfy the needs of different types of walkers. Reebok's strategy is to segment the walking market, recognizing that there is not just one type of walker, and therefore not one shoe to satisfy all walkers' needs. Thus, the Fitness Walker is offered for casual walking, the Power Trainer for workouts, professional racing flats for speed walking, and the Rugged Walker for hiking. The company's slogan is, "We have the shoe for wherever you walk." It accomplishes this by providing a separate marketing mix approach for each of its products with the objective of appealing to every type of walker.

Most firms practice differentiated marketing. Kraft markets a variety of cheeses to appeal to different consumer tastes—Philadelphia Brand cream cheese, Kraft American Singles, Cracker Barrel cheddar, Casino natural cheese, and Velveeta and Cheez Whiz process cheese spreads. The Marriott hotel chain offers different types of lodging to satisfy varying traveler needs—large, full-service hotels; resorts; budget hotels; suite hotels; and Marriott's Courtyard units. VF Corporation reaches all segments of the jeanswear market by offering four brands—Lee, Wrangler, Rustler, and Girbaud. Girbaud is a fashion brand distributed primarily through department and specialty stores, Rustler is marketed as a value brand, and Wrangler is positioned as the "Western original." Jean styles within brand categories are aimed at smaller segments. Lee, for instance, makes jeans for men, women, and children. Some Wrangler products target the leisure jean wearer while others, such as those advertised in Figure 8.12, target the outdoor enthusiast.[48]

By providing increased satisfaction for each of its numerous target markets, the company with a differentiated marketing strategy can produce more sales than would be possible with undifferentiated marketing. In general, however, the costs are greater, too. Production costs usually rise because additional products mean shorter production runs and increased setup time. Inventory costs rise because of added space needs for the products and increases in the necessary recordkeeping. Promotional costs also increase because unique promotional mixes are required for each market segment. Despite the greater costs, a

Figure 8.12   Using a Differentiated Marketing Strategy

Source: Courtesy of Wrangler, a division of VF Corporation.

company may be forced into differentiated marketing in order to remain competitive.

Concentrated Marketing

Rather than attempting to market its product offerings to several market segments, a firm may choose to focus its efforts on profitably satisfying only one market segment. This strategy of **concentrated marketing,** or *niche marketing,* is particularly appealing to small firms that lack the financial resources of their competitors.

Consider the case of tart-tasting Orangina orange soda from France. Packaged in a bulb-shaped bottle, Orangina's gets its unique taste from the fact that it contains 12 percent fruit juice and 2 percent pulp. Only Coke outsells Orangina in France. When Orangina (then named Orelia) was first introduced into the United States, it was targeted at the orange-soda segment of the market. Positioned as a juice-added product, its advertisements criticized the taste of competitive products like Orange Crush. But this attempt at a differentiation strategy failed to accurately assess the taste preferences of American consumers, the majority of whom rejected the French product's tart taste. A four-year

concentrated marketing
Strategy that directs all of a firm's marketing resources toward serving a small segment of the total market.

effort to crack the American mass market cost Personal Ricard, the French beverage producer, some $15 million. As a result, the firm shifted to a concentration strategy that emphasizes Orangina's European heritage.[49]

Concentrated marketing has its dangers. Since the firm's growth is tied to a particular segment, changes in the size of that segment or in customer buying patterns may result in severe financial problems. Sales may also drop if new competitors appeal to the same market segment.

Summary of Chapter Objectives

1. **Explain what is meant by a market.** A market consists of people and organizations with the necessary purchasing power and willingness and authority to buy. Markets may be classified according to product type. Consumer products are purchased by the ultimate consumer for personal use. Industrial products are purchased for use directly or indirectly in the production of other goods and services.

2. **Outline the role of market segmentation in developing a marketing strategy.** Market segmentation refers to the process of dividing the total market into several homogeneous groups. It plays an important role in the development of marketing strategies, because most products are targeted at specific market segments. The segmentation process allows marketers to choose their target markets more accurately.

3. **Explain each of the four bases for segmenting consumer markets.** Consumer markets may be divided on the basis of geographic, demographic, psychographic, or benefit segmentation. Geographic segmentation, one of the oldest forms, is the process of dividing the overall market into homogeneous groups on the basis of population location. The continual shifts in U.S. and foreign populations necessitate considerable effort in identifying the various geographic segments. The most commonly used form of segmentation is demographic segmentation, which classifies the overall market into homogeneous groups based on such characteristics as age, sex, and income level. Psychographic segmentation, a relatively new approach, uses behavioral profiles developed from analyses of consumers' activities, opinions, interests, and lifestyles to identify market segments. Benefit segmentation—sometimes called behavioral segmentation—is perhaps the most useful approach. This approach segments markets on the basis of the perceived benefits consumers expect to derive from a good or service. When this is impossible, benefit segmentation relies on proxy variables like usage rates or brand loyalty.

4. **Describe the three bases for segmenting industrial markets.** There are three bases for industrial market segmentation. Geographic segmentation is commonly used in concentrated industries. Customer-based segmentation focuses on product specifications of industrial buyers. Segmentation by end-use application is based on how industrial purchasers will use the product.

5. **Identify the steps in the market segmentation process.** Market segmentation is the division of large, heterogeneous markets into several relatively homogeneous groups. The segmentation process follows a five-step sequence: identifying the bases on which to segment markets; developing user profiles for appropriate market segments; forecasting the overall market potential for the relevant market segments; estimating market share; and selecting specific market segments.

6. **Explain how target market decision analysis can be used in segmenting markets.** Target market decision analysis is a useful tool in the market segmentation process. It involves identifying the specific characteristics of targeted market segments. All bases for segmenting may be employed in target market decision analysis. The approach can be used for both consumer and industrial markets.

7. **Discuss the three alternative strategies for reaching target markets.** Three alternative strategies exist for matching the firm's offerings to specific target markets. Undifferentiated marketing refers to the strategy of producing only one product and marketing it to the entire market with a single marketing mix. Differentiated marketing refers to the strategy of producing numerous products, each with its own marketing mix, designed to satisfy different segments of the market. Concentrated marketing refers to the strategy of directing all of the firm's marketing resources toward satisfying a small segment of the total market.

Key Terms

market	lifestyle
consumer products	psychographic segmentation
industrial products	AIO statements
market segmentation	VALS 2
geographic segmentation	benefit segmentation
Metropolitan Statistical Area (MSA)	customer-based segmentation
Primary Metropolitan Statistical Area (PMSA)	end-use application segmentation
	end-use application
Consolidated Metropolitan Statistical Area (CMSA)	target market decision analysis
	undifferentiated marketing
demographic segmentation	differentiated marketing
family life cycle	concentrated marketing
Engel's laws	

Review Questions

1. What is a market? Explain the components that are needed in order for a market to exist.

2. Bicycles are consumer goods; iron ore is an industrial good. Are trucks consumer goods or industrial goods? Support your answer.

3. Identify and briefly explain the bases for segmenting consumer markets. Which approach is the oldest? Which one is used most frequently?

4. Identify the major population shifts that have occurred in recent years. How do you account for these shifts?

5. Distinguish among MSAs, PMSAs, and CMSAs. How can marketers use these concepts?

6. Explain the use of usage rates and brand loyalty as segmentation variables. What is meant by a proxy variable in the context of benefit segmentation?

7. What market segmentation base would you recommend for the following?
   a. Portland Trailblazers professional basketball team
   b. Fujitsu fax machine
   c. Listerine mouthwash

8. Identify and briefly explain the bases for segmenting industrial markets. Cite examples of the use of each approach.

9. What is target market decision analysis? Relate it to the concept of market segmentation.

10. Outline the basic features of undifferentiated marketing. Contrast differentiated marketing with concentrated marketing.

Discussion Questions

1. China's Flying Pigeon Bicycle Group had always painted its bicycles black. Eventually it had an inventory of 2 million units. Flying Pigeon then adopted a consumer orientation and began to produce yellow and red bicycles as well as the traditional color. Sales quickly took off.[50] Compare Flying Pigeon's problem to Henry Ford's original approach to segmentation.

2. Kinder-Care targets working women aged 25 to 39 with household incomes of $25,000 to $75,000 and a higher-than-average educational level.[51] What type of market segmentation strategy is Kinder-Care employing? Why do you think Kinder-Care picked this particular market segment?

3. Match the following bases for market segmentation with the appropriate items. Explain your choices.
   a. Geographic segmentation
   b. Demographic segmentation
   c. Psychographic segmentation
   d. Benefit segmentation
      ____ ESPN attracts sports-oriented males, while Lifetime, "The Women's Network," appeals to both career women and contemporary home-makers.[52]
      ____ Campbell Soup decided to divide the U.S. market into 22 regions.
      ____ "7-up, clear, crisp, with no caffeine."
      ____ "This is not your father's Oldsmobile."

4. People over 50 use significantly more aspirin than younger people. As a result, Bristol-Meyers (dropping its heart attack prevention ads) hired actress Angela Landsbury to do commercials with the theme that Bufferin can help people over 50 overcome aches and pains and lead full lives.[53] Is Bristol-Meyers using demographic or benefit segmentation, or both?

5. *American Baby* asks subscribers their baby's actual or prospective birth date. The magazine is then able to divide its 1.1 million readers into postnatal and prenatal stages. This database allows advertisers to target mothers of children of specific age groups. For example, the magazine can insert Gerber ads in copies going to a targeted segment of readers.[54] Relate this illustration to the chapter's discussion of target market decision analysis.

Computer Applications

In one of the earliest reported studies of how consumer expenditure patterns change when household income increases, German statistician Ernst Engel proposed three general conclusions:

1. A smaller percentage of the household budget will be allocated to food purchases.

2. The percentage of the household budget spent on housing, household operations, and clothing will remain constant.

3. The percentage spent on other items (such as education and recreation) and the percentage devoted to savings/investments will increase.

These generalizations became known as *Engel's laws.*

Directions: Use menu item 7 titled "Engel's Laws" to solve each of the following problems.

Problem 1.   Alice Garcia is a single, 26-year-old marketing research analyst at a major consumer goods company in Boston. Last year Alice saved $3,200 and spent the remainder as follows: food, $6,400; housing and clothing, $12,800; and miscellaneous (including entertainment and vacations), $9,600. But a recent promotion and salary increase has prompted Garcia to reevaluate her personal budget. She has decided to use a payroll deduction program to increase her savings to $4,200, go on a diet and cut her food expenditures to $4,600, increase her housing and clothing outlays slightly to $14,000, and spend the rest of next year's $36,000 salary on miscellaneous items (including a short winter vacation). Does Garcia's budget conflict with Engel's laws? If so, how?

Problem 2.   The Martin family of San Antonio uses a budget to monitor and control household expenditures. The family has just prepared this year's budget to reflect the salary increases that both spouses expect at the beginning of the year. The general categories of expenditures and savings and the amounts allocated to each category are shown in the accompanying table. Is the Martins' budget for this year consistent with Engel's laws? With which, if any, of the laws does it conflict?

Budget Category	Last Year's Expenditures	This Year's Budgeted Amount
Food	$18,000	$19,500
Clothing and housing	24,000	29,250
Other	18,000	16,250
Total	$60,000	$65,000

Problem 3.   Sam and Carla Benson of Wilmington, North Carolina, recently consulted a financial planner for assistance in developing a household budget and making investments. In the process, the planner made several suggestions about the Benson's personal expenditures. Noting that the couple's combined income would increase next year by 12 percent, the planner suggested that they purchase the home they had been considering. The planner pointed out that while their monthly housing costs would rise 50 percent above their current rent, most of the increase would be tax deductible as an interest expense. However, Carla was interested in using the additional income to purchase stocks and bonds rather than to serve as a down payment on the house. Last year's expenditures and next year's budget proposals are as follows:

Budget Category	Expenditures	Planner's Proposed Budget for Next Year	Carla's Proposed Budget for Next Year
Food	$ 14,000	$ 15,000	$ 15,000
Beverages	1,000	2,000	2,000
Clothing	20,000	22,000	22,000
Housing	17,000	25,000	17,000
Entertainment	10,000	11,000	11,000
Investments	5,000	5,000	17,000
Other	33,000	32,000	28,000
Total	$100,000	$112,000	$112,000

a.   Does the planner's suggestion conflict with Engel's laws?

b.   How consistent is Carla's proposed budget with Engel's laws?

Problem 4.   Pat and Jan Gardner of Cleveland have never used a formal household budget. But the couple does engage in an annual ritual of sitting in front of their fireplace every New Year's Eve, evaluating the past year and making some general plans for the coming one. The discussion this past December 31 went something like this:

Jan: Well, this year was certainly good to us, with each of us getting a $5,000 raise effective tomorrow.

Pat: Yes, I agree. So maybe it is about time we moved on that condo with the "For Sale" sign that we drive past every day.

Jan: Pat, you read my mind every time! I don't care if it does increase our spending on housing from $15,000 to $19,500 next year. We could make it up somewhere else in our spending plans.

Pat: Well, we still have to eat, but we could stay away from the gourmet section and cut back on our percentage spent on food. My quick tally of the checkbook shows we spent $8,000 on food items this year. We could try to hold our food spending to say, $9,000 next year.

Jan: And I would be willing to spend our vacation in Florida rather than flying to Europe like we planned. According to my mental calculator, that means we would have $3,500 left from our $32,000 take-home pay next year for miscellaneous—including the vacation. That's $500 less than the $4,000 we allocated for miscellaneous spending this past year out of our combined $27,000 in take-home pay.

Pat: Jan, next New Year's Eve, we've just got to start talking about a savings and investment plan. . . .

Do the Gardner's financial plans conflict with Engel's laws? If so, how?

Problem 5. Virgil Romanos is a relief pitcher with the Minnesota Twins. Romanos, who is 23 and single, has just completed the best year of his baseball career, posting a 9-7 win/loss record with 16 saves. His agent has just negotiated a new contract for next year that will boost Romanos to $350,000 from the $280,000 he earned last year. The agent, an attorney and CPA, has also developed a personal budget for Romanos that reflects his raise and the fact that the young pitcher will marry soon. Since the couple plans to start a family right away, the bride-to-be has decided to give up her teaching position in Bloomington. Determine whether the agent's proposed budget coincides with Engel's laws. (Hint: Taxes and the agent's fees should be included in the "other" category.)

Budget Category	Last Year's Expenditures	This Year's Budgeted Amount
Clothing	$ 29,000	$ 35,000
Food	9,000	11,000
Entertainment	23,000	28,000
Travel	10,000	25,000
Housing	37,000	57,000
Professional fees	28,000	35,000
Taxes	84,000	95,000
Savings and investments	60,000	64,000
Total	$280,000	$350,000

VIDEO CASE

8

Irvine Co.

The original 90,000 acres of the Irvine Ranch were purchased by James Irvine and his partners for 35 cents an acre in the 1860s. Running inland 22 miles from the Pacific Ocean, the ranch is located between Los Angeles and San Diego in what is now called Orange County. The tract includes the city of Irvine and sections of several other wealthy Los Angeles suburbs, such as Newport Beach.

For generations, the property was operated as a farm and ranch. In fact, nearly 60,000 acres of this highly fertile land are still used for agricultural pursuits. Major crops include tomatoes, avocados, asparagus, and Valencia oranges.

The area was virtually uninhabited until the 1950s. Then the Los Angeles megapolis spread into the region, and Orange County quickly became one of the fastest-growing areas in the United States. As a result, the land soon became more valuable for housing development than for agricultural purposes. Thus the Irvine Co. set up a project to develop the property by creating planned communities. The Irvine plan was part of the so-called "New Town" concept that was popular at the time. Like developers of such East Coast new towns as Columbia, Maryland, and Reston, Virginia, Irvine's marketing plan involved setting up planned communities that included shopping, schools, churches, and recreational areas along with housing.

Today some 66,500 acres of the Irvine property—15 percent of Orange County—remain undeveloped. As it is one of the largest undeveloped plots of land near a major U.S. city, its future worth is immeasurable.

Irvine's marketers planned to utilize a textbook approach to market segmentation. Since people have differing housing needs based upon their life-cycle stage, the firm should have made alternative housing available to cater to these varying needs. However, the traditional approach to building ignored these needs and treated the housing market as a monolith, recognizing different households' requirements with only variations in the number of bedrooms or overall square footage. The Irvine marketing approach involved an initial analysis of the housing market and the development of a product mix designed to appeal to different types of buyers. Families would live near families, adult households near other adult households, and so forth.

Market segmentation—the process of dividing a market into homogeneous target markets—provided the key to Irvine's planned community concept. Irvine's management felt that market segmentation would allow the firm to meet both social and marketing goals by providing a structure for growth while allowing the development to proceed more rapidly. Market segmentation can be done on geographic, demographic, psychographic, or benefit bases. Irvine's management initially selected psychographic segmentation for characterizing its market. As noted in the chapter, psychographic segmentation is based upon an analysis of consumer lifestyles. The company accumulated all sorts of information, from the cars people drove to the wines they consumed. However, no one could relate this data to the types of housing people desired.

Irvine Co. soon turned to other means of segmenting its market. It began interviewing its home buyers, both to promote public relations and to obtain demographic data that would assist in future segmentation efforts. Builders were persuaded to design homes specifically targeted at given market segments. Thus, demographic segmentation enabled Irvine to build the homes people really wanted. In addition to standard one-, two-, and three-bedroom formats to match various household sizes, it offered options such as a triplex plan, which gave first-time buyers affordable but spacious housing, and nonrelated-adults dwellings with individual master bedrooms.

Irvine's market segmentation efforts hit a snag in the late 1970s. Inflation and substantial in-migration created an unprecedented housing boom in Southern California. Consumer demand soon exceeded product availability, forcing housing prices up 25 to 30 percent per year. Some houses were even being sold through lottery drawings. Also, some homes that cost $80,000 in the 1950s had been sold with 25-year land leases rather than as deeded land. When the leases were reopened in the late 1970s, Irvine Co. sought increases as high as 3,333 percent. It later backed away from this position, offering to sell the land or proposing new leases that were higher priced but far less so than was originally proposed.

If the price hikes did not force buyers out of the housing market, mortgage rates did. A restrictive monetary policy designed to combat double-digit inflation produced interest rates of nearly 20 percent. As a result, new houses remained unsold. Irvine's market segmentation strategy was a shambles, as targeted groups could no longer afford the available housing. In fact, Orange County's industrial growth was stymied as well, since people will not take jobs where they cannot afford to buy homes.

The housing boom began to subside in the early to mid-1980s, when home prices and mortgage rates came into closer balance with consumers' ability to purchase housing. Irvine Co. returned to its segmentation strategy. Once again, the challenge was to provide housing that would accommodate diverse needs and encourage families to remain in the community throughout their life cycles.

More recently, development has expanded to include office parks. Irvine sold 500 acres to the University of California at a cut rate to encourage high-tech commercial and industrial use, which Irvine hopes will attract corporate R&D facilities to adjacent properties. The stagnation of the housing market in the 1990s, however, put severe pressure on the company, and management is investigating alternative plans.

Sources: Gary Hector, "America's Richest Land Baron," *Fortune* (August 27, 1990), pp. 98–102; Harry Hurt III, "Donald Trump, Move Over," *Newsweek* (February 5, 1990), pp. 42–43; Julie Flynn and Mark Frons, "Owning Irvine, Calif., Isn't What It Used to Be," *Business Week* (March 9, 1987), pp. 80, 82; and Gary Hector, "The Land Coup in Orange County," *Fortune* (November 14, 1983), pp. 91–92, 96, 100, 102.

Questions

1. Discuss the importance of market segmentation for Irvine Co.

2. Why was demographic segmentation more effective than psychographic segmentation for Irvine Co.?

3. What specific aspects of demographic segmentation are evident in this case?

Source: Courtesy of H.J. Heinz Company.

The H.J. Heinz Company identifies its varieties of some 3,000 different products marketed on six continents with brand names such as Weight Watchers, StarKist, Ore-Ida, 9-Lives, Chico-San, Orlando, Olivine, and, of course, Heinz. The identification of goods with brand names and symbols is one of many decisions marketers must make in developing product strategies.

PART **4**

Product Strategy

9

Product Strategy

From Belgium to Boston, Post-it brand notes are indispensable in homes and offices around the world. 3M Company pioneered an entirely new product category when it introduced its innovation to American consumers in 1980.

Post-it notes began life as a way of keeping bookmarks from slipping out. Art Fry, a 3M scientist who sang in his church choir, was frustrated because his page markers kept falling out of his hymnal. He remembered another 3M scientist's discovery of a barely sticky adhesive. Fry tried the low-tack adhesive on a piece of paper. It was just what he was looking for.

The 3M product that evolved from this event, Post-it notes, is simply a pad of notepaper with an adhesive strip on the back of each sheet. Because the adhesive is very weak, the strips can be attached to objects without damaging them the way Scotch tape would, for instance. In addition, they do not restrict page turning, as do paper clips, and they don't fall off, as do ordinary paper strips. Post-it notes were an instant success, quickly moving through the introductory stage of the product life cycle.

Fry's idea would never have been converted into a viable product had it not been for 3M's unique corporate culture. Once he had hit upon the idea of Post-it notes, Fry was able to use his "bootlegging" research time on the project—the 15 percent of researchers' work time allowed by 3M for working on anything of personal interest. Fry spent a year and a half perfecting Post-it notes and then convincing the right 3M executives of the idea's commercial possibilities. By late 1975, the product was ready for a market test.

The test proved a failure—but this was the point at which 3M's willingness to exhaust every possibility before abandoning a championed idea paid off. One of 3M's marketing executives suspected that the test failure was due to the testers' inability to get the product into the hands of the right people. A new test was commissioned in Boise, Idaho, this time with the promotional emphasis on free samples. The strategy worked, and Post-it notes were an immediate hit.

The original Post-it notes were little pads of yellow paper. Today there are more than 350 varieties of notes. They come in cubes and pop-up dispensers, different colors and sizes, and printed "creative expression" formats.

3M has increased the number of Post-it note users by marketing the product abroad. Today, about 50 percent of Post-it note sales come from international markets.

One of 3M's goals is to generate 25 percent of each year's annual sales from products introduced within the past five years. That's a tall order, since the 3M product line consists of some 60,000 items. 3M wants to be sure that its researchers are constantly feeding new ideas into the introductory stage of the product life cycle. How does 3M do it? Researchers are pushed to put customers first. "Innovation works from understanding consumer needs," says CEO Allen Jacobson. 3M fosters the spirit of innovation by encouraging researchers to share information and ideas and giving them free rein for developing new products even when the payoff is far down the road. For 3M, the payoff is commercial successes like Post-it notes. And for its successes, 3M has earned the distinction as a "master of innovation."[1]

Photo source: © Steve Niedorf.

Chapter Overview

The first three parts of this book deal with preliminary marketing considerations such as marketing research and buyer behavior aimed at identifying the firm's target market. Now the attention shifts to the firm's marketing mix.

The three chapters in Part 4 focus on the first element of the marketing mix—the goods and services the firm offers to its target market. Planning efforts begin with the choice of products to offer the target market. The other variables of the marketing mix—distribution channels, promotional plans, and pricing structures—must be based on product planning.

This chapter begins with a definition of product. We then present several basic concepts—the classification of products, the product life cycle, and the consumer adoption process—that marketers use in developing successful products such as Post-it brand notes. Finally, we discuss the increasingly important role of customer service in product strategy.

Defining Product

A narrow definition of the word *product* focuses on the physical or functional characteristics of a good or service. For example, a videocassette recorder is a rectangular container of metal and plastic with wires that connect it to a television set, accompanied by a series of special tapes for recording and viewing. But the purchaser has a much broader view of the VCR. Some buyers may want to use it to see soap operas they missed because of work; others may be interested in the warranty and service facilities of the manufacturer; still others may want to rent recently released movies for home viewing.

Marketing decision makers must have this broader conception of product in mind and realize that people buy want satisfaction. For example, most buyers know little about the gasoline they buy. In fact, many view it not as a product but as a price they must pay for the privilege of driving their cars.

A broader view of product extends beyond physical or functional attributes. It is a total product concept that includes package design and labeling, symbols such as trademarks and brand names, and customer service activities that add value to the product. Consequently, a **product** is a bundle of physical, service, and symbolic attributes designed to enhance consumer want satisfaction. The trade advertisement in Figure 9.1 illustrates that General Electric adds value to its appliances by offering "more factory service" than all other appliance firms combined.

product
Bundle of physical, service, and symbolic attributes designed to enhance buyers' want-satisfaction.

An International Perspective

Consumers seek different product benefits in various countries. For example, Japanese and Korean mothers want disposable diapers to be thin, tailored, and available in a relatively small package. Minimal storage space and societally dictated frequent changes are usually cited as the explanation of these mothers' consumer behavior. While Americans now also favor thin diapers, the reason is more likely to be environmental concern about diminishing landfill space. On the other side of the spectrum are Australians, who prefer thick diapers.[2]

Classifying Consumer and Industrial Products

How a firm markets a product depends largely on the product itself. For example, McDonald's uses mass-media advertising to promote its fast-food service at thousands of locations worldwide. Hershey markets its candy products through

Figure 9.1

Service Attributes of a
Product

*It may be hard to believe, but one
appliance company offers more factory*   *service than all the others combined.*
For service, call
800-432-2737

We bring good things to life.

Source: Courtesy of GE Appliances.

candy wholesalers to thousands of supermarkets, convenience stores, discount houses, and vending machine companies. A firm manufacturing and marketing forklifts may use sales representatives to call on industrial buyers and deliver its product either directly from the factory or from regional warehouses.

Product strategy differs for consumer and industrial products. As defined earlier, *consumer products* are destined for use by the ultimate consumer and *industrial products* are used directly or indirectly in producing other products for resale. These two major categories can be further subdivided.

Types of Consumer Products

Several classification systems for consumer products have been suggested. One basic distinction is based on whether or not the buyer perceives a need for the item. Thus, an *unsought product* is one for which the consumer does not yet recognize a need. Examples of unsought products are life insurance and funeral services. In contrast, most consumers recognize the need for various types of consumer goods. The most commonly used classification divides consumer products into three groups: convenience, shopping, and specialty products.[3] This classification is based on consumer buying behavior.

convenience products

Products that consumers want to purchase frequently, immediately, and with a minimum of effort.

Convenience Products. The products that the consumer wants to purchase frequently, immediately, and with a minimum of effort are called **convenience products.** Milk, bread, butter, eggs, and beer (the staples of most 24-hour convenience food stores) are all convenience products. So are newspapers, Post-it brand notes, chewing gum, candy, magazines, cigarettes, and most vending machine items. The products of many service firms such as barber shops, beauty salons, quick-print shops, and dry cleaners may also be purchased on a convenience basis.

Figure 9.2

Promoting a Convenience
Product

Isn't life delicious?

Source: Reprinted with permission of Nabisco Brands, Inc. and Planters Life Savers Company.

Convenience products are usually sold by brand name and are low priced. They fall into three subcategories: staples, impulse items, and emergency items. Many of them—such as bread, milk, and gasoline—are *staple items,* the consumer's supply of which must constantly be replenished. In most cases, the buyer has already decided to purchase a particular brand of gasoline or candy or to buy at a certain store and spends little time deliberating on the purchase decision. Products purchased on the spur of the moment, such as tatoos and ear-piercing, or out of habit when the supply is low are referred to as *impulse products.* For instance, it is estimated that over half of all supermarket purchases are unplanned.[4] The purchase of *emergency items* is prompted by unexpected and urgent needs. A repair kit for a broken water pipe, a visit to a hospital's emergency center for a sprained ankle, or an ice scraper purchased in the midst of an unexpected winter storm are all examples of the final subcategory of convenience products.

The consumer rarely visits competing stores or compares price and quality when purchasing convenience products. The possible gains from such comparisons are outweighed by the costs of acquiring the additional information. This does not mean, however, that the consumer is destined to remain permanently loyal to one brand of beer, candy, or cigarettes. People continually receive new information from radio and television advertisements, billboards, and word-of-mouth communication. Since the prices of most convenience products are low, trial purchases of competing brands or products are made with little financial risk and often create new habits.

Consumers are unwilling to spend much effort in purchasing convenience products, so the manufacturer must strive to make them as convenient as possible. Candy, cigarettes, and newspapers are sold in almost every supermarket, convenience store, and restaurant. Sellers also place vending machines in spots that are convenient for customers, such as office buildings and factories.

Retailers usually carry several competing brands of convenience products and are unlikely to promote any particular one. The promotional burden,

Figure 9.3

Example of a Heterogeneous
Shopping Product

Source: Courtesy of Century Furniture.

therefore, falls on the manufacturer, who must advertise extensively to develop and retain consumer acceptance of the product. The LifeSavers ad in Figure 9.2 is part of Planters LifeSavers Company's promotion to motivate consumers to choose LifeSavers over competing brands. Packaging also plays an important role in the strategy of convenience products marketers. Because most convenience products are bought at the point of purchase, a distinctive package can improve a product's visibility on the store shelf.

shopping products
Products purchased only after the consumer has made comparisons of competing products in competing stores on such bases as price, quality, style, and color.

Shopping Products. In contrast to convenience products, **shopping products** are purchased only after the consumer has made comparisons of competing products in competing stores on such bases as price, quality, style, and color. Shopping products, which typically are more expensive than convenience products, include clothing, furniture, appliances, jewelry, and shoes. Consumers typically shop around for such services as child care and home and auto repair. The purchaser of shopping products lacks complete information prior to the shopping trip and gathers information during it.

A woman intent on adding a new dress to her wardrobe may visit many stores, try on a number of dresses, and spend a weekend making the final choice. She may follow a regular route from store to store in surveying competing offerings and ultimately will select the dress that most appeals to her. New stores carrying assortments of shopping products must ensure that they are located near similar stores so that they will be included in shopping expeditions.

Some shopping products, such as refrigerators and washing machines, are considered *homogeneous;* that is, the consumer views them as essentially the same. Others, such as furniture, are considered *heterogeneous,* or essentially different. For example, the ad in Figure 9.3 shows some of the 160 different styles

Figure 9.4 Advertising a Specialty Product

of dining room chairs available at Century Furniture. Price is an important factor in the purchase of homogeneous shopping products, while quality and styling are relatively more significant in the purchase of heterogeneous products.

Important features of shopping products are physical attributes, service attributes (warranties and after-sale service), price, styling, and place of purchase. The store's name and reputation also have a considerable influence on consumer buying behavior. The brand is often less important, in spite of the large amounts of money firms frequently spend promoting their brands. The personal-selling efforts of salespeople are important in promoting shopping products.

Since buyers of shopping products expend some effort in making their purchases, producers utilize fewer retail stores. Retailers and manufacturers work closely together in promoting shopping products, and retail purchases often are made directly from the manufacturer or its representative rather than the wholesaler. Fashion merchandise buyers for department stores and specialty shops make regular buying trips to regional and national markets in New York, Dallas, Los Angeles, and Seattle. Buyers for furniture retailers often go directly to the factories of furniture manufacturers or attend furniture trade shows.

Specialty Products. The specialty products purchaser is well aware of what he or she wants and is willing to make a special effort to obtain it. The nearest Cartier dealer may be 50 miles away, for example, but the watch purchaser

Table 9.1   Marketing Impact of the Consumer Products Classification System

Factor	Convenience Products	Shopping Products	Specialty Products
Consumer Factors			
Planning time involved in purchase	Very little	Considerable	Extensive
Purchase frequency	Frequent	Less frequent	Infrequent
Importance of convenient location	Critical	Important	Unimportant
Comparison of price and quality	Very little	Considerable	Very little
Marketing Mix Factors			
Price	Low	Relatively high	High
Promotion	Advertising and sales promotion by producer	Personal selling and advertising by both producer and retailer	Personal selling and advertising by both producer and retailer
Distribution channel length	Long	Relatively short	Very short
Number of retail outlets	Many	Few	Very few; often one per market area
Store image	Unimportant	Very important	Important

specialty products
Products with unique characteristics that cause the buyer to prize them and make a special effort to obtain them.

willing to spend several thousand dollars will go there to buy this prestigious timepiece. **Specialty products** possess some unique characteristics that cause the buyer to prize those particular brands. For these products, the buyer has complete information prior to the shopping trip and is unwilling to accept substitutes.

Specialty products typically are high priced and frequently branded. Included in this category are Gucci handbags, the Golden Door health spa, Tiffany jewelry, and Rolls-Royce automobiles. Since consumers are willing to exert considerable effort to obtain them, fewer retail outlets are required. For instance, Mercury outboard motors and Porsche sports cars may be handled by only one or two retailers for every 100,000 people.

Highly personalized service by sales associates and image advertising are used in the promotion of specialty products. Because these products are available in only a few outlets, advertisements frequently list where they can be purchased. For example, the ad in Figure 9.4 includes a list of worldwide boutiques and U.S. retailers where consumers can buy the clothing of French fashion designer Emanuel Ungaro.

Applying the Consumer Products Classification System.

The three-way classification system allows the marketing manager to gain additional information for use in developing a marketing strategy. Consumer behavior patterns differ for each type of consumer product. For example, once a new food product has been classified as a convenience product, insights are gained about marketing needs in branding, promotion, pricing, and distribution methods. Table 9.1 summarizes the impact of the consumer products classification system on the development of an effective marketing mix.

But the classification system also poses problems. The major problem is that it suggests only three categories into which all products must fit. Some products fit neatly into one category, but others fall into the grey areas between categories. For example, how should a new automobile be classified? It is expensive, sold by brand, and handled by a few exclusive dealers in each city. But before classifying it as a specialty product, other characteristics must be considered. Most new-car buyers shop extensively among competing models and auto dealers before deciding on the best deal. A more effective way to utilize the classification system is to consider it as a continuum representing degrees of effort expended by the consumer. At one end of the continuum are convenience products, at the other end lie specialty products, and in the middle fall shopping products. On this continuum, the new-car purchase can be located between the categories of shopping and specialty products but closer to the specialty products end.

A second problem with the classification system is that consumers differ in their buying patterns. One person will make an unplanned purchase of a new Honda Accord, while others will shop extensively before purchasing a car. But one buyer's impulse purchase does not make the Accord a convenience product. Products are classified by the purchase patterns of the majority of buyers.

Types of Industrial Products

Industrial products can be subdivided into six categories: installations, accessory equipment, component parts and materials, raw materials, supplies, and business services.[5] Industrial buyers are professional customers; their job is to make rational, effective purchase decisions. The purchase decision process involved in buying supplies of flour for General Mills, for example, is much the same as that used in buying the same commodity for Pillsbury. Thus, the classification system for industrial products is based on product uses rather than on customer buying behavior.

installations
Major capital items, such as new factories and heavy machinery, that typically are expensive and relatively long-lived.

Installations.
The specialty products of the industrial market are called **installations.** Included in this classification are such major capital items as new factories and heavy machinery, computers, telecommunications systems, Boeing 737s for Air New Zealand, and locomotives for Burlington Northern.

Since installations are relatively long-lived and involve large sums of money, their purchase represents a major decision for an organization. Negotiations often extend over several months and involve the participation of numerous decision makers. In many cases, the selling company must provide technical expertise. When custom-made equipment is involved, representatives of the selling firm work closely with the buyer's engineers and production personnel to design the most feasible product for the buying firm.

Price is almost never the deciding factor in the purchase of installations. The purchasing firm is interested in the product's efficiency and performance over its useful life. It also wants a minimum of breakdowns. "Downtime" is expensive, because employees are nonproductive (but still paid) while the machine is being repaired.

Since most of the factories of firms purchasing installations are geographically concentrated, the selling firm places its promotional emphasis on well-trained salespeople, many of whom have a technical background. Most installations are marketed directly on a manufacturer-to-user basis. Even though a sale may be a one-time transaction, contracts often call for regular product servicing. In the case of extremely expensive installations, such as computer and electronic equipment, some firms lease the installations rather than sell them outright and assign personnel directly to the lessee for operating or maintaining the equipment.

accessory equipment
Capital items, usually less expensive and shorter-lived than installations, such as typewriters, hand tools, and adding machines.

Accessory Equipment.
Fewer decision makers are usually involved in purchasing **accessory equipment**—capital items that typically are less expensive and shorter-lived than installations. Although quality and service are

Figure 9.5

Example of a Component
Material

YOU'RE LOOKING AT A REMARKABLE
GROWTH CURVE. It's a loblolly pine tree seedling.
We're excited about this seedling. It's the latest
generation of special "superior tree" stock that's taken
us 34 years to nurture. We breed these trees to mature
faster, grow straight and tall — and provide twice as
much wood fiber per acre. Since 1980, we've raised
more than one billion. Our work keeps growing.

INTERNATIONAL PAPER
TWO MANHATTANVILLE RD., PURCHASE, NY 10577. 1-(800)-223-1268

important criteria in purchasing accessory equipment, the firm is likely to be much more price conscious. Accessory equipment includes such products as desk calculators, hand tools, portable drills, small lathes, and word processors. Although these products are considered capital items and are depreciated over several years, their useful lives generally are much shorter than that of an installation.

Because of the need for continuous representation and the more widespread geographic dispersion of accessory equipment purchasers, a wholesaler — often called an **industrial distributor** — contacts potential customers in each geographic area. Technical assistance usually is not necessary, and the manufacturer of accessory equipment often can effectively utilize wholesalers in marketing its products. Manufacturers also use advertising more than do installation producers.

Component Parts and Materials. Whereas installations and accessory equipment are used in producing the final product, **component parts and materials** are the finished industrial products of one producer that actually become part of the final product of another producer. Spark plugs complete a new Chevrolet; batteries often are added to Mattel toys; tires are included with a Dodge pickup truck. A digital flight control computer system produced by Allied-Signal is a component part of the F-16 aircraft. Some fabricated materials, such as flour, undergo further processing before the finished product is produced. Textiles, paper pulp, and chemicals are other examples of component materials. The advertisement in Figure 9.5 describes how International Paper breeds a special, superior tree stock that is used in the production of paper, cardboard, and newsprint.

industrial distributor
Wholesaling marketing intermediary that operates in the industrial products market and typically handles small accessory equipment and operating supplies.

component parts and materials
Finished industrial products that actually become part of the final product. Also known as fabricated parts and materials.

Purchasers of component parts and materials need a regular, continuous supply of uniform-quality products. These products generally are purchased on contract for a period of one year or more. Direct sale is common, and satisfied customers often become permanent buyers. Wholesalers sometimes are used for fill-in purchases and in handling sales to smaller purchasers.

Raw Materials.

Farm products—such as cattle, cotton, eggs, milk, pigs, and soybeans—and *natural products*—such as coal, copper, iron ore, and lumber—constitute **raw materials.** They are similar to component parts and materials in that they actually become a part of the final product.

Since most raw materials are graded, the purchaser is assured of standardized products of uniform quality. As with component parts and materials, direct sale of raw materials is common, and sales typically are made on a contractual basis. Wholesalers are increasingly involved in the purchase of raw materials from foreign suppliers.

Price is seldom a deciding factor in the purchase of raw materials, since it is often quoted at a central market and is virtually identical among competing sellers. Purchasers buy raw materials from the firms they consider most able to deliver in the required quantity and quality.

Supplies.

If installations represent the "specialty products" of the industrial market, operating supplies are the "convenience products." **Supplies** are regular expense items that are necessary in the firm's daily operation but are not part of the final product.

Supplies are sometimes called **MRO items,** because they can be divided into three categories: (1) *maintenance items,* such as brooms, floor-cleaning compounds, and light bulbs; (2) *repair items,* such as nuts and bolts used in repairing equipment; and (3) *operating supplies,* such as heating fuel, lubricating oil, Post-it brand notes, and office stationery.

The regular purchase of operating supplies is a routine aspect of the purchasing agent's job. Wholesalers are often used in the sale of supplies due to the items' low unit prices, small sales, and large numbers of potential buyers. Since supplies are relatively standardized, price competition is frequently heavy. However, the purchasing agent spends little time making purchase decisions. He or she frequently places telephone or mail orders or makes regular purchases from the sales representative of the local office supply wholesaler.

Business Services.

The **business services** category includes the intangible products firms buy to facilitate their production and operational processes. Examples of business services are financial, leasing and renting equipment and vehicles, insurance, protection/security, legal, consulting, transportation, and technical.

Price is often a deciding factor in the purchase of a business service. The buying firm must decide whether to buy a service or provide it internally. For example, an industrial buyer may purchase the services of a public relations firm rather than assume the costs of maintaining an in-house public relations department. This decision may be influenced by how frequently the service is used and its degree of specialization. The way business services are purchased varies considerably, depending on the type of service. For example, the purchase of a window-cleaning service is routine and straightforward, similar to that of buying industrial supplies. By contrast, the purchase of a highly specialized engineering or architectural design service is complex and may involve the lengthy negotiations that characterize the purchase of installations. This

---

raw materials
Industrial products, such as farm products (wheat, cotton, soybeans) and natural products (coal, lumber, iron ore), used in producing final products.

supplies
Regular expense items necessary in the firm's daily operation but not part of the final product.

MRO items
Supplies for an industrial firm, categorized as maintenance items, repair items, or operating supplies.

business services
Intangible products firms buy to facilitate their production and operational process.

Table 9.2   Marketing Impact of the Industrial Products Classification System

	Installations	**Accessory Equipment**	**Component Parts and Materials**	**Raw Materials**	**Supplies**	**Business Services**
Industrial Factors						
Planning time involved in purchase	Extensive	Less extensive	Less extensive	Varies	Very little	Varies
Purchase frequency	Infrequent	More frequent	Frequent	Infrequent	Frequent	Varies
Comparison of price and quality	Quality very important	Quality and price important	Quality important	Quality important	Price important	Varies
Marketing Mix Factors						
Price	High	Relatively high	Low to high	Low to high	Low	Varies
Promotion	Personal selling by producer	Advertising	Personal selling	Personal selling	Advertising by producer	Varies
Distribution channel length	Very short	Relatively short	Short	Short	Long	Varies

variability of the marketing mix for business services is outlined in Table 9.2. Business services will be discussed in more depth in Chapter 11.

The Product Life Cycle

product life cycle
Four stages through which a successful product passes—introduction, growth, maturity, and decline.

Products, like individuals, pass through a series of stages. Whereas humans progress from infancy to childhood to adulthood to retirement to death, successful products progress through four basic stages: introduction, growth, maturity, and decline. This progression, known as the **product life cycle,** is depicted in Figure 9.6, along with products in the recording industry that currently fit into each stage. It should be stressed that the product life cycle concept applies to products or product categories within an industry, not to individual product brands.

Figure 9.6

Stages in the Product Life Cycle

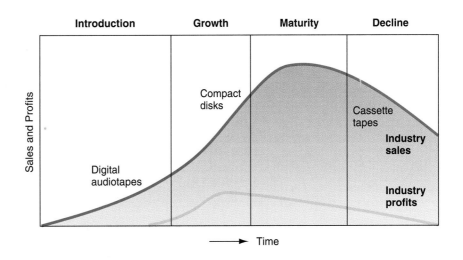

Introductory Stage

The firm's objective in the early stages of the product life cycle is to stimulate demand for the new market entry. Since the product is unknown to the public, promotional campaigns stress information about its features. They also may be directed toward marketing intermediaries in the channel to induce them to carry the product. In this phase, the public becomes acquainted with the product's merits and begins to accept it.

Losses are common during the introductory stage due to heavy promotion and extensive research and development expenditures. But the groundwork is being laid for future profits. Firms expect to recover their costs and begin earning profits when the new product moves into the second phase of its life cycle—the growth stage. Iced coffee, for example, a new product in the beverage industry, is expected to grow to be a $1 billion category by the late 1990s.[6]

Growth Stage

Sales volumes rise rapidly during the growth stage as new customers make initial purchases and early buyers repurchase the product. Word-of-mouth and mass advertising induce hesitant buyers to make trial purchases. As the firm begins to realize substantial profits from its investment during the growth stage, the product attracts competitors. Success breeds imitation, and other firms inevitably rush into the market with competitive products. In fact, the majority of firms in a particular industry enter the market during the growth stage.

Electronic data networks, information services, cellular car phones, and facsimile machines are products in the growth stage in the telecommunications industry. When fax machines were introduced into the American market in the mid-1980s, there were just 7 manufacturers. But as sales grew 22-fold during the next five years, the number of fax makers increased to 25.[7]

Maturity Stage

Industry sales continue to grow during the early part of the maturity stage, but eventually they reach a plateau as the backlog of potential customers dwindles. By this time, a large number of competitors have entered the market, and the firm's profits decline as competition intensifies.

In the maturity stage, differences among competing products diminish as competitors discover the product and promotional characteristics most desired by the market. Heavy promotional outlays emphasize differences among competing products, and brand competition intensifies. Some firms differentiate their products by focusing on attributes such as quality, reliability, and service. For example, in the mature airline industry, American Airlines has differentiated itself from competitors by providing reliable, on-time service. It promoted this distinction of reliability in its "On-time Machine" advertising campaign.

At this stage in the product life cycle, available products exceed industry demand for the first time. Companies attempting to increase their sales and market share must do so at the expense of competitors. As competition intensifies, competitors tend to cut prices in an attempt to attract new buyers. Although a price reduction may be the easiest method of inducing additional purchases, it is also one of the simplest moves for competitors to duplicate. Reduced prices result in decreased revenues for all firms in the industry unless the price cuts produce enough increased purchases to offset the loss in revenue on each item sold.

Figure 9.7

Overlap of Life Cycles for
Products A and B

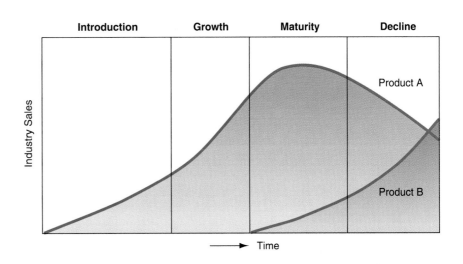

Decline Stage

In the final stage of the product's life, innovations or shifting consumer preferences bring about an absolute decline in industry sales. The safety razor and electric shaver replaced the straight razor years ago. More recently, universal life insurance policies have replaced many whole life insurance policies because of a shift in consumer preferences. As Figure 9.7 indicates, the decline stage of an old product is also the growth stage for a new market entry. In the beverage industry, sales of beer, wine, and hard liquor continue to decline as health-conscious consumers prefer nonalcoholic alternatives such as bottled water, which is expected to be the fastest-growing beverage in the 1990s.

Industry profits decline and in some cases actually become negative as sales fall and firms cut prices in a bid for the dwindling market. Manufacturers gradually begin to leave the industry in search of more profitable products.

The traditional product life cycle needs to be distinguished from fad cycles. Fashions and fads have a profound influence on marketing strategy. *Fashions* are currently popular products that tend to follow recurring life cycles. Women's apparel and accessories provide the best examples. After being out of fashion for over a decade, the miniskirt was reintroduced in the early 1980s and again in the late 1980s. Another example is production-line convertibles. Popular in the 1950s, they disappeared from the market in the late 1960s but were reintroduced in 1982 and have been steadily regaining popularity.[8]

In contrast, *fads* are fashions with abbreviated life cycles. Most fads, such as Pet Rocks and variations of the yellow "Baby on Board" car window stickers, experience short-lived popularity and then quickly fade. However, there are some fads that maintain a residual market among certain market segments.

Using the Product Life Cycle Concept in Marketing Strategy

The product life cycle, with all its variants, is a useful tool in marketing strategy decision making. For instance, the knowledge that profits assume a predictable pattern through the stages and that promotional emphasis must shift from product information in the early stages to brand promotion in the later ones

should allow the marketing decision maker to expand sales and profits in each stage of the product life cycle through appropriate marketing efforts.

A firm's marketing efforts should emphasize stimulating demand at the introductory stage. The focus should shift to cultivating selective demand in the growth period. Market segmentation should be used extensively in the maturity period. During the decline stage, the emphasis should return to increasing primary demand.

Extending the Product Life Cycle.   A frequently used marketing strategy involves taking steps to extend the product life cycle as long as possible. Marketing managers can accomplish this if they take action early in the maturity stage. Product life cycles can be extended indefinitely through actions designed to increase the frequency of use by current customers, add new users, find new uses for the product, and/or change package sizes, labels, or product quality.

Increasing Frequency of Use.   During the maturity stage, the industry sales curve for a product reaches a maximum point as the firm exhausts the supply of customers who previously have not been purchasers. However, if current purchasers increase their purchase frequency, total industry sales will rise even though no new customers enter the market.

By 1986, per-capita pork consumption had dropped to 59 pounds from 68 pounds in 1980. To encourage consumers to eat pork more often, the National Pork Producers Council developed "Pork: The Other White Meat" promotional campaign. The approach emphasized pork's versatility, convenience, healthfulness, and substitution appeal. Many ads, such as the one in Figure 9.8, show how pork can be used in recipes normally made with chicken. Producers also improved the quality of pork. Because of improved feeding and breeding methods, pork is about 50 percent leaner than it was 20 years ago. These efforts have resulted in a steady increase in industry sales and a rise in per-capita consumption to 63 pounds.[9]

Meanwhile, Arkansas-based Tyson Foods, the world's largest poultry firm, is trying to get Europeans to eat more chicken. While U.S. per capita consumption of chicken is 70 pounds annually, Europeans average only 29 pounds. Tyson especially wants to increase the European consumption of processed chicken which carries higher margins than fresh chicken. To prove his commitment to increasing the frequency of use of his product, CEO Don Tyson has moved to Europe. He now resides half of the year near London.[10]

Increasing the Number of Users.   A second strategy for extending the product life cycle is to increase the overall market size by attracting new customers who previously have not used the product. American Home Products increased the number of users of its Woolite laundry detergent by broadening its distribution. For years Woolite was sold only in department stores. Sales tripled after the first year the company introduced the product in food markets. Not only did expanded distribution increase the number of users, it also increased the frequency of use as consumers found it easier to buy the product.[11]

Because products are not always in the same stage of the life cycle in different countries, firms can extend product growth by expanding into new markets. As the cable television industry in the United States has matured, U.S. firms are investing billions of dollars in building cable systems in European and Asian countries where cable is still in its infancy. In Great Britain, for example, the

Figure 9.8

Extending the Product Life
Cycle by Increasing
Frequency of Use

Source: © 1987 National Pork Producers in Cooperation with the National Pork Board.

opportunity for growth is enormous since only 1.3 percent of homes have cable. By the mid-1990s, the number of users is expected to grow to 30 percent.[12]

Finding New Uses. Still another strategy for extending a product's life cycle is to identify new uses for the item. New applications for mature products include oatmeal as a cholesterol-lowerer, wax paper as a food-coverer in microwave cooking, aspirin as an aid in preventing heart disease, and mouthwash as an aid in treating and preventing plaque and gum disease. The teddy bear, marketed for years as a toy for children, is being used by some hospitals as a "primary comfort item" for older patients and traumatized and abused children.[13]

Changing Package Size, Labels, or Product Quality. Many firms implement significant physical changes in their products in an attempt to extend the product life cycle. Many food marketers have introduced smaller-size packages that appeal to one-person households. Other firms offer their products in convenient packages for away-from-home use. An example is the convenient tablet version of Pepto-Bismol shown in the advertisement in Figure 9.9. Consumers may have a bottle of the antacid at home, but the take-along tablets are ideal when indigestion occurs away from home. Similarly, Spam—a product that has been around for a half century—has now been reshaped and repackaged as a lower-fat, vacuum-packed bacon substitute. However, Spam may not have to be repositioned to continue its life cycle in South Korea. In that Pacific Rim country, it is viewed as a delicacy.[14]

Figure 9.9

Extending the Product Life
Cycle through Package
Changes

Source: Courtesy of Procter & Gamble Co.

The Consumer Adoption Process

adoption process
Series of stages in the consumer
decision process regarding a
new product, including awareness, interest, evaluation, trial,
and rejection or adoption.

Consumers also make decisions about a new product offering. In the **adoption process**, potential consumers go through a series of stages from learning of the new product to trying it and deciding to purchase it regularly or to reject it. These stages in the consumer adoption process can be classified as:

1. *Awareness.* Individuals first learn of the new product but lack information about it.
2. *Interest.* They begin to seek information about it.
3. *Evaluation.* They consider whether or not the product is beneficial.
4. *Trial.* They make trial purchases to determine its usefulness.
5. *Adoption/Rejection.* If the trial purchase is satisfactory, they decide to use the product regularly.[15]

The marketing manager needs to understand the adoption process in order to move potential consumers to that stage. Once the manager is aware of a large number of consumers at the interest stage, steps can be taken to stimulate sales by moving consumers through the evaluation and trial stages. For example, Johnson & Johnson enhanced the evaluation and trial of its product innovation—the disposable contact lens—by offering consumers a free trial pair.

By contrast, Polaroid failed when it first entered the French market using the same marketing strategy it had used in the United States. The problem was that the French lacked Americans' 20 years of experience with the benefits of instant

Figure 9.10

Categories of Adopters
Based on Relative Time of
Adoption

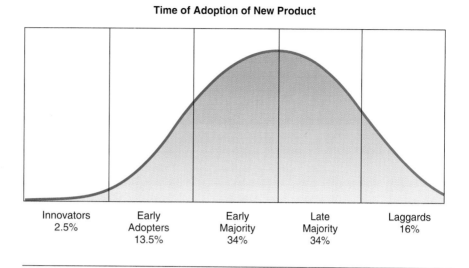

Time of Adoption of New Product

| Innovators 2.5% | Early Adopters 13.5% | Early Majority 34% | Late Majority 34% | Laggards 16% |

photography. Polaroid's promotional efforts did not systematically explain these benefits, and the French rejected the product. Polaroid later changed its strategy and was eventually successful.[16]

Adopter Categories

Some people purchase a new product almost as soon as it is placed on the market. Others wait for additional information and rely on the experiences of **consumer innovators**—first purchasers—before making trial purchases. Consumer innovators are likely to be present in each product area. Some families were the first in the community to buy compact disc players. Some doctors are the first to prescribe new drugs. Some farmers plant new hybrid seeds much earlier than their neighbors.

A number of investigations analyzing the adoption of new products have resulted in the identification of five categories of purchasers based on relative time of adoption. These categories, shown in Figure 9.10, are innovators, early adopters, early majority, late majority, and laggards.

The **diffusion process** is the acceptance of new goods and services by the members of the community or social system. Figure 9.10 shows this process as following a normal distribution. A few people adopt at first; then the number of adopters increases rapidly as the value of the innovation becomes apparent. The adoption rate finally diminishes as fewer potential consumers remain in the nonadopter category.

Since the categories are based on a normal distribution, standard deviations are used to partition them. Innovators are the first 2.5 percent to adopt the new product; laggards are the last 16 percent to do so. Excluded from Figure 9.10 are nonadopters—those who never adopt the innovation.

Identifying First Adopters

Locating first buyers of new products is a challenge for the marketing manager. If first buyers can be reached early in the product's development or introduction, they can serve as a test market, evaluating the products and making suggestions

consumer innovators
First purchasers of a new product.

diffusion process
Acceptance of new products by the members of a community or social system.

for modifications. Since early purchasers are often opinion leaders from whom others seek advice, their attitudes toward new products are quickly communicated to others. Acceptance or rejection of the innovation by these purchasers can help forecast its expected success.

Unfortunately, first adopters of one new product are not necessarily first adopters of other products. A large number of research studies, however, have established some general characteristics of most first adopters. First adopters tend to be younger, have higher social status, be better educated, and enjoy higher incomes than others. They are more mobile than later adopters and change both their jobs and home addresses more often. They are also more likely to rely on impersonal information sources than are later adopters, who depend more on promotional information from the company and word-of-mouth communication.

Rate of Adoption Determinants

Frisbees progressed from the product introduction stage to the market maturity stage in a period of six months. But it took the U.S. Department of Agriculture 13 years to convince corn farmers to use hybrid seed corn—an innovation capable of doubling crop yields. The adoption rate is influenced by five characteristics of the innovation:

1. *Relative advantage*—the degree to which the innovation appears superior to previous ideas. The greater the relative advantage—manifested in terms of lower price, physical improvements, or ease of use—the faster the adoption rate is.

2. *Compatibility*—the degree to which the innovation is consistent with the values and experiences of potential adopters. Consider, for example, the failure of Avert, Kimberly-Clark's germ-killing facial tissue that cost about four times more per tissue than regular tissues. Avert was designed to prevent the spread of colds when used by a sick person, but it did not protect consumers who bought the tissues to avoid catching colds from others. The product failed in the marketplace because consumers were not willing to pay the high price for something used to protect others from getting their colds.[17]

3. *Complexity*—the relative difficulty of understanding the innovation. In most cases, the more difficult a new product is to understand or use, the longer it will take to gain general acceptance.

4. *Possibility of trial use*—the degree to which the innovation can be used on a limited basis. First adopters face two types of risk—financial loss and ridicule from others—if the new product proves unsatisfactory. The option of sampling the innovation on a limited basis reduces these risks and generally accelerates the rate of adoption.

5. *Observability*—the degree to which the results of using the product are observable to others. If the innovation's superiority can be displayed in a tangible form, the adoption rate will increase.[18]

These five characteristics can be implemented to some extent by the marketing manager to accelerate the rate of adoption. Product complexity must be overcome with informative promotional messages. Products should be designed to emphasize their relative advantages and, whenever possible, should be offered on a trial basis to permit sample purchases. If it is physically impossible to offer the product on a trial basis, in-home demonstrations or trial home placements can be used. Positive attempts must also be made to ensure the innovation's compatibility with adopters' value systems.

FOCUS ON ETHICS

CALLER ID—INVASION OF PRIVACY?

Does it make a difference if the people you call know what number you're calling from? You bet it does!

Caller ID is a device that transmits the caller's phone number to an electronic display attached to the receiving phone, enabling the receiver to ignore certain calls. But it's not just a new gadget. It's the subject of a storm of controversy centering on issues of privacy.

Arguments in favor of the new technology emphasize the opportunity for greater protection against invasions of privacy, elimination of obscene and harassing calls, fewer abuses of personal information, and the chance to bring unlawful phone users to justice. Caller ID also makes it easier for businesses to verify orders placed by phone and to handle credit-card orders. When integrated with a computer system, it makes instant retrieval of the caller's file possible—even before the call is answered. One system also captures the phone numbers of callers who receive busy signals or are disconnected before the receiver can answer; the numbers are matched with customer records, and managers can call back and find out what the customer wanted.

Arguments against Caller ID focus on its dangers to marketing research, telemarketing, and other businesses based on telephone use. Because fewer people will answer the phone, it will become more expensive for such businesses to operate effectively. More broadly, it is argued that the new technology invades the *caller's* privacy and that callers should be able to block receivers from identifying their numbers.

Caller ID is opposed by privacy advocates such as the American Civil Liberties Union and, in a 1990 decision the Pennsylvania Commonwealth Court barred Bell Atlantic from selling Caller ID in that state on the grounds that it violates the caller's privacy. The phone company is appealing the ruling while continuing to market the service in five other states and the District of Columbia. The company argues that the service actually enhances privacy because it enables customers to avoid intrusive calls. Meanwhile pending legislation in Congress would require vendors of Caller ID to make available a blocking service for those who wish to prevent their phone number from being recorded.

Many customers who were initially opposed to the service have been persuaded to see its benefits in the long run—especially the dramatic reduction in the number of obscene and harassing phone calls. However, many potential customers may be unwilling to pay the high installation costs and the monthly charge for the service. Caller ID is unlikely to come into widespread use until these issues of ethics and cost have been resolved.

Discussion Questions

1. Advocates of blocking technology point out that some people, such as battered spouses and people calling suicide hotlines, have a strong and legitimate need for anonymity. The telephone company opposes consumer blocking on the ground that it would dilute the value of Caller ID service. Should blocking be made available on a limited basis?

2. Is the privacy argument less potent in the case of calls to an 800 line, which are the equivalent of collect calls?

Sources: Mitch Betts, "Firms Seek Their Magic Number Through ISDN," *ComputerWorld* (February 5, 1990), pp. 67, 75; and Howard Schlossberg, "Caller ID Gets Wires Crossed in Court," *Marketing News* (September 3, 1990), pp. 1, 36.

These actions are based on extensive research studies of innovators in agriculture, medicine, and consumer products. They should pay off in increased sales by accelerating the adoption rate in each adopter category.

Customer Service

As we discussed in the definition of product at the chapter beginning, a product's service attributes are a crucial element of product strategy. According to one survey, 7 of 10 customers who switch from one firm's product to a competitor's

COMPETITIVE EDGE

BRITISH AIRWAYS FOCUS ON THE CUSTOMER

. . . .

BA = British Airways = Bloody Awful.

That's the way people used to think about British Airways. But not any more. Now the airline is ranked among the top three in the world—along with SwissAir and Singapore Airlines—in customer service. What happened?

BA's transformation began in 1983, when Sir Colin Marshall became CEO. Marshall immediately set to work to change the airline's focus from operations to customers. Market surveys showed that passengers place twice as much importance on friendly service as they do on operational factors like fast check-in. But BA was not a customer-oriented organization; even its managers had failed to recognize how highly passengers value sympathy and courtesy. Marshall's greatest challenge was to convince the airline's 35,000 employees that travelers need to be treated like people, not like units or components of a transportation system.

Marshall launched an extensive training program, called "Putting People First," that was designed to teach employees to put themselves in the passenger's shoes. A new motto—"To fly, to serve"—was created, and $80 million was spent upgrading business- and first-class accommodations. Marshall (who was once a steward on a cruise ship) also undertook to "deregiment" the airline: First-class passengers are served meals at times of their choosing; the menu has been broadened; and, on some aircraft, in-flight movies have been replaced by individual video screens with a wide selection of classics and recent box-office hits. Business-class service has been expanded, and passengers may now enjoy such amenities as a separate check-in counter and a departure lounge with comfortable chairs and a free bar. In the airports, sixty trained problem-solvers (called "hunters") roam the terminals and help passengers cope with such matters as lost luggage and missed connections. The airline has also installed Video Point booths, as shown in the photo, in which passengers can tape complaints immediately after leaving the plane.

Perhaps the most significant aspect of British Airways' experience is that management recognized that the entire organization had to improve its performance; simply telling service personnel to "smile" would not do the job. According to Marshall, BA's success is a result of careful goal setting and an overall team effort. The airline as a whole set out "to be the best"—and succeeded.

Discussion Questions

1. Market research indicated that passengers value friendly service more than any other factor. What else could BA's management do to improve its performance in this area?

2. Why is BA focusing on making its existing passengers happy rather than increasing its marketing efforts in order to attract more passengers?

Sources: John Marcom, Jr., "The Middle of the Bus," *Forbes* (July 9, 1990), pp. 96–97; Mark Maremont, "How British Airways Butters Up the Passenger," *Business Week* (March 20, 1990), p. 94; Lois Madison Reamy, "The World's Best Airlines," *Institutional Investor* (June 1989), pp. 195–198; Patricia Sellers, "How to Handle Customers' Gripes," *Fortune* (October 24, 1988); and Michael Thomas, "Coming to Terms with the Customer," *Personnel Management* (February 1987), pp. 24–28. *Photo source:* © Graham Finlayson.

Figure 9.11

Creating Loyal Customers
through Customer Service

We have some very old-fashioned ideas
about cleaning your home.

Source: Courtesy of The ServiceMaster Company.

customer service

Manner in which marketers treat
their customers and the related
activities that enhance the value
of the customers' purchases.

cite poor service, rather than product quality or price, as the main reason.[19] To maintain adopters and attract new customers, consumer and industrial marketers must provide customers with effective and courteous customer service. The term **customer service** refers to the manner in which marketers deal with their customers, and the related activities that enhance the value of the customers' purchases.[20] Dissatisfaction about poor customer service has accelerated in recent years. Complaints about rude and poorly informed personnel, late or no-show deliveries, waiting in long lines while other service windows or cash registers stay closed, and shoddy repairs are alarmingly frequent for a supposedly customer-oriented society.[21]

An increasing number of companies are learning that poor service costs customers. Research studies reveal that it is five times more costly to get a new customer than to keep a current one. A study conducted for the U.S. Office of Consumer Affairs found that while 96 percent of dissatisfied customers never air their complaints to a company, 90 percent of them will not be a repeat customer. Dissatisfied customers can be damaging to a firm's reputation and profits, as they make their complaints known to at least nine other people, according to another study.[22] In contrast, firms that provide superior customer service generate repeat business, can charge higher prices, and often outperform their industry in profits and sales growth.[23] Many marketers believe that customer service is the primary competitive battlefield of the 1990s. Hewlett-Packard, for example, in promoting its personal computers in Europe, emphasizes the extent of its customer service programs rather than the technical attributes of its products.[24] In the advertisement in Figure 9.11, ServiceMaster gives the reasons for its loyal customer base—friendly cleaning crews, on-time delivery at the customer's convenience, and guaranteed total customer satisfaction.

The four major components of customer service are customer relations, delivery, repair service, and warranties. Most aspects of customer service can be placed in one of these categories.

Customer Relations

Marketers must maintain good interpersonal relationships with their customers. The friendliness of customer contact people such as bank tellers, flight attendants, and retail sales personnel is a major factor in one's perception of customer service. A survey of banking, high-tech, and manufacturing firm customers revealed that "the personal touch" is the most important element of service, more than convenience, speed of delivery, and how well a product works. In the past, fast-food customers ranked speed of service as most important, but today they rank courtesy as number one. Business travelers say how much an airline "cares about its customers" is as important to them as efficient check-in and prompt baggage delivery.[25]

Proper handling of customer complaints is an important aspect of good customer relations. Firms should give customers the chance to complain (or compliment) by using comment cards, toll-free 800-number telephone systems, focus groups, and surveys. The use of 800 numbers directly related to customer service has grown about 30 percent a year during the past several years. Answering complaints by phone is faster and more personal than a written response and gives the customer service representative the chance to explain the firm's position and turn a dissatisfied customer into a loyal one. Effective complaint-handling involves empathizing with and rewarding complainers. Hechinger Company, a Maryland-based hardware retailer, sends a dozen roses to particularly unhappy buyers. Listening to customer complaints can alert companies to errors. By using a customer complaint tracking system, Fidelity Bank of Philadelphia discovered a computer programming error that produced incorrect service charges. After the Coca-Cola Company launched New Coke, calls on its 1-800-GET-COKE hotline mushroomed from an average of 400 a day to more than 12,000 a day. Ninety percent of the calls came from customers who preferred old Coke. Hotline calls helped the company realize the depth of its error. The day after old Coke returned as Coca-Cola Classic, 18,000 people, many of whom were earlier complainers, called to say thank you.[26]

Delivery

Delivery is a major customer service component for industrial marketers who supply products to customers using the just-in-time system, in which parts and materials must arrive at the time they are needed for producing other products. Providing exceptional delivery service can add value to undifferentiated products. For example, Premier Industrial Corporation, a Los Angeles distributor of some 250,000 industrial parts, received a call one afternoon from a Caterpillar tractor plant employee in Illinois saying that a $10 electrical relay had broken, shutting down the entire assembly line. Premier put an employee on a plane so the replacement part could be delivered immediately, saving Caterpillar a bundle of money in downtime. "To us, customer service is the main event," says Premier's chairman Morton Mandel. Premier's prompt, personal approach to delivery enables it to charge up to 50 percent more than competitors for the parts it stocks.[27]

Repair Service

Late or poorly done repairs are a source of many customer service complaints. But companies such as Dallas's Sewell Village Cadillac prove that this does not have to be. When a customer buys a Cadillac from Sewell Village, he or she is assigned a personal service adviser for the life of the car. The adviser handles all the aspects of getting the car serviced, even providing 24-hour emergency road service if necessary. In addition, the dealership has a fleet of 150 loaner cars with which to serve its customers.[28]

For IBM customers, quick response to repair work is critical because interruptions in information processing can affect their competitiveness. In Germany, IBM operates mobile service vehicles that can be dispatched to any location in the country within 24 hours to respond to customer repair needs. IBM has set up a countrywide toll-free telephone service in Brazil so customers can receive speedy help in resolving problems. In the United States, IBM has personal computer specialists on call 24 hours a day, 7 days a week, to deal with repair and maintenance problems. IBM also offers repair services for customers' non-IBM equipment. The company recently introduced a new service, Business Recovery Service, to help customers continue operating in the event of a fire, flood, earthquake, or other disaster. This service assures customers that their information processing system will be operational within 24 hours of the time IBM learns of the disaster.[29]

Warranties

warranty

Guarantee to the buyer that the producer will replace or repair a product or refund its purchase price if the product proves defective during a specified time period.

An important feature of many products is the **warranty**—the guarantee to the buyer that the manufacturer or service provider will replace or refund the product's purchase price if it proves defective during a specified time period. Warranties increase consumer purchase confidence and often represent an important means by which to stimulate demand. German automaker Volkswagen offered a money-back guarantee for the Passat in an effort to stimulate the sale of its new sedan, which competes with the popular Honda Accord, Toyota Camry, and Ford Taurus. Under the program, if Passat buyers were not satisfied with the car after owning it for three months or driving 3,000 miles, Volkswagen would refund the purchase price. Volkswagen offered the guarantee because Passat sales fell far short of company projections several months after the car was introduced in early 1990. A Volkswagen official said of the guarantee, "Our goal is to say to the public, 'At least consider us.' "[30]

A warranty trend has permeated many businesses in recent years, including airlines, hotel chains, car manufacturers, computer firms, banks, and appliance companies. "Bugs" Burger Bug Killers (BBBK), a Miami-based pest-extermination company, has made its "100% satisfaction guarantee" the major component of its competitive strategy. When founder Al Burger started the company, he began with the unconditional guarantee of error-free service and structured his entire organization to support the guarantee. While most competitors promise the control of pests to acceptable levels, BBBK guarantees to eliminate them entirely. If hotel and restaurant customers are dissatisfied with BBBK's service, they receive a refund for up to 12 months of service and fees to use another exterminator for the next year. The guarantee is so successful that BBBK charges up to ten times more than competitors and has a disproportionately high market share in the areas where it operates throughout the country.[31]

Summary of Chapter Objectives

1. **Describe the broad view of product.** A narrow view of product focuses on the physical or functional characteristics of a good or service. By contrast, a broad view extends to all aspects of want satisfaction. Therefore, the broader viewpoint defines *product* as a bundle of physical, service, and symbolic attributes designed to enhance consumer want satisfaction.

2. **Identify the classifications of consumer products and briefly describe each category.** The three categories of consumer products are convenience products, shopping products, and specialty products. Convenience products are products that the consumer wants to purchase frequently, immediately, and with a minimum of effort. Shopping products are purchased after extensive comparison on such bases as price, quality, style, and color. Specialty products are those with unique features that will cause the buyer to seek them out.

3. **Identify the types of industrial products.** Industrial products are classified on the basis of product uses rather than on customer's buying behavior. The five categories in the industrial products classification are installations, accessory equipment, component parts and materials, raw materials, and supplies.

4. **Explain the concept of the product life cycle.** Most successful products pass through the four stages of the product life cycle—introduction, growth, maturity, and decline—before their death. The product life cycle concept affects other components of the marketing mix; pricing, distribution, and promotion strategies as well as product strategy must be adjusted in different life cycle stages. Marketers should also attempt to extend life cycles of successful products for as long as possible. This objective can be accomplished by (1) increasing the frequency of use; (2) increasing the number of users; (3) finding new uses; and (4) changing package size, label, or product quality.

5. **Describe how firms can extend the product life cycle.** Marketers can take a variety of actions to extend the product life cycle. In many cases, it can be extended indefinitely. Strategies include increasing the frequency of use by current customers, adding new users, finding new uses for the product, and/or changing package sizes, labels, or product quality.

6. **Identify the determinants of the rate of adoption of a product.** Consumers go through a series of stages in adopting new products: initial product awareness, interest, evaluation, trial purchase, and adoption or rejection. Although first adopters vary among product classes, several common characteristics have been isolated. First adopters are often younger, better educated, and more mobile; they typically have higher incomes and higher social status than later adopters. The rate of adoption for new products depends on five characteristics: (1) relative advantage—the degree of superiority of the innovation over the previous product; (2) compatibility—the degree to which the new product is consistent with the value systems of potential purchasers; (3) complexity of the new product; (4) possibility of trial use—the degree to which small-scale trial purchases are possible; and (5) observability—the degree to which the innovation's superiority can be conveyed to other potential buyers.

7. **Explain the methods for accelerating the speed of adoption.** Product complexity must be overcome by informative promotional messages. Products should be designed to emphasize their relative advantages and, whenever possible, should be available for sample purchases. If it is

physically impossible to offer trial purchases, in-home demonstrations or trial home placements can be used. Positive attempts must also be made to ensure the innovation's compatibility with adopters' value systems. These actions should pay off in increased sales by accelerating the rate of adoption in each adopter category.

8. **Discuss the role of customer service in product strategy and identify the major components of customer service.** Customer service, a crucial element of product strategy, can be defined as the manner in which marketers deal with their customers, and the related activities that enhance the value of the customers' purchases. Customer service—or the lack of it—is the major reason for brand switches and the like. The primary categories of customer service are customer relations, delivery, repair service, and warranties.

Key Terms

product	supplies
convenience products	MRO items
shopping products	business services
specialty products	product life cycle
installations	adoption process
accessory equipment	consumer innovators
industrial distributor	diffusion process
component parts and materials	customer service
raw materials	warranty

Review Questions

1. Compare and contrast the narrow and broader views of *product.* What is meant by a total product concept?

2. Why are some products unsought? Cite examples of products that would fall into this category.

3. Why does the basis used for categorizing industrial products differ from that used for classifying consumer products? Discuss the implication of this difference.

4. Compare a typical marketing mix for convenience products with one for specialty products. What are the primary differences in these mixes?

5. Outline the various categories of industrial products. Discuss the marketing mix for each category.

6. What is included in the business service category? Explain how these intangible products are marketed.

7. Illustrate and explain the product life cycle concept. When does a product move from one stage to the next?

8. How can the product life cycle concept be used in marketing strategy? Explain how the product life cycle can be extended.

9. What is meant by the consumer adoption process? Outline and explain the stages in this process.

10. What is meant by the diffusion process? Describe the determinants of this process.

Discussion Questions

1. For each stage of the product life cycle, select a specific product (other than those mentioned in the text) that fits into it. Explain how marketing strategies vary by life cycle stage for each product.

2. Trace the life cycle of a recent fad. What marketing strategy implications can you derive from your study?

3. DATs (digital audiotapes) are considered to be the eventual replacement for CDs (compact discs). As of 1991, only Sony offered DATs in the United States. What suggestions can you make for accelerating the rate of adoption for DATs?

4. Classify the following consumer products:
    a. Sofa
    b. Nike aerobic shoes
    c. Felt-tip pen
    d. Swimsuit
    e. Acura NSX
    f. Binaca breath freshener
    g. *Modern Maturity* magazine
    h. Original oil painting

5. Classify the following products into the appropriate industrial products category. Briefly explain your choice for each product.
    a. Voice message systems
    b. Land
    c. Light bulb
    d. Cotton
    e. Paper towel
    f. Nylon
    g. Corporate jet
    h. Tire

Computer Applications

The creation of new product offerings for industrial purchasers, organizational buyers, or ultimate consumers is an expensive and risky undertaking. Since marketers usually face a number of alternatives from which to choose a good or service to offer their selected target markets, they need a method for evaluating the most appropriate use of the firm's limited financial and human resources. A commonly used technique for this purpose is *return on investment (ROI)*. This quantitative tool is particularly useful in evaluating proposals for alternative courses of action. ROI equals the rate of profit (net profit divided by sales) multiplied by the firm's turnover rate (sales divided by the required investment):

$$ROI = \frac{Net\ Profit}{Sales} \times \frac{Sales}{Investment}$$

Consider a proposed new product for which the firm's marketers estimate a required investment of $200,000. The company expects to achieve $500,000 in sales, with a projected net profit of $40,000. The proposed product's ROI is calculated as follows:

$$ROI = \frac{\$40,000}{\$500,000} \times \frac{\$500,000}{\$200,000}$$
$$= .08 \times 2.5$$
$$= 20\%.$$

Whether or not the 20 percent return on investment is acceptable depends on similar ROI calculations for alternative uses of company funds. In addition, the marketing decision makers are likely to carefully consider such variables as the fit of the proposed good or service with existing product lines and with long-range marketing plans.

In comparing ROIs of different proposals, it is important to recognize several factors that can affect ROI calculations. In situations in which different depreciation schedules are being used, profits — and therefore ROI — will vary. External conditions can also affect ROI. Favorable economic conditions may be associated with high rates of return, while lower rates may be more common during economic downturns. A third factor affecting ROI is the time period over which product development expenditures are made. The ROI of a product that requires considerable developmental work may be adversely affected.[32]

Directions: Use menu item 8 titled "Return on Investment" to solve each of the following problems.

Problem 1.   The management of Light Manufacturing of Youngstown, Ohio, is considering the development of a new type of industrial shears. The estimated cost of developing the new product is $5 million. The firm expects to sell $20 million of the shears for a profit of $2 million. What is the product's ROI?

Problem 2.   Southern Michigan Industries of Jackson, Michigan, has marketed an industrial drill for years. Current annual sales are $5 million, but last year Southern Michigan earned only $150,000 on the drill because of the rapidly rising cost of component parts. A recent proposal from the production department suggests that shifting to less expensive components would increase profits to $300,000 while maintaining sales at $5 million. However, this would require several plant layout changes costing $1.25 million. What is the ROI of the proposed switch to less expensive parts?

Problem 3.   San Francisco–based Bay Dental Clinics markets franchises to young dentists just starting their practices. The company projects that a franchisee will earn $45,000 in the first year of operation based on $180,000 in professional fees. Total first-year expenses of $135,000 include franchise fees, equipment, personnel, utilities, and other setup costs. In addition, the $135,000 includes interest charges on a special financial arrangement Bay Dental Clinics has developed for new dentists with limited current funds but high future revenue expectations. What is the typical first year's ROI for a dentist who establishes a Bay Dental Clinic?

Problem 4.   Northwoods Industries of Mankato, Minnesota, has developed a new type of ski. Special placement tests at ski instruction schools throughout the United States proved highly successful. In fact, ski instructors preferred the new skis over their current skis by a three-to-one margin. Northwoods' top management estimates that the firm would be able to generate $10 million in revenue from the sale of the skis at wholesale prices. However, development expenses for the prototype skis are estimated at $4 million. Management believes that the new line would add $750,000 to the firm's annual profits. Calculate the ROI for the proposed new line of skis.

Problem 5.   A Lopez Island, Washington, inventor has developed a new fad item about which she refuses to divulge any details until she completes a licensing proposal for a major novelty manufacturer in New York. One part of the proposal is a return-on-investment calculation. The inventor estimates that the manufacturer would have to spend a total of $15 million in production and promotional outlays to successfully launch the fad item. Annual sales are estimated to be $60 million. After subtracting such expenses as shipping, retail price discounts necessary for motivating retailers to carry the item in inventory, and licensing fees, the firm should earn profits of $5 million. What ROI should the inventor include in her proposal to the novelty manufacturer?

Carushka

The bodywear industry has grown by leaps and bounds over the past decade. It began with dancewear, which later was picked up by millions of aerobics class participants. The next step—from aerobics classes to fitness centers—was a logical extension of the product's sales curve. Today bodywear, alternatively called *dancewear* or *exercise wear,* has become acceptable street dress.

Ric Wanetik, a Marshall Field's vice-president, has assessed the reason for this evolution: "I happen to believe people buying this merchandise aren't necessarily doing it to run out and exercise in; they're buying it because it's fashion-smart." Designer Rebecca Moses echoes this view: "People like the way they look in workout clothes, so they incorporated elements of these designs into their everyday wardrobes."

But despite its rapid growth, designer bodywear is a highly volatile market. Designs, labels, and even manufacturers are continually emerging and disappearing as consumer tastes shift. In fact, the entire life cycle of designer bodywear is only about three months.

Firms that seek to compete in this marketplace must have a coherent product strategy. One designer, Carushka, has based her overall product and competitive strategy on innovation: "I am willing to take the step where no one else is. I am a pioneer." Carushka got the idea for her first leotard, a striped model, while watching a Gene Kelly movie. She was the first designer to do stripes, the first to do cottons, and the first to do prints. It is no wonder that the motto of Carushka's company became "Expect the unexpected."

When she began her business, Carushka would load her station wagon with her merchandise and deliver it personally to her first 100 accounts. The leotards were packaged in plastic bags with invoices attached, because Carushka operated on a cash-only basis at the time.

Then her line became popular with specialty boutiques that sold it to the consumer innovators in this marketplace. Since the firm was too small to advertise to such a large market, Carushka developed an alternative marketing strategy: She began sending her designs free to celebrities. The resulting media coverage brought her the broader audience she was seeking. Word-of-mouth promotion then took over, and Carushka became an overnight success. Later she tripled her sales by selling her line through department stores.

The innovative designer applied some unorthodox theories to her company and her lines. A believer in inner personality, numerology, and astrology, Carushka used astrology to pick people for the various functions within the company and numerology to number her garments, avoiding numbers she considered unlucky. But these tactics did not help Carushka when she tried to market a line of men's bodywear. She had teamed up with actor/dancer John Travolta, and the initial response to the line was quite positive, with $1 million of product shipped in the first four months. However, the men's bodywear segment of the industry did not hold up in the long run.

Despite this failure, Carushka remained true to her strategic emphasis on innovation. She refused to test market her new lines, explaining, "This is my look. You either buy it or you don't." But Carushka also admitted that "you have to be crazy to be an entrepreneur."

Entrepreneurial enterprises like Carushka's face two types of risk. First, there is the constant danger that consumers will reject the product offering, as in the case of the Travolta line. Second, in a fashion-oriented industry such as bodywear even the most innovative ideas can be quickly copied. As a result, the pace of innovation becomes a key factor in the long-term success of a firm like Carushka's.

Carushka also believes that the bodywear market will go back to basics. In fact, this is exactly what happened to her own business. The designer was forced to take off for a few years due to health reasons. When she reopened in January 1987, she again concentrated on her original customer base—specialty boutiques. She remarked, "They are more fun than selling to department stores." Carushka no longer uses sales reps; she now sells via consumer and retail mail-orders and through wholesalers. An international sales effort has met with great success, particularly in Japan, where customers expect high quality and are prepared to pay well for it.

While wholesale sales remain the largest portion of the business, Carushka has been working with Catalog Productions of Carlsbad, California, to increase mail and phone order business. And in 1990 Carushka opened her own retail store on Ventura Boulevard in Sherman Oaks, California. Within a year the boutique, with its fantasy-world design, had become a magnet for celebrities and the young and affluent.

Sources: Personal interview with Kim Spath, Carushka, April 1991; Allison Kyle Leopold, "Workout Clothes: From the Gym . . . to the Street," . . . *The New York Times Magazine* (September 28, 1986), pp. 67–68, 110; "Carushka Is Still Shipping, Says Company Won't Close," *Women's Wear Daily* (June 14, 1985), p. 10; and Jim Seale, "Exercise Wear," *Stores* (June 1987), pp. 13–19.

Questions

1. How would you classify Carushka with respect to product life cycle stage?
2. Relate this case to the chapter's discussion of fashions and fads.
3. How did Carushka's product strategy facilitate the consumer adoption process?
4. What part of the consumer goods classification would best match Carushka's product lines?
5. Assess Carushka's decision to increase mail and phone order business.

10

Product Mix Decisions and New-Product Planning

1. To identify the major product mix decisions that marketers must make.

2. To explain why most firms develop a line of related products rather than a single product.

3. To identify alternative new-product development strategies and the determinants of each strategy's success.

4. To explain the various organizational structures for new-product development.

5. To list the stages in the new-product development process.

6. To explain the roles of brands, brand names, and trademarks in a marketing strategy.

7. To describe the major functions of the package.

8. To outline the functions of the Consumer Product Safety Commission and the concept of product liability.

Rubbermaid Incorporated ranks among the elite of new-product innovators. Innovative products made a significant contribution to the company's explosive growth during the 1980s, a decade in which sales quadrupled to $1.5 billion. The continuous rollout of new products and improvements on existing ones keeps

sales and profits growing at about 15 percent each year. That's an impressive feat, considering that housewares, Rubbermaid's major business, is a slow-growing mature industry and intensely competitive. The company's objective is to generate 30 percent of sales each year from products introduced in the previous five years. Realizing that goal requires a planning effort that begins with a steady stream of new-product ideas.

Ideas for the more than 100 new products Rubbermaid launches each year come from inventors, research and development staffers, employees, and consumers. Ideas must meet Rubbermaid's rule that a product be useful, long-lasting, and inexpensive. The idea of Rubbermaid's new line of cleaning tools shown in the accompanying ad sprouted from a consumer focus group in which a woman complained that brooms, mops, and other cleaning tools are poorly designed and make housework "more miserable rather than easier." At the time, Rubbermaid did not make cleaning tools, but listening to the woman's remarks gave executives reasons why it should consider entering the market.

Rubbermaid doesn't exactly take a new-product idea and run with it. For example, before introducing a new line of casual outdoor furniture, product planners spent six years conducting consumer research and lifestyle, demographic, manufacturing, and distribution studies. When the furniture line was launched, it was an immediate success. Rubbermaid's skillful and deliberate approach to planning helps the company achieve an enviable 90 percent new-product success rate. "Our formula for success is very open," says Stanley Gault, Rubbermaid's chairman and CEO. "We absolutely watch the market, and we work at it 24 hours a day."

Rubbermaid used the same market-oriented planning approach in developing its line of cleaning tools.

Focus-group discussions helped planners determine what consumers wanted. Consumers were asked what areas of the house they cleaned and what they used to clean those areas. Employees called consumers at home to find out what cleaning tools they used and the prices they paid for them. Product designers studied data on average height and hand dimensions and then crafted tools with specially designed handles that fit comfortably in the hand and with bristles angled to fit hard-to-reach places. After testing color preferences, Rubbermaid decided on blue because consumers associate blue with freshness and cleanliness.

To test the products, researchers enlisted hundreds of employees, encouraging them to try out the products at home. Rubbermaid never test-markets its products, relying instead on consumer research during product development to predict acceptance in the marketplace. After five years of development, Rubbermaid launched its line of mops, brooms, and brushes with an advertising campaign telling consumers how the tools can make housecleaning easier.

Rubbermaid is a powerful brand name, a "magic name to the minds of consumers," according to one retailing executive. In brand-recognition studies, consumers and retailers list Rubbermaid as the leading housewares brand. Consumers associate the name with well-designed, quality products. Little wonder, then, that the company leveraged its brand equity by extending the Rubbermaid name to its new cleaning tool line and by playing up the "magic" name in promoting the line.[1]

Photo source: Courtesy of Rubbermaid Incorporated.

Chapter Overview

Chapter 9 presented several basic product concepts. This chapter focuses on the decisions organizations make in bringing new products to the marketplace. First we examine the product mix. Then we look at the different approaches firms use in organizing for new-product development and discuss the steps in the development process. Finally we explain how firms identify their products and describe the role of packaging in product strategy.

A **product mix** is the assortment of product lines and individual offerings available from a marketer. Its two primary components are **product line,** a series of related products, and individual offerings that make up the product line. PepsiCo's product mix, shown in Figure 10.1, consists of three basic product lines—soft drinks, snacks, and restaurants—and individual items within the lines such as Pepsi-Cola, Ruffles potato chips, and Pizza Hut restaurants.

Product mixes typically are measured in terms of width, length, and depth of assortment. Selected items from the PepsiCo product mix illustrate these concepts. *Width* of assortment refers to the number of product lines the firm offers. Soft drinks, snacks, and restaurants would be considered the width of PepsiCo's product mix. *Length* refers to the number of products in the mix. For Pepsi it is 12, with 3 brands of soft drinks, 6 snack lines, and 3 restaurant lines. (In reality, PepsiCo markets more brands, but only the major ones are listed in Figure 10.1.) *Depth* refers to variations of each product in the mix. PepsiCo deepened its Doritos brand by adding three flavorings—Nacho Cheese, Cool Ranch, and Salsa Rio.

The Existing Product Mix

An established firm initiates product planning by first assessing its current product mix. What product lines does it now offer? How deep are the offerings within each product line? The marketer looks for gaps in the assortment that can be filled with new products or modified versions of existing ones. PepsiCo, for example, modified Mountain Dew to reach buyers interested in health and fitness. Its new product entry, Mountain Dew Sport, combines the taste of Mountain Dew with the fluid-replacement benefits of sports drinks.[2]

Line Extension

An important rationale for assessing the current product mix is to determine whether line extension is feasible. A **line extension** refers to the development of individual offerings that appeal to different market segments but are closely related to the existing product line. Line extension provides a relatively inexpensive way to increase sales with minimal risk.

An example of successful line extension is Sony Corporation's Walkman headphone stereo cassette player. When Sony introduced the Walkman in 1979, it sold 30,000 units the first year. Since then Sony has extended the line by adding about 70 models. Some versions incorporate technical innovations. The Wireless Walkman, for instance, does not require cords to connect the headphones to the player, thus increasing the listener's freedom of movement. Other models, such as the water-resistant Sport, the impact-resistant Outback, and My First Sony for children, target specific market segments. Today, Walkman sales total about 30,000 units a day.[3]

Cannibalization

A firm wants to avoid a costly new-product introduction that will adversely affect sales of one of its existing products. A product that takes sales from another offering in a product line is said to be **cannibalizing** the line. While it is

---

product mix
Assortment of product lines and individual offerings available from a marketer.

product line
Various related products offered by a firm.

line extension
New product that is closely related to other products in the firm's existing product line.

cannibalizing
Refers to a product that takes sales from another offering in the same product line.

Figure 10.1

The PepsiCo Product Mix

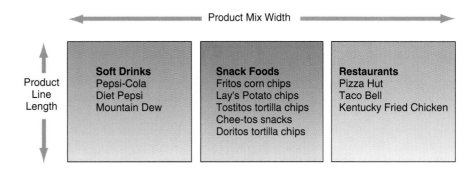

acceptable for the introduction of a new product to take some sales from existing related products, marketing research should ensure that the new offering will guarantee sufficient additional sales to warrant the investment involved in its development and market introduction. M&M/Mars conducted market tests before introducing its new peanut butter version of M&M's because the company wanted to make sure the new candy would not cannibalize chocolate-and-peanut M&M's but would compete instead with Hershey Foods' Reese's Pieces.[4]

The Importance of Product Lines

Firms that market only one product are rare today. Most offer their customers a product line, that is, a series of related products. Reynolds Metals Company, for example, began operations in 1919 by producing lead and tinfoil packaging for the tobacco industry. In 1926 it added aluminum foil to its line of metal-packaging products. Since then, Reynolds has become a producer of aluminum and has developed hundreds of aluminum products for both industrial and consumer markets. These include aluminum cans, Reynolds Wrap household aluminum foil, aluminum siding and other building products, solar hot water heating systems, electrical wire and cable, can and packaging machinery systems, and parts for the automotive, railroad, aircraft, and aerospace industries. With the recent introduction of color plastic wrap and plastic storage bags, Reynolds' line of consumer products totals more than 80 items. Reynolds plans to continue to expand its consumer line as part of the firm's strategy of developing recession-resistant products that provide a hedge against the cycles of the basic aluminum business.[5] Several other factors explain why firms develop complete product lines rather than concentrate on a single product.

Desire to Grow

A company limits its growth potential when it concentrates on a single product. That happened to Baskin-Robbins. The ice-cream chain's sales grew steadily until the mid-1980s, when changing consumer tastes put a dent in company sales and profits. "The market was calling out for lower-calorie, lower-fat desserts, and we weren't in there," says Carol Kirby, the company's vice-president of marketing. Baskin-Robbins developed a line of frozen yogurt products and light frozen dairy desserts that are fat-free or low-fat and have fewer calories than its regular ice cream. "Now 25 percent of our sales come from those products, products we didn't even have four years ago," says Kirby. To overcome its ice-cream-only image, Baskin-Robbins created an advertising campaign with the

Figure 10.2

Adding New Products to Spur
Company Growth

Source: Courtesy of Baskin-Robbins Incorporated.

slogan, "Now there's more to love us for." Ads such as the one in Figure 10.2 showcase the lighter frozen dessert lines.[6]

Firms like Baskin-Robbins introduce new products to boost market growth and company profits. Firms often introduce new products to offset seasonal variations in the sales of their current products. The sale of cranberries, for example, peak during the October through January holiday period. To boost year-round sales of its red berry, Ocean Spray Cranberries, Inc., launched a line of shelf-stable Cran Fruit sauces. Ads for the new product tell consumers how the sauces can be used all year long as a topping for waffles, for instance, or as a complement to a cold chicken sandwich.[7]

Optimal Use of Company Resources

By spreading the costs of its operations over a series of products, a firm may be able to reduce the average production and marketing costs of all of its products. For example, the Honey Nut and Apple Cinnamon line extensions of General Mills' Cheerios brand cereal are economical to produce because they primarily involve flavor changes that attract new consumer segments but share the same manufacturing facilities and distribution channels as the original Cheerios product.

Similarly, production facilities can be used economically in producing related products. Health care marketers are introducing related product lines to optimize the use of their facilities. Health and fitness centers are adding medical components such as body-fat testing, blood pressure screening, and nutritional counseling to their product lines. Some hospitals are expanding beyond their traditional base of corrective treatment by adding preventative medical programs such as stop-smoking clinics, health-education seminars, weight-loss classes, and drug and alcohol abuse programs.[8] The expertise of all of an organization's personnel can be used more economically for a line of products than for a single product.

Increasing Company Importance in the Market

The company with a line of products often is more important to both consumers and marketing intermediaries than is the firm with only one product. A shopper who purchases a tent often buys related camping items. Recognizing this tendency, Coleman Company has developed a complete line of camping products including canoes, sleeping bags, tents, cookers, and camping trailers. The firm would be little known if its only product were lanterns.

Industrial buyers often expect a firm that manufacturers a product to also offer related products. Firms that buy computers, for example, expect computer manufacturers to sell software and computer services. Based on this consumer demand, computer giants such as IBM, Tandem, and NCR are increasingly selling software and services. To reach its goal of deriving 50 percent of its revenues from software and services, IBM introduced a systems integration program for corporate customers called Enterprise Alliance. The service is designed to help firms solve one of the biggest problems in corporate computer systems—the inability to pull together data from different sources on hardware from different companies. Through Enterprise Alliance, IBM hopes to increase its importance in the systems integration market, a $20 billion-a-year market that is growing more than twice as fast as the computer industry as a whole.[9]

Exploiting the Product Life Cycle

As its output enters the maturity and decline stages of the product life cycle, the firm must add new products if it is to prosper. The regular addition of new products to the firm's mix helps ensure that it will not become a victim of product obsolescence. Church & Dwight Company's Arm & Hammer baking soda is in the mature stage of the product life cycle. But the company continues to grow by creating new baking soda–based products such as carpet and room deodorizers, dental care products, and laundry and cleaning products.

New-Product Planning

The product development effort requires considerable advance planning. New products are the lifeblood of any business firm, and a steady flow of new entries must be available if the firm is to survive. Some new products may involve major technological breakthroughs. For example, NutraSweets' Simple Pleasures is a new frozen dairy dessert that is made with Simplesse, the first all-natural fat substitute approved by the U.S. Food and Drug Administration.[10] Other new products are simple product line extensions; in other words, a new product is simply a product new to either the company or the customer. A recent survey

Figure 10.3

Alternative Product
Development Strategies

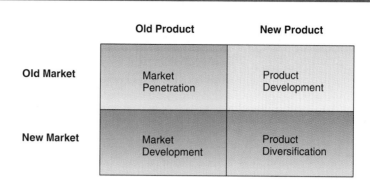

	Old Product	New Product
Old Market	Market Penetration	Product Development
New Market	Market Development	Product Diversification

revealed that only about 10 percent of new-product introductions were truly new products.

Product Development Strategies

The firm's strategy for new-product development varies according to the existing product mix and the extent to which current marketing offerings match overall marketing objectives. The current market position of the firm's products also affects product development strategy. Figure 10.3 identifies four alternative development strategies: market penetration, market development, product development, and product diversification.[11]

A *market penetration strategy* is used to increase sales of existing products in existing markets. Firms attempt to penetrate markets by improving the quality of or modifying their products. Packaged-goods marketers often use this strategy to boost market share for mature products in mature markets. Examples are Procter & Gamble's introduction of no-scent versions of its Charmin bathroom tissue, Bounce fabric softener, and Tide laundry detergent and Colgate's addition of a lemon-lime scent to its Palmolive dishwashing detergent. Product positioning often plays a major role in such a strategy. **Product positioning** refers to the consumer's perception of a product's attributes, use, quality, and advantages and disadvantages relative to competing brands. Marketing research methodology allows marketers to analyze consumer preferences and construct product positioning maps that plot a product in relation to competitive offerings.

product positioning
Buyer's perception of a product's attributes, use, quality, and advantages and disadvantages.

A *market development strategy* concentrates on finding new markets for existing products. Market segmentation, discussed in Chapter 8, is a useful tool in such an effort. A major part of Warner-Lambert's growth plan is expanding the sale of existing products by introducing them in new markets. To broaden the international potential of its Trident gum, the company introduced the product in developing countries with an advertising campaign designed to educate consumers about the benefits of sugarless products.[12] Since opening its first store in Stockholm in 1965, Swedish furniture marketer IKEA has used a market development strategy to become a multinational retailer with 94 stores in 23 countries. Today, almost 75 percent of IKEA's over $3 billion in sales comes from markets outside Scandinavia. The company began tapping the enormous U.S. market in 1985. The advertisement in Figure 10.4 promoted the opening of an IKEA store in Hicksville, Long Island, New York.[13]

Product development strategy, as defined here, refers to the introduction of new products into identifiable or established markets. Sometimes the new product is the firm's first entry in a particular marketplace. Marriott Corporation, a restaurant, hotel, and airline food-service marketer, recently entered the senior

Figure 10.4

Illustrating a Market
Development Strategy

Nancy Reagan styles at Barbara Bush prices.

Now you can easily design a stylish new home at a very practical price. Just select the furniture you want from our range of 12,000 coordinated items displayed in over 100 room settings. From entire living rooms and kitchens to lamps, textiles, cookware, plants and flooring. You'll find quality furniture that's been designed in Sweden, not only to look good, but also to be flat-packed in easy-to-carry boxes. So you can take it home immediately and do the simple, final assembly yourself. That way you save time and money. At IKEA, you don't need to spend 8 years and a lot of money to design a beautiful new home.

It's a big country. Someone's got to furnish it.   **IKEA**

Source: Courtesy of IKEA.

housing market by developing retirement communities and medical care facilities for elderly consumers. In other cases, firms choose to introduce new products into markets in which they already have established positions in an attempt to increase overall market share. These new offerings are called *flanker brands*. Miller Genuine Draft is Miller Brewing Company's flanker to its premium Miller High Life beer. The company introduced the new brand to boost market share of its higher-priced beer.

 Product diversification strategy refers to the development of new products for new markets. In some cases, the new target markets complement existing markets; in others, they do not. Firms often diversify through acquisition. Ford's acquisition of Jaguar represents an important step in the company's goal of developing a luxury-car presence in Europe, Japan, and North America. The purchase is expected to significantly increase Ford's worldwide sales and profits.[14]

New-product planning is a complex area. The critical nature of product planning decisions requires an effective organizational structure.

Organizing for New-Product Development

An effective organizational structure is required in order to stimulate and coordinate new-product development. Most firms assign new-product development to one or more of the following entities: new-product committees, new-product departments, product managers, and venture teams.

New-Product Committees

The most common organizational arrangement for new-product development is the new-product development committee. It is typically composed of representatives of top management in such areas as marketing, finance, manufacturing, engineering, research, and accounting. Committee members are less concerned with the conception and development of new-product ideas than with reviewing and approving new-product plans. Publishing houses, for instance, often have editorial review committees that must approve new project ideas before editors can work with authors in developing new books.

Since members of new-product committees are key executives in the functional areas, their support for any new-product plan is likely to result in approval for further development. However, new-product committees tend to be slow in making decisions and conservative in their views, and sometimes they compromise so that members can get back to their regular company responsibilities.

New-Product Departments

Many companies establish separate, formally organized new-product departments. The departmental structure overcomes the limitations of the new-product committee system and makes new-product development a permanent, full-time activity. The department is responsible for all phases of the product's development within the firm, including screening decisions, developing product specifications, and coordinating product testing. The head of the department has substantial authority and typically reports to the CEO, chief operating officer, or top marketing officer.

An example of the department structure is Alberto-Culver's New Business Development Group. The group researches, develops, tests, and brings to market new products for the company's toiletries, hair-care and beauty, and household/grocery divisions. Innovations launched by the group include Mrs. Dash and Molly McButter, two of Alberto-Culver's fastest-growing product lines.[15]

Product Managers

product manager
Individual in a manufacturing firm assigned a product or product line and given complete responsibility for determining objectives and establishing marketing strategies.

Product managers, also called *brand managers,* are individuals assigned one product or product line and given responsibility for determining its objectives and marketing strategies. Procter & Gamble assigned its first product manager in 1927 when it made one person responsible for Camay soap. The product manager concept was adopted by such marketers as General Foods, Pillsbury, Bristol-Myers, Gillette, and Quaker Oats.

Product managers set prices, develop advertising and sales promotion programs, and work with sales representatives in the field. In multiproduct companies, product managers are key people in the marketing department. They provide individual attention for each product and can utilize the firm's salesforce, marketing research department, and advertising department. Product managers are often responsible for new-product development, creation of new-product ideas, and recommendations for improving existing products.

In recent years, advocates of the product management system have modified the approach to deal with changes in marketing's environment. The system was developed to sell leading brands to mass market consumers with similar tastes. But the increasing fragmentation of the mass market into smaller segments has forced firms to rethink the product management approach. Several firms, including Procter & Gamble, have turned to a team approach, whereby product managers are assigned to a team to work along with research, manufacturing, and sales managers.

Venture Teams

venture team
Organizational strategy for identifying and developing new-product areas by combining the management resources of technological innovation, capital, management, and marketing expertise.

The **venture team** concept is an organizational strategy for developing new-product areas by combining the management resources of technological innovations, capital, management, and marketing expertise. Like new-product committees, venture teams are composed of specialists from different areas of the organization:

☐ Engineering representatives for product design and prototype development.

☐ Marketing staff members for development of product concept tests, test marketing, sales forecasts, pricing, and promotion.

☐ Financial accounting representatives for detailed cost analyses and decisions concerning the concept's probable return on investment.

Unlike committees, venture teams do not disband after every meeting. Team members are assigned a project as a major responsibility, and teams possess the authority necessary for both planning and implementing a course of action. To stimulate product innovation, the venture team typically is linked directly with top management, but it functions as an entity separate from the organization. IBM used a venture team to develop the company's first personal computer. Other firms that have created venture teams are Monsanto, Xerox, Exxon, and Motorola.

The venture team must meet such criteria as prospective return on investment, uniqueness of product, existence of a well-defined need, compatibility of the product with existing technology, and strength of patent protection. Although the venture team is considered temporary, its actual life span is flexible, often extending over a number of years. When the commercial potential of a new product has been demonstrated, the product may be assigned to an existing division, become a division within the company, or serve as the nucleus of a new company. Honda, Monsanto, IBM, and 3M have created separate product development units to develop products more quickly than competitors. Monsanto formed Invitron Corporation to commercialize drugs based on culturing mammalian cells. Honda develops cars in a self-contained subsidiary that performs all research and development and field testing.[16]

Some sources also differentiate venture teams from task forces. A new-product *task force* is an interdisciplinary group on temporary assignment that works through functional departments. Its basic task is to coordinate and integrate the work of the functional departments on a specific project. Colgate formed a multi-country task force to execute the global launch of its first liquid detergent for automatic dishwashers. The task force consisted of employees from research and development, engineering, manufacturing, product management, and Colgate's European Coordination Group. Marketed under the Galaxy or Palmolive Automatic brand name, the new product was introduced in 12 countries, which account for 95 percent of worldwide dishwasher detergent sales. To ensure efficient distribution in these markets, the task force centralized production in three Colgate plants, one in Kansas City to serve North America, one in France to serve all of Europe, and one in Sydney to serve Australia. Through the cooperative efforts of the task force, Colgate was able to penetrate the global marketplace quickly, giving the company an important advantage over competitors.[17]

Once the firm has organized for new-product development, it can establish procedures for moving new products from ideas to the marketplace.

The New-Product Development Process

Developing new products is time-consuming, risky, and expensive. Dozens of new-product ideas are required to produce even one successful product. But most new products are not successful. The failure rate of new products is alarmingly high: about 80 percent. Nearly half of the resources American firms invest in product innovation is spent on products that are commercial failures. Products fail for a number of reasons. Studies reveal that the major ones are inadequate market assessment, the lack of a market orientation, poor screening and project evaluation, product defects, and inadequate launch efforts.[18]

Effective management of the development process increases the likelihood of a product's success. An essential ingredient in new-product success is a six-step development process: (1) idea generation, (2) screening, (3) business analysis, (4) development, (5) testing, and (6) commercialization. At each step, management faces the decision of whether to abandon the project, continue to the next step, or seek additional information before proceeding further. In most cases, each stage of the process is more expensive than the previous one.

Idea Generation

New-product development begins with ideas that emanate from many sources: the salesforce, customers who write letters asking "Why don't you . . . ," employees, research and development specialists, competitive products, suppliers, retailers, and independent inventors. Dow Chemical has set up a six-person Innovation Development Department to identify new-product ideas from the company's basic research. Consumer hotlines are a source of many new-product ideas. Complaints about noisy dishwashers resulted in Whirlpool's new Quiet Wash dishwasher. Other firms, such as Black & Decker, set up dealer advisory panels as a source of new ideas. One panel member's suggestion resulted in Black & Decker's new, heavy-duty reciprocating power saw. Many large companies scan overseas markets for new product ideas. Kellogg got the idea for its Mueslix brand cereal after studying Europe's muesli cereals, a mixture of fruit, grains, and nuts originating in Switzerland.[19] It is important for the firm to develop a system for stimulating new ideas and rewarding their creators.

Screening

The critical screening stage involves separating ideas with potential from those incapable of meeting company objectives. Some organizations use checklists to determine whether product ideas should be eliminated or subjected to further consideration. These checklists typically include such factors as product uniqueness, availability of raw materials, and the proposed product's compatibility with current product offerings, existing facilities, and present capabilities. In other instances, the screening stage consists of open discussions of new-product ideas among representatives of different functional areas in the organization. Toymaker Hasbro Inc. screens new-product ideas by looking for three traits in a toy: lasting play value, ability to be shared, and ability to stimulate the imagination. At Raychem Corporation, a manufacturer of industrial wire and cable, new products must generate a gross profit margin of at least 50 percent.[20]

Business Analysis

Product ideas that survive the initial screening are subjected to a thorough business analysis. The analysis involves an assessment of the new product's potential market, growth rate, and likely competitive strengths. Decisions must be

GETTING CLOSER TO MEN

. . . .

Gillette's new Sensor razor incorporates some revolutionary shaving technology. The razor's twin blades of platinum-hardened chromium are individually mounted on springs. They automatically follow the contours of a man's face and adjust to every irregularity in the skin, making for closer shaves and fewer nicks. Men who use the razor rave about it. Store managers report that it's "flying off the shelves"—5 million units were sold in one month alone.

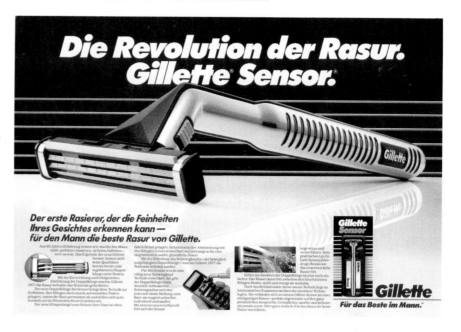

Sensor's success shows that long-term research and development programs can pay off. Gillette spent over $200 million and 13 years developing the new shaving system, which sells for $3.75. Along the way, it applied for 22 patents and developed a new manufacturing process using lasers to weld the blades to the support bar. For television and print advertising during the year in which Sensor was introduced, it budgeted up to $110 million, including $3 million worth of commercials during the Super Bowl. Never before has the company spent so much to launch a single product.

Developing the Sensor was a gamble for Gillette; the idea was to induce users of disposable razors to convert to shaving systems, which are much more profitable. But disposable razors are very popular—they account for 40 percent of men's spending on shaving products—and Gillette ran the risk of cutting into sales of its own disposable brand, Good News. In addition, management was reluctant to make a huge investment in manufacturing and marketing while its existing razors were still making enormous profits.

The level of risk was reduced by careful attention to the needs and opinions of consumers. Gillette spoke with about 10,000 men while it was designing the Sensor. It also tested the product on a panel of 500 employees who came to work unshaven every morning. The decision to launch the product was made when the panel rated the razor as at least 20 percent better than any other. Another important decision was to abandon the disposable version of the razor and to develop a handsome steel handle instead of the plastic handle that had been planned. These decisions seem to have worked: More than 20 million men bought Sensor handles in the first three months after the product was intro-

duced. Retailers also appreciate the new razor, since they make more money on refills than they do on disposables, which also take up more space on display racks.

Sensor is turning out to be a global as well as a national success. It is advertised with the same visuals around the world—only the voice-over changes. The same dialogue (in 26 different languages) is used in Japan, Europe, and the United States. Gillette is building a worldwide mass-market brand while saving millions in packaging, advertising, and other production and marketing costs.

Discussion Questions

1. Despite the time and money it put into development of the Sensor, the introduction of the new razor was a risky venture for Gillette. What problem might the company have faced if its new product had not been so popular?

2. Gillette is planning to introduce a line of upscale products for men, such as aftershave and cologne, building on its advertising theme, "The Best a Man Can Get." How would you evaluate its chances of succeeding in this market?

Sources: James Cox, "Sensor: Five Million Chins and Counting," *USA Today* (February 6, 1990), p. B1; Alison Fahey, "Sensor Sales Sharp," *Advertising Age* (May 7, 1990), p. 60; Jack Falvery, "How the King Maintains His Edge," *The Wall Street Journal* (April 23, 1990), p. A14; Keith H. Hammonds, "How a $4 Razor Ends Up Costing $300 Million," *Business Week* (January 29, 1990), pp. 62–63; Joshua Levine, "Global Lather," *Forbes* (February 5, 1990), pp. 146–148; Ellen Neuborne, "Buyers in a Lather Over Sensor," *USA Today* (February 5, 1990), p. B1; and "Products of the Year," *Fortune* (December 4, 1989), p. 168. *Photo source:* Courtesy of The Gillette Company.

made about the compatibility of the proposed product with such company resources as financial support for necessary promotion, production capabilities, and distribution facilities.

concept testing
Measuring consumer attitudes and perceptions of a product idea prior to its actual development.

Concept testing, or the consideration of the product idea prior to its actual development, is an important aspect of the business analysis stage. **Concept testing** is a marketing research project that attempts to measure consumer attitudes and perceptions relevant to the new-product idea. Focus groups and in-store polling can be effective methods of concept testing. Entrepreneur Mary Anne Jackson tested her new-product concept of nutritional, quick-to-fix children's meals by distributing a survey to 2,000 families. The results showed that a substantial number of parents were interested in the concept if the product could be easily prepared, had no preservatives and additives, and sold for less than $3. Parents indicated they would buy the meals 3.6 times a month. From the survey, Jackson learned what parents wanted their children to eat. Most parents preferred chicken and turkey over beef and were opposed to hot dogs. Jackson concluded her concept was sound and then used trend and census data to determine the size of the market. She figured if the meal were priced at $2.30 and buyers served it 3.6 times a month to their 1.8 million children, the potential annual market would be $500 million. Jackson then proceeded to develop the product, which was introduced to the market a year later as My Own Meals and is now sold nationwide in supermarkets and Toys 'R' Us stores.[21]

The screening and business analysis stages are extremely important because they (1) define the target market and customer needs and wants and (2) determine the product's financial and technical requirements. Several studies indicate that firms spending more time and money in predevelopment activities have a higher rate of product success, have reduced the number of mistakes, and have shortened the time in the development stage.[22]

Development

Financial outlays increase substantially as firms convert product ideas into a physical product. The conversion process is the joint responsibility of the development engineering department, which turns the original concept into a product, and the marketing department, which provides feedback on consumer reactions to product designs, packages, colors, and other physical features. Numerous changes may be necessary before the original mock-up is converted into the final product. Many firms use computer-aided design to reduce the number of prototypes developers must build, thus hastening the development stage. By using computer-aided design, La-Z-Boy Chair has reduced product development from ten months to four months.[23]

The series of tests, revisions, and refinements should ultimately result in the introduction of a product with great likelihood of success. Some firms obtain the reactions of their own employees to proposed new-product offerings. Thom McAn asks its workers to report regularly on shoe wear and fit over an eight-week testing period. Firms test their products in-house or in the field to monitor quality and performance. Brunswick engineers use computers to test how its boats stand up to wind and waves. Timberland chooses athletes to measure performance characteristics of its shoes, boots, and outdoor apparel. The athletes put the products through high endurance tests. For example, by supplying boots to every musher of the Iditarod race, the 1,049-mile sled dog race across Alaska, Timberland tests its boots in temperatures as low as 70 degrees below zero and in winds as high as 100 miles per hour.[24]

The Fit and Finish phase is part of VF Corporation's development of jeanswear, sportswear, intimate apparel, and occupational apparel. Product development involves the fitting of prototype garments on models, who provide feedback on comfort and fit. VF uses this information to make adjustments to designs to meet consumer requirements. During development, VF modifies its garments before final patterns are produced and before manufacturing begins.

Source: Courtesy of VF Corporation.

Testing

To determine consumer reactions to a product under normal conditions, many firms test-market their new-product offerings. Up to this point, they have obtained consumer information by submitting free products to consumers, who then give their reactions. Other information may come from shoppers asked to evaluate competitive products. Test marketing is the first stage at which the product must perform in a real-life environment.

test marketing
Process of selecting a specific city or television coverage area considered reasonably typical of a new market and introducing the product with a marketing campaign in this area.

Test marketing is the process of selecting a specific city or television-coverage area that is considered reasonably typical of the total market and introducing the product with a complete marketing campaign in this area. If the test is carefully designed and controlled, consumers in the test-market city will respond to the new offerings without knowing that a test is being conducted. After the test has been underway for a few months and sales and market shares in the test-market city have been calculated, management can estimate the product's likely performance in a full-scale introduction.

In selecting test-market locations, marketers look for a location with a manageable size. In addition, its residents should represent the overall population in such characteristics as age, education, and income. Finally, the media should be self-contained so that the promotional efforts can be directed to people who represent the target market of the product being tested. The ten most popular U.S. markets for testing food and drug products are shown in Figure 10.5.

Some firms omit test marketing and move directly from product development to full-scale production. These companies cite four problems with test marketing:

1. Test marketing is expensive. It can cost $250,000 to $1 million depending on the size of the test market city and the cost of buying media to advertise the product.[25]

2. Competitors who learn about the test market often disrupt the findings by reducing the prices of their products in the test area, distributing cents-off

Figure 10.5   Top Ten Test Market Locations in the United States

Source: Saatchi & Saatchi DFS Compton, as reported in *The Wall Street Journal* (January 26, 1988), p. 42.

coupons, installing attractive in-store displays, or giving additional discounts to retailers to induce them to display more of their products. In a court settlement, Hartz Mountain once agreed not to engage in advertising designed to disrupt the test of a new pet product by a subsidiary of A. H. Robins.

3. Long-lived durable goods, such as dishwashers, hair dryers, and compact laser disc players, are seldom test marketed due to the major financial investment required for their development, the need to establish a network of dealers to distribute the products, and the parts and servicing required. To develop each silicon chip that performs a single function in an Apple microcomputer costs approximately $100 million and takes at least six months. Producing a prototype for a test market is simply too expensive. Thus, the go/no-go decision for the new, durable product typically is made without the benefit of test market results.

Before adding new products to its menu, McDonald's test-markets them to measure consumer acceptance. In this photo, a new 5½-minute pizza is being test-marketed at a McDonald's in Evansville, Indiana. Results of a seven-month test in 24 outlets in Indiana and Kentucky were so positive that McDonald's expanded the pizza test to three larger cities.

Source: © David Klutho.

4. Test marketing a new product communicates company plans to competitors prior to its introduction. Kellogg Company discovered a new product with sales potential by learning of the test marketing of a new, fruit-filled tart designed to be heated in the toaster and served for breakfast. Kellogg rushed a similar product into full-scale production and became the first national marketer of the product with its Pop Tarts.

The decision to skip the test marketing stage should be based on the conclusion that the new product has an extremely high likelihood of success. The cost of developing a new detergent, for example, from idea generation to national marketing has been estimated at $25 million. Even if a company experiences losses on a product that fails at the test marketing stage, it will save itself from incurring even greater losses and embarrassment in the total market.

Commercialization

The few product ideas that survive all the steps in the development process are ready for full-scale marketing. Marketing programs must be established, outlays for necessary production facilities made, and the salesforce, marketing intermediaries, and potential customers acquainted with the new product.

A systematic approach to new-product development is essential. The traditional method for developing new products, called *phased development,* follows a sequential pattern whereby products are developed in an orderly series of steps. Responsibility for each phase passes from product planners to designers and engineers, then to manufacturers, and finally to marketers. This method works well for firms that dominate mature markets and develop variations on existing products. It is less effective for firms in industries affected by rapidly changing technology or shifts in consumer preference, in which the slow process of phased development is a liability. In the electronics industry, for example, bringing a new product to market nine months late can cost the product half of its potential revenue.

Instead of proceeding sequentially, many firms have adopted the *parallel approach,* which uses teams of design, manufacturing, marketing, sales, and service people who are involved with development from idea generation to commercialization. Venture teams, discussed earlier, are an example of the parallel approach. One of the biggest advantages of this approach is that it reduces the time needed for developing products because team members perform activities concurrently instead of in a series. DowBrands used the parallel approach in developing Spiffits, a line of cleanser-saturated towels designed for quick and convenient household cleaning. The company's consumer research indicated the product had enormous potential. Mike Donohue, new-product development manager, said, "We knew we had a winning concept; the difficult task was to make sure we were the first to market with it." Donohue formed a multidisciplinary "touchdown team" that worked together toward the goal of launching the product ahead of competitors.[26]

Systematic planning of all phases of new-product development and introduction can be accomplished through the use of such scheduling methods as the Program Evaluation and Review Technique (PERT) and the Critical Path Method (CPM). These techniques, originally developed by the U.S. Navy in connection with construction of the Polaris missile and submarine, map out the sequence in which each step must be taken and show the time allotments for each activity. Detailed PERT and CPM flowcharts coordinate all activities entailed in the development and introduction of new products.

Product Deletion Decisions

To avoid waste, product lines must be pruned and old, marginal products eventually eliminated. Marketers typically face this decision during the late maturity and early decline stages of the product life cycle. But some firms have shortened the make-or-break decision period. Campbell Soup Company, for example, decided to withdraw Souper Combos, a soup and sandwich combination, from the market after only a year in national distribution. Campbell also eliminated its fresh produce product line. Campbell dropped these products because they were not profitable.[27] Periodic reviews of weak products should be conducted to eliminate them or justify retaining them. This is a difficult decision for many executives. Often sentimental attachments to marginal products with declining sales preclude objective decisions to drop them.

In some instances, however, a firm continues to carry an unprofitable product in order to provide a complete line of goods for its customers. For example, while most grocery stores lose money on bulky, low-unit-value items such as salt, they continue to carry them to meet shopper demand.

In other instances, shortages of raw materials have prompted some companies to discontinue production and marketing of previously profitable items. Due to such a shortage, Alcoa discontinued its brand of aluminum foil. Or profitable products may be dropped because they fail to fit into the firm's existing product line. The introduction of automatic washing machines necessitated the development of low-sudsing detergents. Monsanto produced the world's first

FOCUS ON ETHICS

DISPOSABLE VERSUS REUSABLE

· ·

In Illinois alone, 900 million dirty diapers, along with 250,000 tons of contaminated waste, are thrown into landfills annually. Throughout the nation, about 16 billion disposable diapers are discarded each year, accounting for as much as 20 percent of the volume in some landfills. The Environmental Protection Agency predicts that by 1995 all landfills will be full.

Disposable diapers have come under attack as environmental awareness has increased among the general public. Both parents and diaper makers have responded in a variety of ways:

☐ Thousands of parents have gone back to cloth diapers, creating a bonanza for diaper services, which witnessed a 39 percent increase in sales in a recent year. The weekly cost of a diaper service is actually lower than that of a week's worth of disposable diapers. But some consumers are unwilling to switch to cloth diapers because disposables are more convenient.

☐ Some makers of disposable diapers (85 percent of the diaper industry) have introduced biodegradable diapers. For example, Rocky Mountain Medical Corp.'s TenderCare diaper uses a special plastic that breaks down within five years. Environmentalists contend, however, that the new diapers do not disintegrate but simply break down into small pieces.

☐ Diaper makers are looking for other ways to address the solid-waste issue. Procter & Gamble, for example, added ultra-absorbents to its Luvs and Pampers; the company claims that this has reduced diaper volume by 50 percent. P&G is also studying ways to recycle and compost diapers. Among the possible uses are flowerpots, plastic garbage bags, cardboard boxes, fertilizer, and insulation.

☐ Illinois Representative Thomas Homer has proposed a tax of a penny a diaper on disposable diapers; the revenues could be used to promote the development and expansion of diaper services. A recent Gallup poll revealed that a large number of consumers favor taxing or even banning disposable diapers in order to protect the environment, and at least 20 states are considering such action.

Arguments can be made on both sides of the diaper issue. Disposable diapers provide fewer opportunities for the spread of infection and are generally more convenient to use than cloth diapers. In addition, while the manufacture of disposable diapers consumes more raw materials, the laundering of cloth diapers consumes more water and energy resources.

One company has attempted to offer a compromise between cloth and disposable: a form-fitted cotton-knit diaper called Cottontails, which is fastened with Velcro tabs and can be reused at least 100 times, with or without a plastic liner. At $6.50 apiece, the product is positioned as an improvement on cloth diapers and an alternative to disposables.

Discussion Questions

1. Disposable diapers account for an average of 2 percent of the volume in landfills. Is it fair to impose a ban or tax on them when so many other products also end up in landfills?

2. In view of the fact that landfill space is finite, what are the long-term prospects for the disposable-diaper industry?

Sources: Christy Fisher and Laurie Freeman, "Disposables Inspire New Cloth Diaper," *Advertising Age* (November 26, 1990), p. 60; Laurie Freeman, "Diaper Image Damaged: Poll," *Advertising Age* (June 11, 1990), pp. 1, 57; Laurie Freeman, "P&G Seeks to Defend Its Diapers," *Advertising Age* (June 11, 1990), pp. 1, 57; Leslie Jay, "Markets Discover the Eco-Consumer," *Management Review* (June 1990), pp. 24–28; Ray Long, "Penny a Diaper," *Journal Star* (Peoria, IL) (April 11, 1990), p. D20; Naushad S. Mehta, "Are You Ready for a Change?" *Time* (April 9, 1990), p. 66; and Brent Felgner, "Baby Needs," *Supermarket Business* (September 1989), pp. 153–154. Laurie Freeman, "Marketers Tout Biodegradable," *Advertising Age* (January 30, 1989), p. 32.

detergent of this sort, All, in the 1950s. All was an instant success, and Monsanto was swamped with orders from supermarkets throughout the nation. The Monsanto salesforce was primarily involved in marketing industrial chemicals to large-scale buyers, and the company would have needed a completely new salesforce to handle the product. Nine months after the introduction of All, Procter & Gamble introduced the world's second low-sudsing detergent, Dash. Because the Procter & Gamble salesforce handled hundreds of products, the company could spread the cost of contacting dealers over all its products. In contrast, Monsanto had only All. Rather than attempt to compete, Monsanto sold All to Lever Brothers, a Procter & Gamble competitor that had a marketing organization capable of handling the product.

Product Identification

Organizations identify their products with brand names, symbols, and distinctive packaging. Almost every product that is distinguishable from another contains a means of identification for the buyer. Sunkist Growers stamps its oranges with the name *Sunkist*. The purchasing agent for a construction firm can turn over a sheet of aluminum and find the Alcoa name and symbol. Prudential Insurance Company uses the Rock of Gibralter as its corporate symbol. Choosing the means of identifying the firm's output represents a major decision for the marketing manager.

Brands, Brand Names, and Trademarks

brand
Name, term, sign, symbol, design, or some combination of these used to identify the products of one firm and differentiate them from competitive offerings.

brand name
Part of the brand consisting of words or letters that comprise a name used to identify and distinguish the firm's offerings from those of competitors.

brand mark
Symbol or pictorial design used to identify a product.

trademark
Brand that has been given legally protected status exclusive to its owner.

A **brand** is a name, term, sign, symbol, design, or some combination used to identify the products of one firm and differentiate them from competitive offerings. The American Marketing Association has defined a **brand name** as the part of the brand consisting of words or letters that comprise a name used to identify and distinguish the firm's offerings from competitors'. It is, therefore, the part of the brand that can be vocalized. A **brand mark** is a symbol or pictorial design. It is the part of the brand that cannot be vocalized. A **trademark** is a brand that has been given legal protection exclusive to its owner. Trademark protection includes the brand name, the brand mark, and any slogan or product name abbreviation, such as "Bud" for Budweiser or "The Met" for the New York Metropolitan Opera. The courts ruled in favor of Budweiser when it claimed that an exterminating company using the slogan "This Bugs for You" constituted trademark infringement. Firms can also receive trademark protection for packaging elements and product features such as color, shape, design, and typeface. Pink, for example, is a protectable color for Owens-Corning's fiberglass insulation. To receive protection, firms must register the brand or brand name with the U.S. Patent and Trademark Office. A trademark should not be confused with a *trade name,* which identifies a company. The Coca-Cola Company is a trade name, but Coke is a trademark of the company. In some cases the trade name is the same as the brand name. For example, Rubbermaid is the brand name of Rubbermaid, Inc.

For the buyer, the process of branding allows repeat purchases of the same product, since the product is identified with the name of its producer. The purchaser thus can associate the satisfaction derived from an ice cream bar, for example, with the brand name Häagen-Dazs. For the marketing manager, the brand serves as the cornerstone of the product's image. Once buyers have been made aware of a particular brand, its appearance becomes additional advertising for the firm. Shell's seashell symbol is instant advertising to motorists who glimpse it while driving.

Well-known brands also allow the firm to escape some of the rigors of price competition. Although any chemists will confirm that all brands of aspirin contain the chemical acetylsalicylic acid, Bayer has developed such a strong reputation that it can successfully market its aspirin at a higher price than competitive products. Well-known gasoline brands typically sell at slightly higher prices than

The Nunes Company, a marketing organization that represents growers of quality lettuce, celery, and cauliflower in California and Arizona, uses the Foxy brand name to identify its produce. To protect the integrity of its brand, Nunes places a label on all consumer packaging of produce grown in the United States that addresses consumer demands for safe food products.

Source: Courtesy of the Nunes Company.

independent brands because many purchasers feel that they are buying higher-quality gasoline. An increasing number of food companies, growers, and distributors are introducing branded produce, which is priced higher than unbranded fruits and vegetables. Dole, for example, has applied its well-known brand name to 20 lines of produce.[28]

Characteristics of Effective Brand Names

Effective brand names are easy to pronounce, recognize, and remember. Short names, such as Bounce, Agree, Raid, and Swatch, meet these requirements. Marketers try to overcome the problem of easily mispronounced brand names by teaching consumers how to pronounce them correctly. For example, advertisements for the Korean car Hyundai explained that the name rhymes with *Sunday.*

Global marketers face a particularly acute problem in selecting brand names; an excellent brand name in one country may prove disastrous in another. Firms marketing a product in many countries must decide whether to use a single brand name universally or tailor the name to individual countries. Every language has *o* or *k* sounds, so *okay* has become an international word. Every language also has a short *a;* thus, Coca-Cola, Kodak, and Texaco are effective brands in any country. Because of language and translation problems, though, some firms create brand names to fit local markets. When Procter & Gamble decided to market its Crest Tartar Control toothpaste in Latin America, it learned there was no Spanish translation for the word *tartar.* Consumer research showed that Latin Americans used the word *sarro* to best express the meaning of tartar. So P&G markets the toothpaste as Crest Anti-Sarro in Latin American countries.[29]

Many firms are taking a global perspective in naming their products. Both Honda Motors and General Motors' Chevrolet division hired NameLab Inc., a firm that specializes in creating brand names, to develop nameplates that would function as global trademarks. NameLab generated Acura for Honda and Geo for GM, brand names that are short, distinctive, and travel well around the world.[30]

Brand names should also give buyers the correct connotation of the product's image. The bicycle brand name Allez carries the image of champion French bicyclists. The Tru-Test name used on the True Value Hardware line of

Figure 10.6   The Rhino Rod: A Name That Promotes the Product's Image

Source: Courtesy of Zebco.

paints suggests reliable performance. Visa suggests a credit card with global use. Zebco, a manufacturer of fishing equipment, chose Rhino as the brand name for a new fishing rod to convey the product's strength. The advertisement in Figure 10.6 is one of a series in a campaign designed to reinforce the Rhino rod's indestructibility.

The brand name must also be legally protectable. The Lanham Act of 1946 states that registered trademarks must not contain words in general use, such as *automobile* or *suntan lotion.* These generic words actually describe a particular type of product and cannot be granted exclusively to any company. A. J. Canfield Company, maker of Diet Chocolate Fudge Soda, sued for trademark infringement when competitors later introduced similar beverages with names that included the words *chocolate fudge.* But the court ruled that those words simply describe a specific drink flavor and are not legally protectable.[31]

generic name
Brand name that has become a generally descriptive term for a product.

When a unique product becomes generally known by its original brand name, the brand name may be ruled as a descriptive **generic name.** If this occurs, the original owner loses exclusive claim to it. For example, in 1989 a federal court ruled that the trademark for The Murphy Door Bed Company's "Murphy bed," a bed that folds up into a wall, was invalid because it had become a generic term. The court decided the company had not done enough to protect its brand name and the name had fallen into common usage.[32] The generic names *nylon, aspirin, escalator, kerosene,* and *zipper* formerly were brand names. Other generic names that were once brand names include *cola, yo-yo, linoleum,* and *shredded wheat.*

There is a difference between brand names that are legally generic and those that are generic in many consumers' eyes. Jell-O is a brand name owned exclusively by General Foods, but to most consumers Jell-O is a descriptive name for gelatin desserts. Legal brand names such as Jell-O are often used by consumers as descriptive names. Many English and Australian consumers use the brand name Hoover as a verb for *vacuuming.* Similarly, Xerox is such a well-known brand name that it is frequently—though incorrectly—used as a verb. To protect its valuable trademark, Xerox Corporation has created advertisements explaining that Xerox is a brand name and registered trademark and should not be used as a verb.

To prevent their brand names from being ruled descriptive and available for general use, owners must take steps to inform the public of their exclusive ownership of the names as Xerox has done. The Lego Group of Billund, Denmark, manufacturer of Lego brand building bricks, uses the ® symbol for registration immediately after the names Lego, Legoland, and Duplo. To preserve its valued trademark, the company informs writers how to use its brand names properly by referring to Lego products as "Lego brand building blocks," "Lego bricks," or "Lego construction sets" rather than "Legos."[33] Since any dictionary name may eventually be ruled generic, some companies create new words for their brand names. Names such as *Tylenol, Keds, Rinso,* and *Kodak* have been created by their owners.

Protecting Trademarks Abroad

A problem that many firms face is the protection of their trademarks in foreign countries. An Indonesian court, for example, ruled that the cartoon character Donald Duck is the property of an Indonesian firm even though Walt Disney Productions claims worldwide rights to it. Many brand name goods, from handbags to computer software, are counterfeited abroad. It is estimated that counterfeiting practices in world trade totals $60 billion each year. Trademark violation is especially prevalent in developing nations such as Taiwan, South Korea, Thailand, and Mexico.[34] In an effort to resolve the problem, the United States, Canada, the European Community, and several other countries are trying to establish a worldwide code for protecting trademarks. It would be enforced by GATT, which could impose severe penalties against countries that permit the manufacture and sale of counterfeit goods.[35]

The United States recently revised its trademark law to help American firms compete against foreign firms. Under the old law, U.S. companies had to first introduce a product to the market before they could register trademarks and brand names. Most other countries, however, do not require use before registration. For example, Japan and European countries require only that firms file a notice of intent to use a new trademark to prohibit its use by others. Firms in these countries can then apply for a U.S. registration based on the registration in their own countries. This put U.S. companies at a disadvantage. The revised law enables U.S. firms to protect new names and trademarks for up to three years without using them.[36]

Measuring Brand Loyalty

Brands vary widely in consumer familiarity and acceptance. While a boating enthusiast may insist on a Johnson outboard motor, one study revealed that 40 percent of U.S. homemakers could not identify the brands of furniture in their own homes. Some brands enjoy worldwide recognition. According to a survey of

Figure 10.7

Building Brand Awareness

Source: Courtesy of Bugle Boy Industries.

10,000 consumers in Japan, the United States, and eight European countries, Coca-Cola ranked first in global "imagepower," a combination of brand recognition and esteem, followed by Sony, Mercedes-Benz, Kodak, Disney, Nestlé, Toyota, McDonald's, IBM, and Pepsi-Cola.[37] Brand loyalty can be measured in three stages: brand recognition, brand preference, and brand insistence.

brand recognition
Stage of brand acceptance at which the consumer is aware of the existence of a brand but does not prefer it to competing brands.

brand preference
Stage of brand acceptance at which the consumer will select one brand over competitive offerings based on previous experience with it.

brand insistence
Stage of brand acceptance at which the consumer will accept no alternatives and will search extensively for the good or service. Also known as brand requirement.

Brand recognition is a company's first objective for its newly introduced products to make them familiar to the consuming public. In 1984 Bugle Boy Industries introduced its line of young men's fashionwear with bus-shelter ads that highlighted the brand's logo. "It met our objectives of getting the brand into the marketplace. It gave us an on-street consistent awareness," says Suzi Sheimann, Bugle Boy's advertising manager. In current ads, such as the billboard in Figure 10.7, Bugle Boy continues to build brand awareness by consistently emphasizing the brand's logo.[38] Brand recognition also is achieved through offers of free samples or discount coupons for purchases. Once consumers have used a product or seen it advertised, it moves from the unknown to the known category, and the probability of its being purchased is increased.

Brand preference is the second stage of brand loyalty. In this stage, consumers, relying on previous experience with the product, will choose it over its competitors if it is available. A college student who prefers Stroh's beer usually will switch to another brand if it is not available at the tavern where he or she meets friends after an evening class. But where Stroh's is available, it will be chosen by that student over other brands. Companies with products at the brand preference stage are in a favorable position for competing in their industry.

Brand insistence, the ultimate stage in brand loyalty, is the situation in which consumers will accept no alternatives and will search extensively for the product. A product at this stage has achieved a monopoly position with that particular group of consumers. Although brand insistence is the goal of many firms, it is seldom achieved. Only the most exclusive specialty goods attain this position with a large segment of the total market.

Figure 10.8

Variations in Brand Loyalty

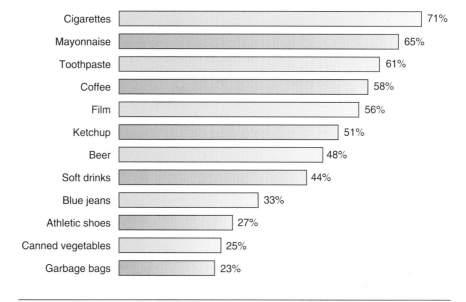

Percentage of users who are loyal to one brand

Cigarettes	71%
Mayonnaise	65%
Toothpaste	61%
Coffee	58%
Film	56%
Ketchup	51%
Beer	48%
Soft drinks	44%
Blue jeans	33%
Athletic shoes	27%
Canned vegetables	25%
Garbage bags	23%

Brand loyalty differs considerably among product categories. Figure 10.8 shows the results of a brand loyalty survey conducted by *The Wall Street Journal.* As the percentages indicate, consumers are most brand-loyal for cigarettes, mayonnaise, and toothpaste and least brand-loyal for athletic shoes, canned vegetables, and garbage bags. The survey revealed that most consumers switch brands, putting price, health and environmental concerns, and other priorities over brand loyalty. More than half of the survey respondents who use 17 of the 25 products listed said they are brand switchers. To increase brand loyalty, many marketers are spending more money on advertising that strengthens the image of their brands.[39]

Brand Extensions and Brand Licensing

brand extension

Decision to use a popular brand name for a new-product entry in an unrelated product category.

Some brands are so popular that they are carried over to unrelated products because of their marketing advantages. The strategy of using a popular brand name for a new-product entry in an unrelated product category is known as **brand extension.** It should not be confused with *line extension,* which refers to new sizes, styles, or related products. Brand extension, in contrast, refers only to carrying over the brand name. Examples of brand extension abound in contemporary marketing. Gerber Products Company, for example, has capitalized on the strong heritage of its Gerber name by extending it beyond baby food to apparel, general merchandise, and a toddler food line. After acquiring RCA, General Electric used the well-established name in consumer electronics on a new line of refrigerators, microwave ovens, washers, dryers, and other household appliances. GE's research indicated that the RCA name had a high level of awareness among consumers and carried positive attributes of quality and reliability.[40]

brand licensing

Practice of allowing other firms to use a brand name for a fee.

A growing number of firms are allowing other companies, for a fee, to use their brand names, a practice known as **brand licensing.** The Walt Disney Company licenses the name Walt Disney, its characters, songs, and music to manufacturers, retailers, printers, and publishers. Worldwide, the company has more than 3,000 licenses for some 16,000 products. Campbell Soup Company recently licensed its brand name to a unit of American Home Products for a line of cooking utensils, and Dr. Scholl's has licensed its name for foot-related products such as shoes, socks, and a foot massager. Harley-Davidson builds and reinforces its name in the motorcycle community by licensing hundreds of products ranging from underwear to an $1,895 curio cabinet. Brand licensing gives firms added exposure in the marketplace and an extra source of income from royalties they receive, which typically range from 4 percent to 8 percent of wholesale sales. However, brand experts advise that firms consider several potential problems of licensing. For example, if a licensee produces a poor-quality product, it could injure the reputation of the brand. Some brand names do not transfer well to certain products because they conflict with consumer perceptions of the brand. For example, Playboy licenses Playboy-brand merchandise from wallpaper in Europe to cooking classes in Brazil and shoes in the United States. But the company decided against a licensing arrangement with a manufacturer of men's suits after discovering in consumer testing that "a college graduate who gets a haircut and a new suit for his first job interview doesn't want to walk in in a Playboy suit," as William Stokken, president of Playboy's licensing group, put it.[41]

Family Brands and Individual Brands

family brand
Name used for several related products, such as the Johnson & Johnson line of baby care products.

Brands can be classified as family brands or individual brands. A **family brand** is a single brand name used for several related products. For example, KitchenAid has a complete line of appliances under the KitchenAid name, and Johnson & Johnson offers a line of baby powder, lotions, disposable diapers, plastic pants, and baby shampoo under one name.

individual brand
Strategy of giving an item in a product line its own brand name rather than identifying it by a single family brand name used for all products in the line.

On the other hand, a manufacturer may choose to utilize **individual brands,** items known by their own brand names rather than by the names of the companies producing them or by an umbrella name covering similar items. Lever Brothers, for example, markets Aim, Close-Up, and Pepsodent toothpastes; All and Wisk laundry detergents; Imperial margarine; Caress, Dove, Lifebuoy, and Lux bath soaps; and Shield and Lever 2000 deodorant soaps. Quaker Oats markets Aunt Jemima breakfast products, Gatorade soft drinks, and Celeste Pizza. Individual brands are more expensive to market because a new promotional campaign must be developed to introduce each new product to its target market. But they are an extremely effective aid in implementing a market segmentation strategy.

When family brands are used, a promotional outlay benefits all the products in the line. For example, a new addition to the Heinz line gains immediate recognition because the family brand is well known. Use of family brands also makes it easier to introduce the product to both the customer and the retailer. Since supermarkets stock thousands of items, they are reluctant to add new products unless they are convinced of potential demand. A marketer of a new brand of black bean soup would have to promise the supermarket buyer huge advertising outlays for promotion and evidence of consumer buying intent before getting the product into the stores. On the other hand, Campbell Soup Company, with its dominant share of the U.S. soup market, could merely add black bean soup to its existing line and secure store placements more easily than could another company offering only individual brand names.

Family brands should be used only when the products are of similar quality, or the firm will risk harming its product image. Using the Rolex name on a new, less expensive watch might severely tarnish the image of the other models in the Rolex product line.

Individual brand names should be used for dissimilar products. Quaker Oats' dog food line is marketed under the Ken-L Ration brand name and its cat food

The Dole Food Company uses a family branding strategy. The Dole brand name and logo appear on a wide array of company products, including canned fruit, nuts, raisins, juices, frozen desserts, fresh fruit, and vegetables.

Source: Courtesy of Dole Food Company.

line under the Puss 'n Boots brand name. Large marketers of grocery products, such as Procter & Gamble, General Foods, and Lever Brothers, employ individual brands to appeal to unique market segments. These brands also enable the firm to stimulate competition within the organization and to increase total company sales. Consumers who do not want Tide can choose Cheer, Dash, or Oxydol—all Procter & Gamble products—rather than a competitor's brand.

Manufacturers' Brands and Private Brands

manufacturer's (national) brand
Brand name owned by a manufacturer or other producer.

private brand
Brand name owned by a wholesaler or retailer.

Most of the brands mentioned in this chapter have been those offered by manufacturers, commonly termed **manufacturers' (national) brands.** But many large wholesalers and retailers also place their own brands on the products they market. The brands offered by wholesalers and retailers are usually called **private brands.** Sears sells its own brands—Kenmore, Craftsman, DieHard, and Harmony House. DieHard is the leading brand of battery today. Safeway shelves are filled with such company brands as Bel Air, Canterbury, Cragmont, Party Pride, Manor House, and Scotch Buy. Private brands and generic products expand the number of alternatives available to consumers.

The growth of private brands is largely attributed to the fact that they allow retailers and wholesalers to maintain control over the products' image, quality, and price. Private brands are usually sold at lower prices than the national brands offered by manufacturers. It is estimated that private brands account for 5 percent to 10 percent of retail sales.

Generic Products

generic product
Food or household item characterized by a plain label, with no advertising and no brand name.

Food and household staples characterized by plain labels, little or no advertising, and no brand names are called **generic products.** These "no-name" products were first sold in Europe, where their prices were as much as 30 percent below brand name products, and introduced in the United States in 1977. Generic products account for 1.5 percent of total store sales. The market share of generic products increases during economic recessions but subsides when the economy improves. Today the most popular generic items are cigarettes and paper products such as towels and tissues. In the pharmaceutical industry, generic drugs account for almost one-third of total drug sales.[42]

Battle of the Brands

Competition between manufacturers' brands and private brands offered by wholesalers and large retailers has been called the "battle of the brands." Although the battle is intensifying, the marketing impact varies widely among industries.

The growth of private brands has paralleled that of chain stores in the United States, most of which has occurred since the 1930s. Chains that market their own brands become customers of the manufacturer, which places the chain's private brand names on its own products. Such leading manufacturers as Westinghouse, Armstrong Rubber, and Heinz are obtaining ever increasing percentages of their total incomes by selling private-label goods. Private-label sales to Sears and other major customers account for about 45 percent of Whirlpool's sales. Polaroid is now manufacturing private-label instant cameras for Sears.

Although some manufacturers refuse to produce private-brand goods, most regard such production as a way to reach another segment of the total market. Except for making tires for Sears, Group Michelin, the French maker of premium tires, refused to produce private-brand tires. But to achieve its goal of doubling its market share in the United States, where private brands account for 50 percent of replacement tire sales, Michelin changed its strategy. Michelin increased its presence in the private-brand market by acquiring Uniroyal Goodrich, a U.S. firm that derives 29 percent of its sales from private-brand production.[43]

Great inroads have been made into the dominance of manufacturers' national brands. Private brands have proven that they can compete with national brands and often have succeeded in effecting price reductions by national brand marketers to make them more competitive. At D'Agostino, a New York supermarket chain, the Decadent Chocolate Chip Cookie from the retailer's President's Choice private brand outsells Nabisco's Chips Ahoy brand cookie.[44]

In Europe private brands are more popular than in the United States. In Great Britain, for example, private brands account for 25 percent of retail sales. British retailer Marks & Spencer holds a dominant market position with its St. Michael brand. Analysts predict that with improvements in product and packaging quality and expansion into more product categories, private brands will continue to grow, throughout the international market.[45]

Packaging

Questions about packaging also must be addressed in a firm's product strategy. Like brand names, a product's package can influence the buyer's purchase decision. Just Born, Inc. learned that kids were not buying its Hot Tamales, Jelly Jos, and Mike and Ike candy because it was packaged in plain black-and-white packages. After the company introduced a new, colorful package, product sales increased 25 percent. "Kids say we went from dull and boring to definitely awesome," says a company official.[46]

Packaging is a vital component of product strategy. Firms increasingly are using scientific approaches in making packaging decisions. Rather than experimenting with physical models or drawings, more and more package designers are using special graphics computers that create three-dimensional images of packages in thousands of colors, shapes, and typefaces. Another computer system helps firms design effective packaging by simulating what shoppers see when they walk down supermarket aisles. Companies use marketing research to evaluate current packages and to test alternative new package designs. Kellogg, for example, tested Nutri-Grain's package as well as the product itself.

The package has several objectives. These can be classified under three general goals:

1. To protect against damage, spoilage, and pilferage
2. To assist in marketing the product
3. To be cost effective

Protection Against Damage, Spoilage, and Pilferage

The original packaging objective was to offer physical protection for the product. The typical product is handled several times between manufacture and consumer purchase, and its package must protect the contents from damage. Furthermore, perishable products must be protected against spoilage in transit, storage, or awaiting consumer selection. Because darkness protects the flavor of beer, Latrobe Brewing Company packages its Rolling Rock bottles in light-tight cardboard containers. Ads for the beer emphasize the important role the package plays in safeguarding flavor. The packaging innovation of temperature-sensitive indicators not only shows consumers when the food is cooked, it also indicates whether the product has been exposed to heat prematurely, and thus has spoiled.

Product tampering has forced many firms to improve package design. Over-the-counter medicinal products now have tamper-resistant packages, many of which warn consumers not to purchase the product if protective seals are broken. SmithKline Beckman redesigned the packaging for its Contac capsules after some were contaminated with rat poison. Capsules are now sealed with gelatin bands to make tampering more difficult and more easily detectable. They are individually sealed in clear plastic blister packs and sold in plastic-wrapped boxes.

Another important safeguard many packages provide for the retailer is prevention of pilferage. At the retail level, customer shoplifting and employee theft costs retailers several billions of dollars each year. Many products are packaged with oversize cardboard backing too large to fit into a shoplifter's pocket or purse. Efficient packaging that protects against damage, spoilage, and theft is especially important for international marketers, who must take into account varying climactic conditions and the added time and stress involved in overseas shipping.

Assistance in Marketing the Product

Packaging is taking on a more important role as a marketing tool. The proliferation of new products, changes in consumer life styles and buying habits, and marketers' emphasis on targeting smaller market segments have increased the importance of packaging as an effective way to promote products. Many firms are addressing consumers' concern about protecting the environment by designing packages that use less material and are biodegradable and recyclable. To let consumers know that they are serious about environmental protection, Procter & Gamble, Coors, McDonald's, Amoco Chemical, and other firms have created ads that describe their efforts in developing environmentally sound packaging.

In a grocery store containing thousands of different items, a product must capture the shopper's attention. Studies show that more consumer buying decisions are being made at the point of purchase and that the time spent during each shopping trip is decreasing.[47] Consequently, many marketers offering product lines are adopting similar package designs to create more visual impact in the store. Packaging Stouffer's frozen foods in orange boxes and the adoption of common package designs by product lines such as Weight Watchers foods and Planters nuts represent attempts to dominate larger sections of retail stores.

Through the use of color, size, shape, graphics, and type, marketers design packages to establish distinct identities that set their products apart from competitors'. Stroh's Brewery Company learned from marketing research that its white beer cans "didn't stand out" against competitors. So Stroh changed its cans and bottle labels to bright blue. The packaging change resulted in increased bottle sales and expanded distribution. Package redesigns are helping private-brand marketers compete against national brands. Without the assistance of advertising, Kroger Company, a grocery store chain, boosted the sales of its private-brand ice cream by 20 percent after redesigning its package by enlarging the type and photo.[48]

Packages can also offer the buyer convenience. Pump dispenser cans facilitate the use of products ranging from mustard to insect repellent. Squeezable bottles of jellies, dessert toppings, and ketchup make the products easier to use and store. Packaging plays a key part in convenience foods such as microwave meals and snacks, juice drinks in small, aseptic packages, and single-serving portions of frozen entrées and vegetables. Firms frequently receive complaints about packages that are inconvenient to open, reseal, and store. Consumer hotline complaints encouraged Procter & Gamble to design a snap-top closure for its Tide detergent package. Oscar Meyer developed a resealable package for its wieners, and Sargento Cheese developed one for its shredded cheese.[49]

Some firms provide increased consumer utility with packages designed for reuse. Peanut butter jars and jelly jars have long been used as drinking glasses. Bubble bath can be purchased in plastic bottles shaped like animals and suitable for bathtub play. Packaging is a major component in Avon's overall marketing strategy. The firm's decorative reuseable bottles have even become collectibles.

Like brand names, packages should evoke the product's image and communicate its value. Colors such as black, gold, and maroon and design elements such as borders and crests help promote a product's premium image. Before introducing his Woodland Pantry brand of gourmet dehydrated mushrooms to American consumers, entrepreneur W. J. Clark realized he needed a package worthy of his product. The pricey mushrooms, most of which are imported from Europe and Japan, sell for between $5 and $13 for a 7/8-ounce package. Clark designed an eye-catching box with illustrations of the mushrooms in lush landscape settings. The package includes a description of the product, how to prepare it, and a gourmet recipe in which it can be used. Retailers gave the new product a try "because they loved our packaging," says Clark. Clark also attributes much of the brand's growth to its enticing and informative package.[50]

Cost-Effective Packaging

Although packaging must perform a number of functions for the producer, marketer, and consumer, it must do so at a reasonable cost. Packaging currently represents the single largest item in the cost of producing a can of beer. It also accounts for 55 percent of the total cost of the single-serving packets of sugar found in restaurants.[51]

Designing a cost-effective package was a major decision facing All American Gourmet Company when it launched its line of Budget Gourmet frozen dinner entrées. Higher-priced frozen dinners such as Le Menu are packaged in expensive boxes, and the food is presented in domed plastic containers. To keep its product in the budget range without sacrificing the quality of the food, All American developed a sturdy, polyester-coated cardboard container that can be used in both conventional and microwave ovens. All American estimates that the package is 30 to 40 percent cheaper than traditional frozen dinner packaging, allowing the firm to keep Budget Gourmet dinners priced at about $2. According to the firm's marketing director, buyers understand that the package, not lack of quality, is the reason they pay less.[52]

The Metric System

U.S. marketers are increasingly adopting the metric measurement system in their packaging and product development decisions. Most soft drinks now come in metric-size containers as a substitute for pints and quarts. Many canned and packaged foods list metric equivalents to ounces and pounds on their labels. General Motors and Ford now design and manufacture their cars to metric specifications alone. About 60 percent of major U.S. firms make some metric products, but most maintain the English system for products sold in the United States and metrics for exports.[53]

 U.S. marketers must make the switch to metrics if they are to compete in the world marketplace. Saudi Arabia recently rejected a shipment of General Electric appliances because they did not conform to metric standards: the products' connecting cords were 6 feet long rather than the required 2 meters, or 6.6 feet. The United States, Liberia, and Burma are the only countries in the world that have not either adopted metrics or mandated its future adoption. Such firms as Caterpillar Tractor, Deere & Company, Navistar, and IBM have been using metrics for years in their foreign trade. The switch to metrics should increase export sales of small U.S. firms that cannot afford to produce two sets of products for different markets. U.S. marketers must also switch to metrics if they want to bid on U.S. government contracts. A provision of the 1988 Omnibus Trade Bill mandates that federal agencies require metric weights and measurements for their purchases.[54]

Labeling

label
Descriptive part of a product's package, listing brand name or symbol, name and address of manufacturer or distributor, ingredients, size or quantity of product, and/or recommended uses, directions, or serving suggestions.

Although in the past the label often was a separate item that was applied to the package, today it is an integral part of most packages. Labels perform both promotional and informational functions. In most instances, a **label** contains the brand name or symbol, the name and address of the manufacturer or distributor, the product composition and size, and recommended uses for the product.

Consumer confusion and dissatisfaction over such incomprehensible descriptions as "giant economy size," "king size," and "family size" led to passage of the Fair Packaging and Labeling Act in 1966. The act requires that a label offer adequate information concerning the package contents and that a package design facilitate value comparisons among competitive products.

The Nutrition Labeling and Education Act of 1990 requires food manufacturers and processors to provide detailed nutritional information on most foods. Figure 10.9 shows a label listing nutritional ingredients. Meat, poultry, and eggs are excluded since they are covered by the U.S. Department of Agriculture

Figure 10.9   Label Showing Nutritional Information and the Universal Product Code

regulations. Also excluded are restaurant meals, infant formulas, and prepared meals sold in supermarkets and delicatessens.

The 1990 legislation also specified that the Food and Drug Administration (FDA) allow only those health claims that were scientifically valid. For instance, the FDA was required to develop standard definitions of health-related terms like *light, low-fat, reduced calories,* and *high-fiber.*[55]

Labeling requirements differ on a country-to-country basis. Countries with two common languages require bilingual labeling. In Canada, for example, labels must be printed in English and French; in Belgium, in French and Flemish; and in Finland, in Finnish and Swedish. The type and amount of information required on labels also varies among nations. International marketers must design labels that conform to the regulations of each country in which they market their products.[56]

Green Labeling.   A recent global trend has been so-called green label-ing—the use of product seals to designate environmentally safe products. Germany's Blue Angel has been around since the 1970s. Examples of U.S. green labels are Green Cross, Green Seal, and Good Earthkeeping.[57]

Universal Product Code (UPC)
Special code on packages that is read by optical scanners.

Universal Product Code.   The Universal Product Code designation is another very important part of a label or package. In other cases, the code lines are printed right into the package, such as on a carton of milk.

The **Universal Product Code (UPC),** introduced in 1974 as a method for cutting expenses in the supermarket industry, is a numerical code read by optical scanners that print the item and its price on the cash register receipt. Virtually all packaged grocery items contain the UPC lines. While UPC scanners are costly, they permit considerable labor savings over manual pricing and improved inventory control. The Universal Product Code is also a major asset for marketing research. For example, some marketing research companies are providing consumer test participants with hand-held wands capable of reading UPC codes, with which the participants record their purchases at home. The Universal Product Code will likely play an even greater role in product management in the 1990s.

Product Safety

If a product is to fulfill its mission of satisfying consumer needs, it must, above all, be safe. Manufacturers must design their products to protect users. Packaging plays an important role in product safety. Aspirin bottle-tops have been made childproof (and virtually parentproof) by St. Joseph's and Bayer since 1968. This safety feature is estimated to have reduced by two-thirds the number of children under five years of age who accidentally swallow overdoses of aspirin.

Prominently placed safety warnings on the labels of such potentially hazardous products as cleaning fluids and drain cleaners inform users of the dangers of these products and urge them to store them out of the reach of children. Changes in product design have reduced the hazards involved in the use of such products as lawn mowers, hedge trimmers, and toys.

Consumer Product Safety Commission

Federal and state legislation have long played a major role in promoting product safety. Many of the piecemeal federal laws passed over a 50-year period were unified by the Consumer Product Safety Act of 1972, which created a powerful regulatory agency—the Consumer Product Safety Commission (CPSC). The agency has assumed jurisdiction over every consumer product except food, automobiles, and a few other products already regulated by other agencies. The CPSC has the authority to ban products without a court hearing, order the recall or redesign of products, and inspect production facilities. It can charge managers of accused companies with criminal offenses.

The Concept of Product Liability

product liability
Concept that manufacturers and marketers are responsible for injuries and damages caused by their products.

Product liability refers to the concept that manufacturers and marketers are responsible for injuries and damages caused by their products. There has been a tremendous increase in product liability suits in recent years. Although many such claims are settled out of court, others are decided by juries, who sometimes have awarded multimillion-dollar settlements.

Not only have marketers stepped up efforts to ensure product safety; product liability insurance has become an essential ingredient in any new or existing product strategy. Premiums for this insurance have risen alarmingly, and in some cases coverage is almost impossible to obtain. A Detroit producer of components for pleasure boats discovered that its liability insurance premiums had increased from $2,500 to $160,000 in a two-year period even though the insurance company had never paid a claim on the firm's behalf.

CPSC activities and the increased number of liability claims have prompted companies to improve their safety standards voluntarily. Safety is now a vital ingredient of product strategy.

Summary of Chapter Objectives

1. **Identify the major product mix decisions that marketers must make.** A product mix is the assortment of product lines and individual offerings available from a marketer. Its two primary components are product line (a series of related products) and individual offerings (single products). Product mixes are assessed in terms of length, width, and depth of assortment. Length refers to the number of products in the mix. Width means the number of product lines the firm offers. Depth refers to variations of each product in the mix.

2. **Explain why most firms develop a line of related products rather than a single product.** Firms usually produce several related products rather than single products to achieve the objectives of growth, optimal use of company resources, and increased company importance in the market, and to exploit the product life cycle.

3. **Identify alternative new-product development strategies and the determinants of each strategy's success.** Many new-product ideas are required in order to produce one commercially successful product. The success of a new product depends on a host of factors and can result from four alternative product development strategies. A market penetration strategy refers to the modification of existing products in existing markets. The finding of new markets for established products is called a market development strategy. The introduction of new products into established or identifiable markets is referred to as a product development strategy. The creation of new products for new markets is called a product diversification strategy.

4. **Explain the various organizational structures for new-product development.** New-product organizational responsibility in most large firms is assigned to new-product committees, new-product departments, product managers, or venture teams. New-product committees are review committees for new-product ideas. New-product departments are organizational units charged with the actual development of new products. Individuals given the responsibility for determining marketing strategies for a product, brand, or product line are called product managers. Venture teams are temporary groups set up to develop a specific product or product line.

5. **List the stages in the new-product development process.** New-product ideas evolve through six stages on the way to their market introduction: idea generation, screening, business analysis, product development, testing, and commercialization.

6. **Explain the roles of brands, brand names, and trademarks in a marketing strategy.** A brand is a name, term, sign, symbol, design, or some combination used to identify the products of one firm and differentiate them from competitive offerings. A brand name is the name part of a brand. A trademark is a brand that has been given legal protection that is granted exclusively to its owner. A trademark includes both the brand's pictorial design and the brand name.

7. **Describe the major functions of the package.** Modern packaging is designed to protect against damage, spoilage, and pilferage; to assist in marketing the product; and to be cost effective.

8. **Outline the functions of the Consumer Product Safety Commission and the concept of product liability.** Product safety has become an increasingly important component of the total product concept. It has evolved through voluntary attempts by product designers to reduce hazards, through various pieces of legislation, and through the establishment of the Consumer

Product Safety Commission. The CPSC was established by the Consumer Product Safety Act of 1972. It has jurisdiction over every consumer product except food, automobiles, and a few other products already regulated by other agencies. It can ban products without a court hearing, order the recall or redesign of products, inspect production facilities, and charge violators of its rules with criminal offenses. The concept of product liability refers to the producer's or marketer's legal responsibility for injuries or damages caused by a defective product. It is becoming an increasingly important factor in contemporary marketing.

Key Terms

product mix	brand recognition
product line	brand preference
line extension	brand insistence
cannibalizing	brand extension
product positioning	brand licensing
product manager	family brand
venture team	individual brand
concept testing	manufacturer's (national) brand
test marketing	private brand
brand	generic product
brand name	label
brand mark	Universal Product Code (UPC)
trademark	product liability
generic name	

Review Questions

1. What is meant by a product mix? How is the concept used in making effective marketing decisions?

2. Explain the concepts of line extension and cannibalization. Why do most business firms market a line of related products rather than a single product?

3. Outline the different product development strategies. Cite an example of each strategy.

4. Outline the alternative organizational structures for new-product development. Identify the steps in the new-product development process.

5. What is the chief purpose of test marketing? What potential problems does it involve?

6. Differentiate among the terms *brand, brand name, brand mark, trademark,* and *trade name.*

7. List the characteristics of an effective brand name. Illustrate each characteristic with an appropriate brand name.

8. Identify and briefly explain each of the three stages of brand loyalty. How does brand loyalty differ among product categories?

9. Differentiate between brand extensions and brand licensing.

10. Explain the chief functions of the Consumer Product Safety Commission. What steps can it take to protect consumers from defective and hazardous products?

Discussion Questions

1. The Coca-Cola Company's line of colas includes Coke, Coca-Cola Classic, Diet Coke, Caffeine Free Diet Coke, Caffeine Free Classic Coke, Cherry Coke, and Diet Cherry Coke. Relate Coca-Cola's lineup to the concept of product mix. What generalizations can you make about the company's product strategies? Discuss.

2. The Western Michigan Research Group (WMRG) includes people from the region's broadcast and print media, advertising agencies, and outdoor advertising companies. WMRG's purpose is to promote the area as a test-market site. The Grand Rapids ADI (area of dominant influence)—the technical name for the test site—includes the cities of Kalamazoo, Battle Creek, and Muskegon. The Grand Rapids ADI, which accounts for about 1 percent of the U.S. population, has a demographic pattern similar to that of the total United States. WMRG estimates that the test marketing of just one new product a month would add $1.5 to $2.0 million to the western Michigan economy.[58] Evaluate WMRG's economic development effort. While obviously self serving, would increased test marketing also benefit the region?

3. Victorinox, the Swiss manufacturer of the well-known Swiss Army Knife, has given a U.S. firm, Forschner Group, permission to use the Swiss Army name for other products. Forschner now markets $115 Swiss Army sunglasses and a Swiss Army watch for $95.[59] What product concept is illustrated by the Victorinox-Forschner arrangement? Discuss.

4. Fred DuLuca, the founder of Subway Sandwiches, always remembered the story of how Henry Ford used special crates to package his Model T engines. A later manufacturing stage took the crates apart and used them for floorboards. Today Subway's meat supplies arrive in cardboard containers that are reused as carryout cartons. Each carton carries the message "Save a box, Save a tree." Participating Subway franchisers deduct a dollar from the next purchase of any customer who brings the carton back. However, DeLuca admits: "Recycling is noble, but it's hard work, very expensive, and a big pain. Sure, it's an ecologically minded promotion, but the real kicker is this way it's not extra work, and franchisers save money on boxes and garbage hauling."[60] Relate this example to the packaging discussion in this chapter.

5. Pasta La Bella is a big seller at Casa di Risparmio, a pasta and bread shop in Parma, Italy. It is not surprising that a quality pasta product would be well-received in a country known for its pasta; what is surprising is that Pasta La Bella is made in Missouri. Packaging has contributed to the American product's success. The original label was a Tuscan hill town surrounded by black packaging, but it was modified by slapping "Made in the U.S.A." across the town.[61] Assess Pasta La Bella's packaging and labeling strategy. Would this strategy be effective on a global basis? Why or Why not?

Computer Applications

In Chapter 6, three approaches to making choices from among alternatives were described. The *overall scoring method* involves scoring or ranking each of the evaluative criteria (or decision factors) used in choosing among alternatives and then selecting the alternative with the highest total score. The *weighted scoring method* involves assigning different weights to the various decision factors according to the decision maker's perception of their relative importance; the weighted scores are then totaled and the alternative with the highest score selected. Finally, the *minimum-score method* establishes a minimum score for one or more decision factors; any alternative with a score below this specified minimum is rejected regardless of its overall score. The minimum-score method can be used in conjunction with either of the other two approaches.

These approaches are described in detail on page 220. While they are used in making consumer purchase decisions, as discussed in Chapter 6, they can also be used to quantify the alternatives in product strategy decisions ranging from selection of package design to choice of brand name.

Directions: Use menu item 5 titled "Evaluation of Alternatives" to solve each of the following problems.

Problem 1. Omaha Industries is trying to pick one of three line extensions for its line of batteries. The alternatives are named Sparky, Big Lite, and Light Forever. Management is evaluating these options on the basis of compatibility with the existing line, production lead time, and potential profitability. The product development group at Omaha Industries has rated each alternative on a system of 3 (excellent), 2 (good), and 1 (fair). The ratings are as follows:

Evoked-Set Alternatives	Evaluative Criteria: Decision Factors		
	(A) Compatibility	(B) Production Lead Time	(C) Profitability
1. Sparky	1	2	3
2. Big Lite	1	3	2
3. Light Forever	2	3	2

a. Which line extension should Omaha Industries select using the overall scoring method?

b. Suppose management considers potential profitability 200 percent more important than any other evaluative factor. Which line extension will it select?

c. Suppose that using the overall scoring method management will not accept any line extension rated less than "good" on any factor. Which line extension will it select?

Problem 2. Toledo Enterprises is considering one of three package designs for its electronic components. It has identified three major factors to consider in this decision: safety, promotional appeal, and ease of storage. Toledo's management has scored each package design on a scale of 1 (poor) to 5 (excellent) for each decision factor. The scores are as follows:

Evoked-Set Alternatives	Evaluative Criteria: Decision Factors		
	(A) Safety	(B) Promotional Appeal	(C) Ease of Storage
Package design 1	4	2	2
Package design 2	2	5	2
Package design 3	5	1	4

a. Which package design would the company select using the overall scoring method?

b. Suppose management considers safety 100 percent more important than any other decision factor. Which package design will it select?

c. Suppose that using the overall scoring method management also decides not to accept any package design that scored less than 2 on any factor. Which package design will it select?

d. Would your response to question c change if management used the weighted scoring method?

Problem 3.   Regina Taylor, marketing vice-president at an Elmira, New York, toy company, must select a brand name for use on a new toy line targeted at preschool children. All five finalists, coded A, B, C, D, and E to maintain their secrecy, have been cleared by the firm's legal department. Taylor's marketing research department has concluded that the marketing impact of the brand names will vary among the parties involved in the toy-buying decision: parents, grandparents, and the children themselves. Each brand name has been evaluated for each group on a five-point scale ranging from excellent (5) to unacceptable (1). The rankings are as follows:

	Evaluative Criteria: Decision Factors		
Evoked-Set Alternatives	(A) Impact with Grandparents	(B) Impact with Parents	(C) Impact with Children
Brand A	4	4	3
Brand B	4	2	5
Brand C	2	5	2
Brand D	3	3	4
Brand E	5	5	2

a.   Which brand name would be selected using the overall scoring method?

b.   Suppose Taylor considers the brand name's marketing impact with children to be 200 percent more important than its impact with parents and grandparents. Which brand name should she select?

c.   Suppose that using the overall scoring method Taylor decides that she will not accept a brand name rated less than 3 by any of the parties who might be involved in a purchase decision. Which brand name should she select?

d.   Would Taylor's decision in question c change if she used the weighted scoring method?

Problem 4.   Miguel Fernandez, director of marketing at San Antonio Industries, wants to add a line extension to his firm's offering of toothbrushes. Various toothbrush configurations are under consideration; these are labeled option 1, 2, 3, 4, and 5. Five factors will be used to evaluate each option: profitability, production lead time, compatibility with the existing product line, adaptability to the standard San Antonio Industries in-store display, and retailer's margin. Fernandez has rated each possible line extension by each variable. His scoring system ranges from 1 (poor) to 5 (excellent). The specific scores are as follows:

	Evaluative Criteria: Decision Factors				
Evoked-Set Alternatives	(A) Profitability	(B) Production Lead Time	(C) Compatibility	(D) Adaptability	(E) Retail Margin
Option 1	2	4	3	2	2
Option 2	5	5	5	2	3
Option 3	3	3	3	3	3
Option 4	3	3	4	3	3
Option 5	5	2	2	5	5

a.   Which line extension option should Fernandez select using the overall scoring method?

b.   Suppose Fernandez decides to assign a weight of 400 percent more to retail margin than to production lead time due to the importance of retailers' acceptance of the new toothbrush line. In addition, he decides to weight adaptability as 300 percent more important than production lead time, profitability as 200 percent more important than production lead time, and compatibility with the existing product line as 100 percent more important than production lead time. Which line extension option should he select?

c. Suppose that using the overall scoring method Fernandez decides to reject any option rated less than 3 on any factor. Which line extension option will he select?

d. Would your response to question c change if Fernandez decided to use the weighted scoring method in making his selection?

Problem 5. Ray Langston, marketing director of a St. Louis garden tool manufacturer, is in the process of choosing one of five new retail display racks. Langston is considering four major factors: promotional appeal, maximum display inventory, cost, and convenient size. He has scored each display design on a scale ranging from 1 (poor) to 5 (excellent) for each decision factor. Langston's ratings are as follows:

	Evaluative Criteria: Decision Factors			
Evoked-Set Alternatives	**(A) Promotional Appeal**	**(B) Maximum Inventory**	**(C) Cost**	**(D) Convenient Size**
Display rack 1	5	3	3	4
Display rack 2	4	4	1	5
Display rack 3	3	5	5	2
Display rack 4	3	3	5	3
Display rack 5	5	5	1	5

a. Which display will Langston select if he uses the overall scoring method?

b. Suppose Langston considers convenient size as the least important of the four decision factors. Promotional appeal and maximum inventory are considered as 100 percent more important than convenient size and cost 400 percent more important than convenient size. Which display rack should Langston select if he applies these weights to the various decision factors?

c. Suppose that using the overall scoring method, Langston also decides that he will not accept any display rack with less than a 3 rating on any decision factor. Which display should he select?

d. Would your response to question c change if Langston decided to use the weighted scoring method in making his decision?

| VIDEO CASE | 10 |

Robert Mondavi

For decades, most Americans thought of wine as either an exotic elixir or something similar to grape juice in a jug. But in the last 25 years, American drinking habits have changed to the point where more than $7 billion worth of wine is sold in the United States each year. While the market did not achieve the 6 to 8 percent annual growth rate that was predicted for the 1980s, its current size is an impressive tribute to the influence of marketing.

To broaden the beverage's appeal, wine marketers had to alter deeply embedded attitudes. The efforts of a few benefitted the industry as a whole. Indeed, until the late 1970s, most wineries portrayed wine as an upscale "tuxedo" drink, one that was not for everyone. The shift in marketing strategies started in 1967, when the Robert Mondavi Winery introduced Fumé Blanc.

Fumé Blanc, a white wine, was a risky proposition since white wines accounted for less than one-fourth of total U.S. wine sales when it was introduced. It is also made from Sauvignon grapes, and Sauvignon wines have traditionally sold poorly in the U.S. market. Robert Mondavi, the firm's founder, decided to go ahead with Fumé Blanc because he sensed that Americans were ready for a dry white wine. Still, the name posed a problem.

"I don't want to call it Sauvignon Blanc, because I know the American people didn't seem to care for the name," said Mondavi. "I had to have something with more appeal."

Marketing provided the breakthrough that Mondavi sought. He thought of Blanc Fumé, a long-established French Sauvignon wine. Mondavi simply reversed the name, and Fumé Blanc went on to become the second best-selling white wine in California. "The only mistake I made was in not copyrighting the name," said Mondavi, who has since seen a number of wineries introduce their own Fumé Blancs.

White wine sales in general have surged, rising from a 25 percent market share in 1970 to a majority market share today. Mondavi wines have shared in this success; the Mondavi winery, opened in 1966, is now one of America's 20 largest wineries.

Mondavi's marketing prowess is considered the best in the wine industry; a high compliment since Ernest Gallo, of the dominant E & J Gallo Winery, is regarded as a marketing genius. But the Mondavi Winery does not advertise. Instead, Mondavi has made a commitment to educate consumers about wine, a complete departure from the former practice of putting wine on the shelf and letting the consumers educate themselves, if they choose.

Robert Mondavi cannot compete head-to-head with Gallo, and it does not attempt to. "We can't be all things to all people," says Michael Mondavi, Robert's son and company president. "The goal is to select a specific niche, then be the best in that niche."

Mondavi's niche is the upper 5 percent of the wine drinking market, which represents the opinion leaders for the rest of the market. No expense is spared to ensure that the wines are of superior quality. Unlike many wineries, Mondavi does not specify a production cost figure for each barrel. This gives Robert's other son and winemaster Tim Mondavi room to make the best wine that he can. The firm also limits its product line and maintains strict control of the product quality. Mondavi Winery uses advanced lab techniques and daily tests of each batch of wine to ensure proper levels of acidity, sugar, and fermentation.

The winery employs some 55 people nationwide to conduct seminars and wine-tasting events, and to meet the wine distributors. But the big push comes at the winery itself. Robert Mondavi designed it for entertaining, and he makes sure the entertainment includes extensive discourses on wine. Every year some 300,000 people visit the vineyards, taking a required tour of the winery. The winery courtyard hosts six jazz concerts a year, starring jazz greats such as Ella Fitzgerald. The Mondavis host a cooking seminar, monthly art shows, and winemaking demonstrations.

Most wineries advertise extensively, spending millions on radio, television, and print ads, although ads for alcohol are increasingly controversial. Others focus on product improvements, challenging Mondavi for innovative supremacy.

For instance, the Benmarl Winery started its Society of Winemakers in 1971. Its wines are given a birth certificate, and the labels are personalized for its members. The concept has worked so well that other wineries have copied it, and some have taken it a step farther, selling the production of particular wines to customers. As another example, St. Julian's, a Michigan winery, operates a chain of stores along an interstate highway, just one of many regional wineries to play to regional ties.

The label of a wine is emphasized by marketers, who discovered that wine drinkers frequently choose wines because of a particularly attractive label. Many wineries invest significant amounts of money in label design.

Even the smallest wineries now issue newsletters, informing wine aficionados and other people included on their mailing lists of their product offerings and the prices of each product and vintage year. Traditionally, wineries were not aggressive marketers, but when Coca-Cola acquired Wine Spectrum in the late 1970s, it brought "cola wars" marketing with it, and consumers responded to the new advertisements. Other wineries took notice, and the big companies, such as Almaden, Inglenook (Heublein), and Paul Masson (Seagrams) are now aggressive marketers.

Mondavi remains a marketing leader; it was the first winery to sell futures on its wine production. Mondavi also introduced a joint venture with the famed French winery Rothschild—Opus One, which debuted at more than $50 a bottle but sold out rapidly.

Sources: "Now, Chateau Cash Flow," *Time* (June 1, 1987), p. 55; Ruth Stroud, "Flat Sales Force Winery Changes," *Advertising Age* (March 12, 1984), p. 3; Eunice Fried, "Sauvignon Blanc," *Black Enterprise* (August 1984), p. 78.

Questions

1. Relate the introduction of Robert Mondavi Fumé Blanc wine to the alternative development strategies shown in Figure 10.3. Which type of strategy was use by the winery?

2. What role has the introduction of new products played in the growth of the Robert Mondavi Winery?

3. Do you agree with the marketing strategy employed by Robert Mondavi? What changes might you make?

4. Robert Mondavi limits the kinds of wine it produces to high quality varieties. What are the advantages and disadvantages of this practice?

11

Marketing of Services

Steel giant Nippon Steel operates an interesting subsidiary in an industrial district of Kitakyushu City, Japan. Space World Inc. is a theme park that includes spaceships, lunar creations, even a space training camp for children, in addition to the usual roller coasters. Lucky and Vicky Rabbit are Space World's mascots. Only a blast furnace reminds visitors of the park's former use. Nippon hopes that the attraction will draw 2 million Japanese annually.

Leisure activities like theme parks are big draws in Japan. Nearly 15 million people have been to Tokyo's Disneyland. Sesame Place, a park featuring Sesame Street characters, is another popular attraction. Even Narita, the site of Tokyo's international airport, offers Japan Village, designed to provide a tour of the country without the two-hour bus ride to Tokyo.

Up to 100 new parks are being planned. However, some of Japan's theme parks are only temporary ventures operated during the summer months. For example, a dinosaur-theme facility was set up in a conventional hall outside Tokyo. Included in the park were the bones of 21 dinosaurs, complete with fossilized droppings, borrowed from a Canadian museum.

Who are the new theme park entrepreneurs? Surprisingly, they are often established Japanese firms — like trading houses, railroads, and shipbuilders — seeking to diversify or expand. The president of Space World once managed Nippon's steel operations. Yuji Nemoto of the Japan Development Bank explains, "They have the land, the people, and the resources to spare." In another interesting twist to the story, Sony-owned Columbia Pictures has announced that it will build Sonyland in the United States.

Some of the ideas for Japanese theme parks are odd by U.S. standards. For instance, Bi-Lingual Co., an English school chain, is planning to build a theme park called Mandaro Bi-Lingual Land featuring a European-style castle. Visitors will go through a make-believe customs and immigration department, and the park's hotel receptionists and waiters will be Japanese who speak only in English. A Mongolian tent village and an indoor windsurfing pool are other examples of future Japanese theme parks.

There is also some duplication among Japanese theme parks. There are two mock Spanish villas and two Scandinavian towns. Four northern Japanese towns quarreled over where to build Santa Land.

Japanese leisure consumers tend to evaluate theme parks critically by comparing them to the immensely successful Tokyo Disneyland. For instance, heat reflected from Space World's metal buildings caused customers to insist that the Nippon subsidiary add water fountains. One disappointed Space World visitor remarked: "The place is rather cheap-looking. If there were real space ships and space shuttles, or even something close, it would have been another thing."[1]

Such theme parks are an example of the growing service sector in industrialized countries. The marketing of services is discussed in the sections that follow.

Photo source: The Stock Market, © 89 Zefa/London.

Chapter Overview

Whether for goods or services, marketing programs are developed in the same manner. They begin with an investigation, analysis, and selection of a particular target market and continue with the creation of a marketing mix designed to satisfy that segment. But while tangible goods and intangible services are both designed to satisfy consumer wants and needs, at some point their marketing requires significant differences in approach. This chapter examines both the similarities and the differences in marketing goods and services.

First, however, the definition of services is addressed, since sometimes the distinction between services and goods is complicated by the fact that a service may provide a good. Consider the retail sector. While all retailing is a service, a

Figure 11.1

Goods-Services Continuum

retailer can be either a "services" retailer or a "goods" retailer. Aaron Rents Furniture offers rentals with an option to purchase. It provides both a service (rental) and a good (a sofa, when ownership is transferred at the time of purchase). Similarly, independent optometrists working in conjunction with Pearle Vision Centers provide eye examinations (service), while Pearle sells eyeglasses and contact lenses (goods).

What Are Services?

goods-services continuum
Method of visualizing the differences and similarities between goods and services.

One approach to defining services is to use a *product spectrum,* or a **goods-services continuum,** like that shown in Figure 11.1. This is a method for visualizing the differences and similarities between goods and services.[2] A dress is a pure good, but the store's alteration service may be sold along with it or included in the total price. Theme parks are pure services, but the parks also sell goods such as toys, hats, and shirts. We place the dress on the "pure good" extreme of the continuum because the service of alteration is less important to the customer than the dress itself, just as the goods sold at the theme park are less important than the service of the rides and exhibits. In the middle range of the continuum is dinner at an exclusive restaurant—an example of equally important good and service components. Satisfaction is derived not only from the food and drink but from the services rendered by the establishment's personnel.

The difficulty of defining *services* is reflected in the current American Marketing Association definition:

Services are products . . . that are intangible, or at least substantially so. If totally intangible, they are exchanged directly from producer to user, cannot be transported or stored, and are almost instantly perishable. Service products are often difficult to identify, since they come into existence at the same time they are bought and consumed. They are composed of intangible elements that are inseparable, they usually involve customer participation in some important way, cannot be sold in the sense of ownership transfer, and have no title.[3]

services
Intangible tasks that satisfy consumer and industrial user needs.

The above definition can be generalized as follows: **services** are intangible tasks that satisfy consumer and industrial user needs.

The Importance of the Service Sector

Expenditures for services have increased considerably during the past decade. Currently services represent approximately three-quarters of the U.S. gross national product, and a similar portion of all new jobs. Virtually all of the gains in female employment have come from this sector. It is also interesting to note that despite the export problems facing the United States (described in Chapter 3),

Figure 11.2   The Growing Importance of Services in International Trade

Guess who didn't send it by Federal Express.

Federal Express deliver over 1.2 million parcels daily in 360 aeroplanes and 25,400 vehicles, to 118 countries worldwide. And we don't just promise to get there, we get there on time. In fact, our unequalled track

record has made us the No. 1 air package carrier in America. Because we understand that if we don't meet our deadlines, you won't meet yours. See Yellow Pages for your nearest Federal Express Office.

Federal Express. When it absolutely, positively has to be there on time.

Source: Courtesy of Federal Express Europlex, Inc. Photo: © Robert Dowling.

services are a bright spot in the U.S. international trade. They now account for about 37 percent of all U.S. exports.[4] Service exports are also very profitable for many organizations. For example, foreign services account for 40 percent of Sheraton's revenue but 73 percent of its operating earnings.[5] Federal Express Corporation expects to increase its revenue base substantially by building a global air express network. The advertisement in Figure 11.2 is part of a campaign created to promote the company's service in European countries.

For most service firms, marketing is emerging as a significant activity for two reasons. First, the growth potential of the service market represents a vast marketing opportunity. Second, increased competition is forcing traditional service industries to emphasize marketing in order to be able to compete in the marketplace.

Characteristics of Services

The preceding discussion suggests the diversity of services. This diversity—far greater than the diversity of goods—is caused by the following characteristics that distinguish services from goods.

1. Services are intangible.
2. Services are inseparable from the service provider.
3. Services are perishable.
4. Standardization of services is difficult.
5. Buyers often are involved in the development and distribution of services.
6. Service quality is highly variable.

Each of these service characteristics is discussed in the following sections. Service marketers must appreciate how each feature uniquely affects their particular service.

Consider the case of the staid banking industry. Once confined to museum-like buildings, banking has now discovered marketing. First National Bank of Jackson, Tennessee converted an armored car into a mobile branch bank that visits factories, nursing homes, and housing projects. Chairman Ernest Vickers II says: "We figured if Federal Express and United Parcel Service are going to folks' front doors to pick up packages, why should bankers demand [that customers come to them?]."[6]

Intangibility

Services do not have tangible features that appeal to consumers' senses of sight, hearing, smell, taste, and touch. Therefore, they are difficult to demonstrate at trade shows, to display in retail stores, to illustrate in magazine advertisements, and to sample. Instead, personal selling and advertising must communicate the benefits of using a service. Tom Bodett's radio commercials for Motel 6 accomplish this task very successfully. In one commercial, Bodett says, "you won't find a treadmill or weight machine like you might at the big fancy hotels, but just take a few laps around the parking lot or up and down the frontage . . . Now you're a lean, mean working machine with a few extra bucks in your pocket." Bodett then closes with what has become his trademark: "We'll leave the light on for you." Bodett has helped tangibilize Motel 6. The firm's research shows that people imagine Bodett to be just like themselves—regardless of age and occupation.[7]

Inseparability

In buyers' minds, those who provide the service are the service. Consumer perceptions of the service provider become their perceptions of the service itself. Thus the Allstate advertisement in Figure 11.3 links the service (fire insurance) to an individual (a compassionate claims adjuster). This advertisement is based on the inseparability principle.

Buyers often are unable to judge the quality of a service prior to purchase. Since they essentially are being asked to buy a promise, the service marketer must attempt to make the service more tangible to them. Here the service vendor's reputation frequently becomes a key factor. Institutional or corporate advertising that promotes the firm's image is helpful to a well-established firm. Consumers often judge the quality of financial institutions on the basis of the intangible concept of strength. For example, a bank rating service once named tiny Cosmopolitan National Bank of Chicago one of 10 safest banks in the United States. Shortly thereafter, Cosmopolitan began using, with good effect, the tagline, "Our little corner of the world may be the safest place on earth" in all of its advertising.[8]

Sheraton hotels believe firmly in the inseparability between the service and its provider. The nation's fourth biggest hotel chain has developed the "Sheraton Guest Satisfaction System," which involves extensive employee training based

Figure 11.3   Inseparability as a Feature of Services

THE SHORTEST DISTANCE BETWEEN TWO POINTS IS OFTEN ONE INDIVIDUAL.

Compassion. You can't teach it. Or place too great a value on it. But you could measure it, down this very road on June 23rd, in the actions of Allstate Claims Adjuster Don Molder, who left his house at five a.m. to drive to the scene of a fire sixty miles away. All just to shorten the distance between a man's loss and his recovery. In times of need, people like Don Molder understand that just one person can make the difference between feelings of despair and feelings of hope. Just one more reason to leave it to The Good Hands People.

A member of the Sears Financial Network

Allstate
You're in good hands.

precisely on this principle of inseparability. Sheraton even uses its system to assign new hires to specific jobs. Job applicants are shown 20 video clips demonstrating situations involving hotel guests. The applicants are then asked to pick the best response to the situation from among those offered by the video. The scores are used to assign new hires to customer contact or behind-the-scenes jobs.

Even Sheraton's non-contact personnel sometimes get involved in responding to customer needs. Ron Wiseman, the head of security at the Sheraton Park Central Hotel in Dallas, rushed into action when a woman called to report she had left $3,000 worth of jewelry at the hotel in a cardboard soap carton. Unable to locate the box at the hotel, Wiseman followed the hotel's trash contractor to the city dump. He then spent three hours sorting through one and a half tons of garbage, ruining his suit and shoes in the process. However, he found the jewelry.[9]

Perishability

Due to their perishability, services cannot be inventoried. During times of peak demand, services may demand high prices that later fall drastically. Consider the hotel rooms in Barcelona priced at $5,500 per person per week during the 1992

Summer Olympics.[10] Vacant seats on an airplane, unsold symphony tickets, idle aerobic instructors, and unused electric generating capacity illustrate the perishable nature of services. Organizations like Italy's Alitalia Airline, the Seattle Symphony, Gold's Gym, and Detroit Edison all must deal with this situation. Some firms use discounts and off-peak pricing to compensate for slow periods. For example, when the North American cruise industry slumped at the beginning of this decade, cruise line operators cut prices as much as 60 percent. They also added fitness cruises and "theme" cruises to fill empty berths.[11] Similarly, vacation resorts feature high- and low-season prices; long-distance telephone calls cost less during evenings and on weekends; and hotels feature lower weekend rates.

Difficulty of Standardization

It is often impossible to standardize offerings among sellers of the same service or even to standardize the service of a single seller. Medical care is often cited as an example of the lack of standardization in the services sector. However, do not tell this to the "alumni" of Toronto's Shouldice Hospital that attend its annual reunion. The Canadian hospital only accepts one type of patient—people requiring hernia operations. Even then Shouldice rejects hernia sufferers with heart problems, those who are overweight, and those who have had other operations in the past 12 months. Once accepted, the Shouldice patient receives very standardized treatment. Shouldice's surgeons do considerably more hernia operations than other physicians, which makes them extremely efficient in the procedure. Shouldice patients also provide much of their own care, which lasts only three and one-half days compared to five to eight days elsewhere. For example, patients shave themselves and walk to the operating room, and then to the recovery room. Meals are served in a central dining room. Every effort is made to get patients to move about on their own, which hastens recovery from hernia operations.[12]

Buyer Involvement

The buyer often plays a major role in the marketing and production of services. The hairstylist's customer may describe the desired look and make suggestions at several stages of the styling process. Clients of tax preparation firms supply relevant information and frequently work closely with the tax specialists. Restaurant customers may put together their entire meals at a well-stocked soup-and-salad bar.

For tangible goods, the only major examples of buyer involvement are the specifications for major capital items like installations. By contrast, the interaction of buyer and seller at the production and distribution stages is a common feature of services.

Variability of Quality

Variability of quality is another characteristic of services. Take the case of restaurants. Posh Jean-Louis in Washington, D.C.'s Watergate complex and your local Pizza Hut are both restaurants. Yet they are considerably different in regard to cuisine, physical surroundings, service standards, and prices.

Service quality, a topic examined in more detail in the next section, is difficult to generalize about, since service providers can be so different from another. Consider the difference between Hyatt Legal Services and a major New York law

Buyer involvement is a key feature of services marketing. Here a couple is involved in planning their wedding with a wedding consultant. Customers of wedding consultants relate what they want and can afford, and the consultant executes the plan by contracting the services of caterers, photographers, florists, and reception facilities. Propelled by changing demographic and lifestyle trends, wedding consulting is a fast-growing new service business. More couples today marry later and have two incomes, allowing them to afford such services. And because they do not have the time to orchestrate their wedding, they are more in need of such services.

Source: © 1990 Jim Stratford/Black Star.

firm, for example. Similarly, service delivery can vary greatly. A 20-minute drive to a crowded post office stands in great contrast to the use of a nearby FAX machine.

Service marketers need to work toward the provision of the quality of service that is expected. Consider the challenge that Marriott faced when it staffed Poland's first Western-owned hotel. Haile Aguilar, the hotel's general manager, noted, "A sense of hospitality is not characteristic of hotels in Poland. We wanted people with no experience and a willingness to learn from us."

Marriott hired 20 Polish managers, none with hotel experience, and flew them to Boston for training. When the new managers returned to Poland, they hired and trained 1,000 people. The new staff quickly learned to deliver the standard of service its Western guests expected. One of the managers, Dorota Kowalska, observed, "Seeing the executive director of food and beverage actually clear tables in the breakfast room was something our people had never experienced before." The Warsaw Marriott now receives higher customer-satisfaction scores than its U.S. counterparts.[13]

Service Quality

service quality
Expected and perceived qualities of a service offering.

Service quality refers to the expected and perceived quality of a services offering. It is the primary determinant of consumer satisfaction or dissatisfaction. Many firms make it a priority to enhance service quality. For example, the Minneapolis Marriott City Center allows its employees to spend $10 to improve guest services. When one traveler mentioned that a particular book was unavailable in the gift shop, a Marriott employee went to a bookstore, bought the item, and delivered it free to the guest. Firms that fail to recognize the importance of service quality generally suffer for it. John Barrier, a long-time customer of a Spokane bank was unable to get his parking validated at a different branch

Figure 11.4

Determinants of Perceived
Service Quality

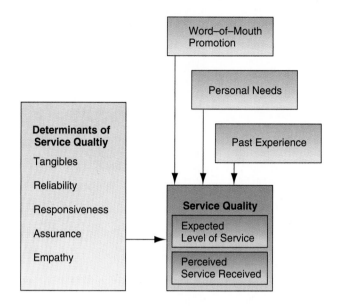

Source: Adapted from Valarie A. Zeithaml, Leonard L. Berry, and A. Parasuraman, "Communication and Control Processes and Delivery of Service Quality," *Journal of Marketing* (April 1988), p. 46; A. Parasuraman, Valarie A. Zeithaml, and Leonard L. Berry, "A Conceptual Model of Service Quality and Its Indications for Future Research," *Journal of Marketing* (Fall 1985), p. 48.

because he had cashed a check, not made a deposit. Refused by the teller and the branch manager, Barrier went to his usual branch and demanded a telephone apology. When the call did not come, Barrier withdrew $1 million.[14]

Determinants of Service Quality

Five variables have been identified as determining service quality: tangibles, reliability, responsiveness, assurance, and empathy.[15] These determinants can be described as follows:

☐ *Tangibles* are the physical evidence of the service. The decor of an attorney's office, a flight attendant's uniform, and a detailed monthly statement from Smith Barney are examples.

☐ *Reliability* refers to the consistency of performance and dependability. GM's "Mr. Goodwrench" advertising campaign emphasizes this determinant in promoting dealership service facilities.

☐ *Responsiveness* involves the willingness and readiness of employees to provide service. The immediate handling of an emergency at a medical center, the prompt recording of frequent flyer mileage, and an attorney who does not wait until the end of the day to return a phone call are examples.

☐ *Assurance* refers to the confidence communicated by the service provider. A physician with a friendly "bedside manner," H&R Block's guarantee, and the warranty provided by Terminex are examples.

☐ *Empathy* refers to the service provider's efforts to understand the customer's needs and then individualize the service delivery. A stockbroker completing a personal profile of a new client is an example.

Figure 11.4 is a model of how service quality is determined. The five determinants listed above—tangibles, reliability, responsiveness, assurance, and empathy—apply both to the expected service and the perceived service. In addition, word-of-mouth promotion, personal needs, and past experiences influence the expected level of service. For example, your expectations of a new Italian restaurant might be higher if your neighbors have given it a rave review. The relationship between expected service and perceived service is the perceived service quality.

Gap Analysis

gaps
Differences between expected service quality and perceived service quality.

Service marketers know that there are sometimes **gaps** between expected service quality and perceived service quality. Gaps can be favorable or unfavorable. A bistro with an excellent new chef and staff might provide better service than expected by the after-theater crowd, providing a favorable gap. By contrast, if the bistro had been reviewed positively in the local newspaper, theatergoers might be disappointed if slow service there caused them to miss the opening curtain—an unfavorable gap. Figure 11.5 illustrates the ways in which gaps might occur. Gap 5—the gap just discussed—is a function of the other four gaps that exist in the delivery of service quality. For instance, Gap 1 could exist if management's perception of what buyers wanted were incorrect. Gap 2 could exist if standards were set too low to meet customers' expectations. Differences between management's intentions and what is actually delivered could produce Gap 3. Finally, Gap 4 could exist if management's communication to buyers about the service were to conflict with what was actually delivered.

The Service Encounter

service encounter
Actual interaction point between the customer and the service provider.

The buyer's perception of service quality is apt to be determined during the **service encounter,** the actual interaction point between the buyer and the service provider.[16] Front-line employees like bank tellers, receptionists, and airline agents determine whether the service encounter will be satisfactory or not. Jan Carlzon, the president of Scandinavian Airlines System (SAS), popularized this concept in his book, *Moments of Truth.* Carlzon pointed out that SAS faced 65,000 moments of truth, or service encounters, per day and that the outcomes of these moments of truth determined the success of SAS.[17]

The outcomes of the service encounter can be classified as word-of-mouth, service switching, and service loyalty.[18] Suppose an executive's family had a particularly satisfying moving experience with North American Van Lines. The executive and his or her spouse are likely to share the experience with another family about to be transferred to Denver. Conversely, one incident with a rude teller might cause a bank customer to switch to another bank, or at least to another branch. A record of satisfying service encounters is likely to build service loyalty among customers. Far East travelers who are impressed with the level of service on Thai Airlines might well become loyal users of that company.

Types of Consumer and Industrial Services

Service firms can serve consumer markets, industrial markets, or both. For example, ServiceMaster's 4,168 worldwide franchises provide cleaning services for both consumer and business markets. Literally thousands of other services are available to both consumer and industrial users. In some instances, they are provided by specialized machinery with almost no personal assistance, such as automated car washes. In other cases, they are performed by skilled profession-

Figure 11.5   Conceptual Model of Service Quality

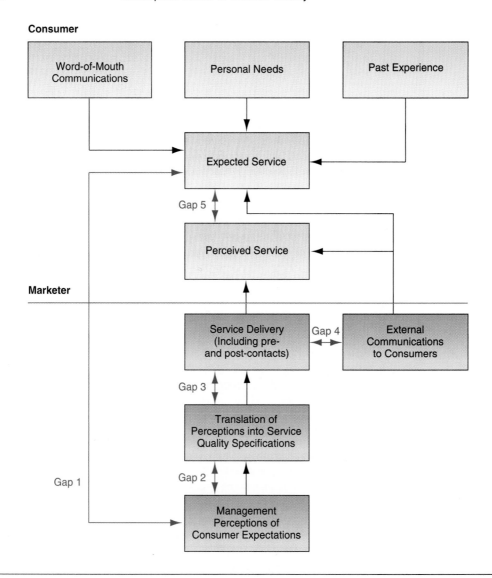

Source: Reprinted from Valarie A. Zeithaml, Leonard L. Berry, and A. Parasuraman, "Communication and Control Processes in the Delivery of Service Quality," *Journal of Marketing* (April 1988), p. 36.

als with little reliance on specialized equipment, such as accountants and management consultants.

Figure 11.6 illustrates a means of classifying services according to two factors: the extent of reliance on equipment in providing the service and the degree of skill possessed by the people who perform it. Thus, the initial classification is based on whether the service is equipment-based or people-based. A movie theater is an equipment-based service, while legal services, obviously, are people-based. The second level of classification is based on the skill levels of the performance. Equipment-based service can be classified as automated, monitored by relatively unskilled workers, or operated by skilled workers. Similarly, people-based services can be provided by unskilled workers, skilled workers, or professionals.

FOCUS ON ETHICS

FREQUENT-FLYER PROGRAMS

Airline frequent-flyer programs, along with other frequent-traveler programs like those of hotel chains and car rental firms, have come in for some criticism. They are charged with enticing members with the promise of free trips to popular locations and then changing the rules when it comes time to deliver on the promise. Although this criticism may be overstated, it is true that each frequent-flyer program is different, and each has restrictions (listed in fine print in the airline's brochures) that can create problems for the unwary traveler. Sometimes it is difficult or impossible to use free tickets the way the traveler wants to use them. One plan, for example, requires travelers who have flown 35,000 miles to make reservations seven days in advance, pick up tickets two days before departure, and fly between noon Monday and noon Friday. Most plans have a long list of "blackout dates" when the free tickets cannot be used — including holidays and the Christmas season, as well as the peak tourist seasons in Europe and Hawaii. And on most airlines there are "capacity controls" that limit the number of seats available for free travel on each flight.

Some disgruntled travelers have filed class-action lawsuits, complaining that because of these restrictions, free seats often are not available when travelers want to cash in their miles. They argue that airlines should make more free seats available and that they should be prevented from implementing capacity controls without notice. The airlines counter that travelers' expectations are too high and that they cannot be expected to fill their planes with nonpaying passengers. Some have tried to alleviate the situation by removing seat restrictions for people willing to cash in more than the normal number of miles and by issuing catalogs that offer merchandise in exchange for mileage points.

Part of the problem is the past generosity of many frequent-flyer programs. So many travelers have accumulated so many free miles (70 billion on American Airlines alone) that there are not enough seats to fly all of them to their desired destinations at the same time. The airlines thus are caught in a bind: Although they reserve the right to end their programs at any time, they cannot risk antagonizing business travelers, whom the programs were designed to attract. Instead, they have set tighter deadlines for taking certain trips, increased the mileage needed for some free trips, and added more blackout dates — thereby adding to the frustration of the nation's 22 million frequent-flyer club members, who see their accumulated mileage as an important reward for all the time they spend on the road.

Discussion Questions

1. According to one travel consultant, "Some of these [mileage] awards are about as good as a three-dollar bill." Have the airlines deceived frequent flyers?

2. Why don't the airlines simply lower their fares and end the cumbersome frequent-flyer programs?

Sources: Gerald A. Michaelson, "Why You Can't (Easily) Get There from Here," *Sales & Marketing Management* (February 1991), pp. 14–15; Jonathan Dahl, "American's Frequent-Flier Plan Poses Some Confusing Choices," *The Wall Street Journal* (April 11, 1990), pp. B1, B6; Jonathan Dahl, "Free Tickets Are Getting Many Frequent Fliers Nowhere," *The Wall Street Journal* (June 25, 1990), pp. B1, B9; Betsy Wade, "Airlines in Retreat from Frequent-Flier Plans," *New York Times* (May 28, 1989), sec. 5, p. 3; Betsy Wade, "Instead of Flights, Gifts or Money for Frequent Fliers," *The New York Times* (December 16, 1990), sec. 5, p. 3; and James T. Yenckel, "Frequent-Flier Update," *Washington Post* (September 23, 1990), pp. E1, E11, E12.

Several other classification schemes have been proposed. For example, one author has proposed using the following five questions to help classify services.

1. What is the nature of the service act?

2. What type of relationship does the service organization have with its customers?

3. How much room is there for customization and judgment on the part of the service provider?

4. What is the nature of demand and supply for the service?

5. How is the service delivered?[19]

Figure 11.6   Types of Service Businesses

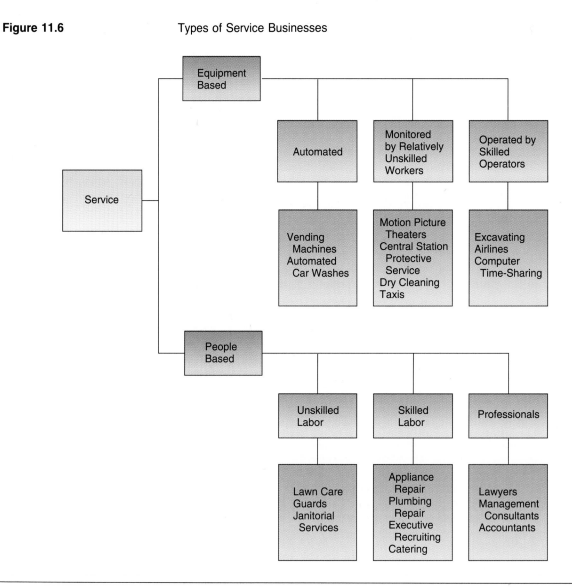

Each of these questions can result in a different classification system. Table 11.1 shows a matrix outlining the options available in service delivery. Multiple- or single-site service outlets are cross-classified by the nature of the interaction between the customer or service organization (customer goes to the service organization, service organization comes to the customer, or some other method of communication).

Environments for Service Firms

The economic, social-cultural, political-legal, technological, and competitive forces vary as much for service firms as they do for goods producers. Private postal centers offer an illustration. These centers allow postal customers the chance to avoid the long lines common at many post offices, as well as the option

Table 11.1

Methods of Service Delivery

Nature of Interaction between Customer and Service Organization	Availability of Service Outlets	
	Single Site	**Multiple Site**
Customer goes to service organization	Theater Hair salon	Bus service Fast-food chain
Service organization comes to customer	Lawn care service Pest control service Taxi	Mail delivery AAA emergency repairs
Customer and service organization transact at arm's length (mail or electronic communications)	Credit-card company Local TV station	Broadcast network Telephone company

Source: Reprinted from Christopher H. Lovelock, "Classifying Services to Gain Strategic Marketing Insights," *Journal of Marketing* (Summer 1983), p. 18.

of using other carriers such as DHL. Private postal centers offer wrapping, box addresses, FAX services, photocopying, money transfers, and in some cases, pickup and delivery service.

Users of private postal centers are attracted by their full range of services and efficiency despite the fact that they must pay 10 to 40 percent more because most carriers do not discount their charges. Recently, however, DHL Worldwide signed an agreement with Mail Boxes Etc. that designates the nation's largest chain of private postal centers as DHL drop-off sites. Mail Boxes Etc. customers get the same price as if they had gone to DHL directly.[20]

Economic Environment

The growth of consumer expenditures for services has been accompanied by further expansion of business and government services to keep pace with the increasing complexity of the American economy. The sharp increase in spending for services and the development of service industries as the major employer of labor have been among the most significant economic trends in the post–World War II economy. Most explanations of this trend are based on the changes associated with a maturing economy and the by-products of rapid economic growth.

A theory developed by economist Colin Clark describes the growth of service industries. In the first (and most primitive) stage, the vast majority of an economy's population is engaged in farming, hunting, fishing, and forestry. As the society becomes more advanced, the emphasis shifts from an agrarian economy to one based on manufacturing activities. The final (and most advanced) stage occurs when the majority of labor is engaged in **tertiary industries**—those involved in the production of services. It should be noted that while some people associate service industries with minimal skills and low pay, many service-sector jobs, such as those in communications and computer software, provide skilled jobs at commensurate pay.

Even more marked than the growth of consumer expenditures for services has been that of business expenditures for services. The servicing of business has become very profitable and has expanded into many areas. In just one field, for example, companies range from suppliers of temporary help to highly specialized management consultation services. Two reasons exist for the rapid growth of business services. First, business service firms frequently are able to perform a specialized function more cheaply than the purchasing company can for itself. Enterprises that provide maintenance, cleaning, and protection services to office buildings and industrial plants are common examples. Second, many

tertiary industry
Service-sector industry.

Figure 11.7   Example of Highly Specialized Business Service

Giving companies
in Chapter 11
a happy ending.

When companies face Chapter 11, many people see only the problems. At Chemical, we see reasons for hope. Our challenge is to help troubled companies and their creditors achieve maximum value.

It's not easy, and the subtlest of advisory skills are required. But while we don't promise a pot of gold, we bring to troubled companies and their creditors a wealth of experience and techniques. Techniques such as Debtor In Possession Financing, which provides breathing room during the reorganization process. Chemical is the nation's leading specialist in this form of finance.

In addition to liquidity, we contribute to efficient management of the reorganization process and help speed it to a sound resolution.

In all cases, guidance from an experienced advisor can provide benefits to more than just a company and its creditors—it can serve employees, customers and our economy as well.

For us, relieving a company's problems is particularly rewarding: Instead of the end of the line, it's often the beginning of the road back.

CHEMICALBANK

Source: Reprinted by permission of Chemical Banking Corp. © 1989 Chemical Banking Corp.

companies do not have the equipment or expertise to perform certain specialized services themselves. Marketing research studies, for example, often require outside specialists. The advertisement in Figure 11.7 illustrates a specialized financial advisory service provided by Chemical Bank for companies in the process of bankruptcy reorganization.

 Consider the case of filmmaking in the Soviet Union. The Soviets are now actively courting the U.S. movie industry to make films there. *Glasnost* and *perestroika* have allowed such endeavors, and the Soviet desire for hard currency has provided the motivation. In the making of "900 Days: The Siege of Leningrad," producer Alberto Grimaldi negotiated a deal whereby the Soviets provided the armies, tanks, and crowds necessary for the film. In return, the Soviets got a 40 percent share of net income and local distribution rights plus those in India and Eastern Europe.[21]

Social-Cultural Environment

The social-cultural environment has a significant impact on the marketing of services, since it helps determine which services customers want. The social-cultural environment changes over time, causing consumer preferences to change also. For instance, the increased use of counselors and consultants has affected many aspects of modern personal, family, and work lives. A few years ago, some of these services were not even available, let alone in demand. Now there are even leisure consultants to advise consumers on what to do with their spare time.

Today's social-cultural environment also provides an opportunity to offer some traditional services in a unique way. Take the case of Tele-Lawyer Inc., a Huntington Beach, California law office. The firm's eight attorneys are equipped with operator-style headsets as they provide legal advice to callers of "900-Infolaw." Tele-Lawyer charges $3 per minute, which appears on the caller's monthly phone bill.[22]

Sunrise Preschools is an example of a service that has surfaced to meet the new needs of a changing social-cultural environment. Located in Phoenix and Hawaii, Sunrise Schools serve the type of parent who, according to Buffy Owens, Sunrise's executive vice-president, "needs a lot of attention." Today's parents, Owens points out, "earn more, they're having fewer children per household than ever before, they're having children much later in life and have more disposable income, so they're looking for a place that can take care of both the parents' and the child's needs." Consequently, Sunrise offers late-night, overnight, and weekend hours. It designs specific programs for employers like McDonnell-Douglas, America West Airlines, the U.S. Postal Service, and the city of Phoenix. Sunrise even has tie-ins with the symphony and local theatre whereby parents can make a child-care reservation at the time they buy their tickets. Sunrise is an excellent example of a service firm adopting to a changing societal environment.[23]

Political-Legal Environment

Some service businesses are more closely regulated than other forms of private enterprise. These firms may be subject to government regulation in addition to the usual taxes, antitrust legislation, and restrictions on promotion and price discrimination. For example, a bus company must have the approval of the local public service commission before adding or dropping a route, and a hairstylist must comply with state licensing requirements.

Many service industries are regulated at the national level by government agencies such as the Federal Power Commission, the Federal Trade Commission (FTC), the Federal Communications Commission (FCC), and the Securities and Exchange Commission (SEC). Other service industries, such as insurance and real estate, are regulated at state and local levels. In addition, many personal and business services are affected at state and local levels by special fees or taxes and certification or licensing requirements. Often included in this category are members of the legal and medical professions, funeral directors, accountants, and engineers.

The international political-legal environment has allowed the so-called "Baby Bells"—the seven regional Bell Telephone companies—to take the first steps toward expanding overseas. For example, Nynex, the regional firm for New York and New England, beat out Japanese, British, and Spanish competitors to run the phone system for Gibraltar.

Selling a service abroad has also required some adaptation on the part of the Baby Bells. Bell South's cellular phone customers in Argentina are billed every ten days in an attempt to keep pace with that nation's rampant inflation.[24]

Technological Environment

productivity
Output produced by each worker.

Historically, two-thirds of the economic growth in the United States has resulted from increases in **productivity**—the output produced by each worker. In the past, technological developments accounted for significant increases in produc-

Union Pacific believes technology is at the heart of its future success as a transportation services company. By adapting technology that improves productivity and enhances customer service, UP plans to leap over its competitors. An example of UP's commitment to technology is its Harriman Dispatching Center in Omaha, the world's largest rail command center. It panoramically displays the entire UP rail system on two video screens, each stretching 300 feet. With a computer/communications network that ties into the railroad's fiber optic and microwave system, the center monitors and controls the 800 trains that run daily over UP's 22,000-mile system. Fully operational in 1991, the new center performs the work of ten regional centers and is expected to generate significant annual savings.

Source: Courtesy of Union Pacific Corporation.

tivity. Cyrus H. McCormick was able to almost triple the output of the average wheat farmer with his new reaper. Henry Ford's innovations made it possible to reduce the average cost of a car by 50 percent. But how are increases in productivity accomplished in a service economy?

Sometimes a simple change in procedure can improve productivity in services as much as a complex technology. Fidelity Investments has benefited itself and its 6 million mutual fund customers by picking up its own mail (15 million pieces annually), and sorting, coding, handling, and delivering its outgoing mail (53 million pieces) to airplanes and U.S. Postal Service trucks. Fidelity's mail trucks run 24 hours a day. This low-tech innovation saves Fidelity $2 million a year, and its customers a day off their mail delivery time.[25]

An example of a high-technology improvement is the system installed by Cincinnati Bell to route telephone calls to backup service representatives. Not only has this system cut the time customers spend waiting, it has allowed the company to operate with 15 percent fewer representatives.[26] Other technological advances abound in the service sector. Sprint now offers a voice-activated calling card, Voice Card, which allows a user to simply say "Call home" to place a call to their home address.[27] ATMs (automated teller machines) are a classic example of technological innovation in a service industry. And now users of ATM cards tied to the Plus or Cirrus networks can get cash on several islands, including Puerto Rico, Guam, and the Virgin Islands.[28]

The technological environment may be the primary determinant of future growth in the service sector. Service marketers are constantly looking for opportunities that will give their firms a technological strategic window.

Competitive Environment

The competitive environment for services represents a paradox in that many services find themselves competing with goods or government services rather than similar business services. In some service industries internal competition is almost nonexistent. And price competition often is limited in such services as communication, legal, and medical services. Moreover, many important service producers such as hospitals, educational institutions, and religious and welfare agencies are nonprofit organizations, which puts a different slant on competition. In addition, many service industries are difficult to enter, requiring a major financial investment or special education or training, and many others are restricted by numerous government regulations.

Competition from Goods.   Direct competition between goods and services is inevitable because competing goods and services often provide the same basic satisfactions. Buyers can often satisfy their service requirements by substituting goods. For example, manufacturers, recognizing buyers' changing needs, have built many services into their products. Consider continuous-cleaning ovens, frost-free refrigerators, and textured-surface appliances that reduce the need for domestic cleaning employees, and VCRs that compete with motion pictures and other forms of entertainment. Buyers often have a choice between goods and services that perform the same general functions.

Competition from Government.   Some services can be provided only by government agencies, but others compete with privately produced goods and services. For example, the U.S. Postal Service's Express Mail competes with Federal Express, Airborne, UPS, and other next-day delivery services.

Outsourcing in the Service Sector.   Outsourcing, moving operations and production abroad, is common in the goods sector and has found a niche in service industries. Consider the following examples. New York Life uses processors in Castleisland, Ireland, to handle claims at least five hours before the U.S. workday starts. American Airlines has 600 workers in Barbados and the Dominican Republic whose job it is to punch flight data into a computer located in Tulsa, Oklahoma. Finally, Asian workers enter court opinions into the Lexis computer service.[29]

The Marketing Mix for Service Firms

Service marketers can use geographic, demographic, psychographic, or benefit segmentation to identify their target markets. As with goods markets, demographic segmentation is the most commonly used segmentation variable for services marketing. As noted in the Competitive Edge feature, American Express has long targeted affluent credit-card users. By contrast, VISA and Mastercard appeal to a wider income range. Now American Express may be in for some stiff competition from abroad. JCB International Credit Card Co. Ltd.—the dominant credit card in Japan—has entered the U.S. market. Some 300,000 American businesses now accept the JCB card. Mitsuo Funayama of JCB's New York office describes his firm's demographic segmentation thus: "Our future market is almost the same as American Express."[30]

AmEx FOCUSES ON QUALITY SERVICES

"Membership has its privileges," goes the American Express slogan. Most of AmEx's card*members* (they're members, not holders) would agree. The company provides an incomparable level of service.

AmEx has built an unbeatable record for quality service with its green, gold, and platinum cards. Now it is trying to build on its reputation to sell new products and services to both existing and potential cardmembers.

With 33 million AmEx cards accepted at 2.7 million establishments in 130 nations, AmEx might have thought twice before changing its highly successful strategy of focusing on higher-income customers and upscale establishments. But this is a company that has never been afraid of change. It has broadened its customer base, which traditionally consisted of upper-middle-class male executives, to include women professionals, senior citizens, small businesses, and students. As the photo shows, movie theaters are a new market for American Express cards. The president of its Consumer Card Group says, "We want people to feel they really can't conduct their business, travel, and personal lives without the American Express card."

A master of market research and segmentation, AmEx is known for its ability to identify customer needs and preferences. On the basis of extensive surveys and test marketing, it segments the credit-card market into groups based on income and lifestyle and then woos them with relevant services: for platinum cardmembers, limousine pickup at airports; for students, a magazine; for senior citizens, extra travel insurance. The company also provides corporate credit cards for large and small businesses—accompanied by a complete travel management service.

Careful targeting is a central feature of AmEx's approach. The company has identified 15 distinct market segments, each of which can be targeted with a high degree of precision. AmEx's computers maintain and constantly update a profile of each customer that includes some 450 attributes. This enables the company to avoid sending out too much direct-marketing material; it sends information about new goods and services only to the people who are most likely to be interested in them. AmEx has used this technique to make its "Global Assist," "Purchase Protection," and "Special Events" programs an unqualified success.

The greatest opportunities may lie overseas. Offices in 150 countries help it attract the business of Americans traveling abroad. And with the exception of Coca-Cola, its name is perhaps the most recognized one in the world. This should give it an edge where the use of charge cards is just beginning to catch on. And in fact, AmEx's international growth rate is faster than its domestic growth rate. Already 10 million AmEx cards are held by foreigners. As CEO James Robinson points out, as people throughout the world become more affluent, they will want to travel more, dine out more, and consume more. AmEx plans to help them do just that—and charge it.

Discussion Questions

1. AmEx believes that it can make each of its targeted segments feel privileged, thereby applying its "membership has its privileges" approach to a broader consumer base. What are the risks in this strategy?

2. How should AmEx go about expanding its customer base overseas?

Sources: "Privileged Plastic," *Forbes* (January 7, 1991), p. 158; "American Express Masters Frequency-Marketing Tactics," *Colloquy* (October 1990), pp. 1, 7; Subrata N. Chakravarty, "A Credit Card Is Not a Commodity," *Forbes* (October 16, 1989), pp. 128–130; Jon Friedman and John Meehan, "Can AmEx Win the Masses—and Keep Its Class?" *Business Week* (October 9, 1989), pp. 134–138; and John Paul Newport, Jr., "American Express: Service That Sells," *Fortune* (November 20, 1989), pp. 80–94. *Photo source:* © Andy Freeberg.

Satisfying buyers' service needs also requires developing an effective marketing mix. Service policies, pricing, distribution, and promotion strategies must be combined into an integrated marketing program. The following sections briefly describe the marketing mix for service firms.

Service Strategy

Like tangible goods, services may be classified according to their intended use. All services are either consumer services or industrial services. Even when the same service (telephone, gas, or electric services, for example) is sold to both consumer and organizational buyers, the service firm often maintains separate marketing groups for each customer segment.

Consumer services may be classified as convenience, shopping, and speciality services. Dry cleaning, shoe repair, and similar personal services are commonly purchased on a *convenience* basis. Automobile repairs and insurance are considered *shopping* services, because they usually involve some shopping effort in comparing prices and quality. *Specialty* services include professional services, such as financial, legal, and medical assistance.

Some service firms have diversified their offerings or combined with other service marketers in an attempt to boost sales. For example, Columbus, Ohio's BankOne offers a Visa card that gives Northwest Airlines' frequent flyers one mile credit for each dollar spent. Similarly, First Chicago's Visa card gives its users credit on United Airlines' frequent-flyer program.

The intangible nature of services makes some of the marketing strategies used with tangible goods of little or no use. For example, packaging and labeling decisions are very limited; service marketers are rarely able to use packages as promotional tools. In addition, the use of sampling as a means of introducing a new service to the market is limited. Sampling is not unheard of, though. Marketers of such services as racquetball clubs and cable television frequently offer trial periods without charge or at greatly reduced rates to move potential customers through the stages of the adoption process and convert them to regular patrons.

Pricing Strategy

Pricing is a major problem for service firms. In developing a pricing strategy, the service marketer must consider the demand for the service; production, marketing, and administrative costs; and the influence of competition. However, price competition is limited for many services. For instance, the prices charged by most utilities are closely regulated by federal, state, and local government agencies.

Price negotiation is an important part of many professional service transactions. Consumer services that sometimes involve price negotiations include auto repairs, physical-fitness programs, and financial, legal, or medical assistance. Specialized business services, such as equipment rental, marketing research, insurance, and maintenance and protection services, are also sometimes priced through direct negotiation.

Price competition has been of particular concern to Federal Express since its acquisition of international freight carrier, Flying Tigers. In addition to competition from other freight handlers like DHL and UPS, Federal Express has to compete with the international airlines, many of them U.S. carriers. Regularly scheduled passenger flights have a price advantage when it comes to freight. Passengers cover the flight costs, so freight can be priced advantageously. The head of American Airlines cargo division says, "Passengers won't ride in the basement.

Figure 11.8

Distribution Channels for
Services

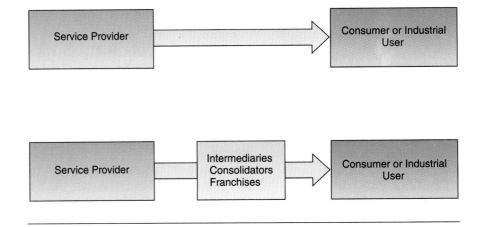

So I have excess capacity, and that's how I price the cargo."[31] In fact, in a recent year, American's passenger load on its European routes was 65.5 percent, while its cargo load factor was over 80 percent.[32]

Distribution Strategy

The distribution channels for services, which are also discussed in Chapter 13, are shown in Figure 11.8. Service channels are often simpler and more direct than those for goods. This is largely due to the intangibility of services. The service marketer is less concerned with storage, transportation, and inventory control and typically employs shorter channels of distribution. Another consideration is the need for continuing personal relationships between performers and users of many services. Consumers will remain clients of the same insurance agents, banks, or travel agents if they are reasonably satisfied. Similarly, companies often retain public accounting firms and lawyers on a relatively permanent basis.

Two major exceptions to direct distribution of services exist, consolidators and franchises. **Consolidators,** commonplace in the air travel business, particularly international flights, purchase seats from airlines at a substantial discount and then re-sell them to travel agents, other consolidators, or to individual consumers directly. For example, if Air India expects vacant seats on the New York to London segment of the flight to Bombay, it might be willing to substantially discount a block of seats on that segment to a consolidator.[33]

Franchises are a distribution channel for services in which production cannot be geographically separated from consumption. Command Performance and Jiffy Lube are examples.

consolidator
Marketing intermediary who acts as a discounter in the travel industry.

Promotional Strategy

The marketing strategy for services includes a promotional mix consisting of the most appropriate blends of personal and nonpersonal selling to inform, persuade, and/or remind individuals or firms that represent the service provider's target market. The intangible nature of services adds to the challenges of developing an effective promotional strategy.

A frequently used promotional strategy is to "tangibilize" the service by linking it to a specific benefit. AT&T, for example, uses a magnetism theme to

Figure 11.9   Promotion That Links a Service to a Customer Benefit

 promote its International 800 Service. As the advertisement in Figure 11.9 illustrates, business customers can benefit from the AT&T service by attracting "more business worldwide." Insurance firms provide numerous examples of tangibilizing their services:

- "CNA—For all the commitments you make."
- "You're in good hands with Allstate."
- "Like a Good Neighbor, State Farm Is There."
- "Get Met, It Pays."
- "Nationwide is on your side."

A second strategy is to attempt to create a favorable image for the service or service company. Among the most commonly used themes by service organizations are efficiency, expertise, status, and friendliness. A third strategy is to show the tangible benefits of purchasing an intangible service. For instance, a local bank shows a retired small-business owner relaxing in Florida thanks to a retirement account she established years ago. These and similar themes help buyers to visualize the benefits of a particular service.

The desire of many service buyers for a personal relationship with a service provider increases the importance of personal selling. Service salespeople should be viewed as "relationship managers." Research has indicated that future sales opportunities depend upon the quality of the relationship between the salesperson and the prospect. **Relationship quality** refers to the customer's trust in and satisfaction with the seller.[34]

Life insurance marketing provides a good illustration of the key role of the sales representative. Because insurance is a confusing, complex subject for the average buyer, the salesperson must be a professional financial advisor and develop a close, personal relationship with the client. Insurance companies and other service firms must develop a well-trained, highly motivated salesforce for providing the relationship quality that customers require.

Summary of Chapter Objectives

1. **Differentiate services from goods.** The American Marketing Association has defined services as follows:

   Services are products . . . that are intangible, or at least substantially so. If totally intangible, they are exchanged directly from producer to user, cannot be transported or stored, and are almost instantly perishable. Service products are often difficult to identify, since they come into existence at the same time they are bought and consumed. They are composed of intangible elements that are inseparable, they usually involve customer participation in some important way, cannot be sold in the sense of ownership transfer, and have no title.

   Contemporary Marketing generalizes this lengthy definition: Services are intangible tasks that satisfy consumer and industrial user needs. Many products have both goods and services components. A continuum from pure services to pure goods is useful in visualizing the differences and similarities between goods and services.

2. **Identify the primary characteristics of services.** Six key elements of services have marketing implications: intangibility, inseparability from the provider, perishability, difficulty in standardization, buyer involvement in the development and distribution of services, and great variability in quality.

3. **Explain the concept of service quality.** Service quality refers to the expected and perceived qualities of a service offering. Gaps can exist between expected service quality and perceived service quality. These gaps can be favorable or unfavorable. Service quality is the major determinant of consumer satisfaction or dissatisfaction. Five factors are involved in the level of service quality: tangibles (physical evidence of the service); reliability (consistency of service performance and dependability); responsiveness (willingness and readiness of employees to provide service); assurance (confidence communicated by the service provider); and empathy (the service provider's efforts to understand the customer's needs and then individualize the service delivery).

4. **Outline the possible outcomes of a service encounter.** A service encounter is the actual interaction point between the customer and the service provider. The outcomes of service encounters fall into three categories: word-of-mouth, service switching, and service loyalty.

5. **Develop a classification for services.** Services can be categorized in a variety of ways. One classification system first determines whether the service is equipment-based or people-based. The second level of classification is based on the skill levels required. Still another system uses a series of five questions concerning the nature of the service, the relationship

between the service organization and customer, the degree of customization, the demand and supply influences, and the method of service delivery.

6. **Explain how environmental factors affect services.** The economic, social-cultural, political-legal, technological, and competitive environments have a profound impact on services in the following ways:

☐ The economic environment has spurred the rapid growth of the service sector.

☐ The social-cultural environment creates changes in consumer tastes for services over time.

☐ The political-legal environment involves closer regulation of many service firms than good producers.

☐ The technological environment produces innovations that lead to increased productivity in the service sector.

☐ The competitive environment for services sometimes comes from goods producers or the government rather than other services.

7. **Discuss market segmentation and the marketing mix for services.** Service marketers can use all four approaches to segmentation: geographic, demographic, psychographic, and benefit segmentation. However, demographic segmentation is the favorite option. The marketing mix for services often differs from that for goods. For example, the intangible nature of services makes it difficult to use some approaches to product strategy such as packaging, labeling, and sampling. Pricing strategy is crucial for service providers. Demand and supply have to be considered. Extensive negotiations are commonplace for professional services. In regard to distribution strategy, service channels are usually simpler and more direct than channels for goods. Finally, promotional strategy tries to do the following: tangibilize the service; create a favorable image for the service or the service firm; and demonstrate the tangible benefits of an intangible service.

Key Terms

goods-services continuum
services
service quality
gaps
service encounter

tertiary industry
productivity
consolidator
relationship quality

Review Questions

1. Explain why services are difficult to define. How is a goods-services continuum useful in defining services?

2. What is the current status of the service sector in the U.S. economy? Why is marketing becoming more important to service firms?

3. Identify the key characteristics of services. Explain how each affects the marketing of services.

4. What is meant by service quality? What are its determinants?

5. Explain gap analysis. What types of gaps can exist in regard to service quality?

6. Define the term *service encounter.* What are the possible outcomes of a service encounter?

7. How can services be classified? Can a service serve both a consumer market and an industrial market? Explain.

8. Name the environments for service firms. Cite examples of environmental factors likely to affect service marketers.

9. Which segmentation approach is used most frequently by service marketers? Identify service examples of each segmentation approach.

10. What are the major differences in the marketing strategies of firms that produce goods and those that produce services? Explain the relative importance of product, pricing, distribution, and promotional strategy for service marketers.

Discussion Questions

1. The U.S. Postal Service has an assistant postmaster general assigned to marketing, and there are marketers in 75 post offices. These people work with the 200 large-scale mailers who account for 20 percent of all U.S. mail volume. Only the U.S. Army—among federal entities—spends more money on advertising than the U.S. Post Office.[35] Why do you think it has become such an aggressive service marketer? Discuss.

2. Blockbuster's 1,200 video rental stores dominate its industry. The firm's wide selection of videos is emphasized in its slogan, "Wow! What a difference." In fact, Blockbuster is bigger than the next 15 video chains combined. Blockbuster is also very profitable; its videos are paid for after just 13 rentals.[36] Why has Blockbuster been so successful? Do any environmental factors threaten its success in the future? Discuss.

3. Nordstrom, the Seattle-based fashion retailer, has stopped discussing its widely acclaimed service quality with the press. The often-repeated stories of employees' efforts to satisfy customers were causing people to have unrealistic expectations for their Nordstrom shopping experience.[37] Relate this example to the chapter's discussion of service quality and gap analysis.

4. Outline a marketing mix for the following service firms:
   a. Local radio station
   b. Independent insurance agency
   c. Janitorial service
   d. Funeral home

5. The Salem Network, a unit of Rupert Murdock's News Corporation, Ltd., offers video programs for beauty salons. The 30-minute tapes include fashion, health, and beauty features adopted from various Murdock publications, as well as 7 to 10 minutes of advertising.[38] Evaluate this service. Could a similar concept be applied elsewhere? Discuss.

Computer Applications

The focus of this chapter is on the marketing of services in both the for-profit and nonprofit sectors. Accordingly, the analytical techniques focus on problems and decisions affecting companies and nonprofit organizations ranging from a financial planning service and a resort to a fund-raising organization and a recycling center. The following problems illustrate the marketing issues facing a diverse array of service firms and the applicability of these analytical techniques for nonprofit organizations as well as profit-seeking service marketers.

Directions: Use menu item 8 titled "Return on Investment" to solve Problems 1 and 2. Use menu item 3 titled "Sales Forecasting" to solve Problem 3. Use menu item 2 titled "Decision Tree Analysis" to solve Problem 4.

Problem 1.   A major New York hotel and entertainment chain is considering buying a highly successful West Virginia lodge and vacation facility for $50 million.

The West Virginia property currently produces a $15 million profit on annual revenues of $60 million. Review the discussion of return on investment (ROI) on page 322, then use menu item 8 titled "Return on Investment" to determine the ROI if this West Virginia resort is purchased.

Problem 2. Lewis & Burns, a Long Beach, California, certified public accounting practice, is considering offering a new financial planning service. The partners believe they will generate $225,000 in professional fees and an annual net profit of $75,000. However, the new service will require purchasing $40,000 in software and an addition to the office costing $72,500. Review the discussion of return on investment (ROI) on page 322, then use menu item 8 titled "Return on Investment" to determine the ROI of the proposed new service.

Problem 3. Annual operations of the Heart Fund of Urbana, Illinois, are funded entirely from contributions from area residents and businesses. A substantial portion of these contributions results from an annual telethon conducted by a local television station. The Heart Fund board of directors bases the annual operating budget on estimated contributions. Contributions for the past eight years are shown below:

Year 1	$ 370,000
Year 2	650,000
Year 3	880,000
Year 4	1,200,000
Year 5	1,600,000
Year 6	2,100,000
Year 7	2,750,000
Year 8	3,500,000

Review the discussion of sales forecasting using trend extension on page 140. Then use menu item 3 titled "Sales Forecasting" to forecast Heart Fund contributions for next year.

Problem 4. Rose Stout, manager of the Los Angeles Recycling Center, has been pleased that recent publicity emphasizing the importance of recycling has greatly increased the amount of materials brought to the center. In fact, she is giving serious consideration to adding two suburban locations in addition to the main center. She estimates a 60 percent likelihood of high growth in the sale of materials for recycling over the next year and a 40 percent chance of moderate growth. Although the expenses associated with operating the proposed new recycling locations would reduce her profits earned on a per-pound basis, the added convenience is certain to generate additional recyclable materials. Stout summarized her two alternatives as follows:

A. Continuing operating at one central location
>   **1.** A high-growth environment will result in 25,000 pounds of materials and generate profits of $.10 per pound.
>   **2.** A moderate-growth environment will result in 15,000 pounds of materials and profits of $.06 per pound.

B. Open two suburban locations
>   **1.** A high-growth environment will result in 40,000 pounds of materials and generate profits of $.06 per pound.
>   **2.** A moderate-growth environment will result in 24,000 pounds of materials and profits of $.01 per pound.

Review the discussion of decision tree analysis on page 75. Then use menu item 2 titled "Decision Tree Analysis" to recommend a course of action for the Los Angeles Recycling Center. Would your recommendation change if the likelihood of high growth were increased to 80 percent?

VIDEO CASE   11

Azure Seas

Cruising is big business. Since 1980, annual passenger growth has averaged 14 percent. Furthermore, research has shown that 30 to 50 million Americans are interested in taking a cruise, including 90 percent of the 10 million people who had previously done so.

What explains the popularity of cruising? Kirk Lanterman, chairman of the Cruise Lines International Association, puts it this way: "Cruising is hot. It's a vacation experience that offers surprising value and affordability and, at the same time, provides the type of luxurious pampering and attention that you might find only in the most expensive and exclusive resorts around the world."

While the growth of cruising over the past decade is impressive, cruise line executives note that 95 percent of all Americans have not sailed. This statistic suggests a tremendous market potential for the industry. As a result, cruise lines have been adding ships and berths since 1980. Some 40 new cruise ships were introduced during the decade. A total of 31,000 new berths were added to the industry's capacity during the 1980s, and 43 older ships were refurbished.

One of these refurbished ships was the Azure Seas, which operated out of Los Angeles. The Azure Seas was purchased by Western Cruise Lines (now known as Admiral Cruises, Inc.) for $30 million and refurbished at a cost of an additional $7 million. The 604-foot long, 78-foot wide vessel has 9 decks and can reach a top speed of 20 knots. The Azure Seas carries over 300 passengers who are served by a crew of 300 to 350.

The company planned to introduce a new concept to West Coast cruising—the short, three- to four-day cruise. The Azure Seas would sail from Los Angeles to Ensenada, Mexico, with varying intermediate stops. The ship's sailing schedule is shown below.

Three-Night Friday Cruise

Depart:	Los Angeles	Friday	7:45 p.m.
Arrive:	Catalina Island	Saturday	9:00 a.m.
Depart:	Catalina Island	Saturday	3:30 p.m.
Arrive:	Ensenada	Sunday	9:00 a.m.
Depart:	Ensenada	Sunday	6:30 p.m.
Arrive:	Los Angeles	Monday	8:00 a.m.

Four-Night Monday Cruise

Depart:	Los Angeles	Monday	4:45 p.m.
Arrive:	San Diego	Tuesday	9:00 a.m.
Depart:	San Diego	Tuesday	3:30 p.m.
Arrive:	Catalina Island	Wednesday	9:00 a.m.
Depart:	Catalina Island	Wednesday	3:30 p.m.
Arrive:	Ensenada	Thursday	9:00 a.m.
Depart:	Ensenada	Thursday	6:30 p.m.
Arrive:	Los Angeles	Friday	8:00 a.m.

Western's management was quite familiar with the short cruise concept. Western's sister company, Eastern Cruise Lines (now also called Admiral Cruises), had long operated short cruises on the East Coast. As Alex Currie, Western's general manager, remarked: "We thought we were the short cruise experts." However, things were different on the West Coast, and the firm had to adapt its service strategy to succeed. Short cruises were sold in the East as a recreational and resort experience, but that idea did not work with West Coast (predominantly California) consumers who were accustomed to such resort areas as Malibu and Tahoe. Management's strategy had to be different for the West Coast market.

Western decided to test market its short cruise concept with area travel agents who would market the cruises. The emphasis was on an affordable, total cruise experience. The travel agents were receptive to the concept, and the Azure Seas venture was launched with extensive advertising in the travel sections of newspapers.

The target market was called the "Golden Core" by Western executives and was defined as the Los Angeles metropolitan area. Western soon discovered that 70 percent of its passengers came from the so-called Golden Core, and 70 percent of these were first-time cruisers. So, the biggest market segment for the Azure Seas was first-time cruisers from Los Angeles, making up about half of all passengers. Western Cruise Lines also used newspaper advertising throughout an 11-state western region. As part of its effort, Western offered a sea-jet program that included air fare to Los Angeles.

While Western's marketing strategy was well planned, the firm encountered some problems a few years later. The Azure Seas' bottom line had not met expectations the previous quarter and fall bookings were also running behind schedule. Furthermore, marketing research revealed that only 4 percent of Los Angeles area travelers recognized the name "Azure Seas." By contrast, Princess Line had an 80 to 90 percent recognition factor. Western's management attributed this difference to the popular "Love Boat" television series, which featured a Princess vessel. The question facing Western's executives was how to better use their $1 million advertising budget to overcome these problems.

In a meeting with its advertising agency, Western's management decided to conduct a two-week test of television advertising as an alternative to traditional newspaper advertising. The television commercials, which were used only in the Los Angeles area, stressed affordability, food, and service. The results of the experiment were impressive. Revenues jumped 40 percent. Still, management decided to be cautious. The company cut the commercials after the initial trial run to see what would happen. The result was that sales declined. When television advertising was reintroduced, sales went up. In fact, during one period, sales actually rose an astounding 80 percent. In addition, a new marketing research study showed that public awareness of the Azure Seas, shot up from 4 percent to 13 percent. As a result of this test, television advertising was continued.

In the late 1980s, Admiral Cruises underwent several changes; it merged with other lines and split off some lines. During the same period competition in the West Coast/Mexico cruise market intensified. As of March 1991, the Azure Seas moved into the Caribbean and had abandoned the short cruise format.

Sources: Personal interview with Paul Bookhorst, Admiral Cruises, Inc., April 1991; William G. Flanagan with Evan McGinn, "Man the Pumps," *Forbes* (December 10, 1990), pp. 116–128; "1988 Shapes Up As Biggest Ever For New Cruise Ships," *Seattle Times* (January 23, 1988), p. 8 (special Travel Show section: Data Source: Cruise Lines International Association); *Supercruise*, 1988 Admiral Seas brochure; "Cruises: TV is Becoming the Industry Medium of Choice." *Adweek* (September 14, 1987), p. F.P.38; and Gail DeGeorge, "Carnival Cruise Lines is Making Waves," *Business Week* (July 6, 1987), p. 34.

Questions

1. How would you place a cruise on the goods-services continuum?

2. What type of segmentation strategy was demonstrated in this video case?

3. How did market segmentation help Western Cruise Lines' marketers?

4. How did Western Cruise Lines attempt to influence the consumer behavior of potential buyers?

Source: Courtesy of Tandy Corporation.

Tandy Corporation controls its own distribution channel by using a fleet of trucks to transport electronics merchandise from warehouses to some 6,900 Radio Shack stores and business computer centers. Marketers must design efficient distribution systems to ensure that goods and services are available to consumers at the right place and at the right time.

PART 5

Distribution Strategy

12

Channel Strategy

1. To explain the role of distribution channels in marketing strategy.

2. To describe the various types of distribution channels.

3. To explain the concept of power as it relates to the distribution channel.

4. To describe the concept of channel leadership.

5. To discuss conflict and cooperation within the distribution channel.

6. To outline the major channel strategy decisions.

7. To identify and discuss the various types of vertical marketing systems.

Bill Rucker of Fort Worth, Texas, is a classic example of a marketing intermediary, or middleman. He performs the crucial functions that make his distribution channel work. The firm he founded, Tracom, Inc., buys and then resells used diesel engines, transmissions, and related parts. In short, Rucker deals in junk. He finds the used engines, buys them for cash, and then sells them to remanufacturers who rebuild them.

Where and how does Rucker find the engines? The annual market for the parts in which Rucker deals is about $1 billion. While trucking companies often have their engines rebuilt, many truck parts end up in junkyards or the repair and maintenance facilities of small truckers. Rucker comments philosophically, "America is a giant scrap yard. Look at how much junk this country has generated in 200 years. We throw off so much excess that it can't be accounted for. So if a trucking guy in Philadelphia puts aside five old engines a year in a warehouse, what's the economic value?" This, of course, is where Rucker comes in. He gets these unused assets back into the economic stream.

Rucker's reward is the profit margin between what he buys and sells the junk for in the aftermarket. One rule in this business is that the sum of the parts is usually worth more than their whole. For example, Rucker typically buys a used diesel engine for $500, then breaks it down into its various parts. If everything is in good shape, he can usually get at least $1,000 for the parts, and sometimes as much as $1,500.

Rucker and his employees regularly call salvage yards, trucking firms, and truck dealers across the country, obtaining about half of the company's parts in this manner. Rucker also uses so-called "bird dogs"—other intermediaries, or middlemen—who buy parts they locate and then resell them to dealers like Rucker.

Tracom tracks its parts inventory by a computer system that monitors about 100,000 items. The company actually owns only a third of these parts. The rest are in what Rucker calls "extended inventory." In other words, the computer has recorded where such parts are available for sale. When an order for an extended inventory item comes in, Rucker negotiates a purchase price with his source and then resells at a higher figure to the customer. This arrangement allows Tracom to minimize its inventory holding expenses. Customers also are offered a computer service whereby they check parts availability directly. This service is particularly important to overseas buyers whose workdays do not overlap those in Fort Worth.

Bill Rucker developed his foreign distribution channels early. When he first went into business, he dealt in used school bus transmissions made by Detroit Diesel Allison Division of General Motors. Then he ran an advertisement in a magazine that made its way to Adelaide, Australia. The net result was an order for 100 used Ford steering boxes, which Rucker quickly filled. Later a California Allison dealer asked to buy not school bus transmissions, but larger ones used in trucks and other industrial equipment. Thus, Tracom was born.

Today, Tracom gets 40 percent of its $3 million sales volume from exports. This foreign growth would not have been possible except for Bristol International, a trade merchant bank, that has financed about 100 overseas deals for Tracom. Bristol acts as a facilitating agency in the international distribution channel. Before teaming up with Bristol, Rucker had been turned down for loans by virtually every bank in the Dallas–Fort Worth metroplex. He recalls the experience: "Can you imagine going into a bank and asking to borrow $3 million to buy *junk* for export?" By contrast, Bristol either takes ownership of, or a security interest in, the exports. It then loans Rucker the money he needs for his deals at 2 to 3 percent per month.

Bill Rucker sums up his success in this way: "We've taken an industry that was disorganized and disjointed and brought a little organization to it."[1] The functions performed by marketing intermediaries like Rucker are explored in this chapter.

Photo source: © Dan Bryant Photographs.

Chapter Overview

This section of the text discusses the activities, decisions, and marketing intermediaries involved in moving goods and services to consumers and industrial users. Bill Rucker's Tracom is an example of a successful intermediary. Basic channel strategy is the starting point for our discussion of the distribution function and its role in the marketing mix.

This chapter analyzes such basic issues as the role and types of distribution channels, channel strategy decisions, and conflict and cooperation in the channel of distribution. Chapters 13 and 14 deal, respectively, with wholesaling and retailing—the marketing institutions in the distribution channel. Although not considered part of the distribution channel, physical distribution is a vital facilitating function that assists regular channel members. It is discussed in Chapter 15. We begin this chapter with an examination of what marketers call distribution channels.

Distribution Channels

Although Tokheim gasoline pumps are made in Fort Wayne, Indiana, they are sold all over the United States. Liz Claiborne clothing sold throughout the United States is usually made in places like Hong Kong, China, Indonesia, Thailand, Korea, Taiwan, Philippines, and Sri Lanka. The Nissan truck bought by someone in Dallas, Texas, was most likely made in Smyrna, Tennessee. In each case, it is necessary to bridge the geographic gap between producer and consumer. Distribution channels do this, providing ultimate users with a convenient means of obtaining the goods and services they desire. **Distribution channels,** therefore, are comprised of the various marketing institutions and the interrelationships responsible for the physical and title flow of goods and services from producer to consumer or industrial user.

distribution channel
Entity consisting of marketing institutions and their interrelationships responsible for the physical and title flow of goods and services from producer to consumer or industrial user.

marketing intermediary
Business firm, either wholesale or retail, that operates between the producer and the consumer or industrial user; sometimes called a middleman.

Marketing intermediaries, or middlemen, are the marketing institutions in the distribution channel; that is, business firms that operate between producers and consumers or industrial purchasers. In this book the terms *jobber* and *distributor* are considered synonymous with *wholesaler*. For example, NAPA is a distributor, or wholesaler, that sells its NAPA-branded products through independently owned retailers.

Some firms operate both wholesaling and retailing operations. Sporting-goods stores, for example, often maintain wholesaling operations to market lines of goods to high schools and sports teams as well as operate retail stores. For simplicity, this text treats these operations as separate entities.

Some retailers claim to be wholesalers and may indeed sell at wholesale prices, but stores that sell goods purchased by individuals for their own use rather than for resale are by definition retailers, not wholesalers. This issue is examined in the ethics box in Chapter 14.

The Role of Distribution Channels in Marketing Strategy

Distribution channels play a key role in marketing strategy because they provide the means by which goods and services are conveyed from producers to consumers and users. Marketing intermediaries exist at both the wholesale and retail levels. As specialists in the performance of marketing functions—rather than producing or manufacturing functions—they perform these activities more

HWC Distribution Corporation is a marketing intermediary in the distribution of specialty wire and cable products. The company inventories some 50,000 reels of wire and cable products it buys from 240 manufacturers. It then resells these products in smaller lengths to 3,000 electrical distributors, who sell to the end user. HWC serves customers nationwide through 12 distribution outlets.

Source: Courtesy of Eric Myer and Alltel Corporation.

efficiently than producers or consumers. The importance of distribution channels and marketing intermediaries can be explained in terms of the utility they create and the functions they perform.

The Creation of Utility

Distribution channels create three types of utility for consumers. *Time utility* is created when distribution channels make products available for sale when the consumer wants to purchase them. *Place utility* is created when goods and services are available at a convenient location. *Ownership* (or *possession*) *utility* is created when title to the products passes from the producer or intermediary to the purchaser. Possession utility can also result from transactions in which the title does not pass to the purchaser, such as in the case of a rental car.

Postit Plus of South El Monte, California, makes a foldable fabric-and-metal shade for car windshields. The firm has been able to overcome the seasonability of its product by selling in markets like Australia, where the seasons are the reverse of the United States. The summer buying season for Australian retailers is June to August, while it is October to March in the United States. Postit Plus's shades are a good Christmas item in Australia. The firm is clearly providing utility to its customers both here and abroad; sales are balanced evenly between the United States and foreign accounts.[2]

Functions Performed by Distribution Channels

The distribution channel performs several functions in the overall marketing system. These functions—originally described by Professor Wroe Alderson—include facilitating the exchange process, sorting to alleviate discrepancies in assortment, standardizing transactions, and the search process.

Figure 12.1   The Sorting Function of Marketing Intermediaries

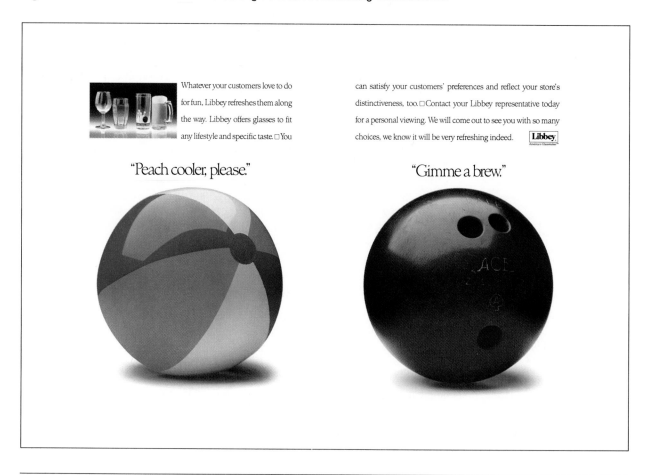

Source: Courtesy of Libbey Glass Inc.

Facilitating the Exchange Process.   The evolution of distribution channels began with the exchange process described in Chapter 1. As market economies grew, the exchange process itself became more complicated. Because there were more producers and potential buyers, marketing intermediaries emerged to facilitate transactions by cutting the number of marketplace contacts. For example, if 10 apple orchards in eastern Washington sell to 6 supermarket chains each, there are a total of 60 transactions. However, if the producers set up and market their apples through a cooperative, the number of contacts declines to 16. This concept is explained in depth in Chapter 13.

Sorting to Alleviate Discrepancies in Assortment.   Another essential function of the distribution channel is to adjust discrepancies in assortment via a process known as *sorting*. A producer tends to maximize the quantity of a limited line of goods, while the buyer needs a minimum quantity of a wide selection of alternatives. Sorting alleviates such discrepancies by adjusting both the buyer's and the producer's needs. The advertisement in Figure 12.1 illustrates the sorting function of retailers in the distribution channel. The producer, Libbey Glass, offers products that satisfy all lifestyle needs, but the retailer must create an assortment by choosing specific styles that match the preferences of customers who patronize the store.

Returning to the apple orchard example, an individual orchard's output can be divided into separate homogeneous categories such as various types and grades of apples. The apples are then combined with similar crops of other orchards—a process known as *accumulation*. These accumulations are broken down into smaller units or divisions, such as boxes of apples. In the marketing literature, this is often called *breaking bulk*. Finally, an assortment is built for the next level in the distribution channel. For example, the eastern Washington state cooperative might prepare an assortment of four boxes of Granny Smith apples and six boxes of Red Delicious apples for a Jewel supermarket in a Chicago suburb.

Standardizing Transactions. If each transaction in a complex market economy were subject to negotiation, the exchange process would be chaotic. Distribution channels standardize exchange transactions in terms of the product, such as the grading of apples and of the transfer process itself. Order points, prices, payment terms, delivery schedules, and purchase lots tend to be standardized by distribution channel members. For example, supermarket buyers might have on-line communications links with the cooperative. Once a certain stock position is reached, more apples are automatically ordered from either current output or controlled-atmosphere storage.

Search Process. Distribution channels also accommodate the search behavior for both buyers and sellers. Buyers search for specific goods and services to fill their needs, while sellers attempt to find out what consumers want. A college student looking for some Granny Smith apples might go to the fruit section of a Chicago-area Jewel store. Similarly, the manager of that department would be able to provide the Washington state cooperative with information about sales trends in his or her marketplace.

Types of Distribution Channels

Literally hundreds of marketing channels exist today, and obviously there is no such thing as one best distribution channel. The best channel for Avon when it entered into a joint venture with China's Guargzhou Cosmetic Factory was its traditional direct-selling route. Today 700 Avon representatives call upon Chinese consumers in much the same way as their American counterparts.[3] By contrast, the best channel for frozen french fries may be from food processor to agent marketing intermediary to merchant wholesaler to supermarket to consumer. Instead of searching for the best channel for all products, the marketing manager must analyze alternative channels in light of consumer needs to determine the most appropriate channel or channels for the firm's goods and services.

Once the proper channels have been chosen and established, however, they may change—like so many marketing variables do. Today's ideal channel may prove inappropriate in a few years.

Consider the case of Tandy Corp. The Fort Worth firm is best known for its Radio Shack outlets, which sell over $3 billion of consumer electronics a year. Tandy is also a major manufacturer of computers as well. Tandy has always sold its personal computers in Radio Shacks, but in the mid-1980s it set up a direct salesforce with 1,500 sales representatives working out of 400 computer centers to tackle the business market. This channel proved unsuccessful, and Tandy was forced to find another distribution channel. Today, Tandy's top-of-the-line personal computers are sold through Grid Systems, a subsidiary acquired in

Figure 12.2   Alternative Distribution Channels

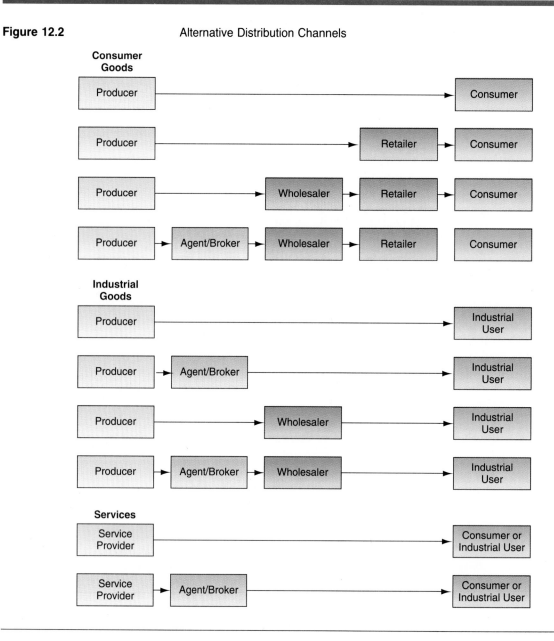

1989. The computers are marketed under the Grid name. Radio Shack no longer deals with firms with revenues in excess of $100 million.[4]

Alternative Distribution Channels

Figure 12.2 depicts the major channels available for marketers of consumer and industrial goods and services. In general, industrial channels tend to be shorter than consumer channels due to geographic concentrations in industrial buying and a relatively limited number of purchasers. Service channels also tend to be short because of the intangibility of services and the need to maintain personal relationships within the channel. Service channels were discussed in the previous chapter.

COMPETITIVE EDGE

AMWAY MAKES A SPLASH IN JAPAN

. . . .

Japanese workers and home-makers have been flocking to Amway in droves, lured by the chance to work for themselves. Amway's Japanese salesforce now numbers in the hundreds of thousands, and Amway (Japan) Ltd.'s $500 million in annual sales accounts for about one-third of Amway's worldwide business.

Many of Amway's Japanese distributors have left jobs in the tightly controlled world of Japanese big business. They are eager to escape from rigid corporate hierarchies and to be paid according to performance rather than seniority. At Amway they receive a 30 percent commission on products they sell and a bonus for each new member they bring in.

In contrast to the door-to-door methods used in the United States, Amway's Japanese salespeople sell the company's detergents, vitamins, and cosmetics through networks of family and friends. Japanese culture, with its emphasis on close personal relationships, is conducive to direct selling: Salespeople work through the *jinmyaku,* the network of human contacts that is at the core of Japanese social life. The norm of *giri,* or obligation, makes it difficult for acquaintances to refuse to buy; and *kuchi-komi,* or word-of-mouth recommendations, have enabled Amway to avoid Japan's costly and import-resistant distribution channels. Before 1989 the company spent nothing on advertising.

The Japanese emphasis on group solidarity also works to Amway's advantage. The company holds meetings and pep rallies for distributors. Salespeople's enthusiasm and group loyalty are so high that they willingly sacrifice as many as two weekends a month to attend corporate meetings at which they share the secrets of their success and vow to reach even higher sales goals.

Some observers believe Amway will be unable to maintain its momentum; *giri* sales cannot be repeated indefinitely, they argue, and the labor shortage will make it harder to recruit salespeople. In addition, competition is intensifying: Daiei Inc., Japan's largest retail chain, has set up a direct-marketing business of its own. Amway is rising to the challenge by modifying its product line to suit Japanese tastes, advertising in magazines and on television, and increasing the productivity of salespeople through improved training and inducements to stay with the company on a long-term basis.

Discussion Questions

1. Amway's Japanese salespeople depend on personal networks to make sales. What can the company do to avoid declining sales when those networks are exhausted?

2. Japanese customers are known for their preference for Japanese products. Can Amway survive increased competition from Japanese companies in the direct-marketing field?

Sources: Gale Eisenstadt with Hiroko Katayama, "Soap and Hope in Tokyo," *Forbes* (September 3, 1990), p. 62; Yumiko Ono, "Amway Translates with Ease into Japanese," *The Wall Street Journal* (September 21, 1990), p. A1. Photo source: © Dennis Budd Gray/Picture Group.

Producer to Consumer or Industrial User. The simplest, most direct distribution channel from producer to consumer, or industrial user, is more common in the industrial setting. When it is used in consumer markets, it can take two forms: **Direct selling** involves direct sales contacts between the buyer and seller, as occurs with Avon, Mary Kay Cosmetics, Tupperware, Amway, and

direct selling
Direct sales contact between buyer and seller.

direct marketing
Direct communication, other than personal sales contacts, between buyer and seller.

Shaklee. **Direct marketing** refers to direct communication other than personal sales contacts between buyer and seller, as occurs in catalog and direct-mail sales. Direct marketing and direct selling are discussed in greater detail in Chapter 14.

Direct channels are considerably more important in the industrial market. Most major installations, accessory equipment, and even component parts and raw materials are marketed through direct contacts between seller and buyer.

Producer to Wholesaler to Retailer to Consumer.

The traditional channel for consumer goods proceeds from producer to wholesaler to retailer to user. It is the method used by small retailers and literally thousands of small producers with limited lines. Small companies with limited financial resources utilize wholesalers as immediate sources of funds and as a means of reaching the hundreds of retailers who will stock their output. Small retailers rely on wholesalers as buying specialists that ensure a balanced inventory of goods produced in various regions of the world.

The wholesaler's salesforce is responsible for reaching the market with the producer's output. Many manufacturers also use specialized sales representatives to contact their retail accounts. These representatives serve as sources of marketing information, but they do not actually sell the product.

Producer to Wholesaler to Industrial User.

Similar characteristics in the organizational market often lead to the utilization of marketing intermediaries between producer and industrial purchaser. The term **industrial distributor** is commonly utilized in the industrial market to refer to intermediaries that take title to the goods they handle. For example, even IBM—long noted for its highly professional salesforce—now uses a variety of intermediaries and 18 different channels to sell its computers.[5]

industrial distributor
Marketing intermediary in an industrial channel.

Producer to Agent to Wholesaler to Retailer to Consumer.

When goods are produced by a large number of small companies, a unique intermediary—the *agent*—performs the basic function of bringing buyer and seller together. The agent is, in fact, a wholesaling intermediary that does not take title to the goods. The agent merely represents the producer or the regular wholesaler (that does take title to the goods) in seeking a market for the manufacturer's output or in locating a source of supply for the buyer. Chapter 13 describes two types of wholesaling intermediaries—merchant wholesalers, which take title to the goods they handle, and agent wholesalers, which do not.

Agents are used in such industries as canning and frozen-food packing. In these industries, many producers supply a large number of geographically scattered wholesalers. The agent wholesaling intermediary performs the service of bringing buyers and sellers together.

Producer to Agent to Wholesaler to Industrial User.

Agents are also used in the industrial market when small producers attempt to market their offerings to large wholesalers. The agent wholesaling intermediary, often called a *manufacturer's representative,* serves as an independent salesforce in contacting the wholesale buyers.

Producer to Agent to Industrial User.

Where the unit sale is small, merchant wholesalers must be used in order to economically cover the market.

By maintaining regional inventories, they achieve transportation economies through stockpiling goods and making final small shipments over short distances. Where the unit sale is large and transportation accounts for a small percentage of the total cost, the producer-agent-industrial user channel is usually employed. The agent wholesaling intermediaries in effect become the company's industrial salesforce.

Service Provider to Consumer or Industrial User. Distribution of services to both consumers and industrial users is simpler and more direct than in the case of industrial and consumer goods. This is partly due to the intangibility of services. The marketer of services is often less concerned with storage, transportation, and inventory control, and typically uses shorter channels.

Another consideration is the need for continuing personal relationships between producers and users of many services. Consumers will remain clients of the same insurance agent, bank, or travel agent as long as they are reasonably satisfied. Similarly, public accounting firms and attorneys are retained on a relatively permanent basis by industrial buyers.

Service Provider to Agent to Consumer or Industrial User. When marketing intermediaries are used by service firms, they are usually agents or brokers. Common examples include insurance agents, securities brokers, travel agents, and entertainment agents. For instance, travel and hotel packages sometimes are created by intermediaries and then marketed at the retail level by travel agents to both vacationers and firms that want to offer employee incentive awards.

Dual Distribution

dual distribution
Network in which a firm uses more than one distribution channel to reach its target market.

Dual distribution refers to the use of two or more distribution channels to reach the same target market. This distribution strategy is usually used to either maximize the firm's coverage in the marketplace or make its marketing effort more cost effective. The first objective is illustrated by automobile parts manufacturers who use both a direct salesforce and independent jobbers. The cost-effectiveness goal, on the other hand, is exemplified by a manufacturer that uses its own salesforce to sell in high-potential areas while relying on manufacturers' representatives (independent, commissioned salespeople) in lower-volume areas.

Fuller Brush now uses a three-part distribution system. The Sara Lee division, which was started in 1906, now has 13,000 door-to-door sales representatives. This distribution channel has long been the way Fuller Brush did business. In recent years Fuller Brush has added a direct-mail catalog that now reaches 10 million households annually. The company also operates factory outlet stores in six states. In contrast to the mid 1980s, when the direct salesforce accounted for all of Fuller Brush's sales, the firm's sales are now divided as follows: direct sales, 60 percent; catalog, 35 percent; and retail, 5 percent.[6]

Similarly, British computer manufacturer Amstrad uses four different channels to reach 4,200 Spanish retailers. The first channel is to large accounts like department stores. The second channel is to buying groups representing electronic stores. The third channel is to Spain's independent stores. Finally, the fourth channel uses wholesalers to reach accounts not covered otherwise.[7]

Distribution Channels for Nonprofit Organizations

Distribution channels for nonprofit organizations tend to be short, simple, and direct. Any marketing intermediaries present in the channel usually are agents such as independent ticket agencies or fund-raising specialists. A major distribution decision involves the specific location of the nonprofit organization.

Nonprofit organizations today are recognizing the need to be creative in going beyond their traditional distribution strategies. For example, many colleges and universities now offer courses off-campus in satellite facilities, plants, offices, at military bases, via correspondence and television, in person, and aboard commuter trains. Similarly, some public agencies, such as health and social welfare departments, have set up branches in neighborhood shopping centers in order to be more accessible to their clientele.

Reverse Channels

reverse channel
Path that goods follow from consumer back to manufacturer.

While the traditional concept of marketing channels involves the movement of goods and services from producer to consumer or industrial user, there is continued interest in **reverse channels**—the backward movement of goods from the user to the producer. In a sense, the opening story about Bill Rucker illustrates such a channel.

Reverse channels have increased in importance as some raw materials have become more expensive, recycling facilities have become more commonplace, and additional laws have been passed. For instance, bottle deposits are required in states like Maine, Michigan, and Oregon. New Jersey requires businesses and households to separate their trash to make recycling more feasible.

For recycling to succeed, four basic conditions must be satisfied:

1. A technology for efficiently processing the material being recycled must be available.

2. A market must be available for the end product—the reclaimed material.

3. A substantial and continuous quantity of secondary products (recycled aluminum, reclaimed steel from automobiles, recycled paper) must be available.

4. A marketing system that can profitably bridge the gap between suppliers of secondary products and end users must be developed.

In some instances the reverse channel consists of traditional marketing intermediaries. In container-law states, retailers and local bottlers perform these functions in the soft-drink industry. In other situations manufacturers establish redemption centers, develop systems to rechannel products for recycling, and create specialized organizations to handle waste disposal and recycling. The Chicago *Tribune,* for example, uses plastic bags for home delivery of its newspaper and has started a recycling program for the bags, as discussed in Figure 12.3. Other reverse-channel participants include community groups that organize cleanup days and develop systems and organizations for handling recycling and waste disposal.

Maine provides a good illustration of how reverse channels work. Maine has the nation's toughest bottle-deposit law. Most non-dairy beverage containers require a deposit in Maine. Aseptic containers, or "juice boxes," are outlawed. Most beer and soft drink companies handle their own bottle collection, refunds, and delivery to recycling centers. By contrast, the juice companies tend to hire intermediaries to pick up their containers from stores and restaurants and then

Figure 12.3

Reverse Channel Marketing

deliver them to recyclers. Finally, bottle drives have become a popular fund-raising activity for Maine's community organizations.[8]

Reverse Channels for Product Recalls and Repairs.

Reverse channels are also used for product recalls and repairs. Ownership of some products is registered so that proper notification can be sent in the event of recalls. For example, in the case of automobile recalls, owners are advised to have the problem corrected at their dealerships. Similarly, reverse channels have been used for repairs for some items. The warranty for a small appliance might specify that if repairs are needed within the first 90 days of sale, the item should be returned to the dealer and after that period to the factory. Such reverse channels are a vital element of product recall and repair procedures.

A reverse channel was established for Kodak instant cameras following a U.S. Supreme Court ruling prohibiting the firm from marketing instant cameras and film. The ruling stemmed from a patent infringement suit initiated by Polaroid. Since owners of the 16.5 million Kodak instant cameras could no longer purchase compatible film, Kodak marketers, within hours of the court ruling, offered camera owners the option of turning in each camera for either a disk camera and film with a retail value of $50, coupons for $50 worth of other Kodak products, or a share of Kodak stock, then selling for about $50. Camera owners were instructed to call a toll-free number, and callers were sent a postage-paid envelope for mailing cameras. Merchandise, coupons, or stock certificates were then mailed to the respondents. Although Eastman Kodak was not legally obligated to make this exchange, the recall was an effective, albeit expensive, method of maintaining the firm's positive image with its customers.[9]

Facilitating Agencies

facilitating agency
Institution, such as an insurance company, bank, or transportation company, that provides specialized assistance for channel members in moving products from producer to consumer.

A **facilitating agency** provides specialized assistance for regular channel members (such as producers, wholesalers, and retailers) in moving products from producer to consumer. Included in the definition of facilitating agencies are insurance companies, marketing research firms, financial institutions, advertising agencies, and transportation firms. In the opening story, Bristol International was a facilitating agency in Tracom's distribution channel.

Facilitating agencies perform a number of special services. Insurance companies assume some of the risks involved in transporting the goods, marketing research firms supply information, financial institutions provide the necessary financing, advertising agencies help sell the goods, and transportation firms store and physically move the goods. In some instances, the major channel members perform these services. Facilitating agencies are not, however, involved in directing the flow of goods and services through the channel.

Power in the Distribution Channel

Some marketing institutions must exercise leadership in the distribution channel if the channel is to be an effective aspect of marketing strategy. Decisions must be made and conflicts among channel members resolved. Channel leadership is a function of a member's power within the distribution channel. For example, strong apparel labels like Anne Klein, Liz Claiborne, and Polo have such appeal that department stores carry them despite the fact that the makers operate their own specialty shops.[10] Channel power is also important in foreign markets. Johnson Wax and 3M have used their financial resources and advertising skills to dominate their channels in Europe and Asia, respectively.[11]

Bases of Power

Most sources cite five bases of power within the distribution channel: reward power, coercive power, legitimate power, referent power, and expert power. These bases were first suggested over 30 years ago by Professors John R. P. French and Bertram Raven. All five bases can be used to establish a position of channel leadership.

Reward Power.   If channel members can offer some type of reward to another member, they possess reward power. Examples are the granting of an exclusive sales territory or franchise.

Coercive Power.   The threat of economic punishment is known as coercive power. For instance, a manufacturer might threaten an uncooperative retailer with loss of its dealership. Another example is Wal-Mart's strength with its suppliers. The Bentonville, Arkansas, retailer's market size is a significant base of power in its distribution channel.

As a channel captain, GTE's Sylvania Lighting Division uses its marketing expertise to help its distributors approach potential customers. One of the company's marketing efforts is this Lightmobile, an "educational program on wheels" that showcases the manufacturer's lighting products and applications. With the Lightmobile, Sylvania can work closely with distributors in demonstrating products that satisfy end users' needs and wants.

Source: Courtesy of GTE.

Legitimate Power. Distribution channels that are linked contractually are examples of legitimate power. For example, a franchisee might be contractually required to perform such activities as maintaining a common outlet facade, contributing to an advertising fund, and remaining open during specified time periods and on weekends.

Referent Power. Agreement among channel members as to what is in their mutual best interests is known as referent power. For instance, many manufacturers maintain dealer councils to help resolve potential problems in distributing a good or service. Both parties have a mutual interest in maintaining effective channel relationships.

Expert Power. Knowledge is the determinant of expert power. For instance, a manufacturer might assist a retailer with store layout or advertising based on its marketing expertise with the product line.

Channel Leadership

channel captain
Dominant and controlling member of a marketing channel.

The dominant and controlling member of a channel is called the **channel captain.** Historically the channel leadership role was performed by the producer or wholesaler since retailers tend to be both small and localized. However, retailers increasingly are taking on the role of channel captain as large chains assume traditional wholesaling functions, even dictating product design specifications to manufacturers. Some manufacturers welcome buyers' involvement in product development. Pentech International, an Edison, New Jersey, maker of inexpensive writing and drawing instruments, invites buyers to dictate product and packaging specifications. On the other hand, Pentech does not start production without an order.[12]

Producers as Channel Captains. Since producers and service providers typically create offerings and enjoy the benefits of large-scale operation, they fill the role of channel captain in many marketing channels. GTE's Sylvania Lighting Division assumed the channel leadership position by establishing Prestige Partnership, a program designed to assist its 2,200 distributors target products at specific market segments. One part of the program is Sylvania Source, a database that helps distributors identify sales prospects within geographic areas. It includes the name, address, and phone number of a prospect plus the name of the person responsible for ordering lighting products, the number of fixtures the firm has, and the annual lighting potential of the prospect. Another part of the program is Techniques for Better Lighting, a package of information distributors can use to educate end users about the economic and performance advantages of Sylvania's lighting products. The Lightmobile in the accompanying photo is yet another way Sylvania assists its independent electric wholesalers in marketing products to potential customers.[13]

Retailers as Channel Captains.   Retailers are often powerful enough to serve as channel captains in many industries. Large chain operations may bypass independent wholesalers and deal directly with manufacturers. Major retailers, such as Wal-Mart, Sears, Kmart, JCPenney, and Montgomery Ward, often act as channel captains in given situations.

Wholesalers as Channel Captains.   Although their relative influence has declined, wholesalers continue to serve as vital members of many marketing channels. Large-scale wholesalers, such as the Independent Grocers Alliance (IGA), serve as channel captains as they assist independent retailers in competing with chain outlets.

The Battle for Shelf Space

On balance, the power in many distribution channels is shifting to the retailer since they control the limited retail space. The advent of scanner research also means that retailers now provide and share in the information needed for crucial marketing decisions.

The battle for shelf space is best illustrated in supermarkets.[14] The nation's 50,000 supermarkets now carry up to 26,000 *stock keeping units* (SKUs) each. The term **SKU** refers to each individual item carried by a store. The typical supermarket has doubled the SKUs it carries over the past decade. Meanwhile manufacturers continue to introduce new products at a brisk pace. In fact, new-product introductions were up over 70 percent in a recent five-year period. Many of these new products are line extensions or items similar to existing SKUs. The net result is cannibalization and a 90 percent failure rate.

This situation has given retailers considerable power in their distribution channel. As a result, manufacturers now spend more promotional money on their channel members—usually referred to as "the trade"—than they do appealing directly to consumers. In fact, some retailers buy only when the manufacturer offers a deal or special promotion. **Forward buying**—as this practice is known—purchases more goods than are required for the promotion. What is not sold during the promotion is held in waiting for later sale at regular prices.

Slotting Allowances.   Many retailers are beginning to demand fees for carrying new products. The fees, called **slotting allowances**, can range from a few thousand dollars up to $80,000. Slotting fees are not demanded of well-established products or new items backed by extensive marketing research and advertising—a fact which may have Robinson-Patman Act implications in the future. From the retailer's perspective, slotting fees cover the costs of inventorying the new items and related accounting costs. From the manufacturer's viewpoint, a refusal to pay slotting allowances can drastically cut the potential market for a new product.

SKU (stock keeping unit)
An individual item carried in inventory by a store.

forward buying
Retailing practice of buying goods only on a deal or special promotion.

slotting allowance
Fees paid by manufacturers to retailers for shelf space.

Other Fees for Shelf Space.   Retailers are now imposing a variety of other fees on manufacturers seeking shelf space. The most common is a failure fee charged if the new SKU does not meet sales projections. This fee is based on the cost of removing the items from inventory as well as the lost revenue from the item. Other fees that have been used by retailers are an annual renewal fee for continuing to carry an SKU, trade allowances, discounts on high-volume purchases, survey fees for research done by the retailer on the new item, and even a fee for a salesperson to present a new item to a buyer. It is estimated that national distribution of a new food item can cost up to $800,000 in fees including slotting allowances.

How Manufacturers Deal with Slotting Allowances and Other Fees.
Manufacturers' responses to demands for payment of slotting allowances and the like are often determined by their own channel power. Kellogg, for instance, can refuse to pay slotting allowances for its popular cereals. By contrast, Carewell Products of Fairfield, New Jersey, knew that it would have to pay high slotting allowances to get its new flexible DenTax toothbrush into U.S. outlets. Therefore, Carewell decided to first market DenTax in Malta, Greece, Malaysia, and Singapore in order to build the cash necessary for a U.S. launch. The American Dental Association seal and "Made in U.S.A." labels and displays were the primary selling points for Carewell in these markets.

Channel Conflict

Channel captains often are called upon to mediate or resolve channel conflicts. Distribution channels must be organized and regarded as cooperative efforts if operating efficiencies are to be achieved. Yet channel members often perform as separate, independent, and even competitive forces. Too often marketing institutions within the channel believe it extends only one step forward or backward. They think in terms of suppliers and customers rather than of vital links within the total channel.

Types of Conflict

Two types of conflict, horizontal or vertical, may hinder the normal functioning of distribution channels.

Horizontal Conflict.   Horizontal conflict develops among channel members at the same level, such as two or more wholesalers or two or more retailers, or among marketing intermediaries of the same type, such as two competing discount stores or several retail florists. More often, however, horizontal conflict occurs among different types of marketing intermediaries that handle similar products. The retail druggist competes with variety stores, discount houses, department stores, convenience stores, and mail-order houses, all of which may be supplied by the producer with identically branded products. Consumer desire for convenient, one-stop shopping has led to multiple channels and the use of numerous outlets for many products.

Horizontal conflict may occur among retailers if a vendor owns competitive outlets. Burger King's 1990 decision to offer Coca-Cola instead of Pepsi gave the world's leading bottler even more dominance in the U.S. fountain-sales market. Although the fast-food operator stated that Coca-Cola offered joint promotions and special advertising campaigns as an enticement, many observers pointed to the conflicts resulting from Pepsi's ownership of numerous fast-food businesses that compete with Burger King. PepsiCo owns Pizza Hut, Taco Bell, and Kentucky Fried Chicken.[15]

Vertical Conflict.   Vertical conflict, which is frequent and often severe, occurs between channel members at different levels—for example, when retailers develop private brands to compete with the producers' brands, or when producers establish their own retail stores or create mail-order operations that compete with retailers. Conflict between producers and wholesalers may occur when producers attempt to bypass wholesalers and make direct sales to retailers or industrial users. In other instances, wholesalers may promote competitive products.

Consider the case of video cassettes: Studios used to sell them for about $65 wholesale, with a retail list price of $89.95. At this price, few consumers would buy them, so most would go to video rental companies that could recover the purchase price in a few months. Recently, studios discovered they could make more money in the "sell-through market"—that is, by selling tapes directly to consumers. Hit videos priced at about $20 can sell more than 2 million units. While video rental firms can now buy their inventory for a lower cost, so can consumers. Thus, the video store is missing a rental. To further complicate the situation, the tapes that video stores used to retail for $89.95 can now be purchased at Wal-Mart or Kmart for less than $20.[16]

Achieving Channel Cooperation

The basic antidote to channel conflict is effective cooperation among channel members. Most channels have more harmonious relationships than conflicting ones; if they did not, they would cease to exist. Cooperation is best achieved by considering all channel members as part of the same organization. Achieving cooperation is the prime responsibility of the dominant member, the channel captain, which must provide the leadership necessary for ensuring the channel's efficient functioning.

WD-40 provides a unique example of channel cooperation. Its San Diego manufacturer has put WD-40 into 75 percent of U.S. households through the astute use of multiple channels. WD-40 is sold everywhere—by mass merchandisers, auto supply stores, farm co-ops, and others. The company has kept its diverse dealers cooperative through competitive pricing, effective point-of-sale displays, and trade deals.[17]

The Gray Market

Another type of channel conflict is represented by the *gray market*. As U.S. manufacturers have licensed their technology and brands abroad, they sometimes must compete domestically against their own brands produced by overseas affiliates. These **gray goods**—sometimes called *parallel goods*—are put into U.S. channels by foreign distributors. While foreign licensees are usually prohibited from selling in the United States, their distributors are not bound by any such rules.

The gray market began a decade ago in the electronics field. It then spread to flashlight batteries, film, and now packaged goods. Gray goods have always been a problem in the apparel industry.

gray goods
Goods manufactured under licenses abroad and then sold in the U.S. market in competition with their U.S.–produced counterparts.

In a legal case involving Cartier and Kmart, Cartier sued the discounter for buying its products from unauthorized sources. Kmart argued that it was just buying from the lowest-cost vendor. In 1988 the Supreme Court ruled in favor of Kmart. The Court held that items made under legitimate license are legal regardless of their country of origin. Thus, retailers may legally buy goods through the gray market.

A few years ago, Lever Brothers lost $5 million in sales because of a gray good. The firm's Shield brand of deodorant soap produced in Great Britain began appearing in U.S. outlets. The lost sales of U.S.–made Shield were one thing, but, also, characteristics of the British version damaged the image of its U.S. counterpart and thus of the product's U.S. manufacturer. British Shield was created for the hard water common in Great Britain, and American showers quickly used up the soap. In addition, it was heavily perfumed, something U.S. buyers disliked.

Walter Volpi, Lever Brothers general counsel, commented, "Consumers wrote in and asked, 'What have you done to my soap?' Our salesforce was demoralized, and retailers began saying, 'Why should we deal with you if we can get the soap elsewhere?' "[18]

Channel Strategy Decisions

Marketers face several channel strategy decisions. The selection of a specific distribution channel is the most basic of these decisions. The level of distribution intensity must also be determined and the issue of vertical marketing systems addressed.

Selection of a Distribution Channel

What makes a franchised retail dealer network best for Ford Motor Company? Why do operating supplies often go through both agents and merchant wholesalers before being purchased by industrial firms? Why do some firms employ multiple channels for the same products? Marketers must answer many such questions in choosing distribution channels. The choice is based on an analysis of market, product, producer, and competitive factors. All factors are important, and often they are interrelated. But the overriding consideration is where, when, and how consumers choose to buy the good or service. Consumer orientation is as important to channel decisions as it is in other areas of marketing strategy.

Market Factors.   A major determinant of channel structure is whether the product is intended for the consumer or industrial market. Industrial purchasers usually prefer to deal directly with the manufacturer (except for supplies or small accessory items), but most consumers make their purchases from retail stores. Often products for both industrial users and consumers are sold through more than one channel.

The needs and geographic location of the firm's market affect channel choice. Direct sales are possible where the firm's potential market is concentrated. A small number of potential buyers also increases the feasibility of direct channels. Consumer goods are purchased by households everywhere. Since these households are numerous and geographically dispersed, and because they purchase a small volume at a given time, marketing intermediaries must be employed for them.

Figure 12.4

Industrial Product Using
Direct Channel Distribution

Source: Courtesy of Akiyama Corporation of America.

A good illustration of how market factors influence distribution is Home Depot's replacement of Lowe's as the leader in the home improvement market. Lowe's traditionally got over 60 percent of its business from professional contractors, but decided to reverse this ratio with its retail business. Half of Lowe's stores were recast in "home design centers," a move that increased the customer home improvement segment to two-thirds. However, the move angered Lowe's industrial customers, so the company opened contractor yards to pacify this market segment.

Meanwhile, Home Depot stuck with the retail customer; only 10 percent of its business comes from contractors. Home Depot has concentrated on large stores that Lowe's did not build until recently. Home Depot's larger inventory and hiring of skilled craftsmen to staff its stores has also made a difference for its retail customers.[19]

Order size also affects the channel decision. Producers are likely to use shorter, more direct channels in cases where retail customers or industrial buyers place relatively small numbers of large orders. Retailers often utilize buying offices to negotiate directly with manufacturers for large-scale purchases, while wholesalers may be used to contact smaller retailers.

Product Factors.   Product factors also play a role in determining optimal distribution channels. Perishable goods, such as fresh produce and fashion products with short life cycles, typically move through relatively short channels directly to the retailer or ultimate consumer. For example, Orlando-based Red Lobster uses air shipments to keep its restaurants around the country stocked with fresh fish. Similarly, Burrito Express in Pasadena, California, regularly sends its burritos to transplanted Southern Californians via Federal Express.[20]

Complex products, such as custom-made installations and computer equipment, typically are sold by the producer to the buyer. Akiyama, a Japanese producer of offset printing presses, uses a direct salesforce supported by trade advertising as shown in Figure 12.4 to market its products to industrial buyers in the United States. In general, the more standardized the product, the longer the channel. Standardized goods usually are marketed by wholesalers. Products that require regular service or specialized repairs normally are not distributed through channels employing independent wholesalers. Automobiles are marketed through a franchised network of retail dealers whose employees receive training on how to properly service the cars.

Another generalization about distribution channels is that the lower the product's unit value is, the longer the channel. Convenience goods and industrial supplies with typically low unit prices frequently are marketed through relatively long channels. Installations and more expensive industrial and consumer goods employ shorter, more direct channels.

Producer Factors.   Companies with adequate financial, managerial, and marketing resources are less compelled to utilize intermediaries in marketing their products. A financially strong manufacturer can hire its own salesforce, warehouse its own goods, and grant credit to retailers or consumers. A weaker firm must rely on marketing intermediaries for these services (although some large retail chains purchase all of the manufacturer's output, thereby bypassing the independent wholesaler). Production-oriented firms may be forced to utilize the marketing expertise of marketing intermediaries to offset their organizations' lack of such skills.

A firm with a broad product line usually is able to market its products directly to retailers or industrial users, since its salesforce can offer a variety of products. High sales volume permits the selling costs to be spread over a number of products and makes direct sales feasible. The single-product firm often discovers that direct selling is an unaffordable luxury.

The manufacturer's need for control over the product also influences channel selection. If aggressive promotion is desired at the retail level, the producer chooses the shortest available channel. For new products, the producer may be forced to implement an introductory advertising campaign before independent wholesalers will agree to handle the items.

Competitive Factors.   Some firms are forced to develop unique distribution channels because of inadequate promotion of their products by independent marketing intermediaries. Popular alternatives are for the manufacturer to add a direct salesforce or set up its own retail distribution network (a concept discussed later in the chapter). Table 12.1 summarizes the factors affecting the selection of a distribution channel and examines the effect of each on the channel's overall length.

Determining Distribution Intensity

Adequate market coverage for some products could mean one dealer for 50,000 people. Mars, Inc., marketers define adequate distribution for Snickers, Milky Way, and Mars candy bars as almost every supermarket, convenience store, drugstore, and variety store, plus many vending machines. The degree of distribution intensity can be viewed as a continuum with three general categories: intensive distribution, selective distribution, and exclusive distribution.

intensive distribution
Policy in which a manufacturer of a convenience item attempts to saturate the market.

Intensive Distribution.   Producers of convenience goods practice **intensive distribution** when they provide saturation coverage of the market, enabling the purchaser to buy the product with a minimum of effort. Examples of goods distributed through this market coverage strategy include soft drinks, candy, gum, and cigarettes.

Table 12.1   Factors Affecting Selection of Distribution Channel

	Characteristics of Short Channels	Characteristics of Long Channels
Market Factors	Industrial user	Consumers
	Geographically concentrated	Geographically diverse
	Technical knowledge and regular servicing required	Technical knowledge and regular servicing not required
	Large orders	Small orders
Product Factors	Perishable	Durable
	Complex	Standardized
	Expensive	Inexpensive
Producer Factors	Manufacturer has adequate resources for performing channel functions	Manufacturer lacks adequate resources for performing channel functions
	Broad product line	Limited product line
	Channel control important	Channel control not important
Competitive Factors	Manufacturer feels that marketing intermediaries are inadequately promoting products	Manufacturer feels that marketing intermediaries are adequately promoting products

The use of intensive distribution can be seen in Fuji's decision to treat floppy disks as a packaged good. Fuji decided that since 30 percent of all U.S. households now have a personal computer, it would be easier to reach floppy disk buyers through food and drug stores. Fuji's six-person salesforce deals with a network of ten brokers that has previous experience with the firm's film and audiotapes. As a result, the company's floppy disks are now sold in chains like Kroger and Shopko.[21] Fuji's efforts to intensify distribution include trade ads such as the one in Figure 12.5, designed to persuade supermarket and drug store buyers to stock its floppy disks.

Japan: The Ultimate in Intensive Distribution.   Japan's multi-tiered distribution system is often accused of screening out U.S. exports. Certainly, Japan provides an ultimate example of intensive distribution. On a per capita basis, Japan has twice as many stores as does the United States. Furthermore, Japan has many more wholesaling stages than do Western countries. The ratio of wholesale to retail sales volume moves up with the levels between the consumer and the manufacturer. In the case of Japan, this ratio is 4.8 to 1. By contrast, the ratio in the United States is 2.1 to 1.[22]

selective distribution
Policy in which a firm chooses only a limited number of retailers to handle its product line.

Selective Distribution.   Another market coverage strategy is **selective distribution,** in which a firm chooses only a limited number of retailers in a market area to handle its line. Price cutting is less likely here, since fewer dealers are handling the firm's line. By limiting the number of retailers, the firm can reduce its total marketing costs while establishing better working relationships within the channel. *Cooperative advertising* (in which the manufacturer pays a percentage of the retailer's advertising expenditures and the retailer prominently displays the firm's products) can be utilized for mutual benefit, and marginal retailers can be avoided. Where service is important, the manufacturer usually provides dealer training and assistance. VW Germany is an example of a company that takes this approach. VW rates its dealers on the basis of customer satisfaction. It knows that if a dealer scores 85 out of 100, on average, 96 percent of German

Figure 12.5 Promotion Designed to Intensify Distribution

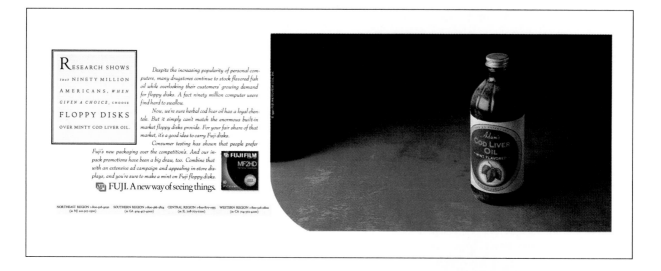

Source: © 1990 Fuji Photo Film U.S.A., Inc.

customers will come back to that dealership for a new car. VW also segments its dealers on the basis of their rankings. The segments are then used in the dealer promotions program.[23]

Exclusive Distribution. When producers grant exclusive rights to a wholesaler or retailer to sell in a specific geographic region, they are practicing **exclusive distribution,** an extreme form of selective distribution. The best example of exclusive distribution is within the automobile industry. For example, a city with a population of 40,000 may have a single Mazda dealer or a single Pontiac dealer. Exclusive-distribution agreements also occur in the marketing of some major appliances and apparel.

Some market coverage may be sacrificed through a policy of exclusive distribution, but this loss is often offset by the development and maintenance of an image of quality and prestige for the product and by the reduced marketing costs associated with a small number of accounts. In exclusive distribution, producers and retailers cooperate closely in decisions concerning advertising and promotion, inventory to be carried by the retailers, and prices.

Legal Problems of Exclusive Distribution. The use of exclusive distribution presents a number of potential legal problems in three areas: exclusive dealing agreements, closed sales territories, and tying agreements. While none of these practices is illegal per se, all may be ruled illegal if they reduce competition or tend to create a monopoly situation.

Exclusive-Dealing Agreements. The use of exclusive distribution may lead to an **exclusive-dealing agreement** prohibiting a marketing intermediary (a wholesaler, or more typically, a retailer) from handling competing products. Producers of high-priced shopping goods, specialty goods, and accessory equipment often require such agreements as assurance by the marketing intermediary of total concentration on the firm's product line. These contracts are

exclusive distribution

Policy in which a firm grants exclusive rights to a wholesaler or retailer to sell in a particular geographic area.

exclusive-dealing agreement

Arrangement between a manufacturer and a marketing intermediary that prohibits the intermediary from handling competing product lines.

F O C U S   O N   E T H I C S

RETAILING IN JAPAN

. . . .

Many American businesspeople consider Japan's complex regulations on the size of retail establishments discriminatory. But there are signs of change in this area, and huge U.S. chains like Toys "R" Us stand to benefit.

Since the 1960s the retailing environment in Japan has been marked by friction between large retailers and smaller ones. In 1974 the Japanese government passed the Large-Scale Retail Stores Law, which heavily regulates domestic distribution. The intent of the law was to protect small retailers by restricting the activities of supermarkets, department stores, and other large retailers. Any store with more than 500 square meters of floor space had to comply with numerous rules governing such matters as store hours and number of holidays. The complex process of gaining approval for the opening of a store took an average of six years. Small retailers effectively had the authority to prevent new large stores from opening in their communities.

As a result of these and other government-imposed restrictions, Japan's distribution system has become a complex, inefficient structure characterized by severe overregulation. This has tended to discourage entry into the market and to increase prices to consumers. In fact, Japanese consumers pay some of the highest prices in the world.

Recently two trends have opened up new opportunities for American retailers in the Japanese market. One is public pressure for changes in distribution that will enable retailers to meet the increasingly diverse and sophisticated needs of Japanese consumers. The other is the set of trade agreements recently negotiated by the United States and Japan.

In 1990 the United States and Japan reached agreement on a set of proposals—the U.S.–Japan

Structural Impediments Initiative (SII)—aimed at removing structural barriers to trade in both countries. Part of the agreement involves relaxing the restrictions on opening large stores in Japan. The time required to license a large retail store would be reduced to 18 months. However, the agreement has met with strong opposition from Japan's Federation of Specialty Stores Association, which charges that it would hurt small store owners in Japan and that the spread of larger stores could destroy local shopping communities.

Discussion Questions

1. Some experts on Japanese retailing stress the importance of preserving shopping communities that form the backbone of residential areas. Others believe that Japanese consumers' desire for more imported goods justifies the new regulations even though some small retailers might suffer. Should social and cultural factors be taken into consideration in the regulation of business? Discuss.

2. Members of Congress have expressed skepticism that Japan will live up to the SII agreements. Should Toys "R" Us adopt a wait-and-see attitude before moving to enter the Japanese market?

Sources: Martin Crutsinger, "U.S. to Closely Monitor Trade Pact with Japan," *Arkansas Democrat* (April 7, 1990), pp. 1A, 13A; "Opportunities in Japan's Changing Retail Market," *Business America* (September 24, 1990), pp. 2–6; Mari Yamaguchi, "Japanese Opposed to Trade Reform; U.S. Must Help Itself, Group Says," *Arkansas Democrat* (April 7, 1990), p. 13A; and Isao Nakauchi, "The Yoke of Regulation Weighs Down on Distribution," *Economic Eye* (Summer 1989), pp. 17–19.

considered violations of the Clayton Act if the producer's or dealer's sales volume represents a substantial percentage of total sales in the market area. The courts have ruled that sellers initially entering a market can use exclusive-dealing agreements as a means of strengthening their competitive positions. However, the same agreements are considered violations of the Clayton Act when used by firms with sizable market shares since they may bar competitors from the market.

closed sales territory
Restricted geographic selling region specified by a manufacturer for its distributors.

Closed Sales Territories.   Producers with **closed sales territories** restrict the geographic territories for each of their distributors. Although the distributors may be granted exclusive territories, they are prohibited from opening new facilities or marketing the manufacturers' products outside their assigned territories. The legality of closed sales territories depends on whe̶ restrictions decrease competition. If competition is lessened, closed ̱ territories are considered as being in violation of the Federal Trade Commissi̶ Act and of provisions of the Sherman Act and Clayton Act.

The legality of closed sales territories is also determined by whether the restrictions are horizontal or vertical. Horizontal territorial restrictions involve agreements by retailers or wholesalers to avoid competition among products from the same producer. Such agreements consistently have been declared illegal. However, the U.S. Supreme Court has ruled that vertical territorial restrictions—those between producers and wholesalers or retailers—may be legal. While the ruling is not clear-cut, such agreements are likely to be legal in cases where the manufacturer occupies a relatively small part of the market. In such instances, the restrictions may actually increase competition among competing brands. The wholesaler or retailer faces no competition from other dealers carrying the manufacturer's brand and therefore can concentrate on effectively competing with other brands.

Tying Agreements. The third legal question of exclusive dealing involves the use of a **tying agreement**—an agreement that requires a dealer that wishes to become an exclusive dealer of an item to also carry other products of that producer. In the apparel industry, for example, such an agreement may require the dealer to carry a line of less popular clothing in addition to the fast-moving items.

Tying agreements violate the Sherman Act and Clayton Act when they lessen competition or create monopoly situations by keeping competitors out of major markets. For this reason, International Salt Company was prohibited from selling salt as a tying product with the lease of its patented salt-dispensing machines for snow and ice removal. The Supreme Court ruled that such an agreement unreasonably eliminated competition among sellers of salt.

tying agreement

Arrangement between a marketing intermediary and a manufacturer that requires the intermediary to carry the manufacturer's full product line in exchange for an exclusive dealership.

Vertical Marketing Systems

Efforts to reduce channel conflict and make distribution more effective have led to the development of vertical marketing systems. These channel systems contrast markedly with earlier distribution channels in the United States. A **vertical marketing system (VMS)** is defined as a planned channel system designed to improve distribution efficiency and cost effectiveness. These objectives are achieved through economies of scale and elimination of duplicated services. There are three types of vertical marketing systems: corporate, administered, and contractual.

vertical marketing system (VMS)

Preplanned distribution channel organized to be cost effective and achieve improved distribution efficiency.

Corporate System

Where there is single ownership of each stage of the distribution channel, a **corporate marketing system** exists. Hartmarx Corp. markets its Hart Schaffner & Marx suits through company-owned stores as well as through independent retailers. AT&T and GTE market telephones and related products through their Phone Centers and Phone Marts, respectively. At one time, Holiday Corp. owned a furniture manufacturer and a carpet mill that supplied its Holiday Inn motels. Other well-known corporate systems include Firestone, Sherwin-Williams, and Singer.

corporate marketing system

VMS in which there is single ownership of each stage in the distribution channel.

The Sherwin-Williams Company has established a corporate vertical marketing system for its Sherwin-Williams branded products (photo at left). These products, which include architectural coatings, industrial maintenance products, industrial finishes, and related items, are produced by the company and distributed exclusively through 1,896 company-operated stores (photo at right). The company also manufactures other brands, such as Dutch Boy, Kem-Tone, and Martin-Senour, which are distributed through independent paint dealers and wholesalers, mass merchandisers, and home centers.

Source: Courtesy of The Sherwin-Williams Company.

Administered System

administered marketing system
VMS in which channel coordination is achieved through the exercise of power by a dominant channel member.

In an **administered marketing system,** channel coordination is achieved through the exercise of power by a dominant channel member. Ethan Allen Inc., for example, closely controls its more than 300 retail stores, determining the stores' displays, layout, and overall appearance. Although the Ethan Allen Home Galleries are independently owned and operated, they carry only furniture that has been manufactured or selected and approved by Ethan Allen Inc. Other examples of manufacturers operating administered channels include McKesson, Sears, Montgomery Ward, and Levitz Furniture.[24]

Contractual System

contractual marketing system
VMS characterized by formal agreements among channel members.

Instead of the common ownership of channel components that characterizes the corporate VMS or the relative power of the component of an administered system, the **contractual marketing system** is characterized by formal agreements among channel members. In practice, there are three types of such agreements: the wholesaler-sponsored voluntary chain, the retail cooperative, and the franchise.

Wholesaler-Sponsored Voluntary Chain.

The wholesaler-sponsored voluntary chain represents an attempt by the independent wholesaler to preserve a market by strengthening the firm's retail customers. To enable the independent retailers to compete with the chains, the wholesaler enters into a formal agreement wherein the retailers agree to use a common name, maintain standardized facilities, and purchase the wholesaler's products. Often the wholesaler develops a line of private brands to be stocked by the members of the voluntary chain.

A common store name and similar inventory allow the retailers to achieve cost savings on advertising, since a single newspaper ad promotes all the retailers in the trading area. IGA (Independent Grocers' Alliance) Food Stores, is a good example of a voluntary chain. Other wholesaler-sponsored chains include Associated Druggists, Sentry Hardware, and Western Auto.

Retail Cooperative.   A second type of contractual VMS is the retail cooperative, a wholesaling operation established by a group of retailers to help them better compete with chains. The retailers purchase ownership shares in the wholesaling operation and agree to buy a minimum percentage of their inventory from it. The members may also choose to use a common store name and develop their own private brands to carry out cooperative advertising. Retail cooperatives such as American Hardware have been extremely successful in rivalling, or even surpassing, corporate chain store systems' sales and service.[25]

franchise

Contractual arrangement in which a wholesaler or retailer (the franchisee) agrees to meet the operating requirements of a manufacturer or other franchiser.

Franchise.   A third type of contractual vertical marketing system is the **franchise** — a contractual agreement in which a wholesaler or dealer (the franchisee) agrees to meet the operating requirements of a manufacturer or other franchiser. Typically the dealers receive a variety of marketing, management, technical, and financial services in exchange for a specified fee. The costs of opening a franchise vary widely. For instance, the total cost of opening a Merry Maids residential cleaning franchise is $28,500 to $33,500, while a McDonald's franchise averages $610,000.[26]

Franchising has become a huge industry, with over 2,500 franchisers and more than 500,000 outlets in the United States. Indeed, franchising is responsible for a third of all U.S. retail sales.[27]

The franchising concept actually began when the Singer Company established franchised sewing machine outlets following the Civil War. Early impetus for the growth of franchising came after 1900 in the automobile industry as automobile travel created a demand for nationwide distribution of gasoline, oil, and tires. Franchises were also created in the soft-drink industry as syrup manufacturers contracted with wholesale bottlers. In recent years, it has dominated the fast-food industry and several service industries. McDonald's, Burger King, KFC, Wendy's, Hardee's, Arby's, Holiday Inn, Weight Watchers, Century 21, and H&R Block are some of the familiar franchise names.

Franchising does not guarantee business success; that depends on the particular business. Certain disclosure information is reported in the *Uniform Franchise Offering Circular (UFOC)* or the Federal Trade Commission's *Disclosure Requirements and Prohibitions Concerning Franchising and Business Opportunities,* which is designed to protect would-be investors by presenting the facts about each franchiser's claims, guarantees, experience, occurrence of bankruptcy, and evidence of the moral character of key personnel. Also specified are the specific terms of the franchising agreement, including all costs involved and services to be provided. In addition to the federal requirements, some 15 states also require that franchisers register or provide certain disclosures.[28]

Franchising Abroad.   Franchising accounts for a growing segment of retail sales abroad — currently 11 percent in the United Kingdom and 10 percent in France, for instance. Approximately 400 U.S. firms franchise overseas, and there are some 300 foreign franchisers. One of the earliest foreign franchisers to operate in the United States was Roche-Bobois USA Ltd., which has 24 U.S. units selling leather seating pieces and French-designed furniture.

master license

Franchiser's license to operate or sub-franchise units in a given geographic area.

Most foreign franchise outlets develop within the framework of a **master license,** granted by the U.S. franchiser as a contractual authorization for a foreign firm or entrepreneur to operate franchise units in a given country or geographic area. The master licensee sub-franchises individual units or owns and operates all of them. The individual unit must meet the franchiser's standard requirements for a franchisee.[29]

Summary of Chapter Objectives

1. **Explain the role of distribution channels in marketing strategy.** Distribution channels refer to the various marketing institutions and the interrelationships responsible for the physical and title flow of goods and services from producer to consumer or industrial user. Wholesalers and retailers are the marketing intermediaries in the distribution channel. Distribution channels bridge the gap between producer and consumer. By making goods and services available when and where the consumer wants to purchase them and by arranging for transfer of title, distribution channels create time, place, and ownership utilities.

2. **Describe the various types of distribution channels.** A host of alternative distribution channels are available for makers of consumer and industrial goods and services. They range from selling directly to consumers or industrial users to using a variety of marketing intermediaries. Multiple channels are also becoming increasingly common today. A unique distribution system is the reverse channel used in recycling, product recalls, and some service situations.

3. **Explain the concept of power as it relates to the distribution channel.** Channel leadership is primarily a matter of relative power within the channel. Five bases for power are reward power, coercive power, legitimate power, referent power, and expert power. The current battle for shelf space in retail stores illustrates how channel power can shift over time.

4. **Describe the concept of channel leadership.** The marketing intermediary that makes the major decisions concerning the operation of a particular channel is called the channel captain. In some channels, the manufacturer or service provider is the channel captain. In others, powerful retailers, such as nationwide operations, may fill this role. In still others, wholesalers serve as channel captains.

5. **Discuss conflict and cooperation within the distribution channel.** Channel conflict is a problem in distribution channels. There are two types of conflict: horizontal (occurring among channel members at the same level) and vertical (occurring among channel members at different levels). Marketers should work toward cooperation among all channel members as the remedy for channel conflict. The advent of gray goods illustrates channel conflict in an international setting.

6. **Outline the major channel strategy decisions.** Basic channel strategy decisions involve channel selection, level of distribution intensity, and use of vertical marketing systems. The selection of a distribution channel is based on market, product, producer, and competitive factors. The decision on distribution intensity involves choosing from among intensive distribution, selective distribution, and exclusive distribution. Another channel strategy decision concerns the use of vertical marketing systems.

7. **Identify and discuss the various types of vertical marketing systems.** Three major types of vertical marketing systems exist: corporate, administered, and contractual. A corporate VMS refers to a situation in which there

is single ownership of each stage of the distribution channel. An administered VMS is one in which a dominant channel member exercises its power to achieve channel coordination. A contractual VMS includes wholesaler-sponsored chains, retail cooperatives, and franchises.

Key Terms

distribution channel	intensive distribution
marketing intermediary	selective distribution
direct selling	exclusive distribution
direct marketing	exclusive-dealing agreement
industrial distributor	closed sales territory
dual distribution	tying agreement
reverse channel	vertical marketing system
facilitating agency	corporate marketing system
channel captain	administered marketing system
SKU (stock keeping unit)	contractual marketing system
forward buying	franchise
slotting allowance	master license
gray goods	

Review Questions

1. How do distribution channels create utility? What specific functions do distribution channels perform?

2. Outline the major categories of distribution channels. Cite an example of a firm that uses each channel.

3. What is meant by dual distribution? Why is it used? How can this practice create channel conflict?

4. What is a reverse channel? Identify the two major uses of reverse channels.

5. Explain the concept of power in the distribution channel. What are the major sources of channel power?

6. What is a channel captain? Under what circumstances do producers, wholesalers, and retailers act as channel captains?

7. Discuss the contemporary battle for shelf space. Explain the role of slotting allowances and other fees.

8. What is meant by channel conflict? Describe the types of channel conflict that can exist.

9. Outline the major categories of channel decision. How might the so-called gray market affect channel decisions?

10. Identify the various vertical marketing systems. Cite an example of each.

Discussion Questions

1. Outline the distribution channel used by a firm in your area. Why did the company select these particular channels?

2. Many people are surprised to learn that Japan is the fastest growing major market for imported cars. By 1995 exports could reach 10 percent of all Japanese

car purchases. The foreign car companies have employed diverse distribution channels to reach Japanese consumers. BMW operates its own dealer network. Chrysler sells its popular Jeep Cherokee through Honda. Volkswagen-Audi has used an independent dealer, but has now opened exclusive VW dealerships. General Motors uses an independent dealer with a separate retail system. Finally, Ford and Mazda sell cars through a cooperative retail organization called Autorama (Ford owns 25 percent of Mazda).[30] Why do you think the car companies have taken such varied approaches to retailing in Japan? What approach would you take?

3. Find a real-world example of channel conflict. Suggest an approach to resolving this conflict.

4. Which degree of distribution intensity is appropriate for each of the following?
    a. *People* magazine
    b. Liz Claiborne sportswear
    c. Camay soap
    d. Hyundai
    e. Waterford crystal

5. The rising value of the yen often allows Japanese consumers to buy Japanese-made products cheaper abroad than they can at home. Shopping trips to Singapore, Hong Kong, and the United States are popular with the Japanese, who use the word *gyakuyunya,* meaning "double-import," to refer to their foreign purchases. However, large-scale importation of foreign-made Japanese brands is limited.[31] Relate *gyakuyunya* to the U.S. gray market. Discuss the similarities and differences. Why do these exist?

Computer Applications

Decision tree analysis, a quantitative technique used in identifying alternative courses of action, assigning probability estimates for the profits or sales associated in each alternative, and indicating the course of action with the highest profit or sales, was first introduced in Chapter 2. Although the technique was used in Chapter 2 to assess the impact of environmental variables on marketing decisions, it can also be applied to channel strategy decisions. The technique is summarized on page 75.

Directions: Use menu item 2 titled "Decision Tree Analysis" to solve each of the following problems.

Problem 1.   A consumer goods company headquartered in Nashville believes it can increase its current $50 million annual sales volume to as much as $65 million if it replaces its current selective distribution arrangement with a strategy of intensive distribution. While the firm's vice-president of marketing believes that the probability of such a sales increase is only 30 percent, she is convinced that sales cannot fall below $50 million if the firm moves to intensive distribution. If the firm elects to continue its selective distribution policy, sales are expected to rise to $55 million. Recommend a course of action for the firm based on the decision tree analysis model.

Problem 2.   A Fresno, California, firm with $10 million in annual sales is considering bypassing its independent wholesaling intermediaries and setting up its own retail outlets. The firm's management estimates that if the new distribution arrangement proves successful, next year's sales will increase to $15 million. Management also feels that sales will decline to $8 million if the new distribution system is unsuccessful. The odds of success are calculated at 60 percent. Should the firm elect to continue its current distribution channel, sales volume is expected to remain at $10 million. Should the firm set up its own retail outlets?

Problem 3. A producer of industrial supplies in Scranton, Pennsylvania, is seriously considering replacing its current network of industrial distributors with its own sales force. The firm's director of marketing believes that the establishment of a quality sales force could increase next year's sales to $30 million, $5 million more than that expected under the current distribution system. In addition, he feels that this sales increase can be achieved with no increase in selling costs. But the marketing director also believes that the conversion to a new distribution channel could cause next year's sales to decline to $10 million unless the firm is successful in attracting, training, and motivating high-quality sales representatives. Since management is confident of its ability to create an effective selling organization, it assigns a 70 percent probability of success. Use the decision tree analysis model to suggest a course of action for the firm.

Problem 4. A Japanese firm has chosen Memphis for its U.S. offices and production facility. The firm's top management is currently evaluating which type of vertical marketing system (VMS) to implement in the United States. Although the firm has eliminated the corporate form of VMS from consideration due to the costs involved, its marketers have concluded that it is possible to establish a contractual VMS or an administered VMS. In response to a request to develop sales forecasts for the firm's products in the United States, an American consulting firm has produced two estimates: an optimistic forecast labeled *Barnburner* and a most-likely forecast labeled *Expected*. The probability of occurrence of each forecast is 30 percent and 70 percent, respectively. The potential sales payoffs for each option are as follows:

Forecast	Administered VMS	Contractual VMS
Barnburner	$50 million	$40 million
Expected	16 million	22 million

Which VMS option should the Japanese firm select?

Problem 5. A Paterson, New Jersey, firm is in the process of choosing one of two possible wholesalers to distribute its Christmas novelty items. A marketing research consultant retained by the firm has prepared both a best-case and worst-case forecast for each wholesaler. The researcher estimates a probability of 50/50 for the occurrence of his "best" and "worst" cases. The potential sales volumes for the two wholesalers are as follows:

Forecast	Wholesaler 1	Wholesaler 2
Best case	$3 million	$5 million
Worst case	2 million	1 million

Which wholesaler should the firm select?

Famous Amos

Today, most of us recognize Wally "Famous" Amos, the man who gave his name to the original gourmet cookie. The company founded by Amos has achieved virtual nationwide distribution of several flavors of its cookies in stores and has scattered retail stores world-wide, with franchises in Japan, Australia, and Canada, as well as the United States.

In 1975, Wally Amos was just another talent agent trying to succeed in Hollywood. However, he soon developed another calling. Friends told him that the cookies he made were so good that he should sell them, and eventually Amos took their advice. Some of these friends backed up their advice by investing $25,000 in his venture, the Famous Amos Chocolate Chip Cookie Company, and the world's first gourmet cookie shop opened in 1975. It was an instant success.

News of Famous Amos spread by word of mouth, and in a classic example of pull-through demand, consumers would walk into stores and ask the owners why they did not stock Famous Amos cookies. The company relied solely on this informal sort of marketing for its first five years.

When Amos started his company, he had made no plans for such growth. His first retail "hot bake" shop appeared to be earning a profit and, after all, in his words, "All I wanted to do was make a living." Consumer demand grew and requests began to pour in from other areas, but Amos did not have the funds to expand his cookie shop concept into a chain. He also wanted to avoid the risk of expanding through borrowing funds. Then the idea struck him—just as it had McDonald's Ray Kroc 20 years earlier: franchising. The firm distributed its frozen dough directly to the franchised "hot bake" shops located in suburban shopping centers and downtown walk-in locations.

Amos also used other distribution alternatives to get the cookies into supermarkets, convenience outlets, "mom-and-pop" stores, and gift shops that make up the Famous Amos market, by contracting with an independent wholesale distributor. This distribution channel saved the company the cost of starting its own network, while giving it access to an already established distribution system, without which the young company might have failed. Even though many store owners were unhappy about doing business with products offering such a low markup, consumer demand was so strong that retailer complaints soon fell to a trickle and distribution became more widespread.

Famous Amos tailored its cookies to its markets. Frozen dough was shipped directly to the firm's franchised "hot bake" shops. For supermarkets, it offered several different sizes of cookies, and sets up racks for the packages in the fresh baked goods section, rather than on the cookie shelf. For convenience stores, one- and two-ounce bags were created to save space and to encourage impulse sales. It now makes several flavors of cookies (oatmeal-based cookies are the nation's best sellers).

Demand was created in part by the cookie's taste. The gourmet cookie shop concept was entirely novel, and to outlast the novelty, Famous Amos cookies had to be good. But while consumers like the taste of the cookies (a recent *Consumer Report's* test rated Famous Amos's chocolate chip cookies one of the best-tasting brands available), much of the success of Famous Amos is based on effective person marketing. Wally Amos's winning grin gleams from each package of Famous Amos cookies, and his presence seems to give the cookies an identity that its competitors lack. John Rosica, a public relations executive with the company, called Wally "a perpetual promotion." In recognition of his role in the company's success, the Smithsonian's Collection of Advertising History includes his Panama hat and brightly patterned Indian gauze shirt.

By the late 1980s, interest in the gourmet cookie had waned so that only a few locations could support bake shops devoted exclusively to cookies. Famous Amos decided to change its placement from gourmet cookie to high-quality family cookie. Package sizes were changed from 2½-, 7-, and 16-ounce packages to a 12-ounce size for wholesale distribution to grocery store outlets and a 30-ounce size for food-club stores. A 2-ounce package was also developed to be sold through vending machines. As of 1991, there were only a few bake shop franchises operating 15 stores, and Famous Amos was restricting itself to making finished cookies.

Even though Amos sold his ownership interest in the firm in 1985, Famous Amos continues to rely solely on promotions that feature Wally. Among the most successful promotions have been its efforts at cause marketing. The company worked in conjunction with literacy councils in several American cities, having stores contribute a percentage of profits to literacy programs. Such promotions resulted in greatly increased sales, including a 38 percent sales jump in Philadelphia.

Sources: Personal interview with Keith Lively, Famous Amos, May 1991. Michael King, "To Sell or Not To Sell . . .," *Black Enterprise* (June 1987), pp. 287–290; Gail Buchetter, "Happy Cookie," *Forbes* (March 10, 1986), pp. 176–178 and *Consumer Reports* (February 1985), pp. 69–72.

Questions

1. What distribution channels are used in the marketing of Famous Amos cookies? Draw each channel and label all components.

2. What changes would be made in the chart in question 1 to reflect the distribution channels existing in the mid-1980s, before the decline of the gourmet cookie concept?

3. Explain the impact of Famous Amos's channel strategy on the firm's growth. How should his strategy be adapted to achieve continued growth?

4. Although Famous Amos has largely ignored mass-market promotions, the firm recently began advertising on television. Explain how such promotion aids the firm's distribution strategy.

13

Wholesaling

CHAPTER OBJECTIVES

1. To identify the functions performed by wholesaling intermediaries.

2. To explain how wholesaling intermediaries improve channel efficiency.

3. To explain the channel options available to a manufacturer that desires to bypass independent wholesaling intermediaries.

4. To identify the conditions under which a manufacturer is likely to assume wholesaling functions rather than use independent wholesaling intermediaries.

5. To distinguish between merchant wholesalers and agents and brokers.

6. To identify the major types of merchant merchant wholesalers and the situations in which each might be used.

7. To describe the major types of agents and brokers and the situations in which each might be used.

8. To outline how a wholesaling strategy is developed.

The home entertainment business is booming, and that's music to the ears of Handleman Company of Troy, Michigan. Handleman is a wholesale rack jobber that specializes in selling four product lines in the home entertainment industry—prerecorded music, prerecorded video cassettes, books, and home computer software—to mass merchandisers such as K Mart, Wal-Mart, and Sears.

Why do giant retailers need an intermediary like Handleman? Mass merchandisers typically carry between 60,000 and 80,000 products. Adding music and video products would increase their inventory by 25,000 to 30,000 items. Craig Ortale, merchandise manager for K Mart, says, "We would have to add enormous staff to our buying department in order to monitor and police all those different titles." Instead, K Mart and other mass merchants rely on Handleman to tell them what's hot and what's not.

The primary services Handleman provides for retailers are the selection of product and the management of inventory risk caused by product obsolescence and changing consumer tastes. Handleman maintains retailers' music, video, book, and computer software departments by supplying and installing in-store fixtures and point-of-purchase advertising. It helps retailers prepare radio, television, and print ads; coordinates product delivery; and allows retailers to exchange slower selling products for best sellers. Handleman creates marketing programs that help retailers maximize sales in other departments; for example, some retailers sell sports videos in their sporting goods department. The wholesaler also develops advertising and displays to promote seasonal, holiday, and event themes, such as "Scary Movies" for Halloween and an "Exercise" promotion in January.

Handleman's 800-person salesforce and its computerized Retail Inventory Management System (RIMS) ensure that retailers have the right product at the right time. Sales representatives who visit stores two to four times a month use portable optical scanners to check inventory and transmit the data to a central computer for processing. Orders are sent to regional distribution cen-

ters where they are packaged and delivered to customers. RIMS enables Handleman to tailor the inventories of individual stores to reflect the customer profile of each store and to adjust inventory levels, product mix, and selections according to seasonal and current selling trends.

Starting in business as a pharmaceuticals wholesaler in the early 1930s, Handleman moved into music in the 1950s. Today, music products account for about 60 percent of company sales. Successfully managing the dramatic changes in product format in the music industry during the past 40 years—from vinyl records to eight-tracks to cassettes to compact discs—has spurred Handleman's growth.

Another factor contributing to growth is Handleman's ability to identify consumer trends. The number of prerecorded videos sold jumped from 3 million in 1980 to 52 million in 1985, the year that Handleman started selling videos as a test program. Video is now the company's second-largest and fastest-growing product line, accounting for 33 percent of sales. Handleman's video and compact disc sales have grown from $2.8 million in 1985 to more than $270 million today.

Through acquisitions and joint ventures, Handleman is extending its customer base beyond mass merchandisers and entering new markets. It acquired a video rack jobber that services drugstores and supermarkets, and it formed a joint venture to duplicate and sell videos in Canada. The purchase of one of its largest suppliers, a firm that acquires licenses to duplicate and distribute low-cost videos, extended Handleman's customer base to other rack jobbers, wholesalers, and music and video specialty stores. The company entered retailing by opening Entertainment Zone, a music and video store, which also provides the wholesaler with a setting to test new marketing concepts, fixtures, signing, and products for other customers. And Handleman is tapping into another growth opportunity by testing video sales through regional and national video rental chain stores.[1]

Photo source: Courtesy of Handleman Company, Troy, Michigan.

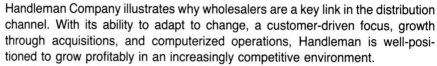

Chapter Overview

wholesaler
Wholesaling intermediary that takes title to the goods it handles; also called *jobber* or *distributor*.

wholesaling intermediary
Broad term describing both wholesalers and agents and brokers that perform important wholesaling activities without taking title to the goods.

Handleman Company illustrates why wholesalers are a key link in the distribution channel. With its ability to adapt to change, a customer-driven focus, growth through acquisitions, and computerized operations, Handleman is well-positioned to grow profitably in an increasingly competitive environment.

Wholesaling involves the activities of persons or firms that sell primarily to retailers or to other wholesalers or industrial users and only in insignificant amounts to ultimate consumers. The term **wholesaler** applies only to wholesaling intermediaries that take title to the products they handle. **Wholesaling intermediaries** is a broader term that describes not only marketing intermediaries that assume title to the goods they handle but agents and brokers that perform important wholesaling activities without taking title to the goods. Under this definition, then, a wholesaler is a wholesaling intermediary. Handleman Company is a wholesaler because it takes title to the goods purchased from producers of movies, music, books, and computer software.

Wholesaling activity also exists in the marketing of some services. For example, wholesaling intermediaries operate in the travel industry. They are largely responsible for the GIT (group-inclusive tour) marketing in which "land packages" (hotels and meals) are offered to retail travel agents that combine them with air travel for their customers as a complete, prepaid vacation.

The most recent U.S. Census of Wholesale Trade lists 469,539 wholesaling establishments with a total sales volume of $2.5 trillion. New York City alone accounts for 7.4 percent of all wholesale trade.

But it is important to note that wholesaling activity varies considerably from country to country. A nation's stage of economic development, its political and legal system, and its culture all influence the size, structure, and role of wholesaling. The United States and Canada have sophisticated and competitive systems in place. Under the Soviet Union's centralized economic system, wholesaling did not exist, and even after years of economic reform efforts, wholesale trade in the Soviet Union remains negligible.[2] In Finland, four wholesaling establishments control the distribution of most goods. Marketers who want to distribute their goods across national boundaries must have knowledge of the unique wholesale structure of each host country.

Functions and Costs of Wholesaling Intermediaries

The route that goods follow on the way to the consumer or industrial user is actually a chain of marketing institutions. Goods that "bypass" the marketing intermediaries in the chain and move directly from manufacturer to consumer constitute only 3 percent of the total in the consumer goods market. Some consumers complain that marketing intermediaries are an unnecessary cost in the distribution system. Many discount retailers claim lower prices as a result of direct purchases from manufacturers. Moreover, chain stores often assume wholesaling functions and bypass independent wholesalers.

Are wholesaling intermediaries indeed still appropriate today? The answer to this question can be found by considering the functions and costs of these marketing intermediaries.

Services Provided by Wholesaling Intermediaries

A marketing institution can continue to exist only as long as it performs a service that fulfills a need. Its demise may be slow, but it is inevitable once other channel members discover they can survive without it. Table 13.1 lists a number of

Table 13.1 Wholesaling Services for Customers and Producer-Suppliers

Service	Service Provided	
	Customers	Producer-Suppliers
Buying Anticipates customer demands and possesses knowledge of alternative sources of supply; acts as purchasing agent for customers.	●	
Selling Provides a salesforce to call on customers that serves as a low-cost method of servicing smaller retailers and industrial users.		●
Storing Provides a warehousing function at lower cost than most individual producers or retailers could provide. Reduces risk and cost of maintaining inventory for producers and provides customers with prompt delivery service.	●	●
Transporting Customers receive prompt delivery in response to their demands, reducing their inventory investments. Wholesalers also break-bulk by purchasing in economical carload or truckload lots, then reselling in smaller quantities to their customers, thereby reducing overall transportation costs.	●	●
Providing Market Information Serves as important marketing research input for producers through regular contacts with retail and industrial buyers. Provides customers with information about new products, technical information about product lines, reports on competitors' activities, industry trends, and advisory information concerning pricing changes, legal changes, and so forth.	●	●
Financing Aids customers by granting credit that might be unavailable if customers purchased directly from manufacturers. Provides financing assistance to producers by purchasing products in advance of sale and through prompt payment of bills.	●	●
Risk Taking Assists producers by evaluating credit risks of numerous distant retail customers and small industrial users. Extends credit to customers that qualify. Wholesaler responsible for transporting and stocking products in inventory assumes risk of spoilage, theft, or obsolescence.	●	●

services provided by wholesaling intermediaries. It is important to note that numerous types of wholesaling intermediaries exist and that not all of them provide every service listed in the table. Producer-suppliers and their customers, who rely on wholesaling intermediaries for distribution, select those that will provide the desired combination of services.

The list of services clearly indicates the marketing utilities—time, place, and possession or ownership—that wholesaling intermediaries provide. The services also reflect the provision of the basic marketing functions of buying, selling, storing, transporting, risk taking, financing, and supplying market information.

Sometimes the wholesaler is the difference between success and failure in the marketplace. British-made MacLaren strollers are popular purchases for American parents. The secret of the product's success seems to lie in the modifications made by its U.S. distributor, Marshall Electronics, Inc. of Chicago. The American wholesaler replaced the standard British components with brighter fabrics and bigger wheels. Marshall also added seat belts to comply with U.S. safety rules.[3]

An increasing number of wholesalers are using computer systems and electronic data interchange to provide customers with faster and more efficient service and to help customers manage their businesses. FoxMeyer, a pharmaceuticals wholesaler, developed an on-line computer system that gives hospital pharmacy customers instantaneous data on their purchase history and inventory, FoxMeyer's inventory, prices, brands of various drugs, and product usage trends. Instant access to such data helps pharmacists place orders, monitor prices, manage inventory, and better serve the needs of hospital patients.[4]

The critical marketing functions listed in Table 13.1 form the basis for evaluating the efficiency of any marketing intermediary. The risk-taking function is present in each service the wholesaling intermediary provides.

Transportation and Storage.   Wholesalers transport and store goods at locations convenient for customers. Manufacturers ship goods from their warehouses to numerous wholesalers, which in turn ship smaller quantities to retail outlets in locations convenient for purchasers. A large number of wholesalers assume the inventory function (and cost) for manufacturers. They benefit through the convenience afforded by local inventories. The manufacturer benefits through reduced cash needs, since its goods are sold directly to the retailer or wholesaler.

Costs can be reduced at the wholesale level by making large-volume purchases from the manufacturer. The wholesaler receives quantity discounts from the manufacturer and incurs lower transportation costs because economical carload or truckload shipments are made to the wholesaler's warehouse. At the warehouse, the wholesaler divides the goods into smaller quantities and ships them to the retailer over a shorter distance (but at a higher rate) than would be the case if the manufacturer filled the retailer's order directly from a central warehouse.

The economics of small-scale shipments places a premium on efficient warehousing at the wholesale level. For example, McKesson Drug installed an automated sorting system at its Memphis distribution center to increase warehousing and transportation efficiency. A programmed bar code scanner reads bar codes affixed to customer orders as they move to the loading dock for shipment. The scanner works in harmony with more than two miles of conveyor belts, automatically sorting orders and routing them to one of 30 holding lanes. The system groups each order and releases it directly onto the appropriate truck according to a last-stop-first, first-stop-last delivery route plan. The system has reduced driver overtime by 60 percent and truck loading to a minimum, and it has improved accuracy.[5]

Lowering Costs through Reduced Contacts.   As the Computer Applications in Chapter 1 demonstrate, when a marketing intermediary represents numerous producers, the costs involved in buying and selling often decrease. The transaction economies are shown in Figure 13.1. In this illustration, five manufacturers are marketing their outputs to four different retail outlets. A total of 20 transactions result if no intermediary is utilized. By adding a wholesaling intermediary, the number of transactions is reduced to nine.

Source of Information.   Because of their central position between manufacturers and retailers or industrial buyers, wholesalers serve as important information links. Wholesalers give their retail customers useful information about new products and promotions. In addition, they supply manufacturers with information about market acceptance of their product offerings.

To provide reliable and timely delivery to its customers, United Stationers, an office products wholesaler, maintains an extensive truck fleet that extends the reach of 12 regional distribution centers and 42 local distribution points. United's computer-based physical distribution network provides 12,000 dealers with products from 400 manufacturers within 24 hours.

Source: Courtesy of United Stationers, Gerald C. Borek, Photographer.

Computer technology is increasing the wholesaler's role as a source of information. Book wholesalers, for example, now use electronic communication and on-line computer systems to speed the ordering and distribution of books to library customers. Traditionally libraries ordered books based entirely on reviews and then mailed the book orders to wholesalers. But today libraries order books prepublication and before reviews to satisfy patron demand. This has dramatically changed the wholesaler's role. "We have become information brokers," says Michael Strauss of Baker & Taylor, a book wholesaler that gives libraries software to link their orders by modem with the wholesaler's computers. The technology gives librarians immediate access to the wholesaler's inventories so they can tell if a book is in print and in stock. Computers also enable distributors to track sales information and report it back to publishers, helping them gauge book demand for reprint decisions.[6]

Source of Financing.   Wholesalers also serve a financing function. They often provide retailers with goods on credit, allowing the retailers to minimize their cash investments in inventory and pay for most of the goods as they are sold. This allows them to benefit from the principle of leverage, whereby spending a minimum amount on goods in inventory inflates the return on invested funds. Some wholesalers extend financing beyond inventory. Wetterau, a food wholesaler, provides retailers with funding support to finance store equipment, fixtures, and improvements and also leases buildings and equipment to store operators.

Wholesalers of industrial goods provide similar services for customers. In the steel industry, intermediaries referred to as *metal service centers* currently market one-fourth of all steel shipped by U.S. mills. The Earle M. Jorgensen Company of Los Angeles, which operates 24 metal service centers nationwide, warehouses, processes, and delivers metal to small-volume buyers and to major metal users that buy in large quantities directly from the steel mills but turn to service centers for quick delivery of special orders. While an order from the mills may take several weeks to deliver, a service center can usually deliver locally within 24 hours. The cost and risk of maintaining the stock are assumed by the service center, saving money for both the mills and the buyers. A metal buyer for

Figure 13.1

Achieving Transaction
Economy with Wholesaling
Intermediaries

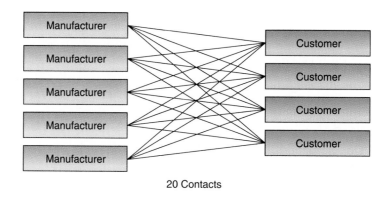

20 Contacts

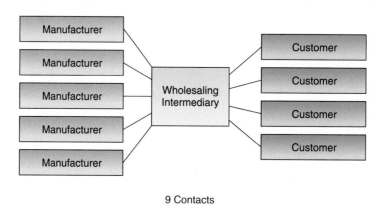

9 Contacts

Hewlett-Packard put it this way: "We use service centers because of the cost-of-metal-ownership. We don't want to own metal in unworked form any longer than we have to."[7]

Marketing Channel Functions: Who Should Perform Them?

While wholesaling intermediaries often perform a variety of valuable functions for their manufacturer, retailer, and other wholesaler clients, these operations could be performed by other channel members. Manufacturers may choose to bypass independent wholesaling intermediaries by establishing networks of regional warehouses, maintaining large salesforces to provide market coverage, serving as sources of information for their retail customers, and assuming the financing function. In some instances, they may decide to push the responsibility for some of these functions through the channel on to the retailer or the ultimate purchaser. Large retailers that choose to perform their own wholesaling operations face the same choices.

A fundamental marketing principle applies to marketing channel decisions:

Marketing functions must be performed by some member of the channel. They can be shifted, but they cannot be eliminated.

Large retailers that bypass wholesalers and deal directly with manufacturers can assume the functions previously performed by wholesaling intermediaries, or

Value-added services are an important part of the marketing strategy of Van Waters & Rogers Inc., a wholesale distributor of industrial chemicals in the United States. To meet the needs of many customers, Van Waters & Rogers provides value-added services such as the custom blending of chemicals and laboratory analysis for quality control. Many Van Waters & Rogers facilities have on-site laboratories to ensure that these services are performed quickly and professionally.

Source: Reprinted with permission of Univar Corporation, parent company of Van Waters & Rogers Inc.

these activities can be performed by the manufacturers. Similarly, manufacturers that deal directly with the ultimate consumer or industrial buyer can assume the functions of storage, delivery, and marketing information previously performed by marketing intermediaries. Intermediaries can be eliminated from the channel, but someone must perform the channel functions.

Independent wholesaling intermediaries earn a profit for the services they provide manufacturers and retailers. Their profit margins are low, ranging from 1 percent for food wholesalers to 5 percent for durable goods wholesalers.[8] These profits could be realized by manufacturers and retailers—or the savings could be used to reduce retail prices—if the manufacturer or retailer could perform the distribution functions as efficiently as the independent intermediaries.

A trend toward consolidation of wholesaling intermediaries partially explains their low profit margins. Since 1979 the number of U.S. drug wholesalers has dropped from 133 to 86 and the number of food service distributors from 6,000 to 3,500. The increased competition resulting from the acceleration of mergers is credited with reducing wholesalers' slim profit margins even more.[9]

To grow profitably in this competitive environment, wholesalers must provide better service at less cost than the manufacturer or retailer can provide for themselves. Modern technology—computerization and automation—is one competitive tool wholesalers use to make ordering, inventory handling, and delivery more efficient.[10] By reducing operating expenses as a percentage of sales, the wholesaler can improve its profit margin.

Another competitive tool used by wholesalers to improve profit margins is *value-added services.* Sysco, a food service wholesaler, has expanded its services to include menu consultation and kitchen design for its restaurant, hotel, school, and hospital customers. Sysco also helps manufacturers develop products that food service customers would buy.[11] United Stationers, an office products wholesaler, recently added a new wrap and label service to reduce organizational customers' need to rehandle merchandise for shipment to their own customers. To use the service, office product dealers give their customer orders directly to United Stationers, which packs the orders, puts the dealer's labels on the package, and ships them directly to the dealer's customers. This

FOCUS ON ETHICS

TRADE LOADING

. . . .

First comes the push: The manufacturer offers wholesalers inducements, such as price discounts, to buy more of a product than they really need. Then comes the pull: The manufacturer finances promotions at the retail level to help the wholesalers move the extra supply to retailers' shelves. The result: High costs for the manufacturer, excessive inventories for the wholesalers, and overstated operating profits in reports to shareholders.

This practice, known as *trade loading,* may not actually be illegal, but it is certainly deceptive, and in the long run it creates more problems than benefits. Consider the case of RJR Nabisco's tobacco division.

In the early 1980s RJR's managers were obsessed with maintaining the company's 32 percent market share—at least on paper—in the face of intensified competition and declining sales in the cigarette industry. Trade loading was already common in the industry, but RJR began engaging in this practice on a vast scale. It established a pattern in which it raised its cigarette prices every June and December, and wholesalers developed the habit of buying huge quantities of its brands before each price increase in order to resell them later at the higher price. Not all of the product "sold through" to retailers, however, and as time went by the excess inventories in wholesalers' warehouses grew by leaps and bounds. By 1988 RJR's "trade load"—the number of excess units stored by wholesalers—was estimated at 14 billion! Meanwhile the manufacturer was providing quarterly reports to investors showing sales, profits, and

market share based on the number of units sold to wholesalers, not the number actually sold at retail. According to a *Fortune* estimate, its operating profits were overstated by some $250 million.

The problem with trade loading is that it is addictive. Once a manufacturer has indulged in the practice and reported inflated sales and profits, in subsequent years there is a powerful temptation to repeat the process in order to show continued good performance. Wholesalers also become addicted to trade loading. RJR's wholesalers began building the expectation of price increases into their budgets.

This kind of smoke screen cannot be maintained indefinitely. In RJR's case, trade loading was becoming increasingly costly; it created peaks and valleys in production, and the push and pull promotions were enormously expensive. In September 1989 management decided to quit cold turkey. The company would forgo $340 million in reported operating profits that year, and the wholesalers would lose the quarterly surge in profits that had become a way of life.

Discussion Questions

1. Trade loading is not explicitly illegal; it appears to be simply a way of manipulating numbers. Is anyone actually hurt by the practice?

2. What are the implications of RJR's decision for its wholesalers?

value-added service allows United's dealer customers to complete a sale without absorbing the cost of inventorying or handling the merchandise.[12]

Types of Wholesaling Intermediaries

Various types of wholesaling intermediaries are present in different marketing channels. Some provide a wide range of services or handle a broad line of goods, while others specialize in a single service, good, or industry. Figure 13.2 classifies wholesaling intermediaries by two characteristics: *ownership* (whether the wholesaling intermediary is independent, manufacturer owned, or retailer owned) and *title flows* (whether title passes from the manufacturer to the wholesaling intermediary). The three basic types of ownership are: (1) manufacturer-owned sales offices and branches, (2) independent wholesaling intermedi-

Figure 13.2

Major Types of Wholesaling
Intermediaries

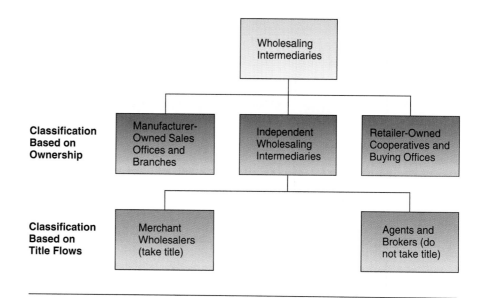

aries, and (3) retailer-owned cooperatives and buying offices. The two types of independent wholesaling intermediaries are merchant wholesalers, which take title to goods, and agents and brokers, which do not.

Manufacturer-Owned Facilities

For several reasons, manufacturers may distribute their goods directly through company-owned facilities. Some goods are perishable; others require complex installation or servicing; some need aggressive promotion; still others are high-unit-value goods that the manufacturer can profitably sell to the ultimate purchaser.

To gain entry into foreign markets, firms may initially use independent wholesaling intermediaries and then shift to company-owned facilities. For example, when Sony and Panasonic first entered the U.S. market, they dealt with American importers who handled radios. As product acceptance and distribution grew, they switched from importers to exclusive distributors. When the marketplace expanded more, they eliminated distributors and established their own distribution network.[13]

Sales Branches and Offices. The basic distinction between a company's sales branches and sales offices is that a **sales branch** carries inventory and processes orders to customers from available stock. Branches duplicate the storage function of independent wholesalers and serve as offices for sales representatives in the territory. They are prevalent in the marketing of chemicals, commercial machinery and equipment, motor vehicles, and petroleum products. Operating expenses for the 21,935 sales branches in the United States average 10.8 percent of sales. General Electric has sales branches in every major U.S. city. Its subsidiary, General Electric Supply Corporation, provides regular contacts and overnight delivery to GE retailers and industrial purchasers.

Since warehouses represent a substantial investment in real estate, small manufacturers and even large firms developing new sales territories may choose

sales branch
Establishment maintained by a manufacturer that serves as a warehouse for a particular sales territory, thereby duplicating the services of independent wholesalers; carries inventory and processes orders to customers from available stock.

public warehouse
Independently owned storage facility that stores and ships products for a rental fee.

sales office
Manufacturer's establishment that serves as a regional office for salespeople but does not carry inventory.

trade fair
Periodic show at which manufacturers in a particular industry display wares for visiting retail and wholesale buyers.

merchandise mart
Permanent exhibition facility in which manufacturers rent showrooms to display products for visiting retail and wholesale buyers, designers, and architects.

to use **public warehouses** — independently owned storage facilities. For a rental fee, manufacturers can store their goods in any of the more than 10,000 public warehouses in the United States for shipment by the warehouses to customers in the area. Warehouse owners will package goods into small quantities to fill orders and even handle billing for manufacturers by issuing warehouse receipts for inventory. Manufacturers can use these receipts as collateral for bank loans.

A **sales office,** in contrast, does not carry inventory but serves as a regional office for the firm's sales personnel. Sales offices located close to the firm's customers help reduce selling costs and improve customer service. For example, numerous offices in various suburbs, serve Detroit's automobile industry. A firm's listing in the local telephone directory often results in new sales for the local representative. Many buyers prefer to telephone the office of a supplier rather than take the time to write to distant suppliers. Since the nation's 14,375 sales offices do not carry inventory, store, or deliver goods, their operating expenses are relatively low, averaging 3.7 percent of total sales.

Other Outlets for Manufacturers' Products.   In addition to using sales forces and regionally distributed sales branches, manufacturers often market their goods through trade fairs and merchandise marts.

A **trade fair** (or *trade exhibition*) is a periodic show at which manufacturers in a particular industry display their wares for visiting retail and wholesale buyers. The annual New York City Toy Fair and the yearly computer and information technology trade fair in Hanover, West Germany, are examples. The cost of making a face-to-face contact with a prospective customer at a trade fair is only 44 percent of the cost of a personal sales call.

Trade fairs are effective means of generating additional sales. For thousands of small firms that produce consumer goods such as toys, gifts, hardware, and sporting goods, trade exhibitions are critical to survival. For example, Tedco, Inc., a small manufacturer of gyroscopes and educational toys and games, generates much of its sales from orders placed at the Toy Fair by specialty retail stores, museums, grocery stores, and catalog companies.[14] Also, exhibiting at trade fairs in foreign countries is an effective way in which both large and small firms can cultivate new customers abroad. For example, in the advertisement in Figure 13.3, Clarks of England invites retailers to visit its exhibit of new men's and women's shoe designs at several shoe trade shows in the United States. Trade fairs are particularly important in Eastern Europe, where there are few other forms of promotion. For instance, Procter & Gamble's participation in a Moscow trade fair led to a large order for toothpaste, soap, and detergent. As a result, P&G's sales of Crest toothpaste in the Soviet Union now equal its sales in Canada.[15]

A **merchandise mart** provides space for permanent exhibits at which manufacturers rent showrooms to market their goods. The Mart Center in Chicago is the largest wholesale buying center in the world. This 7-million-square-foot complex consists of the Merchandise Mart, the Apparel Center, and Expocenter/Chicago. The center hosts 33 seasonal buying markets each year and accounts for more than 3 million buyer visits by retailers, designers, architects, and industrial purchasers. Industries represented here include residential and commercial furnishings, floor coverings, giftware, apparel, and information technology. The Mart Center enables exhibitors from around the world to display their latest goods in a central location. Over 1 million items are on permanent exhibit in the 1,800 showrooms. To ensure that manufacturers receive maximum benefits from their showrooms, the Mart Center conducts an ongoing marketing program that includes advertising, direct mail, and publicity.[16]

Figure 13.3   A Trade Fair Advertisement

Source: Courtesy of Goodby, Berlin, and Silverstein.

Independent Wholesaling Intermediaries

As Figure 13.4 indicates, independent wholesaling intermediaries account for 92 percent of the wholesale establishments and 69 percent of the wholesale sales in the United States. They can be divided into two categories: merchant wholesalers and agents and brokers.

merchant wholesaler

Wholesaling intermediary that takes title to the goods it handles.

Merchant Wholesalers.
The **merchant wholesaler** takes title to the goods it handles. Merchant wholesalers account for slightly more than 59 percent of all sales at the wholesale level, with sales of about $1.5 trillion. They can be further classified as full-function or limited-function wholesalers, as indicated in Figure 13.5.

Full-Function Merchant Wholesalers.
A complete assortment of services for retailers and industrial purchasers is provided by full-function merchant wholesalers. These wholesalers store merchandise in convenient locations, thereby allowing their customers to make purchases on short notice and minimize their inventory requirements. They also usually maintain salesforces

Figure 13.4

Comparison of Wholesale Trade by Sales Volume and Number of Establishments

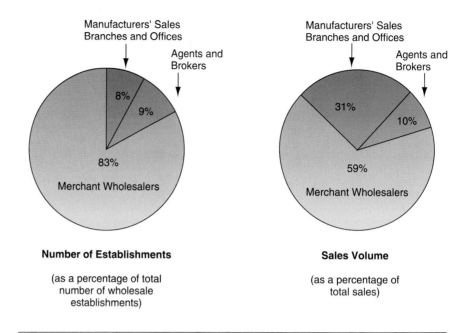

Manufacturers' Sales Branches and Offices

Agents and Brokers

8%

9%

83%

Merchant Wholesalers

Manufacturers' Sales Branches and Offices

Agents and Brokers

31%

10%

59%

Merchant Wholesalers

Number of Establishments

(as a percentage of total number of wholesale establishments)

Sales Volume

(as a percentage of total sales)

Source: Census of Wholesale Trade (Washington, D.C.: Government Printing Office, 1989), p. 9.

that call regularly on retailers, make deliveries, and extend credit to qualified buyers. In the industrial goods market, full-function merchant wholesalers (often called *industrial distributors*) usually market machinery, inexpensive accessory equipment, and supplies.

Full-function merchant wholesalers prevail in industries in which retailers are small and carry large numbers of relatively inexpensive items, none of which they stock in depth. The drug, grocery, and hardware industries traditionally have been serviced by full-function merchant wholesalers. Fleming Companies, for example, is a full-function merchant food wholesaler that serves more than 5,000 retailers. Fleming has 38 distribution centers, operates a 5,000-unit truck fleet, and provides customers with more than 100 support services, including marketing research, financing, advertising, consumer education, and store planning and development.

A unique type of service wholesaler emerged after World War II as grocery retailers began to stock high-profit-margin nonfood items. Because food store managers knew little about health and beauty items, housewares, paperback books, and toys, rack jobbers provided the necessary expertise. A **rack jobber** supplies the racks, stocks the merchandise, prices the goods, and makes regular visits to refill the shelves. In essence, rack jobbers rent space from retailers on a commission basis. They have expanded into discount, drug, hardware, and variety stores.

Since full-function merchant wholesalers perform a large number of services, their operating expenses average nearly 14.5 percent, and sometimes as high as 30 percent, of sales. Attempts to reduce the costs of dealing with these wholesalers have led to the development of a number of limited-function intermediaries.

Limited-Function Merchant Wholesalers. Four types of limited-function merchant wholesalers are cash-and-carry wholesalers, truck wholesalers, drop shippers, and mail-order wholesalers.

rack jobber
Full-function merchant wholesaler that markets specialized lines of merchandise to retail stores and provides the services of merchandising and arrangement of goods, pricing, maintenance, and stocking of display racks.

Figure 13.5

Classification of Independent Wholesaling Intermediaries

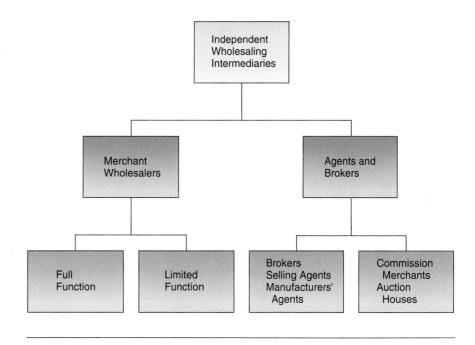

cash-and-carry wholesaler
Limited-function merchant wholesaler that performs most wholesaling functions except financing and delivery.

The **cash-and-carry wholesaler** performs most wholesaling functions except for financing and delivery. These wholesalers first appeared on the marketing scene in the grocery industry during the Depression era of the 1930s. In an attempt to reduce costs, retailers began driving to wholesalers' warehouses, paying cash for their purchases, and making their own deliveries. By eliminating the delivery and financing functions, cash-and-carry wholesalers were able to reduce their operating costs to approximately 9 percent of sales.

Although feasible for small stores, this kind of wholesaling generally is unworkable for large-scale grocery stores. Chain store managers are unwilling to perform the delivery function, and today cash-and-carry is typically one department of a regular, full-service wholesaler. However, the cash-and-carry wholesaler has proven successful in the United Kingdom, where 600 such operators produce over $1 billion a year in sales.

truck wholesaler
Limited-function merchant wholesaler that markets perishable food items; also called *truck jobber*.

A **truck wholesaler,** or *truck jobber,* markets perishable food items such as bread, tobacco, potato chips, candy, and dairy products. Truck wholesalers make regular deliveries to retail stores and perform the sales and collection functions. They also aggressively promote their product lines. The high costs of maintaining delivery trucks and the low dollar volume per sale mean relatively high operating costs of 15 percent.

drop shipper
Limited-function merchant wholesaler that receives orders from customers and forwards them to producers, which ship directly to the customers.

A **drop shipper** receives orders from customers and forwards them to producers, which ship directly to the customers. Although drop shippers take title to the goods, they never physically handle or even see them. Since they perform no storage or handling functions, their operating costs are a relatively low 4 to 5 percent of sales.

Drop shippers operate in industries in which goods are bulky and customers make their purchases in carload lots. Transportation and handling costs represent a substantial percentage of the total cost of goods such as coal and lumber. Drop shippers do not maintain an inventory of goods, which eliminates the expenses of loading and unloading carload shipments. Their major service is developing a complete assortment of goods. Since various types and grades of

Table 13.2   Wholesaling Services for Customers and Producer-Suppliers

Services	Full-Function Wholesalers	Limited-Function Wholesalers			
		Cash-and-Carry Wholesalers	Truck Wholesalers	Drop Shippers	Mail-Order Wholesalers
Anticipates customer needs	Yes	Yes	Yes	No	Yes
Carries inventory	Yes	Yes	Yes	No	Yes
Delivers	Yes	No	Yes	No	No
Provides market information	Yes	Rarely	Yes	Yes	No
Provides credit	Yes	No	No	Yes	Sometimes
Assumes ownership risk by taking title	Yes	Yes	Yes	Yes	Yes

mail-order wholesaler
Limited-function merchant wholesaler that utilizes catalogs instead of a salesforce to contact customers in an attempt to reduce transportation costs.

coal and lumber are produced by different companies, drop shippers can assemble a complete line to fill any customer's order.

The **mail-order wholesaler** is a limited-function merchant wholesaler that relies on catalogs rather than a salesforce to contact retail, industrial, and institutional customers. Purchases are then made by mail or telephone by relatively small customers in outlying areas. Mail-order operations are found in the hardware, cosmetics, jewelry, sporting goods, and specialty foods lines as well as in general merchandise.

Table 13.2 compares the various types of merchant wholesalers in terms of services provided. Full-function merchant wholesalers and truck wholesalers are relatively high-cost intermediaries due to the number of services they perform, while cash-and-carry wholesalers, drop shippers, and mail-order wholesalers provide fewer services and have relatively lower operating costs.

Agents and Brokers.

agents and brokers
Independent wholesaling intermediaries that may or may not take possession of goods but never take title to them.

A second group of independent wholesaling intermediaries—**agents and brokers**—may or may not take possession of the goods, but they never take title. They normally perform fewer services than merchant wholesalers and typically are involved in bringing buyers and sellers together. Agent wholesaling intermediaries can be classified into five categories—commission merchants, auction houses, brokers, selling agents, and manufacturers' agents.

commission merchant
Agent wholesaling intermediary that takes possession of goods when they are shipped to a central market for sale, acts as the producer's agent, and collects an agreed upon fee at the time of sale.

The **commission merchant,** which predominates in the marketing of agricultural products, takes possession when the producer ships goods such as grain, produce, and livestock to a central market for sale. Commission merchants act as the producer's agents and receive an agreed-upon fee when the sale is made. Since customers inspect the products and prices fluctuate, commission merchants receive considerable latitude in making decisions. The owner of the goods may specify a minimum price, but the commission merchant will sell them on a "best-price" basis. The commission merchant's fee is deducted from the price and remitted to the original owner.

auction house
Establishment that brings buyers and sellers together in one location for the purpose of permitting buyers to examine merchandise before purchase.

Auction houses bring buyers and sellers together in one location and allow potential buyers to inspect merchandise before purchasing it. Auction house commissions typically are based on a specified percentage of the sales prices of the auctioned items. The auction method of marketing is common in the distribution of tobacco, used cars, artworks, livestock, furs, and fruit.

An example of an auction house is Sotheby's, which specializes in the auction of art and antiques. Sotheby's holds about 600 auctions a year, covering more than 70 collecting areas, and has offices in 37 countries. Its principal auction centers are in New York and London, but sales are also held in 18 other

Auction houses serve as intermediaries between the buyers and sellers of classic automobiles. This 1962 Ferrari G.T.O. 250, owned by an American collector, was sold by Sotheby's at an auction in Monte Carlo. The buyer, an automobile collector from Sweden, purchased the car for $10.8 million, the highest price paid to date at auction for an automobile. To promote interest in the sale and provide would-be buyers with information, Sotheby's took the car on a global tour before the sale.

Source: © 1990 Sotheby's, Inc.

locations worldwide. Through innovative services and marketing, Sotheby's has broadened the scope of art auctions from a select few to an international marketplace. Each of its auctions has telephone hookups to facilitate worldwide bidding. It prepares catalogs and promotion materials to provide information to a wide global audience. Sotheby's also presents art education courses to make the market more understandable and accessible to buyers and sellers.[17]

broker
Agent wholesaling intermediary that does not take title to or possession of goods and whose primary function is to bring buyers and sellers together.

Brokers bring buyers and sellers together. They represent either the buyer or the seller in a given transaction but not both, and they receive fees from their clients when the transactions are completed. Since the only service they perform is negotiating for exchange of title, their operating expense is low, averaging 3–4 percent of sales. Those who specialize in arranging buying and selling transactions between domestic producers and foreign buyers are called *export brokers.* Brokers operate in industries characterized by a large number of small suppliers and purchasers, for example, real estate, frozen foods, and used machinery.

Because brokers operate on a one-time basis for sellers or buyers, they cannot serve as an effective marketing channel for manufacturers seeking regular, continuing service. A manufacturer that seeks to develop a more permanent channel utilizing agent wholesaling intermediaries might consider instead the use of the selling agent or manufacturer's agent.

selling agent
Agent wholesaling intermediary responsible for the total marketing program of a firm's product line.

Selling agents often are referred to as *independent marketing departments,* because they can be responsible for the total marketing program of a firm's product line. Typically a **selling agent** has full authority over pricing decisions and promotional outlays and often provides financial assistance for the manufacturer. The manufacturer can then concentrate on production and rely on the selling agent's expertise for all marketing activities. Selling agents are common in the coal, lumber, and textile industries. In the coal industry, for example, A. T. Mossey Company of Richmond, Virginia, and Primary Coal, Inc., of New York are selling agents. For small, poorly financed, production-oriented firms, they may prove the ideal marketing channel.

manufacturer's agent
Agent wholesaling intermediary who represents a number of manufacturers of related but noncompeting products and receives a commission based on a specified percentage of sales.

While manufacturers may utilize only one selling agent, they typically use a number of **manufacturers' agents,** who often refer to themselves as *manufac-*

Table 13.3   Services Provided by Agents and Brokers

Services	Commission Merchants	Auction Houses	Brokers	Manufacturers' Agents	Selling Agents
Anticipates customers needs	Yes	Some	Some	Yes	Yes
Carries inventory	Yes	Yes	No	No	No
Delivers	Yes	No	No	Some	No
Provides market information	Yes	Yes	Yes	Yes	Yes
Provides credit	Some	No	No	No	Some
Assumes ownership risk by taking title	No	No	No	No	No

turers' reps. These independent salespeople work for a number of manufacturers of related but noncompeting products and receive commissions based on a specific percentage of sales. Although some commissions are as high as 22.5 percent of sales, most average between about 5 and a little over 15 percent.[18] Unlike selling agents, who may be given exclusive world rights to market a manufacturer's product, manufacturers' agents operate in specified territories.

Manufacturers' agents reduce their total selling costs by spreading the cost per sales call over a number of different products. An agent in the plumbing supplies industry, for example, may represent a dozen manufacturers.

Manufacturers develop their marketing channels through the use of manufacturers' agents for several reasons. First, when they are developing new sales territories, the costs of adding salespeople to "pioneer" the territories may be prohibitive. Agents, who are paid on a commission basis, can perform the sales function in these territories at a much lower cost.

Second, firms with unrelated lines may need to employ more than one channel. One product line may be marketed through the company's sales force and another through independent manufacturers' agents. This is particularly common where the unrelated product line is a recent addition and the firm's salesforce has had no experience with it.

Finally, small firms with no existing salesforce may turn to manufacturers' agents to gain access to their markets. Mac Equipment, a small firm that manufactures filters and conveying equipment, uses 45 manufacturers' agents to sell to industrial customers. Chuck Copenhaver, Mac's vice-president of marketing, says, "For us to field a direct salesforce of a hundred or so people to cover the same territory would be crazy. Rep selection is the most important business decision we make."[19]

The importance of selling agents has declined since 1940, because manufacturers desire to better control their marketing programs. In contrast, the volume of sales by manufacturers' agents has more than doubled and now comprises 37 percent of all sales by agent wholesaling intermediaries. The nation's 24,427 agency firms account for more than $98 billion in sales. Table 13.3 compares the major types of agents and brokers on the basis of the services they perform.

Retailer-Owned Facilities

Retailers also assume numerous wholesaling functions in an attempt to reduce costs or provide special services. Independent retailers occasionally band together to form buying groups to achieve cost savings through quantity purchases. Other groups of retailers establish retailer-owned wholesale facilities

Figure 13.6

Operating Expenses of
Wholesaling Intermediaries
as a Percentage of Sales

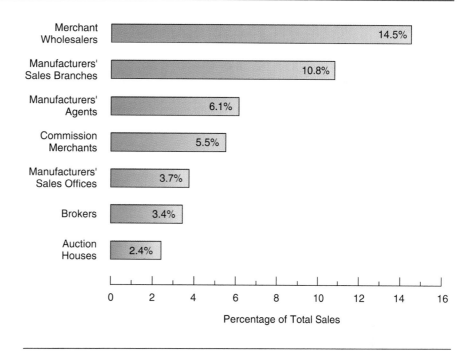

Source: U.S. Department of Commerce, *Census of Wholesale Trade* (Washington, D.C.: Government Printing Office, 1989), p. 9.

as a result of the formation of a cooperative chain. Large-size chain retailers often establish centralized buying offices to negotiate large-scale purchases directly with manufacturers for the chain members.

Certified Grocers of California, Ltd. is a statewide, retailer-owned wholesaler that provides data processing, financing, accounting, and insurance services for its independent retailers. To help them increase their share of the market, Certified offers retailers a promotional pricing program, advertising support, and store design and development counseling.[20]

Costs of Wholesaling Intermediaries

Costs of the various wholesaling intermediaries are calculated as a percentage of total sales. Figure 13.6 lists the costs for each major category. The chief conclusion to be drawn from the chart is that expense variations result from differences in the number of services each intermediary provides. Cost ratios are highest for merchant wholesalers and manufacturers' sales branches because both provide such services as maintenance of inventories, market coverage by a salesforce, and transportation. Auction houses perform only one service: bringing buyers and sellers together. As a consequence, they have the lowest expense ratios. Of course, these ratios are averages and will vary among firms within each category depending on the actual services provided.

Trends in Wholesaling

Many marketing observers of the 1920s felt that the end had come for independent wholesaling intermediaries as chain stores grew in importance and threatened to bypass them. Over the ten-year period from 1929 to 1939,

Figure 13.7

Wholesaling in the United States: A Long-Term Perspective

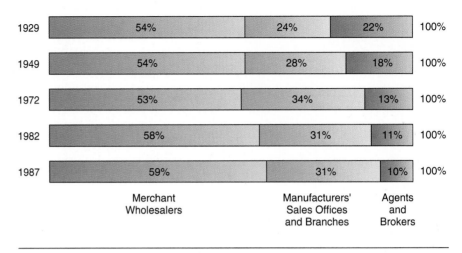

Year	Merchant Wholesalers	Manufacturers' Sales Offices and Branches	Agents and Brokers	
1929	54%	24%	22%	100%
1949	54%	28%	18%	100%
1972	53%	34%	13%	100%
1982	58%	31%	11%	100%
1987	59%	31%	10%	100%

Source: U.S. Department of Commerce, *Census of Wholesale Trade,* and previous census reports.

independent wholesalers' sales volume indeed dropped, but it has increased since then. Figure 13.7 shows how the relative shares of total wholesale trade have changed since 1929.

After the decade of the 1920s, agents and brokers began to decline in importance while company-owned channels and merchant wholesalers began to increase. As they continued to improve the efficiency of their operations and expand their services to meet changing customer needs, merchant wholesalers became an increasingly important link in the distribution channel. Their share of goods distribution is expected to grow to 63 percent by 1995.[21] A number of wholesalers are becoming vertically integrated by operating retail outlets. For example, Genuine Parts Company, a distributor of automotive replacement parts, serves about 6,000 auto parts stores, 562 of which are company owned.[22]

In recent years, wholesalers have extended their geographic reach, mostly through mergers and acquisitions. The wholesaling industry has evolved from local and regional businesses to national and international operations. Like the manufacturing sector, the wholesaling industry now operates in the global marketplace. For example, Wolseley PLC of Great Britain has doubled its presence in the United States by purchasing plumbing and heating supply wholesalers in California and Oregon.[23] During the past decade, several large food wholesalers have set up international divisions to export goods directly to foreign retailers. Wakefern Food Corporation exports 3,500 items to 150 supermarkets in 25 countries in the Middle East, the Far East, Scandinavia, and the Caribbean. To facilitate its expansion worldwide, Fleming Companies installed a computer system designed for international business transactions. U.S. food wholesalers are also targeting the European marketplace as a future source of growth.[24]

Another trend in wholesaling is increased cooperation between wholesalers and their suppliers and customers. To improve their competitive positions, many producers and retailers are cutting costs by switching to just-in-time (JIT) delivery systems, whereby goods are delivered just as producers and retailers need them. Servicing these customers requires that wholesalers be fully stocked at all times and provide error-free and on-time delivery. Adapting to these changing market needs, some wholesalers are forming single-source partnership arrangements with suppliers. For example, Darter Inc., a distributor of paper goods to industrial customers, discontinued buying from three paper companies and now buys

COMPETITIVE EDGE

McKESSON CORP.

. . . .

The company has had its ups and downs, but now it's going strong. Service improvements and international expansion are paying dividends.

Things were looking gloomy when McKesson lost its largest account, Wal-Mart, which brought in more than $400 million a year. But after a brief lapse, it won back the account. It also had a stroke of luck: Its $5 million VSAT (very small aperture terminal) communications project, which uses satellites and small dish antennas, enabled the company to continue filling cus-

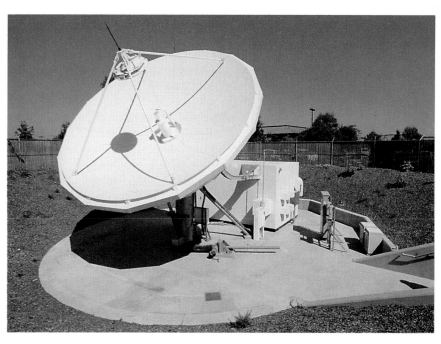

tomer orders following a major telephone switching station fire in Hinsdale, Illinois, and a distribution center roof cave-in in Las Vegas. Without VSAT (which is linked to McKesson's electronic data interchange system), many orders would have been lost.

McKesson is a leading drug distribution company providing products to retail and health-care outlets. It is the nation's largest wholesale distributor of ethical and proprietary drugs; it also distributes medical-surgical and first-aid products, health and beauty aids, and toiletries to drugstores, food stores, and mass merchandisers. The company has also expanded into health-related services.

McKesson's international enterprises include the acquisition of a half-interest in Montreal-based Medis Health & Pharmaceutical, which holds a 50 percent share of the Canadian drug-distribution market. The company is also exploring opportunities in Europe. Its managers are convinced that the pharmaceutical distribution industry will follow the lead of the pharmaceutical manufacturers and go through a period of international expansion and consolidation. They hope to be in the vanguard of this trend.

Several other factors are likely to work in McKesson's favor in coming years. One is that the drug distribution business is almost recession-proof; another is

that the population is aging and its need for prescription drugs is increasing. The growing tendency of manufacturers to rely on wholesalers rather than handle their own distribution will also work to McKesson's advantage.

Discussion Questions

1. Recently McKesson's management decided to focus on a few core businesses, and the company sold off some of the businesses it had acquired in the 1960s. At the same time, the company is poised to expand internationally. Are these two moves contradictory?

2. Why was it so important for McKesson to avoid the interruptions in service that would have resulted from the Hinsdale fire and the Las Vegas cave-in?

Sources: Harlan S. Byrne, "Investment News & Views: McKesson Corp.," *Barron's* (June 25, 1990), pp. 51–52; G. Pierre Goad, "McKesson to Buy Canada's Largest Drug Distributor," *The Wall Street Journal* (January 22, 1990), p. C18; "McKesson Begins PCS Offer," *The Wall Street Journal* (March 14, 1990), p. A6; McKesson Corp., *Annual Report,* 1990; "Satellite Keeps Watchful Eye on McKesson," *Chain Store Executive* (October 1990), pp. 81–82. *Photo source:* Courtesy of McKesson Corporation.

exclusively from one supplier to assure customers of product availability and faster delivery. Other wholesalers are forming partnership relationships with customers, which can spur wholesalers' growth because they reduce competition, provide a predictable market, and deliver larger-volume contracts. For example, when the market for new construction projects slows down, Noland Company, a building-products wholesaler, can rely on DuPont Company to purchase a large volume of maintenance goods for its plants.[25]

The wholesaling field has become more customer oriented and more professional, boasting computerization, automation, and vertical integration. Wholesalers' willingness to innovate in response to changing market needs explains much of their continuing ability to compete with alternative channels. Their market size proves that they continue to fill a need in many marketing channels.

Wholesaling Strategy

Wholesaling intermediaries, like other Channel members, must develop an effective marketing strategy. They do this by determining a target market and then creating an appropriate marketing mix with which to reach it.

Target Market

A wholesaling intermediary's target market can be defined in terms of product lines, customer size, customer needs, and promotional strategy employed. The following types of wholesaling intermediaries illustrate each of these dimensions:

- ☐   Product line: Food broker
- ☐   Customer size: Cash-and-carry wholesaler
- ☐   Customer needs: Rack jobber
- ☐   Promotional strategy employed: Mail-order wholesaler

Once the target market has been specified, the wholesaling intermediary's attention shifts to the marketing mix.

Product Strategy

The wholesaling intermediary's product strategy is primarily a matter of the width, length, and depth of its assortment. As noted earlier, some wholesaling intermediaries, such as manufacturers' reps, carry no inventory, while others, such as many merchant wholesalers, carry an extensive product line. For the most part, a wholesaling intermediary's product strategy is largely a function of the target market it has chosen.

Distribution Strategy

Distribution strategies vary among wholesaling intermediaries. Drop shippers can work through a combination of post office boxes and public warehouses. In contrast, a food broker would be required to have an extensive warehousing and delivery operation.

Promotional Strategy

Personal selling is the primary ingredient of a wholesaling intermediary's promotional strategy. Advertising is limited to trade publications that reach their particular marketplaces.

Pricing Strategy

The pricing strategy of these channel members depends on the extent of service they provide for their customers. Merchant wholesalers perform many services; as a result, the prices they charge retail customers are higher than those charged by wholesaling intermediaries that perform only a few functions.

Summary of Chapter Objectives

1. **Identify the functions performed by wholesaling intermediaries.** Wholesaling intermediaries provide time, place, and ownership utilities. They do this by performing the basic marketing functions of buying, selling, storing, transporting, risk taking, financing, and supplying market information.

2. **Explain how wholesaling intermediaries improve channel efficiency.** Wholesaling intermediaries improve channel efficiency by cutting the number of buyer-seller transactions required. For example, if 4 manufacturers marketed their output to 4 different retail outlets, a total of 16 transactions would be needed. Using a wholesaling intermediary, however, would reduce the total number of transactions to eight.

3. **Explain the channel options available to a manufacturer that desires to bypass independent wholesaling intermediaries.** The most commonly used approach to bypassing independent wholesaling intermediaries is to establish a salesforce to call on retail customers and industrial purchasers. This may involve the establishment of regional sales branches from which orders are filled from inventory carried in stock at the branch. Other approaches include the establishment of sales offices, the use of permanent exhibits of company products in merchandise marts, or the periodic display of the manufacturer's offerings in trade fairs.

4. **Identify the conditions under which a manufacturer is likely to assume wholesaling functions rather than use independent wholesaling intermediaries.** Products are marketed directly by manufacturers through company-owned wholesaling facilities for a variety of reasons. Some products are perishable, either in terms of physical perishability or a limited life due to rapid fashion changes. Some products require complex installation or servicing; others require aggressive promotion; still others are high-unit-value goods that the manufacturer can sell profitably to the ultimate purchaser.

5. **Distinguish between merchant wholesalers and agents and brokers.** Merchant wholesalers take title to the goods they handle. Agents and brokers may take possession of the goods, but they do not take title.

6. **Identify the major types of merchant wholesalers and the situations in which each might be used.** The two major categories of merchant wholesalers are full-function merchant wholesalers, such as rack jobbers, and limited-function merchant wholesalers, including cash-and-carry wholesalers, truck wholesalers, drop shippers, and mail-order wholesalers.

Full-function wholesalers are common in the drug, grocery, and hardware industries. Limited-function wholesalers are sometimes used in the food, coal, lumber, cosmetics, jewelry, sporting goods, and general-merchandise industries.

7. **Describe the major types of agents and brokers and the situations in which each might be used.** Commission merchants, auction houses, brokers, selling agents, and manufacturers' agents are classified as agent wholesaling intermediaries because they do not take title to the products they sell. Commission merchants are common in the marketing of agricultural products. Auction houses are used to sell tobacco, used cars, art, livestock, furs, and fruit. Brokers are prevalent in the real estate, frozen foods, and used machinery industries. Selling agents are used in the coal, lumber, and textile industries. Finally, manufacturers' agents are used by companies to develop new sales territories, firms with unrelated lines, and smaller firms.

8. **Outline how a wholesaling strategy is developed.** Like other marketing strategies, a wholesaling strategy starts with determining the target market, which can be defined in terms of product line, customer size, customer needs, and promotional strategy employed. After the target market is set, a marketing mix is developed. The wholesaling intermediary's product strategy is primarily a matter of the width, length, and depth of its inventory assortment. Wholesaling pricing strategy depends on the extent of the services offered. Distribution strategies employed vary among wholesale intermediaries. Finally, promotional strategy basically emphasizes personal selling.

Key Terms

wholesaler	truck wholesaler
wholesaling intermediary	drop shipper
sales branch	mail-order wholesaler
public warehouse	agents and brokers
sales office	commission merchant
trade fair	auction house
merchandise mart	broker
merchant wholesaler	selling agent
rack jobber	manufacturer's agent
cash-and-carry wholesaler	

Review Questions

1. What is meant by a wholesaling intermediary? How do their activities differ from country to country?

2. In what ways do wholesaling intermediaries assist manufacturers? How do they help retailers?

3. Who should perform the various marketing channel functions? How has this assignment changed over time?

4. Distinguish between sales offices and sales branches. Under what conditions might each type be used?

5. Distinguish between a trade fair and a merchandise mart. Why do manufacturers use these outlets to reach wholesale and retail buyers?

6. Distinguish merchant wholesalers from agents and brokers. What are the major subclassifications of each of these categories?

7. How do commission merchants and brokers differ? Cite examples of industries that would use each.

8. Distinguish between a manufacturer's agent and a selling agent. Under what circumstances would each be used?

9. Why are the operating expenses of the merchant wholesaler higher than those of the typical agent or broker? Also explain how these expenses are measured.

10. What are the major trends in wholesaling activity? Which ones will have the greatest impact on marketing?

Discussion Questions

1. In outlying areas of Central America, packaged food products are distributed by wholesaling intermediaries on three to five different levels. The first intermediary buys the products in lots of several cases and then breaks bulk by selling to other wholesalers in smaller quantities. They, in turn, resell in smaller quantities to other intermediaries. The products continue to be resold until finally a peddler on a mule travels into the jungles with a couple of cans and several other manufacturers' products for resale to small retailers. Discuss the contributions made by this unique wholesaling system.

2. Match each of the following industries with the most appropriate wholesaling intermediary:
   ____ Hardware
   ____ Perishable foods
   ____ Lumber
   ____ Wheat
   ____ Used cars
   a. Drop shipper
   b. Truck wholesaler
   c. Auction house
   d. Full-function merchant wholesaler
   e. Commission merchant

3. Comment on the following statement: "Drop shippers are good candidates for elimination. All they do is process orders; they do not even handle the products they sell."

4. Chow Yei Chang has become a multimillionaire selling Toshiba fax machines and other office equipment. His firm, Chevalier (OA) Holdings Ltd., is Toshiba's sole agent in Hong Kong.[26] Where would you place Chow's company on the spectrum of wholesaling activity? Explain the rationale for your classification.

5. List the following wholesaling intermediaries in ascending order on the basis of operating expense percentages:
   a. Full-function merchant wholesaler
   b. Cash-and-carry wholesaler
   c. Broker
   d. Manufacturer's sales branch
   e. Truck wholesaler

Computer Applications

Inventory turnover, the number of times the dollar value of the firm's average inventory is sold annually, is an important ratio in evaluating the performance of wholesaling intermediaries and their retailer customers. Since trade associations publish average inventory turnover rates for different types of firms, products, and geographic areas, a comparison of the firm's turnover with those of similar organizations provides tangible evidence of the firm's performance. In addition, comparing current turnover rates with those for prior years enables marketers to evaluate changes in performance over time.

Inventory turnover rates are also likely to be reflected in the markups of a wholesaling intermediary. In most instances, wholesaling intermediaries with relatively low turnover rates charge higher average markups than those with higher turnover rates. (Exceptions are instances in which a wholesaler performs few services relative to another wholesaler that might have a similar annual turnover rate but performs a large number of services for its customers.)

To calculate the rate of inventory turnover for a wholesaling intermediary, the firm's average inventory for the year must be known. Average inventory can be determined by adding beginning and ending inventories and dividing by 2. Inventory turnover is then calculated with one of the following formulas depending on whether the firm's inventory is recorded at *retail* (the prices at which the products will be sold to the wholesaler's customers) or *cost* (the prices paid for the products in inventory):

$$\text{Inventory Turnover Rate (at retail)} = \frac{\text{Sales}}{\text{Average Inventory}}$$

$$\text{Inventory Turnover Rate (at cost)} = \frac{\text{Cost of Goods Sold}}{\text{Average Inventory}}$$

The following example illustrates the two methods of determining annual inventory turnover rates. Wholesaler A, with $100,000 in sales and an average inventory of $20,000 at retail, has an annual turnover rate of 5. Wholesaler B, with a cost of goods sold of $120,000 and an average inventory of $30,000 at cost, has an annual turnover rate of 4:

Wholesaler A:

$$\text{Inventory Turnover Rate (at retail)} = \frac{\text{Sales}}{\text{Average Inventory}}$$

$$= \frac{\$100,000}{\$20,000} = 5$$

Wholesaler B:

$$\text{Inventory Turnover Rate (at cost)} = \frac{\text{Cost of Goods Sold}}{\text{Average Inventory}}$$

$$= \frac{\$120,000}{\$30,000} = 4$$

In cases in which average inventory is recorded at cost and only the inventory's selling price is known, the markup percentage must be subtracted from the selling price to calculate the inventory turnover rate on a cost basis. For example, consider the operations of a small wholesaler that carries an average inventory at a cost of $750,000, generates annual sales of $3,850,000, and operates on a 15 percent markup percentage on the selling price. To calculate the firm's inventory turnover rate, the $3,850,000 total sales must be reduced by the 15 percent markup for a total of $3,272,500. The second formula can then be used to determine the firm's turnover rate:

$$\text{Inventory Turnover Rate (at cost)} = \frac{\text{Cost of Goods Sold}}{\text{Average Inventory}}$$

$$= \frac{\$3,272,500}{\$750,000}$$

$$= 4.4$$

Directions: Use menu item 10 titled "Inventory Turnover" to solve each of the following problems.

Problem 1.   A Columbia, South Carolina, wholesaling intermediary carries an average inventory recorded at cost of $6 million. Its total cost of goods sold is $42 million. What is the firm's inventory turnover rate?

Problem 2.   Tucson Mart is a merchandise mart in Tucson, Arizona. Retailers can order displayed merchandise for shipment directly from the factories of the exhibiting firms. But since many of the manufacturers' factories are located in distant cities, Tucson Mart requires its tenants to carry modest inventories. Total inventories at Tucson Mart average $1,200,000 (at retail). The mart's management estimates that about $9,600,000 in merchandise (at retail) is sold out of these inventories each year. What is the annual inventory turnover rate for the inventories carried at Tucson Mart?

Problem 3.   Coleman Brothers, Inc. is a book jobber (wholesaler) in York, Pennsylvania. The firm carries an average inventory at a cost of $1 million. Its annual sales are approximately $7 million. Coleman Brothers operates on a 30 percent markup percentage on selling price. What is the firm's annual turnover rate?

Problem 4.   A wholesaler in Flint, Michigan, had a $10 million cost-based inventory on January 1, but was able to reduce it to $9 million by the end of the year. The firm had a 24 percent markup percentage on selling price. Its yearly sales volume was $50 million. Calculate the year's inventory turnover rate for the Flint wholesaler.

Problem 5.   A Wilmington, Delaware, wholesaler began the year with an inventory of $4 million at retail. During the year, the wholesaler decided to increase its overall inventory position to better serve its customers. The firm ended the year with a $5 million inventory (at retail). Sales were $27 million. What was the wholesaler's inventory turnover rate for the year?

VIDEO CASE   **13**

Northern Produce Co./Mushrooms, Inc.

It is 4:00 a.m. on a Monday morning when Joey Weiss arrives at the Central Produce Market in Los Angeles. With the eye of an experienced buyer, Joey moves quickly from stall to stall, assessing the quality and quantity of fresh fruits and vegetables displayed by many suppliers. The produce he buys in large volume must fill the orders of hundreds of restaurant, hotel, and grocery-store customers that expect delivery of their daily supply of fresh produce within a few hours.

Joey Weiss is president of Northern Produce Co./Mushrooms, Inc. of Los Angeles. As a full-function merchant wholesaler, Northern takes title to the produce it distributes and provides a broad range of services for customers and suppliers. Joey and his brother Barry are third-generation owners of a family business, set up by their father and grandfather in 1938, as a wholesaler of fresh produce. In the 1950s, the Weiss family expanded their business by distributing cultivated mushrooms. During the late 1970s, they moved into specialty produce, buying and selling fresh herbs and such exotic fare as miniature vegetables, edible flowers, and unusual varieties of wild and cultivated mushrooms. Today the company has 85 employees and rings up annual sales of $20 million.

Northern buys produce to service more than 400 customers, including Von's, Safeway, and other major retail food stores; Irvine Ranch specialty markets; Hilton and Sheraton hotels; Royal Viking cruise ships; and some of Southern California's most fashionable restaurants.

To satisfy diverse customer needs, Joey buys from alternative supply sources. Buying decisions take into account fluctuating market conditions and the seasonal availability of many produce items. Joey buys about half of the firm's inventory during his early morning trips to three produce markets in Los Angeles. He frequently revisits the markets at the end of the day to plan his buying strategy for the following day. Fruits and vegetables in plentiful supply at the end of a day means that he will have more bargaining power the next morning.

Joey buys many specialty and off-season items directly from food brokers, shippers, and growers in other countries. To reduce the air freight costs on some imported produce, Joey has imported seeds from Europe and lined up farmers in the United States to grow such crops as edible flowers, white carrots, haricots verts (a French green bean), and radiccio (a red Italian lettuce).

Each produce shipment arriving at Northern's two warehouses is inspected carefully to ensure that the merchandise is not damaged or spoiled. The quality check reduces the company's risk of taking title to produce it may not be able to sell to customers. Fruits and vegetables passing inspection are moved to refrigerated areas and placed on pallets. Warehouse workers continually rotate inventory, a task that helps alleviate confusion about which produce is brought in to be cooled and which is going out to be delivered to customers. Other warehouse workers sort through bulk packages of produce and repack them so that customers receive produce that is uniform in size, color, and degree of ripeness.

The high quality of Northern's produce is especially important to its cruise ship customers, who have proliferated in recent years. Not only must the ships have top-quality produce to satisfy their discriminating clientele, but there is no way for Northern to make good on defective produce when the ship is at sea. Joey is justly proud of the large amount of repeat business he gets from the ships.

Northern maintains a fleet of 25 refrigerated delivery trucks, each one hand-painted with a giant mural of different fruits and vegetables. For many customers, prompt delivery is as important as produce quality and price. A cruiseship customer says, "We need to be able to ensure that the product is delivered to us when the wholesaler says he will deliver to us. A truck stopped on the freeway is of no use to us because the ship must sail on time."

Northern Produce takes pride in its reputation of being a service-oriented wholesaler. Says Joey, "We tell our customers that if they need two or three deliveries a day, they will have them." The company also sends out several delivery trucks to the same geographic area to ensure that produce is delivered to customers when they want it. Produce is shipped by air to customers in faraway places—for example, the Grand Hyatt Hotel in New York and cruise ships in Europe, Peru, Tahiti, Hawaii, and Japan.

Another service Northern provides for customers is financing. Customers are given up to 30 days to pay for produce. If they bought directly from brokers or the market, they would have to pay within a week.

Keeping customers informed is a top priority of Northern's eight full-time salespeople. Because Northern specializes in exotic produce, much of which may be unfamiliar to many customers, salespeople regularly contact customers, explaining new items in detail so that customers understand their features and uses. In addition to servicing existing accounts, salespeople continually monitor the opening of new hotels, restaurants, and specialty food stores in an effort to bring in new business.

Source: Personal interview with Joey Weiss, May 1991; telephone interviews with Joey and Barry Weiss, February 18 and 19, 1988.

Questions

1. Explain why Northern Produce is classified as a full-function merchant wholesaler.

2. How does Northern Produce attempt to reduce the risks it assumes in taking title to goods?

3. What functions does Northern Produce perform in linking producers with customers?

4. Competition among chic restaurants in Los Angeles is fierce. To remain competitive, chefs constantly look for new ideas to attract their upscale clientele. Do you think Northern Produce could make a difference in the success or failure of a restaurant? Why or why not?

5. Which marketing mix elements do you think contributed most to the growth of Northern Produce? Which elements will be most important to the wholesaler's future growth and expansion?

14

Retailing

CHAPTER OBJECTIVES

1. To describe the evolution of retailing.

2. To outline the various elements of retailing strategy.

3. To identify and explain each of the five bases for categorizing retailers.

4. To explain the concept of scrambled merchandising.

On the bulletin board behind Anita Roddick's desk are 12 words that serve as a constant reminder of the challenge ahead: "To be a success in business, be daring, be first, be different." Roddick has lived this motto as she built The Body Shop, the Littlehampton, England-based company she founded in 1976, from a storefront to an international business empire operating in 37 countries, including the United States. Although like many other stores, The Body Shop purveys hair- and skin-care products, its similarity to the competition ends there, for it is Roddick's conviction that success comes not from focusing on profits but from humanizing the company. How does Roddick do this? By linking social activism with day-to-day business, by making employees care about the company through a sense of excitement that transcends profits, by establishing credibility through information, and by nurturing consumer loyalty.

While, on the surface, social activism appears to have little to do with business success, it is a cornerstone of Anita Roddick's marketing strategy. In the United Kingdom, The Body Shop is known as much for its passionate commitment to the environment as it is for the quality of its cosmetics. Not only does the company offer biodegradable products and refillable containers, it also conducts campaigns to stop the burning of the rain forests and to save the whales. Such environmental concerns take center stage at The Body Shop by means of window displays, posters, T-shirts, brochures, and even videotapes. And when need arises, Roddick also puts herself and her staff on the picket line. With about 250 of her employees, she picketed the Brazilian embassy in London to draw attention to the plight of the Yanomami Indians, a Stone Age tribe on the brink of extinction. To spread the message she turned the sides of company trucks into environmental billboards: "The Indians are the custodians of the rain forest. The rain forests are the lungs of the world. If they die, we all die. The Body Shop says immediate urgent action is needed." Few bystanders forget this message as company trucks drive by.

Although Roddick minimizes the public relations value of her environmental activism, she admits being perceived as an environmentalist increases profits — but not for the reasons most people expect. In her view, this strategy succeeds by motivating employees to care about the company and its products.

"I'd never get that kind of motivation if we were just selling shampoos and body lotion. I'd never get that sort of. . . . bonding to customers. [And] it's a way for people to bond to the company. They're doing what I'm doing. They're learning. Three years ago I didn't know anything about the rain forest. Five years ago I didn't know anything about the ozone layer. It's a process of learning to be a global citizen. And what it produces is a sense of passion you simply won't find in a Bloomingdale's department store."

Whether Roddick is talking about the rain forest or product ingredients, she believes that the more customers and employees know, the better for business. Thus, a crucial part of her marketing strategy is education. Through brochures, product packaging, in-store displays and videos, customers learn where products come from and how they are used. Customers also learn about Roddick's trips to Third World countries to find natural ingredients and to talk to natives about their methods of skin and hair care. The result is intensely loyal customers who believe that Body Shop products are different from anything they will find elsewhere.

Roddick has taken advantage of consumer loyalty to spread the reputation of her business. She has no advertising budget. Amazingly, the act of one person telling another has fueled the company's phenomenal growth. And although it operates in one of the most marketing-intense industries in the world, The Body Shop has no marketing department!

With Princess Diana and Sting among its loyal customers, and with the possibility of becoming a $1 billion company by 1995, the electricity and passion that are corporate mainstays at The Body Shop are strong. All of this is no small achievement for Anita Roddick — a woman who talks in terms of "soaring spirits," a "sense of fun," and doing business "in an honorable way."[1]

Photo source: © Dudley Reed/Onyx.

Chapter Overview

The nation's 2 million retail outlets serve as contact points between channel members and the ultimate consumer. In a very real sense, retailers are the distribution channel for most consumers, since the typical shopper has little contact with manufacturers and virtually none with wholesaling intermediaries. Retailers determine location, store hours, quality of salespeople, store layout, product selection, and return policies—which are often more important than the physical item in developing consumers' images. Consider the case of The Body Shop in the opening story. The products produced by the manufacturers are less important than Anita Roddick's ways of providing them. Both large and small retailers perform the major channel activities: creating time, place, and ownership utilities.

Retailers are both customers and marketers in the channel. They market products to ultimate consumers and at the same time are customers of wholesalers and manufacturers. Because of their critical location in the channel, retailers often perform an important feedback role: They obtain information from customers and transmit it to manufacturers and other channel members.

Retailing may be defined as all of the activities involved in the sale of goods and services to the ultimate consumer. Although the bulk of all retail sales occurs in retail stores, the definition of retailing also includes several forms of non-store retailing, which involves such activities as telephone and mail-order sales, vending machine sales, and direct selling.

retailing
All activities involved in the sale of goods and services to the ultimate customer.

Evolution of Retailing

Early retailing can be traced to the establishment of trading posts such as the Hudson Bay Company and to pack peddlers who carried their wares to outlying settlements. The first type of retail institution in the United States was the general store, which stocked merchandise to meet the needs of a small community or rural area. Here customers could buy clothing, groceries, feed, seed, farm equipment, drugs, spectacles, and candy. General stores flourished for many years, but the basic needs that had created them also doomed them to a limited existence. Since storekeepers attempted to satisfy customers' needs for all types of goods, they carried a small assortment of each item. As communities grew, new stores opened; these concentrated on specific product lines, such as drugs, dry goods, groceries, and hardware. The general stores could not compete, and their owners either converted them into more limited-line stores or closed them. Most of the few hundred general stores still operating today serve customers in rural areas.

The development of retailing illustrates the marketing concept in operation. Innovations in retail institutions have emerged to satisfy changing consumer wants and needs. Supermarkets appeared in the early 1930s in response to consumers' desire for lower prices. The 1950's innovation of discount department stores in suburban locations offered consumers convenient parking and lower prices in exchange for reduced services. The emergence of convenience food stores in the 1960s satisfied consumer demand for fast service, convenient location, and expanded hours of operation. The development of off-price retailers in the 1980s reflected consumer demand for brand-name merchandise at price levels considerably lower than those of traditional retailers. Similarly, the 1990s are seeing a continuation of retailing innovations. In addition, the 1990s are seeing the expansion of some retailers, like the discount chain Wal-Mart, and the decline of others, like department stores. Let's look at the concept behind this evolution.

Blockbuster Video superstores make shopping convenient by remaining open from 10 a.m. to midnight seven days a week. Blockbuster's focus on developing service policies and programs that give customers what they want is key to its success as the world's leading video retailer. Other store services include a 24-hour Quik Drop depository, a selection of more than 10,000 videos, computerized check-in and check-out, a Youth Restricted Viewing Program, and Kids' Clubhouses, where children can play and watch videos while their parents shop.

Source: Courtesy of Blockbuster Entertainment Corporation.

Wheel of Retailing

wheel of retailing
Hypothesis stating that new types of retailers gain a competitive foothold by offering lower prices through reduction or elimination of services. Once established, they add more services, gradually raise their prices, and then become vulnerable to the emergence of a new, low-price retailer with minimum services.

The **wheel of retailing** is an attempt to explain the patterns of change in retailing. According to this hypothesis, new types of retailers gain a competitive foothold by offering their customers lower prices through the reduction or elimination of services. Once established, however, they add more services, and their prices gradually rise. They then become vulnerable to a new, low-price retailer that enters with minimum services—and so the wheel turns.

Most of the major developments in retailing appear to fit the wheel pattern. Early department stores, chain stores, supermarkets, discount stores, hypermarkets, and catalog retailers emphasized limited service and low prices. For most of these retailers, price levels gradually increased as services were added. There have been some exceptions. Suburban shopping centers, convenience food stores, and vending machines were not built around low-price appeals. However, the wheel pattern has been evident sufficiently in the past to enable it to serve as a general indicator of future retailing developments.

Retailing Strategy

Like manufacturers and wholesalers, retailers develop marketing strategies based on overall organizational goals and strategic plans. They monitor environmental factors and assess organizational strengths and weaknesses to ascertain marketing opportunities and constraints. Retailers' marketing decisions center on the two fundamental steps of (1) analyzing, evaluating, and selecting a target market and (2) developing a marketing mix designed to profitably satisfy the chosen market. Components of retailing strategy, presented in Figure 14.1,

Figure 14.1   Components of Retailing Strategy

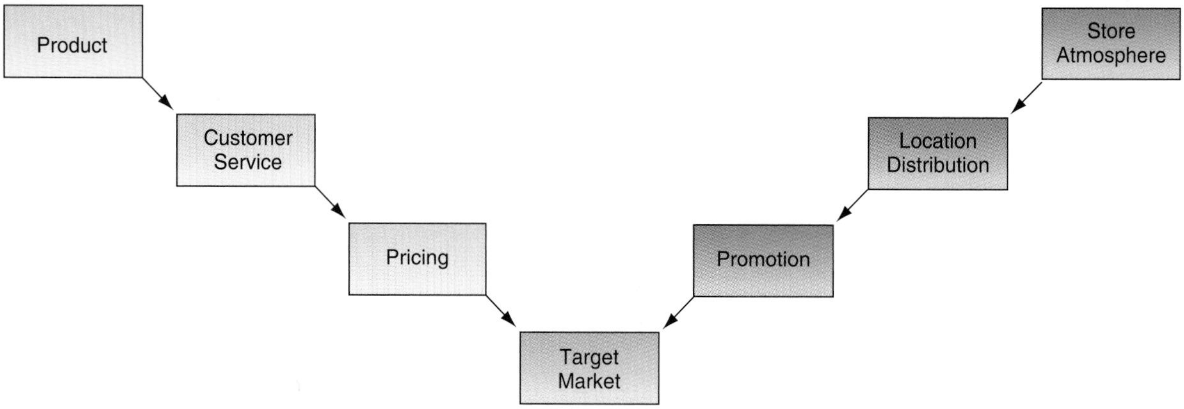

retail image
Consumers' perception of the store and the shopping experience it provides.

include product, customer service, pricing, target market, promotion, location/distribution, and store atmosphere. The combination of these elements projects the **retail image**—the consumer's perception of the store and the shopping experience it provides. Retail image communicates to consumers whether the store is, say, economical, prestigious, conservative, or contemporary. All components of retailing strategy must work together to create the desired image—that is, an image that appeals to the target market.

Target Market

Retailers must start by selecting a market. Factors to take into account are its size and profit potential and the level of competition. In recent years, for example, department stores have realized the growth potential in the petite clothing market. Compared to a 35 percent gain in the overall women's apparel market during a recent seven-year period, sales of petite lines grew 108 percent. To attract the petite shopper, most stores have begun buying clothing cut specially for the shorter figure and setting aside departments to present these designs. No longer faced with the necessity of buying and altering clothing designed for taller women, petites have responded by purchasing nearly three times as much as their non-petite counterparts.[2]

Retailers segment markets according to demographic, geographic, and psychographic bases. Kmart, for example, targets middle-income families who earn between $15,000 and $60,000 a year. Fiesta Mart, Inc., a Houston grocery store chain, targets a multicultural clientele—Southeast Asians, Hispanics, Chinese, Koreans, Filipinos, Indians, and immigrants of other nationalities. Capitalizing on the current baby boom, many retailers are opening stores targeted specifically at children. The Gap, Inc., has opened GapKids apparel shops to serve children age 2 to 12, and Waldenbooks, Inc., is targeting the for-kids-only segment through its new chain of Waldenkids bookstores.

One of the most dominant trends in retailing is that of increased market segmentation. Retailers that traditionally sought to serve the mass market have shifted their strategy to target more narrowly defined segments. General merchandisers such as F.W. Woolworth are placing more emphasis on specialty store formats because they provide greater sales per square foot and thus higher profit margins and returns on investment than do general merchandise stores. Woolworth's shoe business, for example, began with Kinney shoe stores, which sell a full range of casual and dress shoes, boots, and accessories for men, women, and children. Later, Kinney opened its first Foot Locker athletic shoe store to cater to Americans' growing interest in physical fitness. In recent years, Kinney has further segmented its shoe business by opening Lady Foot Locker and Kids Foot Locker stores.

After identifying a target market, retailers position themselves among competitors by developing a marketing plan consisting of a blend of the retailing strategy components. These strategies are outlined below.

Product Strategy

Product strategy involves making decisions about what type of merchandise the retailer will offer that target customers want to buy. In developing a product mix, the retailer must decide on general product categories, product lines, specific products within lines, and the depth and width of assortment. Here are several examples:

□ Sears groups its merchandise into seven so-called "power formats": women's apparel, appliances and electronics, home improvement, children's clothes, automotive, men's fashions, and furniture. Each format is sold in a setting resembling a specialty shop, and some departments are actually freestanding stores. Sears Brand Central, for example, sells appliances and electronics in an atmosphere that looks like an electronics discounter.

□ At Home Depot, retailers maintain their product focus by selling only do-it-yourself supplies. Rather than displaying pantyhose or candybars at the front registers, they concentrate on home-improvement products related to their plumbing and electrical supplies, hardware, gardening equipment and supplies, lumber, cabinetry, paint, wallcoverings, floor and ceiling tiles, insulation, replacement doors and windows, and roofing supplies.

□ JC Penney narrowed its product mix when it decided to concentrate on apparel and home furnishings and do away with home electronics, appliances, sporting goods, and photography equipment.

□ To differentiate itself from the glut of general entertainment video stores on the market, Video Vault in Alexandria, Virginia, specializes in hard-to-find cult movie classics and advertises itself as having the "guaranteed worst movies in town."[3]

In deciding which products to include in the merchandise assortment, retailers must consider the competitive environment. Sales of many department stores have eroded in recent years due to increased competition from specialty and discount stores. To improve their profitability, many department stores have narrowed their traditionally broad product lines by eliminating high-overhead, low-profit categories such as toys, appliances, sporting goods, and furniture. Department stores are now focusing on expanding their assortment of women's clothing, men's and women's sportswear, jewelry, cosmetics, and linens product categories that bring higher returns on investment.[4]

Understanding target customers' wants and needs is vital to developing a successful product strategy. By conducting marketing research, retailers can determine what their customers expect and adjust their product offerings accordingly. Marketing research is a crucial part of JC Penney's retail marketing strategy. Working through its own private broadcast network, Penney executives

The product strategy of Pier 1 Imports is to offer targeted customers with household incomes of $50,000 unique, handmade merchandise from 44 countries around the world. The company's wide assortment of decorative home furnishings, specialty gifts, and casual clothing differentiates it from other retailers. Pier 1 uses a variety of marketing research tools, including demographic and psychographic studies, focus groups, and customer advisory groups to tailor its merchandise to customer needs and wants. Of the 4,500 products Pier 1 stores carry, about 40 percent are new each year.

Source: Courtesy of Pier 1 Imports.

screen merchandise samples in front of focus groups in 16 cities for immediate consumer response. After a recent buying trip to the Far East, men's sportswear buyers used this system to learn consumer response in advance of making costly commitments to suppliers.[5]

Marketing research was also crucial to the development of Staples, a Connecticut-based office supply warehouse that buys directly from manufacturers and passes substantial savings on to business customers and ultimately consumers. Before opening his first store, company founder Tom Sternberg surveyed 100 small businesses to learn how much they were spending on office supplies and how much they could save through his proposed Staples discount plan. Survey results told Sternberg that small businesses were not spending enough on supplies to care about saving money. Skeptical about the accuracy of these responses, Sternberg asked to examine the respondents' office supply invoices and found that the companies were spending about twice as much as they estimated. This information told Sternberg that he had a viable retailing idea, but that to make it work, he had to educate customers about their current costs and potential savings.[6]

Marketing research sometimes encourages retailers to try something new. Despite the fact that McDonald's does not sell frankfurters in the United States, the 700 outlets in Japan offer franks on their menus. Marketing research told management that the trend-conscious Japanese "are very taken with hot dogs."[7]

Customer Service Strategy

Retailers may provide shoppers with a variety of customer services. Examples are gift wrapping, alterations, return privileges, bridal registries, consultants, interior designers, merchandise delivery and installation—and, recently, electronic shopping via gift-ordering machines in airports. In developing a customer service strategy, the retailer must determine which services to offer and whether

A customer service innovation at Fred Meyer, Inc., stores is Freddy's Playland, an enclosed and supervised babysitting area for the children of parents shopping in the huge, one-stop stores that range in size up to 200,000 square feet and offer 225,000 food and other products such as apparel, shoes, fine jewelry, home electronics, housewares, sporting goods, and home improvements. Freddy's Playland enables parents to shop at their leisure knowing their children are safe with CPR-trained employees. When Fred Bear, the retailer's ambassador of goodwill, is in a store, he always stops by to visit.

Source: Courtesy of Fred Meyer, Inc.

to charge customers for them. Those decisions are influenced by several factors: store size, type, and location; merchandise assortment; level of service offered by competitors; customer expectations; and financial resources.

The basic objective of all customer services is to attract and retain target customers, thus increasing store sales, profits, and market share. Some services, such as restrooms, lounges, complimentary coffee, and drinking fountains, are designed for shoppers' comfort. Quicksilver, a children's clothing store, has set aside a store area for parents that has a rocking chair, bottle warmer, and diaper kits.

Other examples of customer service are abundant. Vision-care giants Pearle and Lenscrafters provide one-hour eyeglass service. Direct Tire Sales, a Watertown, Massachusetts, tire, brake, and alignment shop, also gives one-hour service. Customers who cannot wait have the option of borrowing one of the company's seven loaner cars for the day. To make shopping easier, Florida's Palm Beach Milk Co., installed a computer that accepts customer orders as late as 10:00 p.m. for delivery by 7:00 a.m. the next morning. And for those customers who have run out of the ingredients for a full breakfast, the company also delivers such nondairy products as bacon, eggs, juice, and bread.[8]

A customer service strategy can also be used to build demand for a line of merchandise. In an attempt to upgrade its image from a no-frills discount store to a retailer of fashionable merchandise, K Mart has hired food and entertainment expert Martha Stewart to promote its new kitchen, bed, bath, and home decorating merchandise available in its home departments. As a shoppers' consultant, Stewart makes personal appearances in K Mart stores nationwide.[9]

Recognizing the importance of customer service as a competitive tool, some retailers have established companywide customer-service programs. Wal-Mart and Nordstrom are known for their high levels of customer service. When customers enter Wal-Mart, they are greeted by smiling personnel who give them a shopping cart. Credit-card purchases are verified in less than four seconds through credit-card magnetic machines that eliminate the need for any other credit check. Nordstrom's customers receive service far beyond that offered by other department stores as salespeople make phone calls in search of hard-to-find merchandise, make personal deliveries (a saleswoman once delivered hose to a businesswoman in time for an important meeting), and write notes of thanks. Stew Leonard's, a supermarket in Norwalk, Connecticut, has its customer-service motto on a boulder at the store's front entrance. "Rule 1," says the motto, "The customer is always right. Rule 2: When the customer is wrong, reread rule 1." To make sure his 700-person staff understands the importance of customer service, Leonard enrolls all in Dale Carnegie courses.[10]

Although the concept of customer service is new to Poland, it is quickly becoming a valued commodity. With the privatization of the Polish economy has come the recognition that good service draws customers. Pewex, a growing department store chain, improved retail service by reducing the amount of time customers stand in line. While customers in traditional Polish stores are forced to queue up for shopping baskets and for every item they want to buy, Pewex offers the advantage of Western-style self-service that eliminates all but one check-out line.[11]

Pricing Strategy

Prices play a major role in the consumer's perception of the retailer. Consumers realize, for example, that Bijan, the exclusive men's clothier on Rodeo Drive and Fifth Avenue, caters to the ultra-rich with a selection of $250 ties, $800 shirts, and $5,000 off-the-rack suits. They also know that when they walk into Step Ahead, a chain of 14 discount retailers in West Sacramento, California, they will find a selection of products ranging from hoze nozzles to brewer's yeast, all for under 98 cents. Wal-Mart has gained a reputation for its direct-from-the-factory prices, often cheaper than the wholesale prices local merchants pay.[12] And The Gap name has become synonymous with casual contemporary clothing, such as the bike shorts advertised in Figure 14.2, at affordable prices.

Prices reflect the retailer's price-setting objectives and policies described in Chapters 19 and 20. Because prices are based on the cost of merchandise, efficient and timely buying is an essential part of the retailer's pricing strategy. Realizing this, Dillard's, the Little Rock, Arkansas-based department store chain, relies on sophisticated computer technology to electronically reorder goods based on the previous week's sales. This so-called Quick Response program has cut turnaround time from a month to 12 days and increased sales on electronically reordered items by 50 percent.[13]

As the channel member directly responsible for the prices consumers pay, retailers can use two methods for setting and adjusting prices: markups and markdowns.

markup
Amount added to the cost of an item to determine its selling price.

Markups.   The amount the retailer adds to the product's cost to determine the selling price is the **markup.** The amount of the markup typically results from two factors:

1. The services performed by the retailer. (Other things being equal, the greater the number of services provided for customers, the larger is the markup required for covering their cost.)

2. The inventory turnover rate. (Other things being equal, the greater the turnover rate, the smaller is the markup required for covering the retailer's costs and generating a profit.)

Markups are important factors in the retailer's image among its present and potential customers. In addition, they affect the retailer's ability to attract shop-

Figure 14.2

The Role of Pricing in the Consumer's Perception of the Retailer

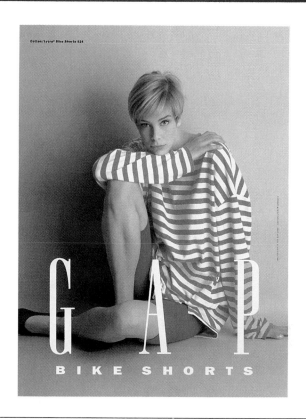

Source: Courtesy of Gap.

pers. Excessive markups may result in the loss of customers; inadequate markups may not generate sufficient funds to cover the cost of operations and return a profit.

Markups typically are stated as a percentage of either the product's selling price or its cost. The formulas for calculating markups follow:

$$\text{Markup Percentage on Selling Price} = \frac{\text{Amount Added to Cost (Markup)}}{\text{Selling Price}}.$$

$$\text{Markup Percentage on Cost} = \frac{\text{Amount Added to Cost (Markup)}}{\text{Cost}}.$$

Consider a product with an invoice cost of $.60 and a selling price of $1.00. The total markup (selling price less cost) is $.40. The two markup percentages are calculated as follows:

$$\text{Markup Percentage on Selling Price} = \frac{\$.40}{\$1.00} = 40\%.$$

$$\text{Markup Percentage on Cost} = \frac{\$.40}{\$.60} = 66.7\%.$$

To determine the selling price when only the cost and markup percentage on selling price are known, the following formula is used:

$$\text{Price} = \frac{\text{Cost in Dollars}}{100\% - \text{Markup Percentage on Selling Price}}.$$

In the previous example, the correct selling price of $1.00 could be determined as follows:

$$\text{Price} = \frac{\$.60}{100\% - 40\%} = \frac{\$.60}{60\%} = \$1.00.$$

Similarly, the markup percentage can be converted from one basis (selling price or cost) to the other using the following formulas:

$$\frac{\text{Markup Percentage}}{\text{on Selling Price}} = \frac{\text{Markup Percentage on Cost}}{100\% + \text{Markup Percentage on Cost}}.$$

$$\frac{\text{Markup Percentage}}{\text{on Cost}} = \frac{\text{Markup Percentage on Selling Price}}{100\% - \text{Markup Percentage on Selling Price}}.$$

Again using the data from the previous example, the following conversions can be made:

$$\frac{\text{Markup Percentage}}{\text{on Selling Price}} = \frac{66.7\%}{100\% + 66.7\%} = \frac{66.7\%}{166.7\%} = 40\%.$$

$$\frac{\text{Markup Percentage}}{\text{on Cost}} = \frac{40\%}{100\% - 40\%} = \frac{40\%}{60\%} = 66.7\%.$$

Markups are based partly on the marketer's judgment regarding the amounts consumers will be willing to pay for a given product. But when buyers refuse to pay the price or when improved products or fashion changes render current merchandise less saleable, the marketer must seriously consider reducing the product's price in the form of a markdown.

Markdowns. The amount by which the retailer reduces the original selling price of a product is the **markdown.** The markdown percentage—the discount amount typically advertised for the "sale" item—can be computed as follows:

markdown

Amount by which the retailer reduces the original selling price of an item.

$$\text{Markdown Percentage} = \frac{\text{Dollar Amount of Markdown}}{\text{"Sale" (New) Price}}.$$

Returning to the above example, suppose no one has been willing to pay $1.00 for the item. The marketer has therefore decided to reduce the selling price to 79 cents. Advertisements for the special "sale" item might emphasize that the product has been marked down 27 percent:

$$\text{Markdown Percentage} = \frac{\$.21}{\$.79} = 26.6\%.$$

Markdowns are sometimes used for evaluative purposes. For example, store managers or buyers in a large department store may be evaluated partly on the basis of the average markdown percentage on the product lines for which they are responsible.

Location/Distribution Strategy

Real estate professionals often point out that location may be the determining factor in the success or failure of a retail business. Retailers may choose to locate at an isolated site, in a central business district, or in a planned shopping center. The location decision depends on many factors, including the type of merchandise sold, the retailer's financial resources, characteristics of the target market, and site availability.

Extending the location of its frozen yogurt stores beyond traditional sites in shopping centers and metropolitan areas is an important part of TCBY's growth strategy. The company is introducing a double drive-through store, shown here, in high-traffic areas and smaller population-based markets. TCBY also developed a soft-serve pushcart to distribute cups and cones in satellite locations such as airports, toll road plazas, and sports arenas.

Source: Courtesy of TCBY Enterprises, Inc.

When Galeries Lafayette, France's leading department store chain, decided to enter the U.S. market, it chose Fifth Avenue and 57th Street, one of New York City's most exclusive corners, as its location. Its reason, according to chairman Georges Meyer, is the company's decision to target luxury shoppers. Instead of locating stores in places compatible with its merchandise, Long Drug Stores, a chain of 234 retail drug stores in six western states, adapts to its locations. Its store near a Walnut Creek, California, retirement community stocks few diapers and baby-food products, concentrating instead on aspirins, laxatives, and other products used by senior citizens. In contrast, its store located in an upper-income family community in the same town, has plenty of diapers and stocks stereos, cameras, and other expensive electronic equipment.[14]

Planned Shopping Centers.

planned shopping center
Group of retail stores planned, coordinated, and marketed as a unit to shoppers in a geographic trade area.

The pronounced shift of retail trade away from the traditional downtown retailing districts and toward suburban shopping centers has been underway since 1950. A **planned shopping center** is a group of retail stores planned, coordinated, and marketed as a unit to shoppers in their geographical trade areas. These centers have followed population shifts to the suburbs with the intent of avoiding many of the problems associated with shopping in downtown business districts. They provide a convenient location for shoppers as well as free parking facilities based on the number and types of stores. Shopping is facilitated by uniform hours of operation and evening and weekend shopping hours.

Types of Shopping Centers.

There are three main types of planned shopping centers. The smallest is the *neighborhood shopping center,* which most often is composed of a supermarket and a group of smaller stores such as a drugstore, a laundry and dry cleaner, a small-appliance store, and perhaps a beauty shop and barber shop. These centers provide convenient shopping for perhaps 5,000 to 50,000 shoppers who live within a few minutes' commuting time. They typically contain 5 to 15 stores, and the product mix is usually confined to convenience goods and some shopping goods.

Community shopping centers serve 20,000 to 100,000 persons in a trade area extending a few miles. These centers are likely to contain from 10 to 30 retail stores and a branch of a local department store or a large variety store as the primary tenant. In addition to the stores found in a neighborhood center, the community center is likely to have more stores featuring shopping goods, some professional offices, and a branch bank.

The *regional shopping center* is a large shopping district of at least 400,000 square feet of shopping space. It is usually built around one or more major department stores and includes as many as 200 smaller stores. In order to be successful, regional centers must be located in areas in which at least 250,000 people reside within 30 minutes' driving time. Regional centers provide a wide assortment of convenience, shopping, and specialty goods, plus many professional and personal service facilities.

Planned shopping centers generate about $725 billion in annual sales, or more than 55 percent of total nonautomotive U.S. retail sales.[15] The growth of planned shopping centers has slowed in recent years, because the most lucrative locations are already occupied and the market is becoming saturated in many areas. As a result, several new shopping center strategies are being pursued. A new regional mall approach, for example, combines shopping with entertainment. Cincinnati's Forest Fair mall includes an 18-hole miniature golf course, baseball batting range, basketball shooting area, and carousel. Its live entertainment area seats 1,600. At Bloomington, Minnesota's Mall of America, the largest regional mall in the United States (the mall covers 78 acres and includes four department stores, 400 specialty shops, and 12,000 parking spaces), an indoor theme park is inspired by the cartoon dog Snoopy. The mall has hotels, miniature golf courses, movie theaters, and about 100 nightclubs and restaurants.[16]

With business slowing, malls are also trying to attract customers through a wider range of customer services. At the Galleria at Tysons II in McLean, Virginia, 16 purple-clad concierges help customers locate hard-to-find gifts and order theater tickets. At the Del Amo Fashion Center in Torrance, California, 14 interactive electronic video directories help lost customers find stores. In addition, many malls offer valet parking, parking lot shuttle buses, child care, and diaper-changing rooms. Realizing that parents will spend more time in stores if their school-aged children are entertained, American Cartoon Theaters now operates three Kids Only Cartoon Theaters in midwestern malls and is rapidly expanding.[17]

Another trend gaining popularity is the *specialty store shopping center*. Unlike community or regional centers, specialty store centers are not anchored by a department store; they consist only of specialty shops and restaurants and target the upscale consumer. The Galleria in Edina, Minnesota, is a specialty-store shopping center consisting of fashion retailers, home furnishings stores, jewelers, gift shops, and restaurants. A newspaper called Galleria Globe, shown in Figure 14.3, is distributed to targeted upscale consumers in the Minneapolis–St. Paul area to inform them of the stores' merchandise and the availability of international products. Outlet malls, selling brand-name merchandise at discount prices, are also gaining in popularity as they target upscale bargain hunters. For example, shoppers at Liberty Village in Flemington, New Jersey, can find their favorite Anne Klein outfits at discount prices.[18]

Other Distribution Decisions.   Retailers also face a variety of other distribution decisions, many of which ensure that adequate quantities of stock are available when consumers want to buy. Realizing the importance of an effective

Figure 14.3

Promoting Retailers in a Specialty Store Shopping Center

Source: Courtesy of Galleria Merchants Association.

inventory system, retailers such as Wal-Mart, Dillard's, and Dayton Hudson have adopted a "quick response" strategy, similar to the "just-in-time" inventory system developed by the Japanese. QR, as the system is called, uses the scanner tracking capabilities of store computers to monitor sales and arrange for speedy store deliveries from manufacturers. The $180 million cookie chain Mrs. Fields relies on this type of computer technology to tell store managers how many cookies to bake to meet customer demand.[19]

Promotional Strategy

The objective of the retailer's promotional strategy is to work together with the other components of the retailing mix in establishing the store image. Retailers meet this goal by designing advertisements, staging special events, and developing sales promotions aimed at the target market.

Recent promotional strategies include the following:

☐ Chief Auto Parts Inc. sells "environmentally safe and biodegradable" windshield washer fluid and antifreeze products in response to customer concern about the environment.

☐ Catalog retailer Esprit de Corp prints its catalogs on recycled paper, urging consumers, "Be good to our Earth."

☐ To attract a new upscale buyer, recent JC Penney magazine ads have focused on "The Spirit of the American Woman" with black-and-white photos suggestive of those used by more exclusive retailers.

The value of innovative promotional strategies is becoming clear to some retailers in Eastern Europe. Poland's Pewex department store chain advertises heavily on television. It promotes a line of toys, for example, by sponsoring the He-Man cartoon series. It has also backed 60 performances in Poland of the

Disney-character ice show and has offered a trip to Disney World to a child attending each show. As a result of these and other strategies, sales at Pewex climbed 68 percent in a recent year.[20]

Through promotional efforts, retailers communicate information about their stores—their locations, merchandise, store hours, and prices. Also, retailers selling merchandise that changes frequently due to fashion trends can effectively use advertising to promote current styles. In addition, retailers can use the promotional component to persuade and motivate. Waldenbooks, the national bookstore chain with about 1,300 locations, has begun a "Preferred Readers" program that rewards consumer loyalty with a 10 percent discount on nearly every item. Store executives hope this promotion will motivate customers to continue shopping at Waldenbooks. Jordan Marsh, New England's largest department store chain, hopes to persuade customers that it offers services not found in other department stores through a new advertising campaign that asks the question, "Why Jordan Marsh?" and then explains the store's unique features. For example, in a Carole Little sportswear ad, the store becomes a fashion advisor as it demonstrates how to mix and match eight apparel items to make twenty-five different outfits.[21]

Retail salespeople are an important promotional tool in communicating store image and persuading shoppers to buy. To serve as a source of information, they must be knowledgeable about such store policies and procedures as credit, discounts, special sales, delivery, layaways, and returns. To increase store sales, they must be able to persuade customers that what they are selling is what the customers need. To this end, salespeople should be trained to use *selling up* and *suggestion selling* techniques.

selling up
Retail sales technique of convincing the customer to buy a higher priced item than he or she originally intended.

Selling up means convincing the customer to buy a higher-priced item than he or she originally intended. For example, an automobile salesperson might convince a customer to buy a more expensive model than the person originally considered. It is important that the practice of selling up always be used within the constraints of the customer's real needs. If the salesperson sells the customer something that he or she really does not need, the potential for repeat sales by that seller will be substantially diminished.

suggestion selling
Form of retail selling that attempts to broaden the customer's original purchase with related items, special promotions, and holiday or seasonal merchandise.

Suggestion selling seeks to broaden the customer's original purchase with related items, special promotions, or holiday and seasonal merchandise. Here, too, the idea is to help the customer recognize true needs rather than to sell him or her unwanted merchandise. Suggestion selling is one of the best methods of increasing retail sales and should be practiced by all sales personnel.

Customers' attitudes toward a retailer are greatly influenced by the impression made by sales personnel. Increasing customer complaints about unfriendly, inattentive, and unknowledgeable salespeople have prompted many retailers to pay more attention to training and motivating salespeople.

At Tower Records, the compact disc, record, and tape chain, salespeople are chosen partially on the basis of their enthusiasm for and knowledge of music. At Tres Mariposas, an El Paso, Texas, fashion specialty shop, salespeople are expected to be courteous and knowledgeable in dealing with upscale consumers shopping for sportswear, furs, and fashion jewelry. After greeting customers with casual conversation and an offer of refreshments, they lead them to the merchandise floor. The store prides itself on its staff's ability to answer questions about every item in the store. Some retailers, like Nordstrom and Brooks Brothers, motivate employees by paying sales commissions.[22]

Store Atmospherics

atmospherics
Combination of physical store characteristics and amenities provided by the retailer that contributes to the retail image.

While store location, merchandise selection, customer service, pricing, and promotional activities all contribute to a store's overall image, its personality is also projected by **atmospherics**—the physical characteristics and amenities that

Sales counselors at Circuit City, a superstore retailer of consumer electronics and major appliances, receive ongoing training to improve their product knowledge and selling techniques. Circuit City attributes its success as the leader in a highly competitive industry characterized by rapidly changing technology to its skilled salesforce that delivers on the company's advertising theme, "Circuit City—Where Service Is State of the Art."

Source: © Jeff Zaruba for Circuit City.

attract customers and satisfy their shopping needs. Atmospherics include both a store's exterior and interior.

A store's exterior, which includes architectural design, window displays, signs, and entryways, helps identify the retailer and attract its target market. The Saks Fifth Avenue script logo on storefronts and McDonald's golden arches are exterior elements that readily identify these retailers. Bookstores and fashion retailers often attempt to draw customers inside stores by creating exciting window displays.

The interior of a store should complement the retailer's image, be responsive to customers' interests, and, most important, induce the shopper to buy. Interior elements include store layout, merchandise presentation, lighting, color, sounds, scents, and cleanliness. With live plants, waterfall, stocked trout pond, and special sound effects, the interior of L. L. Bean's store in Freeport, Maine, creates an outdoor environment that appeals to its clientele and matches the type of merchandise it sells—outdoor sports clothing and accessories. Every detail inside the Polo/Ralph Lauren Store on New York's Madison Avenue, enhances the store's image of gentility, high style, and "the good life." In keeping with the refined tastes of its clientele, the store plays jazz, Vivaldi, and Frank Sinatra recordings.[23] T. J. Cinnamons, a Kansas City–based gourmet bakery chain specializing in cinnamon buns, locates its bakeries close to escalators in shopping malls and installs glass roofs so that prospective customers can see and smell the fresh baked goods as they travel between floors.[24]

When Tandy Corp. opened The Edge in Electronics, a new consumer electronics chain that targets women, it used atmospherics to help women feel comfortable in the stores. Mahogany paneling, curved glass cases, and marble tiling make the atmosphere reminiscent of a fine jewelry store. There is little evidence of the hardware-heavy environment found in Tandy's other electronics chain, Radio Shack.[25]

Retailers often use atmospherics to change a store's image perhaps to attract a new group of buyers. Many auto parts, hardware, and consumer electronics stores are shedding their traditional for-men-only image by redesigning interiors and adding amenities that appeal to the growing number of female buyers. To boost its womens' clothing sales, Sears is overhauling its image through the use of unified color motifs with names like Breakaway Brights and Indian Summer, reinforced by theme posters and special display props. To make sure every detail is right, store personnel receive special instructions on how to dress the mannequins that appear near the theme posters. With its reputation based on DieHard batteries and Kenmore washers, Sears is waging an uphill battle to change its image. The corporate goal is to use atmospherics, along with trendier merchandise, to make women as comfortable wearing Sears cocktail dresses as they are buying Kenmore dishwashers.[26]

Sometimes retailers design new store environments to better serve their target markets. When executives at Royal Farms, a mid-Atlantic convenience store chain, saw the convenience store industry evolving from 7-Eleven look-alikes to chains whose survival depended on a distinct personality, they re-designed their stores so that the deli and fried chicken sections were among the first things customers saw when they entered the store. The simple act of moving the fried chicken section from the back room to the front of the store had a positive impact on sales as customers observed the fresh preparation of products. Placing the deli section nearby encouraged people to buy salads and other deli products to make a full meal.[27]

Shoppers' behavior has fueled the retailing trend of creating environments that entertain and has elevated the importance of atmospherics in retail im-age-making. Recent studies indicate that most people shop for reasons other than purchasing needed items. According to one marketing research survey of 34,000 mall shoppers nationwide, only 25 percent of the respondents said they came to buy a specific item. Common reasons given for shopping were to dispel boredom, alleviate loneliness, relieve depression, escape the routine of daily life, and fulfill fantasies. Challenged to satisfy these broad-based needs and desires, retailers increasingly are turning to atmospherics.[28] Consider the atmosphere of the Disney stores, which transports customers into a little corner of the Magic Kingdom. At the back of the store, hundreds of stuffed Mickeys and Minnies, Donalds and Dumbos invite the attention of small hands as they sit below a large video screen showing Disney animated movies. Theatrical lighting and the happy sounds of Disney music create an atmosphere of fantasy for both children and adults.[29]

Types of Retailers

Since new types of retail operations continue to evolve in response to changing consumer demands, no universal classification has been devised. The following bases can be used in categorizing them: (1) shopping effort expended by cus-tomers, (2) services provided to customers, (3) product lines, (4) location of retail transactions, and (5) form of ownership.

Any retailing operation can be classified according to each of the five bases. A 7-Eleven food store may be classified as a convenience store (category 1), self-service (category 2), relatively broad product line (category 3), store-type retailer (category 4), and a member of a corporate chain (category 5).

Classification by Shopping Effort

In Chapter 9, consumer goods were classified as convenience goods, shopping goods, or specialty goods based on consumer purchase patterns in securing a particular good or service. This three-way classification system can be extended to retailers by considering the reasons consumers shop at particular retail outlets. The result is a classification scheme in which retail stores are categorized as convenience, shopping, or specialty retailers.[30] This determination has a significant influence on the marketing strategies a retailer selects.

Convenience retailers focus on accessible locations, long store hours, rapid checkout service, and adequate parking facilities. Local food stores, gasoline stations, and some barber shops may be included in this category.

Shopping stores typically include furniture stores, appliance retailers, clothing outlets, and sporting goods stores. Consumers usually compare prices, assortments, and quality levels of competing outlets before making purchase decisions. Consequently, managers of shopping stores attempt to differentiate their outlets through advertising, window displays, in-store layouts, well-trained knowledgeable salespeople, and appropriate merchandise assortments.

Specialty retailers provide a combination of product lines, services, or reputation that attempts to convince consumers to expend considerable effort to shop at their stores. Nordstrom, Neiman-Marcus, Lord & Taylor, and Saks Fifth Avenue have accomplished this task to a sufficient degree to be categorized as specialty retailers.

Classification by Services Provided

Some retailers seek to develop an advantage by creating a unique combination of service offerings for the customers in their target market. It is possible to distinguish these various retailer types by focusing on whether they offer self-service, self-selection, or full service.

Since *self-service* and *self-selection* retailers provide few services for their customers, retailer location and price are important considerations. These retailers tend to specialize in staple convenience goods that are purchased frequently and require little product service or advice from retail personnel. The term limited service is also sometimes used to refer to sellers who provide minimal services.

Full-service retail establishments focus on fashion-oriented shopping goods and specialty items and offer a wide variety of services for their clientele. As a result, their prices tend to be higher than those of self-service retailers due to the higher operating costs these services generate.

Classification by Product Lines

Retail strategies can also be based on the product lines carried. Grouping retailers by product line produces three major categories: specialty stores, limited-line retailers, and general merchandise retailers.

Specialty Stores

A specialty store typically handles only part of a single product line. However, this portion is stocked in considerable *depth* (meaning variety) for the store's customers. Specialty stores include fish markets, men's and women's shoe stores, bakeries, and furriers. Although some are run by chains, most are independent, small-scale operations. They are perhaps the greatest stronghold of independent retailers that develop expertise in providing a very narrow line of products for their local markets.

In recent years, large retailers like Montgomery Ward and Woolworth have become specialty merchants. Under the Woolworth corporate umbrella are more than 40 different specialized stores, including Champs, a sporting goods retailer, and Kids Mart, a children's clothing store. Similarly, Montgomery Ward currently operates such free-standing stores as the Kids Store—a children's apparel specialist—Auto Express, and Home Ideas.[31]

Specialty stores should not be confused with specialty goods. Specialty stores typically carry convenience and shopping goods. The label "specialty" comes from the practice of handling a specific, narrow line of merchandise.

limited-line store
Retail establishment that offers a large assortment of one-product line or just a few related product lines.

A large assortment of one product line or a few related lines of goods are offered in the **limited-line store.** This type of retail operation has developed where population size has been sufficient to support it. Examples of limited-line stores are IKEA (home furnishings and housewares), Levitz (furniture), Handy Dan and Handy Man (home repair products), and The Gap (clothing). These retailers cater to the needs of people who want to select from a complete line in purchasing a particular product.

category killer
Retailer that combines huge selection and low prices in a single product line.

In recent years, a new kind of limited-line retailer has emerged. Known as **category killers,** these stores combine huge selection and low price in a single product line. Stores like Toys "R" Us, Soft Warehouse, a Philadelphia computer technology supermarket, Streamers, a discount party-supply chain, and Office Depot, an office-supply discounter are among the fastest growing retailers in the nation. Toys "R" Us has taken its marketing clout abroad and now has 74 international toy stores. Category killers have taken business away from general merchandise discounters, who cannot compete in selection or price.

With profit margins averaging only about 1 percent of sales after taxes, supermarkets compete through careful planning of retail displays in order to sell a large amount of merchandise each week and thereby retain a low investment in inventory. Product location within the store is carefully studied to expose the consumer to as much merchandise as possible and thus increase impulse purchases. In Europe, supermarket strategists believe that bigger is better as chains combine to increase buying power, streamline distribution, and promote their own house brands. Eight European chains including Britain's Safeway Food Stores Ltd. and France's Casino, now operate under the umbrella of Associated Marketing Services.[32]

Supermarkets carry nonfood products, such as magazines, records, small kitchen utensils, toiletries, and toys, for two reasons: Consumers have displayed a willingness to buy such items in supermarkets, and supermarket managers like the profit margins on these items, which are higher than those on food products.

Three trends are evident in the supermarket industry. First, several chains, such as Safeway, have built so-called *superstores*—large-square-footage stores that carry a broad range of food and nonfood items along with specialty sections such as a deli. Second, upscale or upgraded supermarkets now operate in many marketplaces. For example, in an attempt to capture a greater share of the take-out food business, Ohio-based Kroger hired an in-store chef to oversee all food preparation and to give cooking suggestions to shoppers. Kroger also offers popular microwave cooking classes.[33] Third, supermarkets are adding services. For instance, at the Safeway store on Market Street in San Francisco, shoppers have access to a bank cash machine, a Federal Express drop box, a photo finishing service, fresh pizza, and pet care.[34]

This level of supermarket service is not present in other parts of the world. In Germany, for example, stores are open only from 8 a.m. to 6:30 p.m. Monday through Friday and from 7 a.m. to 2 p.m. on Saturday. (In Bonn, service has been extended to 8:30 on Thursday nights.) In addition, many supermarkets close on 12 holidays. Service at the check-out counter also falls below U.S. standards. Customers do their own bagging and must either bring their own bags or buy them from the store.[35]

COMPETITIVE EDGE

IKEA MAKES FURNITURE SHOPPING EASY AND FUN

. . . .

IKEA's home furnishings stores have been described as "Disneyland for adults." The company uses every possible inducement to get customers to come in and stay. As a result, almost no one leaves empty-handed.

The idea behind IKEA (rhymes with idea) is simple: to sell quality Scandinavian furniture at prices that almost anyone can afford. This idea is so universally appealing that in 1990 IKEA attracted 100 million customers to its 94 stores in 23 countries. Nearly, 75 percent of the company's sales come from countries outside Scandinavia.

Since 1985 IKEA has launched seven stores in the United States, and it plans to add two or three a year. The stores are huge warehouse-style buildings covering an average of over 200,000 square feet, decorated in bold blue and yellow (the colors of the Swedish flag) and filled with china, plants, wallpaper, flooring, carpets, lighting, and furniture that customers assemble themselves. About 12,000 items are available.

IKEA attracts customers in a variety of ways. It sells well-designed merchandise in self-service stores at extremely low prices. All purchases are available on the spot—usually. (Out-of-stock items are the company's main problem.) Once the customer is in the store, all obstacles to purchase are removed: Catalogs, tape measures, pencils and paper, and shopping carts are provided; strollers are available, or children may be left in a supervised play area; a "baby care" room, which provides free diapers; a restaurant/cafe serves Swedish food at moderate prices; there are automatic teller machines in the stores; and customers can borrow automobile roof racks. By encouraging customers to take their purchases home with them, IKEA saves money on shipping, storage, and assembly.

IKEA's cut-rate pricing is combined with mass mailings and multimedia advertising. Whenever it opens a new store, IKEA blitzes the area with billboards and sends catalogs to all homes within a 40-mile radius. It spends nearly half of its annual marketing budget on direct mail, publishing 29 different editions of the catalog in 13 languages.

Discussion Questions

1. IKEA is classified as a "category killer." Are there any risks associated with this approach to retailing?

2. One observer remarks that "IKEA is not just selling Swedish furniture; it's selling Swedish lifestyle." Should the company attempt to appeal to customers with other tastes in home furnishings?

Sources: Cara Appelbaum, "How IKEA Blitzes a Market," *Marketing Week* (June 11, 1990), pp. 18–19; Seth Chandler, "Swedish Marketers Going Global," *Advertising Age* (April 16, 1990), p. 38; and Diane Harris, "Money's Store of the Year," *Money* (December 1990), pp. 144–150. Janet Bamford with A. Dunlap Smith, "Why Competitors Shop for Ideas at IKEA. "*Business Week* (October 9, 1989), p. 88. *Photo source:* Courtesy of IKEA U.S., Inc., Plymouth Meeting, PA.

General Merchandise Retailers

General merchandise retailers may be distinguished from limited-line and specialty retailers by the large number of product lines they carry. The general store described earlier in this chapter is a primitive form of **general merchandise retailer**—a retail establishment that carries a wide variety of product lines, all stocked in some depth. Included in this category are variety stores, department stores, and mass merchandisers such as catalog retailers, discount stores, hypermarkets, and off-price retailers.

Variety Stores.   A retail firm that offers an extensive range and assortment of low-priced merchandise is called a **variety store.** Less popular than they once were, many of these stores have evolved into or been replaced by other retailing categories such as discount stores. The nation's variety stores now account for less than 1 percent of all retail sales. However, variety stores remain very popular in Western Europe. Woolworth, for example, currently has about 284 Woolworth variety stores in this area and recently moved into the East German market.[36]

Department Stores.   The **department store** is actually a series of limited-line and specialty stores under one roof. By definition, it is a large retail firm that handles a variety of merchandise, including men's and boy's wear, women's wear and accessories, household linens and dry goods, home furnishings, and furniture. It serves the consumer as a one-stop shopping center for almost all personal and household items.

Department stores are known for offering their customers a wide variety of services, such as charge accounts, delivery, gift wrapping, and liberal return privileges. As a result, they have relatively high operating costs, averaging from 45 to 60 percent of sales.

Department stores have faced intensified competition over the past several years. Their relatively high operating costs have made them vulnerable to retailing innovations such as discount stores, catalog merchandisers, and hypermarkets. In addition, department stores were traditionally located in downtown business districts and experienced the problems associated with limited parking, traffic congestion, and population migration to the suburbs.

However, department stores have been willing to adapt to changing consumer desires. They have added bargain basements and expanded parking facilities in attempts to compete with discount operations and suburban retailers. They have also followed the population movement to the suburbs by opening major branches in shopping centers. They have attempted to revitalize downtown retailing in many cities by modernizing their stores, expanding store hours, making a special effort to attract the tourist and convention trade, and focusing on urban residents.

Japanese retailers, such as Yaohan and Jusco, have concentrated in recent years on building department stores in Taiwan, Hong Kong, Singapore, Bangkok, Jakarta, and other major Asian cities. With department store sales in some Southeast Asian countries growing 30 percent a year, Japanese retailers see an opportunity to tap the needs and wants of middle-class consumers. In Hong Kong, the Japanese currently operate 19 department stores that account for half of all department store sales. Interestingly, the Japanese see fewer opportunities at home as low profit margins, exorbitant land costs, and market saturation discourage their retailing efforts there.[37]

Mass Merchandisers.   Mass merchandising has made major inroads in department stores' sales during the past two decades by emphasizing lower prices for well-known brand name products, high turnover of goods, and reduced

general merchandise retailer
Establishment that carries a wide variety of product lines, all of which are stocked in some depth.

variety store
A retail firm that offers an extensive range and assortment of low-price merchandise.

department store
Large retail firm that handles a variety of merchandise, including clothing, household goods, appliances, and furniture.

mass merchandiser
Store that stocks a wider line of goods than a department store but usually does not offer the same depth of assortment.

discount house
Store that charges lower-than-normal prices but may not offer typical retail services such as credit, sales assistance, and home delivery.

services. The **mass merchandiser** often stocks a wider line of products than department stores but usually does not offer depth of assortment within each line. Discount houses, off-price retailers, hypermarkets, and catalog retailers are all mass merchandisers.

Discount Houses. The birth of the modern **discount house** came at the end of World War II when a New York–based company called Masters discovered that a large number of customers were willing to shop at a store that charged lower-than-usual prices and did not offer such traditional services as credit, salesperson assistance, and delivery. Soon retailers throughout the country were following the Masters formula, either changing over from their traditional operations or opening new stores dedicated to discounting. At first discount stores sold mostly appliances, but they have expanded into furniture, soft goods, drugs, and even food.

Discount operations had existed before World War II, but they sold goods chiefly from manufacturers' catalogs; they kept no stock on display and often had limited potential customers. Today's discounters operate large stores, advertise heavily, emphasize low prices for well-known brands, and are open to the public. Elimination of many of the "free" services provided by traditional retailers has allowed these operations to keep their markups 10 to 25 percent below their competitors'. After consumers became accustomed to self-service by shopping at supermarkets, they responded in great numbers to this retailing innovation. Conventional retailers such as Kresge joined the discounting practice by opening its own K Mart stores. Some of the early discounters have since added services, begun to stock name brands, and boosted their prices; in fact, they now resemble traditional department stores.

The newest wave of true discounters is the *warehouse club.* These stores are no-frills, cash-and-carry outlets that offer consumers access to name-brand items at deep-discount prices. The selection includes fax machines, peanut butter, luggage, and sunglasses in a setting that looks like a retail warehouse. Customers must buy club memberships in order to shop at warehouse clubs (fees range from $25 to $35 a year). Wal-Mart's Sam's Wholesale Clubs and Seattle-based Costco are examples of this type of retailer. Since the warehouse club concept began in 1980, sales have grown at an annual rate of 30 percent and are now estimated at $22 billion.[38]

off-price retailer
Retailer that sells designer labels or well-known brand name clothing at less than typical retail prices.

outlet mall
Shopping center consisting entirely of off-price retailers.

Off-Price Retailers. Another version of the discount house is the **off-price retailer.** These retailers buy only designer labels or well-known brand name clothing at regular wholesale prices or less and pass the cost savings along to the consumer. Their inventory frequently changes as they take advantage of special price offers from manufacturers desiring to sell excess merchandise. Off-price retailers such as Loehmann's, Marshalls, T. J. Maxx, and Hit or Miss tend to keep their prices below traditional retailers' by purchasing fashion merchandise at lower-than-normal wholesale prices and offering fewer services. Consumer acceptance has been dramatic, making off-price retailing a major retail growth trend. Currently, the 350 outlet chains in the United States generate nearly $6 billion in sales.[39]

While many off-price retailers are located in downtown areas or freestanding buildings, a growing number are concentrating in **outlet malls**—shopping centers consisting entirely of off-price merchandisers. At the Potomac Mills outlet mall outside Washington, D.C., for example, more than 200 stores sell men's and women's clothing, furniture, toys, and gifts. Manufacturers operate many of the stores including Calvin Klein, Anne Klein, Laura Ashley, and Nike at prices that are 20 percent to 60 percent off regular retail prices.[40]

WHOLESALE(?) CLUBS

A new form of retailing—wholesale clubs, also called warehouse clubs—is growing rapidly and generating controversy as well as profits. The clubs charge membership dues of about $25 a year and offer high-quality merchandise at minimal markups in huge, warehouse-like stores. Club members take merchandise directly from shelves or pallets without sales help. Although food accounts for about half of their total sales, the clubs sell everything from fresh produce to office furniture, jewelry, and tires. Some have begun to offer services such as optical departments. The goods are sold at near-wholesale prices, and payment is in cash only.

Wholesale clubs are the fastest-growing sector of the retail industry, with an annual growth rate of 30 percent. They now number over 600 and have total sales estimated at $22 billion annually.

Unlike discount stores, which stock about 50,000 items, wholesale clubs stock about 4,000 items geared to the needs of small businesses—especially items such as paper products, soft drinks, frozen foods, and trash bags. They combine wholesaling and retailing by buying items in bulk for business customers and carrying a few high-turnover items for retail customers. The typical customer of a wholesale club is a small business, a church, or a nonprofit organization. These customers often use the clubs as a substitute for holding inventories of needed items.

One problem faced by wholesale clubs is how to avoid becoming too much like ordinary discount stores while maintaining their low-price mystique. Some critics believe that club members have the illusion of saving a great deal of money but that club prices are not necessarily lower than those of supermarkets. Another problem is the use of the word *wholesale* by large organizations like Sam's Wholesale Club (a subsidiary of Wal-Mart), which sell mainly to consumers. Four states—Illinois, North Carolina, Kentucky, and Alabama—have required the clubs to drop the word *wholesale* from their names on the grounds that they are primarily retail businesses.

Discussion Questions

1. Although it has been barred from using the word *wholesale* in four states, Sam's intends to continue to use it elsewhere. Comment on this practice.

2. Wholesale clubs create an atmosphere of no-frills cost-saving by piling merchandise on pallets and selling goods in bulk quantities. Still, they carry fewer SKUs than competitive outlets. Also, small quantities can often be purchased at comparable prices elsewhere. What ethical considerations are involved in this situation?

Sources: Steve Weinstein, "The Power of the Club," *Progressive Grocer* (February 1991), pp. 26–32; Martha T. Moore, "Warehouse Clubs Lead Retail Pack," *USA Today* (June 26, 1990), p. B1; Joya L. Wesley, "Warehouse Clubs Fastest Growing Segment of the Retail Industry," *Mobile Press Register* (May 27, 1990), p. C1; and Andrew Kupfer, "The Final Word in No-Frills Shopping?" *Fortune* (March 13, 1989), p. 30.

---

hypermarket
Giant mass merchandiser of soft goods and groceries that operates on a low-price, self-service basis.

Hypermarkets.   Another retailing innovation is the **hypermarket**—a giant, one-stop shopping facility that offers a wide selection of grocery items and general merchandise at discount prices. Safeway's superstores, mentioned earlier, are an example. Store size is the major difference between hypermarkets and supermarkets. Hypermarkets typically have 200,000 or more square feet of selling space compared to about 44,000 for the average new supermarket.

The hypermarket concept originated with Carrefour in France and then spread to Canada and South America as well as the United States. At Michigan- and Ohio-based Meijers Thrifty Acres, consumers can buy food, hardware, soft goods, building materials, auto supplies, appliances, and prescription drugs in a 245,000-square-foot store. When they are done shopping, they can visit the restaurant, beauty salon, barbershop, bank branch, and bakery that are part of the facility.

Although hypermarkets were expected to make major inroads in U.S. retailing in the 1990s, they have run into problems and have generated lower than expected sales. Consumer complaints about having to do too much walking, limited brand selection (on items like electronics, consumers prefer conventional discounters where the choice is greater and the staff more knowledgeable), higher than expected building maintenance costs, and difficulty finding large enough land parcels for the building and adjacent parking lots have discouraged the expansion of these stores. K Mart and Wal-Mart, for example, currently operate seven hypermarkets between them but do not intend to build additional units.

 Hypermarkets have been more successful in Europe for several reasons. Because there are fewer retail outlets in Europe, these stores draw customers in search of a variety of merchandise. Often shoppers travel between 25 and 30 miles to the hypermarket. In addition, with fewer automobiles per capita, European consumers plan major shopping trips, often by bus, to take advantage of the hypermarket's one-stop shopping convenience. When Carrefour expanded to northeast Philadelphia, it encountered the same problems as U.S.–based retailers. It learned that to Americans, bigger is not necessarily better and that what makes good marketing sense in Europe and Latin America does not necessarily make sense here.[41]

Catalog Retailers: Catalog, Showroom, and Warehouse.   Catalog retailers mail catalogs to their customers and operate from showrooms that display samples of each product they handle. Orders are filled from backroom warehouses. Price is an important factor for catalog store customers. Low prices are made possible by few services, warehouse storage of most inventory, reduced shoplifting losses, and handling of long-lived products such as luggage, small appliances, gift items, sporting equipment, toys, and jewelry. Best Products and Service Merchandise are examples of catalog retailers.

Classification by Location of Retail Transactions

Some retailers choose to implement marketing strategies outside the store environment. Although the overwhelming majority of retail transactions occur in retail stores, non-store retailing is important for many products. Non-store retailing includes direct selling, direct-response selling, and automatic merchandising.

Direct Selling

The concept of direct selling, introduced in Chapter 12, is to provide maximum convenience for the consumer and allow the manufacturer to control its distribution channels. A number of merchandisers use direct selling, including manufacturers of bakery products, dairy products, and newspapers. Amway distributors market a variety of consumer products directly to their customers, who often are friends and acquaintances. Firms emphasizing product demonstrations also tend to use the direct-selling channel. Among them are companies that sell vacuum cleaners (Electrolux Corporation), household items (Fuller Brush Company), encyclopedias (The World Book Encyclopedia), and insurance. Some firms, such as Stanley Home Products, use a variation called *party selling,* in which a customer hosts a party to which neighbors and friends are invited. During the party, an independent salesperson makes a presentation of the products. The salesperson receives a commission based on the amount of products sold. In recent years, direct sellers like Tupperware and Avon have begun doing business in the workplace. During lunch-time and coffee-break presentations held in offices, conference rooms, and cafeterias, salespeople seek customers among working women. Avon now makes 25 percent of its sales in business settings.[42] The largest direct-selling retailers are Amway Corporation, Avon Products, Electrolux Corporation, Encyclopedia Britannica, Home Interiors & Gifts, Mary Kay Cosmetics, Princess House, Scott Fetzer (The Kirby Company, World Book), Shaklee Corporation, and Tupperware.

Direct-Response Selling.   The customers of direct-response retailers can order merchandise by mail, via telephone, by visiting the mail-order desk of a retail store or via computer or FAX machine. Goods are then shipped to the customer's home or to the local retail store. Many department and specialty stores issue catalogs to create telephone and mail-order sales and to promote in-store purchases of items featured in the catalogs.

Mail-order selling actually began in 1872, when Montgomery Ward issued its first catalog to rural midwestern families. That catalog contained only a few items, mostly clothing and farm supplies. Today mail-order houses offer a wide range of products, from alluring lingerie (Victoria's Secret) to upscale clothing (J. Crew) casual apparel and luggage (Lands' End) to home furnishings (Conran's Habitat). Many mail-order catalog organizations also generate retail sales by having consumers buy from retail outlets of their catalog stores.

Mail-order sellers, which now produce 14 billion pieces of mail a year, are trying to attract more shoppers through customer service (toll-free 800 numbers are common, and computer shopping services like CompuServe are becoming more popular) and their catalogs' unique look. Victoria's Secret, for example, uses British affectations (prices are in pounds as well as dollars; models are seen reading the *Financial Times;* the word "pajamas" is spelled "pyjamas"). Department stores like Sears are also dividing their large catch-all catalogs into slimmer, more accessible specialized books targeting such items as home furnishings, casual apparel, uniforms, and infants furniture. In addition, as department store strategies have shifted from a wide range of merchandise to a narrow focus on upscale apparel, the stores have moved the sales of many nonapparel items to catalogs. JC Penney, for example, now sells consumer electronics only through its catalog.[43]

Direct-response retailing also includes **home shopping**—the use of cable television networks to sell merchandise through telephone orders. One form of home shopping has existed for years, namely, the late-night, 30-second commercials featuring products such as K-Tel Records and Veg-O-Matic. Similarly, interactive cable television, such as Warner-Amex's QUBE system, was an early effort at home shopping. The home shopping boom, however, began with the launching of the Home Shopping Network, Inc., which spawned numerous competitors. Today half of all U.S. households with television sets will watch one or more home shopping networks. Sales statistics indicate that over 9 percent of those who watch will buy via this type of direct-response retailing.

Programming ranges from 24-hour-a-day commercials to call-in shows to game-show formats. In fact, nearly a quarter of all TV shoppers report that entertainment is the primary reason they watch these shows. Shoppers are given an 800 number to call for products they wish to purchase, and goods are delivered to the buyers' homes. A recent trend is specialization of home shopping channels by merchandise category, thus allowing viewers to tune into only those items that interest them. Home shoppers tend to be heavy users of this form of retailing, averaging six orders a year. In fact, in many ways they are similar to catalog shoppers.[44]

home shopping
Use of cable television to sell products via telephone orders.

Most vending machines in Japan are located on city sidewalks rather than in offices and factories as in the United States. One machine can sell 10,000 drinks a year, comparable to that sold in a U.S. convenience store. About half of Japan's soft drink sales are made through vending machines, compared to 10 percent in the United States. Some machines are high-tech. Equipped with special microchips, they play tunes or talk to buyers while dispensing soda, fruit ice, sports drinks, and canned coffee and tea.

Source: © David Wade.

Automatic Merchandising

The world's first vending machines dispensed holy water for a five-drachma coin in Egyptian temples around 215 B.C. However, the period of most rapid growth came after World War II when coffee and soft-drink vending machines were introduced in the nation's offices and factories. Today automatic merchandising machines are a convenient way to purchase a vast array of convenience goods ranging from Pepsi-Cola to Marlboros to Michigan lottery tickets, and they are a $24.5 billion industry.

In search of upscale consumers, the industry is experimenting with cappuccino and espresso vending machines as well as machines that dispense microwave pizza. To pay for these higher-priced items, some vendors are giving customers the option of using a debit-card system. After feeding a $10 bill into the machine, customers receive a magnetic-strip credit card. Each purchase is deducted from the customer's balance. A 75-cent candy bar, for example, would leave a $9.25 balance on the card. This idea is geared to college campuses and other settings that attract regular customers.[45]

Although vending machines are a national institution in the United States, they are not as welcome in parts of Europe. In Bordeaux, France, for example, merchants protested the installation of 60 Coca-Cola vending machines on public sidewalks by refusing to serve Coca-Cola to their customers. They objected to the impersonal nature of this distribution system and to the placement of the machines too close to their cafes, thus creating what they claimed was unfair competition. With machine-dispensed Cokes costing about 90 cents compared to about $2.50 in a restaurant, the merchants lost considerable business as a result of the machines. Although Coca-Cola eventually agreed to move these particular machines, the company has not changed its plan to install another 20,000 machines throughout France.[46]

Where does the vending machine dollar go? According to the National Automatic Merchandising Association, 45.4 cents of each dollar goes for the product, 52 cents for operating expenses, and 2.6 cents for profit. Typically the owner of the building receives more money from a machine just for allowing it on the premises than does the owner of the machine for installing, stocking, and servicing it.[47]

Classification by Form of Ownership

A final method of categorizing retailers is by ownership. The two major types are corporate chain stores and independent retailers. In addition, independent retailers may join a wholesaler-sponsored voluntary chain, band together to form a retail cooperative, or enter into a franchise arrangement through contractual agreements with a manufacturer, wholesaler, or service organization. Each type of ownership has its own unique advantages and strategies.

Chain Stores

chain store
Group of retail stores that are centrally owned and managed and handle essentially the same product lines.

Chain stores are groups of retail stores that are centrally owned and managed and handle the same product lines. One major advantage that chain operations have over independent retailers is economies of scale. Volume purchases through a central buying office allow chains to pay lower prices than independents. Since chains may have thousands of retail stores, they can use layout specialists, sales training, and computerized merchandise-ordering, inventory, forecasting, and accounting systems to increase efficiency. Also, the large sales volume and wide geographic expanse of many chains enable them to advertise in a variety of media, including television and national magazines.

For years, Sears was the nation's largest retailer. However, by the end of 1990, Sears had been replaced by Wal-Mart, which reported sales of $32.6 billion. Sears' $32 billion placed it in a virtual dead heat with K Mart. While Wal-Mart and Sears compete in only 30 percent of their product offerings, it is interesting to note that a decade earlier, Sears was more than eight times Wal-Mart's size. What's more, the Bentonville, Arkansas–based discounter operates in only 35 states, so it has considerable future growth potential.[48]

Independent Retailers

Although most retailers are small, independent operators, the larger chains dominate a number of fields. The U.S. retailing structure can be characterized as having a large number of small stores, many medium-size stores, and a small number of large stores. According to the Department of Commerce, independent retailers account for about 43 percent of all retail sales, or an estimated $780 billion annually.

In many industries independents are a force to be reckoned with. Independent "mom and pop" supermarkets account for about $152 billion in sales, over 42 percent of the industry total, and independent drug stores are responsible for more than a third of the industry's $68 billion annual sales. Independent video retailers make up 85 percent of the industry.[49]

Independents have attempted to compete with chains in a number of ways. Some have been unable to do so efficiently and are now out of business. Others have joined retail cooperatives, wholesaler-sponsored voluntary chains, or franchise operations. Still others have concentrated on a traditional advantage of independent stores: friendly, personalized service. Cooperatives like Ace Hardware and Valu-Rite Pharmacies give independents the ability to compete with chains by providing volume buying power as well as nationwide advertising and marketing programs.

Scrambled Merchandising

scrambled merchandising
Retailing practice of carrying dissimilar product lines in an attempt to generate additional sales volume.

It is becoming increasingly difficult to classify retailers, because in many cases the traditional differences no longer exist. Anyone who recently has filled a physician's prescription has been exposed to the concept of **scrambled merchandising**—the retail practice of carrying dissimilar lines in an attempt to generate additional sales volume. The drugstore carries not only prescription and proprietary drugs but garden supplies, gift items, groceries, hardware, housewares, magazines, records, and even small appliances.

Scrambled merchandising was born out of retailers' willingness to add dissimilar merchandise lines to satisfy consumer demand for one-stop shopping. Consider Sears's purchase of Coldwell Banker, a real estate firm, and Dean Witter Reynolds Inc., a stock brokerage firm. Sears already had an insurance company, Allstate, operating within its stores. Other examples of scrambled merchandising include the following:[50]

- Shoppers at Winn-Dixie supermarkets in Florida can also bank at branches of the Crossland Savings Bank.
- When renting a movie at the West Coast Video franchise in Whitehall, Pennsylvania, customers can also buy candy, chips, pretzels, and soda.
- Stew Leonard's supermarket in Norwalk, Connecticut has a year-round ice cream and frozen yogurt concession as well as seasonal garden and Christmas tree shops.

Scrambled merchandising complicates manufacturers' channel decisions. In most cases, their attempts to maintain or increase market share will require them to develop multiple channels in order to reach the diverse variety of retailers handling their products.

Summary of Chapter Objectives

1. **Describe the evolution of retailing.** Retailing institutions generally have evolved in accordance with the wheel of retailing, which holds that new types of retailers gain a competitive foothold by offering their customers lower prices through reduction or elimination of services. Once established, however, they add more services and increase their prices, thus becoming vulnerable to the next low-price retailer.

2. **Outline the various elements of retailing strategy.** A retailer must first identify a target market and then develop a product strategy. Next, it must establish a customer service strategy. Retail pricing strategy involves decisions on markups and markdowns. Location is often the determining factor in a retailer's success or failure. A retailer's promotional strategy, along with store atmosphere, plays an important role in establishing a store's image.

3. **Identify and explain each of the five bases for categorizing retailers.** Retailers can be categorized on five bases: shopping effort expended by customers, customer services provided, product lines, location of retail transactions, and form of ownership. Retailers, like consumer goods, may be divided into convenience, shopping, and specialty categories based on the effort shoppers are willing to expend in purchasing products. A second method of classification categorizes retailers on a spectrum ranging from self-service to full-service. The third method divides retailers into three categories: limited-line stores, which compete by carrying a large assortment

of one or two product lines; specialty stores, which carry a very large assortment of only part of a single product line; and general merchandise retailers, including department stores, variety stores, and mass merchandisers such as discount houses, off-price retailers, hypermarkets, and catalog retailers, all of which handle a wide variety of products. A fourth classification method distinguishes between retail stores and non-store retailing. While most U.S. retail sales take place in retail stores, such non-store retailing activities as direct selling, direct-response retailing, and automatic merchandising machines are important in marketing many types of goods and services. The fifth method of classification categorizes retailers by form of ownership. The major types include corporate chain stores, independent retailers, and independents that have banded together to form retail cooperatives or join wholesaler-sponsored voluntary chains or franchises.

4. **Explain the concept of scrambled merchandising.** Scrambled merchandising refers to retailers' practice of carrying dissimilar product lines in an attempt to generate additional sales volume. Scrambled merchandising has made it increasingly difficult to classify retailers.

Key Terms

retailing	general merchandise retailer
wheel of retailing	variety store
retail image	department store
markup	mass merchandiser
markdown	discount house
planned shopping center	off-price retailer
selling up	outlet mall
suggestion selling	hypermarket
atmospherics	home shopping
limited-line store	chain store
category killer	scrambled merchandising

Review Questions

1. Describe the evolution of retailing. What role does the wheel of retailing concept have in this evolution?

2. How do retailers identify target markets? Explain the major retailing strategies used to reach the target market.

3. A Syracuse, New York, discount store purchases garden hoses for $6 each and sells them for $9 each. What are its markup percentages on selling price and on cost?

4. A Taos, New Mexico, arts and crafts shop purchases decorative wooden carvings for $10 each and sells them for $30 each. What are the shop's markup percentages on selling price and cost?

5. A carpet store in Flint, Michigan, uses a markup percentage on cost of 66.67 percent. If the store decided to convert to basing markup on retail, what would be the equivalent markup percentage on retail?

6. What is the current status of shopping-center development in the United States? Describe the major types of shopping centers.

7. Outline the five bases for categorizing retailers. Cite examples of each of the subclassifications.

8. Identify the major types of general merchandise retailers. Cite examples of each type.

9. Differentiate between direct selling and direct-response retailing. Cite examples of both.

10. What is meant by scrambled merchandising? Why has this practice become so common in retailing?

Discussion Questions

1. Give several examples of the wheel of retailing in operation. Also identify situations that do not conform to this hypothesis. What generalizations can be drawn from this exercise?

2. Many European retailers are now seeking to become mass-market retailers, spanning nations rather than just regions, to take advantage of manufacturers' discounts for volume buying. With experts expecting European retailing to grow in a pattern similar to that of the United States, how do you think retailers will deal with the distinct regional tastes that prevail throughout Europe? Do you see different short-term and long-term solutions?

3. In the tough retailing environment of the early 1990s, off-price retailers have been facing new competition from department store chains like Bloomingdale's and Saks seeking to unload merchandise. To counter the competition, Newark, California–based Ross Stores is offering current fashions at discount prices. Gone is last year's merchandise and irregulars. Instead of a bargain-basement atmosphere, Ross now offers full service and readily accessible designer labels.[51] What do you think will happen to this strategy as department store business improves? What role will consumer perception of Ross's marketing strategy play? Do you think consumers adapt easily to a series of marketing shifts?

4. Research and then classify each of the following retailers:
   a. Dollar Stores
   b. Lane Bryant
   c. AM-PM Mini Marts
   d. Taco Bell
   e. Levitz Furniture Stores
   f. JC Penney

5. Back-to-basics is the marketing strategy of Rally's, a 240-outlet fast-food chain based in Louisville, Kentucky. Rally's operates under the strategy that instant, cheap service is what people want. With market research to support its point of view, Rally's is adding 100 instant-service stands. Their marketing research encouraged Rally's to go against the prevailing retailing trend by offering a limited menu, no seating, and a store only about one-fifth the size of the average McDonald's. Rally's high volume and small outlets translate into annual sales that run about $1,300 per square foot, compared with $400 for the average McDonald's.[52] Do you think Rally's success is linked to economic conditions, or is its marketing research predicting a longer-lasting trend?

Computer Applications

A *markup* is the amount added to a product's cost to determine its selling price. The amount of the markup usually depends on (1) the *services* the retailer performs (the more services provided, the larger the markup required) and (2) the *inventory turnover rate* (the higher the turnover rate, the smaller the markup needed).

By contrast, a *markdown* is the amount by which the retailer reduces the product's original selling price. Detailed explanations for calculating markups and markdowns are included on pages 465 and 466.

Directions: Use menu item 11 titled "Markups" to solve Problems 1 through 5. Use menu item 12 titled "Markdowns" to solve Problems 6 through 8.

Problem 1.   Suppose that the Eastern Michigan University bookstore uses a markup percentage on selling price of 50 percent for its line of EMU T-shirts. What would be the markup percentage on cost for the T-shirts?

Problem 2.   A Jackson, Mississippi, shoe store always adds a 40 percent markup (based on selling price) for its shoes. A shipment of shoes just arrived carrying an invoice cost of $54 per pair. What should the retail selling price be for each pair of shoes?

Problem 3.   At a recent meeting of the management committee of Litman and Daughter, a Newark, New Jersey, retailer, one of the buyers reported that a new line of dresses carried a markup percentage on cost of 66.67 percent. The firm's president asked the buyer to determine the markup percentage on the line's selling price. How should the buyer respond?

Problem 4.   A Louisville, Kentucky, florist sells a special gift arrangement for $30. The florist's costs are $15. What are the florist's markup percentage on selling price and markup percentage on cost?

Problem 5.   The Fish Market, a Santa Barbara, California, seafood restaurant, sells a house wine for $7.50 a carafe. The wine actually costs the restaurant $2.50 per carafe. What are the restaurant's markup percentages on selling price and cost?

Problem 6.   A Missoula, Montana, retailer pays $156 per dozen for a particular brand of men's shirts. The store attempted to sell these shirts at $30, but sales have been disappointing. In an effort to stimulate additional sales, the store manager decides to mark the shirts down to $25. Determine the store's markdown percentage on the shirts.

Problem 7.   A Joliet, Illinois, bookstore has been selling a collection of local recipes for $9.95. The store buys the books from a local gourmet club for $5 each. No returns are allowed. The recipe collection has sold well, and only 19 copies remain. Management recently decided to make space for new inventory by putting the recipe books on the store's discount table at $5.95 each. Determine the bookstore's markdown percentage on the books.

Problem 8.   A local economic downturn has adversely affected the sales of a store's line of $150 dresses. The manager decides to mark the dresses down to $120. What markdown percentage should it feature in advertising the sale items?

. . . .

South Coast Plaza

Over the past fifty years the rapid increase in automobile ownership has combined with the tremendous pace of urbanization to favor the proliferation of shopping malls. Two characteristics of shopping malls have given them distinct advantages over the traditional "downtown" retail districts: being newly developed on vacant land, they can provide the parking facilities desired by car-dependent consumers, and because they have a single owner, the facilities can be developed and occupied very rapidly with an appropriate mix of retailers. Typically, shopping mall development hinges on the establishment of a flagship or anchor store, often a large department store, to draw shoppers and as an inducement to other businesses to locate in the mall. The remaining land is leased to other retailers. By retaining ownership, the developers can control the mix of businesses, their location, and the amenities provided by the mall.

South Coast Plaza, in Costa Mesa, California, was developed in this way in the early 1960s by Henry Segerstrom, whose family had owned land in Orange County since the late nineteenth century. South Coast's strategy was cautious. A conventional mix of businesses was developed, based on anchor operations by Sears and the May Company. This approach proved to be a sound one, and the Plaza's operations provided higher-than-expected profits.

By the late 1970s, the population and affluence of Orange County had risen to the point where South Coast officials felt it was time to expand. Since South Coast Plaza was no longer the only mall in the area, Segerstrom saw the expansion as an opportunity to reposition South Coast to attract the most affluent segments of the population and thus distinguish the Plaza from other malls. High-end retailers were courted; I Magnin opened in 1977, Nordstrom in 1978, and Saks in 1979. At the same time, elite stores like Cartier, Mark Cross, and Rizzoli were attracted to the mall. South Coast Plaza had established itself as a unique, high-quality shopping mall.

South Coast Plaza chooses its retailers carefully, and the price tags on their goods are not the main criterion in this choice. South Coast looks for retailers with a strong commitment to customer service who view South Coast Plaza as a very desirable location. The mall's management handles its own leasing, shunning brokers in order to retain control. "It is my opinion you shouldn't lease sitting behind the desk answering a telephone," says Segerstrom. "You should be out in the market seeing what's going on, finding the retailers that are exciting and new, and we try to do that."

That is precisely how Segerstrom found Nordstrom. Years earlier during a visit to Seattle he had discovered the Nordstrom store and came away very favorably impressed by it. The Nordstrom family was considering expansion outside the Northwest but did not think Southern California was the right area; moreover, Nordstrom was usually the anchor store when located in a mall. After four years of discussions, Segerstrom finally convinced the family to bring a store to South Coast Plaza. Today the South Coast Nordstrom has the highest volume of sales per square foot of any store over 100,000 square feet in California.

Nordstrom is a perfect match for South Coast Plaza. Founded in 1901, it has always stressed service, value, and quality. When salespeople are trained, instead of merely being given a book of instructions they are taught how to make the customer happy. They are taught to go from department to department with the customer and to record purchases so that they can better advise the same customer in the future. Nordstrom also offers a personal shopper service in which sellers are available by appointment and stay with their customers as long as they are needed. This service is particularly helpful at rush times, such as the Christmas season.

It is apparent that the anchor store concept is no longer applicable to South Coast Plaza. Each of the stores has to draw customers in its own right. South Coast is careful to maintain a mix of stores, and this mix is dynamic because leases are usually for relatively short five-year periods. The range of stores in the mall is considerable, from a tool retailer (Brookstone) and a foreign exchange and precious metals dealer (Deak-Pereira) to an art museum store (New York's Metropolitan Museum of Art), as well as highly respected clothiers (Barney's) and athletic clothing retailers (Foot Locker).

While the mix is controlled, in some instances the location of stores within the mall has more to do with space availability than with planning. Three toy stores—FAO Schwartz, Sesame Street, and Disney—are in close proximity to each other and to the mall's carousel and other children's stores. Although it was not planned as such, the result is an immensely successful mini-mall for children. Parents with children, especially children in strollers, do not like walking the length of the mall to get to the next store. The proximity of the stores makes it possible to buy the kids some clothing and mollify them with a trip to the toy store without taking all day to do it.

South Coast Plaza functions like a huge department store. Each shopper experiences the mall differently: A family hurries past; a group of teenagers searches for friends; a man buys a book and stands under a light reading intently; a middle-aged couple buys a wedding gift for a nephew and then has dinner at a gourmet restaurant. Each shopper feels that South Coast was made for him or her, that it is the right place to go to satisfy his or her needs. Because so many of the retailers are target stores and because of its size, South Coast can offer amenities beyond those available to a single department store—including a branch of the Laguna Art Museum.

Once a pioneer in the fledgling shopping mall industry, South Coast Plaza today maintains its leadership by going beyond the real estate management philosophy of its competitors. It is not unreasonable to call South Coast Plaza a retail operations manager because of its control of its tenant mix and its careful shaping of its image. As long as its owners continue to monitor the pulse of retailing sensitively, South Coast should continue to prosper.

Sources: Mary Ann Galante, "Barneys N.Y. to Open South Coast Plaza Store," *Los Angeles Times* (May 23, 1989), pp. 2, 3; Anne Michaud, "Met Museum to Open Store in Costa Mesa Mall," *Los Angeles Times* (July 4, 1990), pp. D1, D4; John Needham, "Mall Accidentally Corners the Toy Scene," *Los Angeles Times* (November 23, 1990), p. E14.

Questions

1. Identify the advantages of regional shopping centers such as South Coast Plaza over traditional downtown retailers. What steps have downtown retailers taken in recent years to overcome their competitive disadvantages?

2. Discuss the following methods of categorizing retailers as each applies to South Coast Plaza:
   a. Shopping effort expended by customers
   b. Services provided to customers
   c. Product lines
   d. Location of retail transactions
   e. Form of ownership

3. What does South Coast Plaza offer its tenants that they would not get from a competing mall?

4. Discuss the importance of location within South Coast Plaza to its retailers. Is the importance of location the same for retailers that are anchor stores as it is for those that draw customers from the mall traffic?

15

Physical Distribution

CHAPTER OBJECTIVES

1. To explain the role of physical distribution in an effective marketing strategy.

2. To identify and compare the major components of a physical distribution system.

3. To outline the suboptimization problem in physical distribution.

4. To explain the impact of transportation deregulation on physical distribution activities.

5. To compare the major transportation alternatives on the basis of factors such as speed, dependability, cost, frequency of shipments, availability in different locations, and flexibility in handling products.

Among the definitions of *logistics* in *Webster's Collegiate Dictionary* is this: the aspects of military science dealing with the procurement, maintenance, and transportation of military material, facilities and personnel; the handling of the details of an operation.

Never has there been a logistical challenge to equal the 1991 Persian Gulf War. Involved in the deployment and maintenance of the 523,000 U.S. troops stationed in the Persian Gulf were supplies enough for the daily war effort, including:

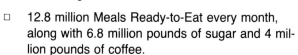

- ☐ 12.8 million Meals Ready-to-Eat every month, along with 6.8 million pounds of sugar and 4 million pounds of coffee.
- ☐ 5.2 million camouflage trousers and 376,000 pairs of goggles.
- ☐ 6 million gallons of fresh water a day.
- ☐ 18 million gallons of fuel a day, almost all of which were furnished by Saudi Arabia via a fleet of 1,500 tanker trucks.

In total, the military logistics effort transported the equivalent of a city the size of Richmond, Virginia, to the Saudi desert—an effort that was essential for the Allied Forces' victory over Saddam Hussein.

"Good logistics is combat power," is the motto of Lieutenant General William G. "Gus" Pagonis, head of the Army's Central Support Command in Saudi Arabia, the largest military logistics operation in history. As logistics commander, Pagonis made sure that all 350,000 U.S. ground forces were fully supplied—a mission that involved a distribution network of 50,000 workers, 100,000 trucks, huge open-air warehouses, and operating costs approaching $1 billion. Also involved was the cooperative effort of the military and private industry. Airlines like Northwest and rail haulers like the CSX Corp., as well as private truck and water carriers, contributed to the deployment effort.

Pagonis's logistics operation was complicated from the start. When several crews on foreign ships refused to sail into the war zone, the general was forced to find replacements or have supplies dropped off at distant ports and trucked to key Saudi supply points. In addition, many of the older Ready Reserve ships used steam turbine power, and few crews knew how to oper-

ate them. Pagonis took these and other problems in stride. "Hey, everything goes wrong every minute. What you do is fix it." To help minimize logistical problems, four computer models, developed at the Oak Ridge National Laboratories in Tennessee, automated the movement of buses, trucks, trains, planes, and ships throughout every link in the supply line.

The war's greatest logistical challenge occurred during the deployment of allied troops in preparation for the ground war. Pagonis was given the job of moving more than 200,000 troops west along a 300-mile route without alerting the Iraqi military. Using only a single highway and starting only 10 days before the ground assault, Pagonis deployed a 24-hour-a-day convoy consisting of volving 4,500 trucks traveling at a rate of 18-a-minute past any given spot. The deployment worked; the Iraqis had no warning of the flanking attack.

In an equal victory of sorts, Pagonis and his food service manager, Chief Warrant Officer Wesley C. Wolf, managed to prepare and deliver to most Desert Storm troops two fresh meals a day. Hot dog and hamburger stands were set up in the desert, supplied, at one point, by a cargo plane delivering 200,000 pounds of frankfurters.

Although logistics is often considered the tedious side of war, without a carefully planned logistical effort even the most brilliant military strategy will fail. A case in point: During World War II, General George Patton's tanks were in hot pursuit of a retreating German army division when they ran out of fuel. With no supply trucks in sight, U.S. forces had little choice but to sit and watch the enemy escape.[1]

Photo source: Todd Buchanan D. O. D. pool/Philadelphia Inquirer.

Chapter Overview

Chapters 12, 13, and 14 concentrated on distribution channel strategy and the marketing activities of wholesaling and retailing. This chapter focuses specifically on the physical flow of goods. Improving customer service through more efficient physical distribution remains an important aspect of any organization's marketing strategy.

physical distribution

Activities concerned with efficient movement of finished goods from the end of the production line to the buyer.

Physical distribution involves a broad range of activities aimed at efficient movement of finished goods from the end of the production line to the consumer. Although the terms *transportation* and *physical distribution* are sometimes used interchangeably, they do not mean the same thing. Physical distribution, or *logistics,* includes such important decision areas as customer service, inventory control, materials handling, protective packaging, order processing, transportation, warehouse site selection, and warehousing. American President Company's relationship with the Ford Motor Company demonstrates several of the extended functions of physical distribution. APC uses double-stack container rail service to transport automobile parts from Woodhaven, Michigan, to Ford's auto assembly plant in Hermosillo, Mexico. APC coordinates inventory information and handling so it can deliver vendor parts on a just-in-time basis in the sequence necessary for production. APC controls the movement of goods over four railroads and the coordination of deliveries with Mexican customs officials to avoid border delays. When the shipments arrive at the Ford plant, APC's cranes and people break down the containers and help deliver parts, as needed, onto the assembly line.[2] The opening story about Operation Desert Storm gives another example of logistics.

Importance of Physical Distribution

In recent years, physical distribution activities have received increasing attention. A major reason is that these functions represent almost half of total marketing costs.

Historically, management's focal point for cost cutting was production. These attempts began with the Industrial Revolution of the 1700s and 1800s, when businesses emphasized efficient production, continually attempting to decrease production costs and improve the output levels of factories and production workers. But managers now recognize that production efficiency has reached a point at which further cost savings are difficult to achieve. Increasingly, managers are turning to physical distribution activities as a possible cost-saving area. Currently, total physical distribution costs amount to approximately 20 percent of the nation's GNP.[3]

A second—and equally important—reason for the increased attention on physical distribution activities is their role in providing customer service. By storing goods in convenient locations for shipment to wholesale and retail customers, firms create time utility. Place utility is created primarily by transportation.

Customer satisfaction depends heavily on the reliable movement of products to ensure availability—even in a crisis. When Hurricane Hugo struck South Carolina, Pearlstine Distributors Inc., a distributor for Anheuser Busch, needed a way to continue its day-to-day operations. With electrical power to the region—and to company computers—interrupted, the distributor devised a method to continue tracking inventory, sales, and distribution using its portable hand-held route automation system. "We discovered that the hand-held units charge off our truck batteries," explained a company vice-president. "With the hand-helds powered up, we went ahead and delivered to customers in our usual way. It was critical that there were absolutely no interruptions in customer deliveries during the crisis." This focus on getting goods to market enabled

Pearlstine to surmount a serious obstacle. Pearlstine's beer sales increased by 75 percent during the post-hurricane period because of a shortage of potable water and because of the influx of disaster workers to the area.[4]

Failure to pay attention to logistics can result in major problems and added costs for suppliers and customers. At the Five Star Beer brewery in Beijing, China, a government-owned facility, plant managers hoped to raise the level of exports to North America from 30,000 to 500,000 cases. Although a large investment had been made in the brewing technology, the Chinese paid little attention to the process of packaging goods for shipment. As a result, the shipping boxes, provided by an outside supplier, were the wrong size for the bottles. Hours of additional labor were required to retrofit the boxes so that shipment was possible.[5]

When the firm delivers an intangible service rather than a physical good, information is often a key component of the offering. Fidelity Investor Centers achieved a competitive edge over other discount brokers by increasing its telephone operator-to-client ratio. A few years ago the Dow Jones Industrial Average tumbled more than 500 points in a single day—often called Black Monday. Several discount brokers reportedly dealt with the influx of telephone calls by leaving their phones off the hook. But Fidelity had recently tripled its staff of operators. As a result, each of the 580,000 calls logged that day was answered within 48 seconds on average.[6]

Giving customers what they need when they need it may require firms to shift their physical distribution focus to customer service. The Motors Division of General Electric made this move when it created a new computer-based order/ delivery system driven by each customer's specific delivery date. Involved was a restructuring of the company, with every department, except sales, reporting to customer service. For example, instead of reporting to manufacturing as they worked to support production schedules, the transportation and physical distribution departments are now considered part of customer service. By removing internal bureaucratic obstacles, GE Motors can now focus on whether deliveries are made when the customer wants them—an orientation that eventually will be reflected in company profitability.[7]

Improved customer service can be expensive since companies may have to carry increased inventories to meet customers' needs. To evaluate the wisdom of increasing inventory costs, companies must assess the trade-off between a lower purchase price at the expense of customer service versus better service at the expense of higher prices. In addition to inventory, other factors may push prices up. Intel Corp., a manufacturer of microcomputers, decided that in order to maintain its preferred supplier status with a key customer, it would locate a warehouse near the customer's plant in the Northeast, enabling Intel to supply needed components, manufactured in Manila, on time. Although the cost of this facility and its inventory are high, Intel has saved considerable money by shipping many components via truck rather than air.[8]

In recent years, a new concept has been added to this mix of physical distribution components—that of *value-added service,* defined by one warehouse operator as "the ability and motivation to take two steps when the customer expects you to take only one." Following are examples of some attempts to improve service at the same or reduced prices:

☐   Realizing the importance of customer service, North American Van Lines has signed a $12 million contract with QUALCOMM, Inc. to outfit its fleet with a two-way communication unit called WorldTRAC. This system will allow North American to track vehicles and communicate directly with fleet drivers, thus eliminating costly vehicle stops and improving equipment use and driver responsiveness.[9] Figure 15.1 describes the communications system.

Figure 15.1   Tracking System for Long-Haul Trucking

Source: Courtesy of McQUERTERGROUP—A High-Tech Business to Business Advertising and Public Relations Firm in San Diego, California.

☐ CTI, a contract warehousing and transportation company, warehouses parts for General Motors' Truck & Bus Group plant near Janesville, Wisconsin. As an added service, it performs subassembly of wheel units prior to delivering them to the production line. Although CTI is paid for this service, the cost is less than GM would incur had its own employees done the work.

☐ Air Products and Chemicals, Inc. ships cargoes of liquid helium to hospitals. Since these cargoes are extremely sensitive and cumbersome, lift-gate trucks are required, something which most less-than-truckload carriers do not have. Truckers that are willing to rent lift-gate trailers provide the company with a value-added service.[10]

Involved in many of these value-added services are logistics alliances that were virtually unheard of a decade ago but are today reducing distribution and inventory storage costs. In many of these cases, goods producers work with logistics services, in innovative, customized ways, to speed goods through the manufacturing and distribution pipeline. Although outsourcing of transportation and warehousing functions has long been common, today's alliance partners combine operations for mutual benefit. A growing part of the logistics service industry is made up of full-support companies, like Roadway Logistics and

Trammell Crow Distribution Corporation, that do everything from order processing to customer-order delivery.[11]

By providing consumers with time and place utilities, physical distribution contributes to implementing the marketing concept. Robert Woodruff, former president of The Coca-Cola Company, emphasized the role of physical distribution in his firm's success when he stated that its policy is to "put Coke within an arm's length of desire."

Physical Distribution System

The study of physical distribution is one of the classic examples of the systems approach to business problems. The basic notion of a *system* is that of a set of interrelated parts. The word is derived from the Greek word *systema,* which refers to an organized relationship among components. The firm's components include such interrelated areas as production, finance, and marketing. Each component must function properly if the system is to be effective and organizational objectives are to be achieved.

system
Organized group of components linked according to a plan for achieving specific objectives.

A **system** may be defined as an organized group of components linked according to a plan for achieving specific objectives. The physical distribution system contains the following elements:

1. *Customer service:* What level of customer service should be provided?
2. *Transportation:* How will the products be shipped?
3. *Inventory control:* How much inventory should be maintained at each location?
4. *Protective packaging and materials handling:* How can efficient methods be developed for handling goods in the factory, warehouse, and transport terminals?
5. *Order processing:* How should the orders be handled?
6. *Warehousing:* Where will the goods be located? How many warehouses should be utilized?

In Figure 15.2, the Atchison, Topeka, and Santa Fe Railway Company advertises how it handles several of the system components with its Quality Distribution Center program.

The above components are interrelated; decisions made in one area affect the relative efficiency of others. Attempts to reduce transportation costs by using low-cost, relatively slow water transportation may increase inventory costs because the firm may have to maintain large inventory levels because of the large volumes required to ship by that mode and to compensate for longer delivery times. The physical distribution manager must balance each component so that no single aspect is stressed to the detriment of the system's overall functioning.

The Problem of Suboptimization

The objective of an organization's physical distribution system may be stated as follows: to establish a specified level of customer service while minimizing the costs involved in physically moving and storing a good from its production point to its ultimate purchase. Marketers must first agree on the necessary level of customer service and then seek to minimize the total costs of moving the good to the buyer. All physical distribution elements must be considered as parts of a

Figure 15.2

Santa Fe's Quality
Distribution Center Program

Setting Up A Distribution System Is Even Simpler Than It Looks.

All it takes is a single phone call. To find out about Santa Fe's Quality Distribution Center (QDC) Program.

It's a system that lets you buy smarter. Ship bigger. And deliver faster. With savings.

Here's how it works. We pick up your shipment by truck and take it to a QDC in your city. When it's time to ship, we send it in Santa Fe railcars.

At your destination city, shipments may again be warehoused in a QDC where they can be broken down and delivered as needed. At the end of the month you get just one bill.

So Call Santa Fe at 1-800-234-9568 and find out how easy it is to put your distribution system on the right track. With QDC.

Super Fleet
Setting the track record in transportation.

The Atchison, Topeka, and Santa Fe Railway Company, 80 E. Jackson Boulevard, Chicago, Illinois 60604-2401

© 1990 The Atchison, Topeka, and Santa Fe Railway Company

suboptimization
Condition in which individual objectives are achieved at the expense of broader organizational objectives.

maquiladoras
Mexican assembly plants located near U.S. border.

whole rather than individually when attempting to meet customer service levels at minimum cost. But this does not always happen.

Suboptimization is a condition in which the manager of each physical distribution function attempts to minimize costs but, due to the impact of one physical distribution task on the others, obtains less than optimal results. The analogy of a military unit with well-trained personnel and the latest equipment that nonetheless loses major battles will help explain suboptimization.

Why does suboptimization frequently occur in physical distribution? The answer lies in the fact that each logistics activity is often judged by its ability to achieve certain management objectives, some of which are at cross-purposes with other goals. For example, in an attempt to reduce import tariffs on goods entering the United States, companies like Sony, Hitachi, and Panasonic have assembly plants in Mexico known as *maquiladoras,* close to the U.S. border. These facilities attract American companies because of their ready supply of low-cost labor. Companies also realize that by adding enough Mexican-made content to their products, they will benefit from the lower-tariff structure imposed on goods entering the United States from lesser-developed countries. The attraction to increase local content is strong, but it has its risks. Although Mexican-made components reduce company operating expenses, the quality of these components is often poor and their delivery unreliable—both of which can jeopardize customer service and loyalty.[12]

Effective management of the physical distribution function requires some cost trade-offs. Some of the firm's functional areas will experience cost increases and others cost decreases, resulting in minimization of total physical distribution costs. Of course, the reduction of any physical distribution cost should be made with the goal of maintaining the required level of customer service.

SPEED VERSUS SAFETY

Domino's Pizza Inc. is famous for its pledge to deliver pizzas to customers within 30 minutes. But some people criticize this policy on the grounds that it has resulted in a high rate of accidents involving Domino's delivery personnel. According to the critics, the firm's guarantee encourages delivery people to drive recklessly. Domino's management denies that there is any connection between its fast-delivery policy and accidents involving its drivers. The company's delivery system is geared to give drivers ample time to deliver: Pizzas are usually ready for delivery in 12 minutes, and delivery areas average 2 miles or less.

To those who believe the driver is held responsible when a pizza is delivered late, the company responds that the $3.00 refund to the customer is paid by Domino's, not by the delivery person. Domino's management also points out that each of the company's deliverers drive about 450 miles a year. In total, they deliver an estimated 275 million pizzas in all kinds of weather.

Despite these arguments, the Lafayette, California, city council voted to deny a business license to a Domino's franchisee, citing the high rate of traffic accidents,

some of them fatal, involving Domino's delivery people. (Domino's drivers were involved in about 100 accidents in 1989, and in 1988 twenty people were killed in accidents involving Domino's vehicles.)

In the Los Angeles area, Domino's has attempted to deflect some of the criticism by airing public-service radio spots on safe driving. The campaign features police officers discussing safety tips and warning people not to drive when they are drunk, upset, or tired.

Discussion Questions

1. Domino's drivers are widely perceived as having a poor safety record. Is this perception justified?

2. Should Domino's eliminate or modify its 30-minute delivery guarantee?

Sources: Bruce Horovitz, "Domino's Airing Public Service Spots on Safe Driving," *Los Angeles Times* (June 16, 1990), p. D2; Chip Johnson, "Domino's Craps Out as a Suburb Refuses to Gamble on Safety," *The Wall Street Journal* (September 4, 1990), p. A3; and "Domino's Pizza to Stress Safety over Speed," *Washington Post* (December 18, 1989), p. D4.

Customer Service Standards

customer service standards
Quality of service that a firm wants its customers to receive.

Customer service standards are the quality of service determined by a firm that its customers should receive. For example, a customer service standard for one firm might be that 60 percent of all orders are shipped within 48 hours after they are received, 90 percent in 72 hours, and all within 96 hours.

Realizing how customer service is affected by inventory control, Burger King Distribution Services, which supplies food to 65 percent of the 5,355 Burger King restaurants in the United States, introduced an Electronic Support System (ESS) to computerize the supply-ordering process. The goal of this system is to reduce inventory-ordering errors, especially those involving perishable foods. Automating the system also gives managers more time to focus on management issues and problems.[13]

Today, customer service improvements often involve the use of computerized logistics analysis. Burlington Northern, a rail carrier, helps customers improve service through a computerized logistics planning tool known as ShipSmart. A company using ShipSmart can simultaneously analyze all the routes and transportation modes available to determine the fastest, most cost-effective way to deliver goods.[14]

A vital assignment of the physical distribution specialist is to delineate the costs involved in fulfilling proposed standards. Increased service levels typically cost more, and all employees must be aware of the costs of providing the ser-

Table 15.1   Customer Service: A Physical Distribution Perspective

Definition: Non-price and non-product features of one vendor/firm over those of another. It is often *the* reason for the sale.

Components:

A. Product Availability
   1. Product availability
   2. Percent of orders shipped complete

B. Order Cycle Time
   3. Length of order cycle time
   4. Reliability of order cycle time

C. Order Handling/Shipping
   5. Adherence to customer's special shipping instructions
   6. Ability to expedite orders for customers
   7. Order entry procedures
   8. Order entry personnel
   9. Transportation policy
   10. Speed and accuracy in billing
   11. Expedient handling of billing errors and credits
   12. Handling of adjustment claims
   13. Availability of technical information

D. Financial Terms
   14. Cash discounts

   15. Payment period
   16. Pricing policy

E. General Marketing Support
   17. Knowledgeable sales representatives
   18. Availability of product information
   19. Availability of promotion and pricing items
   20. Knowledgeable technical service

F. Information Availability
   21. Order status information
   22. Advance information on price changes
   23. Advance information on new products
   24. Availability of inventory status
   25. Advance information on shipping delays
   26. Advance information on order deletions and substitutions
   27. Back order status

G. Physical Condition
   28. Product information
   29. Order filling accuracy
   30. Procedure for returned goods

Source: Reprinted from Joseph Cavinato, "How to Keep Customers Coming Back for More," *Distribution* (December 1989), p. 61.

vice levels necessary for maintaining both satisfied customers and profitable operations.

Table 15.1 indicates the specific components of customer service. It illustrates the wide range of logistics functions involved in achieving minimum customer service standards.

Elements of the Physical Distribution System

The physical distribution function requires the establishment of a standard of acceptable levels of customer service. The physical distribution system should then be designed to achieve this standard at the lowest possible *total* cost of the following components: (1) transportation; (2) warehousing, (3) inventory control, (4) order processing, and (5) protective packaging and materials handling. Relative costs for each component are shown in Figure 15.3.

Transportation

Transportation costs are the largest expense item in physical distribution. Moreover, for many products—particularly perishable goods—transportation is the key to satisfactory customer service. Realizing this, British retailer Marks & Spencer ensures its close relationship with farms and factories by deploying daily its own specially designed trucks from suppliers to its 264 stores across Great Britain. This trucking network has helped Marks & Spencer maintain its position as a leading prepackaged refrigerated food retailer. Sales of such specialty food items as *salmon en croute* with cream sauce and spaghetti carbonara account for 37 percent of the retailer's total sales.[15]

Figure 15.3

Where the Physical
Distribution Dollar Goes

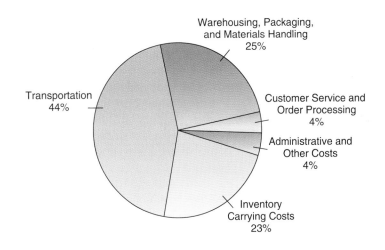

Warehousing, Packaging,
and Materials Handling
25%

Transportation
44%

Customer Service and
Order Processing
4%

Administrative and
Other Costs
4%

Inventory
Carrying Costs
23%

Source: Data provided by Herbert W. Davis and Company, Englewood Cliffs, N.J., *Physical Distribution Costs for 1990.*

A fast, efficient transportation system gives manufacturers a competitive edge. To break into the newly opened East German market within days of the destruction of the Berlin Wall, Coca-Cola executives loaded thousands of cases of Coke onto fleets of waiting trucks and sent the trucks to key crossing points. At one checkpoint, truckers gave eager East Germans over 70,000 cans of free Coke in a few hours. Border crossers in cars received free cases. To Heinz Wiezorek, president of Coca-Cola's German division, this rapid distribution was crucial. "There won't be two colas in restaurants and small outlets," he said. "They'll choose the one that's first in the market."[16]

Rate Determination.   The U.S. Transportation system historically has been a regulated industry, much like the telephone and electrical utilities. The railroads were first regulated under the Interstate Commerce Act of 1887. This act established the Interstate Commerce Commission (ICC), the first regulatory body in the United States. The ICC regulates some rates and services of railroads, slurry pipelines, motor carriers, and inland water carriers. The Federal Maritime Commission regulates U.S. ocean carriers.

class rate
Standard transportation rate established for shipping various commodities.

There are two basic types of freight rates; class and commodity. The **class rate** is the standard rate for every commodity moving between any two destinations. The class rate is the higher of the two rates. The **commodity rate** is sometimes called a *special rate,* since it is given by carriers to shippers as a reward for either regular use or large-quantity shipments. It is used extensively by railroads and inland water carriers.

commodity rate
Special transportation rate granted by carriers to shippers as a reward for either regular use or large-quantity shipments.

A third type of rate commonly used in the railroad and motor carrier industries today is the *negotiated,* or *contract rate.* This type of rate, which became popular following the deregulation of these industries in 1980, allows the shipper and carrier to negotiate a rate for a particular service. The terms of the rate, service, and other variables are then finalized in a contract between the two parties.

Transportation Deregulation.   The deregulation of the U.S. transportation industry began in 1977 with the removal of regulations for cargo air carriers not engaged in passenger transportation. The next year, the Airline Deregulation Act was passed. It granted passenger airlines considerable freedom in establishing fares and choosing new routes.

In 1980 the Motor Carrier Act and the Staggers Rail Act significantly deregulated the trucking and railroad industries, respectively. These laws enabled transportation carriers to negotiate rates and services, eliminating much of the bureaucracy that traditionally had hampered the establishment of new and innovative rates and services.

Transporters now have added flexibility in designing services and rates to match shippers' unique needs. For example, rail carrier Burlington Northern worked with glass manufacturers who needed an alternate way to ship millions of pounds of soda ash, a key raw material, from mines to company processing plants. With railroad tracks almost 200 miles away from the nearest mines, the transporter and manufacturers jointly built a truck loading facility and developed a system for transferring the cargo from trucks to Burlington's waiting railroad cars.

Deregulation has brought with it real cost savings that benefit U.S. producers, distributors, and, ultimately, consumers. Logistics costs in 1986 were 21 percent below the level of 1980. In real dollars, this amounts to an annual savings of some $60 billion. In large part, these savings were brought about by the efficiency of the deregulated transportation system. Before deregulation, no truck carrier served the contiguous 48 states; today, more than 4,000 carriers have that authority. The service of such companies as West Point Pepperill, MS Carriers, and Contract Freighters is so fast and reliable that channel members often choose them as an alternative to air freight service. In addition, the trucking industry is now far more efficient, with many carriers reducing empty mileage by two-thirds.

Railroads have responded to the greater efficiency in the trucking industry by dramatically reducing costs. To streamline operations, 500,000 rail cars and 8,000 locomotives have been taken out of service, thousands of miles of tracks have been abandoned, and the workforce reduced. In addition, such new competitive services as intermodal transportation, which will be discussed later in the chapter, have allowed railroads to compete with longhaul truckers. This service alone grew from $2 billion to $6 billion during the past decade.[17]

Massive deregulatory changes will occur in Europe after January 1, 1993. For the first time, there will be no barriers among the 12 European Economic nations—a situation that promises to dramatically improve logistics efficiency and reduce costs. As national borders open, multiple distribution operations will no longer be necessary. Warehouse locations can be chosen on the basis of efficiency rather than national borders with the result, for example, that German and French warehouses located close to one another can be consolidated into a single operation. This will benefit companies that can choose a central—rather than a country-specific—location for their European operations.[18]

Qualified trucking companies will be issued international licenses that allow them to cross national borders without being stopped. According to transportation strategist Robert V. Delaney, "Europe is headed toward a system in which trucks and trailers will eventually operate between and among countries with the speed and efficiency of operations throughout North America today."[19]

The new transportation environment has increased the importance of physical distribution managers, because their areas of responsibility are even more complex than in a highly regulated situation. It is now possible to simultaneously increase service levels and decrease transportation costs. For example, the transportation director of the diagnostic division of Abbott Laboratories works with an international agent from Integrated Traffic Systems (ITS), a logistics consulting firm, to handle overseas airline shipments. The advantage to Abbott is a direct link to ITS's airline computer system and to the most efficient—and least expensive—air transportation combinations possible. Since the ITS agent can book flights on a same-day rather than a next-day basis, Abbott also benefits through inventory cost savings and reduced customer back orders.[20]

Classes of Carriers. Freight carriers are classified as common, contract, and private. Common carriers, sometimes called the backbone of the transportation industry, are for-hire carriers that serve the general public. Their rates and services are regulated, and they cannot conduct their operations without permission of the appropriate regulatory authority. Common carriers exist for all modes of transport.

Contract carriers are for-hire transporters that do not offer their services to the general public. Instead, they establish specific contracts with certain customers and operate exclusively for a particular industry (most commonly the motor freight industry). These carriers are subject to much less regulation than are common carriers.

Private carriers are not-for-hire carriers. Their operators transport products only for a particular firm and traditionally have been prohibited from soliciting other transportation business. Since the transportation they provide is solely for their own use, there is no rate or service regulation. The ICC permits private carriers to also operate as common or contract carriers. Many private carriers have taken advantage of this rule to operate their trucks fully loaded at all times.

Major Transportation Modes. The physical distribution manager has five major transportation alternatives: railroads, motor carriers, water carriers, pipelines, and air freight. Figure 15.4 indicates the percentage of total intercity ton-miles shipped by each major mode from 1940 to 1989. The term *ton-mile* refers to moving one ton of freight one mile. Thus, a 3-ton shipment moved 8 miles equals 24 ton-miles.

The water carriers' percentage has gradually declined, stabilizing at a lower level. Railroads have experienced a significant decrease, and pipelines and motor carriers have experienced substantial increases. Air carriers are dwarfed by the other transportation alternatives, accounting for fewer than 1 percent of all shipments.

Railroads—The Nation's Leading Transporter. Railroads continue to control the largest share of the ton-mile market by a margin of about 1.4 to 1 over their nearest competitors. They represent the most efficient mode for the movement of bulky commodities over long distances. For instance, two-thirds of domestic coal and about 60 percent of new automobiles are transported by rail. Chemicals, grain, nonmetallic minerals, and lumber and wood products are other major commodity groups that the railroads carry. Rail carriers such as Burlington Northern, Union Pacific, Santa Fe Southern Pacific, and Norfolk Southern transport three-eighths of all goods shipped in the United States.

In recent years, the railroads have launched a drive to improve their service standards to attract more business and have introduced a number of innovative concepts in pursuit of these objectives. Unit trains, run-through trains, intermodal (piggyback) operations and double-stack container trains, have played a major role in improving the efficiency and reducing the cost of rail transport.

The unit train, now widely used in coal, grain, and other high-volume movements, runs back and forth between a single loading point (such as a mine) and a single destination (such as a power plant) to deliver one commodity. The run-through train, which bypasses intermediate terminals to speed up schedules, is similar in concept. The difference between them is that the run-through may carry a variety of commodities.

Figure 15.4

Share of Intercity
Ton-Miles by Mode

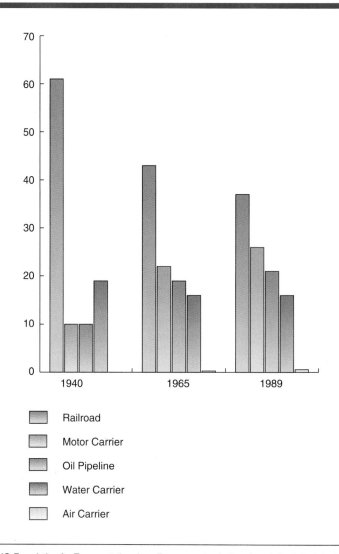

Railroad

Motor Carrier

Oil Pipeline

Water Carrier

Air Carrier

Source: ENO Foundation for Transportation, Inc., *Transportation in America: A Statistical Analysis of Transportation in the United States,* May 1990, p. 7; 1989 data from December 1990 supplement, p. 6.

In piggyback operations, highway trailers and containers ride on rail flatcars, thus combining the long-haul capacity of the train with the door-to-door flexibility of the truck. In contrast, double-stack container trains involve two containers stacked on top of one another in bathtub-shaped wells that ride on special rail cars. By nearly doubling train capacity and slashing costs 25 percent, this system offers enormous advantages to rail customers. Realizing this, Procter & Gamble is now using double-stack trains instead of trucks for many of its shipments of potato chips, peanut butter, and liquid detergent from its Midwestern plants to the West Coast. Double-stack train service was initiated in 1984 by American President Co. Today, CSX Corp., Burlington Northern Inc., Union Pacific Railroad, and Santa Fe Pacific Corp. are also double-stack carriers.[21]

Railroads provide other innovative equipment as well, including covered hopper cars, which may be loaded with 100 tons of grain in twelve minutes and unloaded in three. Dual-mode vehicles with two sets of wheels—flanged-steel wheels for use on rails and rubber-tired wheels for use on highways—may be driven away from rail terminals within minutes. Automatic identification systems, using radio-triggered devices mounted on the sides of freight cars, are now being used to track freight-car movement. Thus, the need to manually enter identification codes into a computer has been eliminated. In the past, manual identification has produced an error rate of between 1 percent and 3 percent, resulting in freight cars ending up on the wrong train headed for the wrong destination.[22]

With the completion of the Channel Tunnel, also referred to as the "Chunnel" or the "Eurotunnel," connecting England and France, a railway system will change the nature of the physical distribution process in Western Europe. The Channel Tunnel beneath the English Channel consists of three separate 30-mile tunnels, two of which will transport passenger and cargo rail traffic. Approximately 6 million to 7 million tons of freight are expected to be shipped annually.

The Channel Tunnel symbolizes Europe's economic integration. Not only are tariffs removed for goods traveling among the 12 European Community countries, the physical barrier—namely the English Channel—separating Great Britain from the Continent will also be minimized. Connecting rail lines feeding into the tunnel are part of the project as are rail terminals in Folkstone, England, and Sagatte, France. In addition, to meet the increased traffic, existing rail lines in both countries are being extended and modernized.

The Channel Tunnel has broad-ranging implications for European and international trade. Companies operating within Europe will have easier, less expensive access to the entire European Community. Exporters in the United States and other non-European nations may need to reevaluate how their goods enter Europe.[23]

Motor Carriers—Flexible and Growing.   The trucking industry has shown dramatic growth over the past decades. Its primary advantage over the other transportation modes is its relatively fast, consistent service for both large and small shipments. Motor carriers concentrate on manufactured products, while railroads haul more bulk and raw-material goods. Motor carriers therefore receive greater revenue per ton shipped—more than 23 cents per ton-mile—than do railroads, which earn less than 3 cents per ton-mile.

To reduce costs, the trucking industry now uses double 28-foot trailers and single 48-foot trailers. In addition, some companies are pulling the 53-foot trailers that are permitted in some states. These longer rigs travel on interstates and other major highways, especially on the East and West coasts. The industry is also proposing the use of 100-foot triple-trailer rigs resembling truck trains. Although trucking costs would decrease by a third by reducing the number of cabs and drivers needed, they have met with stiff opposition from traffic-safety experts who warn of dangers to automobiles and the deterioration of highways caused by such heavy trucks.[24]

Deregulation, specifically the Motor Carrier Act of 1980, has spurred the growth of the trucking industry. For example, after deregulation, Arkansas-based J. B. Hunt Transport, Inc. obtained unlimited ICC authority for expansion. Today the carrier has more than 4,000 tractors and 9,000 trailers and is the largest truckload carrier in the country.[25]

The removal of regulatory barriers in the European Community greatly reduced the cost of truck transportation. With truck drivers spending an average of 30 percent of their time waiting or doing paperwork (as many as 200 forms at border crossings), the removal of barriers is expected to reduce overall prices on goods by about 2 percent.[26]

Water Carriers—Slow but Inexpensive.   There are two basic types of water carrier: inland or barge lines and oceangoing deepwater ships. Barge lines are efficient transporters of bulky, low-unit-value commodities such as grain,

Figure 15.5

Cast Container Shipping

Volume Leader.

Cast moves
more cargo, more frequently,
than any container fleet on
the North Atlantic.

CAST

The Blue Box System of Container Shipping

gravel, lumber, sand, and steel. A typical lower Mississippi River barge line may be more than a quarter-mile in length and 200 feet wide.

Oceangoing ships operate in the Great Lakes, transporting goods among U.S. port cities, and in international commerce. For example, the container-carrying vessel pictured in Figure 15.5 operates in the North Atlantic. Water carrier costs average one cent per ton-mile.

 International sea shipments are an important part of foreign trade. Although usually reliable, the schedules for these shipments were disrupted during the Persian Gulf War. For example, Dow Chemical reported that some shipments from Europe to Hong Kong were three weeks late as ships that normally traveled through the Suez Canal were diverted through the Panama Canal, a longer route.[27]

Pipelines—Specialized Transporters.   Although the pipeline industry ranks third after railroads and motor carriers in number of ton-miles transported, many people are barely aware of its existence. More than 214,000 miles of pipelines crisscross the United States. Pipelines serve as extremely efficient transporters of natural gas and oil products, as evidenced by the latter's average revenue per ton-mile of 1.3 cents. Oil pipelines carry two types of commodities: crude (unprocessed) oil and refined products, such as gasoline, jet fuel, and kerosene. A so-called slurry pipeline also exists. In this method of transport, a product such as coal is ground up into a powder, mixed with water, and transported in suspension through the pipeline.

Although pipelines represent a low-maintenance, dependable method of transportation, they have a number of characteristics that limit their use. Their availability in different locations is even more limited than that of water carriers, and their use is restricted to a small number of products. Finally, pipelines rep-

Table 15.2   Comparison of Transport Modes

	Factor					
Mode	Speed	Dependability in Meeting Schedules	Frequency of Shipments	Availability in Different Locations	Flexibility in Handling	Cost
Rail	Average	Average	Low	Extensive	High	Medium
Water	Very slow	Average	Very low	Limited	Very high	Very low
Truck	Fast	High	High	Very extensive	Average	High
Pipeline	Slow	High	High	Very limited	Very low	Low
Air	Very fast	High	Average	Average	Low	Very high

resent a relatively slow method of transportation; liquids travel through pipelines at an average speed of only three to four miles per hour.

Air Freight—Fast but Expensive.   The use of air carriers as a transportation alternative has been growing significantly. In 1961 U.S. domestic airlines flew about 1 billion ton-miles. By 1989 this figure had jumped to 9.8 billion ton-miles. As a result, the air freight industry currently generates about $20 billion in revenue.[28] However, air freight is still a relatively insignificant percentage of the total ton-miles shipped, amounting to less than four-tenths of 1 percent in a recent year.

Because of air freight's relatively high cost, it is used primarily for valuable or highly perishable products. Typical shipments consist of computers, furs, fresh flowers, high-fashion clothing, and live lobsters. Shippers of this type of freight are often able to offset the high cost of air transportation with reduced inventory holding costs and faster customer service. During an economic recession, many companies move away from air freight for all but the most urgent shipments, returning once more when times improve. According to McDonnell-Douglas, by the year 2000, international air freight will make up nearly 85 percent of all air cargo traffic, up from nearly 77 percent in 1987. Among the reasons for this growth are increased demand for fresh produce and fish and reliance on just-in-time inventory control systems, which require immediate shipments as needed.[29]

International air freight service is expected to grow substantially in Asia and the Pacific Rim. This was one of the reasons behind Federal Express's purchase of Flying Tigers—a company with valuable route rights into Japan. Air freight business in and out of the 12-member European Community will grow as a result of the economic integration. The elimination of customs clearance speeds up air-freight service and, ultimately, lowers costs.[30]

Table 15.2 compares the five transport modes on several bases. Although shippers are likely to consider such items as reliability, speed, and cost in choosing the most appropriate transportation method, these factors will vary in importance for different products. For example, while motor carriers rank highest in availability in different locations, shippers of petroleum products frequently choose the lowest-ranked alternative, pipelines, due to factors such as cost.

Examples of types of products most often handled by the various transport modes include the following:

☐   *Railroads:* Lumber, iron and steel, coal, automobiles, grain, chemicals.

☐   *Motor carriers:* Clothing, furniture and fixtures, lumber and plastic products, food products, leather and leather products, machinery.

□ *Water carriers:* fuel, oil, coal, chemicals, minerals, petroleum products.

□ *Pipelines:* Oil, diesel fuel, jet fuel, kerosene, natural gas.

□ *Air carriers:* Flowers, technical instruments and machinery, high-priced specialty products.

Freight Forwarders—Transportation Intermediaries.

Freight forwarders are considered transportation intermediaries, because their function is to consolidate shipments to get lower rates for their customers. The transport rates on less-than-truckload (LTL) and less-than-carload (LCL) shipments often are twice as high on a per-unit basis as the rates on truckload (TL) and carload (CL) shipments. Freight forwarders charge less than the higher rates but more than the lower rates. They make their profit by paying the carriers the lower rates. By consolidating shipments, freight forwarders offer their customers two advantages: lower costs on small shipments and faster delivery service than LTL and LCL shippers provide.

Supplemental Carriers.

The physical distribution manager can also utilize a number of auxiliary, or supplemental carriers that specialize in transporting small shipments. These carriers include bus freight services, United Parcel Service, Federal Express, DHL International, and the U.S. Postal Service.

Kansas City–based Hallmark Cards ships approximately 70 percent of its goods via United Parcel Service. The remainder is handled by such LTL truckers as Roadway Express and St. Johnsbury. To make sure that it is getting the best shipping deal, Hallmark's computer system compares the cost of shipping each parcel via UPS and LTL truckers. Those parcels that are shipped via UPS are placed on a conveyer belt that feeds directly into a UPS trailer. Hallmark ships an average of five trailerloads a day on UPS. An additional two trailers are sent to UPS drop-shipping points in Pittsburgh and Atlanta—a shipping strategy that saves Hallmark more than $200,000 a year.[31]

Intermodal Coordination.

The various transport modes often combine their services to give shippers the service and cost advantages of each. Piggyback, discussed earlier, is the most widely accepted form of intermodal coordination. The combination of truck and rail services generally gives shippers faster service and lower rates than either mode does individually, since each method is used where it is most efficient. Shipper acceptance of piggybacking has been tremendous. In 1965, 1.7 million trailers and containers were shipped via piggyback railcars; by 1990 that figure had jumped to 6.3 million.[32] The ICC has exempted piggyback service from government regulation, a move that is expected to increase competition and improve growth prospects for this concept.

In a recent development, J. B. Hunt Transport Services and the Santa Fe Railway established daily intermodal freight service between Chicago and Los Angeles, serving such customers as Ralston Purina and United Parcel Service. In this joint transportation program, J. B. Hunt will pick up freight from the shippers and deliver it to the railroad. When the rail trip is over, Hunt will reload the freight onto its trucks for final delivery.[33]

Another form of intermodal coordination is *birdyback*. Here motor carriers deliver and pick up a shipment, and air carriers take it over a longer distance. *Fishyback* is the form of intermodal coordination between motor carriers and water carriers.

Multimodal Transportation Companies.

Another form of intermodal coordination is performed by *multimodal* transportation companies. Piggyback generally is done by two separate companies—a railroad and trucking company. A

At Baltimore's Seagirt Marine Terminal, giant cranes load containers aboard a ship. The intermodal terminal boasts the world's largest, fastest, most automated cranes. At the truck terminal, customized computer software makes it possible to keep track of thousands of containers, which are loaded from ship to truck to rail and vice versa.

Source: Insight Magazine/Brig Cabe.

multimodal firm provides intermodal service in which all, or some, of the transportation modes are owned and operated by one company. The advantage to the shipper is that the one-carrier service has responsibility from origin to destination. There can be no argument over which carrier caused the shipment to be late or is responsible for a loss or damage. In addition, major U.S. carriers are increasingly looking toward vertical integration to provide coordinated door-to-door service. For example, an ocean shipping company may also operate warehouses and distribution centers, freight forwarders, customs brokers, and rail and motor carriers.[34] United Parcel Service is an example of a multimodal carrier with its own fleet of trucks and airplanes. Currently, UPS owns 162 jets and charters 251 more. It operates 119,000 trucks. UPS delivers 11.5 million packages daily, making it the largest package delivery system in the world.[35]

Warehousing

storage warehouse
Warehouse in which products are stored prior to shipment.

distribution warehouse
Facility designed to assemble and then redistribute products to facilitate rapid movement of products to purchasers.

Two types of warehouses exist: storage and distribution. A **storage warehouse** stores products for moderate to long term periods in an attempt to balance supply and demand for producers and purchasers. They are most often used by firms whose products' supply or demand are seasonal. A **distribution warehouse** assembles and redistributes products, keeping them on the move as much as possible. Many distribution warehouses or centers physically store goods for fewer than 24 hours before shipping them on to customers.

In an attempt to reduce transportation costs, manufacturers have developed central distribution centers. A manufacturer located in Philadelphia with custom-

An employee of Toshiba America Information Systems Inc. scans bar codes from a forklift. Scanners such as this enable warehouses to keep track of inventory electronically. By using such a system, a company has ready access to information for adjusting production levels to meet demand and for scheduling deliveries and shipments.

Source: Courtesy of Toshiba America Information Systems, Inc.

ers in the Illinois-Wisconsin-Indiana area could send each customer a direct shipment. But if each customer placed small orders, the transportation charges for the individual shipments would be relatively high. A feasible solution is to send a large, consolidated shipment to a *break-bulk center*—a central distribution center that breaks down large shipments into several smaller ones and delivers them to individual customers in the area. For the manager in Philadelphia, the feasible break-bulk center might be located in Chicago.

Conversely, the *make-bulk center* consolidates several small shipments into one large shipment and delivers it to its destination. For example, a large retailer may operate several satellite production facilities in a given area. Each plant can then send shipments to a storage warehouse in Dallas. This, however, could result in a large number of small, expensive shipments. If a make-bulk center were created in San Francisco and each supplier sent its shipments there, all Dallas-bound deliveries could be consolidated into a single, economical shipment.

The top ten distribution center cities in the United States are Los Angeles, Atlanta, Chicago, Dallas, New York, Philadelphia, San Francisco, Houston, Denver, and Boston. Atlanta, Orlando, and Portland, Oregon are the fastest growing distribution sites.[36] Hallmark Cards serves 21,000 retail outlets nationwide from two distribution centers in Liberty, Missouri, and Enfield, Connecticut.[37]

Automated Warehouses.

Warehouses lend themselves well to automation, with the computer as the heart of the operation. At Control Data Corporation's emergency and spare parts warehouse in Arden Hills, Minnesota, sophisticated computer software translates orders into bar codes and determines the most efficient inventory picking sequence. The same information is available in the hand-held scanners warehouse employees use to fill orders. Order information is keyboarded only once and also generates labels, bills of lading, and shipping documents. Using this system, CDC's rate of inventory error has dropped from 14

Table 15.3

Considerations in Site
Selection for Distribution
Centers

Factor	Overall	Manufacturer	Retailer	Distributor
Transportation access	1	1	2	1
Outbound transportation	2	2	3	5
Customer proximity	3	3	6	6
Labor availability	4	5	1	3
Labor costs	5	6	7	4
Inbound transportation	6	4	4	2
Union environment	7	7	5	9
Taxes	8	8	10	7
State incentives/laws	9	10	—	—
Land costs	10	—	8	8
Utilities	—	—	9	10
JIT requirements	—	9	—	—

Source: Les B. Artman and David A. Clancy, "Distribution Follows Consumer Movement," *Transportation and Distribution* (June 1990), p. 19.

percent to 3 percent and picking errors have been virtually eliminated. In addition, to speed parts to customers whose computer systems are down, the CDC software is able to distinguish between routine and emergency orders and to fulfill priority needs within two hours. CDC's Arden Hills warehouse is a 50,000-square-foot facility that stocks some 75,000 parts valued at $45 million.[38]

Although automated warehousing costs are expensive, they can provide major savings for high-volume distributors such as grocery chains. They can "read" computerized store orders, choose the correct number of cases, and move them in the desired sequence to loading docks. These warehouses reduce labor costs, worker injuries, pilferage, fires, and breakage; they also assist in inventory control.

Location Factors.   A major decision each company faces concerns the number and location of its storage facilities. The two general factors involved are (1) warehousing and materials-handling costs and (2) delivery costs from warehouse to customer. The first type of costs are subject to economies of scale; therefore, on a per-unit basis they decrease as volume increases. Delivery costs, on the other hand, rise as the distance from the warehouse location to the customer increases.

The specific location of the firm's warehouse and distribution centers presents a complicated problem. Factors that must be considered are analyzed in Table 15.3. Site selection factors are analyzed from the point of view of manufacturers, retailers, and distributors.[39]

Inventory Control System

Inventory control is a major component of the physical distribution system. Current estimates of inventory holding costs are about 23 percent per year. This means that $1,000 of inventory held for a single year costs the company $230. Inventory costs include funds invested in inventory, depreciation, and possible obsolescence of the goods. Total business inventories currently equal some $777 billion—a figure that would have been significantly higher had it not been for deregulation. Analysts estimate that deregulation has saved an additional $200 billion a year in inventory investments.[40]

Figure 15.6

Determining the Economic
Order Quantity

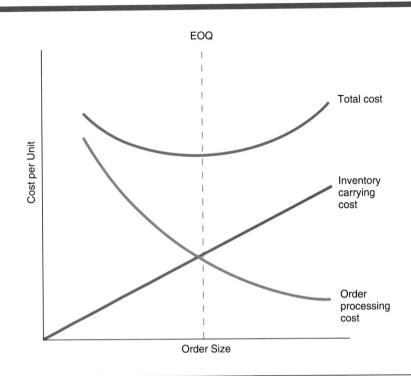

Inventory control analysts have developed a number of techniques for helping the physical distribution manager effectively control inventory. The most basic is the **economic order quantity (EOQ) model.** This technique revolves around the cost trade-off between two fundamental inventory costs: inventory-carrying costs, which increase with the addition of more inventory, and order-processing costs, which decrease as the quantity ordered increases. As Figure 15.6 indicates, these two cost items are traded off to determine the optimal order quantity for each product. Here the EOQ point is the one at which total cost is minimized. By placing orders for this amount as needed, firms can minimize their inventory costs.

economic order quantity (EOQ) model
Technique used to determine the costs of holding inventory versus the costs involved in placing orders in order to arrive at the optimal order quantity.

Inventory control systems in Eastern Europe are primitive compared to those in the West, resulting in considerable waste and lost productivity. For example, in Kiskunhalas, Hungary, employees at Texcoop, a state-owned sweater factory, are often forced to sit idle for lack of goods to work on. In contrast, U.S. manufacturer Levi Strauss, which recently opened a factory in Hungary, uses a computerized inventory control system to ensure that huge rolls of imported denim arrive as needed.[41]

The Just-in-Time System

just-in-time (JIT) system
Inventory control system designed to minimize inventory.

The **just-in-time (JIT) inventory system,** borrowed from the Japanese, has rapidly gained acceptance in the United States. It involves minimizing inventory at each production facility. Manufacturers prefer this system because it greatly reduces their inventory-carrying costs. Often parts arrive the same day they are used in the production process. Just-in-time inventory control requires precise delivery schedules with heavy emphasis on coordination between the purchaser's traffic department and carriers to ensure timely delivery. The seller also must have efficient personnel to ensure that products arrive as scheduled. Just-in-time inventory systems are especially important in the food industry, where wholesalers and retailers guarantee freshness.

Inherent in the JIT system is the expectation that deliveries will be made at the time they are needed. In Japan, meeting precise delivery requirements is made easier because suppliers are located close to their customers, and because many Japanese industrial companies own controlling interests in key suppliers, thus guaranteeing greater service and loyalty. It is difficult to duplicate the Japanese system in the United States because of our larger land mass and because few U.S. manufacturers own controlling interests in their suppliers. As a result, intermediaries whose business it is to manage the flow of supplies on a just-in-time basis from producers to customers are an essential part of the U.S. physical distribution system.[42]

The just-in-time system is particularly effective with products that have relatively few variations. Consequently, heavy users of this approach, such as Toyota, offer a number of "luxury" features on their cars as standard equipment. U.S. auto manufacturers, which previously charged extra for such options, are beginning to duplicate the Japanese approach by offering fewer options and many more standard features. Using this strategy, Nissan's plants in the expanding European market operate with just three days inventory of locally supplied parts, only one day more than the company requires in Japan.[43]

In 1987 Rank Xerox, Xerox Corporation's European subsidiary, put into effect a just-in-time inventory system. The system was badly needed; for every $1 billion worth of equipment stored at the company's Venray, Netherlands distribution facility, $300 million was spent to move the equipment to the various operating companies. With the goal of reducing by one-third its annual logistics spending, Rank Xerox made a number of important changes including (1) centralizing stock in one location in France rather than in 15 branch warehouses—a move that cut inventory needs by half—and (2) shipping against actual customer orders rather than forecasted orders, a change that helped employees focus on customer service. "This changed the mission of the people working [in the warehouse]," said Jackie Soulas, Xerox's manager of equipment development in Europe. "Matching an order with a piece of equipment for an end customer triggers greater responsibility." Following its success in France, Xerox implemented similar just-in-time distribution plans throughout Europe. The result was a reduction of stock from a 30-day to a 7-day supply and logistics cost savings of $150 million a year.[44]

Despite the advantages of the just-in-time system, under extraordinary circumstances it can cause problems. During the Persian Gulf War, for example, companies that relied on just-in-time inventory fed to them from overseas suppliers were placed in a vulnerable position. With normal air and freight shipments disrupted, distribution managers at Nissan Motor Co.'s U.S. plant in Smyrna, Tennessee, found it difficult to locate space on cargo planes for emergency shipments from Japan. As a result, express air shipping services such as Skyway Freight Systems of Watsonville, California, a specialist in just-in-time deliveries, reported a 20 percent surge in "rush" air-service orders during the war.[45]

Order Processing

The physical distribution manager is concerned with order processing, another logistics function, because it directly affects the firm's ability to meet its customer service standards. If the order-processing system is inefficient, the company may have to compensate by using costly premium transportation or by increasing the number of field warehouses in all major markets.

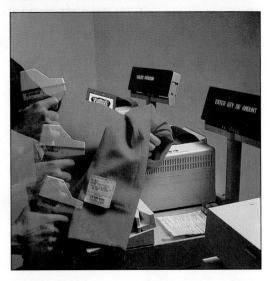

COMPETITIVE EDGE

THE IMPACT OF EDI

. . . .

EDI is not only enhancing productivity, flexibility, and competitiveness, but also revolutionizing the relationship between suppliers and purchasers. In fact, EDI capability may soon become a requirement for a long-term relationship with a supplier.

EDI, or electronic data interchange, allows computers at two different locations to exchange business documents in machine-readable format, employing strictly defined industry standards. Instead of exchanging paper documents through the mail, business partners trade documents electronically over data communications lines. Purchase orders, invoices, remittance slips, and the like can be exchanged electronically, thereby eliminating duplication of data entry, dramatically reducing errors, and speeding up the procurement cycle. EDI differs from electronic mail in that it is concerned with specific documents used for the transaction of business.

The data embedded in an EDI message can automatically initiate a series of actions: Inventories can be updated, customers invoiced, and suppliers paid, all without human intervention. The potential for savings and streamlining of operations in such areas as order administration, distribution, and purchasing is enormous. EDI can also improve customer service. But perhaps the most important effect of EDI is the forging of closer and more efficient working relationships between business partners. As one analyst puts it, "The edges between trading partners begin to blur, creating a new interrelated organization that begins to function like a single organism."

In the long run, EDI can result in substantial increases in productivity and savings in the millions. For this reason, many industries have required their suppliers to invest in EDI hardware and software (a personal computer, specialized translation software, and a subscription to a network). The railroad industry adopted EDI across the board in the mid-1970s, and the grocery industry estimates overall savings from EDI at $300 million per year. Internationally, EDI is in widespread use to reduce the cost of international documentation (paperwork can account for 8 percent of the cost of an international transaction). Indeed, EDI is rapidly becoming essential for participation in the global business environment.

One firm that is using EDI to gain a competitive edge is Mercantile Stores Company, which operates several department store chains as well as numerous beauty salons and specialty stores. Mercantile's EDI system, called Quick Response, has been installed at cash registers in its department stores. Product information contained on bar-coded merchandise tags is collected by electronic scanners at the point of sale (see photo). The data are then transmitted to manufacturers, who send it along to their suppliers. The system links together retailers' and manufacturers' computers, making possible the instant receipt and shipping of orders. Since orders can be placed much closer to the time the merchandise will be sold, inventories and out-of-stock situations can be reduced and customer service improved. With benefits like these, it's hard to imagine how companies ever got along without EDI.

Discussion Questions

1. Is there any reason not to invest in EDI?

2. As purchasers and suppliers become increasingly interdependent, what issues of control are likely to arise?

Sources: Ronald A. Margulis, "The Food Industry Turns to EDI for Efficiency," *U.S. Distribution Journal* (March 1990), p. 16; "Productivity through Messaging," *Fortune* (December 3, 1990), pp. 155–176; and "The Strategic Link Between Business Partners," *Business Week* (November 12, 1990), pp. 137–149; Mercantile Stores Company, Inc., *Annual Report,* 1988. *Photo source*: Courtesy of Mercantile Stores Company, Inc.

Order processing typically consists of four major activities: (1) a credit check; (2) recording the sale, such as crediting a sales representative's commission account; (3) making the appropriate accounting entries; and (4) locating the item, shipping, and adjusting inventory records. An item that is not available for shipment is known as a **stockout.** The order-processing unit must advise the customer of a stockout and offer a choice of alternative actions.

Technological innovations such as increased use of the Universal Product Code are contributing to greater efficiency in order processing. Quill Corporation, the largest independent distributor of office products in the United States, recently installed a bar-code scanning system to aid order processing. With $240 million in sales, Quill ships more than 12,000 boxes a day and pays $16 million in annual freight costs. The bar-code system gave Quill the ability to route customer orders efficiently and reduce the need for manual handling. The coded information includes all the data necessary to generate customer invoices, thus eliminating the need for repeated keypunching. Although the price tag for Quill's order processing system was about $1 million, it has helped reduce company freight bills by about the same amount each year. An added advantage is that carriers like Roadway Package Service can read Quill's bar codes via hand-held computers and track shipments through the system.[46]

Protective Packaging and Materials Handling

All of the activities associated with moving products within the manufacturer's plants, warehouses, and transportation company terminals comprise the **materials handling** component of physical distribution. These activities must be thoroughly coordinated for both intracompany and intercompany activities. The efficiency of plants and warehouses depends on an effective system.

Two important innovations in the area of materials handling have occurred. One is known as **unitizing**—combining as many packages as possible into one load, preferably on a *pallet* (a platform, generally made of wood, on which goods are transported). Unitizing can be accomplished by using steel bands to hold the unit in place or by *shrink packaging.* A shrink package is constructed by placing a sheet of plastic over the unit and then heating it. As the plastic cools, it shrinks, enabling it to hold the individual packages together securely. Unitizing is advantageous because it requires little labor per package, promotes rapid movement, and minimizes damage and pilferage.

The second innovation is **containerization**—the combining of several unitized loads. The container is typically a big box, 8 feet wide, and 10, 20, 30, or 40 feet long. Such a container facilitates intertransport mode changes. A container of oil rig parts, for example, can be loaded in Tulsa and trucked to Kansas City, placed on a high-speed, run-through train to New York City, and then placed on a ship to Saudi Arabia.

Containerization also markedly reduces the time involved in loading and unloading ships. Container ships often can be unloaded in fewer than 24 hours—a task that otherwise could take up to two weeks. In-transit damage is also reduced, because individual packages are not handled en route to the purchaser.

One shipping company currently has container ships that can make a round trip between New York, Bremerhaven, and Rotterdam in 14 days. Only four days are needed for crossing the Atlantic and another six days for three port calls. This speed allows U.S. exporters to provide competitive delivery schedules for European markets.

When unitizing and containerization are added at the warehouse, they are considered value-added services. These services may also move goods from bulk packaging to consumer packaging. For example, a tank car filled with anti-

stockout
Inventory item that is unavailable for shipment or sale.

materials handling
All activities involved in moving goods within a manufacturer's plants, warehouses, and transportation company terminals.

unitizing
Process of combining as many packages as possible into one load in order to expedite product movement and reduce damage and pilferage.

containerization
Process of combining several unitized loads of products into a single load to facilitate intertransport changes in transportation modes.

freeze may arrive at a distribution warehouse, where it is unloaded into a filling bin and then dispensed into consumer containers. This system provides a cost advantage to the manufacturer, who is able to ship the product in bulk from factory to distribution center, avoiding, in the process, the more costly shipping of consumer packages.[47]

Summary of Chapter Objectives

1. **Explain the role of physical distribution in an effective marketing strategy.** The goal of the physical distribution function is to produce a specified level of customer service while minimizing the costs involved in physically moving and storing the product from its production point to its ultimate purchase.

2. **Identify and compare the major components of a physical distribution system.** Physical distribution involves a broad range of activities concerned with efficient movement of finished goods from the end of the production line to the consumer. As a system, physical distribution consists of six elements: (1) customer service, (2) transportation, (3) inventory control, (4) protective packaging and materials handling, (5) order processing, and (6) warehousing. These elements are interrelated and must be balanced to create a smoothly functioning distribution system and avoid suboptimization.

3. **Outline the suboptimization problem in physical distribution.** Suboptimization refers to a situation in which each manager of a physical distribution activity attempts to minimize his or her costs, resulting in a negative impact on other physical distribution activities. The objective of the physical distribution function is to focus on total distribution costs to minimize the degree of suboptimization.

4. **Explain the impact of transportation deregulation on physical distribution activities.** Deregulation has had a profound effect on transportation in recent years. Many transporters now are free to develop unique solutions to shippers' needs. Deregulation has been particularly important for motor carriers, railroads, and air carriers.

5. **Compare the major transportation alternatives on the basis of factors such as speed, dependability, cost, frequency of shipments, availability in different locations, and flexibility in handling products.** Railroads rank high on flexibility in handling products and availability in different locations; average on speed, dependability in meeting schedules, and cost; and low on frequency of shipments. Motor carriers are relatively high in cost but are ranked high on speed, dependability, shipment frequency, and availability in different locations. Water carriers balance their slow speed, low shipment frequency, and limited availability with very low costs. The special nature of pipelines makes them rank relatively low on availability, flexibility, and speed but also low in cost. Air transportation is high in cost but offers very fast and dependable delivery schedules.

Key Terms

physical distribution	customer service standards
system	class rate
suboptimization	commodity rate
maquiladoras	storage warehouse

distribution warehouse   materials handling

economic order quantity (EOQ) model   unitizing

just-in-time (JIT) inventory system   containerization

stockout

Review Questions

1. Why has physical distribution been one of the last areas in most companies to be carefully studied and improved?

2. Outline the basic reasons for the increased attention to physical distribution management. Pay special attention to increased pressure from foreign competitors.

3. What are the basic objectives of physical distribution in a corporation? Compare and contrast them to the logistics objectives in a military operation like Operation Desert Storm.

4. Explain the role of customer service standards in the physical distribution system. Why are some companies placing more emphasis on customer service?

5. What factors should be considered in locating a new distribution warehouse? What are some of the cost trade-offs a company must consider in its location decision?

6. Who should be ultimately responsible for determining the level of customer service standards? Explain. Do you agree or disagree with the statement that an orientation toward customer service should permeate all levels of the organization?

7. Outline the basic strengths and weaknesses of each mode of transport. Describe the relative importance of each mode in terms of ton-miles.

8. What do freight forwarders do? Under what circumstances are they used by business?

9. Identify the major forms of intermodal coordination, and give an example of a good for which each is likely to be used. Why have piggyback railcars become so popular?

10. Explain the advantages and potential problems of the just-in-time system of inventory control. Relate your answer to the need to control and lower carrying costs.

Discussion Questions

1. Suggest the most appropriate method of transportation for each of the following products. Defend your choices.
   a. Iron ore
   b. Dash detergent
   c. Heavy earth-moving equipment
   d. Crude oil
   e. Orchids
   f. Lumber

2. Project ten years after the economic integration of the European Community in 1992. What changes do you foresee in the region's system of physical distribution with regard to transportation, the location of warehouses, inventory control, and customer service? How will these changes affect European business? How will they affect U.S. firms doing business in Western Europe?

3. Explain why the study of physical distribution is one of the classic examples of the systems approach to business problems.

4. Which mode of transportation do you believe will experience the greatest ton-mile percentage during the 1990s? Why?

5. Analyze the concept of value-added services as it applies to physical distribution management. How does improved technology in the form of sophisticated, computerized inventory tracking and order placement and fulfillment systems relate to the demand for value-added services?

Computer Applications

The physical distribution manager must balance two types of costs involved in inventory: (1) inventory holding costs, which increase with the addition of more inventory, and (2) order costs, which decrease as the quantity ordered increases. The *economic order quantity (EOQ)* model is a particularly useful quantitative technique for determining the order size that will most closely balance these two types of costs. It is described in more detail on pages 510 and 511.

The following formula is used to determine the economic order quantity:

$$EOQ = \sqrt{\frac{2RS}{IC}}$$

where

EOQ = economic order quantity (in units)
R = annual usage rate
S = cost of placing an order
I = annual inventory carrying costs expressed as a percentage
C = item's cost per unit (the "unit" may consist of a single item or a prepackaged box containing a dozen items, a gross, or even more)

In the above formula, R is an estimate based on the demand forecast for the item; S is calculated from the firm's cost records; and I is an estimate based on the costs of such items as handling, insurance, interest, storage, depreciation, and taxes. Since the item's per-unit cost may vary over time, C is also likely to be an estimate. The EOQ can be determined by inserting specific data into the formula. Consider, for example, the following:

$$R = 6,000$$
$$S = \$8.50$$
$$I = 15\%$$
$$C = \$14.50$$

$$EOQ = \sqrt{\frac{(2)(6,000)(8.50)}{(14.50)(.15)}}$$
$$= 216.56$$

The calculation often results in a fractional quantity that must be rounded to the next whole number to determine the economic order quantity. Thus, the EOQ in the above example would be rounded to 217 units.

Although the exact EOQ calculation has been determined at 217 units, other factors may have to be considered. For instance, suppliers may place additional constraints on the ordering firm. In some cases, orders may be limited to even dozens or multiples of 100. The economic order quantity must be adjusted to match such constraints.

Directions: Use menu item 13 titled "Economic Order Quantity (EOQ)" to solve the following problems.

Problem 1.   Appliance Mart of Salisbury, Maryland, sells 160 refrigerators annually. The store pays an average of $300 for each unit, and each order costs $25 to place. The annual inventory carrying cost is 10 percent. What is the appropriate EOQ for Appliance Mart?

Problem 2.   An Erie, Pennsylvania, retailer sells about 220 dozen of a certain brand of men's shirts each year. The wholesale cost is $145 per dozen. The retailer tries to keep the inventory as low as possible because of the 26 percent annual carrying cost. Each order costs the store $30 to place. Calculate the EOQ for this retailer.

Problem 3.   A souvenir shop in Myrtle Beach, South Carolina, pays 12 cents for each of the 30,000 postcards it sells annually. Inventory carrying costs are a modest 5 percent, and placing an order costs only $5. Calculate this retailer's EOQ.

Problem 4.   The owner of a Bridgeport, Connecticut, sporting goods retail store wants to calculate the EOQ for a certain line of tennis racquets. The racquets cost the store $20 and have an average inventory carrying cost of 25 percent. Each order costs $25. The store sells 600 of these racquets each year.

a.   Determine the economic order quantity for the tennis racquets.

b.   Suggest the most appropriate order size if the manufacturer insists that orders be placed in multiples of 10.

Problem 5.   A Birmingham, Alabama, motorcycle shop has an order placement cost of $50 for its $75 (wholesale cost) helmets. Its average annual inventory carrying cost is 15 percent. The shop sells 250 helmets each year.

a.   Determine the EOQ for the motorcycle helmets.

b.   Determine the most appropriate order size if the shop's supplier decides to require that all orders be placed in multiples of one dozen.

Arrowhead Drinking Water Co.

Bottled water got a big boost in the late 1970s when the importers of Perrier launched a $4 million advertising campaign in the United States promoting their sparkling spring water as an alternative to soft drinks and alcoholic beverages. The campaign spoke to a receptive audience—a growing number of health-conscious and fitness-minded Americans concerned about water pollution and purity, and showing a preference for low-calorie, alcohol-free beverages.

The advertising blitz not only helped Perrier become the market leader in U.S. bottled water sales; it also fueled an explosive growth in the industry, as other bottled water marketers began aggressively promoting their mineral water, club soda, seltzer, and sparkling water. Americans responded by buying bottled water in record numbers. Per-capita consumption grew from 1.5 gallons in 1976 to 7.9 gallons in 1990.

Today the $2.35 billion bottled water market is the fastest growing segment of the beverage business. According to the Beverage Marketing Corporation, bottled water sales increased 173% during the past decade and are expected to continue growing at an annual rate of 16 percent through 2000. The bottled water business in the United States is highly regionalized, but the market's growth during the past decade has attracted competitors such as PepsiCo and other national soft-drink, beer, and spirits marketers. Perrier, eager to maintain its market leadership and increase its market share, acquired Arrowhead Drinking Water Co. from Beatrice Foods in 1987. The acquisition not only doubled Perrier's market share to 21 percent, it also broadened the firm's presence in the nonsparkling water market.

Arrowhead, based in Monterey Park, California, is a major regional distributor of jug water. Jug water is marketed primarily as a substitute for tap water through two channels: through supermarkets in 1- and 2.5-gallon containers, and delivered directly to consumers in 5-gallon bottles for their water coolers. Though jug water lacks the sparkle of its specialty counterparts, it accounts for the lion's share—77 percent—of all U.S. bottled water sales. In 1985, Arrowhead entered the sparkling water market by introducing Arrowhead Springs Sparkling Water in 1.5-liter bottles and six-packs of 10-ounce bottles. A year later, the company extended the line by adding Ozarka Sparkling Water.

Perrier's marketing success in the United States can be attributed to its promotional efforts, but Arrowhead's accomplishments as a bottled water marketer are tied mainly to a superior product and an efficient distribution system that brings mountain spring water to customers' homes and offices and to supermarkets in Arizona, California, Hawaii, and Nevada.

Arrowhead's beginnings date to the early 1800s when David Smith built a health spa at Arrowhead Springs. Visitors flocked there to bathe in—and drink—the supposedly restorative mineral water. As customer demand for the drinking water increased, Smith began piping water down the mountainside and, in 1905, started bottling it in the basement of the spa's hotel and shipping it to customers.

Today, Arrowhead gathers water from seven springs in the San Bernardino Mountains. From these sources, water flows through 7-mile pipelines to storage reservoirs, where it is loaded by gravity within 25 minutes into 64,000-gallon-capacity tanker trucks that transport it to Arrowhead's bottling plant. The tankers operate 24 hours a day, seven days a week. While alternative methods such as railroad and pipeline have been tried, trucks have proven to be the most efficient way to transport the water supply needed to satisfy Arrowhead's customer demand.

At the bottling plant, water is pumped through several filtration stages to produce three different products: spring, distilled, and fluoridated water. In a computer-controlled bottling room, sanitized bottles are rapidly filled and capped. Five-gallon bottles are individually crated, while smaller containers are packed in boxes. Boxes and crates are unitized to ensure that forklift operators can move them safely and efficiently from the production line to the warehouse or delivery yard.

Arrowhead generates most of its sales from the delivery of 5-gallon water bottles directly to consumers. Satisfying these customers is the firm's top priority, and Arrowhead's route salespeople do more than deliver water. They are responsible for soliciting new business and completely servicing existing accounts. They control their own truck inventory and make daily adjustments to accommodate last-minute customer requests, collect money, update orders, and balance their books. Route salespeople receive support from telephone operators in the order processing department who answer customer inquiries, transmit called-in orders, and set up delivery schedules. Because deliveries are scheduled at 14-day intervals, route salespeople must ensure that each delivery will satisfy a two-week demand. "The route salesperson is really the backbone of the company," says Larry Balarsky. "If it weren't for the route salespeople, Arrowhead wouldn't even exist. They're the most important part of the company."

Since home delivery involves high transportation and labor costs, it takes up a large part of Arrowhead's expense budget. To contain delivery costs, Arrowhead marketers chose a different approach for grocery-store customers. Rather than investing in a fleet of delivery trucks, Arrowhead offers the grocery trade a freight allowance as an incentive for retailers to pick up products at Arrowhead's warehouse.

To compete profitably with other bottled water companies and municipal water systems and yet maintain its high level of customer service, Arrowhead marketers strive for operating efficiency in inventory control, materials handling, packaging, and warehousing. Marketers plan for inventory needs by preparing detailed 1-, 5-, and 10-year forecasts of consumer demand, which enable them to estimate the type of water and number of bottles that will be needed. These estimates assist planners in the purchase of bottles, containers, boxes, crates, and other operating equipment and supplies, and in determining future warehousing needs.

Arrowhead marketers balance their large capital investment expenses by maintaining a minimum inventory of 5-gallon bottles. The manager of production operations states that the inventory plan operates on the principle of one day for empty bottles to be filled, one day for full bottles on the route trucks to be delivered, and a quarter- to a half-day for bottles on hand as backup. To the extent possible, bottles are taken directly from the production line and loaded on delivery trucks to avoid double handling.

Because the production process for the bottled water sold to supermarkets is slower than that for the 5-gallon bottles, these products are warehoused to ensure that enough is available when the retailers need them. To balance production output with retail demand, Arrowhead marketers try to maintain a three- to four-day supply of 1- and 2.5-gallon bottles and several weeks' supply of sparkling water. They move inventory on a first-in, first-out basis to keep the product as fresh as possible on supermarket shelves. They also encourage retailers to keep their own backroom inventories of high-volume drinking water to meet customer demand.

As Arrowhead's distribution requirements have increased through the years, so have their costs for loading and unloading delivery trucks—a process that originally required route salespeople to stay with their trucks during the one to one and a half hours of loading. To reduce loading expenses, Arrowhead marketers asked their engineers to develop a more cost-efficient system. They designed a straddle trailer that moves hundreds of bottles at one time. The straddle trailer allows for a 15-minute turnaround time, so between an hour and an hour and 15 minutes is being saved, not only of the drivers' time, but the capital investment on $150,000 worth of equipment that can be kept on the road.

In making packaging decisions, Arrowhead marketers consider production-line efficiency as well as the rate of product turnover. All aspects of marketing home-delivered bottled water are geared to the 5-gallon size—the industry standard since the turn of the century. Changes in bottle size would involve millions of dollars of new production equipment. Without changing the size, Arrowhead has significantly improved 5-gallon productivity by changing from a 14-pound glass bottle to a 3-pound polycarbonate bottle. With the lighter bottle, route salespeople carry one ton less a day in weight and have fewer lifting-related injuries, while delivery trucks get much better gas mileage.

When Arrowhead introduced its sparkling water, marketers decided to package the 1.5-liter plastic bottles in eight-bottle cases, even though the industry standard for sparkling water in glass bottles was 12 per case. Their decision, which took into account the advice of industry suppliers and other experts, was based on providing the best distribution economies throughout the system.

Sources: Personal interview with Larry Balarsky, Arrowhead Drinking Water Co., June 1991. Beverage Marketing Corp., *1987 Annual Industry Survey;* Marcy Magiera, "Bottled Waters Spring Up," *Advertising Age* (September 21, 1987), pp. 24, 83; and "Water, Water Everywhere," *Consumer Reports* (January 1987), pp. 42–47.

Questions

1. Arrowhead marketers use multiple distribution channels in reaching the firm's customers. Draw a diagram of each channel used and label each part.

2. Relate each of the components of the physical distribution system to the way that Arrowhead provides mountain spring water to customers.

3. What are Arrowhead's physical distribution objectives? Identify several possible sources for suboptimization to occur and explain how the total-cost approach is used by Arrowhead marketers to avoid the occurrence of suboptimization.

4. Which transportation factors discussed in the chapter might have affected Arrowhead's decision to switch from the use of railroad cars to trucks in transporting water from its source to the bottling plant?

5. Which of Arrowhead's marketing decisions have improved the effectiveness and efficiency of the firm's physical distribution system?

Source: Robert Deutsch/USA TODAY.

PART **6**

Promotional Strategy

CHAPTER 16
Introduction to Promotion

CHAPTER 17
Advertising, Sales Promotion, and
Public Relations

CHAPTER 18
Personal Selling and Sales
Management

16

Introduction to Promotion

CHAPTER OBJECTIVES

1. To explain the relationship of promotional strategy to the process of communication.

2. To list the objectives of promotion.

3. To explain the concept of the promotional mix and its relationship to the marketing mix.

4. To identify the primary determinants of a promotional mix.

5. To contrast the two major alternative promotional strategies.

6. To compare the primary methods of developing a promotional budget.

7. To defend promotion against common public criticisms.

Ken Meyers and two partners developed a unique snack food that fit the bill for consumers' increasing desire for healthy foods. They called their product Smartfood, a brand name signaling to consumers that it was a healthy alternative to junk snack food. This all-natural prepopped popcorn coated with white cheddar cheese powder differed from other cheese-popcorn products that had preservatives and artificial flavorings and colorings. Smartfood's package—a shiny black bag featuring a bright green cornstalk with popped yellow kernels spilling out the top—was

visually different from the see-through packages of other popcorn products on the market.

The small Marlborough, Massachusetts, firm had a distinctive product but little money to promote it. Shortly after launching the product in 1985, Smartfoods, Inc., quickly used up its annual $100,000 promotional budget by running radio ads for several weeks in one city. First-year sales, projected at $1 million, fell $965,000 short of the mark. Meyers says, "Clearly, this wasn't acceptable. We had to find a different way of getting our message across."

The entrepreneurs decided to try guerrilla marketing—promotional methods that cost less than major media advertising yet are unusual enough to make the brand stand out. Smartfood was targeted at young, active consumers, so the company devised promotions to reach their target audience, who are considered to be opinion leaders for this type of consumer good. To build visibility and stimulate sales of Smartfood, the company formed marketing teams that promoted the popcorn directly to consumers and distributed product samples. Ski teams handed out samples on the slopes of New England ski areas, and windsurfing teams gave away samples to beach crowds. The company bought an old ice cream truck, put a stage on the top, and turned it into a comedy cruiser named the Smartfood Yuk Truck, from which comics and other performers entertained crowds of people and team members threw bags of Smartfood. A team of mountain bikers hit the road, pulling Smartfood billboards on trailers behind them.

"We decided that our product and package were our best advertising tools," says Meyers. "The product

was, for us, easy and relatively cost-effective to give away." To help build its brand image, each element of Smartfoods' promotions—including windsurfer sails, marketing team costumes, point-of-purchase displays in stores, and company delivery trucks—was designed to carry through the package theme of the cornstalk graphic on a black background.

The promotional strategy attracted attention to and sparked interest in Smartfood, enabled consumers to try it, produced positive feedback, and created credible word-of-mouth advertising. Meyers says, "It's more valuable for 10 or 100 people to see us on the ski slopes doing silly things than for many times that number to flip past us in a magazine. If a friend tells you, 'You won't believe it. I saw three bags of popcorn skiing down a mountainside,' you're going to listen to that more than you would to a radio ad." Consumers who liked Smartfood asked for it at retail stores and complained when they couldn't find it, which motivated more retailers to carry the new brand.

Smartfoods' promotions were so effective that sales soared to $20 million in 1989 from $35,000 in 1985. In 1989 Smartfoods was purchased by Frito-Lay, whose national salesforce and excellent distribution system helped expand it from a regional to a national brand. Smartfoods now advertises in major media but plans to continue its zany promotions that have become a company hallmark. "Field marketing is still our main thing," says Meyers. "We're working continuously to make sure our field activities are effective and fresh."[1]

Photo source: Copyright 1991 by Seth Resnick.

Chapter Overview

Thus far we have examined two of the four broad variables of the marketing mix. In Part 6, we analyze the third marketing mix variable—promotion. This chapter introduces promotion and briefly describes the elements comprising a firm's promotional mix—personal and nonpersonal selling—and the factors that determine the optimal mix. It identifies the objectives of promotion and describes the importance of developing promotional budgets and measuring the effectiveness of promotions. Finally, the chapter discusses the importance of the business, economic, and social aspects of promotion. Chapter 17 discusses advertising, sales promotion, and the other nonpersonal selling elements of the promotional mix. Chapter 18 completes this section by focusing on personal selling.

A good place to begin the discussion of promotion is by defining the term. **Promotion** is the function of informing, persuading, and influencing the consumer's purchase decision. Consider how this definition applies to Smartfoods. Its promotions informed the target market of the availability of the new product, persuaded consumers to try it by giving away free samples, and influenced consumers to buy Smartfood at retail stores or request it where it was unavailable.

The marketing manager sets the goals and objectives of the firm's promotional strategy in accordance with overall organizational objectives and the goals of the marketing organization. Based on these objectives, the various elements of the strategy—personal selling, advertising, sales promotion, publicity, and public relations—are formulated into a coordinated promotional plan. This becomes an integral part of the total marketing strategy for reaching selected market segments. The feedback mechanism, including marketing research and field reports, completes the system by identifying any deviations from the plan and suggesting modifications for improvement.

Promotional strategy is closely related to the process of communication. A standard definition of *communication* is the transmission of a message from a sender to a receiver. **Marketing communications,** then, are those messages that deal with buyer-seller relationships. Marketing communication is a broader concept than promotional strategy, because it includes word-of-mouth advertising and other forms of unsystematic communication. A planned promotional strategy, however, is certainly the most important part of any marketing communications.

promotion
Function of informing, persuading, and influencing the consumer's purchase decision.

marketing communications
Transmission from a sender to a receiver of messages dealing with buyer-seller relationships.

The Communications Process

Figure 16.1 shows a general communications process and its application to promotional strategy. The *sender* is the source of the communications system, since he or she seeks to convey a *message* (a communication of information, advice, or request) to a *receiver* (the recipient of the communication). The message must accomplish three tasks in order to be effective:

1. It must gain the receiver's attention.
2. It must be understood by both receiver and sender.
3. It must stimulate the receiver's needs and suggest an appropriate method of satisfying them.

The three tasks are related to the **AIDA concept** (attention-interest-desire-action) proposed by E. K. Strong over 60 years ago as an explanation of the steps an individual must go through before making a purchase decision. First, the potential consumer's attention must be gained. Then the promotional message

AIDA concept
Acronym for attention-interest-desire-action, the traditional explanation of the steps an individual must take prior to making a purchase decision.

Figure 16.1   Relating Promotion to the Communications Process

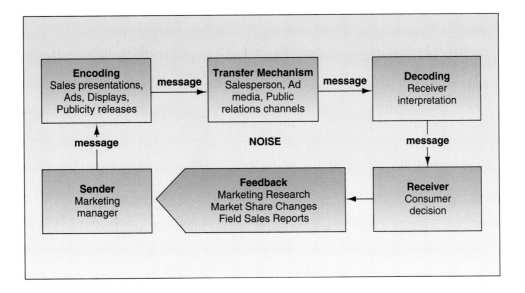

seeks to arouse interest in the good or service. The next stage is to stimulate desire by convincing the would-be buyer of the product's ability to satisfy his or her needs. Finally, the sales presentation, advertisement, or sales promotion technique attempts to produce action, in the form of a purchase or a more favorable attitude, that may lead to future purchases.

The message must be *encoded,* or translated into understandable terms, and transmitted through a communications medium. *Decoding* is the receiver's interpretation of the message. The receiver's response, known as *feedback,* completes the system. Throughout the process, *noise* can interfere with the transmission of the message and reduce its effectiveness.

The marketing manager is the sender in the system, as shown in Figure 16.1. The message is encoded in the form of sales presentations, advertising, displays, or publicity releases. The *transfer mechanism* for delivering the message may be a salesperson, a public relations channel, or an advertising medium. The decoding step involves the consumer's interpretation of the sender's message. This is often the most troublesome aspect of marketing communications, because consumers do not always interpret a promotional message in the same way the sender does. Since receivers are likely to decode messages according to their own frames of reference or experiences, the sender must be careful to ensure that the message is encoded correctly so that it will match the frame of reference of the target audience.

Feedback is the receiver's response to the message. Federal Savings Bank in Columbia, South Carolina, has received an incredible amount of positive feedback from an advertising campaign featuring the antics of Sunshine, an orangutan, who shakes her head, sticks out her tongue, and covers her eyes with her hands while a voice-over promotes the bank's services. Not only do new and existing customers tell bank personnel how much they love the campaign, but marketers worldwide have responded to the promotion by buying syndication rights to the visual and dubbing in a different voice-over. The Christian Democrat Party of the Federal Republic of Germany, for example, used one of Federal's television commercials and supplied a new voice-over for its election campaign

Figure 16.2

Promotion Designed to
Produce Feedback in Form
of Purchase

in 1990. Syndication sales have paid for the production of Federal's campaign and one year's worth of media buying.[2]

Feedback may take the form of attitude change, purchase, or nonpurchase. In some instances, organizations use promotion to create a favorable attitude toward their goods or services in the hope that such attitude changes will result in future purchases. In other instances, the objective of the promotional communication is to directly stimulate consumer purchases. The Norwest Banks ad in Figure 16.2 was part of a promotional campaign introducing the bank's electronic filing service for taxpayers. The promotion, which included radio ads and transit and in-bank posters, was so effective that consumer demand exceeded expectations one week after the campaign started. Note how the ad accomplishes the major tasks of effective communications: it is attention-getting, easily understood by both sender and receiver, stimulates the receiver's need or desire of getting a speedy tax refund, and suggests how to satisfy the need. Even nonpurchases may serve as feedback to the sender. Failure to purchase may result from ineffective communication in which the message was not believed or not remembered. Alternatively, the message may have failed to persuade the receiver that the firm's goods or services are superior to its competitors'. Feedback can be obtained from techniques such as marketing research studies and field sales reports.

Noise represents interference at some stage in the communications process. It may result from such factors as transmission of competitive promotional messages over the same communications channel, misinterpretation of a sales presentation or advertising message, receipt of the promotional message by the wrong person, or random noise factors such as people conversing during a television commercial or leaving the room. Noise in the forms of a mechanical problem, receiver decoding, and negative publicity interfered with Coca-Cola USA's $100 million "Magic Summer '90" promotion for Coca-Cola Classic. The

Table 16.1   Examples of Marketing Communications

Type of Promotion	Sender	Encoding	Transfer Mechanism	Decoding by Receiver	Feedback
Personal selling	Canon business products	Sales presentation on new model of office copier	Canon sales representative	Office manager and employees in local firm discuss Canon sales presentation and those of competing suppliers	Order placed for Canon copier
One-dollar-off coupon (sales promotion)	Popeye's chicken	Popeye's marketing department and advertising agency	Coupon insert in Sunday newspaper	Newspaper reader sees coupon for chicken and saves it	Chicken purchased by consumers using coupon
Television advertising	Walt Disney Enterprises	Advertisement for a new, "G"-rated animated movie is developed by Disney's advertising agency	Network television during programs with high percentage of viewers under 12 years old	Children see ad and ask parents to take them; parents see ad and decide to take children	Movie tickets purchased

promotion offered specially designed MagiCans that, when opened, popped up cash or prize coupons. The prize cans were filled with chlorinated water not meant for consumption. Some cans malfunctioned and didn't pop up as they should have, some consumers were confused by the surprise prizes, and one child drank the chlorinated water. After receiving consumer complaints, the company ran ads to alert consumers of possible malfunctions and to warn them not to drink the liquid inside MagiCans. But due to lingering perception problems about the safety of the promotion, Coca-Cola ended the promotion two months earlier than planned.[3]

In some instances, the noise produced by misinterpretations of faulty communications results in amusing examples of miscommunications. Here are four recent international examples:[4]

□ *On a sign in a Bucharest hotel lobby:* The lift is being fixed for the next day. During that time we regret that you will be unbearable.

□ *From a Japanese information booklet about using a hotel air conditioner:* Cooles and Heates: If you want just condition of warm in your room please control yourself.

□ *In an Acapulco hotel:* The manager has personally passed all the water served here.

□ *In a Yugoslavian hotel:* The flattening of underwear with pleasure is the job of the chambermaid.

Table 16.1 illustrates the steps in the communications process with several examples of promotional messages. Although the types of promotion may vary from a highly personalized sales presentation to such nonpersonal promotions as television advertising and one-dollar-off coupons, each goes through every stage in the communications model.

Objectives of Promotion

Determining the precise objectives of promotion has always been a perplexing problem for management. What specific tasks should promotion accomplish? The answer to this question seems to be as varied as the sources one consults.

Generally, however, the following are considered objectives of promotion: (1) to provide information, (2) to increase demand, (3) to differentiate the product, (4) to accentuate the product's value, and (5) to stabilize sales.

Providing Information

The traditional function of promotion was to inform the market about the availability of a particular good or service. Indeed, a large part of current promotional efforts is still directed at providing product information for potential customers. For example, the typical newspaper advertisement for a university or college extension course program emphasizes informative features, such as the availability, time, and location of different courses. Industrial salespeople inform buyers of new products and how they work. Retail advertisements provide information about merchandise, prices, and store location and hours.

Providing information is a promotional objective of firms introducing their goods and services in new foreign markets. N.V. Philips, the Dutch consumer electronics firm, placed ads in newspapers to introduce its electric ice cream machine to East German consumers. The ads included a coupon that consumers were asked to fill out and name the three appliances they would most like to buy, such as a vacuum cleaner or toaster. Consumers who mailed in the coupon were eligible for a sweepstakes with a grand prize for a trip for two to Venice. The promotion included in-store product demonstrations that showed crowds of curious shoppers how to operate the ice cream maker.[5]

Increasing Demand

An objective of most promotions is to increase demand for a good or service. Some promotions are aimed at increasing *primary demand,* the desire for a general product category. For example, the main objective of Honda's long-term, $75 million "Come Ride With Us" campaign is to expand the market beyond bike enthusiasts by communicating to new market segments that motorcycling is a fun, wholesome activity. The promotion includes television and print advertisements, special events such as Family Fun Days, and a rider training and education program. Most promotions, however, are aimed at increasing *selective demand,* the desire for a specific brand. Part of Honda's promotion includes advertisements promoting specific Honda models. One television commercial, for example, promotes Honda's new Pacific Coast sport touring bike.[6]

Differentiating the Product

A frequent objective of the firm's promotional effort is *product differentiation.* Homogeneous demand means consumers regard the firm's output as virtually identical to its competitors' products. In these cases, the individual firm has almost no control over marketing variables such as price. A differentiated demand schedule, in contrast, permits more flexibility in marketing strategy, such as price changes. For example, the high quality and distinctiveness of Cross pens are widely advertised, which has enabled Cross's marketers to ask for and obtain a price 100 times those of some disposable pens. The Giro Sport Design advertisement in Figure 16.3 points out how the company's lightweight cycling helmets differ in design and manufacture from those of competitors. Mentioning that Greg LeMond, winner of the celebrated Tour de France cycling race, wears Giro helmets and helped design one model gives credibility to the top-quality image presented and helps justify the high-end pricing.

Figure 16.3   Communicating Product Differentiation

Source: Courtesy of Stein Robaire Heim (Los Angeles) Agency for Giro Sport Design.

Accentuating the Product's Value

Promotion can explain the greater ownership utility of a product to buyers, thereby accentuating its value and justifying a higher price in the marketplace. For example, when industrial marketer GAF introduced ShipShape, a new reusable resin cleaner for cleaning equipment and tools, its promotional efforts in personal selling and trade magazine advertisements focused on the product's reusability, and also its distinctiveness as an alternative to competitors' cleaning solvent acetone, which has been criticized as an environmental and health hazard. An advertisement shows that one pail of reusable ShipShape replaces 17 or more pails of competitors' cleaners. ShipShape is priced much higher than the competition. But Tony Durante, marketing manager of GAF Chemicals engineered products, explains, "The high value that our customer attaches to reusability, which we emphasize in the ad, allows us to price it higher per unit than our competition."[7]

Stabilizing Sales

For the typical firm, sales are not uniform throughout the year. Sales fluctuations may be caused by cyclical, seasonal, or irregular demand. Stabilizing these variations is often an objective of the firm's promotional strategy. Coffee sales, for example, follow a seasonal pattern, with purchases and consumption increasing during the winter months. To stimulate summer sales of the Sanka brand of decaffeinated coffee, General Foods has created advertisements that include a recipe for making instant iced coffee, promoting it as a refreshing, caffeine-free summer beverage. Hotels and motels, which have high occupancy during the week from business travelers, often promote special weekend packages at lower room rates to boost occupancy on weekends. Some firms sponsor sales contests during slack periods that offer prizes to sales personnel who meet sales goals.

The Promotional Mix

promotional mix
Blending of personal selling and nonpersonal selling (including advertising, sales promotion, and public relations) by marketers in an attempt to achieve promotional objectives.

Like the marketing mix, the **promotional mix** involves the proper blending of numerous variables to satisfy the needs of the firm's target market and achieve organizational objectives. While the marketing mix is comprised of product, pricing, promotion, and distribution elements, the promotional mix is a subset of the overall marketing mix. With the promotional mix, the marketing manager attempts to achieve the optimal blending of various promotional elements to attain promotional objectives. The components of the promotional mix are personal selling and nonpersonal selling, including advertising, sales promotion, and public relations.

Personal selling, advertising, and sales promotion are the most significant elements, because they usually account for the bulk of a firm's promotional expenditures. However, all factors contribute to efficient marketing communications. A detailed discussion of each of these elements is presented in the following chapters. Here we will simply define the elements and discuss their advantages and disadvantages.

Personal Selling

personal selling
Interpersonal influence process involving a seller's promotional presentation conducted on a person-to-person basis with the prospective buyer.

Personal selling, the original form of all promotion, may be defined as a seller's promotional presentation conducted on a person-to-person basis with the buyer. It is a direct form of promotion that may be conducted face to face, over the telephone, through videoconferencing, or through interactive computer links between the buyer and seller. Today about 14 million people in the United States are employed in personal selling. Its cost is very high. The median cost is $224 for an industrial sales call, $196 for a consumer goods sales call, and $165 for a service industry sales call.[8]

Nonpersonal Selling

Nonpersonal selling includes advertising, sales promotion, and public relations. Advertising and sales promotion are usually regarded as the most important forms of nonpersonal selling. About one-third of marketing dollars is spent on media advertising and two-thirds on trade and consumer promotions.

advertising
Paid, nonpersonal communication through various media by business firms, nonprofit organizations, and individuals who are identified in the advertising message and hope to inform or persuade members of a particular audience.

Advertising may be defined as paid, nonpersonal communications through various media by business firms, nonprofit organizations, and individuals that are in some way identified in the advertising message and hope to inform or persuade members of a particular audience.[9] Advertising primarily involves the mass media, such as newspapers, television, radio, magazines, and billboards. Also included are less traditional forms such as commercials on videotapes, videoscreens in supermarkets, and messages on signs pulled by airplanes. Businesses have come to realize the tremendous potential of this form of

Figure 16.4

A Burger King Sales
Promotion

Source: Courtesy of Burger King Corporation.

sales promotion
Marketing activities other than
personal selling, advertising, and
publicity that stimulate consumer
purchasing and dealer effectiveness; includes displays, trade
shows, coupons, premiums, contests, product demonstrations,
and various nonrecurrent selling
efforts.

public relations
Firm's communications and relationships with its various publics.

promotion, and advertising is a major promotion mix component for thousands of organizations. Mass consumption and geographically dispersed markets make advertising particularly appropriate for goods and services that rely on sending the same promotional message to large audiences.

Sales promotion consists of marketing activities other than personal selling, advertising, and publicity that stimulate consumer purchasing and dealer effectiveness. These include displays, trade shows, coupons, contests, samples, premiums, product demonstrations, and various nonrecurrent selling efforts used on an irregular basis. Sales promotion is a short-term incentive and is usually combined with other forms of promotion to emphasize, assist, supplement, or otherwise support the objectives of the promotional program. Figure 16.4 shows one of Burger King's sales promotions that was targeted to kids. The company used a character called Captain Planet, a crusader dedicated to cleaning up the environment, to give away toys with the purchase of one of its Kids Club meals.

Public relations is a firm's communications and relationships with its various publics. These publics include customers, suppliers, stockholders, employees, the government, the general public, and the society in which the organization operates. Public relations programs can be either formal or informal. The critical point is that every organization, whether or not it has a formally organized program, must be concerned about its public relations.

Table 16.2   Comparison of the Four Promotional Mix Elements

	Personal Selling	Advertising	Sales Promotion	Public Relations
Advantages	□ Permits measurement of effectiveness □ Elicits a more immediate response □ Allows tailoring of the message to fit the customer	□ Reaches a large group of potential consumers for a relatively low price per exposure □ Allows strict control over the final message □ Can be adapted to either mass audiences or specific audience segments □ Can be successfully used to create instant product awareness	□ Produces a more immediate consumer response □ Attracts attention and creates product awareness □ Easier measurement of results □ Provides short-term sales increases	□ Is effective in creating a positive attitude toward a product or company □ Can enhance credibility of the product or company
Disadvantages	□ Relies almost exclusively upon the ability of the salesperson □ Involves high cost per contact	□ Does not permit totally accurate measurement of results □ Usually cannot close sales □ Is nonpersonal in nature	□ Is nonpersonal in nature □ Is difficult to differentiate from competitive efforts	□ May not permit accurate measurement of effect on sales □ Involves much effort directed toward nonmarketing-oriented goals

publicity
Stimulation of demand for a good, service, place, idea, person, or organization by disseminating commercially significant news or obtaining favorable media presentation not paid for by the sponsor.

Publicity is an important part of an effective public relations effort. It can be defined as the nonpersonal stimulation of demand for a good, service, person, cause, or organization by placing significant news about it in a published medium or by obtaining favorable presentation of it through radio, television, or the stage that is not paid for by an identified sponsor. Compared to personal selling, advertising, and even sales promotion, expenditures for public relations are usually low in most firms. Since they don't pay for it, companies have less control over the publication by the press or electronic media of good or bad company news. For this reason, a consumer may find this type of news source more believable than if the information were disseminated directly by the company.

As Table 16.2 indicates, each type of promotion has both advantages and shortcomings. Although personal selling entails a relatively high per-contact cost, there is less wasted effort than in nonpersonal forms of promotion such as advertising. Personal selling often is more flexible than the other forms because the salesperson can tailor the sales message to meet the unique needs—or objections—of each potential customer.

The major advantages of advertising are that it can create instant awareness of a good, service, or idea; build brand equity; and deliver the marketer's message to mass audiences for a relatively low cost per contact. Major disadvantages of advertising include the difficulty in measuring its effectiveness and high media costs. Sales promotions, by contrast, can be more accurately monitored and measured than advertising, produce an immediate consumer response, and provide short-term sales increases. Public relations efforts such as publicity frequently have a high degree of believability compared to other promotional techniques. The task confronting the marketer is to determine the

FOCUS ON ETHICS

FREEBIES

. . . .

As automotive magazines have grown in size and influence, auto makers have taken to wooing the writers who review their products with freebies and consulting fees. Not only are reporters for magazines like *Car and Driver* and *Motor Trend* invited on all-expense-paid "press trips" to exotic locations, but they are showered with gifts such as luggage, binoculars, compact-disc players, and cassette recorders. The manufacturers sometimes go to great lengths in the hope of a favorable review that could give them an edge in a crowded market.

Recently the editor of *Car and Driver* instructed staff members to cease accepting consulting fees from automobile manufacturers; he also sent a letter to the auto makers asking them to limit their gifts to souvenirs and mementos. Reporters may attend press trips to test drive new cars, but they no longer may bring their spouses along at a manufacturer's expense.

Journalism experts applauded *Car and Driver's* move, noting that it is inappropriate for reporters to accept consulting work in the industry they cover. Other automotive magazines, on the other hand, stated that their staff members are not influenced by gifts and free trips and do not accept consulting work from car makers. The editor of *Road and Track* said that gifts are "an anachronism" and that the auto makers should stop giving them, but acknowledged that writers for the magazine continue to accept the gifts.

A spokesman for Nissan Motor Corp. said that *Car and Driver's* policy is a valid one but that Nissan will continue to hold its product reviews in scenic locations. The purpose is to "put the vehicle in an environment that's complementary." Of course, it may also put reporters in a nice place and improve the chances of favorable reviews in the automotive magazines.

Discussion Questions

1. Is there a difference between accepting a consulting fee and accepting a gift?

2. Are "press trips" a legitimate part of the job of reviewing automotive products?

Source: Neal Templin, "Car Magazine Signals End to Auto Makers' Freebies," *The Wall Street Journal* (February 5, 1991), p. B1.

appropriate blend of promotional mix elements in marketing the firm's goods and services.

Developing an Optimal Promotional Mix

The blending of advertising, personal selling, sales promotion, and public relations to achieve marketing objectives is the promotional mix. Since quantitative measures for determining the effectiveness of each mix component in a given market segment are not available, the choice of a proper mix of promotional elements is one of the most difficult tasks facing the marketing manager. Factors affecting the promotional mix are (1) the nature of the market, (2) the nature of the product, (3) the stage in the product life cycle, (4) price, and (5) funds available for promotion.

Nature of the Market

The marketer's target audience has a major impact on the type of promotion to be used. In cases in which there are a limited number of buyers, personal selling may prove highly effective. However, markets characterized by a large number of potential customers scattered over a sizable geographical area may make the cost of contact by personal salespeople prohibitive. In such instances, advertising may be used extensively. The type of customer also affects the promotional mix. A target market made up of industrial purchasers or retail and wholesale buyers is more likely to be served by firms that rely heavily on personal selling than is a target market consisting of ultimate consumers. Similarly, pharmaceutical firms use large salesforces to sell prescription drugs directly to physicians and hospitals but use consumer advertising to promote over-the-counter drugs for the consumer market. When a prescription drug receives FDA approval to be sold over the counter, the drug firm must switch its promotional strategy from personal selling to consumer advertising.

Nature of the Product

A second important factor in determining an effective promotional mix is the product itself. Highly standardized products with minimal servicing requirements are less likely to depend on personal selling than are custom products that are technically complex and/or require frequent servicing. Consumer goods are more likely to rely heavily on advertising than are industrial goods.

Promotional mixes vary within each product category. For example, installations typically involve heavy reliance on personal selling compared to the marketing of operating supplies. In contrast, the marketing mix for convenience goods is likely to involve more emphasis on manufacturer advertising and less on personal selling. On the other hand, personal selling plays an important role in the marketing of shopping goods, and both personal and nonpersonal selling are important in the marketing of speciality goods. A personal-selling emphasis is also likely to be more effective in the marketing of products involving trade-ins.

Stage in the Product Life Cycle

The promotional mix must be tailored to the product's stage in the product life cycle. In the introductory stage, heavy emphasis is placed on personal selling to inform the marketplace of the merits of the new good or service. Salespeople contact marketing intermediaries to secure interest in and commitment to handling the offering. Trade shows are frequently used to inform and educate prospective dealers and ultimate consumers. Advertising and sales promotion are also emphasized at this stage to create awareness and stimulate initial purchases. For example, informative advertising and sales promotion played a vital role in Sony's promotional strategy when the company introduced its smaller format 8mm video products such as the Video Walkman shown in the ad in Figure 16.5. Advertising for this portable VCR/TV stressed the product's usage in a wide range of places outside the home. Sony encouraged consumer trial by setting up rental programs for the Video Walkman at dealers located near commuter trains, and the product was offered on Virgin Air flights.[10]

As the good or service moves into the growth and maturity stages, advertising becomes relatively more important in persuading consumers to make purchases. Personal-selling efforts continue to be directed at marketing intermediaries in an attempt to expand distribution. As more competitors enter the marketplace, advertising begins to stress product differences to persuade consumers to purchase the firm's brand. In the maturity and early decline stages, firms frequently reduce advertising and sales promotion expenditures.

Price

The price of the good or service is the fourth factor that affects the choice of a promotional mix. Advertising is the dominant promotional mix component for low-unit-value products due to the high per-contact costs in personal selling. As

Figure 16.5   Promotion Tailored to Stage in the Product Life Cycle

Source: Courtesy Sony Corporation of America.

a result, it has become unprofitable to promote lower-value goods and services through personal selling. Advertising, in contrast, permits a low promotional expenditure per sales unit because it reaches mass audiences. For low-value consumer goods, such as chewing gum, soft drinks, and snack foods, advertising is the most feasible means of promotion.

Funds Available for Promotion

A real barrier to implementing any promotional strategy is the size of the promotional budget. A single 30-second television commercial on the most recent Super Bowl telecasts cost the advertiser $800,000! Although the message may be received by millions of viewers and the cost per contact is relatively low, such an expenditure exceeds the entire promotional budget of thousands of firms. For many new or small firms, the cost of mass advertising is prohibitive, and they are forced to seek less expensive methods. Kransco, a small manufacturer of toy vehicles called Power Wheels that children sit in and drive, had a pre-Christmas promotional budget of less than $75,000 compared to the million-dollar budgets of competitors who advertise heavily in major media. To

Table 16.3   Factors Influencing Choice of Promotional Mix

	Factor	Emphasis	
		Personal Selling	**Advertising**
Nature of the Market	Number of buyers	Limited number	Large number
	Geographic concentration	Concentrated	Dispersed
	Type of customer	Industrial purchaser	Ultimate consumer
Nature of the Product	Complexity	Custom-made, complex	Standardized
	Service requirements	Considerable	Minimal
	Type of good	Industrial	Consumer
	Use of trade-ins	Trade-ins common	Trade-ins uncommon
Stage in the Product Life Cycle		Often emphasized at every stage; heavy emphasis in the introductory and early growth stages in acquainting marketing intermediaries and potential consumers with the good or service	Often emphasized at every stage; heavy emphasis in the latter part of growth stages, as well as the maturity and early decline stages to persuade consumers to select specific brands
Price		High unit value	Low unit value

reach its target audience, Kransco sponsored a special holiday event in the center of 63 shopping malls. It included a sweepstakes contest for kids in which winners drove Power Wheels they won in a mall parade that coincided with Santa's arrival. The event gave Kransco six weeks of visibility in the malls, reached 46 million shoppers, and prompted more retailers to carry Power Wheels. Kransco received about $8,000 of free publicity in each market and benefited from more than $600,000 of advertising from participating malls.[11]

Table 16.3 summarizes the factors that influence the determination of an appropriate promotional mix: nature of the market, nature of the product, stage in the product life cycle, and price.

Pulling and Pushing Promotional Strategies

Essentially marketers may use two promotional alternatives: a pulling strategy and a pushing strategy. A **pulling strategy** is a promotional effort by the seller to stimulate final-user demand, which then exerts pressure on the distribution channel. When marketing intermediaries stock a large number of competing products and exhibit little interest in any one of them, a pulling strategy may be necessary for motivating them to handle the product. In such instances, this strategy is implemented with the objective of building consumer demand so that consumers will request the product when they go to retail stores. Smartfoods, for example, successfully used a pulling strategy by stimulating the demand of targeted consumers, who then asked for its brand at retail outlets.

Advertising and sales promotion are the most commonly used elements of promotion in a pulling strategy. Two sales promotion techniques—sponsoring of special events and unusual sampling settings—have become popular with food marketers as means of gaining consumer support. New York Seltzer marketers, for example, have distributed samples of their beverage at dentist conventions,

pulling strategy
Promotional effort by a seller to stimulate demand by final users, who will then exert pressure on the distribution channel to carry the good or service, thereby "pulling" it through the marketing channel.

Figure 16.6

Implementing a Push
Strategy

Source: Courtesy of Foods From Spain.

garlic festivals, and sailing races. Atlantis Dairy Products sponsored some 50 special events at which it used mobile sampling centers to promote its Bon Lait brand of *fromâge frais* — a yogurtlike blend of cheese and fruit popular in European markets. When Atlantis launched its new market entry in Southern California, many retailers were reluctant to stock the product due to their lack of familiarity with it. But the consumer promotions worked. According to Atlantis' marketing manager, "Being able to show retailers crowds of people eating the product really helped to get shelf space."[12]

In contrast, a **pushing strategy** relies more heavily on personal selling. Here the objective is promoting the product to the members of the marketing channel rather than to the final user. This can be done through cooperative advertising allowances, trade discounts, personal-selling efforts by the firm's salesforce, and other dealer supports. Such a strategy is designed to gain marketing success for the firm's products by motivating representatives of wholesalers and/or retailers to spend extra time and effort promoting the products to customers.

pushing strategy
Promotional effort by a seller to members of the marketing channel to stimulate personal selling of the good or service, thereby "pushing" it through the marketing channel.

While pulling and pushing strategies are presented here as alternative methods, it is unlikely that many companies depend entirely on either one. Most firms use a combination of the two methods. For example, the Commercial Office of Spain uses both pushing and pulling strategies to promote Spanish olive oil. The ad in Figure 16.6, placed in food trade magazines, is part of a push strategy to convince retailers to carry Spanish brands. The office also uses a pulling strategy by advertising in magazines such as *Bon Appetit* to stimulate consumer demand.

Usually marketers emphasize one strategy more than the other, depending on which one best meets their marketing goals. Food and consumer goods marketers generally spend a greater percentage of their promotional budget on

COMPETITIVE EDGE

SINGIN' IN THE SHOWER

"My heart belongs to Dove. I love my Dove and W-N-E-W!"

The scene is Grand Central Terminal in New York City. The singer is on a stage that looks like a shower stall. Nearby, a radio station DJ is handing out free soap.

Lever Brothers' "Singin' in the Shower" promotion began with an on-air radio contest in which contestants (women aged 18 to 45) sang shower songs incorporating the names of Lever bar-soap brands and the radio station's call letters. Winners won a trip to Jamaica and clean-up kits containing a shower radio, soap, a scrub brush, and a rubber duckie. In the second phase, contestants or groups were selected to perform "in the tub." Lever provided a set that included running water, a tub and shower, curtains featuring its brands, and a sound system. The events took place at high-visibility locations and were supported by press kits, media alerts, and phone follow-ups, as well as on-site public relations efforts in the top markets. The winners of the local events were flown to Universal Studios in Hollywood to compete for the $5,000 grand prize; this event was aired on network television.

Six months before the promotion began, Lever's salespeople were at work describing the event to grocery buyers and obtaining space for point-of-purchase displays. During the radio phase of the promotion, retail stores carried an interactive display that "sang" the contest jingle and carried sweepstakes entry forms; the participating radio station was identified. The results were impressive: Lever beat all competitors to become the most displayed company during the promotional period; the sweepstakes generated a 10 percent response; and the publicity resulted in widespread print and television coverage for the company.

The "Singin' in the Shower" promotion successfully applied several principles of effective special-events promotion: grassroots involvement, tie-in with local media, coordination at the point of sale, a push from the salesforce, public relations support, and a chance for everyone to win something. Push and pull strategies were integrated to increase awareness of all the company's soap brands, as well as the Lever name. Most important, the company maintained consumer involvement throughout, thereby not only increasing immediate sales but boosting brand image in the long run.

Discussion Questions

1. Why was it so important for Lever Brothers to select the "right" radio station in each market?

2. Would the promotion have been as effective if the salesforce had not been involved?

Sources: Martin Everett, "Why Special Events Wash Well with Lever Brothers," *Sales & Marketing Management* (September 1989), pp. 86, 90; and "Spray It Again, Sam," *Marketing Week* (September 18, 1989), p. 44. *Photo source:* Reprinted with the permission of *Adweek's Marketing Week.*

---

efforts that push products through the retailing system to gain shelf space amid the increasing number of new products. Some, however, are shifting away from trade promotions and focusing more on consumer advertising. After losing market share to competitors, Kellogg changed its promotional emphasis to consumer advertising in an attempt to rebuild brand loyalty for Rice Krispies, Corn Flakes, and other brands. Kellogg continues to spend millions on trade promotions, but "there's growing emphasis on the pull side of the business, to get the consumer," says Joseph M. Stewart, Kellogg's senior vice-president of corporate affairs.[13]

Timing is another factor to consider in developing a promotional strategy. The relative importance of advertising and selling changes during the various phases of the purchase process. Prior to the actual sale, advertising usually is more important than personal selling. It is often argued that one of the primary advantages of a successful advertising program is that it assists the salesperson in approaching the prospect. Selling then becomes more important than advertising at the time of purchase. In most situations, personal selling is the actual mechanism for closing the sale. In the post-purchase period, advertising regains primacy in the promotional effort. It affirms the customer's decision to buy a particular good or service and reminds him or her of the product's favorable qualities in an attempt to reduce any cognitive dissonance (discussed earlier) that might occur.

The promotional strategies used by car marketers illustrate the timing factor. During the pre-purchase period, car makers spend heavily on consumer advertising to create awareness. At the time of the purchase decision, the personal-selling skills of dealer salespeople is most important in closing the sale. And in the post-purchase stage, consumer advertising frequently cites awards such as *Motor Trend* Car of the Year or results of customer-satisfaction surveys to affirm buyers' decisions.

Budgeting for Promotional Strategy

Promotional budgets may differ not only in amount but in composition. Industrial firms generally invest a larger proportion of their budgets for personal selling than for advertising, while the reverse is usually true of most producers of consumer goods.

Evidence suggests that sales initially lag behind promotion for structural reasons — filling up retail shelves, low initial production, and lack of buyer knowledge. This produces a threshold effect whereby there may be few sales but substantial initial investment in promotion. A second phase might produce returns (sales) proportionate to a given promotional expenditure; this would be the most predictable range. Finally, the area of diminishing returns is reached when an increase in promotional spending fails to produce a corresponding increase in sales.

For example, an initial expenditure of $40,000 may result in the sale of 100,000 product units for a consumer goods manufacturer. An additional $10,000 expenditure may generate sales of 30,000 more units and another $10,000 sales of an additional 35,000 units. The cumulative effect of the expenditures and repeat sales will have resulted in increasing returns from the promotional outlays. However, as the advertising budget moves from $60,000 to $70,000, the marginal productivity of the additional expenditure may fall to 28,000 units. At some later point, the return may actually become zero or negative as competition intensifies, markets become saturated, and less effective advertising media are employed.

To test the thesis that a saturation point for promotion exists, Anheuser-Busch marketers once quadrupled their advertising budget in several markets. After three months, the company's distributors demanded an advertising cut. Many claimed that beer consumers were coming into their stores demanding, "Give me anything *but* Bud."

The ideal method of allocating a promotional budget is to increase the budget until the cost of each additional increment equals the additional incremental revenue received. In other words, the most effective allocation procedure is to increase promotional expenditures until each dollar of promotional expense is matched by an additional dollar of profit. This procedure — referred to as *marginal analysis* — results in maximization of the input's productivity. The difficulty arises in identifying the optimal point, which requires a precise balancing of marginal expenses for promotion and the resulting marginal receipts.

Table 16.4

Promotional Budget
Determination

Method	Description	Example
Percentage of sales	Promotional budget is set as a specified percentage of either past or forecasted sales.	"Last year we spent $10,500 on promotion and had sales of $420,000. Next year we expect sales to grow to $480,000, and we are allocating $12,000 for promotion."
Fixed sum per unit	Promotional budget is set on the basis of a predetermined dollar amount of each unit sold or produced.	"Our forecast calls for sales of 14,000 units, and we allocate promotion at the rate of $65 per unit."
Meeting competition	Promotional budget is set to match competitors' promotional outlays on either an absolute or a relative basis.	"Promotional outlays average 4 percent of sales in our industry."
Task-objective	Once marketers determine their specific promotional objectives, the amount (and type) of promotional spending needed to achieve them is determined.	"By the end of next year, we want 75 percent of the area high school students to be aware of our new, highly automated fast-food prototype outlet. How many promotional dollars will it take, and how should they be spent?"

percentage-of-sales method
Promotional budget allocation method in which the funds allocated for promotion during a given time period are based on a specified percentage of either past or forecasted sales.

fixed-sum-per-unit method
Promotional budget allocation method in which promotional expenditures are a predetermined dollar amount for each sales or production unit.

meeting competition method
Promotional budget allocation method that matches competitors' promotional outlays on either an absolute or relative basis.

task-objective method
Promotional budget allocation method in which a firm defines its goals and then determines the amount of promotional spending needed for achieving them.

Traditional methods for creating a promotional budget are percentage of sales, fixed sum per unit, meeting the competition, and task-objective. Each method is briefly examined in Table 16.4.

The **percentage-of-sales method** is perhaps the most common way of establishing promotional budgets. The percentage can be based on either past (such as the previous year) or forecasted (estimated current year) sales. While this plan is appealing in its simplicity, it is not an effective way to achieve basic promotional objectives. Arbitrary percentage allocations, whether applied to historical or future sales figures, fail to provide the required flexibility. Further, such reasoning is circular, since the promotional allocation depends on sales rather than vice versa, as it should. Consider, for example, the implications of a decline in sales, an occurrence that would force the marketer to further curtail the firm's promotional outlays.

The **fixed-sum-per-unit method** differs from percentage of sales in only one respect: It applies a predetermined allocation to each sales or production unit. This can also be based on either historical or forecasted figures. Producers of high-value, consumer durable goods, such as automobiles, often use this budgeting method.

Another traditional approach is **meeting competition,** or simply matching competitors' outlays on either an absolute or a relative basis. However, this kind of approach usually leads to a status quo situation with each company retaining its percentage of total sales. Meeting the competition's budget does not necessarily pertain to promotional objectives and, therefore, seems inappropriate for most contemporary marketing programs.

The **task-objective method** of developing a promotional budget is based on a sound evaluation of the firm's promotional objectives and, as a result, is better attuned to modern marketing practices. It involves two sequential steps:

1. The firm's marketers must *define the realistic communication goals* they want the promotional mix to achieve; for example, a 25 percent increase in brand awareness or a 10 percent rise in the number of consumers who realize that the product has certain specific, differentiating features. The key

is to specify in quantitative terms the objectives to be attained. These in turn become an integral part of the promotional plan.

2. Marketers must *determine the amount (as well as type) of promotional activity required for achieving each objective that has been set.* Combined, these units become the firm's promotional budget.

A crucial assumption underlies the task-objective approach—that the productivity of each promotional dollar is measurable. That is why the objectives must be carefully chosen, quantified, and accomplished through promotional efforts. Generally an objective such as "We wish to achieve a 5 percent increase in sales" is a marketing objective, because a sale is a culmination of the effects of *all* elements of the marketing mix. Therefore, an appropriate promotional objective might be "to make 30 percent of the target market aware of the one-hour optical service concept."

While promotional budgeting is always difficult, recent research studies and more frequent use of computer-based models have made it less of a problem than it used to be.

Measuring the Effectiveness of Promotion

It is widely recognized that part of a firm's promotional effort is ineffective. John Wanamaker, a successful nineteenth-century retailer, observed: "I know half the money I spend on advertising is wasted, but I can never find out which half."

Measuring the effectiveness of promotional expenditures has become an extremely important research issue, particularly among advertisers. Studies aimed at this measurement dilemma face several major obstacles, one of them being the difficulty of isolating the effect of the promotional variable.

Most marketers would prefer to use a *direct-sales-results* test to measure the effectiveness of promotion. Such an approach would reveal the specific impact on sales revenues for each dollar of promotional spending. This type of technique has never been possible, however, due to the marketer's inability to control for other variables operating in the marketplace. A firm may experience $20 million in additional sales following a new, $1.5 million advertising campaign, but the success may have resulted from price increases of competing products rather than from the advertising outlays.

Because of the difficulty of isolating the effects of promotion from the other marketing elements and outside environmental variables, many marketers have simply abandoned all attempts at measurement. Others, however, turn to indirect evaluation. These researchers concentrate on the factors that are quantifiable, such as *recall* (how much is remembered about specific products or advertisements) and *readership* (size and composition of the audience). The basic problem is the difficulty of relating these variables to sales—for example, does extensive ad readership lead to increased sales?

Frequently used assessment methods for determining promotional effectiveness include sales inquiries and research studies aimed at determining changes in consumer attitudes toward the product and/or improvement in public knowledge and awareness. General Foods marketers developed a unique approach to consumer sales inquiries for its Ronzoni pasta products by offering free membership in its newly formed Sono Buoni Club. Club members were promised coupons, a newsletter, cook-offs, and other premiums. The benefits for General Foods were an extensive database indicating who uses Ronzoni pasta products and the ability to encourage brand loyalty through coupons and continued contacts.[14]

Measuring promotion effectiveness in foreign markets can be especially challenging. In the Federal Republic of Germany, television commercials run in four blocks of seven minutes each, rather than throughout the programs as in the United States. To gain experience in this format, Procter & Gamble conducted a consumer contest called "Remember the Brands" that tested the recall of its commercials. P&G bought entire seven-minute blocks to air commercials for ten products. Half of the commercials were altered in some way. For example, in one commercial for Ariel detergent a woman soiled her sweatsuit while jogging and in another while riding an elephant. Viewers who correctly identified the brands with altered commercials were eligible to win an Opel Corsa automobile.[15]

The technological innovation that has revolutionized evaluation of consumer advertising and sales promotion is the *single-source* research system. It combines scanner-generated buying information at supermarkets with consumer demographics and the television advertising and in-store promotions to which those consumers are exposed. From this data, marketers can measure the effectiveness of their advertising and sales promotion, determine why or why not sales increase, discover which consumers respond to which promotions, and test the short- and long-term profitability of advertising and sales promotion. With single-source data marketers can avoid wasting money on ineffective communications.[16]

The Value of Promotion

Promotion has often been the target of criticism. Common complaints are

- □   "Promotion contributes nothing to society."
- □   "Most advertisements and sales presentations insult my intelligence."
- □   "Promotion 'forces' consumers to buy products they cannot afford and do not need."
- □   "Advertising and selling are economic wastes."
- □   "Salespersons and advertisers are usually unethical."

Consumers, public officials, and marketers agree that too many of these complaints are true.[17] Some salespeople do use unethical sales tactics. Some product advertising indeed is directed at consumer groups that can least afford the particular item. Many television commercials do contribute to the growing problem of cultural pollution.

While promotion can certainly be criticized on many counts, it is important to remember that promotion plays a crucial role in modern society. This point is best understood by examining the importance of promotion at the social, business, and economic levels.

Social Importance

Criticisms such as "most promotional messages are tasteless" and "promotion contributes nothing to society" sometimes ignore the fact that no commonly accepted set of standards or priorities exist within our social framework. We live in a varied economy characterized by consumer segments with differing needs, wants, and aspirations. What is tasteless to one group may be quite appealing to another. Promotional strategy faces an "averaging" problem that escapes many of its critics. The one generally accepted standard in a market society is freedom of choice for the consumer. Consumer buying decisions eventually determine what is acceptable practice in the marketplace.

Figure 16.7

Promotion Addressing a
Social Concern

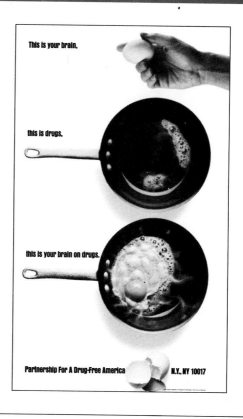

Source: Courtesy of Partnership for a Drug-Free America.

Promotion has become an important factor in the campaigns to achieve socially oriented objectives, such as stopping smoking, family planning, physical fitness, and elimination of drug abuse. The advertisement in Figure 16.7 is one of hundreds in an anti-drug campaign developed by the Partnership for a Drug-Free America, which pledged $1 million a day in anti-drug advertising. The campaign's creative work and media time and space are donated by members of the advertising and media industries. Tracking surveys conducted by the partnership indicate that the advertising has had a positive influence on discouraging the use of illicit drugs.[18]

Promotion performs an informative and educational task that makes it crucial to the functioning of modern society. As with everything else in life, what is important is *how* promotion is used rather than whether it is used.

Business Importance

Promotional strategy has become increasingly important to both large and small business enterprises. The long-term increase in funds spent on promotion is well documented and certainly attests to management's faith in the ability of promotional efforts to produce attitude changes, brand loyalty, and additional sales. It is difficult to conceive of an enterprise that would not attempt to promote its product or service in some manner. Most modern institutions simply cannot survive in the long run without promotion. Business must communicate with its publics.

Nonbusiness enterprises also recognize the importance of promotional efforts. The U.S. government spends about $300 million a year on advertising and ranks thirty-sixth among all U.S. advertisers. The Canadian government is the leading advertiser in Canada, promoting many concepts and programs. Religious organizations have acknowledged the importance of promoting what they do. Even labor organizations have used promotional channels to make their viewpoints known to the public at large.

Economic Importance

Promotion has assumed a degree of economic importance if for no other reason than it provides employment for thousands of people. More important, however, effective promotion has allowed society to derive benefits not otherwise available. For example, the criticism that promotion costs too much isolates an individual expense item and fails to consider the possible beneficial effect of promotion on other categories of expenditures.

Promotional strategies that increase the number of units sold permit economies in the production process, thereby lowering the production costs associated with each unit of output. Lower consumer prices in turn make these products available to more people. Similarly, researchers have found that advertising subsidizes the informational content of newspapers and the broadcast media.[19] In short, promotion pays for many of the enjoyable entertainment and educational aspects of contemporary life as well as lowering product costs.

Summary of Chapter Objectives

1. **Explain the relationship of promotional strategy to the process of communication.** Communication is the transmission of a message from a sender (or source) to a receiver (or recipient). Marketing communications are those messages that deal with buyer-seller relationships. Promotional strategy focuses on the appropriate blending of the promotional mix elements—personal and nonpersonal selling—to inform, persuade, and remind present and potential customers and to achieve overall objectives. *Marketing communications* is a broader term than *promotional strategy,* because it includes other forms of communication. A planned promotional strategy, however, is certainly the most important part of marketing communications.

2. **List the objectives of promotion.** The five basic objectives of promotion are to provide information, stimulate demand, differentiate the product, accentuate the product's value, and stabilize sales.

3. **Explain the concept of the promotional mix and its relationship to the marketing mix.** The promotional mix, like the marketing mix, involves the proper blending of numerous variables in order to satisfy the needs of the firm's target market and achieve organizational objectives. While the marketing mix is comprised of product, pricing, promotion, and distribution elements, the promotional mix is a subset of the overall marketing mix. In the case of the promotional mix, the marketing manager attempts to achieve the optimal blending of personal and nonpersonal selling to attain promotional objectives.

4. **Identify the primary determinants of a promotional mix.** Developing an effective promotional mix is complex. The elements of promotion are related to the type and value of the product or service being promoted, the nature of the market, the stage of the product life cycle, and the funds available for promotion as well as to the timing of the promotional effort. Personal selling is used primarily for industrial goods and services, for higher-value items,

and during the decision phase of the purchasing process. Advertising, in contrast, is used mainly for consumer goods and services, for lower-value items, during the later stages of the product life cycle, and during the pre-purchase and post-purchase phases.

5. **Contrast the two major alternative promotional strategies.** A pushing strategy relies heavily on personal selling and attempts to promote the product to the members of the marketing channel rather than to the final user. A pulling strategy concentrates on stimulating final-user demand, primarily in the mass media through advertising and sales promotion.

6. **Compare the primary methods of developing a promotional budget.** The percentage-of-sales method bases the promotional budget on a percentage of either past or forecasted sales. The fixed-sum-per-unit method uses a predetermined allocation for each sales or production unit; this can be done on either a historical or forecasted basis. The approach of meeting competitors' promotional expenses can be used on either an absolute or percentage basis. The task-objective approach first defines realistic goals for the promotional effort and then determines the amount and type of promotional activity required for achieving each objective.

7. **Defend promotion against common public criticisms.** Criticisms of promotion range from lack of social contribution to unethical promotional practices. Marketers acknowledge that many of the criticisms are justified, but they also point out the considerable contributions promotion makes via its business, economic, and social roles.

Key Terms

promotion

marketing communications

AIDA concept

promotional mix

personal selling

advertising

sales promotion

public relations

publicity

pulling strategy

pushing strategy

percentage-of-sales method

fixed-sum-per-unit method

meeting competition method

task-objective method

Review Questions

1. Relate the steps in the communications process to promotional strategy. Cite examples of each step in the process.
2. Explain the concept of the promotional mix. What is its relationship to the marketing mix?
3. Identify the major determinants of a promotional mix. Describe how they affect the selection of an appropriate blending of promotional techniques.
4. Compare the five basic objectives of promotion. Cite specific examples.
5. Explain the concept and causes of noise in marketing communications. How can marketers deal with noise?
6. Under what circumstances should a pushing strategy be used in promotion? When would a pulling strategy be effective?
7. What is meant by AIDA? Relate the concept to the marketing communications process.

8. Identify and briefly explain the alternative methods of developing a promotional budget. Which is the best approach?

9. How can a firm attempt to measure the effectiveness of its promotional efforts? Which techniques are most effective?

10. Identify the major public criticisms of promotion. Prepare a defense for each criticism.

Discussion Questions

1. "Perhaps the most critical promotional question facing the marketing manager concerns when to use each component of promotion." Comment on this statement. Relate your response to the good's classification, product value, marketing channels, price, and timing of the promotional effort.

2. What mix of promotional variables would you use for each of the following?
   a. Champion spark plugs
   b. Weedeater lawn edgers
   c. Management consulting service
   d. Industrial drilling equipment
   e. Women's sportswear
   f. Customized business forms

3. Develop a hypothetical promotion budget for the following firms. Ignore dollar amounts by using percentage allocations for the various promotional variables (such as 30 percent for personal selling, 60 percent for advertising, and 10 percent for public relations).
   a. National Car Rental
   b. Ramada Inn
   c. Manufacturer of industrial chemicals
   d. Allstate Insurance Company

4. Trace the history of advertising done by physicians, dentists, and lawyers. How do these professionals currently promote their services? What restrictions apply to their promotional efforts?

5. When paperback book sales suffered a downturn, several of the major publishers adopted new promotional strategies. One firm began using 30-cents-off coupons to promote its romantic series. Another company, on the other hand, established a returns policy that rewarded dealers with high sales. The new policy also contained penalties to discourage low volume by retail book outlets. Relate these promotional strategies to the material discussed in the chapter.

Computer Applications

This chapter describes a number of traditional methods for allocating a promotional budget. These include the percentage-of-sales, fixed-sum-per-unit, meeting the competition, and task-objective methods. The following problems focus on the various methods of promotional budgeting.

Directions: Use menu item 14 titled "Promotional Budget Allocations" to solve each of the following problems. To solve Problem 5, also use menu item 3 titled "Sales Forecasting" to calculate the necessary data.

Problem 1.   Terry Simpson, manager of Fairfax Import Motors, has decided to use the fixed-sum-per-unit method to determine the appropriate promotional budget amount for the following year. He plans to base the precise sum on the average for other automobile dealers in his market area. Available data reveal the following:

Dealer	Per-Car Promotional Expenditures
A	$ 37
B	48
C	65
D	85
E	110

Simpson forecasts next year's sales to amount to 1,400 cars. How much should he allocate to promotion on a per-unit basis in the coming year? What will his total promotional budget be for next year?

Problem 2.   Jeffcoat Clothiers of Pawtucket, Rhode Island, has allocated $27,000 for next year's promotional budget. It calculated the allocation by basing the budget on the same percentage allocation used during the previous year. Last year the store generated sales of $400,000 and spent a total of $24,000 on promotion. How much sales revenue does Jeffcoat Clothiers expect to generate during the coming year?

Problem 3.   Golden Bear Enterprises was founded six years ago in Oakland, California. Its growth has been substantial, and the firm has expanded into several cities in northern California. Sales and annual promotional expenditures for the past six years were as follows:

Year	Annual Sales	Promotional Expenditures
1	$1,400,000	$ 58,800
2	2,300,000	92,000
3	3,000,000	135,000
4	3,700,000	185,000
5	4,500,000	243,000
6	5,700,000	302,000

The sales forecast for next year is $6,500,000. The firm's four major competitors have the following annual sales and promotional outlays:

Competitor	Estimated Current Annual Sales	Estimated Promotional Budget
A	$3,800,000	$159,600
B	4,200,000	298,200
C	6,700,000	335,000
D	9,200,000	496,800

a.   What percentage of next year's sales should Golden Bear Enterprises include in its promotional budget if it bases the budget on the percentage allocated for Year 6 sales? How many dollars would it allocate to promotion?

b.   Suppose the firm's marketers decide to use the average percentage allocated for promotion over the past six years. They determine this average by calculating total sales and total promotional outlays since Year 1 and then dividing total promotional outlays by total sales. What percentage would they include in the promotional budget for next year? How many dollars would they allocate to promotion?

c.   The firm's marketers are also considering simply meeting competition by basing their promotional budget on the average percentage of promotional outlays for each of the four major competitors. What percentage would they use for promotion if they implemented this approach?

Problem 4.   Len Berne, marketing manager for New York Fashions, is in the process of developing a promotional budget for next year. Total expected sales amount to $675,000. Berne has collected the following historical sales and promotional expenditures data for the firm:

Year	Annual Sales	Promotional Outlays
1	$520,000	$33,800
2	580,000	38,860
3	620,000	37,200
4	640,000	37,760
5	652,000	32,600

Berne has also collected data on sales and promotional outlays of his three major competitors. Last year Town & Country Fashions spent $37,560 on promotion and generated sales of approximately $820,000. The promotional budget at Miss Patti's was $75,400, and total sales amounted to $1.4 million. The Style Shop, New York Fashions' largest competitor, generated $1.5 million in sales last year and spent $80,000 on promotion.

a.   What percentage of next year's sales should Berne include in his promotional budget if he bases it on the percentage used for Year 5 sales? How many dollars would he allocate to promotion?

b.   Suppose Berne decides to use the average percentage allocated for promotion over the past five years. He determines this average by calculating total sales and total promotional outlays since Year 1 and then dividing total promotional outlays by total sales. What percentage would he include in his next year's promotional budget using this method? How many dollars would he allocate to promotion?

c.   Berne is also considering meeting competition by basing his promotional budget on the average promotional outlays of each of his three major competitors. What percentage would he use for promotion if he utilized this approach? How many dollars would he allocate to promotion next year?

Problem 5.   Liz Seimais, marketing vice-president of Allan Designs, plans to allocate 6.5 percent of next year's sales to promotion. To develop her budgets, she needs to forecast sales for the coming year. Annual sales for each of the nine previous years were as follows:

Year	Annual Sales
1	$ 7,200,000
2	8,100,000
3	8,800,000
4	9,500,000
5	10,000,000
6	10,600,000
7	11,200,000
8	11,800,000
9	12,800,000

Estimate next year's sales by using menu item 3 titled "Sales Forecasting" (this sales forecasting technique is described on page 140). After you have next year's estimated sales, calculate the amount of funds Seimais should allocate for promotion for the coming year.

VIDEO CASE 16

Apple Computer, Inc.

"I've always believed that marketing must begin with a great product. So now, wouldn't you like to see one? Ladies and gentlemen, inside this small, handsome case rests one of the great visions of our company—the Apple IIc."

With those words, John Sculley, president and chief executive officer of Apple Computer, Inc., introduced the company's newest personal computer to 4,000 dealers, industry analysts, and members of the press during a product roll-out extravaganza in San Francisco back in 1984. The big, splashy event, complete with rock music and laser lights, was Apple's way of generating excitement for its new product. "We think we can put on great events," says Del Yocam, executive vice-president, "and so we like the idea of capturing individuals' entire attention—their focus whether it's for a day or a period of time. It helps them concentrate on Apple, whether it's the Macintosh group or the Apple II group, it is Apple. They feel a part of the family."

Event marketing—expensive, unconventional promotions in advertising, sales promotion, and personal selling—and innovative product design have helped Apple stay afloat in the high-risk personal computer market. Apple co-founders Steven Jobs and Steven Wozniak, who designed the first Apple personal computer in 1976, are credited with developing this multibillion dollar market. Apple sales grew rapidly during the late 1970s and early 1980s. But by 1983, the company was in trouble, losing market share to IBM, who entered the personal computer market in 1981. Two years later, IBM dominated the market, driving out many large and small competitors and causing others to reposition their products as IBM-compatibles.

Apple intended to survive the shakedown. In 1983, John Sculley was recruited from PepsiCo to bring professional management to Apple, consistency to its product line, and order to its marketing efforts. Under Sculley's direction, Apple changed its entire product line in 100 days, increased its advertising budget of $15 million in 1983 to $100 million in 1984, and embarked on an attention-getting promotional campaign. Sculley says, "We couldn't have taken that big risk of changing our products and gone with technology that was radically different from where IBM and the rest of the industry were headed unless we had the boldness and voice of big events."

Sculley's promotional plan of staging big events was based on an assessment of Apple's products and the industry. In the early 1980s, the personal computer industry was in its infancy. The products were expensive, in the introductory stage of the product life cycle, and embodied high technology that most people did not understand. Sculley believed that advertising for personal computers was ineffective because it was filled with high-tech jargon that baffled almost everyone other than computer experts. He planned to increase Apple sales by using big events that would differentiate Apple from other computer companies and communicate a single message to consumers and retailers: Apple was a winning company with vision and bold products.

In promoting the Apple IIc to consumers, Apple marketers faced the considerable problem of how to communicate the small, compact computer's tremendous power, which was impossible to explain simply in a 30-second commercial. To show the computer's power, Apple's advertising agency created a commercial illustrating how the IIc could control all of the operating systems—air conditioning, security, fire alarms, elevators, and turbines—in a 50-story office building, which require far more power than a typical personal computer purchaser would need for home or classroom use.

"Apple will use advertising in outrageous ways to communicate very fundamental messages," says Sculley. In 1984, the company had an important message to communicate. Apple had developed the Macintosh, an innovative computer with its own proprietary operating system, and decided to position it as an alternative to the IBM PC, whose MS/DOS operating system was the standard in the personal computer industry. To launch the Macintosh, Apple marketers used a single advertising event. They bought $2 million worth of Super Bowl advertising on January 22 to air "1984," a television commercial that likened IBM to the Big Brother in George Orwell's futuristic novel *1984*. Apple's message was: "On January 24th, Apple Computer will introduce Macintosh. And you'll see why 1984 won't be like *1984*."

Like all of Apple's big events, the "1984" commercial was designed to make people curious about the product before it actually hit the marketplace. For the first Macintosh promotion, Mike Murray, director of marketing, says, "We needed to have a message that was so strong and so radical that people would say, 'What was that?'. . . . We needed to use IBM as almost a punching bag during 1984 so we could draw attention to why we were saying Macintosh could be positioned as an alternative to the IBM PC." The commercial did indeed draw attention. It was given much of the credit for generating $100 million in Macintosh sales within the 10 days following the commercial's one-time airing.

To back its advertising claim that Macintosh was "the first personal computer anyone can learn to use overnight," Apple marketers ran the promotion "Test Drive a Macintosh," which invited consumers to visit one of Apple's more than 2,000 authorized dealers and take a Macintosh home overnight to try it out.

Since the firm's beginning, Apple marketers targeted their products at the home and educational markets. They have given hundreds of computers to elementary and high schools as part of their long-term strategy of converting student users into future buyers. But with the Macintosh, Apple marketers aimed at appealing to a new target group—business users. The business market, according to Sculley, comprises "the biggest market with the highest profit and the fastest growth in the personal computer industry."

In order to sell to the business market, Apple marketers refocused their promotional efforts on personal selling and publicity, changing the flavor of their advertising. Apple formed a new national sales force by recruiting 350 salespeople to sell Macintosh products to corporations. To generate favorable publicity, Apple managers held meetings for industry analysts and business consultants, during which new products were explained well in advance of their launch. Advertisements directed at business users emphasized detailed product information and solutions to problems. To communicate this information effectively, Apple marketers decided to use more print advertising rather than television commercials. As Apple added new Macintosh software and equipment aimed at business users, the timing of promotions became an important factor, so that promises made in advertising and public events were translated into meeting product delivery deadlines.

In 1990, Apple introduced three new low-price models, providing a new generation of entry-level machines promoted by a $25 million television and print advertising campaign. By the next year, orders were outstripping an already expanded production facility. Apple also recognized that most of its sales to consumers were for business or educational uses, and it concentrated its promotional efforts on those segments.

In the summer of 1991, Apple and IBM announced that they were forming a joint venture that would share technologies. By that time Apple's share of the PC market had dropped from 18 percent to 15 percent, and IBM's share had decreased from about 46 percent to 23 percent.

Today, largely owing to its ability to promote its products effectively, Apple is a successful corporation. It is maintaining its leadership position in the educational market while gaining widespread acceptance in the business market.

Source: Thomas McCarroll, "Love at First Byte," *Time* (July 15, 1991), pp. 46–47. Apple Computer, Inc., 1990 Annual Report; 1991 First Quarter Report; Christy Fisher, "Battle Moves to the Home Front," *Advertising Age* (November 12, 1990), pp. 51–52; Bradley Johnson, "Mac Leaves Home," *Advertising Age* (October 15, 1990), p. 6; Brenton R. Schlender, "Yet Another Strategy for Apple," *Fortune* (October 22, 1990), pp. 81–87. Apple Computer, Inc., *1987 Annual Report,* p. 24; Brian O'Reilly, "Growing Apple Anew for the Business Market," *Fortune* (January 4, 1988), pp. 36–37; and Katherine M. Hafner, "Apple Goes for a Bigger Bite of Corporate America," *Business Week* (August 24, 1987), pp. 74–75.

Questions

1. Give examples of how Apple marketers have used both pushing and pulling promotional strategies in their marketing efforts.

2. Explain how the nature of Apple's product and the industry influenced the firm's promotional strategy.

3. Relate the promotional elements discussed in the chapter to Apple's different target markets.

4. What are Apple's promotional objectives in targeting the consumer market? The business market?

5. The chapter discussed several methods marketers use in setting promotional budgets. Which method did John Sculley use when he raised Apple's advertising budget to $100 million? Discuss Sculley's decision in terms of Apple's competition and personal computers' position in the product life cycle.

6. What promotional strategies would you suggest for the new Apple–IBM joint venture and its parent companies?

17 Advertising, Sales Promotion, and Public Relations

CHAPTER OBJECTIVES

1. To explain the current status and historical development of advertising, sales promotion, and public relations.

2. To identify the major types of advertising.

3. To list and discuss the major advertising media.

4. To explain how advertising effectiveness is determined.

5. To outline the organization of the advertising function.

6. To describe the process of creating an advertisement.

7. To identify the principal methods of sales promotion.

8. To explain the role of public relations and publicity in an organization's promotional strategy.

Breaking into a new market is difficult, especially when the market is dominated by formidable and well-entrenched competitors such as Nike and Reebok. That was the marketing situation when Champion Products, Inc., of Rochester, New York, entered the retail market in 1985. For more than 70 years, Champion has supplied athletic apparel to the institutional market, primarily uniforms for school and professional sports teams. The Champion brand has a strong athletic heritage, known for its quality, durability, and authenticity. But to promote its new line of T-shirts, shorts, and other fashion activewear, Champion had to create a strong brand identity at the retail level to make its brand stand out from competitors'. Champion's challenge was to persuade consumers and retailers that its activewear line was as fashionable as competitors' yet more authentic and durable.

Champion selected advertising agency Rumrill Hoyt to plan and develop the advertising campaign. Objectives were to build retail sales and distribution. Target markets included

☐ Serious athletes—predominantly male, age 13 to 49, single and married, middle to upper income

☐ Occasional athletes and emulators—age 13 to 49, single and married, middle to upper income

☐ Store buyers—activewear decision makers and buying influencers at sporting goods, sports specialty, and department stores.

With a budget of $1.5 million, the agency designed print ads and selected media that would effectively reach Champion's target audiences. Four-fifths of the ad budget were devoted to the consumer target market, with ads placed in sports and consumer magazines such as *Sports Illustrated, Women's Sports & Fitness, Rolling Stone, People, Gentlemen's Quarterly,* and *The New York Times Magazine.* Promotion to store buyers included ads in athletic apparel trade publications, a direct-mail campaign to key trade buyers, and participation in trade shows such as the National Sporting Goods Association show.

The ad shown here is an example of Champion's recent "Winning Attitude" campaign. The creative strategy of the campaign is to position Champion as a leader in authentic athletic wear and also make authentic athletic wear sexy and exciting. The ads present lifestyle situations of an athletic endeavor and the drive to win. Copy is introspective, reflecting a winning attitude and presenting a story of achievement, with which both serious athletes and emulators can identify. Dominating the ads are striking photographs, a critical element in gaining impact in print advertising. Champion's portrayal of amateur athletes differs from competitors' use of top-name professionals.

The visibility created by Champion's advertising significantly changed the perception of the brand and increased retail sales and distribution. Since its first year in retail, activewear sales have jumped from $30 million to $150 million, and the Champion line is now sold in more than 500 retail outlets. The ad campaign also is credited with contributing to Champion's success in gaining favorable publicity in business publications such as *The Wall Street Journal, Fortune,* and *Adweek's Marketing Week.*

Building on these initial successes, Champion is beefing up its promotional efforts by focusing on sporting event promotions, moving into television advertising, and investing more in print media, especially those that reach the college market.[1]

Photo source: Courtesy of Champion Products, Inc.

Chapter Overview

As Chapter 16 explained, promotion consists of both personal and nonpersonal elements. This chapter examines the nonpersonal elements of promotion: advertising, sales promotion, and public relations. These components play critical roles in the promotional mixes of thousands of organizations.

For many organizations, including Champion Products, advertising represents the most important type of nonpersonal promotion. This chapter examines advertising objectives, the importance of planning for advertising, and the different types of advertisements and media choices. It discusses both retail advertising and manufacturer (national) advertising and examines alternative methods of assessing an advertisement's effectiveness. Finally, the chapter discusses sales promotion and public relations, including publicity.

Advertising

If you sought to be the next member of the U.S. Senate, you would have to communicate with every possible voter in your state. If you developed new computer software and went into business to market it, your chances of success would be slim without informing and persuading students, businesspeople, and other potential customers of the usefulness of your offering. In these situations you would discover, as have countless others, the need to use advertising to communicate to buyers. As defined in Chapter 16, **advertising** is paid, nonpersonal communication through various media and by business firms, nonprofit organizations, and individuals who are in some way identified in the advertising message and hope to inform or persuade members of a particular audience.

advertising
Paid, nonpersonal communication through various media by business firms, nonprofit organizations, and individuals who are identified in the advertising message and hope to inform or persuade members of a particular audience.

Today's widespread markets make advertising an important part of business. Since the end of World War II, U.S. advertising and related expenditures have risen faster than the gross national product and most other economic indicators. Furthermore, about 212,000 workers are employed in advertising.

The nation's leading advertiser is Philip Morris Companies, spending over $2 billion. Procter & Gamble, General Motors, and Sears, Roebuck each spend more than $1 billion a year on advertising. The total annual expenditure for advertising in the United States exceeds $123 billion or approximately $500 for every man, woman, and child.[2]

Advertising expenditures vary among industries and companies. Cosmetic companies often are cited as examples of firms that spend a high percentage of their funds on advertising and promotion. Schonfeld & Associates studied 5,700 firms in 400 industry sectors and calculated their average advertising expenditures as a percentage of sales. Estimates for selected industries are given in Figure 17.1. As shown in the figure, wide differences exist among industries. Advertising spending can range from 0.7 percent in the carpet and rugs industry to more than 16 percent of sales in the industrial inorganic chemicals industry.

Evolution of Advertising

It is likely that some form of advertising has existed since the development of the exchange process. Most early advertising was vocal. Criers and hawkers sold various products, made public announcements, and chanted advertising slogans such as this:

One-a-penny, two-a-penny, hot-cross buns
One-a-penny, two for tuppence, hot-cross buns.

Figure 17.1   Estimated Average Advertising Expenditures as Percentage of Sales in Ten Industries

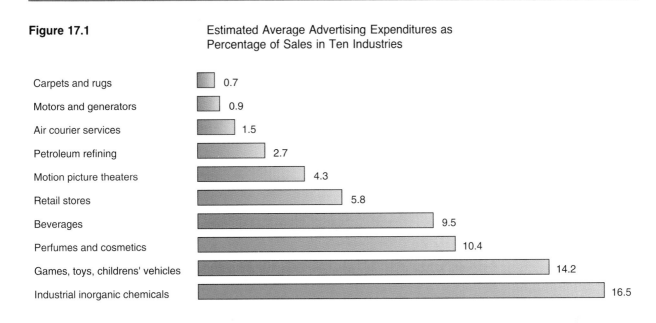

Carpets and rugs	0.7
Motors and generators	0.9
Air courier services	1.5
Petroleum refining	2.7
Motion picture theaters	4.3
Retail stores	5.8
Beverages	9.5
Perfumes and cosmetics	10.4
Games, toys, childrens' vehicles	14.2
Industrial inorganic chemicals	16.5

Source: Schonfeld & Associates, "Advertising Ratios and Budgets," as reported in "Ratios Indicate Hikes in Ad Levels," *Advertising Age* (November 13, 1989), p. 32.

Criers were common in colonial America. The cry "Rags! Any rags? Any wool rags?" filled the streets of Philadelphia in the 1700s. Signs were also used in early advertising. Most used symbolism in their identification of products or services. In Rome, a goat signified a dairy, a mule driving a mill implied a bakery, and a boy being whipped suggested a school.

Later the development of the printing press greatly expanded advertising's capabilities. A 1710 advertisement in the *Spectator* billed one dentifrice as "The Incomparable Powder for cleaning Teeth, which has given great satisfaction to most of the Nobility and Gentry in England." Colonial newspapers such as Benjamin Franklin's *Gazette* also featured advertising—in fact, many newspapers carried it on their front pages. Most of these advertisements would be called "classified ads" today. A few national advertisers, such as Lorillard, a producer of tobacco products, also began to use newspaper advertising in the late 1700s.

Volney Palmer organized the first advertising agency in the United States in 1841. George P. Rowell was another advertising pioneer. Originally advertising agencies simply sold ad space; services such as advertising research, copywriting, and planning came later. In the early 1900s, Claude C. Hopkins used a large-scale consumer survey on home-baked beans before launching a campaign for Van Camp's Pork and Beans. Hopkins claimed that home-baked beans were difficult to digest and suggested that consumers try Van Camp's. He advocated the use of "reason-why copy" to persuade people to buy the product.

Some early advertising promoted products of questionable value, such as patent medicines. An example was an advertisement promoting Pratt's Healing Ointment "for man and beast." As a result, a reform movement in advertising developed during the early 1900s, and some newspapers began to screen their advertisements. *Saturday Evening Post* publisher Cyrus Curtis began rejecting certain types of advertising, such as medical copy that claimed cures and advertisements for alcoholic beverages. In 1911, the forerunner of the American Advertising Federation drew up a code of improved advertising.

Figure 17.2

International Advertisement
Aimed at Increasing Cereal
Sales

Source: Courtesy of Kellogg (Australia) Pty. Ltd. and Leo Burnett Pty. Limited, Sydney.

One identifying feature of advertising in the twentieth century is its concern
for researching its target markets. Originally advertising research dealt primarily
with media selection and the product. Then advertisers became increasingly
concerned with determining the appropriate *demographics*—characteristics
such as the ages, sex, and income levels of potential buyers. Understanding
consumer behavior is now an important aspect of advertising strategy. Behavioral influences in purchase decisions, often called *psychographics,* can be
useful in describing potential markets for advertising appeals. As discussed in
Chapter 8, these influences include factors such as lifestyle and personal
attitudes. Increased information about consumer psychographics has led to
improved advertising decisions.

The emergence of the marketing concept, with its emphasis on a companywide consumer orientation, expanded the role of advertising as marketing
communications assumed greater importance in business. Today consumers are
exposed to thousands of advertising messages each day. Advertising provides
an efficient, inexpensive, and fast method of reaching the much sought after
consumer. It currently rivals sales promotion and personal selling in extent of use.
Indeed, advertising has become a key ingredient in the effective implementation
of the marketing concept.

Since the mid-1980s, advertising in foreign markets has outpaced the growth
in the U.S. market. In 1989 foreign advertising expenditures increased 12
percent, to $136 billion, while spending in the United States increased only 5
percent, to $123 billion.[3] The leading advertisers in foreign markets are Unilever
(London/Rotterdam), spending more than $1 billion in 24 countries; Procter &
Gamble, spending more than $900 million in 18 countries; and Nestlé (Switzer-
land), spending about $600 million in 19 nations. Kellogg Company spends about
one-fifth of its advertising dollars in nine foreign countries.[4] The advertisement in
Figure 17.2 is part of an Australian print campaign for Kellogg Special K cereal.
The ad targets teenagers, the second-largest consumers of weight-maintenance
cereal in Australia.

Major reasons for the growth in international advertising include the increased number of multinational corporations and global brands, increased trade among nations, worldwide improvement in living standards, and innovations in communication and transportation.[5] An example of international advertising on a grand scale is PepsiCo's global debut of its "Make a Wish" commercial featuring pop singer Madonna. At a cost of $5 million, the two-minute commercial aired in 40 countries, reaching an audience of 250 million viewers. Placed on the top-rated evening show in each country, the ad appeared first in Japan and followed the time zones around the world.[6]

Advertising Objectives

Traditionally advertising objectives were stated in terms of direct sales goals. A more realistic approach, however, is to view advertising as having communications objectives that seek to inform, persuade, and remind potential customers of the product. Advertising attempts to condition the consumer to adopt a favorable viewpoint toward the promotional message. The goal is to improve the likelihood that the customer will buy a particular good or service. In this sense, advertising illustrates the close relationship between marketing communications and promotional strategy.

Recent findings have confirmed the ability of effective advertising to enhance consumer perceptions of quality in a good or service. The results of these quality perceptions are stronger customer loyalty, more repeat purchases, and less vulnerability to price wars. In addition, perceived superiority pays off in the ability to raise prices without losing market share.[7]

Where personal selling is the primary component of a firm's marketing mix, advertising may be used in a support role—to assist salespeople. Much of Avon's advertising is aimed at assisting the neighborhood salesperson by strengthening the image of Avon, its products, and its salespeople. New York Life developed an advertising campaign to change the image consumers have of insurance salespeople as annoying policy pushers. Featuring company agents, the ads portray New York Life's salespeople as helpful and friendly next-door neighbors. Because agents are the only way insurance firms can sell life policies, the campaign attempts to persuade consumers to respond favorably to agent phone calls and visits.[8]

Translating Advertising Objectives into Advertising Plans

Advertising planning begins with the marketing objectives and strategies derived from the firm's overall objectives. These general marketing objectives and strategies are the basis for marketing communications objectives and strategies. Effective research is essential for both marketing and advertising planning. The results of the research allow management to make strategic decisions that are translated into tactical areas such as budgeting, copywriting, scheduling, and media selection. Post-tests are used to measure the effectiveness of advertising and form the basis for feedback concerning needs for possible adjustment. The elements of advertising planning are shown in Figure 17.3.

There is a real need for following a sequential process in advertising decisions. Novice advertisers often are overly concerned with the technical aspects of advertisement construction and ignore the more basic steps, such as market analysis. The type of advertisement to be used in a particular situation is largely related to the planning phase of this process.

Figure 17.3 Elements of Advertising Planning

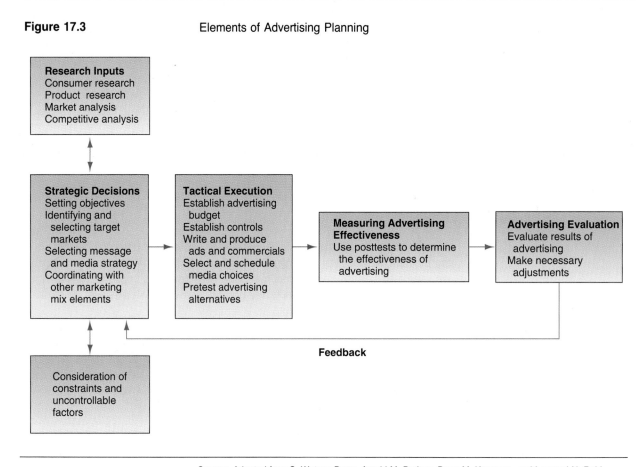

Source: Adapted from S. Watson Dunn, Arnold M. Barban, Dean M. Krugman, and Leonard N. Reid, *Advertising: Its Role in Modern Marketing* (Hinsdale, IL: The Dryden Press, 1990), p. 200.

Positioning

positioning

Developing a marketing strategy aimed at a particular market segment and designed to achieve a desired position in the prospective buyer's mind.

The concept of **positioning** involves developing a marketing strategy aimed at a particular market segment and designed to achieve a desired position in the prospective buyer's mind. Marketers use a positioning strategy to distinguish their good or service from the competition and create advertisements to communicate the desired position.

As Professors David A. Aaker and J. Gary Shansby point out, a variety of positioning strategies are available to the advertiser.[9] Advertising messages can position a good or service by

1. Attributes *(Crest is a cavity fighter.)*
2. Price/quality *(Sears is a value store.)*
3. Competitors *("Avis is only number two in rent-a-cars, so why go with us? We try harder.")*
4. Application *("Raid kills bugs dead.")*
5. Product user *(Miller is for the blue-collar, heavy beer drinker.)*
6. Product class *(Carnation Instant Breakfast is a breakfast food.)*

A common positioning technique is to position some aspect of the firm's marketing mix against the leading competitors. When Richard Cronin joined MTV Networks' Nickelodeon *(Nick at Nite)* as vice-president of marketing, the classic comedy programs for adults lacked a strong brand identity. Cronin developed an advertising campaign to position the cable network programming as a nutty alternative to that of broadcast TV. The ads had to follow Cronin's three marketing criteria of being funny, typical of TV-land, and silly. One ad for *Car 54, Where Are You?* showed a giant iguana swallowing police officers Toody and Muldoon. Promotion for *Mr. Ed* included mock scratch-and-sniff ads pitching Mr. Ed aftershave (a nonexistent product) with fragrances such as "bouquet of pasture" and "essence of stall." The positioning campaign was so successful that within a year viewership among the targeted audience (age 19 to 49) increased 127 percent.[10]

Success in positioning requires a careful, well-researched plan:

The selection of a positioning strategy involves identifying competitors, relevant attributes, competitor positions, and market segments. Research-based approaches can help in each of these steps by providing conceptualization even if the subjective judgments of managers are used to provide the actual input information to the position decision.[11]

Types of Advertising

product advertising
Nonpersonal selling of a good or service.

institutional advertising
Promoting a concept, an idea, a philosophy, or the goodwill of an industry, company, organization, place, person, or government agency.

Two broad types of advertisements exist: product and institutional. **Product advertising** deals with the nonpersonal selling of a particular good or service. It is the type that comes to the average person's mind when he or she thinks about advertisements. **Institutional advertising,** in contrast, is concerned with promoting a concept, an idea, a philosophy, or the goodwill of an industry, company, organization, person, geographic location, or government agency. It is a broader term than *corporate advertising,* which is typically limited to nonproduct advertising sponsored by profit-seeking firms. Institutional advertising is often closely related to the public relations function of the enterprise. Figure 17.4 shows examples of Anheuser-Busch's product and institutional advertising. The Family Talk About Drinking Program described in the institutional ad is one of many public relations programs developed by Anheuser-Busch to discourage alcohol abuse and driving while intoxicated.

Advertising can be subdivided into three categories, depending on the primary objective of the message: informative, persuasive, and reminder. **Informative advertising** seeks to develop initial demand for a good, service, organization, person, place, idea, or cause. It tends to characterize the promotion of any new market entry because the objective often is simply to announce its availability. Informative advertising is used in the introductory stage of the product life cycle.

informative advertising
Promotion that seeks to announce the availability of and develop initial demand for a good, service, organization, person, place, idea or cause.

persuasive advertising
Competitive promotion that seeks to develop demand for a good, service, organization, person, place, idea, or cause.

reminder advertising
Promotion that seeks to reinforce previous promotional activity by keeping the name of the good, service, organization, person, place, idea, or cause in front of the public.

Persuasive advertising attempts to develop demand for a good, service, organization, person, place, idea, or cause. It is a competitive type of promotion used in the growth stage and early in the maturity stage of the product life cycle.

Reminder advertising strives to reinforce previous promotional activity by keeping the name of the good, service, organization, person, place, idea, or cause before the public. It is used in the latter part of the maturity stage as well as throughout the decline stage of the product life cycle.

Figure 17.5 gives examples of informative, persuasive, and reminder ads. Penn, well-known for its tennis balls, created this informational ad to introduce its new market entry — tennis shoes. Tetley uses a persuasive approach to build brand preference and encourage consumers to switch to its brand. The Walt Disney ad reminds consumers where to go for a vacation in the sun.

Figure 17.4   Product and Institutional Advertising

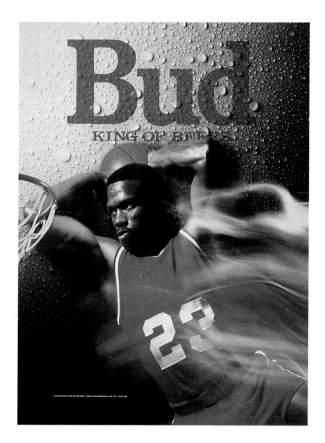

Source: Courtesy of Anheuser-Busch, Inc.

Advocacy Advertising

advocacy advertising

Paid public communication or message that presents information on a point of view bearing on a publicly recognized, controversial issue.

One form of persuasive institutional advertising that has increased during the past decade is advocacy advertising. **Advocacy advertising,** sometimes referred to as *cause advertising,* can be defined as any kind of paid public communication or message, from an identified source and in a conventional advertising medium, that presents information or a point of view bearing on a publicly recognized, controversial issue. Such advertising is designed to influence public opinion, affect current and pending legislation, and gain a following.

Advocacy advertising, described in the discussion of idea marketing in Chapter 1, has been effectively utilized by nonprofit organizations such as The Partnership for a Drug-Free America, Mothers Against Drunk Driving (MADD), and the National Rifle Association. In recent years, profit-seeking companies (particularly energy and resource firms) with a stake in some issue have turned to advocacy advertising. Among the firms that have attempted to convince the public of their viewpoints by this means are Mobil Oil, Exxon, and Bethlehem Steel.

Figure 17.5   Advertisements to Inform, Persuade, and Remind

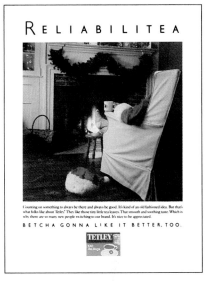

Sources: Courtesy of Fallon McElligott (*top left*); reprinted with the permission of Tetley, Inc. (*top right*).

Media Selection

One of the most important decisions in developing an advertising strategy is the media to be used for transmitting the firm's message. A mistake at this point can cost a company literally millions of dollars in ineffective advertising. The media the marketer selects must be capable of accomplishing the communications objectives of informing, persuading, and reminding potential customers of the good, service, person, or idea.

Research should identify the target market to determine its size and characteristics and then match the target with the audience and the effectiveness of the available media with that particular audience. The objective is to achieve adequate media coverage without advertising beyond the identifiable limits of the potential market. Finally, alternative costs should be compared to determine the best possible media purchase.

The major advertising media are compared on the bases of their shares of overall advertising expenditures as well as their major strengths and weaknesses in Table 17.1.[12] *Broadcast media* include television and radio. Newspapers, magazines, outdoor advertising, and direct mail represent the major types of *print media*. As Table 17.1 reveals, newspapers and television are the leading advertising media; and radio, magazines, and outdoor advertising rank at the bottom. Since 1950 newspapers, radio, and magazines have experienced declines in their market shares, while television has grown tremendously.

Television

Even though only 29 cents of every advertising dollar is spent in the broadcast media of television and radio, the television medium contains so many characteristics favorable to effective advertising that it has grown to the point where it rivals newspapers as the dominant advertising medium. Although television ranks second to newspapers, with a 22 percent share of over-all advertising revenues, the relative attractiveness of the two media differs in local and national markets. Most newspaper advertising revenues come from local advertisers. In contrast, television is the dominant medium for national advertising.

Television advertising can be divided into four categories: network, national, local, and cable. Columbia Broadcasting System, National Broadcasting Company, and American Broadcasting Company are the three major national networks. Their programs accounted for about one-third ($9 billion) of total television advertising expenditures of $26.9 billion in a recent year. A national "spot" is nonnetwork broadcasting used by a general advertiser. Local advertising spots, used primarily by retailers, consist of locally developed and sponsored commercials. Cable television is a rapidly growing medium, currently installed in half of U.S. households. Total cable advertising revenues were $1.3 billion in 1989. By 1995, it is estimated that 70 percent of homes will subscribe to a cable system, and ad revenues will reach $4 billion.[13]

Television advertising offers the advantages of impact, mass coverage, repetition, flexibility, and prestige. Its disadvantages include loss of control of the promotional message to the telecaster (who can influence its impact), high costs, high mortality rates for commercials, some public distrust, and lack of selectivity in the ability of specific television programs to reach precisely defined target market consumers without a significant degree of wasted coverage.

Radio

Advertisers who use radio can also be classified as network, national, and local. Radio accounts for about 7 percent of total advertising revenue and 10 percent of local expenditures. Its advantages are immediacy (studies show most people regard radio as the best source for up-to-date news), low cost, flexibility, practical and low-cost audience selection, and mobility. Its disadvantages include fragmentation, the temporary nature of messages, and less research information than for television.

Table 17.1   Advertising Media Alternatives

Media	Percentage of Total Advertising Expenditures[a]	Advantages	Disadvantages
Broadcast Media			
Television	22%	Great impact Mass coverage Repetition Flexibility Prestige	Temporary nature of message High cost High mortality rate for commercials Distrust Lack of selectivity
Radio	7	Immediacy Low cost Flexibility Practical audience selection Mobility	Fragmentation Temporary nature of message Little research information
Print Media			
Newspapers	26	Flexibility Community prestige Intensive coverage Reader control of exposure Coordination with national advertising Merchandising service Special techniques	Short life span Hasty reading Relatively poor reproduction
Direct mail	18	Selectivity Intense coverage Speed Flexibility of format Complete information Personalization	High per-person cost Dependency on quality of mailing list Consumer resistance
Magazines	5	Selectivity Quality reproduction Long life Prestige associated with some magazines Extra services offered by some publications	Lack of flexibility
Outdoor advertising	1	Communication of quick and simple ideas Repetition Ability to promote products available for sale locally	Brevity of message Public concern over aesthetics

[a]An additional 21 percent is spent on a variety of miscellaneous advertising media, including Yellow Pages advertising, business papers, transit advertising, point-of-purchase displays, cinema advertising, and regional farm papers.
Source: Based on S. Watson Dunn, Arnold M. Barban, Dean M. Krugman, and Leonard N. Reid, *Advertising: Its Role in Modern Marketing,* 7th ed. (Hinsdale, Ill.: Dryden Press, 1990), pp. 393–458. Relative shares of total advertising expenditures from Robert J. Coen, "U.S. Advertising Volume," *Advertising Age* (May 6, 1991), p. 16.

Newspapers

Newspaper advertising continues to dominate local markets. It accounts for 26 percent of total advertising revenues. Newspapers' primary advantages are flexibility (advertising can be varied from one locality to the next), community prestige (newspapers have a deep impact on their communities), intensive coverage (in most locations, 90 percent of the homes can be reached with a single newspaper), reader control of exposure to the advertising message (unlike with electronic media, readers can refer back to newspapers), coordination with national advertising, merchandising services (such as promotional and research support), and special techniques such as singlesheet or multipage insert ads. The disadvantages are a short life span, hasty reading (the typical reader spends about 40 minutes reading the newspaper), and relatively poor reproduction.

Magazines

Magazines, which are divided into three basic categories—consumer, farm, and business publications—account for about 5 percent of national advertising, 42 percent of which appears in weekly magazines. The primary advantages of magazine advertising are their selectivity in reaching precise target markets, quality reproduction, long life, the prestige associated with some magazines, and the extra services many publications offer. The primary disadvantage is that magazines lack the flexibility of newspapers, radio, and television.

Modern Maturity is the nation's leading magazine in terms of annual paid subscriptions, with 20 million. Other leading magazines include *Reader's Digest, TV Guide, National Geographic,* and women's magazines such as *Better Homes & Gardens, Family Circle, Good Housekeeping,* and *McCall's.*

Direct Mail

Sales letters, postcards, leaflets, folders, broadsides (which are larger than folders), booklets, catalogs, and house organs (periodical publications issued by organizations) are forms of direct-mail advertising. The advantages of direct mail are selectivity, intensive coverage, speed, format flexibility, completeness of information, and personalization of each mailing piece. Disadvantages of direct mail are its high cost per reader, its dependence on the quality of mailing lists, and some consumers' resistance to it.

Consumer objections to receipt of unsolicited direct mail led the Direct Mail/Marketing Association to establish its Mail Preference Service in 1971. This consumer service sends name-removal forms to people who do not wish to receive direct-mail advertising. It also provides add-on forms for those who like to receive a lot of mail. Approximately 18 percent of total advertising is spent on direct mail.

Outdoor Advertising

Posters (commonly called *billboards*), painted bulletins or displays (such as those that appear on the walls of buildings), and electric spectaculars (large, illuminated, and sometimes animated signs and displays) make up the outdoor-advertising medium. This form of advertising has the advantages of ready communication of quick and simple ideas, repetition, and the ability to promote products that are available for sale locally. Outdoor advertising is particularly effective in metropolitan and other high-traffic areas. Its disadvantages are the brevity of its messages and public concern over aesthetics. The Highway Beautification Act of 1965, for example, regulates the placement of outdoor advertising near interstate highways. This medium accounts for approximately 1 percent of all advertising.

Other Types of Advertising Media

In addition to the major media, firms use many other vehicles to communicate their messages. Transit advertising includes ads placed both inside and outside of buses, subways, and commuter trains. Some firms place ads on taxi tops, bus shelters and benches, telephone enclosures, and parking meters. A growing but controversial form of advertising in the United States is cinema advertising, which has been popular in European countries for many years. About half of the 23,000 movie theatres in the United States accept commercials.[14] Ads appear in printed programs of live-theater productions, and firms such as PepsiCo and Chrysler advertise on video cassette movies. Directory advertising includes the familiar yellow pages in telephone books and thousands of other types of directories, most of which are business related. Some firms use hot air balloons, blimps, banners behind airplanes, and scoreboards at sporting events for advertising purposes. An Israeli firm, Eggvert International, is promoting advertising on eggs. Eggs with ads sell well in Israel, and Eggvert intends to extend the concept globally.[15]

Advertising is moving into the electronic age. One firm has developed a system of electronic advertising on supermarket shopping carts whereby commercials are triggered by the aisle in which the consumer is shopping.[16] Several firms have introduced video networks in shopping malls that air commercials along with entertainment and other programming.[17] An advertising medium expected to grow in the next decade is videotex, an interactive electronic system that transmits data and graphics from a computer network over telephone lines and displays it on a subscriber's television or computer screen. Prodigy, a computer information services videotex system developed jointly by IBM and Sears, has attracted more than 200 advertisers since it started selling ad space in 1987.[18]

Media Scheduling

media scheduling
Timing and sequencing of advertisements.

Once the advertiser has selected the media that best match its advertising objectives and promotional budget, attention shifts to **media scheduling**—the timing and sequencing of advertisements. A variety of factors influence this decision as well. Sales patterns, repurchase cycles, and competitive activities are the most important variables.

Seasonal sales patterns are common in many industries. For example, an airline might reduce advertising during peak travel periods and boost its media schedule during low travel months (see the discussion of promotion as a variable for stabilizing sales in Chapter 16). Repurchase cycles may also play a role in media scheduling—the shorter the repurchase cycle, the more likely it is that the media schedule will be consistent throughout the year. Competitive activity is still another influence on media scheduling. For instance, a small firm may elect to avoid advertising during periods of heavy competitive advertising.

Seasonal sales patterns and competitive activities have considerable influence on the media scheduling of photo-film makers. December is the busiest film-buying month of the year, accounting for about 30 percent of annual U.S. film sales. Makers of photo film—Kodak, Polaroid, Fuji, and Konica—spend almost half their multimillion-dollar annual advertising budgets in December to persuade consumers to purchase their brand. They use television commercials and print ads in newspapers and magazines to reach the mass market.[19]

Advertisers use the concepts of reach, frequency, and gross rating points to measure the effectiveness of media scheduling plans. *Reach* refers to the

Figure 17.6   Hypothetical Media Schedule for a New Auto Model

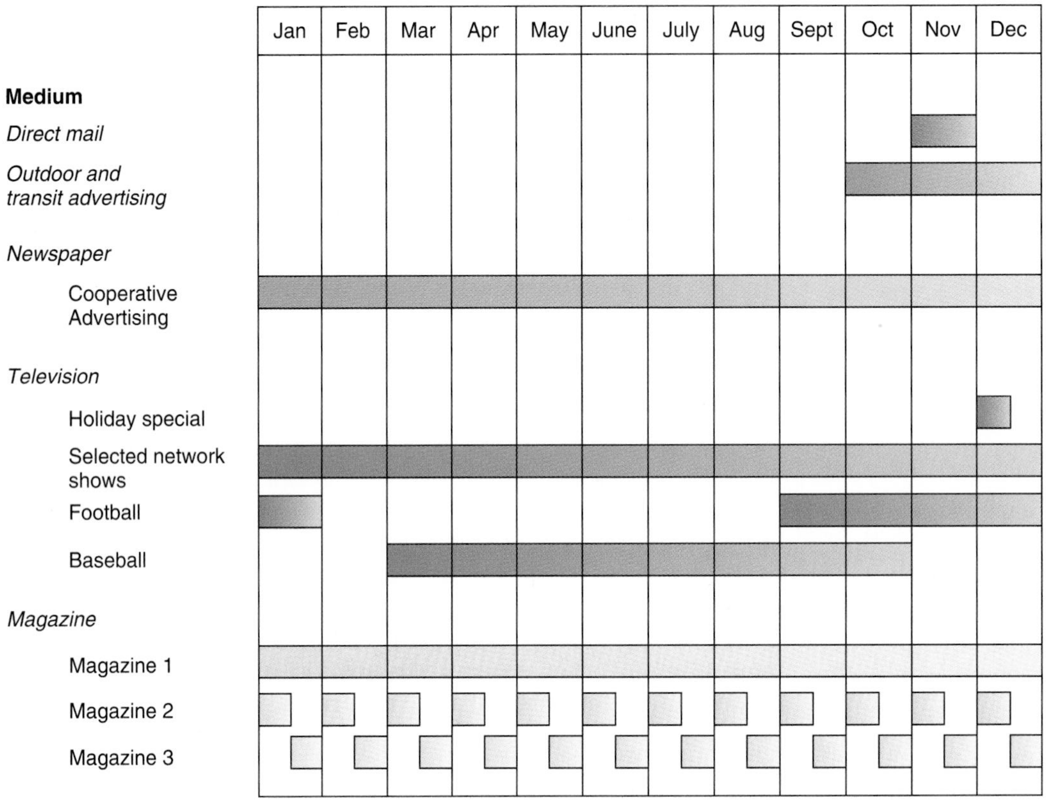

	Jan	Feb	Mar	Apr	May	June	July	Aug	Sept	Oct	Nov	Dec

Medium

Direct mail

Outdoor and transit advertising

Newspaper

    Cooperative Advertising

Television

    Holiday special

    Selected network shows

    Football

    Baseball

Magazine

    Magazine 1

    Magazine 2

    Magazine 3

number of different persons or households exposed to an advertisement at least once during a certain time period, typically four weeks. *Frequency* refers to the number of times a person is exposed to an advertisement during a certain time period. By multiplying reach times frequency, advertisers can quantitatively describe the total weight of a media effort, which is called the *gross rating point.*[20]

Hypothetical Media Schedule

Figure 17.6 shows a hypothetical media schedule for the introduction of a new automobile designed to appeal primarily to male buyers. The model is introduced in November with a direct-mail piece offering recipients test drives. It is supported by extensive outdoor and transit advertising during a three-month introductory period and is featured in the firm's commercials shown during a Christmas television special early in December.

This particular manufacturer also advertises in selected network shows throughout the year, as well as on football and baseball telecasts. The manufacturer is an extensive user of magazines as well. Since women are expected to purchase 40 percent of the total number of models sold, one women's publication is used every month and two national magazines are used on an alternating basis: one for the first two weekly issues and the second for the last two weeks each month. Finally, newspapers are used for cooperative advertising, in which the manufacturer and dealer share the advertising costs.

Organization of the Advertising Function

Although the ultimate responsibility for advertising decision making often rests with top marketing management, the organization of the advertising function varies among companies. A producer of a technical industrial product may be served by one person within the company whose primary task is writing copy for submission to trade publications. A consumer goods company, on the other hand, may have a large department staffed with advertising specialists.

The advertising function is usually organized as a staff department reporting to the vice-president (or director) of marketing. The director of advertising is an executive position that heads the functional activity of advertising. The individual in this position must be not only a skilled and experienced advertiser but an effective communicator within the organization. The success of a firm's promotional strategy depends on the advertising director's willingness and ability to communicate both vertically and horizontally. The major tasks typically organized under advertising include advertising research, design, copywriting, media analysis, and, in some cases, sales promotion.

Advertising Agencies

advertising agency
Marketing specialist firm used to assist advertisers in planning and implementing advertising programs.

Many major advertisers use an independent **advertising agency,** a marketing specialist firm that assists advertisers in planning and preparing advertisements. There are several reasons why most large advertisers use agencies for at least a portion of their advertising. Agencies typically are staffed with highly qualified specialists who provide a degree of creativity and objectivity that is difficult to sustain in a corporate advertising department. In some cases, they also reduce the cost of advertising because the advertiser can avoid many of the fixed expenses associated with maintaining an internal advertising department.

Effective use of an advertising agency requires a close relationship between the advertiser and the agency. The agency must have thorough knowledge of the advertiser's good or service and channels of distribution, competitors' strategy, and available media that can be used to reach the consumer and trade markets.

Traditionally agencies were compensated by receiving a 15 percent commission based on media and production billings. Today only about 35 percent of advertisers use the standard 15 percent commission. About one-third of advertisers have adopted a guaranteed-profit system in which the advertiser negotiates a fee with the agency based on the cost of producing the ads and the agency's profits. Other advertisers have adopted performance-based compensation plans. For example, General Foods has lowered the base rate percentage to 14 percent and installed a rating system that allows agencies to earn up to three additional percentage points in commission for outstanding and effective advertising.[21]

Figure 17.7 shows the organization chart for a large advertising agency. While the titles may vary among agencies, the major operational functions may be classified as creative services; account services; marketing services in the forms of media services, marketing research, and sales promotion; and finance and management. The top agencies in the world, ranked by worldwide billings, are Dentsu of Tokyo ($10 billion) and U.S.–based Young & Rubicam ($6.2 billion), Saatchi & Saatchi Advertising Worldwide ($6 billion), Backer Spielvogel Bates Worldwide ($5.1 billion), Ogilvy & Mather Worldwide ($4.8 billion), and McCann-Erickson Worldwide ($4.7 billion). Of the world's largest 100 agencies, 46 are based in the United States, 28 in the Pacific's western rim (primarily Tokyo), and 18 in Europe.[22]

Figure 17.7   Advertising Agency Organization Chart

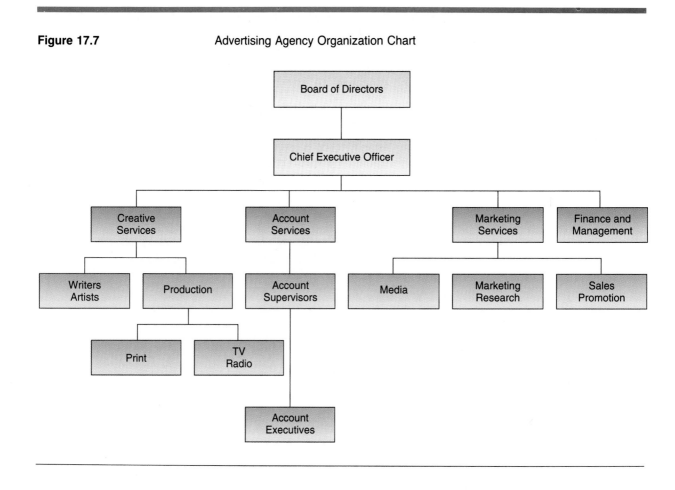

Creating an Advertisement

The final step in the advertising process—the development and preparation of an advertisement—should flow logically from the promotional theme selected. It should be a complementary part of the marketing mix and its role in the total marketing strategy carefully determined. Major factors to consider when preparing an advertisement are its creativity, its continuity with past advertisements, and possibly its association with other company products.

What should an advertisement accomplish? Regardless of the chosen target, an advertisement should (1) gain attention and interest, (2) inform and/or persuade, and (3) eventually lead to buying action.

Gaining attention should be productive; that is, it should instill some recall of the good or service. Otherwise, it will not lead to buying action. Consider Gillette Company, which once had a chimpanzee shave a man's face in a commercial. After testing the commercial in two cities, one Gillette spokesperson lamented, "Lots of people remembered the chimp, but hardly anyone remembered our product. There was fantastic interest in the monkey, but no payoff for Gillette."[23]

An advertisement should also inform and/or persuade. For example, many insurance advertisements are informative—they typically specify the policy's features—and they are persuasive—they may use testimonials in attempting to persuade prospective purchasers.

Stimulating buying action is often difficult because an advertisement cannot actually close a sale. Nevertheless, if the ad gains attention and informs or persuades, it is probably well worthwhile. Too many advertisers fail to suggest

Figure 17.8

Elements of a Typical Advertisement

how the receiver can purchase a product if he or she so desires. This is a shortcoming that should be eliminated.

The Birds Eye advertisement in Figure 17.8 identifies the four major elements of a print advertisement: headline, illustration, body copy, and signature. *Headlines* and *illustrations* (photographs, drawings, or other artwork) should work together to generate interest and attention. *Body copy* serves to inform, persuade, and stimulate buying action. The *signature,* which may include company name, address, phone number, slogan, trademark, or product photo, names the sponsoring organization. An ad may also have a *subhead*—a heading subordinate to the main headline that either links the main headline to the body copy or subdivides sections of the body copy.

In developing a creative strategy, advertisers must decide how the message should be communicated. Should the tone of the advertisement be rational or should it evoke an emotional response of, say, fear, humor, or fantasy? In recent years, the use of fear appeals in advertising has escalated. Ads for Prestone antifreeze, Michelin tires, Mercedes-Benz automobiles, Allstate and Liberty Mutual insurance, and American Express's Global Assist program all carry the message that incorrect buying decisions endanger the well-being of consumers and in many cases their children. For example, a Prestone commercial shows a young hockey player waiting on the side of a road for a ride from his dad. The setting is nighttime, the boy is cold, and the dad is stranded somewhere with bad antifreeze. The boy blows on his hands to warm them up and woefully asks, "Where are you, dad?"[24]

The creation of each advertisement in a campaign is an evolutionary process that begins with an idea and ultimately results in a finished product in the form of print and electronic media advertising. The idea itself must first be converted into

H.J. HEINZ MOVES INTO CHINA

. . . .

As the U.S. food market has matured and competition has stiffened, H.J. Heinz has begun looking elsewhere for growth. It has converted its dominant products, ketchup and Weight Watchers diet meals, into global brands and has entered new markets around the world. In 1991, 40 percent of its revenues came from overseas. But perhaps its most innovative move has been to make and sell an instant rice cereal for babies in China.

Heinz has a lot going for it in the Chinese market. For one thing, 22 million babies are born in China each year—six times the number born in the United States. For another, under China's one-child-per-family policy a child born in that nation stands a good chance of being an only child and the apple of its parents' eye—or, as the Chinese say, their "little emperor."

For the parents of these infants, a Western baby food high in vitamins and minerals is well worth the relatively high price of 75 cents a box (an expensive purchase for a worker earning $40 a month). To attract their attention, Heinz has produced high-quality television commercials in a market where most advertising is done via newspapers and billboards. The commercials show happy babies being cuddled by their mothers, with a message assuring viewers of the product's nutritional value. The fact that Heinz's cereal is precooked and instant—in contrast to less expensive products that need to be cooked—makes it more appealing to families in which both parents work.

Heinz began making instant cereal in a small plant in Guangzhou (formerly Canton) in 1986. The venture is already profitable—a surprise in a country where it usually takes a decade to turn a profit. In fact, its margins are comparable to those of the parent company, prompting Heinz to begin a search for a second factory site.

Discussion Questions

1. Nestlé, a long-time marketer of baby food throughout the world, recently opened its own factory in China. Does this spell the end of Heinz's profitable venture there?

2. Would Heinz sell more baby cereal to Chinese families if it lowered the price of its product?

Sources: Alicia Swasy, "Heinz's O'Reilly Drives Hard for Growth," *The Wall Street Journal* (February 7, 1991), p. A4; Patrice Duggan, "Feeding China's 'Little Emperors'" *Forbes* (August 6, 1990), pp. 84–85; Gregory L. Miles, "Heinz Ain't Broke, but It's Doing a Lot of Fixing," *Business Week* (December 11, 1989), pp. 84, 85, 88. *Photo Source:* © L. Ka Tai/Woodfin Camp & Associates.

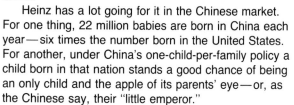

a thought sketch, a tangible summary of the intended message. The next step involves refinement of the thought sketch into a rough layout. Continued refinements of the rough layout eventually produce the final version of the advertisement that is ready to print or record.

Comparative Advertising

comparative advertising
Nonpersonal-selling efforts that make direct or indirect promotional comparisons with competitive brands.

Comparative advertising is an advertising strategy in which the firm's advertising messages make direct or indirect promotional comparisons with competitive brands. A comparative advertising strategy is often employed by firms whose goods and services do not lead their markets. Most market leaders do not acknowledge in their advertising that competitive products even exist. Procter & Gamble and General Foods, for example, traditionally have devoted little of their huge promotional budgets to comparative advertising. But many firms use it extensively. Here are some examples:

☐ Ad for diet Coke: "Discover The One-Calorie Real Cola Taste Worth Leaving Pepsi For."

☐ "GE Rechargeable Batteries can't be beaten. Not even by a hare." (The hare refers to the pink drum-banging bunny in Eveready Battery Company's Energizer commercials.

☐ Ad for U.S. Sprint: "Who Is AT&T Kidding When They Say Their Rates Are Competitive?"

Comparative advertising has become commonplace in automobile and truck advertising. General Motors Chevrolet division ran an ad comparing its pickup truck to Ford's by standing them up side by side on their front ends. Ford retaliated by developing a similar ad showing the Chevrolet truck sinking into the ground. Foreign and domestic automakers have created a blitz of comparative ads in an attempt to gain a larger share of the U.S. market. In one ad, Volvo claims its sedan model outclasses Mercedes. A Saab ad boasts that its 9000 model is roomier than a BMW and safer than Mercedes and Volvo. Ads in Chrysler's "Meet the Americans that beat the Hondas" campaign give results of a survey of car owners in California who ranked Chrysler's Spirit, Acclaim, and Shadow models higher than the market leaders, Honda's Accord and Civic. Chrysler's campaign targets young, affluent buyers who own domestic vehicles but are considering switching to an import.[25]

Marketers who contemplate using comparative advertising in their promotional strategies should take care to ensure that they can substantiate their claims. Comparative advertising has the potential to produce lawsuits. Also, advertising experts disagree on the long-term effects of comparative advertising. It may be a useful strategy in only a limited number of circumstances.

Celebrity Testimonials

In attempting to improve the effectiveness of their advertising, a number of marketers utilize celebrities to present their advertising messages. Well-known examples include rap artist M.C. Hammer for British Knights athletic footwear, singer Paula Abdul for Coca-Cola, Chicago Bears football coach Mike Ditka for Budget Rent-A-Truck, and singers Madonna, Tina Turner, and Michael Jackson for Pepsi. Foreign firms also use the star status of U.S. celebrities to promote goods and services in their countries. In Japan, for example, actor Paul Newman is spokesperson for Fuji Card Service's FujiCard, movie director George Lukas for Panasonic Technics, and actor Mickey Rourke for Daihatsu's Charade automobile.[26]

The primary advantage of using big-name personalities is that they may improve product recognition in a promotional environment filled with hundreds of competing 15- and 30-second commercials. (Advertisers use the term *clutter* to describe this situation.) In order for this technique to succeed, the celebrity must be a credible source of information for the item being promoted. Bill Cosby dressed up as an ice cream vendor to promote Jello-O Pudding Pops is an effective spokesperson. He was equally convincing when he discussed quality and integrity in advertising for Ford Motor Company. But actress Cybill Shepherd proved to be a less than believable spokesperson in ads for The Beef Industry Council and L'Oreal hair-care products after she revealed in magazine interviews

Figure 17.9

Effective Use of Celebrity
Advertising

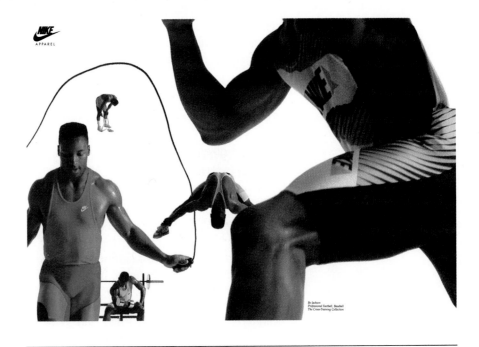

Source: Courtesy of NIKE.

that one of her beauty tips is not eating red meat and that she never colors her hair.[27]

Celebrity advertisements are most effective when there is a relevant link between the celebrity and the advertised good or service. An excellent example is the use of versatile athlete Bo Jackson to promote Nike's cross-training athletic shoe, as shown in the ad in Figure 17.9. Another example is General Mills's use of top athletes such as Olympic gold medalist Mary Lou Retton, tennis great Chris Evert, and basketball star Michael Jordan to promote its Wheaties "The Breakfast of Champions" cereal. In a recent year, Coke, Diet Coke, Pepsi, and Diet Pepsi used nearly three dozen movie stars, athletes, musicians, and television personalities in their efforts to increase cola sales.[28]

Millions of people around the world are very sports and celebrity oriented. Therefore, there is opportunity for firms to profitably sponsor athletes or sporting events. However, such promotions should be clear adjuncts to existing promotional programs. There are several principles that corporate sponsors should consider before getting involved. First, they must be selective and specific. A target market should be pinpointed and a sport or celebrity carefully matched to that target and objective. Second, they should follow sports interest trends carefully; too often firms get involved without assessing the trend's strength. Third, they must be original and look for a special focus. Is it possible to come up with a unique concept? Fourth, they should analyze the results in both the short and long terms. Sponsorship is a business decision that should pay off in profits.[29]

Retail Advertising

retail advertising
Nonpersonal selling by stores that offer goods or services directly to the consuming public.

Retail advertising is all advertising by stores that sell goods or services directly to the consuming public. While it accounts for a sizable portion of total annual advertising expenditures, retail advertising varies widely in its effectiveness. One study showed that consumers are often suspicious of retail price advertisements.

Source, message, and shopping experience seem to affect consumer attitudes toward these advertisements.[30]

The basic problem is that retail stores often treat advertising as a secondary activity. Except for some retail giants, they rarely use advertising agencies. Instead, store managers are usually given the responsibility of advertising along with their normal functions. The basic step in correcting this deficiency is to give one individual both the responsibility and the authority for developing an effective retail advertising program.

Cooperative Advertising. The sharing of advertising costs between the retailer and the manufacturer or wholesaler is called **cooperative advertising.** For example, an apparel marketer may pay a percentage of the cost of a retail store's newspaper advertisement featuring its product lines.

Cooperative advertising resulted from the media's practice of offering lower rates to local advertisers than to national ones. Later cooperative advertising was seen as a way to improve dealer relations. From the retailer's viewpoint, it permits a store to secure advertising that would be otherwise unobtainable.

cooperative advertising
Sharing of advertising costs between the retailer and the manufacturer of the good or service.

Assessing the Effectiveness of an Advertisement

Because advertising represents a major expenditure for many firms, it is imperative to determine whether a chosen campaign is accomplishing its promotional objectives. Advertisers are well aware of the number of advertising messages to which consumers are exposed daily and their ability to practice *selective perception* by simply screening them out. Novel forms of advertising, such as inserting ads in video cassettes and cinema advertising, are aimed at increasing the likelihood that the messages will be seen and heard.

Three-dimensional pop-up ads for Disney World, Dodge trucks, and Honeywell computers in magazines are designed to stand out—and be remembered. Absolut vodka marketers inserted musical microchips in magazine ads so that the ads would play songs when readers turned to them. Trifari Krussman & Fischel, a maker of costume jewelry, ran a pop-out, try-on ad of a gold necklace, earrings, and a pin so readers could punch them out, try them on, and match them with outfits at home. Advertisers of cigarettes, diapers, cars, and computers create magazine foldout ads (called *gatefolds*) of up to 16 pages to catch readers' attention. Nissan's unconventional commercials showing trees and rocks were designed to pique consumers' curiosity and create awareness of its new Infiniti automobiles.[31]

The objective of these novel approaches is to enhance the likelihood that the advertisement message will be received and remembered. However, determining whether an advertising message has achieved its intended objective is one of the most difficult undertakings in marketing. Assessment of advertising effectiveness consists of two primary elements: pretesting and post-testing.

Pretesting

pretesting
Assessment of an advertisement's effectiveness before it is actually used.

Pretesting is the assessment of an advertisement's effectiveness before it is actually used. It includes a variety of evaluative methods. To test magazine advertisements, the Batten, Barton, Durstine & Osborn ad agency cuts ads out of advance copies of magazines and then "strips in" the ads it wants to test. Interviewers later check the impact of the advertisements on readers who receive free copies of the revised magazine.

| FOCUS ON ETHICS |

PROMOTING CIGARETTES AND ALCOHOL

Community activists, angry at the targeting of minority groups, are painting over billboards advertising tobacco and liquor products in minority neighborhoods. Congress is considering a bill that would require alcohol ads to carry health warnings, and a significant number of consumers favor an outright ban on ads for alcoholic beverages. California has mounted a slick advertising campaign in which commercials show tobacco company executives callously dismissing health concerns and seeking ways to replace the 3,100 American smokers who quit or die each year.

Promotion as well as advertising of these products has come under fire. Led by Louis Sullivan, Secretary of Health and Human Services, antismoking activists have attacked the sponsorship of sports events by tobacco and brewing companies. Athletic events like the Virginia Slims tennis tournament are accused of pushing "a product that, when used as intended, causes death." According to Sullivan, "The sponsorship itself uses the vigor and energy of athletes as a subtle but incorrect and dishonest message that smoking is compatible with good health."

Tobacco companies claim that sponsorship of sports is a form of good citizenship. "What we are promoting is tennis, not smoking. . . . We only hope that those who attend who do smoke will smoke our brand," says a spokesperson for Philip Morris. In response to the claim that the tobacco industry is deliberately targeting young people, a salesperson for the Tobacco Institute points out that "advertising doesn't get people to smoke. High school kids haven't seen ads for marijuana."

Efforts to prohibit sponsorship of sports and to ban alcohol and tobacco ads are also criticized on the grounds that they violate the First Amendment protection of freedom of speech. The American Civil Liberties Union has sided with the tobacco marketers on this issue, and many observers have pointed out that bans on the advertising of tobacco and alcohol could lead to restrictions in other areas of free speech. The First Amendment, they note, "does not exist to protect non-controversial speech."

Nevertheless, the idea of curbing the advertising of legal vices is gaining support. Congress is considering 72 bills that would inhibit tobacco use. A bill introduced by Senator Edward Kennedy of Massachusetts calls for the establishment of a Center for Tobacco Products to organize federal efforts to dissuade people from smoking. Other legislation would require spoken health warnings in all TV and radio ads for beer and wine. The movement is gaining strength in Europe as well: The French government plans to ban all tobacco advertising by 1993 and to restrict alcohol ads to print media.

Some brewers, stung by criticism of their aggressive college marketing, have attempted to forestall restrictive legislation by undertaking campaigns to promote moderation—"Know when to say when"; "Think when you drink." Several billboard companies have voluntarily limited the placement of certain ads, avoiding locations near schools and churches. But these moves may not be enough to deflect a public that is increasingly irritated by advertising it perceives as socially irresponsible.

Discussion Questions

1. "He may call it civil disobedience in the spirit of Martin Luther King, but I call it book-burning in the spirit of Adolf Hitler," says the president of the American Association of Advertising Agencies, referring to the leader of the movement to paint over billboards advertising alcohol and cigarettes in minority neighborhoods. Is his claim justified? Are the activists' actions a legitimate form of protest?

2. Antismoking activists believe that if a tennis player participates in the Virginia Slims tournament she becomes "a walking billboard for a cigarette company," but many athletes disagree with the idea that they implicitly endorse the products of the companies that sponsor sports events. Is either of these claims justified?

Source: Stephen Barlas, "Bill Poses Threat to Cigarette Ads," *Marketing News* (February 19, 1990), pp. 1–2; Erik Brady, "The Face-off: Free Ads vs. Fair Promotion," *USA Today* (March 28, 1990), pp. 1A–2A; Janice Castro, "Volunteer Vice Squad," *Time* (April 23, 1990), pp. 60–61; Alison Fahey, "Outdoor Reacts to Assaults," *Advertising Age* (March 26, 1990), p. 47; John E. Gallagher, "Under Fire from All Sides," *Time* (March 5, 1990), p. 41; Mark Landler, "Consumers are Getting Mad, Mad, Mad, Mad at Mad Ave," *Business Week* (April 30, 1990), pp. 70–72; Tom Morganthau, "Sullivan: Bush's Aide Makes Waves," *Newsweek* (March 5, 1990), p. 19; Joseph M. Winski, "Consumers Support Bill: Poll," *Advertising Age* (April 9, 1990), pp. 1, 64; Howard H. Bell, "Any Ad Ban Will Harm All," *Advertising Age* (February 20, 1989), p. 24.

Another ad agency, McCann-Erickson, uses a *sales conviction test* to evaluate magazine advertisements. Interviewers ask heavy users of a particular item to pick one of two alternative advertisements that would convince them to purchase it.

Potential radio and television advertisements often are screened by consumers who sit in a studio and press two buttons, one for a positive reaction to the commercial and the other for a negative reaction. Sometimes proposed ad copy is printed on a postcard that also offers a free product; the number of cards returned is viewed as an indication of the copy's effectiveness. *Blind product tests* are also often used. In these tests, people are asked to select unidentified products on the basis of available advertising copy.

Mechanical means of assessing how people read advertising copy are yet another method. One mechanical test uses a hidden eye camera to photograph how people read ads. The results help determine headline placement and advertising copy length. Another mechanical approach is the galvanic skin response, which measures changes in the electrical resistance of the skin produced by emotions.

Posttesting

posttesting
Assessment of an advertisement's effectiveness after it has been used.

Posttesting is the assessment of advertising copy after it has been used. Pretesting generally is a more desirable testing method than posttesting because of its potential cost savings. However, posttesting can be helpful in planning future advertisements and in adjusting current advertising programs. For example, a posttest conducted by the Partnership for a Drug-Free America revealed that one ad showing a drug addict playing Russian roulette had sent a dangerously incorrect message — that suicide is the only escape for heavy drug users. The test helped the Partnership avoid making the same mistake in creating new ads.[32]

In one of the most popular posttests, the *Starch Readership Report,* interviewers ask people who have read selected magazines whether they have read various ads in them. A copy of the magazine is used as an interviewing aid, and each interviewer starts at a different point in the magazine. For larger ads, respondents are also asked about specifics, such as headlines and copy. Figure 17.10 shows an advertisement for Bounce fabric softener with the actual Starch scores. All such *readership,* or *recognition,* tests assume that future sales are related to advertising readership.

Unaided recall tests are another method of posttesting advertisements. Here respondents are not given copies of the magazine but must recall the ads from memory. Interviewers for the Gallup and Robinson marketing research firms require people to prove they have read a magazine by recalling one or more of its feature articles. The people who remember particular articles are given cards with the names of products advertised in the issue. They then list the ads they remember and explain what they recall about them. Finally, the respondents are asked about their potential purchase of the product. A readership test concludes the Gallup and Robinson interview. Burke Research Corporation uses telephone interviews the day after a commercial has aired on television to test brand recognition and the advertisement's effectiveness. Another unaided recall test is adWatch, a joint project of *Advertising Age* magazine and the Gallup Organization. It measures ad awareness by polling consumers by telephone and asking them to name the advertisement that first comes to mind of all the ads they have seen, heard, or read in the past 30 days.

Inquiry tests are another popular form of posttest. Advertisements sometimes offer a gift — generally a sample of the product — to people who respond to them. The number of inquiries relative to the advertisement's cost is used as a measure of its effectiveness.

Figure 17.10   Magazine Advertisement with Starch Scores

The "Ad-As-A-Whole" label indicates the percentage of readers interviewed who "Noted" the ad in the issue, "Associated" it with a specific advertiser or product, and "Read Most" (more than 50%) of the ad copy. This label summarizes the ad's total readership.

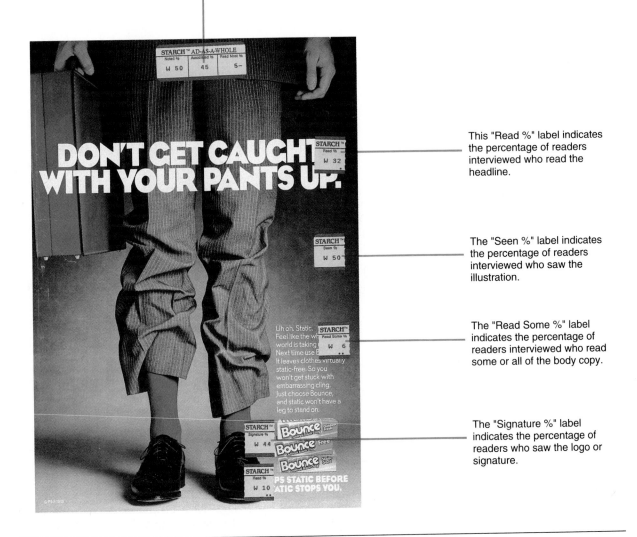

This "Read %" label indicates the percentage of readers interviewed who read the headline.

The "Seen %" label indicates the percentage of readers interviewed who saw the illustration.

The "Read Some %" label indicates the percentage of readers interviewed who read some or all of the body copy.

The "Signature %" label indicates the percentage of readers who saw the logo or signature.

Source: Courtesy of Starch INRA Hooper.

Split runs allow advertisers to test two or more ads at the same time. Although they have traditionally been used in newspapers and magazines, split runs are frequently used with cable television systems to test the effectiveness of TV ads. With this method, the cable TV audiences or a publication's subscribers are divided in two: Half would view advertisement A and the other half would view advertisement B. The relative effectiveness of the alternatives is then determined through inquiries or recall and recognition tests.

Regardless of the exact method used, marketers must realize that pretesting and posttesting are expensive and, as a result, they must plan to use them as effectively as possible.

Sales Promotion

sales promotion

Marketing activities other than personal selling, advertising, and publicity that stimulate consumer purchasing and dealer effectiveness; includes displays, trade shows and expositions, demonstrations, and various nonrecurrent selling efforts.

Although sometimes mistakenly relegated to a secondary role in a firm's overall promotional strategy, the second type of nonpersonal selling is actually double the size of advertising in terms of promotional dollar outlays. **Sales promotion** may be defined as those marketing activities, other than personal selling, advertising, and publicity, that enhance consumer purchasing and dealer effectiveness. Approximately $250 billion is spent each year on such sales promotion activities as displays, trade shows and exhibitions, demonstrations, and various nonrecurrent promotional efforts.

Sales promotion techniques were originally intended as short-term incentives aimed at producing an immediate consumer buying response. Traditionally they were viewed as a supplement to other elements of the firm's promotional mix. Today however, they are an integral part of many marketing plans, and their focus has shifted from short-term to longer-term goals of building brand equity and continuity of purchase.[33] For example, frequent-flyer programs have enabled airlines to build a base of loyal customers where none existed before.

Sales promotion techniques may be used by all members of a marketing channel: manufacturers, wholesalers, and retailers. Sales promotion activities typically are aimed at specific target markets. For example, Kraft USA's "Cheese & Macaroni Club" is a fully integrated sales promotion and advertising program targeted at children. Kids can join the club for $2.95 and three proofs of purchase from Kraft Macaroni and Cheese. As club members, kids receive shoelaces, stickers, and other goodies. From the membership, Kraft will build a database to be used for other promotions targeted at children.[34]

Marketers using sales promotion can choose from various methods—point-of-purchase advertising; specialty advertising; trade shows; samples, coupons, and premiums; contests; and trading stamps. More than one option is frequently used in a single promotional strategy, but probably no promotional strategy has ever used all of them in a single program. While they are not mutually exclusive, promotions generally are employed on a selective basis.

Point-of-Purchase Advertising

point-of-purchase advertising

Displays and other promotions located near the site of the actual buying decision.

Point-of-purchase advertising refers to displays and other promotions located near the site of the actual buying decision. The in-store promotion of consumer goods is a common example. Such advertising may be useful in supplementing a theme developed in another area of promotional strategy. A life-size display of a celebrity used in television advertising is a very effective in-store display.

In addition to displaying merchandise, some point-of-purchase promotions are designed to educate and assist shoppers. Campbell Soup has electronic displays that show videos on cooking, give shoppers recipes, and dispense discount coupons. Ryder Rental Truck has touch-screen kiosk displays in shopping centers that give consumers tips on the best way to pack and help them select the best moving method based on their individual needs. The system includes an automatic-dialing phone so consumers can reserve rental trucks without leaving the mall.[35]

Specialty Advertising

specialty advertising

Sales promotion technique that involves the use of articles such as key rings, calendars, and ballpoint pens that bear the advertiser's name, address, and advertising message.

Specialty advertising is a sales promotion technique that utilizes useful articles carrying the advertiser's name, address, and advertising message to reach target consumers. The origin of specialty advertising has been traced to the Middle

Ages, when wooden pegs bearing artisans' names were given to prospects to be driven into their walls and serve as a convenient place on which to hang armor.

Specialty advertising has grown to a $3-billion-a-year business. Wearables, including T-shirts, baseball caps, and jackets, are the most popular products, followed by writing instruments. Other popular forms of contemporary advertising specialties that carry the sponsoring firm's name include desk and business accessories, calendars, and glassware/ceramics.

Advertising specialties help reinforce previous or future advertising and sales messages. A study by Gould/Pace University in New York found the use of advertising specialties generates a greater response to direct mail and three times the dollar volume of sales of those produced by direct mail alone.[36]

Trade Shows

To influence channel members and resellers in the distribution channel, it has become common for sellers to participate in *trade shows.* These shows are often organized by an industry's trade association and may be part of the association's annual meeting or convention. Vendors serving the industry are invited to the show to display and demonstrate their products for the association's membership. The National Restaurant Association, for example, holds the annual National Restaurant/Hotel-Motel Show in Chicago each May, which attracts more than 100,000 attendees from all 50 states and 70 countries and almost 2,000 exhibitors.

Shows are also used to reach the ultimate consumer. Home, recreation, and automobile shows, for instance, allow businesses to display and demonstrate home-care, recreation, and other consumer products to entire communities.

Samples, Coupons, and Premiums

The distribution of samples, coupons, and premiums is probably the best-known sales promotion technique. *Sampling* is the free distribution of a product in an attempt to obtain future sales. Price Choppers, a chain of discount supermarkets, increased its sales of Canfield's Diet Chocolate Fudge soda from 80 to 250 cases per week after it ran a five-week sampling promotion.[37] Samples may be distributed on a door-to-door basis, by mail, via demonstrations, or by inclusion in packages containing other products. Sampling is especially useful in promoting new or unusual products.

A *coupon* offers a discount—usually some specified price reduction—on the next purchase of a good or service. Coupons are redeemable at retail outlets that receive a handling fee from the manufacturer. Mail, magazine, newspaper, and package insertions are the standard methods of distributing coupons. Packaged-good marketers spend more than $900 million a year distributing some 277 billion coupons through print media. The redemption rate, however, is low—under 3 percent. Because the mass market is suffering from coupon clutter, and usage is declining, the distribution of coupons is shifting away from print media to in-store coupons, door-to-door delivery, and direct mail. Quaker Oats has developed the Quaker Direct program that targets households on an individual basis. Each of 20 million homes receives a package of coupons for Quaker products based on a database profile of the home.[38]

Premiums are items given free or at a reduced cost with the purchase of another product. They have proven effective in motivating consumers to try new products or different brands. Premiums should have some relationship with the purchased item. For example, the service department of an auto dealership might offer its customers ice scrapers. Similarly, many fast-food franchises offer

Nabisco Brands Inc. installed automatic product sampling machines, such as the one shown here, in supermarkets to introduce its new Harvest Crisp-Crackers and Honey Graham Bites snacks. Nabisco's strategy in using machines is to sustain sampling for several weeks so all shoppers in a particular store have a chance to try the new products. After dispensing the crackers and snacks, the talking machine says "Thank you."

Source: Frederick Charles/Time Magazine.

premiums tied to popular movies. McDonald's gave away windup toy animals featured in Walt Disney's Jungle Book with its popular Happy Meals. The value of such premium giveaways runs into billions of dollars each year.

Contests

Firms often sponsor contests to introduce new goods and services and to attract additional customers. Contests, sweepstakes, and games offer substantial prizes in the form of cash or merchandise as inducements to potential customers. Planters Life Savers Company sponsored a contest for its Care*free Sugarless Gum that targeted high school and junior high students. Students in nine markets were challenged to save their gum wrappers. The prize for the school that saved the most wrappers was a live concert at the school by British rock group The Escape Club plus a $1,000 check. The contest was publicized on radio, in mailings sent to schools, and on posters in record stores.[39]

In recent years, a number of court rulings and legal restrictions have limited the use of contests. As a result, firms contemplating using this promotional technique should engage the services of a specialist.

Trading Stamps

A sales promotion technique similar to premiums is *trading stamps.* Customers receive trading stamps with their purchases in various retail establishments. The stamps can be saved and exchanged for gifts, usually at special redemption centers operated by the trading-stamp company.

Although the trading stamps were originated by Sperry & Hutchison in 1896, the height of their popularity as a sales promotion tool occurred in 1969, when some 400 stamp companies operated, and 75 percent of all groceries and supermarkets, in addition to thousands of retail gas stations, issued them. Since then, their U.S. market has declined substantially. Sperry & Hutchison now offers Green Seals, equaling 50 stamps, and electronic cards that hold the equivalent of 20 books of stamps for customers' convenience. Stamp redemption rates are high—about 90 percent.[40]

Public Relations

public relations
Firm's communication and relationships with its various publics.

In Chapter 16, **public relations** was defined as the firm's communications and relationships with various publics, including customers, employees, stockholders, suppliers, government, and the society in which it operates. Public relations efforts date back to 1889, when George Westinghouse hired two people to publicize the advantages of alternating current to refute arguments for direct-current electricity.

Public relations is an efficient indirect communications channel for promoting products, although its objectives are broader than those of other components of promotional strategy. It is concerned with the prestige and image of all parts of the organization. A major objective is to build goodwill between the firm and its various publics. Through a massive communication effort, Pacific Gas and Electric strengthened its goodwill with employees, customers, shareholders, the community, and the press following the San Francisco earthquake in 1989. The earthquake disrupted gas and electric supplies to 1.4 million customers, but PG&E not only restored service to most customers within 48 hours, it also ran ads in 60 daily newspapers and 160 weekly publications to publicize its efforts and sent personal letters of assurance to 106,000 shareholders. It set up a hotline for employees, so they could get current information on the situation. It published a special edition of the staff newspaper. CEO Dick Clarke contacted local and national politicians and became personally involved in the restoration effort by assessing damage first-hand and talking to employee work crews and customers. The community applauded PG&E's handling of the crisis by hanging "Thank you PG&E" signs in windows and sending letters of gratitude to the utility.[41]

Other examples of nonmarketing-oriented public relations objectives include a company's attempt to gain favorable public opinion during a long strike and an open letter to Congress published in a newspaper during congressional debate on a bill affecting a particular industry. Although the public relations departments of some companies are not part of the marketing divisions, their activities invariably have an impact on promotional strategy.

Approximately 160,000 people are employed in public relations in both the nonprofit and profit-oriented sectors. Some 1,800 public relations firms currently operate in the United States. The largest are Hill & Knowlton, Burson-Marsteller, Ogilvy Public Relations Group, and Fleishman-Hillard. In addition, there are thousands of smaller firms and one-person operations.

Public relations is in a period of major growth as a result of increased public pressure on industry regarding corporate ethical conduct, environmentalism, and internationalism. Internationally, public relations is growing more rapidly than advertising and sales promotion. Worldwide, public relations accounts for 33 percent of marketing service expenditures, but it is growing at 20 percent a year and, in some countries, more than twice as fast as advertising and sales promotion.[42]

Many top executives are becoming more involved in public relations, as illustrated by Lee Iacocca's efforts to publicize the need for increased competitiveness on the part of U.S. firms. The public expects top managers to take greater responsibility for company actions. Those who do not are widely criticized.

Publicity

publicity
Stimulation of demand for a good, service, place, idea, person, or organization by disseminating commercially significant news or obtaining favorable media presentation not paid for by the sponsor.

The aspect of public relations that is most directly related to promoting a firm's products is publicity. **Publicity** can be defined as the nonpersonal stimulation of demand for a good, service, place, idea, person, or organization by placing significant news about it in a print or broadcast medium without having to pay for the time or space. Firms generate publicity by creating special events, holding press conferences, and preparing news releases and media kits.

Since publicity is designed to familiarize the general public with the characteristics and advantages of a good, service, place, idea, person, or organization, it is an informational activity of public relations. While its associated costs are minimal compared to those of other forms of promotion, publicity is not entirely cost-free. Publicity-related expenses include the costs of employing marketing personnel assigned to create and submit publicity releases, printing and mailing costs, and other related expense items.

Some publicity is used to promote a company's image or viewpoint. Other publicity involves corporate activities such as plant expansions, mergers and acquisitions, management changes, and research and development. A significant amount of publicity, however, provides information about goods and services, particularly new ones. For example, Downey Community Hospital in southern California launched a public relations campaign through its advertising and public relations agency, Ripley-Woodbury, to publicize the opening of the hospital's new $6 million heart-care center. To attract attention to the center months before it opened, a billboard ad featured a 16-foot-high inflatable heart that visibly pulsed at a rate of 60 beats per minute. The company invited journalists and cameramen from Los Angeles television stations, major newspapers, and business and trade magazines to attend a press conference on the day of the center's opening. After the opening it mailed photos of the event and press releases to 45 additional publications. These efforts resulted in extensive local and national publicity, with coverage on television and radio news programs and articles in magazines and newspapers including *USA Today.*[43]

Because many consumers accept information in a news story more readily than they do that in an advertisement, publicity releases are often sent to media editors for possible inclusion in news stories. In some cases, the information in a publicity release about a new good or service provides valuable assistance for a television, newspaper, or magazine writer and eventually is broadcast or published. Publicity releases are sometimes used to fill voids in a publication and at other times are used in regular features. In either case, they are a valuable supplement to advertising.

Today public relations must be considered an integral part of promotional strategy even though its basic objectives extend far beyond the attempt to influence the purchase of a particular good or service. Public relations programs—especially publicity—make a significant contribution to the achievement of promotional goals.

Summary of Chapter Objectives

1. **Explain the current status and historical development of advertising, sales promotion, and public relations.** Some forms of the nonpersonal-selling elements of promotion have probably existed since the beginnings of the exchange process. The origins of advertising, for instance, can be traced to the vocal chants of criers and hawkers. Symbolic signs were an early form of sales promotion. Today these promotional elements enjoy professional status and are vital aspects of most for-profit and nonprofit organizations.

2. **Identify the major types of advertising.** Advertising may be divided into two broad categories. Product advertising involves the nonpersonal selling of a good or service. Institutional advertising is the nonpersonal promotion of a concept, idea, philosophy, or goodwill of an industry, company, organization, person, geographic area, or government agency. Each of these types can be further subdivided into informative, persuasive, and reminder-oriented product or institutional advertising.

3. **List and discuss the major advertising media.** A variety of media exist for the advertiser: broadcast media, such as television and radio, and print media, including newspapers, magazines, outdoor advertising, and direct mail, along with assorted alternative media ranging from transit advertising to ads placed in video cassettes. Each type possesses its own distinct advantages and disadvantages. Newspapers are the dominant local medium, while television is the most significant national advertising medium.

4. **Explain how advertising effectiveness is determined.** The effectiveness of advertising can be measured by both pretesting and posttesting. Pretesting is the assessment of an ad's effectiveness before it is actually used. It includes such methods as sales conviction tests and blind product tests. Posttesting is the assessment of the advertisement's effectiveness after it has been used. Commonly used posttests include readership tests, unaided recall tests, inquiry tests, and split runs.

5. **Outline the organization of the advertising function.** Within a firm, the advertising department is usually a staff group that reports to a vice-president (or director) of marketing. Advertising departments typically include the following capabilities: research, art and design, copywriting, and media analysis. In many instances, they also include a sales promotion function. Many advertisers use independent advertising agencies to provide the creativity and objectivity that might be missing in their own organizations and to reduce advertising costs. Such marketing specialist firms are typically divided into the functions of creative services; account services; marketing research and sales promotion; and, finance and management.

6. **Describe the process of creating an advertisement.** Effective advertisements must accomplish the following: (1) gain attention and interest; (2) inform, persuade, and/or remind; and (3) eventually lead to buying action. An advertisement evolves from initial ideas to a thought sketch, which is then converted into a rough layout. The layout is further refined until the final version of the advertisement is ready to print or record.

7. **Identify the principal methods of sales promotion.** Expenditures for sales promotion exceed total spending on advertising each year. A variety of methods are used, including (1) point-of-purchase advertising (in-store displays), (2) specialty advertising (giveaway items bearing the advertiser's name), (3) trade shows (large-scale product demonstrations), (4) samples (product giveaways), (5) coupons (one-time price reductions), (6) premiums (gift items given with a product purchase), (7) contests, and (8) trading stamps.

8. **Explain the role of public relations and publicity in an organization's promotional strategy.** Public relations consists of the firm's communications and relationships with its various publics, including customers, employees, stockholders, suppliers, government, and the society in which it operates. Publicity, the aspect of public relations that is most closely linked to promotional strategy, is the dissemination of newsworthy information about a product or organization. This information activity of public relations is frequently used in new-product introductions.

Key Terms

advertising	comparative advertising
positioning	retail advertising
product advertising	cooperative advertising
institutional advertising	pretesting
informative advertising	posttesting
persuasive advertising	sales promotion
reminder advertising	point-of-purchase advertising
advocacy advertising	specialty advertising
media scheduling	public relations
advertising agency	publicity

Review Questions

1. Explain the wide variation in advertising expenditures as a percentage of sales in the industries shown in Figure 17.1

2. Describe the primary objectives of advertising. Offer a local example of an advertising campaign, and explain how the campaign seeks to accomplish specific objectives.

3. Identify the six basic types of advertising. Give a specific example of each.

4. Discuss the relationship between advertising and the product life cycle. What type of advertising matches up with specific product life cycle stages?

5. What are the major advantages and disadvantages associated with using each of the advertising media? Give examples of types of advertisers most likely to use each medium.

6. Discuss the organization of the advertising function. Consider all the major activities associated with advertising.

7. Under what circumstances are celebrity spokespersons in advertising likely to be effective? Give recent examples of effective and ineffective use of spokespersons in advertisements.

8. Why is retail advertising so important today? Relate cooperative advertising to the discussion of alternative promotional strategies in Chapter 16.

9. Distinguish between advertising and sales promotion. Explain the principal methods of sales promotion, and give an example of each.

10. Describe the public relations components of a firm's promotional mix. Do you agree with the statement that publicity is free advertising?

Discussion Questions

1. Many states have government-operated lotteries. Suggest a promotional plan for marketing lottery tickets with particular emphasis on the nonpersonal-selling aspects of the promotional mix.

2. Choose a candidate who ran for political office during the most recent election. Assume that you were in charge of advertising for this person's campaign. Develop an advertising strategy for your candidate. Select a campaign theme and the media to be employed. Finally, design an advertisement for the candidate.

3. Review the changes in the relative importance of the various advertising media during the past 40 years that are mentioned in the chapter. Suggest likely explanations for these changes.

4. Present an argument favoring the use of comparative advertising by a marketer who is currently preparing an advertising plan. Make any assumptions necessary.

5. Develop a sales promotion program for each of the following. Justify your choice of each sales promotion method employed.
    a. Independent insurance agent
    b. Retail furniture store
    c. Interior decorator
    d. Local radio station

Computer Applications

Since advertising frequently represents a substantial portion of total marketing costs, marketers are continually seeking more efficient methods of achieving their promotional objectives. Advertisers not only seek to communicate with and persuade prospective customers; they also want to accomplish this at the lowest possible cost. In evaluating alternative advertising media, marketers attempt to match the characteristics of their target market customers with the audiences for radio and television programs, newspapers, magazines, and so on. But the advertising costs of specific media vary greatly according to such factors as market coverage, size or length of the advertisement, and location of the advertising message. Consequently, some common denominator with which to compare available alternatives is needed.

One commonly used method for comparing alternative vehicles within a single advertising medium is the *cost-per-thousand* criterion. Since M is the Roman numeral for 1,000, "cost per thousand" is frequently abbreviated *CPM*. For magazines, the following formula is used:

$$\frac{\text{Cost Per}}{\text{Thousand (CPM)}} = \frac{\text{Magazine Page Cost} \times 1{,}000}{\text{Circulation}}.$$

For radio or television, the CPM formula is modified as follows:

$$\frac{\text{Cost Per}}{\text{Thousand (CPM)}} = \frac{\text{Cost of Commercial} \times 1{,}000}{\text{Circulation}}.$$

Since circulation and program audience data are available from independent research sources, CPM calculations can easily be made and updated regularly. Circulation data for magazines are available from research specialists such as Standard Rate & Data Service. Program audience data for television and radio can be obtained from firms such as A. C. Nielsen or Arbitron.

Assume that a magazine has a circulation of 8 million and charges $75,000 for a one-page, full-color advertisement. Its CPM could be calculated as follows:

$$\text{CPM} = \frac{\$75{,}000 \times 1{,}000}{8{,}000{,}000} = \frac{\$75{,}000{,}000}{8{,}000{,}000} = \$9{,}375.$$

In addition to the basic CPM calculation, a potential advertiser may be able to more precisely evaluate different advertising vehicles by focusing solely on the percentage of the magazine's readers, radio program's listeners, or television program's viewers who match the demographic and geographic profiles of the firm's target market. The denominator in the CPM formulation would be changed to include only the target market members in the advertising medium's audience. If the advertiser feels that only one-eighth of the total circulation of *Modern Maturity* matches the precise profiles of the firm's target market, the CPM calculation will be made as follows:

$$\text{CPM} = \frac{\begin{array}{c}\text{Advertisement}\\\text{Cost} \times 1{,}000\end{array}}{\begin{array}{c}\text{Number of Target}\\\text{Market Members}\\\text{in Audience}\end{array}} = \frac{75{,}000{,}000}{1{,}000{,}000} = \$75.$$

However, CPM is of little use in comparing different *types* of advertising media: "You can't compare a CPM figure for a page in *Reader's Digest* with a CPM for a 30-second commercial . . . because there's no basis for comparing the value of a magazine ad to the value of a TV commercial. The communications approaches are totally different, as are audience attention and involvement." Nevertheless, such comparisons may be extremely useful in evaluating alternative vehicles within a single advertising medium.

Once the advertiser has established a common denominator for making such comparisons, it can make qualitative judgments about the leading candidates' relative merits. One author suggests four factors that should be considered before deciding where to place the advertisements:

First, the measure should be adjusted for audience quality. *For a baby lotion advertisement, a magazine read by one million young mothers would have an exposure value of one million, but if read by one million old men would have a zero exposure value. Second, the exposure value should be adjusted for the* audience attention probability. *Readers of some magazines pay more attention to ads than readers of others. Third, the exposure value should be adjusted for the* editorial quality *(prestige and believability) that one magazine [or broadcast program] might have over another. Fourth, the exposure value should be adjusted for the magazine's [or broadcaster's] ad placement policies and extra services.*

Directions: Use menu item 15 titled "Advertising Evaluations" to solve each of the following problems.

Problem 1. Cynthia Faulkner is in charge of placing advertisements for Long Island–based National Consumer Goods, Inc. She is currently in the process of comparing seven major magazines. The cost of a one-page, four-color advertisement is shown below. Which magazine has the lowest CPM? Which has the lowest CPM for male readers? For female readers?

Magazine	Four-Color Page Rate	Total Readers	Male Readers	Female Readers
Amazing World	$62,750	12,375,000	3,473,000	8,902,000
Weekly Facts	80,675	10,335,000	5,575,000	4,760,000
Sunday Digest	53,175	7,300,000	4,220,000	3,080,000
52	82,400	19,940,000	8,790,000	11,150,000
SportWeek	45,550	5,365,000	4,045,000	1,320,000
Viewer	70,775	8,180,000	4,645,000	3,535,000
Contemporary Homes	70,000	16,650,000	7,590,000	9,060,000

Problem 2. After comparing the readership profiles of the seven magazines discussed in Problem 1, Cynthia Faulkner has developed the following estimates of the numbers of male and female readers for each magazine who match the profile of National's target market customers:

Magazine	Readers in Target Market	
	Male Readers	Female Readers
Viewer	1,750,000	1,800,000
Contemporary Homes	1,900,000	1,600,000
Amazing World	1,000,000	800,000
Weekly Facts	2,200,000	3,700,000
Sunday Digest	1,350,000	225,000
SportWeek	1,200,000	900,000
52	1,900,000	2,300,000

a. Which magazine has the lowest CPM for male readers who match National's target market profile? Which has the highest CPM?

b. Which magazine has the lowest CPM for female readers who match National's target market profile? Which has the highest CPM?

Problem 3.   Vicky Ballow is senior branch manager for the snacks division of Best Treats of Richmond, Virginia. She is in the process of narrowing the number of magazines under consideration for next year's advertising campaign and has prepared the following table for eight magazines whose readership appears to best match the characteristics of Best Treats' target market. Ballow has also included her estimate of the percentage of each magazine's readers who precisely match the demographic characteristics of her firm's market.

Magazine	Four-Color Page Rate	Total Readers	Estimated Number of Magazine Readers Matching Best Treats' Market Profile
21st Century Homes	$11,500	1,800,000	520,000
Elan	17,500	2,200,000	440,000
Family	13,000	1,900,000	380,000
Gotham Lady	36,000	8,500,000	850,000
Happy Home	28,000	5,700,000	800,000
Modern Homemaker	7,500	900,000	250,000
Single Parent	34,500	8,000,000	450,000
Suburban Garden	26,000	4,900,000	100,000

a. Which magazine has the lowest CPM if total readers are considered? Which has the highest CPM?

b. Which magazine has the lowest CPM if only target market readers are considered? Which has the highest CPM?

Problem 4.   Dave Putnam is brand manager for LongDrive golf balls, one of more than 50 brand names produced and marketed by Bluegrass Sporting Goods Company of Louisville, Kentucky. Putnam has analyzed six likely magazines for use in advertising the LongDrive brand. He has collected the following data:

Magazine	Black-and-White Page Rate	Total Readers	College Graduates	Managerial, Administrative
SportView	$18,800	1,900,000	700,000	1,100,000
Modern Golf	13,500	1,000,000	300,000	500,000
Links	16,300	2,600,000	400,000	1,300,000
Golf Tips	9,750	600,000	200,000	300,000
18 Holes	38,200	4,000,000	800,000	900,000
Golf Pro	12,960	2,200,000	400,000	600,000

a. Which magazine has the lowest overall CPM? Which is most expensive in terms of overall CPM?

b. If Putnam defines his target market as consisting of only college graduates, which magazine will offer him the lowest CPM?

c. If Putnam decides to focus solely on persons holding managerial or administrative positions, which magazine will allow him to reach his target at the lowest CPM? Which will be the most expensive in terms of CPM?

Problem 5.   Joe Ed Anderson is in charge of advertising for Cajun Video Rentals in New Orleans. He is targeting his advertising message at persons aged 18 to 49 in the New Orleans metropolitan area and plans to use radio during morning and afternoon drive times. He has assembled the following data on four radio stations that offer the programming blend designed to attract his target market listeners:

Radio Station	Cost of 30-Second Commercial	Total Audience	Listeners Age 18–34	Listeners Age 35–49
WZED	$100	25,000	6,500	6,000
WZZZ	90	28,000	5,600	7,000
WNEL	220	42,000	16,800	12,600
WBBB	250	70,000	21,000	17,500

a. Which radio station has the lowest overall CPM? Which is the most expensive in terms of overall CPM?

b. Which station has the lowest CPM for listeners between the ages of 18 and 34? Which is the most expensive for this age category?

c. Which would reach Anderson's targeted customers at the lowest CPM?

Santa Anita Park

Thoroughbred horse racing is the most heavily attended sports activity in the United States. Robert Strub, president of Southern California's Santa Anita Park, explains why: "One of the interesting things about thoroughbred racing, [is that] it's a participation sport. The public actually participates because they make their wagers. They affect the odds and, therefore, affect the amount of money that's going to be bet on this horse or that horse. I think the best thing we have to offer the public is a great sport. People who like horses, people who like to see a real contest and have the excitement of watching the horses pound down the stretch, and root for the horses they put their wagers on, is one of the most exciting things you can do. Once in a while, I turn around to look back at the crowd and take my eyes off the race course just to see what the people are doing. And they're jumping up and down, they're screaming, they're yelling, they're pounding their friends on the back, doing everything they can to root their horse home. I think this is exciting for people."

Strub knows, however, that Santa Anita needs to do more than just race horses to survive. "We live in a community here with a tremendous population base," he says, "but it's also one of the great sports capitals of the world, so it's very competitive. People have lots of things to do and we have to offer something that they want to come out and see and participate in." Because of that competition, which comes from virtually every other known leisure activity, Santa Anita must sell itself to the public in order to encourage its current patrons to return and to attract new patrons.

To achieve these goals, Santa Anita uses sales promotions, heavy advertising, and direct selling through a group sales department. Effective use of sales promotion requires knowledge of the population segments to which a service or product appeals. Horse racing appeals to a mix that represents the entire population, though with a low proportion of the younger segments and a high proportion of the older ones. To increase patronage both now and in the future, therefore, a promotion should be aimed at the younger segments of the population.

The specific sales promotion programs used by Santa Anita marketers include premium giveaways, discount admission coupons, entertainment events, and contests. Promotions are carefully integrated into Santa Anita's advertising program and are fully analyzed for their effectiveness. Moreover, the costs of each promotion are compared to any increases in profit or attendance that can be attributed to the promotion. Records are kept on a daily basis. Thus, a promotion that brings new customers to the park but costs more than those customers spend can be analyzed for its long-term effects on patronage and profit. Careful planning of sales promotion and advertising resources is especially important because of the short (four-month) season.

Sports facilities frequently use premium giveaway programs to attract repeat patronage. Hollywood Park, one of Santa Anita's major competitors, offers giveaways once or twice a week. Patrons there have come to expect a low-value giveaway every time they enter the park. Santa Anita uses higher-quality merchandise, such as an all-leather key case with a pocket for parimutuel tickets or money. Like most of the giveaways, the case has Santa Anita's name on it and is of high enough quality to be actually used after the patron's visit.

Although giveaway promotions occur roughly every two weeks, they are carefully timed. Holidays are prime candidates for giveaways because they attract families that might choose some other pasttime without the added inducement of the gift. The giveaways are distributed at the race track by members of local PTAs or charities, and Santa Anita sends a check to the organization involved. The volunteers are friendly and cheerful, and Santa Anita's contribution to a worthy cause enhances its public image.

Discount admission coupons printed in newspapers and distributed to about 200,000 previous patrons by direct mail also serve to attract repeat customers. The redemption rate for the direct mail is higher than the rate for the newspaper ads. The loss of 50 or 75 cents off the $2.25 admission price is not significant, since the park obtains 80 percent of its income from betting.

Unlike giveaways and discount admission coupons, entertainment events attract new patrons. Such events have been particularly effective in attracting families, young people, and Hispanic patrons. The Hispanic community in Southern California is growing rapidly, and drawing these customers not only increases patronage but adds to its diversity. Entertainment events are typically held before and between races in the infield section of the park. Both comedy shows and a "Latin Fiesta" have been effective. Advertising for the latter event was carried on Spanish-speaking radio and television.

Entertainment events at Santa Anita are not expected to make money. It is even expected that the costs of running them will exceed the earnings from the new patrons, especially in view of the fact that customers in the target segments are less likely than regular patrons to place bets. However, it is hoped that the new visitors will return in the future and that as they age and become more affluent they will become profitable patrons.

Contests appeal to both new and repeat patrons. As originally presented, a contest called "The Key to the Mint" awarded between $10,000 and $25,000 to the winners. After a number of contests had been held, Santa Anita changed the event so that the winnings are no longer fixed in advance. Instead, five winners are selected and invited to the track's winner's circle. There they choose their own prize from 100 identical money bags. All the bags contain at least $1,000, but a few contain larger amounts ranging up to $100,000. It is felt that this approach generates more excitement.

The future is almost certain to bring further increases in competition for discretionary spending, as well as further competition for the land on which Santa Anita Park is located, resulting in proportionately higher taxes. The park will probably have to further expand its patronage in order to survive. By maintaining a flexible promotional mix, Santa Anita can hold and expand its existing market segments and appeal to new ones.

Source: Off and Running: A Case Study in Promotional Strategy, produced by KOCE-TV. John Helyar, "Race Tracks Try New Marketing Tricks," *The Wall Street Journal* (June 7, 1991), p. B1.

Questions

1. Horse racing generates its own publicity in the form of sportscasts and newspaper sports pages. What does Santa Anita do, or what could it do, to generate additional publicity?

2. Betting, which generates most of Santa Anita's income, is an adult activity. Why would the track want to attract families?

3. What advantages does Santa Anita's giveaway program have over Hollywood Park's?

4. Since most of Santa Anita's income is generated by betting, why not lower the admission fee instead of using one-time discount admission coupons?

18

Personal Selling
and Sales Management

CHAPTER OBJECTIVES

1. To explain the factors affecting the relative importance of personal selling in the promotional mix.

2. To contrast field selling, over-the-counter selling, and telemarketing.

3. To identify the three basic sales tasks.

4. To outline the steps in the sales process.

5. To describe sales management's boundary-spanning role.

6. To list the functions of sales management.

In 1983 Eiji Toyoda, chairman of Toyota Motor Corporation, challenged his engineers to "develop the best car in the world." Using Mercedes and BMW as benchmarks, Toyota spent six years and more than $500 million in developing the Lexus LS 400, a $40,000 luxury sedan aimed at young, affluent American consumers. The new Japanese nameplate marked Toyota's entry into the highly competitive luxury-car market.

Toyota's relationship with potential Lexus buyers began long before the car debuted in September 1989. Using a computerized prospect-identification system based on consumer demographics, Toyota identified some 400,000 prospects to be the target of a pre-launch direct-mail campaign. "Hot prospects" were those providing Toyota with a phone number and expressing a desire to try out Lexus. They received a videotape and a personalized invitation to take a test drive when the car arrived at dealers. The prospect-identification system was so exact that "more than 90 percent of the audience we're mailing to is truly a prospect," said Bob Neuman, Lexus marketing operations manager.

Advertising played a key role in Toyota's preselling strategy. Introductory ads were designed to build awareness and develop a prestigious image for the new brand. To persuade consumers that Lexus was a worthy competitor of well-established luxury cars, Toyota chose "the relentless pursuit of perfection" as its advertising theme and developed ads describing the company's six-year pursuit of perfecting the Lexus in luxury, performance, and safety.

Confident that Lexus would perform as planned and that advertising would bring consumers into showrooms, Toyota executives realized their success in selling the best car in the world now depended on developing the best salesforce to sell it. The baby boom consumers of the Lexus target market often base their car-buying decisions on how they are treated and how dealers satisfy their service needs. For them, the quality of dealerships and salespeople make a big difference. For Toyota, this meant pioneering a new way of selling to and servicing Lexus prospects.

Toyota created a new dealer network for Lexus, separate from existing dealers selling the company's economy models. From a pool of 1,200 applicants, the company selected 100 dealers based on their customer-satisfaction ratings. To learn from competitors, Toyota hired anthropologists to observe the selling styles of other luxury-car salespeople. The company staffed its dealerships by recruiting sales and service people who had previously worked at European, Japanese, and domestic dealers.

Before beginning work, recruits received extensive training that reinforced the Lexus goal: "Complete customer satisfaction." Trainees were told they were not mere car salespeople but a new breed of professionals working in an often despised industry. (Indeed, surveys reveal that Americans consider car salespeople the least trustworthy of all professions, often describing them as con artists and thieves.)

Through lectures, tests, and role-playing exercises, Lexus trainees learned how to conduct honest negotiations with buyers, how to treat customers with respect and courtesy, and how to tailor a presentation to a customer's specific interest. Training included in-depth knowledge about Lexus and competing models, but personal attitudes rather than product knowledge was stressed. "The most important single factor in the Lexus division is what is in the hearts and minds of the people who make up the organization," says J. Davis Illingworth, Jr., Lexus division general manager. The Lexus way of selling appealed to recruits. One said, "I've been waiting for this style of selling for 10 years. I never did like beating on people."[1]

Photo source: © 1989 Steve Leonard.

Chapter Overview

Chapters 16 and 17 focus on the concept of promotion, the promotional mix, and the use of advertising and other nonpersonal promotion in achieving marketing objectives. This chapter examines the second major variable of the promotional mix: personal selling. The opening story shows the significant role of personal selling in a firm's promotional strategy.

personal selling
Interpersonal influence process involving a seller's promotional presentation conducted on a person-to-person basis with the prospective buyer.

Personal selling was defined in Chapter 16 as an interpersonal influence process. Specifically it involves a seller's promotional presentations conducted on a person-to-person basis with the buyer. It is an inherent function of any enterprise. Accounting, engineering, personnel, production, and other organizational activities are useless unless the firm's good or service matches the need of a client or customer. The nearly 14 million people employed in sales occupations in the United States testify to selling's importance in the 1990s. While the average firm's advertising expenses may represent from 1 to 3 percent of total sales, selling expenses are likely to equal 10 to 15 percent. In many firms, personal selling is the single largest marketing expense.

Personal selling is likely to be the primary component of a firm's promotional mix when consumers are geographically concentrated; when orders are large; when the goods or services are expensive, are technically complex, and require special handling; when trade-ins are involved; when channels are short; and when the number of potential customers is relatively small. Table 18.1 summarizes the factors that influence the importance of personal selling in the overall promotional mix according to the type of variable involved: consumer, product, price, or distribution channels.

The Evolution of Personal Selling

Selling has been a standard business activity for thousands of years. The earliest peddlers were traders who had some type of ownership interest in the goods they sold after manufacturing or importing them. In many cases, these people viewed selling as a secondary activity.

Selling later became a separate function. The peddlers of the eighteenth century sold to the farmers and settlers of the vast North American continent. In the nineteenth century, salespeople called *drummers* sold to both consumers and marketing intermediaries. These early sellers sometimes used questionable sales practices and techniques and earned undesirable reputations for themselves and their firms. Negative stereotypes persist today. To some people, the term *salesperson* conjures up unpleasant visions of Arthur Miller's antihero Willy Loman in *Death of a Salesman:*

You don't understand: Willy was a salesman. . . . He don't put a bolt to a nut. He don't tell you the law or give you medicine. He's a man way out there in the blue, riding on a smile and a shoeshine. And when they start not smiling back—that's an earthquake.[2]

But selling is far different from what it was in its early years. Far from the fast-talking, joke-telling, back-slapping caricatures in some novels and comic strips, today's salesperson is usually a professional. Professors Thomas Ingram and Raymond LaForge define *sales professionalism* as "a customer-oriented approach that employs truthful, nonmanipulative tactics to satisfy the long-term needs of both the customer and the selling firm."[3] Professional salespeople are problem solvers, focusing on satisfying the needs of customers before, during, and after the sale. They are armed with knowledge about their firm's goods or services, those of competitors, and their customer's business. As competitive pressures mount, more firms are emphasizing **relationship selling**, whereby

relationship selling
Establishment of a sustained seller-buyer relationship.

Table 18.1

Factors Affecting the Importance of Personal Selling in the Promotional Mix

Variable	Factors Increasing the Relative Importance of Personal Selling	Factors Increasing the Relative Importance of Advertising
Consumer	Geographically concentrated	Geographically dispersed
	Relatively few in number	Relatively large in number
Product	Expensive	Inexpensive
	Technically complex	Simple to understand
	Custom made	Standardized
	Requires special handling	Does not require special handling
	Frequently involves trade-ins	Does not involve trade-ins
Price	Relatively high	Relatively low
Channels	Relatively short	Relatively long

salespeople build mutually beneficial relationships with customers on a regular basis over an extended period. To create strong, long-lasting bonds with customers, salespeople must meet buyer expectations. Several recent surveys indicate what buyers expect of professional salespeople.[4] A compilation of the results of these surveys appears in Table 18.2.

Personal selling today is a vital, vibrant, dynamic process. And with the increased emphasis on productivity resulting from domestic and foreign competition, personal selling is taking on a more prominent role in the corporate marketing mix. Salespeople must be able to communicate the subtle advantages of their firms' goods and services over competitors'. Mergers and acquisitions and a host of new products and promotions have expanded the scope and complexity of many selling jobs. Even the way in which salespeople perform their jobs is changing as more and more firms integrate computer and communications technology into the salesforce. Salespeople's use of such technologies as laptop and hand-held computers, electronic mail, fax machines, cellular phones, and expert software systems will continue to increase as firms aim to improve salesforce productivity and respond more quickly to customer needs.[5]

Personal selling is an attractive career choice for today's college and university students. Approximately 60 percent of all marketing graduates choose sales as their first marketing position. Job prospects in selling are also attractive. The Bureau of Labor Statistics projects that jobs in selling and marketing occu-

Table 18.2

What Buyers Expect from Salespeople

Buyers prefer to do business with salespeople who:

☐ Can orchestrate events and bring to bear whatever resources are necessary to satisfy.

☐ Can provide counseling to the customer based on in-depth knowledge of the product, the market, and the customer's needs.

☐ Can engage in problem solving with a high degree of proficiency that ensures satisfactory customer service over extended time periods.

☐ Can demonstrate high ethical standards and are honest in all communications.

☐ Are willing to advocate the customer's wishes within the selling organization.

☐ Are imaginative in meeting buyers' needs.

☐ Are well-prepared for sales calls.

Source: Thomas N. Ingram, ''Improving Sales Force Productivity: A Critical Examination of the Personal Selling Process,'' *Review of Business* (Summer 1990), p. 12.

pations that require a college degree will show faster than average rates of growth of all occupations for the remainder of the twentieth century.[6]

Sales jobs are attracting an increasing number of women. During the past decade, the proportion of women in selling has increased from 7 percent to 18 percent. Industries in which women comprise about half of the salesforce include textiles, utilities, financial services, publishing, and housewares. Because most selling jobs offer compensation based on salary plus commission or bonus, sales is one of the few occupations in which women can overcome the 40 percent pay gap. Sales statistics indicate that women, as a group, are successful in the customer-oriented, relationship-building selling jobs of the 1990s.[7]

A sales background provides visibility for the individual and serves as an excellent route to the top of the corporate hierarchy. Giant corporations such as Reebok International, Union Camp, Xerox, Bear Stearns, Capital Cities/ABC, CPC International, Texaco, and Subaru of America are all headed by executives who began their careers in sales.

The Three Selling Environments

field selling
Sales presentations made at prospective customers' homes or businesses on a face-to-face basis.

The personal-selling process may occur in a variety of environments. **Field selling** involves sales calls to customers at their homes or businesses. Some situations, such as in-home sales of encyclopedias and insurance or industrial sales of major computer installations, involve considerable creative selling. In other cases, such as calling on already established customers in such industries as food, textiles, or wholesaling, processing of customer orders is the chief selling task.

team selling
Use of specialists from other functional areas to sell a product.

An emerging trend in field selling is **team selling,** in which the salesperson is joined by specialists from other functional areas of the firm during the selling process. For 20 years Reynolds Metals used traditional one-on-one field selling in an effort to convince Campbell Soup Company to switch from the steel cans it made for its tomato juice products to Reynolds's recyclable aluminum cans. In the mid-1980s, Dick Holder, Reynolds' president and a former field salesman, assembled a team of salespeople, marketers, graphic designers, and engineers to educate a Campbell buying team on the benefits of aluminum as a packaging material. After a five-year team-selling effort, Reynolds won Campbell as a customer. In many industries team selling has become the standard for successful selling, especially to large and important customers.[8]

over-the-counter selling
Personal selling conducted in retail and some wholesale locations in which customers come to the seller's place of business.

The second approach, **over-the-counter selling,** typically describes selling in retail locations. Customers take the initiative to come to the seller's location —sometimes in response to direct mail or personal letters of invitation from store personnel or to take advantage of advertised sales, special events, or the introduction of new product lines. This type of selling typically involves providing product information and arranging for completion of the sales transaction.

telemarketing
Promotional presentation involving the use of the telephone on an outbound basis by salespeople or an inbound basis by customers who initiate calls to obtain information and place orders.

Both field selling and over-the-counter selling sometimes utilize the telephone in such activities as prospecting for new customers and following up with existing accounts. The telephone is also the basis for a third approach to personal selling, **telemarketing,** in which selling is conducted entirely by telephone. It can be classified as either outbound or inbound. *Outbound telemarketing* involves a salesforce that uses only the telephone to contact customers. This approach is designed to reduce the substantial costs entailed in making personal visits to customers' homes or businesses. *Inbound telemarketing* typically involves a toll-free 800 number that customers can call to obtain information and make purchases. This form of selling provides maximum convenience for customers who initiate the sales process.

The inbound telemarketing approach is used by many mail-order companies. The telemarketing associates shown here take orders called in by customers using a toll-free telephone number.

Source: © Leng/Leng/Westlight.

 Telemarketing is growing in importance in the selling strategies of many firms in the United States and other developed countries. Two European department stores, Galeries Lafayette in Paris and Harrods in London, use inbound telemarketing to sell apparel and other merchandise to U.S. consumers. Most firms use telemarketing as a support to field selling in presale and postsale activities and to sell to smaller accounts. Some firms, however, use telemarketing in place of field selling. Allegiance Distribution, for example, utilizes only telemarketers to sell semiconductor chips nationwide. The 2 million telemarketers in the United States generate sales exceeding $100 billion. The usage of telemarketing is growing about 25 percent a year, and it is estimated that telemarketing jobs will increase to 10 million by the year 2000.[9]

Sales Tasks

Today's salesperson is more concerned with helping customers select the correct products for meeting their needs than with simply selling whatever is available. Professional salespeople advise and assist customers in their purchase decisions. Where repeat purchases are common, the salesperson must be certain that the buyer's purchases are in his or her best interest; otherwise, no future sales will be made. The seller's interests are tied to the buyer's in a symbiotic relationship.

Not all selling activities are alike. While all sales activities assist the customer in some manner, the exact tasks that are performed vary from one position to another.[10] Three basic sales tasks can be identified: (1) order processing, (2) creative selling, and (3) missionary sales. These tasks form the basis for a sales classification system.

It should be observed, however, that most sales personnel do not fall into a single category. Instead, salespersons often perform all three tasks to a certain extent. A sales engineer for a computer firm may be doing 50 percent missionary sales, 45 percent creative selling, and 5 percent order processing. Most selling jobs, however, are classified on the basis of the primary selling task performed.

Order Processing

order processing
Selling at the wholesale and retail levels; specifically, identifying customer needs, pointing them out to customers, and completing orders.

Order processing, which can involve both field selling and telemarketing, is most often typified by selling at the wholesale and retail levels. For instance, a Pepsi-Cola route salesperson who performs this task must take the following steps:

1. *Identify customer needs.* The route salesperson determines that a store that normally carries an inventory of 40 cases has only 7 cases left in stock.
2. *Point out the need to the customer.* The route salesperson informs the store manager of the inventory situation.
3. *Complete (write up) the order.* The store manager acknowledges the situation. The driver unloads 33 cases, and the manager signs the delivery slip.

Order processing is part of most selling positions. It becomes the primary task in situations in which needs can be readily identified and are acknowledged by the customer. Even in such instances, however, salespersons whose primary responsibility involves order processing will devote some time to seeking to convince their wholesale or retail customers to carry more complete inventories of their firms' products or handle additional product lines. They also are likely to try to motivate purchasers to feature some of their firms' products, increase the amount of shelf space devoted to their products, and improve product location in the stores.

Creative Selling

creative selling
Personal selling involving situations in which a considerable degree of analytical decision making on the buyer's part results in the need for skillful proposals of solutions for the customer's needs.

When a considerable amount of analytical decision making is involved in purchasing a good or service, the salesperson must use **creative selling** techniques to solicit an order. While the order processing task deals mainly with maintaining existing business, creative selling generally is used to develop new business either by adding new customers or introducing new goods and services. New products often require a high degree of creative selling. The salesperson must first identify the customer's problems and needs and then propose a solution, in the form of the good or service being offered. Creative selling may occur in telemarketing, over-the-counter selling, and field selling. It may be the most demanding of the three sales tasks.

New-equipment salespeople at City International Trucks, a Navistar dealer in Chicago, use creative selling during their lengthy negotiations with buyers. Like many other equipment purchasers, truck buyers are concerned with lowering the total cost of ownership, which includes repairs and replacement parts. City salespeople try to find out from buyers the age of trucks in their firm's fleet and what problems they are having. They prepare computer printouts that show comparative data on such factors as repair frequency. During the many months it takes to get an order, salespeople emphasize City's solution to buyers' repair

COMPETITIVE EDGE

SHORTENING THE BUSINESS CYCLE

· · · · · · · · · · · ·

Frito-Lay salespeople are using computer technology to give management almost instant feedback and to dramatically shorten the business cycle. Information that sometimes took months to reach headquarters is now available immediately.

At the end of each workday, each route salesperson plugs a handheld computer into a minicomputer at the local sales office (or into a modem at home) and transmits a report of the day's activities to company headquarters in Dallas. Instead of spending several hours every week filling out forms and reports, the salesperson can spend that time selling. Specific sales and marketing information is available to management on a daily basis. The computer network also enables management to transmit instructions and information to salespeople almost instantaneously.

The salespeople's handheld computers automatically print sales receipts and record sales, eliminating paperwork. The market information provided to headquarters allows sales managers to spot problems, take advantage of opportunities, and react quickly to competitive situations. The system gives Frito-Lay the advantages of a local business—speed and flexibility—combined with a national perspective and the expertise of analysts at company headquarters.

Management is delighted. Distribution costs are lower than ever, and sales are increasing by 10 to 12 percent a year without the addition of more salespeople. Decisions are being made faster too. For example, quick feedback on the local success of Frito-Lay's line of low-fat snacks speeded the decision to introduce the new line nationally.

The handheld computers have been so effective that Frito-Lay is experimenting with a new information tool: A system that condenses the vast quantities of information received from salespeople and automatically highlights problem areas.

Discussion Questions

1. Are there any risks associated with the use of computers instead of written reports to obtain information from salespeople?

2. Could the almost instantaneous availability of information from salespeople cause Frito-Lay's management to react prematurely to changes in its marketing environment?

Sources: Jeremy Main, "Frito-Lay Shortens Its Business Cycle," *Fortune* (January 15, 1990), p. 11; PepsiCo, *Annual Report,* 1989. *Photo source:* © 1990 Jay Brousseau.

and service needs: City is open 24 hours a day and promises fast replacement parts delivery.[11]

Missionary Sales

missionary sales
Indirect type of selling in which specialized salespeople promote the firm's goodwill, often by assisting customers in product use.

Missionary sales are an indirect type of selling: Salespeople sell the firm's goodwill and provide their customers with information and technical or operational assistance. For example, a toiletries company salesperson may call on retailers to check on special promotions and overall stock movement, even

Figure 18.1

The AIDA Concept and the
Personal-Selling Process

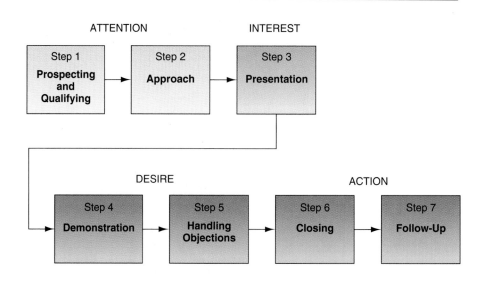

though a wholesaler is used to take orders and deliver merchandise. The medical detail salesperson seeks to persuade doctors, the indirect customers, to specify the pharmaceutical company's product brand in prescriptions. However, the company's actual sales ultimately are made through a wholesaler or directly to the pharmacists who fill prescriptions.

Missionary sales may involve both field selling and telemarketing. In recent years, technical and operational assistance, such as that provided by a systems specialist, also have become a critical part of missionary selling. Team selling often includes technical support salespeople who help design, install, and maintain equipment and train customers' employees.

The Sales Process

What are the steps involved in selling? While the terminology may vary, most authorities agree on the following sequence: (1) prospecting and qualifying, (2) approach, (3) presentation, (4) demonstration, (5) handling objections, (6) closing, and (7) follow-up.

As Figure 18.1 indicates, the steps in the personal selling process follow the attention-interest-desire-action (AIDA) concept discussed in Chapter 16. Once a sales prospect has been qualified, an attempt is made to secure his or her attention. The presentation and demonstration steps are designed to generate interest and desire. Successful handling of buyer objections should arouse further desire. Action occurs at the close of the sale.

Prospecting and Qualifying

prospecting
Personal-selling function of identifying potential customers.

Prospecting, the identification of potential customers, is difficult work involving many hours of diligent effort. Prospects may come from many sources: computerized databases, trade show exhibits, previous customers, friends and neighbors, other vendors, nonsales employees in the firm, suppliers, and social and professional contacts. While a firm may emphasize personal selling as the

Figure 18.2   Use of Advertising to Identify Sales Prospects

Source: Courtesy of Norfolk Southern Corporation. Created by J. Walter Thompson Company, USA.

primary component of its overall promotional strategy, direct mail and advertising campaigns may be effective in identifying prospective customers. The advertisement in Figure 18.2 is designed to motivate global marketers in need of transportation services within the United States and Canada to call one of Norfolk Southern's 50 sales offices. A Norfolk Southern sales representative will contact prospects to discuss their transportation needs and Norfolk Southern's capabilities in satisfying them.

New sales personnel may find prospecting frustrating, because there is usually no immediate payback. But without prospecting, there are no future sales. Firms must seek out potential users of new and existing goods and services. Prospecting is a continuous process because of the inevitable loss of some customers over time as well as the emergence of new potential customers or first-time prospects.

Many sales management experts consider prospecting to be the very essence of the sales process. Karl Gerlinger, president of BMW of North America, agrees. Berlinger warned his 400 U.S. dealers not to rely solely on advertising to bring buyers into their showrooms but to actively seek out prospects. "We're moving from the passive approach to the active," he says. It is a strategy used successfully by dealers in European countries. BMW gave its dealers manuals on how to find new customers. Suggestions include making cold calls to potential customers, sending prospects promotional videotapes, dropping off cars for test drives at a potential buyer's home or business, and sending salespeople and sample cars to events, such as a convention for private airplane owners, that attract affluent consumers who qualify to purchase a luxury car.[12]

qualifying
Determining that a prospect has the needs, income, and purchase authority necessary for being a potential customer.

Qualifying—determining that the prospect really is a potential customer—is another important sales task. Not all prospects are qualified to become customers. Qualified customers are those with both the money and the authority to make purchase decisions. A person with an annual income of $25,000 may wish to own a $200,000 house, but his or her ability to actually become a customer is questionable. Many firms use telemarketers as a cost-effective approach to prospecting and qualifying. They pass on qualified leads to field salespeople who can concentrate on prospects most likely to buy.[13]

Approach

approach
Salesperson's initial contact with a prospective customer.

Once the salesperson has identified a qualified prospect, he or she collects all available relevant information and plans an **approach**—the salesperson's initial contact with the prospective customer. Collecting information prior to the initial contact is invaluable for telemarketers and field salespeople. Information can be gathered from secondary sources (magazine or newspaper articles) or directly from the prospect. In collecting information, the salesperson must be sensitive to the issue of invading the prospect's privacy. The professional salesperson does not use unethical tactics to obtain personal information about the prospect.[14]

precall planning
Use of information collected during the prospecting and qualifying stages of the sales process and during previous contacts with the prospect to tailor the approach and presentation to match the customer's needs.

The information-gathering component of personal selling makes **precall planning** possible. Salespeople who have gathered relevant information about their prospects are prepared for the opening discussions that may ultimately result in a purchase. Effective precall planning permits the salesperson to make an initial contact armed with knowledge about the prospect's purchasing habits; his or her attitudes, activities, and opinions; and commonalities between the salesperson and the prospect.

Precall planning is usually not possible for retail salespeople, but they can compensate by asking leading questions to learn more about the prospect's purchase preferences. Business marketers have far more data available, and they should make use of it before scheduling the first sales contact.

Presentation

presentation
Describing a product's major features and relating them to a customer's problems or needs.

When the salesperson gives the sales message to a prospective customer, he or she makes a **presentation.** The seller describes the product's major features, points out its strengths, and concludes by citing illustrative successes. The seller's objective is to talk about the good or service in terms meaningful to the buyer—benefits rather than technical specifications. Thus, the presentation is the stage in which the salesperson relates product features to customer needs.

The presentation should be well-organized, clear, and concise, and it should emphasize the positive. To enhance the clarity and effectiveness of presentations, salespeople use printed sales support materials (charts, product literature, research papers, product reviews), laptop computers, and audiovisual aids such as videotapes.[15]

canned approach
Memorized sales talk used to ensure uniform coverage of the selling points that management has deemed important.

The traditional approach to sales presentations, the canned approach, originally was developed by John H. Patterson of National Cash Register Company during the late 1800s. The **canned approach** is a memorized sales talk used to ensure uniform coverage of the points management deems important. While canned presentations are still used in such areas as door-to-door *cold canvassing*—making unsolicited sales calls on a random group of people —most salesforces have long since abandoned them. Flexible presentations are

Product demonstrations increase the effectiveness of personal selling. Hewlett-Packard Company opened this medical marketing center in Boeblingen, Germany, where customers and prospects from across Europe can try out all of the company's medical products. Patient responses can be simulated electronically, allowing medical personnel to test the equipment in mock-emergency situations.

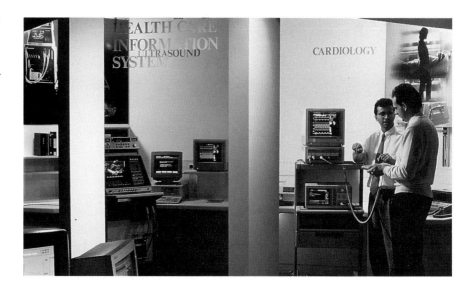

Source: Courtesy of Hewlett-Packard Company.

nearly always needed to match the unique circumstances of each purchase decision. Proper planning, of course, is an important part of tailoring a presentation to each prospective customer.

Demonstration

One important advantage of personal selling over most advertising is its ability to actually demonstrate the good or service to the potential buyer. Print advertisements and television commercials are sometimes capable of simulating a product demonstration. But a static magazine advertisement or even a quasi-demonstration of a product in action on a television screen is a far cry from the real thing. A demonstration ride in a new automobile, for example, allows the prospect to become involved in the presentation. It awakens customer interest in a way that no amount of verbal presentation can.

Demonstrations supplement, support, and reinforce what the sales representative has already told the prospect. Some firms use demonstration vans or trains to bring their products to potential customers. Rank Xerox, for example, used a railroad car to demonstrate its copiers and office equipment to prospects in Europe. Other firms have set up demonstration centers. Digital Equipment Corporation (DEC) has demonstration centers where prospects can see its computers run software for specific industries.

The key to a good demonstration—one that gains the customer's attention, keeps his or her interest, is convincing, and stays in the customer's memory—is planning. The salesperson should check and recheck all aspects of the demonstration prior to its delivery.

Handling Objections

A vital part of selling involves handling objections. *Objections* are expressions of sales resistance by the prospect, and it is reasonable to expect them: "Well, I really should check with my spouse." "Perhaps I'll stop back next week." "I like everything except the color." Objections typically involve the product's features, its price, and services to be provided by the selling firm.

The professional salesperson uses each objection as a cue for providing additional information for the prospect. In most cases, an objection such as "I don't like the color of the interior" is really the prospect's way of asking what other choices or product features are available. A customer's question reveals an interest in the product and gives the seller an opportunity to expand a presentation by supplying additional information. For instance, testimonials from satisfied customers may be effective in responding to product objections. Also, providing a copy of the warranty and the dealer's service contract may resolve the buyer's doubts about product service.

During this stage of the selling process, salespeople often are confronted with objections concerning competitors' products. Professional salespeople avoid badmouthing the competition. Instead, they view such objections as an opportunity to provide more information about their good or service. An example of how salespeople should respond to competitive objections is provided by Steve Shilling, director of sales in New York City for Northern Telecom, an international telecommunications company. In response to a bidding invitation, Shilling called on a communications manager of an industrial firm. The manager handed Shilling a long list of drawbacks of Northern Telecom's equipment. The list was prepared by a competitor whom the manager favored. With thorough knowledge of his own firm's and competitors' products, Shilling responded to each item on the list. He admitted the truth about claims that were valid and gave information that disproved false claims. This positive, honest, and straightforward approach to handling objections earned Shilling the buyer's trust. The buyer then told Shilling what he needed, Shilling offered a solution, and after several months of negotiations he won the $1 million contract.[16]

Closing

closing
Stage of personal selling where the salesperson asks the customer to make a purchase decision.

The moment of truth in selling is the **closing** — the point at which the salesperson asks the prospect for an order. If the sales representative has made an effective presentation based on applying the product to the customer's needs, the closing should be the natural conclusion. However, a surprising number of sales personnel find it difficult to actually ask for an order. To be effective, they must overcome this difficulty. Commonly used methods of closing a sale include the following:

1. The *"If-I-can-show-you . . ."* technique first identifies the prospect's major concern in purchasing the good or service and then offers convincing evidence of the offering's ability to resolve it. ("If I can show you how the new heating system will reduce your energy costs by 25 percent, would you be willing to let us install it?")

2. The *alternative-decision technique* poses choices for the prospect where either alternative is favorable to the salesperson. ("Will you take this sweater or that one?")

3. The *SRO (standing-room-only) technique* warns the prospect that a sales agreement should be concluded now because the product may not be available later or an important feature, such as price, will soon be changed.

4. *Silence* can be used as a closing technique, since a discontinuance of a sales presentation forces the prospect to take some type of action (either positive or negative).

5. An *extra-inducement close* offers special incentives designed to motivate a favorable buyer response. Extra inducements may include quantity discounts, special servicing arrangements, or layaway options.

Customer care is the primary mission of the nearly 15,000 people who sell and service Pitney Bowes office equipment. Follow-up is an important part of that care. Here, a Pitney Bowes saleswoman makes an early-morning follow-up call to discuss business with a facsimile machine customer. The customer, a board director of a regional agricultural cooperative, is one of 90 members who own a Pitney Bowes machine in a facsimile network used by members to communicate with each other and the cooperative's headquarters.

Source: Courtesy of Pitney Bowes.

Follow-up

The word *close* can be misleading, since the point at which the prospect accepts the seller's offer is where much of the real work of selling begins. In the competitive sales environment of the 1990s, the successful salesperson seeks to ensure that today's customers will be future purchasers. Jacques Murphy, who sells the marketing research services of the Gallup Organization to banks, savings and loans, and credit unions, says, "When we win a contract for Gallup, that's when the selling *really* starts. We're constantly reinforcing the buying decisions by keeping ahead on deadlines and showing how the research is useful to the buyer. In market research, you're in for ten weeks and you're gone. There's no guarantee you'll get the next project."[17]

follow-up

Postsales activities that often determine whether an individual who has made a recent purchase will become a repeat customer.

The postsales activities that often determine whether a person will become a repeat customer constitute the sales **follow-up.** To the maximum extent possible, the sales representative should contact customers to find out whether they are satisfied with their purchases. This step allows the salesperson to psychologically reinforce the customer's original decision to buy. It gives the seller an opportunity to correct any sources of discontent with the purchase as well as to secure important market information and make additional sales. Also, follow-up helps to strengthen the bond salespeople try to build with customers in relationship selling. Automobile dealers often keep elaborate records of their previous customers so that they can promote new models to individuals who already have shown a willingness to buy from them. One successful travel agency never fails to telephone customers upon their return from a trip. Proper follow-up is a logical part of the selling sequence.

Effective follow-up also means that the salesperson should conduct a critical review of every call made by asking, "What was it that allowed me to close that sale?" or "What caused me to lose that sale?" Such continuous review results in significant sales dividends.

NORDSTROM

Until recently, Seattle-based Nordstrom Inc. was widely viewed as a model for department stores everywhere, with a level of service that has been described as legendary. Then some disturbing information was made public.

Nordstrom clerks are famous for providing special services to customers, such as dropping off purchases at shoppers' homes and writing thank-you notes to loyal customers. But it turns out that they have been providing those services on their own time. The United Food and Commercial Workers Union collected more than 1,000 complaints from Nordstrom employees who said they worked between eight and ten hours a week "off the clock," and the Washington Department of Labor and Statistics ruled that Nordstrom had violated state law by not keeping accurate records of employee overtime.

These charges came at a bad time for the retailer. Nordstrom is planning to open twenty new stores in thirteen states during the next few years: by 1995, this once-modest chain will be a retailing giant, with 80 stores and sales of more than $5 billion. The union announced that it would picket the store openings.

According to Nordstrom's management, its hourly employees receive a commission that compensates them for extra duties such as home deliveries and company meetings. However, the union is suing the retailer to force it to pay for such work even if the employee also receives a commission.

Nordstrom has made some changes in response to the union's charges. It has modified its record-keeping methods to ensure that all time worked by employees is properly recorded and has set up a $15 million fund to resolve claims for back pay from employees outside the state of Washington. The company has accused the union of exaggerating the seriousness of what is really a minor record-keeping problem.

Discussion Questions

1. A union official contends that Nordstrom's employees are discouraged from reporting overtime hours because it reduces their sales-per-hour figure, on which promotions and shift assignments are based. A Nordstrom executive counters that the sales-per-hour figure is weighed equally with customer service and team effort. Is the union exaggerating or should Nordstrom change its methods of evaluating employees?

2. If Nordstrom's employees know when they are hired that they will be expected to do "extra" work that will not be paid for directly, is this a legitimate arrangement?

Sources: Cyndee Miller, "Labor Strife Clouds Store's Service Policy," *Marketing News* (May 28, 1990), pp. 1, 18; Dori Jones Yang and Laura Zinn, "Will 'The Nordstrom Way' Travel Well?" *Business Week* (September 3, 1990), pp. 82–83.

Managing the Sales Effort

sales management
Activities of planning, organizing, staffing, motivating, compensating, and evaluating and controlling a salesforce to ensure its effectiveness.

boundary-spanning role
Role performed by a sales manager in linking the salesforce to other elements of the organization's internal and external environments.

The overall direction and control of the personal-selling effort is in the hands of **sales management,** which is organized on a hierarchical basis. For example, in a typical geographical sales structure, a district or divisional sales manager might report to a regional or zone manager, and these people, in turn, may report to a national sales manager or vice-president of sales.

Sales managers perform what is known as a **boundary-spanning role;** that is, they link the salesforce to other elements of the internal and external environments. The internal organizational environment consists of top management, other functional areas in the firm, and other internal information sources. The external environment includes trade groups, competitors, customers, suppliers, and regulatory agencies.

The sales manager's job requires a unique blend of administrative and sales skills, depending on the specific level in the sales hierarchy. Sales skills are very important for first-level sales managers, since these managers must train and

Figure 18.3 How Salespeople and Sales Managers Spend Their Time

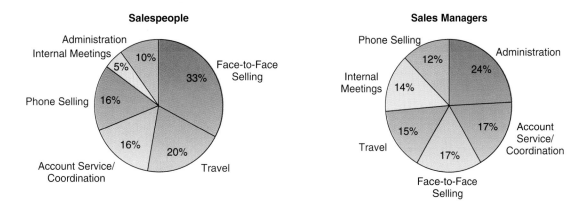

Source: William A. O'Connell and William Keenan, Jr., "The Shape of Things to Come," *Sales & Marketing Management* (January 1990), p. 39.

directly lead the salesforce. But as one rises in the sales management structure, more managerial skills and fewer sales skills are required for performing the job. A recent survey of 192 U.S. firms employing almost 10,000 sales representatives revealed that 75 percent of a typical salesperson's time is devoted to face-to-face selling, telephone selling, or travel. By contrast, sales managers devote 55 percent of their time to administration, internal meetings, and coordinating account service. The time allocations are shown in Figure 18.3.

Sales management is the administrative channel for sales personnel; it links individual salespersons to general management. The sales manager performs seven basic managerial functions: (1) recruitment and selection, (2) training, (3) organization, (4) supervision, (5) motivation, (6) compensation, and (7) evaluation and control.

For sales managers in the 1990s, the performance of these tasks is becoming more demanding and complex. They must manage an increasingly diverse salesforce that includes more women and minorities. They must select and train people to fill a growing number of selling positions such as product specialists, sales consultants, telemarketers, and customer service and sales support representatives. The expansion of firms into global markets challenges the sales manager to develop salesforces in other countries. A study of U.S. firms that derive half or more of their total revenues from foreign sales revealed that cultural and economic obstacles make it difficult to recruit and retain native salesforces. For example, recruiting local sales reps in Hong Kong is difficult because many natives of Chinese descent are leaving to take jobs in Japan and Taiwan in anticipation of Hong Kong's return to Chinese rule in 1997. The social caste system and many languages of India make it difficult for sales reps to sell outside their own social levels.[18]

Recruitment and Selection

Recruiting and selecting successful salespeople is one of the sales manager's greatest challenges. The turnover rate of salespeople is the highest of all white-collar professions.[19] Sources of new salespeople include colleges and

Figure 18.4   Average Annual Compensation for Salespeople

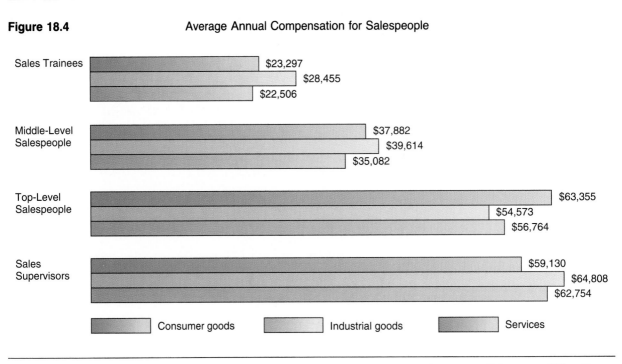

Source: "1990 Survey of Selling Costs," *Sales & Marketing Management* (February 26, 1990), p. 75.

universities, trade and business schools, sales and nonsales personnel in other firms, and the firm's current nonsales employees.

Not all of these sources are equally productive. One problem area involves the reluctance of some high school guidance counselors and college instructors to promote the advantages of a selling career to students. But in fact, a successful sales career offers satisfaction in all five areas that a person generally considers when deciding on a profession:

1. *Opportunity for advancement.* Studies have shown that successful sales representatives advance rapidly in most companies. Advancement can come either from within the sales organization or laterally to a more responsible position in some other functional area of the firm.

2. *High earnings.* The earnings of successful salespersons compare favorably with those of successful people in other professions. As Figure 18.4 indicates, the average top-level consumer goods salesperson earns more than $63,000 per year.

3. *Personal satisfaction.* A salesperson derives satisfaction from achieving success in a competitive environment and helping customers satisfy their wants and needs.

4. *Security.* Contrary to what many students believe, selling provides a high degree of job security. Experience has shown that economic downturns affect personnel in sales less than they do people in most other employment areas. In addition, there is a continuing need for good sales personnel.

5. *Independence and variety.* Salespersons most often operate as "independent" businesspeople or as managers of sales territories. Their work is quite varied and provides an opportunity for involvement in numerous business functions.

The careful selection of salespeople is important for two reasons. First, the selection process involves substantial amounts of money and management time. Second, selection mistakes are detrimental to customer relations and salesforce performance as well as costly to correct.

A seven-step process typically is used in selecting sales personnel: application, screening interview, in-depth interview, testing, reference checks, physical examination, and analysis and hiring decision. An application screening is followed by an initial interview. If there is sufficient interest, an in-depth interview is conducted. During the interview, sales managers look for personal characteristics that enhance the effectiveness of salespeople in the competitive selling environment. Among the characteristics are enthusiasm, good organizing skills, ambition, persuasiveness, the ability to follow instructions, and sociability.[20]

Next, the company may use testing in its selection procedure, including aptitude, intelligence, interest, knowledge, and/or personality tests. One testing approach gaining in popularity is the assessment center. This technique, which uses situational exercises, group discussions, and various job simulations, allows the sales manager to measure a candidate's skills, knowledge, and ability. Assessment centers enable managers to see what potential salespeople can do rather than what they say they can do.[21] After testing, references are checked to ensure that job candidates have represented themselves accurately. A physical examination is usually included before the final analysis and hiring decision.

Training

In order to shape new sales recruits into an efficient sales organization, management must conduct an effective training program. The principal methods used in sales training are on-the-job training, individual instruction, in-house classes, and external seminars. Popular training techniques include videotapes, lectures, role-playing exercises, slides, films, and interactive computer programs. Some firms use experienced salespeople to mentor new recruits. For example, Georgia-Pacific has a formal mentoring program to train its new field and in-house salespeople. In addition to teaching new hires about the products and the Georgia-Pacific style of selling, mentors offer them counseling on adapting to the firm's culture.[22]

Ongoing sales training is also important for veteran salespeople. Much of this type of training is conducted by sales managers in an informal manner. A standard format is for the sales manager to travel with a field sales representative periodically and then compose a critique of the person's work. Sales meetings and training tapes are other important parts of training for experienced personnel. Northwestern Mutual Life offers its experienced salespeople some 100 different courses and seminars each year covering topics such as customer relations and new laws and regulations affecting the insurance industry. "Our whole training program is based on one premise," says Dennis Tamcsin, vice-president of sales, " 'He who stops getting better ceases being good.' "[23]

Organization

Sales managers are responsible for the organization of the field salesforce. General organizational alignments, which are usually made by top marketing management, may be based on geography, products, types of customers, or some combination of these factors. Figure 18.5 presents simplified organizational charts illustrating each of these alignments.

Learning about the technical aspects of medicine is an integral part of Merck & Company's sales training. Here a sales trainer (standing) shows an associate professional representative how to use an interactive video program designed to teach new reps about the physiological processes of heart disease. This training helps salespeople describe to physicians how Merck's medications meet the needs of patients.

Source: Bob Krist/Black Star. Courtesy of Merck & Co., Inc.

A product sales organization would have specialized salesforces for each major category of the firm's products. This approach is common among industrial product companies such as Alcoa that market large numbers of similar but separate products of a very technical or complex nature, sold through different marketing channels.

A customer organization would use different salesforces for each major type of customer served. Some firms use separate salesforces to sell to consumer and organizational customers. Others have salesforces for specific industries, such as financial services, educational, and automotive. Salesforces can also be organized by customer size, with a separate salesforce assigned to large, medium, and small accounts. A growing trend is the **major accounts organization,** which is designed to strengthen a firm's relationship with large and important customers. Procter & Gamble, which previously had a salesforce for each product division, has reorganized its national salesforce into teams assigned to major retail accounts. P&G's key account teams are composed of salespeople from each grocery division: soap and detergent, food and beverage, and paper and household products. The new organization is intended to create better partnerships with all customers, both large and small. An industry analyst said, "Their attitude now is what can P&G do, together with the retailer, to meet . . . sales goals."[24]

The final approach, geographic specialization, is a widely used approach for firms marketing similar products throughout a large territory. For example, multinational corporations may have different sales divisions in different continents. CPC International, a U.S.–based consumer foods firm that markets in 47 countries, is organized geographically, with European, Latin American, and Far East

major accounts organization
Assignment of sales teams to a firm's largest accounts.

Figure 18.5   Basic Approaches to Organizing the Salesforce

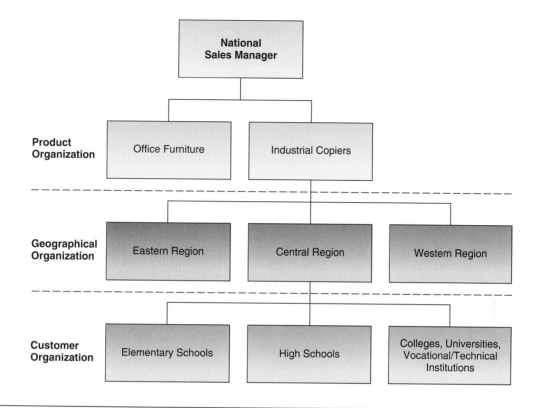

divisions.[25] Geographic organization may also be combined with other organizational methods, such as customer or product.

The individual sales manager also has the task of organizing the sales territories within his or her area of responsibility. Factors such as sales potential, strengths and weaknesses of available personnel, and workloads are considered in territory allocation decisions. The workload method of salesforce allocation is described in the "Computer Applications" at the end of the chapter.

Supervision

A source of constant debate among sales managers concerns the supervision of the salesforce. It is impossible to pinpoint the exact amount of supervision that is correct in each situation, since this varies with the individuals involved and the environments in which they operate. However, the concept of the *span of control* can be used in reaching some generalizations. The span of control refers to the number of sales representatives who report to the first level of sales management. The optimal span of control is affected by such factors as complexity of work activities being performed, ability of the individual sales manager, degree of interdependence among individual salespersons, and the extent of training each salesperson receives. Johnson, Kurtz, and Scheuing suggest a 6-to-1 ratio as the optimal span of control for first-level sales managers supervising technical or industrial salespeople. In contrast, they suggest a 12-to-1 ratio if the sales representatives are calling on wholesale and retail accounts.[26]

Figure 18.6   Monetary Award Used as Sales Incentive

Source: Courtesy of United Airlines.

Motivation

The sales manager's responsibility for motivating the salesforce cannot be taken lightly. Because the sales process is a problem-solving one, it often leads to considerable mental pressures and frustrations. Often sales are achieved only after repeated calls on customers and may, especially with new customers and complex technical products, involve a long completion period. Motivation of salespeople usually takes the form of debriefings, information sharing, and both psychological and financial encouragement. Appeals to emotional needs, such as ego needs, recognition, and peer acceptance, are examples of psychological encouragement. Monetary rewards and fringe benefits, such as club member- ships and sales contest awards, are types of financial incentives. A popular incentive for salespeople is travel awards, such as those described in the United Airlines ad in Figure 18.6.

Sales managers can improve salesforce productivity by understanding what motivates individual salespeople. They can gain insight into the subject of motivation by studying the various theories of motivation developed over the years. One theory that has been applied effectively to salesforce motivation is the **expectancy theory** proposed by Victor Vroom. According to this theory, motivation depends on the expectations an individual has of his or her ability to perform the job and how performance relates to attaining rewards that the individual values.

Sales managers can apply the expectancy theory of motivation by following a five-step process.[27] First, they must let each salesperson know in detail what

expectancy theory
Theory that motivation depends on an individual's expectations of his or her ability to perform a job and how that performance re- lates to attaining rewards the in- dividual values.

is expected in terms of selling goals, service standards, and other areas of performance. Second, they should make the work valuable by assessing the needs, values, and abilities of each salesperson and then assigning tasks that match them. Third, the sales manager must make the work doable. As leaders, they must inspire self-confidence in their salespeople and offer training and coaching to reassure them. Fourth, they must provide immediate and specific feedback, guiding those who need improvement and giving positive feedback to those doing well. Finally, sales managers should offer rewards that reinforce the values of each salesperson. By following these steps, sales managers can help motivate salespeople to performance levels that meet individual needs as well as company expectations.

Compensation

Because monetary rewards are an important factor in motivating subordinates, compensating sales personnel is a critical matter for managers. Basically, sales compensation can be based on a straight salary plan, a commission plan, or some combination of these.

commission

Incentive compensation directly related to the sales or profits achieved by a salesperson.

A **commission** is a payment tied directly to the sales or profits that a salesperson achieves. For example, a sales representative might receive a 5 percent commission on all sales up to a specified quota and 7 percent on sales beyond that point. While commissions provide a maximum selling incentive, they may cause some salesforce members to shortchange nonselling activities, such as completing sales reports, delivering sales promotion materials, and normal account servicing. A **salary** is a fixed payment made periodically to an employee. For example, a firm that has decided to use salaries rather than commissions might pay a salesperson a set amount every week.

salary

Fixed compensation payments made periodically to an employee.

There are both benefits and disadvantages in using predetermined salaries to compensate management and sales personnel. A straight salary plan gives management more control over how sales personnel allocate their efforts, but it reduces the incentive to expand sales. As a result, many firms use compensation programs that combine features of both salary and commission plans. When retailer Dayton Hudson added a bonus plan for exceeding sales quotas to a base salary, salespeople's annual wages increased from a range of $10,000 to $14,000 to $16,000 to $20,000.[28] According to a survey of compensation practices, most firms offer a salary-plus-bonus plan (46 percent) or a salary-plus-commission program (46 percent). A small percentage pay salary only (4 percent) or commission only (4 percent).[29]

Evaluation and Control

Perhaps the most difficult tasks required of sales managers are evaluation and control. The basic problems are setting standards and choosing instruments with which to measure sales performance. Sales volume, profitability, and investment return are the usual means of evaluating sales effectiveness. They typically involve the use of a **sales quota**—a specified sales or profit target that a salesperson is expected to achieve. For example, a particular sales representative might be expected to sell $300,000 in territory 414 during a given year. In many cases, the quota is tied to the compensation system.

sales quota

Level of expected sales for a territory, product, customer, or salesperson against which actual results are compared.

Regardless of the key elements in the evaluation program, the sales manager must follow a formal system of decision rules. The purpose of such a system is to supply information to the sales manager for action. What the sales manager needs to know are the answers to three general questions.

First, what are the rankings of the salesperson's performance relative to the predetermined standards? In making this comparison, full consideration should be given to the effect of uncontrollable variables on sales performance. Preferably, each adjusted ranking should be stated in terms of a percentage of the standard. This simplifies evaluation and facilitates converting the various rankings into a single, composite index of performance.

Second, what are the salesperson's strong points? One way to answer this question is to list areas of the salesperson's performance in which he or she has surpassed the respective standard. Another way is to categorize a salesperson's strong points in three areas of the work environment:

1. *Task,* or the person's technical ability. This is manifested in knowledge of the product (end uses), customer, and company, as well as selling skills.

2. *Process,* or the sequence of work flow. This pertains to the actual sales transaction—the salesperson's application of technical ability and interaction with customers. Personal observation frequently is used for measuring process performance. Other measures are sales calls and expense reports.

3. *Goal,* or the end results or output of sales performance. Usually this aspect of the salesperson's work environment is stated in terms of sales volume and profits.

Third, what are the weaknesses or negatives in the salesperson's performance? These should be categorized to the same degree as the salesperson's strong points.

In making the evaluation summary, the sales manager should follow a set procedure:

1. Each aspect of sales performance for which a standard exists should be measured separately. This helps prevent the *halo effect,* whereby the rating given on one factor is carried over to other performance variables.

2. Each salesperson should be judged on the basis of actual sales performance rather than potential ability. This emphasizes the importance of rankings in the evaluation.

3. Each salesperson should be judged on the basis of sales performance for the entire period under consideration rather than for particular incidents. As the rater, the sales manager should avoid reliance on isolated examples of the salesperson's success or failure.

4. Each salesperson's evaluation should be reviewed for completeness and evidence of possible bias. Ideally this review would be made by the sales manager's immediate superior.

While the evaluation step includes both revision and correction, the sales manager must focus his or her attention on correction. This translates into adjusting actual performance to predetermined standards. Corrective action, with its obviously negative connotations, typically poses a substantial challenge for the sales manager.

Summary of Chapter Objectives

1. **Explain the factors affecting the relative importance of personal selling in the promotional mix.** Personal selling is likely to be relatively more important in the following instances: (1) when consumers are concentrated geographically and relatively small in number; (2) when the products or services are expensive, are technically complex, require special handling,

or typically involve trade-ins; (3) when channels are relatively short; and (4) when the price of the product is relatively high.

2. **Contrast field selling, over-the-counter selling, and telemarketing.** Field selling involves sales calls to customers at their homes or businesses for the purpose of providing demonstrations or information about the good or service. Over-the-counter (retail) selling involves providing product information and arranging for completion of the sales transaction to customers at the retail location. Telemarketing is used to reduce the substantial cost involved in maintaining a sales force for making personal calls at customers' homes or businesses. It involves personal selling conducted entirely by telephone, either outbound (when salespeople contact customers) or inbound (when customers call to obtain information and make purchases).

3. **Identify the three basic sales tasks.** Order processing is basically the routine handling of an order; it characterizes a sales setting in which the need is made known to and is acknowledged by the customer. Creative selling is persuasion aimed at making the prospect see the value of the good or service being presented. Missionary sales are indirect selling, such as making goodwill-type calls and providing technical or operational assistance.

4. **Outline the steps in the sales process.** The basic steps in the sales process are prospecting and qualifying, approach, presentation, demonstration, handling objections, closing, and follow-up.

5. **Describe sales management's boundary-spanning role.** Sales managers link the salesforce to other aspects of the internal and external environments. The internal environment consists of top management, other functional units in the firm, such as advertising, and other internal information sources. The external environment includes trade groups, customers, competitors, suppliers, and regulatory agencies.

6. **List the functions of sales management.** Sales management involves seven basic functions: recruitment and selection, training, organization, supervision, motivation, compensation, and evaluation and control.

Key Terms

personal selling	precall planning
relationship selling	presentation
field selling	canned approach
team selling	closing
over-the-counter selling	follow-up
telemarketing	sales management
order processing	boundary-spanning role
creative selling	major accounts organization
missionary sales	expectancy theory
prospecting	commission
qualifying	salary
approach	sales quota

Review Questions

1. What is meant by *relationship selling?* Why is it becoming such a factor in personal selling?

2. Discuss the benefits of a sales career. What is the BLS projection for sales jobs?

3. How does personal selling differ among the three major selling environments? Give examples of local firms that operate in each environment.

4. What is meant by *team selling?* Why is it important?

5. Cite two local examples of each of the three basic sales tasks.

6. Explain the AIDA concept and its relationship to the steps in the personal-selling process.

7. Under what conditions is the canned approach to selling likely to be used? What are the major problems with this method?

8. Give an example of each function performed by sales managers in an organization.

9. Compare the alternative sales compensation plans. Point out the advantages and disadvantages of each.

10. Explain how a sales manager's problems and areas of emphasis might change in dealing with each of the following:
    a. Telephone salespeople
    b. Over-the-counter retail salespeople
    c. Field sales representatives
    d. Missionary salespeople

Discussion Questions

1. As marketing vice-president of a large paper company, you are asked to address a group of university students about selling as a career. List the five most important points you would make in your speech.

2. Explain and offer examples of how the following factors affect the decision to emphasize personal selling or advertising:
    a. Geographic market concentration
    b. Length of marketing channels
    c. Degree of product technical complexity
    d. Price
    e. Number of customers
    f. Prevalence of trade-ins

3. What sales tasks are involved in selling the following products?
    a. IBM office equipment
    b. United Way (to an employee group)
    c. Arby's fast-food restaurant
    d. Ed's Used Cars
    e. Cleaning compounds for use in plant maintenance

4. How would you describe the job of each of the following salespersons?
    a. Salesperson in a retail record store
    b. Century 21 real estate sales representative
    c. Route driver for Frito-Lay snack foods (sells and delivers to local food retailers)
    d. Sales engineer for Wang computers.

5. Suppose that you are the local sales manager for the telephone company's Yellow Pages and you employ six representatives who call on local firms to solicit advertising space sales. What type of compensation system would you use? How would you suggest that these sales personnel be evaluated?

Computer Applications

Although a quality salesforce may represent the difference between marketing success and failure, the salaries and direct expenses needed for supporting a field sales force may be the largest single component of total marketing expenses.

Table 1 Determination of Total Number of Hours Required for Sales Calls for Each Type of Account

Type of Account	Number of Contacts per Year	×	Minutes per Sales Call	=	Time Required for Planned Calls	+	Time Required for Unplanned Emergency Calls[a]	=	Total Minutes	=	Total Hours
A	52		40		2,080		208		2,288		38.13
B	26		30		780		78		858		14.30
C	12		20		240		24		262		4.40

[a]Estimated by management at 10 percent of total time required for planned calls.

Consequently, one important marketing decision involves determining the optimal number of salespersons. This decision often is made by using the *workload* method. It consists of the following steps:[30]

1. *Classify the firm's customers into categories.* Because customers vary greatly in terms of sales, servicing costs, and profitability, they should be divided into categories. One writer estimates that the top 15 percent of a firm's customers will account for 65 percent of its sales, the next 20 percent for 20 percent, and the remaining 65 percent for only 15 percent. The first group might be labeled *type A accounts,* the second *type B accounts,* and the third *type C accounts.* A firm with 5,200 accounts might categorize them as follows:

   800 type A accounts (high sales, high profitability)
   1,400 type B accounts (medium sales, moderate profitability)
   3,000 type C accounts (low sales, low profitability)

2. *Specify the desired number of annual calls for each account type and the average length of each call.* These specifications can be based on analyses of sales call reports submitted by the field sales force. In addition, they are likely to involve the judgment and experience of sales management. Suppose that sales management decides on weekly contacts for type A accounts, biweekly contacts for type B accounts, and monthly contacts for type C accounts. In addition, the desired length of an average sales call is set at 40 minutes for A, 30 minutes for B, and 20 minutes for C. Finally, an additional 10 percent is included for emergency or other unplanned calls in each account category. The number of hours required for each type of account is calculated in Table 1.

3. *Calculate the total hours required for contacting all accounts.* This step is accomplished by multiplying the total number of hours required for servicing each account type by the number of customers in each category. In this example, the calculation would be:

   800 type A accounts × 38.13 hours = 30,504 hours
   1,400 type B accounts × 14.30 hours = 20,020 hours
   3,000 type C accounts × 4.40 hours = 13,200 hours
   Total = 63,724 hours

4. *Calculate the time available for each salesperson.* This step is accomplished by multiplying the number of hours the typical salesperson works each week by the average number of weeks worked per year. If the typical salesperson works 40 hours per week for 46 weeks, the average number of hours per year is 1,840 (40 × 46).

5. *Allocate each salesperson's time to assigned tasks.* A considerable percentage of the typical salesperson's time is spent on activities other than calling on established accounts, such as traveling between accounts. In addition, the

Table 2

Allocation of Salesperson's
Time to Assigned Tasks

Activity	Percentage of Available Time	Number of Hours per Year
Sales/service calls on established accounts	40%	736
Sales calls on potential accounts	10	184
Travel	30	552
Other nonselling activities	20	368
Total	100%	1,840 hours

typical representative is responsible for such nonselling activities as preparing reports and attending sales meetings. Finally, the salesperson may devote additional time to contacting potential customers. For example, the salesperson working an average of 1,840 hours per year may divide his or her hours as shown in Table 2.

6. *Determine the required number of salespersons.* The final step can be accomplished by dividing the total number of hours required for servicing all accounts by the average number of hours each salesperson devotes to sales and servicing established accounts. The formula is:

$$\frac{\text{Required Number}}{\text{of Salespersons}} = \frac{\text{Total Number of Hours Required for Servicing Accounts}}{\text{Total Number of Hours Each Salesperson Devotes to Calling on Established Accounts}}$$

$$= \frac{63,724 \text{ hours}}{736 \text{ hours}}$$

$$= 86.6 \text{ or } 87 \text{ salespersons.}$$

Directions: Use menu item 16 titled "Sales Force Size Determination" to solve each of the following problems.

Problem 1.   Gwen Finney is a Tampa-based manufacturer's agent in the clothing industry. Over the years, the number of salespersons in her organization has grown along with the number of her firm's retail accounts. Finney divides her 3,500 retail store accounts as follows: 525 type A, 700 type B, and 2,275 type C. She expects each type A account to be contacted once a month and the sales call to last 60 minutes. Type B accounts should be contacted every other month, with the average call lasting 45 minutes. The less profitable type C accounts should be contacted once in the spring, summer, autumn, and winter, with each call lasting an average of 40 minutes. Unplanned/emergency calls add another 5 percent to the total. Finney estimates that her average sales representative works 40 hours each week and 45 weeks each year. Approximately 40 percent of a sales representative's time is spent contacting established accounts, 30 percent on potential accounts, 15 percent on travel, and 15 percent on nonselling activities. How many salespersons does Finney need for covering her market?

Problem 2.   John Brodski is vice-president of sales at Ohio-based Springfield Industrial Supplies. Brodski uses three classifications for his firm's 1,600 accounts: 220 type A firms, 580 type B firms, and 800 type C firms. He estimates that type A accounts should be called on 26 times per year and types B and C 20 and 15 times per year, respectively. The length of time for each sales call should be 30 minutes for type A and type B accounts and 15 minutes for type C accounts. Another 15 percent is to be added to each type of account for unplanned/emergency calls. The typical

Springfield Industrial Supplies sales representative works a 40-hour week for 48 weeks each year and devotes 50 percent of his or her time calling on established accounts, 20 percent on potential accounts, 20 percent on travel, and 10 percent on nonselling activities. How many salespersons should Brodski have in his department?

Problem 3. Lynn Victor's salesforce calls on 4,000 beauty shops and hairstyling salons throughout Missouri, Kansas, Oklahoma, and Nebraska from her Tulsa headquarters. She estimates that she currently has 800 type A accounts for her firm's beauty supplies, 1,000 type B accounts, and 2,200 type C accounts. Each type A account is contacted every other week for 30 minutes per call, type B accounts are contacted monthly for 30 minutes per call, and type C accounts are contacted every other month for 20 minutes per call. An additional 10 percent of the time involved in contacting established accounts is included for unplanned/emergency calls. Victor's sales representatives work 48 weeks per year with an average workweek of 40 hours. Each sales representative spends approximately 40 percent of his or her time contacting established accounts, 15 percent on potential accounts, 30 percent on travel, and 15 percent on nonselling activities.

a. How many sales representatives should Victor employ to service her accounts?

b. What effect would reducing the number of weeks worked per year from 48 to 45 have on the size of her sales force?

c. What effect would increasing the amount of time spent on a type C account sales call from 20 to 30 minutes and increasing the number of contacts from 6 to 12 have on the size of Victor's sales force?

Problem 4. Len Gordon is sales manager for a Providence-based industrial distributor. Gordon categorizes 100 of his 600 accounts as type A, 125 as type B, and 375 as type C. Type A accounts are contacted every other week and type B and C accounts once a month. Average sales calls last 30 minutes for type A and B accounts and 20 minutes for type C accounts. An additional 15 percent of the time involved in contacting each account is included for unplanned/emergency calls. Gordon's sales representatives work 40-hour weeks for an average of 47 weeks each year. Gordon estimates that they spend 35 percent of their time on actual sales calls on established accounts, 20 percent on potential accounts, 15 percent on travel, and 30 percent on nonselling activities.

a. How many sales representatives does Gordon need for servicing his accounts?

b. Gordon is considering several methods of reducing sales expenses. Since type C accounts generate smaller sales and profits than do types A and B, he is contemplating reducing the number of contacts from 12 to 6 and lowering the average sales call time from 20 to 15 minutes. What effect would these changes have on the number of sales representatives required?

c. One of Gordon's senior sales representatives has argued that the percentage of time spent on sales calls on established accounts could be increased from 35 to 50 percent by reducing the frequency and amount of reports and other paperwork each salesperson must prepare. Assuming the sales representative is correct, what effect would this change have on the number of sales representatives needed for servicing the firm's accounts?

Problem 5. Tomas Sanchez has gradually increased the market coverage of his Fort Worth-based wholesaling firm; currently it serves retail accounts throughout Texas. His type A accounts represent 15 percent (165) of the firm's 1,100 accounts. Another 25 percent (275) of his accounts are categorized as type B and the remaining 60 percent (660) as type C. Type A accounts are contacted weekly, type B accounts biweekly, and type C accounts monthly. The average length of sales calls for each account type is 40 minutes, 30 minutes, and 20 minutes, respectively. An additional 10 percent is added to the time spent on each type of account as a result of unplanned/emergency calls. Sanchez's sales representatives work 40-hour weeks for an average of 46 weeks each year and spend approximately 35 percent of their time contacting established accounts, 25 percent on potential accounts, 20 percent on travel, and 20 percent on nonselling activities.

a. How many salespersons should Sanchez employ?

b. Sanchez is considering increasing the number of sales calls on type C retail customers from 12 to 24 in order to stimulate additional sales. What impact would this have on the number of salespersons he needs?

c. Rather than attempting to stimulate purchases by type C customers, Sanchez is considering using his current salesforce to contact prospective customers. To accomplish this, he would have to reallocate the current usage of time by his sales force. He estimates that he would have to reduce the time spent on established accounts from 35 to 25 percent. What impact would this change have on the number of salespersons needed?

Lipton & Lawry's

Top management at Lipton & Lawry's raves about the firm's sales force. After all, the L&L sales organization is largely responsible for generating annual sales of more than $1.3 billion for the Unilever subsidiary and maintaining market shares of more than 80 percent for several L&L products. Admittedly, the strong consumer franchise enjoyed by such buyer favorites as Lipton's teas and dried soups, Lawry's blended seasonings, and Wishbone salad dressings is a decided advantage, but the marketing leadership at Lipton & Lawry's works hard to ensure that its salespeople are well-prepared to meet customer needs.

Newly hired field sales personnel must complete a rigorous 27-week training program. The first week of training is spent orienting the new sales representatives, giving them a broad understanding of L&L and the markets it serves. The second week takes them into the field to observe experienced salespeople in action. This is followed by another week of specialized training sessions on selling skills, including three days where they engage in simulated selling situations. Their performances are recorded on videotape and critiqued by experienced sales representatives who conduct the training activities. The next 24 weeks constitute a period of gradually increased responsibility for the trainees. During this period they accompany various L&L sales representatives in calling on established accounts and prospects. At the end of six months, the new sales representatives attend a week-long L&L national training seminar. Here they work on fine-tuning their sales and customer-service skills.

The training program is heavily weighted toward time spent in the field with experienced sales representatives. The approach is a logical one, since the L&L salespeople spend most of their workdays there, representing the company to the retail merchants they call on.

Periodic sales meetings are a fact of life for today's professional salesperson, but poorly planned or unnecessary meetings are blamed as timewasters by the sales forces of many firms. This is not the case at Lipton & Lawry's. "We never have a sales meeting unless there is a reason to have a meeting," says Frank Cleveland, L&L's Los Angeles district sales manager. "The two primary reasons you have sales meetings are, one, to discuss the work plan and the strategies that surround it, and the other reason would be due to motivation: challenging people and showing them how they can accomplish the things that need to be accomplished if the programs we have are properly implemented."

Such programs may involve heavy increases in seasonal advertising, special in-store promotions, use of recipe giveaways, and coupons. To make certain that the sales force believes in the products it represents, members of the L&L sales organization frequently travel to company headquarters, where they participate in blind taste tests of new products. Such participation is useful in involving them in the product development process, providing conviction about product strengths, and supplying them with information about the strengths and weaknesses of competing brands.

Each sales representative is responsible for selling the entire Lipton & Lawry's product line—approximately 250 items—ranging from seasoning salts to taco shells. The L&L sales organization is divided into four regions: West, Midwest, East, and South. Within each region are four or five districts, which are in turn divided into business units.

At the national level, the national sales manager is responsible for direct sales to grocery chains, such as Kroger's, Safeway, and A&P. (Separate divisions are used to market the L&L lines to company buyers for mass merchandisers and drug store chains.)

Each sales unit is staffed by a business manager who calls on the major accounts located in its geographic area, and a retail unit manager who oversees between 6 and 10 of the approximately 35 salespersons in each district. Some units also have senior sales representatives who are responsible for calling on smaller chain-store accounts located in the unit's territory. Each district also has a district sales administrator to handle computer-related activities and a district sales trainer, who is responsible for coordinating training activities for newly hired salespeople and continuing training activities for experienced sales reps.

L&L sales representatives are compensated on a straight salary basis. However, they can earn bonuses of up to an additional 25 percent of their base salaries, depending on total sales in the district. Merchandisers, approximately 10 in each district, receive hourly wages, but they can also earn bonuses of up to 10 percent of their annual wages depending on district sales.

Selling at Lipton & Lawry's is a two-phase operation. First, the national sales manager and the various unit business managers must sell the product to headquarters buyers of various food chain retailers. Then the retail sales force takes over to meet the needs of the individual stores.

L&L salespeople frequently work in two-person teams consisting of the sales representative and a merchandiser. The latter's responsibilities consist of replacing the physical stock on store shelves, setting up special cardboard displays (known as shippers) of L&L products, and checking inventory, thereby saving the store manager both time and labor costs. Both the merchandiser and the salesperson are trained to spot display opportunities for L&L brands within the store.

The unit retail sales manager performs a number of functions, including sales assistance, motivation, and performance evaluation. Several days will be spent in the field with each sales representative over a three-month period, during which the unit sales manager will assist the salesperson in making difficult sales, handling problems, and conducting on-the-spot performance reviews through what L&L calls *curbstone review.* Such reviews take place immediately following a sales call and consist of a summarization by the manager of positive components of the sales call and suggestions for improvement. The intent, of course, is to aid the sales professional in becoming even more effective. As district sales manager Frank Cleveland points out, "If you're with us a year or 15 years, you're still always learning and growing."

Techniques such as the taste tests and curbstone reviews are intended to enhance motivation. Financial rewards such as the potential bonus are also used. Sales rewards are also part of the salesperson motivation formula, and L&L marketers give them on national, regional, district, and business unit levels. All phases of the sales representative's job — selling, merchandising, and customer service — are evaluated in choosing the award winners. Suzanne Valker, a senior sales representative who has won the salesperson of the year award, summed up her goal as a Lipton & Lawry's salesperson, "You want to help the customer."

Sources: 'Tis the Season: A Case Study in Selling, produced by KOCE-TV; personal interview with John Heil, Lawry/Lipton Foods, May 1991.

Questions

1. Draw the Lipton & Lawry's, Inc. sales organization chart. Evaluate the basis used for aligning the L&L sales organization. Why do you feel that one of the other alternative bases for sales force organization was not used?

2. Categorize the L&L salesperson on the following bases described in Chapter 18: (a) personal selling environment and (b) sales tasks. What contributions might result from adding telemarketing to the current use of salespeople?

3. Evaluate the L&L compensation method for its salespeople. Would the use of sales commissions be warranted for this company?

4. Describe the functions performed by the L&L district sales manager and give an example from the case of each function. Propose a performance evaluation method based on the text discussion of sales tasks, process, and goals using the performance evaluation summary shown in the chapter.

Source: Courtesy of A. & P. Tea Co., Inc.

*At A&P's Sav-A-Center su-
perstore in New York, bold
in-store banners emphasize
low prices that appeal to the
store's target market—suburban shoppers with moderate
incomes. Determining pricing
strategies for goods and services is influenced by a host of
factors, including a firm's marketing objectives, costs, competition, and consumer demand.*

PART 7

Pricing Strategy

CHAPTER 19
Price Determination

CHAPTER 20
Managing the Pricing Function

19

Price Determination

CHAPTER OBJECTIVES

1. To outline the legal constraints on pricing.

2. To identify the major categories of pricing objectives.

3. To explain the concept of price elasticity and its determinants.

4. To list the practical problems involved in applying price theory concepts to actual pricing decisions.

5. To explain the major cost-plus approaches to price setting.

6. To list the major advantages and shortcomings of using breakeven analysis in pricing decisions.

7. To explain the superiority of modified breakeven analysis over the basic breakeven model.

David and Linda "Charlie" West have a great product. Their San Luis Sourdough Co. sells sourdough bread in San Luis Obispo, California, halfway between Los Angeles and San Francisco. When the Wests started their company, they planned to market to local restaurants and to have one or two small retail shops of their own. Their plans changed when area supermarket executives found out how good their bread was and wanted to stock it on their store shelves.

Lacking the financial resources to go head to head with huge national bread companies, the Wests realized that they had to compete on the basis of quality, not service level, and that their pricing system had to reflect that fact. They brainstormed pricing strategies with Carol Rounsaville, their Administrative Manager, who is a local California State Polytechnic University graduate. She developed a three-tiered, cost-plus pricing system designed to cover the cost of the different levels of customer service. The Wests used this strategy to remain competitive.

For Level 1 service, where bread is dropped off at the store's delivery entrance, the supermarket pays 97 cents for each one-pound loaf. For Level 2 service, which accommodates the return of day-old bread for full credit, the charge is $1.02. And for Level 3 service, which includes shelf-stocking and shelf and bread price-labeling, the price climbs to $1.05.

This pricing strategy covers the cost of the service the Wests provide and nothing more. That is, they make as much profit on Level 1 service as they do on Levels 2 and 3. For example, even though there is an 8-cent-per-loaf premium for full-service Level 3 treatment, after the Wests pay the cost of the driver's salary and benefits for the 30 minutes it takes to stock the shelves, company profits are the same as when the driver simply drops the bread off at the store's back door. Dave West explains, "We don't care which pricing option you choose; they're all the same to us."

Why not charge everyone $1.05 a loaf? Although if they did this, the Wests would make a profit on their service (only 20 percent of their customers choose the most expensive Level 3 option, while 60 percent choose Level 2 and the remaining 20 percent Level 1), they saw problems with this strategy. "Our bread costs more to begin with," says Charlie, "and we don't want to be accused of gouging."

Despite its accounting complexity, the West's three-tiered system has another advantage. By passing on the cost of service to their customers instead of absorbing it themselves, they are reducing their own operating expenses and boosting company profits. The result: San Luis Sourdough Co. has pretax margins of 10 percent.

How do customers feel about the company's pricing system? If Costco Wholesale Inc., a national chain that maintains a low-price policy, is typical, they are delighted. "To be honest with you, I'm happy as hell," explains Randy Cochrane, perishable buyer for Costco who chose San Luis Sourdough's Level 3 service. "We don't have the manpower here to stock the shelves, price, and handle returns. As long as I'm still able to offer the lowest price on their bread, it's a very workable arrangement."

This pricing strategy has helped the Wests build San Luis Sourdough into a $3 million company. What also helped is a commitment to administering the policy fairly, no matter the customer. "If we started providing Level 3 service to one company for the price of Level 2 or even Level 1, pretty soon we'd have to do it for everybody," explains Dave West. "By handling every customer the same way, we don't run the risk of alienating anyone."[1]

Chapter Overview

Although each marketing mix variable is examined in considerable detail in separate sections of the text, all are clearly interrelated. In our opening story about the San Luis Sourdough Company, pricing strategy was linked to customer service. A recent strategy by Quaker Oats Co., on the other hand, linked pricing with promotion. During the late 1980s, actor Wilford Brimley told consumers that eating Quaker Oats was "the right thing to do." Sales grew to $500 million under this campaign marketing Quaker Oats as a "healthy" product. During the last economic recession, though, the company shifted its promotion emphasis to reflect consumers' search for value. Although the product price did not change, Brimley now told consumers that Quaker Oats cost "one nickel and four pennies" a bowl, linking this price to the value of nickels and pennies in the past. Realizing that to many consumers, stressing price by itself connotes cheapness, however, the company continued to emphasize value. The idea promoted was quality at a reasonable cost. Advertising executive James Jordan explained, "The more weight placed on value, the more likely the brand will retain its franchise in the competition for a purchasing decision."

Holiday Inn took a similar value-oriented tack, this time involving pricing and product decisions. The chain launched a line of economy-class hotels named Holiday Inn Express. Although the rooms are standard Holiday Inn fare and guests have the benefit of an express checkout desk and a breakfast buffet, there are no pools, room service, or other amenities. Consequently, room rates are about 20 percent less than at full-service Holiday Inns. Using this product and pricing strategy, the chain plans to open 250 Express hotels within five years.[2]

price
Exchange value of a good or service.

The starting point for examining pricing strategy is to understand the meaning of the term *price*. **Price** is the exchange value of a good or service, meaning what it can be exchanged for in the marketplace. In earlier times, the price of an acre of land might have been 20 bushels of wheat, 3 head of cattle, or 1 boat. When the barter process was abandoned in favor of a monetary system, *price* came to mean the amount of funds required to purchase an item.

The factors involved in determining a profitable but justifiable (fair) price are the subject of this chapter. Chapter 20 focuses on management of the pricing function and discusses pricing strategies, price-quality relationships, and pricing in both the industrial and public sectors.

Legal Constraints in Pricing

Pricing decisions are subject to a variety of legal constraints at both the federal and state levels. Pricing is also regulated by the general constraints of U.S. antitrust legislation (outlined in Chapter 2). Some of the most important pricing legislation is discussed in the following sections.

Robinson-Patman Act

Robinson-Patman Act
Federal legislation prohibiting price discrimination that is not based on a cost differential; also prohibits selling at an unreasonably low price to eliminate competition.

The **Robinson-Patman Act** (1936) typifies Depression-era legislation. Known in some circles as the *Anti-A&P Act,* it was inspired by price competition from the developing grocery store chains—in fact, the original draft was prepared by the United States Wholesale Grocers Association. The country was in the midst of the Depression, and legislative interest was primarily in saving jobs. The developing chain stores were seen as a threat to traditional retailing and employment, and this act was a government effort designed to counteract it.

The Robinson-Patman Act, which technically was an amendment to the Clayton Act, prohibits price discrimination in sales to wholesalers, retailers, and other producers that is not based on cost differentials. It also disallows selling at an unreasonably low price in order to eliminate competition. The Clayton Act had applied only to price discrimination by geographic area, which injured local sellers. The rationale for the Robinson-Patman legislation was that the chain stores

COMPETITIVE EDGE

PERSEVERANCE PAYS OFF FOR PEPSICO

. . . .

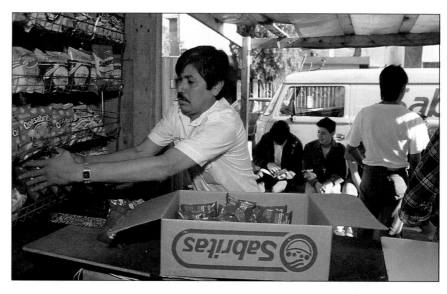

In 1982 Mexico's economy collapsed; price controls and the devaluation of the peso caused most foreign companies to cut back their Mexican operations sharply. However, PepsiCo decided to expand instead. Now the Mexican economy is thriving, and PepsiCo is Mexico's largest consumer products company.

When the peso was devalued, PepsiCo's Mexican subsidiary started exporting wheat, then taco shells, frozen juices, and pineapples. In 1984 it added candy and gum to its line of soft drinks and chips. Recently it expanded still more by buying 80 percent of Empresas Gamesa, Mexico's largest cookie company. Now that the peso has strengthened and price controls are easing, foreign investment in Mexico is looking more attractive—but with an estimated $1.2 billion in sales, PepsiCo is years ahead of other multinational companies in the Mexican market.

PepsiCo's Mexican subsidiary, Sabritas, was acquired in 1967. At the time the company had sales of under $1 million and a rudimentary distribution system: Bicyclists were hired to deliver bags of potato chips to small mom-and-pop stores. Sabritas now has a sophisticated distribution network that uses vans to carry its snack line directly from its four plants in Mexico to supermarkets as well as to the mom-and-pop stores. It controls over 70 percent of the salty snack market.

PepsiCo spent $300 million to buy its controlling interest in Gamesa and will spend another $200 million to introduce new products and more efficient technology in the next five years. Gamesa's products are the perfect complement to Sabritas' snack line.

What about the future? Easy. PepsiCo will export Sabritas and Gamesa products to South America, especially Venezuela and Brazil. Taking the same long-term view that produced success in Mexico, PepsiCo International's chairman thinks these countries, too, are on the road to economic recovery. If the company's Mexican experience is any guide, this strategy will yield still more profits for PepsiCo.

Discussion Questions

1. What risks does PepsiCo run in expanding into countries whose economies are undergoing major changes?

2. As the Mexican economy strengthens, other multinational companies will be attracted to this market. How might this affect Sabritas' plans?

Sources: Claire Poole, "Pepsi's Newest Generation," *Forbes* (February 18, 1991), pp. 88, 92; Anthony Ramirez, "PepsiCo Increases Role in the Mexican Market," *New York Times* (October 3, 1990), p. D3. *Photo source:* © 1990 Will Van Overbeek.

might be able to secure supplier volume discounts that were unavailable to small, independent stores.

The major defenses against charges of price discrimination are that price differentials are used to meet competitors' prices and that they are justified by cost differences. When a firm asserts that price differentials are used in good faith to meet competition, the logical question is, "What constitutes good-faith pricing behavior?" The answer depends on the particular situation.

When cost differentials are claimed as a defense, the price differences must not exceed the cost differences resulting from selling to various classes of buyers. A major problem with this defense is that of justifying the differences; indeed, many authorities consider this one of the most confusing areas in the Robinson-Patman Act.

The varying interpretations of the act certainly qualify it as one of the vaguest marketing laws.[3] For the most part, charges brought under the act are handled on an individual basis. Therefore, domestic marketers must continually evaluate their pricing actions to avoid potential Robinson-Patman violations.

The Robinson-Patman Act does not cover export markets, though. A U.S. firm is not prohibited from selling a product to a foreign customer at a price significantly lower than the domestic wholesale price.

Unfair-Trade Laws

unfair-trade laws
State laws requiring sellers to maintain minimum prices for comparable merchandise.

Unfair-trade laws are state laws requiring sellers to maintain minimum prices for comparable merchandise. Enacted in the 1930s, these laws were intended to protect small specialty shops, such as dairy stores, from the *loss-leader pricing* used by chain stores for some products. Such stores might sell a certain product below cost to attract customers. Typically a state law would set retail price floors at cost plus some modest markup. Although some of these laws remain on the books, they have become less important in recent years.

Fair-Trade Laws

fair-trade laws
Statutes enacted in most states that permit manufacturers to stipulate a minimum retail price for a product.

Fair trade is a concept that affected pricing decisions for decades. **Fair-trade laws** allowed manufacturers to stipulate minimum retail prices for products and to require their retail dealers to sign contracts agreeing to abide by these prices.

The basic argument behind this legislation is that a product's image, which is implied by its price, is a property right of the manufacturer, which should have the authority to protect its asset by requiring retailers to maintain a minimum price. Fair-trade legislation can be traced to lobbying by organizations of independent retailers who feared chain store growth. The economic mania of the Depression years were clearly reflected in these statutes.

In 1931, California became the first state to enact fair-trade legislation. Most other states soon followed suit; only Missouri, the District of Columbia, Vermont, and Texas failed to adopt such laws.

A U.S. Supreme Court decision holding fair-trade contracts illegal in interstate commerce led to the passage of the *Miller-Tydings Resale Price Maintenance Act* (1937), which exempted interstate fair-trade contracts from compliance with antitrust requirements. The states were thus authorized to keep these laws on their books if they so desired.

Over the years, fair-trade laws declined in importance as discounters emerged and price competition became a more important aspect of marketing strategy. These laws became invalid with the passage of the *Consumer Goods Pricing Act* (1975), which halted all interstate use of resale price maintenance, an objective long sought by consumer groups.

The Role of Price in the Marketing Mix

Ancient philosophers recognized the importance of price in the functioning of an economic system. Some of their early written accounts refer to attempts to determine a fair or just price. Price continues to serve as a means of regulating economic activity. Employment of any or all of the four factors of production—land, capital, human resources, and entrepreneurship—depends on the prices each factor receives. Also, for an individual firm, prices and the corresponding quantities purchased by its customers represent the revenue to be received. Prices, therefore, influence a firm's profit as well as its employment of the factors of production.

Pricing Objectives

Just as price is a component of the total marketing mix, so are pricing objectives a component of the organization's overall objectives. As Chapter 4 explained, marketing objectives represent the outcomes that executives hope to attain. They are based on the overall objectives of the organization. The objectives of the firm and of the marketing organization provide the basis for developing pricing objectives, which in turn are used to develop and implement the more specific pricing policies and procedures.

A firm's major overall objective might be to become the dominant factor in the domestic market. Its marketing objective might then be maximum sales penetration in each region and the related pricing objective sales maximization. These objectives might lead to the adoption of a low-price policy implemented with the highest price discounts to channel members of any firm in the industry.

While pricing objectives vary from firm to firm, they can be classified into four major groups: (1) profitability objectives, (2) volume objectives, (3) meeting competition objectives, and (4) prestige objectives. Profitability objectives include profit maximization and target-return goals. Volume objectives can be categorized as either sales maximization or market-share goals.

A study of U.S. businesses asked marketers to identify their firms' primary and secondary pricing objectives. Meeting competitors' prices was most often mentioned as a primary or secondary pricing objective. This was followed closely by two profitability-oriented objectives: a specified return on investment and particular total profit levels. These two objectives ranked first and second, respectively, as primary pricing objectives.[4] The findings are shown in Table 19.1.

Profitability Objectives

Classical economic theory is based on certain assumptions, one of them being that firms will behave rationally and that rational behavior will result in an effort to maximize gains and minimize losses. Thus, *profit maximization* is assumed to be the basic objective of a firm.

Radisson Hotels International made profitability a major pricing objective when the company developed its own brand of pizza. Executives had noticed that hotel trash containers were filled with empty pizza boxes from Domino's, Pizza Hut, and local chains, despite the fact that the hotel sold its own pizza. To overcome the negative stereotype of hotel food and to get a larger share of guests' pizza orders, the company introduced its own "Napolizza Pizza" with a unique marketing strategy. Guests wanting to order pizza were instructed to dial a special room service phone number dedicated to these orders alone. To give guests the impression that the pizza was made in an Italian pizzeria, the hotel had it delivered by room service waiters wearing white Napolizza Pizza sports shirts, windbreakers, and baseball caps. Radisson justified the expense of this separate marketing program by the profits that were earned. While gross profits on normal food and beverage sales average around 15 percent, pizza profits range between 70 and 75 percent. Now Radisson is pushing pizza sales for

A casually dressed server (right) delivers Napolizza Pizza to guests of Radisson Hotels, in contrast to the traditional formal attire (left) associated with room service. Higher gross margins make pizza a profitable offering at Radisson.

Source: © Steve Woit.

another reason as well. Most people who order room-service pizza are single guests who would probably order a sandwich or hamburger if pizza were not available. Yet the bill for pizza is in the $8 to $10 range, much higher than the price of a sandwich or hamburger. Radisson hopes that its new marketing strategy will increase its share of all pizza orders made in its hotels from 25 percent to 50 percent.[5]

Profits are a function of revenue and expenses:

$$\text{Profits} = \text{Revenue} - \text{Expenses}.$$

Revenue is determined by the product's selling price and number of units sold:

$$\text{Total Revenue} = \text{Price} \times \text{Quantity Sold}.$$

Price, therefore, should be increased to the point at which it will cause a disproportionate decrease in the number of units sold. A 10 percent price increase that results in only an 8 percent cut in volume will add to the firm's revenue. However, a 10 percent price hike that results in an 11 percent sales decline will reduce revenue. Manufacturers of high-fashion neckties such as those advertised in Figure 19.1 feared that price increases for Chinese raw silk would result in an unacceptable decrease in the number of units sold. With top-of-the-line neckties now priced at between $60 and $100, marketers worry that even wealthy consumers may cut back on the number of new ties they buy.

Economists refer to this approach as *marginal analysis.* They identify **profit maximization** as the point at which the addition to total revenue is just balanced by the increase in total cost. The basic problem is how to achieve this delicate balance. Relatively few firms actually do. A significantly larger number prefer to direct their efforts toward more achievable goals.

Consequently, **target return objectives** — short-run or long-run goals usually stated as a percentage of sales or investment — have become common in industry. This is particularly true among the larger firms in which pressure prohibits use

profit maximization
Point at which the additional revenue gained by increasing the price of a product equals the increase in total costs.

target return objectives
Short-run or long-run pricing objectives of achieving a specified return on either sales or investment.

Figure 19.1

Richel's Fashionable Neckties: Would a Price Increase Generate a Revenue Increase?

of the profit maximization objective. A specified rate of return on investment is the most commonly reported primary pricing objective in Table 19.1. Target return objectives offer several benefits for the marketer. They serve as a means for evaluating performance. They also are designed to generate a "fair" profit as judged by management, stockholders, and the public.

Volume Objectives

Many business executives argue that a more accurate explanation of actual pricing behavior is that firms strive for *sales maximization* within a given profit constraint. In other words, they set a minimum acceptable profit level and then seek to maximize sales (subject to this profit constraint) in the belief that the increased sales are more important than immediate high profits to the long-run competitive picture. The companies continue to expand sales as long as their total profits do not drop below the minimum return acceptable to management. General Motors Corp.'s Pontiac division adopted this strategy when it priced a special two-door Grand Prix at about $17,000, $9,000 cheaper than a look-alike model it sold the previous year. Similarly, sales at PepsiCo Inc.'s Taco Bell jumped 15 percent in response to a "value" menu offering 15 items priced between 39 cents and 99 cents.[6]

Another volume-related pricing objective is the *market share objective* — the goal set for the control of a portion of the market for a firm's good or service. The company's specific goal may be either to maintain its share of a particular market or to increase its share, say, from 10 to 20 percent. As Table 19.1 indicates, almost two-thirds of all responding firms list volume objectives as either a primary or secondary pricing objective.

Table 19.1   Primary and Secondary Pricing Objectives of U.S. Firms

Pricing Objective	Percentage of Respondents Ranking the Item[a]		
	As Primary Objective	As Secondary Objective	As Either Primary or Secondary Objective
Profitability Objectives			
Specified rate of return on investment	61%	17%	78%
Specified total profit level	60	17	77
Increased total profits above previous levels	34	38	72
Specified rate of return on sales	48	23	71
Volume Objectives			
Increased market share	31	42	73
Retaining existing market share	31	36	67
Serving selected market segments	27	39	66
Specified market share	16	41	57
Meeting Competition Objectives			
Meeting competitive price level	38	43	81
Prestige Objectives			
Creation of a readily identifiable image for the firm and/or its products	22	41	63

[a]Totals exceed 100 percent because most firms list multiple pricing objectives.
Source: Louis E. Boone and David L. Kurtz, *Pricing Objectives and Practices in American Industry: A Research Report.* All rights reserved.

Profit Impact of Market Strategies (PIMS) project
Research that discovered a strong positive relationship between a firm's market share and its return on investment.

The PIMS Studies.   Market share objectives may prove critical to the achievement of other organizational objectives. High sales, for example, often mean more profits. The extensive **Profit Impact of Market Strategies (PIMS) project,** conducted by the Marketing Science Institute, analyzed more than 2,000 firms and revealed that two of the most important factors influencing profitability were product quality and market share.

The linkage between market share and profitability is clear. PIMS data reveal an average 32 percent return on investment for firms with market share of over 40 percent. In contrast, average ROI decreases to 24 percent for firms whose market share is between 20 and 40 percent. Firms with a minor market share (less than 10 percent) generate average pretax investment returns of approximately 13 percent.[7]

The relationship also applies to individual brands offered by the firm. In comparing the top four brands in a market segment, PIMS research data revealed that the leading brand generates after-tax returns on investment of 18 percent, considerably higher than the second-ranked brand. Weaker brands, on average, fail to earn adequate returns.

The underlying explanation of the positive relationship between profitability and market share appears to be the greater operating experience and lower overall costs of high-market-share firms relative to competitors with smaller market shares. Accordingly, segmentation strategies might focus on obtaining larger shares of smaller markets and avoiding smaller shares of larger ones. The financial returns may be greater for a major competitor in several smaller market segments than for a relatively minor competitor in a larger market. Most companies are concerned with their products' market share. (To automakers, for example, each market share percentage point is worth about $1.4 billion.[8]) When Tyson Foods Inc. bought Holly Farms Corp, it did so, in part, because Holly holds a 19 percent share of brand-name chicken sales and is the national market leader.[9] Caterpillar realized the importance of holding onto its market share when threatened by Japan's Komatsu heavy construction machinery company, which undercut Caterpillar's prices by 40 percent. Between 1981 and 1986, Komatsu captured 11 percent of the U.S. market while Caterpillar lost $950 million. But Caterpillar's market-share maintenance strategy, which emphasized new products, improved quality, and aggressive factory automation, enabled the company to meet Komatsu's challenge and return to its pre-1981 profitability levels. While at its high, Komatsu's market share reached 15 percent, it is now down to 9 percent.[10]

Meeting Competition Objectives

The third pricing objective, that of meeting competitors' prices, is met simply by matching the prices of the established industry price leader. As Table 19.1 indicates, four out of five respondents listed this as a primary or secondary objective, making meeting competition the most frequently mentioned pricing objective.

The net result of this objective is to deemphasize the price element of the marketing mix and focus more strongly on nonprice competition. Although pricing is a highly visible mix component and an effective method of obtaining a differential advantage over competitors, a price reduction is an easily duplicated move. The airline price competition of recent years exemplifies the actions and reactions of competitors in this marketplace. Because of the direct impact of such price changes on overall profitability, many firms attempt to promote stable prices by utilizing the objective of simply meeting competition and competing for market share by focusing on product strategies, promotional decisions, and distribution—the non-price elements of the marketing mix.

An emphasis on the non-price elements of the marketing mix is often initiated by consumers. That is, when discounts become the norm, consumers may look for other features in choosing a good or service. For example, like its competitors, Choice Hotels International (with 1,570 inns) the parent company to Clarion Hotels and Quality, Comfort, Rodeway, and Sleep Inns, has traditionally targeted the senior market with heavy discounts to attract frequent travelers. After using this strategy for years. Clarion's research showed that seniors also value consistency, credibility, and reliability. With this in mind, the chain developed a new marketing plan that included reserving first-floor and nonsmoking rooms for senior citizens' use. The result was a dramatic increase in sales in this segment of the market.[11]

Prestige Objectives

The final category of pricing objectives, unrelated to either profitability or sales volume, is prestige objectives. Prestige objectives involve establishing relatively high prices to develop and maintain an image of quality and exclusiveness that appeals to status-conscious consumers. Such objectives reflect marketers' recognition of the role of price in creating an overall image for the firm and its goods and services.

Prestige pricing is used for such products as Baccarat crystal, Louis Vuitton luggage, Rolls-Royce automobiles, Rolex watches, and Tiffany jewelry. Perfume that costs $135 or more an ounce reflects the marketers emphasis on image far more than the cost of ingredients. Analyses have shown that ingredients account for only 4 percent of a perfume's cost.[12] Thus, advertisements for Joy that

Figure 19.2

Advertisement Emphasing Prestige

promote the fragrance as the "costliest perfume in the world" are using price to promote product prestige.

In contrast to low-price strategies used by some discount jewelry chains, Cartier marketers emphasize the store's special image. The ad in Figure 19.2 targets a "clientele which, like Cartier itself, is unique in all the world." To increase Cartier's prestige, the ad refers to the work of "Cartier artists" who are "masters of imagination" and to a 140-year-long heritage. Ads like this appear in such upscale magazines as *Vanity Fair* and *Architectural Digest*.

Many French manufacturers have targeted the ultra-high-end of the luxury goods market and priced their goods accordingly. Prestige pricing is used to sell Yves Saint Laurent dresses, Limoges china, Christofle silverware, and Chateau Lafite-Rothschild champagne. French companies sell nearly half of the world's luxury goods—a high-margin market that totals some $52 billion a year. Despite its comfortable position, the French are feeling pressure from manufacturers in Italy, West Germany, Great Britain, and the United States who are marketing their own goods at prestige prices. To maintain their image of exclusivity, the challenge ahead for French manufacturers is to maintain the highest quality possible at whatever price necessary. The urge to expand by bringing out a lower-priced line may dilute—and even cheapen—a company's distinctive label.[13]

Pricing Objectives of Nonprofit Organizations

Pricing typically is a very important element of the marketing mix for nonprofit organizations. Pricing strategy can be used to achieve a variety of organizational goals in nonprofit settings:

1. *Profit maximization.* While nonprofit organizations by definition do not cite profitability as a primary goal, there are numerous instances in which they do try to maximize their returns on single events or series of events. A $1,000-a-plate political fund raiser is a classic example.

2. *Cost recovery.* Some nonprofit organizations attempt to recover only the actual cost of operating the unit. Mass transit, publicly supported colleges, and bridges are common examples. The amount of recovered costs is often dictated by tradition, competition, and/or public opinion.

3. *Providing market incentives.* Other nonprofit groups follow a lower than average pricing policy or offer a free service to encourage increased usage of the good or service. Seattle's bus system offers free service in the downtown area in an attempt to reduce traffic congestion, encourage retail sales, and minimize the effort required to use downtown public services.

4. *Market suppression.* Price is sometimes used to discourage consumption. In other words, high prices are used to accomplish societal objectives and are not directly related to the costs of providing the good or service. Illustrations include tobacco and alcohol taxes, parking fines, tolls, and gasoline excise taxes.[14]

How Prices Are Determined

The determination of price may be viewed in two ways—the theoretical concepts of supply and demand and the cost-oriented approach that characterizes current business practice. During the first part of this century, most discussions of price determination emphasized the classical concepts of supply and demand. Since World War II, however, the emphasis has shifted to a cost-oriented approach. Hindsight reveals that both concepts have certain flaws.

customary prices

In pricing strategy, the traditional prices that customers expect to pay for certain goods and services.

Another concept of price determination—one based on the impact of custom and tradition—is often overlooked. **Customary prices** are retail prices that consumers expect as a result of tradition and social habit. Candy makers' attempt to hold the line on the traditional price levels led to considerable reduction in product size. Similar practices have prevailed in the marketing of soft drinks as bottlers attempt to balance consumer expectations of customary prices with the realities of rising costs.

Wm. Wrigley Jr. Co., manufacturer of such chewing gum standards as Juicy Fruit, Doublemint, and Big Red, took advantage of the weakness in the industry's customary pricing strategy by introducing a smaller-quantity pack at a lower price. While Wrigley's competitors continued to offer only seven-piece packs for 35 cents, Wrigley's five-piece packs were priced at 25 cents. To spur impulse buying, the company prominently displayed the price on the package, as shown in Figure 19.3. The strategy was so successful that within two years of its inception, Wrigley discontinued selling seven-stick gum packs.[15]

At some point in time, someone has to set initial prices for products. In addition, competitive moves and changes in costs necessitate periodic review of price structures. The remainder of this chapter discusses the traditional and current concepts of price determination. It also considers how best to integrate the concepts to develop a realistic pricing approach.

PRODUCT DOWNSIZING

A box of Luvs used to contain 88 diapers; now it contains 80. A can of Brim used to contain 13 ounces of coffee; now it contains 11.5. A box of Rice-A-Roni used to hold 8 ounces; now it holds 6.9. Similar changes can be observed in packages of Knorr soup mix, StarKist tuna, and Lipton instant tea.

But the price hasn't changed.

Such "downsizing"—reducing package size or contents without changing the price—can result in a hidden price increase of as much as 10 percent. Critics like New York State Attorney General Robert Abrams believe that this practice is deceptive (Abrams calls it "package-shorting") and are calling for legislation to require manufacturers to announce such changes, either on the package or by posting a sign where the item is displayed. Manufacturers claim that there is no deception and that their packages are clearly labeled with the volume and weight information required by law. It's up to the consumer to read the label.

Downsizing is done for a variety of reasons, usually economic. The marketer may be trying to offset higher raw-materials costs or to raise profit margins by lowering unit costs. Sometimes the purpose is to keep prices from rising beyond the psychological barriers for particular products. The practice is most frequent in boxed and canned foods and for household products such as coffee, detergent, rice, pasta, canned meats, jellies, and peanut butter.

According to critics, downsizing is equivalent to a nearly invisible price increase. It is done quietly and subtly so that consumers will not notice the difference. In effect, the consumer pays more without knowing it. Manufacturers defend the practice in a variety of ways: They claim that smaller packages place less of a burden on the environment, or that the product has been reformulated so that a smaller amount has the same yield (e.g., the same number of cups of coffee), or that the changes are intended to bring a product more in line with competitors' products. These arguments do not convince the critics, who claim that downsizing is "sneaky" and "misleading."

Discussion Questions

1. Consumers purchase many packaged goods out of habit, without looking at the labels. Since manufacturers know this, are they deceiving consumers when they practice product downsizing?

2. Would posting signs in stores noting changes in package sizes make a difference in the behavior of either manufacturers or consumers?

Sources: John B. Hinge, "Critics Call Cuts in Package Size Deceptive Move," *Wall Street Journal* (February 5, 1991), pp. B1, B8; David Kiley, "N.Y. Attorney General Probes Product 'Downsizing,' " *Marketing Week* (January 7, 1991), p. 7; "Manufacturers Cut Volumes, Not Prices of Food Products," *Northwest Arkansas Times* (January 6, 1991), p. 7C; Harriet Nolan, "Incredible Shrinking Products," *USA Today* (February 7, 1991), p. 8B.

---

demand
Schedule of the amounts of a firm's product that consumers will purchase at different prices during a specified time period.

supply
Schedule of the amounts of a good or service that a firm will offer for sale at different prices during a specified time period.

pure competition
Market structure characterized by homogeneous products in which there are so many buyers and sellers that none has a significant influence on price.

Price Determination in Economic Theory

The microeconomic approach to price determination assumes a profit-maximization objective and leads to the derivation of correct equilibrium prices in the marketplace. This approach considers both supply and demand factors, thus providing a more complete analysis than that typically utilized by business firms.

Demand refers to a schedule of the amounts of a firm's good or service that consumers will purchase at different prices during a specified period. **Supply** refers to a schedule of the amounts of a good or service that will be offered for sale at different prices during a specified time period. These schedules may vary for different types of market structures. Four types of market structures exist: pure competition, monopolistic competition, oligopoly, and monopoly.

Pure competition is a market structure in which there are so many buyers and sellers that none has a significant influence on price. Other characteristics of pure competition are a homogeneous product and ease of entry for sellers due

Figure 19.3

Package Showing an Alternative to Customary Prices

monopolistic competition
Market structure involving a heterogeneous product and product differentiation among competing suppliers, allowing the marketer some degree of control over prices.

oligopoly
Market structure involving relatively few sellers and barriers to new competitors due to high start-up costs.

monopoly
Market structure involving only one seller of a good or service for which no close substitutes exist.

to low start-up costs. This marketing structure is largely theoretical today; however, the agricultural sector exhibits many of the characteristics of a purely competitive market and provides the closest example of it.

Monopolistic competition, which typifies most retailing, is a market structure with large numbers of buyers and sellers. It involves a heterogeneous product and product differentiation, which allows the marketer some degree of control over prices.

An **oligopoly** is a market structure in which there are relatively few sellers. Each seller may affect the market, but no one seller controls it. Because of high start-up costs, new competitors encounter significant barriers to entry. The demand curve facing each firm in an oligopolistic market contains a unique "kink" at the current market price. Because of the impact of a single competitor on total industry sales, any attempt by one firm to reduce prices in an effort to generate additional sales is likely to be matched by competitors. The result of total industry price cutting is a reduction in total industry revenues. Oligopolies frequently occur in the petroleum refining, automobile, and tobacco industries.

A **monopoly** is a market structure with only one seller of a product and no close substitutes for the product. Antitrust legislation has nearly eliminated all but temporary monopolies, such as those created through patent protection, and regulated monopolies, such as utility companies. The government allows regulated monopolies in markets in which competition would lead to an uneconomical duplication of services. In return for this license, government reserves the right to regulate the monopoly's rate of return.

Table 19.2 compares the four types of market structures on the following bases: number of competitors, ease of entry into the industry by new firms, similarity of competing products, degree of control over price by individual firms,

Table 19.2   Distinguishing Features of the Four Market Structures

	Type of Market Structure			
Characteristics	**Pure Competition**	**Monopolistic Competition**	**Oligopoly**	**Monopoly**
Number of competitors	Many	Few to many	Few	No direct competitors
Ease of entry into industry by new firms	Easy	Somewhat difficult	Difficult	Regulated by government
Similarity of goods or services offered by competing firms	Similar	Different	Can be either similar or different	No directly competing goods or services
Control over price by individual firms	None	Some	Some	Considerable
Demand curve facing individual firms	Totally elastic	Can be either elastic or inelastic	Kinked; inelastic below kink; more elastic above	Can be either elastic or inelastic
Examples	160-acre farm	JC Penney store	Texaco	Commonwealth Edison

and the elasticity or inelasticity of the demand curve facing the individual firm. Elasticity—the degree of consumer responsiveness to changes in price—is discussed in more detail in a later section.

Cost and Revenue Curves

The price set for a product must be sufficient to cover the costs involved in producing and marketing it. Total cost is composed of total variable costs and total fixed costs. *Variable costs* are the costs that change with the level of production (such as labor and raw materials costs), while *fixed costs* are those that remain stable regardless of the production level achieved (such as lease payments or insurance costs). *Average total costs* are calculated by dividing total variable and fixed costs by the number of units produced. Finally, *marginal cost* is the change in total cost that results from producing an additional unit of output.

The demand side of the pricing equation focuses on revenue curves. *Average revenue* is calculated by dividing total revenue by the quantity associated with these revenues. Average revenue is actually the demand curve facing the firm. *Marginal revenue* is the change in total revenue that results from selling an additional unit of output. As Figure 19.4 shows, the point of profit maximization occurs where marginal costs are equal to marginal revenues.

Table 19.3 illustrates why the intersection of the marginal cost and marginal revenue curves is the logical point at which to maximize revenue for the organization. Although the firm can earn a profit at several different prices, the price at which it earns maximum profits is $22. At a price of $24, $66 in profits are earned—$4 less than the $70 profit at the $22 price. If a price of $20 is set to attract additional sales, the marginal costs of the extra sales ($7) are greater than the marginal revenues received ($6), and total profits decline.

The Concept of Elasticity in Pricing Strategy

Although the intersection of the marginal cost and marginal revenue curves determines the level of output, the impact of changes in price on sales varies

Figure 19.4   Determining Price by Combining Marginal Revenue and Marginal Cost

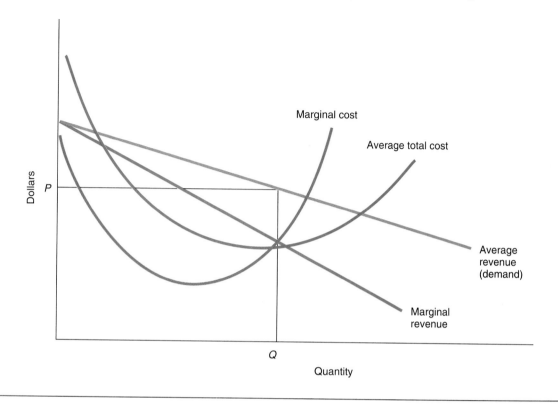

greatly. In order to understand why it fluctuates, it is necessary to understand the concept of elasticity.

elasticity

Measure of responsiveness of purchasers and suppliers to a change in price.

Elasticity is the measure of responsiveness of purchasers and suppliers to price changes. The price elasticity of demand (or elasticity of demand) is the percentage change in the quantity of a good or service demanded divided by the percentage change in its price. A 10 percent increase in the price of eggs that results in a 5 percent decrease in the quantity of eggs demanded yields a price elasticity of demand for eggs of 0.5. The price elasticity of supply of a product is the percentage change in the quantity of a good or service supplied divided by the percentage change in its price. A 10 percent increase in the price of shampoo that results in a 25 percent increase in the quantity supplied yields a price elasticity of supply for shampoo of 2.5.

Consider a case in which a 1 percent change in price causes more than a 1 percent change in the quantity supplied or demanded. Numerically that means an elasticity greater than 1.0. When the elasticity of demand or supply is greater than 1.0, that demand or supply is said to be *elastic*. If a 1 percent change in price results in less than a 1 percent change in quantity, a product's elasticity of demand or supply will be less than 1.0. In that case, the demand or supply is called *inelastic*. For example, the demand for cigarettes is relatively inelastic; research studies have shown that a 10 percent increase in cigarette prices results in only a 4 percent sales decline.

In Latin American countries like Peru and Venezuela, which suffer from astoundingly high annual inflation rates, marketers find it necessary to raise product prices by as much as 20 to 30 percent every two weeks. Procter & Gamble found that these price increases for products like Ace detergent and Crest toothpaste resulted in elastic demand on the wholesale and retail levels,

Table 19.3   Price Determination Using Marginal Analysis

Price	Number Sold	Total Revenue	Marginal Revenue	Total Costs	Marginal Costs	Profits (Total Revenue − Total Costs)
—	—	—	—	$ 50	—	($50)
$34	1	$ 34	$34	57	$ 7	(23)
32	2	64	30	62	5	2
30	3	90	26	66	4	24
28	4	112	22	69	3	44
26	5	130	18	73	4	57
24	6	144	14	78	5	66
22	**7**	**154**	**10**	**84**	**6**	**70**
20	8	160	6	91	7	69
18	9	162	2	100	9	62
16	10	160	(2)	110	11	50

not because the prices are perceived as too high but because inflationary pressures will push prices even higher within a short time. To distribute goods to small suppliers, P&G hired a fleet of delivery people in Volkswagen vans, some of whom deliver orders as small as 12 tubes of toothpaste.[16]

Determinants of Elasticity.   Why is the elasticity of supply or demand high for some products and low for others? What determines demand elasticity? One major factor influencing the elasticity of demand is the availability of substitutes or complements. If a good or service has close substitutes, demand for it tends to be elastic. The demand for olive oil, for instance, is more elastic than it would be if other salad oils were not available as substitutes. The demand for motor oil tends to be inelastic, because it is a complement to the more important product, gasoline.

When a product price is below that of major competitors, the demand for the product tends to be elastic. General Motors priced its basic Saturn sedan at $7,995, considerably less than similar vehicles marketed by Toyota, Nissan, and Isuzu in the hope that consumers' positive response would result in greater numbers of vehicles sold.[17]

Elasticity of demand also depends on whether a product is a necessity or a luxury. For example, high-fashion clothes such as the Chanel suits depicted in Figure 19.5 are a luxury for most people. If prices for designer outfits increase, people can respond by wearing more lower priced items instead. In contrast, medical and dental care are considered necessities, so price changes will have little effect on the frequency of medical or dental visits. However, under the influence of higher prices, some necessities may be perceived as luxuries as demand decreases. For example, although Australians are known for their love affair with the automobile, gasoline sales dropped 10 percent in September 1990 compared to the same period a year earlier. The elasticity of demand was in response to skyrocketing gasoline prices, which jumped more than 30 percent from $1.95 (U.S.) per gallon to $2.45 at the height of the Persian Gulf Crisis.[18]

Elasticity is further influenced by the portion of a person's budget that is spent on a good or service. Matches, for example, are no longer really a necessity; good substitutes exist. Nonetheless, the demand for matches is thought to be very inelastic because people spend so little on them that they hardly notice a price change. In contrast, the demand for housing and transportation is not

Figure 19.5

Advertising a Luxury

totally inelastic, even though these are necessities, because both occupy a large part of people's budgets.

Elasticity of demand is also affected by the time perspective. Demand is less often elastic in the short run than in the long run. Consider the demand for home heating fuel. In the short run, when the prices go up people find it difficult to cut back on the quantity used. They are accustomed to living with a specific temperature setting, dressing in a certain way, and so forth. Given time, though, they may find ways to economize. They can better insulate their homes, dress more warmly, or even move to a warmer climate.

Sometimes the usual patterns do not hold true, though. Alcohol and tobacco, which are not necessities but do occupy a large share of some personal budgets, also are subject to inelastic demand.

Elasticity and Revenue.

There is an important relationship between the elasticity of demand and the way in which total revenue varies as the price of a good or service changes. Assume, for example, that New York City officials are considering alternative methods of raising more money for the city budget. One possible fund-raising method is to change the subway fare. But should it be raised or lowered? The correct answer depends on the elasticity of demand for subway rides. A 10 percent decrease in fares should attract more riders, but unless there is more than a 10 percent increase in riders, total revenue will fall. A 10 percent increase in fares will bring in more money per rider, but if more than 10 percent of the riders stop using the subway, total revenue will fall. A price cut will increase revenue only if demand is elastic, and a price increase will raise revenue only if demand is inelastic. New York City officials seem to believe that the demand for subway rides is inelastic; they raise fares when they need more money for the city budget.

Practical Problems of Price Theory

From the marketer's viewpoint, price theory concepts are sometimes difficult to apply in practice. What, then, are their practical limitations?

First, many firms do not attempt to maximize profits. Economic analysis is subject to the same limitations as the assumptions on which it is based—for example, the proposition that all firms attempt to maximize profits. Second, it is difficult to estimate demand curves. Modern accounting procedures provide managers with a clear understanding of cost structures so managers can readily comprehend the supply side of the pricing equation. But they find it difficult to estimate demand at various price levels. Demand curves must be based on marketing research estimates that often are less exact than cost figures. Although the demand element can be identified, it is often difficult to measure in real-world settings.

Price Determination in Practice

cost-plus pricing
Practice of adding a percentage of specified dollar amount (markup) to the base cost of a product to cover unassigned costs and to provide a profit.

The practical limitations inherent in price theory have forced practitioners to turn to other techniques. **Cost-plus pricing,** the most popular method, uses a base-cost figure per unit and adds a markup to cover unassigned costs and to provide a profit. The only real difference among the multitude of cost-plus techniques is the relative sophistication of the costing procedures employed. For example, a local apparel shop may set prices by adding a 45 percent markup to the invoice price charged by the supplier. The markup is expected to cover all other expenses and permit the owner to earn a reasonable return on the sale of clothes.

In contrast to this rather simple pricing mechanism, a large manufacturer may employ a complex pricing formula that uses a computer program to make the necessary calculations. However, this is only a sophisticated procedure for calculating costs. In the end, the formula still requires someone to make a decision about the markup. The apparel shop and the large manufacturer may differ with respect to the cost aspect, but they are remarkably similar when it comes to the markup side of the equation.

An International Comparison

Marketing experts point out that while U.S. manufacturers have traditionally priced their products based on what it costs to produce them, Japanese manufacturers use a *market-price approach.* That is, they determine the price necessary to penetrate and capture a large share of a market, then they figure out how to manufacture the product for that cost. This approach has the advantage of creating pressure within a company to meet the target price through efficiency and cost-cutting. It also helps the company focus on market share.[19]

Alternative Pricing Procedures

The two most common cost-oriented pricing procedures are the full-cost method and the incremental-cost method. *Full-cost pricing* uses all relevant variable costs in setting a product's price. In addition, it allocates those fixed costs that cannot be directly attributed to the production of the specific item being priced. Under the full-cost method, if job order 515 in a printing plant amounts to .000127 percent of the plant's total output, .000127 percent of the firm's overhead expenses are charged to that job. This approach allows the marketer to recover all costs plus the amount added as a profit margin.

The full-cost approach has two basic deficiencies. First, there is no consideration of competition or of demand for the item. Perhaps no one wants to pay the price the firm has calculated! Second, any method of allocating overhead (fixed expenses) is arbitrary and may be unrealistic. In manufacturing, overhead allocations often are tied to direct labor hours. In retailing, the square footage of each profit center is sometimes the factor used in computations. Regardless of the technique employed, it is difficult to show a cause-effect relationship between the allocated cost and most products.

One way to overcome the arbitrary allocation of fixed expenses is with *incremental-cost pricing,* which attempts to use only those costs directly attributable to a specific output in setting prices. Consider a small-scale manufacturer with the following income statement:

Sales (10,000 units at $10)		$100,000
Expenses:		
Variable	$50,000	
Fixed	40,000	90,000
Net profit		$ 10,000

Suppose the firm is offered a contract for an additional 5,000 units. Since the peak season is over, these items can be produced at the same average variable cost. Assume that the labor force would be idle otherwise. How low should the firm price its product in order to get the contract?

Under the full-cost approach, the lowest price would be $9 per unit. This figure is obtained by dividing the $90,000 in expenses by an output of 10,000 units. The incremental approach, on the other hand, could permit any price above $5, which would significantly increase the possibility of securing the additional contract. This price would be composed of the $5 variable cost associated with each unit of production plus a $.10-per-unit contribution to fixed expenses and overhead. With a $5.10 proposed price, the income statement now looks like this:

Sales (10,000 at $10; 5,000 at $5.10)		$125,500
Expenses:		
Variable (15,000 × $5)	$75,000	
Fixed	40,000	115,000
Net profit		$ 10,500

Profits thus are increased under the incremental approach.

Admittedly the illustration is based on two assumptions: (1) the ability to isolate markets such that selling at the lower price will not affect the price received in other markets and (2) the absence of legal restrictions on the firm. The example, however, does illustrate that profits can sometimes be enhanced by using the incremental approach.

Breakeven Analysis

breakeven analysis
Pricing technique used to determine the number of products that must be sold at a specified price in order to generate revenue to cover total cost.

Breakeven analysis is a means of determining the number of goods or services that must be sold at a given price in order to generate sufficient revenue to cover total costs. Figure 19.6 graphically depicts the process. The total cost curve includes both fixed and variable segments, and total fixed cost is represented by a horizontal line. Average variable cost is assumed to be constant per unit as it was in the example for incremental pricing.

The breakeven point is the point at which total revenue just equals total cost. In the example in Figure 19.6, a selling price of $10 and an average variable cost

Figure 19.6

Breakeven Chart

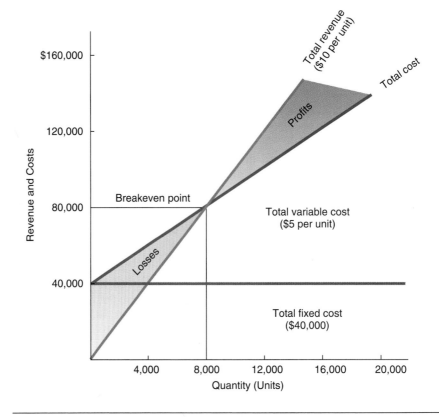

of $5 result in a per-unit contribution to fixed cost of $5. The breakeven point in terms of units is found by using the following formula:

$$\text{Breakeven Point (in Units)} = \frac{\text{Total Fixed Cost}}{\text{Per-Unit Contribution to Fixed Cost}}$$

$$\text{Breakeven Point (in Units)} = \frac{\$40,000}{\$5} = 8,000 \text{ units,}$$

where the per-unit contribution equals the product's price less the variable cost per unit. The breakeven point in dollars is found with the following formula:

$$\text{Breakeven Point (in Dollars)} = \frac{\text{Total Fixed Cost}}{1 - \dfrac{\text{Variable Cost per Unit}}{\text{Price}}}$$

$$\text{Breakeven Point (in Dollars)} = \frac{\$40,000}{1 - \dfrac{\$5}{\$10}} = \frac{\$40,000}{.5} = \$80,000.$$

Once the breakeven point has been reached, sufficient revenues will have been obtained from sales to cover all fixed costs. Any additional sales will generate per-unit profits equal to the difference between the product's selling price and the variable cost of each unit. As Figure 19.6 reveals, sales of 8,001 units (1 unit above the breakeven point) will produce net profits of $5 ($10 sales price less per-unit variable cost of $5). Once all fixed costs have been covered, the per-unit contribution will become the per-unit profit.

Target Returns. Although breakeven analysis indicates the sales level at which the firm will incur neither profits nor losses, most firms' managers include some target profit in their analyses. In some instances, management sets a desired dollar return when considering a proposed new product or other marketing action. A retailer may set a desired profit of $250,000 in considering whether to expand to a second location. In other instances, the target return may be expressed in percentages, such as a 15 percent return on sales. These target returns can be included in the breakeven calculations.

A specified dollar target return can be treated as an addition to total fixed cost in the breakeven equation. Using the example of the firm with a total fixed cost of $40,000, a selling price of $10, and an average variable cost of $5, assume that management specifies a $15,000 return. In this case, the basic breakeven formula can be modified as follows:

$$\begin{matrix} \text{Breakeven Point} \\ \text{(including specified} \\ \text{dollar target return)} \end{matrix} = \frac{\text{Total Fixed Cost} + \text{Profit Objective}}{\text{Per-Unit Contribution}}$$

$$= \frac{\$40,000 + \$15,000}{\$5}$$

$$= 11,000 \text{ units.}$$

If the target return is expressed as a percentage of sales, it can be included in the breakeven formula as a variable cost. Suppose the marketing manager in the above example seeks a 10 percent return on sales. The desired return is $1 for each product sold (the $10 per unit selling price multiplied by the 10 percent return on sales). In this case, the basic breakeven formula will remain unchanged, although the variable cost per unit will be increased to reflect the target return. In this problem, the current variable cost of $5 will be raised by the $1-per-unit target return and the per-unit contribution to fixed cost will be reduced to $4. As a result, the breakeven point will increase from 8,000 to 10,000 units:

$$\text{Breakeven Point} = \frac{\$40,000}{\$4} = 10,000 \text{ units.}$$

Evaluation of Breakeven Analysis. Breakeven analysis is an effective tool for marketers in assessing the sales required for covering costs and achieving specified profit levels. It is easily understood by both marketing and nonmarketing executives and may help them decide whether required sales levels for a certain price are in fact realistic goals. However, it has its shortcomings.

First, the model assumes that costs can be divided into fixed and variable categories. Some costs, such as salaries and advertising outlays, may be either fixed or variable depending on the particular situation. In addition, the model assumes that per-unit variable costs do not change at different levels of operation. However, these may vary because of quantity discounts, more efficient utilization of the work force, or other economies resulting from increased levels of production and sales. Finally, the basic breakeven model does not consider demand. It is a cost-based model and does not directly address the crucial question of whether consumers will actually purchase the product at the specified price and in the quantities required for breaking even or generating profits. The marketer's challenge is to modify breakeven analysis and the other cost-oriented pricing approaches to incorporate demand analysis. Pricing must be examined from the buyer's perspective. Such decisions cannot be made in a management vacuum in which only cost factors are considered.

Toward Realistic Pricing

Traditional economic theory considers both costs and demand in determining an equilibrium price. The dual elements of supply and demand are balanced at the point of equilibrium. In actual practice, however, most pricing approaches are largely cost oriented. Since purely cost-oriented approaches to pricing violate the marketing concept, modifications that will add demand analysis to the pricing decision are required.

Consumer research on such issues as degree of price elasticity, consumer price expectations, existence and size of specific market segments, and buyer perceptions of strengths and weaknesses of substitute products is necessary for developing sales estimates at different prices. Because much of the resulting data involves perceptions, attitudes, and future expectations of present and potential customers, such estimates are likely to be less precise than cost estimates.

The Modified Breakeven Concept

modified breakeven analysis
Pricing technique used to evaluate consumer demand by comparing the number of products that must be sold at a variety of prices in order to cover total cost with estimates of expected sales at the various prices.

The breakeven analysis in Figure 19.6 is based on the assumption of a constant $10 retail price regardless of quantity. But what happens when different retail prices are considered? **Modified breakeven analysis** combines the traditional breakeven analysis model with an evaluation of consumer demand.

Table 19.4 summarizes both the cost and revenue aspects of a number of alternative retail prices. The $5 unit variable cost and the $40,000 total fixed cost are based on the costs utilized in the basic breakeven model. The expected unit sales for each specified retail price are obtained from marketing research. The table contains the information necessary for calculating the breakeven point for each of the five retail price alternatives. These points are shown in Part A of Figure 19.7.

The data shown in the first two columns of Table 19.4 represent a demand schedule by indicating the number of units consumers are expected to purchase at each of a series of retail prices. As Part B of the figure shows, these data can

Table 19.4   Revenue and Cost Data for Modified Breakeven Analysis

	Revenues			Costs		Breakeven Point (Number of Sales Required to Break Even)	Total Profit (or Loss)
Price	Quantity Demanded	Total Revenue	Total Fixed Cost	Total Variable Cost	Total Cost		
$15	2,500	$ 37,500	$40,000	$12,500	$ 52,500	4,000	$(15,000)
10	10,000	100,000	40,000	50,000	90,000	8,000	10,000
9	13,000	117,000	40,000	65,000	105,000	10,000	12,000
8	14,000	112,000	40,000	70,000	110,000	13,334	2,000
7	15,000	105,000	40,000	75,000	115,000	20,000	(10,000)

Figure 19.7   Modified Breakeven Chart (a) Showing Different Sales Prices
                                   and (b) Reflecting Consumer Demand

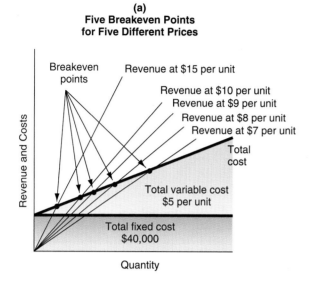

**(a)
Five Breakeven Points
for Five Different Prices**

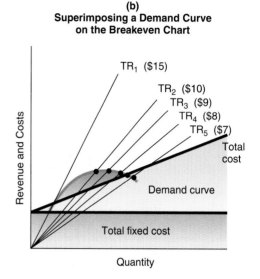

**(b)
Superimposing a Demand Curve
on the Breakeven Chart**

be superimposed onto a breakeven chart to identify the range of feasible prices for the marketer to consider.

Figure 19.7 reveals that the range of profitable prices exists from a low of approximately $8 ($TR_4$) to a high of $10 ($TR_2$), with a price of $9 ($TR_3$) generating the greatest projected profits. Changing the retail price produces a new break-even point. At a relatively high $15 ($TR_{12}$) retail price, the breakeven point is 4,000 units; at a $10 retail price, it is 8,000 units; and at the lowest price considered, $7 ($TR_5$), it is 20,000 units.

The contribution of modified breakeven analysis is that it forces the marketer to consider whether the consumer is likely to purchase the number of units of a good or service required for achieving breakeven at a given price. It demonstrates that a large number of units sold does not necessarily produce added profits, since—other things equal—lower prices are necessary for stimulating additional sales. Consequently, it is important to consider both costs and consumer demand in determining the most appropriate price.

Pricing Goods for Export to the Soviet Union and Eastern Europe

Since the currency in the Soviet Union and many Eastern European countries is practically worthless in the United States and other Western countries, businesses face the dilemma of how to price the goods and services they export there. As was shown in Chapter 3, many companies use countertrade—the practice of conducting foreign trade in the form of barter. As this practice becomes more prevalent, companies are learning how to employ it more effectively. However, the need for countertrade may disappear in the Soviet Union by the year 2000 as the Soviet economy moves toward a market-driven economy that will make the ruble convertible into Western currencies.[20]

Bottles of Pepsi with labels like these are being sold in the Soviet Union. Rather than taking payment in rubles, PepsiCo has signed countertrade agreements specifying that the company will receive other goods in exchange for the soft drink. For example, the company receives Stolichnaya vodka, which it then sells in the United States.

Source: Vladmir Vyatkin. Time Magazine.

Summary of Chapter Objectives

1. **Outline the legal constraints on pricing.** A variety of laws affect pricing decisions. The antitrust legislation outlined in Chapter 2 provides a general set of constraints. The Robinson-Patman Act amended the Clayton Act to prohibit price discrimination in sales to wholesalers, retailers, and other producers that is not based on a cost differential. This law does not cover export markets.

    At the state level, unfair-trade laws require sellers to maintain minimum prices for comparable merchandise. These laws have become less important in recent years. Fair-trade laws were one legal barrier to competition that has been removed. These laws permitted manufacturers to set minimum retail prices for products and to require their dealers to sign contracts agreeing to abide by such prices. The Consumer Goods Pricing Act banned interstate usage of fair trade.

2. **Identify the major categories of pricing objectives.** Pricing objectives should be the natural consequence of overall organizational goals and more specific marketing goals. They can be classified into four major groups: (1) profitability objectives, including profit maximization and target returns; (2) volume objectives, including sales maximization and market share; (3) meeting-competition objectives; and (4) prestige objectives.

3. **Explain the concept of price elasticity and its determinants.** Elasticity is an important element in price determination. The degree of consumer re-

sponsiveness to price changes is affected by such factors as availability of substitute or complement goods, a good's or service's status as a necessity or a luxury, the portion of a person's budget being spent, and the time perspective.

4. **List the practical problems involved in applying price theory concepts to actual pricing decisions.** In practice, there are three problems in using price theory. First, many firms do not attempt to maximize profits, a basic assumption of price theory. Second, it is difficult to actually estimate demand curves. Finally, inadequate training of managers and poor communication between economists and managers make it difficult to apply price theory in the real world.

5. **Explain the major cost-plus approaches to price setting.** Cost-plus pricing uses a base-cost figure per unit and adds a markup to cover unassigned costs and to provide a profit. It is the most commonly used method of setting prices today. There are two primary cost-oriented pricing procedures. Full-cost pricing uses all relevant variable costs in setting a product's price and allocates those fixed costs that cannot be directly attributed to the production of the specific item being priced. Incremental-cost pricing attempts to use only those costs directly attributable to a specific output in setting prices to overcome the arbitrary allocation of fixed expenses. The basic limitation of cost-oriented pricing is that it does not adequately account for product demand.

6. **List the major advantages and shortcomings of using breakeven analysis in pricing decisions.** Breakeven analysis is a means of determining the number of goods or services that must be sold at a given price to generate revenue sufficient for covering total costs. It is easily understood by both marketing and nonmarketing executives and may help them decide whether required sales levels for a certain price are realistic goals. Its shortcomings are as follows. First, the model assumes that cost can be divided into fixed and variable categories and ignores the problems of arbitrarily making some allocations. Second, it assumes that per-unit variable costs do not change at different levels of operation, ignoring the possibility of quantity discounts, more efficient utilization of the workforce, and other possible economies. Third, the basic breakeven model does not consider demand. It is a cost-based model and fails to directly address the crucial question of whether consumers will actually purchase the product at the specified price and in the quantities required for breaking even or generating profits.

7. **Explain the superiority of modified breakeven analysis over the basic breakeven model.** The modified breakeven model combines the traditional breakeven analysis model with an evaluation of consumer demand. Consumer surveys, input by marketers and channel members, and actual field tests may be used in assessing consumer reactions to different prices. These data can then be superimposed onto a breakeven chart to identify the range of feasible prices for consideration by the marketer. Thus, the modified model provides a more realistic basis for deciding on final prices.

Key Terms

price

Robinson-Patman Act

unfair-trade laws

fair-trade laws

profit maximization

target return objectives

Profit Impact of Market Strategies (PIMS) project

customary prices   monopoly

demand   elasticity

supply   cost-plus pricing

pure competition   breakeven analysis

monopolistic competition   modified breakeven analysis

oligopoly

Review Questions

1. Distinguish between fair-trade laws and unfair-trade laws. As a consumer, do you support such laws? Would your answer change if you were the owner of a small retail store?

2. Identify the major categories of pricing objectives. Give an example of each.

3. How do the pricing objectives of nonprofit organizations differ from those of profit-seeking firms?

4. What are the major price implications of the PIMS studies? Suggest possible explanations for the relationships they reveal.

5. Explain the concept of elasticity. Identify each factor influencing elasticity, and give a specific example of how it affects the degree of elasticity in a good or service.

6. Explain the advantages of using incremental-cost pricing rather than full-cost pricing. What potential drawbacks exist?

7. Why do many firms choose to deemphasize pricing as a marketing tool and instead concentrate on the other marketing mix variables in seeking to achieve a competitive advantage?

8. What do economists mean by the term *marginal analysis?* Discuss.

9. How can locating the breakeven point assist in price determination? What are the primary dangers in relying solely on breakeven analysis in pricing decisions?

10. What is the breakeven point for a product with a selling price of $35, average variable cost of $18, and related fixed cost of $25,500? What impact would a $2-per-unit profit requirement have on the breakeven point?

Discussion Questions

1. Categorize each of the following as a specific type of pricing objective. Suggest a company or product likely to utilize each pricing objective.
   a. A 6 percent increase in profits over the previous year
   b. Prices no more than 4 percent higher than prices quoted by independent dealers
   c. A 10 percent increase in market share
   d. A 20 percent return on investment (before taxes)
   e. Following the price set by the most important competitor in each market segment
   f. Setting the highest prices in the product category to maintain favorable brand image

2. Describe the market situations that exist for the following products. Defend your answers.
   a. Telephone service
   b. U.S.–made cigar
   c. Golf clubs
   d. Steel
   e. Soybeans
   f. Dishwasher

g. Compact disks
h. Skis

3. How are the following prices determined, and what do they have in common?
    a. Ticket to a movie theater
    b. Your college tuition fee
    c. Local property tax rate
    d. Printing of graduation announcements

4. "Firms whose sales reach the magic breakeven point should increase their promotional budgets to earn greater and greater amounts of profitable above-breakeven-point profits." Do you agree with this statement? Why or why not?

5. Do you agree or disagree with the following statement? "The emerging free-market economies of Eastern Europe and the Soviet Union offer opportunities for U.S. businesses, despite these countries' currency conversion problems." Explain your answer in the light of the need for U.S. exporters to use countertrade as payment for their products.

Computer Applications

Breakeven analysis, described on pages 645–647, is a useful technique for determining the sales volume, in either dollars or units, that must be achieved at a specified price in order to generate revenues sufficient to cover total production and marketing costs. Target profit returns, in either absolute dollar amounts or percentages of sales, can also be included in the breakeven model. *Modified breakeven analysis* is a technique for incorporating assessments of consumer demand into the basic breakeven model. By considering estimated sales at several different possible prices, modified breakeven analysis helps the marketer determine the volume needed for breaking even at various prices. It also shows whether such sales can be achieved.

Directions: Use menu item 9 titled "Breakeven Analysis" to solve each of the following problems.

Problem 1.   Guy Pinchot, Inc., of New Orleans manufactures a line of women's swimsuits. The swimsuits wholesale for $15. Variable cost per unit is $4. Total fixed cost of the line is $180,000.

a. How many swimsuits must be produced and sold in order to break even?

b. How much revenue must be generated from the product line in order to reach the breakeven point?

c. Pinchot's marketing director, Beth Dwyer, wants to generate profits equal to 12 percent of sales for the swimsuit line. How many units must be produced and sold in order to both break even and achieve this target return?

d. Dwyer is also considering using a cooperative advertising allowance of $1 per swimsuit to motivate retailers to push the Pinchot brand. What impact, if any, will Dwyer's proposal have on the swimwear's breakeven point if the target return is *not* included?

Problem 2.   Texas Industries of Dallas is considering the possible introduction of a new product proposed by its research and development staff. The firm's marketing director estimates that the product can be marketed at a price of $25. Total fixed cost is $132,000, and average variable cost is calculated at $19.

a. What is the breakeven point in units for the proposed product?

b. The firm's president has suggested a target profit return of $100,000 for the proposed product. How many units must be sold in order to both break even and achieve this target return?

c. Texas Industries' marketing director has made a counterproposal of a 10 percent return on sales as a realistic expectation for the proposed new product. How many units must be sold in order to both break even and achieve the return specified by the marketing director?

d. How would your answers to questions a, b, and c change if the proposed price were increased to $28?

Problem 3. The marketing research staff at Milwaukee-based Consolidated Novelties has developed the following sales estimates for a proposed new item designed to be marketed through direct-mail sales:

Proposed Selling Price	Sales Estimate (Units)
$ 8	55,000
10	22,000
15	14,000
20	5,000
24	2,800

The new product has a total fixed cost of $60,000 and a $7 variable cost per unit.

a. Which of the proposed selling prices would generate a profit for Consolidated Novelties?

b. Consolidated Novelties' director of marketing also estimates that an additional $.50-per-unit allocation for extra promotion will produce the following increases in sales estimates: 60,000 units at an $8 unit selling price, 28,000 units at $10, 17,000 units at $15, 6,000 units at $20, and 3,500 units at $24. Indicate the feasible range of prices if this proposal is implemented and results in the predicted sales increases.

c. Indicate the feasible price or prices if the $.50-per-unit additional promotion proposal is not implemented but management insists on a $25,000 target return.

Problem 4. Maureen D'Angelo, vice-president of marketing at Upstate Manufacturing in Buffalo, has assembled the following estimates of per unit variable cost for a proposed new product:

Labor	$2.52
Materials	3.60
Packaging	0.08
Sales commissions	1.00
Transportation	0.18
Other	0.62

Her calculations of fixed costs include $30,000 for manufacturing overhead, $112,000 for marketing, and $58,000 for miscellaneous fixed costs. Sales estimates for each possible price are as follows:

Proposed Selling Price	Sales Estimates (Units)
$ 9	150,000
12	55,000
15	40,000
18	25,000
20	18,000
25	8,000

a. Indicate the range of feasible prices for the new product.

b. Which price(s) is feasible if a target return of 10 percent of sales is included?

c. Which price(s) is feasible if a $40,000 target return is included?

Problem 5.   Rocky Mountain Foods of Denver is in the process of evaluating the feasibility of introducing Happy Puppy, a new canned dog food. Variable-cost estimates include the following:

Labor	$.24
Materials	.32
Transportation	.02
Packaging	.06
Sales commissions	.08
Other	.04

Fixed costs include $50,000 for manufacturing overhead outlays such as salaries, general office expenses, rent, utilities, interest charges, and depreciation; $200,000 on marketing, which includes expenditures such as salaries and advertising expenditures contracted at the beginning of the operating period; and $50,000 for research and development on the product. The proposed sales price for the firm's channel customers is 92 cents.

a. What is the breakeven point in units for Happy Puppy? How much sales in dollars is required for the firm to break even?

b. A compromise has been reached by the various members of top management at Rocky Mountain Foods concerning target profit returns for the proposed dog food. Rather than adhering to a specific dollar profit return recommended by the firm's chief financial officer, a decision has been reached to use 10 percent of sales as the target return. How many units of Happy Puppy must be sold in order to both break even and achieve the specified target return?

VIDEO CASE   19

Yamaha Motorcycles

When marketers at Japan's second largest motorcycle maker decided to create the world's fastest, most exciting motorcycle, they were all too aware of the impact their decision would have on the firm's future sales and profits. Their company, Yamaha, had suffered greatly during the 1982 to 1984 downturn in the motorcycle market, losing billions of yen during this period. High tariffs, aimed at protecting Harley-Davidson, the sole U.S. motorcycle maker, from bankruptcy, had worsened Yamaha's competitive position. If the new bike proved to be a mistake, it could cripple the company. Consequently, months of intensive planning went into the new product's development.

A total of 14 different focus groups were used to review preliminary plans for the motorcycle that would be called the V-MAX. Feedback from these groups revealed that consumers who rode the big 1200cc motorcycles wanted a "muscle car" machine, a motorcycle that would rekindle the imagery of the hot rods of the 1950's era. Focus group participants were excited about the V-MAX design; they stated that it looked like it was powerful, a machine that would impress others *if* it could deliver on its promise of power.

The power issue was in the hands of Yamaha engineers, who responded by developing an engine that would produce 135 to 140 horsepower, one of the most powerful on the market. The new bike had the right name, the right look, and it delivered the necessary power. Now it was time to move on to another major—but difficult—decision: the price tag to attach to the V-MAX.

In early planning meetings, John Porter, Yamaha's assistant product manager for the V-MAX, emphasized his belief that consumers in this market segment "want the fastest and are prepared to pay for it—they volunteered prices of $4,000, $5,000, $5,500. If it can deliver the performance, and it is executed in quality, $5,500 is not going to be unreasonable."

"Usually the customer has a pretty specific idea of what he wants in terms of price to pay, and usually that price is about 25 percent lower than the actual cost," said Dennis Stefani, Yamaha USA's manager of product planning. "Usually [we have] to look for ways to get the cost down and give him the kind of features he's looking for, or ways to make that motorcycle as exciting as possible, so that he's more willing to pay the extra money for that motorcycle."

Yamaha marketers had to consider a number of elements in deciding how to price the new product. In addition to consumer expectations concerning the price for this type of motorcycle, they had to consider the prices of competing brands offered by such companies as Honda, Kawasaki, Suzuki, BMW, and Harley-Davidson, as well as the retail prices of other products in their own motorcycle line. Production costs, as well as the costs of transporting the V-MAX from Japan to the U.S., set a floor for price considerations. Another factor involved margins for dealers who handled the line in the United States. Marketing expenses, including distribution and promotion, represented additional costs to consider. Another factor involved pricing objectives and whether relatively high prices should be used as a component of the product's overall image and to achieve prestige objectives. Finally, all of these factors had to be calculated in terms of the yen-dollar exchange rate and the impact of the tariff. After considering all the factors, Yamaha marketers decided to price the V-MAX at $5,299, which placed it near, but not at, the top of the market.

Promotional activities were designed to emphasize the unique appearance of the V-MAX, whose "muscle-car" look made it as different from other motorcycles as Ferraris are from other cars. At the same time, the advertising had to portray the bike's ability to deliver on its performance promise.

The advertising campaign featured ads set in a 1950's-era carhop drive-in, complete with the muscle cars after which it is styled. In the advertisements, though, all eyes are on the V-MAX. The ads and the bike itself succeeded in bringing an increased number of shoppers to Yamaha retail dealerships. Marketing research revealed that they liked the V-MAX's combination of unique styling and high performance, and the image the ad conveyed of V-MAX owners. Interviews with actual purchasers showed that all the agonizing over price had paid off: Most purchasers thought the bike was reasonably priced.

Although first-year sales of the V-MAX exceeded expectations, Harley-Davidson has proven to be a formidible competitor in the 700cc or larger engine market. Yamaha assistant product manager John Porter summarizes the recent sales results: "While sales initially were quite good, somewhere on the order of 5,000 bikes, we overproduced in the second year." In 1988, the decision was made to offer the V-MAX in a limited edition of only 1,500 bikes at higher prices. The combination of restricted supply and higher prices was intended to further enhance the V-MAX image.

At its September 1990 sales meeting, Yamaha announced an innovative option for the V-MAX: full insurance coverage for the first year of ownership included in the price of $7,999. Without the insurance, the bike is available for $7,414. Thus, the option is highly desirable both because of the tremendous savings over outside insurance coverage (which can range up to $2,500) and because it is amortized over the life of the vehicle loan. Although it is not available in all states, the option has proven popular where it is available and underscores Yamaha's innovative spirit.

Sources: Personal interview with Dave Ahlers, Yamaha Motor Company, May 1991. John A. Conway, "Harley Back in Gear," *Forbes* (April 20, 1987), p. 8; Norman Mayersohn, "Brute Bikes," *Popular Mechanics* (December 1985), pp. 106–112; "Yamaha Plays a Different Tune," *The Economist* (November 9, 1985), pp. 96–97; and Beth Bogart, "Harley Davidson Trades Restrictions for Profits," *Advertising Age* (August 10, 1987), p. S-27.

Questions

1. Relate the discussion of Yamaha's pricing decision for the V-MAX to the chapter discussion of price determination.

2. What pricing objectives are involved in the Yamaha pricing decision?

3. What is the relationship between costs and the final price set for the V-MAX? Do you feel that demand for the motorcycle is price elastic? Defend your answer.

4. Yamaha marketers are attempting to increase the motorcycling marketplace by attracting families to motorcycling. Is the V-MAX likely to assist them in these efforts? Why or why not?

5. Some people argue that Yamaha marketers could have expanded the sales potential of the V-MAX significantly had they selected a lower retail price. Do you agree? Explain your answer.

20

Managing the Pricing Function

1. To explain the organizational structure for pricing decisions.

2. To compare the alternative pricing strategies and explain when each strategy is most appropriate.

3. To describe how prices are quoted.

4. To identify the various pricing policy decisions that marketers must make.

5. To relate price to consumer perceptions of quality.

6. To contrast competitive bidding and negotiated prices.

7. To explain the importance of transfer pricing.

There's nothing typical about Dallas-based Southwest Airlines. Not its service, nor its attitude, nor its pricing policies. Examples prove the point: During the company's first eight years, Southwest's flight attendants wore the then fashionable shorts called "hot pants" as part of a marketing campaign stressing friendly—and somewhat irreverent—service, an attitude that came from the top. Herb Kelleher, Southwest's CEO, sets the company's tone. "We take our competition seriously," said Kelleher, "but we don't take ourselves too seriously." Thus, when a competing airline in Phoenix suggested that people might be too embarrassed to fly Southwest, Kelleher aired a commercial emphasizing low fares. Kelleher can also be found serving cocktails to passengers or working a ticket counter. When the federal government banned smoking from airline flights, the chain-smoking chairman passed out lollipops to passengers in need.

Started in 1971 as a commuter airline linking Dallas, Houston, and San Antonio, Southwest follows the simple strategy of "low fares, lots of flights, and loads of fun." The result today is a $1 billion airline providing service to 33 cities in the Midwest, Southwest, and West. Focusing on short-haul trips of an hour or less, Southwest keeps operating costs and customer fares low.

The airline makes money by going against conventional wisdom. Except for peanuts, it offers no in-flight meals, nor does it assign seats or transfer baggage to other carriers. It also avoids computer reservations systems that drain $1.85 per ticket. Instead, to book a flight, travelers or travel agents call Southwest directly. Finally, it relies on employees, motivated by profit sharing and per-mile pay, to turn its planes around in record time. (They do it in as little as 10 minutes.) These strategies have given Southwest the lowest cost structure in the industry. With expenses of 5.8 cents per available seat mile, it beats the industry average by 1.3 cents.

The result is passenger fares as low as $19 between San Diego and Phoenix and $38 for a round trip between Houston and Dallas. This penetration pricing strategy is not likely to change, because the company sees the automobile—not other airlines—as its major competitor. Kelleher is convinced that in the short-haul market, a consistent low-price policy is crucial.

Southwest also wins points because of its simple fare structure. While consumers need their own computers to figure out the complex fares and rules of other airlines, Southwest offers everyday low fares with few restrictions. Unlimited coach fares are offered on a "peak/off peak" basis, which means that weekend and evening travelers pay less. Further discounts are available to passengers who book in advance. To keep business travelers happy, Southwest started its own frequent-flyer program in 1987. The program awards travelers for the number of flights they take rather than for total mileage—a strategy that benefits the short-haul traveler.

The success of Southwest's pricing policy speaks for itself. Company experience shows that within 12 months of Southwest's arrival in a city, air travel tends to double. "We breed traffic," explains Kelleher, through frequent flights and low fares. Not surprisingly, company earnings have grown 8 percent annually in recent years.[1]

Photo source: Courtesy of Southwest Airlines Co.

Chapter Overview

In translating pricing objectives into pricing decisions, two major steps must be followed. First, someone must be assigned responsibility for making pricing decisions and administering the pricing structure. Second, the overall pricing structure—that is, the selected price and appropriate discounts for channel members as well as for various quantities and for geographic and promotional considerations—must be set.

A survey of marketing executives found that the people or groups most commonly chosen to set price structures were (1) a pricing committee composed of top executives, (2) the CEO of the company (as in the case of Southwest Airlines), and (3) the chief marketing officer. According to this survey, the pricing structure is most often administered by marketers. As Figure 20.1 indicates, the chief marketing officer is the person responsible for pricing in 51 percent of the firms surveyed. In all, marketers administered the pricing structure in over 68 percent of the companies.

In another survey, Princeton economist Alan Binder asked business managers how often their companies change prices on major products. He found that most businesses are slow to change the amount they charge customers even when demand is strong. While half of the companies questioned typically change prices once a year or less than once a year, only one out of ten has a price change more than once a month. Businesses may be slow to shift prices for a number of reasons. When demand is strong, instead of raising prices they may choose to scale down customer service and incentives. They may also take a wait-and-see attitude to avoid raising prices before their competitors do. (Few businesses want the distinction of being the first to charge more.) Since many businesses base their prices on manufacturing costs rather than consumer

Figure 20.1   Executives Responsible for Setting and Administering Price Structures

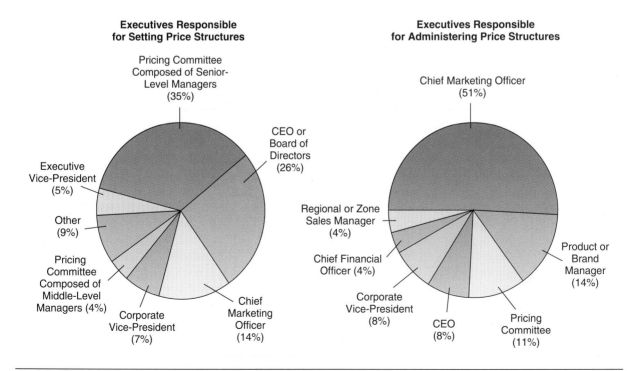

demand, they may wait for cost increases before responding with price changes. These increases are generally slower to emerge than changes in consumer demand. Finally, since many business executives believe that steady prices will help preserve a long-term relationship with customers, they are reluctant to raise prices even when demand is strong.[2]

Chapter 19 introduced the concept of price and its role in the economic system and in marketing strategy. This chapter considers who should be responsible for the pricing decision and the sequential approach to such decisions. It examines alternative pricing strategies and the administration of price structures. Finally, it considers other pricing practices such as negotiated prices, competitive bidding, and pricing in the public sector.

Alternative Pricing Strategies

The specific strategies firms use in pricing their goods and services are the result of the marketing strategies formulated to assist in accomplishing overall organizational objectives. For example, to attract value-conscious consumers, Subaru changed the marketing strategy for its Loyale line. While in 1990 a no-frills Loyale sold for $9,299, in 1991 the car sold for $200 more—but now was equipped with air conditioning, power locks, tinted glass, a rear-window defroster, and cloth seats. To reduce the price even further, the company offered a $1,000 rebate. As a result of this marketing shift, sales doubled to 2,400 cars a month. Attracting large numbers of buyers is important to Subaru since its value-pricing strategy has resulted in narrower profit margins.[3]

In contrast, in launching super-premium pet-food lines, Ralston Purina Co., Kal Kan Foods, and Quaker Oats Co. are aiming at a small segment of the pet-food market. With products such as Quaker's New Cycle, shown in Figure 20.2, the companies are using price to enhance their products' image of prestige and exclusivity. All three companies are focusing on health-conscious Americans who also want to take better care of their pets' nutritional needs. Thus, the slogan for New Cycle is "A Veterinarian's Idea of Advanced Nutrition." To enhance product image, these companies are asking retailers to create pet-nutrition centers where pet-care pamphlets are available. All three companies see enormous potential in this high-priced market segment. While pet owners outside the United States spend an average of $95 a year on each pet, Americans spend only $60, reflecting the popularity of inexpensive pet foods and the opportunity for upscale marketers.[4]

The Subaru example on the one hand and the premium pet-food makers on the other illustrate two of the three major pricing strategies. Subaru uses a penetration pricing strategy, while Ralston Purina, Kal Kan, and Quaker Oats favor a skimming strategy. The third pricing strategy alternative is one of simply meeting competition by pricing the firm's products at a level comparable to those of the primary competitors.

Skimming Pricing Strategy

skimming pricing strategy
Pricing strategy involving the use of a high price relative to competitive offerings.

A **skimming pricing strategy** is sometimes referred to as a *market-plus* approach to pricing, because it involves the use of a high price relative to prices of competing products. The name is derived from the expression *skimming the cream.*

A skimming strategy is commonly used as a market-entry price for distinctive goods or services with little or no initial competition. For example, when Lone Star

Figure 20.2

Super-Premium Pet Food:
Using High Prices to
Enhance a Prestige Image

Industries developed a super-strong, fast-drying cement called Pyrament, it priced the cement between $120 and $180 a ton, more than double the per-ton price for regular concrete. Lone Star believed that despite its premium price, Pyrament would sell in two-major markets: airports (for runway repairs) and interstate expressway systems. While regular concrete cures in seven to fourteen days, Pyrament sets in just four hours and requires 30 percent less concrete to obtain the same strength.[5]

Some firms continue to use a skimming strategy throughout most stages of the product life cycle—a decision that sometimes works and sometimes does not. When Genentech, a biotechnology company, first introduced tissue plasminogen activator (TPA), a fast-acting drug that dissolves blood clots after heart attacks, it priced the agent at $2,200 a dose. It has continued to market the drug at this price even though streptokinase, a competing agent made by Germany's Hoechst, sells for only $200. Continued sales growth for TPA has proved the effectiveness of this skimming strategy.[6]

In contrast, when Quaker State Corp. decided that the quality of its motor oil justified higher prices in an extremely competitive market, its market share dropped to 14 percent, well below the 22 percent market share it held a decade earlier. The skimming strategy failed because consumers were not convinced that Quaker State Motor Oil was a superior product, deserving a premium price. Marketing specialist Richard Winger explains, "To take a commodity out of the pricing fray you have to find a way to add some unique value. It's something that has to be built up very carefully."[7]

One benefit of a skimming strategy is that it allows the firm to quickly recover its research and development costs. The assumption is that competition will eventually drive down the price. Such was the case with VCRs and personal computers. A skimming strategy for many new products, therefore, attempts to

Figure 20.3   Advertising a Laser Printer to Additional Market Segments

 maximize the revenue received from the sale of a new product before the entry of competition. This approach is particularly important for pharmaceutical companies operating in the Republic of Korea. Since the Korean health care system does not permit price increases for drugs, Upjohn and other companies are forced to introduce products at the highest possible price—a price that ultimately will erode as competition increases.[8]

A skimming strategy is also useful in segmenting the overall market on a price basis. In the case of new products that represent significant innovations, relatively high prices convey an image of distinction and appeal to buyers who are less sensitive to price. Laser printers were introduced in the last decade at a price in the thousands. Today the best-selling laser printers, such as the one in Figure 20.3, are priced at close to $1,000. Other examples of products that were introduced using a skimming strategy include television sets, Polaroid cameras, digital watches, and pocket calculators. Subsequent price reductions have allowed the marketers of these products to appeal to additional, more price-sensitive market segments.

A third advantage of a skimming strategy is that it permits the marketer to control demand in the introductory stages of the product's life cycle and adjust its productive capacity to match demand. One danger in low initial prices for a new product is that demand may outstrip the firm's production capacity, resulting in consumer and retailer complaints and possibly permanent damage to the product's image. Excess demand occasionally results in poor-quality products, as the firm strives to satisfy consumer desires with inadequate production facilities.

During the late growth and early maturity stages of the product life cycle, the price is typically reduced for two reasons: (1) the pressure of competition and (2) the desire to expand the product's market. Figure 20.4 shows that 10 percent of the market for product X would buy the item at $10, another 20 percent for $8.75. Successive price declines will expand the firm's market as well as meet new competition.

A skimming strategy has one chief disadvantage: It attracts competition. Potential competitors see that the innovating firms receive large financial returns and thus decide to enter the market. This forces the price even lower than what it might be under a sequential skimming procedure. However, if a firm has patent protection, or a proprietary ability to exclude competition, it may use a skimming strategy for a relatively long period.

Figure 20.4

Use of Price Reductions to
Expand Total Market

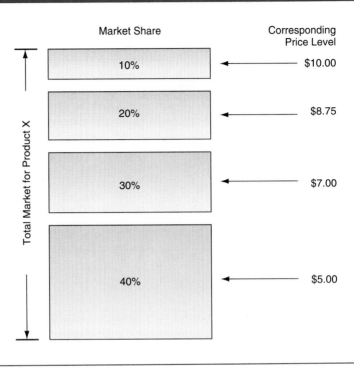

One-sixth of the respondents in the study of pricing practices cited earlier reported frequent use of a skimming strategy. Skimming appears to be more common in industrial markets than in consumer markets.

Penetration Pricing Strategy

penetration pricing strategy
Pricing strategy involving the use of a relatively low entry price as compared with competitive offerings; based on the theory that this initial low price will help secure market acceptance.

A **penetration pricing strategy** uses low prices as a major marketing weapon. Products are priced noticeably lower than competing offerings. In some instances, penetration pricing is used to introduce new products in industries characterized by dozens of competing brands. Once the product has achieved some market recognition as a result of consumer trial purchases stimulated by the lower prices, marketers may increase the price to the level of competitive products. Consumer products such as toothpaste and detergents often use this strategy. In other cases, a penetration pricing strategy may be used throughout several stages of the product life cycle as the firm seeks to maintain a reputation as a low-price competitor.

A penetration pricing strategy is sometimes called a *market-minus* approach because it is based on the premise that a lower-than-market price will attract buyers and move the brand from the "unknown" category to at least the brand-recognition stage—or even the brand-preference stage. Since in many instances the firm intends to increase the price in the future, large numbers of consumer trial purchases are critical to the success of a penetration strategy. One advantage of this strategy is that it discourages competition, since the prevailing low price does not suggest the attractive financial returns associated with a skimming strategy. General Motors used this strategy when it introduced its new line of automobile, the Saturn. The Saturn SL sports sedan sells for $2,000 less than the Toyota Corolla DLX and $1,500 less than the Honda Civic DX.[9]

COMPETITIVE EDGE

JAN BELL COMPETES ON PRICE

Conventional wisdom says you can't compete solely on price. Jan Bell Marketing Inc. doesn't believe it. Jan Bell, based in Sunrise, Florida, sells private-label jewelry to wholesale clubs for about one-third of what other manufacturers charge.

Competing on price is especially difficult today, when consumers no longer take seriously phrases like "manufacturer's list price," "discount," or "special sale." Consistency in pricing is a must—otherwise consumers will be confused or will simply wait for a sale or rebate. The only way you can compete effectively on price is by consistently selling at a noticeably lower price than everyone else, which means producing and distributing the product more cheaply than everyone else. This is Jan Bell's strategy.

Jan Bell doesn't have a magic formula for cutting costs. The company just keeps its costs to a minimum at every step of the way in every way possible. For example, it buys raw materials in bulk direct from the source, and it always pays cash. More important, it buys raw materials throughout the year, unlike other manufacturers, which buy mostly in the fall; this policy allows it to save between 10 and 15 percent on total raw-materials costs.

Jan Bell also keeps its inventory to an absolute minimum. It immediately converts its gold and diamonds into jewelry that will sell quickly, such as gold chains. It also keeps its overhead low by contracting out almost all of its assembly work. As soon as finished goods arrive, they are inspected and shipped out by Federal Express.

By basing all its decisions on price, Jan Bell has shown that competing on price alone is not impossible—just tricky. It requires total commitment and detailed information about every aspect of costs.

Discussion Questions

1. As jewelry retailers increasingly compete on factors other than price, Jan Bell's market becomes increasingly limited. How can it cope with this situation?

2. What risks are involved in Jan Bell's strategy of being the lowest-cost supplier?

Source: Paul B. Brown, "How to Compete on Price," *Inc.* (May 1990), pp. 105, 107. *Photo source:* © Michael I. Price.

Only in the last few years have U.S. manufacturers been able to use price to their advantage in the Japanese market. Before then, tariffs and quotas on items ranging from automobiles to chocolates made penetration pricing impossible. In addition, Japanese middlemen inflated the cost of imports even more. Today, companies like Toys "R" Us are opening discount chains in Japan with the result that price-based competition from U.S. exports is growing. The ability to compete on price is also affected by a new trend toward discounting. At a suburban Japanese discount store, American designer jeans sell for $39, compared to $63 at a full-priced Tokyo department store. Similarly, Reebok sneakers sell for $47 versus $67 downtown.

Penetration pricing is likely to be used when demand for the good or service is highly elastic. In such cases, large numbers of consumers are highly price sensitive. The strategy is also likely to be used when large-scale operations and long production runs result in substantial reductions in the firm's production and marketing costs. Finally, penetration pricing may be appropriate in market situations in which a new product is likely to attract strong competitors when it is introduced. Such a strategy may allow it to reach the mass market quickly and capture a large share of it prior to entry by competitors. The survey cited earlier

Shoppers examine televisions at an electronics discount store in suburban Tokyo. At such outlets, services are minimal, and so are prices. For example, a 19-inch color TV that a Japanese discounter has on sale for $93 might sell for $500 at a posh department store.

Source: Robert Wallis/SIPA.

revealed that 21 percent of the responding companies frequently use a penetration pricing strategy.

Competitive Pricing Strategy

competitive pricing strategy
Pricing strategy designed to de-emphasize price as a competitive variable by pricing a good or service at the general level of comparable offerings.

Although a number of organizations use price extensively as a competitive weapon, an even larger number prefer to use a **competitive pricing strategy.** This approach shifts the emphasis to non-price competition by concentrating marketing efforts on the product, distribution, and promotional elements of the marketing mix. As pointed out earlier, price is not only a dramatic means of achieving a competitive advantage; it is also the easiest variable for competitors to match. In fact, in industries in which competitors' offerings are relatively homogeneous, competitors are forced to match price reductions in order to maintain market share and remain competitive.

Retailers like Wal-Mart and Montgomery Ward & Company use the same strategy. Both stores advertise a price-matching pledge, assuring consumers that they will meet—and better—the competition's prices.[10] For example, Woolworth allows managers at its 1,100 variety stores to raise and lower the prices on hundreds of key items to make sure they are locally competitive.[11]

Even when product offerings are relatively heterogeneous, competitors analyze the prices of major competing offerings so that their own prices will not markedly differ. When IBM entered the personal computer market, its marketing efforts emphasized the versatility and power of the IBM computer line. However, the firm's marketers were quick to point out that each product in their personal computer line was competitively priced.

What happens when a price reduction is matched by other firms in the industry? Unless the lower prices can expand the overall market enough to offset the ensuing lost per-unit revenue, the result will be less revenue for all competitors. Nearly two-thirds of all firms surveyed in the authors' study used pricing at the level of comparable products as their primary pricing strategy.

By pricing their products at the general levels of competitive offerings, marketers largely negate the price variable in their marketing strategies. They then must emphasize non-price variables in seeking to develop areas of distinctive competence and in attracting customers. Tyco uses this approach in Figure 20.5, telling consumers that although Tyco Super Blocks and Lego Basic

Figure 20.5

Advertising a Distinctive
Difference

Blocks sell for the same price, the Tyco set contains 61 more pieces and thus is a better competitive value.

Price Quotations

The method for quoting prices depends on many factors, including cost structures, traditional industry practices, and policies of individual firms. In this section, the reasoning and methodology behind price quotations is examined.

Consider the situation facing Ford Motor Company. To reduce the cost of its cars while maintaining quality, Ford is focusing on such engineering changes as the substitution of palladium for the more expensive platinum in its catalytic converters. Similarly, Caterpillar has maintained its competitive prices by automating and consolidating many of its factories. A machine clutch that used to take 20 days to assemble is now completed in just four hours. These types of cost-cutting efforts force companies to focus on such internal operations as purchasing, manufacturing, sales, and marketing—an approach that, ultimately, results in lower product prices.[12] This strategy is becoming increasingly important in the face of competition from Japanese manufacturers whose efficiency and productivity results in low-priced quality merchandise.[13]

list price
Established price normally
quoted to potential buyers.

The basis on which most price structures are built is the **list price**—the rate normally quoted to potential buyers. List price is usually determined by one or a combination of the methods discussed in Chapter 19. The sticker price on a new automobile is a good example: It shows the list price for the basic model and then adds the prices of all options that are included.

Reductions from List Price

market price
Price a consumer or marketing intermediary actually pays for a product after subtracting any discounts, allowances, or rebates from the list price.

The amount that a consumer pays—the **market price**—may or may not be the same as the list price. In some cases, discounts or allowances reduce the list price. List price is often used as the starting point from which discounts that set the market price are taken. Discounts can be classified as cash, trade, or quantity.

Cash Discounts.   Reductions in price offered to consumers, industrial purchasers, or channel members for prompt payment of bills are known as **cash discounts.** These discounts usually specify an exact time period, such as 2/10, net 30. This means that the bill is due within 30 days, but if it is paid within 10 days the customer may subtract 2 percent from the amount due.

cash discount
Price reduction offered to a consumer, industrial user, or marketing intermediary in return for prompt payment of a bill.

Cash discounts have been a traditional pricing practice in many industries. They are legal provided they are offered to all customers on the same terms. Such discounts originally were instituted to improve the liquidity position of sellers, lower bad-debt losses, and reduce expenses associated with bill collection. Whether these advantages outweigh the relatively high cost of capital involved in cash discounts depends on the seller's need for liquidity as well as alternative sources (and costs) of funds.

Trade Discounts.   Payments to channel members for performing marketing functions are known as **trade discounts,** or *functional discounts.* The services performed by various channel members and the related costs were discussed in earlier chapters. A manufacturer's list price must incorporate the costs incurred by channel members in performing required marketing functions and expected profit margins for each member.

trade discount
Payment to a channel member or buyer for performing marketing functions; also known as a *functional discount.*

Trade discounts initially were based on the operating expenses of each category, but they have become more or less a custom in some industries. They are legal under the Robinson-Patman Act as long as all buyers in the same category, such as wholesalers and retailers, receive the same discount privileges.

Figure 20.6 shows how a chain of trade discounts works. In the first instance, the trade discount is "40 percent, 10 percent off list price" for wholesalers. In other words, the 40 percent discount on the $40 product is the trade discount the retailer receives to cover operating expenses and earn a profit. The wholesaler receives 10 percent of the $24 price to retailers to cover expenses and earn a profit. The manufacturer receives $21.60 from the wholesaler for each order.

In the second example, the manufacturer and retailer decide to bypass the wholesaler, and a trade discount of 45 percent is offered to the retailer. In this

---

Figure 20.6

Chain of Trade Discounts

"40 Percent, 10 Percent Off" Trade Discount

List Price	−	Retail Trade Discount	−	Wholesale Trade Discount	=	Manufacturer Proceeds
$40	−	$16 ($40 × 40%)	−	$2.40 ($24 × 10%)	=	$21.60 ($40 − $16 − $2.40)

"45 Percent" Trade Discount

List Price	−	Retail Trade Discount	=	Manufacturer Proceeds
$40	−	$18 ($40 × 45%)	=	$22 ($40 − $18)

instance, the retailer receives $18 for each product sold at its list price and the manufacturer receives the remaining $22. The services previously performed by the wholesaler are assumed by either the retailer or the manufacturer or shared between them.

Quantity Discounts.

quantity discount
Price reduction granted for a large-volume purchase.

Price reductions granted because of large-volume purchases are known as **quantity discounts.** These discounts are justified on the grounds that large orders reduce selling expenses and may shift a portion of the storing, transporting, and financing to the buyer. Quantity discounts are lawful provided they are offered on the same basis to all customers.

Quantity discounts may be either noncumulative or cumulative. *Noncumulative quantity discounts* are one-time reductions in list price. For example, a firm might offer the following discount schedule for a product priced at $1,000 per unit:

1 unit	$1,000
2–5 units	List less 10%
6–10 units	List less 20%
Over 10 units	List less 25%

Cumulative quantity discounts are reductions determined by purchases over a stated time period. Annual purchases of at least $25,000 might entitle the buyer to a 3 percent rebate, while purchases exceeding $50,000 would mean a 5 percent refund. These reductions are really patronage discounts, since they tend to bind the customer to a single source of supply.

Many businesses have come to expect quantity discounts in their dealings with suppliers. A resistance to these discounts has created competitive trouble for United Parcel Service with its large clients like DuPont Co., which pays more than $60 million a year for UPS shipping service. Seeing an opportunity to capture some of UPS's business, Roadway Package System Inc. has begun offering widespread discounting.[14]

Allowances.

trade-in
Credit allowance given for a used item when a customer purchases a new item.

promotional allowance
Advertising or sales promotion funds provided by a manufacturer to other channel members in an attempt to integrate promotional strategy within the channel.

Allowances are similar to discounts in that they are deductions from the price the purchaser must pay. The major categories of allowances are trade-ins and promotional allowances. **Trade-ins** are often used in the sale of durable goods such as automobiles. They preserve the new item's basic list price while reducing the amount the customer must pay by allowing credit on a used object—usually the kind being purchased. **Promotional allowances** are attempts to integrate promotional strategy within the channel. For example, manufacturers often provide advertising and sales-support allowances for channel members. Automobile manufacturers frequently offer allowances to retail dealers so that the dealers can reduce prices to stimulate sales.

Rebates.

rebate
Refund for a portion of the purchase price, usually granted by the product's manufacturer.

Still another way to reduce the consumer's cost is to offer a **rebate** —a refund of a portion of the purchase price. Rebates have been most prominently used by automobile manufacturers eager to move models during periods of slow sales. However, they are also offered in product categories ranging from appliances and sports equipment to grocery products and cigarettes. When Lorillard Inc. introduced a new brand of cigarettes called Heritage, it chose a full-price strategy but offered an immediate $4 rebate with a coupon attached to every carton. This decision was based on the fact that since many consumers consider discount cigarettes inferior, lowering the price would probably lower demand.[15]

Rebates averaging about $1,000 for every car and light truck cost Ford Motor Co. about $4 billion a year. Although these incentives have enabled Ford to hold onto its nearly 29 percent domestic market share, they have eroded profits.[16]

In a recent marketing shift, Ford decided to eliminate direct-to-customer cash rebates on most of its models. Instead, it will give the same dollar discounts to dealers, who may use the money to fund their own customer rebates or for advertising. Ford's move is in response to complaints that corporate rebates interfere with dealer marketing strategies.[17] Auto executives, including those at Ford, also question the psychological impact rebates have on consumers. They fear that consumers may be getting the message that sticker prices are too high to begin with and that they do not represent honest value. Perhaps in response to this, the GM Saturn has a ceiling price of only $12,000—a price lower than originally expected and one not likely to be reduced further through consumer rebates.[18]

Geographic Considerations

Geographic considerations are important in pricing when the shipment of heavy, bulky, low-unit-cost materials is involved. The transportation component of a product's price may be handled in several ways: (1) The buyer pays all transportation charges; (2) the seller pays all transportation charges; or (3) the buyer and the seller share the charges. This is particularly important in the case of a firm seeking to expand its geographic coverage to distant markets. How can it compete when local suppliers in the distant markets are able to avoid the considerable shipping costs that it faces? The seller has several alternatives for handling transportation costs.

FOB plant, or *FOB origin,* pricing includes no shipping charges. The buyer must pay all the freight charges. The seller pays only the cost of loading the merchandise aboard the carrier selected by the buyer. The abbreviation *FOB* means "free on board." Legal title and responsibility pass to the buyer after the purchase is loaded and a receipt is obtained from the representative of the common carrier. Phoenix-based Kiva Container Corp., a manufacturer of plastic containers, insists on FOB terms when shipping goods overseas in order to protect itself from the taxes imposed by foreign countries.[19]

Prices may also be shown as *FOB origin—freight allowed.* In this case, the seller permits the buyer to subtract transportation expenses from the bill. The amount the seller receives varies with the freight charged against the invoice. This alternative, called **freight absorption,** is commonly used by firms with high fixed costs because it permits considerable expansion of their market since the same price is quoted regardless of shipping expenses.

The same price, including transportation expenses, is quoted to all buyers when a **uniform delivered price** is the firm's policy. Such pricing is the exact opposite of FOB pricing. This system is often compared to the pricing of mail service; hence, it is sometimes called *postage-stamp pricing.* The price that is quoted includes an average transportation charge per customer, meaning that distant customers actually pay a smaller share of shipping costs while nearby customers pay what is known as *phantom freight* (the amount by which the average transportation charge exceeds the actual cost of shipping).

In **zone pricing,** which is simply a modification of a uniform delivered pricing system, the market is divided into different zones and a price is established within each zone. By including average transportation costs for shipments within each zone as part of the delivered price of goods sold within it, phantom freight is reduced but not eliminated. The primary advantage of zone pricing is that it is easy to administer and enables the seller to be more competitive in distant markets. The U.S. Postal Service's package rates depend on zone pricing.

FOB plant
"Free on board" price quotation that does not include shipping charges; also called *FOB origin.*

freight absorption
System for handling transportation costs under which the buyer may deduct shipping expenses from the cost of the goods.

uniform delivered price
System for handling transportation costs under which all buyers are quoted the same price, including transportation expenses.

zone pricing
System for handling transportation costs under which the market is divided into geographic regions and a different price is set in each region.

RESALE-PRICE MAINTENANCE

· ·

On one side are the manufacturers, who want to make sure their products are sold at or above a certain minimum price. On the other side are the retailers, who want to be free to sell products at whatever price they choose.

Resale-price maintenance is generally prohibited by federal antitrust laws, but there are numerous exceptions that enable manufacturers to dictate higher prices. As long as manufacturers impose price ranges unilaterally—that is, without consulting retailers—the practice is legal and they may suspend shipments to retailers that set prices below the required level. Retailers who violate a manufacturer's price rules may find themselves cut off—meaning that they are barred from selling the manufacturer's products.

Discounters are especially vulnerable to this practice. When a manufacturer receives complaints from full-price retailers who say they are being undersold, it may impose minimum resale prices or simply cut off the discounter. Some observers believe that manufacturers actually conspire with some retailers to eliminate others

through illegal price fixing, but the existence of such conspiracies is extremely hard to prove.

Manufacturers claim that resale-price maintenance is a legitimate means of ensuring that retailers make healthy profits, which in turn ensure that consumers receive expert sales advice and service. But critics claim that the practice is harmful to consumers as well as to discounters; according to the chair of the House Judiciary Committee, resale-price maintenance costs U.S. consumers $20 billion a year.

Discussion Questions

1. Some manufacturers set price levels because many retailers want them. Why might retailers want to have price guidelines imposed on them?

2. Do consumers really lose when retailers make "healthy" profits?

Source: Paul M. Barrett, "Anti-Discount Policies of Manufacturers Are Penalizing Certain Cut-Price Stores," *The Wall Street Journal* (February 27, 1991), pp. B1, B8.

---

basing point system
System for handling transportation costs used in some industries during the early twentieth century in which the buyer's costs included the factory price plus freight charges from the basing point city nearest the buyer.

In a **basing point system,** the price to the customer includes the price at the factory plus freight charges from the basing point city nearest the buyer. The *basing point* is the point from which freight charges are determined and is not necessarily the point from which the goods are shipped. In either case, the actual shipping point is not considered in the price quotation. The idea when this system was introduced was to permit distant marketers to compete, since all competitors will quote identical transportation rates. Few buyers would accept a basing point system today.

The best-known basing point system was the *Pittsburgh-plus* pricing procedure, which was used in the steel industry for many years. Steel price quotations contained freight charges from Pittsburgh regardless of where the steel was produced. As the industry matured, other steel centers emerged in Chicago, Gary, Cleveland, and Birmingham. Pittsburgh, however, remained the basing point for steel pricing. This meant that a buyer in Atlanta who purchased steel from a Birmingham mill had to pay phantom freight from Pittsburgh.

Pricing Policies

pricing policy
General guidelines based on pricing objectives and intended for use in specific pricing decisions.

Pricing policies are an important ingredient in the firm's total image. They provide the overall framework and consistency needed in pricing decisions. A **pricing policy** is a general guideline, based on pricing objectives, that is intended for use in specific pricing decisions.

Decisions concerning price structure generally tend to be more technical than decisions concerning pricing policies. Price structure decisions take the

Figure 20.7

Advertisement Featuring
Odd Pricing

Source: Courtesy of Wal-Mart Inc.

selected pricing policy as a given and use it to specify the applicable discounts. Pricing policies are more important strategically, particularly with respect to competitive considerations. They are the bases on which pricing decisions are made.

Pricing policies must deal with various competitive situations. The type of pricing policy used depends on the environment within which the pricing decision must be made. The types of policies firms consider are psychological pricing, unit pricing, one-price policy versus price flexibility, product line pricing, and promotional prices.

Psychological Pricing

psychological pricing
Pricing policy based on the belief that certain prices or price ranges make a good or service more appealing than others to buyers.

Psychological pricing is based on the belief that certain prices or price ranges make products more appealing to buyers than others. There is, however, no consistent research foundation for such thinking, and studies often report mixed findings. Prestige pricing, discussed in Chapter 19, is one of many forms of psychological pricing. Another is **odd pricing,** in which prices are set at odd numbers just under round numbers. A price of $4.99 is assumed to be more appealing than $5, supposedly because the buyer interprets it as $4 and change.

odd pricing
Pricing policy based on the belief that a price ending with an odd number just under a round number is more appealing—for instance, $9.99 rather than $10.

Odd pricing originally was used to force clerks to make change, thus serving as a cash control device within the firm. Now it has become a customary feature of contemporary price quotations. Moreover, some retailers use prices ending in digits other than 5, 8, or 9 in the belief that customers regard price tags of $5.95, $6.98, or $7.99 as regular retail prices but would consider $6.77 a discount price. This may be the rationale for the $96.94 price on the lawn mower in Figure 20.7.

unit pricing
Pricing policy in which prices are stated in terms of a recognized unit of measurement or a standard numerical count.

Consumer advocates often have pointed out the difficulty of comparing consumer products that are available in different package or container sizes. **Unit pricing,** in which all prices are stated in terms of some recognized unit of measurement (such as grams and liters) or a standard numerical count, is a response to this problem. It may also be considered a form of psychological pricing. Some supermarket chains have come to regard unit pricing as a competitive tool on which to base extensive advertising. However, unit pricing has not improved the shopping habits of low-income consumers as originally envisioned. Research studies have shown that it is most likely to affect purchases by better-educated consumers with higher earnings.

Price Flexibility Policies

price flexibility
Pricing policy permitting variable prices for goods and services.

Marketing executives must also determine company policy with respect to **price flexibility**—that is, will the firm have just one price or pursue a variable-price policy in the market? Generally, one-price policies characterize situations in which mass selling is employed, whereas variable pricing is more common where individual bargaining typifies transactions.

A one-price policy is common in retailing, because it facilitates mass merchandising. For the most part, once the price is set, the manager can direct attention to other aspects of the marketing mix. The $5 Clothing Store is a good example of a firm using a one-price policy. This West Coast chain sells discounted and overstocked lines of brand-name, top-quality clothing at a single price whether the garment had an original price tag of $60 or $10.[20] By contrast, Kinsey Baker, the owner of the Book Haven, an out-of-print book store in Lancaster, Pennsylvania, shaves his prices—and profits—when customers ask him to. "I want business, so I make concessions in hopes of building a long-term relationship," he said. Baker's variable pricing policy has reduced his profits by 10 percent.[21]

While variable pricing has the advantage of flexibility in selling situations, it may conflict with Robinson-Patman Act provisions. It may also lead to retaliatory pricing by competitors, and it is not well received by those who have paid the higher price.

Product Line Pricing

product line pricing
Practice of marketing different lines of merchandise at a limited number of prices.

Since most firms market several different lines, an effective pricing strategy must consider the relationship among all of these products instead of viewing each in isolation. **Product line pricing** is the practice of marketing merchandise at a limited number of prices. For example, a clothier might have three lines of men's suits—one priced at $375, a second at $525, and the most expensive at $695. These price points are important factors in achieving product line differentiation and in trading up and trading down by the firm's customers.

Product line pricing is used extensively in retail marketing. The old five-and-dime variety stores were operated using this approach. It can be an advantage to both retailer and customer. Shoppers can choose the price range they desire and then concentrate on other product variables such as color, style, and material. Retailers can purchase and offer specific lines at a limited number of price categories instead of more general assortments with dozens of different prices.

Product line pricing requires identifying the market segment or segments to which the firm is appealing. Taco Bell, for example, has rewritten its menu, grouping items by price instead of by types of food. The four main price tiers—39 cents, 59 cents, 79 cents, and 99 cents—are designed to appeal to budget-conscious fast-food customers.[22]

One problem with a product line pricing decision is that once it is made, retailers and manufacturers may have difficulty adjusting it. Rising costs, therefore, force the seller to either change the price lines, which results in confusion, or reduce costs through production adjustments, which opens the firm to the complaint that "XYZ Company's merchandise certainly isn't what it used to be!"

Promotional Pricing

promotional pricing
Pricing policy in which a lower than normal price is used as a temporary ingredient in a firm's marketing strategy.

In **promotional pricing,** a lower-than-normal price is used as a temporary ingredient in a firm's selling strategy. In some cases, promotional prices are recurrent, such as the annual shoe store "buy one pair, get the second pair for one cent" sale. Another example is a new pizza restaurant that has an opening special to attract customers. In other situations, a firm may introduce a promotional model or brand to allow it to compete in another market.

loss leaders
Product offered to consumers at less than cost to attract them to stores in the hope that they will buy other merchandise at regular prices.

Most promotional pricing occurs at the retail level. One type is **loss leaders**—goods priced below cost to attract customers who, the retailer hopes, will then buy other, regularly priced merchandise. The use of loss leaders can be effective. However, loss-leader pricing is not permitted in states with unfair-trade acts, which were discussed in Chapter 19.

Richard Portillo uses close to loss-leader prices to attract customers to his 11 Portillo's Hot Dogs restaurants in Chicago. He sells all-beef, natural-casing hot dogs at only $1.29—a few pennies above cost. Other menu items account for the chain's profitability. For example, every time a customer buys a $3.29 beef-n-cheddar croissant, Portillo makes $2.47. Such high-margin items as sandwiches, fries, soft drinks, beer, and wine account for more than half of Portillo's revenues.[23]

The potential pitfalls should be considered when making a promotional pricing decision:

1. Some consumers are little influenced by promotional pricing.

2. Continuous use of an artificially low price may result in its being accepted as customary for the product. For example, poultry, which was used as a loss leader during the 1930s and 1940s, has long suffered from this phenomenon. Airlines may suffer a similar fate. Ticket discounting is so pervasive that few consumers expect to pay full fare. According to a recent Gallup report released by the Air Transport Association, more than nine out of ten domestic air trips involved a discount ticket, which, on average, was 65 percent below full fare.[24]

Price-Quality Relationships

One of the most researched aspects of pricing is the relationship between price and the consumer's perception of product quality. In the absence of other cues, price is an important indicator of how the consumer perceives the product's quality. Many buyers believe that higher prices mean better-quality products.

The relationship between price and perceived quality is widely used in contemporary marketing. Marketers of Michelin's tires stress the price-quality link in Figure 20.8. The ad's headline and copy tell readers that the higher price for Michelin tires is justified by the company's emphasis on quality control and the durability of its tires. A similar price-quality approach was taken by Otis Elevator. The headline in a recent advertisement said, "Low bid got the service contract," while the picture showed 13 business people stuck several feet below floor level

Figure 20.8   Advertising Based on Relationship between Price and Perceived Quality

A LOT OF TIRES COST LESS THAN A MICHELIN.
THAT'S BECAUSE THEY SHOULD.

To everyone out there looking to save a few dollars on a set of tires, let's not mince words. You buy cheap, you get cheap.

There may be a lot of tires out there that cost less than a Michelin.

The only question is, what do you have to give up if you buy one?

Do they handle like a Michelin?

Do they last like a Michelin?

Are they as reliable as a Michelin?

Then ask yourself this: Do you really want to find out?

At Michelin, we make only one kind of tire. The very best we know how.

Because the way we see it, the last place a compromise belongs is on your car.

As a matter of fact, we're so obsessed with quality we make the steel cables that go into our steel-belted radials.

We even make many of the machines that make and test Michelin tires.

And our quality control checks are so exhaustive that they even include x-rays.

These and hundreds of other details, big and small (details that may seem inconsequential to others), make sure that when you put a set of Michelin tires on your car, you get all the mileage Michelin is famous for.

True, there may be cheaper tires. But if they don't last like a Michelin, are they really less expensive?

So the next time someone tries to save you a few dollars on a tire, tell him this: It's not how much you pay that counts. It's what you get for your money.

And then *he'll* know that *you* know that there's only one reason a tire costs less than a Michelin.

It deserves to.

MICHELIN
BECAUSE SO MUCH IS RIDING ON YOUR TIRES.

Source: Courtesy of Michelin Tire Corporation.

in an elevator. The aim of the ad was to convince building owners that despite its higher price, Otis's service made it the best buy.[25]

Probably the best price-quality conceptualization is the idea of *price limits.*[26] It is argued that consumers have limits within which their product-quality perceptions vary directly with price. A price below the lower limit is regarded as too cheap, whereas a price above the higher limit is perceived as too expensive. Marketers at Taco Bell realized this when they dramatically lowered their menu prices. John Martin, president and CEO of Taco Bell Corp., explains, "Even if it made money, we couldn't sell tacos at 39 cents on an ongoing basis, because consumers wouldn't think highly of the quality."[27]

Due to hyperinflation that is running at an astounding annual rate of 34,000 percent, there is little relationship between price and quality in Brazil. At one point, a consumer could buy a deluxe ice-cream sundae or two kitchen blenders for 950 cruzados ($15). Prices for the same item also vary tremendously from store to store. For example, at the point in time referred to above, the price of a simple pencil eraser ranged from 2 cruzados (3 cents) to 21 cruzados.[28]

Competitive Bidding and Negotiated Prices

Many situations involving government and organizational procurement are not characterized by set prices, particularly in cases of nonrecurring purchases such as a weapon system for the Department of Defense. Competitive bidding is a process in which buyers ask potential suppliers to give price quotations on a proposed purchase or contract. Specifications describe the item (or job) that the government or organization wishes to acquire. One of the most important tasks in purchasing management is to accurately describe what the organization seeks to buy. This generally requires the assistance of the firm's technical personnel, such as engineers, designers, and chemists.

In some cases, industrial and government purchasers use negotiated contracts instead of inviting competitive bidding for a project. In these situations, the terms of the contract are set through agreement between the buyer and the seller.

Where only one available supplier exists or where contracts require extensive research and development work, negotiated contracts are likely to be employed. In addition, some state and local governments permit their agencies to negotiate purchases under a certain limit—say, $500 or $1,000. This policy is an attempt to eliminate the economic waste involved in obtaining bids for relatively minor purchases.

The Transfer Pricing Dilemma

transfer price

Cost assessed when a product is moved from one profit center in a firm to another.

profit center

Any part of an organization to which revenue and controllable costs can be assigned.

A pricing problem peculiar to large-scale enterprises is the determination of an internal **transfer price**—the price for moving goods between **profit centers,** which are any part of the organization to which revenue and controllable costs can be assigned, such as a department. As companies expand, they tend to decentralize management and set up profit centers as a control device in the newly decentralized operation.

In large companies, profit centers might secure many of their resource requirements from within the corporate structure. The pricing problem becomes, what rate should profit center A (maintenance department) charge profit center B (sales department) for the cleansing compound used on B's floors? Should the price be the same as it would be if A did the work for an outside party? Should B receive a discount? The answers to these questions depend on the philosophy of the firm involved.

Setting an acceptable transfer pricing policy proved difficult for Bellcore, the centralized organization supporting the seven regional telephone holding companies. When Bellcore's charge-back system was first designed in 1983, it was considered equitable to all of the holding companies. Within a few years, however, it became clear that the fees charged by the word processing, graphics, technical publications, and secretarial departments were so high that researchers and engineers in the holding companies were typing their own documents and making their own overhead slides to avoid excessive transfer charges. When Bellcore executives studied this situation, they found that these four service areas were paying too high an allocation for overhead and rent, which in turn forced them to charge too much for their services. With efficiency improvements and accounting changes to more fairly determine the cost of rent and other services, Bellcore was able to correct its troubled transfer system.[29]

Sometimes transfer pricing can be manipulative. Recently, Congress has been focusing on measures that would give the Internal Revenue Service power to crack down on foreign companies and their U.S. distributors that use transfer

Figure 20.9   Transfer Pricing

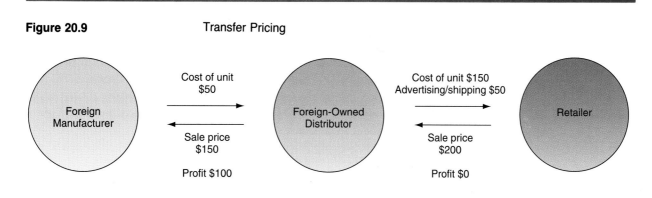

Source: Howard Gleckman, "Can Uncle Sam Mend this Hole in His Pocket?" *Business Week,* September 10, 1990, p. 48.

pricing to avoid taxes. Figure 20.9 shows how this type of pricing manipulation works. In this example, a South Korean VCR manufacturer sells its machines to its U.S. subsidiary for distribution to dealers. Although each unit costs $50 to build, the manufacturer charges its distributor $150. In turn, the distributor sells the VCRs to retailers for $200. By charging off $50 for advertising and shipping costs, the distributor is left with no profits and no tax liability. In contrast, the South Korean manufacturer has earned a $100 profit on each machine and pays taxes only in South Korea.[30]

Summary of Chapter Objectives

1. **Explain the organizational structure for pricing decisions.** Two basic steps in making pricing decisions are (1) to assign someone to administer the pricing structure and (2) to set the overall structure. The person or groups in the firm most commonly chosen to set pricing structures are (1) a pricing committee composed of top executives, (2) the company CEO, or (3) the chief marketing officer. In one study, the chief marketing executive was responsible for administering the price structure in 51 percent of the firms surveyed, while overall marketers administered the pricing structure in over 68 percent.

2. **Compare the alternative pricing strategies and explain when each strategy is most appropriate.** The alternative pricing strategies are a skimming pricing strategy, a penetration pricing strategy, and a competitive pricing strategy. Skimming pricing is commonly used as a market-entry price for distinctive products with little or no initial competition. Penetration pricing is used when there is a wide array of competing brands. Competitive pricing is employed when the marketers wish to concentrate their competitive efforts on marketing variables other than price. More than two-thirds of the firms surveyed in a recent study used the competitive pricing approach.

3. **Describe how prices are quoted.** Methods for quoting prices depend on such factors as cost structures, traditional practices in the particular industry, and policies of individual firms. Prices quoted can involve list prices, market prices, cash discounts, trade discounts, quantity discounts, and allowances such as trade-ins, promotional allowances, and rebates.

Shipping costs often figure heavily in the pricing of goods. A number of alternatives for dealing with these costs exist: FOB plant, in which the price includes no shipping charges; freight absorption, which allows the buyer to deduct transportation expenses from the bill; uniform delivered price, in which the same price, including shipping expenses, is charged to all buyers; and zone pricing, in which a set price exists within each region.

4. **Identify the various pricing policy decisions that marketers must make.** A pricing policy is a general guideline based on pricing objectives and is intended for use in specific pricing decisions. Pricing policies include psychological pricing, unit pricing, price flexibility, product line pricing, and promotional pricing.

5. **Relate price to consumer perceptions of quality.** The relationship between price and consumer perceptions of quality has been the subject of considerable research. In the absence of other cues, price is an important indicator of how the consumer perceives the product's quality. A well-known and accepted concept is that of *price limits*—limits within which the perception of product quality varies directly with price. The concept of price limits suggests that extremely low prices may be considered too cheap, thus indicating inferior quality.

6. **Contrast competitive bidding and negotiated prices.** Competitive bidding and negotiated prices are pricing techniques used primarily in the industrial sector and in government and organizational markets. Sometimes prices are negotiated through competitive bidding, in which several buyers quote prices on the same service or good. Buyer specifications describe the item that the government or industrial firm wishes to acquire. Negotiated contracts are another possibility in many procurement situations. The terms of the contract are set through talks between buyer and seller.

7. **Explain the importance of transfer pricing.** A phenomenon in large corporations is transfer pricing, in which a company sets prices for transferring goods or services from one company profit center to another. A *profit center* refers to any part of the organization to which revenue and controllable costs can be assigned. In large companies whose profit centers acquire resources from other parts of the firm, the prices charged by one profit center to another have a direct impact on the cost and profitability of the output of both profit centers.

Key Terms

skimming pricing strategy	uniform delivered price
penetration pricing strategy	zone pricing
competitive pricing strategy	basing point system
list price	pricing policy
market price	psychological pricing
cash discount	odd pricing
trade discount	unit pricing
quantity discount	price flexibility
trade-in	product line pricing
promotional allowance	promotional pricing
rebate	loss leaders
FOB plant	transfer price
freight absorption	profit center

Review Questions

1. What is meant by the price structure? Who in the organization is most likely to be responsible for setting the price structure? Who is most likely to administer the price structure?

2. What is a skimming price strategy? What are the benefits of using it?

3. What is meant by penetration pricing? Under what circumstances is penetration pricing most likely to be used?

4. Explain why most marketing executives choose meeting competitors' prices as a pricing strategy.

5. Contrast the freight absorption and uniform delivery pricing systems. Cite examples of each.

6. What is meant by a basing point system? Discuss the Pittsburgh-plus case.

7. Define pricing policy. List and discuss the reasons for establishing pricing policies.

8. When does a price become a promotional price? What are the pitfalls in promotional pricing?

9. What is the relationship between price and consumer perceptions of quality? Give examples of what you consider acceptable price ranges for a common consumer good or service, such as toothpaste, a haircut, or mouthwash. How might a price outside this range affect the product's quality image?

10. What is a transfer price? How is it used in the management of large organizations?

Discussion Questions

1. Skimming pricing, penetration pricing, and competitive pricing are the three alternative pricing strategies. Which of the three appears most appropriate for the following items? Defend your answers.
   a. Spreadsheet software package
   b. CD player
   c. Fuel additive that substantially increases automobile mileage
   d. Ultrasensitive burglar, smoke, and fire alarm
   e. New brand of toothpaste

2. Frequent-flyer programs are discount schemes designed by airlines to attract and reward consumer loyalty. What type of discount plan describes these programs? Explain. What are the potential dangers of such programs?

3. How are prices quoted for each of the following?
   a. Delta Airlines ticket to Orlando
   b. Installation of aluminum siding by a local contractor
   c. Jogging suit from a sportswear retailer
   d. New Acura Legend automobile

4. Assume that a product sells for $100 per ton and that Pittsburgh is the basing point city for transportation charges. Per-ton shipping from Pittsburgh to a potential customer in Cincinnati costs $10 per ton. The actual shipping costs of suppliers in three other cities are $8 per ton for supplier A, $11 per ton for supplier B, and $10 per ton for supplier C. Using this information, answer the following questions.
   a. What delivered price would a salesperson for supplier A quote to the customer?
   b. What delivered price would a salesperson for supplier B quote to the customer?
   c. What delivered price would a salesperson for supplier C quote to the customer?

d. How much would each supplier net (after subtracting actual shipping costs) per ton on the sale?

5. Interview one or more administrators at your school. Can you find any examples of transfer prices in use? Discuss.

Computer Applications

Problems 1 through 4 deal with situations involving competitive bidding by firms offering goods and services to industrial purchasers or government organizations. The description of the *expected net profit (ENP)* approach to competitive bidding on pages 253 and 254 should be reviewed before attempting to solve these problems.

Problems 5 and 6 focus on the application of two pricing strategies discussed in the chapter: skimming strategies and penetration pricing. The discussion of breakeven analysis on pages 645–647 should be reviewed before attempting to solve these problems.

Directions: Use menu item 6 titled "Competitive Bidding" to solve Problems 1–4. Use menu item 9 titled "Breakeven Analysis" to solve Problems 5 and 6.

Problem 1.   The manager of Rochester, New York–based Empire State Construction hopes to earn an expected net profit (ENP) of $9,000 on a job with an estimated cost of $4,000.

a. What probability of acceptance is being assigned if the manager submits a bid of $20,000?

b. What probability of acceptance is being assigned if the manager submits a bid of $14,000?

Problem 2.   Joe Worthington, marketing manager at Washington, D.C.–based Capitol Construction, wants to submit a bid for a job that he estimates will cost $80,000. He has prepared two preliminary proposals: (1) a bid for $120,000 and (2) a bid for $105,000. If Worthington estimates a 40 percent chance of the buyer accepting the first bid and a 60 percent chance of his accepting the second bid, which bid will yield the higher expected net profit?

Problem 3.   Jane Dawson is owner/manager of Hawkeye Contractors based in Des Moines, Iowa. She has estimated the probability of acceptance of her firm's bid on a state contract at 70 percent. Since her planned bid is $60,000 and the estimated cost of completing the project is $36,000, Dawson has calculated the expected net profit as $16,800.

a. What would the expected net profit be if the cost estimate turned out to be $2,000 too low?

b. What would the expected net profit be if total costs could be held to only $35,000?

Problem 4.   Houston Suppliers' marketing executive, Charlie Robbins, has spent a number of days developing a bidding strategy for two bid invitations his firm recently received from Harris County. The cost of each bid is estimated as $18,000.

a. What bid should Robbins submit in order to ensure an expected net profit of $15,000 if he estimates the expected probability of acceptance of bid 1 at 65 percent?

b. The owner of Houston Suppliers has specified a minimum acceptable expected net profit of $15,000. Robbins estimates the probability of acceptance of bid 2 at 55 percent. What bid should he submit?

c. What bid should Robbins submit if Houston Suppliers' owner requires a minimum acceptable expected net profit of $15,000 and also asks Robbins to lower the probability of bid 2's acceptance to 45 percent?

Problem 5. Midwest Industries of Kansas City is considering the possible introduction of a new service. Focus group research has revealed that consumers expect the service to be priced at approximately $50. Total fixed costs are $620,000, and average variable costs are calculated as $22.

a. What is the breakeven point (in units) for the proposed service?

b. The firm's director of marketing has suggested a target profit return of $100,000 for the service. How many units must be sold in order to both break even and achieve the target return?

c. Another proposal is to use a 12 percent return on sales as a target return instead of a fixed dollar amount. How many units must be sold in order to both break even and achieve the 12 percent return?

d. How would your answers to questions a, b, and c change if the firm's marketing director decided to implement a skimming strategy and price the service at $85?

e. How would your answers to questions a, b, and c change if the firm's marketing director decided to implement a penetration strategy and price the service at $35?

Problem 6. Ole Johansen is marketing vice-president of Seattle-based Puget Sound Manufacturing, a major appliance manufacturer with its own chain of retail outlets. Johansen is evaluating a product development department proposal for a new portable washer. Fixed costs are estimated at $1.2 million, variable costs are expected to be $40 per unit, and typical retail prices on similar products are $125.

a. What is the breakeven point for Puget Sound Manufacturing if Johansen decides to meet competition by choosing the $125 price for the portable washer?

b. Johansen is also considering a skimming strategy for the new washer and a price of $160. This strategy will help improve the image of other Puget Sound appliances and will assist Johansen in adjusting his production level to match consumer demand. However, he feels that the firm will have to spend an additional $500,000 on advertising, store displays, and other promotional materials in order to ensure the new washer's success if he decides to implement the price-skimming strategy. Determine the breakeven point if these expenditures are made and the skimming strategy is used.

c. Johansen's national sales manager feels that a penetration pricing strategy might prove effective in gaining quick consumer acceptance for the new product and in attracting to the firm's retail stores customers who might purchase additional appliances with higher margins. He suggests $100 as a retail price. How many units of the new portable washer will have to be sold in order to break even if the firm chooses the penetration strategy?

d. Suppose that Puget Sound Manufacturing selects the penetration strategy but also establishes a minimum target return of 15 percent of sales. How many units must be sold in order to both break even and achieve the target return?

VIDEO CASE   20

Looking Good Calendar Co.

Pricing a product seems a relatively simple task: add up the production and marketing costs, then pick a price that will guarantee a profit. But costs do not determine prices and control over the price frequently does not rest with the producer—the caprices of the market set the price.

"There is no relation between what it costs to make a product and what it sells for," confirms Dr. Richard Buskirk, marketing professor and director of the University of Southern California's entrepreneurship program. Therefore, it should come as no surprise that pricing is at the same time one of the most important and trickiest parts of developing a marketing mix for a good or service. If the price is too high, the product may remain on store shelves. A too-low price means lost profit opportunities and the possibility of consumer demand too great for supply.

Jim and Nick Colachis, founders of Looking Good Calendar Co., recognized the importance of pricing from the time they founded their company. They paid special attention to the price variable when they developed their initial business plan. Their overriding company objective was to make money, and they thought they had an infallible method to achieve their goal.

"Back then, it was a beginning thing: no one had heard of a male calendar," said Nick. "It was brand new, and while some people said 'Why is it going to sell?' that didn't matter to us, because we knew the co-eds wanted it."

As it turned out the Colachis brothers underestimated consumer demand. They approached the USC bookstore manager about ordering some Looking Good calendars, hoping for an initial order of five or six dozen. The manager examined the calendar carefully and ordered 3,500.

"We left the room in shock," said Nick. "We printed 5,000, so we could sell 1,500 to the fraternities and sororities, the bookstore took 3,500, and we made $12,000 in about a minute. It was a good feeling."

First-year sales for Looking Good amounted to $30,000. In recent years, sales have soared to $2 million a year and Looking Good has expanded into a company with six full-time and two part-time employees. Jim Colachis feels that much of the credit goes to a clever pricing strategy that he and his brother have used from the start. Even though they felt the market would support a considerably higher price, they deliberately priced the calendar low in order to achieve maximum market penetration.

"We've made, in our first few years, very little money, in order to promote that name," said Jim. "Sell the calendar a little bit cheaper, give someone a better deal, because we had to get the name out there, because that's valuable when it comes time to do things like posters. . . ."

To get an idea of what the market might bear in terms of price, the Looking Good partners conducted their own very informal, very unscientific marketing research. They showed the calendar to female students at USC and then asked them what they would pay for it. Nick summarized the results of the research: "Some said $4, and some said $5, and some said $6. . . . When they saw [cover model Mike Flynn's] picture they'd die, they'd say 'I want this now!' "

Jim and Nick chose to price their first calendar at $5.95 because "most of the other calendars in the store were selling for $6.95, so why not be $1 cheaper?" said Nick. By the late 1980s, the firm was offering 14 different calendars, both in color and in black and white, ranging in size from 11 to 13 inches square, and in price from $7.95 to $9.95. Since most calendars are now priced at $8.95, the typical Looking Good calendar continues to be priced one dollar below the average competitor's price.

"We undercut the market in terms of price and value," says David Gothard, Looking Good's vice president. "We use more expensive materials than other calendar companies, higher-quality photography, more expensive paper, metal spiral binding, and special processing."

Today the calendars have worldwide distribution through some 24 independent representatives. Expansion into international markets has just begun and 95 percent of current sales are generated in the United States.

Even though the success of Looking Good is impressive, even more impressive is the fact that the Colachis twins planned for this kind of growth when they started their company. "You have to plan from the beginning that you're going to be national, you're going to be the best, and you're going to put money into making your calendar stay on top," said Nick.

Looking Good's founders and their associates continue to work extended hours in pursuit of their growth and profit objectives. The acquisition of another calendar company enabled them to double the previous year's sales.

Source: Great Expectations: A Case Study in Marketing and Forecasting and What the Market Will Bear: Great Moments in Pricing, produced by KOCE-TV; telephone interviews with Nick Colachis and David Gothard.

Questions

1. What pricing strategy is being used by Looking Good for its calendars? Justify the choice of this strategy.

2. Suggest methods by which the Colachis brothers can continue to grow and protect their product concept from competitors.

3. Relate the following pricing concepts to the material in this case:
   a. trade discounts
   b. promotional allowances
   c. psychological pricing
   d. product-line pricing

4. Discuss the price-quality relationship as it relates to Looking Good pricing decisions. What other factors might serve to offset this relationship?

5. Discuss the impact of increased production costs on the ability of Looking Good to continue its current pricing strategy.

Careers in Marketing

How can someone get on a marketing career path like the one that led Evette Beckett to considerable professional and personal accomplishments? The starting point is to prepare for an entry-level position in marketing. Some basic information follows. Specifically, this appendix focuses on the following aspects of careers in marketing:

1. The kinds of positions available and the responsibilities attached to each.

2. The career ladder for the various functional areas within marketing.

3. Marketing employment trends and opportunities.

4. The marketing employment status of women and minorities.

Marketing Positions

Marketing is the single largest employer in the U.S. civilian labor force. Students intending to pursue a marketing career may be bewildered at the range of employment opportunities in the field. How can they find their way through the maze of marketing occupations and concentrate on the ones that best match their interests and talents? The starting point is to understand the duties of the different positions.

Of course, these duties may differ among organizations and industries. Certain marketing tasks may be undertaken in-house by company marketing personnel in one firm but subcontracted to outside sources by another. Indeed, a large number of agencies are available for supporting in-house marketing efforts, including advertising agencies, public relations firms, and marketing research companies. Marketing employment can thus be found in a variety of organizations: manufacturing firms, nonprofit organizations, distributive enterprises such as retailers and wholesalers, service suppliers, and research agencies.

People come to marketing careers in a variety of ways.[1] Take the case of Evette Beckett. When she graduated from Tufts University with majors in English and Drama, Beckett was best known for founding the school's first black drama group. She then went on to earn an MBA from Columbia University, specializing in marketing and finance. Having decided to establish a career in finance, she went to work for Bankers Trust. But a year with the bank's automotive accounts convinced Beckett that marketing might be a better calling for her. So she shifted over to Avon in the U.S. direct-selling consumer merchandising department, where she was responsible for developing product offers in the sales brochures.

Today, Evette Beckett is director of fragrance marketing, the largest product category in Avon's direct-selling division. In her limited spare time (Beckett is married and has a four-year-old daughter), she has won

the company's Outstanding Volunteer Award for her work with various black and professional organizations. "I've always been the kind of person who likes to juggle a lot of things at once," she says, adding, "It's important to give back to the community you live and work in. I think that helps you grow as a person as well."[2]

Photo source: © James Joern.

All of these organizations offer managerial positions in marketing, the specific duties of which vary with the organization's size, the nature of its business, and the extent to which marketing operations are departmentalized or centralized. Marketing management jobs generally involve a role in formulating the organization's marketing policies and the responsibility to plan, organize, coordinate, and control marketing operations and resources. Some typical marketing management positions are described below. (Specific titles of positions may vary among companies.)

Chief Marketing Executive.   The chief marketing executive, often called vice-president of marketing, oversees all marketing activities and is ultimately responsible for the success of the marketing function. All other marketers report through channels to this person.

Marketing Research Director.   The marketing research director determines the organization's marketing research needs and plans and directs the various stages of its marketing research projects. On the basis of this research, the director helps formulate marketing policies and strategies.

Product Manager.   The product manager is in charge of marketing operations for a particular product category or brand. The titles *brand manager* or *marketing manager* are sometimes used to describe this position.

Sales Manager.   The person responsible for managing the salesforce is the sales manager. Some of the manager's specific duties are (1) establishing sales territories; (2) deploying the salesforce; (3) recruiting, hiring, and training salespeople; and (4) setting sales quotas.

Advertising Manager.   The advertising manager plans and arranges for promotion of the company's goods or services. Among this person's duties are formulating advertising policy, selecting advertising agencies, evaluating creative promotional ideas, and setting the advertising budget.

Public Relations Officer.   The public relations officer directs all the activities that project and maintain a favorable image for the organization. This person arranges press conferences, exhibitions, news releases, and the like.

Purchasing or Procurement Manager.   The purchasing or procurement manager controls all the activities involved in acquiring merchandise, equipment, and materials for the organization.

Retail Buyer.   The retail buyer is responsible for purchasing merchandise from various sources—manufacturers, wholesalers, and importers, among others—for resale through retail outlets.

Wholesale Buyer.   The wholesale buyer purchases products from manufacturers, importers, and others for resale through wholesale channels. This buyer's duties are similar to that of the retail buyer but within the specific context of wholesale distribution.

Physical Distribution Manager.   The trend for firms to consolidate physical distribution activities under a single managerial hierarchy has significantly increased the importance of the physical distribution manager. This person—sometimes called a *logistics manager*—is involved with activities such as transportation, warehousing, inventory control, order processing, and materials handling.

Preparing for a Marketing Career

What are the requirements for obtaining a marketing job? At which positions do marketing careers typically begin? What is the usual sequence of progression to the top spots in marketing management?

The starting point is a sound education. Of course, college course work does not guarantee entry into any career field. But the more you know about business, careers, employment trends, and the like, the better prepared you will be when entering the labor force. In fact, business administration is now the most popular major on most U.S. campuses.

The Marketing Career Ladder

The career ladder to top marketing management involves a series of marketing positions.[3] These positions require varying amounts of education, but a college degree is becoming increasingly necessary, and for some positions an M.B.A.

like the one Evette Beckett obtained, is important. Opportunities for work abound both in-house and in firms that supply marketing services to other organizations, such as direct-mail companies and advertising agencies. Opportunities for marketers exist in almost all industries—in today's business environment, all firms must effectively market their goods and services in order to survive.

Following are some of the positions that aspiring marketers might hold at some point in their careers. Most companies will not offer all of these positions, and some combine positions. For example, a small firm or in-house operation probably can make do with a single copywriter who performs duties that a large firm would divide between an assistant and a senior copywriter.

Sales. Every business has to sell something. The people responsible for this activity go by a variety of titles, such as sales representative, account executive, or bank loan officer. Sales positions are equivalent to marketing "one on one." Sales representatives still go into the field to deal directly with organizational buyers, distributors, and other corporate and individual users. Sales can be a career in itself or a starting point for moving on to other kinds of marketing jobs, since working directly with a product gives the salesperson firsthand opportunities to see how it might best be marketed.

Marketing Research. Research can make the difference between a successful product or promotion and a failure. In most marketing research organizations, "researcher" is an entry-level position, for either moving on in research or expanding into another aspect of marketing. Marketing research departments operate as microcosms of the corporate hierarchy: a project manager oversees the research process, an account executive solicits business and keeps the research focused on the client's needs, a project director moves the research along the appropriate avenues, and a marketing research specialist does the actual work.

Product Management. The position of product or brand manager is a common one at firms that sell consumer goods, such as Procter & Gamble (which originated the brand manager position) and Johnson & Johnson. Major firms tend to employ teams of product managers composed of an associate and assistant product manager as well as a product manager, a group manager who oversees several teams, and a division head above the group managers. The product management team essentially operates as a self-contained marketing department; thus, each team member performs extensive marketing duties.

Advertising. The major advertising agencies employ people in every marketing position, from the direct-sales function of the account executive to the public relations expert. Yet no one walks out of college into a position of account executive or art director, or even copywriter, unless a firm is extremely small or the individual performed well as an intern somewhere. In advertising, a hierarchy exists at every position—assistant and associate copywriters, art directors, and media buyers toil to become full-fledged copywriters, art directors, and media buyers. People in "name" positions, such as account executive, art director, copywriter, and sales promotion manager, have two, three, or four steps to go before reaching the top level.

Nonprofit Organizations. Nonprofit institutions are increasingly employing marketing directors to help them solicit grants and contributions or to attract

Table A.1

Employment Projections for Selected Marketing Positions through Year 2000

Marketing Occupation	Recent Employment	Projected through Year 2000
Insurance sales workers	423,000	AFA
Manufacturers' and wholesale sales reps	1,883,000	FTA
Marketing, advertising, and PR managers	406,000	FTA
Purchasing agents and managers	458,000	AFA
Real estate agents, brokers, and appraisers	422,000	AFA
Reservation agents and ticket clerks	133,000	FTA
Retail sales workers	4,571,000	FTA
Securities and financial service sales reps	200,000	MFTA
Service sales reps	481,000	MFTA
Travel agents	142,000	MFTA
Wholesale and retail buyers	207,000	MSTA

MFTA = much faster than average; FTA = faster than average; AFA = about as fast as average; MSTA = more slowly than average.

Source: U.S. Department of Labor, Bureau of Labor Statistics, *Occupational Outlook Handbook,* 1990–1991 edition, pp. 47, 61, 231–243, 261–262.

more people to see exhibits, attend performances, and the like. There is no real hierarchy in the field, and responsibilities vary widely among nonprofit groups.

Retailing.   Retailing employs sales personnel, buyers, and operations people. A store manager directs the retail outlet's overall operations, while a general merchandising manager oversees the work performed by buyers.

Physical Distribution.   While sometimes overlooked by people seeking jobs in marketing, physical distribution, or logistics, is an essential segment of the marketing process. Logistics offers an extensive number of positions—from traffic coordinator to inventory control—all of which require the ability to think independently and coordinate effectively.

Trends and Opportunities

Table A.1 reports the Bureau of Labor Statistics employment projections through the year 2000 for selected marketing occupations. Some sales positions, such as those in the financial and service sectors, are forecasted to do particularly well during the current decade.

Marketing Salaries

In a recent year, Robert Bardagy, the chief marketing executive at ComDisco, earned $1.4 million. Dozens of other marketing executives earned six-figure incomes. The median compensation level for top sales and marketing executives was $168,700.[4]

Table A.2

Female and Minority
Employment in Selected
Marketing Occupations

Occupation	Percentage of Total		
	Female	Black	Hispanic
Purchasing managers	24.4	5.6	2.8
Managers, marketing, advertising, and public relations	32.0	3.6	2.6
Sales occupations:	48.9	6.1	5.3
Supervisors and proprietors	33.5	4.3	4.8
Sales representatives, finance and business services	41.2	4.0	3.4
Insurance sales	39.7	4.5	4.3
Real estate sales	48.5	3.2	2.6
Securities and financial services sales	27.5	2.5	2.3
Advertising and related sales	47.8	5.4	3.3
Sales representatives, commodities, except retail	19.2	3.1	3.7
Sales workers, retail and personal services	68.6	8.9	6.8

Source: U.S. Bureau of the Census, *Statistical Abstract of the United States: 1990,* 110th ed. (Washington, D.C.: Government Printing Office, 1990), pp. 389–390.

These examples illustrate the income potential of marketing careers. As for the beginning salary level, most marketing and sales graduates are hired within a range of approximately $22,000 to $25,000.[5]

Status of Women and Minorities in Marketing

Advertising, marketing research, and retailing are marketing occupations in which women traditionally have held jobs. Women often enter marketing by way of retail and personal services sales, where they outnumber men by a ratio of more than two to one, as shown in Table A.2. Women also account for nearly half of real estate sales employees.

Although there have been gains in women's employment in recent years, an earnings gap between men and women employees still exists, and a similar situation confronts minorities. Employment of blacks in marketing often constitutes less than 5 percent of a marketing job category, as Table A.2 illustrates. As in the female marketing employment situation, a higher proportion of blacks (8.9 percent) are employed as retail sales workers. The marketing employment situation for Hispanics mirrors that of women and blacks. For example, Hispanics hold only 5.3 percent of all sales jobs. However, considerable progress has been made in recent years. Female, black, and Hispanic participation in marketing employment are all expected to climb still further in the remaining years of the twentieth century.

Notes

Chapter 1

1. Doron P. Levin, "Hot Wheels," *New York Times Magazine* (September 30, 1990), pp. 32ff; Jim Treece, "A Ragtop Time Machine," *Business Week* (September 18, 1989), p. 130; and Kim B. Clark and Takahiro Fujimoto, "The Power of Product Integrity," *Harvard Business Review* (November–December 1990), pp. 107–118.

2. Matthew Grimm, "To Munich and Back with Nike and L.A. Gear," *Adweek's Marketing Week* (February 18, 1991), pp. 21–22.

3. "France's Largest Retailer Signs Trump Tower Lease," *The Wall Street Journal* (July 10, 1990), p. A4.

4. Damon Darlin, "South Koreans Crave American Fast Food," *The Wall Street Journal* (February 22, 1991), p. B1.

5. Peter F. Drucker, *The Practice of Management* (New York: Harper & Row, 1954), p. 37.

6. Joseph P. Guiltinan and Gordon W. Paul, *Marketing Management,* 4th ed. (New York: McGraw-Hill, 1990), pp. 3–4.

7. "AMA Board Approves New Marketing Definition," *Marketing News* (March 1, 1985), p. 1.

8. Wroe Alderson, *Marketing Behavior and Executive Action* (Homewood, IL: Richard D. Irwin, 1957), p. 292.

9. Robert J. Keith, "The Marketing Revolution," *Journal of Marketing* (January 1960), p. 36.

10. The company's experience is described in Chester M. Woolworth, "So We Made a Better Mousetrap," *The President's Forum* (Fall 1962), pp. 26–27.

11. Keith, "The Marketing Revolution," p. 38.

12. Theodore Levitt, *Innovations in Marketing* (New York: McGraw-Hill, 1962), p. 7.

13. General Electric Company, *Annual Report,* 1952, p. 21.

14. "From Boxes to Solutions: A Company in Transition," *Benchmark* (a Xerox Corporation magazine), VI, No. 2 (Summer 1989), pp. 1–6.

15. Susan Dillingham, "Milk Industry Moves into Promotional Wear," *Insight* (September 24, 1990), p. 43.

16. Theodore Levitt, "Marketing Myopia," *Harvard Business Review* (July–August 1960), pp. 45–56. For a different perspective, see David J. Morris, Jr., "The Railroad and Movie Industries: Were They Myopic?" *Journal of the Academy of Marketing Science* (Fall 1990), pp. 279–284.

17. Howard Schlossberg, "Electric Utilities Finally Discover Marketing," *Marketing News* (November 20, 1989), pp. 1, 2.

18. Philip Kotler and Sidney J. Levy, "Broadening the Concept of Marketing," *Journal of Marketing* (January 1969), pp. 10–15.

19. David J. Luck, "Broadening the Concept of Marketing—Too Far," *Journal of Marketing* (July 1969), pp. 53–55.

20. This interesting series of exchanges appears in the *Journal of the Academy of Marketing Science* (Summer 1979). See Gene R. Laczniak and Donald A. Michie, "The Social Disorder of the Broadened Concept of Marketing," pp. 214–232; Sidney J. Levy and Philip Kotler, "Toward a Broader Concept of Marketing's Role in Social Order," pp. 232–239; and Laczniak and Michie, "Broadening Marketing and Social Order: A Reply," pp. 239–242.

21. Gifford Claiborne, "How Marketing Rescued an L.A. Rescue Mission," *Marketing News* (December 18, 1989), p. 13.

22. James T. Bennett and Thomas J. DiLorenzo, *Unfair Competition: The Profits of Nonprofits* (Lanham, Maryland: Hamilton Press, 1989), pp. 11–16.

23. "Selling of Self," *Marketing News* (August 14, 1987), pp. 4, 11.

24. Howard Schlossberg, "Surviving in a Cause-Related World: Social Agencies Grow into Sophisticated Markets," *Marketing News* (December 18, 1989), pp. 1, 12.

25. Karen Schwartz, "Nonprofits' Bottom Line: They Mix Lofty Goals and Gutsy Survival Strategies," *Marketing News* (December 13, 1989), pp. 1, 2.

26. Philip Kotler, *Marketing for Nonprofit Organizations* (Englewood Cliffs, N.J.: Prentice-Hall, 1982), p. 9.

27. "Eye on: Packaging," *Adweek's Marketing Week* (January 8, 1990), pp. 76, 77.

28. Doron P. Levin, "Olds Offers Full Credit to Unhappy Buyers," *The New York Times* (September 8, 1989), pp. 25, 27.

29. Patricia Sellers, "Busch Fights to Have It All," *Fortune* (January 15, 1990), p. 81.

30. Clare Ansberry, "Jolt Is Aiming to Be More Than a Flash in the Can," *The Wall Street Journal* (February 3, 1989), p. B2.

31. Laurie Freeman and Laurel Wentz, "P&G's First Soviet TV Spot," *Advertising Age* (March 12, 1990), pp. 56, 57.

32. "How 'I Can't Believe It's Yogurt' Became a Frozen Favorite," *Adweek's Marketing Week* (September 4, 1989), pp. 52, 53.

33. "Business's Green Revolution," *U.S. News & World Report* (February 19, 1990), pp. 45, 46; and David Kirkpatrick, "Environmentalism: The New Crusade," *Fortune* (February 12, 1990), pp. 44–53.

34. "Wal-Mart's 'Green' Campaign to Emphasize Recycling Next," *Adweek's Marketing Week* (February 12, 1990), pp. 60, 61.

35. Dan Koeppel, "Colgate Goes 'Green' with Palmolive in a Bag," *Adweek's Marketing Week* (October 23, 1989), p. 3; and Laurie Freeman, "The Green Revolution: Procter & Gamble," *Advertising Age* (January 29, 1991), pp. 16, 24.

Chapter 2

1. John B. Hinge, "Fur Industry, Under Fire, Shows Its Claws," *The Wall Street Journal* (January 3, 1991), p. B5; Jeffrey A. Trachtenberg, "Slump Leads Furriers to Cut Prices Early," *The Wall Street Journal* (December 5, 1990), pp. B1, B8; David Kiley, "The Whole World Is Watching," *Ad Week's Marketing Week* (July 23, 1990), pp. 18–21; Jeffrey A. Trachtenberg, "Fur Industry Braces for a Rough Season," *The Wall Street Journal* (November 6, 1989), p. B1; J.D. Reed, "The Furor over Wearing Furs," *Time* (December 18, 1989), p. 72; and Cyndee Miller, "The Fur Flies as Fashion Foes Pelt It Out Over Animal Rights," *Marketing News* (December 4, 1989), pp. 2, 8.

2. Scott Hume, "KFC 'Skins' the Fat Off New Chicken Entry," *Advertising Age* (January 28, 1991), p. 9; "Bad

News for Swedish Smokers," *The Wall Street Journal* (January 11, 1991), p. A6; Stuart Elliott, "War Makes Self-Censors of Advertisers," *USA Today* (January 21, 1991), p. 2B; and Scott Hume, "The Green Revolution: McDonald's," *Advertising Age* (January 29, 1991), p. 32.

3. Louis Kraar, "Your Rivals Can Be Your Allies," *Fortune* (March 27, 1989), pp. 66–76; and *Corning International, 1989 Annual Report,* pp. 1, 10, 11.

4. Frederick H. Katayan, "Who's Fueling the Fax Frenzie," *Fortune* (October 23, 1989), pp. 151–156.

5. "Winning in the '90s," *General Mills, 1989 Annual Report,* p. 4; and Walter Kiechel III, "Corporate Strategy for the 1990s," *Fortune* (February 29, 1988), pp. 34–42.

6. George Stalk, Jr., "Time—The Next Source of Competitive Advantage," *Harvard Business Review* (July–August 1988), pp. 41–51.

7. Catherine Toups, "X-Rated Satellite Fare Leads to Penalty," *Insight* (November 26, 1990), p. 50.

8. "Environmentally Conscious Maine Bans Fruit Juice Box," *Arkansas Democrat* (August 31, 1990), p. 3A; and Russell Mitchell, "A Word of Advice, Benjamin: Stay Out of Plastics," *Business Week* (April 17, 1989), p. 23.

9. Joanne Lipman, "FTC Zaps Misleading Infomercials," *The Wall Street Journal* (June 1, 1990), pp. B1, B6.

10. Joann S. Lublin, "Volvo Settles With Texas," *The Wall Street Journal* (November 6, 1990), p. B10.

11. Robert Taylor, "Velsicol Agrees with EPA to Halt Sales of Anti-Termite Chemicals Pending Test," *The Wall Street Journal* (August 12, 1987), p. 20.

12. Robert E. Norton, "Can Business Win in Washington?" *Fortune* (December 3, 1990), pp. 75–84.

13. "The Consumer's Role: Large and Worrisome," *The Wall Street Journal* (August 10, 1987), p. 1.

14. Brian DuMaine, "How to Manage in a Recession," *Fortune* (November 5, 1990), pp. 58–72; Alecia Swasey, "Firms Change Pitch as Economy Falters,"*The Wall Street Journal* (November 9, 1990), pp. B1, B5; and " 'Value' Strategy to Battle Recession," *Advertising Age* (January 7, 1991), pp. 1, 44.

15. Hartmarx 1987 Annual Report, p. 13, and 1989 Annual Report, p. 10; Michael Oneal, "A Retailored Hartmarx Still Needs Some Altering," *Business Week* (March 9, 1987), p. 109.

16. "The Consumer's Role: Large and Worrisome," *The Wall Street Journal* (August 10, 1987), p. 1.

17. *The Story of Chewing Gum and the Wm. Wrigley Jr. Company.*

18. Elaine Underwood, "Three Strategies for Reaching Older Consumers in the 1990s," *Adweek's Marketing Week* (December 3, 1990), pp. 30–31.

19. Stephen Kreider Yoder, "Superconductivity Electrifies Japan, Inc." *The Wall Street Journal* (August 12, 1987), p. 6.

20. "Chrysler Plans Electric Minivan by '95," *Pensacola News Journal* (January 12, 1991), p. 6E.

21. Alecia Swasey, "How Innovation at P&G Restored Luster To Washed-Up Pert and Made It No. 1," *The Wall Street Journal* (December 6, 1990), pp. B1, B3.

22. Paul B. Carroll, "Computers Cut Through the Service Maze," *The Wall Street Journal* (May 1, 1990), pp. B1, B5.

23. Ronald A. Margulis, "The food industry turns to EOI for efficiency," *U.S. Distribution Journal* (March 1990), p. 16.

24. Gene Bylinsky, "America's Hot Young Scientists," *Fortune* (October 8, 1990), p. 56; and Hewlett-Packard, *1989 Annual Report,* p. 9.

25. Gene Bylinsky, "Turning R&D into Real Products," *Fortune* (July 2, 1990), pp. 72–77; Alan Murray and Urban C. Lehner, "What U.S. Scientists Discover, the Japanese Convert—Into Profit," *The Wall Street Journal* (June 25, 1990), pp. 1, A16; and Hewlett-Packard, *1989 Annual Report,* p. 9.

26. Joshua Levine, "Fantasy, Not Flesh," *Forbes* (January 22, 1990), pp. 118, 119.

27. Christy Fisher, "Hispanic influence to 'explode,' " *Advertising Age* (August 3, 1990), p. 55.

28. Michael J. McCarthy, "Coke's French Sales Lack Much Fizz Because of Cultural and Health Fears," *The Wall Street Journal* (December 19, 1989), p. A6.

29. David W. Cravens and Gerald G. Hills, "Consumerism: A Perspective for Business," *Business Horizons* (August 1970), p. 21.

30. The examples cited are from Matthew Grimm, "Reebok Retires Bungee II," *Adweek's Marketing Week* (April 30, 1990), p. 8; "Merchants of Death," *The Animal's Agenda* (July–August 1990), p. 40; Seth Mydans, "America's Tuna Fleet Is Jolted by Drive to Rescue Dolphins," *The New York Times* (May 10, 1990), pp. A1, A17; and Janice Castro, "One Big Mac, Hold the Box!: McDonald's Faces a Children's Crusade against Polystyrene," *Time* (June 25, 1990), p. 44.

31. Michael Oneal, "Anheuser-Busch: The Scandal May Be Small Beer After All," *Business Week* (May 11, 1987), p. 72.

32. Laura Bird, "Marketing in Big Brother's Shadow," *Adweek's Marketing Week* (December 10, 1990), pp. 26–30.

33. Mark Landler, "Consumers Are Getting Mad, Mad, Mad, Mad at Mad Ave," *Business Week* (April 30, 1990), pp. 70–72.

34. James F. Engel and Roger D. Blackwell, *Consumer Behavior,* 6th ed. (Hinsdale, Ill.: The Dryden Press, 1990), p. 783.

35. "Made Just for Him," *Time* (April 16, 1990), p. 49; and Rick Hampson, "Gerber Hears Family Plea, Makes Formula for Teen," *Arkansas Democrat* (April 6, 1990), pp. 1D, 3D.

36. "Selling Environmentally Friendly Products," *Inc.* (September 1990), p. 117; and Stuart Elliott, "Nike Jumps from Gym to Classroom," *USA Today* (April 18, 1990).

37. Emily T. Smith, Vicki Cahan, Naomi Freundlich, James E. Ellis, and Joseph Weber, "The Greening of Corporate America," *Business Week* (April 23, 1990), pp. 96–103.

38. For these and other examples of pollution reduction programs, see "Directory of 'Who's Who' in Environmental Marketing," *Advertising Age* (January 29, 1991), pp. 36–43; Kenneth R. Sheets, "Business's Green Revolution," *U.S. News & World Report* (February 19, 1990), pp. 45–48; David Kirkpatrick, "Environmentalism: The New Crusade," *Fortune* (February 12, 1990), pp. 44–54; David Walker, "Ridding the Nation of Polystyrene Peanuts," *Adweek's Marketing Week* (October 22, 1990), p. 17; Robert McMath, "Foods with a Social Conscience," *Adweek's Marketing Week* (April 16, 1990), p. 49; and "Painting the Town Green," *Adweek's Marketing Week* (April 16, 1990), p. 3.

39. James S. Hirsch, "Heinz to Unveil Recyclable Bottle for Its Ketchup," *The Wall Street Journal* (April 4, 1990), p. B3; Michael J. McCarthy, "Recycled Plastic Wins Converts," *The Wall Street Journal* (December 5, 1990), pp. B1, B6; Stratford P. Sherman, "Trashing a $150 Billion Business," *Fortune* (August 28, 1989), pp. 89–98; and William J. Cook, "A Lot of Rubbish," *U.S. News & World Report* (January 1, 1990), pp. 60–61.

Chapter 3

1. "The Beauty Part," *Time* (April 22, 1991), p. 61; Alecia Swasy, "At Procter & Gamble, Change Under Artzt Isn't Just Cosmetic," *The Wall Street Journal* (March 5, 1991), pp. A1, A8; and Zachary Schiller, Ted Holden, and Mark Maremont, "P&G Goes Global by Acting Like a Local," *Business Week* (August 28, 1989), p. 58; Procter & Gamble's *1990 Annual Report,* pp. 1–7; Laurie Freeman, "Japan rises to P&G's No. 3 market," *Advertising Age* (December 10, 1990), p. 42; and Laurie Freeman, "P&G products immigrate to U.S.," *Advertising Age* (October 30, 1989), p. 24.

2. "U.S. Firms with the Biggest Foreign Revenues," *Forbes* (July 23,

1990), pp. 362, 364; and Rueben Mark, "Partnerships Will Be the Thrust of the 1990s," *Fortune* (March 26, 1990), p. 32.

3. "Global Goliath: Coke Conquers the World," *U.S. News & World Report* (August 13, 1990), p. 52.

4. "U.S. Firms with the Biggest Foreign Revenues," *Forbes* (July 23, 1990), pp. 362, 364, 365.

5. "All Exports Aren't Created Equal," *The Wall Street Journal* (July 3, 1989), p. 41.

6. "Japan Upsets Computer Applecart," *Insight* (October 22, 1990), pp. 44–45.

7. Sylvia Nasar, "America Still Reigns in Services," *Fortune* (June 5, 1989), pp. 64–68.

8. "Back to Basics," *Business Week Special 1989 Bonus Issue* (1989), p. 17; and Joseph M. Sakach, "Can We Compete?" *Business Marketing* (September 1987), p. 86.

9. Jacob Park, "Overseas Sales Take Off At Last," *Fortune* (July 16, 1990), p. 77.

10. Thomas A. Stewart, "How To Manage in the New Era," *Fortune* (January 15, 1990), p. 59.

11. Randy McClain, "U.S. Execs Pick up on East German Market," *The Stars and Stripes* (April 8, 1990), p. 1.

12. Kamran Kashani and John A. Quelch, "Can Sales Promotion Go Global?" *Business Horizons* (May–June 1990), p. 38.

13. Damon Darlin, "Myth and Marketing in Japan," *The Wall Street Journal* (April 6, 1989), p. B1.

14. Richard S. Teitelbaum, "CPC's Global Spread," *Fortune* (October 22, 1990), p. 106.

15. Robin T. Peterson, "Screening Is First Step in Evaluating Foreign Market," *Marketing News* (July 9, 1990), p. 13.

16. Robert Guenther, "Citicorp Pushes Its Bank Cards Overseas," *The Wall Street Journal* (August 20, 1990), p. B1.

17. John Borrell, "Living with Shock Therapy," *Time* (June 11, 1990), p. 31.

18. Shawn Tully, "Poland's Gamble Begins to Pay Off," *Fortune* (August 27, 1990), pp. 91–96.

19. Philip Revzin, "Stalled Revolution: Romanian Elections Portend More Strife, Even Before the Count," *The Wall Street Journal* (May 21, 1990), p. 1.

20. "Borders, Barriers, and Walls," *Marketing Insights* (Spring 1990), p. 112.

21. Shawn Tully, "Full Throttle Toward a New Era," *Fortune* (November 20, 1989), pp. 131–134.

22. Ralph E. Winter, "U.S. Exporters Find the Party's Not Over," *The Wall Street Journal* (October 4, 1989), p. A2.

23. Louis Uchitelle, "Dollar's Decline as Export Engine," *The New York Times* (February 26, 1991), p. D2.

24. "Condom Ads Get Hit in Spain," *Advertising Age* (November 26, 1990), p. 44.

25. Robert Guenther, "Citicorp Pushes Its Bank Cards Overseas," *The Wall Street Journal* (August 20, 1990), p. B1.

26. Steven C. Levi, "Hong Kong Tense as Red China Takeover Nears," *Marketing News* (July 9, 1990), p. 8; and Andrew Geddes, "Ads Return to Chinese Market," *Advertising Age* (July 4, 1990), p. 41.

27. Kamran Kashani and John A. Quelch, "Can Sales Promotion Go Global?" *Business Horizons* (May–June 1990), p. 39.

28. Shawn Tully, "What the 'Greens' Mean for Business," *Fortune* (October 23, 1989), p. 159.

29. Edward O. Welles, "Being There," *Inc.* (September 1990), p. 145.

30. "Insuring Success Abroad," *Forbes* (January 7, 1991), p. 177.

31. "Y&R Fined in Jamaica Case," *Marketing News* (March 19, 1990), p. 5.

32. Stephen Phillips, "That 'Vroom!' You Hear Is Honda Motorcycles," *Business Week* (September 3, 1990), pp. 74–76; and Beth Bogart, "Harley-Davidson Trades Restrictions for Profits," *Advertising Age* (August 10, 1987), p. S-27.

33. "Taking Japan Off the Hit List," *Newsweek* (May 7, 1990), p. 50; "Japan Makes the Hit List," *Newsweek* (June 5, 1989), p. 48; and "Getting Tough with Tokyo," *Time* (June 5, 1989), pp. 50–52.

34. "Lee's Lament," *Fortune* (November 20, 1989), p. 213.

35. Mark Memmott, "U.S. Goods in Japan: Look Hard and Pay Up," *USA Today* (March 29, 1990), p. B1.

36. Clyde H. Farnsworth, "Revival of Trade Talks Stirs Political Fight in U.S.," *The New York Times* (February 25, 1991), p. D1.

37. Dom Del Prete, "Free Trade Treaty Seen as Boom for Most U.S., Canadian Firms," *Marketing News* (July 9, 1990), p. 4.

38. "Inching Toward a North American Market," *Business Week* (June 25, 1990), p. 40.

39. "The European Market Juggernaut Is on Track," *Update Magazine*, No. 3 (1990), pp. 29–31; and John Hillkirk, "The EC in 1992: 12 Nations, United," *USA Today* (May 7, 1990), p. 8E. See also John K. Ryans, Jr., and Pradeep A. Rau, *Marketing Strategies for the New Europe* (New York: American Marketing Association, 1990); and Brian Reading, "A Greater European Century," *Across the Board* (December 1989), pp. 17–20.

40. Mindy Fetterman, "Exports Rise as Trade Barriers Fall," *USA Today* (May 7, 1990), p. E1.

41. Gerhard Gschwandtner, "Robert Mosbacher's Global Selling Secrets: Five Reasons Why You Should Sell Overseas," *Personal Selling Power* (January–February 1991), p. 19.

42. Paul B. Brown, "Over There," *Inc.* (April 1990), p. 105.

43. "Going Global? Here's How," *Business Week* (July 2, 1990), p. 88.

44. Shelly Liles-Morris, "Culture to Be Hot Ticket," *USA Today* (May 7, 1990), p. E1.

45. Craig Forman, "U.S. Firms Plunk Down Cash in East Bloc," *The Wall Street Journal* (June 1, 1990), p. A12.

46. G. Pascal Zachary, "Businessland Enters Japan, Aided by 4 Big Local Firms," *The Wall Street Journal* (June 6, 1990), p. B1.

47. "New Kids on the Bloc," *Time* (July 2, 1990), p. 44.

48. Janet Meyers, "Hearst, Soviets to Test Joint Paper," *Advertising Age* (May 28, 1990), p. 59.

49. "Cowboy Capitalism Goes East," *U.S. News & World Report* (January 22, 1990), p. 35.

50. "Mad Ave. Takes the Perestroika Challenge," *Business Week* (March 5, 1990), p. 68.

51. "The Piroshki Has Landed," *Fortune* (May 7, 1990), p. 17.

52. Jeremy Main, "Making Global Alliances Work," *Fortune* (December 17, 1990), p. 121.

53. "The Stateless Corporation," *Business Week* (May 14, 1990), pp. 98–105; Alex Taylor III, "Japan's New U.S. Car Strategy," *Fortune* (September 10, 1990), pp. 65–80; and Robert B. Reich, "Who Is Us?" *Harvard Business Review* (January–February 1990), pp. 53–64.

54. Philip R. Cateora, *International Marketing,* 7th ed. (Homewood, IL: Irwin, 1990), p. 2.

55. John Hilkirk, "Matsushita to Build Huge Texas Facility," *USA Today* (May 25, 1990), p. B1.

56. "Ted Levitt Is Back in the Trenches," *Business Week* (April 9, 1990), pp. 82–84.

57. "Coke Spins Same Sell All Around the World," *USA Today* (December 28, 1988), p. 6B.

58. John F. Magee, "1992: Moves Americans Must Make," *Harvard Business Review* (May–June 1989), p. 81.

59. Lynn W. Adkins, "Think Globally, Act Locally," *World Trade* (Winter 1989), p. 24.

60. Damon Darlin, "Myth and Marketing in Japan," *The Wall Street Journal* (April 6, 1989), p. B1.

61. Laurie Peterson, "1992 and Promotion," *Adweek's Promote* (November 6, 1989), p. P7.

62. Damon Darlin, "Myth and Marketing in Japan," *The Wall Street Journal* (April 6, 1989), p. B1.

63. "Ship Me a Pepsi, Please," *Time* (April 23, 1990), p. 64; and Roger Enrico, "It's Not How Much You Sell But What You Earn," *Fortune* (March 26, 1990), pp. 124–125.

64. Sheila J. Witherington, "Where Square Pegs Fit Round Holes," *International Marketing*, no. 4 (1990), p. 15.

65. Ibid. See also Aspy P. Palia, "Worldwide Network of Countertrade Services," *Industrial Marketing Management* (February 1990), pp. 69–76.

Chapter 4

1. Todd Vogel and Chris Perry, "How Japan Is Beating the Others Cold," *Business Week* (September 3, 1990), p. 79.

2. Alfred D. Chandler, *Strategy and Structure* (Cambridge, MA: MIT Press, 1962), p. 13. See also Paul F. Anderson, "Marketing, Strategic Planning, and the Theory of the Firm," *Journal of Marketing* (Spring 1982), pp. 15–26.

3. David Kiley, "Geo Solves an Identity Crisis for Chevrolet," *Adweek's Marketing Week* (October 29, 1990), pp. 34–35.

4. Ibid.

5. Phone interview with Edith Weiner, March 4, 1991.

6. See Paul B. Brown, "What Business Are You In?" *INC* (May 1989), pp. 125–126; and Jolie Soloman, "Defining Values, Not Just Goods," *The Wall Street Journal* (January 30, 1989), p. B1.

7. *Johnson & Johnson Annual Report.*

8. *Saturn Corporation: Face to Face with the Future.*

9. Ronald Henkoff, "How to Plan for 1995," *Fortune* (December 31, 1990), pp. 74, 76.

10. David Kiley, "Toyota Hits the Passing Lane and Guns for Number Three," *Adweek's Marketing Week* (July 2, 1990), p. 4.

11. "25 Executives To Watch: Richard LeFauve," *The 1990 Business Week 1000* (April 13, 1990), p. 130.

12. "Can Maurizio Gucci Bring the Glamour Back?" *Business Week* (February 5, 1990), p. 83.

13. Andrew Tanner, "What's Wrong with This Picture?" *Forbes* (November 26, 1990), p. 154.

14. "Coca-Cola Sets Invasion of East Germany, Plans $140 Million in Investments There," *The Wall Street Journal* (April 24, 1990), p. A2.

15. Thomas C. Hayes, "The Job of Fighting Kuwait's Infernos," *The New York Times* (February 28, 1991), pp. D1 and D5.

16. John Birmingham, "Can Kodak Hold on to Its Share in a Rapidly Changing Market?" *Adweek's Marketing Week* (January 1, 1990), p. 18.

17. Derek F. Abell, "Strategic Windows," *Journal of Marketing* (July 1978), pp. 21–26. See also John K. Ryans, Jr., and William L. Shanklin, *Strategic Planning: Concepts and Implementation* (New York: Random House, 1985), p. 11.

18. Steve Lohr, "U.S. Corporations Win Kuwait Rebuilding Jobs," *The New York Times* (February 28, 1991), p. A11.

19. "Can Perrier Purify Its Reputation?" *Business Week* (February 26, 1990), p. 45; and Laura Bird, "Will Perrier's Recall Cast a Pall on Other Water Brands?" *Adweek's Marketing Week* (February 19, 1990), p. 3.

20. Chemical Banking Corporation, *1989 Annual Report.*

21. Matthew Grim, "Reebok, Reorganizing, Tries to Rediscover Its True Soul," *Adweek's Marketing Week* (January 29, 1990), p. 7.

22. Marcia Berss, "Marching to Its Own Drummer," *Forbes* (September 17, 1990), p. 95.

23. Kathryn Graven and Bradley A. Stertz, "Toyota Is Gearing Up to Expand Output, Extend Global Research," *The Wall Street Journal* (July 20, 1990), p. A1.

24. Alecia Swasey, "At Procter & Gamble, Change under Artist Isn't Just Cosmetic," *The Wall Street Journal* (March 5, 1991), p. A1.

25. Alecia Swasey, "Diaper's Failure Shows How Poor Plans, Unexpected Woes Can Kill New Products," *The Wall Street Journal* (October 9, 1990), p. B1.

26. Ely S. Lurin, "Audit Determines the Weak Link in the Marketing Chain," *Marketing News* (September 12, 1986), pp. 35, 37.

27. Dan Koeppel, "McDonald's Big Mac-Over: Looking Beyond Fast Food," *Adweek's Marketing Week* (June 25, 1990), pp. 20–21.

28. Henkoff, "How to Plan for 1995," p. 72.

29. George J. Church, "So Far, So Good," *Time* (January 28, 1991), p. 18.

30. Appendix text is adapted from Stephen K. Keiser, Robert E. Stevens, and Lynn J. Loudenback, *Contemporary Marketing Study Guide,* 5th ed. (Hinsdale, IL: The Dryden Press, 1986), pp. 482–487. A more detailed discussion of marketing plans can be found in W. Douglas Johnstone, *Planning for Corporate Growth: The Annual Marketing Plan* (Washington, D.C.: Direct Selling Association, n.d.).

Chapter 5

1. Helene Diamond, "Lights, Cameras . . . Research!," *Marketing News* (September 11, 1989), pp. 10–11.

2. Peter Bennett (ed.) *Dictionary of Marketing Terms* (Chicago: American Marketing Association, 1988), p. 184.

3. For information about how Saturn used marketing research to develop its prelaunch advertising, see Cleveland Horton, "Saturn Takes to the Air as Debut Nears," *Advertising Age* (October 1, 1990), pp, 1, 54; and Raymond Horton, Patricia Strnad, and Cleveland Horton, "Kudos for Saturn," *Advertising Age* (November 12, 1990), p. 6.

4. Nancy R. Gibbs, "You Want Me to Eat This?" *Time* (March 13, 1989), p. 76.

5. Toni Mack, "Let the Computer Do It," *Forbes* (August 10, 1987), p. 94.

6. Howard Schlossberg, "Simulated vs. Traditional Test Marketing," *Marketing News* (October 23, 1989), p. 2.

7. Martha T. Moore, "Kid Does Adult Job By Researching Toys," *USA Today* (February 13, 1990).

8. Thomas C. Kinnear and Ann R. Root (eds.) 1988 *Survey of Marketing Research* (Chicago: American Marketing Association, 1989), p. 10.

9. Jack Honomichl, "The Honomichl 50," *Marketing News* (May 28, 1990), p. 144.

10. The classification and definitions of marketing research companies are based on William G. Zikmund, *Exploring Marketing Research,* 4th ed. (Hinsdale, IL: The Dryden Press, 1992).

11. John S. Blyth, "Designers Become Enlightened About the Value of Research," *Marketing News* (September 11, 1989), p. 33.

12. Philip R. Cateora, *International Marketing,* 6th ed. (Homewood, IL: Richard D. Irwin, Inc., 1990), p. 372.

13. Gretchen Morgenson, "The Buyout That Saved Safeway," *Forbes* (November 12, 1990), pp. 88–90, 92.

14. Johnny K. Johanson and Ikujiro Nonaka, "Market Research the Japanese Way," *Harvard Business Review* (May–June, 1987), pp. 16–22. Reported in Michael R. Czinkota and Ilkaa A. Ronkainen, *International Marketing,* 2d ed. (Hinsdale, IL: The Dryden Press, 1990), p. 509.

15. Anita Gates, "Avis, Sidestepping Price Wars, Focuses on the Drive It-self," *Adweek's Marketing Week* (February 12, 1990), p. 24.

16. Jerry Goodbody, "Hallmark Wants to Sell 'Just How I Feel' all Year Long," *Adweek's Marketing Week* (November 20, 1989), p. 30.

17. Trachtenberg, "Beyond the Hidden Persuaders," pp. 135, 138.

18. Cateora, *International Marketing,* pp. 389–390.

19. Jeremy Main, "Computers of the World, Unite!," *Fortune* (September 24, 1990), p. 116.

20. BPI is defined in "1990 Survey of Buying Power—Part II, *Sales & Marketing Management* (November 12, 1989), p. 17.

21. Honomichl, "Information Resources Inc., Honomichl 50," p. H10. Also see Susan Caniniti, "What the Scanner Knows About You," *Fortune* (December 3, 1990), pp. 51–52; Martin Mayer, "Scanning the Future," *Forbes* (October 15, 1990), pp. 114–117; and Betsey Spethmann, "Software Softens Scanner Data Deluge," *Advertising Age* (May 14, 1990), p. 44.

22. Kenneth Labich, "American Takes on the World," *Fortune* (September 24, 1990), pp. 42, 44; and Jennifer Lawrence, "American Air Aims at Global Lead," *Advertising Age* (April 30, 1990), p. 52.

23. Passive people meters are discussed in Wayne Walley, "People Meter Changes Proposed," *Advertising Age* (December 18, 1990), p. 45.

24. Cateora, *International Marketing,* p. 384.

25. "Privacy Is Chic in L.A.," *Adweek's Marketing Week* (February 13, 1989), p. 2.

26. Jack Honomichl, "Answering Machines Threaten Survey Research," *Marketing News* (August 6, 1990), p. 11.

27. Harold Schlossberg, "Caller ID Gets Wires Crossed in Court," *Marketing News* (September 3, 1990), p. 1, 36.

28. William Band, "Customers Satisfaction Research Can Improve Decision Marketing," *Marketing News* (February 5, 1990), p. 13.

29. Czinkota and Ronkainen, *International Marketing,* pp. 510–511.

30. Katherine T. Smith, "Most Marketing Researchers Use Mall Intercepts," *Marketing News* (September 11, 1989), p. 16.

31. Cateora, *International Marketing,* p. 384.

32. Czinkota and Ronkainen, *International Marketing,* p. 513.

33. Jody Becker, "Good-Buy Lemon Yellow, Hello Vivid Tangerine," *McCall's* (August, 1990), p. 63.

34. Kathleen Vyn, "Nonprofits Learn How-To's of Marketing," *Marketing News* (August 14, 1989), p. 1.

35. Paul B. Brown, "The Company Store," *Inc.* (November, 1989), pp. 153–155.

36. Cateora, *International Marketing,* pp. 388–389.

37. Jeffrey Roth Feder, Jim Bartimo, Lois Therrien, and Richard Brandt, "How Software is Making Food Sales a Piece of Cake," *Business Week* (July 2, 1990), pp. 54–55.

38. Louis A. Waller, *Decision Support Systems for Marketing* (New York: The Conference Board, Inc., 1989), pp. 1, 9–10.

39. Christopher Winans, "Gallop Will Start Ringing Doorbells in Russia Soon," *The Wall Street Journal* (January 27, 1989), p. B6.

40. "An All-American Snapshot: How We Count and Why," *U.S. News & World Report* (April 2, 1990), p. 10; "They Count By Night," *Time* (February 5, 1990), p. 25; and David Wessel, "Counting the Homeless Will Tax the Ingenuity of 1990 Census Takers," *The Wall Street Journal* (November 18, 1989), p. A1, A16.

41. Kevin Maney, "Japanese Take Cues from U.S. Culture," *USA Today* (March 21, 1990), p. 2B.

42. Annetta Miller and Dody Tsiantar, "Psyching Out Consumers," *Newsweek* (February 27, 1989), p. 46–47.

43. Reprinted from Peter Banting, "Languages in International Marketing," *AMS News* (October 1990), p. 12.

Chapter 6

1. Jon Berry, "Help Wanted," *Marketing Week* (July 9, 1990), pp. 28–38.

2. This definition is adapted from James F. Engel, Roger D. Blackwell, and Paul W. Miniard, *Consumer Behavior,* 6th ed. (Hinsdale, IL: The Dryden Press, 1990), p. 3.

3. Eleanor Yy, "Asian-American Market Often Misunderstood," *Marketing News* (December 4, 1989), p. 11.

4. Engel, Blackwell, and Miniard, *Consumer Behavior,* p. 63.

5. "Japan Wants More Babies," *Parade Magazine* (May 20, 1990), p. 39.

6. For a more complete discussion of other American core values and their influence on consumer behavior, see Leon Shiffman and Leslie Kanuk, *Consumer Behavior,* 4th ed. (Englewood Cliffs, NJ: Prentice-Hall, 1991), pp. 410–424.

7. Anne B. Fisher, "What Consumers Want in the 1990s," *Adweek's Marketing Week* (January 29, 1990), p. 108.

8. Ronald Beatson, "Reaching United Europe Won't Be a Simple Task," *Advertising Age* (April 9, 1990), p. 31.

9. Michael R. Czinkota and Ilkka A. Ronkainen, *International Marketing,* 2d ed. (Hinsdale, IL: The Dryden Press, 1990), pp. 143–144.

10. Elizabeth Roberts, "Nicaraguans," *Adweek's Marketing Week* (November 13, 1989), p. 25; and David J. Wallace,

"How to Sell Yuccas to Yugas," *Advertising Age* (February 13, 1989), p. 5–6.

11. William A. Henry III, "Beyond the Melting Pot," *Time* (April 9, 1990), pp. 31–38.

12. "The Nation," *The Chronicle of Higher Education Almanac* (September 5, 1990), p. 3; Bryant Rubeg, "Understanding a Changing America," *Adweek's Marketing Week* (April 16, 1990), p. 40; Chester A. Swenson, "Marketing to Ethnics in a Long-Term Commitment," *Marketing News* (April 24, 1989), p. 7; Leon E. Winter, "Marketing to Blacks Needs Wider Range," *The Wall Street Journal* (May 7, 1990), p. B6D; and Cyndee Miller, "Upwardly Mobile Blacks Keep Strong Sense of Industry," *Marketing News* (February 19, 1990), p. 10.

13. Robey, "Understanding a Changing America," p. 40.

14. William O'Hare, "Blacks and Whites: One Market or Two?" *American Demographics* (March 1987), pp. 44–48.

15. The Conference Board report is cited in "Blacks and Whites."

16. Joseph Cosco, "African-Americans," *Adweek* (January 21, 1991), pp. 18–21; and Trudy Gallant-Stokes, "Black Marketing Marks Manship," *Black Enterprise* (February 1990).

17. "Hispanics on the Rise," *Time* (October 23, 1989), p. 43; James Peltz, "Neilson to Count Hispanic Viewers," *Satellite TV Week* (October 15, 1989), p. 3; and Robey, "Understanding a Changing America," p. 40.

18. "The Pick for Power," *Newsweek* (April 9, 1990), p. 18.

19. This study by Strategy Research Corporation is profiled in Joe Schwartz, "Hispanic Opportunities," *American Demographics* (May 1987), pp. 56, 58–59.

20. "Promotion Is Life at Tiangris," *Promote* (September 25, 1989), p. 7.

21. Joanne Lipman, "Marketers Resort More to Promotions to Woo Hispanics," *The Wall Street Journal* (September 21, 1989), p. B6.

22. Mike Czary, "Reaching the New Immigrants," *Adweek's Marketing Week* (September 11, 1989), pp. 20, 24–25, 28.

23. Michola Zaklan, "The Art of Reaching Asian Immigrants," *Adweek's Marketing Week* (January 1, 1990), p. 23.

24. Fay Rice, "Yuppie Spending Gets Serious," *Fortune* (March 27, 1989), pp. 147–149.

25. Ford S. Worthy, "Asia's New Yuppies," *Fortune* (June 4, 1990), pp. 224–235.

26. John P. Shields, Jr., "Recession Psychology," *Marketing Insights* (Spring 1990), pp. 37–40.

27. Jon Berry, "Forever Single," *Adweek's Marketing Week* (October 15, 1990), pp. 20–24.

28. Scott Donation, "Study Boosts Men's Buying Role," *Advertising Age* (December 4, 1989), p. 48.

29. "Business Bulletin," *The Wall Street Journal* (May 17, 1990), p. A1.

30. Engel, Blackwell, and Miniard, *Consumer Behavior,* pp. 174–177.

31. "In Dining, Kids Look for More Than Just Food," *The Wall Street Journal* (September 19, 1988), p. 37.

32. Peter Newcomb, "Hey, Dude, Let's Consume," *Forbes* (June 11, 1990), pp. 126–131.

33. Alecia Swasey, "Family Purse Strings Fall into Young Hands," *The Wall Street Journal* (February 2, 1990), p. B1.

34. "Resources," *Adweek's Marketing Week* (May 7, 1990), p. 49.

35. Patricia Sellers, "The ABC's of Marketing to Kids," *Fortune* (May 8, 1989), pp. 114–120.

36. Jon Berry, "Asia Minors," *Marketing Week* (July 17, 1989), pp. 32–43.

37. David Kiley, "Hallmark's Cards Address Modern Family Problems," *Adweek's Marketing Week* (March 27, 1989), p. 26.

38. Thomas Forbes, "Clutter Kills: The Junk Bonding of America," *Adweek's Marketing Week* (June 18, 1990), pp. 24–28.

39. William Bunch, "New York Waterline Personnel Prepare for 'Super Bowl Flush'," *Arkansas Democrat* (January 26, 1991), p. 3B.

40. Cyndee Miller, " 'Talkies' Take Print Ads a Step Further Than Pop-Ups," *Marketing News* (May 22, 1989), p. 13.

41. Michael J. McDermott, "For Bic, What Worked in Pens, Doesn't Do It in Perfumes," *Adweek's Marketing Week* (December 4, 1989), pp. 20–21.

42. Michael J. McCarthy, "Rewarding 'Frequent Buyer' for Loyalty," *The Wall Street Journal* (June 21, 1989), p. B1.

43. This section is based on Michael L. Rothschild and William C. Gaidis, "Behavioral Learning Theory: Its Relevance to Marketing and Promotions," *Journal of Marketing* (Spring 1981), pp. 70–78.

44. Laurie Petersen, "The Pavlovian Syndrome," *Adweek's Marketing Week* (April 9, 1990), pp. 6–9.

45. Michael Wahl, "Eye Popping Persuasion," *Marketing Insights* (June 1989), pp. 130–135.

46. Engel, Blackwell, and Miniard, *Consumer Behavior,* pp. 522–523.

47. Ibid., pp. 514–516.

48. Debra Goldman, "Spotlight: Automobiles," *Adweek's Marketing Week* (August 27, 1990), pp. 37–40.

49. George Dixon, "Keep 'em Satisfied," *Marketing News* (January 2, 1989), pp. 1, 14.

50. These categories were originally suggested in John A. Howard, *Marketing Management: Analysis and Planning* (Homewood, IL: Richard D. Irwin, Inc., 1963). This discussion is based on Donald R. Lehmann, William L. Moore, and Terry Elrod, "The Development of Distinct Choice Process Segments Over Time: A Stochastic Modeling Approach," *Journal of Marketing* (Spring 1982), pp. 48–50.

51. Ted Holden and Suzanne Woolley, "The Delicate Art of Doing Business in Japan," *Business Week* (October 2, 1989), p. 120.

52. William F. Allman, "Science 1, Advertisers 0," *U.S. News & World Report* (May 1, 1989), p. 61.

53. "Down to the Last Drop," *Time* (July 9, 1990), p. 54.

54. "Selling Goes to the Movies," *Sales & Marketing Management* (February 1990), p. 29.

55. Similar approaches are discussed in David L. Kurtz and H. Robert Dodge, *Professional Selling,* 6th ed. (Homewood, IL: Richard D. Irwin, 1991), pp. 82–83.

Chapter 7

1. Leslie Brokaw, "Anatomy of a Start-up Revisited," *Inc.* (March 1991), p. 89; Arian Sains, "MicroFridge Goes to College (and Hotels)," *Adweek's Marketing Week* (May 14, 1990), p. 26; Robert A. Mamis, "The Small Chill," *Inc.* (February 1990), pp. 66–68, 71–73; and "No 'Me Too' ", *Marketing News* (May 14, 1990), pp. 1, 10; "Where Are They Now?" *Inc.* (April 1991), p. 62.

2. Doris Jones Yany, Michael O'Neal, Stewart Ton, Mark Maremont, and Robert Neff, "How Boeing Does It," *Business Week* (July 9, 1990), p. 46.

3. Philip R. Cateora, *International Marketing,* 7th ed. (Homewood, IL: Richard D. Irwin, Inc., 1990), p. 430.

4. Christopher Payne-Taylor, "Manufacturer's New Ad Campaign is a Classic," *Marketing News* (July 31, 1989), p. 2.

5. Gerald Reisberg, "Using Data to Increase Marketing Effectiveness," *Sales & Marketing Management* (June 1990), pp. 132, 134.

6. Samuel Gilbert, "Who Your Potential Customers Are: A Marketing Application," *Sales & Marketing Management* (June 1990), p. 137.

7. See for example, Lise Heroux, "A Cross Cultural Comparison of American and Canadian Industrial Buying and Selling Processes," *Proceedings of the Southern Marketing Association* (1990).

8. Scott Payne and Karen Lowry Miller, "For Shipbuilders, It's Full Speed Ahead," *Business Week* (July 9, 1990), p. 56.

9. See David L. Kurtz, Thomas J. Steele, James P. Jolly, and M. Blaine McCormick III, "The Role of J.I.T. in Corporate Philosophy: Implications for Marketers," *Journal of Managerial Issues* (Winter 1989), pp. 133–141.

10. Paul A. Dion, Peter M. Banting, and Loretta M. Hasey, "The Impact of J.I.T. on Industrial Marketers," *Industrial Marketing Management* (February 1990), p. 44.

11. Marc Beauchamp, "No More Weekend Stands," *Forbes* (September 17, 1990), p. 191.

12. Arthur Bragg, "How to Sell In the Big Time," *Sales & Marketing Management* (February 1990), p. 42; and Arthur Bragg, "Corporations Spread the Welcome Mat," *Sales & Marketing Management* (February 1990), p. 46.

13. Bragg, "Corporations Spread the Welcome Mat," pp. 44, 46; and Bragg, "How to Sell In the Big Time," p. 44.

14. Edith Cohen, "A View From the Other Side," *Sales & Marketing Management* (June 1990), pp. 108, 112.

15. Ibid., pp. 112, 114.

16. Beauchamp, "No More Weekend Stands," pp. 191–192.

17. "Why the Long Sell May Get Shorter," *Sales & Marketing Management* (August 1989), p. 30.

18. This discussion follows Michael D. Hutt and Thomas W. Speh, *Business Marketing Management,* 3d ed. (Hinsdale, IL: The Dryden Press, 1988), pp. 75–81.

19. "Arkansans Among Guardsmen to Get Trucks Made for Sand," *Arkansas Democrat* (October 9, 1990), p. 8A.

20. Ibid., pp. 78–80, 113–122.

21. Adapted from Frederick E. Webster, Jr. and Yoram Wind, *Organizational Buying Behavior* (Englewood Cliffs, NJ: Prentice-Hall, 1972), pp. 77–80. This adaptation is modified and reprinted from Hutt and Speh, *Business Marketing Management,* p. 119. Used by permission of Prentice-Hall, Inc., and The Dryden Press.

22. Bill Kelley, "When Your Customer Base Changes," *Sales & Marketing Management* (February 1990), pp. 72–74.

23. Jean-Pierre Jeannet and Hubert D. Hennessay, *International Marketing Management* (Boston: Houghton-Mifflin, 1988), pp. 188–189.

24. Herbert E. Brown and Roger W. Brucker, "Charting the Industrial Buying

Stream," *Industrial Marketing Management* (February 1990), p. 58.

25. Paul A. Dion and Peter M. Banting, "What Industrial Marketers Can Expect from U.S.–Canadian Free Trade," *Industrial Marketing Management* (February 1990), pp. 79–80.

26. U.S. Bureau of the Census, *Statistical Abstract of the United States: 1990* (110th edition), Washington, D.C., pp. 272, 303, 326.

27. Mark R. Goldstein, "Customer No. 1: Federal Government Has Voracious Appetite," Supplement to *Advertising Age* (June 11, 1990), p. M-13.

28. Jeannet and Hennessay, *International Marketing Management,* p. 192.

29. Rick Wartzman, "Boeing Gets Order By China For 33 Aircraft," *The Wall Street Journal* (June 1, 1990), p. A6.

30. Goldstein, p. M-14, and Bruce Auster, "A Healthy Military-Industrial Complex," *U.S. News & World Report* (February 12, 1990), p. 42.

31. Goldstein, pp. M-13, M-14.

32. "K Mart Specials to Protect U.S. Soldiers," *Arkansas Democrat* (August 15, 1990), p. 11A.

33. John C. Franke, "Marketing to the Government: Contracts There For Those Who Know Where to Look," *Marketing News* (October 9, 1989), pp. 1, 7.

34. Warren H. Suss, "How to Sell to Uncle Sam," *Harvard Business Review* (November–December 1984), pp. 136–144.

35. Auster, "Healthy Military-Industrial Complex," p. 43.

36. "Octoberfest," *U.S. News & World Report* (September 24, 1990), p. 14.

Chapter 8

1. Fred Pfaff, "How Health & Tennis Corp. Segmented the New York Market," *Adweek's Marketing Week* (October 2, 1989), pp. 22–23.

2. This story is told in Richard S. Tedlown, *New and Improved: The Story of Mass Marketing in America* (New York: Basic Books, 1990), and elsewhere.

3. Selwyn Feinstein, "Koenig Finds Customers Where None Existed Before," *The Wall Street Journal* (December 29, 1989), p. 82.

4. Philip Kotler, *Marketing Management,* 7th ed. (Englewood Cliffs, NJ: Prentice-Hall, 1991).

5. Diane Crispell, Thomas Exter, and Judith Waldrop, "Snapshots of the Nation," *The Wall Street Journal Reports* (March 9, 1990), p. R12.

6. Michael Hiestand, "California's Population Bomb," *Adweek's Marketing Week* (February 20, 1989), p. 3.

7. Judith Waldrop, "2010," *American Demographics* (February, 1989), p. 18.

8. Bryant Robey, "Smaller Populations Expected for Industrial States," *Adweek's Marketing Week* (February 13, 1989), p. 48.

9. Ford S. Worthy, "A New Mass Market Emerges," *Fortune* (Pacific Rim, 1990), p. 54.

10. Patrick Rupinski, "Public Needs Education on Catfish," *Arkansas Democrat* (February 25, 1990), p. 6H; and Thomas U. Osborne, "An American Mosaic," *Marketing Insights* (June 1989), p. 82.

11. Osborne, "An American Mosaic," p. 82.

12. Reno Bartos, "The Quiet Revolution," *Marketing Insights* (June 1989), pp. 64, 71.

13. Peter Waldman, "Tobacco Firms Try Soft, Feminine Sell," *The Wall Street Journal* (December 29, 1989), p. B2.

14. "For Bargain Hunters, Life Begins at 50," *Business Week* (April 2, 1990), p. 118.

15. Melinda Beck, "Going for the Gold," *Newsweek* (April 23, 1990), p. 74; and Ken Pychtwold, "Madison Avenue Apparently Doesn't Trust Anyone Over 50," *Mobile Register* (April 10, 1990), p. 8B.

16. Beck, "Going for the Gold," p. 75.

17. "Notes on Research," *The Chronicle of Higher Education* (April 11, 1990), p. A13.

18. Jeff Ostoroff, "Tracking the Global Market," *Adweek's Marketing Week* (July 31, 1989), p. 24; and Blaise Waguespack and M. Wayne DeLozier, "Marketing to the Aging Population: The International, Private, and Public Sectors," *Advances in Marketing* (1990), pp. 280–281.

19. Information provided by J. Walter Thompson (November 1990).

20. "Average Household Slips to Record Low of About 2½ People," *The Wall Street Journal* (May 5, 1989), p. B5; and William Dunn, "Size of USA Households Hits New Low," *USA Today* (December 7, 1989), p. 1A.

21. "Singles Savings Down, Then Up," *Sales & Marketing Management* (November 1990), p. 34.

22. Worthy, "A New Mass Market Emerges," p. 54.

23. Kathleen Hughes, "California Retailer Amen Wardy Stresses Glamour to Leisure Well-Heeled Customers," *The Wall Street Journal* (January 31, 1989), p. B1.

24. David Kiley, "Western Union, On the Edge of Insolvency, Targets a Growing Base of Poor Customers," *Adweek's Marketing Week* (December 4, 1989), p. 5.

25. Donald B. Pittenger, "Gathering Foreign Demographics Is No Easy Task," *Marketing News* (January 8, 1990), pp. 23–25.

26. Judith Graham, "Research 'Finds' Fickle Consumers," *Advertising Age* (June 26, 1989), 31.

27. The discussion of VALS 2 is from Martha Farnsworth Riche, "Psychographics for the 1990s," *American Demographics* (July 1989), pp. 24–26, 30–31, 53–54.

28. Reprinted from "Ad Agency Finds 5 Global Segments," *Marketing News* (January 8, 1990), pp. 9, 17.

29. Frieda Curtindale, "A Red Hot Mustang," *American Demographics* (March 1989), p. 56.

30. Ronald Alsop, "The Shame of Smelly Clothes Makes Lever Detergent a Hit," *The Wall Street Journal* (July 2, 1987), p. 21.

31. "A Well Seated Look," *The Wall Street Journal* (January 19, 1989), p. 1.

32. Julie Liesse, "Kellog Puts $300m on Kids," *Advertising Age* (April 9, 1990), p. 1.

33. Worthy, "A New Mass Market Emerges," p. 55.

34. Worthy, "A New Mass Market Emerges," p. 57.

35. "Rich Folks Don't Fish, and Old Timers Stay Away from Softball," *Adweek's Marketing Week* (January 1, 1990), p. 26.

36. Julie Liesse and Iran Teinowitz, "Data Bases Uncover Brands' Biggest Fans," *Advertising Age* (February 19, 1990), pp. 3, 73; and "The Great Turnaround: Selling to the Individual," *Adweek's Marketing Week* (August 27, 1990), pp. 23–24. (Based on Stan Rapp and Thomas L. Collins, *The Great Marketing Turnaround: The Age of the Individual—and How to Profit From It,* Englewood Cliffs, NJ: Prentice-Hall, 1990).

37. Lawrence Hooper, " 'Segment' Is New Buzzword for PC Sellers," *The Wall Street Journal* (June 21, 1990), p. B1.

38. Subhash C. Jain, *International Marketing Management* (Boston: PWS KENT, 1990), p. 355.

39. Information provided by R.C. Cunningham of AFG Industries (November 19, 1990).

40. This section is adapted from M. Dale Beckman, Louis E. Boone, and David L. Kurtz, *Foundations of Marketing,* 5th ed. (Toronto: Holt, Rinehart, and Winston of Canada, 1991). The materials were originally prepared by Professor J.D. Forbes of the University of British Columbia and are reprinted by permission of the authors and publisher.

41. Laurie Petersen, "Aiming at the Household," *Adweek's Marketing Week* (February 27, 1989), p. 21.

42. Information provided by the American Dental Association (November 1990).

43. John Marcom, Jr., "Cola Attack," *Forbes* (November 26, 1990), p. 48.

44. Nancy Youman, "Re-Mapping the American People, Block by Block," *Adweek's Marketing Week* (April 9, 1990), pp. 2–3.

45. Julie Liesse, "Alpo Eats into Cat Food Market," *Advertising Age* (October 1, 1990), p. 51; and Grand Metropolitan, *1989 Annual Report,* p. 15.

46. "International Newsletter," *Sales & Marketing Management* (April 1987), p. 86.

47. Paula Span, "Have Idea, Will Travel," *Savvy* (January 1987), pp. 24, 26, 76.

48. VF Corporation, *1989 Annual Report,* pp. 7–8.

49. Roula Kholef, "The Niche Word," *Forbes* (January 8, 1990), p. 307.

50. Susan V. Lawrence, "The Revolt of the Chinese Consumer," *U.S. News & World Report* (December 3, 1990), p. 62.

51. Nancy Youman, "Post Boomlet Kinder-Care Makes Parents a Priority," *Adweek's Marketing Week* (July 9, 1990), p. 20.

52. Penny Taylor, "Microtargeting Key Element Behind Cable TV Appeals," *Puget Sound Business Journal* (June 26, 1989), p. 25.

53. Patricia Winters, "Bufferin Aims at 50-Plus," *Advertising Age* (October 23, 1989), p. 4.

54. John Mohavalli, "Toward an Age of Customerized Magazines," *Adweek Special Report* (February 12, 1989), pp. 36–37.

Chapter 9

1. Brian Dumaine, "Ability to Innovate," *Fortune* (January 29, 1990), pp. 43–44; Russell Mitchell, "Masters of Innovation," *Business Week* (April 10, 1989), pp. 58–63; 3M 1988 and 1989 annual reports; "The Case of the Glue That Didn't Stick Right," *Training* (February 1985), p. 38; "The 'Blunders' Making Millions for 3M," *Business Week* (July 18, 1984), p. 118; and "Post-it Notes Click Thanks to Entrepreneurial Spirit," *Marketing News* (August 31, 1984), p. 21.

2. Rosalind Klein Berlin, "Picky! Picky! Picky! Meet the World's Toughest Customers," *Fortune* (December 3, 1990), p. 45.

3. This three-way classification of consumer goods was first proposed by Melvin T. Copeland. See his *Principles of Merchandising* (New York: McGraw-Hill, 1924), Chapters 2 through 4.

4. Laurie Petersen, "Study Confirms Impulse Buying on Rise," *Promote* (October 12, 1987), p. 6.

5. Robert W. Haas, *Industrial Marketing Management,* 4th ed., (Boston: PWS-KENT Publishing Co., 1989), pp. 11–21.

6. Judann Dagnoli, "GF Ices Cappuccino: New Adult Beverage Market Seen," *Advertising Age* (July 23, 1990), p. 49.

7. Frederick H. Katayama, "Who's Fueling the Fax Frenzy," *Fortune* (October 23, 1989), pp. 151–156.

8. Sue Woodman, "Gone Yesterday, Here Today," *Adweek's Marketing Week* (November 7, 1988), pp. H.P. 40–41.

9. Joshua Levine, "Cluck, Cluck, Oink," *Forbes* (April 16, 1990), pp. 126–128; and Julie Liesse Erickson, "Pork Ads Rib Its Meat Rivals," *Advertising Age* (January 16, 1989), p. 54.

10. "Chicken King Tyson To Perch in London," *Fortune* (November 5, 1990), p. 166.

11. Gerald Schoenfeld, "Treat Old Products Like New," *Marketing News* (July 31, 1989), p. 15.

12. William C. Symonds and Richard A. Melcher, "American Cable Is Lassoing Foreign Markets," *Business Week* (August 14, 1989), pp. 70–71.

13. Sue Woodman, "From Hats to Harley-Davidsons, Marketers Find New Uses for Old Products," *Adweek's Marketing Week* (November 7, 1988), p. H.P. 42.

14. "Eye on the 90s," *U.S. News & World Report* (December 10, 1990), p. 20.

15. Everett M. Rogers and F. Floyd Shoemaker, *Communication of Innovation* (New York: Free Press, 1971), pp. 135–157. Rogers later re-labeled his model on an innovation-decision process. The five steps were then called knowledge, persuasion, decision, implementation, and confirmation. See Everett M. Rogers, *Diffusion of Innovations,* 3d ed. (New York: The Free Press, 1983), pp. 164–165.

16. Philip R. Cateora, *International Marketing,* 7th ed. (Homewood, IL: Richard D. Irwin, 1990), p. 419.

17. Cynthia F. Mitchell, "How Kimberly-Clark Wraps Its Bottom Line in Disposable Huggies," *The Wall Street Journal* (July 23, 1987), pp. 1, 25.

18. Rogers, *Diffusion of Innovations,* pp. 210–232.

19. The survey conducted by Forum Corp., a Boston consulting firm, is cited in Amanda Bennett and Carol Humowitz, "For Customers, More Than Lip Service?" *The Wall Street Journal* (October 6, 1989), p. B1.

20. Customer service definitions are discussed in Richard Germain and M. Bixby Cooper, "How A Customers Mission Statement Affects Company Performance," *Industrial Marketing Management* (February 1990), pp. 47–54.

21. David Wessel, "Sure Ways to Annoy Customers," *The Wall Street Journal* (November 6, 1989), p. B1.

22. The study is cited in William Band, "Build Competitive Advantage Through Customer Service," *Marketing News* (December 5, 1988), p. 16.

23. Stephen Phillips, Amy Dunkin, James B. Treece, and Keith H. Hammonds, "King Customer," *Business Week* (March 12, 1990), pp. 88–94.

24. Charlotte Klopp, "Customer Satisfaction Just Catching On In Europe," *Marketing News* (May 28, 1990), p. 5.

25. Patricia Sellers, "What Customers Really Want," *Fortune* (June 4, 1990), p. 58.

26. Sharyn Hunt and Ernest F. Cooke, "It's Basic But Necessary: Listen To the Customer," *Marketing News* (March 5, 1990), p. 22; Brent Bowers, "Companies Draw More on 800 Lines," *The Wall Street Journal* (November 9, 1989), pp. B1, B6; and Patricia Sellers, "How To Handle Customer Gripes," *Fortune* (October 24, 1988), pp. 87–100.

27. "King Customer," p. 88.

28. Joseph P. Kahn, "Caddy Shack," *inc.* (May 1987), p. 80.

29. IBM *1989 Annual Report,* p. 16.

30. Bradley A. Stertz, "VW Offers Money-Back Guarantee," *The Wall Street Journal* (August 9, 1990), p. B1.

31. Christopher W.L. Hart, "The Power of Unconditional Service Guarantees," *Harvard-Business Review* (July–August 1988), pp. 54–62.

32. These factors are suggested in J. Fred Weston and Eugene F. Brigham, *Essentials of Managerial Finance,* 9th ed. (Hinsdale, IL: The Dryden Press, 1991).

Chapter 10

1. David Walker, "Rubbermaid Tries Its Hand at Bristles and Wood," *Adweek's Marketing Week* (March 5, 1990), pp. 20–21; Maria Mallory, "Profits on Everything But the Kitchen Sink," *Business Week,* Special Edition: Innovation in America, p. 122; "Seventy Years of Success," Rubbermaid Inc., *1989 Annual Report,* pp. 10–11; and Alex Taylor III, "Why the Bounce at Rubbermaid?" *Fortune* (April 13, 1987), pp. 77–78.

2. PepsiCo, Inc. *1989 Annual Report,* p. 10.

3. Phil Patton, "Why Sony Is Betting So Big on Such a Small Format," *Adweek's Marketing Week* (February 12,

1990), pp. 20–21; and Sony Corporation *1989 Annual Report,* p. 9.

4. Janet Meyers, "M&M's go Peanut Butter," *Advertising Age* (July 23, 1990), p. 17.

5. "Consumer Products Sales Top $700 Million Marlo," Reynolds Metals Company *1989 Annual Report,* pp. 10–11; and "Aluminum's Centennial: Reynolds' Role," Reynolds Metals Company *1985 Annual Report,* pp. 1–12.

6. Michola Zaklan, "Baskin-Robbins Scoops Up Healthier Fare," *Adweek's Marketing Week* (June 4, 1990), pp. 30–31.

7. Christine Donahue, "Can Ocean Spray Sell Cranberry Sauce Off-Season?" *Adweek's Marketing Week* (June 26, 1989), p. 25.

8. Larry M. Strum, "Health Care Marketers Eye Hot Topics," *Marketing News* (February 27, 1989), pp. 1, 10; and James W. Busbin, "Employee Wellness Emerges as Major Health Product," *Marketing News* (February 27, 1989), pp. 2, 10.

9. Paul B. Carroll, "IBM Seeking a Source of Renewal, Turns to Services," *The Wall Street Journal* (June 12, 1990), p. B4.

10. Dan Koepell, "With Simplesse Ok'd, Can NutraSweet Market Its Own Ice Cream?" *Adweek's Marketing Week* (February 26, 1990), p. 5; and Richard Koenig and Alix M. Freedman, "FDA Clears Monsanto Fat Substitute, Gives It a Jump On the Competition," *The Wall Street Journal* (February 23, 1990), pp. B1, B5.

11. These alternative strategies were first suggested in H. Igor Ansoff, "Strategies for Diversification," *Harvard Business Review* (September–October 1957), pp. 113–124; and later in H. I. Ansoff, *Corporate Strategy* (New York: McGraw-Hill Book Company, 1965), p. 109.

12. Warner-Lambert Company, *1988 Annual Report,* p. 23.

13. Seth Chandler, "Swedish Marketers Going Global," *Advertising Age* (April 16, 1990), p. 38; and Cara Appelbaum, "How IKEA Blitzes a Market," *Adweek's Marketing Week* (June 11, 1990), pp. 18, 19.

14. Ford Motor Company, *1989 Annual Report,* p. 3.

15. Alberto-Culver Company, *1989 Annual Report,* p. 9.

16. Bro Uttal, "Speeding New Ideas to Market," *Fortune* (March 12, 1987), pp. 62–66.

17. Colgate-Palmolive Company, *1987 Annual Report,* p. 8.

18. Several studies on product success and failure are cited in Robert G. Cooper, "Stage-Gate Systems: A New Tool for Managing New Products," *Business Horizons* (May–June 1990), pp. 44–54.

19. Michael J. McCarthy, "More Companies Shop Abroad for New-Product Ideas," *The Wall Street Journal* (March 14, 1990), pp. B1, B4; Susan Voyles, "Calls Help Companies Give Us What We Want," *USA Today* (May 21, 1987), p. 7B; and Christopher S. Zklund, "How Black & Decker Got Back in the Black," *Business Week* (July 13, 1987), pp. 86, 90.

20. Lois Therrieu, "Has Hasbro Become King of the Toymakers?" *Business Week* (September 22, 1986), p. 90; and William Taylor, "The Business of Innovation: An Interview with Paul Cook," *Harvard Business Review* (March–April 1990), pp. 97–105.

21. Tom Richman, "The New American Start-Up," *Inc.* (September 1988), pp. 54–75, and "Food Fit for Kicks," *Business Week* (January 8, 1990), p. 136.

22. "Stage-Gate Systems: A New Tool for Managing New Products," pp. 47–49.

23. Andrew Kupfer, "Success Secrets of Tomorrow's Stars," *Fortune* (April 23, 1990), pp. 77–82.

24. John Hillkirk, "Firms Learn That Quick Development Means Big Profits," *USA Today* (November 22, 1989), p. 10B; and Timberland, *1988 Annual Report,* pp. 4–5.

25. Ronald Alsop, "Companies Get on Fast Track to Roll Out Hot New Brands," *The Wall Street Journal* (July 10, 1986), p. 27.

26. Lori Beth Skigen, "Mike Donahue: New-Product Development," *Adweek's Marketing Week* (November 27, 1989), p. M.R.C. 28; and Dan Koeppel, "Dow Gives K-C the Once Over," *Adweek's Marketing Week* (April 17, 1989), p. 2.

27. Judann Dagnoli, "Campbell: Back on Profits Track," *Advertising Age* (October 15, 1990), pp. 3, 71.

28. Dan Koeppel, "Dole Wants The Whole Produce Aisle," *Adweek's Marketing Week* (October 22, 1990), pp. 20–26; David Kiley, "Finally, Branded Vegetables Are On the Shelves," *Adweek's Marketing Week* (October 30, 1990), pp. 20–24; and Lynn W. Adkins, "How Nunes Got Brooke Shields to Sell Lettuce," *Adweek's Marketing Week* (October 30, 1990), pp. 20–21.

29. "Crest Earns Smiles to the North and South," Procter & Gamble, *1988 Annual Report,* p. 15.

30. Casey McCabe, "What's in a Name?" *Adweek's Marketing Week* (April 16, 1990), p. 22.

31. Alan L. Unikel, "Imitation Might Be Flattering, But Beware of Trademark Infringement," *Marketing News* (September 11, 1987), pp. 20–21.

32. "The Trademark That Fell Asleep," *U.S. News & World Report* (May 15, 1989), pp. 16–17; and "Trademarks: What Makes a Real Murphy," *Time* (May 15, 1989), p. 59.

33. "Lego Trademark Usage," The Lego Group publicity release, January 1, 1990.

34. Damon Darlin, "Where Trademarks Are Up For Grabs," *The Wall Street Journal* (December 5, 1989), pp. B1, B5; and "The Counterfeit Trade," *Business Week* (December 16, 1985), p. 64.

35. Edwardo Lachica, "Trade Thievery: U.S. Companies Curb Pirating of Some Items But by No Means All," *The Wall Street Journal* (March 16, 1989), pp. 1, A8.

36. Milo Geyelin and Ann Hagedorn, "Trademark Law Change Is Taking Effect," *The Wall Street Journal* (November 15, 1989), p. B9; and Vincent N. Palladino, "New Trademark Law Aids U.S. in Foreign Markets," *Marketing News* (February 13, 1989), p. 7.

37. The Landor Associates "Image Power" Survey/1990 is cited in Mary Lord, "Global Brands," *U.S. News & World Report* (September 24, 1990), p. 19.

38. Howard Ruben, "Bugle Boy's Guerilla Tactics," *Adweek's Marketing Week* (June 11, 1990), p. 22.

39. Ronald Alsop, "Brand Loyalty Is Rarely Blind Loyalty," *The Wall Street Journal* (October 19, 1989), pp. B1, B12.

40. "No Brand Like an Old Brand," *Forbes* (June 11, 1990), pp. 179–180; and Michael J. McDermott, "A New Spin on the RCA Name," *Adweek's Marketing Week* (July 3, 1989), pp. 18–22.

41. Howard Schlossberg, "Slashing Through Market Clutter: Brand Equity Seen as a Major New Force for the 1990s," *Marketing News* (March 5, 1990), p. 1; "But In The Office, No," *Forbes* (October 16, 1989), pp. 272–273; and The Walt Disney Company, *1988 Annual Report,* pp. 24, 41.

42. Reginald Rhein, Joseph Weber, and Michael O'Neal, "Drugs: What's in a Name Brand? Less and Less," *Business Week* (December 5, 1988), pp. 172, 176.

43. Stewart Toy and Zachary Schiller, "That Screeching Is Michelin Doing a U-Turn," *Business Week* (October 9, 1989), p. 50.

44. "The Chill Wind From Canada," *Forbes* (May 29, 1989), pp. 308–310.

45. Ibid., p. 310.

46. Alecia Swasey, "Sales Lost Their Vim? Try Repackaging," *The Wall Street Journal* (October 11, 1989), p. B1.

47. The DuPont/Point-of-Purchase Advertising Institute study is cited in Noreen O'Leary, "Making The Package a Product Benefit," *Adweek* (October 3, 1988), p. A.D. 18.

48. "Sales Lost Their Vim? Try Repackaging."

49. "Making the Package a Product Benefit."

50. John Duggleby, "Into the Woods to Start a Food Company," *Adweek's Marketing Week* (January 23, 1989), p. 26.

51. National Confectioners Association for the United States.

52. Betsey Sharkey, "Budget Gourmet's Downscale Look (and Its Upscale Taste) Whetted Consumers' Appetites," *Adweek* (August 3, 1987), p. M.R.C. 30.

53. Kenneth R. Sheets, "A New Measure of Success," *U.S. News & World Report* (March 12, 1990), p. 61.

54. Ibid.

55. Andrea Dorfman, "Less Baloney On The Shelves," *Time* (November 5, 1990), p. 79.

56. Michael R. Czinkota and Ilkka A. Ronkainen, *International Marketing,* 2d ed. (Hinsdale, IL: The Dryden Press, 1990), p. 288.

57. John Schwartz, Karen Springer, and Mary Hager, "It's Not Easy Being Green," *Newsweek* (November 19, 1990), pp. 51–52.

58. "Michigan ADI Markets Itself as a Testing Site," *Marketing News* (October 29, 1990), p. 9.

59. "But Will They Open Cans," *Time* (September 10, 1990), p. 63.

60. Elizabeth Conlin, "A New Twist," *Inc.* (November 1990), p. 24.

61. "Yankee noodles dandy," *Forbes* (November 12, 1990), p. 310.

Chapter 11

1. Yumiko Ono, "Theme Parks Boom in Japan as Investors and Consumers Rush to Get in on the Ride," *The Wall Street Journal* (August 8, 1990), p. B.1; and "Move Over, Mickey," *U.S. News & World Report* (January 21, 1991), p. 13.

2. The concept of a goods-services continuum is suggested in G. Lynn Shostack, "Breaking Free from Product Marketing," *Journal of Marketing* (April 1977), p. 77. See also John M. Rathmell, "What Is Meant by Services," *Journal of Marketing* (October 1980), pp. 32–36.

3. Peter Bennett (ed.), *Dictionary of Marketing Terms* (Chicago: American Marketing Association, 1988), p. 184.

4. Michael R. Czinkota and Ilkka A. Ronkainen, *International Marketing,* 3d ed. (Hinsdale, IL: The Dryden Press, 1990), p. 679.

5. Brian Bremmer, "Sheraton: Swanky Abroad, Ho-Hum Here," *Business Week* (August 13, 1990), p. 106.

6. "Banks Take the Road in Search of Customers," *The Wall Street Journal* (May 11, 1990), p. B.1.

7. Joshua Levine, "Drive Time," *Forbes* (March 1990), pp. 144, 146.

8. Lynn W. Atkins, "How A Small Chicago Bank Went Wild and Raised Interest," *Adweek's Marketing Week* (June 5, 1989), p. 41.

9. David Walker, "At Sheraton, The Guest Is Always Right," *Adweek's Marketing Week* (October 23, 1989), pp. 20–21.

10. Rick Christie, "Cruise Operators Hope Marketing Push Will Put the Wind Back in Their Sails," *The Wall Street Journal* (April 3, 1990), p. B.1.

11. James Popkin and Martha Williams, "Hotel Heroics for the '92 Olympics," *U.S. News & World Report* (January 11, 1990), p. 69.

12. William H. Davidow and Bro Uttal, "Service Companies: Focus or Falter," *Harvard Business Review* (July–August 1989), pp. 77–85. Copyright © 1989 by William H. Davidow and Bro Uttal.

13. Patricia Sellers, "What Customers Really Want," *Fortune* (June 4, 1990), pp. 60–61.

14. Christopher W. L. Hart, James L. Heskett, and W. Earl Sasser, Jr., "The Profitable Art of Service Recovery," *Harvard Business Review* (July–August 1990), pp. 150, 155.

15. Valarie A. Zeithaml, Leonard L. Berry, and A. Parasuraman, "Communication and Control Processes in the Delivery of Service Quality," *Journal of Marketing* (April 1988), p. 46. Some of the definitions come from A. Parasuraman, Valarie A. Zeithaml, and Leonard L. Berry, "A Conceptual Model of Service Quality and Its Implications for Future Research," *Journal of Marketing* (Fall 1985), p. 47.

16. A similar definition appears in Mary Jo Bitner, Bernard H. Booms, and Mary Stanfield Tetreault, "The Service Encounter: Diagnosing Favorable and Unfavorable Incidents," *Journal of Marketing* (January 1990), p. 71.

17. Carlzon's book is discussed in "Business Service Now a Long-Term Affair," *Marketing News* (September 25, 1989), p. 1.

18. Mary Jo Bitner, "Evaluating Service Encounters: The Effects of Physical Surroundings and Employee Responses," *Journal of Marketing* (April 1990), pp. 69–82.

19. Christopher H. Lovelock, "Classifying Services to Gain Strategic Marketing Insights," *Journal of Marketing* (Summer 1983), p. 10.

20. John A. MacLeod, "Consumers Pay More but Get More at Private Postal Centers," *Marketing News* (October 1, 1990), p. 8.

21. Kathleen A. Hughes, "Hollywood Turns to Russia, with Love," *The Wall Street Journal* (June 1990), p. B.1, B.7.

22. Larry Armstrong and Peter Coy, "900 Numbers Are Being Born Again," *Business Week* (September 17, 1990), p. 144.

23. Cathryn Trost, "Marketing-Minded Child-Care Centers Become More Than 9-to-5 Baby Sitters," *The Wall Street Journal* (June 18, 1990), p. B.1.

24. "The Baby Bells Take Their Show on the Road," *Business Week* (June 25, 1990), pp. 104–106.

25. Jaclyn Fierman, "How Fidelity Beats the Post Office," *Fortune* (May 7, 1990), p. 92.

26. Joseph Spiers, "Services: They Can Too Be Provocative," *Fortune* (June 4, 1990), p. 24.

27. Judith D. Schwartz, "Sprint Dials T for Technology in Its Battle with AT&T, MCI," *Adweek's Marketing Week* (May 14, 1990), pp. 42–43.

28. John Waggoner, "Automated Tellers Get Easier to Find Overseas," *USA Today* (June 27, 1990), p. b.1.

29. Mack Memmott, "Big Four Export Their Paperwork," *USA Today* (June 6, 1988), p. 1. Reprinted from Czinkota and Ronkainen, *International Marketing,* p. 675.

30. "Japan Exports Plastic to U.S.," *Marketing News* (April 30, 1990), p. 5.

31. Erick Calonius, "Federal Express's Battle Overseas," *Fortune* (December 3, 1990), p. 137.

32. Bridget O'Brian, "American Air Expands into Three Continents, Flexing Its U.S. Muscle," *The Wall Street Journal* (June 8, 1990), p. A4.

33. Everett Potter, "How to Beat the Cost of Air Travel to Terrific Destinations," *Money* (January, 1991), pp. 135–136.

34. Lawrence A. Crosby, Kenneth R. Evans, and Deborah Cowles, "Relationship Quality in Services Selling: An Interpersonal Influence Perspective," *Journal of Marketing* (July 1990), pp. 68–81.

35. Nancy Nichols, "Walking Up a Sleeping Giant," *Adweek's Marketing Week* (June 12, 1989), p. 20.

36. Erick Calonius, "Meet the King of Video," *Fortune* (June 4, 1990), p. 208.

37. Davidow and Uttal, "Service Companies: Focus or Falter," p. 84.

38. Susan Dillingham, "Video Beauty Tips Come with the Rinse," *Insight* (March 12, 1990), p. 44.

Chapter 12

1. Stephen D. Soloman, "The Accidental Trader," *INC.* (March 1990), pp. 84–87, 89.

2. Martha Woodward, "When Domestic Markets Are Down," *INC.* (November 1990), p. 100.

3. Jennifer Reese, "Avon's Knocking on China's Door," *Fortune* (December 17, 1990), p. 12; and Laura Bird, "Avon Rings Up Sales, Despite the Threat of Hostile Investors," *Adweek's Marketing Week* (May 7, 1990), p. 12.

4. Alyssa A. Lappen, "We're Still Here," *Forbes* (November 26, 1990),

pp. 191, 194–195; and Kevin Kelly, "What's in a Name? A Lot, Says Tandy," *Business Week* (February 27, 1989), p. 109.

5. Rowland T. Moriarty and Ursula Moran, "Managing Hybrid Marketing Systems," *Harvard Business Review* (November–December, 1990), p. 146.

6. Eric N. Berg, "At Fuller Brush, New Ways to Get Foot in the Door," *The New York Times* (May 18, 1989), p. 25.

7. "How Amstrad Successfully Set Up a Distribution Channel in Spain," *Business International/Ideas in Action* (March 14, 1988), pp. 4–6. Reported in Michael Czinkota and Ilkka A. Ronkainen, *International Marketing*, 2d ed. (Hinsdale, IL: The Dryden Press, 1990), p. 345.

8. "Maine Will Recycle 50% More Bottles as Toughest U.S. Deposit Law Expands," *Arkansas Democrat* (December 25, 1990), p. 4A.

9. "Kodak 'Stands Tall' with Consumers While Demarketing Instant Photo Line," *Marketing News* (January 31, 1987), p. 1; and "Coping with 16.5 Million Headaches," *Fortune* (March 3, 1987), p. 38.

10. Teri Ogins, "Clothing Makers Don Retailers' Garb," *The Wall Street Journal* (July 13, 1989), p. B1.

11. Bert Rosenbloom, "Motivating Your International Channel Partners," *Business Horizons* (March–April, 1990), p. 55.

12. "Customer as Partner," *INC.* (May, 1990), p. 101.

13. Cyndee Miller, "Sylvania Targets Brightest Prospects with 'Prestige Partnership' Marketing," *Marketing News* (March 4, 1991), p. 12.

14. This section is based on David Kiley, "America's Next Test Market? Singapore," *Adweek's Marketing Week* (February 4, 1991), p. 22; Robert D. Buzzell, John A. Quelch, and Walter J. Salomon, "The Costly Bargain of Trade Promotion," *Harvard Business Review* (March–April, 1990), pp. 141–149; Christine Donahue, "Getting Them Going and Coming," *Adweek's Marketing Week* (September 4, 1989), pp. 20–21; Lois Therrien, "Want Shelf Space at the Supermarket? Ante Up," *Business Week* (August 7, 1989), pp. 60–61; and Brent H. Felgner, "Retailers Grab Power, Control Marketplace," *Marketing News* (January 16, 1989), pp. 1–2.

15. "Why Burger King Canned Pepsi," *Business Week* (May 14, 1990), p. 45.

16. Peter Newcomb, "Can Video Stores Survive?" *Forbes* (February 5, 1990).

17. Allan Magrath, "Crystallizing a Marketing Vision," *Marketing News* (May 14, 1990), p. 18.

18. Dan Koeppel, "Brands Dressed in Gray," *Adweek's Marketing Week* (March 20, 1989), pp. 10–20, 24.

19. Seth Lubove, "A Chain's Weak Link," *Forbes* (January 21, 1991), pp. 76, 80.

20. Mary Paige-Royer, "Fast Food," *Express Magazine* (Winter 1989), p. 15.

21. Martin Everett, "When There's More Than One Route to the Customer," *Sales & Marketing Management* (August 1990), p. 50.

22. Isao Nakaucho, "The Yoke of Regulation Weighs Down on Distribution," *Economic Eye* (Summer 1989), pp. 17–18. Translated and abridged from *Economic Today* (Winter 1989).

23. Wolfgang Muller, "European Firms Set Management Principles for Customer Satisfaction," *Marketing News* (February 4, 1991), p. 6.

24. Bert Rosenbloom, *Marketing Channels*, 4th ed. (Hinsdale, IL: The Dryden Press, 1991), p. 444.

25. Ibid., p. 448.

26. "10 Top Franchises For the 1990s," *Money Extra* (1990), p. 40.

27. Peter J. Brennan, "Franchising Overseas," *World Trade* (April–May 1990), pp. 99–100.

28. Ronsleen R. Roha, "The Elusive Affordable Franchise," *Changing Times* (October 1989), pp. 60–65.

29. This section is based on Michael Selz, "Europe Offers Expanding Opportunities to Franchisers," *The Wall Street Journal* (July 20, 1990), p. B2; Jefferey A. Tannenbaum, "Foreign Franchisors Entering U.S. in Greater Numbers," *The Wall Street Journal* (June 11, 1990), p. B2; and Brennan, "Franchising Overseas," p. 100.

30. Susan Moffat, "Foreign Car Sales Go Vroom in Japan," *Fortune* (April 9, 1990), p. 10.

31. "'Gyakuyunya' Takes Hold In Japan," *Adweek's Marketing Week* (March 20, 1989), p. 22.

Chapter 13

1. Michael McBride, "Entertainment Center," *Michigan Business* (October 1989), pp. 33–34; and "The Tape's the Thing," *U.S. News & World Report* (April 2, 1990), p. 68; Handleman Company 1989 and 1990 annual reports; Lisa Gubernick, "We Are a Society of Collectors," *Forbes* (July 24, 1989), p. 80.

2. Peter Gumbel, "Wholesale Trade in U.S.S.R. Remains Negligible After 5 Years of Perestroika," *The Wall Street Journal* (November 20, 1989), p. A14.

3. Steven P. Galante, "Distributors Switch Strategies to Survive Coming Shakeout," *The Wall Street Journal* (July 20, 1987), p. 25.

4. National Intergroup, *1989 Annual Report*, pp. 10–11.

5. *McKesson Today* (June 1989), p. 10.

6. Robert Burroughs, "Full Speed Ahead: Book Wholesaling in the 1990s," *Library Journal* (February 15, 1990), pp. 157–159.

7. "Jorgensen Steel's Approach to Success: Keep it Simple, Do it Right," *Purchasing* (May 21, 1987), pp. 47–49.

8. Joseph Weber, "Mom and Pop Move Out of Wholesaling," *Business Week* (January 9, 1989), p. 91.

9. Ibid., and "Perspectives on Food Service Distribution," *Processed Poultry* (November–December 1988), p. 40.

10. Gene R. Tyndall, "Four Strategies Key to Success in Wholesale Distributor Industry," *Marketing News* (March 13, 1989), pp. 22–23.

11. Suzanne Loeffelholz, "Voracious Appetite," *Financial World* (April 18, 1989), pp. 72–73.

12. United Stationers, Inc., *1988 Annual Report*, p. 8.

13. This story is told in John E. Richardson (ed.), *Marketing 89–90* (Guilford, CT: Dushkin Publishing Group, 1989), pp. 233–236.

14. Barbara Marsh, "Small Firms Try for Good Show at Trade Fairs," *The Wall Street Journal* (March 5, 1990), p. B1.

15. Nancy Giges, Laurie Freeman, and Elena Bowes, "Trade Fairs Offer Entree to Eastern Markets," *Advertising Age* (February 19, 1990), p. 45.

16. *The Mart Center Fact Sheet.*

17. Sotheby's *1989 Annual Report*, pp. 2, 4.

18. Manufacturers' Agents National Association, *MANA's 1990 Survey of Sales Commissions.*

19. Martin Everett, "What to Do When You're Tenth Out of the Bag," *Sales & Marketing Management* (January 1989), p. 37.

20. Certified Grocers of California, Ltd., *1988 Annual Report.*

21. Tyndall, "Four Strategies Key to Success in Wholesale Distribution Industry," p. 22.

22. Genuine Parts Company, *1989 Annual Report*, p. 6.

23. Weber, "Mom and Pop Move out of Wholesaling."

24. Ronald A. Margulis, "Food Distributors go Sightseeing Overseas," *U.S. Distribution Journal* (January 1990), pp. 16–25.

25. Joseph Weber, "Getting Cozy with Their Customers: Partnerships are Transforming Wholesaling," *Business Week* (January 8, 1990), p. 86.

26. Doris Jones Yang, "A First Ride on Hong Kong's High-Tech Wave," *Business Week* (May 22, 1989), p. 111.

Chapter 14

1. Bo Buflingham, "This Woman Has Changed Business Forever," *Inc.* (June 1990), pp. 34–38, 41–42, 44–46.

2. Cara Appelbaum, "Small Is Beautiful—and Big," *Adweek's Marketing Week* (July 9, 1990), p. 17.

3. "At Sears, the More Things Change . . ." *Business Week* (November 12, 1990), p. 66; "Retailing Perestroika," *Newsweek* (September 3, 1990), p. 52; Susan Caminite, "The New Champs of Retailing," *Fortune* (September 24, 1990), pp. 85–90; and Eugene Carlson, "Video Stores Try Sharper Focus in Market Glut," *The Wall Street Journal* (July 2, 1990), p. B1.

4. Susan Caminiti, "The New Champs of Retailing," *Fortune* (September 24, 1990), pp. 85–100.

5. David Kiley, "Can J.C. Penney Change Its Image without Losing Customers?" *Adweek's Marketing Week* (February 26, 1990), p. 21.

6. Stephen D. Solomon, "Born to Be Big," *Inc.* (June 1989), p. 95.

7. Mark Memmott and Martha Moore, "McDonald's Puts Dogs Under Arches in Japan," *USA Today* (March 28, 1990), p. 48.

8. Debra Nussbaum, " 'SuperOpticals' Edge Out the Corner Optician," *Adweek's Marketing Week* (October 1, 1990), p. 36; Paul B. Brown, "The Real Cost of Customer Service," *Inc.* (September 1990), pp. 48–60; and "The Milkman Cometh with More Services," *Insight* (September 10, 1990), p. 47.

9. Information provided by Steve Pagnoni, KMart Corp., February 19, 1991.

10. Michael J. McDermott, "Retailing," *Adweek's Marketing Week* (September 11, 1989), p. 126; David Smith, "Satellite Scans Wal-Mart Empire," *Arkansas Democrat* (December 3, 1989), p. G1; "Customer Satisfaction: The Strategic Edge for the 1990s," *Adweek's Marketing Week* (September 3, 1990), p. 22; Bob Baker, " 'All That Glitters Isn't Gold' for Nordstrom Workers," *Arkansas Democrat* (February 4, 1990), p. H1; and Susan C. Faludi, "At Nordstrom Stores, Service Comes First—But at a Big Price," *The Wall Street Journal* (February 20, 1990), p. 1.

11. Steve Weiner, "Epitaph for a Spy," *Forbes* (February 4, 1991), pp. 48–49.

12. John Davidson, "The King of Wretched Excess," *California* (August 1990), p. 117; "Buy the Buy," *Inc.* (December 1989), p. 127; and "How Wal-Mart Hits Main St." *U.S. News & World Report* (March 13, 1989), p. 53.

13. Susan Caminiti, "A Quiet Superstar Rises in Retailing," *Fortune* (October 23, 1989), pp. 167–168.

14. "Sashaying into a Retail Slump," *Business Week* (July 23, 1990), p. 28; and Ellen Paris, "Managers as Entrepreneurs," *Forbes* (October 31, 1988), p. 62.

15. Robert E. O'Neill, "Planning Ahead for 1990," *Monitor Magazine* (November 1990), p. 26.

16. Michael Hiestand, "Cincinnati Gets an 18-Hole Mall," *Adweek's Marketing Week* (February 13, 1989), p. 2; Jeffrey A. Trachtenberg, "Largest of All Malls in the U.S. Is a Gamble in Bloomington, Minn.," *The Wall Street Journal* (October 30, 1990), p. 1; and "The Minnesota Mallers," *U.S. News & World Report* (June 26, 1989), p. 12.

17. Marco R. della Cava, "Decking the Malls with Customer Services," *USA Today* (December 4, 1989), p. D1; and Adrienne Ward, "The Gap Opens Door to New Mall Concept," *Advertising Age* (January 21, 1991), p. 39.

18. Ward, "The Gap Opens Door to New Mall Concept," p. 39; and "Retailing: Who Will Survive," *Business Week* (November 26, 1990), p. 140.

19. Michael McDermott, "Using Scanners for the 'Store of the Future,' " *Adweek's Marketing Week* (July 9, 1990), p. 58; and Stephen D. Solomon, "Use Technology to Manage People," *Inc.* (May 1990), p. 124.

20. Francine Schwadel, "Retailers Latch on to the Environment," *The Wall Street Journal* (November 13, 1989), p. B1; Adrienne Ward, "Esprit Catalogs Catching the Recycling Spirit," *Advertising Age* (February 19, 1990), p. 49; David Kiley, "Can J.C. Penney Change Its Image without Losing Customers?" *Adweek's Marketing Week* (February 26, 1990), p. 21; and Steve Weiner, "Epitaph for a Spy," *Forbes* (February 4, 1991), pp. 48–49.

21. Maureen J. O'Brien, "Charting the Course for Waldenbooks," *Publisher's Weekly* (March 2, 1990), pp. 52–53; and Alison Fahey, "Jordan Marsh Refines Its Image," *Advertising Age* (August 20, 1990), p. 49.

22. Gail Bushalter, "Profiting Well Is the Best Revenge," *Forbes* (October 22, 1990), pp. 80–86; and "One Store Where Selling Is Still in Style," *Sales & Marketing Management* (September 1989), p. 31.

23. Information provided by Don Fish, Publicity Associate, Polo/Ralph Lauren, February 14, 1991.

24. Cara Appelbaum, "T.J. Cinnamons Makes the Sticky Buns as Down Home as Apple Pie," *Adweek's Marketing Week* (February 19, 1990), p. 25.

25. Dawn Smith, "Tandy Seeks a Feminine Edge," *Adweek's Marketing Week* (November 12, 1990), p. 42.

26. Francine Schwadel, "Its Earnings Sagging, Sears Upgrades Line of Women's Apparel," *The Wall Street Journal* (May 9, 1990), p. 1; and "Retailing Perestroika," *Newsweek* (September 3, 1990), p. 52.

27. Michael J. McDermott, "How a Convenience-Store Chain Made Its Units More Convenient," *Adweek's Marketing Week* (January 23, 1989), pp. 39, 42.

28. Betsy Morris, "As a Favored Pastime, Shopping Ranks High with Most Americans," *The Wall Street Journal* (July 30, 1987), p. 1, 13.

29. "Every Store Is a Stage," *Fortune* (December 4, 1989), p. 132.

30. Louis P. Bucklin, "Retail Strategy and the Classification of Consumer Goods," *Journal of Marketing* (January 1963), pp. 50–55, published by the American Marketing Association.

31. Bill Saporito, "Woolworth to Rule the Malls," *Fortune* (June 5, 1989), p. 145; Cyndee Miller, "Ward's to Extend 'Specialty' Strategy with New Kids Stores," *Marketing News* (October 9, 1989), p. 6.

32. "Supermarket Darwinism; The Survival of the Fattest," *Business Week* (July 9, 1990), p. 42.

33. Ruth Hamel, "Food Fight," *American Demographics* (March 1989), p. 39.

34. Ibid., p. 38.

35. "Shopping Hell," *Time* (July 9, 1990), p. 82.

36. Alison Fahey, "Woolworth Charts Major Expansion," *Advertising Age* (August 20, 1990), p. 49.

37. Andrew Tanzer, "Selling the Japanese Way of Life," *Forbes* (September 3, 1990), pp. 58–60.

38. Martha T. Moore, "Warehouse Clubs Lead Retail Pack," *USA Today* (June 26, 1990), p. B1; Joya L. Wesley, "Warehouse Clubs Fastest Growing Segment of the Retail Industry," *Mobile Press Register* (May 27, 1990), p. C1; and "Retailing: Who Will Survive?" *Business Week* (November 26, 1990), p. 140.

39. Marybeth Nibley, "Discount Malls a Booming Business," *Chicago Sun-Times* (August 5, 1990), p. 54.

40. Teri Agins, "Upscale Retailers Head to Enemy Turf," *The Wall Street Journal* (August 25, 1989), p. B1.

41. Chris Burritt, "A Gargantuan Letdown," *The Atlanta Journal* (August 8, 1990), p. C1; "Wal-Mart Gets Lost in the Vegetable Aisle," *Business Week* (May 28, 1990), p. 48; Michael J. McDermott, "Retailing," *Adweek's Marketing Week*

(September 11, 1989), p. 126; and Diana Fong, "Cherchez La Store," *Forbes* (January 9, 1989), pp. 311, 314.

42.   Kate Ballen, "Get Ready for Shopping at Work," *Fortune* (February 15, 1988), pp. 95, 98.

43.   "Retailing: Who Will Survive?" *Business Week* (November 26, 1990), p. 135; James S. Hirsch, "Victoria's Secret? Keep Earnings Up with Garter Belts," *The Wall Street Journal* (May 29, 1990), p. A1; Francine Schwadel, "Sears Struggles to Save Catalog Business," *The Wall Street Journal* (September 4, 1990), p. B1; and David Kiley, "Can J.C. Penney Change Its Image without Losing Customers?" *Adweek's Marketing Week* (February 26, 1990), p. 24.

44.   This discussion of home shopping is based on Judann Dagnoli, "Merger Trend Hits TV Home Shopping," *Advertising Age* (January 26, 1987), pp. 1, 68; Syndey P. Fresdberg, "Home Shopping Shakeout Forces Survivors to Find Fresh Approach," *The Wall Street Journal* (November 4, 1987), p. 33; and Mark Ivey, Mary J. Pitzer, Kenneth Dreylock, and Mark N. Vamos, "Home Shopping," *Business Week* (December 14, 1986), pp. 62–64, 68–69.

45.   "Vending Machines of the 1990s to Offer Cappuccino and Hot Pizza," *Marketing News* (December 18, 1989), p. 5.

46.   "Bordeaux to Coke: 'Non' on Machines," *Fortune* (July 30, 1990), p. 18.

47.   National Automatic Merchandising Association, *Operating Ratio Report: 1990.*

48.   Janell Blount, "Wal-Mart Takes Over No. 1 Spot," *Arkansas Democrat* (February 16, 1991), pp. A1, 11; and Janice Castro, "Mr. Sam Stuns Goliath," *Time* (February 25, 1991), pp. 62–63.

49.   Mike McDermott, "The Revenge of the Little Guy," *Adweek's Marketing Week* (September 17, 1990), pp. 21–27; and Eugene Carlson, "Video Stores Try Sharper Focus in Market Glut," *The Wall Street Journal* (July 2, 1990), p. B1.

50.   Robert Guenther, "At Last, Success Arrives for Financial Supermarkets," *The Wall Street Journal* (June 7, 1989), p. B1; and Ariane Sains, "Video Stores Emerge as Food Marts," *Adweek's Marketing Week* (June 5, 1989), p. 25.

51.   Ellen Paris, "A Touch of Class," *Forbes* (February 5, 1990), pp. 148–150.

52.   John Harris, "I Don't Want Good, I Want Fast," *Forbes* (October 1, 1990), p. 186.

Chapter 15

1.   "Desert Storm Express," *U.S. News & World Report* (February 11, 1991), pp. 49–50; "Half Audie Murphy, Half Jack Welch," *Business Week*

(March 4, 1991), pp. 42–43; Thomas Mathews, "The Secret History of the War," *Newsweek* (March 18, 1991), p. 38; Frank Munger, "4 Computer Models Aided Deployment," *Arkansas Democrat* (January 19, 1991), p. 8A; Paul Hoversten, "Logistics Crucial at the Front," *USA Today* (February 18, 1991), p. 4A; and David A. Howard, "Ever Try to Define Logistics?" *American Shipper* (June 1989), p. 128.

2.   Donald J. Bowersox, "The Strategic Benefits of Logistics Alliances," *Harvard Business Review* (July–August 1990), p. 36.

3.   George Gecowets, National Council of Physical Distribution Management, telephone interview, April 1, 1991.

4.   "Hugo No Match for Handheld Data Terminals," *Transportation & Distribution* (March 1990), pp. 44, 46.

5.   Robert McMath, "China's Long March to Free Markets," *Adweek's Marketing Week* (May 7, 1990), p. 19.

6.   Bro Uttal, "Companies That Serve You Best," *Fortune* (December 7, 1987), p. 112.

7.   E. J. Muller, "The Corporate Crossroads," *Distribution* (September 1989), pp. 32, 34.

8.   Ibid., pp. 28–29.

9.   "Growth Strategies: Prime Time," *Inc.* (December 1989), p. 125.

10.   E. J. Muller, "The Strange Case of Added Value," *Distribution* (January 1990), pp. 32–36.

11.   Donald J. Bowersox, "The Strategic Benefits of Logistics Alliances," pp. 36–45.

12.   Juanita Darling, "An Export Platform," *World Trade* (Winter 1989), pp. 62–67.

13.   Mary Versprille Yetter, "Computers: Logistics' Productivity Tool," *Distribution* (April 1990), pp. 66–68.

14.   James F. Watson, "Integrated Logistics Management: Challenges and Opportunities," *Traffic World* (November 13, 1989), pp. 16–18.

15.   Barbara Toman, "Will U.S. Warm to Refrigerated Dishes?" *The Wall Street Journal* (August 18, 1989), p. B1.

16.   Patricia Sellers, "Coke Gets Off Its Can in Europe," *Fortune* (August 13, 1990), p. 72.

17.   Robert V. Delaney, "Deregulated Transportation Drives U.S. Towards More Efficient Business Logistics," *Traffic World* (November 13, 1989), pp. 7–12.

18.   Perry A. Trunick, "Prepare for Changes in European Logistics," *Transportation & Distribution* (September 1989), pp. 21–26.

19.   Delaney, "Deregulated Transportation Drives U.S. Towards More Efficient Business Logistics," pp. 7–12. See also Joel A. Bleeke, "Strategic Choices for

Newly Opened Markets," *Harvard Business Review* (September–October 1990), pp. 158–165.

20.   E. J. Muller, "The Strange Case of Added Value," *Distribution* (January 1990), p. 33.

21.   Daniel Machalaba, "Trains Double Up to Get Truck Business," *The Wall Street Journal* (July 28, 1989), p. B3.

22.   Daniel Machalaba, "Radio Tags Trigger Train Identification," *The Wall Street Journal* (May 10, 1990), p. B1.

23.   Mark M. Nelson and Susan Carey, "New EC Train System Burrows Forward," *The Wall Street Journal* (November 6, 1989), p. A12; M. Katherine Glover, *Business America* (July 3, 1989); and David Black, "Channel Tunnel Construction Moves Along," *Europe* (May 1989).

24.   Daniel Machalara, "Push for Long Trucks Hits Bumpy Road," *The Wall Street Journal* (May 9, 1990), p. B1.

25.   "J. B. Hunt Transport, Inc." *Rural Arkansas* (June 1990), pp. 10–11.

26.   Saeed Samiee, "Strategic Considerations of the EC 1992 Plan for Small Exporters," *Business Horizons* (March–April 1990), p. 50.

27.   Thomas F. O'Boyle, "Gulf War Affects Firms as Shipments Lag," *The Wall Street Journal* (January 31, 1991), p. A2.

28.   "Airfreight May Hit Some Turbulence After a Banner Year in 1989," *Distribution* (January 1990), p. 24.

29.   David A. Clancy, "Demand Drives Air Cargo," *Transportation & Distribution* (January 1990), p. 42.

30.   Ibid., pp. 42–44.

31.   Jay Gordon, "Managing Small Shipments Is Big Business at Hallmark," *Distribution* (September 1989), pp. 54–56.

32.   Association of American Railroads, *Railroad Facts: 1990.*

33.   Bowersox, "The Strategic Benefits of Logistics Alliances," p. 38.

34.   Helen L. Richardson, "Vertical Integration Guides Ocean Shipping," *Transportation & Development* (January 1990), p. 38.

35.   United Parcel Service, March 28, 1991.

36.   Les B. Artman and David A. Clancy, "Distribution Follows Consumer Movement," *Transportation & Distribution* (June 1990), pp. 17–20.

37.   Gordon, "Managing Small Shipments Is Big Business at Hallmark," pp. 54–56.

38.   Robert Bowman, "Casebook: Control Data," *Distribution* (April 1990), pp. 68–70.

39.   Artman and Clancy, "Distribution Follows Consumer Movement," pp. 17–20.

40. Delaney, "Deregulated Transportation Drives U.S. Towards More Efficient Business Logistics," p. 7.

41. Philip Revzin, "Ventures in Hungary Test Theory That West Can Uplift East Bloc," *The Wall Street Journal* (April 5, 1990), p. A1.

42. Frank V. Cespedes and E. Raymond Corey, "Managing Multiple Channels," *Business Horizons* (July–August 1990), pp. 69–70.

43. Shawn Tully, "Now Japan's Autos Push into Europe," *Fortune* (January 29, 1990), p. 99.

44. Jennifer E. Beaver, "Getting It There—Just in Time," *Benchmark* (Summer 1990), pp. 18–20.

45. O'Boyle, "Gulf War Affects Firms as Shipments Lag," p. A2.

46. "Streamlining the Logistics Pipeline," *Distribution* (December 1989), pp. 46, 48.

47. Kenneth B. Ackerman, "Value-Added Warehousing Cuts Inventory Costs," *Transportation & Distribution* (July 1989), pp. 32–35.

Chapter 16

1. Ken Meyers is quoted in Judith D. Schwartz, "Smartfood's Expansion Hasn't Diminished Its Sense of Whimsy," *Adweek's Marketing Week* (January 29, 1990), pp. 34, 35. See also Joseph P. Kahn, "The Snack Food That's Eating America: Portrait of a Very Hot Product," *Inc.* (August 1988), pp. 34–40.

2. Hannah Miller, "Going Ape Over Ads," *Advertising Age* (August 6, 1990), p. 8.

3. Michael J. McCarthy, " 'The Real Thing' Could Be a Buck Instead of a Coke," *The Wall Street Journal* (March 14, 1990), p. A9; Patricia Winters, "MagiCan Maladies," *Advertising Age* (May 21, 1990), p. 3; "Coke and Gadgetry's Pitfalls," *Advertising Age* (June 4, 1990), p. 20; and Scott Hume, "Perrier Factor Doomed MagiCan," *Advertising Age* (June 4, 1990), p. 52.

4. Reported in "Travelers' Tales II," *Forbes* (October 15, 1990), p. 24.

5. Kevin Cote, "Promotions, Sampling Sweeping E. Germany," *Advertising Age* (July 9, 1990), pp. 3, 42.

6. "Honda Hopes to Win New Riders by Emphasizing 'Fun' of Cycles," *Marketing News* (August 28, 1989), p. 6.

7. Bristol Voss, "Business Advertising: Cutting through the Clutter," *Sales & Marketing Management* (February 1990), pp. 19–20.

8. "1990 Survey of Selling Costs," *Sales & Marketing Management* (February 26, 1990), p. 75.

9. S. Watson Dunn, Arnold M. Barban, Dean M. Krugman, and Leonard N. Reid, *Advertising: Its Role in Modern Marketing,* 7th edition (Hinsdale, IL: The Dryden Press, 1990), p. 9.

10. Phil Patton, "Why Sony is Betting So Big on Such a Small Format," *Adweek's Marketing Week* (February 12, 1990), pp. 20, 21.

11. "Power Wheels Christmas," *Adweek's Marketing Week* (September 18, 1989), p. 47.

12. Michael Hiestand, "Been to Any Garlic Festivals Lately?" *Adweek* (August 3, 1987), p. 43.

13. Richard Gibson, "Kellogg Shifts Strategy to Pull Consumers In," *The Wall Street Journal* (January 22, 1990), pp. B1, B4.

14. "Notebook: A Review of Current Promotions," *Marketing Week* (May 11, 1987), p. 8.

15. Dagmar Mussey, "P&G: Remember Our Ads," *Advertising Age* (March 6, 1989), p. 48.

16. Magid M. Abraham and Leonard M. Lodish, "Getting the Most Out of Advertising and Sales Promotion," *Harvard Business Review* (May–June 1990), pp. 50–60; Thomas Exter, "Advertising and Promotion: The One-Two Punch," *American Demographics* (March 1990), pp. 18–21; and Scott Hume, "Scanner Research Snared in Discounting Web," *Advertising Age* (June 11, 1990), p. S-10.

17. Richard W. Pollay, "The Distorted Mirror: Reflections on the Unintended Consequences of Advertising," *Journal of Marketing* (April 1986), pp. 18–36.

18. Thomas A. Hedrick, Jr., "Pro Bono Anti-Drug Ad Campaign Is Working," *Advertising Age* (June 25, 1990), p. 22; and Steven W. Colford, "Anti-Drug Victory: Donated Ad Media Near $1M a Day," *Advertising Age* (April 30, 1990), p. 22.

19. Francis X. Callahan, "Does Advertising Subsidize Information?" *Journal of Advertising Research* (August 1978), pp. 19–22. See also Morris B. Holbrook, "Mirror, Mirror on the Wall, What's Unfair in the Reflections on Advertising?" *Journal of Marketing* (July 1987), pp. 95–103.

Chapter 17

1. Rumrill Hoyt advertising agency and Warren Berger, "Champion Starts to Show Its True Colors Off the Field," *Adweek's Marketing Week* (April 23, 1990), pp. 20, 21.

2. R. Craig Endicott, "Philip Morris Ad Spending Muscles Past $2 Billion," *Advertising Age* (September 27, 1989), p. 1; and "U.S. Advertising Volume," *Advertising Age* (May 14, 1990), p. 12.

3. Julie Skur Hill, "Euro, Pacific Spending Spree: Ad Budgets for '89 Lag in U.S.," *Advertising Age* (April 10, 1989), pp. 4, 55.

4. Julie Skur Hill, "Unilever Triumphs as Top Ad Spender," *Advertising Age* (December 4, 1989), p. S-1; see also "Top 100 Agencies Worldwide," *Advertising Age* (December 24, 1990), p. 16; and Alan T. Shao, "To What Extent Do Multinational Advertising Agencies Perform Global Campaigns?" *Proceedings of the Southern Marketing Association* (Orlando: Southern Marketing Association, 1990).

5. S. Watson Dunn, Arnold M. Barban, Dean M. Krugman, and Leonard N. Reid, *Advertising: Its Role in Modern Marketing* (Hinsdale, IL: The Dryden Press, 1990), pp. 555–559.

6. "Pepsi Buys Time Globally for Ad with Madonna," *Mobile Register* (March 2, 1989), p. 30; and James Cox, "Pepsi's Madonna Ad Premières Tonight," *USA Today* (March 3, 1989), p. B1.

7. Sarah Stiansen, "Ogilvy Study: Advertising Works," *Marketing Week* (December 14, 1987), p. 2.

8. Stephen J. Simurda, "New York Life Gets Its Foot in the Door," *Adweek's Marketing Week* (March 19, 1990), p. 46.

9. David A. Aaker and J. Gary Shansby, "Positioning Your Product," *Business Horizons* (May–June 1982), p. 62.

10. Matthew Grimm, "If It Ain't 'Stupid,' Then It Ain't Good Enough for Nick at Nite," *Adweek's Marketing Week* (July 10, 1989), p. 23.

11. Aaker and Shansby, "Positioning Your Product."

12. Dunn, Barban, Krugman, and Reid, *Advertising: Its Role in Modern Marketing,* pp. 393–458.

13. John Motavalli, "Media in the 90s: Cable TV," *Adweek's Marketing Week* (September 11, 1989), pp. 158–159.

14. Thomas R. King, "Warner Bros. Plans an Offensive Against Ads in Movie Theaters," *The Wall Street Journal* (April, 18, 1990), p. B4.

15. "Which Came First? Adman or Egg?" *Fortune* (April 9, 1990), p. 11.

16. David Kiley, "After a Successful Test, VideOcart Rolls East," *Adweek's Marketing Week* (November 12, 1990), p. 46.

17. Alison Fahey, "Malls Open Up to Video Nets," *Advertising Age* (January 15, 1990), p. 37.

18. Maria Shao, "The Following Floppy Is Brought to You By. . . ," *Business Week* (December 4, 1989), pp. 64, 65.

19. Peter Pae, "For Makers of Photo Film, Holidays Are War Days," *The Wall Street Journal* (December 13, 1989), p. B1.

20. Dunn, Barban, Krugman, and Reid, *Advertising: Its Role in Modern Marketing,* pp. 370–371.

21. Jeffrey L. Seglin, "The New Era of Ad Measurement," *Adweek's Marketing Week* (January 23, 1989), p. 24; and

Walecia Konrad, "A Word from the Sponsor: Get Results—or Else," *Business Week* (July 4, 1988), p. 66.

22. R. Craig Endicott, "Ad Age 500 Grows 9.7%, Billings Top $85 Billion," *Advertising Age* (March 26, 1990), pp. S-1, S-6.

23. William M. Carley, "Gillette Co. Struggles as Its Rivals Slice Fat Profit Margins," *The Wall Street Journal* (February 2, 1972), p. 1.

24. Kevin Kerr, "Buy Our Brands or You Die!: Consumers Are Assaulted with an Avalanche of 'Fear Ads,'" *Adweek's Marketing Week* (December 18, 1989), p. 36.

25. Jacqueline Mitchell, "More Car Ads Challenge Rivals Head-On," *The Wall Street Journal* (June 25, 1990), pp. B1, B6, and Melinda Grenier Guiles, "With Sales Falling, Chrysler Takes On Honda in New Ads," *The Wall Street Journal* (May 8, 1990), pp. B1, B4.

26. "U.S. Stars Sell in Japan," *Advertising Age* (January 23, 1989), p. 43.

27. Andrea Gabor, "Star Turns That Can Turn Star-Crossed," *U.S. News & World Report* (December 7, 1987), p. 57.

28. Regis McKenna, "Marketing Is Everything," *Harvard Business Review* (January–February 1991), p. 74.

29. M. Daniel Rosen, "Big-Time Plugs on Small-Company Budgets," *Sales & Marketing Management* (December 1990), pp. 48–55. For a report on sponsorship in the USSR, see Michael Hiestand, "Soviet Sponsors Learn the Meaning of Marketing," *USA Today* (October 23, 1990), p. 2C.

30. Joseph N. Fry and Gordon H. McDougall, "Consumer Appraisal of Retail Price Advertisements," *Journal of Marketing* (July 1974), pp. 64–67.

31. Marc Myers, "Trifari's New Ad Lets Consumers Try on Jewelry at Home," *Adweek's Marketing Week* (August 14, 1989), p. 35; Martha T. Moore, "Ad Execs, Readers Reach for Fold-Outs," *USA Today* (March 30, 1989), p. 8B; and Cleveland Horton, "Infiniti Ads Trigger Auto Debate," *Advertising Age* (January 22, 1990), p. 49.

32. Eva Pomice, "Misery Loves Madison Ave.," *U.S. News & World Report* (June 11, 1990), p. 53.

33. Laurie Petersen, "Sales Promotion," *Adweek's Marketing Week* (September 11, 1989), pp. 231–232.

34. Laurie Petersen, "The Medium *Is* the Message—Including Promotions," *Adweek's Marketing Week* (March 26, 1990), p. 61.

35. "New P-O-P Displays Take Customers in Hand," *Sales & Marketing Management* (January 1990), p. 31.

36. Nancy Bishop, "Specialty Advertising Embarks on Second Century," *Marketing Week* (January 4, 1988), p. 32.

37. Alix M. Freedman, "Use of Free Product Samples Wins New Favor as Sales Tool," *The Wall Street Journal* (August 26, 1986), p. 17.

38. Scott Hume, "Redeeming Feature," *Advertising Age* (February 4, 1991), p. 35; and Laurie Petersen, "Quaker Bets Direct Promotion Is the Right Thing to Do," *Adweek's Marketing Week* (January 8, 1990), pp. 4, 5.

39. "Now Playing in Your H.S. Gym," *Adweek's Marketing Week* (September 18, 1989), p. 46.

40. "Electronic Cards Replacing Green Stamps at Grocery Stores," *Marketing News* (January 30, 1989), p. 16.

41. "A Quake Response," *Adweek's Marketing Week* (December 18, 1989), p. 5.

42. Paul Holmes, "Public Relations," *Adweek's Marketing Week* (September 11, 1989), pp. 234, 235.

43. See Christel K. Beard and H.J. Dalton, Jr., "The Power of Positive Press," *Sales & Marketing Management* (January 1991), pp. 37–43.

Chapter 18

1. Alex Taylor III, "Here Come the Hot New Luxury Cars," *Fortune* (July 2, 1990), pp. 58–65; David Kiley, "The New Deal in Cars," *Adweeks' Marketing Week* (August 13, 1990), pp. 18–20; Wendy Zeller, "Two Days in Boot Camp—Learning to Love Lexus," *Business Week* (September 4, 1989), p. 87; Alex Taylor III, "Here Comes Japan's New Luxury Cars," *Fortune* (August 14, 1989), pp. 62–66; Janice Steinberg, "Exhaustive Research Lines Up Infiniti, Lexus Prospects," *Advertising Age* (July 24, 1989), p. 5–6; and Raymond Serafin, "Lexus Ads Sidestep Japanese Heritage," *Advertising Age* (August 7, 1989), p. 59.

2. Arthur Miller, *Death of a Salesman* (New York: Viking, 1949).

3. Thomas N. Ingram and Raymond W. LaForge, *Sales Management: Analysis and Decision Making* (Hinsdale, IL: The Dryden Press, 1989), p. 21.

4. "Good Salespeople Make the Difference," *Purchasing* (February 23, 1989), pp. 19–20; "What Buyers Really Want," *Sales & Marketing Management* (October 1989), p. 30; and Kate Bertrand, "What Makes a Winning Sales Rep," *Business Marketing* (March 1989), p. 42.

5. David J. Good, "Sales in the 1990s: A Decade of Development," *Review of Business* (Summer 1990), pp. 3–6; and William A. O'Connell and William Keenan, Jr., "The Shape of Things to Come," *Sales & Marketing Management* (January 1990), pp. 36–41.

6. Ronald E. Kutscher, "Outlook 2000: The Major Trends," *Occupational Outlook Quarterly* (Spring 1990), pp. 3–7.

7. Beth Brophy, "The Birth of a Saleswoman," *U.S. News & World Report* (February 6, 1989), pp. 40–42.

8. William Keenan, Jr., "America's Best Sales Forces: Six at the Summit," *Sales & Marketing Management* (June 1990), pp. 72–73.

9. Rawlie R. Sullivan, "New Trends in Business-to-Business Sales Require Interdynamic Integration," *Review of Business* (Summer 1990), pp. 25–30; and William C. Moncrief, Shannon H. Shipp, Charles W. Lamb, Jr., and David W. Cravens, "Examining the Roles of Telemarketing in Selling Strategy," *The Journal of Personal Selling & Sales Management* (Fall 1989), pp. 1–11.

10. See William C. Moncrief III, "Selling Activity and Sales Position Taxonomies for Industrial Salesforces," *Journal of Marketing Research* (August 1986), pp. 261–270.

11. Martin Everett, "This Is the Ultimate in Selling," *Sales & Marketing Management* (August 1989), pp. 28–38.

12. Bruce Hager and John Templeman, "Now, They're Selling BMWs Door-to-Door—Almost," *Business Week* (May 14, 1990), p. 65.

13. Richard Bnock, "How to Get Quality Sales from Qualified Leads," *Sales & Marketing Management* (August 1990), pp. 94–96.

14. Thomas N. Ingram, "Improving Sales Force Productivity: A Critical Examination of the Personal Selling Process," *Review of Business* (Summer 1990), pp. 7–12.

15. Ibid., p. 9.

16. Edward Doherty, "How to Steal a Satisfied Customer," *Sales & Marketing Management* (March 1990), pp. 40–45.

17. Martin Everett, "Selling's New Breed: Smart and Feisty," *Sales & Marketing Management* (October 1989), pp. 52–64.

18. "Native Sales Staffs Pose Problems for U.S. Firms," *Marketing News* (May 8, 1989), p. 7.

19. William A. O'Connell and William Keenan, Jr., "The Shape of Things to Come," p. 40.

20. Mark W. Johnston, Joseph F. Hair, Jr., and James Boles, "Why Do Salespeople Fail?" *The Journal of Personal Selling & Sales Management* (Fall 1989), p. 53.

21. E. James Randall, "Selecting That Successful Salesperson," *Review of Business* (Summer 1990), pp. 19–24.

22. Arthur Bragg, "Is a Mentor Program in Your Future?" *Sales & Marketing Management* (September 1989), pp. 54–63.

23. "America's Best Sales Forces," *Sales & Marketing Management* (June 1989), pp. 40–41.

24. Laurie Freeman, "P&G Rolls Out Retailer Sales Teams," *Advertising Age* (May 21, 1990), p. 18.

25. John S. Hill and Richard R. Still, "Organizing the Overseas Sales Force: How Multinationals do it," *The Journal of Personal Selling & Sales Management* (Spring 1990), pp. 57–66.

26. Eugene M. Johnson, David L. Kurtz, and Eberhard Scheuing, *Sales Management* (New York: McGraw-Hill, 1986).

27. Thomas L. Quick, "Motivation: The Best-Kept Secret for Increasing Productivity," *Sales & Marketing Management* (July 1989), pp. 34–38.

28. Francine Schwadel, "Chain Finds Incentives a Hard Sell," *The Wall Street Journal* (July 5, 1990), pp. B1, B4.

29. A.S. Hansen, Inc., Sales Compensation Survey 1986, as reported in *Sales & Marketing Management* (February 16, 1987), p. 57.

30. The workload method was first described in Walter J. Talley, Jr., "How to Design Sales Territories," *Journal of Marketing* (January 1961), pp. 7–13. The steps are described in Douglas J. Dalrymple, *Sales Management* (New York: Wiley, 1988), pp. 477–478, and Gilbert A. Churchill, Jr., Neil M. Ford, and Orville C. Walker, Jr., *Sales Force Management,* 3d ed. (Homewood, Ill.: Irwin, 1990), pp. 213–216.

Chapter 19

1. Paul B. Brown, "You Get What You Pay For," *Inc.* (October 1990), pp. 155–156.

2. Amy E. Gross, " 'Value' Brands Head for Shelves," *Adweek's Marketing Week* (October 29, 1990), p. 6.

3. Kenneth C. Schneider and James C. Johnson, "Marketing Managers and the Robinson-Patman Act: How Large Is the Fog Factor?" In *1985 AMA Educators Proceedings,* ed. Robert F. Lusch et al. (Chicago: American Marketing Association, 1985), pp. 317–323.

4. Research by Professor Saeed Samiee ranked "satisfactory return on investment" first among a similar list of objectives. Samiee correctly points out the difficulties in making the meeting competition objective operational. See "Pricing in Marketing Strategies of U.S.—and Foreign-Based Companies," *Journal of Business Research,* 15 (1987), pp. 17–30.

5. Bill Stack, "Radisson Fights the Competition with Its Own 'Pizzeria,' " *Marketing News* (December 4, 1989), p. 7.

6. Joseph B. White, " 'Value Pricing' Is Hot as Shrewd Consumers Seek Low-Cost Quality," *The Wall Street Journal* (March 12, 1991), p. A1.

7. Robert D. Buzzell and Frederick D. Wiersema, "Successful Share Building Strategies," *Harvard Business Review* (January–February 1981), pp. 135–144.

8. Alex Taylor II, "Why U.S. Carmakers Are Losing Ground," *Fortune* (October 23, 1989), p. 96.

9. "Don Tyson Wins Holly Farms, but His Debts Aren't Chicken Feed," *Business Week* (July 10, 1989), pp. 29–30.

10. Allan J. Magrath, "8 Timeless Truths About Pricing," *Sales & Marketing Management* (October 1989), pp. 78–79.

11. "Niche Marketing Replacing Discounts Based on Age," *Marketing News* (October 15, 1990), p. 9.

12. Teri Agins, "A Celebrity's Name Can Make Scents—Especially If It's Liz," *The Wall Street Journal* (November 10, 1989), p. A1.

13. Philip Revzin, "French Luxury-Goods Makers Bid Adieu to Days When Market Was All Theirs," *The Wall Street Journal* (June 25, 1990), p. B1.

14. These pricing objectives are suggested in Philip Kotler, *Marketing For Nonprofit Organizations* (Englewood Cliffs, NJ: Prentice-Hall, 1982), pp. 306–309.

15. "Companies to Watch: Wm. Wrigley Jr., Co.," *Fortune* (August 13, 1990), p. 90.

16. Alecia Swasey, "Procter & Gamble Fixes Aim on Tough Market: The Latin Americans," *The Wall Street Journal* (June 15, 1990), p. A1.

17. George Leaming, "Saturn Strategy: On Solid Ground or up in the Stars?" *Marketing News* (November 26, 1990), p. 8.

18. "Gas up 30%; Australians Buy 10% Less," *Arkansas Democrat* (October 18, 1990), p. 6A.

19. John Norton, "Lessons Learned from the Masters of Pricing," *World Trade* (Winter 1988–89), p. 75.

20. Jim Heintz, "Making Ruble Convertible Is a Complex Problem," *Mobile Press Register* (September 9, 1990), p. D1.

Chapter 20

1. Jim Bartimo, "Dallas' Love Field Could Become a Battleground," *Business Week* (June 11, 1990), p. 25; Southwest Airlines Co., *1989 Annual Report;* Southwest Airlines Co., *1988 Annual Report;* Suzanne Loeffelholz, "The Love Line," *Financial World* (March 21, 1989), pp. 26–28; and Frank Gibney, Jr. and Suzanne Loeffelholz, "Southwest's Friendly Skies," *Newsweek* (May 30, 1988), p. 49.

2. David Wessel, "The Price Is Wrong, and Economists Are in an Uproar," *The Wall Street Journal* (January 2, 1991), p. B1.

3. Joseph B. White, " 'Value Pricing' Is Hot as Shrewd Consumers Seek Low-Cost Quality," *The Wall Street Journal* (March 12, 1991), pp. A1, A9.

4. Julie Liesse and Bradley Johnson, "New Pet Food Scrap in Supermarkets," *Advertising Age* (January 28, 1991), p. 3.

5. Allan J. Magrath, "8 Timeless Truths About Pricing," *Sales & Marketing Management* (October 1989), p. 79.

6. "Genetech: A Textbook Case of Medical Marketing," *Business Week* (August 13, 1990), pp. 96–97.

7. Dana Milbank, "Quaker State Slips in Marketing Battle," *The Wall Street Journal* (February 13, 1991), p. A4.

8. The Upjohn Company, *1988 Annual Report.*

9. S. C. Gwynne, "The Right Stuff," *Time* (October 29, 1990), pp. 74–84. See also George Leaming, "Saturn Strategy: On Solid Ground or Up in the Stars?" *Marketing News* (November 26, 1990), p. 8.

10. Ellen Neuborne, "Wal-Mart Wins with Folksy Approach," *USA Today* (December 12, 1990), p. 1B; and Francine Schwadel, "Are Price-Matching Policies Largely PR?" *The Wall Street Journal* (March 16, 1989), p. B1.

11. Francine Schwadel, "Ferocious Competition Tests the Pricing Skills of a Retail Manager," *The Wall Street Journal* (December 11, 1989), p. A1.

12. Magrath, "8 Timeless Truths About Pricing," p. 79.

13. John Norton, "Lessons Learned From the Masters of Pricing," *World Trade* (Winter 1988–1989), p. 75.

14. "Can UPS Deliver the Goods in a New World?" *Business Week* (June 4, 1990), p. 81.

15. "Bright Sales Expected for 'Value' Cigarettes," *Insight* (November 26, 1990), p. 46.

16. "Incentives Cost Ford $4 Billion," *USA Today* (May 11, 1990), p. B1.

17. Krystal Miller, "Ford Will Shift Rebates on Most Models to Its Dealers," *The Wall Street Journal* (December 11, 1990), p. B1.

18. David Kiley, "Automakers and Car Values Suffer from a Rash of Rebates," *Adweek's Marketing Week* (January 15, 1990), p. 2.

19. Jill Andresky Fraser, "Innocents Abroad," *Inc.* (May 1990), p. 116.

20. Robert A. Mamis, "Take It Off, Take Most of It Off," *Inc.* (June 1987), p. 10.

21. Jeffrey A. Trachtenberg, "A Buyer's Market Has Shoppers Demanding and Getting Discounts," *The Wall Street Journal* (February 5, 1991), p. A1.

22. Stuart Elliott, "Taco Bell Sounds New Round in Price War," *USA Today* (October 29, 1990), p. B1.

23. Janis Bultman, "Hot Dogs with Mustard and Glitz," *Forbes* (December 12, 1988), p. 122.

24. Elaine Underwood, "Fly the Discounted Skies," *Adweek's Marketing Week* (January 21, 1991), p. 15.

25. Fergus O'Daly, "The Heart of Any Great Ad: Engagement," *Sales & Marketing Management* (September 1989), p. 72.

26. Rustan Kosenko and Don Rahtz, "Buyer Market Price Knowledge Influence on Acceptable Price Range and Price Limits," in *Advances in Consumer Research,* ed. Michael J. Houston (Association for Consumer Research, 1987); and Anthony D. Cox, "New Evidence Concerning Consumer Price Limits," in *Advances in Consumer Research,* ed. Richard Lutz (Association for Consumer Research, 1986), pp. 268–271.

27. Elliott, "Taco Bell Sounds New Round in Price War," p. B1.

28. "Living With Hyperinflation," *U.S. News & World Report* (March 5, 1990), p. 61.

29. Edward J. Kovac and Henry P. Troy, "Getting Transfer Prices Right: What Bellcore Did," *Harvard Business Review* (September–October 1989), pp. 148–154.

30. "Can Uncle Sam Mend This Hole in His Pocket?" *Business Week* (September 10, 1990), pp. 48–49.

Appendix

1. The authors would like to thank Dinoo Vanier and Michael Fitzgerald for their contribution to this appendix.

2. "Evette Beckett: Market Sensitive," *Sales & Marketing Management* (January 1991), pp. 22–23.

3. This section is partly based on David Rosenthal and Michael A. Powell, *Careers in Marketing* (Englewood Cliffs, NJ: Prentice-Hall, 1984).

4. William Kennan, Jr., "The Executive Pay: The Good News and The Bad," *Sales & Marketing Management* (November 1990), pp. 38, 46.

5. Data from College Placement Council *CPC Salary Survey* (September 1990), p. 4.

Glossary

accessory equipment Capital items, usually less expensive and shorter-lived than installations, such as typewriters, hand tools, and adding machines. (p. 304)

administered marketing system VMS in which channel coordination is achieved through the exercise of power by a dominant channel member. (p. 420)

adoption process Series of stages in the consumer decision process regarding a new product, including awareness, interest, evaluation, trial, and rejection or adoption. (p. 312)

advertising Paid, nonpersonal communication through various media by business firms, nonprofit organizations, and individuals who are identified in the advertising message and hope to inform or persuade members of a particular audience. (p. 532)

advertising agency Marketing specialist firm used to assist advertisers in planning and implementing advertising programs. (p. 569)

advocacy advertising Paid public communication or message that presents information on a point of view bearing on a publicly recognized, controversial issue. (p. 562)

agents and brokers Independent wholesaling intermediaries that may or may not take possession of goods but never take title to them. (p. 442)

AIDA concept Acronym for attention-interest-desire-action, the traditional explanation of the steps an individual must take prior to making a purchase decision. (p. 526)

AIO statements Collection of statements in a psychographic study to reflect the respondents' activities, interests, and opinions. (p. 273)

approach Salesperson's initial contact with a prospective customer. (p. 602)

Asch phenomenon The effect of a reference group on individual decision making. (p. 196)

atmospherics Combination of physical store characteristics and amenities provided by the retailer that contributes to the retail image. (p. 470)

attitudes One's enduring favorable or unfavorable evaluations, emotional feelings, or pro or con action tendencies. (p. 206)

auction house Establishment that brings buyers and sellers together in one location for the purpose of permitting buyers to examine merchandise before purchase. (p. 442)

basing point system System for handling transportation costs used in some industries during the early twentieth century in which the buyer's costs included the factory price plus freight charges from the basing point city nearest the buyer. (p. 671)

benefit segmentation Dividing a population into homogeneous groups on the basis of benefits consumers expect to derive from a product. (p. 277)

bids Written sales proposals from vendors. (p. 248)

boundary-spanning role Role performed by a sales manager in linking the salesforce to other elements of the organization's internal and external environments. (p. 606)

brand Name, term, sign, symbol, design, or some combination of these used to identify the products of one firm and differentiate them from competitive offerings. (p. 344)

brand extension Decision to use a popular brand name for a new-product entry in an unrelated product category. (p. 349)

brand insistence Stage of brand acceptance at which the consumer will accept no alternatives and will search extensively for the good or service. Also known as brand requirement. (p. 348)

brand licensing Practice of allowing other firms to use a brand name for a fee. (p. 349)

brand mark Symbol or pictorial design used to identify a product. (p. 344)

brand name Part of the brand consisting of words or letters that comprise a name used to identify and distinguish the firm's offerings from those of competitors'. (p. 344)

brand preference Stage of brand acceptance at which the consumer will select one brand over competitive offerings based on previous experience with it. (p. 348)

brand recognition Stage of brand acceptance at which the consumer is aware of the existence of brand but does not prefer it to competing brands. (p. 348)

breakeven analysis Pricing technique used to determine the number of products that must be sold at a specified price in order to generate revenue to cover total cost. (p. 645)

broadening concept Expanded view of marketing as a generic function to be performed by both profit-seeking and non-profit organizations. (p. 15)

broker Agent wholesaling intermediary that does not take title to or possession of goods and whose primary function is to bring buyers and sellers together. (p. 443)

business services Intangible products firms buy to facilitate their production and operational process. (p. 306)

buyer's market Marketplace characterized by an abundance of goods and/or services. (p. 10)

buying center Participants in the organizational buying action. (p. 244)

canned approach Memorized sales talk used to ensure uniform coverage of the selling points that management has deemed important. (p. 602)

cannibalizing Refers to a product that takes sales from another offering in the same product line. (p. 328)

cash-and-carry wholesaler Limited-function merchant wholesaler that performs most wholesaling functions except financing and delivery. (p. 441)

cash discount Price reduction offered to a consumer, industrial user, or marketing intermediary in return for prompt payment of a bill. (p. 668)

category killer Retailer that combines huge selection and low prices in a single product line. (p. 474)

census Collection of data from all possible sources in a population or universe. (p. 174)

chain store Group of retail stores that are centrally owned and managed and handle essentially the same product lines. (p. 482)

channel captain Dominant and controlling member of a marketing channel. (p. 409)

class rate Standard transportation rate established for shipping various commodities. (p. 499)

closed sales territory Restricted geographical selling region specified by a manufacturer for its distributors. (p. 418)

closing Stage of personal selling where the salesperson asks the customer to make a purchase decision. (p. 604)

cluster sample Probability sample in which geographic areas or clusters are selected and all of or a sample within them become respondents. (p. 174)

cognitive dissonance Post-purchase anxiety that results when an imbalance exists among an individual's cognitions (knowledge, beliefs, and attitudes). (p. 215)

commission Incentive compensation directly related to the sales or profits achieved by a salesperson. (p. 613)

commission merchant Agent wholesaling intermediary that takes possession of goods when they are shipped to a central market for sale, acts as the producer's agent, and collects an agreed upon fee at the time of sale. (p. 442)

commodity rate Special transportation rate granted by carriers to shippers as a reward for either regular use or large-quantity shipments. (p. 499)

comparative advertising Nonpersonal-selling efforts that make direct or indirect promotional comparisons with competitive brands. (p. 572)

competitive environment Interactive process that occurs in the marketplace among marketers of directly competitive products, marketers of products that can be substituted for one another, and marketers competing for the consumer's purchasing power. (p. 43)

competitive pricing strategy Pricing strategy designed to de-emphasize price as a competitive variable by pricing a good or service at the general level of comparable offerings. (p. 666)

component parts and materials Finished industrial products that actually become part of the final product. Also known as fabricated parts and materials. (p. 305)

concentrated marketing Strategy that directs all of a firm's marketing resources toward serving a small segment of the total market. (p. 286)

concept testing Measuring consumer attitudes and perceptions of a product idea prior to its actual development. (p. 338)

Consolidated Metropolitan Statistical Area (CMSA) Major population concentration, including the 25 or so urban giants. (p. 263)

consolidator Marketing intermediary who acts as a discounter in the travel industry. (p. 386)

consumer behavior All the acts of individuals in obtaining, using, and disposing of economic goods and services, including the decision processes that precede and determine these acts. (p. 190)

consumer innovators First purchasers of a new product. (p. 313)

consumerism Social force within the environment designed to aid and protect the consumer by exerting legal, moral, and economic pressures on business and government. (p. 61)

consumer orientation Business philosophy incorporating the marketing concept of first determining unmet consumer needs and then designing a system for satisfying them. (p. 10)

consumer products Products purchased by the ultimate consumer for personal use. (p. 260)

consumer rights As stated by President Kennedy in 1962, the consumer's right to choose freely, to be informed, to be heard, and to be safe. (p. 61)

containerization Process of combining several unitized loads of products into a single load to facilitate intertransport changes in transportation modes. (p. 513)

contractual marketing system VMS characterized by formal agreements among channel members. (p. 420)

convenience products Products that consumers want to purchase frequently, immediately, and with a minimum of effort. (p. 299)

convenience sample Nonprobability sample based on the selection of readily available respondents. (p. 175)

cooperative advertising Sharing of advertising costs between the retailer

and the manufacturer of the good or service. (p. 575)

corporate marketing system VMS in which there is single ownership of each stage in the distribution channel. (p. 419)

cost-plus pricing Practice of adding a percentage of specified dollar amount (markup) to the base cost of a product to cover unassigned costs and to provide a profit. (p. 644)

countertrade Form of exporting whereby goods and services are bartered rather than sold for cash. (p. 106)

creative selling Personal selling involving situations in which a considerable degree of analytical decision making on the buyer's part results in the need for skillful proposals of solutions for the customer's needs. (p. 598)

cue Any object existing in the environment that determines the nature of the response to a drive. (p. 209)

culture Complex of values, ideals, attitudes, and other meaningful symbols that help people communicate, interpret, and evaluate as members of society. (p. 190)

customary prices In pricing strategy, the traditional prices that customers expect to pay for certain goods and services. (p. 637)

customer-based segmentation Dividing a business market into homogeneous groups on the basis of product specifications identified by organizational buyers. (p. 279)

customer service Manner in which marketers treat their customers and the related activities that enhance the value of the customers' purchases. (p. 317)

customer service standards Quality of service that a firm wants its customers to receive. (p. 497)

data Statistics, opinions, facts, or predictions categorized on some basis for storage and retrieval. (p. 176)

database Collection of data that are retrievable through a computer. (p. 164)

Delphi technique Qualitative sales forecasting method that involves several rounds of anonymous forecasts and ends when a consensus of the participants is reached. (p. 133)

Demand Schedule of the amounts of a firm's product that consumers will purchase at different prices during a specified time period. (p. 638)

demarketing Process of reducing consumer demand for a good or service to a level that the firm can supply. (p. 54)

demographic segmentation Dividing a population into homogeneous groups based on characteristics such as age, sex, and income level. (p. 266)

department store Large retail firm that handles a variety of merchandise, including clothing, household goods, appliances, and furniture. (p. 476)

derived demand Demand for an industrial product that is linked to the demand for a consumer product. (p. 234)

differentiated marketing Strategy employed by organizations that produce numerous products and use different marketing mixes designed to satisfy market segments. (p. 285)

diffusion process Acceptance of new products by the members of a community or social system. (p. 313)

direct marketing Direct communication, other than personal sales contracts, between buyer and seller. (p. 404)

direct selling Direct sales contact between buyer and seller. (p. 403)

discount house Store that charges lower-than-normal prices but may not offer typical retail services such as credit, sales assistance, and home delivery. (p. 477)

distribution channel Entity consisting of marketing institutions and their interrelationships responsible for the physical and title flow of goods and services from producer to consumer or industrial user. (p. 398)

distribution strategy Element of marketing decision making comprising activities and marketing institutions involved in getting the right good or service to the firm's customers. (p. 24)

distribution warehouse Facility designed to assemble and then redistribute products to facilitate rapid movement of products to purchasers. (p. 24)

drive Strong stimulus that impels action. (p. 209)

drop shipper Limited-function merchant wholesaler that receives orders from customers and forwards them to producers, which ship directly to the customers. (p. 441)

dual adaptation International product and promotional strategy in which modifications of both product and promotional strategies are employed in the foreign market. (p. 104)

dual distribution Network in which a firm uses more than one distribution channel to reach its target market. (p. 405)

dumping Controversial practice of selling a product in a foreign market at a price lower than what it receives in the producer's domestic market. (p. 95)

economic environment Factors that influence consumer buying power and marketing strategies, including stage of the business cycle, inflation, unemployment, resource availability, and income. (p. 51)

economic order quantity (EOQ) model Technique used to determine the costs of holding inventory versus the costs involved in placing orders in order to arrive at the optimal order quantity. (p. 510)

Elasticity Measure of responsiveness of purchasers and suppliers to a change in price. (p. 641)

embargo Complete ban on the import of specified products. (p. 95)

end-use application segmentation Dividing a business market into homogeneous groups on the basis of precisely how different industrial purchasers will use the product. (p. 279)

Engel's laws Three general statements on spending behavior: As a family's income increases, (1) a smaller percentage of income goes for food; (2) the percentage spent on household operations, housing, and clothing remains constant; and (3) the percentage spent on other items increases. (p. 272)

environmental forecasting Broad-based economic forecasting that focuses on the impact of external factors on the firm's markets. (p. 136)

environmental management Attainment of organizational objectives by predicting and influencing the competitive, political-legal, economic, technological, and social-cultural environments. (p. 42)

evaluative criteria Features considered in a consumer's choice of alternatives. (p. 213)

evoked set Number of brands that a consumer actually considers before making a purchase decision. (p. 213)

exchange control Method used to regulate the privilege of international trade among importing organizations by controlling access to foreign currencies. (p. 95)

exchange process Process by which two or more parties give something of value to each other to satisfy perceived needs. (p. 7)

exchange rates Price of one nation's currency in terms of other countries' currencies. (p. 88)

exclusive-dealing agreement Arrangement between a manufacturer and a marketing intermediary that prohibits the intermediary from handling competing product lines. (p. 417)

exclusive distribution Policy in which a firm grants exclusive rights to a wholesaler or retailer to sell in a particular geographical area. (p. 417)

expectancy theory Theory that motivation depends on an individual's expectations of his or her ability to perform a job and how that performance relates to attaining rewards the individual values. (p. 612)

experiment Scientific investigation in which a researcher controls or manipulates a test group(s) and compares these results with those of a group(s) that did not receive the controls or manipulations. (p. 173)

exploratory research Process of discussing a marketing problem with informed sources within the firm as well as with outside sources such as wholesalers, retailers, and customers and examining secondary sources of information. (p. 159)

exponential smoothing Quantitative forecasting technique that assigns weights to historical sales data, giving greater weight to the most recent data. (p. 135)

exporting Selling of domestically produced goods and services in foreign countries. (p. 83)

facilitating agency Institution, such as an insurance company, bank, or transportation company, that provides specialized assistance for channel members in moving products from producer to consumer. (p. 408)

fair-trade laws Statutes enacted in most states that permit manufacturers to stipulate a minimum retail price for a product. (p. 630)

family brand Name used for several related products, such as the Johnson & Johnson line of baby care products. (p. 350)

family life cycle Stages of family formation and dissolution that can be used in demographic segmentation. (p. 269)

field selling Sales presentations made at prospective customers' homes or businesses on a face-to-face basis. (p. 596)

fixed-sum-per-unit method Promotional budget allocation method in which promotional expenditures are a predetermined dollar amount for each sales or production unit. (p. 542)

FOB plant "Free on board" price quotation that does not include shipping charges; also called *FOB origin*. (p. 670)

focus group interview Information-gathering procedure in marketing research that typically brings eight to twelve individuals together in one location to discuss a given subject. (p. 172)

follow-up Postsales activities that often determine whether an individual who has made a recent purchase will become a repeat customer. (p. 605)

foreign licensing Agreement in which a firm permits a foreign company to either produce or distribute the firm's goods in a foreign country or gives it the right to utilize the firm's trademark, patent, or processes in a specified geographic area. (p. 98)

forward buying Retailing practice of buying goods only on a deal or special promotion. (p. 410)

franchise Contractual arrangement in which a wholesaler or retailer (the franchisee) agrees to meet the operating requirements of a manufacturer or other franchiser. (p. 421)

freight absorption System for handling transportation costs under which the buyer may deduct shipping expenses from the cost of the goods. (p. 670)

friendship, commerce, and navigation (FCN) treaties International agreements that deal with many aspects of commercial relations among nations. (p. 91)

gaps Differences between expected service quality and perceived service quality. (p. 375)

General Agreement on Tariffs and Trade (GATT) International trade agreement that has helped reduce world tariffs. (p. 94)

general merchandise retailer Establishment that carries a wide variety of product lines, all of which are stocked in some depth. (p. 476)

generic name Brand name that has become a generally descriptive term for a product. (p. 346)

generic product Food or household item characterized by a plain label, with no advertising or no brand name. (p. 351)

geographic segmentation Dividing a population into homogeneous groups on the basis of location. (p. 262)

global marketing strategy Standardized marketing mix with minimal modifications that a firm uses in all of its foreign markets. (p. 102)

goods-services continuum Method of visualizing the differences and similarities between goods and services. (p. 368)

gray goods Goods manufactured under licenses abroad and then sold in the U.S. market in competition with their U.S. produced counterparts. (p. 412)

home shopping Use of cable television to sell products via telephone orders. (p. 480)

hypermarket Giant mass merchandiser of soft goods and groceries that operates on a low-price, self-service basis. (p. 478)

hypothesis Tentative explanation about some specific event; statement about the relationship among variables, including clear implications for testing it. (p. 163)

iceberg principle Theory suggesting that collected data in summary form often obscures important evaluative information. (p. 161)

idea marketing Identification and marketing of a cause to chosen consumer segments. (p. 18)

importing Purchasing of foreign products and raw materials. (p. 83)

import quota Trade restriction that limits the number of units of certain goods that can enter a country for resale. (p. 95)

individual brand Strategy of giving an item in a product line its own brand name rather than identifying it by a single family brand name used for all products in the line. (p. 350)

industrial distributor Wholesaling marketing intermediary that operates in the industrial products market and typically handles small accessory equipment and operating supplies. (p. 305)

industrial market Individuals and firms that acquire goods and services to be used, directly or indirectly, to produce other goods and services. (p. 228)

industrial products Products purchased for use directly or indirectly in the production of other products for resale. (p. 260)

information Data relevant to marketing decision making. (p. 176)

informative advertising Promotion that seeks to announce the availability of and develop initial demand for a good, service, organization, person, place, idea, or cause. (p. 561)

infrastructure A nation's communication systems, transportation networks, and energy facilities. (p. 88)

installations Major capital items, such as new factories and heavy machinery, that typically are expensive and relatively long-lived. (p. 304)

institutional advertising Promoting a concept, an idea, a philosophy, or the goodwill of an industry, company, organization, place, person, or government agency. (p. 561)

intensive distribution Policy in which a manufacturer of a convenience item attempts to saturate the market. (p. 415)

joint demand Demand for an industrial product as related to the demand for another industrial product that is necessary for the use of the first item. (p. 234)

joint venture Agreement in which a firm shares the risks, costs, and management of a foreign operation with one or more partners who are usually citizens of the host country. (p. 99)

jury of executive opinion Qualitative sales forecasting method that combines and averages the sales expectation of various executives. (p. 132)

just-in-time (JIT) inventory system Inventory control system designed to minimize inventory. (p. 510)

label Descriptive part of a product's package, listing brand name or symbol, name and address of manufacturer or distributor, ingredients, size or quantity of product, and/or recommended uses, directions, or serving suggestions. (p. 355)

learning Changes in behavior, immediate or expected, that occur as a result of experience. (p. 209)

lifestyle The way people decide to live their lives, including family, job, social activities, and consumer decisions. (p. 273)

limited-line store Retail establishment that offers a large assortment of one-product lines or just a few related product lines. (p. 474)

line extension New product that is closely related to other products in the firm's existing product line. (p. 328)

list price Established price normally quoted to potential buyers. (p. 328)

loss leaders Product offered to consumers at less than cost to attract them to stores in the hope they will buy other merchandise at regular prices. (p. 667)

mail-order wholesaler Limited-function merchant wholesaler that utilizes catalogs instead of a salesforce to contact customers in an attempt to reduce transportation costs. (p. 674)

major accounts organization Assignment of sales teams to a firm's largest accounts. (p. 610)

manufacturer's agent Agent wholesaling intermediary who represents a number of manufacturers of related but noncompeting products and receives a commission based on a specified percentage of sales. (p. 443)

manufacturer's (national) brand Brand name owned by a manufacturer or other producer. (p. 350)

maquiladoras Mexican assembly plants located near U.S. border. (p. 496)

markdown Amount by which the retailer reduces the original selling price of an item. (p. 466)

market Group of people who possess purchasing power and the authority and willingness to purchase. (p. 260)

marketing Process of planning and executing the conception, pricing, promotion, and distribution of ideas, goods, and services to create exchanges that will satisfy individual and organizational objectives. (p. 6)

marketing audit Objective evaluation of an organization's marketing philosophy, goals, policies, tactics, practices, and results. (p. 131)

marketing communication Transmission from a sender to a receiver of messages dealing with buyer-seller relationships. (p. 526)

marketing concept Companywide consumer orientation with the objective of achieving long-run success. (p. 11)

marketing cost analysis Evaluation of such items as selling costs, billing, and advertising to determine the profitability of particular customers, territories, or product lines. (p. 161)

marketing ethics Marketer's standards of conduct and moral values. (p. 64)

marketing information system (MIS) Planned, computer-based system designed to provide managers with a continuous flow of information relevant to their specific decision areas. (p. 176)

marketing intermediary Business firm, either wholesale or retail, that operates between the producer and the consumer or industrial user; sometimes called a middleman. (p. 398)

marketing mix Blending the four strategy elements of marketing decision making—product, pricing, distribution, and promotion—to satisfy chosen consumer segments. (p. 22)

marketing myopia Term coined by Theodore Levitt in his argument that

executives in many industries fail to recognize the broad scope of their businesses; according to Levitt, future growth is endangered because the executives lack a marketing orientation. (p. 14)

marketing planning process of anticipating the future and determining the courses of action necessary for achieving marketing objectives. (p. 118)

marketing research Information function that links the marketer and the marketplace. (p. 154)

marketing strategy Selection of a target market and the related blending of marketing mix elements. (p. 127)

market price Price a consumer or marketing intermediary actually pays for a product after subtracting any discounts, allowances, or rebates from the list price. (p. 668)

market segmentation Process of dividing the total market into several relatively homogeneous groups with similar product interests based on such factors as demographic or psychographic characteristics, geographic location, or perceived product benefits. (p. 261)

market share/market growth matrix Matrix that classifies a firm's products in terms of the industry growth rate and its market share relative to competitive products. (p. 128)

market test Quantitative forecasting method in which a new product, price, promotional campaign, or other marketing variable is introduced in a relatively small test market location in order to assess consumer reactions. (p. 134)

markup Amount added to the cost of an item to determine its selling price. (p. 464)

mass merchandiser Store that stocks a wider line of goods than a department store but usually does not offer the same depth of assortment. (p. 477)

master license Franchiser's license to operate or sub-franchise units in a given geographic area. (p. 422)

materials handling All activities involved in moving goods within a manufacturer's plants, warehouses, and transportation company terminals. (p. 513)

MDSS Marketing decision support system that links a decision maker with relevant databases. (p. 177)

media scheduling Time and sequencing of advertisements. (p. 567)

meeting-competition method Promotional budget allocation method that matches competitors' promotional out-

lays on either an absolute or relative basis. (p. 542)

merchandise mart Permanent exhibition facility in which manufacturers rent showrooms to display products for visiting retail and wholesale buyers, designers, and architects. (p. 438)

merchant wholesaler Wholesaling intermediary that takes title to the goods it handles. (p. 439)

Metropolitan Statistical Area (MSA) Large, freestanding area for which detailed marketing-related data are collected by the Bureau of the Census. (p. 263)

mission General enduring statement of organizational purpose. (p. 122)

missionary sales Indirect type of selling in which specialized salespeople promote the firm's goodwill, often by assisting customers in product use. (p. 599)

modified breakeven analysis Pricing technique used to evaluate consumer demand by comparing the number of products that must be sold at a variety of prices in order to cover total cost with estimates of expected sales at the various prices. (p. 648)

modified rebuy Situation in which purchasers are willing to reevaluate available options in a repurchase of the same good or service. (p. 243)

monopolistic competition Market structure involving a heterogeneous product and product differentiation among competing suppliers, allowing the marketer some degree of control over prices. (p. 639)

monopoly Market structure involving only one seller of a good or service for which no close substitutes exist. (p. 639)

motive Inner state that directs a person toward the goal of satisfying a felt need. (p. 201)

MRO items Supplies for an industrial firm, categorized as maintenance items, repair items, or operating supplies. (p. 306)

multinational corporation Firm with significant operations and marketing activities outside its home country. (p. 101)

multinational marketing strategy Application of market segmentation to foreign markets by tailoring the firm's marketing mix to match specific target markets in each nation. (p. 102)

multiple sourcing Using several vendors in a purchasing situation. (p. 238)

need Lack of something useful; a discrepancy between a desired state and the actual state. (p. 201)

new-task buying First-time or unique purchase situation that requires considerable effort on the decision makers' part. (p. 243)

nonprobability sample Arbitrary sample in which most standard statistical tests cannot be applied to the collected data. (p. 175)

odd pricing Pricing policy based on the belief that a price ending with an odd number just under a round number is more appealing—for instance, $9.99 rather than $10. (p. 672)

off-price retailer Retailer that sells designer labels or well-known brand name clothing at less than typical retail prices. (p. 477)

oligopoly Market structure involving relatively few sellers and barriers to new competitors due to high start-up costs. (p. 639)

opinion leader Individual in a group who serves as an information source for other group members. (p. 198)

order processing Selling at the wholesale and retail levels; specifically, identifying customer needs, pointing them out to customers, and completing orders. (p. 598)

organization marketing Marketing by mutual benefit organizations, service organizations, and government organizations that seek to influence others to accept their goals, receive their services, or contribute to them in some way. (p. 19)

outlet mall Shopping center consisting entirely of off-price retailers. (p. 477)

over-the-counter selling Personal selling conducted in retail and some wholesale locations in which customers come to the seller's place of business. (p. 596)

penetration pricing strategy Pricing strategy involving the use of a relatively low entry price as compared with competitive offerings; based on the theory that this initial low price will help secure market acceptance. (p. 664)

percentage-of-sales method Promotional budget allocation method in which the funds allocated for promotion during a given time period are based on a specified percentage of either past or forecasted sales. (p. 542)

perception Manner in which an individual interprets a stimulus; the often highly subjective meaning that one attributes to an incoming stimulus or message. (p. 203)

perceptual screen Filtering process through which messages must pass. (p. 203)

personal selling Interpersonal influence process involving a seller's promotional presentation conducted on a person-to-person basis with the prospective buyer. (p. 532)

person marketing Marketing efforts designed to cultivate the attention, interest, and preference of a target market toward a person (typically a political candidate or celebrity). (p. 17)

persuasive advertising Competitive promotion that seeks to develop demand for a good, service, organization, person, place, idea, or cause. (p. 561)

physical distribution Activities concerned with efficient movement of finished goods from the end of the production line to the buyer. (p. 492)

place marketing Marketing efforts to attract people and organizations to a particular geographic area. (p. 17)

planned shopping center Group of retail stores planned, coordinated, and marketed as a unit to shoppers in a geographic trade area. (p. 467)

planning Process of anticipating the future and determining the courses of action necessary for achieving organizational objectives. (p. 118)

point-of-purchase advertising Displays and other promotions located near the site of the actual buying decision. (p. 579)

political-legal environment Component of the marketing environment consisting of laws and interpretations of laws that require firms to operate under competitive conditions and to protect consumer rights. (p. 46)

population (universe) Total group that the researcher wants to study. (p. 174)

positioning Developing a marketing strategy aimed at a particular market segment and designed to achieve a desired position in the prospective buyer's mind. (p. 560)

posttesting Assessment of an advertisement's effectiveness after it has been used. (p. 577)

precall planning Use of information collected during the prospecting and qualifying stages of the sales process and during previous contacts with the prospect to tailor the approach and presentation to match the customer's needs. (p. 602)

presentation Describing a product's major features and relating them to a customer's problems or needs. (p. 602)

pretesting Assessment of an advertisement's effectiveness before it is actually used. (p. 575)

price Exchange value of a good or service. (p. 628)

price flexibility Pricing policy permitting variable prices for goods and services. (p. 673)

pricing policy General guidelines based on pricing objectives and intended for use in specific pricing decisions. (p. 671)

pricing strategy Element of marketing decision making that deals with the methods of setting profitable and justifiable exchange values for goods and services. (p. 24)

primary data Information or statistics collected for the first time during a marketing research study. (p. 164)

Primary Metropolitan Statistical Area (PMSA) Major urban area within a CMSA. (p. 263)

private brand Brand name owned by a wholesaler or retailer. (p. 351)

probability sample Sample in which every member of the population has a known chance of being selected. (p. 174)

product Bundle of physical, service, and symbolic attributes designed to enhance buyers' want-satisfaction. (p. 298)

product adaptation International product and promotional strategy wherein product modifications are made for the foreign market, but the same promotional strategy is used. (p. 104)

product advertising Nonpersonal selling of a good or service. (p. 561)

product invention In international marketing, the development of a new product combined with a new promotional strategy to take advantage of unique foreign opportunities. (p. 104)

production orientation Business philosophy stressing efficiency in producing a quality product; attitude toward marketing is "a good product will sell itself." (p. 8)

productivity Output produced by each worker. (p. 381)

product liability Concept that manufacturers and marketers are responsible for injuries and damages caused by their products. (p. 357)

product life cycle Four stages through which a successful product passes—introduction, growth, maturity, and decline. (p. 307)

product line Various related products offered by a firm. (p. 328)

product line pricing   Practice of marketing different lines of merchandise at a limited number of prices. (p. 673)

product manager   Individual in a manufacturing firm assigned a product or product line and given complete responsibility for determining objectives and establishing marketing strategies. (p. 334)

product mix   Assortment of product lines and individual offerings available from a marketer. (p. 328)

product positioning   Buyer's perception of a product's attributes, use, quality, and advantages and disadvantages. (p. 332)

product strategy   Element of marketing decision making comprising activities involved in developing the right good or service for the firm's customers; involves package design, branding, trademarks, warranties, product life cycles, and new-product development. (p. 22)

profit center   Any part of an organization to which revenue and controllable costs can be assigned. (p. 676)

Profit Impact of Market Strategies (PIMS) project   Research that discovered a strong positive relationship between a firm's market share and its return on investment. (p. 634)

profit maximization   Point at which the additional revenue gained by increasing the price of a product equals the increase in total costs. (p. 632)

promotion   Function of informing, persuading, and influencing the consumer's purchase decision. (p. 526)

promotion adaptation   International product and promotional strategy in which the same product is introduced in a foreign market with a unique promotional strategy for the new market. (p. 104)

promotional allowance   Advertising or sales promotion funds provided by a manufacturer to other channel members in an attempt to integrate promotional strategy within the channel. (p. 669)

promotional mix   Blending of personal selling and nonpersonal selling (including advertising, sales promotion, and public relations) by marketers in an attempt to achieve promotional objectives. (p. 532)

promotional pricing   Pricing policy in which a lower than normal price is used as a temporary ingredient in a firm's marketing strategy. (p. 674)

promotional strategy   Element of marketing decision making that involves appropriate blending of personal selling, advertising, and sales promotion for use

in communicating with and seeking to persuade potential customers. (p. 26)

prospecting   Personal-selling function of identifying potential customers. (p. 600)

psychographic segmentation   Dividing a population into homogeneous groups on the basis of behavioral and lifestyle profiles developed by analyzing consumer activities, opinions, and interests. (p. 273)

psychological pricing   Pricing policy based on the belief that certain prices or price ranges make a good or service more appealing than others to buyers. (p. 672)

publicity   Stimulation of demand for a good, service, place, idea, person, or organization by disseminating commercially significant news or obtaining favorable media presentation not paid for by the sponsor. (p. 534)

public relations   Firm's communications and relationships with its various publics. (p. 533)

public warehouse   Independently owned storage facility that stores and ships products for a rental fee. (p. 438)

pulling strategy   Promotional effort by a seller to stimulate demand by final users, who will then exert pressure on the distribution channel to carry the good or service, thereby "pulling" it through the marketing channel. (p. 538)

pure competition   Market structure characterized by homogeneous products in which there are so many buyers and sellers that none has a significant influence on price. (p. 638)

pushing strategy   Promotional effort by a seller to members of the marketing channel to stimulate personal selling of the good or service, thereby "pushing" it through the marketing channel. (p. 539)

qualifying   Determining that a prospect has the needs, income, and purchase authority necessary for being a potential customer. (p. 602)

quantity discount   Price reduction granted for a large-volume purchase. (p. 669)

quota sample   Nonprobability sample that is divided so that different segments or groups are represented in the total sample. (p. 175)

rack jobber   Full-function merchant wholesaler that markets specialized lines of merchandise to retail stores and provides the services of merchandising and arrangement of goods, pricing, maintenance, and stocking of display racks. (p. 440)

raw materials   Industrial products, such as farm products (wheat, cotton, soybeans) and natural products (coal, lumber, iron ore), used in producing final products. (p. 306)

rebate   Refund for a portion of the purchase price, usually granted by the product's manufacturer. (p. 669)

reciprocity   Practice of extending purchasing preference to suppliers who are also customers. (p. 247)

reference groups   Group with which an individual identifies to the point where it dictates a standard of behavior. (p. 196)

reinforcement   Reduction in drive that results from an appropriate response. (p. 209)

relationship quality   Buyer's trust in and satisfaction with a seller. (p. 388)

relationship selling   Establishment of a sustained seller-buyer relationship. (p. 594)

reminder advertising   Promotion that seeks to reinforce previous promotional activity by keeping the name of the good, service, organization, person, place, idea, or cause in front of the public. (p. 561)

research design   Series of advanced decisions that, when taken together, comprise a master plan or a model for conducting marketing research. (p. 163)

retail advertising   Nonpersonal selling by stores that offer goods or services directly to the consuming public. (p. 574)

retail image   Consumers' perception of the store and the shopping experience it provides. (p. 460)

retailing   All activities involved in the sale of goods and services to the ultimate customer. (p. 458)

reverse channel   Path that goods follow from consumer back to manufacturer. (p. 406)

Robinson-Patman Act   Federal legislation prohibiting price discrimination that is not based on a cost differential; also prohibits selling at an unreasonably low price to eliminate competition. (p. 628)

roles   Behavior that members of a group expect of individuals who hold a specific position within it. (p. 196)

salary   Fixed compensation payments made periodically to an employee. (p. 613)

sales analysis   In-depth evaluation of a firm's sales. (p. 160)

sales branch Establishment maintained by a manufacturer that serves as a warehouse for a particular sales territory, thereby duplicating the services of independent wholesalers; carries inventory and processes orders to customers from available stock. (p. 437)

salesforce composite Qualitative sales forecasting method in which sales estimates are based on the combined estimates of the firm's salesforce. (p. 133)

sales forecast Estimate of company sales for a specified future period. (p. 132)

sales management Activities of planning, organizing, staffing, motivating, compensating, and evaluating and controlling a salesforce to ensure its effectiveness. (p. 606)

sales office Manufacturer's establishment that serves as a regional office for salespeople but does not carry inventory. (p. 438)

sales orientation Business philosophy assuming that consumers will resist purchasing nonessential goods and services; attitude toward marketing is that creative advertising and personal selling are required in order to overcome consumer resistance and convince them to buy. (p. 9)

sales promotion Marketing activities other than personal selling, advertising, and publicity that stimulate consumer purchasing and dealer effectiveness; includes displays, trade shows, coupons, premiums, contests, product demonstrations, and various nonrecurrent selling efforts. (p. 579)

sales quota Level of expected sales for a territory, product, customer, or salesperson against which actual results are compared. (p. 161)

scrambled merchandising Retailing practice of carrying dissimilar product lines in an attempt to generate additional sales volume. (p. 438)

secondary data Previously published data. (p. 164)

selective distribution Policy in which a firm chooses only a limited number of retailers to handle its product line. (p. 416)

self-concept Mental conception of one's self, comprised of the real self, self-image, looking-glass self, and ideal self. (p. 211)

seller's market Marketplace characterized by a shortage of goods and/or services. (p. 10)

selling agent Agent wholesaling intermediary responsible for the total marketing program of a firm's product line. (p. 443)

selling up Retail sales technique of convincing the customer to buy a higher priced item than he or she originally intended. (p. 470)

service encounter Actual interaction point between the customer and the service provider. (p. 375)

service quality Expected and perceived qualities of a service offering. (p. 373)

services Intangible tasks that satisfy consumer and industrial user needs. (p. 368)

shopping products Products purchased only after the consumer has made comparisons of competing products in competing stores on such bases as price, quality, style, and color. (p. 300)

simple random sample Basic type of probability sample in which every item in the relevant universe has an equal opportunity to be selected. (p. 174)

skimming pricing strategy Pricing strategy involving the use of a high price relative to competitive offerings. (p. 661)

SKU (stock-keeping unit) An individual item carried in inventory by a store. (p. 410)

slotting allowance Fees paid by manufacturers to retailers for shelf space. (p. 410)

social-cultural environment Component of the marketing environment consisting of the relationship between the marketer and society and its culture. (p. 59)

social responsibility Marketing philosophies, policies, procedures, and actions that have the enhancement of society's welfare as a primary objective. (p. 67)

sole sourcing Using just one vendor in a purchasing situation. (p. 236)

specialty advertising Sales promotion technique that involves the use of articles such as key rings, calendars, and ballpoint pens that bear the advertiser's name, address, and advertising message. (p. 579)

specialty products Products with unique characteristics that cause the buyer to prize them and make a special effort to obtain them. (p. 301)

specifications Written descriptions of a good or service needed by a firm. (p. 248)

spreadsheet analysis Marketing planning tool that uses a decision-oriented computer program to answer "what if" questions posed by marketing managers. (p. 130)

Standard Industrial Classification (SIC) Government classification system that subdivides the industrial marketplace into detailed market segments. (p. 232)

status Relative position of any individual in a group. (p. 196)

stockout Inventory item that is unavailable for shipment or sale. (p. 513)

storage warehouse Warehouse in which products are stored prior to shipment. (p. 507)

straight extension International product and promotional strategy whereby the same product marketed in the home market is introduced in the foreign market using the same promotional strategy. (p. 103)

straight rebuy Recurring purchase decisions in which an item that has performed satisfactorily is purchased again by a customer. (p. 242)

strategic business unit (SBU) Related product groupings of businesses within a multiproduct firm with specific managers, resources, objectives, and competitors; structured for optimal planning purposes. (p. 128)

strategic planning Process of determining an organization's primary objectives, allocating funds, and then initiating actions designed to achieve those objectives. (p. 118)

strategic window Limited periods during which the "fit" between the key requirements of a market and the particular competencies of a firm is optimal. (p. 126)

stratified sample Probability sample that is constructed so that randomly selected subsamples of different groups are represented in the total sample. (p. 174)

subculture Subgroup of a culture with its own distinct mode of behavior. (p. 193)

subliminal perception Receipt of information at a subconscious level. (p. 205)

suboptimization Condition in which individual objectives are achieved at the expense of broader organizational objectives. (p. 496)

suggestion selling Form of retail selling that attempts to broaden the customer's original purchase with related items, special promotions, and holiday or seasonal merchandise. (p. 470)

supplies   Regular expense items necessary in the firm's daily operation but not part of the final product. (p. 306)

supply   Schedule of the amounts of a good or service that a firm will offer for sale at different prices during a specific time period. (p. 638)

survey of buyer intentions   Qualitative sales forecasting method in which sample groups of present and potential customers are surveyed concerning their purchase intentions. (p. 134)

SWOT analysis   Study of organizational resources and capabilities to assess the firm's strengths and weaknesses and scanning the external environments to identify opportunities and threats. (p. 125)

system   Organized group of components linked according to a plan for achieving specific objectives. (p. 495)

systems integration   Centralization of the procurement function within an internal division or external supplier. (p. 241)

tactical planning   Implementation of activities that are necessary for the achievement of the firm's objectives. (p. 119)

target market   Group of people toward whom a firm markets its goods, services, or ideas with a strategy designed to satisfy their specific needs and preferences. (p. 21)

target market decision analysis   Evaluation of potential market segments on the basis of relevant characteristics. (p. 283)

target return objectives   Short-run or long-run pricing objectives of achieving a specified return on either sales or investment. (p. 632)

tariff   Tax levied against imported goods. (p. 92)

team selling   Use of specialists from other functional areas to sell a product. (p. 596)

technological environment   Applications to marketing of knowledge based on discoveries in science, inventions, and innovations. (p. 56)

telemarketing   Promotional presentation involving the use of the telephone on an outbound basis by salespeople or an inbound basis by customers who initiate calls to obtain information and place orders. (p. 596)

tertiary industry   Service-sector industry. (p. 379)

test marketing   Process of selecting a specific city or television coverage area considered reasonably typical of a new total market and introducing the product with a marketing campaign in this area. (p. 339)

time-based competition   Strategy of developing and distributing goods and services more quickly than competitors. (p. 46)

trade discount   Payment to a channel member or buyer for performing marketing functions; also known as a *functional discount.* (p. 668)

trade fair   Periodic show at which manufacturers in a particular industry display wares for visiting retail and wholesale buyers. (p. 438)

trade-in   Credit allowance given for a used item when a customer purchases a new item. (p. 669)

trade industries   Retailers or wholesalers that purchase products for resale to others. (p. 228)

trademark   Brand that has been given legally protected status exclusive to its owner. (p. 344)

transfer price   Cost assessed when a product is moved from one profit center in a firm to another. (p. 676)

trend analysis   Quantitative sales forecasting method in which estimates of future sales are determined through statistical analyses of historical sales patterns. (p. 134)

truck wholesaler   Limited-function merchant wholesaler that markets perishable food items; also called *truck jobber.* (p. 441)

tying agreement   Arrangement between a marketing intermediary and a manufacturer that requires the intermediary to carry the manufacturer's full product line in exchange for an exclusive dealership. (p. 419)

undifferentiated marketing   Strategy used by organizations that produce only one product and market it to all customers using a single marketing mix. (p. 284)

unfair-trade laws   State laws requiring sellers to maintain minimum prices for comparable merchandise. (p. 630)

uniform delivered price   System for handling transportation costs under which all buyers are quoted the same price, including transportation expenses. (p. 670)

unitizing   Process of combining as many packages as possible into one load in order to expedite product movement and reduce damage and pilferage. (p. 513)

unit pricing   Pricing policy in which prices are stated in terms of a recog-nized unit of measurement or a standard numerical count. (p. 673)

Universal Product Code (UPC)   Special code on packages that is read by optical scanners. (p. 356)

utility   Want-satisfying power of a good or service. (p. 4)

VALS 2   Commercially available psychographic segmentation system. (p. 274)

value added by manufacturing   Differences between the price charged for a manufactured product and the cost of the raw material and other inputs. (p. 230)

value analysis   Systematic study of the components of a purchase to determine the most cost-effective way to acquire the item. (p. 238)

variety store   A retail firm that offers an extensive range and assortment of low-price merchandise. (p. 476)

vendor analysis   Assessment of the supplier's performance in areas such as price, back orders, timely delivery, and attention to special requests. (p. 240)

venture team   Organizational strategy for identifying and developing new-product areas by combining the management resources of technological innovation, capital, management, and marketing expertise. (p. 335)

Vertical Marketing System (VMS)   Preplanned distribution channel organized to be cost effective and achieve improved distribution efficiency. (p. 419)

warranty   Guarantee to the buyer that the producer will replace or repair a product or refund its purchase price if the product proves defective during a specified time period. (p. 319)

wheel of retailing   Hypothesis stating that new types of retailers gain a competitive foothold by offering lower prices through reduction or elimination of services. Once established, they add more services, gradually raise their prices, and then become vulnerable to the emergence of a new, low-price retailer with minimum services. (p. 459)

wholesaler   Wholesaling intermediary that takes title to the goods it handles; also called *jobber* or *distributor.* (p. 430)

wholesaling intermediary   Broad term describing both wholesalers and agents and brokers that perform important wholesaling activities without taking title to the goods. (p. 430)

zone pricing   System for handling transportation costs under which the market is divided into geographic regions and a different price is set in each region. (p. 670)

Name and Company Index

Subject Index

Key terms and the page number(s) on which they are defined appear in boldface type.